Oct '95

1995

Mobil
Travel
Guide.

Frequent Traveler's
Guide to Major Cities

Fodor's Travel Publications, Inc.

Frequent Traveler's Guide to Major Cities is published by Fodor's Travel Publications, Inc., in collaboration with Mobil Corporation, which has sponsored the books since 1958. The aim of the Mobil Travel Guide is to provide the most comprehensive, up-to-date, and useful city guide at the lowest possible price. All properties listed are inspected by trained, experienced field representatives. There is no charge to any establishment for inclusion in Frequent Traveler's Guide to Major Cities, and only establishments that meet the Mobil Travel Guide criteria are listed.

Every effort has been made to select a variety of all types of lodging and dining establishments available in a given locale. However, space limitations make it impossible to include every fine establishment, and the fact that some omissions occur does not imply adverse criticism or inferiority to listed establishments.

Information in the Mobil Travel Guide is revised and updated yearly. Ratings are reviewed annually on the basis of reports from our field representatives, senior staff evaluators and careful analysis of all available relevant material, including more than 100,000 opinions from users of the Mobil Travel Guide. All ratings are impartial, and every effort is made to rate fairly and consistently.

At the time of inspection, all establishments were clean, well-managed and met Mobil Travel Guide standards. Occasionally an establishment may go out of business or change ownership after date of publication. By calling ahead readers can avoid the disappointment of a closed or changed establishment.

By revising our listings yearly, we hope to make a contribution to maintaining and raising the standards of restaurants and accommodations available to travelers across the country. We are most interested in hearing from our readers about their experiences at the establishments we list, as well as any other comments about the quality and usefulness of the Mobil Travel Guide. Every communication from our readers is carefully studied with the object of making the Mobil Travel Guide better. Please address suggestions or comments about attractions, accommodations, or restaurants to Mobil Travel Guide, Fodor's Travel Publications, Inc., 4709 W. Golf Road, Suite 803, Skokie, IL 60076.

THE EDITORS

Guide Staff

Managing Director and Editor-in-Chief: Alice M. Wisel
Inspection Manager: Diane E. Connolly
Editorial Coordinator: Thomas W. Grant
Inspection Assistant: Adam Blieberg
Editorial Assistant: Mary Beth Doyle
Staff Assistant: Douglas M. Weinstein
Creative Director: Fabrizio LaRocca
Cover Design: John Olenyik
Cover Photograph: H. Mark Weidman

Acknowledgements

We gratefully acknowledge the help of our 100 field representatives for their efficient and perceptive inspection of every hotel, motel, motor hotel, inn, resort and restaurant listed; the proprietors of these establishments for their cooperation in showing their facilities and providing information about them; our many friends and users of previous editions of Mobil Travel Guide; and the thousands of Chambers of Commerce, Convention and Visitors' Bureaus, city, state and provincial tourism offices and government agencies for their time and information.

Note

Information about prices and hours has been obtained directly from the establishments listed. However, some changes are inevitable, and the publishers cannot be responsible for any variations from the information printed in the guide.

Mobil 🐎
and Pegasus,

Published in 1995 by Fodor's Travel Publications, Inc.
201 E. 50th St.
New York, NY 10022

ISBN 0-679-02858-7
ISSN 1075-5926

Manufactured in the United States of America
10 9 8 7 6 5 4 3 2 1

Contents

Cities

Introduction

The *Mobil Travel Guide: Frequent Traveler's Guide to Major Cities* offers complete travel planning information for recreational and business travelers alike. Whether you are planning an extended trip, getting away for the weekend or dining close to home, you will find all the current detailed information you need to know in this guide. By planning ahead, you can save money, and when you arrive you won't waste valuable time deciding what to do.

An outstanding feature of the *Mobil Travel Guide: Frequent Traveler's Guide to Major Cities* is its valuable quality ratings and information on more than 4,000 lodgings and restaurants. **There is no charge to an establishment for inclusion in *Mobil Travel Guide* publications.**

Cities are arranged alphabetically by name. Following each city name are population figures taken from the most recent census of the Bureau of Census, Department of Commerce. In addition, time zone and area code information is noted.

A brief overview of the city is given, followed by general references and phone numbers for information sources, points of interest, attractions, and much more. Quality-Rated listings of lodgings and restaurants follow this information. Also, street maps, airport maps and neighborhood maps are provided.

The Introduction section explains the features of the *Mobil Travel Guide: Frequent Traveler's Guide to Major Cities* in more detail and provides useful travel advice.

Please keep in mind that every effort has been made to ensure that the information in this publication was accurate at the time it was printed. Neither Fodor's Travel Publications, Inc., nor Mobil Corporation can be held responsible for changes that occurred after publication. We regret any inconvenience you may incur due to improper information being listed.

Rating System

The star symbols and check marks are used in rating hotels, motor hotels, lodges, motels, inns, resorts, and restaurants:

★	**Good, better than average**
★★	**Very good**
★★★	**Excellent**
★★★★	**Outstanding—worth a special trip**
★★★★★	**One of the best in the country**
✔	**In addition, an unusually good value, relatively inexpensive**

Listing Symbols

Pegasus, the Flying Red Horse, is a trademark of Mobil Oil Corporation. This symbol next to a town name indicates the presence of one or more Mobil service stations in the area.

D   Disabled facilities available

Pets allowed

Fishing on property

Horseback riding on premises

Snow skiing nearby

Golf, 9-hole minimum, on premises or privileges within 10 miles

Tennis court(s) on premises or privileges within 5 miles

Swimming on premises

Exercise equipment or room on premises

Jogging on premises

Major commercial airport within 2 miles of premises

No-smoking rooms

SC   Senior citizen rates

Smoke detector and/or sprinkler system

Note: During the inspection of establishments, field representatives identify fire protection equipment in lodgings. The inspection does not extend to every room nor does it determine whether the equipment is working properly. The symbol appearing at the end of a lodging listing indicates the presence of smoke detectors and/or sprinkler systems. This symbol does not appear in our restaurant listings because the presence of this equipment is assumed. Travelers wishing to gain more information on fire protection systems at properties should contact the establishment directly to verify the installation and working condition of their systems.

Credit Cards

The major credit cards honored by each establishment are indicated by initials at the end of the listing. When credit cards are not accepted, the listing will say "no cr cds accepted."

Please remember that Mobil Corporation credit cards cannot be used for payment of meals and room charges. Be sure the credit cards you plan to use in your travels are current and will not expire before your trip is over. If you should lose one, report the loss immediately.

The following letters indicate credit cards that are accepted by the listed establishments:

> A-American Express
> C-Carte Blanche
> D-Diners Club
> DS-Discover
> ER-En Route
> MC-MasterCard
> V-Visa
> JCB-Japanese Credit Bureau

Discount Coupons

The Mobil Travel Guide is pleased to offer discounts from major companies for products and services. These coupons can be found at the back of this book.

The Mobil Travel Guide and Fodor's Travel Publications, Inc., may not be held responsible for the failure of any participating company to honor these discounts

How to Read the Lodging & Restaurant Listings

Each listing of a motel, lodge, motor hotel, hotel, inn and resort gives the quality rating, name, address, directions (when there is no street address), phone number (local and 800), room rates, seasons open (if not year-round) and number and type of rooms available. Facsimile (FAX) numbers appear immediately following an establishment's phone number for properties offering this service to all of their guests.

Listings in major cities include the neighborhood and/or directions from downtown as an aid to finding your way around. Maps showing these neighborhoods can be found immediately following the city name. Geographic descriptions of the neighborhoods are given under the "City Neighborhoods" heading. These are followed by a list of restaurants arranged by neighborhood, in alphabetical order. The listings also include information on recreational and dining facilities on or adjacent to the establishment and credit card information. Some hotels and motor hotels offer **LUXURY LEVELS**. You will find specific information on these special accommodations within the listing.

Restaurant listings give the quality rating, name, address, directions (when there is no street address), phone number, hours and days of operation, price range for each meal served and cuisine specialties. Additionally, special features such as chef ownership, ambience, entertainment, and credit card information are noted.

Some listings may be located out of town, in a suburb or a nearby community. In these cases, the address and town appear in parentheses immediately following the name of the establishment.

In large cities, lodgings located within 5 miles of major, commercial airports are listed under a separate "Airport" heading, following the city listings.

Mobil Travel Guide makes every effort to select a variety of lodging and dining establishments in a given locale. Occasionally, an establishment may go out of business or change ownership just after our publication deadline. By calling ahead for reservations, you can avoid the disappointment of discovering a closed or changed establishment. Space limitations necessitate the omission of many fine places; however, no adverse criticism is implied or should be inferred.

Neither Fodor's Travel Publications, Inc., nor Mobil Corporation can be held responsible for changes in prices, name, management or deterioration in services. There is no contractual agreement between management and the Mobil Travel Guide to guarantee prices or services. **There is no charge to an establishment for inclusion in Mobil Travel Guide publications.**

Motels and Lodges

Motels and lodges provide accommodations in low-rise structures with rooms easily accessible to parking areas. They have outdoor room entry and small, functional lobbies. Shops and businesses will be found only in the higher-rated properties.

Service is often limited and dining may not be offered in lower-rated motels and lodges. However, higher-rated properties will offer such services as bellmen, room service and restaurants serving three meals daily.

Lodges differ from motels primarily in their emphasis on outdoor recreational activities and in location. They are often found in resort and rural areas rather than in major cities and along highways.

Motor Hotels

Motor hotels offer the convenience of motels as well as many of the services of hotels. They range from low-rise structures offering limited services to multistoried buildings with a wide range of services and facilities. Dual building entry, elevators, inside hallways and parking areas near access doors are some of the features of a motor hotel.

Lobbies offer sitting areas and 24-hour desk and switchboard services. Often bellman and valet services are found in motor hotels as well as restaurants serving three meals a day. Expanded recreational facilities and more than one restaurant will be available in higher-rated properties. Because the following features and services apply to most establishments, they are not shown in the listing of motels and motor hotels:

- Year-round operation with a single rate structure
- European plan (meals not included in room rate)

- Bathroom with tub and/or shower in each room
- Air-conditioned/heated, often with individual room control
- Cots
- Daily maid service
- Free parking
- Phones in rooms
- Elevators

The distinction between motor hotels and hotels in metropolitan areas is minor.

Hotels

To be categorized as a hotel, the establishment must have most of the following facilities and services: multiple floors, a restaurant and/or coffee shop, elevators, room service, bellhops, valet services, spacious lobby and some recreational facilities.

A hotel offers its guests a broad spectrum of lodging experiences. Because the following features and services apply to most establishments, they are not shown in the listing:

- Year-round operation with a single rate structure
- European plan (meals not included in room rate)
- Bathroom with tub and/or shower in each room
- Air-conditioned/heated, often with individual room control
- Daily maid service
- Valet service (one-day laundry/cleaning service)
- Room service during hours restaurant is open
- Elevator
- Phones in rooms
- Bellhops
- Oversize beds available

LUXURY LEVEL: Many hotels offer their guests increased luxury accommodations on floors or towers that operate as a separate unit from the main establishment.

A boldface title, **LUXURY LEVEL(S),** follows the principal hotel listing with information pertinent to that level. There is no separate rating for this listing; the rating given applies to the overall hotel.

The criteria used to determine the qualifications for this distinctive listing are:

1. A minimum of one entire floor of the total structure must be devoted to the luxury level.

2. Management must provide no less than three of these four services:

- Separate check-in and check-out services
- Concierge services
- Private lounge
- Private elevator service (key access)

Complimentary breakfast and snacks are commonly offered on these floors as well as upscale amenities and services.

Resorts

Resorts are establishments specializing in stays of three days or more. They usually offer American Plan and/or housekeeping accommodations, with an emphasis on recreational facilities, and often provide the services of a social director.

Food services are of primary importance at a resort. Guests must be able to obtain three meals a day on the premises or be provided with grocery stores to enable them to obtain food for meal preparation without leaving the premises.

When horseback riding is indicated, phone ahead to inquire about English saddle availability; Western style is assumed.

Inns

Frequently thought of as a small hotel, an inn is a place of homelike comfort and warm hospitality. It is often a structure of historic significance, located in an equally interesting setting.

Meals are a special occasion at an inn and frequently tea and drinks are served in the late afternoon. Rooms are usually individually decorated, featuring antiques or furnishings representative of the locale. Phones, bathrooms, and TVs may not be available in every room.

Restaurants

Unless otherwise specified, restaurants listed:

- Are open daily, year-round
- Offer chiefly American cooking

Prices for an *a la carte* menu are given for entrees or main dishes only. Prices for *semi-a la carte* meals include vegetable, salad, soup, appetizer or other accompaniments to the main dish. *Table d'hôte* means a full meal for a stated price, with no *a la carte* selections available. *Prix fixe* indicates a fixed price for any meal on the menu.

By carefully reading the detailed restaurant information and comparing prices, you can easily determine whether the restaurant is formal and elegant or informal and comfortable for families. When children's meals are offered, you will find it noted in the listing.

Unrated Dining Spots

Chosen for their unique atmosphere, specialized menu and local flavor, restaurants listed under the Unrated Dining Spots category appear without a *Mobil Travel Guide* rating. However, they have been inspected by our team of field representatives and meet our high standards of cleanliness and maintenance.

These establishments feature a wide range of dining, from pizza, ice cream, sandwiches and health food to cafeterias and English tea service in fine hotels. They often offer extraordinary values, quick service and regional flavor and are worth a visit when traveling to a city offering these special listings. Unrated Dining Spots can be found after restaurant listings in many cities.

Prices and Taxes

All prices quoted in *Mobil Travel Guide* publications are expected to be in effect at the time of publication and during the entire year; however, prices cannot be guaranteed.

In some localities there may be short-term price variations because of special events or holidays. Whenever possible, these price changes are noted. Certain resorts have complicated rate structures that vary with the time of year; it's a good idea to contact the management to confirm specific rates.

State and city sales taxes as well as special room taxes can increase your room rates as much as 25% per day. We are unable to bring this specific information into the listings, but we strongly urge that you ask about these taxes when placing reservations with establishments. Another charge that is often overlooked by travelers is that of telephone usage. Frequently, hotels charge a service fee for unanswered phone calls and credit card calls as well as long distance calls. It is advised that you read the information offered by the establishment before placing phone calls from your room. It is not unusual for a hotel to send bills for telephone calls to your home after you have checked out. Be certain to take the time to read your bill carefully before checking out. You will not be expected to pay for charges that were not explained in the printed matter given to you at the time of check-in. The use of public telephones in hotel lobbies should not be overlooked since the financial benefits may outweigh the inconvenience.

Explaining the Ratings

The *Mobil Travel Guide* has been rating motels, lodges, motor hotels, hotels, inns, resorts and restaurants since the first edition was published in 1958. For years it was the only guidebook to provide such ratings on a national basis, and *Mobil Travel Guide* remains one of the few guidebooks to rate restaurants across the country.

The rating categories, ★ through ★★★★★, apply nationally. The rating for each establishment—motel, lodge, motor hotel, hotel, inn, resort, guest ranch, or restaurant—is measured against others of the same type. The criteria for rating accommodations are related to the number and quality of facilities, guest services, luxury of appointments and attitude and professionalism of staff and management. Restaurant evaluations emphasize quality of food, preparation, presentation, freshness of ingredients, quality of service, attitude and professionalism of staff/management. Each type of establishment is viewed also in terms of its own style, unique characteristics, decor and ambience. Climate, historic, cultural and artistic variations representative of regional differences are also major factors in each rating. No rating is ever final and, since each is subject to annual review, each establishment must continue to earn its rating and has a chance to improve it as well.

Every establishment listed in *Mobil Travel Guide* publications is inspected by experienced field representatives who submit detailed reports to the editorial offices. From these reports, the editors extract information for listings and ascertain that establishments to be recommended are clean, well-maintained, well-managed and above average.

Ratings are based upon the inspection reports, written evaluations of staff members who stay and dine anonymously at establishments throughout the year, and an extensive review of guest comments received by the *Mobil Travel Guide*.

Every effort is made to assure that ratings are fair and accurate; the designated ratings are published to serve as an aid to travelers and should not be used for any other purpose.

A further rating designation exists: Unrated. When major changes have occurred during the one-year period prior to publication, there will be no star rating. These changes may be in management, ownership, general manager and master chef. If an establishment is undergoing major renovation/refurbishment or has been in operation less than one year, it will also appear unrated. The decision to list an establishment "unrated" is the responsibility of the Rating Committee.

Good Value Check Mark

The check mark (✔) designation appearing in front of the star rating of an establishment listing indicates "an unusually good value, relatively inexpensive." It will appear with the listing in the following manner:

✔ ★ FODOR'S MOTOR INN

Lodging establishments rated with a good value check mark have been determined to be clean and well-maintained, offering some appointments such as room phones, free television, pools and breakfast on or adjacent to the premises, at economical prices. Restaurants rated with a good value check mark have been determined to be clean and well-maintained, offering good food at economical prices.

Because prevailing rates vary regionally, we are able to be more selective in our good value rated establishments in some areas than in others. However, you will find a wide range of these properties to visit in all locales.

In major cities and resort areas, prices tend to be higher than in outlying areas. The following price range has been used to determine those properties awarded the good value check mark:

Lodging and Restaurant Listings

Lodging—single, average $75–$90 per night
double, average $90–$105 per night

Restaurants—lunch, average $18, complete meal
dinner, exclusive of beverages and gratuities, average $30, complete meal

Terms and Abbreviations

The following terms and abbreviations are used consistently throughout the listings.

AP American plan (lodging plus all meals)

Bar Liquor, wine and beer are served at a bar or in a cocktail lounge and usually with meals unless otherwise indicated (e.g., "wine, beer")

Ck-in; ck-out Check-in time; check-out time

Coin lndry Self-service laundry

Complete meal Soup and/or salad, entree, dessert and non-alcoholic beverage

Continental bkfst Usually coffee and a roll or doughnut

Cover "Cover" is a fee added to the actual cost of food and drink in restaurants

D Followed by a price; indicates room rate for two people in one room (one or two beds; charge may be higher if two double beds are offered)

Each addl Extra charge for each additional person beyond the stated number of persons for a given price

Early In referring to season openings or closings, approximately the first third of a month (May 1 to May 10); check with management for exact date

Early-bird dinner A meal served at specified hours, at a reduced price

EP European plan (lodging only)

Exc Except

Exercise equipt Two or more pieces of exercise equipment on the premises

Exercise rm Both exercise equipment and room, with an instructor on the premises

FAX Facsimile machines available to all guests

Golf privileges Privileges at a course within 10 miles

Hols Holidays

In-rm movies Video cassette player available for use with video tapes

Kit. or kits. A kitchen or kitchenette with stove or microwave, sink, and refrigerator that is either part of the room or a separate room. If the kitchen is not fully equipped, the listing will indicate "no equipt" or "some equipt"

Late In referring to season openings or closings, approximately the last third of a month (May 21 to May 31); check with management for exact date

MAP Modified American plan (lodging plus two meals)

Mid In referring to season openings or closings, approximately the middle third of a month (May 11 to May 20); check with management for exact date

No elvtr In a hotel with more than two stories, it is assumed there is an elevator, so it is not noted; only its absence is noted

No phones Only the absence of phones is noted

Parking There is a parking lot on the premises

Private club A cocktail lounge or bar available to members and their guests (in motels and hotels where these clubs exist, registered guests can usually use the club as guests of the management; frequently the same is true of restaurants)

Prix fixe A full meal for a stated price; usually one price is quoted

Res Reservations

S Followed by a price; indicates room rate for one person

Serv bar A service bar, where drinks are prepared for dining patrons only

Serv charge Service charge is the amount added to the restaurant check in lieu of a tip

Snow skiing downhill/x-country Downhill and/or cross-country skiing within 20 miles of property

Table d'hôte A full meal for a stated price dependent upon entree selection

Tennis privileges Privileges at tennis courts within 5 miles

TV Indicates color television; B/W indicates black-and-white television

Under 18 free Children under a specific age not charged if staying in room with one or both parents

Valet parking An attendant is available to park and retrieve a car

Information for Travelers with Disabilities

The *Mobil Travel Guide* symbol Ⓓ shown in accommodation and restaurant listings indicates establishments that are at least partially accessible to people with mobility problems. Facilities providing for the needs of travelers with disabilities are noted in the listings.

The *Mobil Travel Guide* Criteria for accessibility are unique to our publication and were designed to meet the standards developed by our editorial staff. Please do not confuse them with the universal symbol for wheelchair accessibility. Travelers wishing to gain more information on facilities and services for travelers with disabilities should contact the establishments directly.

When the Ⓓ symbol appears following a listing, the establishment is equipped with facilities to accommodate persons in wheelchairs as well as on crutches and the aged in need of easy access to doorways and restroom facilities. Persons with severe mobility problems, as well as the hearing and visually impaired, should not assume establishments bearing our symbol will offer facilities to meet their needs. We suggest travelers with disabilities phone an establishment before their visit to ascertain if their particular needs will be met.

The following facilities must be available at all lodging properties bearing our Ⓓ symbol:

Public Areas

- ISA-designated parking near access ramps
- Level or ramped at entryways to buildings
- Swinging entryway doors minimum 3'-0"
- Restrooms on main level with room to operate a wheelchair; handrails at commode areas
- Elevators equipped with grab bars and lowered control buttons
- Restaurants with accessible doorways; restrooms with room to operate wheelchair; handrails at commode areas

Rooms

- Minimum 3'-0" width entryway to rooms
- Low-pile carpet
- Telephone at bedside and in bathroom
- Bed placed at wheelchair height
- Minimum 3'-0" width doorway to bathroom
- Bath with open sink—no cabinet; room to operate wheelchair
- Handrails at commode areas; tub handrails
- Wheelchair accessible "peep" hole in room entry door
- Wheelchair accessible closet rods and shelves

Restaurants

- ISA-designated parking beside access ramps
- Level or ramped front entryways to building
- Tables to accommodate wheelchairs
- Main-floor restrooms; minimum 3'-0" width entryway
- Restrooms with room to operate wheelchair; handrails at commode areas

Tips for Travel

The passage of the Americans with Disabilities Act (ADA) of 1990 means that all hotels and motels in the US have to make their facilities and services accessible to all guests. Although this law went into effect early in 1992, it will take some time for the more than 40,000 hotels and motels to implement the renovation programs and make their facilities totally accessible to every guest.

Any facility opened after January 26, 1993, must be designed and built totally in accordance with ADA Accessibility Guidelines. This means that a certain percentage of the rooms must be accessible to guests who have mobility, vision, hearing or speech impairments. In addition, all public spaces must be accessible to all guests to use and enjoy.

While all existing hotels and motels will not be totally accessible, you can expect all properties to be aware of the ADA and to make efforts to accommodate the special needs of any guest who has a physical disability.

To get the kind of service you need and have a right to expect, do not hesitate when making a reservation to:

- Ask about the availability of accessible rooms, parking, entrances, restaurants, lounges or any other facilities that are important to you.
- Inquire about any special equipment, transportation or services you may need.
- Ask for details about the accessibility of the room. For example, do both the room entry and bathroom doors have 30" of clear width? Is there a 5' diameter turning space in the bedroom and bathroom? For the hearing impaired, are fire alarms indicated by blinking lights?

When your stay is over, fill out the guest comment card and let the management know about the facilities, equipment and services that worked for you and those that need to be improved.

Additional Publications

Fodor's *Great American Vacations for Travelers with Disabilities* ($18) covers 38 top US travel destinations, including parks, cities and popular tourist regions. It's available from bookstores or by calling 1-800/533-6478.

The most complete listing of published material for travelers with disabilities is available from *The Disability Bookshop,* Twin Peaks Press, PO Box 129, Vancouver, Washington 98666; phone 206/694-2462.

A comprehensive guidebook to the national parks is a 1992 publication, *Easy Access to National Parks: The Sierra Club Guide for People with Disabilities;* Sierra Club, distributed by Random, $16 (paperback). Local public libraries should have relevant books on travel for people with disabilities. Individuals should contact the reference librarian at their public library for assistance.

The Reference Section of the National Library Service for the Blind and Physically Handicapped (NLS), Library of Congress, provides information and resources for persons with mobility problems and hearing and vision impairments, as well as information about the NLS talking-book program. For further information, contact: Reference Section, National Library Service for the Blind and Physically Handicapped, Library of Congress, Washington, DC 20542; phone 202/707-9275 or 202/707-5100.

Travel Tips

Lodging

Many hotels in major metropolitan areas have special weekend package plans. These plans offer considerable savings on rooms and may include breakfast, cocktails and some meal discounts as well. Prices for these specials are not included because they change frequently throughout the year. We suggest you phone to obtain such information prior to your trip.

LUXURY LEVEL accommodations, which appear within some hotel and motor hotel listings, frequently offer good value because many of them provide breakfast, cocktails, newspapers and upgraded amenities in the price of the room.

Dining

Reservations are important at most major city restaurants. Many restaurants will ask you to confirm your reservation by calling back the day you are to dine. Should you fail to do so, your reservation will not be held for you.

In fine restaurants the pace is leisurely, the service is professional and the prices are above average. Most of the dishes are cooked to order, and patrons' requests for special preparation are handled graciously.

Four-Star and Five-Star establishments are usually quite expensive because they offer higher quality food, superior service and distinctive decor. Read the listing and see if they are open for lunch. While the lunch prices are considerably higher than those at other restaurants, you may still enjoy the ambience, service and cuisine of a famous establishment for about half the cost of a dinner.

"Early bird" dinners are popular in many parts of the country and offer considerable savings on dinner prices. Information on the availability of these dinners has been given to us by restaurant management, but we suggest you phone ahead and ask if they still offer this special plan.

Tipping

Lodgings: Doormen in major city hotels are usually given $1 for getting you into a cab. Bellmen expect $1 per bag, usually never less than a $2 tip if you have only one bag. Concierges are tipped according to the service they perform. Suggestions on sightseeing or restaurants, as well as making reservations for dining, are standard services often requiring no tip. However, when reservations are obtained at restaurants known to be difficult to get into, a gratuity of $5 should be considered. If theater or sporting event tickets are obtained, a tip is expected, often $5 to $10. Maids, often overlooked by guests, may be tipped $1 to $2 per each day of your stay.

Restaurants: Coffee shop and counter service wait staff are usually given 8 to 10 percent of the bill. In full service restaurants, 15 percent of the bill, before sales tax, is suggested. In fine dining restaurants, where the staff is large and share the gratuity, 18 to 20 percent is recommended. The number of restaurants adding service charges to the bill is increasing. Carefully review your bill to make certain an automatic gratuity was not charged.

Airports: Curbside luggage handlers expect $1 per bag. Car rental shuttle drivers who help with your luggage appreciate a $1 or $2 tip. **Remember, tipping is an expression of appreciation for good service. You need not tip if service is poor—tipping is discretionary.**

10 Tips for Worry-Free Travel

1. Be sure to notify local police and leave a phone number where you can be contacted in case of emergency.

2. Lock doors and windows, but leave shades up and lights on (or on an automatic timer).

3. Stop newspaper deliveries and discontinue garbage pickups.

4. Remove food and defrost refrigerator; store valuables in a safe place; disconnect electrical appliances; turn off gas jets, including hot water heater; turn off water faucets and drain pipes in severe weather.

5. Remember to pack personal medicines and duplicate prescriptions; spare eyeglasses or the prescription; sunglasses; suntan lotion; first-aid kit; insect spray; towels and tissues; writing materials.

6. Make sure that proof of car insurance is in your glove compartment; also take along your driver's license and those of other passengers (check expiration dates); car registration; copies of birth certificates (if driving outside US); traveler's checks. Be sure you have a duplicate set of car keys.

7. Check to see that you have a jack, spare tire, repair kit, emergency tools, flashlights, tire chains, spare fan belt, windshield scraper, auto fuses, lug wrench and work gloves. A pre-trip tune-up won't hurt—and, of course, be sure to "fill up" before you start out.

8. Also check vehicle's battery, oil and air filters, cooling system, brakes and lights.

9. Remember "extras" like hunting/fishing licenses and equipment; camera and film; bathing suits, beach accessories, sports equipment; portable radio and/or TV; picnic accessories.

10. Buckle up your seat belt, and have a nice trip!

Savings for Seniors

Mobil Travel Guide publications note senior citizen rates in lodgings, restaurants and attractions. Always call ahead to confirm that the discount is being offered. Carry proof of age, such as a passport, birth certificate or driver's license. Medicare cards are often accepted as proof. Contact the following organizations for additional information:

1. American Association of Retired Persons (AARP)
   Financial and Special Services Dept
   601 E Street NW
   Washington, DC 20049
   Phone 202/434-2277

2. National Council of Senior Citizens
   1331 F Street NW
   Washington, DC 20004
   Phone 202/347-8800

The mature traveler on a limited budget should look for the senior citizen discount symbol in Lodging and Restaurant listings. Also, pay special attention to all listings in the guide highlighted by a check mark (✔). (See Federal Recreation Areas for Golden Age Passport information.)

Car Care

Familiarize yourself with the owner's manual for your car. It provides valuable advice for service and maintenance. Before you travel, get a lubrication and oil change, an inspection of tires, fan belts and cooling system, and a check of engine performance, lights and brakes. Other inspections recommended by the car manufacturer should be made as well.

Once your car is ready for the road, make certain your insurance is paid up—and don't forget your registration certificate, insurance information, driver's license and an extra set of keys.

Keep your seat belt and harness fastened. Watch your instrument panel closely—your panel gauges or indicators will alert you to potential problems. If a problem arises, get to a service station as soon as possible.

A world of convenience is yours with a Mobil credit card. Mobil's gasoline, oil and tires, as well as many other products and services, may be charged at Mobil dealers in the United States as well as at certain other dealers throughout Canada.

Road Emergencies

The best insurance against an emergency is proper maintenance of your car. Despite care, however, the unexpected can happen. Here are a few tips for handling emergencies:

Accidents. If you should have an accident, observe the following:

- Do not leave accident scene
- Help the injured but don't move them unless necessary
- Call police—ask for medical help if needed
- Get names, addresses, license numbers and insurance companies of persons involved
- Get names and addresses of at least two witnesses
- Get description and registration number(s) of car(s) involved
- Report accident to your insurance company
- Diagram the accident, showing cars involved

Breakdowns. If your car breaks down, get out of traffic as soon as possible, pulling off the road if you can. Turn on your emergency flashers and raise the hood. If you have no flashers, tie a white cloth to the roadside door handle or antenna. Stay near your car but off the road. Carry and use flares or reflectors to keep your car from being hit.

Blowout. Do not overreact if you have a tire blowout. Hold the wheel steady—do not jerk it. Gradually let up on the gas pedal, steer straight and coast to a stop. If you have to brake, do so very gently.

Collision. "If a collision is imminent, you will need to make these split-second decisions," advises the National Safety Council's Defensive Driving Course. "Drive right, away from the oncoming vehicle. Drive with control, don't skid off the road. If you are forced to drive off the road, look for either something soft, like bushes or small trees, or something fixed, like a breakaway pole or a fence to break your impact. A fixed object has no momentum, and the crash will be less intense than if you had hit the oncoming vehicle. If you are unable to ride off the road, try to collide with the oncoming vehicle at an angle. A glancing blow is less dangerous than hitting a vehicle head on."

Flat tire. Drive off the road, even if you risk ruining your tire. Set the parking brake firmly, but remember it may not hold if a rear wheel is off the ground. Put wooden blocks, bricks or stones tightly against the front and rear of the tire diagonally opposite the flat. After removing the hubcap, loosen each wheel nut about one-half turn. Position the jack exactly as the instructions indicate, then raise the car an inch or two to determine how the jack fits. (If it appears to be about to slip, stop and wait for help.)

Jack the car until the flat is about three inches off the ground, remove the wheel nuts and put them in the hubcap. Keep your body away from the car. Handle the tire from the sides; never put your hand above or underneath the tire.

Slide the spare tire into place, using the wrench as a lever. You may have to raise the jack a little farther. Screw the nuts on firmly, and jack the car down, standing at the side, not in front of the car. Finally, fully tighten the wheel nuts and leave the hubcap off as a reminder to have the flat fixed.

Skids. When your car skids, let up on the gas gently, keeping some power going to the wheels. Steer into the direction of the skid, and brake only after you have the car under complete control.

Stuck wheels. If you get stuck in the mud or snow, don't spin the wheels. Rock the car by gently accelerating ahead and back in rhythm with the car's natural tendency.

Equipment. The following checklist describes the necessary equipment to carry at all times:

- ☐ Spare tire; tool kit; first-aid kit; flashlight
- ☐ Road flares; jumper cables; gloves
- ☐ Container of motor oil; a can opener
- ☐ Empty one-gallon container (Note: Check local laws governing type of container to use for gasoline.)
- ☐ Spare parts, fan belt and fuses
- ☐ In winter: chains, ice scraper, de-icer in spray can, shovel, "liquid chain" or a bag of sand
- ☐ Major credit card and auto club identification

HOW TO SURVIVE A HOTEL FIRE

The chances are quite slim that you will ever encounter a hotel or motel fire. In addition, should you hear an alarm or see smoke, the danger is almost always less than you think it to be. But in the event you do encounter a fire, **ENSURE YOUR SURVIVAL WITH BASIC PREPARATION AND CALM ACTION.**

PREPARATION IS QUICK AND EASY

WHEN YOU CHECK INTO YOUR ROOM, DO THE FOLLOWING SAFETY CHECK:
- *Where are the fire exits?* Walk to at least two, counting the doors along the way in case you need to find the exit in the dark.
- *Where are the fire extinguishers and alarms?* Walk to them quickly.
- *Where is the "off switch" on your room's air conditioner?* In case of fire, turn off the air conditioner to prevent smoke from being sucked into your room.
- *Where is your room key?* Keep your key with you so you may reenter your room.

IF THERE'S A FIRE . . . STAY CALM

Keep in mind that smoke, poisonous gases, and panic are the greatest threats. The fresh air you need to breathe is at or near the floor. Get on your hands and knees; stay low, keep calm and react as follows:

If you find a fire,
- pull the nearest fire alarm;
- then use a fire extinguisher *if the fire is small;*
- leave the building through the fire exit.

    Never enter an elevator when fire is threatening.

If you hear an alarm from your room,
- take your room key;
- check the door for heat, but *do not open a hot door;*
- open the door a crack if it is cool;
- use the fire exit if the hall is clear of thick smoke, but *slam the door shut if the hall is smoky.*

If your exit is blocked,
- try another exit;
- or if all exits are smoky, go back to your room—it's the safest place;
- and if you cannot get to your room, go to the roof.

If you must stay in your room because thick smoke blocks the fire exits,
- turn off the air conditioner;
- stuff wet towels under the door and in air vents to keep smoke out;
- fill your bathtub with water and keep wastebaskets or ice buckets nearby to remoisten the clothes or toss water on heating walls;
- phone your location to the front desk or directly to the fire department;
- *stay low, below smoke and poisonous gases, and await assistance;*
- tie a wet towel around your nose and mouth—it's an effective filter.

Hotel/Motel Toll-Free '800' Numbers

This selected list is a handy guide for hotel/motel toll-free reservation numbers. You can save time and money by using them in the continental United States and Canada; Alaska and Hawaii are not included. Although these '800' numbers were in effect at press time, the *Mobil Travel Guide* cannot be responsible should any of them change. Many establishments do not have toll-free reservation numbers. Consult your local telephone directory for regional listings. The toll-free numbers designated 'TDD' are answered by a telecommunications service for the deaf. *Don't forget to dial "1" before each number.*

Best Western International, Inc.
800-528-1234 Cont'l USA & Canada
800-528-2222 TDD

Budgetel Inns
800-4-BUDGET Cont'l USA

Budget Host
800-BUD-HOST

Clarion Hotels
800-CLARION

Comfort Inns
800-228-5150 Cont'l USA

Courtyard by Marriott
800-321-2211 Cont'l USA

Days Inn
800-325-2525 Cont'l USA

Doubletree Hotels
800-222-8733 Cont'l USA

Drury Inns
800-325-8300 Cont'l USA

Econo Lodges of America
800-446-6900 Cont'l USA & Canada

Embassy Suites
800-362-2779 Cont'l USA

Exel Inns of America
800-356-8013 Cont'l USA

Fairfield Inn by Marriott
800-228-2800

Fairmont Hotels
800-527-4727 Cont'l USA

Four Seasons Hotels
800-332-3442 Cont'l USA & Canada

Friendship Inns of America Int'l
800-453-4511 Cont'l USA

Guest Quarters
800-424-2900 Cont'l USA
800-PICKETT

Hampton Inn
800-HAMPTON Cont'l USA

Hilton Hotels Corp
800-HILTONS Cont'l USA
800-368-1133 TDD

Holiday Inns
800-HOLIDAY Cont'l USA & Canada
800-238-5544 TDD

Howard Johnson
800-654-2000 Cont'l USA & Canada
800-654-8442 TDD

Hyatt Corp
800-228-9000 Cont'l USA & Canada

Inns of America
800-826-0778 USA

Inter-Continental Hotels
800-327-0200 Cont'l USA, HI & Canada

La Quinta Motor Inns, Inc.
800-531-5900 Cont'l USA
800-426-3101 TDD

Loews Hotels
800-223-0888 Cont'l USA exc NY

Marriott Hotels
800-228-9290 Cont'l USA

Master Hosts Inns (Hospitality)
800-251-1962 Cont'l USA & Canada

Omni Hotels
800-843-6664 Cont'l USA & Canada

Park Inns Int'l
800-437-PARK

Quality Inns
800-228-5151 Cont'l USA & Canada

Radisson Hotel Corp
800-333-3333 Cont'l USA & Canada

Ramada Inns
800-2-RAMADA Cont'l USA
800-228-3232 TDD

Red Carpet/Scottish Inns (Hospitality)
800-251-1962 Cont'l USA & Canada

Red Lion-Thunderbird
800-547-8010 Cont'l USA & Canada

Red Roof Inns
800-843-7663 Cont'l USA & Canada

Residence Inn By Marriott
800-331-3131

Ritz-Carlton
800-241-3333 Cont'l USA

Rodeway Inns International
800-228-2000 Cont'l USA

Sheraton Hotels & Inns
800-325-3535 Cont'l USA & Canada

Shilo Inns
800-222-2244

Signature Inns
800-822-5252

Stouffer Hotels and Resorts
800-HOTELS-1 Cont'l USA & Canada

Super 8 Motels
800-843-1991 Cont'l USA & Canada
800-800-8000 Cont'l USA & Canada

Susse Chalet Motor Lodges & Inns
800-258-1980 Cont'l USA & Canada

Travelodge International Inc./Viscount Hotels
800-255-3050 Cont'l USA & Canada

Trusthouse Forte Hotels
800-225-5843 Cont'l USA & Canada

Vagabond Hotels Inc.
800-522-1555 Cont'l USA

Westin Hotels
800-228-3000 Cont'l USA & Canada

Wyndham Hotels
800-822-4200

Car Rental Toll-Free '800' Numbers

Advantage Rent A Car
800-777-5500 Cont'l USA

Agency Rent-A-Car
800-321-1972 Cont'l USA

Alamo Rent-A-Car
800-327-9633 Cont'l USA,
Canada

Allstate Rent-A-Car
800-634-6186 Cont'l USA

Avis-Reservations Center
800-331-1212 Cont'l USA,
Canada

Budget Rent-A-Car
800-527-0700 Cont'l USA,
Canada

Dollar Rent-A-Car
800-800-4000 Cont'l USA,
Canada

Enterprise Rent-A-Car
800-325-8007 Cont'l USA

Hertz Corporation
800-654-3131 Cont'l USA
800-654-3001 Canada

National Car Rental
800-CAR-RENT Cont'l USA,
Canada

Payless Rent-A-Car Inc.
800-237-2804 Cont'l USA

Sears Rent-A-Car
800-527-0770 Cont'l USA

Thrifty Rent-A-Car
800-367-2277 Cont'l USA,
Canada

U-Save Auto Rental of America
800-272-USAV

Value Rent-A-Car
800-327-2501 Cont'l USA,
Canada

Airline Toll-Free '800' Numbers

American Airlines, Inc. (AA)
800-433-7300

Canadian Airlines Intl, LTD
800-426-7000

Continental Airlines (CO)
800-231-0856

Delta Air Lines, Inc. (DL)
800-221-1212

Northwest Airlines, Inc. (NW)
800-225-2525

Southwest Airlines (WN)
800-435-9792

Trans World Airlines, Inc. (TW)
800-221-2000

United Air Lines, Inc. (UA)
800-241-6522

USAir (US)
800-428-4322

Atlanta

Founded: 1837

Pop: 394,017

Elev: 1,050 feet

Time zone: Eastern

Area code: 404

Peachtree Plaza, 73 stories of iron and glass dominating the city skyline, symbolizes one side of this nerve center of the New South. Atlanta is a booming city. Strikingly modern skyscrapers, busy streets and varied entertainments give a sense of boundless energy. Yet Atlanta, rebuilt on the ashes left by General Sherman's march to the sea, holds to its Southern traditions.

After Georgia's secession from the Union on January 19, 1861, the city became a manufacturing, storage, supply and transportation center for the Confederate forces. This made Atlanta the target and last real barrier on General Sherman's march. Atlanta finally surrendered after four months of seige. Although the terms promised protection of life and property, all but 400 of the 3,600 houses and commercial buildings were destroyed in the subsequent burning. Many citizens had returned to the city by January of 1865; by June, steps had been taken to reorganize business and repair wrecked railroad facilities. Atlanta was made the federal headquarters for Reconstruction in the area in 1866. It became the state capital two years later. Atlanta's recovery and expansion received a large boost in 1872, when two more railroads met here.

Eager for growth, Atlanta launched a "Forward Atlanta" program in 1960, with the largest national advertising campaign of any American city up to that time. Designed to attract industries and commercial firms, it was very successful—nearly 600 branches of national companies were established within 3 years.

Business

Conventions and tourism are foremost in the business of Atlanta. The city is also a retail/wholesale trade and distribution center and has one of the world's busiest airports, Hartsfield Atlanta International. Service jobs, manufacturing and government service also rank high. Many Fortune 500 corporations have offices here. The city is a financial center as well, with dozens of banking and investment firms.

"Forward Atlanta" brought great changes to the city in the 1960s. Its population increased by almost a third; 50 new downtown office buildings were constructed; hotel and motel space more than doubled; the face of the downtown area was lifted by a new stadium, civic center, merchandising mart and art center.

Peachtree Center, in downtown Atlanta, has proven to be a model of urban development. Designed by architect John Portman, the center contains office towers, hotels and a variety of shops and stores. It features open garden plazas punctuated with contemporary sculpture and glass-enclosed skyways connecting the buildings—a beautiful, modern city within a city. The center was expanded to include more shopping, entertainment and the 1,674-room Marriott Marquis.

Other imaginative complexes following the lead of Peachtree Center include Colony Square, at Peachtree and 14th streets, and CNN Center, across International Boulevard from the Georgia World Congress Center. The building boom in Atlanta during the last quarter of this century has made this one of the most dynamic and prosperous cities in the nation and a center of activity for the entire Southeast.

Convention Facilities

The Georgia World Congress Center provides 640,000 square feet of exhibit space. It has 70 meeting rooms of various sizes, a 33,000-square-foot ballroom and a 2,000-seat auditorium. Permanent simultaneous interpretation equipment in six languages is available. The Atlanta Market Center, designed by John Portman, contains the Atlanta Merchandise and Apparel Mart, the Atlanta Decorative Arts Center and Inforum, a high-technology showcase area. There are 280,000 square feet of exhibit space. Skywalks connect the facility to Peachtree Center across the street.

The Georgia International Convention and Trade Center provides 40,000 square feet of exhibit space with 17 meeting rooms of various sizes. An ongoing expansion project will create an additional 80,000 square feet of exhibit space.

The Omni Coliseum at CNN Center is also available for conventions. It seats 17,000 people. There are 51,000 guest rooms in the metropolitan Atlanta area, 11,000 located in the center of the city.

Sports and Recreation

Crowds flock to Atlanta-Fulton County Stadium in spring and summer to watch the national baseball league Atlanta Braves; and in fall crowds fill the Georgia Dome for Falcons football. The Hawks round out the year with basketball at the Omni Coliseum.

South of the city is the Atlanta Motor Speedway, where the NASCAR Winston Cup and Busch Grand National draw racing enthusiasts from all over the country.

Golfers enjoy the BellSouth Golf Classic in early May and the many public courses throughout the city. Tennis facilities are numerous.

For those interested in outdoor recreation, the Appalachian Trail is only about a two-hour drive from the city. There is camping, backpacking and hiking throughout the area. There is boating on lakes Lanier and Allatoona, just north of the city. The Chattahoochee River is a major attraction for summer activities. Water excitement can also be found at White Water theme park, located north of Atlanta in Marietta.

Entertainment

Music, drama and visual arts provide cultural enrichment for residents and visitors. The Robert W. Woodruff Arts Center is home to the Atlanta Symphony Orchestra and the Alliance Theater Company. The symphony season runs from September to May and mid-June-mid-August. Theater of the Stars presents a summer play season. Other repertory groups offer year-round productions.

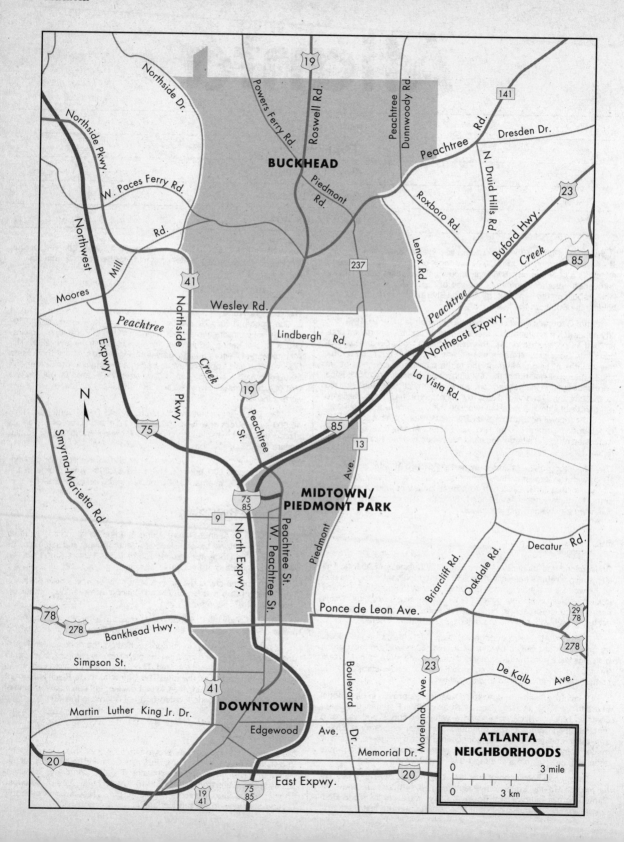

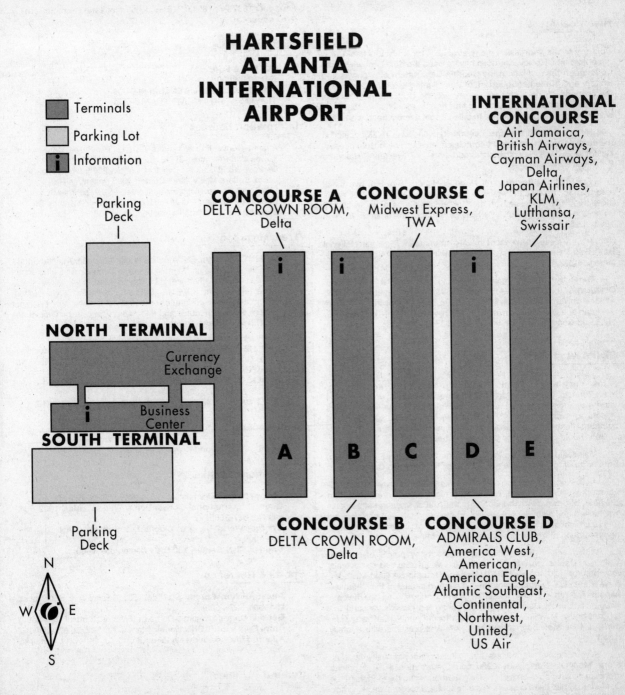

HARTSFIELD ATLANTA INTERNATIONAL AIRPORT

Terminals
Parking Lot
i Information

INTERNATIONAL CONCOURSE
Air Jamaica,
British Airways,
Cayman Airways,
Delta,
Japan Airlines,
KLM,
Lufthansa,
Swissair

Parking Deck

CONCOURSE A
DELTA CROWN ROOM,
Delta

CONCOURSE C
Midwest Express,
TWA

NORTH TERMINAL

Currency Exchange

i Business Center

SOUTH TERMINAL

A   B   C   D   E

Parking Deck

CONCOURSE B
DELTA CROWN ROOM,
Delta

CONCOURSE D
ADMIRALS CLUB,
America West,
American,
American Eagle,
Atlantic Southeast,
Continental,
Northwest,
United,
US Air

N
W   E
S

Nightclubs, jazz clubs, pubs, dancing spots, cabarets, comedy clubs and the like are scattered throughout the city. Like any metropolitan area, Atlanta is constantly changing. Consult local arts and entertainment magazines for current information.

Historical Areas

Contrary to the impression many strangers have about Atlanta, it is not an old city. However, it does have a past, the details of which can be found in the exhibits at the Georgia Department of Archives and History and at the headquarters of the Atlanta Historical Center. On the grounds of the Historical Center are the beautiful neoclassical Swan house and a restored 1840s farmhouse, as well as outbuildings where exhibits are displayed and traditional craft demonstrations are held.

Historic Roswell is a small community founded in 1830. Located in the north Atlanta metro area, it contains numerous antebellum houses, including Bulloch Hall, the childhood home of President Theodore Roosevelt's mother.

The Martin Luther King, Jr National Historic Site is a two-block area that serves as a memorial to the famed leader of the civil rights movement. The gravesite with the eternal flame is here, as are King's birthplace and the church at which he was co-pastor from 1960 to 1968.

Twenty miles northwest of the city is Kennesaw Mountain National Battlefield Park, site of a crucial encounter in General Sherman's Atlanta campaign.

The city boasts many venerable educational institutions: Oglethorpe University was founded in 1835, Emory University in 1836, Atlanta University in 1865, Morehouse in 1867, Clark in 1869, both Spelman and Morris Brown in 1881, Georgia Institute of Technology in 1885 and Georgia State University in 1913.

Sightseeing

Areas in and around Atlanta offer a wide variety of sightseeing. For many tourists, a walk through the ultramodern downtown complexes can be an interesting experience. The Cyclorama in Grant Park gives visitors a multimedia history of the Battle of Atlanta. (One word of caution: Atlanta is notorious for its rush-hour traffic congestion. Sightseeing should, therefore, be planned accordingly.)

Major shopping areas include Lenox Square and Phipps Plaza, both north of town. There is also shopping in Peachtree Center.

A six-block area known as Underground Atlanta provides a "festival marketplace" of shops, restaurants, nightclubs and attractions in the heart of downtown. Abandoned in the 1920s, when the street level was raised, the district's below-ground storefronts have been rescued and refurbished; its Victorian-era cobblestone streets are now linked to above-ground plazas, promenades and fountains.

Within one to three hours' drive are many points of interest. Visitors to Dahlonega, a boomtown in 1828 when gold was discovered, may pan for gold and visit the Dahlonega Courthouse Gold Museum. New Echota is a restoration of the last eastern capital of the Cherokee nation. The Little White House, at Warm Springs, was the favorite refuge of Franklin Delano Roosevelt during his presidency, and the modest house in which he died is open to the public. Callaway Gardens, at Pine Mountain, combines a botanical preserve with a family resort.

Several tourist attractions near Atlanta are nationally famous. Stone Mountain Park, with 3,200 acres, surrounds a huge granite monolith on which a deep relief carving memorializing the leaders of the Confederacy has been created. It is a beautiful place for picnicking and exploring nature trails. Six Flags Over Georgia, just beyond the city limits, is a 331-acre family entertainment center where Georgia's history under the flags of England, France, Spain, the Confederacy, Georgia and the United States is featured.

General References

Founded: 1837 Pop: 394,017 Elev: 1,050 feet Time zone: Eastern Area code: 404

Phone Numbers

POLICE & FIRE: 911
FBI: 679-9000
POISON CONTROL CENTER: 616-9000
TIME: 455-7141   WEATHER: 762-6151

Information Sources

Atlanta Convention & Visitors Bureau, Peachtree Center/Harris Tower, 233 Peachtree St NE, Suite 2000, 30303; 222-6688.
Georgia World Congress Visitors Center, 285 International Blvd.
Lenox Square Mall Visitors Center, 3393 Peachtree Rd.
Peachtree Center Mall Visitors Center, 231 Peachtree St.
Underground Atlanta Visitors Center, 65 Upper Alabama St.
Department of Parks & Recreation, 817-6788.

Transportation

AIRLINES: Air Jamaica; America West; American; Atlantic Southeast; British Airways; Cayman Airways; Continental; Delta; Japan Airlines; KLM (Netherlands); Lufthansa (Germany); Midwest Express; Northwest; SABENA (Belgium); Swissair; TWA; United; USAir; and other commuter and regional airlines. For the most current airline schedules and information consult the *Official Airline Guide,* published twice monthly.

AIRPORT: Hartsfield Atlanta International, 530-6600.
CAR RENTAL AGENCIES: (See Toll-Free Numbers) Avis 530-2700; Budget 530-3000; Dollar 766-0244; Hertz 530-2900; National 530-2800.
PUBLIC TRANSPORTATION: Metropolitan Atlanta Rapid Transit Authority (MARTA), 848-4711.
RAILROAD PASSENGER SERVICE: Amtrak 800/872-7245.

Newspapers

Atlanta Constitution; Atlanta Daily World; Atlanta Journal.

Convention Facilities

Atlanta Market Center, 240 Peachtree St NW, 220-3000.
Georgia International Convention & Trade Center, 1902 Sullivan Rd, 997-3566.
Georgia World Congress Center, 285 International Blvd NW, 223-4000.
Omni at CNN Center, 100 CNN Center, 659-0000.

Sports & Recreation

Atlanta-Fulton County Stadium, 521 Capitol Ave SE (Braves, baseball, 522-7630).
Georgia Dome, 1 Georgia Dome Dr (Falcons, football, 261-5400).
Omni Coliseum, 1 CNN Center (Hawks, basketball, 827-3800).
Atlanta Motor Speedway, 27 mi S on I-75, 946-4211 (auto racing).

Cultural Facilities

Theaters
Alliance Theater (Robert W. Woodruff Arts Center), 1280 Peachtree St NE, 892-2414.
Civic Center, 395 Piedmont Ave NE, 523-6275.

Onstage Atlanta, 420 Courtland St, 897-1802.
Theater of the Stars, Fox Theater, 660 Peachtree St NE, 252-8960.

Concert Halls

Center Stage Theater, W Peachtree at 17th St, 874-1511.
Civic Center, 395 Piedmont Ave NE, 523-6275.
Fox Theatre, 660 Peachtree St NE, 881-2100.
Symphony Hall, Robert W. Woodruff Arts Center, 1280 Peachtree St NE (Atlanta Symphony Orchestra, 892-2414).

Museums

Georgia State Museum of Science and Industry, State Capitol (fourth floor), 656-2844.
High Museum of Art (Robert W. Woodruff Arts Center), 1280 Peachtree St NE, 892-HIGH.
Museum of the Jimmy Carter Library, One Copenhill Ave, 331-0296.
SciTrek-the Science and Technology Museum of Atlanta, 395 Piedmont Ave NE, 522-5500.
World of Coca-Cola, Underground Atlanta, 55 Martin Luther King, Jr Dr SW, 676-5151.

Points of Interest

Historical

Atlanta Heritage Row, Underground Atlanta, 55 Upper Alabama St, 584-7879.
Atlanta History Center: Swan House & Tullie Smith House, 130 W Pacesferry Rd NW, 814-4000.
Fort McPherson, main gate on Lee St, US 29, about 3 mi SW via I-75 & Lakewood Frwy, 752-2204.
Kennesaw Mt Natl Battlefield Park, 25 mi NW off US 41, 427-4686.
Little White House, approx 70 mi SW in Warm Springs, 706/655-5870.
Martin Luther King, Jr National Historic Site, Auburn Ave NE, 524-1956.
New Echota Historic Site, approx 60 mi NW on I-75 near Calhoun, 706/629-8151.
State Capitol, Capitol Sq, 656-2844.
Stone Mountain Park, 19 mi E on US 78, 498-5600.
Wren's Nest, 1050 Ralph D. Abernathy Blvd SW, 753-8535.

Other Attractions

Atlanta State Farmers' Market, 10 mi S on I-75 in Forest Park, 366-6910.
Atlanta Zoo, Grant Park, Cherokee Ave SE, 624-5600.
Callaway Gardens, approx 65 mi SW on US 27 in Pine Mountain, 706/663-2281 or 800/282-8181.
Chastain Memorial Park, between Powers Ferry Rd & Lake Forest Dr, 252-2027 or 526-1042.
Fernbank Science Center, 156 Heaton Park Dr NE, 378-4311.
Lake Lanier Islands, 35 mi NE off I-85, 932-7200.
Piedmont Park, Piedmont Ave at 14th St NE, 658-6016.
Six Flags Over Georgia, 12 mi W via I-20, 948-9290.
Underground Atlanta, bounded by Wall, Central, Peachtree Sts and Martin Luther King Jr Dr, 523-2311.

Sightseeing Tours

Atlanta Preservation Center, (Feb-Nov) 156 7th St NE, Suite 3, 30308; 876-2040.
Gray Line bus tours, 370 Leef Mill Rd, 30050; 767-0594.

Annual Events

Atlanta Steeplechase, Seven Branches Farm in Cumming, 237-7436. 1st Sat Apr.
Atlanta Dogwood Festival, 952-9151. Early-mid-Apr.
Georgia Renaissance Festival. 8 wkends late Apr-mid-June.
BellSouth Golf Classic, Atlanta Country Club, Atlanta Country Club Dr, Marietta, 951-8777. Early May.

City Neighborhoods

Many of the restaurants, unrated dining establishments and some lodgings listed under Atlanta include neighborhoods as well as exact street addresses. A map showing these neighborhoods can be found immediately following the city introduction. Geographic descriptions of these areas are given, followed by a table of restaurants arranged by neighborhood.

Buckhead: South of the northern city limits, west of Lenox and Peachtree Rds, north of Wesley Rd and east of Northside Dr.
Downtown: South of North Ave, west of I-75/85, north of I-20 and east of Northside Dr. **North of Downtown:** North of North Ave.
East of Downtown: East of I-75/I-85.
Midtown/Piedmont Park: South of I-85, west of Piedmont Park, north of North Ave and east of I-75/85.

Lodgings and Food

ATLANTA RESTAURANTS BY NEIGHBORHOOD AREAS

(For full description, see alphabetical listings under Restaurants)

DOWNTOWN

City Grill. 50 Hurt Plaza

Dailey's. 17 International Blvd

Fisherman's Cove. 201 Courtland St

Hsu's Gourmet Chinese. 192 Peachtree Center Ave

Lombardi's. 94 Upper Pryor St

Mick's Underground. 75 Upper Alabama St

Morton's Of Chicago. 245 Peachtree Center Ave

Nikolai's Roof (Hilton & Towers Hotel). 255 Courtland St NE

Pittypat's Porch. 25 International Blvd

The Restaurant (The Ritz-Carlton). 181 Peachtree St NE

NORTH OF DOWNTOWN

Cafe Chanterelle. 4200 Paces Ferry Rd NE

Capri. 5785 Roswell Rd NE

La Paz. 6410 Roswell Rd

Old Vinings Inn. 3011 Paces Mill Rd

Patio By The River. 4199 Paces Ferry Rd NW

Piccadilly Cafeteria. 5647 Peachtree Industrial Blvd

Ray's On The River. 6700 Powers Ferry Rd

Ruth's Chris Steak House. 5788 Roswell Rd

Winfield's. 1 Galleria Pkwy

EAST OF DOWNTOWN

Harry & Sons. 820 N Highland Ave

MIDTOWN/PIEDMONT PARK

The Abbey. 163 Ponce de Leon Ave NE

Ciboulette. 1529 Piedmont Ave

Country Place. 1197 Peachtree St NE

The Mansion. 179 Ponce de Leon Ave

Mary Mac's Tearoom. 224 Ponce de Leon Ave

Peggy's Cafe. 1821 Piedmont

Royal Bagel. 1544 Piedmont NE

Taste Of New Orleans. 889 W Peachtree St NE

Varsity. 61 North Ave

Veni Vidi Vici. 41 14th St

Note: *When a listing is located in a town that does not have its own city heading, it will appear under the city nearest to its location. In these cases, the address and town appear in parenthesis immediately following the name of the establishment.*

Motels

✔★ **BEST WESTERN BRADBURY SUITES.** *4500 Circle 75 Pkwy (30339), I-75 exit 110, north of downtown. 404/956-9919; FAX 404/955-3270.* 242 rms in 2 bldgs, 3-5 story. S, D $39.95-$74.95; each addl $5; suites $69.95-$74.95; under 12 free; wkly, wkend rates. Crib $10. TV; cable. Pool; whirlpool. Complimentary full bkfst buffet. Restaurant nearby. Ck-out noon. Coin lndry. Meeting rms. Health club privileges. Some refrigerators. Theme suites. Cr cds: A, C, D, DS, ER, JCB, MC, V.

D ➤ ≈ ✕ 🐾 🔥 SC

✔★ **COMFORT INN-FOREST PARK.** *3701 Jonesboro Rd SE (30354), south of downtown. 404/361-1111; FAX 404/366-0294.* 73 rms, 2 story. S $40-$60; D $45-$65; each addl $5; suites $65-$75; under 18 free. Crib $5. TV; cable. Pool. Complimentary continental bkfst, coffee. Restaurant nearby. Ck-out 11 am. Coin lndry. Meeting rms. Valet serv. Sundries. Cr cds: A, C, D, DS, ER, JCB, MC, V.

D ➤ ≈ ✕ 🐾 SC

★★★ **COURTYARD BY MARRIOTT-NORTHLAKE.** *4083 La Vista Rd (30084), adj to Northlake Festival Mall, east of downtown. 404/938-1200; FAX 404/934-6497.* 128 units, 20 suites, 2 story. S $74-$84; D $84-$89; suites $79-$89; under 18 free; wkly, wkend rates. Crib free. TV; cable. Heated pool. Complimentary coffee in rms. Restaurant 6:30-10 am; Sat, Sun from 7 am-noon. Bar 4-11 pm. Ck-out noon. Coin lndry. Meeting rms. Valet serv. Airport transportation. Exercise equipt; weights, bicycles, whirlpool. Some refrigerators. Private patios, balconies. Picnic tables. Cr cds: A, C, D, DS, MC, V.

D ≈ ✕ 🐾 SC

★★ **EMORY INN.** *1641 Clifton Rd NE (30329), north of downtown. 404/712-6700; res: 800/933-6679; FAX 404/712-6701.* 107 rms, 2 story. S $87-$97; D $97-$107; under 12 free. Crib free. TV; cable. Pool; poolside serv. Restaurant 7 am-2 pm, 5-10 pm; Sat 7-10 am, 5-10 pm. Ck-out noon. Meeting rms. Bellhops. Valet serv. Airport, RR station transportation avail. Exercise equipt; weight machine, stair machine, whirlpool. Antiques. Library/sitting rm. Cr cds: A, C, D, DS, ER, MC, V.

D ≈ ✕ 🐾 SC

★★ **EXECUTIVE VILLAS HOTEL.** *5735 Roswell Rd NE (30342), at I-285 Roswell Rd exit 17, north of downtown. 404/252-2868; res: 800/241-1013.* 130 kit. suites, 1-3 stories. 1-bedrm $99; 2-bedrm $129; 3-bedrm $159; wkend plans; wkly & monthly rates. Crib free. Pet accepted, some restrictions; $150. TV; cable. Pool. Complimentary continental bkfst. Restaurant nearby. Ck-out 11 am. Coin lndry. Meeting rms. Valet serv. Health club privileges. Private patios, balconies. Picnic tables, grills. Cr cds: A, C, D, DS, MC, V.

D 🐾 ≈ ✕ 🔥 SC

★★ **HAWTHORN SUITES-ATLANTA NORTHWEST.** *1500 Parkwood Circle (30339), I-75 exit 110, north of downtown. 404/952-9595; FAX 404/984-2335.* 200 kit. suites, 2-3 story. Suites $105-$145; each addl $10; under 18 free; wkend, monthly rates. Crib free. TV; cable. Heated pool. Complimentary continental bkfst. Restaurant nearby. Ck-out noon. Coin lndry. Meeting rms. Valet serv. Lighted tennis. Exercise equipt; weights, bicycles, whirlpool. Refrigerators. Private patios, balconies. Picnic tables, grills. Elaborate landscaping, flowers. Cr cds: A, C, D, DS, MC, V.

D 🐾 ≈ ✕ 🔥 SC

✔★ **RED ROOF INN-DRUID HILLS.** *1960 N Druid Hills Rd (30329), I-85 exit 31, north of downtown. 404/321-1653; FAX 404/321-1653, ext. 444.* 115 rms, 3 story. S $37-$46; D $46.99-$51.99; each addl $6; under 18 free. Crib free. Pet accepted, some restrictions. TV; cable. Restaurant nearby. Ck-out noon. Cr cds: A, C, D, DS, MC, V.

D 🐾 🔥

★★ **RESIDENCE INN BY MARRIOTT-DUNWOODY.** *1901 Savoy Dr (30341), I-285 at Chamblee-Dunwoody exit, north of downtown. 404/455-4446; FAX 404/451-5183.* 144 kit. suites, 2 story. S, D $79-$99; wkend rates. Crib free. Pet accepted; $35. TV; cable. Heated pool; whirlpool, hot tubs. Complimentary continental bkfst. Ck-out noon. Coin lndry. Meeting rms. Valet serv. Health club privileges. Many fireplaces. Private patios, balconies. Picnic tables, grills. Cr cds: A, C, D, DS, MC, V.

D ⛵ ≈ ⊠ 🔥 SC

★ ★ ★ **STONE MOUNTAIN INN.** *(Box 775, Stone Mountain 30086) 16 mi E on US 78, Stone Mountain Park exit. In Stone Mountain Park.* 404/469-3311; res: 800/277-0007; FAX 404/498-5691. 92 rms, 2 story. $5 parking fee (required to reach motel). April 1-early Sept: S $65-$89; D $75-$99; under 12 free; lower rates rest of yr. Crib free. TV; cable. Pool. Restaurant 7 am-9 pm (hrs vary off-season). Ck-out 11 am. Coin lndry. Meeting rms. Bellhops. Gift shop. Lighted tennis. 36-hole golf, pro. Balconies; private patios for poolside rms. Cr cds: A, D, DS, MC, V.

⛵ 🎿 🏊 ≈ 🏃 🎿 ⊠ 🔥 SC

★ ★ **SUMMERFIELD SUITES.** *760 Mt Vernon Hwy (30328), north of downtown.* 404/250-0110; res: 800/833-4353; FAX 404/250-9335. 122 kit. suites, 2-3 story. 1-bedrm $119; 2-bedrm $159; family, wkly, wkend rates. Crib free. TV; cable, in-rm movies. Heated pool. Complimentary continental bkfst. Complimentary coffee in rms. Ck-out noon. Coin lndry. Meeting rms. Sundries. Airport, MARTA transportation. Exercise equipt; weights, bicycles, whirlpool. Health club privileges. Picnic tables, grills. Cr cds: A, C, D, DS, JCB, MC, V.

D ≈ 🏃 ⊠ 🔥 SC

★ **TRAVELODGE-DOWNTOWN.** *311 Courtland St NE (30303), downtown.* 404/659-4545; FAX 404/659-5934. 71 rms, 3 story. S $70-$84; D $78-$84; each addl $8; under 18 free; wkend rates. Crib free. TV; cable, in-rm movies avail. Pool. Coffee in rms. Restaurant adj open 24 hrs. Ck-out noon. Valet serv. Health club privileges. Some balconies. Cr cds: A, C, D, DS, ER, JCB, MC, V.

D ≈ ⊠ 🔥 SC

Motor Hotels

★ ★ **COURTYARD BY MARRIOTT-CUMBERLAND.** *3000 Cumberland Circle (30339), I-285 Cobb Pkwy exit, north of downtown.* 404/952-2555; FAX 404/952-2409. 182 rms, 8 story. S $79; D $89; under 12 free; wkly rates. Crib free. TV; cable, in-rm movies avail. Indoor pool. Complimentary coffee in rms. Restaurant 6:30 am-2 pm, 5-10 pm; wkends 7 am-noon. Bar 4-11 pm. Ck-out noon. Meeting rms. Bellhops. Valet serv. Sundries. Exercise rm; instructor, weights, bicycles, whirlpool, sauna. Some refrigerators, wet bars. Balconies. Cr cds: A, C, D, DS, MC, V.

D ≈ 🏃 ⊠ 🔥 SC

✔ ★ ★ **QUALITY INN-NORTHEAST.** *2960 NE Expressway (I-85) (30341), at Shallowford Rd, north of downtown.* 404/451-5231; FAX 404/454-8704. 157 rms, 2 story. S, D $36-$49; family, wkly rates. Crib free. TV; cable. Pool; poolside serv. Continental bkfst 7-10 am. Ck-out noon. Coin lndry. Meeting rms. Bellhops. Cr cds: A, C, D, DS, MC, V.

D ≈ ⊠ 🔥 SC

✔ ★ ★ **RAMADA INN-SIX FLAGS.** *4225 Fulton Industrial Blvd (30336), I-20W exit 14, west of downtown.* 404/691-4100; FAX 404/261-2117. 229 rms, 4-5 story. Apr-mid-Sept: S, D $58-$78; each addl $10; lower rates rest of yr. Crib free. TV; cable. Pool. Restaurant open 24 hrs. Rm serv. Bar 3 pm-1:30 am; entertainment, dancing Thurs-Sat. Ck-out 11 am. Coin lndry. Meeting rms. Valet serv. Game rm. Grill. Cr cds: A, D, DS, MC, V.

D ≈ ⊠ 🔥 SC

★ ★ ★ **WYNDHAM GARDEN.** *2857 Paces Ferry Rd (30339), I-285 exit 12, north of downtown.* 404/432-5555; FAX 404/436-5558. 159 rms, 4 story. S, D $109-$119; suites $119-$129; under 18 free; wkend rates. Crib free. TV; cable. Heated pool; whirlpool, poolside serv. Restaurant 6:30 am-2:30 pm, 5-10 pm. Rm serv from 5 pm. Bar 11:30 am-midnight. Ck-out noon. Meeting rms. Valet serv. Tennis privi-

leges. Health club privileges. Private patios, balconies. Cr cds: A, C, D, DS, ER, JCB, MC, V.

D 🎿 ≈ ⊠ 🔥 SC

Hotels

★ ★ **BILTMORE INN.** *30 5th St NE (30308), at W Peachtree St, in Midtown/Piedmont Park.* 404/874-0824; res: 800/822-0824; FAX 404/458-5384. 60 kit. suites, 10 story. Kit. suites $95-$225; monthly rates. Crib free. Covered parking $5. TV; cable. Complimentary continental bkfst. Restaurant nearby. Ck-out noon. Airport transportation avail. Health club privileges. Wet bars, in-rm whirlpools. Some balconies. Built 1924; Georgian design with vaulted ceilings, skylights, and limestone detailing. Cr cds: A, C, D, DS, MC, V.

⊠ 🔥

★ ★ **COMFORT INN-DOWNTOWN.** *101 International Blvd (30303), downtown.* 404/524-5555; FAX 404/221-0702. 260 rms, 11 story. S $59-$199; D $59-$209; each addl $10; under 12 free; wkend rates. Crib free. Garage in/out $6. TV; cable. Pool; whirlpool. Restaurant 6:30-10:30 am, 11:30 am-1:30 pm, 5:30-10 pm. Bar 4 pm-12:30 am. Ck-out noon. Meeting rms. Gift shop. Health club privileges. Adj to Atlanta Market Center and World Congress Center. Cr cds: A, C, D, DS, ER, JCB, MC, V.

D ≈ ⊠ 🔥 SC

★ ★ **DAYS INN-DOWNTOWN.** *300 Spring St (30308), downtown.* 404/523-1144; FAX 404/577-8495. 262 rms, 10 story. S $59-$119; D $69-$129; each addl $10; suites $175; under 18 free. Crib free. Garage $5/day. TV. Pool. Restaurant 6:30 am-10 pm. Bar 5 pm-midnight. Ck-out 11 am. Meeting rms. Gift shop. Airport, RR station, bus depot transportation $8-$15. Some refrigerators. Balconies. Cr cds: A, C, D, DS, ER, MC, V.

D ≈ ⊠ 🔥 SC

★ ★ ★ **DOUBLETREE.** *7 Concourse Pkwy (30328), north of downtown.* 404/395-3900; FAX 404/395-3935. 370 rms, 20 story. S $119-$139; D $129-$149; each addl $15; suites $250-$850; under 17 free; wkend rates. Crib free. TV; cable. Heated pool; whirlpool, sauna, poolside serv. Restaurants 6:30 am-11 pm. Rm serv 24 hrs. Bar 4:30 pm-1 am, Sun to 12:30 am; entertainment. Ck-out noon. Convention facilities. Free covered parking; valet. Tennis privileges. 18-hole golf privileges, greens fee, pro. Some refrigerators. **LUXURY LEVEL : CONCIERGE LEVEL.** 40 rms, 2 floors. S, D $149-$169. Concierge. Private lounge, honor bar. Complimentary continental bkfst, refreshments, newspaper. Cr cds: A, C, D, DS, ER, JCB, MC, V.

D 🎿 🏃 ≈ 🏃 ⊠ 🔥 SC

★ ★ ★ **EMBASSY SUITES-GALLERIA.** *2815 Akers Mill Rd (30339), north of downtown.* 404/984-9300; FAX 404/955-4183. 261 suites, 9 story. S $99-$139 D $109-$149; each addl $10; under 18 free; wkend rates. Crib free. TV; cable. Indoor pool; whirlpool, sauna. Complimentary full bkfst. Restaurant 11 am-11 pm. Bar to 1 am. Ck-out noon. Meeting rms. Gift shop. Airport transportation avail. Health club privileges. Game rm. Refrigerators. Garden atrium, glass elvtrs. Cr cds: A, C, D, DS, MC, V.

D ≈ ⊠ 🔥 SC

★ ★ ★ **FRENCH QUARTER SUITES.** *2780 Whitley Rd (30339), I-285 Cobb Pkwy exit, north of downtown.* 404/980-1900; res: 800/843-5858; FAX 404/980-1528. 155 suites, 8 story. Suites $99-$119; under 12 free; wkly, wkend rates. Crib free. TV; cable. Pool. Complimentary full bkfst. Complimentary coffee in rms. Restaurant 5 am-11 pm. Rm serv 24 hrs. Bar 11-1 am, Sun to 12:30 am; entertainment, dancing Fri-Sat. Ck-out noon. Meeting rms. Exercise equipt; weights, bicycles, sauna. Health club privileges. Bathrm phones, in-rm whirlpools; some refrigerators. Some private patios, balconies. Cr cds: A, C, D, DS, ER, JCB, MC, V.

D ≈ 🏃 ⊠ 🔥 SC

★ ★ ★ **GUEST QUARTERS SUITE HOTEL-ATLANTA PERI-METER.** *6120 Peachtree-Dunwoody Rd (30328), north of downtown.* 404/668-0808; FAX 404/668-0008. 224 suites, 6 story. Suites $99-$149; under 18 free; wkend rates. Crib free. TV; cable. Indoor/outdoor pool. Restaurant 6:30-10 am, 11 am-10:30 pm. Bar 11:30-2 am. Ck-out noon. Coin lndry. Meeting rms. Airport transportation. Exercise equipt; weight machine, bicycles, whirlpool, sauna. Health club privileges. Refrigerators. Cr cds: A, C, D, DS, ER, JCB, MC, V.

D ≈ ✗ ⊠ 🔥 SC

★ ★ ★ **HILTON & TOWERS.** *255 Courtland St NE (30303), at Harris St, downtown.* 404/659-2000; FAX 404/222-2868. 1,224 rms, 29 story. S $135-$200; D $155-$220; each addl $20; suites from $350; family, wkend rates. Crib free. Valet parking, in/out $9, garage avail. TV; cable. Pool; poolside serv. Restaurant open 24 hrs; dining rm (see NIKOLAI'S ROOF). Bars 11:30-2 am, Sun 12:30 pm-midnight; entertainment, dancing. Ck-out 11 am. Convention facilities. Shopping arcade. Airport transportation. Lighted tennis, pro. Exercise rm; instructor, weights, bicycles, whirlpool, sauna. Some bathrm phones. Balconies on 4th floor. Built around 5-story atrium; glass-enclosed elvtrs. *LUXURY LEVEL : THE TOWERS.* 113 rms, 17 suites, 3 floors. S $215; D $235; suites from $350. Concierge. Private lounge, honor bar. Complimentary continental bkfst, refreshments, newspaper. Cr cds: A, C, D, DS, ER, JCB, MC, V.

D 🏋 ≈ ✗ ⛷ ⊠ 🔥 SC

★ ★ ★ **HOLIDAY INN.** *(1075 Holcomb Bridge Rd, Roswell 30076) N on GA 400 to exit 7B, then NW on Holcomb Bridge Rd.* 404/992-9600; FAX 404/993-6539. 174 rms, 7 story. S $94-$104; D $104-$114; each addl $10; suites $158-$237; under 18 free; wkend rates. Crib free. TV; cable. Pool. Complimentary coffee in lobby. Restaurant 6:30 am-10:30 pm. Bar 4:30 pm-2 am. Ck-out noon. Meeting rms. Gift shop. Airport, RR station, bus depot transportation avail. Health club privileges. Refrigerators avail. Cr cds: A, C, D, DS, JCB, MC, V.

D ≈ ⊠ 🔥 SC

★ ★ ★ **HOLIDAY INN-CROWNE PLAZA.** *4355 Ashford-Dunwoody Rd (30346), 1 blk N I-285 exit 21, north of downtown.* 404/395-7700; FAX 404/392-9503. 495 rms, 15 story, 29 suites. S $160-$180; D $170-$190; each addl $10; suites $225-$950; under 18 free; wkend rates. Crib free. Valet parking $7. TV; cable. Indoor pool. Restaurants 6 am-10:30 pm. Rm serv to 1:30 am. Bar; entertainment exc Sun. Ck-out noon. Convention facilities. Concierge. Gift shop. Free covered parking. Airport transportation. Lighted tennis. Exercise equipt; weights, bicycles, whirlpool, sauna. Refrigerator in suites. 3-story greenhouse atrium with waterfalls. On 42 acres, 10 wooded. Adj Perimeter Mall. *LUXURY LEVEL : CROWNE PLAZA CLUB.* 25 rms, 3 suites, 1 floor. S $180; D $190; suites $225-$950. Private lounge, honor bar. Minibars. Bathrm phones. Complimentary continental bkfst, refreshments, newspaper. Cr cds: A, C, D, DS, JCB, MC, V.

D 🏋 ≈ ✗ ⛷ ⊠ 🔥 SC

★ ★ ★ **HYATT REGENCY ATLANTA.** *265 Peachtree St NE (30303), in Peachtree Center, downtown.* 404/577-1234; FAX 404/588-4137. 1,279 rms, 23 story. S $205; D $230; each addl $25; suites $360-$725; under 18 free; wkend plans. Crib free. Garage, in/out $13. TV; cable, in-rm movies avail. Pool; poolside serv. Restaurant 6-1 am. Bar from 11 am. Ck-out noon. Convention facilities. Concierge. Gift shop. Airport transportation. Exercise equipt; weights, bicycles, whirlpool, sauna, steam rm. Minibars. Refrigerator in suites. Many balconies. Built around 23-story atrium lobby; glass-enclosed elvtr. Revolving Polaris dining rm & bar atop roof; panoramic view of city. *LUXURY LEVEL : REGENCY CLUB.* 30 rms, 3 suites. S $240 D $265; suites $425-$700. Private lounge. Bathrm phone in suites. Complimentary continental bkfst, refreshments. Cr cds: A, C, D, DS, ER, JCB, MC, V.

D ≈ ✗ ⊠ 🔥 SC

★ ★ ★ **HYATT REGENCY SUITES-PERIMETER NORTH-WEST.** *2999 Windy Hill Rd NE (30067), I-75N to Windy Hill exit, north of downtown.* 404/956-1234; FAX 404/956-9479. 200 suites, 7 story. S $69-$126; D $69-$151; under 18 free; wkend rates. Crib free. TV (3 per unit); cable. Heated pool. Complimentary coffee in rms. Restaurant 6:30 am-11 pm. Bar 11:30 am-midnight. Ck-out noon. Meeting rms. Tennis privileges. Exercise equipt; weights, bicycles, whirlpool, sauna. Health club privileges. Refrigerators. Atop hill with view of downtown Atlanta. Cr cds: A, C, D, DS, ER, JCB, MC, V.

D 🏋 ≈ ✗ ⊠ 🔥 SC

★ **INN AT THE PEACHTREES.** *330 W Peachtree St NW (30308), downtown.* 404/577-6970; res: 800/242-4642; FAX 404/659-3244. 101 rms, 4 story. S $120; D $135; each addl $10; under 12 free. TV; cable. Ck-out 11 am. Meeting rm. Covered parking. Airport transportation. Health club privileges. Near Merchandise Mart & Apparel Mart. Cr cds: A, C, D, DS, JCB, MC, V.

⊠ 🔥 SC

★ ★ ★ **THE MARQUE OF ATLANTA.** *111 Perimeter Center West (30346), north of downtown.* 404/396-6800; res: 800/683-6100; FAX 404/399-5514. 276 rms, 12 story, 156 kit. suites. S $115; D $139; each addl $10; kit. suites $119; under 12 free; wkend rates. Crib free. TV; cable. Pool; poolside serv. Complimentary continental bkfst. Restaurant 6-10 am, noon-2 pm, 6-10 pm. Rm serv 6 am-midnight. Bar. Ck-out noon. Coin lndry. Meeting rms. Concierge. Airport transportation. Exercise equipt; weight machine, bicycles, whirlpool, sauna. Balconies. Situated in park-like setting. Cr cds: A, C, D, DS, MC, V.

D ≈ ✗ ⊠ 🔥 SC

★ ★ ★ **MARRIOTT MARQUIS.** *265 Peachtree Center Ave (30303), downtown.* 404/521-0000; FAX 404/586-6299. 1,674 rms, 50 story. S, D $200; each addl $20; suites from $350; under 18 free; wkend, honeymoon rates. Crib free. Garage $12 in/out. TV; cable. Indoor/outdoor pool; lifeguard, poolside serv. 5 restaurants. Rm serv 24 hrs. Bar 11-1 am, Sun from 12:30 pm; entertainment. Ck-out noon. Convention facilities. Shopping arcade. Barber, beauty shop. Exercise equipt; weight machines, bicycles, whirlpool, sauna. Game rm. Rec rm. Some refrigerators. Bathrm phone in suites. *LUXURY LEVEL : CONCIERGE LEVEL.* 80 rms, 10 suites, 2 floors. S, D $225; suites $450-$950. Private lounge, honor bar. Complimentary continental bkfst, refreshments. Cr cds: A, C, D, DS, ER, JCB, MC, V.

D ≈ ✗ ⊠ 🔥 SC

★ ★ ★ ★ **OCCIDENTAL GRAND HOTEL.** *75 Fourteenth St (30309), Grand Bldg, in Midtown/Piedmont Park.* 404/881-9898; res: 800/952-0702; FAX 404/873-4692. 246 rms, 19 story, 18 suites. S, D $147-$265; each addl $25; suites $395-$1,500; under 16 free; wkend rates. Crib free. Pet accepted, some restrictions; deposit required. Garage parking, valet $12.50. TV; cable. Indoor pool; poolside serv. Restaurant 6 am-11 pm. Rm serv 24 hrs. Bar 11:30-1 am; entertainment. Ck-out noon. Convention facilities. Concierge. Sundries. Barber, beauty shop. Airport, RR station transportation. Exercise rm; instructor, weight machine, bicycles, whirlpool, sauna, steam rm. Masseuse. Spa/health club. Refrigerators, minibars. Complimentary newspaper. Occupies first 20 floors of the Grand Bldg. Three-story grand entry with dramatic grand staircase. Grand ballroom on 4th floor. A 5th-floor terrace provides scenic view of skyline. Luxury hotel combines Old-World traditions with hospitality of the New South. Cr cds: A, C, D, DS, ER, JCB, MC, V.

D 🐾 ≈ ✗ ⛷ ⊠ 🐾 SC

★ ★ ★ **OMNI HOTEL AT CNN CENTER.** *100 CNN Center (30335), downtown.* 404/659-0000; FAX 404/525-5050. 466 rms, 15 story. S $170; D $190; each addl from $20; suites $250-$1,200; under 18 free; wkend rates. Crib free. Garage $12-$15 in/out. TV; cable. Restaurant 7 am-11 pm. Rm serv 6-2 am. Bars 11-1 am; entertainment Tues-Sat. Ck-out noon. Convention facilities. Concierge. Shopping arcade. Barber, beauty shop. Valet parking. Airport, RR station, bus depot transportation. Health club privileges. Minibars. Bathrm phone, wet bar. Balconies. Omni Sports Coliseum, Georgia World Congress Center adj. Underground Atlanta nearby. Cr cds: A, C, D, DS, ER, JCB, MC, V.

D 🏃 ⊠ 🐾 SC

★ ★ **RADISSON HOTEL.** *165 Courtland St (30303), downtown.* 404/659-6500; FAX 404/524-1259. 754 rms, 12 story. S $109-$119; D $129-$145; each addl $10; suites $189-$650; under 18 free; wkend rates. Crib free. Pet accepted, some restrictions; $25 refundable. Covered parking $8.75. TV; cable. Indoor/outdoor pool; poolside serv. Restaurant 6:30 am-11 pm. Bar 11-2 am, Sun to 12:30 am; entertainment Fri-Sat, dancing. Ck-out noon. Convention facilities. Concierge. Shopping arcade. Barber, beauty shop. Exercise equipt; weights, bicycles, whirlpool, sauna. Health club privileges. Game rm. Some bathrm phones. Some private patios, some balconies. Cr cds: A, C, D, DS, ER, JCB, MC, V.

D ⚹ ≋ 🏃 ⤢ 🔥 SC

★ ★ **REGENCY SUITES.** *975 W Peachtree St NE (30309), at 10th St, in Midtown/Piedmont Park.* 404/876-5003; res: 800/642-3629. 96 kit. suites, 9 story. Suites $89-$244; under 18 free; wkend, monthly rates. Crib free. Garage, covered parking ($6). TV; cable. Complimentary continental bkfst, coffee. Ck-out 11 am. Coin lndry. Meeting rms. Exercise equipt; weight machines, bicycles. Adj to MARTA station. Cr cds: A, C, D, DS, MC, V.

D 🏃 ⤢ 🔥 SC

★ ★ ★ **RENAISSANCE.** *590 W Peachtree St NW (30308), at North Ave, in Midtown/Piedmont Park.* 404/881-6000; res: 800/633-0000; FAX 404/815-5010. 504 rms, 25 story, 24 suites. S $140-$160; D $155-$175; suites $265-$640; under 12 free; wkend rates. Crib free. Garage parking; valet $9, in/out $7.50. TV; cable. Pool; poolside serv. Restaurant 6:30-1 am. Bar 11-1 am; entertainment. Ck-out noon. Meeting rms. Concierge. Gift shop. Airport, RR station, bus depot transportation. Exercise equipt; weights, bicycles. Health club privileges. Bathrm phones, minibars; some refrigerators, wet bars. Balconies. Luxurious rms; European-style personal service. *LUXURY LEVEL :* **EXECUTIVE LEVEL.** 48 rms, 2 floors. S $185; D $200; each addl $15; 2-bedrm suite $640. Concierge. Private lounge. Complimentary continental bkfst, refreshments, newspapers. Cr cds: A, C, D, DS, ER, JCB, MC, V.

D ≋ 🏃 ⤢ 🔥 SC

★ ★ ★ ★ **THE RITZ-CARLTON.** *181 Peachtree St NE (30303), downtown.* 404/659-0400; FAX 404/688-0400. 447 rms, 25 story. S, D $159-$219; suites $450-$785; under 12 free; wkend, hol rates. Crib free. Valet parking $12.50, in/out $8. TV; cable. Restaurant (see THE RESTAURANT). Rm serv 24 hrs. Bar 11:30-2 am; entertainment. Ck-out noon. Convention facilities. Concierge. Gift shop. Airport, RR station transportation. Lighted tennis privileges. 18-hole golf privileges; greens fee $42. Exercise equipt; weight machine, treadmill, steam rm. Massage therapy. Health club privileges. Refrigerators, minibars. *LUXURY LEVEL :* **CLUB LEVEL.** 37 rms, 2 floors, 2 suites. S, D $249; suites $850 & $950. Concierge. Private lounge, honor bar. Complimentary continental bkfst. Complimentary refreshments. Cr cds: A, C, D, DS, ER, JCB, MC, V.

D ⚹ 🏃 ⤢ 🔥 SC

★ ★ ★ **SHERATON CENTURY CENTER.** *2000 Century Blvd NE (30345), in Century Center Park, north of downtown.* 404/325-0000; FAX 404/325-4920. 283 rms, 15 story. S $79-$109; D $89-$119; each addl $10; suites from $200; under 18 free; wkend rates. Crib free. TV; cable, in-rm movies avail. Heated pool; poolside serv. Restaurant 6:30 am-2 pm, 5-10 pm. Bar noon-midnight. Ck-out 1 pm. Convention facilities. Gift shop. Barber. Lighted tennis. Exercise equipt; weights, bicycles. Some refrigerators. Cr cds: A, C, D, DS, ER, JCB, MC, V.

D 🏃 ≋ 🏃 ⤢ 🔥 SC

★ ★ ★ **SHERATON COLONY SQUARE.** *188 14th St NE (30361), in Midtown/Piedmont Park.* 404/892-6000; FAX 404/872-9192. 461 rms, 27 story. S, D $149; suites $350-$800; under 18 free; wkend, summer hol plans. Crib free. Valet parking $10 in/out. TV; cable. Pool; poolside serv. Restaurant 6:30-1 am. 2 bars 11-2 am, Sun to midnight. Ck-out noon. Convention facilities. Concierge. Shopping arcade. Airport transportation. Tennis & golf privileges. Exercise equipt; weight machine, bicycles. *LUXURY LEVEL :* **COLONY CLUB.** 44 rms, 2 story.

S, D $159. Private lounge. Complimentary continental bkfst, refreshments, newspaper. Cr cds: A, C, D, DS, ER, JCB, MC, V.

D 🏃 ⚹ ≋ 🏃 ⤢ 🔥 SC

★ ★ ★ **SHERATON SUITES-CUMBERLAND.** *2844 Cobb Pkwy SE (30339), north of downtown.* 404/955-3900; FAX 404/916-3165. 278 suites, 17 story. Suites $99-$159; each addl $15; under 18 free; wkend rates. Crib free. TV; cable, in rm movies. 2 pools, 1 indoor; poolside serv. Complimentary full bkfst. Complimentary coffee in rms. Restaurant 6:30 am-10:30 pm. Bar 11 am-midnight. Ck-out noon. Coin lndry. Convention facilities. Gift shop. Free garage parking. Airport, RR station transportation avail. Exercise equipt; weights, bicycles, whirlpool, sauna. Refrigerators. Minibars. Cr cds: A, C, D, DS, ER, MC, V.

D ≋ 🏃 ⤢ 🔥 SC

★ ★ ★ **STOUFFER WAVERLY.** *2450 Galleria Pkwy (30339), north of downtown.* 404/953-4500; FAX 404/953-0740. 521 rms, 14 story, 24 suites, 12 conference parlors. S $159-$179; D $179-$199; each addl $20; suites $325-$425; under 18 free; wkend rates. Crib free. TV; cable. 2 pools, 1 indoor. Complimentary coffee. Restaurant open 24 hrs. Rm serv 24 hrs. 3 bars 11:30-1 am. Ck-out noon. Convention facilities. Concierge. Shopping arcade. Airport transportation. Exercise equipt; weight machines, bicycles, whirlpool, sauna, steam rm. Bathrm phones; refrigerator in suites. *LUXURY LEVEL :* THE CLUB LEVEL. 36 rms, 4 suites. S $189; D $209; suites $425-$1,200. Private lounge. Minibars. Complimentary continental bkfst, refreshments, magazines. Cr cds: A, C, D, DS, ER, JCB, MC, V.

D ≋ 🏃 🏃 ⤢ 🔥 SC

★ ★ ★ **SUITE HOTEL-UNDERGROUND.** *54 Peachtree St (30303), at Underground Atlanta, downtown.* 404/223-5555; res: 800/477-5549; FAX 404/223-0467. 156 suites, 17 story. S $135-$200; D $145-$210; each addl $10; under 16 free; wkend rates. Crib free. Valet parking $12. TV; cable. Restaurant 11 am-11 pm. Ck-out noon. Meeting rms. Airport, RR station, bus depot transportation. Health club privileges. Bathrm phones, minibars. Cr cds: A, C, D, DS, ER, JCB, MC, V.

D ⤢ 🔥 SC

★ ★ ★ **THE WESTIN PEACHTREE PLAZA.** *210 Peachtree St (30303), at International Blvd, downtown.* 404/659-1400; FAX 404/589-7424. 1,068 rms, 73 story. S $165-$185; D $190-$210; each addl $25; suites $360-$1,360; under 18 free; wkend rates. Crib free. Pet accepted, some restrictions. Garage $12.50, valet, in/out $13. TV; cable. Indoor/outdoor pool; poolside serv. Restaurants 6 am-11 pm. Rm serv 24 hrs. Bars (1 revolving rooftop) 11-2 am; entertainment. Ck-out 1 pm. Convention facilities. Concierge. Shopping arcade. Airport, RR station, bus depot transportation. Exercise equipt; weights, bicycles, sauna. Many bathrm phones; some refrigerators. 73-story circular tower built around 8-story atrium. *LUXURY LEVEL :* EXECUTIVE CLUB. 88 rms, 6 suites, 5 floors. S $210; D $235; suites $675. Private lounge, honor bar. Minibar in suites. Bathrm phones. Complimentary continental bkfst, refreshments, newspaper, shoeshine. Cr cds: A, C, D, DS, ER, JCB, MC, V.

D ⚹ 🏃 ≋ 🏃 ⤢ 🔥

★ ★ ★ **WYNDHAM MIDTOWN.** *125 10th St (30309), at Peachtree St, in Midtown/Piedmont Park.* 404/873-4800; FAX 404/870-1530. 191 rms, 11 story, 5 suites. S $182; D $202; each addl $10; suites $250-$500; under 18 free; wkly, wkend rates. Crib free. Covered parking $7.50, in/out; valet parking $9.50. TV; cable. Indoor pool. In rm coffee avail. Restaurant 6:30 am-11 pm. Bar 4:30 pm-11 pm, Fri, Sat to 1 am. Ck-out noon. Meeting rms. Exercise rm; instructor, weight machines, whirlpool, sauna, steam rm. Many refrigerators. Cr cds: A, C, D, DS, ER, MC, V.

D ≋ 🏃 ⤢ 🔥

Inns

★ ★ **ANSLEY INN.** *253 15th St NE (30309), north of downtown.* 404/872-9000; res: 800/446-5416; FAX 404/892-2318. 15 rms, 3 story. S, D $100-$250; wkly, monthly rates. TV; cable. Complimentary continental bkfst, coffee. Restaurant nearby. Ck-out 11 am, ck-in 3 pm. Bellhops. Valet serv. Concierge. Airport transportation. Tennis privileges. Health club privileges. In-rm whirlpools. Turn-of-the-century English Tudor house; art gallery. Cr cds: A, C, D, DS, ER, MC, V.

✔★ ★ **SHELLMONT.** *821 Piedmont Ave NE (30308), in Midtown/Piedmont Park.* 404/872-9290. 4 rms, 2 story, carriage house. Some rm phones. S $65-$70; D $79-$100; each addl $20; carriage house $87-$97. Children under 12 in carriage house only. Crib free. Complimentary full bkfst. Restaurant nearby. Ck-out 11 am, ck-in 3 pm. Some patios, balconies. Restored Victorian house (1891); Tiffany windows, hardwood floors, antiques, artwork. Cr cds: A, D, MC, V.

🔥 SC

Resort

★ ★ ★ **EVERGREEN CONFERENCE CENTER.** *(1 Lakeview Dr, Stone Mountain 30086) W on US 78, in Stone Mountain State Park.* 404/879-9900; res: 800/722-1000; FAX 404/464-9013. 238 rms, 5 story. $5 park entrance fee (required to reach resort). Apr-Sept: S $120; D $140; each addl $20; suites $200-$300; family, wkend, wkly & hol rates; AP, MAP avail; golf plans; wkends; higher rates Super Bowl wkend; lower rates rest of yr. Crib free. TV; cable. 2 pools, 1 indoor; wading pool, poolside serv, lifeguard. Restaurant 6 am-11:30 pm. Box lunches. Snacks. Picnics. Rm serv 24 hrs. Bar; entertainment, dancing (in season). Ck-out noon, ck-in 4 pm. Gift shop. Grocery, coin lndry 1 mi. Bellhops. Concierge. Valet serv. Sports dir. Lighted tennis. 36-hole golf, pro, putting green, driving range, greens fee $38. Swimming beach; boats. Horse stables on premises. Hiking. Bicycles (rentals). Social dir. Game rm. Exercise rm; instructor, weight machine, bicycles, whirlpool. Masseuse. Refrigerators. Many balconies. Picnic tables. Situated on lake within Stone Mountain State Park. Cr cds: A, C, D, DS, ER, MC, V.

Restaurants

★ ★ ★ **THE ABBEY.** *163 Ponce de Leon Ave NE, at Piedmont Rd & North Ave, in Midtown/Piedmont Park.* 404/876-8831. Hrs: 6-10 pm. Closed major hols. Res accepted. Continental menu. Bar from 5 pm. Wine cellar. A la carte entrees: dinner $17-$25. Specializes in seafood, chicken, veal. Own baking, desserts. Harpist. Valet parking. Former church; 50-ft arched and vaulted ceiling. Costumed servers. Cr cds: A, C, D, DS, ER, JCB, MC, V.

✔★ ★ **CAFE CHANTERELLE.** *4200 Paces Ferry Rd NE, north of downtown.* 404/433-9775. Hrs: 11:30 am-3 pm, 6-10 pm; Fri & Sat to 11 pm. Closed some major hols. Res accepted. Continental menu. Bar. A la carte entrees: lunch $4.95-$8.95, dinner $7.95-$15.95. Specializes in veal dishes, seafood. Parking. Cr cds: A, MC, V.

D

✔★ ★ **CAPRI.** *5785 Roswell Rd NE, north of downtown.* 404/255-7222. Hrs: 11:30 am-2 pm, 6-10:30 pm; Fri, Sat to 11 pm. Closed Sun; major hols. Res accepted. Italian menu. Bar. Semi-a la carte: lunch $5.50-$11.95. A la carte entrees: dinner $8.95-$16.50. Specializes in veal, pasta, northern Italian dishes. Parking. Intimate atmosphere. Cr cds: A, C, D, DS, MC, V.

D

★ ★ ★ **CIBOULETTE.** *1529 Piedmont Ave, in Midtown/Piedmont Park.* 404/874-7600. Hrs: 6-10 pm; Fri, Sat to 11 pm. Closed Sun; major hols. French menu. Bar. Semi-a la carte: dinner $14.95-$21.95. Specialties: nage of fish "Mediterranean-style," duck liver pâté. Own desserts. Parking. Open kitchen. Casual dining in elegant atmosphere. Cr cds: A, D, MC, V.

D

★ ★ ★ **CITY GRILL.** *50 Hurt Plaza, in the Hurt Bldg, downtown.* 404/524-2489. Hrs: 11:30 am-2:30 pm, 5:30-10 pm. Closed most major hols. Res accepted. Contemporary Amer menu. Bar. Wine cellar. A la carte entrees: lunch $5-$15, dinner $17-$26. Specializes in crab cakes, chicken. Own pastries. Valet parking (dinner). Rotunda entrance, bronze chandeliers, marble columns, wall murals. Jacket (dinner). Cr cds: A, C, D, DS, MC, V.

D

★ ★ **COUNTRY PLACE.** *1197 Peachtree St NE, Colony Square Complex, in Midtown/Piedmont Park.* 404/881-0144. Hrs: 11:30 am-3 pm, 5:30-11 pm; Fri to midnight; Sat 5:30 pm-midnight; Sun brunch 11 am-3 pm. Closed Thanksgiving, Dec 25. Bar. Semi-a la carte: lunch $5.95-$10.50, dinner $9.95-$19.95. Sun brunch $5.95-$10.50. Pianist Tues-Sat. Parking. Cr cds: A, C, D, DS, MC, V.

D

★ ★ **DAILEY'S.** *17 International Blvd, downtown.* 404/681-3303. Hrs: 11 am-3:30 pm, 5:30-11 pm; Fri & Sat to midnight. Closed major hols. Res accepted. Bar. Semi-a la carte: lunch $4.95-$10.50, dinner $11.95-$22. Specialties: New Zealand rack of lamb, swordfish au poivre. Dessert bar. Pianist 5:30-9:30 pm. Converted warehouse; vaulted ceiling. Cr cds: A, C, D, DS, MC, V.

D

✔★ ★ **EMBERS SEAFOOD GRILLE.** *(234 Hilderbrand Dr, Sandy Springs 30328) N on GA 9.* 404/256-0977. Hrs: 11:30 am-3 pm, 6-11 pm; Sat from 6 pm; Sun 6-9:30 pm. Res accepted. Bar. Semi-a la carte: lunch $3-$10.95, dinner $5.95-$15.95. Child's meals. Specializes in seafood, steak. Parking. Outdoor dining. Modern wall hangings. Cr cds: A, C, D, DS, MC, V.

D

★ ★ **FISHERMAN'S COVE.** *201 Courtland St, downtown.* 404/659-3610. Hrs: 5-10 pm; Fri & Sat to 10:30 pm. Closed Thanksgiving, Dec 25. Res accepted. Bar from 5 pm. A la carte entrees: dinner $12.75-$21.95. Child's meals. Specializes in lobster bouillabaisse, Maine lobster, shrimp scampi. Parking. New England fish house decor. Cr cds: A, C, D, DS, JCB, MC, V.

✔★ **HARRY & SONS.** *820 N Highland Ave (30306), east of downtown.* 404/873-2009. Hrs: 11:30 am-10:30 pm; Fri to 2 am; Sat & Sun 10 am-11 pm. Closed Jan 1, Dec 25. Thai, Italian menu. Bar. Semi-a la carte: lunch $3.95-$15, dinner $4.95-$15. Specializes in kiev-wone, chicken curry, pasta. Parking. Split-level. Cr cds: A, DS, MC, V.

D

★ ★ ★ **HSU'S GOURMET CHINESE.** *192 Peachtree Center Ave, downtown.* 404/659-2788. Hrs: 11:30 am-11 pm; Sun 5-10 pm. Closed Sun; July 4, Thanksgiving, Dec 25. Res accepted. Chinese menu. Bar. Wine list. A la carte entrees: lunch $5.75-$10.95, dinner $10.95-$17.95. Specialties: Peking Duck, asparagus shrimp in black bean sauce, steamed salmon with ginger sauce. Parking (dinner). Chinese decor. Cr cds: A, C, D, DS, MC, V.

D

★ **LA PAZ.** *6410 Roswell Rd, north of downtown.* 404/256-3555. Hrs: 11 am-10 pm; Fri to 11 pm; Sat 5-11 pm; Sun from 5 pm. Southwestern menu. Bar. A la carte entrees: dinner $3.95-$15. Child's meals. Own desserts. Parking. Outdoor dining. Cr cds: A, C, D, DS, MC, V.

D

★ ★ **LOMBARDI'S.** *94 Upper Pryor St, downtown.* 404/522-6568. Hrs: 11 am-10 pm; Fri to 11 pm; Sat 5-11 pm; Sun 5-10 pm. Closed some major hols. Res accepted. Italian menu. Bar. A la carte entrees: lunch $7-$10.95, dinner $9.50-$15.95. Specializes in pasta, veal, seafood. Parking. Cr cds: A, C, D, MC, V.

D

★ ★ ★ **THE MANSION.** *179 Ponce de Leon Ave, in Midtown/Piedmont Park.* 404/876-0727. Hrs: 11 am-2 pm, 6-10 pm; Sun brunch 11 am-2:30 pm. Closed some major hols. Res accepted. Continental menu. Bar 11 am-midnight. Wine list. Semi-a la carte: lunch $8.50-$14.95, dinner $15.95-$26.95. Sun brunch $19.95. Specializes in fresh seafood, veal, lamb. Own baking, desserts. Parking. Shingle-style Victorian mansion (1885) with garden, gazebo. Cr cds: A, C, D, DS, ER, JCB, MC, V.

D

✔★ **MARY MAC'S TEAROOM.** *224 Ponce de Leon Ave, in Midtown/Piedmont Park.* 404/876-1800. Hrs: 11 am-3 pm, 5-9 pm. Closed major hols. Serv bar. Complete meals: lunch $5-$7, dinner $6-$12. Child's meals. Specializes in baked and fried chicken, fresh vegetables. Own desserts. Parking. Informal neighborhood cafe. Family-owned. No cr cds accepted.

D

✔★ **MICK'S UNDERGROUND.** *75 Upper Alabama St, downtown.* 404/525-2825. Hrs: 11 am-11 pm; Fri, Sat to 1 am; Sun noon-10:30 pm. Closed Thanksgiving, Dec 25. Bar. Semi-a la carte: lunch, dinner $3.50-$12.95. Child's meals. Specializes in hamburgers, chicken, pasta. Own desserts. Cr cds: A, C, D, DS, MC, V.

D

★ ★ **MORTON'S OF CHICAGO.** *245 Peachtree Center Ave, in Marquis One Tower office building, downtown.* 404/577-4366. Hrs: 5:30-11 pm; Sun 5-10 pm. Closed major hols. Res accepted. Bar. A la carte entrees: dinner $25-$55. Specializes in prime aged steak, veal, lobster. Valet parking. Cr cds: A, C, D, MC, V.

D

★ ★ **NIKOLAI'S ROOF.** *(See Hilton & Towers Hotel)* 404/659-2000. Sittings: 6:30 & 9:30 pm; open seating wkdays. Res accepted. Classic French menu with Russian flair. Extensive wine list. Prix fixe: five-course dinner $60. Specialties (sample only, menu varies): turbot à la vapeur sur un lit de chanterelles, la coupe royale de gibier aux airells et poivres, piroshkis & borsht. Own baking, desserts. Menu recited. Valet parking. Elegant decor; on 29th floor of hotel. Jacket, tie. Cr cds: A, C, D, DS, ER, JCB, MC, V.

✔★ **OLD VININGS INN.** *3011 Paces Mill Rd (30339), north of downtown.* 404/438-2282. Hrs: 11:30 am-2:30 pm, 5:30-10 pm. Closed Mon. Bar from 5:30 pm. Semi-a la carte: lunch $6.50-$10, dinner $10-$16. Child's meals. Specializes in modern American cooking. Parking. Outdoor dining. In 1830s house. Original fireplace. Oil paintings. Cr cds: A, C, D, DS, MC, V.

D SC

★ ★ **PATIO BY THE RIVER.** *4199 Paces Ferry Rd NW, north of downtown.* 404/432-2808. Hrs: 11:30 am-2:30 pm, 6-10 pm; Sat from 6 pm; Sun brunch 11:30 am-2:30 pm. Closed most major hols. Res accepted. French menu. Bar. Semi-a la carte: lunch $4-$10, dinner $16-$21. Sun brunch $4-$11. Specializes in lamb chops, trout, grilled salmon. Parking. Patio dining. View of Chattahoochee River. Cr cds: A, C, D, DS, MC, V.

D

✔★ **PEGGY'S CAFE.** *1821 Piedmont (30324), in Midtown/Piedmont Park.* 404/875-5017. Hrs: 11 am-11 pm; Fri to midnight; Sat 8 am-midnight; Sun 8 am-10 pm. Closed Thanksgiving, Dec 25. Bar. Semi-a la carte: bkfst $2.95-$5.95, lunch $3.95-$6.75, dinner $4.95-$6.95. Child's meals. Specializes in hamburgers, chicken. Parking. Outdoor dining. 1950s diner decor & atmosphere. Cr cds: DS, MC, V.

★ ★ **PITTYPAT'S PORCH.** *25 International Blvd, downtown.* 404/525-8228. Hrs: 5-11 pm. Closed Labor Day, Dec 25; also 1 wk in Dec. Res accepted. Southern menu. Bar. Semi-a la carte: dinner $16.95-$19.95. Child's meals. Specializes in fresh coastal fish, Savan- nah crab cakes, coastal venison pie. Own desserts. Pianist. Parking. Collection of rocking chairs in lounge. Cr cds: A, C, D, DS, MC, V.

D

★ ★ **RAY'S ON THE RIVER.** *6700 Powers Ferry Rd, north of downtown.* 404/955-1187. Hrs: 11 am-3 pm, 5:30-10:30 pm; Fri, Sat to midnight; Sun 10 am-3 pm, 5-10 pm. Closed Dec 25. Res accepted. Bar 11 am-midnight; Fri & Sat 11-1 am; Sun 12:00-10 pm. Semi-a la carte: lunch $4.95-$9.50, dinner $9.95-$16.95. Sunday brunch $14.95. Child's meals. Specializes in mesquite-grilled seafood, prime rib. Jazz eves Tues-Sat. Valet parking. View of Chattahoochee River. Cr cds: A, C, D, DS, MC, V.

D

★ ★ ★ **THE RESTAURANT.** *(See The Ritz-Carlton)* 404/659-0400. Hrs: 11:30 am-2:30 pm, 6-11 pm; Sat, Sun from 6:30 pm. Res accepted. French, continental menu. Bar 11:30-2 am. Wine cellar. Buffet lunch $11.50. A la carte entrees: dinner $18-$26. Child's meals. Specialties: sautéed duck foie gras, seared gulf red snapper, baby lamb loin. Own baking, ice cream, pasta. Entertainment Tues-Sat evenings. Valet parking. Private club atmosphere; objets d'art. Jacket. Cr cds: A, C, D, DS, ER, JCB, MC, V.

D

★ ★ ★ **RUTH'S CHRIS STEAK HOUSE.** *5788 Roswell Rd, north of downtown.* 404/256-2922. Hrs: 5-11 pm. Closed July 4, Dec 25. Res accepted. Bar. Wine list. A la carte entrees: dinner $15.95-$29.95. Specializes in prime beef, fresh seafood. Valet parking. Cr cds: A, C, D, DS, MC, V.

D

✔★ ★ **TASTE OF NEW ORLEANS.** *889 W Peachtree St NE, in Midtown/Piedmont Park.* 404/874-5535. Hrs: 11:30 am-2 pm, 6-10 pm; Fri 11:30 am-2 pm, 5:30-11 pm; Sat 5:30-11 pm. Closed Sun; most major hols. Res accepted. Cajun, Creole menu. Bar. Semi-a la carte: lunch $5.99-$7.95, dinner $8.95-$16.95. Specializes in gumbo, seafood etouffee. Parking. Cr cds: A, C, D, MC, V.

★ ★ ★ **VAN GOGH'S.** *(70 W Crossville Rd, Roswell 30075) N on GA 400 to exit 7B, then approx 3 mi NW.* 404/993-1156. Hrs: 11:30 am-midnight. Closed some major hols. Res accepted. Continental menu. Bar. Wine list. Semi-a la carte: lunch $4.95-$10.95, dinner $9.95-$24.95. Sun brunch $3.95-$14.95. Child's meals. Specializes in seafood, grilled portobello mushrooms, crab cakes. Parking. European ambiance. Cr cds: A, C, D, DS, MC, V.

D

★ ★ **VENI VIDI VICI.** *41 14th St, at W Peachtree, in Midtown/Piedmont Park.* 404/875-8424. Hrs: 11:30 am-11 pm; Fri to midnight; Sat 5 pm-midnight; Sun 5-10 pm. Closed Jan 1, Thanksgiving, Dec 25. Res accepted. Italian menu. Bar 11:30 am-midnight. A la carte entrees: lunch $6-13, dinner $9.50-$22. Specializes in Northern Italian cooking. Own pasta. Valet parking. Outdoor dining. Vaulted ceilings. Open kitchen. Cr cds: A, C, D, DS, MC, V.

D

★ ★ **WINFIELD'S.** *1 Galleria Pkwy, north of downtown.* 404/955-5300. Hrs: 11:30 am-3 pm, 5:30-10 pm; Fri & Sat to 11 pm; Sun 5-9 pm; Sun brunch 11:30 am-3 pm. Closed Thanksgiving, Dec 25. Bar. Semi-a la carte: lunch $7.50-$10.50, dinner $10.50-$19.95. Sun brunch $5.50-$9.50. Child's meals. Specializes in hickory charcoal-grilled meats & seafoods, homemade desserts. Pianist Tues-Sat evenings. Parking. Cr cds: A, C, D, DS, MC, V.

D

Unrated Dining Spots

BOYCHIK'S DELI. *4520-A Chamblee-Dunwoody Rd, in Georgetown Shopping Center, north of downtown.* 404/452-0516. Hrs: 10 am-9 pm; Sat, Sun from 9 am. Closed Dec 25. Semi-a la carte: bkfst $2.25-$4.65, lunch $3.50-$5.25, dinner $5.50-$7.50. Child's meals.

Specializes in chopped liver, hot pastrami. New York-style deli. Cr cds: A, MC, V.

PICCADILLY CAFETERIA. *5647 Peachtree Industrial Blvd, north of downtown.* 404/451-5364. Hrs: 11 am-8:30 pm. Closed Dec 25. Res accepted. Avg ck: lunch $4.50, dinner $5. Child's meals. Specializes in fried chicken. Parking. Cr cds: A, C, D, DS, MC, V.

D

ROYAL BAGEL. *1544 Piedmont NE (30324), Ansley Mall, Midtown.* 404/876-3512. Hrs: 7 am-5 pm; Sun to 4 pm. Closed most major hols. Semi-a la carte: bkfst $2.25-$5.95, lunch $2.25-$7.50. Specializes in bagels, pastries, soups. Outside dining. No cr cds accepted.

VARSITY. *61 North Ave, in Midtown/Piedmont Park.* 404/881-1706. Hrs: 7-12:30 am; Fri, Sat to 2 am. Specializes in hot dogs, hamburgers, fried peach pie. Avg ck: $4-$4.50. Parking. View of some preparation areas. One of world's largest drive-ins. Graffitiesque decor; tiered seating. Adj Georgia Tech campus. No cr cds accepted.

Atlanta Hartsfield Airport Area

Motels

✔★★ **COMFORT INN-ATLANTA AIRPORT.** *(1808 Phoenix Blvd, College Park 30349)* S on I-85 to I-285, E on I-285, exit 43 (Riverdale Rd S), then W on Phoenix Blvd. 404/991-1099; FAX 404/991-1076. 194 rms, 4 story. S $39-$89; D $44-$94; each addl $5; under 17 free; wkend rates; higher rates Atlanta "500." Crib free. TV; cable. Heated pool; poolside serv. Complimentary coffee in lobby. Restaurant 6-10:30 am, 11:30 am-2 pm, 6-10 pm; Sat, Sun 7-11:30 am, 5:30-10 pm. Rm serv. Bar 5-10 pm. Ck-out 11 am. Coin lndry. Meeting rms. Valet serv. Sundries. Free airport transportation. Balconies. Cr cds: A, C, D, DS, ER, JCB, MC, V.

D ≋ ✈ ⊼ 🔥 SC

★★★ **COURTYARD BY MARRIOTT.** *(2050 Sullivan Rd, College Park 30337)* S on I-85 to Riverdale Rd, E to Best Rd, S to Sullivan Rd. 404/997-2220; FAX 404/994-9743. 144 rms, 3 story. S $77; D $87; each addl $10; suites $87-$97; under 12 free; wkly, wkend rates. Crib free. TV; cable. Indoor pool. Coffee in rms. Restaurant 6:30-10 am, 6-10 pm. Bar 4-11 pm. Ck-out noon. Coin lndry. Meeting rms. Valet serv. Sundries. Free airport transportation. Exercise equipt; weights, bicycles, whirlpool. Some private patios, balconies. Cr cds: A, C, D, DS, MC, V.

D ≋ ⫩ ✈ ⊼ 🔥 SC

✔★★ **HAMPTON INN.** *(1888 Sullivan Rd, College Park 30337)* S via I-85 exit 18, E on Riverdale Rd to Sullivan Rd. 404/996-2220; FAX 404/996-2488. 130 units, 4 story. S, D $53-$67; under 18 free. Crib free. TV; cable. Pool. Complimentary continental bkfst, coffee. Restaurant adj 6-2 am. Ck-out noon. Meeting rms. Free airport transportation. Public park adj. Cr cds: A, C, D, DS, MC, V.

D ≋ ✈ ⊼ 🔥 SC

Motor Hotels

★★ **DAYS INN.** *(4601 Best Rd, College Park 30337)* S on I-85, exit Riverdale Rd W, then N on Best Rd. 404/761-6500; FAX 404/763-3267. 160 rms, 6 story. S, D $62-$82; each addl (after 4th person) $10. Crib free. TV; cable. Pool. Playground. Restaurant 6 am-10 pm. Rm serv. Bar 5 pm-midnight. Ck-out noon. Meeting rms.

Valet serv. Free airport transportation. Exercise equipt; weights, bicycle. Many refrigerators. Cr cds: A, C, D, DS, MC, V.

D ≋ ⫩ ✈ ⊼ 🔥 SC

★★ **RAMADA-ATLANTA AIRPORT.** *(1419 Virginia Ave, Atlanta 30337)* N on I-85, exit Virginia Ave W. 404/768-7800; FAX 404/767-5451. 245 rms, 6 story. S $58-$78, D $68-$88; each addl $10; suites $85-$131; under 12 free. Crib $10. TV; cable. Pool. Restaurant 6 am-2 pm, 5-9 pm. Rm serv. Bar 5 pm-1 am. Ck-out noon. Coin lndry. Meeting rms. Bellhops. Valet serv. Free airport transportation. Exercise equipt; weight machines, bicycles, sauna. Cr cds: A, C, D, DS, MC, V.

D ≋ ⫩ ✈ ⊼ 🔥 SC

Hotels

★★★ **ATLANTA RENAISSANCE HOTEL INTERNATIONAL AIRPORT.** *(4736 Best Rd, Atlanta 30337)* S on I-85, exit Riverdale Rd W. 404/762-7676; FAX 404/763-4199. 496 units, 10 story. S $110-$170; D $125-$185; each addl $15; suites $175-$600; wkend plans. Crib free. Pet accepted, some restrictions. TV; cable. Indoor/outdoor pool; poolside serv. Restaurant 6:30 am-2:30 pm, 5:30-11 pm. Rm serv 6-1 am. Bar 11-2 am. Ck-out noon. Convention facilities. Gift shop. Free airport transportation. Exercise equipt; weights, bicycles, whirlpool, sauna. Minibars; some bathrm phones. *LUXURY LEVEL : CONCIERGE LEVEL.* 55 units, 4 suites. S $170; D $185; suites $250-$700. Concierge. Private lounge, honor bar. Complimentary continental bkfst, refreshments, newspaper. Cr cds: A, C, D, DS, ER, JCB, MC, V.

D ⫞ ≋ ⫩ ✈ ⊼ 🔥 SC

★★★ **HILTON & TOWERS.** *(1031 Virginia Ave, Atlanta 30354)* N on I-85, exit 19 Virginia Ave E. 404/767-9000; FAX 404/768-0185. 503 rms, 17 story. S $127-$152; D $142-$167; each addl $15; suites $350-$450; family, wkend rates. Crib free. TV; cable. 2 pools, 1 indoor; poolside serv. Coffee in rms. Restaurant 6 am-midnight. Rm serv 24 hrs. Bar 11:30-1 am; entertainment. Ck-out noon. Convention facilities. Concierge. Gift shop. Barber, beauty shop. Free valet parking. Free airport, RR station, bus depot transportation. Lighted tennis. Exercise rm; instructor, weight machines, bicycles, whirlpool, sauna. Massage. Minibars; some bathrm phones, wet bars. Refrigerators avail. *LUXURY LEVEL : TOWERS.* 63 rms, 4 suites, 2 floors. S $142; D $167. Private lounge, honor bar. Complimentary continental bkfst, refreshments, newspaper. Cr cds: A, C, D, DS, ER, JCB, MC, V.

D ⫨ ≋ ⫩ ✈ ⊼ 🔥 SC

★★★ **MARRIOTT-ATLANTA AIRPORT.** *(4711 Best Rd, College Park 30337)* S on I-85, exit Riverdale Rd W. 404/766-7900; FAX 404/209-6808. 638 rms, 15 story. S $140; D $155; suites $200-$600; under 18 free; wkly, wkend, hol rates. Crib free. TV; cable. Indoor/outdoor pool; poolside serv. Restaurant 6:30 am-midnight. Bar 5 pm-2 am, Sun 12:30 pm-midnight; entertainment, dancing. Ck-out noon. Convention facilities. Concierge. Gift shop. Barber, beauty shop. Free airport transportation. Lighted tennis. Exercise equipt; weight machines, bicycles, whirlpool, sauna. Game rm. Refrigerators avail. Some balconies. *LUXURY LEVEL : CONCIERGE FLOOR.* 72 rms. S $150; D $165. Private lounge, honor bar. Complimentary continental bkfst, refreshments. Cr cds: A, C, D, DS, JCB, MC, V.

D ⫞ ≋ ⫩ ✈ ⊼ 🔥 SC

★★★ **STOUFFER CONCOURSE.** *(One Hartsfield Centre Pkwy, Atlanta 30354)* I-85 exit 20, at Hartsfield Centre. 404/209-9999; FAX 404/209-8934. 387 rms, 11 story. S $130-$165; D $150-$185; each addl $20; suites $225-$825; family, baseball wkend rates. Crib free. Valet parking $5. TV; cable. 2 pools, 1 indoor; poolside serv. Complimentary coffee in rms. Restaurant 6 am-11 pm. Rm serv 24 hrs. Bar; entertainment, dancing exc Sun. Ck-out 1 pm. Convention facilities. Concierge. Gift shop. Free airport transportation. Exercise rm; instructor, weight machine, bicycles, whirlpool, sauna. Health club privileges. Refrigerators, minibars. Balconies. *LUXURY LEVEL : CLUB LEVEL.* 40 rms, 1 suite. S $165; D $185; suite $825. Concierge. Private lounge, honor bar. Complimentary continental bkfst, refreshments. Cr cds: A, C, D, DS, ER, JCB, MC, V.

D ≈ 兀 ✈ ⊁ ⽕ SC

Buckhead

Motels

✔★ ★ **HAMPTON INN-BUCKHEAD.** 3398 Piedmont Rd NE (30305). 404/233-5656; FAX 404/237-4688. 154 rms, 6 story. S $59-$77; D $66-$84; under 18 free. Crib free. TV; cable. Pool. Complimentary continental bkfst, coffee. Restaurant adj 11 am-11 pm. Ck-out noon. Meeting rms. Valet serv. Health club privileges. Cr cds: A, C, D, DS, MC, V.

D ≈ ⊁ ⽕

★ ★ **SUMMERFIELD SUITES.** 505 Pharr Rd NE (30305). 404/262-7880; res: 800/833-4353; FAX 404/262-3734. 88 suites, 3 story. No elvtr. S, D $124-$164; wknd rates. Crib $15. Pet accepted, some restrictions. TV; cable, in-rm movies. Heated pool. Complimentary continental bkfst. Complimentary coffee in rms. Restaurant opp 11 am-midnight. Ck-out 11 am. Coin lndry. Meeting rms. Valet serv. Exercise equipt; weights, bicycles, whirlpool. Refrigerators. Balconies. Picnic tables, grills. Cr cds: A, C, D, DS, JCB, MC, V.

D ⽊ ≈ 兀 ⊁ ⽕ SC

Motor Hotel

✔★ ★ **LENOX INN.** 3387 Lenox Rd NE (30326). 404/261-5500; res: 800/241-0200; FAX 404/261-6140. 180 rms, 2-3 story. S $65; D $70; each addl $5; suites $79-$205; under 18 free. Crib free. TV. 2 pools. Complimentary continental bkfst. Restaurant 6:30-9:30 am, Sat & Sun 7-11 am. Bar 5:30-8 pm. Ck-out noon. Meeting rms. Valet serv. Some refrigerators. Cr cds: A, C, D, MC, V.

≈ 千 ⊁ ⽕ SC

Hotels

★ ★ ★ **EMBASSY SUITES.** 3285 Peachtree Rd (30305). 404/261-7733; FAX 404/261-6857. 328 suites, 16 story. Suites $129-$169; under 19 free; wknd rates; higher rates special events. Crib free. TV; cable. 2 pools, 1 indoor. Complimentary full bkfst. Complimentary coffee in rms. Restaurant 11 am-2 pm, 5-10 pm. Bar 11-1 am. Ck-out noon. Coin lndry. Meeting rms. Gift shop. Airport transportation. Exercise equipt; weights, bicycles, whirlpool, sauna. Refrigerators, wet bars. Cr cds: A, C, D, DS, JCB, MC, V.

D ≈ 兀 ⊁ ⽕ SC

★ ★ **HOLIDAY INN-ATLANTIC CENTRAL.** 418 Armour Dr NE (30324). 404/873-4661; res: 800/282-8222; FAX 404/872-1292. 282 units, 5 story. S, D $79-$89; suites $150-$300; under 19 free; wknd rates. Crib free. TV; cable. Pool; poolside serv. Restaurant 6:30 am-2 pm, 5-10 pm. Bar 11-1 am. Ck-out noon. Coin lndry. Convention facilities. Concierge. Gift shop. Barber, beauty shop. Airport, RR station, bus depot transportation. Health club privileges. Refrigerators avail. In-rm whirlpool, refrigerator, wet bar, fireplace in suites. Balconies. Cr cds: A, C, D, DS, ER, JCB, MC, V.

D ≈ ⊁ ⽕ SC

★ ★ **HOTEL NIKKO.** 3300 Peachtree Rd (30305). 404/365-8100; FAX 404/233-5686. 440 rms, 25 story. S $145-$185, D $165-$205; each addl $25; suites $435-$1,500; wknd rates. TV; cable, in-rm movies. Pool. Restaurants 6:30 am-11 pm. Rm serv 24 hrs. Bars 11-1 am; entertainment, pianist. Ck-out noon. Convention facilities. Concierge. Gift shop. Garage, valet parking. Airport transportation avail. Tennis & golf privileges. Exercise equipt; bicycles, treadmill, sauna.

Bathrm phones, minibars. Tri-level Japanese garden; 35-ft cascading waterfall. *LUXURY LEVEL : THE NIKKO FLOORS.* 43 rms, 5 suites, 3 floors. S $215, D $235; suites $435-$750. Private lounge. Complimentary continental bkfst, refreshments, newspapers. Cr cds: A, C, D, DS, ER, JCB, MC, V.

D ⽊ 千 ≈ 兀 ⊁ ⽕

★ ★ ▲ **J W MARRIOTT.** 3300 Lenox Rd NE (30326), at Peachtree Rd. 404/262-3344; FAX 404/262-8689. 371 units, 25 story. 43 suites. S, D $105-$200; suites $225-$500; under 18 free. Crib free. Garage $7, valet $9. TV; cable. Indoor pool. Restaurant 6:30 am-11 pm. Rm serv 24 hrs. Bar 11:30-1 am, Fri, Sat to 2 am; entertainment Wed-Sat. Ck-out 1 pm. Convention facilities. Concierge. Shopping arcade. Airport transportation. Tennis privileges. Exercise equipt; weight machine, bicycles, whirlpool, sauna. Health club privileges. Bathrm phones, minibars. *LUXURY LEVEL : CONCIERGE LEVEL.* 28 rms, 6 suites, 3 floors. S $155; D $200; suites $225-$500. Private lounge, honor bar. Minibars. Complimentary continental bkfst, refreshments. Cr cds: A, C, D, DS, JCB, MC, V.

D ⽊ 千 ≈ 兀 ⊁ ⽕ SC

★ ★ ★ **THE RITZ-CARLTON, BUCKHEAD.** 3434 Peachtree Rd NE (30326). 404/237-2700; res: 800/241-3333; FAX 404/239-0078. 553 rms, 22 story. S, D $159-$229; suites $425-$1,100; under 12 free; wknd, honeymoon plans. Crib free. Valet parking $12; self-park in/out $8. TV; cable. Indoor pool; poolside serv. Restaurant 6:30 am-midnight (also see THE CAFE and THE DINING ROOM). Rm serv 24 hrs. Bar 11-2 am; entertainment. Ck-out noon. Convention facilities. Concierge. Shopping arcade. Airport transportation. Tennis privileges, pro. Golf privileges, greens fee $40-$100. Exercise rm; instructor, weight machines, bicycles, whirlpool, sauna, steam rm. Massage. Bathrm phones, minibars. *LUXURY LEVEL : THE RITZ-CARLTON CLUB.* 52 rms, 10 suites, 2 floors. S, D $249. Private lounge. Complimentary continental bkfst, refreshments, afternoon tea. Cr cds: A, C, D, DS, ER, JCB, MC, V.

D ⽊ 千 ≈ 兀 ⊁ ⽕ SC

★ ★ **SWISSÔTEL ATLANTA.** 3391 Peachtree Rd NE (30326). 404/365-0065; res: 800/253-1397; FAX 404/365-8787. 364 rms, 22 story. S $165-$215; D $185-$240; suites $380-$1,000; under 16 free; wkend rates. Crib free. Garage $6, valet $7, in/out $10. TV; cable. Indoor pool; poolside serv. Restaurant 6:30 am-11 pm. Rm serv 24 hrs. Bar 11 am-midnight, Fri-Sat to 1 am; entertainment. Ck-out 1 pm. Meeting rms. Concierge. Gift shop. Beauty shop. Airport, RR station, bus depot transportation. Tennis privileges. Golf privileges. Exercise rm, instructor, stair machine, weight machine. Bathrm phones, minibars. Art and photo collection. *LUXURY LEVEL : EXECUTIVE LEVEL.* 35 rms, 4 suites, 2 floors. S $210-$260; D $235-$285. Private lounge, honor bar. Complimentary continental bkfst, refreshments, newspaper, shoeshine. Cr cds: A, C, D, DS, ER, JCB, MC, V.

D ⽊ 千 ≈ 兀 ⊁ ⽕ SC

★ ★ **TERRACE GARDEN INN.** 3405 Lenox Rd NE (30326). 404/261-9250; res: 800/866-7666; FAX 404/848-7391. 364 rms, 8 story. S $135-$175; D $150-$190; suites $185-$220; under 14 free; wkend rates. Crib free. Covered parking $4. Pet accepted, some restrictions. TV; cable. 2 pools, 1 indoor; wading pool, poolside serv. Restaurant 6 am-2 pm, 6-10 pm. Bars noon-2 am. Ck-out noon. Convention facilities. Concierge. Gift shop. Exercise equipt; weight machines, bicycles, whirlpool, sauna. Some refrigerators, wet bars; bathrm phone in suites. Some balconies. *LUXURY LEVEL : CLUB LEVEL.* 69 rms, 2 floors. S $175; D $190. Private lounge. Complimentary continental bkfst, refreshments, newspaper. Cr cds: A, C, D, DS, MC, V.

D ⽊ ≈ 兀 千 ⊁ ⽕ SC

✔★ ★ **TRAVELODGE.** 2061 N Druid Hills Rd NE (30329), at I-85 exit 31. 404/321-4174; FAX 404/636-7264. 180 rms, 9 story. S $49-$59; D $59-$80; each addl $10; suites to $175; under 18 free; wkend rates. Crib free. TV; cable. Pool. Restaurant 6:30 am-1:30 pm, 5:30-9:30 pm. Bar 5 pm-midnight. Ck-out 11 am. Meeting rms. Exercise equipt; weights, bicycles, sauna. Near Lenox Sq. *LUXURY*

LEVEL : CLUB LEVEL. 24 rms, 1 suite. S, D $59-$80; suite $175. Private lounge. Complimentary continental bkfst, refreshments, magazines. Cr cds: A, C, D, DS, ER, JCB, MC, V.

★ ★ **THE WYNDHAM GARDEN HOTEL-BUCKHEAD.** 3340 Peachtree Rd NE (30326). 404/231-1234; FAX 404/231-5236. 221 rms, 6 story. S, D $99-$109; each addl $10; suites from $149; under 16 free; wkend rates. Crib $10. TV; cable. Pool; poolside serv. Restaurant 6:30 am-10 pm, Sat & Sun from 7 am. Bar 11:30 am-midnight, Sun from noon. Ck-out noon. Meeting rms. Sundries. Airport, bus depot transportation. Health club privileges. Some refrigerators. Cr cds: A, C, D, DS, JCB, MC, V.

Inn

✔★ **BEVERLY HILLS.** 65 Sheridan Dr (30305). 404/233-8520; res: 800/331-8520; FAX 404/233-8520, ext. 18. 18 kit. suites, 3 story. S $65-$74; D $80-$120; each addl $10-$15; wkly, monthly rates. Crib avail. Pet accepted, some restrictions. TV. Pool privileges. Complimentary continental bkfst, sherry. Restaurant nearby. Ck-out noon, ck-in 1 pm. Health club privileges. Balconies. European-style hotel restored to 1929 ambiance. Cr cds: A, C, D, DS, ER, JCB, MC, V.

Restaurants

★ ★ ★ ★ **103 WEST.** 103 W Paces Ferry Rd. 404/233-5993. Hrs: 6-11 pm; Fri, Sat from 5:30 pm. Closed Sun; major hols. Res accepted. French, Amer menu. Bar. Wine cellar. A la carte entrees: dinner $15.50-$29.50. Child's meals. Specialties: all lump crab cake, roast breast of duck, broiled noisettes of lamb. Own baking, desserts. Pianist. Valet parking. Victorian and Renaissance decor; 18th- & 19th-century antiques. Chef-owned. Jacket. Cr cds: A, C, D, DS, MC, V.

★ ★ **ABRUZZI RISTORANTE.** 2355 Peachtree Rd NE, at Peachtree Battle Shopping Center. 404/261-8186. Hrs: 11:30 am-2:30 pm, 5:30-10:30 pm; Sat 5:30-11 pm. Closed Sun; some major hols. Res required. Italian menu. Bar. Semi-a la carte: lunch from $15, dinner $25. Specialties: Capellini alla Nico, homemade spinach ravioli, osso buco. Parking. Understated Florentine decor. Jacket. Cr cds: A, D, MC, V.

★ ★ **ANNE MARIE'S.** 3340 Peachtree Rd (30326). 404/237-8686. Hrs: 11:30 am-2:30 pm, 6:30-10:30 pm; Fri & Sat to 11 pm. Closed Sun; Jan 1, Dec 25. Res accepted. French menu. Bar. Semi-a la carte: lunch $3.75-$9.95, dinner $15.50-$21.75. Specialities: Dover sole Veronique, carre' d'Agneau. Own desserts. Parking. Outdoor dining. Replica of 300-yr old house in southern France. Many French artifacts. Cr cds: MC, V.

★ ★ ★ **ANTHONY'S.** 3109 Piedmont Rd NE. 404/262-7379. Hrs: 6-11 pm. Closed Sun; major hols. Res accepted. Continental menu. Bar. Wine cellar. A la carte entrees: dinner $14.95-$24.95. Specializes in beef, lamb. Own baking. Valet parking. Plantation house (1797); antiques. Cr cds: A, C, D, DS, JCB, MC, V.

★ ★ **AZALEA.** 3167 Peachtree Rd NE. 404/237-9939. Hrs: 5-11 pm; Fri, Sat to midnight; Sun to 10 pm. Closed July 4, Thanksgiving, Dec 25. Continental menu. Serv bar. A la carte entrees: dinner $7.95-$22.95. Specializes in fresh seafood, pasta. Valet parking. West coast atmosphere. Cr cds: A, D, DS, MC, V.

★ ★ ★ **BACCHANALIA.** 3125 Piedmont Rd (30305). 404/365-0410. Hrs: 6-9:30 pm; Fri & Sat to 10 pm. Closed Sun, Mon; some major hols. Res required. Wine, beer. Prix fixe: dinner $27.50 & $32.50.

Specializes in seafood, game. Parking. Many antiques. Austrian crystal chandeliers, Oriental rugs. Totally nonsmoking. Cr cds: A, D, MC, V.

✔★ ★ **BASIL'S MEDITERRANEAN CAFE.** 2985 Grandview Ave. 404/233-9755. Hrs: 11:30 am-2:30 pm, 6-10 pm; Fri to 11 pm; Sat noon-4 pm, 6-11 pm. Closed Sun & Mon; some major hols. Res accepted. Mediterranean menu. Bar. A la carte entrees: lunch $4.50-$7.25, dinner $8.25-$16.95. Specializes in Middle Eastern cooking. Parking. Outdoor dining. Mediterranean decor. Cr cds: A, D, DS, MC, V.

★ ★ **THE BISTRO.** 56 E Andrews Dr NW (30305). 404/231-5733. Hrs: 6-11 pm. Closed Sun, Mon; Jan 1, Thanksgiving, Dec 25. Res accepted. French menu. Bar. A la carte entrees: dinner $12.95-$22.95. Child's meals. Specializes in lamb chops, salmon, filet mignon. Parking. Outdoor dining. Many paintings; antique German mirrors. Cr cds: A, C, D, DS, MC, V.

★ ★ ★ **BONE'S.** 3130 Piedmont Rd NE, at Peachtree Rd. 404/237-2663. Hrs: 11:30 am-2:30 pm, 6-11 pm; Sat & Sun from 6 pm. Closed major hols. Res accepted. Bar. Wine cellar. Semi-a la carte: lunch $8.95-$16.95. A la carte entrees: dinner $18.95-$36. Specializes in aged prime beef, seafood, live Maine lobster. Own desserts. Valet parking. Club atmosphere; wood paneling, fireplace. Cr cds: A, C, D, MC, V.

★ ★ **BUCKHEAD DINER.** 3073 Piedmont Rd. 404/262-3336. Hrs: 11 am-midnight; Sun to 10 pm. Closed Jan 1, Thanksgiving, Dec 25. Bar. A la carte entrees: lunch $4.25-$12.95, dinner $4.25-$17.50. Specializes in sautéed grouper, veal meat loaf, white chocolate banana cream pie. Valet parking. Update of classic, stainless steel-wrapped diner. Cr cds: A, C, D, DS, MC, V.

★ ★ ★ **THE CAFE.** (See The Ritz-Carlton, Buckhead Hotel) 404/237-2700. Hrs: 6:30 am-midnight; Sun brunch 11:30 am-2:30 pm. Bar. A la carte entrees: bkfst $7-$15, lunch $10-$22, dinner $15-$30. Sun brunch $32. Child's meals. Specializes in grilled meat, seafood, local dishes. Own pastries. Pianist. Valet parking. Antiques, original art. Cr cds: A, C, D, DS, ER, JCB, MC, V.

✔★ ★ **CAFE TU TU TANGO.** 220 Pharr Road. 404/841-6222. Hrs: 11:30 am-closing. Eclectic menu. Bar. A la carte entrees: lunch, dinner $3.95-$7.95. Specializes in stir-fry, salad, pizza. Valet parking. Outdoor dining. Artist's studio decor; painters at work. Cr cds: A, MC, V.

★ ★ ★ **CARBO'S CAFE.** 3717 Roswell Rd. 404/231-4433. Hrs: 5-11:30 pm. Closed major hols. Res accepted. Continental menu. Bar 5 pm-3 am. Wine cellar. Complete meals: dinner $14.95-$28.95. Specializes in seafood, veal, steak. Own baking. Piano bar. Valet parking. Outdoor dining. European decor; antiques, fireplaces, fountain. Cr cds: A, C, D, MC, V.

★ ★ ★ **CHOPS.** 70 W Paces Ferry Rd. 404/262-2675. Hrs: 11:30 am-2:30 pm, 5:30-11 pm; Fri, Sat 5:30-midnight; Sun 5:30-10 pm. Closed some major hols. Res accepted. Bar. A la carte entrees: lunch $6.50-$13.95, dinner $14.50-$29.50. Specializes in steak, fresh seafood. Own pastries. Valet parking. Art deco motif. Cr cds: A, C, D, DS, MC, V.

★ ★ ★ **COACH AND SIX.** 1776 Peachtree Rd NW. 404/872-6666. Hrs: 5:30-10 pm; Fri & Sat to 10:30 pm. Closed Jan 1, Dec 25. Res accepted. Continental menu. Bar. Wine cellar. Semi-a la carte: dinner $16.95-$24.95. Child's meals. Specializes in steak, Maine lobster, fresh fish, triple-cut lamb chops. Own baking, desserts. Valet parking. English club decor; painting collection. Cr cds: A, C, D, DS, MC, V.

D

★ ★ **DANTE'S DOWN THE HATCH.** *3380 Peachtree Rd NE, across from Lenox Square. 404/266-1600.* Hrs: 4-11:30 pm; Fri & Sat to 12:30 am; Sun 5-11 pm. Closed Jan 1. Res accepted. Bar. Semi-a la carte: dinner $11.90-$23.70. Specializes in mixed fondue dinners. Own desserts. Classical guitarist; jazz trio. Parking. Nautical decor. Antique English, Polish ship figureheads. Ship-board dining within multilevel vessel. Family-owned. Cr cds: A, C, D, DS, MC, V.

D

★ ★ ★ **THE DINING ROOM.** *(See The Ritz-Carlton, Buckhead Hotel) 404/237-2700.* Hrs: 6-10 pm. Closed Sun; major hols. Res accepted. Traditional European menu with American regional influences. Bar. Extensive wine cellar. Semi-a la carte: dinner $58-$80. Specializes in light contemporary cuisine. Own baking, pasta, ice cream. Menu changes daily. Valet parking. Elegant decor; Waterford chandeliers, original artwork, antiques. Exquisite paneling. Jacket, tie. Cr cds: A, C, D, DS, ER, JCB, MC, V.

D

✔★ **GEORGIA GRILLE.** *2290 Peachtree Rd (30309). 404/352-3517.* Hrs: 6-10 pm; Fri & Sat to 11 pm. Closed Mon; most major hols. Southwestern menu. Bar. Semi-a la carte: dinner $3.95-$15.95. Child's meals. Specializes in grilled beef, chicken, seafood. Parking. Outdoor dining. Southwestern decor. Cr cds: A, MC, V.

D

★ ★ **HEDGEROSE HEIGHTS INN.** *490 E Paces Ferry Rd NE. 404/233-7673.* Hrs: 6:30-10 pm. Closed Sun, Mon; major hols. Res accepted. French, continental menu. Bar. Wine cellar. A la carte entrees: dinner $16-$24. Specializes in seafood, seasonal game dishes, veal. Own pastries. Parking. Restored 1915 house featuring English woodwork. Jacket. Totally nonsmoking. Cr cds: A, C, D, MC, V.

D

★ ★ **LA GROTTA.** *2637 Peachtree Rd NE. 404/231-1368.* Hrs: 6-10:30 pm. Closed Sun; major hols; also last wk June-1st wk July. Res required. Northern Italian menu. Bar. Wine list. Semi-a la carte: dinner $15-$23.50. Specialties: vitello tonnato/carpaccio, veal scaloppine. Own pasta, sauces, desserts. Valet parking. Seasonal outdoor dining. Jacket. Totally nonsmoking. Cr cds: A, C, D, DS, MC, V.

D

★ ★ **LA TOUR.** *3209 Paces Ferry Place. 404/233-8833.* Hrs: 6-11 pm. Closed Sun; some major hols. Res accepted. Continental menu. Bar. Wine cellar. Semi-a la carte: dinner $16.95-$26.95. Child's meals. Specializes in seafood, veal. Own pastries, desserts. Pianist. Valet parking. Classic architectural details, faux marbling in formally decorated dining rms. Jacket. Cr cds: A, C, D, DS, ER, MC, V.

D

★ ★ **McKINNON'S LOUISIANE.** *3209 Maple Dr. 404/237-1313.* Hrs: 6-10 pm; Fri, Sat to 10:30 pm. Closed Sun; major hols. Res accepted. Cajun, Creole menu. Bar. Semi-a la carte: dinner $12.95-$16.95. Specializes in fresh seafood. Parking. Pianist (wkends). Country French decor. Family-owned. Cr cds: A, C, D, DS, MC, V.

D

★ ★ **NAKATO.** *1776 Cheshire Bridge Rd NE. 404/873-6582.* Hrs: 5:30-10 pm; Fri & Sat to 11 pm; Sun 5-10 pm. Res accepted.

Japanese menu. Bar. Semi-a la carte: dinner $11-$35. Child's meals. Specializes in sushi, teppan, sashimi. Valet parking. Japanese garden. Cr cds: A, C, D, JCB, MC, V.

D

✔★ **NINO'S.** *(1931 Cheshire Bridge Rd, Atlanta 30306) 404/874-6505.* Hrs: 5:30-11 pm. Closed Mon; Jan 1, Dec 25. Res accepted. Italian menu. Bar. Semi-a la carte: dinner $8.95-$16.95. Child's meals. Specializes in veal, pasta. Parking. Outdoor dining. Oil paintings, Italian sculpture. Cr cds: A, C, D, DS, MC, V.

D

✔★ **OK CAFE.** *(1284 W Paces Ferry Rd, Atlanta) 404/233-2888.* Open 24 hrs. Closed Mon from 11 pm to 6 am Tues. Closed some major hols. Wine, beer. Semi-a la carte: bkfst $4-$8, lunch $4-$10, dinner $6-$12. Parking. Diner atmosphere. Totally nonsmoking. Cr cds: A, MC, V.

D

★ ★ ★ **PANO'S AND PAUL'S.** *1232 W Paces Ferry Rd. 404/261-3662.* Hrs: 6-10:30 pm; Fri & Sat 5:30-11 pm. Closed Sun; major hols. Res accepted. Continental, Amer menu. Bar from 5 pm. Wine cellar. Semi-a la carte: dinner $15-$27. Specialties: fried lobster tail, thick prime veal chop, creative continental/American dishes, white and dark chocolate mousse. Own baking, desserts. Pianist Fri & Sat. Parking. Victorian decor. Chef-owned. Jacket. Dining rm totally nonsmoking. Cr cds: A, C, D, DS, MC, V.

D

★ ★ **PRICCI.** *500 Pharr Rd. 404/237-2941.* Hrs: 11 am-11 pm; Fri to midnight; Sat 5 pm-midnight; Sun 5-10 pm. Closed Jan 1, Dec 25. Res accepted. Italian menu. Bar. Semi-a la carte: lunch $7-$12, dinner $9-$25. Own breads. Parking. Cr cds: A, C, D, DS, MC, V.

D

★ ★ **SOUTH OF FRANCE.** *2345 Cheshire Bridge Rd. 404/325-6963.* Hrs: 11:30 am-2 pm, 6-10:30 pm; Fri to 11:30 pm; Sat 6-11:30 pm. Closed Sun; major hols. Res accepted. Country French menu. Bar. A la carte entrees: lunch $7.95-$12.95, dinner $12.95-$22.95. Specialties: bouillabaise à la Marseillaise, rack of lamb, duck with orange sauce. Parking. Entertainment Wed-Sat. Country French decor. Cr cds: A, C, D, DS, MC, V.

D SC

★ ★ ★ **SUNTORY.** *3847 Roswell Rd NE. 404/261-3737.* Hrs: 11:45 am-2 pm, 6-10 pm. Closed Sun; most major hols. Res accepted. Japanese menu. Bar. Wine list. Semi-a la carte: lunch $5-$16.50, dinner $12.95-$22.95. Complete meals: lunch $6.95-$25, dinner $31.25. Sushi bar. Parking. Tableside preparation. Elegant Japanese dining with view of Japanese garden; multiple dining areas featuring traditional Japanese service. Cr cds: A, C, D, DS, JCB, MC, V.

D

Unrated Dining Spot

THE VARSITY JR. *(1085 Lindbergh Dr NE, Atlanta 30324) 404/261-8843.* Hrs: 10 am-11 pm; Fri & Sat to midnight; Sun from 11 am. Closed Thanksgiving, Dec 25. Semi-a la carte: lunch, dinner $.75-$2.90. Specializes in hot dogs. Parking. Outdoor dining. 1950s drive-in. Family-owned. No cr cds accepted.

D

Baltimore

Settled: 1661	
Pop: 736,014	
Elev: 32 feet	
Time zone: Eastern	
Area code: 410	

Baltimore, a major East Coast manufacturing center and world seaport, is one of the nation's oldest cities. It began to expand rapidly in the early 19th century, first as a result of the opening of the National Road, which encouraged trade with Midwestern cities, and later as the terminus of the nation's first railroad, the Baltimore & Ohio (incorporated 1827). In 1904, a disastrous fire destroyed 140 acres of the business district and waterfront area, causing losses of more than $50 million. But the city revived rapidly, and during World Wars I and II it was a major shipbuilding and repair center.

The economic health of Baltimore was threatened again during the 1950s and 1960s; buildings decayed and were not replaced, and both people and businesses left for the suburbs. In an effort to revitalize the city, area businessmen, aided by local government and bold city planners, launched a major redevelopment program. Hundreds of acres of slums were cleared to make way for new apartment, office and public buildings; rotting wharves and warehouses were removed to turn Inner Harbor over to public use for the first time in 200 years. Today, festivals, museums, shops and restaurants bring millions of tourists and residents downtown.

Business

Baltimore is the largest city in Maryland and one of the most populous in the nation; it is the heart of a five-county metropolitan area. The city thrives, as it has for two centuries, because of its world seaport. In the 1960s, Baltimore's marine terminals pioneered the use of container shipping. The Port Authority continues to expand in this direction today.

Baltimore has traditionally been one of the East Coast's major industrial and manufacturing centers; virtually all major manufacturing groups are represented. It is best known for its steel mills, automotive assembly plants, can companies, electronics firms and clothing, tool, spice and cosmetic factories. Baltimore is also a financial, retail and transportation hub, with overland shipping of port cargo by rail and truck.

The city's urban renaissance has been applauded and emulated by city planners around the world. The most important business development is the 33-acre Charles Center project, which consists of major office buildings, apartment towers, restaurants, boutiques, theaters, European-style plazas and an elevated walkway system that allows pedestrians to walk 14 blocks without crossing a street.

Convention Facilities

The Baltimore Convention Center/Festival Hall in the Inner Harbor area contains 142,000 square feet of exhibit space and 60,000 square feet of meeting room space, as well as full banquet facilities.

The Baltimore Arena, a 14,000-seat entertainment arena, hosts concerts, circuses, ice and horse shows, meetings and sporting events. The arena is equipped with a permanent stage, modern concessions, dressing room facilities and a sophisticated sound system.

Sports and Recreation

The Pimlico Race Course conducts its annual meet in spring, highlighted on the third Saturday in May by the Preakness Stakes, middle and richest jewel in racing's Triple Crown for three-year-old Thoroughbreds. Between Baltimore and Washington, DC, is Laurel Race Track, with racing in the fall and winter. Timonium's half-mile track in Baltimore County operates during the Maryland State Fair in the late summer.

Oriole Park at Camden Yards hosts Orioles' baseball from April through September. The Baltimore Arena hosts the Major Indoor Soccer League's Baltimore Blast, the Baltimore Skipjacks, who take to the ice for hockey action between October and March, and the Thunder, a world championship box lacrosse team.

Facilities for boating, jogging, swimming, biking and many other activities can be found throughout the city.

Entertainment

The Baltimore Symphony Orchestra season runs from October through May at Meyerhoff Symphony Hall, and the Baltimore Opera Company performs at the Lyric Opera House. Nightclub entertainment is provided at major hotels and clubs. Broadway shows come to the Morris Mechanic Theatre, and repertory plays are performed at Center Stage.

Baltimore hosts many annual festivals, including more than a dozen ethnic festivals and the Preakness Celebration. In June, the Harbor Expo celebrates the city's salty roots with seafood, rowing regattas and visits by antique and modern ships. In July and August, the Inner Harbor's Pier 6 Concert Pavilion presents entertainment four nights a week. The La Provence Concert Series, a series of free outdoor concerts, runs from May to September in Hopkins Plaza. Held the third weekend in September, the City Fair transforms a section of the downtown area into a carnival with more than 100 neighborhood exhibits, a midway and 4 entertainment stages.

Some major department stores are located in suburban malls, such as Security Square and Golden Ring. Chic shopping is found around Harborplace and the Gallery at the Inner Harbor, as well as such neighborhood developments as Cross Keys, Old Town Mall and the Rotunda. Seven city markets, including historic Lexington Market, abound with fresh meats, seafood and produce.

Historical Areas

Many of Baltimore's historically and architecturally significant neighborhoods are undergoing extensive private restoration. Fell's Point, the

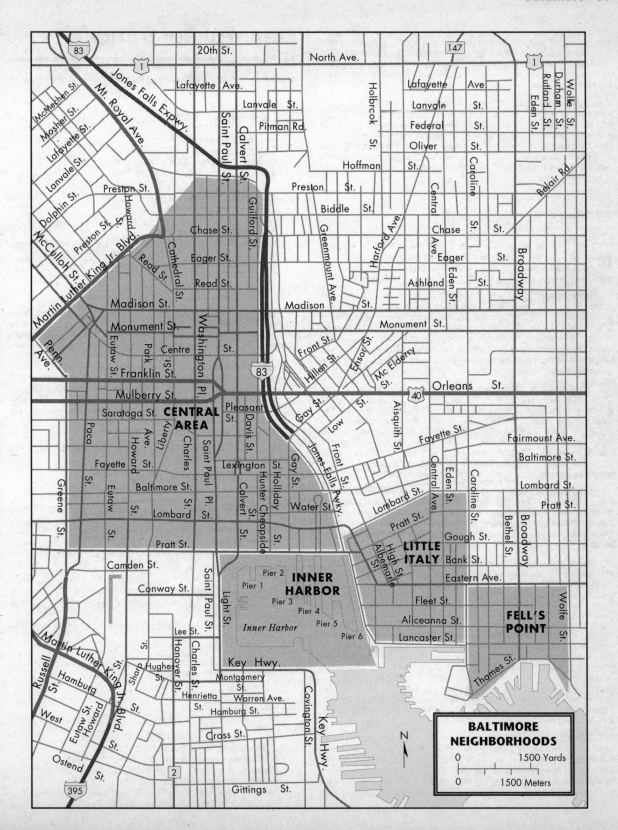

BALTIMORE
NEIGHBORHOODS

0   1500 Yards

0   1500 Meters

city's 18th-century shipbuilding center, retains its nautical character and colonial charm with picturesque houses, shops, bistros and new urban inns. Nearby in Little Italy, churches and restaurants reflect the residents' ethnic heritage. Federal Hill provides a beautiful skyline view of downtown Baltimore; while Bolton Hill has stately town houses, mansions and churches dating from the late 1860s.

Tyson Street, Seton Hill and Charles Village, with Victorian buildings and student residences, are areas worth exploring. Along Stirling Street, Otterbein and Barre Circle are former tenements that were purchased from the city for $1 in a lottery and then renovated by the new owners. Mount Vernon Place, downtown on Monument St, has splendid houses, institutions and a hotel built along formal squares extending from the nation's first major monument, erected in honor of George Washington.

Sightseeing

Many areas of Baltimore have great charm and interest for walkers. Visitors are invited to stop at the visitors information centers, located at 300 West Pratt Street and the kiosk on the West Shore promenade of the Inner Harbor (summer only), to pick up maps and literature.

Inner Harbor, just south of the city center on the basin of the Patapsco River, is one of Baltimore's major accomplishments. Cleared of warehouses and rotting piers, it is a spectacular combination of public and commercial facilities covering 95 acres. The harborside boasts a promenade, the Maryland Science Center, which houses the Davis Planetarium and IMAX Theater, the National Aquarium and Harborplace, a unique mall housing 140 small shops and restaurants in 2 glass pavilions.

The World Trade Center extends out over the water and has an observation deck and exhibits on the 27th floor. Docked along the promenade and open to the public are the US Frigate *Constellation*, the navy's oldest warship; the *Minnie V.,* a Chesapeake Bay skipjack; and the World War II submarine USS *Torsk.* Throughout the summer and early fall, the *Baltimore Patriot,* takes visitors on narrated cruises around the harbor. The *Lady Baltimore* cruises to Annapolis and other Chesapeake Bay destinations, while the *Clipper City,* one of the harbor's largest sailing crafts, offers luxurious excursions.

Baltimore is famous for its many educational institutions. Foremost is Johns Hopkins University, with its world-renowned medical facilities. The downtown campus of the University of Maryland includes Davidge Hall, the oldest medical school building in the country. Morgan State University is one of the nation's finest predominantly black universities.

Many of the city's museums are located in historic buildings. Mount Clare Station, the first passenger station built in the US, houses the B & O Railroad Museum. Edgar Allan Poe's house and grave remind visitors of the poet's life and mysterious death. The Maryland Science Center, National Aquarium, Baltimore Zoo and city parks and gardens provide journeys into the world of nature.

A full history of early Baltimore is gathered into an outstanding group of lithographs, photographs, paintings, artifacts and furniture in the Peale Museum, the oldest museum building in the country. The Maryland Historical Society has a vast collection of American art and literature, including the original manuscript of "The Star-Spangled Banner." Outstanding examples of archaeological art are found at the Walters Art Gallery, and many fine 19th- and 20th-century paintings, including an extensive collection of French Impressionist works, are on display at the Baltimore Museum of Art.

Baltimore is a prime gateway to many of the attractions in the mid-Atlantic region. To the north are Gettysburg and the Pennsylvania Dutch region; to the west are Harper's Ferry, Antietam National Battlefield and the Appalachians. Washington, DC (see) and historic Annapolis are a short drive south; to the east lies the great Chesapeake Bay and the Eastern Shore, with its poultry and produce farms and bustling ocean resorts.

General References

Settled: 1661 **Pop:** 736,014 **Elev:** 32 feet **Time zone:** Eastern **Area code:** 410

Phone Numbers

POLICE & FIRE: 911
FBI: 265-8080
POISON CONTROL CENTER: 528-7701
TIME: 844-1212 **WEATHER:** 936-1212

Information Sources

Baltimore Area Convention and Visitors Association, 1 Light St, 21202; 659-7300.
Visitors Information Centers, 300 W Pratt St, 21201, or Kiosk, West shoreline of Inner Harbor; 837-INFO or 800/282-6632.
Department of Parks & Recreation, 396-7900.

Transportation

AIRLINES: Air Canada; Air Jamaica; American; America West; Cayman; Delta; Northwest; TWA; United; USAir; and other commuter and regional airlines. For the most current airline schedules and information consult the *Official Airline Guide,* published twice monthly.
AIRPORT: Baltimore-Washington International, 859-7100.
CAR RENTAL AGENCIES: (See Toll-Free Numbers) Avis 859-1680; Budget 859-0850; Hertz 850-7400; National 859-8860.
PUBLIC TRANSPORTATION: Mass Transit Administration, 539-5000; Metro Rail Subway, 539-5000; Baltimore Trolley Works, 396-4259.
RAILROAD PASSENGER SERVICE: Amtrak 800/872-7245.

Newspapers

Afro-American; City Paper; The Sun.

Convention Facilities

Convention Center/Festival Hall, 1 W Pratt St, 659-7000.
Baltimore Arena, 201 W Baltimore St, 347-2020.

Sports & Recreation

Major Sports Facilities

Baltimore Arena, 201 W Baltimore St, 347-2020 (Blast, soccer; Skipjacks, hockey).
Oriole Park at Camden Yards, at Inner Harbor, 685-9800 (Orioles, baseball).

Racetrack

Pimlico, Hayward & Winner Aves, 542-9400.

Cultural Facilities

Theaters

Arena Players, Inc, 801 McCulloh St, 728-6500.
Center Stage, 700 N Calvert St, 332-0033.
Fell's Point Corner Theatre, 251 S Ann, 276-7837.
Morris A. Mechanic, Hopkins Plaza, 625-1400.
Spotlighters, 817 St Paul St, 752-1225.
Theatre Project, 45 W Preston St, 752-8558.
Vagabond Players, 806 S Broadway, 563-9135.

Concert Halls

Lyric Opera House, 140 W Mt Royal Ave, 685-5086.
Meyerhoff Symphony Hall, 1212 Cathedral St, 783-8100.
Peabody Institute of the Johns Hopkins University, Friedberg Hall, 1 E Mt Vernon Pl, 659-8165.
Pier 6 Concert Pavilion, Pier 6, 625-1400.

Museums

Baltimore & Ohio Railroad Museum, Pratt & Poppleton Sts, 752-2464.
Baltimore Maritime Museum (USS *Torsk,* Coast guard cutter *Taney* and lightship *Chesapeake*), Pier 3, Pratt St, 396-3854.
Baltimore Museum of Industry, 1415 Key Hwy, 727-4808.
Baltimore Streetcar Museum, 1901 Falls Rd, 547-0264.
Cloisters Children's Museum, 8 mi N, 10440 Falls Rd, Brooklandville, 823-2550.
Johns Hopkins Archaeological Collection, 3400 N Charles St, Gilman Hall, Rm 129, Johns Hopkins University, 516-7561.
Lovely Lane Methodist Church Museum, 2200 St Paul St, 889-1512.
Maryland Historical Society, 201 W Monument St, 685-3750.
Mount Clare Mansion, Carroll Park at Monroe St & Washington Blvd, 837-3262.
Public Works Museum & Streetscape Sculpture, 751 Eastern Ave, 396-5565.
Star-Spangled Banner Flag House and 1812 Museum, 844 E Pratt St, 837-1793.

Art Museums and Galleries

Baltimore Museum of Art, Art Museum Dr near N Charles & 31st Sts, 396-7100 or -7101.
Maryland Institute, College of Art, 1300 W Mount Royal Ave at W Lanvale St, 669-9200.
Peale Museum, 225 Holliday St, 396-1149.
Walters Art Gallery, 600 N Charles St at Centre St, 547-9000.

Points of Interest

Historical

Babe Ruth Birthplace/Baseball Center, 216 Emory St, 727-1539.
Basilica of the Assumption of the Blessed Virgin Mary, Cathedral & Mulberry Sts, 727-3564.
Battle Monument, Calvert & Fayette Sts.
Carroll Mansion, 800 E Lombard St, 396-3523.
City Courthouse, St Paul & Fayette Sts.
City Hall, 100 N Holliday St, 396-3190.
Edgar Allan Poe Grave, Westminster Burying Ground, Fayette & Greene Sts, 706-2070.
Edgar Allan Poe House, 203 N Amity St, 396-7932.
Eubie Blake Cultural Center, 34 Market Pl, 396-8128.
First Unitarian Church, Charles & Franklin Sts, 685-2330.
Fort McHenry National Monument and Historic Shrine, E end of Fort Ave, 962-4299.
Hampton National Historic Site, 535 Hampton Lane, Towson, 962-0688.
H.L. Mencken House, 1524 Hollins St, 396-7997.
Jewish Historical Society of Maryland, 15 Lloyd St, 732-6400.
Minnie V. Skipjack, near Constellation Dock, 522-4214.
Mother Seton House, 600 N Paca St, 523-3443.
Old Otterbein United Methodist Church, Conway & Sharp Sts, 685-4703.
Patterson Park, Baltimore St, Eastern & Patterson Park Aves.
Shot Tower, Fayette & Front Sts.
US Frigate *Constellation,* Pier 1 (Constellation Dock), Pratt St, 539-1797.
Washington Monument, Charles & Monument Sts, 396-7939.

Other Attractions

Baltimore Zoo, Druid Hill Park, 396-7102.
Charles Center, bounded by Lombard, Saratoga, Charles, Liberty Sts.

Cylburn Arboretum, 4915 Greenspring Ave, 396-0180.
Enoch Pratt Free Library, 400 Cathedral St, 396-5430.
Federal Hill Park, Warren St & Battery Ave.
Fell's Point, E of Inner Harbor, S of Fleet St, W of Wolfe St and E of Caroline St.
Harborplace, 200 E Pratt St at Inner Harbor, 332-4191.
Holocaust Memorial, Water & Gay Sts.
Inner Harbor, just S of city center, bordered by Light & Pratt Sts.
Johns Hopkins Medical Institutions, Broadway & Monument Sts.
Lacrosse Hall of Fame, 113 W University Pkwy, 235-6882.
Lexington Market, 400 W Lexington St between Eutaw & Paca Sts, 685-6169.
Maryland Science Center & Davis Planetarium, 601 Light St at Key Hwy, 685-5225.
Morgan State University, Cold Spring Lane & Hillen Rd, 319-3333.
National Aquarium, Pier 3, Pratt St, 576-3800.
Sherwood Gardens, Highfield Rd & Greenway, 366-2572.
William D. Schaefer Conservatory, Druid Hill Park, 396-0180.
World Trade Center Top of the World Observation Deck, Pratt St at the harbor, 837-4515.

Sightseeing Tours

Baltimore Patriot, Inner Harbor, 685-4288.
Baltimore Trolley Tours, 752-2015.
Clipper City, Inner Harbor, 575-7930.
Maryland Classics, 252-0632.
Spirit of Baltimore, Inner Harbor, 752-7447.

Annual Events

Atlantic Crafts Council Crafts Fair, Convention Center/Festival Hall. Late Feb.
Maryland House and Garden Pilgrimage, 1105-A Providence Rd, 21204; 821-6933. Late Apr-early May.
Flower Mart, Mt Vernon Pl. Early May.
Preakness Celebration, 837-3030. 10 days preceding 3rd Sat May.
Showcase of Nations Ethnic Festivals, downtown, 752-8632. June-Sept.
Baltimore International Jumping Classic, Baltimore Arena, 347-2020. Early Oct.
New Year's Eve Extravaganza, Convention Center/Festival Hall and Inner Harbor.

City Neighborhoods

Many of the restaurants, unrated dining establishments and some lodgings listed under Baltimore include neighborhoods as well as exact street addresses. A map showing these neighborhoods can be found immediately following the city introduction. Geographic descriptions of these areas are given, followed by a table of restaurants arranged by neighborhood.

Central Area: South of Mt Royal Ave, west of I-83, north of the Inner Harbor and Pratt St and east of Martin Luther King Jr Blvd and Greene St. **North of Central Area:** North of Chase. **East of Central Area:** East of I-83.
Fell's Point: Waterfront area east of Inner Harbor; south of Fleet St, west of Wolfe St and east of Caroline St.
Inner Harbor: Waterfront area south of Central Baltimore at Pratt St, west of E Falls Ave and east of Light St.
Little Italy: East of Inner Harbor; south of Lombard St, west of Caroline St, north of Lancaster St and the waterfront and east of E Falls Ave.

Lodgings and Food

BALTIMORE RESTAURANTS BY NEIGHBORHOOD AREAS

(For full description, see alphabetical listings under Restaurants)

CENTRAL AREA

Light House. 10 Park Ave

Louie's Bookstore Cafe. 518 N Charles St

Maison Marconi's. 106 W Saratoga

Prime Rib. 1101 N Calvert St

Tio Pepe. 10 E Franklin St

NORTH OF CENTRAL AREA

Angelina's. 7135 Harford Rd

Brass Elephant. 924 N Charles St

Jeannier's. 105 W 39th St

Thai Restaurant. 3316 Greenmount Ave

EAST OF CENTRAL AREA

Haussner's. 3244 Eastern Ave

Ikaros. 4805 Eastern Ave

Karson's Inn. 5100 Holabird Ave

FELL'S POINT

Henninger's Tavern. 1812 Bank St

Obrycki's. 1727 E Pratt St

Waterfront Hotel. 1710 Thames St

INNER HARBOR

City Lights. 301 Light St

Hampton's (Harbor Court Hotel). 550 Light St

Taverna Athena. 201 E Pratt St

Water Street Exchange. 110 Water St

Wayne's Bar-B-Que. 301 Light St

LITTLE ITALY

Capriccio. 846 Fawn St

Chiapparelli's. 237 S High St

Dalesio's. 829 Eastern Ave

Germano's Trattoria. 300 S High St

Giuseppe Ristorante Italiano. 248 Albermarle St

Velleggia's. 829 E Pratt St

Note: *When a listing is located in a town that does not have its own city heading, it will appear under the city nearest to its location. In these cases, the address and town appear in parenthesis immediately following the name of the establishment.*

Motels

(In this area I-95 is Kennedy Memorial Hwy; I-695 is the Beltway)

(Rates may be much higher Preakness wkend, mid-May)

✔★ **CHRISTLEN.** *8733 Pulaski Hwy (US 40) (21237), I-695 exit 35B, east of Central Area. 410/687-1740.* 28 rms. S $32-$38; D $38-$42; each addl $5. Crib $5. TV; cable. Restaurant adj open 24 hrs. Ck-out 11 am. Refrigerators. Picnic tables. Cr cds: A, D, DS, MC, V.

D 🐾 🎇

★ **ECONO LODGE.** *5801 Baltimore Natl Pike (21228), on US 40, just E of I-695 exit 15A, west of Central Area. 410/744-5000; FAX 410/788-5197.* 217 rms, 2-3 story, 38 kits. No elvtr. S $42.95-$48.95; D $45.95-$55.95; each addl $5; kit. units $52.95; under 18 free. Crib free. Pet accepted. TV; cable. Pool; lifeguard. Restaurant 7 am-2 pm, 5-10 pm. Rm serv. Ck-out noon. Coin lndry. Meeting rms. Sundries. Cr cds: A, C, D, DS, JCB, MC, V.

D 🐾 ≋ 🏊 🎇 SC

★★ **HOLIDAY INN SECURITY/BELMONT.** *1800 Belmont Ave (21244), north of Central Area. 410/265-1400; FAX 410/281-9569.* 135 units, 2 story. S, D $59-$83; each addl (after 3 persons) $10; under 18 free; monthly rates. Crib free. Pet accepted. TV; cable. Pool; wading pool, lifeguard. Restaurant 6 am-2 pm, 5-10 pm; Sat & Sun from 7 am. Rm serv. Bar 5 pm-midnight; Sun to 10 pm. Ck-out noon. Meeting rms. Valet serv. Sundries. Health club privileges. Some refrigerators. Cr cds: A, C, D, DS, ER, JCB, MC, V.

D 🐾 ≋ 🏊 🎇 SC

✔★ **SUSSE CHALET.** *4 Philadelphia Court (21237), I-695 exit 34, north of Central Area. 410/574-8100; FAX 410/574-8204.* 132 rms, 5 story. S $48.70; D $55.70; each addl $3. Crib free. TV; cable. Pool; lifeguard. Complimentary continental bkfst. Restaurant nearby. Ck-out 11 am. Coin lndry. Sundries. Cr cds: A, C, D, DS, MC, V.

D ≋ 🏊 🎇 SC

Motor Hotels

★★ **BEST WESTERN-EAST.** *5625 O'Donnell St (21224), I-95 exit 57, east of Central Area. 410/633-9500; FAX 410/633-6314.* 175 rms, 12 story. S $69-$74; D $79-$84; each addl $10; suites $189-$225. Crib avail. Pet accepted; some restrictions; $25 deposit. TV; cable. Indoor pool; lifeguard. Complimentary continental bkfst. Restaurant 6:30 am-10 pm. Rm serv. Bar. Ck-out noon. Coin lndry. Meeting rms. Gift shop. Airport, bus depot transportation. Exercise equipt; weights, treadmill, sauna. Game rm. Cr cds: A, DS, MC, V.

D 🐾 ≋ 🏃 🏊 🎇 SC

★★ **CROSS KEYS INN.** *5100 Falls Rd (21210), north of Central Area. 410/532-6900; res: 800/532-5397; FAX 410/532-2403.* 148 rms, 4 story. S $79-$129; D $99-$139; each addl $10; suites $140-$340; under 16 free; wkend rates. Crib $10. TV; cable. Pool; poolside serv, lifeguard. Restaurant 7 am-10 pm. Rm serv. Bar 11 am-midnight. Ck-out noon. Meeting rms. Shopping arcade. Barber, beauty shop. Free city transportation. Tennis privileges. Bathrm phones. Some private balconies. Cr cds: A, C, D, DS, MC, V.

D 🏌 ≋ 🏃 🏊 🎇 SC

★★ **DAYS INN INNER HARBOR.** *100 Hopkins Pl (21201), in Central Area. 410/576-1000; FAX 410/576-9437.* 250 rms, 9 story. S $75-$95; D $85-$115; each addl $10; suites $115-$130; under 12 free. Crib free. Garage $7. TV; cable. Pool; poolside serv, lifeguard. Restaurant 7 am-10 pm. Rm serv. Bar. Ck-out noon. Meeting rms. Bellhops. Concierge. Sundries. Health club privileges. Some refrigerators. Cr cds: A, D, DS, MC, V.

D ≋ 🏊 🎇 SC

★★ **HOLIDAY INN TIMONIUM.** *(2004 Greenspring Dr, Timonium 21093) I-83 exit 16. 410/252-7373; FAX 410/561-0182.* 250 rms, 5 story. S $99; D $109; each addl $10; suites $150; family, wkly, wkend, hol rates. Crib free. TV; cable. Indoor/outdoor pool; whirlpool, sauna, poolside serv. Restaurant 6 am-10 pm. Bars; entertainment. Ck-out noon. Coin lndry. Meeting rms. Bellhops. Gift shop. Valet serv. Health club privileges. Cr cds: A, C, D, DS, JCB, MC, V.

[D] [≈] [✕] [🔥] [SC]

✔★ **HOWARD JOHNSON.** *5701 Baltimore Natl Pike (21228), 1/2 mi E of I-695 exit 15A, west of Central Area.* 410/747-8900; FAX 410/744-3522. 145 rms, 7 story. S $40-$50; D $48-$60; each addl $8; under 18 free. Crib free. TV; cable. Pool; whirlpool, lifeguard. Restaurant open 24 hrs. Ck-out noon. Coin lndry. Meeting rms. Sundries. Some refrigerators, balconies. Cr cds: A, C, D, DS, ER, JCB, MC, V.

[D] [≈] [✕] [🔥] [SC]

Hotels

★★ **BROOKSHIRE INNER HARBOR SUITE HOTEL.** *120 E Lombard St (21202), Inner Harbor.* 410/625-1300; res: 800/647-0013 (exc MD); FAX 410/625-0912. 90 suites, 12 story. S $145-$185; D $155-$195; each addl $10; children free; wkend rates. Valet parking $15. TV; cable. Restaurant 7 am-10 pm. Bar 11 am-9 pm. Ck-out noon. Meeting rms. Concierge. Health club privileges. Bathrm phones, refrigerators, minibars. Cr cds: A, C, D, DS, MC, V.

[D] [✕] [🔥] [SC]

★★★ **CLARION INN-HARRISON'S PIER 5.** *711 Eastern Ave (21202), Inner Harbor.* 410/783-5553; FAX 410/783-1787. 71 rms, 3 story. May-Oct: S $139-$169; D $149-$179; each addl $10; suites $199-$350; under 18 free; lower rates rest of yr. Crib free. TV; cable. Restaurant 7 am-11 pm. Bar 11-1 am; entertainment. Ck-out noon. Meeting rms. Shopping arcade. Airport transportation. Exercise equipt; weight machines, bicycles. Bathrm phones, minibars. Some balconies. Mahogany furnishings. Atrium lobby with 40-ft skipjack boat. On Inner Harbor. Cr cds: A, C, D, DS, ER, MC, V.

[D] [✕] [✕] [🔥] [SC]

✔★★ **DAYS HOTEL.** *(9615 Deereco Rd, Timonium 21093) I-83 exit 17, Padonia Rd.* 410/560-1000; FAX 410/561-3918. 146 rms, 7 story. S $45-$75; D $45-$90; each addl $5; suites $90-$125; family, hol rates. Crib avail. TV; cable. Pool. Complimentary continental bkfst. Restaurant open 24 hrs. Rm serv 7 am-10 pm. Bar. Ck-out noon. Lndry facilities. Meeting rms. Exercise equipt; weights, treadmill. Health club privileges. Game rm. Cr cds: A, C, D, DS, MC, V.

[D] [≈] [✕] [✕] [🔥] [SC]

★★★ **DOUBLETREE INN AT THE COLONNADE.** *4 West University Pkwy (21218), north of Central Area.* 410/235-5400; FAX 410/235-5572. 125 units, 11 story, 31 suites. S, D $109-$149; each addl $15; suites $135-$475; family rates; wkend, honeymoon plans. Crib free. Pet accepted. TV; cable, in-rm movies. Indoor pool; whirlpool, poolside serv. Restaurant 6 am-11 pm. Rm serv to midnight. Ck-out noon. Meeting rm. Concierge. Gift shop. Barber, beauty shop. Free RR station, bus depot, downtown transportation. Exercise equipt; bicycles, treadmill. Video library. Some wet bars. Balconies. Biedermeier-inspired furnishings; extensive collection of 18th-century European masters. Adj to Johns Hopkins University. Cr cds: A, C, D, DS, ER, JCB, MC, V.

[D] [✔] [≈] [✕] [✕] [🔥] [SC]

★★ **EMBASSY SUITES.** *(213 International Circle, Hunt Valley 21030) I-83N to exit 20A, Shawan Rd E.* 410/584-1400; FAX 410/584-7306. 223 kit. suites, 8 story. S $109-139, D $119-149; each addl $5; under 12 free; wkend rates; higher rates special events. Crib free. Pet accepted. TV; cable. Indoor pool; whirlpool, sauna, steam rm. Complimentary full bkfst. Restaurant 11 am-10 pm. Bar to 2 am. Ck-out noon. Meeting rms. Gift shop. Built around 8-story atrium; glass-enclosed elvtrs. Cr cds: A, C, D, DS, JCB, MC, V.

[D] [✔] [≈] [✕] [🔥] [SC]

★★★ **HARBOR COURT.** *550 Light St (21202), Inner Harbor.* 410/234-0550; res: 800/824-0076; FAX 410/659-5925. 203 rms, 8 story, 25 suites. S $205-$245; D $220-$260; suites $375-$2,000; under 18 free; wkend rates; some package plans. Crib free. Covered parking: self-park $9; valet $12. TV; cable. Heated pool; poolside serv, lifeguard. Restaurant 7 am-11 pm (also see HAMPTON'S). Rm serv 24 hrs. Bar 11-2 am; entertainment exc Sun. Ck-out noon. Meeting rms. Concierge. Airport transportation. Tennis. Exercise rm; instructor, weight machines, bicycles, whirlpool, sauna. Massage. Handball, racquetball courts. Lawn games. Bathrm phones, refrigerators. Elegant retreat located on Inner Harbor; panoramic view of city. Cr cds: A, C, D, DS, ER, JCB, MC, V.

[D] [✕] [≈] [✕] [✕] [✕] [🔥] [SC]

★★ **HOLIDAY INN BALTIMORE-INNER HARBOR.** *301 W Lombard St (21201), in Central Area.* 410/685-3500; FAX 410/727-6169. 375 rms, 10 & 13 story. Apr-Sept: S $109; D $119; each addl $10; suites $250; under 13 free; lower rates rest of yr. Crib free. Pet accepted, some restrictions. Garage parking $6. TV; cable. Indoor pool; lifeguard. Complimentary coffee in rms. Restaurant 6:30 am-11 pm. Bar 11-1 am. Ck-out noon. Convention facilities. Gift shop. Exercise equipt; weight machine, bicycles, sauna. Some balconies. Cr cds: A, C, D, DS, ER, JCB, MC, V.

[D] [✔] [≈] [✕] [✕] [🔥] [SC]

★★★ **HYATT REGENCY.** *300 Light St (21202), adj to Inner Harbor.* 410/528-1234; FAX 410/685-3362. 487 rms, 14 story. S $119-$180; D $145-$200; each addl $25; suites $250-$1,000; under 18 free; wkend plan. Crib free. Valet parking $12. TV; cable. Pool. Restaurant 6:30-1 am. Bar 11:30-2 am; entertainment. Ck-out noon. Convention facilities. Concierge. Gift shop. Tennis. Exercise rm; instructor, weight machines, bicycles, whirlpool, sauna. Minibars. *LUXURY LEVEL :* 54 rms. S, D $175-$225. Private lounge, honor bar. Complimentary continental bkfst, refreshments. Cr cds: A, C, D, DS, ER, JCB, MC, V.

[D] [✕] [≈] [✕] [✕] [✕] [🔥] [SC]

★★★ **LATHAM.** *612 Cathedral St (21201), at Mt Vernon Pl, north of Central Area.* 410/727-7101; res: 800/528-4261; FAX 410/789-3312. 104 rms, 14 story, 2 suites, 5 kits. S $135-$155; D $155-$175; each addl $20; suites $250-$350; under 18 free; wkend, honeymoon packages. Crib free. Valet parking $10. TV; cable. Pool privileges. Restaurants 6:30 am-11 pm. Rm serv to midnight. Bar. Ck-out 1 pm. Meeting rms. Concierge. Health club privileges. Bathrm phones, minibars; some in-rm whirlpools. Restored hotel built 1927. Marble floors & stairs in lobby. Period furnishings, artwork, crystal chandeliers. Cr cds: A, C, D, DS, ER, JCB, MC, V.

[D] [✕] [🔥] [SC]

★★★ **MARRIOTT INNER HARBOR.** *Pratt & Eutaw Sts (21201), Inner Harbor.* 410/962-0202; FAX 410/962-0202, ext. 2044. 525 units, 10 story. S, D $195; suites $195-$650; under 18 free; wkend rates. Crib free. Pet accepted, some restrictions. Covered parking $8. TV; cable. Indoor pool; lifeguard. Restaurant 6 am-11 pm. Bar noon-2 am; entertainment, dancing. Ck-out noon. Convention facilities. Concierge. Exercise rm; instructor, weights, bicycles, whirlpool, sauna. Opp baseball stadium at Camden Yards. *LUXURY LEVEL : CONCIERGE FLOOR.* 70 units. S, D $195; suites $195-$625. Private lounge. Wet bars. Complimentary continental bkfst 7-10 am, refreshments. Cr cds: A, C, D, DS, ER, JCB, MC, V.

[D] [✔] [≈] [✕] [✕] [🔥] [SC]

★★★ **OMNI INNER HARBOR.** *101 W Fayette St (21201), Inner Harbor.* 410/752-1100; FAX 410/625-3805. 703 rms, 2 towers, 23 & 27 story. S $135-$160; D $155-$180; each addl $20; suites $200-$750; under 17 free; wkend rates. Crib free. Garage $9; valet parking $14. TV; cable. Pool; poolside serv, lifeguard. Restaurant 6:30 am-midnight. Bars noon-2 am. Ck-out noon. Convention facilities. Inner Harbor transportation. Exercise equipt; weights, bicycles. Minibars; some refrigerators. Cr cds: A, C, D, DS, ER, MC, V.

[D] [≈] [✕] [✕] [🔥] [SC]

★★ **RADISSON PLAZA-LORD BALTIMORE.** *20 W Baltimore St (21201), in Central Area.* 410/539-8400; FAX 410/625-1060. 419 rms, 23 story. S $129; D $144; each addl $15; suites $199-$350;

kit. units $600-$800; under 17 free; wkend rates. Crib free. Valet parking $12. TV; cable. Restaurants 6:30 am-10 pm. Bar 11-2 am. Ck-out noon. Meeting rms. Concierge. Airport transportation. Exercise equipt; weight machines, bicycles, whirlpool, sauna. Historic landmark; near harbor. Cr cds: A, C, D, DS, ER, JCB, MC, V.

⊡ ⚹ ⟿ 🔥 SC

★ ★ ★ **SHERATON INNER HARBOR.** *300 S Charles St (21201), in Inner Harbor.* 410/962-8300; FAX 410/962-8211. 337 rms, 14 story. Mar-June & Sept-Dec: S, D $155-$185; each addl $15; suites $325-$1,300; under 17 free; wkly, wkend rates; lower rates rest of yr. Crib free. Pet accepted. Covered parking $10. TV; cable. Indoor pool; lifeguard. Restaurant 6:30 am-11 pm. Bar 11:30-2 am. Ck-out noon. Convention facilities. Concierge. Gift shop. Exercise equipt; bicycles, treadmill, sauna. Minibars; some bathrm phones, refrigerators. Cr cds: A, C, D, DS, ER, JCB, MC, V.

⊡ ⚹ ≈ ⚹ ⟿ 🔥 SC

★ ★ ★ **STOUFFER HARBORPLACE.** *202 E Pratt St (21202), Inner Harbor.* 410/547-1200; FAX 410/539-5780. 622 rms, 12 story. S $180-$210; D $200-$230; each addl $20; suites $300-$1,000; under 18 free; wkend rates. Covered parking $8; valet $11. Crib free. TV; cable. Indoor pool; poolside serv, lifeguard. Restaurant 6:30 am-11 pm. Rm serv 24 hrs. Bar 11-1:30 am; entertainment. Ck-out noon. Convention facilities. Concierge. Shopping arcade. Tennis privileges. Exercise rm; instructor, weight machines, bicycles, whirlpool, sauna. Minibars; many bathrm phones. Opp harbor. *LUXURY LEVEL : CLUB FLOOR.* 94 units, 7 suites. S $210-$230; D $230-$250; suites $300-$1,000. Private lounge. Complimentary bkfst, refreshments, newspaper. Cr cds: A, C, D, DS, ER, JCB, MC, V.

⊡ ⚹ ≈ ⚹ ⟿ 🔥 SC

✔ ★ ★ **TREMONT.** *8 E Pleasant St (21202), in Central Area.* 410/576-1200; res: 800/873-6668; FAX 410/244-1154. 58 kit. suites, 13 story. S $89-$119; D $109-$139; each addl $20; under 16 free; wkend rates. Crib free. Pet accepted; $3 per night. Valet parking $8.50. Pool privileges. TV; cable. Restaurant 7 am-2 pm, 5-10 pm. Bar 5 pm-2 am. Ck-out noon. Meeting rms. Health club privileges. Cr cds: A, C, D, DS, MC, V.

⊡ ⚹ ⟿ 🔥 SC

Inns

★ ★ ★ **ADMIRAL FELL.** *888 S Broadway (21231), in Fell's Point.* 410/522-7377; res: 800/292-4667 (exc MD); FAX 410/522-0707. 37 rms, 4 story. S, D $115-$175; each addl $15; wkly rates. TV; cable. Complimentary continental bkfst 7-11 am. Dining rm 11 am-3 pm, 5-9 pm; Sat to 10 pm. Bar 11-2 am. Ck-out noon, ck-in 3 pm. Meeting rms. Concierge. Some in-rm whirlpools. Cr cds: A, D, DS, MC, V.

⊡ ⟿ 🔥 SC

★ ★ ★ **CELIE'S WATERFRONT BED & BREAKFAST.** *1714 Thames St (21231), in Fell's Point.* 410/522-2323; res: 800/432-0184; FAX 410/522-2324. 7 rms (1 with shower only), 3 story. 2-day min: S $90-$140; D $100-$160; hol & wkend rates. Children over 9 yrs only. TV. Complimentary continental breakfast. Complimentary coffee in room. Restaurant adj 11 am-10 pm. Ck-out 11 am, ck-in 3 pm. Refrigerators. On harbor; many antiques. Totally nonsmoking. Cr cds: A, D, MC, V.

⊡ ⟿ 🔥

★ ★ ★ **GOVERNMENT HOUSE.** *1125 N Calvert St (21202), north of Central Area.* 410/539-0566; FAX 410/539-0567. 20 rms, 4 story. S, D $125-$150; wkly rates; Preakness (2-day min). TV. Complimentary continental bkfst, afternoon tea & wine. Restaurant nearby. Ck-out noon, ck-in 2 pm. Part of complex of several Federal and Victorian mansions and town houses (1888). Totally nonsmoking. Cr cds: A, C, D, MC, V.

⟿ 🔥 SC

★ ★ **THE INN AT HENDERSON'S WHARF.** *1000 Fell St (21231), in Fell's Point.* 410/522-7777; res: 800/522-2088; FAX 410/522-7087. 38 rms. S, D $95-$135; each addl $15; under 16 free; higher rates special events. Crib free. TV; cable, in-rm movies avail. Complimentary continental bkfst. Restaurant nearby. Ck-out noon, ck-in 3 pm. Coin lndry. Meeting rms. Bellhops. Valet serv. Sundries. Gift shop. Exercise equipt; weight machine, bicycles. Some refrigerators, minibars. On waterfront. 19th-century tobacco warehouse. Cr cds: A, C, D, MC, V.

⊡ ⚹ ⟿ 🔥 SC

★ ★ ★ **MR MOLE BED & BREAKFAST.** *1601 Bolton St (21217), north of Central Area.* 410/728-1179; FAX 410/728-3379. 5 rms, 5 story, 2 suites. S $75-$100; D $90-$115; each addl $15; suites $100-$145; higher rates wkends (2-day min); children over 16 yrs only. Complimentary continental bkfst. Restaurant nearby. Ck-out 11 am, ck-in 4-6 pm. Free RR station transportation. Built 1867; furnished with 18th- and 19th-century antiques. Library in each rm. Totally nonsmoking. Cr cds: A, DS, MC, V.

⟿ 🔥

✔ ★ **SOCIETY HILL-58 WEST.** *58 W Biddle St (21201), west of Central Area.* 410/837-3630; res: 800/676-3630; FAX 410/837-4654. 15 rms, 4 story. S, D $90-$140. TV; cable. Complimentary continental bkfst. Dining rm 11 am-10 pm; Fri, Sat to midnight. Bar to midnight; Fri, Sat to 2 am; pianist Wed-Sat. Ck-out noon, ck-in 1 pm. Turn-of-the-century building in the heart of the Mt Vernon district; original antique furnishings. Cr cds: A, C, D, MC, V.

🔥 SC

★ ★ ★ **SOCIETY HILL-HOPKINS.** *3404 St Paul St (21218), north of Central Area.* 410/235-8600; FAX 410/235-7051. 26 rms, 4 story. S, D $107-127; suites $127-$135; wkly rates. Crib free. TV. Complimentary continental bkfst, tea & wine. Restaurant nearby. Ck-out 11 am, ck-in 1 pm. Meeting rms. Covered parking. 1920's Spanish-revival apartment building. Rms individually furnished in variety of styles. Cr cds: A, C, D, MC, V.

⟿ 🔥 SC

Restaurants

★ ★ **ANGELINA'S.** *7135 Harford Rd, north of Central Area.* 410/444-5545. Hrs: 11:30 am-10 pm; Fri, Sat to 11:30 pm. Closed Mon; Thanksgiving, Dec 25. Italian menu. Bar. Semi-a la carte: lunch $5-$15, dinner $9-$26. Child's meals. Specializes in crab cakes, seafood. Entertainment Fri. Cr cds: A, DS, MC, V.

★ ★ ★ **BRASS ELEPHANT.** *924 N Charles St, north of Central Area.* 410/547-8480. Hrs: 11:30 am-2 pm, 5:30-9:30 pm; Fri to 11 pm; Sat 5:30-11 pm; Sun 5-9 pm. Closed major hols & Dec 24. Res accepted. Northern Italian menu. Bar 5 pm-1 am. Semi-a la carte: lunch $4.25-$10., dinner $10.50-$22. Complete meals: lunch $7, dinner $15.95. Specializes in homemade pasta, seafood, veal. Own pastries. Braille menu. Historic town house (1861); floor-to-ceiling stained-glass windows, marble fireplace. 6 dining areas, individually decorated. Totally nonsmoking. Cr cds: A, C, D, MC, V.

★ ★ **CAPRICCIO.** *846 Fawn St, Little Italy.* 410/685-2710. Hrs: 11:30 am-10:30 pm; Fri & Sat to 11:30 pm. Closed Thanksgiving, Dec 25. Res accepted. Northern Italian menu. Bar. Semi-a la carte: lunch $6.25-$12, dinner $9.95-$26. Child's meals. Specialties: fettucine frutta de mare (white or red), veal Capriccio, seafood. Own pasta. Cr cds: A, C, D, MC, V.

★ ★ **CHIAPPARELLI'S.** *237 S High St, Little Italy.* 410/837-0309. Hrs: 11 am-11 pm; Fri, Sat to midnight. Closed Thanksgiving, Dec 25. Res accepted. Italian menu. Semi-a la carte: lunch $7-$14, dinner $10-$24. Child's meals. Specialty: Piatto Napolitano. Built 1870; original brick walls, oak paneling. 7 dining rms on 2 levels. Family-owned. Cr cds: A, C, D, DS, MC, V.

⊡

★ ★ **CITY LIGHTS.** 301 Light St, Light St Pavilion, Inner Harbor. 410/244-8811. Hrs: 11:30 am-10 pm; Fri & Sat to midnight. Closed Thanksgiving, Dec 24 & 25. Res accepted. Bar. A la carte entrees: lunch, dinner $5-$18. Child's meals. Specializes in Chesapeake Bay seafood. Own desserts. Outdoor dining. Cr cds: A, C, D, DS, MC, V.

★ ★ **DALESIO'S.** 829 Eastern Ave, Little Italy. 410/539-1965. Hrs: 11:30 am-3 pm, 5-10 pm; Sun 4-9 pm. Closed Thanksgiving. Res accepted. Northern Italian menu. Bar. A la carte entrees: lunch $5.25-$10.95, dinner $9.75-$22.95. Specializes in Northern Italian spa cuisine. Own cakes, pasta. Cr cds: A, D, MC, V.

★ ★ **GERMANO'S TRATTORIA.** 300 S High St, Little Italy. 410/752-4515. Hrs: 11:30 am-11 pm; Fri, Sat to midnight. Closed Thanksgiving, Dec 25. Res accepted. Italian menu. Bar. Semi-a la carte: lunch $4-$8.95, dinner $7.50-$19.75. Child's meals. Specializes in Tuscan cuisine. Cr cds: A, C, D, MC, V.

★ ★ **GIUSEPPE RISTORANTE ITALIANO.** 248 Albermarle St, Little Italy. 410/685-1859. Hrs: 11 am-11 pm. Closed Thanksgiving, Dec 25. Res accepted; required Fri & Sat. Italian menu. Bar. A la carte entrees: lunch $6.50-$13.50, dinner $8.50-$23. Child's meals. Specialties: linguine pescatore, veal involtino. Traditional decor. Cr cds: A, D, MC, V.

D

★ ★ **HAMPTON'S.** (See Harbor Court Hotel) 410/234-0550. Hrs: 5:30-11 pm; Sun to 10 pm; Sun brunch 10:30 am-3 pm. Closed Mon. Res required. Serv bar. Wine list. A la carte entrees: dinner $20-$36. Sun brunch $19.95-$27.95. Specializes in seafood, veal, game, regional dishes. Own pastries. Valet parking $12. Dining rm decor similiar to that of 18th-century mansion. Scenic view of harbor. Jacket. Cr cds: A, C, D, DS, ER, JCB, MC, V.

D

★ ★ **HAUSSNER'S.** 3244 Eastern Ave, east of Central Area. 410/327-8365. Hrs: 11 am-10 pm. Closed Sun, Mon; Dec 25. Res accepted. German, Amer menu. Bar. Semi-a la carte: lunch, dinner $8-$24.50. Specializes in seafood, sauerbraten, strawberry pie. Own baking. Braille menu. Large display of original artwork. Old-world atmosphere. Family-owned. Cr cds: A, C, D, DS, MC, V.

D

★ **HENNINGER'S TAVERN.** 1812 Bank St, in Fell's Point. 410/342-2172. Hrs: 5-10 pm; Fri, Sat to 11 pm. Closed Sun, Mon; Jan 1, Dec 25. Bar to 1 am. A la carte entrees: dinner $13.95-$18.95. Specializes in seafood. Late 1800s atmosphere. Cr cds: A, MC, V.

✔★ ★ **IKAROS.** 4805 Eastern Ave, east of Central Area. 410/633-3750. Hrs: 11 am-10 pm; Fri, Sat to 11 pm. Closed Tues; Thanksgiving, Dec 25. Greek, Amer menu. Serv bar. Semi-a la carte: lunch $4-$9, dinner $8-$15. Specializes in lamb, squid, fresh whole fish. Cr cds: A, C, D, DS, MC, V.

★ ★ **JEANNIER'S.** 105 W 39th St, north of Central Area. 410/889-3303. Hrs: 11:30 am-2:30 pm, 5:30-9:30 pm; Fri to 10 pm; Sat 5:30-10 pm; early-bird dinner 5:30-7 pm. Closed Sun; most major hols. French, continental menu. Bar 11:30 am-11 pm. Wine cellar. A la carte entrees: lunch $6-$11, dinner $13.95-$25. Complete meals: dinner $13 & $22. Specializes in seafood, country-French cuisine. Own pastries, desserts. Country chateau decor. Cr cds: A, MC, V.

★ ★ **KARSON'S INN.** 5100 Holabird Ave, east of Central Area. 410/631-5400. Hrs: 11 am-10 pm; Sat 4-11 pm; Sun noon-9 pm. Closed major hols. Res accepted; required hols. Bar. Semi-a la carte: lunch $4.95-$10.50, dinner $10.95-$32. Child's meals. Specializes in steak, seafood. Parking. Family-owned. Cr cds: A, DS, MC, V.

D

✔★ **LIGHT HOUSE.** 10 Park Ave, in Central Area. 410/727-3814. Hrs: 7-2 am. Closed Thanksgiving, Dec 25. Bar. Semi-a la carte: bkfst $3-$6, lunch $4.50-$9, dinner $9.95-$14. Child's meals. Special-izes in Maryland seafood, Greek shish kebab. Valet parking. Built 1890; former hotel. Cr cds: A, C, D, MC, V.

SC

★ **MAISON MARCONI'S.** 106 W Saratoga, in Central Area. 410/727-9522. Hrs: 11:30 am-3:30 pm, 5-8 pm; Fri & Sat to 9 pm. Closed Sun, Mon; major hols. Res accepted. Continental menu. Serv bar. A la carte entrees: lunch, dinner $7-$19. Specialties: lobster Cardinal, seafood. Complimentary valet parking. Early 19th-century town house. Jacket. Cr cds: A, MC, V.

★ ★ **OBRYCKI'S.** 1727 E Pratt St, in Fell's Point. 410/732-6399. Hrs: noon-11 pm; Sun to 9:30 pm. Closed mid-Dec-Mar. Bar. Semi-a la carte: lunch $5.50-$17.95, dinner $13.25-$24.95. Child's meals. Specializes in steamed crab, crabmeat entrees. Cr cds: A, C, D, DS, MC, V.

D

★ ★ ★ **PRIME RIB.** 1101 N Calvert St (21202), in Central Area. 410/539-1804. Hrs: 5 pm-midnight; Sun 4-11 pm. Closed Thanksgiving. Res accepted. Wine list. A la carte entrees: dinner $15-$25. Specializes in steak, seafood, lamb. Pianist. Parking. Black laquered walls. Paintings and prints displayed. Jacket. Family-owned. Cr cds: A, C, D, MC, V.

★ ★ **TAVERNA ATHENA.** 201 E Pratt St, in Pratt St Pavilion, Inner Harbor. 410/547-8900. Hrs: 11:30 am-10:30 pm; wkends to 11 pm. Closed Thanksgiving, Dec 25. Res accepted; required July 4 & Dec 31. Greek menu. Bar to 11 pm. Semi-a la carte: lunch $4.95-$13.95, dinner $5.95-$26.95. Specializes in seafood, lamb, veal. Outdoor dining. Cr cds: A, C, D, DS, MC, V.

✔★ **THAI RESTAURANT.** 3316 Greenmount Ave, north of Central Area. 410/889-7304. Hrs: 11:30 am-3 pm, 5-10:30 pm; Sun from 5 pm. Closed July 4 & Dec 25. Thai menu. Serv bar. Semi-a la carte: lunch $5.50-$7, dinner $6.95-$14. Specializes in traditional Thai curry dishes. Cr cds: A, MC, V.

★ ★ ★ **TIO PEPE.** 10 E Franklin St, in Central Area. 410/539-4675. Hrs: 11:30 am-2:30 pm, 5-10:30 pm; Fri to 11:30 pm; Sat 5-11:30 pm; Sun 4-10:30 pm. Closed most major hols. Res required. Spanish, continental menu. Bar. Wine cellar. Semi-a la carte: lunch $7-$12, dinner $13.75-$22. Specialties: shrimp in garlic sauce, suckling pig. Spanish casa atmosphere. Jacket. Cr cds: A, C, D, DS, MC, V.

D

★ ★ **VELLEGGIA'S.** 829 E Pratt St, Little Italy. 410/685-2620. Hrs: 11 am-11 pm; Fri, Sat to 1 am. Closed Dec 24 & 25. Res accepted. Italian menu. Bar. A la carte entrees: lunch $4.50-$9.50, dinner $8.50-$19.95. Child's meals. Specializes in veal, seafood. Own pasta. Family-owned. Cr cds: A, D, MC, V.

✔★ ★ **WATER STREET EXCHANGE.** 110 Water St, Inner Harbor. 410/332-4060. Hrs: 11:30 am-11 pm; major hols. Res accepted. Bar to 2 am. Semi-a la carte: lunch, dinner $5-$15. Specializes in salad, sandwiches. Own desserts. Outdoor dining. Victorian decor. Cr cds: A, C, D, DS, MC, V.

★ **WATERFRONT HOTEL.** 1710 Thames St, in Fell's Point. 410/327-4886. Hrs: 11 am-10 pm; Fri, Sat to 11 pm. Closed Dec 25. Res accepted. Continental menu. Bar 10-2 am. Semi-a la carte: lunch $4.50-$9.95, dinner $11.95-$24.95. Child's meals. Specializes in seafood, beef. Restored building (1772) located on waterfront; 3-story brick fireplace, stained-glass windows. Cr cds: A, C, D, MC, V.

✔★ **WAYNE'S BAR-B-QUE.** 301 Light St, in Light St Pavilion, Inner Harbor. 410/539-3810. Hrs: 8 am-midnight; Fri, Sat to midnight. Closed Thanksgiving. Res accepted. Bar to 2 am. A la carte entrees: bkfst $4.50-$7.95, lunch, dinner $5-$12.95. Child's meals. Specializes in barbecue dishes, desserts. Outdoor dining. Cr cds: A, C, D, MC, V.

SC

Unrated Dining Spot

LOUIE'S BOOKSTORE CAFE. *518 N Charles St, in Central Area.* 410/962-1224. Hrs: 11:30-1 am; Mon to midnight; Fri, Sat to 2 am; Sun 10:30 am-midnight; Sun brunch to 3:30 pm. Closed major hols. Bar. Semi-a la carte: lunch $3.50-$8.95, dinner $3.95-$14.75. Sun brunch $3.25-$7. Specializes in Maryland seafood, desserts. Own pastries. Chamber music. Enter through bookstore; cafe in rear. Original artwork. Cr cds: A, MC, V.

Baltimore/ Washington Intl Airport Area

Motel

✔★ **HOLIDAY INN-SOUTH.** *(6600 Ritchie Hwy, Glen Burnie 21061)* I-195 to I-695, E to MD 2 (Ritchie Hwy). 410/761-8300; FAX 410/760-4966. 100 rms, 3 story. S, D $69; each addl $10; under 18 free. Crib free. Pet accepted, some restrictions. TV; cable. Pool; lifeguard. Restaurant 6 am-2 pm, 5-10 pm; Sat, Sun from 7 am. Rm serv. Bar 4 pm-midnight. Ck-out noon. Meeting rms. Valet serv. Mall opp. Cr cds: A, C, D, DS, ER, JCB, MC, V.

Motor Hotels

✔★ ★ **BEST WESTERN AT BWI AIRPORT.** *(6755 Dorsey Rd, Dorsey 21227)* I-295 S to MD 176. 410/796-3300; FAX 410/379-0471. 134 rms, 4 story. S $69; D $74; each addl $5; under 18 free. Crib free. TV; cable. Indoor pool; lifeguard. Complimentary coffee in lobby. Restaurant adj 7 am-11 pm; Sat, Sun to 10 pm. Ck-out noon. Meeting rms. Valet serv. Free airport transportation. Exercise equipt; weight machines, bicycles, whirlpool, sauna. Cr cds: A, C, D, DS, ER, MC, V.

★ ★ **COMFORT INN-AIRPORT.** *(6921 Baltimore Annapolis Blvd, Baltimore 21225)* N on MD 170 to Baltimore Annapolis Blvd. 410/789-9100; FAX 410/355-2854. 188 rms, 6 story. S $70; D $78; each addl $8; suites $125-$225; studio rms $68-$78; under 12 free; wkend rates. Pet accepted. TV; cable. Restaurant 6:30 am-11 pm. Bar 11 am-midnight. Ck-out 11 am. Meeting rms. Bellhops. Valet serv. Free airport transportation. Exercise equipt; weights, bicycles, whirlpool, sauna. Game rm. Cr cds: A, C, D, DS, ER, JCB, MC, V.

✔★ **HAMPTON INN.** *(829 Elkridge Landing Rd, Linthicum 21090)* From I-95 or I-295 take I-195E to exit 1A (MD 170N). 410/850-0600; FAX 410/850-0600, ext. 607. 139 rms, 5 story. S $64; D $68; under 18 free. Crib free. TV; cable. Complimentary continental bkfst, coffee. Restaurant nearby. Ck-out noon. Meeting rms. Bellhops. Valet serv. Free airport, local transportation. Some refrigerators. Cr cds: A, C, D, DS, MC, V.

★ ★ ★ **SHERATON INTERNATIONAL AT BWI AIRPORT.** *(7032 Elm Rd, Baltimore 21240)* N of terminal. 410/859-3300; FAX 410/859-0565. 196 rms, 2 story. S $117-$129; D $129-$149; each addl $10; suites $165-$225; under 16 free; wkend rates. Crib free. TV; cable. Pool; poolside serv, lifeguard. Coffee in rms. Restaurant 6:30 am-3 pm, 5-10:30 pm. Rm serv 24 hrs. Bar 11-2 am; entertainment, dancing. Ck-out noon. Meeting rms. Bellhops. Sundries. Gift shop. Free airport transportation. Exercise equipt; weights, bicycles. Cr cds: A, C, D, DS, MC, V.

★ **SUSSE CHALET.** *(1734 W Nursery Rd, Linthicum 21090)* 410/859-2333; FAX 410/859-2357. 128 rms, 5 story. S $58.70-$65.70; D $61.70-$76.70; each addl $5; suites $79.70-$104.70; under 18 free. Crib free. TV; cable. Pool; lifeguard. Complimentary continental bkfst. Restaurant nearby. Ck-out 11 am. Coin lndry. Meeting rms. Bellhops. Valet serv. Free airport, RR station transportation. Cr cds: A, C, D, DS, MC, V.

Hotel

★ ★ ★ **GUEST QUARTERS-AIRPORT.** *(1300 Concourse Dr, Linthicum 21090)* N on MD 170 to Elkridge Landing Rd, NW 1 1/2 mi to Winterson Rd, W to Concourse Dr; or I-295 to W Nursery Rd exit, then to Winterson Rd. 410/850-0747; FAX 410/859-0816. 251 suites, 8 story. S $140-$170; D $160-$190; each addl $20; under 18 free; wkend rates. Crib free. TV; cable. Indoor pool; lifeguard. Complimentary coffee in rms. Restaurant 6:30 am-11 pm. Bar 11-1 am. Ck-out noon. Convention facilities. Gift shop. Airport transportation. Exercise equipt; weights, bicycles, whirlpool, sauna. Bathrm phones, refrigerators, wet bars. Cr cds: A, C, D, DS, ER, JCB, MC, V.

Pikesville

Motels

✔★ **COMFORT INN NORTHWEST.** *10 Wooded Way, at I-695 exit 20.* 410/484-7700; FAX 410/653-1516. 103 rms, 2-3 story. No elvtr. S $40-$69; D $53-$75; each addl $7; under 18 free; wkly, monthly rates. Crib free. TV; cable. Pool; wading pool, lifeguard. Complimentary continental bkfst. Restaurant adj 6:30 am-11:30 pm. Ck-out 11 am. Coin lndry. Meeting rms. Valet serv Mon-Fri. Cr cds: A, C, D, DS, ER, JCB, MC, V.

★ ★ **HOLIDAY INN PIKESVILLE.** *1721 Reisterstown Rd, at I-695 exit 20.* 410/486-5600; FAX 410/484-9377. 108 rms, 2 story. S, D $49-$79; under 18 free; higher rates Preakness. Crib free. Pet accepted. TV; cable. Pool; poolside serv, lifeguard. Restaurant 6:30 am-2 pm, 5-10 pm; Sat, Sun from 7 am. Rm serv. Bar 4 pm-midnight. Ck-out noon. Meeting rms. Valet serv. Some refrigerators. Cr cds: A, C, D, DS, ER, JCB, MC, V.

Motor Hotel

★ ★ ★ **HILTON INN.** *1726 Reisterstown Rd, at I-695 exit 20S.* 410/653-1100; FAX 410/484-4138. 165 rms, 5 story. S $72-$118; D $82-$128; each addl $10; suites $150-$425; wkend plans; family rates. Crib $10. TV; cable. Pool; lifeguard. Restaurant 7 am-11 pm. Rm serv. Bar 11-2 am; entertainment Fri & Sat, dancing. Ck-out noon. Meeting rms. Bellhops. Valet serv. Gift shop. Barber, beauty shop. Airport transportation. Indoor tennis, pro. Exercise rm; instructor, weight machines, bicycles, sauna. Bathrm phones. Cr cds: A, C, D, DS, ER, MC, V.

Inn

★ ★ ★ **GRAMERCY.** *(1400 Greenspring Valley Rd, Stevenson 21153)* I-695 exit 23N, Falls Rd to 2nd light, left on Greenspring Valley Rd. 410/486-2405. 2 rms, 3 story, 2 suites. No rm phones. D $90-$150; each addl $25; suites $100-$150; family rates. Crib $10. TV. Pool; whirlpool. Complimentary full bkfst. Ck-out noon, ck-in after 3-6 pm. Bellhop. Tennis. Lawn games. Picnic tables. Mansion (1902) on 45-acre wooded estate. Flower, herb gardens. Totally nonsmoking. Cr cds: DS, MC, V.

Restaurant

★ ★ ★ **FIORI.** *(100 Painters Mill Rd, Owings Mills)* From I-695 exit 19, 4 mi NW on MD 795, then right on Owings Mill Blvd, then right on Dolfield Rd S, at jct Painters Mill Rd. 410/363-3131. Hrs: 11:30 am-2:30 pm, 5-9 pm; Sat 5-10 pm; Sun 4-8:30 pm; early-bird dinner Mon-Fri 5-6:30 pm. Closed Jan 1, July 4, Dec 25. Res accepted. Italian menu. Bar. Wine list. A la carte entrees: lunch $4.50-$8.25, dinner $14-$20. Specializes in fresh seafood, homemade pasta, veal. Parking. In Owings mansion (1767), house of proprietor of Owings mills, for which town was named. Cr cds: A, MC, V.

Boston

Founded: 1630

Pop: 574,283

Elev: 0-330 feet

Time zone: Eastern

Area code: 617

No city in the United States attracts more historically interested visitors than venerable, picturesque, dynamic Boston. Named the capital of Massachusetts Bay Colony in 1630, the Boston settlement soon grew to be the largest town in New England. By the middle of the 18th century, Boston was a thriving cultural and political center.

The American Revolution began in Boston, when British troops, in 1770, fired on an angry mob, killing six citizens. The "Boston Massacre," as it came to be known, was followed by the Boston Tea Party in 1773 and the midnight ride of Paul Revere in 1775.

In the years following the Revolution, Boston's prominence continued to grow as many fortunes were made in shipbuilding and international trade. Greater Boston has been a leader in education since 1636, when Harvard College was founded in Newtowne. Today, this area has a tremendous concentration of institutions of higher learning, including Massachusetts Institute of Technology, Tufts, Boston University and Northeastern University.

The Boston metropolitan area, populated by more than 3 million people, is an interesting combination of old and new. It continues to be regarded by many of its natives as the "hub of the universe."

Business

Investment in construction of commercial structures, medical, educational and cultural facilities and housing has increased in Boston during the last few years. The economy of the city is heavily diversified, with a base of finance and insurance, business services, higher education, medical services, recreation and tourism, retail trade and industry.

Boston's harbor, which covers more than 30,000 acres, is one of the world's largest and busiest, and millions of tons of cargo are handled at this port. The harbor has been a major economic asset to the city since its founding.

Hundreds of manufacturing firms make Boston a major industrial center as well.

Convention Facilities

Boston is a favorite city for conventions because it has so much to offer visitors. Its many educational, medical and scientific institutions are a magnet for scholars, researchers and scientists, and the city's varied industrial and commercial activities draw in the business community. In addition, Boston's historical heritage, sightseeing, cultural activities and entertainment make up an urban package that is difficult to match.

The John B. Hynes Veterans Memorial Convention Center has more than 193,000 square feet of exhibit space; a 5,000-seat auditorium with complete stage facilities and dressing rooms; 38 permanent meeting rooms, the largest of which seats up to 1,200, several modular rooms with seating capacities ranging from 125 to 375 and smaller rooms for groups of 25 to 50. There is direct access on the first floor to the Prudential Plaza and on the second to an adjacent hotel.

The 865,000-square-foot World Trade Center on Commonwealth Pier houses meetings, conferences and exhibitions.

Sports and Recreation

Boston has something for everyone in the recreation category. There are the Red Sox for baseball, the Celtics for basketball, the New England Patriots for football and the Bruins for hockey. Visitors can choose among greyhound, Thoroughbred and harness racing. Within a few miles are many lovely Atlantic beaches and several amusement parks.

For the very energetic, a 15-mile jogging trail offers runners not only an opportunity to train for the famed Boston Marathon in April, but also spectacular scenery and attractive sights along its course. It stretches westward from the city along the Charles River, past sailboats and sculling crews, past Massachusetts Institute of Technology, Boston University and Harvard.

Entertainment

Boston has many museums, a planetarium and an aquarium. Symphony concerts, opera and theater are also here to enjoy.

The Boston Symphony season extends from October through April with performances at Symphony Hall. The Boston Ballet season is October, December and February through May. The Boston Pops performs at Symphony Hall from May to mid-July and give free outdoor concerts at the Edward Hatch Memorial Shell on and in the week of July 4th. The Opera Company of Boston season is fall to early spring.

Boston is home to restaurants of every imaginable type, including some of the country's best seafood places, which keep alive the city's heritage as a fishing port.

Many entertainment spots are available throughout Greater Boston, but one of the charms of the city is that a great many of them are within walking distance of the major hotels. Boston is a pedestrian's city, and to enjoy it fully visitors must do some exploring on foot.

Historical Areas

Almost all of Boston could be classified as a "historical area," but the most famous and interesting of its many sights have been marked for walking and bus tours as the Freedom Trail. A map and the official guidebook to Boston are available at Boston information centers and at the Greater Boston Convention and Visitors Bureau.

Before taking the trail, visit the Custom House Observation Tower to scan downtown Boston and the harbor and locate points of interest found on the maps and brochures. The ornate stone tower is 500 feet tall; for many years it was the highest vantage point in Boston.

The Freedom Trail begins at Boston Common, an area used by the residents of the town since 1634, originally for the grazing of cattle and

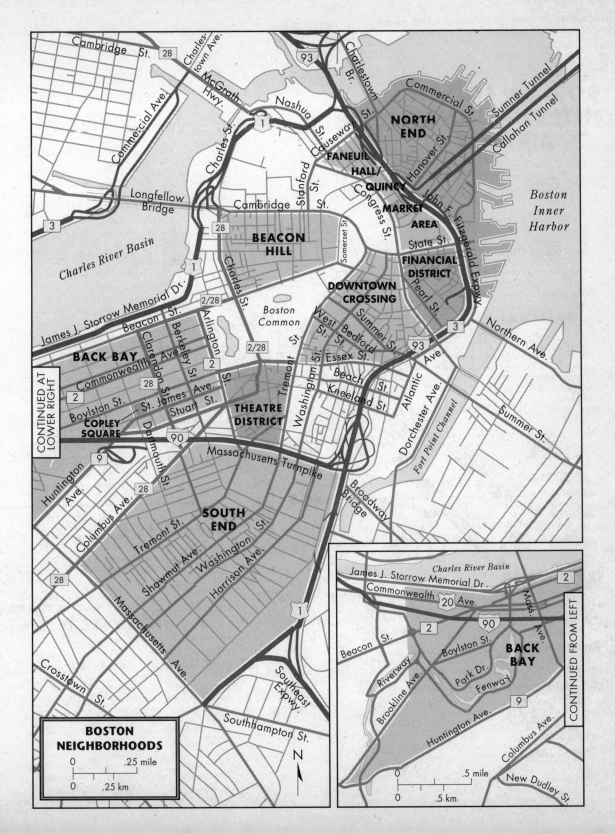

BOSTON NEIGHBORHOODS

0   .25 mile

0   .25 km

N

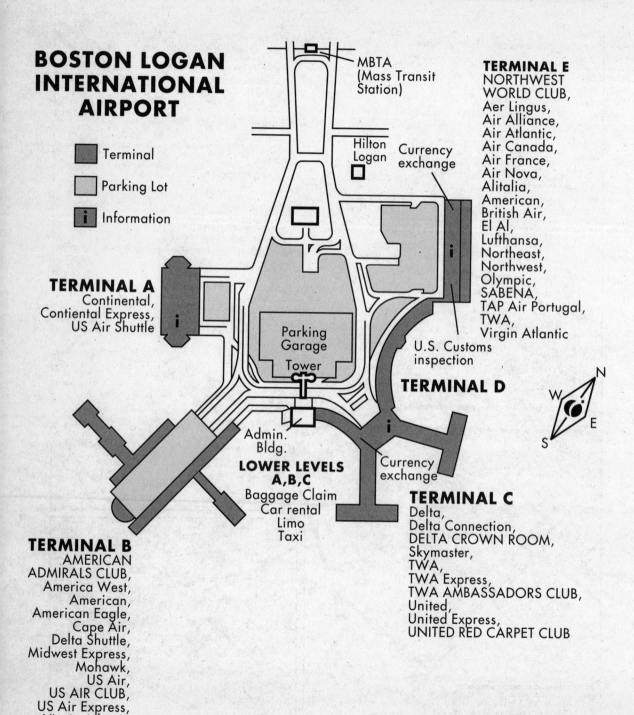

BOSTON LOGAN INTERNATIONAL AIRPORT

- ■ Terminal
- ■ Parking Lot
- **i** Information

MBTA (Mass Transit Station)

Hilton Logan

Currency exchange

TERMINAL E
NORTHWEST WORLD CLUB,
Aer Lingus,
Air Alliance,
Air Atlantic,
Air Canada,
Air France,
Air Nova,
Alitalia,
American,
British Air,
El Al,
Lufthansa,
Northeast,
Northwest,
Olympic,
SABENA,
TAP Air Portugal,
TWA,
Virgin Atlantic

U.S. Customs inspection

TERMINAL A
Continental,
Contiental Express,
US Air Shuttle

Parking Garage

Tower

TERMINAL D

Admin. Bldg.

LOWER LEVELS A,B,C
Baggage Claim
Car rental
Limo
Taxi

Currency exchange

TERMINAL C
Delta,
Delta Connection,
DELTA CROWN ROOM,
Skymaster,
TWA,
TWA Express,
TWA AMBASSADORS CLUB,
United,
United Express,
UNITED RED CARPET CLUB

TERMINAL B
AMERICAN
ADMIRALS CLUB,
America West,
American,
American Eagle,
Cape Air,
Delta Shuttle,
Midwest Express,
Mohawk,
US Air,
US AIR CLUB,
US Air Express,
Virgin Atlantic

N
W E
S

the training of militia. The following spots are designated: the State House, built in 1795 by architect Charles Bulfinch; Park Street Church, where William Lloyd Garrison gave his first antislavery speech in 1829; Granary Burying Ground, where John Hancock, Samuel Adams, Paul Revere and many others are buried; King's Chapel, built in 1749; the site of the nation's first public school, built in 1635; a statue of Benjamin Franklin, dating from 1856; the Globe Corner Book Store Building, located on the site of Anne Hutchinson's house, and once a gathering place for such scholars and writers as Emerson, Longfellow, Holmes, Whittier, Hawthorne, Stowe and Howe.

Also along the Trail are Old South Meeting House, from which the group of patriots left to launch the Boston Tea Party; the Old State House, built in 1713; the site of the Boston Massacre, just outside the Old State House; Faneuil Hall, public marketplace, meeting place and "cradle of liberty"; Paul Revere House, built ca 1680, the oldest building in the city; Old North Church, 1723, an architectural gem, oldest standing church in Boston and the place where the two lanterns were hung on the night of April 18, 1775; the USS *Constitution*, "Old Ironsides," a 44-gun frigate built in 1797; a replica of the brig *Beaver*, scene of the Boston Tea Party on the night of December 16, 1773; and finally, the Bunker Hill Monument in Charlestown, commemorating the first major battle of the Revolution on June 17, 1775.

Although a good many of the city's historical sites are situated along the Freedom Trail, the entire Boston area is filled with places that preserve the nation's past. The Black Heritage Trail walking tour covers much of the Beacon Hill section that relates to the history of 19th-century black Boston. To take this walking tour start at the African Meeting House. An informal walking tour of the Back Bay area can lead to many interesting sites of early Boston.

Information centers are located on the Boston Common, the Visitor Center in Prudential Plaza West and at the National Park Visitor Hospitality Center at 15 State St. For information phone 536-4100.

Sightseeing

Boston is a gateway to many New England destinations. Among them are the north woods and rugged seacoast of Maine, the breathtaking scenery of the White Mountains, the serene Green Mountains, ski resorts in all directions and the charming and scenic old Rhode Island cities of Providence and Newport.

But close enough for Boston to serve as your headquarters are four major regions: the North Shore, the South Shore, Cape Cod and the suburbs of Boston.

The North Shore includes Rockport, a seacoast art colony with more than 60 shops, galleries and craft studios; Gloucester, once one of the nation's largest fishing ports and still one of the finest places for seafood; and the "bewitched" city of Salem, now a quiet sea town, home of the House of Seven Gables and interesting mansions built by captains of the clipper ships.

On the South Shore, which runs from Boston to Cape Cod, are two places not to be missed. One is Quincy, home of John Adams and John Quincy Adams, where three 17th- and 18th-century houses in which the two presidents lived are open to the public. The second town is Plymouth, where there is enough to see and do for at least one full day. The tiny rock on which the Pilgrims landed is enshrined in an observation cupola, and nearby is a full-scale replica of the *Mayflower*. South of town is Plimoth Plantation, a 100-acre reproduction of the first settlement. Other points of interest are the Antiquarian House, Major John Bradford House, Burial Hill, Cole's Hill, Harlow Old Fort House, Howland House, Pilgrim Hall Museum, Pilgrim Village, Plymouth National Wax Museum, Spooner House and Richard Sparrow House.

Cape Cod is a mecca for artists and sailing enthusiasts. Swimmers, scuba divers, sunbathers and sand-lovers have more than 300 miles of shoreline to enjoy. Most of the outer cape is preserved by the National Seashore Park and is open for public recreation.

The suburbs of Boston are as interesting as the city itself. Cambridge, home of Harvard University, Radcliffe College and the Massachusetts Institute of Technology, has been an intellectual community for centuries. Homes of many famous scholars are here, and the

museums of Harvard University are among the most varied and interesting on the continent.

Lexington and Concord, where the American Revolution actually began, have numerous memorials to the past. A stroll through these communities will take the visitor past dozens of markers, monuments, restored historic houses and buildings open to the public; guides stand ready to tell fascinating stories of the early days of the Revolution and of 19th-century Concord, when the city was the home of Emerson, Thoreau, Hawthorne and the Alcotts.

General References

Founded: 1630 **Pop:** 574,283 **Elev:** 0-330 feet **Time zone:** Eastern **Area code:** 617

Phone Numbers

POLICE & FIRE: 911
FBI: 742-5533
POISON CONTROL CENTER: 800/682-9211 or 232-2120.
TIME: 637-1234 **WEATHER:** 936-1234

Information Sources

Greater Boston Convention & Visitors Bureau, Prudential Tower, PO Box 490, 02199; 536-4100.
Boston Common Information Center, Boston Common, Tremont St, 426-3115.
National Park Visitor Center, 15 State St, 02109; 242-5642.
Parks & Recreation Department, 10 Massachusetts Ave, 635-4505.

Transportation

AIRLINES: Aer Lingus (Ireland); Air Canada; Air France; Alitalia; American; America West; British Airways; Cape Air; Continental; Delta; El Al (Israel); Lufthansa (Germany); Midwest Express; Mohawk; Northwest; QANTAS (Australia); SABENA (Belgium); Skymaster; TWA; United; USAir; and other commuter and regional airlines. For the most current airline schedules consult the *Official Airline Guide,* published twice monthly.
AIRPORT: Logan International, 800/235-6426.
CAR RENTAL AGENCIES: (See Toll-Free Numbers) Avis 561-3500; Budget 787-8200; Hertz 569-7272; National 569-6700.
PUBLIC TRANSPORTATION: Massachusetts Bay Transportation Authority, 722-3200.
RAILROAD PASSENGER SERVICE: Amtrak 800/872-7245.

Newspapers

Boston Globe; Boston Herald; Christian Science Monitor.

Convention Facilities

John B. Hynes Veterans Memorial Convention Center, 900 Boylston St, 424-8585.
World Trade Center, 164 Northern Ave, 439-5000.

Sports & Recreation

Major Sports Facilities
Boston Garden, 150 Causeway St, 227-3200 (Celtics, basketball; Bruins, hockey).
Fenway Park, Jersey St at Brookline Ave, 267-1700 (Red Sox, baseball).

Sullivan Stadium. US 1, Foxboro, 508/543-1776 (New England Patriots, football).

Racetrack

Wonderland, US 1A, Revere, 284-1300 (greyhound racing).

Cultural Facilities

Theaters

(Bostix, Faneuil Hall Marketplace, 723-5181, offers half-price tickets for same-day theater, music and dance performances)

American Repertory Theater, 64 Brattle St, Cambridge, 547-8300.
Boston Ballet Co, 19 Clarendon St, 695-6950.
Boston Center for the Arts, 539 Tremont St, 426-5000.
Charles Playhouse Theatre, 74 Warrenton St, 426-5225.
Colonial Theatre, 106 Boylston St, 426-9366.
Opera Laboratory Theatre, 162 Boylston St, 426-4943.
Shubert Theatre, 265 Tremont St, 426-4520.

Concert Halls

Berklee Performance Center, 136 Massachussetts Ave, 266-7455.
Boston Center for the Arts, 539 Tremont St, 426-5000.
Symphony Hall, 301 Massachusetts Ave, 266-1492.

Museums

African Meeting House, Museum of Afro-American History, 46 Joy St, on Beacon Hill, 742-1854.
Bell's Laboratory, New England Telephone Bldg, 185 Franklin St, in lobby, 743-9800.
Blue Hills Trailside Museum, 1904 Canton Ave, Milton, 333-0690.
Boston Tea Party Ship and Museum, Congress St Bridge on Harborwalk, 338-1773.
Cape Ann Historical Museum, 27 Pleasant St, Gloucester, 508/283-0455.
Children's Museum, Museum Wharf, 300 Congress St, 426-8855.
Computer Museum, Museum Wharf, 300 Congress St, 423-6758.
Concord Museum, 200 Lexington Rd, Concord, 508/369-9609.
DeCordova Museum, 51 Sandy Pond Rd, Lincoln, 259-8355.
Gibson House Museum, 137 Beacon St, 267-6338.
Harvard University Museums of Cultural and Natural History, 24 Oxford St, Cambridge, 495-2341.
Longyear Museum, 120 Seaver St, Brookline, 277-8943.
Museum at the John Fitzgerald Kennedy Library, University of Massachusetts Columbia Point campus, 929-4523.
Museum of Our National Heritage, 33 Marrett Rd, Lexington, 861-6559.
Museum of Science and Charles Hayden Planetarium, Science Park, Charles River Dam Bridge, 723-2500 or 523-6664.
Museum of Transport, 15 Newton St, Lars Anderson Park, 522-6547.
New England Aquarium, Central Wharf, 973-5200.
Nichols House Museum, 55 Mt Vernon St, 227-6993.
Peabody Museum, East India Square, Salem, 508/745-9500 or -1876.
Salem Witch Museum, 19½ Washington Square N, Salem, 508/744-1692.
USS Constitution, Boston National Historical Park, 426-1812 or 242-5670.

Art Museums

Boston Center for the Arts, 539 Tremont St, 426-5000.
Concord Art Association, 37 Lexington Rd, Concord, 508/369-2578.
Fogg Art Museum, 32 Quincy St, Harvard University, Cambridge, 495-9400.

Guild of Boston Artists, 162 Newbury St, 536-7660.
Institute of Contemporary Art, 955 Boylston St, 266-5151.
Isabella Stewart Gardner Museum, 280 The Fenway, 566-1401 or 734-1359.
Museum of Fine Arts, 465 Huntington Ave, 267-9300.
Sackler Art Museum, 485 Broadway, Harvard University, Cambridge, 495-9400.

Points of Interest

Historical

Battle Green, center of town, Lexington.
Beauport, 75 Eastern Point Blvd, Gloucester, 508/283-0800.
Black Heritage Trail, start at African Meeting House, Smith Ct, 742-1854 or -5415.
Boston Common, Beacon & Tremont Sts.
Boston Massacre Monument, Boston Common.
Boston Massacre Site, 30 State St.
Boston National Historical Park, visitor center located at 15 State St, 242-5642.
Boston Public Library, 666 Boylston St, 536-5400.
Buckman Tavern, 1 Bedford St, Lexington, 862-5598.
Bunker Hill Monument, Monument Square, Lexington & High Sts, Charlestown, 242-5641.
Central Burying Ground, Boston Common.
Copley Square, Boylston St, west of Trinity Cathedral (Trinity St), north of St James Ave and east of the Public Library.
Copp's Hill Burying Ground, Hull & Snow Hill Sts.
Faneuil Hall, Merchants Row & Faneuil Hall Square, 227-1638.
Frederick Law Olmstead National Historic Site, 99 Warren St, Brookline, 566-1689.
The Freedom Trail, downtown Boston. Follow signs and red brick sidewalk line.
Globe Corner Book Store, School & Washington Sts, 523-6658.
Gloucester Fisherman, off Western Ave on the harbor, Gloucester.
Granary Burying Ground, Tremont St, opposite end of Bromfield St.
Hammond Castle Museum, 80 Hesperus Ave, Gloucester, 508/283-7673.
Hancock-Clarke House, 36 Hancock St, Lexington, 861-0928.
Harrison Gray Otis House, 141 Cambridge St, 227-3956.
House of Seven Gables, 54 Turner St, at Derby St, Salem, 508/744-0991.
Isaac Royall House, 15 George St, Medford, 396-9032.
John F. Kennedy National Historic Site, 83 Beals St, Brookline, 566-7937.
King's Chapel, Tremont & School Sts, 227-2155.
Longfellow National Historic Site, 105 Brattle St, Cambridge, 876-4491.
Louisburg Square, Mount Vernon St.
Minute Man National Historical Park, North Bridge Unit, 174 Liberty St, Concord, 508/369-6993.
Munroe Tavern, 1332 Massachusetts Ave, Lexington, 862-1703.
The Old Manse, Monument St at the North Bridge, Concord, 508/369-3909.
Old North Church, 193 Salem St, 523-6676.
Old South Meeting House, 310 Washington St, 482-6439.
Old State House, 206 Washington St, at State St, 720-3290.
Orchard House and School of Philosophy, 399 Lexington Rd, Concord, 508/369-4118.
Park Street Church, 1 Park St, 523-3383.
Paul Revere House, 19 North Square, 523-2338.
Peabody Essex Museum, East India Sq, Salem, 508/744-3390.
Plimoth Plantation, MA 3A (Warren Ave), Plymouth, 508/746-1622.
Plymouth Rock, Water St, Plymouth.
Ralph Waldo Emerson House, 28 Cambridge Tpke, at Lexington Rd, Concord, 508/369-2236.
Sargent House Museum, 49 Middle St, Gloucester, 508/281-2432.

Site of the First Public School, School St.
Sleepy Hollow Cemetery, Bedford St, Concord.
State House, Beacon St at head of Park St.
Statue of Benjamin Franklin, School St, near Old City Hall.
Trinity Church, Copley Square, 536-0944.
USS Constitution, Boston National Historical Park, 426-1812 or 242-5670.
Walden Pond State Reservation, 915 Walden St, Concord, 508/369-3254.
The Wayside, Lexington Rd, Concord, 508/369-6975.

Other Attractions

Back Bay Area, Commonwealth Ave.
Cape Cod, SE of Boston.
Copley Place, 100 Huntington Ave, Copley Square, 375-4477.
Franklin Park Zoo, S on Jamicaway, then E on MA 203, in Dorchester area, 442-2002.
Harvard University, Harvard Square, Cambridge, 495-1573.
John Hancock Observatory, 200 Clarendon St, at Copley Square, 572-6429.
Market District, Haymarket Square.
The Mother Church, The First Church of Christ, Scientist, Christian Science Center, Huntington & Massachusetts Aves, 450-3790.
Prudential Center, 800 Boylston St, 236-3318.
Public Garden, Charles St.
The Skywalk, Prudential Tower.
"Whites of their Eyes," Bunker Hill Pavilion, 55 Constitution Rd, Charlestown, 241-7575.

Sightseeing Tours

Bay State Cruise Company, 67 Long Wharf, 723-7800.
Boston by Foot, 77 N Washington St, 367-2345.
Boston Tours, 56 William St, Waltham, 899-1454.
Brush Hill Tours, Prudential Center, 236-2148.
Massachusetts Bay Lines, 60 Rowes Wharf, 542-8000.
Old Town Trolley Tours, 329 W 2nd St, 269-7010.

Annual Events

Chinese New Year. Feb.

St Patrick's Day & Evacuation Day. Mid-Mar.
Patriots Day. 3rd Mon Apr.
Boston Marathon. 3rd Mon Apr.
Bunker Hill Day. Mid-June.
Harborfest, Hatch Shell on the Esplanade. Late June-July 4.
Esplanade Concerts. Late June-early July.
Charles River Regatta. 3rd Sun Oct.
First Night Celebration. New Year's Eve.

City Neighborhoods

Many of the restaurants, unrated dining establishments and some lodgings listed under Boston include neighborhoods as well as exact street addresses. A map showing these neighborhoods can be found immediately following the city introduction. Geographic descriptions of these areas are given, followed by a table of restaurants arranged by neighborhood.

Back Bay: South of Memorial Dr along the Charles River Basin, west of Arlington St, north of Stuart St and Huntington Ave and east of Boston University campus and Brookline.
Beacon Hill: South of Cambridge St, west of Somerset St, north of Beacon St and east of St Charles St.
Copley Square: South of Boylston St, west of Trinity Cathedral (Trinity St), north of St James Ave and east of the Public Library (Dartmouth St).
Downtown Crossing: At intersection of Washington St and Winter and Summer Sts; area south of State St, north of Essex St, east of Tremont St and west of Congress St.
Faneuil Hall/Quincy Market Area: South and west of the John F. Fitzgerald Expy (I-93), north of State St and east of Congress St.
Financial District: South of State St, west and north of the John F. Fitzgerald Expy (I-93) and east of Congress St.
North End: Bounded by Boston Harbor and the John F. Fitzgerald Expy (I-93).
South End: South of I-90, west of John F. Fitzgerald Expy (I-93), north of Massachusetts Ave and east of Columbia Ave.
Theatre District: South of Boylston St, west of Tremont St, north of I-90 and east of Arlington St.

Lodgings and Food

BOSTON RESTAURANTS
BY NEIGHBORHOOD AREAS

(For full description, see alphabetical listings under Restaurants)

BACK BAY

Aujourd'hui (Four Seasons Hotel). 200 Boylston St
Cactus Club. 939 Boylston St
Casa Romero. 30 Gloucester St
Charley's. 284 Newbury St
Ciao Bella. 240A Newbury St
The Dining Room (The Ritz-Carlton, Boston Hotel). 15 Arlington St
Grill 23. 161 Berkley St
Harvard Book Store Cafe. 190 Newbury St
L'Espalier. 30 Gloucester St
The Lounge (The Ritz-Carlton, Boston Hotel). 15 Arlington St
Mirabelle. 85 Newbury St
Morton's Of Chicago. One Exeter Plaza
Mr. Leung. 545 Boylston St
Small Planet Bar & Grill. 565 Boylston St
Spasso. 160 Commonwealth Ave
Top of the Hub. 800 Boylston St

BEACON HILL

Hungry I. 71½ Charles St
Library Grill at the Hampshire House. 84 Beacon St
Rebecca's. 21 Charles St
Ristorante Toscano. 47 Charles St

COPLEY SQUARE

Cafe Budapest (Copley Square Hotel). 47 Huntington Ave

DOWNTOWN CROSSING AREA

Locke Ober. 3 Winter Place
Maison Robert. 45 School St
Parker's (Omni Parker House). 60 School St

FANEUIL HALL/QUINCY MARKET AREA

Bay Tower Room. 60 State St
Cricket's. 101 S Faneuil Hall Marketplace
Durgin Park. 30 N Market St
Ye Olde Union Oyster House. 41 Union St
Zuma's Tex Mex Cafe. 7 N Market St

FINANCIAL DISTRICT

Jimmy's Harborside. 242 Northern Ave
Julien (Meridien Hotel). 250 Franklin St
Rowes Wharf (Boston Harbor Hotel). 70 Rowes Wharf

NORTH END

Davide. 326 Commercial St

Felicia's. 145A Richmond St
Jasper's. 240 Commercial St
Joe Tecce's. 61 N Washington St
Mamma Maria. 3 North Square
Michael's Waterfront. 85 Atlantic Ave
No Name. 15½ Fish Pier
Sally Ling's. 256 Commercial St

SOUTH END

Icarus. 3 Appleton St
St Cloud. 557 Tremont St

THEATRE DISTRICT

Kyoto. 201 Stuart St

Note: *When a listing is located in a town that does not have its own city heading, it will appear under the city nearest to its location. In these cases, the address and town appear in parenthesis immediately following the name of the establishment.*

Motel

✔★ **SUSSE CHALET.** 800 Morrissey Blvd (02122), 3 mi S of Downtown Crossing Area. 617/287-9100. 176 rms, 2-3 story. S $49.70-$67.70; D $59-$73; each addl $3-$7; under 18 free. Crib $3. TV; cable. Pool; lifeguard. Restaurant adj 6:30 am-10:30 pm. Ck-out 11 am. Coin lndry. Meeting rms. Gift shop. Refrigerators avail. Cr cds: A, C, D, DS, MC, V.

D 🏊 🚫 🔥 SC

Hotels

★★ **BEST WESTERN BOSTON-THE INN AT CHILDREN'S.** 342 Longwood Ave (02115), in Back Bay. 617/731-4700; FAX 617/731-6273. 152 rms, 8 story. S $79-$215; D $89-$225; each addl $15; kits. $119-$225; under 18 free. Crib free. Covered parking $12. TV. Restaurant 7 am-10 pm, dining rm 11:30 am-2:30 pm, 5-10 pm. Bar; entertainment. Ck-out noon. Meeting rm. Shopping arcade. Health club privileges. Cr cds: A, C, D, DS, ER, MC, V.

D 🚫 🔥 SC

★★★★ **BOSTON HARBOR.** 70 Rowes Wharf (02110), on the waterfront, in Financial District. 617/439-7000; res: 800/752-7077; FAX 617/330-9450. 230 rms, 16 story, 26 suites. S $195-$330; D $225-$375; each addl $50; suites $425; under 18 free; wkend packages. Crib free. Pet accepted, some restrictions; kennel facilities also available. Garage parking, valet $23 or self-park. TV; cable. Indoor pool; poolside serv. Restaurant 6 am-11 pm (also see ROWES WHARF). Rm serv 24 hrs. Bar 11:30-2 am; entertainment. Ck-out 1 pm. Meeting rms. Concierge. Airport transportation. Complimentary transportation throughout the greater Boston area. Exercise rm; instructor, weight machines, bicycles, whirlpool, sauna, steam rm. Masseuse. European-style spa. Bathrm phones, minibars. Balconies. On waterfront; water shuttle service to and from Logan airport. Copper-domed observatory provides panoramic view of city. Extensive art collection in public areas. Cr cds: A, C, D, DS, JCB, MC, V.

D ⛵ 🏊 🏋 🚫 🔥

★★ **BOSTON PARK PLAZA HOTEL & TOWERS.** 64 Arlington St (02116), in Back Bay. 617/426-2000; res: 800/225-2008; FAX 617/426-5545. 974 rms, 15 story. S $155-$195; D $175-$215; each addl $20; suites $375-$595; family, wkend rates. Garage $18; valet. TV. Pool privileges. Restaurant 6:30 am-9 pm. Rm serv 24 hrs. Bar 11-2 am; piano bar exc Sun. Ck-out noon. Convention facilities. Concierge. Shopping arcade. Barber, beauty shop. Airport transportation. Exercise equipt; stair machine, bicycles. Health club privileges. Some bathrm phones, refrigerators. *LUXURY LEVEL : PLAZA TOWERS.* 617/426-2345. 82 rms, 5 suites. S $195-$245; D $215-$265; suites $595-$2,000.

Private lounge. Complimentary continental bkfst, refreshments, newspapers. Cr cds: A, C, D, DS, ER, JCB, MC, V.

D 🏊 🌊 🚶 🎿 🔥 SC

★ ★ ★ **THE COLONNADE.** *120 Huntington Ave (02116), in Back Bay.* 617/424-7000; res: 800/962-3030; FAX 617/424-1717. 288 rms, 11 story. Apr-June & Sept-Nov: S $205-$265; D $230-$290; suites $435-$1,400; under 12 free; wkly, wkend & hol rates; higher rates: marathon, graduation; lower rates rest of yr. Crib free. Pet accepted, some restrictions. Valet parking $20. Pool; poolside serv. Restaurant 7 am-11 pm. Rm serv 24 hrs. Bar; entertainment Tues-Sat. Ck-out noon. Meeting rms. Concierge. Airport transportation. Exercise equipt; weights, bicycles. Health club privileges. Refrigerators avail. Minibars. Cr cds: A, C, D, DS, ER, JCB, MC, V.

D 🏊 🌊 🚶 🎿 🔥 SC

★ ★ ★ ★ **COPLEY PLAZA WYNDHAM.** *138 St James Ave (02116), in Copley Square.* 617/267-5300; FAX 617/267-7668. 373 rms, 7 story. S $160-$245; D $185-$265; each addl $25; suites $375-$1,200; under 17 free; special wkend rates. Crib free. Pet accepted, some restrictions. Valet parking $20. TV; cable. Pool privileges. Restaurant 6:30 am-11:30 pm. Rm serv 24 hrs. Bars 11:30-2 am; pianist. Ck-out 1 pm. Meeting rms. Concierge. Shopping arcade. Barber, beauty shop. Airport, RR station transportation. Tennis privileges. Health club privileges. Old world elegance. Cr cds: A, C, D, DS, ER, JCB, MC, V.

D 🏊 🏃 🎿 🌊 🔥 SC

★ ★ **COPLEY SQUARE.** *47 Huntington Ave (02116), in Copley Square.* 617/536-9000; res: 800/225-7062; FAX 617/267-3547. 143 rms, 7 story. S $105-$145; D $120-$165; each addl $10; suites $250; under 17 free. Crib free. Garage $12; in/out $5. TV; cable. Complimentary coffee in rms. Restaurant 7 am-11 pm (also see CAFE BUDAPEST). Bar 11:30-2 am. Ck-out noon. Meeting rms. Concierge. Airport transportation. Family-owned hotel; established 1891. Cr cds: A, C, D, DS, ER, JCB, MC, V.

D 🌊 🔥 SC

★ ★ ★ **FOUR SEASONS.** *200 Boylston St (02116), in Back Bay.* 617/338-4400; FAX 617/423-0154. 288 rms, 15 story. S $240-$415; D $280-$455; each addl $40; suites $375-$2,600; under 18 free; wkend rates. Crib free. Pet accepted, some restrictions. Valet, garage parking $20. TV; cable. Indoor pool; poolside serv. Restaurant 7 am-11 pm (also see AUJOURD'HUI). Rm serv 24 hrs. Bar 11-1 am; entertainment. Ck-out 1 pm. Convention facilities. Concierge. Gift shop. Free transportation downtown 7 am-10 pm. Exercise equipt; weights, bicycles, whirlpool, sauna. Bathrm phones, refrigerators. Classic elegance. Overlooks public gardens. Cr cds: A, C, D, ER, JCB, MC, V.

D 🏊 🌊 🚶 🎿 🔥 SC

★ ★ ★ **GUEST QUARTERS SUITES.** *400 Soldiers Field Rd (02134), west of Back Bay, north of Brookline.* 617/783-0090; FAX 617/783-0897. 310 suites, 15 story. S, D $189-$219; each addl $20; under 18 free; wkend packages. Crib free. TV; cable. Indoor pool. Complimentary coffee in rms. Restaurant 6:30 am-10 pm. Bar 11:30-12:45 am; entertainment Tues-Sat. Ck-out noon. Meeting rms. Coin lndry. Concierge. Downtown Boston, Cambridge transportation. Exercise equipt; bicycles, stair machine, whirlpool, sauna. Game rm. Bathrm phones, refrigerators, minibars. Some private patios, balconies. On river. Cr cds: A, C, D, DS, ER, JCB, MC, V.

D 🌊 🚶 🎿 🔥 SC

★ ★ **HILTON-BACK BAY.** *40 Dalton St (02115), in Back Bay.* 617/236-1100; FAX 617/267-8893. 335 rms, 26 story. S $160-$190; D $180-$210; each addl $20; suites $410-$615; family, wkend rates. Pet accepted, some restrictions. Garage $15. TV; cable. Indoor pool. Restaurant 7 am-midnight. Bar 5:30 pm-12:30 am. Ck-out noon. Convention facilities. Concierge. Gift shop. Airport transportation avail. Exercise equipt; weight machine, bicycles. Some balconies. Cr cds: A, C, D, DS, ER, JCB, MC, V.

D 🏊 🌊 🚶 🎿 🔥 SC

★ ★ ★ **HILTON-LOGAN AIRPORT.** *Logan Intl Airport (02128), east of Downtown Crossing Area.* 617/569-9300; FAX 617/569-3981. 541 rms, 14 story. S $110-$185; D $130-$205; each addl $20; suites $400; family, wkend rates. Crib free. Pet accepted, some restrictions. TV; cable. Pool; poolside serv, lifeguard. Restaurant 5:30 am-10:30 pm. Bar 11-2 am. Ck-out noon. Meeting rms. Concierge. Free airport transportation. Exercise equipt; treadmill, stair machine. Bathrm phone in suites. Cr cds: A, C, D, DS, ER, JCB, MC, V.

D 🏊 🌊 🚶 ✈ 🎿 🔥 SC

★ ★ ★ **HOLIDAY INN-GOVERNMENT CENTER.** *5 Blossom St (02114), at Cambridge St, Downtown Crossing Area.* 617/742-7630; FAX 617/742-4192. 303 rms, 15 story. Apr-Nov: S, D $169-$235; each addl $20; under 20 free; wkly, wkend rates; higher rates graduation wkends; lower rates rest of yr. Crib free. Garage $15.50. TV; cable. Heated pool. Restaurant 6:30 am-midnight. Bar. Ck-out noon. Coin lndry. Exercise equipt; weights, bicycles. Overlooks Charles River. **LUXURY LEVEL : EXECUTIVE ADDITION.** 47 rms, 2 suites, 2 floors. S $189-$205; D $209-$225; suites $460. Concierge. Private lounge. Bathrm phones. Coffee in rms. Complimentary continental bkfst, refreshments. Refrigerators. Cr cds: A, C, D, DS, JCB, MC, V.

D 🌊 🚶 🎿 🔥 SC

✔ ★ ★ **HOWARD JOHNSON/THE 57 PARK PLAZA.** *200 Stuart St (02116), in Theatre District.* 617/482-1800; FAX 617/451-2750. 350 rms, 24 story. S, D $90-$185; each addl $15; suites $230-$350; under 18 free; wkend rates. Crib free. Pet accepted, some restrictions. TV; cable. Indoor pool; sauna. Restaurant 6:30 am-10 pm; dining rm 11:30 am-11 pm, Sun noon-10 pm. Bar. Ck-out noon. Free garage parking. Barber. Airport transportation. Cr cds: A, C, D, ER, JCB, MC, V.

🏊 🌊 🎿 🔥 SC

★ ★ ★ **HYATT HARBORSIDE.** *101 Harborside Dr (02128), at Logan Intl Airport, east of downtown.* 617/568-1234; FAX 617/567-8856. 270 rms, 14 story. S $195; D $220; suites $275. Crib free. TV; cable. Indoor pool. Restaurant 6 am-11 pm. Bar. Ck-out noon. Meeting rms. Concierge. Free airport, RR station transportation. Exercise equipt; weights, bicycles, whirlpool, sauna. Refrigerator in suites. Cr cds: A, C, D, DS, ER, JCB, MC, V.

🌊 🚶 ✈ 🎿 🔥 SC

★ ★ ★ **LENOX.** *710 Boylston St (02116), at Exeter St; Prudential Center, in Back Bay.* 617/536-5300; res: 800/225-7676; FAX 617/267-1237. 214 rms, 11 story. S $140-$235; D $150-$235; each addl $20; suites $350; under 18 free. Parking $22. TV; cable. 2 restaurants 7-1:30 am. Rm serv to midnight. Bars 11:30-1:30 am; pianist Tues-Sat. Ck-out noon. Meeting rms. Barber. Airport transportation avail. Many decorative and wood-burning fireplaces. Cr cds: A, C, D, DS, ER, JCB, MC, V.

D 🎿 🔥 SC

★ ★ ★ **MARRIOTT-COPLEY PLACE.** *110 Huntington Ave (02116), in Copley Square.* 617/236-5800; FAX 617/236-5885. 1,147 rms, 38 story. S, D $179; suites $300-$950; under 18 free; wkend rates. Crib free. Valet parking $21. TV; cable. Pool. Restaurant 6:30-1 am. Rm serv 24 hrs. Bar 11-2 am; entertainment, dancing. Ck-out noon. Convention facilities. Concierge. Shopping arcade. Airport, RR station, bus depot transportation. Exercise rm; instructor, weights, bicycles, whirlpool, sauna. Massage therapy. Game rm. **LUXURY LEVEL : CONCIERGE LEVEL.** 69 rms, 2 floors. S, D $199. Private lounge, honor bar. Complimentary continental bkfst, refreshments. Cr cds: A, C, D, DS, ER, JCB, MC, V.

D 🌊 🚶 🎿 🔥 SC

★ ★ ★ **MARRIOTT-LONG WHARF.** *296 State St (02109), on waterfront, in Faneuil Hall/Quincy Market Area.* 617/227-0800; FAX 617/227-2867. 400 rms, 7 story. S, D $189-$250; suites $300-$1,200; under 18 free; wkend rates. Crib free. Valet parking $21. TV; cable. Indoor pool; poolside serv. Restaurant 6:30 am-11 pm. Bar; dancing. Ck-out noon. Coin lndry. Convention facilities. Gift shop. Exercise equipt; weights, bicycles, whirlpool, sauna. **LUXURY LEVEL : CONCI-**

ERGE LEVEL. 49 rms, 5 suites. S $239; D $259; suites $350-$475. Concierge. Private lounge. Bathrm phones. Complimentary continental bkfst, refreshments, newspaper. Cr cds: A, C, D, DS, ER, JCB, MC, V.

D ⛵ ≋ ✕ ✕ 🔥 SC

★ ★ ★ **MERIDIEN.** 250 Franklin St (02110), in Financial District. 617/451-1900; FAX 617/423-2844. 326 rms, 9 story. S, D $220-$240; each addl $25; suites $400-$790; under 12 free; wkend plans. Crib free. Pet accepted, some restrictions. Valet parking $24. TV; cable. Pool. Restaurant 7 am-10 pm (also see JULIEN). Rm serv 24 hrs. Bar 11-2 am; pianist. Ck-out 1 pm. Convention facilities. Concierge. Shopping arcade. Exercise rm; instructor, weights, treadmill, sauna. Massage. Bathrm phones, minibars; some refrigerators. Cr cds: A, C, D, DS, JCB, MC, V.

D ⛵ ≋ ✕ ✕ 🔥

★ ★ **OMNI PARKER HOUSE.** 60 School St (02108), 1 blk N of Boston Common, Downtown Crossing Area. 617/227-8600; FAX 617/742-5729. 535 rms, 14 story. June, early Sept-mid-Nov: S, D $99-$205; suites $245-$325; under 17 free; wkend rates; lower rates rest of yr. Crib free. Garage $22. TV; cable. Restaurant (see PARKER'S). Bar 6:30 am-midnight; entertainment, dancing exc Sun. Ck-out noon. Convention facilities. Concierge. Shopping arcade. Health club privileges. Some bathrm phones. Oldest continuously operating hotel in the US. Cr cds: A, C, D, DS, JCB, MC, V.

D ✕ 🔥 SC

✔ ★ ★ **RAMADA HOTEL-AIRPORT.** 225 McClellan Hwy (02128), near Logan Intl Airport, east of Downtown Crossing Area. 617/569-5250; FAX 617/569-5159. 350 rms, 12 story. S $79-$109; D $89-$119; each addl $10; under 18 free. Crib free. TV; cable. Pool. Restaurant 6 am-10 pm. Bar 11-2 am; entertainment, dancing. Ck-out noon. Meeting rms. Gift shop. Free airport transportation. Exercise equipt; weight machine, stair machine. Cr cds: A, C, D, DS, JCB, MC, V.

D ≋ ✕ ✕ ✕ 🔥 SC

★ ★ ★ ★ **THE RITZ-CARLTON, BOSTON.** 15 Arlington St (02117), at Newbury St, in Back Bay. 617/536-5700; res: 800/241-3333; FAX 617/536-1335. 278 rms, 17 story. S $220-$320; D $260-$360; each addl $25; 1-2 bedrm suites $325-$1,500; under 12 free; wkend rates. Crib free. Pet accepted, some restrictions. Garage $20. TV; in-rm movies. Restaurant 6:30 am-midnight (also see THE DINING ROOM; and see THE LOUNGE, Unrated Dining). Rm serv 24 hrs. Bar noon-1 am. Ck-out noon. Convention facilities. Concierge. Barber. Exercise equipt; weights, bicycles, sauna. Masseuse. Health club privileges. Bathrm phones, refrigerators. Fireplace in suites. Overlooks Public Garden. **LUXURY LEVEL : RITZ-CARLTON CLUB.** 33 rms, 7 suites. S $340; D $380; suites $375-$775. Private lounge. Minibars. Complimentary continental bkfst, afternoon tea, refreshments. Cr cds: A, C, D, DS, ER, JCB, MC, V.

D ⛵ ✕ ✕ 🔥

★ ★ ★ **SHERATON BOSTON HOTEL & TOWERS.** 39 Dalton St (02199), at Prudential Ctr, in Back Bay. 617/236-2000; FAX 617/236-6061. 1,208 rms, 29 story. S $165-$230; D $185-$250; each addl $20; suites from $250; under 18 free; wkend rates. Crib free. Garage $18. TV; cable. Indoor/outdoor pool; poolside serv. Coffee in rms. Restaurant 6:30-1:30 am. Bars 11:30-2 am; entertainment, dancing. Ck-out 1 pm. Convention facilities. Gift shop. Airport transportation avail. Exercise rm; instructor, weights, bicycles, whirlpool. **LUXURY LEVEL : SHERATON TOWERS.** 25 rms, 7 suites. S, D $230-$250; suites from $350. Concierge. Private lounge. Some wet bars. Butler serv. Complimentary bkfst, refreshments, newspapers. Cr cds: A, C, D, DS, ER, JCB, MC, V.

D ≋ ✕ ✕ 🔥 SC

★ ★ ★ **SWISSÔTEL.** 1 Avenue de Lafayette (02111), in Financial District. 617/451-2600; res: 800/621-9200; FAX 617/451-0054. 500 rms, 22 story. S, D $205-$225; each addl $25; under 14 free; wkend rates. Crib free. Pet accepted, some restrictions. Garage $15, valet parking $19. TV; cable. Indoor pool. Restaurant 7 am-11 pm. Rm serv

24 hrs. Bar 11-1 am; entertainment. Ck-out 1 pm. Concierge. Airport transportation. Gift shop. Exercise equipt; bicycles, rowers. **LUXURY LEVEL : SWISS BUTLER.** 125 rms, 10 suites, 4 floors. S, D $265; suites $300-$475. Private lounge, honor bar. Concierge. Minibars. Bathrm phones. Complimentary continental bkfst, refreshments, newspaper. Cr cds: A, C, D, DS, ER, JCB, MC, V.

D ⛵ ≋ ✕ ✕ 🔥 SC

★ ★ **TREMONT HOUSE.** 275 Tremont St (02116), in Theatre District. 617/426-1400; res: 800/331-9998; FAX 617/482-6730. 281 rms, 15 story. S $105-$120; D $115-$130; each addl $15; under 18 free. Crib free. Valet parking $15. TV; cable. Restaurant 6:30 am-11:30 pm. Bar 4-11 pm; entertainment, dancing Thurs-Sat. Ck-out noon. Meeting rms. Airport transportation. Crystal chandelier, grand piano in lobby. Cr cds: A, C, D, DS, ER, JCB, MC, V.

D ✕ 🔥 SC

★ ★ ★ **THE WESTIN HOTEL, COPLEY PLACE.** 10 Huntington Ave (02116), in Copley Square. 617/262-9600; FAX 617/424-7483. 800 rms, 36 story. S $195-$220; D $220-$245; each addl $25; suites $480-$1,500; under 18 free. Crib free. TV; cable. Indoor pool. Restaurant 7:30 am-11:30 pm. Rm serv 24 hrs. Entertainment. Ck-out 1 pm. Concierge. Airport transportation. Exercise rm; instructor, weights, bicycles, whirlpool, sauna. Masseuse. Many minibars. Copley Place shopping gallery across skybridge. **LUXURY LEVEL : EXECUTIVE CLUB.** 617/424-7498. 59 rms, 6 suites, 2 floors. S $230; D $250; suites $250-$270. In-rm movies. Concierge. Private lounge, honor bar. Minibars. Complimentary continental bkfst, refreshments. Cr cds: A, C, D, DS, ER, JCB, MC, V.

D ≋ ✕ ✕ 🔥 SC

Inn

★ **NEWBURY GUEST HOUSE.** 261 Newbury St (02116), in Back Bay. 617/437-7666; res: 800/437-7668; FAX 617/262-4243. 32 rms, 4 story. Mar-Dec: S $85-$115; D $95-$125; each addl $10; under 3 free; higher rates: marathon, graduations; lower rates rest of yr. Parking $10. TV; cable. Complimentary continental bkfst. Ck-out noon, ck-in 3 pm. Sitting rm. Built 1882. Original art. Cr cds: A, C, D, DS, MC, V.

D 🔥

Restaurants

★ ★ ★ **AUJOURD'HUI.** (See Four Seasons Hotel) 617/338-4400. Hrs: 6:30 am-2:30 pm, 5:30-10:30 pm; Sat 7 am-noon, 5:30-10:30 pm; Sun 7-11 am, 5:30-10:30 pm; Sun brunch 11:30 am-2:30 pm. Res accepted. Bar. Wine cellar. A la carte entrees: bkfst $10-$18, lunch $14.50-$22, dinner $28-$42. Sun brunch $35. Child's meals. Menu changes seasonally. Own baking. Valet parking. View of Boston Public Garden. Jacket (dinner). Cr cds: A, C, D, ER, JCB, MC, V.

D

★ ★ ★ **BAY TOWER ROOM.** 60 State St, 33rd floor, in Faneuil Hall/Quincy Market Area. 617/723-1666. Hrs: 5:30-10 pm; Fri, Sat to 11 pm. Closed Sun; Dec 25. Res accepted. Bar 4:30 pm-1 am; Fri, Sat to 2 am. Wine list. A la carte entrees: dinner $18-$36. Parking. Harbor view. Jacket. Cr cds: A, C, D, DS, MC, V.

D

✔ ★ **CACTUS CLUB.** 939 Boylston St, in Back Bay. 617/236-0200. Hrs: 11:30 am-10:30 pm; Sun brunch 11 am-4 pm. Closed Dec 25. Res accepted. Mexican, Native American menu. Bar. Semi-a la carte: lunch $4.50-$7.95, dinner $7.95-$13.95. Sun brunch $4.50-$7.95. Child's meals. Specializes in Southwestern cuisine. Valet parking. Outdoor dining. Mexican, Southwestern decor. Cr cds: A, C, D, DS, MC, V.

★ ★ ★ **CAFE BUDAPEST.** (See Copley Square Hotel) 617/266-1979. Hrs: noon-3 pm, 5-10:30 pm; Fri, Sat to midnight; Sun 1-10:30 pm. Closed Jan 1, Dec 25; also wk of July 4. Res accepted. Hungarian, continental menu. Bar. Semi-a la carte: lunch $14.50-$20, dinner $20-$33. Specialties: veal goulash, cherry soup, chicken paprikash, stuffed mushrooms. Own baking. Original paintings. Old World atmosphere. Family-owned. Jacket. Cr cds: A, C, D, DS, MC, V.

D

✔★ ★ **CASA ROMERO.** 30 Gloucester St (02115), in Back Bay. 617/536-4341. Hrs: 5-10 pm; Fri & Sat to 11 pm. Closed some major hols. Res accepted. Mexican menu. Serv bar. Semi-a la carte: dinner $12-$16. Specialties: marinated tenderloin of pork, giant shrimp in cilantro and tomatillos. Outdoor dining. Authentic Mexican decor. Family-owned. Totally nonsmoking. Cr cds: C, D, DS, MC, V.

★ ★ **CHARLEY'S.** 284 Newbury St, in Back Bay. 617/266-3000. Hrs: 11:30-12:30 am; Sat & Sun from 11 am. Res accepted. Bar. Semi-a la carte: lunch $5.99-$10.99, dinner $5.99-$22.95. Child's meals. Specializes in fresh seafood, baby-back ribs, blackened chicken pasta. Valet parking (dinner exc Sun). Outdoor dining. Renovated Victorian school. Cr cds: A, DS, MC, V.

D

★ ★ **CIAO BELLA.** 240A Newbury St, in Back Bay. 617/536-2626. Hrs: 11:30 am-11 pm; Thurs-Sat to 11:45 pm; Sun brunch to 3:30 pm. Closed Thanksgiving, Dec 25. Res accepted. Italian menu. Bar. A la carte entrees: lunch $6.50-$14.95, dinner $8.95-$25. Sun brunch $4.95-$11.50. Specializes in mozzarella alla Caprese, veal chops, swordfish chops. Valet parking (Tues-Sat evening). Outdoor dining. European decor. Cr cds: A, C, D, DS, MC, V.

★ ★ **CRICKET'S.** 101 S Faneuil Hall Marketplace, in Faneuil Hall/Quincy Market Area. 617/720-5570. Hrs: 11-2 am. Closed Dec 25. Continental menu. Bar; entertainment. Semi-a la carte: lunch $6.95-$12.95, dinner $6.50-$17.95. Specializes in fresh seafood. Entertainment. Outdoor dining. Cr cds: A, D, DS, MC, V.

D

★ ★ **DAVIDE.** 326 Commercial St, in the North End. 617/227-5745. Hrs: 11:30 am-3 pm, 5-11 pm; Sat, Sun from 5 pm; July-Aug from 5 pm. Northern Italian menu. Bar. A la carte entrees: lunch $9-$12, dinner $12-$23. Specialties: potato gnocchi, veal chop with fontina and prosciutto. Own pasta, ice cream. Valet parking. Cr cds: A, C, D, MC, V.

★ ★ **DAVIO'S.** (204 Washington St, Brookline) W on Beacon St. 617/738-4810. Hrs: 11:30 am-3 pm, 5-9:30 pm; Sat 5-10:30 pm; Sun brunch (Sept-May) 11:30 am-3 pm; early-bird dinner Sun-Fri 5-6:30 pm. Closed some major hols. Res accepted. Italian menu. Bar. A la carte entrees: lunch $7.95-$10.95, dinner $13.95-$19.95. Semi-a la carte: lunch $4.95-$10.95, dinner $4.95-$18.95. Sun brunch $4.95-$10.95. Specializes in veal scallopine, Caesar salad, home-made desserts. Valet parking. Cr cds: A, D, DS, MC, V.

D

★ ★ ★ **THE DINING ROOM.** (See The Ritz-Carlton, Boston Hotel) 617/536-5700. Hrs: noon-2:30 pm, 5:30-10 pm; Fri & Sat to 11 pm. Res accepted; required wkends. Continental, New England regional menu. Bar. Wine cellar. A la carte entrees: lunch $19.50-$29, dinner $30-$43. Table d'hôte: lunch $29-$38, dinner $42-$55. Sun brunch $42. Child's meals. Specializes in lobster au whiskey, Boston clam chowder, roast rack of lamb. Own baking. Pianist. Valet parking. Formal atmosphere, French Provincial decor. Jacket, tie. Cr cds: A, C, D, DS, ER, JCB, MC, V.

D

✔★ ★ **DURGIN PARK.** 30 N Market St, in Faneuil Hall/Quincy Market Area. 617/227-2038. Hrs: 11:30 am-10 pm; Sun 11:30 am-9 pm. Closed Dec 25. Some A/C. Bar to 2 am; entertainment. A la carte entrees: lunch $3.95-$15.95, dinner $4.95-$15.95. Specializes in prime rib, Indian pudding, strawberry shortcake. Own soups. Near Faneuil Hall. Established 1826. Cr cds: A, D, DS, MC, V.

D

✔★ ★ **FELICIA'S.** 145A Richmond St, on 2nd floor, in the North End. 617/523-9885. Hrs: 4-9:30 pm; Fri & Sat to 10:30 pm; Sun 2-9:30 pm. Closed Easter, Thanksgiving, Dec 24, 25. Italian menu. Wine, beer. Semi-a la carte: dinner $7.95-$14.95. Specialties: shrimp scampi, chicken verdicchio. Own pasta. Italian antique furnishings; paintings. Cr cds: A, C, D, DS, MC, V.

D

★ ★ **GRILL 23.** 161 Berkley St (02116), in Back Bay. 617/542-2255. Hrs: 5:30-10:30 pm; Fri & Sat to 11 pm. Closed major hols. Res accepted. Bar from 4:30 pm. A la carte entrees: $16.75-$26.75. Specializes in aged beef, New England seafood. Valet parking. Open kitchen. 1920s decor. Cr cds: A, D, DS, MC, V.

D

★ ★ **HUNGRY I.** 71½ Charles St, on Beacon Hill. 617/227-3524. Hrs: 6-9:30 pm; Sat to 10 pm; Sun brunch 11 am-2 pm. Closed July 4, Thanksgiving, Dec 25. Res accepted. European menu. Wine, beer. A la carte entrees: dinner $17-$26. Sun brunch $9-$15. Specialties: maison paté, venison au poivre. Patio dining. 1840s house in historic district. Fireplace. Cr cds: A, C, D, MC, V.

★ ★ **ICARUS.** 3 Appleton St, in the South End. 617/426-1790. Hrs: 6-10 pm; Fri & Sat to 11 pm; Sun brunch 11 am-3 pm (exc June-Aug). Closed most major hols. Res accepted; required wkends. Bar from 5:30 pm. Semi-a la carte: dinner $17-$25. Sun brunch $6-$9. Specialties: clam roast, rack of lamb. Valet parking (Mon-Sat). Converted 1860s building. Cr cds: A, C, D, MC, V.

★ ★ **JASPER'S.** 240 Commercial St, in the North End. 617/523-1126. Hrs: 6-10 pm. Closed Sun & Mon; some major hols. Res accepted. Bar from 5 pm. A la carte entrees: dinner $20-$36. Specialties: duck salad, pan-roasted lobster. Raw bar. Valet parking. Glass sculpture by Dan Dailey. On waterfront. Cr cds: A, DS, MC, V.

D

★ ★ **JIMMY'S HARBORSIDE.** 242 Northern Ave, adj to Financial District. 617/423-1000. Hrs: noon-9:30 pm; Sun 4-9 pm. Closed Dec 25. Res accepted. Bar. A la carte entrees: lunch $9-$22, dinner $10-$32. Child's meals. Specializes in shrimp, lobster, broiled fish. Valet parking. Nautical decor. Family-owned. Cr cds: A, C, D, MC, V.

D

★ ★ **JOE TECCE'S.** 61 N Washington St, in the North End. 617/742-6210. Hrs: 11:30 am-3 pm, 4-11 pm; Fri & Sat from 4 pm; Sun 3-10 pm. Closed Jan 1, Thanksgiving, Dec 25. Res accepted. Italian menu. Bar. Semi-a la carte: lunch $5.95-$8, dinner $7-$22.50. Child's meals. Specialties: antipasto, steak mafia alla marinara. Family-owned. Cr cds: A, D, MC, V.

D

★ ★ ★ **JULIEN.** (See Meridien Hotel) 617/451-1900. Hrs: noon-2 pm, 6-10 pm; Sat 6-10:30 pm. Closed Sun; wk of July 4. Res accepted. French, English menu. Bar 5 pm-midnight, closed Sun. Wine list. A la carte entrees: lunch $16.50-$21, dinner $21-$45. Complete meals: lunch $21, 5-course dinner $65. Specializes in seafood, lamb, breast of duck. Own baking. Entertainment. Valet parking. Elegant surroundings; carved wood, high celings, crystal chandeliers. Jacket. Cr cds: A, C, D, DS, JCB, MC, V.

★ ★ **KYOTO.** 201 Stuart St, in Theatre District. 617/542-1166. Hrs: 11:30 am-2 pm, 5-10 pm; Fri to 11 pm; Sat 4-11 pm; Sun 4-9 pm. Closed some major hols. Res accepted. Japanese menu. Bar. Complete meals: lunch $5.50-$9.95, dinner $11.25-$19.95. Child's meals. Specialties: hibachi swordfish, Kyoto turkey breast. Sushi bar. Parking. Japanese decor. Teppan-yaki grill. Cr cds: A, C, D, DS, JCB, MC, V.

D

★ ★ ★ **L'ESPALIER.** 30 Gloucester St, in Back Bay. 617/262-3023. Hrs: 6-10 pm. Closed Sun; most major hols. Res accepted. Contemporary French menu. Bar. Wine cellar. Prix fixe: dinner $56. Menu dégustation (Mon-Fri): dinner $72/person. Specialties: roast smoked duck, steamed Maine lobster. Own baking. Valet parking. Daily menu. Elegant dining in 19th-century Back Bay town house. Cr cds: A, D, DS, MC, V.

★ ★ **LIBRARY GRILL AT THE HAMPSHIRE HOUSE.** *84 Beacon St, on Beacon Hill.* 617/227-9600. Hrs: 5-10:30 pm; Sun brunch 10:30 am-2:30 pm; July-Aug 6-11 pm. Res accepted. Continental menu. Bar. A la carte entrees: dinner $16-$24. Sun brunch $9-$15. Jazz Sun. Valet parking. In 1910 town house. Cr cds: A, C, D, DS, MC, V.

★ ★ **LOCKE OBER.** *3 Winter Place, Downtown Crossing Area.* 617/542-1340. Hrs: 11:30 am-10 pm; Sat, Sun from 5:30 pm. Closed major hols; also Sun in July & Aug. Continental menu. Bar. Semi-a la carte: lunch $12-$18, dinner $18-$45. Specialties: Wienerschnitzel, baked lobster Savannah. Built in 1875. Old World atmosphere. Jacket. Cr cds: A, C, D, DS, MC, V.

★ ★ **MAISON ROBERT.** *45 School St (02108), Downtown Crossing Area.* 617/227-3370. Hrs: 11:30 am-2:30 pm, 5:30-10 pm; wkend hrs vary. Closed some major hols. Res accepted. French menu. Bar. Semi-a la carte: lunch $9-$22, dinner $17-$32. Specializes in rack of lamb, fresh fish, seafood. Jazz Thurs & Fri. Valet parking. Outdoor dining in courtyard of former city hall. Jacket. Cr cds: A, C, D, MC, V.

[D]

★ ★ **MAMMA MARIA.** *3 North Square, in the North End.* 617/523-0077. Hrs: 11:30 am-2 pm, 5-11 pm; Sun 5-10 pm; Mon 5-10 pm. Closed Jan 1, Thanksgiving, Dec 24, 25. Res accepted. Northern Italian menu. Serv bar. A la carte entrees: lunch $8-$10, dinner $14-$22. Specialties: sautéed Norwegian salmon, tenderloin of veal. Valet parking. Upper rm overlooks historic area; Paul Revere house across square. Cr cds: A, C, D, DS, MC, V.

★ ★ **MICHAEL'S WATERFRONT.** *85 Atlantic Ave, on Commercial Wharf, in the North End.* 617/367-6425. Hrs: 5:30-10 pm; Fri & Sat to 10:30 pm. Closed Jan 1, Dec 24 & 25. Res accepted. Bar from 4 pm. A la carte entrees: dinner $14.95-$19.95. Specializes in rack of lamb, swordfish, lobster. Valet parking. Outdoor dining. Several dining areas on 2 floors of historic Commercial Wharf. Cr cds: A, C, D, DS, MC, V.

★ ★ **MIRABELLE.** *85 Newbury St (02116), in Back Bay.* 617/859-4848. Hrs: 11 am-4 pm, 5:30-11 pm; Sat from 9 am; Sun 9 am-3 pm, 5:30-11 pm. Closed Thanksgiving, Dec 25. Res accepted. Bar. A la carte entrees: bkfst $7-$11, lunch $10-$15, dinner $18-$25. Serv charge 15%. Specializes in prime meats, seafood, organic vegetables. Valet parking Mon-Sat, dinner. Outdoor dining. Casual atmosphere. Totally nonsmoking. Cr cds: A, C, D, DS, MC, V.

★ ★ ★ **MORTON'S OF CHICAGO.** *One Exeter Plaza, at Boyleston St, in Back Bay.* 617/266-5858. Hrs: 11:30 am-2:30 pm, 5:30-11 pm; Sat from 5:30 pm; Sun 5-10 pm. Closed major hols. Res accepted. Bar. A la carte entrees: lunch $5.95-$17.50, dinner $16.95-$29.95. Specializes in prime dry-aged beef, fresh seafood. Valet parking. Menu recited. Cr cds: A, C, D, MC, V.

[D]

★ ★ **MR. LEUNG.** *545 Boylston St, in Back Bay.* 617/236-4040. Hrs: noon-3 pm, 6-10 pm; Fri to 11 pm; Sat 6-11 pm; Sun 6-10 pm. Closed Thanksgiving. Res accepted. Chinese menu. Bar. A la carte entrees: lunch $8-$10, dinner $18-$24. Specialties: Peking duck, paradise shrimp, black pepper filet mignon. Valet parking. Cr cds: A, D, MC, V.

[D]

★ ★ ★ **PARKER'S.** *(See Omni Parker House)* 617/725-1600. Hrs: 6:30 am-2:30 pm, 5:30-10 pm; Mon-Wed to 2:30 pm; wkend hrs vary. Res accepted. Continental menu. Bar. Wine cellar. Complete meal: bkfst $3.25-$10.75. A la carte entrees: lunch $11-$18.50, dinner $16-$28. Specialties: Parker House rolls, Boston cream pie, seafood. Pianist dinner. Valet parking. Victorian setting with modern accents. Totally nonsmoking. Cr cds: A, C, D, DS, JCB, MC, V.

[D]

★ **REBECCA'S.** *21 Charles St, on Beacon Hill.* 617/742-9747. Hrs: 11:30 am-10:30 pm; Fri & Sat 10:30 am-11:30 pm; Sat & Sun brunch 11 am-4 pm. Closed Dec 25. Continental menu. Wine, beer. Semi-a la carte: lunch $6-$12, dinner $6.50-$19. Sat & Sun brunch $6-$12. Valet parking. Cr cds: A, MC, V.

★ ★ **RISTORANTE TOSCANO.** *47 Charles St, on Beacon Hill.* 617/723-4090. Hrs: 11:30 am-2:30 pm, 5:30-10 pm; Fri, Sat to 10:30 pm; Sun 5:30-10 pm. Closed some major hols. Res accepted. Northern Italian menu. Bar. A la carte entrees: lunch $7.50-$10.50, dinner $15-$22. Specializes in veal, fish, pasta, steak. Valet parking (dinner). Italian decor. Cr cds: A.

[D]

★ ★ ★ **ROWES WHARF.** *(See Boston Harbor Hotel)* 617/439-3995. Hrs: 6:30 am-10 pm; Sun brunch 11 am-2:30 pm. Res accepted. Bar 11:30-2 am. Wine cellar. A la carte entrees: bkfst $6-$11, lunch $11-$19, dinner $18-$30. Complete meals: dinner $28-$42. Sun brunch $35. Child's meals. Specialties: roast rack of Vermont lamb, Maine lobster sausage over lemon pasta, seared yellowfin tuna. Own baking. Valet parking. View of Boston Harbor. Jacket. Cr cds: A, C, D, DS, JCB, MC, V.

[D]

★ ★ **SALLY LING'S.** *256 Commercial St, in the North End.* 617/720-1188. Hrs: noon-10 pm, Sat & Sun noon-11 pm. Closed Thanksgiving. Res accepted. Chinese menu. Bar. A la carte entrees: lunch $6-$8, dinner $12-$18. Specialties: filet mignon in black pepper sauce, Peking duck. On waterfront. Cr cds: A, C, D, DS, MC, V.

✔ ★ ★ **SMALL PLANET BAR & GRILL.** *565 Boylston St, in Back Bay.* 617/536-4477. Hrs: 11:30 am-midnight; Sun from 5 pm. Closed Thanksgiving, Dec 25. Varied menu. Bar. A la carte entrees: lunch $3.95-$7.95, dinner $7.95-$15.95. Specializes in fresh seafood. Cr cds: A, C, D, DS, MC, V.

[D]

✔ ★ ★ **SPASSO.** *160 Commonwealth Ave (02116), in Back Bay.* 617/536-8656. Hrs: 11:30 am-10 pm; wkends to 11 pm; Sun brunch to 3 pm. Closed Thanksgiving, Dec 25. Italian menu. Bar 11-1 am. A la carte entrees: lunch $6.95-$8.95, dinner $9.95-$15.95. Sun brunch $12.95. Child's meals. Specialty: di strutto. Valet parking. Outdoor dining. Colorful Italian atmosphere. Cr cds: A, D, DS, MC, V.

[D]

★ ★ **ST CLOUD.** *557 Tremont St, at Clarendon St, in the South End.* 617/353-0202. Hrs: 11:30 am-3 pm, 5:30 pm-midnight; Sat 5:30-midnight; Sun brunch 11 am-3 pm. Closed July 4, Thanksgiving, Dec 25. Bar to 12:45 am. A la carte entrees: lunch $7.50-$9.50, dinner $12-$22. Sun brunch $13. Specializes in duck, roast rack of lamb, salmon. Valet parking. Cr cds: A, C, D, DS, MC, V.

[D]

★ ★ **TOP OF THE HUB.** *800 Boylston St, at top of Prudential Bldg, in Back Bay.* 617/536-1775. Hrs: 11:30 am-2:30 pm, 5:30-10 pm; Fri to 11 pm; Sat noon-3 pm, 5:30-11 pm; Sun brunch 10 am-2:30 pm. Closed Dec 25. Res accepted. Bar. A la carte entrees: lunch $6-$15, dinner $15-$25. Jazz quartet or vocalist Tues-Sat. View of Charles River and downtown Boston. Cr cds: A, C, D, DS, MC, V.

[D]

★ **YE OLDE UNION OYSTER HOUSE.** *41 Union St, in Faneuil Hall/Quincy Market Area.* 617/227-2750. Hrs: 11 am-9:30 pm; Fri, Sat to 10 pm; Sun brunch 11 am-3 pm. Closed Thanksgiving, Dec 25. Res accepted. Bar. Semi-a la carte: lunch $7-$10, dinner $11.50-$45. Sun brunch $9.95. Child's meals. Specializes in shore dinner, seafood platter. Valet parking. Historic oyster bar established 1826; originally a silk & dry goods shop (1742). Family-owned. Cr cds: A, C, D, DS, JCB, MC, V.

[D]

✔★ **ZUMA'S TEX MEX CAFE.** *7 N Market St, in Faneuil Hall/Quincy Market Area.* 617/367-9114. Hrs: 11:30 am-11 pm; Fri, Sat to midnight; Sun noon-10 pm. Closed Dec 25. Mexican menu. Bar. Semi-a la carte: lunch, dinner $4-$11. Specializes in fajitas, neon margaritas. Cr cds: A, C, D, DS, MC, V.

Unrated Dining Spots

HARVARD BOOK STORE CAFE. *190 Newbury St, at Exeter, in Back Bay.* 617/536-0097. Hrs: 8 am-11 pm; Fri, Sat to midnight; Sun brunch noon-4 pm. Closed Jan 1, Thanksgiving, Dec 25. International menu. Serv bar. A la carte entrees: bkfst $2-$5, lunch, dinner $5-$12. Sun brunch $9-$11. Outdoor dining. Bookstore. Cr cds: A, MC, V.

THE LOUNGE. *(See The Ritz-Carlton, Boston Hotel)* 617/536-5700. Hrs: 11:30-12:30 am. Res accepted. Bar. English-style tea menu. Complete tea $12.50-$16.50. A la carte entrees: lunch, dinner $9-$35. Child's meals. Features sandwiches, chowders, seafood, scones, tea breads, pastries, desserts. Own baking. Entertainment (evenings). Valet parking. Jacket. Cr cds: A, C, D, DS, ER, JCB, MC, V.

NO NAME. *15½ Fish Pier, in the North End.* 617/338-7539. Hrs: 11 am-10 pm; Sun to 9 pm. Closed Thanksgiving, Dec 25. Wine, beer. A la carte entrees: lunch $1.50-$0.50, dinner $1.75-$9.95. Specializes in fresh seafood, steak, hamburgers. View of ocean, fishing boats. Family-owned. No cr cds accepted.

 SC

RUBIN'S DELICATESSEN. *(500 Harvard St, Brookline)* W on Beacon St. 617/731-8787. Hrs: 10 am-8 pm; Fri 9 am-3 pm; Sun 9 am-8 pm. Closed Sat; Jewish hols. Kosher deli menu. Semi-a la carte: lunch $3.50-$12, dinner $6.50-$15. Parking. Family-owned. Totally nonsmoking. No cr cds accepted.

Buffalo

Founded: 1803

Pop: 328,123

Elev: 600 feet

Time zone: Eastern

Area code: 716

Niagara Falls

Settled: 1806

Pop: 61,840

Elev: 610 feet

Time zone: Eastern

Area code: 716

The Buffalo/Niagara Falls area was strategically important to the government during both World Wars because of its enormous industrial production. Much of this stemmed from the hydroelectric power generated by the falls. The development of Niagara power began in 1852, when construction was started on a canal to carry the water from the upper river around the falls. Electric power was first made available in Niagara Falls in 1895; by the late 1890s, power was available in great quantities for the entire region. With a flow of more than 200,000 cubic feet of water per second, Niagara has a power potential of approximately 4 million horsepower. Electrical production is controlled by agreements between the United States and Canada so each nation receives a full share, while the beauty of the cataracts is preserved.

Transportation has played an important role in the Buffalo area's development. In 1679, when Buffalo was claimed by the French, La Salle built the wooden *Griffon,* the first large boat to sail the Great Lakes. In 1818, *Walk-in-the-Water,* the first steamboat on Lake Erie, was launched with the opening of the Erie Canal in 1825. The area became the major transportation break between East and West. In later years Buffalo became one of the largest railroad centers in the nation; today, 2 passenger and 14 freight rail offices handle thousands of trains annually. Since the completion of the St. Lawrence Seaway in 1959, Buffalo has become one of the top Great Lakes ports in import-export tonnage.

Tourism is an extremely important component of the Niagara Falls economy. Both sides of the international border at the falls cater to the tourist trade with numerous motels, hotels, souvenir shops and variety of attractions.

Business

Buffalo is one of the largest manufacturing centers in New York State. Its grain-processing industry began with Joseph Dart's invention of a steam-powered grain elevator in 1843.

The transportation equipment industry is the area's largest manufacturing employer. Buffalo ranks among the nation's top 30 manufacturing areas in a diversity of products. Major products are automobile parts, iron and steel, metal alloys and abrasives, tires, food products, silk and rayon, chemicals and dyes, cellophane, aircraft and missile components and industrial machinery.

Research is also a major activity in the Buffalo manufacturing area, with more than 150 industrial research laboratories covering such diverse fields as nuclear power, aerosystems and health care.

Agriculture is significant to the area, but it is overshadowed by the manufacturing complex. Dairy farming is the chief agricultural pursuit in the eight-county area, but fruit orchards and vineyards are also important.

Convention Facilities

The Buffalo Convention Center, downtown, has 75,000 square feet of exhibition space, including the main floor with 66,500 square feet and 22 meeting rooms with a total of 26,550 square feet of space. The center is viewed as the cornerstone of downtown Buffalo redevelopment.

The Niagara Falls Convention and Civic Center can accommodate approximately 7,000 persons for a 3-ring circus, some 9,000 for a basketball game or about 11,000 for a concert within the main arena. Another 4,500 to 5,000 persons can at the same time be using the various peripheral meeting and function rooms. There is a total exhibition space of 83,520 square feet, banquet capacity of 6,000, a 1,700-seat double balcony ballroom and a portable 60-by-40 foot stage.

A seven-acre public plaza, named in honor of former Niagara Falls Mayor E. Dent Lackey, abuts the main entrance of the convention center; it includes an outdoor amphitheater. There is also a 1,800-foot pedestrian mall that connects the convention center with Prospect Point, brink of the American Falls, only 6 blocks away. Several full-service hotels are within a short walk of both the convention center and falls. The downtown capacity is 2,000 rooms, and the city's total is 4,500 rooms.

Sports and Recreation

In the Buffalo/Niagara Falls area, both participants and spectators enjoy a wide range of sports, including hockey, football, basketball, baseball, skiing, auto racing, horse racing, sailing, fishing, hunting, bowling, rowing, horseback riding, curling and skating. Facilities for tennis and golf are abundant.

Hockey fans root for the Buffalo Sabres at the Memorial Auditorium. Rich Stadium in Orchard Park, seating 80,000, is the home of the Buffalo Bills football team. The Bisons represent the city in minor league baseball at the downtown stadium, Pilot Field. There are also six local colleges that have exciting basketball seasons.

Harness racing at the Buffalo Raceway in Hamburg is also popular, as well as boating on the Niagara River. There are boat launching ramps on both the upper and lower river. The Erie County Fair, which has been held annually for more than a century, is one of the largest county fairs in the nation.

Entertainment

The Buffalo Philharmonic Orchestra presents both symphony and pop concerts at Kleinhans Music Hall. Many cultural events are offered within the city's revitalized downtown Theater District, featuring Shea's Buffalo Theater, Studio Arena Theatre and several smaller establishments. Programs include dance, opera, film series, orchestra and organ recitals and popular music concerts. More than 100 nightclubs cater to the varied interests of both residents and visitors, as do several dinner theaters.

Many popular entertainers are brought to Artpark, at Lewiston on the Niagara River. This 172-acre state park is devoted to the visual and performing arts, with outdoor musical, theatrical and dance events held in the summer. It is also a showcase for contemporary art.

The Shaw Festival Theatre, Niagara-on-the-Lake, Ontario, presents a summer theater season of plays by Shaw and his contemporaries.

E. Dent Lackey Plaza is the site of the annual Niagara Summer Experience, a series of free entertainment events and ethnic festivals held every weekend in July and August. The annual "Festival of Lights" draws nearly a million visitors to Niagara Falls each Christmas season.

Sightseeing

Sightseeing in the Buffalo/Niagara Falls area begins, of course, with the magnificent Niagara Falls. The falls drain the waters of half a continent over a sheer cliff; two hundred thousand cubic feet of water per second flow over the brink into the lower Niagara River. The power of the water has caused constant erosion; the falls have, therefore, been receding at the rate of about one foot every ten years. Geologists believe that about 12,000 years ago the falls were nearly 7 miles downstream at Lewiston. The concern of the American and Canadian government has prompted several remedial projects to preserve the shape of the falls.

Vantage points vary, and most overlooks reached on foot are free. From Prospect Point, on the American side, the visitor can see the 1,000-foot crest of the American Falls and beyond to the Bridal Veil Falls and beyond that to the Horseshoe Falls, all enveloped in high-rising spray. Colored lights illuminate the rushing waters and provide a spectacular evening view.

For a small fee the visitor can be lifted to a platform 180 feet above the pool on the Prospect Point Observation Tower and then lowered to river level. Sightseeing tours can be arranged via limousine or motor coach, and horse-drawn surreys carry visitors around the area. A Viewmobile train takes people around Goat Island and Prospect Point, with three stops. Helicopter flights offer air views of the panorama. The closest possible access to both falls is afforded from Goat Island State Park, which lies in the middle of the falls themselves.

Other islands provide access to the rapids above the falls. Several observation towers on both sides of the border offer excellent views of the falls, along with shops, restaurants and amusements.

A one-of-a-kind experience offered at the falls is a boat ride on the *Maid of the Mist,* which leaves either shore every 20 minutes. This excursion has been world famous for decades. Visitors are taken from the lower river to as close as possible to the foot of Horseshoe Falls, which thunders above.

The famous 100-year-old Cave of the Winds trip invites visitors to don yellow slickers and descend in an elevator. A short tunnel connects the walkways at the base of the American Falls, and visitors proceed to Hurricane Deck, just 25 feet from the roaring cataract.

On the Canadian side, at the Table Rock House Scenic Tunnels, south of the Rainbow Bridge in Queen Victoria Park, it is possible to descend by elevator to a point about 25 feet above the river, which offers an excellent view of the falls from below and behind; waterproof garments are supplied. At Great Gorge Adventure, at the narrowest point of the Niagara River, an elevator and tunnel take visitors to the boardwalk at the edge of whirlpool rapids, while the Spanish Aero Car takes passengers across the whirlpool and rapids for an exciting ride, suspended on 1,800-foot cables.

At the Niagara Power Project Visitors Center, four miles north of Niagara Falls, an animated power plant, models of transmission lines, terrain map, motion pictures and slides explain to visitors the $737-million hydroelectric development of the State Power Authority. From 350 feet above the river there are balcony views of the American and Canadian power plants and of Niagara Gorge.

The Aquarium in Niagara Falls is the first oceanarium to use synthetic seawater in all its exhibits. The aquarium is specially designed to interest children. Dolphins and sea lions perform, and electric eel demonstrations are presented hourly. Marineland in Canada has the King Waldorf Aqua Theater Show with performing killer whales, dolphins and sea lions. It also has wildlife displays and an amusement park.

Some of the more interesting museums in the Niagara Falls area include the Native American Center for the Living Arts, in its unusual turtle-shaped building, the Schoelkopf Geological Museum and the Niagara Falls Museum in Canada, which is one of the oldest museums in North America and includes "Niagara's Original Daredevil Hall of Fame."

The Buffalo Museum of Science houses the Kellogg Observatory, the Bell Hall of Space Exploration, the Gibson Hall of Space, Insect World, Dinosaurs and Co and the Discovery Room for children, as well as exhibits on mummies, endangered species, botany, geology, zoology, anthropology and natural sciences.

The Albright-Knox Gallery has an extensive collection of 18th-century English, 19th-century French and American and 20th-century European and American paintings, as well as sculpture from 3,000 B.C. to the present. The Western New York Forum for American Art, at the Burchfield Art Center of the State University College at Buffalo, displays works and memorabilia of Charles Burchfield and works of major western New York artists.

Among the many architecturally interesting buildings in Buffalo are the $7 million city hall, state and federal buildings, the Guaranty Building by Louis Sullivan and several Frank Lloyd Wright residences. In Allentown, a historic preservation district, there are many Victorian structures, ethnic restaurants, antique stores, art galleries and boutiques.

The Buffalo and Erie County Histrical Society is housed in a white marble building constructed for the 1901 Pan-American Exposition. The society was organized in 1862, and Millard Fillmore was its first president. On the lower floor of the museum, an 1870 street of shops re-creates the Buffalo of the mid-Victorian era, and the Turn-of-the-Century Street presents a slightly later look at the city. On the upper floor are exhibits relating to the major ethnic groups that settled in the area, the Indians of the Niagara Frontier, the opening of the Erie Canal and the Pan-American Exposition.

Also operated by the Historical Society, on behalf of the National Park Service, is the Theodore Roosevelt Inaugural National Historic Site. Here in the library of a house owned by lawyer Ansley Wilcox, Theodore Roosevelt was sworn in as 26th president of the United States after the assassination of William McKinley.

Buffalo is ringed with 3,000 acres of parks, which offer swimming, boating, tennis, golf and horseback riding. The Buffalo Zoological Gardens, located in the city's largest park, is one of the top-ranked zoological exhibits in the country and is home to more than 1,600 animals. The Buffalo and Erie County Botanical Gardens feature 12 greenhouses with palms, ferns, cacti, many exotic plants and seasonal shows.

Darien Lake, a theme park east of Buffalo in Darien Center, features a giant triple roller coaster, Adventureland for children and one of the largest Ferris wheels in North America, as well as waterslides, sand beach and a petting zoo.

Beaver Island State Park, a 952-acre park on the southern tip of Grand Island, northwest of Buffalo, has a wide range of activities including, swimming from a sand beach, fishing, golfing, hiking and boating from a marina, as well as many winter sports.

The Buffalo and Erie County Naval and Servicemen's Park, the only inland naval park in the nation, displays ships, aircraft and other World War II equipment. The *Miss Buffalo II* departs from the park for afternoon or evening charter cruises on the harbor, the Niagara River and Lake Erie. The Niagara River is crossed at Buffalo by the Peace Bridge, built in 1927 to celebrate 100 years of peace between the US and Canada. Just south of the bridge is La Salle Park, which has in its central plaza a statue of Oliver Hazard Perry, hero of the Battle of Lake Erie.

Shopping

Within minutes of the falls are more than 50 variety stores, plus various other types of shopping. The Galleria Mall in Buffalo and Summit Park and Rainbow Center malls in Niagara Falls offer a large selection of shops, restaurants and movie theaters. The Factory Outlet mall features name-brand outlets. Historic Lewiston, seven miles north of Niagara Falls, is a Federal-era village with vintage shops and restaurants. The Broadway Market, near Fillmore Avenue in Buffalo, sells fresh food products in an indoor, Old-World atmosphere.

General References
Buffalo

Founded: 1803 **Pop:** 328,123 **Elev:** 600 feet **Time zone:** Eastern **Area code:** 716

Phone Numbers

POLICE & FIRE: 911
FBI: 856-7800
POISON CONTROL CENTER: 878-7654
TIME & WEATHER: 844-1717

Information Sources

Greater Buffalo Convention & Visitors Bureau, 107 Delaware Ave, 14202-2801; 852-0511.
Department of Parks & Recreation, 851-5806.

Transportation

AIRLINES: American; Continental; Delta; Northwest; United; USAir; and other commuter and regional airlines. For the most current airline schedules and information consult the *Official Airline Guide,* published twice monthly.
AIRPORT: Greater Buffalo International, 632-3115.
AIRPORT TRANSPORTATION: Taxi $10; Limo $30; Shuttle bus $5.
CAR RENTAL AGENCIES: (See Toll-Free Numbers) Avis 632-1808; Budget 632-4662; Hertz 632-4772; National 632-0203; Payless 631-9880.
PUBLIC TRANSPORTATION: Metro Bus/Metro Rail 855-7211.
RAILROAD PASSENGER SERVICE: Amtrak 800/872-7245.

Newspaper

Buffalo News.

Convention Facilities

Buffalo Memorial Auditorium, 140 Main St, 851-5663.
Convention Center, Convention Center Plaza, 855-5555.

Sports & Recreation

Major Sports Facilities
Memorial Auditorium, 140 Main St, 856-7300 (Sabres, hockey).
Pilot Field, 275 Washington St, 846-2003 (Bisons, baseball).
Rich Stadium, Abbott Rd & US 20, 15 mi SE in Orchard Park, 648-1800 (Buffalo Bills, football).

Racetrack
Buffalo Raceway, 5600 McKinley Pkwy, 12 mi S off NY State Thrwy (I-90) exit 56, Erie County Fairgrounds in Hamburg, 649-1280 (harness racing).

Cultural Facilities

Theaters
Lancaster Opera House, 21 Central Ave, Lancaster, 683-1776.
Pfeifer Theatre, State University of NY at Buffalo, 681 Main St, 847-6461.
Shaw Festival Theatre, Wellington & Picton Sts, Niagara-on-the-Lake, ON, Canada, 905/468-2172.
Shea's Buffalo Theater, 646 Main St, 847-0850.
Studio Arena Theatre, 710 Main St, 856-5650.

Concert Hall
Kleinhans Music Hall, Pennsylvania & Porter Sts, 885-4632 (Buffalo Philharmonic Orchestra, 885-5000).

Museums
Buffalo & Erie County Historical Society, 25 Nottingham Ct, 873-9644.
Buffalo Museum of Science, 1020 Humboldt Pkwy, 896-5200.
Millard Fillmore House & Museum, 24 Shearer Ave, East Aurora, 652-8875.

Art Galleries
Albright-Knox Art Gallery, 1285 Elmwood Ave, 882-8700.
Burchfield Art Center, State University College at Buffalo, 1300 Elmwood Ave, 878-6012.

Points of Interest

Historical
Allentown Historic Preservation District, 881-1024.
Forest Lawn Cemetery, 1411 Delaware Ave, 885-1600.
Theodore Roosevelt Inaugural National Historic Site (Wilcox Mansion), 641 Delaware Ave, 884-0095.
Williamsville Water Mills, 56 Spring St, Williamsville, 632-1162.

Other Attractions
Broadway Market, 999 Broadway, 893-0705.
Buffalo and Erie County Botanical Gardens, 4 mi SE, 2 mi off Dewey Thrwy exit 55 in South Park, 828-1040.
Buffalo and Erie County Naval & Servicemen's Park, 1 Naval Park Cove, 847-1773.
Buffalo City Hall/Observation Tower, Niagara Square, 851-5891.
Buffalo Zoological Gardens, Jewett & Parkside Aves, 837-3900.
Darien Lake Theme Park, NY 77, off I-90 exit 48A in Darien Center, 599-4641.
Delaware Park, Lincoln Pkwy.
Fantasy Island Theme Park, I-190 exit N19 in Grand Island at 2400 Grand Island Blvd, 773-7591.
Q-R-S Music Rolls, Inc, 1026 Niagara St, 885-4600.

Sightseeing Tours
Buffalo Charters, Inc, *Miss Buffalo II* departs Naval & Servicemen's Park, foot of Main St; *Niagara Clipper* departs River Rd in North Tonawanda; 856-6696.
Buffalo Guide Service, 170 Franklin St, 852-5201.
Gray Line bus tours, 5355 Junction Rd, Lockport 14094; 625-9214.
Niagara Scenic Tours, 5220 Camp Rd, in Hamburg, 648-1500.
Silent Partners, 175 Cleveland, 883-1784.
Smoke Creek Carriages, 533 Fisher in West Seneca, 824-2838.

Annual Events
Hellenic Festival, W Utica St & Delaware Ave, 882-9485. 3rd wkend May.
Erie County Fair, 12 mi S off NY State Thrwy (I-90) exit 56, in Hamburg, 649-3900. Mid-Aug.

Niagara Falls

Settled: 1806 **Pop:** 61,840 **Elev:** 610 feet **Time zone:** Eastern **Area code:** 716

Phone Numbers
POLICE & FIRE: 911
FBI: 285-9215
POISON CONTROL CENTER: 878-7654

Information Sources
Niagara Falls Convention and Visitors Bureau, 310 4th St, 14303; 285-2400.
Dept of Parks & Recreation, 286-4943.

Transportation
AIRLINES: Served by regional airlines. For the most current airline schedules and information consult the *Official Airline Guide,* published twice monthly.
AIRPORT: Niagara Falls International, 297-4494.

AIRPORT TRANSPORTATION (from Greater Buffalo International): Taxi $35; Shuttle bus $15.
CAR RENTAL AGENCIES: (See Toll Free Numbers) Brown 297-2474; National 285-5008.
RAILROAD PASSENGER SERVICE: Amtrak 800/872-7245.

Newspaper
Niagara Gazette.

Convention Facility
Convention & Civic Center, 305 4th St, 286-4769.

Cultural Facilities

Museums
Castellani Art Museum, Niagara University, 285-1212.
Native American Center for the Living Arts, 25 Rainbow Blvd, 284-2427.
Schoellkopf Geological Museum, off Robert Moses Pkwy near Main St, 278-1780.

Points of Interest

Historical
Devil's Hole State Park, 4 1/2 mi N of falls, 278-1770.
Fort George, 18 mi W on Niagara Pkwy, Niagara-on-the-Lake, ON, Canada, 905/468-4257.
Fort Niagara, Fort Niagara State Park, 14 mi N on Robert Moses Pkwy, Youngstown, 745-7273.

Other Attractions
Aquarium of Niagara Falls, 701 Whirlpool St at Pine Ave, 285-3575.
Artpark, 7 mi N on Robert Moses Pkwy, 754-9000.
E. Dent Lackey Plaza, Convention & Civic Center.
Goat Island, separates the Canadian & American Falls.
Historic Lewiston, 8 mi N via Robert Moses Pkwy.
Historic Lockport, 15 mi E via NY 31, 433-4762.
Marineland, 7657 Portage Rd, Niagara Falls, ON, Canada, 905/356-8250.
Native American Center for the Living Arts, 25 Rainbow Blvd, 284-2427.
Niagara Falls Museum, 5651 River Rd, Niagara Falls, ON, Canada, 905/356-2151.
Niagara Power Project Visitor Center, 5777 Lewiston Rd (NY 104), 4 1/2 mi N, 285-3211.
Niagara Reservation State Park, 4 mi W of I-190 via Robert Moses Pkwy, foot of Falls St, 278-1770.
Niagara Splash Water Park, 701 Falls St, 282-5132.
Niagara's Wax Museum of History, 303 Prospect St at Old Falls St, 285-1271.
Prospect Point Observation Tower, Prospect Park, 278-1770.
Reservoir State Park, Witmer Rd, 4 mi NE at jct NY 31, 265, 278-1762.
Spanish Aero Car, on Niagara Pkwy in Niagara Falls, ON, Canada, 905/354-5711.
Table Rock House Scenic Tunnels, Queen Victoria Park, Niagara Falls, ON, Canada, 905/354-1551.
Whirlpool State Park, 3 mi N of falls on Robert Moses Pkwy, 278-1770.
Wintergarden, Rainbow Blvd, 285-8007.

Sightseeing Tours
Cave of the Winds, Goat Island, 278-1730.
Maid of the Mist, 151 Buffalo Ave, 284-4233.
Niagara Viewmobile, Prospect Point, 278-1730.

Rainbow Helicopters, 454 Main St, 284-2800.

Annual Events

Niagara Summer Experience, E. Dent Lackey Plaza, 284-6188. Wkends June-mid-Aug.

Festival of Lights. Sat after Thanksgiving-Sun after Jan 1.

Lodgings and Food
Buffalo

Motels

★ ★ **COMFORT SUITES.** *901 Dick Rd (14225), near Greater Buffalo Intl Airport.* 716/633-6000; FAX 716/633-6858. 100 suites, 2 story. S $67-$80; D $72-$88; each addl $7; family rates; ski plan; higher rates sporting events. Crib free. TV. Indoor pool; lifeguard. Complimentary continental bkfst. Complimentary coffee in rms. Restaurant nearby. Ck-out noon. Coin lndry. Meeting rms. Bellhops. Sundries. Valet serv. Free airport, RR station transportation. Tennis privileges. Golf privileges. Downhill/x-country ski 20 mi. Exercise equipt; bicycles, rowers, whirlpool. Game rm. Refrigerators. Cr cds: A, C, D, DS, ER, JCB, MC, V.

⊡ 🏊 🏃 ⛷ ≈ 🏃 ✈ 🚫 🔥 **SC**

★ ★ **HAMPTON INN.** *10 Flint Rd, Amherst 14226) N on I-290 to exit 5B, left at Flint Rd.* 716/689-4414; FAX 716/689-4382. 199 rms, 4 story. S $63-$72; D $70-$79; under 18 free. Crib free. TV; cable. Pool; lifeguard. Complimentary continental bkfst. Restaurant opp 7 am-midnight. Ck-out noon. Meeting rms. Free airport, RR station transportation. Cr cds: A, D, DS, MC, V.

⊡ ≈ 🚫 🔥 **SC**

✔ ★ **MOTEL 6.** *(4400 Maple Rd, Amherst 14226) E on NY 33, N on I-290, exit 5B.* 716/834-2231; res: 505/891-6161. 94 rms. S $36.99; D $42.99; each addl $3-$6; under 18 free. Crib free. Pet accepted, some restrictions. TV; cable. Restaurant nearby. Ck-out noon. Cr cds: A, C, DS, MC, V.

⊡ 🐾 🚫 🔥

★ ★ ★ **RAMADA INN-BUFFALO AIRPORT.** *6643 Transit Rd (14221), I-90 exit 49.* 716/634-2700; FAX 716/634-1644. 123 rms, 2 story. Mid-Apr-mid-Oct: S $79-$94; D $89-$104; each addl $10; under 18 free; wknd plans; lower rates rest of yr. Crib free. TV; cable. Heated pool; poolside serv, lifeguard. Playground. Restaurant 6:30-1 am. Rm serv to 11 pm. Bar 11:30-4 am. Ck-out 11 am. Meeting rms. Valet serv. Sundries. Free airport, RR station transportation. Cr cds: A, C, D, DS, ER, JCB, MC, V.

≈ ≈ 🚫 🔥 **SC**

✔ ★ **RED ROOF INN-AMHERST.** *(42 Flint Rd, Amherst 14226) NE on I-290, Millersport exit to Flint Rd.* 716/689-7474; FAX 716/689-2051. 109 rms. S from $42; D from $44.95; each addl $8; under 18 free. Crib free. Pet accepted, some restrictions. TV; cable. Complimentary coffee. Restaurant nearby. Ck-out noon. Cr cds: A, C, D, DS, MC, V.

⊡ 🐾 🚫 🔥 **SC**

★ ★ **RESIDENCE INN BY MARRIOTT.** *(100 Maple Rd, Williamsville 14221) NE via I-290, NY 263 exit to Maple Rd.* 716/632-6622; FAX 716/632-5247. 112 kit. suites, 2 story. Kit. suites $120-$150. Crib free. Pet accepted, some restrictions; $6 per day. TV; cable. Heated pool. Complimentary continental bkfst. Ck-out noon. Coin lndry. Valet serv. Free airport transportation. Health club privileges. Cr cds: A, C, D, DS, MC, V.

⊡ 🐾 ≈ 🚫 🔥

★ **SUPER 8.** *(1 Flint Rd, Amherst 14226) E on NY 5, N on I-290, exit 5B.* 716/688-0811; FAX 716/688-2365. 104 rms, 4 story. Late May-Sept: S $47.88; D $55.88; each addl $5; under 12 free; lower rates rest of yr. TV; cable. Complimentary coffee. Restaurant nearby. Ck-out 11 am. Cr cds: A, C, D, DS, JCB, MC, V.

⊡ 🚫 🔥 **SC**

★ ★ **VILLAGE HAVEN.** *(9370 Main St, Clarence 14031) E on NY 5.* 716/759-6845. 30 rms, 7 kits. Late May-early Sept: S $40-$60; D $50-$77; each addl $6; kit. units $6 addl; wkly rates off-season; higher rates hols; lower rates rest of yr. Crib $6. TV. Pool; lifeguard. Playground. Complimentary continental bkfst in season. Complimentary coffee in rms. Restaurant nearby. Ck-out 11 am. Refrigerators. Picnic tables. Cr cds: A, MC, V.

≈ 🚫 🔥 **SC**

★ **WELLESLEY INN.** *(4630 Genesee St, Cheektowaga 14225) E on NY 33 to jct I-90, exit 51.* 716/631-8966; FAX 716/631-8977. 84 rms, 4 story. S $50; D $57-$65; each addl $5; under 18 free. Crib free. Pet accepted, some restrictions. TV; cable, in-rm movies. Complimentary continental bkfst in lobby. Restaurant adj. Ck-out 11 am. Valet serv. Free airport transportation. Some refrigerators. Cr cds: A, D, DS, ER, MC, V.

⊡ 🐾 🚫 🔥 **SC**

Motor Hotels

★ ★ **BEST WESTERN INN DOWNTOWN.** *510 Delaware Ave (14202), I-190 exit N-9 Niagara St.* 716/886-8333. 61 rms, 5 story. S $72-$74; D $78-$80; each addl $6; suites $198-$250; under 12 free. Crib $7. TV; cable. Ck-out noon. Meeting rm. Valet serv. Wet bar in suites. Cr cds: A, C, D, DS, JCB, MC, V.

🚫 🔥 **SC**

★ ★ **DAYS INN.** *4345 Genesee St (14225), near from Greater Buffalo Intl Airport.* 716/631-0800; FAX 716/631-7589. 130 rms, 6 story. S $55-$65; D $65-$79; each addl $8; family rates. Crib free. TV; cable. Pool; lifeguard. Restaurant 6:30 am-10:30 pm. Rm serv. Ck-out noon. Meeting rms. Free airport, RR station transportation. Cr cds: A, D, DS, MC, V.

⊡ ≈ ✈ 🚫 🔥 **SC**

★ ★ **HOLIDAY INN-DOWNTOWN.** *620 Delaware Ave (14202).* 716/886-2121; FAX 716/886-7942. 168 rms, 8 story. S $64-$89; D $72-$97; each addl $8; under 18 free; ski plans. Crib free. Pet accepted, some restrictions. TV; cable. Heated pool; wading pool, lifeguard. Restaurant 6:30 am-10 pm. Rm serv. Bar 11 am-midnight. Ck-out noon. Coin lndry. Meeting rms. Bellhops. Valet serv. Some free indoor parking. Free airport transportation. Health club privileges. Cr cds: A, C, D, DS, JCB, MC, V.

⊡ 🐾 ≈ 🚫 🔥 **SC**

★ **LORD AMHERST.** *(5000 Main St, Amherst 14226) E on NY 5 to jct I-290, near Greater Buffalo Intl Airport.* 716/839-2200; FAX 716/839-2200, ext. 458. 101 rms, 2 story. May-Sept: S $53-$65; D $63-$85; each addl $7; kit. units $65-$130; under 18 free; lower rates rest of yr. Crib free. Pet accepted, some restrictions. TV; cable. Heated pool; lifeguard. Complimentary full bkfst. Restaurant 7 am-9 pm. Bar 11 am-midnight. Ck-out 1 pm. Coin lndry. Meeting rms. Valet serv. Game rm. Colonial decor. Cr cds: A, C, D, DS, MC, V.

🐾 ≈ ✈ 🚫 🔥 **SC**

★ ★ **MARRIOTT.** *(1340 Millersport Hwy, Amherst 14221) N on I-290, exit Millersport.* 716/689-6900; FAX 716/689-0483. 356 rms. S $122; D $132; each addl $10; suites $275; under 18 free; wknd plans. Crib free. Pet accepted, some restrictions; $50. TV; cable. Indoor/outdoor pool; poolside serv, lifeguard. Restaurant 6:30 am-10:30 pm; Fri & Sat 7 am-11 pm; Sun 7 am-10:30 pm. Bar 11:30-3 am, Tues, Fri & Sat to 4 am, Sun noon-2 am; dancing. Ck-out noon. Convention facilities. Bellhops. Valet serv. Concierge. Gift shop. Free airport transportation. Exercise equipt; weights, bicycles, whirlpool, sauna. Game rm. Some bathrm phones; refrigerators avail. Some poolside patios. *LUXURY LEVEL : CONCIERGE LEVEL.* 37 rms. S $129; D $139; honeymoon plan. Honor bar. Bathrm phones. Complimentary continental bkfst, refreshments. Cr cds: A, C, D, DS, ER, JCB, MC, V.

⊡ 🐾 ≈ 🏃 ✈ 🚫 🔥 **SC**

★ ★ ★ **SHERATON AIRPORT.** *(2040 Walden Ave, Cheektowaga 14225) At I-90 exit 52E.* 716/681-2400; FAX 716/681-8067. 300 rms, 8 story. S $124-$139; D $139-$154; each addl $10; bi-level suites $325; under 18 free; wkend rates. Crib free. TV; cable. Indoor pool; poolside serv, lifeguard. Restaurant 6:30 am-10 pm. Rm serv. Bars noon-2 am; dancing Tues-Sat. Ck-out noon. Meeting rms. Bellhops. Valet serv. Sundries. Gift shop. Free airport, RR station transportation. Exercise equipt; weights, bicycles, sauna. *LUXURY LEVEL :* **PREFERRED QUARTERS.** 56 rms. S $139; D $154. Private lounge. Refrigerators. Complimentary continental bkfst, refreshments. Cr cds: A, C, D, DS, MC, V.

Hotels

★ ★ ★ **HILTON.** *120 Church St (14202), at Terrace St, on Lake Erie.* 716/845-5100; FAX 716/845-5377. 475 rms, 9 story. S $100-$125; D $112-$137; each addl $12; suites $160-$700; family, wkend rates. Crib free. Garage parking (fee). TV; cable. Indoor pool; poolside serv. 3 restaurants 6:30 am-midnight. 2 bars; entertainment, dancing. Ck-out 11 am. Convention facilities. Concierge. Gift shop. Airport transportation. 6 indoor tennis courts, pro. Exercise equipt; weight machine, bicycles, sauna, steam rm. Raquetball. Game rm. Refrigerator avail in some suites. Some private patios, balconies. *LUXURY LEVEL :* **EXECUTIVE LEVEL.** 55 rms, 5 suites. S $135; D $147; suites $250-$700. Ck-out 1 pm. Private lounge. Complimentary continental bkfst. Cr cds: A, C, D, DS, ER, JCB, MC, V.

★ ★ ★ **HYATT REGENCY.** *Two Fountain Plaza (14202), corner of Pearl & Huron Sts.* 716/856-1234; FAX 716/856-6734. 400 rms, 16 story. S $99-$133; D $124-$158; each addl $10; suites $210-$375; under 18 free; wkend rates. Crib free. Garage $7.50. TV; cable. Restaurant 6:30-11 pm. Bar 11:30-2 am, Sat & Sun from noon. Ck-out noon. Convention facilities. Gift shop. Beauty shop. 1923 building with glass atrium addition; in theater district. Bathrm phone, whirlpool in suites. Cr cds: A, C, D, DS, ER, JCB, MC, V.

✔★ ★ **LENOX.** *140 North St (14201), just off Delaware Ave, I-190 exit N-9.* 716/884-1700; FAX 716/885-8636. 149 rms, 9 story, 129 kits. S $59; D $69; each addl $10; suites $70-$100; under 12 free; wkly, monthly rates. Crib free. TV. Restaurant 7 am-7 pm. Ck-out noon. Coin lndry. Meeting rms. Airport transportation. Built in late 1800s. Cr cds: A, C, D, DS, MC, V.

★ ★ ★ **RADISSON HOTEL.** *(4243 Genesee St, Cheektowaga 14225) I-90, exit 51 E, near Greater Buffalo Intl Airport.* 716/634-2300; FAX 716/632-2387. 274 rms, 4 story, 54 suites. S $122-$132; D $132-$142; each addl $10; suites $142-$152; under 18 free; wkend rates. Crib free. TV; cable. Indoor/outdoor pool; poolside serv, lifeguard. Restaurant 6 am-midnight. Bar 8 pm-4 am; entertainment, dancing. Ck-out noon. Convention facilities. Concierge. Gift shop. Free airport, RR station transportation. Exercise equipt; weights, bicycles, whirlpool, sauna. Many bathrm phones; some wet bars. *LUXURY LEVEL :* **CLUB LEVEL.** 54 suites, 2 floors. Suites $142-$500. Private lounge, honor bar. Bathrm phones; some in-rm whirlpools. Complimentary continental bkst, refreshments. Cr cds: A, C, D, DS, ER, JCB, MC, V.

Inn

★ ★ ★ **ASA RANSOM HOUSE.** *(10529 Main St, Clarence 14031) E on NY 5.* 716/759-2315; FAX 716/759-2791. 6 rms, 1 with shower only, 2 story, 3 suites. Apr-Oct: S $75-$135; D $85-$150; each addl $15; suites $150-$160; higher rates hols; lower rates Nov & Feb-Mar. Closed Jan. Crib free. TV. Complimentary full bkfst; coffee in library. Restaurant (see ASA RANSOM HOUSE). Ck-out 11 am, ck-in 2 pm. Bellhop. Free RR Station transportation. Many fireplaces, balconies. Built 1853; antiques. Each rm decorated to distinctive theme. Totally nonsmoking. Cr cds: DS, MC, V.

Restaurants

★ ★ ★ **ASA RANSOM HOUSE.** *(See Asa Ransom House Inn)* 716/759-2315. Hrs: 4-8:30 pm; Wed also 11:30 am-2:30 pm; early-bird dinner Mon-Thurs 4-5:30 pm. Closed Fri; Dec 25; also Jan-mid-Feb. Res accepted; required hols. Semi-a la carte: lunch $6-$12, dinner $9.95-$19.95. Child's meals. Specialties: salmon pond pie, raspberry chicken, smoked corned beef with apple raisin sauce. Own baking, ice cream. Parking. Outdoor dining. Built in 1853. Early Amer decor; library-sitting rm, antiques. Fresh herb garden. Braille menu. Jacket. Cr cds: DS, MC, V.

★ ★ ★ **COACHMAN'S INN.** *(10350 Main St, Clarence 10350) I-90 exit 49.* 716/759-6852. Hrs: 11:30 am-10 pm; early-bird dinner Mon-Thurs 3-5:30 pm. Closed Dec 24-25. Res accepted; required hols. Semi-a la carte: lunch $4.95-$10.95, dinner $8.95-$24.95. Child's meals. Specializes in steak, prime rib, lobster tail. Pianist Fri, Sat. Parking. Fireplaces, beamed ceilings; old-time inn. View of countryside, gardens. Family-owned. Cr cds: A, C, D, DS, ER, MC, V.

★ ★ ★ **DAFFODIL'S.** *(930 Maple Rd, Williamsville) NE via I-290, NY 263 exit.* 716/688-5413. Hrs: 11:30 am-2:30 pm, 5-11 pm; Sun 4-9 pm; Sun brunch 11 am-2 pm. Closed major hols. Res suggested. Bar. Semi-a la carte: lunch $5.95-$9.95, dinner $13.95-$32.95. Child's meals. Specializes in seafood, Angus beef, rack of lamb. Own pastries. Pianist Fri, Sat. Valet parking. Victorian decor. Jacket. Cr cds: A, D, MC, V.

★ ★ **OLD RED MILL INN.** *(8326 Main St, Williamsville) E on I-90, exit 49.* 716/633-7878. Hrs: 11:30 am-10 pm; Fri & Sat to 11 pm; early-bird dinner 4-5:30 pm. Closed Dec 25. Res accepted. Bar. Semi-a la carte: lunch $3.95-$9.25, dinner $8.75-$22.95. Child's meals. Specializes in prime rib, steaks & seafood combination plates. Parking. Fireplaces; country inn built in 1858. Caboose & Union Pacific dining cars. Cr cds: A, C, D, DS, MC, V.

★ ★ ★ **RUE FRANKLIN WEST.** *341 Franklin St, I-190 Church St exit.* 716/852-4416. Hrs: 5:30-10 pm. Closed Sun, Mon; July 4, Thanksgiving, Dec 25. Res accepted. French menu. Bar to 12:30 am. Wine list. A la carte entrees: dinner $14-$19.50. Seasonal specialties. Own pastries, sauces, soups. Parking. Built 1880s. Family-owned. Cr cds: A, C, D, MC, V.

★ ★ ★ **SALVATORE'S ITALIAN GARDENS.** *6461 Transit Rd, I-90 exit 49, near airport.* 716/683-7990. Hrs: 5-11 pm; Sun from 3 pm. Closed Dec 24, 25. Res accepted. Italian, Amer menu. Bar. Wine list. Semi-a la carte: dinner $10.95-$28.95. Child's meals. Specializes in steak, prime rib, lobster, veal, rack of lamb. Own pastries. Jazz combo Fri, Sat. Parking. Courtyard & gardens. Family-owned. Cr cds: A, C, DS, MC, V.

★ ★ ★ **SCOTT'S.** *(7740 Transit Rd, Amherst) 1/4 mi N of Eastern Hills Mall.* 716/634-8888. Hrs: 11:30 am-2:30 pm, 5-10 pm; Fri, Sat to 11 pm. Closed Sun. Res accepted. Bar to 1 am. Wine list. Semi-a la carte: lunch $4.95-$7.95, dinner $12.95-$18.95. Child's meals. Specializes in rack of lamb, veal, seafood. Own baking, soups. Parking. Some tableside cooking. Cr cds: A, C, D, MC, V.

✔★ ★ **SIENA.** *4516 Main St.* 716/839-3108. Hrs: 11:30 am-3 pm, 5-10 pm; Fri & Sat to midnight; Sun 4:30-9 pm. Closed some major hols. Res accepted. Italian menu. Bar. A la carte entrees: lunch $6.25-$8.75, dinner $6.50-$16. Specializes in pizza, pasta, osso buco. Parking. Outdoor dining. Wood-burning pizza oven. Totally nonsmoking. Cr cds: A, MC, V.

✔★ **VITO'S GOURMET MARKET.** *206 S Elmwood Ave.* 716/852-5650. Hrs: 10 am-9 pm; Fri to midnight; Sat to 3 pm. Closed Sun; Easter, Thanksgiving, Dec 25. Res accepted Fri. Bar. A la carte entrees: lunch, dinner $2.50-$8.25. Child's meals. Specializes in deli fare. Parking. Outdoor dining. Cr cds: A, MC, V.

Unrated Dining Spots

JENNY'S ICE CREAM. *78 E Spring St, Williamsville)* 1 mi E of I-290/90 exit 50. 716/633-2424. Hrs: 11 am-9:30 pm; July-Aug to 11 pm. Closed Jan 1, Thanksgiving, Dec 25. A la carte entrees: salad, soup & sandwiches $3-$5. Specializes in homemade ice cream creations, yogurt, sorbet. Former stable, built in 1807. Old-fashioned decor. Totally nonsmoking. No cr cds accepted.

OLD MAN RIVER. *(375 Niagara St, Tonawanda)* 190 N exit River Rd. 716/693-5558. Hrs: 7 am-11 pm; Oct-Apr to 9 pm. Closed Jan 1, Thanksgiving, Dec 25. A la carte entrees: bkfst, lunch, dinner $3-$6. Child's meals. Specializes in charcoal-broiled hot dogs, chicken & sausage, sweet potato french fries. Clam & lobster bar in summer. Own apple dumplings, soups, cookies. All counter serv. Lobster tank. Player piano. Parking. Overlooks Niagara River; reproduction of 18th-century sailing ship for children to play on. No cr cds accepted.

PRIMA PIZZA PASTA. *396 Pearl St, at Chippewa.* 716/852-5555. Hrs: 9:30 am-midnight; Thurs 9-1 am; Fri, Sat to 3 am; Sun 3 pm-midnight. Closed Dec 25. Italian, Amer menu. Serv bar. A la carte entrees: lunch, dinner $2.75-$10. Specializes in pizza, calzones, chicken wings. Two-story; cafe style downstairs, upstairs dining area overlooking street. Cr cds: DS, MC, V.

Niagara Falls

Motels

★ **BEL-AIRE.** *9470 Niagara Falls Blvd (14304).* 716/297-2250; FAX 716/297-8712. 25 rms. Late June-Labor Day: S $58; D $68; each addl $7; higher rates hol wkends; lower rates rest of yr. TV; cable. Heated pool. Restaurant adj 7 am-11 pm. Ck-out 11 am. Tours. Cr cds: A, C, D, DS, MC, V.

✔★ **BUDGET HOST AMERI-CANA.** *9401 Niagara Falls Blvd (14304).* 716/297-2660; FAX 716/297-3188. 50 rms, 14 with shower only. Many rm phones. June-Labor Day: S $39-$69; D $45-$75; each addl $5; kit. suites $69-$125; under 18 free; higher rates Amer & Canadian hols; lower rates rest of yr. Crib free. TV; cable. Heated pool. Complimentary coffee in lobby. Restaurant opp 7-3 am. Ck-out 11 am. Coin lndry. Some refrigerators. Picnic tables. Cr cds: A, C, D, DS, MC, V.

★ **CHATEAU MOTOR LODGE.** *(1810 Grand Island Blvd, Grand Island 14072)* S on I-190 exit 19. 716/773-2868. 17 rms, 4 kits. June-Sept: S $59; D $69; under 8 free; wkly rates; lower rates rest of yr. Crib free. Pet accepted, some restrictions. TV. Restaurant nearby. Ck-out 11 am. Refrigerators. Cr cds: A, DS, MC, V.

✔★ **DRIFTWOOD.** *2754 Niagara Falls Blvd (14304).* 716/692-6650. 20 rms. No rm phones. Mid-June-mid-Sept: S $32; D

$37-$54; each addl $10; higher rates hol wkends; lower rates rest of yr. TV. Pool. Restaurants nearby. Ck-out 10:30 am. Cr cds: A, DS, MC, V.

★ **ECONO LODGE.** *7708 Niagara Falls Blvd (14304).* 716/283-0621; FAX 716/283-2121. 70 rms, 2 story. June-Labor Day: S $59-$79; D $59-$99; each addl $10; under 13 free; wkly rates; higher rates hols; lower rates rest of yr. Crib $10. TV. Heated pool. Complimentary coffee in lobby. Restaurant nearby. Ck-out 11 am. Gift shop. Picnic tables. Cr cds: A, DS, JCB, MC, V.

★ **PORTAGE HOUSE.** *(280 Portage Rd, Lewiston 14092)* 7 mi N on NY 104, at entrance to Artpark. 716/754-8295. 21 rms, 2 story. No rm phones. May-Labor Day: S $49; D $56; each addl $7; under 12 free; lower rates rest of yr. Crib free. TV; in-rm movies avail. Complimentary coffee. Restaurant adj 6 am-8 pm. Ck-out 11 am. Cr cds: A, MC, V.

✔★ **RAMADA INN.** *219 4th St (14303),* at Rainbow Blvd. 716/282-1734. 112 rms, 2 story. Apr-Oct: S, D $45-$120; each addl $8-$12; lower rates rest of yr. Crib free. TV; in-rm movies avail. Indoor pool. Restaurant 6:30 am-11 pm. Ck-out 11 am. Coin lndry. Airport transportation. Cr cds: A, C, D, DS, ER, MC, V.

★ **SUMMIT PARK COURT.** *2305 Niagara Falls Blvd (14304).* 716/731-5336. 12 rms, 3 suites, 1 kit. June-Sept: S $45-$60; D $55-$70; each addl $5; suites $85-$145; kit. unit $8 addl; higher rates hol wkends; lower rates rest of yr. Crib free. TV; cable. Heated pool. Complimentary coffee in rms. Restaurant nearby. Ck-out 11 am. Gift shop. Refrigerators. Cr cds: DS, MC, V.

Motor Hotels

★★ **BEST WESTERN RED JACKET INN.** *7001 Buffalo Ave (14304).* 716/283-7612; FAX 716/283-7631. 150 rms, 8 story. Late May-Sept: S $68-$108; D $78-$118; each addl $10; under 18 free; mid-wk, wkend plans; lower rates rest of yr. Crib free. TV. Pool; lifeguard. Restaurant 7 am-2 pm, 4:30-9 pm. Rm serv. Bar noon-midnight; entertainment, dancing Fri, Sat. Ck-out noon. Coin lndry. Meeting rms. Airport transportation. Game rm. Boat docking. On Niagara River. Cr cds: A, C, D, DS, ER, JCB, MC, V.

★★ **COMFORT INN-THE POINTE.** *1 Prospect Point (14303).* 716/284-6835; FAX 716/284-5177. 116 rms, 6 story. June-Oct: S $75-$129; D $85-$139; each addl $10; suites $150-$265; under 18 free; lower rates rest of yr. Crib free. TV; cable. Restaurant 7 am-11 pm. Bar 4 pm-3 am; dancing Fri, Sat. Ck-out 11 am. Meeting rms. Sundries. Gift shop. Game rm. Retail complex adj. Cr cds: A, C, D, DS, ER, JCB, MC, V.

★★★ **HOLIDAY INN-DOWNTOWN.** *114 Buffalo Ave (14303).* 716/285-2521; FAX 716/285-0963. 194 rms, 7 story. June-Aug: S $119-$149; D $129-$149; each addl $10; suites $175-$279; under 19 free; varied lower rates rest of yr. Crib free. TV; cable. Indoor pool; whirlpool, sauna, lifeguard. Supervised child's activities (mid-June-Aug, daily; rest of yr, wkends). Restaurant 6:30 am-10 pm. Rm serv. Bar noon-2 am. Ck-out noon. Coin lndry. Bellhops. Valet serv. Holidome. Game rm. Cr cds: A, C, D, DS, ER, JCB, MC, V.

★★ **HOWARD JOHNSON-DOWNTOWN.** *454 Main St (14301).* 716/285-5261; FAX 716/285-8536. 75 rms, 5 story. June-Labor Day: S $75-$125; D $80-$135; each addl $8; under 18 free; wkly, wkend rates; higher rates: hols, special events; lower rates rest of yr. Crib free. TV; cable. Indoor pool; sauna, lifeguard. Restaurant 6:30

am-11 pm. Serv bar. Ck-out noon. Coin lndry. Sundries. Airport transportation. Game rm. Near falls. Helicopter tours. Cr cds: A, C, D, DS, ER, JCB, MC, V.

[icons] SC

★ ★ **INN AT THE FALLS.** *240 Rainbow Blvd (14303). 716/282-1212; res: 800/223-2557; FAX 716/282-1216.* 217 rms, 4 story, 8 suites. Memorial Day-Labor Day: S, D $69-$139; each addl $10; suites $119-$249; under 16 free; lower rates rest of yr. TV. Indoor pool; whirlpool. Complimentary morning coffee avail. Restaurant 7 am-10 pm. Rm serv. Bar 3 pm-1 am; entertainment, dancing wkends. Ck-out 11 am. Meeting rms. Bellhops. Shopping mall adj; falls 1½ blks. Cr cds: A, D, DS, MC, V.

D [icons] SC

★ **QUALITY INN RAINBOW BRIDGE AT THE FALLS.** *443 Main St (14301). 716/284-8801; FAX 716/284-8633.* 168 rms, 8 story. Mid-June-mid-Sept: S, D $89-$129; each addl $10; under 16 free; wkend rates; lower rates rest of yr. Crib free. TV. Indoor pool; sauna. Restaurant 7 am-10 pm. Bar 11-2 am. Ck-out 11 am. Meeting rms. Valet serv. Sundries. Gift shop. Airport transportation. Game rm. Guided tours. Cr cds: A, C, D, DS, ER, JCB, MC, V.

D [icons] SC

Hotels

★ ★ **DAYS INN FALLS VIEW.** *201 Rainbow Blvd (14303), 1 blk E of Falls. 716/285-9321; FAX 716/285-2539.* 200 rms, 12 story. Mid-June-early Sept: S, D $59-$118; each addl $8; under 16 free; lower rates rest of yr. Crib free. TV. Restaurant 6:30 am-10 pm. Bar 11-2 am; entertainment, dancing Fri, Sat. Ck-out 11 am. Meeting rms. Game rm. Some refrigerators. Overlooks rapids. Tours. Cr cds: A, D, DS, MC, V.

D [icons] SC

★ ★ ★ **HOLIDAY INN-GRAND ISLAND.** *(PO Box 430, Grand Island 14072) S on I-190, exit 19. 716/773-1111; FAX 716/773-9386.* 262 rms, 6 story. Mid-June-early Sept: S, D $70-$120; each addl $10; under 19 free; wkend plan; lower rates rest of yr. Crib free. TV; cable, in-rm movies. 2 pools, 1 indoor; wading pool, lifeguard. Playground. Restaurant 6:30 am-10 pm. Bar noon-2 am; dancing wkends. Ck-out noon. Meeting rms. Gift shop. Tennis. 18-hole golf, driving range. Exercise rm; instructor, weights, bicycles, whirlpool, sauna. Masseuse. Rec rm. Lawn games. Balconies. Resort-type hotel; on Niagara River. Marina. *LUXURY LEVEL :* 30 rms. S $80-$120; D $90-$130. Complimentary continental bkfst, refreshments. Cr cds: A, C, D, DS, ER, JCB, MC, V.

D [icons] SC

★ ★ ★ **RADISSON.** *PO Box 845 (14303), Third & Old Falls Sts. 716/285-3361; FAX 716/285-3900.* 401 rms, 6 story. Mid-June-mid-Sept: S, D $109; each addl $10; suites $175-$375; lower rates rest of yr. Crib free. Pet accepted, some restrictions; $50 refundable. Garage parking $6/night. TV; cable. Indoor/outdoor pool; sauna. Restaurant 6:30 am-10 pm. Bar 11-2 am, Fri, Sat to 3 am. Ck-out noon. Convention facilities. Gift shop. Airport transportation. Game rm. Some refrigerators. Walkway to Intl Convention Center & Rainbow Center. Cr cds: A, C, D, DS, ER, JCB, MC, V.

D [icons] SC

Inn

★ ★ ★ **RED COACH INN.** *2 Buffalo Ave (14303). 716/282-1459; FAX 716/282-2650.* 7 rms, 3 story, 5 kit. suites. D $95; kit. suites $125-$175; wkly, monthly rates; lower rates winter. TV. Complimentary continental bkfst. Complimentary coffee in rms. Restaurant (see RED COACH INN). Rm serv. Bar to 2 am. Ck-out noon, ck-in 2 pm. Meeting

rms. Airport transportation. X-country ski 5 mi. View of Upper Rapids. Built 1923; authentic Old English atmosphere. Cr cds: A, C, D, DS, JCB, MC, V.

[icons] SC

Restaurants

✔ ★ **ALPS CHALET.** *1555 Military Rd. 716/297-8990.* Hrs: 11-2 am; Sat noon-3 am. Closed Mon. Res accepted. Greek, Amer menu. Bar. Semi-a la carte: lunch $3-$5, dinner $5.50-$13. Child's meals. Specializes in steak, seafood. Own baklava. Parking. Chalet-type decor. Family-owned. Cr cds: A, C, MC, V.

D SC

★ ★ **CLARKSON HOUSE.** *(810 Center St, Lewiston) N on Robert Moses Pkwy, Lewiston exit. 716/754-4544.* Hrs: 5-11 pm; Sun 4-10:30 pm. Closed Mon; Dec 25. Res accepted; required Sat, Sun. Bar. Semi-a la carte: dinner $9.40-$28.95. Child's meals. Specializes in charbroiled steak, lobster. Parking. Open-hearth cooking. 1818 house. Family-owned. Cr cds: A, MC, V.

✔ ★ ★ **COMO.** *2220 Pine Ave. 716/285-9341.* Hrs: 11:30 am-11 pm; early-bird dinner Mon-Thurs 3-6 pm. Closed Dec 25. Res accepted. Italian, Amer menu. Bar. Semi-a la carte: lunch $4-$7, dinner $7-$12. Child's meals. Specializes in veal parmigiana, fettucine Alfredo, ravioli. Parking. Statuary reproductions. Family-owned. Cr cds: A, MC, V.

D SC

★ ★ **JOHN'S FLAMING HEARTH.** *1965 Military Rd, 6 mi NE of Falls. 716/297-1414.* Hrs: 11:30 am-11 pm; Sun from noon; early-bird dinner Mon-Sat 4-6 pm. Res accepted. Bar. Semi-a la carte: lunch $3-$7.50. Complete meals: dinner $11.95-$27.95. Child's meals. Specializes in steak, lobster, pumpkin ice cream pie. Own ice cream. Entertainment Sat. Parking. Family-owned. Cr cds: A, C, D, MC, V.

D SC

★ **MACRI'S PALACE.** *755 W Market St. 716/282-4707.* Hrs: 11 am-11 pm; Fri, Sat to midnight. Closed July 4, Thanksgiving, Dec 25. Res accepted. Italian, Amer menu. Bar 11:30-2:30 am; Fri, Sat to 3:30 am. Semi-a la carte: lunch $3.50-$6, dinner $7-$15. Child's meals. Specializes in pasta, steak, seafood. Contemporary decor. Cr cds: A, DS, MC, V.

✔ ★ **POLISH NOOK.** *2242 Cudaback Ave. 716/282-6712.* Hrs: 11 am-11 pm; Mon, Tues to 2 pm. Closed most major hols. Polish, Amer menu. Bar. Semi-a la carte: lunch $2.50-$5.50, dinner $4.50-$8. Specialties: golambki, pierogi. Parking. Old World decor. Family-owned. No cr cds accepted.

★ ★ **RED COACH INN.** *(See Red Coach Inn) 716/282-1459.* Hrs: 11:30 am-10 pm; Fri & Sat to 11 pm. Closed Dec 25. Bar. Semi-a la carte: lunch $3.95-$8.95, dinner $5.75-$19.95. Child's meals. Specializes in prime rib. Parking. Glassed-porch dining overlooking Upper Rapids. English inn decor & atmosphere. Cr cds: A, C, D, DS, MC, V.

SC

★ ★ **RIVERSIDE INN.** *(115 S Water St, Lewiston) N on Robert Moses Pkwy, Lewiston exit. 716/754-8206.* Hrs: 11:30 am-3 pm, 4-11 pm; Fri & Sat to midnight; winter hrs vary; early-bird dinner Mon-Thurs 4-6 pm; Sun brunch 10 am-3 pm. Res accepted. Bar. Semi-a la carte: lunch $4.95-$8.95, dinner $10.95-$16.95. Sun brunch $10.95. Child's meals. Specializes in fresh seafood, steak, prime rib. Salad bar. Entertainment Thurs-Sat; also Sun in summer. Parking. Outdoor dining. Built 1871; riverboat atmosphere. Family-owned. Cr cds: A, D, DS, MC, V.

D SC

Charlotte

Settled: 1748

Pop: 395,934

Average temperature: (January) 43°F, (July) 77°F

Time zone: Eastern

Area code: 704

The largest city in North Carolina, Charlotte combines the charm of a Southern community with the opportunities of a modern metropolis. An old and dignified city, Charlotte is also a lively business center serving the entire Southeast.

When the first European settlers came to the lower Piedmont region, they found fertile valleys and hills, lovely streams and the friendly Catawba Indians. Before the California Gold Rush of 1848, the area around Charlotte was the nation's major gold producer. A branch of the US Mint was established here, operating from 1837 to 1861.

Although chiefly agricultural prior to the Civil War, after Appomattox the Charlotte region took eagerly to industry. The Catawba River's abundant water power, used for generating electricity, has been a principal reason for the city's rapid growth.

Business

In recent years, Charlotte has been among the country's top 25 cities in new construction. Today, some of the nation's largest banks are located in the city, making Charlotte a major financial center of the South.

Convention Facilities

The Charlotte Convention Center has a total exhibition floor space of 134,000 square feet; 2 auditoriums, when not being used for exhibits, can seat 11,000 people, and 2 banquet areas can serve 7,700. Meeting rooms can accommodate from 200 to 700 people each. A new convention center is under construction and scheduled to be completed in 1994.

The Merchandise Mart offers 224,000 square feet of meeting and exhibit space, divided among 3 exhibit halls; the Charlotte International Trade Center has an additional 100,000 square feet of space. The hotels and motels of the area have a combined total of more than 16,000 rooms.

Sports and Recreation

There are more than 120 parks and playgrounds in the Charlotte metropolitan area, offering tennis, fishing and boating, nature trails, picnic areas and ball fields.

Automobile races are held at Charlotte Motor Speedway throughout the year. The Coca-Cola 600 on the Winston Cup circuit, the longest-running NASCAR-sponsored stock car race, and the All Pro Auto Parts 300 and 500 are run here. Another major sporting event in Charlotte is the Paine Webber Invitational Golf Tournament.

The Charlotte Hornets play home basketball games at the 23,500-seat Coliseum. The Charlotte Knights play their home baseball games in the Knights' Castle ballpark.

Nearby lakes abound with largemouth bass, bluegill, catfish, carp and bream, and there is hunting for small game in season. Several ski areas are only a few hours' drive from the city.

Entertainment

Charlotte is a musical city. Its opera is the only professional company between Washington and Atlanta; the season lasts from October to November and January to early May. The Charlotte Symphony Orchestra gives performances featuring solo artists and choral groups from late September to mid-April.

The Oratorio Singers of Charlotte present various two-concert series throughout the year. Other concerts are given by the American Guild of Organists and the Charlotte Choral Society.

Theatre Charlotte and Children's Theater entertain playgoers, and activities at the University of North Carolina's Charlotte campus and four area colleges round out a rich schedule of cultural events. Charlotte Repertory Theatre also offers a full season of plays.

Historical Areas

The Mint Museum of Art is a reminder of the days before the California Gold Rush of 1848, when Charlotte was the nation's major gold producer. A branch of the US Mint, which operated here from 1837 to 1861 and from 1867 to 1913, has been remodeled into a museum of art.

About 17 miles northeast of Charlotte, off NC 24, the state has opened the old Reed Gold Mine. Guided tours include a demonstration of placer-mining techniques. It was near here, in 1799, that 12-year-old Conrad Reed stumbled on a 17-pound gold nugget while wading in Meadow Creek. Not realizing the stone's value, his family used it as a doorstop for several years. Once the "pretty rock" was identified, the nation's first gold rush was on. The area is now a state historic site.

Forty-two miles northeast of the city is the historic town of Salisbury. First settled in the 1720s, it was involved in both the American Revolution and the Civil War. The town is home to many historic structures, including the restored Old Stone House (1766), the Rowan Museum in the Maxwell Chambers house (1819) and the restored Grimes Mill (1896). During the Civil War, Salisbury was the site of a Confederate prison for Union soldiers; most of the 5,000 men who died in the prison are buried in the town's National Cemetery.

Southeast of Charlotte, near Waxhaw, an outdoor monument commemorates the birthplace of President Andrew Jackson. Another president, James K. Polk, was born a half-mile south of Pineville; a museum, visitor center and replica of the log cabin Polk was born in are located at the site.

Sightseeing

Southwest of Charlotte, just over the line in South Carolina, is Kings Mountain National Military Park, site of a crucial battle of the American Revolution. Near the center of the park is the battlefield ridge with several monuments, including the Centennial Monument, dedicated in 1880. A self-guided trail leads to key features of the battlefield. Living history demonstrations are held daily during the summer months.

Just south of the city, on the state line and built in both North and South Carolina, is Paramount's Carowinds, a family entertainment complex with 10 theme areas. The park features rides, shows, water attractions, restaurants and shops.

The spectacular Blue Ridge Mountains lie several hours west of Charlotte. In Asheville, 112 miles northwest of the city, stands Biltmore, an elegant 250-room mansion on a 10,000-acre estate, built in 1895 by George W. Vanderbilt. This impressive estate includes 35 acres of formal gardens and numerous varieties of azaleas and roses.

General References

Settled: 1748 **Pop:** 395,934 **Av temp:** (January) 43°F, (July) 77°F **Time zone:** Eastern **Area code:** 704

Phone Numbers

POLICE, FIRE & AMBULANCE: 911
FBI: 377-9200.
POISON CONTROL CENTER: 355-4000.
TIME: 375-6711 **WEATHER:** 359-8466

Information Sources

Charlotte Convention & Visitors' Bureau, 122 E Stonewall St, 28202; 334-2282, 331-2700 or 800/231-4636.
Charlotte Chamber of Commerce, 129 W Trade St, 28202; 378-1300.
Dept of Parks & Recreation, 336-2884.

Transportation

AIRLINES: American; Delta; TWA; United; USAir and other commuter and regional airlines. For the most current airline schedules and information consult the *Official Airline Guide,* published twice monthly.
AIRPORT: Charlotte/Douglas International Airport, 359-4013.
CAR RENTAL AGENCIES: (See Toll-Free Numbers) Avis 359-4580; Budget 359-5000; Dollar 359-4700; Enterprise 391-0061 Hertz 359-0114.
PUBLIC TRANSPORTATION: Charlotte Transit System 336-3366.
RAILROAD PASSENGER SERVICE: Amtrak 800/872-7245.

Newspapers

Charlotte Observer; Charlotte Post.

Convention Facilities

Charlotte International Trade Center, 200 N College St, 335-9100.
Charlotte Convention Center, 101 S College St, 332-5051.
Merchandise Mart, 2500 E Independence Blvd, 333-7709.

Sports & Recreation

Major Sports Facilities

Charlotte Coliseum, 100 Paul Buck Blvd, 357-4700.

Knights Stadium, S on I-77, exit 88, 2280 Deerfield Dr, Fort Mill, 332-3746 (Knights, baseball).

Racetrack

Charlotte Motor Speedway, 12 mi N on US 29 or off I-85, Harrisburg, 455-3200.

Cultural Facilities

Theaters

Charlotte Repertory Theatre, Blumenthal Performing Arts Center, 130 N Tryon St, 375-4796.
Children's Theater, 1017 E Morehead St, 333-8983 or 376-5745.
Theatre Charlotte, 501 Queens Rd, 376-3777.

Concert Halls

Ovens Auditorium, 2700 E Independence Blvd, 372-3600.
Spirit Square Center for the Arts, 345 N College St, 372-7469 or -9664.

Museums

The Charlotte Museum of History and Hezekiah Alexander Home Site, 3500 Shamrock Dr, 568-1774.
Discovery Place, Charlotte Observer Omnimax Theater & Kelly Space Voyager Planetarium, 301 N Tryon St, 372-6261.
Nature Museum, 1658 Sterling Rd, 337-2660.
Schiele Museum of Natural History & Planetarium, 1500 E Garrison Blvd, Gastonia, 866-6900 or -6903.

Art Museums

Afro-American Cultural Center, 401 N Myers St, 374-1565.
Mint Museum of Art, 2730 Randolph Rd, 337-2000.
Spirit Square Center for the Arts, 345 N College St, 372-9664.

Points of Interest

Historical

Andrew Jackson Birthplace, 25 mi S on US 521, near Waxhaw.
Fourth Ward, uptown, near central business district.
James K. Polk Memorial State Historic Site, 12 mi S on US 521, Pineville, 889-7145.
Kings Mountain National Military Park, 40 mi W on I-85 in SC, 803/936-7921.
Latta Place, Latta Plantation Park, 5225 Sample Rd, Huntersville, 875-2312 (house) or -1391 (park).
Reed Gold Mine State Historic Site, 20 mi E off NC 24, Stanfield, 786-8337.
Salisbury, 42 mi NE via I-85, 636-0103.

Other Attractions

Backing Up Classics Memory Lane Museum, 12 mi N on US 29, adj Charlotte Motor Speedway, Harrisburg, 788-9494.
Paramount's Carowinds, 10 mi S off I-77, 588-2600 or 800/888-4FUN.
Charlotte Symphony Orchestra, Blumenthal Performing Arts Center, 130 Tryon St, 332-6136.
Glencairn Garden, 725 Crest St, Rock Hill, SC, 803/329-7009.
Opera Carolina, Blumenthal Performing Arts Center, 130 Tryon St, 332-7177.

Annual Events

Springfest, Uptown. Phone 332-0126. Last wkend Apr.
Coca-Cola 600 Winston Cup, Charlotte Motor Speedway, 455-3200. Memorial Day wkend.
Paine Webber Invitational Golf Tournament, Tournament Players Club, Piper Glen, 846-4699. Late May.
Festival in the Park, Freedom Park. Late Sept.

Lodgings and Food

Motels

✔★ **COMFORT INN AIRPORT.** 4040 I-85 S (28208), exit 32 (Little Rock Rd), near Douglas Intl Airport. 704/394-4111. 117, 2 story. S $41.95; D $46.95; each addl $5; under 18 free; higher rates stock car races. Crib $5. TV; cable. Pool. Complimentary continental bkfst. Restaurant adj 7 am-10 pm. Bar 5-11 pm. Ck-out 11 am. Meeting rms. Free airport transportation. Exercise equipt; stair machine, rowers. Refrigerators avail. Cr cds: A, C, D, DS, JCB, MC, V.

🅳 ≋ 🏃 ✈ 🛇 🔥 SC

✔★ **COMFORT INN-SUGAR CREEK.** 5111 N Sugar Creek Rd (28269). 704/598-0007; FAX 704/598-0007, ext. 302. 87 rms, 2 story. S $37.95; D $41-$53; each addl $6; under 18 free; higher rates special events. Crib free. Pet accepted, some restrictions. TV; cable. Pool. Complimentary continental bkfst, coffee. Restaurant nearby. Ck-out 11 am. Meeting rms. Valet serv. Exercise equipt; weight machine, bicycles, whirlpool. Cr cds: A, C, D, DS, ER, JCB, MC, V.

🅳 🐾 ≋ 🏃 🔥 SC

★★ **COURTYARD BY MARRIOTT.** 800 E Arrowwood Rd (28217), I-77 exit 3. 704/527-5055; FAX 704/525-5848. 146 rms, 3 story. S $62.95; D $72.95; under 6 free; wkend rates. Crib free. TV; cable. Pool. Bkfst avail. Bar 5-9 pm. Ck-out noon. Meeting rms. Coin lndry. Valet serv. Exercise equipt; weights, bicycles, whirlpool. Some refrigerators. Private patios, balconies. Cr cds: A, C, D, DS, MC, V.

🅳 ≋ 🏃 🛇 🔥 SC

★★ **COURTYARD BY MARRIOTT-UNIVERSITY.** 333 W Harris Blvd (28262). 704/549-4888; FAX 704/549-4946. 152 rms, 4 story. S, D $57; suites $69.95-$72.95; under 12 free; wkend rates; higher rates special events. Crib free. TV; cable. Pool. Complimentary coffee in rms. Bkfst avail. Bar. Ck-out noon. Coin lndry. Meeting rms. Exercise equipt; weight machine, bicycles, whirlpool. Refrigerator in suites. Near University of NC at Charlotte. Cr cds: A, C, D, DS, MC, V.

🅳 ≋ 🏃 🛇 🔥 SC

★ **CRICKET INN.** 1200 W Sugar Creek Rd (28213). 704/597-8500; res: 800/274-2538; FAX 704/598-1815. 132 rms, 2 story. S $36; D $41; suites $42-$49; under 18 free; higher rates special events. Crib free. TV; cable. Pool. Complimentary coffee in lobby. Restaurant opp 24 hrs. Ck-out 11 am. Refrigerator in suites. Cr cds: A, C, D, DS, MC, V.

🅳 ≋ 🛇 🔥 SC

✔★ **FAIRFIELD INN BY MARRIOTT.** 5415 N I-85 Sevice Rd (28262), I-85 exit 41. 704/596-2999; FAX 704/596-2999, ext. 709. 133 rms, 3 story. S $34-$40; D $43-$46; under 18 free; higher rates special events. Crib free. TV; cable. Pool. Complimentary continental bkfst in lobby. Restaurant nearby. Ck-out noon. Meeting rm. Cr cds: A, C, D, DS, MC, V.

🅳 ≋ 🛇 🔥 SC

★★ **HAMPTON INN.** 440 Griffith Rd (28217), approx 6 mi S via I-77, Tyvola Rd exit 5. 704/525-0747; FAX 704/522-0968. 161 rms, 4 story. S $51-$58; D $57-$64; under 18 free. Crib free. TV; cable. Pool. Complimentary continental bkfst. Ck-out noon. Valet serv. Airport transportation. Exercise equipt; weights, bicycles, sauna. Cr cds: A, C, D, DS, MC, V.

🅳 ≋ 🏃 🛇 🔥 SC

✔★ **INNKEEPER.** 305 Archdale Drive (28217). 704/525-3033; res: 800/822-9899. 70 rms, 2 story. S $32.95-$36.95; D $39.95-$42.95; each addl $5; under 16 free; higher rates special events. Crib

free. TV; cable. Pool. Complimentary continental bkfst, coffee. Restaurant nearby. Ck-out 11 am. Cr cds: A, C, D, DS, MC, V.

🅳 ≋ 🛇 🔥 SC

★★ **LA QUINTA-SOUTH.** 7900 Nations Ford Rd (28217), S via I-77 to exit 4 (Nations Ford Rd). 704/522-7110; FAX 704/521-9778. 118 rms, 3 story. S, D $43-$51; each addl $6; under 18 free; higher rates auto race wkends. Crib free. Pet accepted, some restrictions. TV; cable. Heated pool. Continental bkfst. Restaurant adj open 24 hrs. Ck-out noon. Valet serv. Cr cds: A, C, D, DS, MC, V.

🅳 🐾 ≋ 🛇 🔥 🐾 SC

✔★ **RED ROOF INN-COLISEUM.** 131 Red Roof Dr (28217), I-77 S to exit 4 (Nations Ford Rd). 704/529-1020; FAX 704/529-1020, ext. 444. 116 rms, 3 story. S $27-$31; D $34.99-$42.99; up to 5, $44.99; under 18 free. Crib free. Pet accepted, some restrictions. TV; cable. Complimentary coffee in lobby. Ck-out noon. Cr cds: A, C, D, DS, MC, V.

🅳 🐾 🛇 🔥

★★ **RESIDENCE INN BY MARRIOTT.** 5800 Westpark Dr (28217), off I-77S at Tyvola Rd exit 5. 704/527-8110; FAX 704/521-8282. 80 kit. suites, 1-2 story. S, D $99-$119. Crib free. Pet accepted; $50 deposit and $5 per day. TV; cable. Heated pool; whirlpool. Complimentary continental bkfst. Restaurant adj 7 am-10 pm. Coin lndry. Ck-out noon. Valet serv. Health club privileges. Lawn games. Private patios, balconies. Cr cds: A, C, D, DS, MC, V.

🅳 🐾 ≋ 🛇 🔥 SC

✔★ **RODEWAY INN.** 1416 W Sugar Creek Rd (28213). 704/597-5074. 56 rms, 2 story. S $35.95; D $40.95; each addl $2; under 12 free. Crib free. TV; cable. Pool. Complimentary continental bkfst. Restaurant adj open 24 hrs. Ck-out 11 am. Cr cds: A, C, D, DS, MC, V.

🅳 ≋ 🛇 🔥 SC

Motor Hotels

★★ **HOLIDAY INN-WOODLAWN.** 212 Woodlawn Rd (28217), at I-77S exit 6A. 704/525-8350; FAX 704/522-0671. 425 rms, 4 story. S, D $60-$84; each addl $8; suites $120-$150; under 12 free; wkend rates; higher rates special events. Crib free. TV; cable. Pool. Restaurant 6 am-10 pm. Rm serv. Bar 4 pm-1 am; entertainment, dancing exc Sun. Ck-out noon. Meeting rms. Bellhops. Valet serv. Sundries. Airport transportation. Exercise equipt; weight machine, bicycle, whirlpool. Refrigerator in suites. Cr cds: A, C, D, DS, JCB, MC, V.

🅳 ≋ 🏃 🛇 🔥 SC

★★ **HOMEWOOD SUITES.** 4920 S Tryon St (28217). 704/525-2600; FAX 704/521-9932. 144 suites, 5 story. S $95; D $95-$149. Crib free. Pet accepted; $8 per day. TV; cable, in-rm movies. Heated pool. Complimentary continental bkfst. Restaurant adj 8 am-10 pm. Ck-out noon. Coin lndry. Meeting rms. Bellhops. Sundries. Free airport transportation. Exercise equipt; weights, bicycles, whirlpool. Refrigerators. Cr cds: A, C, D, DS, JCB, MC, V.

🅳 🐾 ≋ 🏃 🛇 🔥 SC

★★ **SHERATON AIRPORT PLAZA.** 3315 S I-85 (28208), at Billy Graham Pkwy, near Douglas Intl Airport, I-85 exit 33. 704/392-1200; FAX 704/393-2207. 225 rms, 8 story. S $87-$115; D $97-$125; each addl $10; suites $150-$175; under 16 free; wkend rates. Crib free. Pet accepted. TV; cable. Indoor/outdoor pool; poolside serv. Complimentary continental bkfst. Coffee in rms. Restaurant 6:30 am-10:30 pm. Rm serv. Bar 11-2 am; entertainment Wed, dancing exc Sun. Ck-out noon. Meeting rms. Bellhops. Valet serv. Gift shop. Free airport transportation. Exercise equipt; weights, bicycles, whirlpool, sauna. Bathrm phones. Cr cds: A, C, D, DS, MC, V.

🅳 🐾 ≋ 🏃 ✈ 🛇 🔥 SC

★★ **WYNDHAM GARDEN HOTEL.** 2600 Yorkmont Rd (28208), off Billy Graham Pkwy at Tyvola Rd & Coliseum exit. 704/357-

9100; FAX 704/357-9159. 173 rms, 3 story. S $99; D $109; each addl $10; suites $109-$119; under 12 free; wkend rates; higher rates special events. Crib free. Pet accepted, some restrictions; $50. TV; cable. Heated pool. Complimentary coffee in rms. Restaurant 6:30 am-2:30 pm, 5-10 pm. Rm serv from 5 pm. Bar 4 pm-midnight. Ck-out noon. Meeting rms. Bellhops. Valet serv. Free airport transportation. Exercise equipt; weight machine, bicycles, whirlpool. Refrigerator in some suites. Situated on well-landscaped grounds. Cr cds: A, C, D, DS, ER, MC, V.

`D` `♥` `≈` `🏋` `🏃` `🏊` `🔥` `SC`

Hotels

★ ★ ★ **ADAM'S MARK.** 555 S McDowell St (28204), at jct US 74. 704/372-4100; FAX 704/846-4645. 598 rms, 18 story, 37 suites. S $79-$109; D $89-$119; each addl $15; suites $275-$350; under 18 free; wkend rates. Crib free. TV; cable. Heated pools, 1 indoor. Restaurant 6 am-midnight. Bars 11-1 am; entertainment, dancing. Ck-out noon. Convention facilities. Concierge. Gift shop. Exercise equipt; weights, bicycles, whirlpool, sauna. Some refrigerators. Wet bar in some suites. Opp park. Cr cds: A, C, D, DS, ER, MC, V.

`D` `≈` `🏋` `🏃` `🏊` `🔥` `SC`

★ ★ ★ **DOUBLETREE CLUB.** 895 W Trade St (28202). 704/347-0070; FAX 704/347-0267. 187 rms, 8 story. S $109-$119; D $119-$129; each addl $10; under 12 free; wkend rates; higher rates auto races (May & Oct). TV; cable. Pool. Complimentary continental bkfst, coffee. Restaurant 6-9 am, 5-10 pm. Bar 5 pm-1 am. Ck-out 1 pm. Meeting rms. Covered parking. Free downtown transportation. Exercise equipt; weight machine, bicycles, whirlpool, sauna. Cr cds: A, C, D, DS, ER, JCB, MC, V.

`D` `≈` `🏋` `🏊` `🔥` `SC`

★ ★ ★ **DUNHILL.** 237 N Tryon St (28202). 704/332-4141; res: 800/354-4141; FAX 704/376-4117. 60 rms, 10 story. S $99; D $109; each addl $10; under 16 free; wkend rates; higher rates special events. Crib free. TV; cable. Restaurant 6:30 am-10:30 pm. Bar; pianist Mon-Thurs. Ck-out noon. Meeting rms. Concierge. Free garage parking. Free airport transportation. Exercise equipt; stair machine, treadmill. Health club privileges. Refrigerators. European-style hotel built circa 1920; 18th-century furnishings, original artwork. Cr cds: A, C, D, DS, MC, V.

`D` `🏊` `🔥` `SC`

★ ★ ★ **EMBASSY SUITES.** 4800 S Tryon St (28217). 704/527-8400; FAX 704/527-7035. 274 units, 8 story. Suites $124-$160; each addl $20; under 12 free; wkend rates; higher rates special events. Crib free. TV; cable. Indoor pool; poolside serv. Complimentary coffee in rms. Restaurant 11 am-10 pm. Bar 10-2 am; entertainment, dancing. Ck-out noon. Coin lndry. Meeting rms. Gift shop. Covered parking. Free airport transportation. Tennis privileges. Exercise equipt; treadmill, bicycles, whirlpool, sauna. Refrigerators, wet bars; some bathrm phones. Cr cds: A, C, D, DS, MC, V.

`D` `🏃` `≈` `🏋` `🏊` `🔥` `SC`

★ ★ ★ **HILTON AT UNIVERSITY PLACE.** 8629 J M Keynes Dr (28262), off I-85, exit 45A (Harris Blvd). 704/547-7444; FAX 704/548-1081. 243 rms, 12 story. S $75-$135; D $85-$135; each addl $10; family, wkend rates. Crib free. TV; cable. Heated pool; poolside serv. Restaurant 6:30 am-10 pm. Bar 11:30-1 am; entertainment, dancing (May-Sept). Ck-out noon. Convention facilities. Exercise equipt; weights, bicycles. Cr cds: A, C, D, DS, MC, V.

`D` `≈` `🏋` `🏊` `🔥` `SC`

★ ★ ★ **HYATT.** 5501 Carnegie Blvd (28209), opp South Park Mall. 704/554-1234; FAX 704/554-8319. 262 rms, 7 story. S $125-$150; D $150-$175; suites $350-$750; under 18 free. Crib free. Free valet parking. Pet accepted, some restrictions. TV; cable. Indoor pool; poolside serv. Restaurant 6 am-10:30 pm. Rm serv 24 hrs. Bar 11-1 am. Ck-out noon. Convention facilities. Gift shop. Free airport transportation. Exercise equipt; weights, bicycles, whirlpool, sauna. Some

bathrm phones, refrigerators. Some balconies. *LUXURY LEVEL :* 41 rms. Suites $550-$650. Private lounge. Complimentary continental bkfst. Cr cds: A, C, D, DS, ER, JCB, MC, V.

`D` `♥` `≈` `🏋` `🏃` `🏊` `🔥` `SC`

★ ★ ★ **MARRIOTT-CITY CENTER.** 100 W Trade St (28202). 704/333-9000; FAX 704/342-3419. 431 rms, 19 story. S $130; D $140; suites $200-$350; under 12 free. Crib free. TV; cable. Covered parking, valet $10. TV; cable. Heated pool; poolside serv. Restaurant 6:30 am-10 pm. Bar 11:30-1 am. Ck-out noon. Coin lndry. Convention facilities. Concierge. Gift shop. Airport transportation. Exercise equipt; weights, bicycles, whirlpool. Refrigerators. Shopping adj. *LUXURY LEVEL : CONCIERGE LEVEL.* 67 rms, 4 suites, 2 floors. S $119; D $145; suites $300-$350. Private lounge, honor bar. Complimentary continental bkfst, refreshments. Cr cds: A, C, D, DS, ER, JCB, MC, V.

`D` `≈` `🏋` `🏊` `🔥` `SC`

★ ★ ★ **OMNI.** 222 E Third St (28202). 704/377-6664; FAX 704/377-4143. 410 rms, 22 story. S $109-$149; D $124-$164; each addl $10; suites $189; under 18 free; wkend rates. Crib free. Garage parking; valet $10. Pool privileges adj. Restaurant 6 am-11 pm; wkends from 7 am. Bar 11-1:30 am. Ck-out noon. Convention facilities. Concierge. Shopping arcade. Airport transportation. Tennis privileges. 18-hole golf privileges. Health club privileges. Minibars; some bathrm phones. Refrigerators avail. Wet bar in suites. Elegant hotel in heart of city's financial center. Cr cds: A, C, D, DS, JCB, MC, V.

`D` `🏌` `🏃` `🏊` `🔥` `SC`

★ ★ ★ ★ **THE PARK HOTEL.** 2200 Rexford Rd (28211). 704/364-8220; res: 800/334-0331; FAX 704/365-4712. 194 rms, 6 story. S $115-$135; D $125-$145; each addl $10; suites $325-$625; under 18 free; wkend rates. Crib free. TV; cable. Heated pool; poolside serv. Restaurant (see MORROCROFTS). Rm serv 24 hrs. Bars 11-2 am; entertainment, dancing. Ck-out noon. Meeting rms. Concierge. Free valet parking. Airport, RR station, bus depot transportation. Tennis & golf privileges. Exercise equipt; weight machines, bicycles, whirlpool, steam rm. Some refrigerators. Elegant decor. Cr cds: A, C, D, DS, JCB, MC, V.

`D` `🏌` `🏃` `≈` `🏋` `🏊` `🔥` `SC`

★ ★ ★ **RADISSON EXECUTIVE PARK.** 5624 Westpark Dr (28217), I-77 exit 5. 704/527-8000; FAX 704/527-4278. 178 rms, 7 story, 34 suites. S $100; D $110; each addl $10; suites $120; under 18 free. Crib free. Pet accepted; $50 ($30 refundable). TV; cable. Heated pool. Complimentary full bkfst. Restaurant 6:30 am-2 pm, 5-10 pm. Bar 2 pm-midnight. Ck-out noon. Meeting rms. Free airport, RR station transportation. Exercise equipt; weight machine, treadmill, whirlpool. Refrigerator in suites. Cr cds: A, C, D, DS, MC, V.

`D` `♥` `≈` `🏋` `🏊` `🔥` `SC`

★ ★ ★ **RADISSON PLAZA.** 5624 Westpark Dr (28217), at jct Trade & Tryon Sts. 704/377-0400; FAX 704/347-0649. 365 rms, 15 story. S, D $109; each addl $10; suites $119-$325; under 18 free; wkend rates. Crib free. TV; cable. Heated pool; poolside serv. Restaurant 6:30 am-10:30 pm. Bar 6:30 am-midnight. Ck-out noon. Convention facilities. Concierge. Shopping arcade. Barber, beauty shop. Covered parking. Exercise equipt; weights, stair machine, sauna. Health club privileges. Refrigerator, wet bar in suites. *LUXURY LEVEL : PLAZA CLUB.* 69 rms. S, D $119; suite $325. Private lounge. Complimentary bkfst, refreshments, newspaper. Cr cds: A, C, D, DS, ER, MC, V.

`D` `≈` `🏋` `🏊` `🔥` `SC`

★ ★ ★ **SOUTHPARK.** 6300 Morrison Blvd (28211), near South Park Mall. 704/364-2400; res: 800/647-8483; FAX 704/362-0203. 208 kit. suites, 3-6 story. S $95-$125; D $105-$250; under 18 free; wkend rates. Crib avail. TV; cable. Pool; poolside serv. Restaurant 6:30 am-11 pm. Bar 4 pm-midnight. Ck-out noon. Lndry facilities avail. Meeting rms. Gift shop. Airport transportation. Exercise equipt; weights, bicycles, whirlpool, sauna. Private patios, balconies. Cr cds: A, C, D, DS, MC, V.

Restaurants

★ ★ ★ **EPICUREAN.** *1324 East Blvd. 704/377-4529.* Hrs: 6-10 pm. Closed Sun; major hols; also 1st 2 wks July. Res accepted. Continental menu. Serv bar. Wine list. Semi-a la carte: dinner $11.50-$19.95. Child's meals. Specializes in prime beef, fresh seafood, lamb. Own baking. Parking. Family-owned. Cr cds: A, C, D, MC, V.

[D]

★ ★ **THE FISHMARKET.** *6631 Morrison Blvd. 704/365-0883.* Hrs: 11:30 am-2 pm, 6-10 pm; Sat, Sun from 6 pm. Closed major hols. Res accepted. Bar 4 pm-1 am. Semi-a la carte: lunch $6.25-$10.95, dinner $13.95-$28.95. Specializes in seafood, pasta, desserts. Cr cds: A, D, MC, V.

★ ★ **HEREFORD BARN STEAK HOUSE.** *4320 N I-85, on service road between Sugar Creek Rd & Graham St. 704/596-0854.* Hrs: 5-10 pm; Fri & Sat to 11 pm. Closed Sun; major hols. Serv bar. Semi-a la carte: dinner $9.95-$33.95. Child's meals. Specializes in steak, prime rib, chicken. Parking. Country-barn decor; farm implements; fireplace. Family-owned. Cr cds: A, C, D, DS, MC, V.

[SC]

★ ★ ★ **LA BIBLIOTHEQUE.** *1901 Roxborough Rd (28211), in Morrison office bldg. 704/365-5000.* Hrs: 11:30 am-2:30 pm, 5:30-10:30 pm. Closed Sun; Jan 1, Dec 25. Res required. French menu. Serv bar. A la carte entrees: lunch $7.50-$8.95, dinner $19-$26. Specializes in seafood, beef, veal. Parking. Terrace dining. Traditional decor; oil paintings. Jacket (dinner). Cr cds: A, C, D, DS, MC, V.

★ ★ ★ **LAMP LIGHTER.** *1065 E Morehead St. 704/372-5343.* Hrs: 5:30-10 pm; Fri, Sat to 10:30 pm. Closed Jan 1, Thanksgiving, Dec

25. Res accepted. Bar. Extensive wine list. Semi-a la carte: dinner $14.50-$26.95. Specializes in fresh seafood, wild game, Maine lobster. Own baking. Valet parking. In Spanish-colonial house built 1926. Jacket. Cr cds: A, C, D, MC, V.

[D]

★ ★ ★ **MORROCROFTS.** *(See The Park Hotel) 704/364-8220.* Hrs: 6:30 am-11 pm; early-bird dinner 5-6:30 pm; Sun brunch 9:30 am-2 pm. Res accepted. Bar. Wine list. Semi-a la carte: bkfst $2.50-$6.95, lunch $5-$8, dinner $12.95-$21.95. Sun brunch $11.95. Child's meals. Specializes in fresh seafood, regional cuisine. Own baking. Pianist. Valet parking. Outdoor dining. English club decor. Cr cds: A, C, D, DS, JCB, MC, V.

[D]

✔★ **OLD SPAGHETTI FACTORY.** *911 E Morehead St. 704/375-0083.* Hrs: 11:30 am-2 pm, 5-9:30 pm; Fri to 10:30 pm; Sat 5-10:30 pm; Sun noon-9 pm. Closed Dec 25. Italian menu. Bar. Semi-a la carte: lunch $2.95-$5.35, dinner $4.10-$9.25. Child's meals. Specializes in lasagne, chicken Mediterranean-style. Parking. In former skating rink. Cr cds: DS, MC, V.

[D]

★ **RANCH HOUSE.** *5614 Wilkinson Blvd (28208). 704/399-5411.* Hrs: 5-11 pm. Closed Sun; major hols. Serv bar. Semi-a la carte: dinner: $9.50-$19.50. Child's meals. Specializes in steak, seafood, chicken. Parking. Western decor. Family-owned. Cr cds: A, D, DS, MC, V.

★ ★ ★ **TOWNHOUSE.** *1011 Providence Rd. 704/335-1546.* Hrs: 6-10 pm. Closed Sun; some major hols. Res accepted. Bar from 5 pm. Wine list. Semi-a la carte: dinner $12.95-$29.95. Specializes in fowl, seafood, prime beef. Own baking, pasta. Parking. 18th-century English decor. Cr cds: A, C, D, MC, V.

[D]

Chicago

Settled: 1803	
Pop: 2,783,726	
Elev: 596 feet	
Time zone: Central	
Area code: 312 (city); 708 (suburbs)	

Chicago was incorporated as a city in 1837. Only four years later, in 1841, grain destined for world ports began to pour into the city. Almost immediately, Chicago became the largest grain market in the world. In the wake of the grain came herds of hogs and cattle for the Chicago slaughterhouses. Tanneries, packing plants, mills and factories soon sprang up. The completion of the Illinois and Michigan Canal in 1848 quadrupled imports and exports, and the railroads fanned out from the city, transporting merchandise throughout the nation and bringing new produce to Chicago. By the 1850s the city included 18 square miles of boom town and quagmire—its streets more bog than thoroughfare. The Civil War doubled grain shipments from Chicago, and in 1865 the square-mile Union Stock Yards were established.

Chicago was riotously prosperous, and its population had skyrocketed when, on October 8, 1871, fire erupted in a West Side barn. It roared through the city, destroying 15,768 buildings, killing approximately 300 persons and leaving a third of the population homeless. But temporary and permanent rebuilding started at once, and Chicago emerged from the ashes to take advantage of the rise of industrialization. The labor unrest of the period produced the Haymarket Square Riot as well as the Pullman and other strikes. In the 1880s and 1890s Chicago witnessed the development of a new urban architectural form for which the term skyscraper was coined. The World's Columbian Exposition of 1893, a magnificent success, was followed by a depression and municipal corruption. Nevertheless, Chicago's fantastic rate of growth continued into the 20th century, while Al Capone, the prohibition gangster, and Samuel Insull, the financial finagler whose stock manipulations left thousands penniless, were the symbols of the times. The stock market crash of 1929 brought down the shakier financial pyramids; the repeal of prohibition quieted the rackets; and a soberer Chicago produced the Century of Progress Exposition in 1933-34. The city's granaries and steel mills helped carry the country through the Second World War. Today the city is still booming as of old, with the world's largest inland port and the largest concentration of rail, truck and air transportation.

Business

Metropolitan Chicago has more than 10,000 factories with a sales volume of $98 billion. Chicago ranks as one of the top cities in the United States in the marketing of furniture and in the production of candy, canned and frozen foods, metal products, machinery, tool and die making, petroleum products, railroad equipment, printing and office equipment, musical instruments, telephones, housewares and lampshades. It has the world's busiest airport, largest commodity futures exchange and biggest mail-order business. It is a great educational center (58 institutions of higher learning, 800 technical schools); the world's largest convention and trade-show city; and a marketplace, shopping and financial center. Wholesale trade volume is over $90 billion annually, retail trade about $15 billion. Tourism is a significant industry in Chicago, which attracts more than 8 million visitors annually.

Convention Facilities

Chicago's McCormick Place, overlooking Lake Michigan, is one of the largest convention complexes in the world. Its statistics are staggering: 1,680,000 square feet of exhibit space; seating for 40,000 people at one time in the Don Maxwell Hall; parking for 12,000 cars (2,200 of them under roof); 8 restaurants that can feed a total of 20,000 people; banquet capacity of 25,000; 28 meeting rooms holding from 50 to more than 4,000 people; and the Arie Crown theater, with a seating capacity of 4,319.

Some of the annual exhibitions and trade shows draw more than a million people over a short period of time. Waiting in line for any type of service is seldom necessary, even when more than 100,000 people are on the premises.

Chicago's Apparel Center and Expocenter/Chicago are located downtown on the Chicago River. The Apparel Center marks Chicago's emergence as a major fashion design center. Expocenter/Chicago contains 140,000 square feet of exhibition space; parking and many amenities are available on the premises.

Rosemont Convention Center, near O'Hare International Airport, has 450,000 square feet of exhibition space on one level, 48,000 square feet of meeting space and 25 meeting rooms; parking is available for 5,000 cars.

In addition, there are many hotels in the Chicago area that provide extensive meeting facilities.

Sports and Recreation

For baseball, there are the Cubs (National League), who play at Wrigley Field, and the White Sox (American League), whose home field is Comiskey Park. The city's professional football team, the Bears, play at Soldier Field. The Blackhawks play hockey and the Bulls play basketball at the Chicago Stadium.

College sports include the DePaul Blue Demons, the Loyola Ramblers and the Northwestern Wildcats.

Horse racing is another popular spectator sport; local racetracks around the city include Arlington International Racecourse, Balmoral Park Race Track, Hawthorne Race Course, Maywood Park Race Track and Sportsman's Park.

For those athletes who wish to participate, Lake Michigan is a mecca for all water sports during warm months, and the city's enormous park areas can be enjoyed year-round.

Entertainment

This is a city known for its excellence in the arts of all types. Especially noteworthy are the Chicago Symphony and the Lyric Opera. Theater companies in Chicago and surrounding areas are too numerous to list; however, major theaters within the city proper are the Goodman, Royal

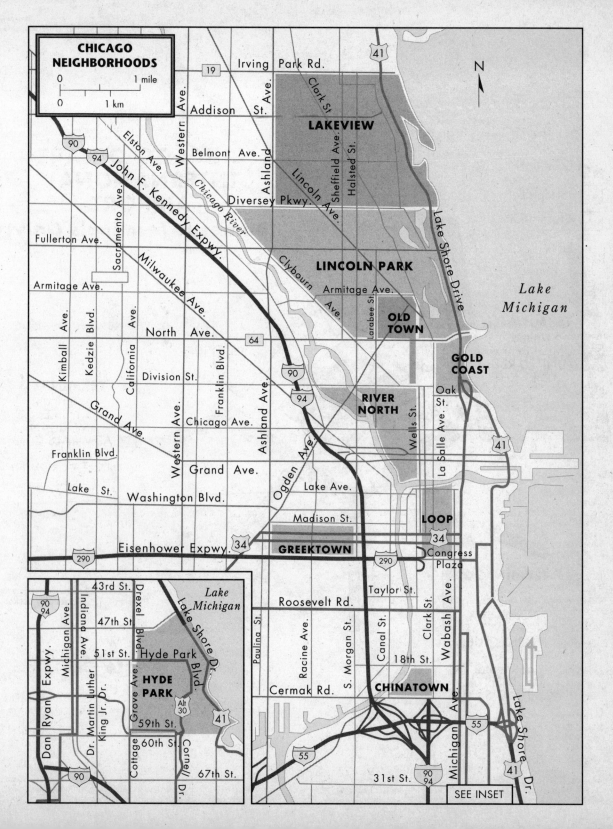

CHICAGO NEIGHBORHOODS

0   1 mile
0   1 km

19   Irving Park Rd.

41

Western Ave.

Clark St.

Addison St.

LAKEVIEW

90

94

Belmont Ave.

Ashland

Sheffield Ave.

Halsted St.

John F. Kennedy Expwy.

Elston Ave.

Chicago River

Diversey Pkwy.

Lincoln Ave.

Fullerton Ave.

Sacramento Ave.

LINCOLN PARK

Lake Michigan

Milwaukee Ave.

Clybourn

Ave.

Armitage Ave.

Larabee St.

Lake Shore Drive

Armitage Ave.

Kimball Ave.

Kedzie Blvd.

California Ave.

North Ave.

Franklin Blvd.

OLD TOWN

GOLD COAST

64

Division St.

Ashland Ave.

90

94

Oak St.

Grand Ave.

Western Ave.

Chicago Ave.

Ogden Ave.

RIVER NORTH

Wells St.

La Salle Ave.

41

Franklin Blvd.

Grand Ave.

Lake Ave.

Lake St.

Washington Blvd.

Madison St.

LOOP

34

Eisenhower Expwy.

34

GREEKTOWN

290

Congress Plaza

290

Taylor St.

Roosevelt Rd.

Paulina St.

Racine Ave.

S. Morgan St.

Canal St.

Clark St.

18th St.

Wabash Ave.

Cermak Rd.

CHINATOWN

55

31st St.

90 94

Michigan Ave.

Lake Shore Dr.

41

SEE INSET

Lake Michigan

90 94

Michigan Ave.

Indiana Ave.

43rd St.

47th St.

51st St.

Drexel Blvd.

Lake Shore Dr.

Hyde Park Blvd.

Dan Ryan Expwy.

Dr. Martin Luther King Jr. Dr.

Grove Ave.

Cottage

HYDE PARK

Hyde Park

Alt 30

59th St.

41

60th St.

Cornell Dr.

90

67th St.

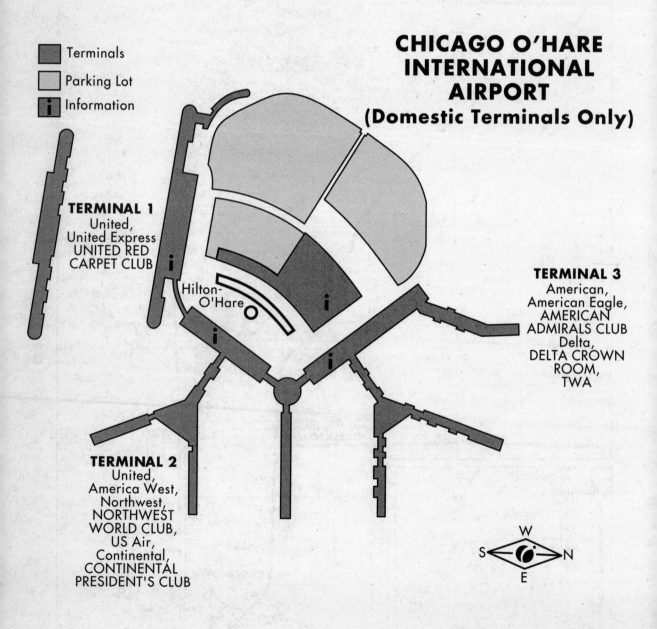

Legend:
- Terminals
- Parking Lot
- **i** Information

CHICAGO O'HARE INTERNATIONAL AIRPORT
(Domestic Terminals Only)

TERMINAL 1
United,
United Express
UNITED RED
CARPET CLUB

Hilton-
O'Hare

TERMINAL 3
American,
American Eagle,
AMERICAN
ADMIRALS CLUB
Delta,
DELTA CROWN
ROOM,
TWA

TERMINAL 2
United,
America West,
Northwest,
NORTHWEST
WORLD CLUB,
US Air,
Continental,
CONTINENTAL
PRESIDENT'S CLUB

George and the Auditorium. Theater companies are thriving, offering productions ranging from Second City's satirical reviews to Steppenwolf's award-winning dramas.

Chicago is teeming with night spots of every style imaginable. The city, though, is probably best known for jazz and blues. Step into almost any lounge or nightclub on the Near North Side, Lincoln Avenue in the Lincoln Park area or on Halsted Street in New Town for superb live entertainment.

Historical Areas

Old Prairie Avenue, once known as "Millionaires' Row," caught the attention of preservation-minded citizens. This area, known as the Prairie Avenue Historic District, has undergone some renovation. On the far South Side, most of the original buildings still stand in the Pullman House District, the famous industrialist's visionary model company town.

The Chicago school of architecture has had a great influence on international building design. World famous landmarks in the Loop, as well as many neighborhoods, are well worth visiting. The ArchiCenter features exhibits and tours of the city's architectural highlights.

Sightseeing

A one-week vacation does not allow sufficient time to see this great city, but for a start, either head for the observation floors of the John Hancock Building (100 stories), the world's tallest office-residential skyscraper, or the Sears Tower (110 stories), the world's tallest building, for an unforgettable experience. *Here's Chicago*, located in the Water Tower Pumping Station, presents a multimedia introduction to the city along with cultural exhibits. During summer months, boat cruises on the river provide a different view of the city. Visitors should also not miss the Art Institute on Michigan Avenue, which includes world-renowned collections of American and European art; the Field Museum of Natural History on Roosevelt Road at Lake Shore Drive; the John G. Shedd Aquarium on Lake Shore Drive; and the Museum of Science and Industry on 57th Street and Lake Shore Drive, featuring more than 2,000 displays, many hands-on, showing how science and industry have contributed to modern-day life.

General References

Settled: 1803 **Pop:** 2,783,726 **Elev:** 596 feet **Time zone:** Central **Area code:** 312 (city); 708 (suburbs)

Phone Numbers

POLICE, FIRE & AMBULANCE: 911
FBI: 431-1333
POISON CONTROL CENTER: 800/942-5969
TIME & WEATHER: 976-1616

Information Sources

Chicago Convention & Tourism Bureau, McCormick Place on the Lake, 567-8500.
Chicago Office of Tourism, Historic Water Tower, 806 N Michigan Ave, 744-2400.
Cultural Information Hotline, 346-3278.
Hot Tix, theater information line, 977-1755.
Department of Cultural Affairs, Cultural Information Booth in the east lobby of Richard J. Daley Center, Randolph & Dearborn Sts.
Chicago Park District, 294-2200.

Transportation

AIRLINES: *O'Hare International:* Aer Lingus; Air Canada; Air France; Alitalia; American; American Trans Air; America West; Austrian; British Airways; Continental; Czechoslovak; Delta; El Al; JAL; KLM; Korean; Lot Polish; Lufthansa; Mexicana; Northwest; Olympic; Russian Intl; SABENA; SAS; Swissair; TWA; United; USAir; and other commuter and regional airlines. *Midway:* American; Continental; Northwest; Qantas; Southwest; Sun Country; TWA; United; USAir; and other commuter and regional airlines. *Meigs Field:* commuter airlines. For the most current airline schedules and information consult the *Official Airline Guide,* published twice monthly.
AIRPORTS: O'Hare International, 686-2200; Midway, 767-0500; Meigs Field, 744-4787.
CAR RENTAL AGENCIES: (See Toll Free Numbers) Avis 694-5600; Budget 686-4950; Hertz 686-7272; National 694-4640.
PUBLIC TRANSPORTATION: RTA/CTA Public Transportation Travel Center provides information for buses, rapid transit & trains regarding schedules, fares & routing; CTA and RTA 836-7000.
RAILROAD PASSENGER SERVICE: Amtrak 800/872-7245.

Newspapers

Chicago Sun-Times; Chicago Tribune; Crain's Chicago Business; Wall Street Journal (Midwest Edition); Chicago Reader.

Convention Facilities

McCormick Place, E 23rd St & S Lake Shore Dr, 791-7000.
Rosemont Convention Center, 5555 N River Rd, Rosemont, 708/692-2220.

Sports & Recreation

Major Sports Facilities
Chicago Stadium, 1800 W Madison St, (Blackhawks, hockey, 733-5300; Bulls, basketball, 455-4000).
Comiskey Park, 333 W 35th St, 924-1000 (White Sox, baseball).
Rosemont Horizon, 6920 N Mannheim Rd, in Rosemont, 708/635-6600 (Loyola, DePaul college basketball).
Soldier Field, Lake Shore Dr at McFetridge Dr, 663-5100 (Bears, football).
Wrigley Field, 1060 W Addison St, 404-2827 (Cubs, baseball).

Racetracks
Arlington International Racecourse, Wilke & Euclid Rds, Arlington Heights, 708/255-4300.
Balmoral Park Race Track, IL 394 & Elmscourt Lane, Crete, 568-5700 or 708/672-7544.
Hawthorne Race Course, 3501 S Laramie Ave, Cicero, 708/780-3700.
Maywood Park Race Track, 8600 W North Ave, Maywood, 708/343-4800.
Sportsman's Park, 3301 S Laramie Ave, Cicero, 242-1121.

Cultural Facilities

Theaters
HOT TIX, 108 N State St, half-price (cash only), day-of-performance theater tickets when available, 977-1755.
Apollo, 2540 N Lincoln Ave, 935-6100.
Arie Crown, McCormick Place, 791-6000.
Auditorium Theater, 50 E Congress Pkwy, 922-4046.
Body Politic, 2261 N Lincoln Ave, 871-3000.
Briar Street, 3133 N Halsted St, 348-4000.
Centre East, 7701 N Lincoln Ave, Skokie, 708/673-6300.
Goodman, 200 S Columbus Dr, at the Art Institute, 443-3800.
Mayfair, *Shear Madness,* 636 S Michigan Ave, 786-9120.
Royal George, 1641 N Halsted, 988-9000.

Second City, 1616 N Wells, in Old Town, 337-3992.
Shubert, 22 W Monroe St, 977-1700.
Steppenwolf, 1650 N Halsted, 335-1650.

Concert Halls

Lyric Opera of Chicago, 20 N Wacker Dr, 332-2244.
Orchestra Hall, 220 S Michigan Ave, 435-6666.
Poplar Creek Music Theater, Northwest Tollway (I-90), Barrington Rd exit, Hoffman Estates, 708/426-1222.
Ravinia, Green Bay Rd at Lake Cook Rd, Highland Park, 728-4642.
Rosemont Horizon, 6920 N Mannheim Rd, Rosemont, 708/635-6600.

Museums

Adler Planetarium, 1300 S Lake Shore Dr, 322-0300 or -0304.
Balzekas Museum of Lithuanian Culture, 6500 S Pulaski Rd, 582-6500.
Cernan Earth and Space Center, 20 mi W, 2000 N 5th Ave, River Grove, 708/456-5815.
Chicago Academy of Sciences, 2001 N Clark St, in Lincoln Park, 871-2668.
Chicago Children's Museum, 435 E Illinois St, 527-1000.
Chicago Fire Academy, 558 W DeKoven St, 747-8151.
Chicago Historical Society, Clark St at North Ave, 642-4600.
DuSable Museum of African-American History, 740 E 56th Pl, 947-0600.
Field Museum of Natural History, Roosevelt Rd at Lake Shore Dr, 922-9410.
International Museum of Surgical Science, 1524 N Lake Shore Dr, 642-6502.
Morton B. Weiss Museum of Judaica, 1100 E Hyde Park Blvd, 924-1234.
Museum of Broadcast Communications, 78 E Washington St, at Michigan Ave, 629-6000.
Museum of Holography/Chicago, 1134 W Washington Blvd, 226-1007.
Museum of Science and Industry and Crown Space Center, E 57th St & S Lake Shore Dr, 684-1414.
Oriental Institute Museum, 1155 E 58th St, 702-9521.
Peace Museum, 350 W Ontario St, 440-1860.
Polish Museum of America, 984 N Milwaukee Ave, 384-3352.
Spertus Museum of Judaica, 618 S Michigan Ave, 922-9012.

Art Museums

Art Institute of Chicago, 111 S Michigan Ave at Adams St, 443-3600.
Museum of Contemporary Art, 237 E Ontario St, 280-2660 or -5161.
Terra Museum of American Art, 666 N Michigan Ave, 664-3939.

Points of Interest

Historical

Glessner House, 1800 S Prairie Ave, headquarters of Chicago Architecture Foundation, 922-3432.
Jane Addams' Hull House, 800 S Halsted St, on University of Illinois at Chicago campus, 413-5353.
Monadnock Building, 53 W Jackson Blvd, 922-1890.
Prairie Ave Historic District, Prairie Ave between 18th and Cullerton Sts.
Pullman Historic District, Visitor Center, 11141 S Cottage Grove, 785-8181.
Robie House, 5757 S Woodlawn Ave, 702-8374.
The Rookery, 209 S LaSalle St, 553-6150.
Water Tower, Michigan Ave at Chicago Ave, 440-3160

Other Attractions

Brookfield Zoo, 14 mi SW at 31st St & 1st Ave, Brookfield, 242-2630 or 708/485-0263.
Buckingham Fountain, foot of Congress St in Grant Park.

Chicago Botanic Garden, 21 mi N off I-94 in Glencoe, 708/835-5440.
Chicago Cultural Center, 78 E Washington St, at Michigan Ave, 346-3278.
Chicago Mercantile Exchange, 30 S Wacker Dr, 930-8249.
Garfield Park and Conservatory, 300 N Central Park Blvd, 533-1281.
Greektown, Halsted St from Madison St S to Van Buren.
Here's Chicago, Water Tower Pumping Station, Michigan & Chicago Aves, 467-7114.
John Hancock Center Observatory, 875 N Michigan Ave, 751-3681.
Lincoln Park, stretches along almost entire N end of the city on the lake.
Lincoln Park Zoo, Farm and Conservatory, west entrance Lincoln Park, Webster Ave & Stockton Dr, 294-4660 or 935-6700.
Magnificent Mile, Michigan Ave, Chicago River north to Oak St.
Marshall Field & Co, 111 N State St, 781-4882.
Navy Pier, E end of Grand Ave at the lake.
Newberry Library, 60 W Walton St, 943-9090.
New Town, area of Lakeview S of Addison St, W of the lake, N of Diversey Pkwy and E of Clark St.
Old Town, area of Wells St between Division St on the S and North Ave on the N; also area of Lincoln Park S of Armitage Ave, W of Clark St, N of North Ave and E of Larrabee St.
Richard J. Daley Center and Plaza, Washington, Randolph, Clark & Dearborn Sts.
River North, area N of the Merchandise Mart and Chicago River, W of LaSalle St, S of Division St and E of the river's North Branch.
Rockefeller Memorial Chapel, 5850 S Woodlawn Ave, on University of Chicago campus, 702-8374.
John G. Shedd Aquarium, 1200 S Lake Shore Dr, 939-2438.
Sears Tower, 233 S Wacker Dr, 875-9696.
Tribune Tower, 435 N Michigan Ave, 222-3994.
University of Chicago, 5801 S Ellis Ave, 702-8374.
Water Tower Place, 835 N Michigan Ave, 440-3165.
Wrigley Building, 400 N Michigan Ave.

Sightseeing Tours

American Sightseeing, 530 S Michigan Ave, 427-3100.
Chicago Architecture Foundation, 224 S Michigan Ave, 922-3432.
CTA Culture Buses, 836-7000.
Gray Line bus tours, 427-3107.
Mercury, the Skyline Cruiseline, Wacker Dr & Michigan Ave, S side of Chicago River at Michigan Ave bridge, 332-1353.
Wendella Sightseeing Boats, 400 N Michigan Ave, at Wrigley Building, N side of Chicago River at Michigan Ave bridge, 337-1446.

Annual Events

Chicago Auto Show, McCormick Place. Early Feb.
St Patrick's Day Parade. Mar 17.
Blues Festival, Grant Park. Early or mid-June.
Old Town Art Fair, N Lincoln Park W. Usually 2nd wkend June.
Concert & Fireworks, Grant Park. July 3.
Taste of Chicago, Grant Park. Late June-early July.
Air & Water Show, North Ave Beach. July.
Chicago to Mackinac Race, on Lake Michigan. 3rd wkend July.
Venetian Night, Monroe St harbor & along lakefront. Aug.
Jazz Festival, Grant Park. Late Aug-early Sept.
Chicago International Film Festival. 3 wks Oct.

City Neighborhoods

Many of the restaurants, unrated dining establishments and some lodgings listed under Chicago include neighborhoods as well as exact street addresses. A map showing these neighborhoods can be found immediately following the city introduction. Geographic descriptions of these areas are given, followed by a table of restaurants arranged by neighborhood.

Chinatown: South of the Loop on Wentworth St at Cermak Rd.

Gold Coast: South of North Ave, west of the lake, north of Oak St and east of LaSalle St.

Greektown: West of the Loop on Halsted St between Van Buren St on the south and Madison St on the north.

Hyde Park: South of the Loop; south of 47th St, west of the lake, north of the Midway Plaisance (60th St) and east of Cottage Grove Ave.

Lakeview: Includes New Town and Wrigleyville, south of Irving Park Rd, west of the lake, north of Diversey Pkwy and east of Ashland Ave.

Lincoln Park: Old Town and DePaul, south of Diversey Pkwy, west of the lake, north of North Ave and east of Clybourn Ave.

Loop: Area within the "loop" of the elevated train tracks; south of Lake St, west of Wabash Ave, north of Congress Pkwy and east of Wells St. **North of the Loop:** North of Lake St. **South of the Loop:** South of Congress Pkwy.

Old Town: Wells St between Division St on the south and North Ave on the north; also area of Lincoln Park south of Armitage Ave, west of Clark St, north of North Ave and east of Larrabee St.

River North: Area north of the Merchandise Mart and Chicago River, west of LaSalle St, south of Division St and east of the river's North Branch.

Lodgings and Food

CHICAGO RESTAURANTS
BY NEIGHBORHOOD AREAS

(For full description, see alphabetical listings under Restaurants)

CHINATOWN

Cantonese Chef. 2342 S Wentworth Ave
Emperor's Choice. 2238 S Wentworth Ave
Haylemon. 2201 S Wentworth Ave
Mandar-Inn. 2249 S Wentworth Ave

GOLD COAST

Biggs. 1150 N Dearborn Pkwy
Brasserie Bellevue (Le Meridien). 21 E Bellevue Place
Costa d'Oro. 1160 N Dearborn Pkwy
Le Mikado. 21 W Goethe St
Pump Room (Omni Ambassador East Hotel). 1301 N State Parkway
Waterfront. 16 W Maple St

GREEKTOWN

Greek Islands. 200 S Halsted St
Parthenon. 314 S Halsted St
Santorini. 800 W Adams St

LAKEVIEW

Ann Sather. 929 W Belmont Ave
Arco de Cuchilleros. 3445 N Halsted St
Bella Vista. 1001 W Belmont Ave
El Jardin. 3335 N Clark St
Genesee Depot. 3736 Broadway St
Mia Francesca. 3311 N Clark St
Schulien's. 2100 W Irving Park Rd

LINCOLN PARK

Ambria. 2300 N Lincoln Park West
Blue Mesa. 1729 N Halsted St
Café Ba Ba Reeba. 2024 N Halsted St
Carlucci. 2215 N Halsted St
Charlie Trotter's. 816 W Armitage Ave
Geja's. 340 W Armitage Ave
Golden Ox. 1578 N Clybourn Ave
Jackie's. 2478 N Lincoln Ave
Jerome's. 2450 N Clark St
La Llama. 2666 N Halsted St
La Risotteria. 2324 N Clark St
Pockets. 2618 N Clark St
Relish. 2044 N Halsted St
Shine Garden. 901 W Armitage Ave
Sole Mio. 917 W Armitage Ave
Stefani's. 1418 W Fullerton Ave

Un Grand Cafe. 2300 Lincoln Park West
Vinci. 1732 N Halsted St
Vinny's. 2901 N Sheffield Ave

THE LOOP

Austin Koo's. 318 W Adams St
Berghoff. 17 W Adams St
Binyon's. 327 S Plymouth Court
City Tavern. 33 W Monroe St
Everest. 440 S La Salle St
La Strada. 155 N Michigan Ave
Nick's Fishmarket. 1 First National Plaza
Russian Tea Cafe. 63 E Adams St
Trattoria No. 10. 10 N Dearborn St
Vivere. 71 W Monroe St

NORTH OF THE LOOP

Arun's. 4156 N Kedzie Ave
Avanzare. 161 E Huron St
Bice. 158 E Ontario St
Bistro 110. 110 E Pearson St
Blackhawk Lodge. 41 E Superior St
Bukhara. 2 E Ontario St
Cafe Gordon (Tremont). 100 E Chestnut St
Cape Cod Room (The Drake Hotel). 140 E Walton Place
Chez Paul. 660 N Rush St
Cielo (Omni Chicago Hotel). 676 N Michigan Ave
Como Inn. 546 N Milwaukee Ave
Cuisines (Stouffer Riviere Hotel). 1 W Wacker Dr
D.B. Kaplan's. 845 N Michigan Ave
Eli's The Place For Steak. 215 E Chicago Ave
Entre Nous (Fairmont At Illinois Center). 200 N Columbus Dr
The Greenhouse (The Ritz-Carlton Hotel). 160 E Pearson St
Gypsy. 215 E Ohio St
Hamburger Hamlet. 1024 Rush St
Hatsuhana. 160 E Ontario St
Heidelberger Fass. 4300 N Lincoln Ave
House of Hunan. 535 N Michigan Ave
Jimmy's Place. 3420 N Elston Ave
Lawry's The Prime Rib. 100 E Ontario St
Lutz's Continental Cafe & Pastry Shop. 2458 W Montrose Ave
Mare. 400 N Clark St
Morton's. 1050 N State St
Old Carolina Crab House. 455 E Illinois St
Papagus. 620 N State St
Pasteur Cafe. 45 E Chicago Ave
Pizzeria Uno. 29 E Ohio St
Ritz-Carlton Dining Room (The Ritz-Carlton Hotel). 160 E Pearson St
Ruth's Chris Steak House. 431 N Dearborn Ave
The Saloon. 200 E Chestnut
Sayat Nova. 157 E Ohio St
Seasons (Four Seasons Hotel). 120 E Delaware Place
Seasons Lounge (Four Seasons Hotel). 120 E Delaware Place

Shaw's Crab House. 21 E Hubbard St

Signature Room at the 95th. 875 N Michigan Ave

Spiaggia. 980 N Michigan Ave

Streeterville Grill & Bar. 301 E North Water St

Su Casa. 49 E Ontario St

Suntory. 11 E Huron St

Tucci Benucch. 900 N Michigan Ave

Tucci Milan. 6 W Hubbard St

SOUTH OF THE LOOP

Buckingham's (Hilton & Towers Hotel). 720 S Michigan Ave

New Rosebud Cafe. 1500 W Taylor St

Prairie (Hyatt On Printers Row Hotel). 500 S Dearborn St

Printer's Row. 550 S Dearborn St

Tuscany. 1014 W Taylor St

RIVER NORTH

Benkay (Hotel Nikko Chicago). 320 N Dearborn St

Big Bowl Cafe. 159½ W Erie St

Butcher Shop. 358 W Ontario St

Celebrity Cafe (Hotel Nikko Chicago). 320 N Dearborn St

Centro. 710 N Wells St

Chicago Chop House. 60 W Ontario St

Club Gene & Georgetti. 500 N Franklin St

Coco Pazzo. 300 W Hubbard St

The Eccentric. 159 W Erie St

Ed Debevic's. 640 N Wells St

Frontera Grill. 445 N Clark St

Gordon. 500 N Clark St

Hard Rock Cafe. 63 W Ontario St

Harry Caray's. 33 W Kinzie St

Hat Dance. 325 W Huron St

Kinzie Street Chophouse. 400 N Wells St

Klay Oven. 414 N Orleans St

Michael Jordan's. 500 N La Salle St

Planet Hollywood. 633 N Wells St

Topolobampo. 445 N Clark St

Tuttaposto. 646 N Franklin St

Note: *When a listing is located in a town that does not have its own city heading, it will appear under the city nearest to its location. In these cases, the address and town appear in parenthesis immediately following the name of the establishment.*

Motel

★ ★ **HAMPTON INN.** *(6540 S Cicero Ave, Bedford Park 60638) Near Midway Airport, southwest of the Loop.* 708/496-1900; FAX 708/496-1997. 171 rms, 5 story. S $68; D $74; under 18 free. Crib free. TV; cable. Complimentary continental bkfst. Restaurant nearby. Rm serv. Ck-out noon. Meeting rms. Valet serv. Free Midway Airport transportation. Health club privileges. Cr cds: A, C, D, DS, MC, V.

Motor Hotels

★ **BEST WESTERN RIVER NORTH.** *125 W Ohio St (60610), west of N Michigan Ave, River North.* 312/467-0800; FAX 312/467-1665. 148 rms, 7 story. S $107-$127; D $117-$137; each addl

$8; suites $150-$170; under 18 free; wkend rates; higher rates special events. Crib free. TV; cable, in-rm movies. Indoor pool. Restaurant 6:30 am-11 pm. Rm serv. Ck-out noon. Meeting rm. Bellhops. Airport transportation. Exercise equipt; weights, bicycles, sauna. Some refrigerators. Cr cds: A, C, D, DS, JCB, MC, V.

✔ ★ **COMFORT INN.** *601 W Diversey Pkwy (60614), Lincoln Park.* 312/348-2010. 74 rms, 5 story. S $60-$92; D $65-$100; each addl $10; suites $185; under 18 free. TV; cable. Complimentary continental bkfst. Ck-out noon. Meeting rm. Health club privileges. Some in-rm whirlpools, saunas. Cr cds: A, C, D, DS, ER, JCB, MC, V.

★ ★ **HOLIDAY INN-MIDWAY AIRPORT.** *7353 S Cicero Ave (IL 50) (60629), near Midway Airport, south of the Loop.* 312/581-5300; FAX 312/581-8421. 161 rms, 5 story. S $65-$85; D $75-$90; each addl $10; under 18 free; wkend rates. Crib free. TV; cable. Pool. Complimentary full bkfst. Restaurant 6 am-10 pm. Rm serv. Bar noon-2 am; entertainment, dancing Fri & Sat. Ck-out noon. Meeting rms. Bellhops. Free Midway Airport transportation. Cr cds: A, C, D, DS, JCB, MC, V.

★ ★ **INN AT UNIVERSITY VILLAGE.** *625 S Ashland Ave (60607), at Rush-Presbyterian-St Luke's Medical Center, west of the Loop.* 312/243-7200; res: 800/662-5233; FAX 312/243-1289. 114 rms, 4 story. S $145; D $155; each addl $10; suites $165-$525; under 18 free; wkend, wkly, monthly rates. Crib free. Pet accepted. TV. Pool privileges. Complimentary continental bkfst wkends. Restaurant 6:30 am-10 pm. Rm serv. Bar 11 am-11 pm. Ck-out noon. Meeting rms. Bellhops. Valet serv. Valet parking. Airport transportation. Tennis privileges. Exercise equipt; weight machine, bicycles. Health club privileges. Refrigerator in suites. Near University of Illinois Chicago campus. Cr cds: A, C, D, DS, MC, V.

✔ ★ **MIDWAY AIRPORT INN.** *5400 S Cicero Ave (60638), at edge of Midway Airport, south of the Loop.* 312/581-0500; res: 800/621-0127 (exc IL), 800/238-0638 (IL); FAX 312/581-9868. 200 rms, 2 story. S $55-$65; D $60-$65; each addl $5; suites $68-$75; under 16 free; wkend rates. Crib $5. TV; cable. Heated pool; lifeguard. Restaurant 7 am-10 pm. Rm serv. Bar to 4 am; dancing. Ck-out noon. Meeting rms. Free Midway Airport transportation. Exercise equipt; weight machine, bicycle. Refrigerators avail. Cr cds: A, C, D, DS, MC, V.

RAMADA INN LAKE SHORE. *(New manager, therefore not rated) 4900 S Lake Shore Dr (60615), Hyde Park.* 312/288-5800; FAX 312/288-5745. 182 rms, 2-4 story. S $75-$95; D $85-$105; each addl $10; suites $155; under 19 free; wkend rates. Crib free. Pet accepted, some restrictions. TV; cable. Pool; poolside serv. Restaurant 6:30 am-11 pm. Bar 11-1 am. Ck-out 11 am. Meeting rms. Bellhops. Valet serv. Many rms with view of Lake Michigan. Cr cds: A, C, D, DS, MC, V.

Hotels

AMBASSADOR WEST. *(New general manager, therefore not rated) 1300 N State Pkwy (60610), at Goethe St, Gold Coast.* 312/787-3700; FAX 312/640-2999. 219 rms, 12 story. S $109-$179; D $109-$189; each addl $20; suites $800; under 18 free; wkend rates; package plans. Crib free. Valet parking $19.50. TV; cable, in-rm movies avail. Restaurant 6:30 am-10:30 pm. Bar from 4:30 pm. Ck-out noon. Meeting rms. Barber. Airport transportation. Minibars; wet bars in suites. Cr cds: A, C, D, DS, JCB, MC, V.

★ ★ **BARCLAY.** *166 E Superior St (60611), north of the Loop.* 312/787-6000; res: 800/621-8004; FAX 312/787-4331. 119 suites, 29 story, some kits. S $145-$195; D $165-$215; each addl $20; kit. suites

$175-$195; under 12 free; wkend rates; package plans. Crib free. Valet parking $17. TV; cable, in-rm movies. Pool. Restaurants 6:30 am-11 pm. Bars 11-1 am. Ck-out noon. Meeting rms. Barber. Tennis privileges. Health club privileges. Refrigerators; many minibars, bathrm phones; some wet bars. Exercise equipt avail in guest rms. Cr cds: A, C, D, DS, JCB, MC, V.

D ⌨ ⩘ ⤢ ⚲ SC

★ ★ **BEST WESTERN INN OF CHICAGO.** *162 E Ohio St (60611), north of the Loop. 312/787-3100; FAX 312/573-3140.* 357 rms, 22 story. S $99-$129; D $119-$139; suites $235-$405; under 17 free; wkend package plans. Valet parking $11. TV; cable. Restaurant 6:30 am-10:30 pm; Fri & Sat to midnight. Bar 11-2 am. Ck-out noon. Lndry facilities. Meeting rms. Gift shop. Airport transportation. Indoor tennis privileges. Health club privileges. Sun deck on top floor. Cr cds: A, C, D, DS, JCB, MC, V.

D ⌨ ⤢ ⚲ SC

★ ★ **CLARIDGE.** *1244 N Dearborn Pkwy (60610), Gold Coast. 312/787-4980; res: 800/245-1258; FAX 312/266-0978.* 168 rms, 14 story. S $109-$165; D $125-$165; each addl $15; suites $244-$450; under 18 free; wkend packages. Crib free. Pet accepted, some restrictions. Valet parking $15.50. TV. Complimentary continental bkfst. Restaurant 6:30 am-10:30 pm. Bar noon-2 am. Ck-out noon. Meeting rms. Concierge. Airport transportation. Health club privileges. Minibars. Fireplace in some suites. Exercise equipt avail in guest rms. Library. In historic residential area. Cr cds: A, C, D, DS, JCB, MC, V.

D ⌨ ⤢ ⚲ SC

★ ★ **COURTYARD BY MARRIOTT.** *30 E Hubbard St (60611), north of the Loop. 312/329-2500; FAX 312/329-0293.* 334 rms, 15 story. S, D $79-$149; suites $109-$169; under 18 free; wkly, wkend rates. Crib free. Garage parking $17, in/out $17. TV; cable. Indoor pool; poolside serv. Complimentary coffee in rms. Restaurant 6:30 am-11 pm. Bar 4 pm-midnight. Ck-out 1 pm. Coin lndry. Meeting rms. Gift shop. Airport transportation avail. Tennis privileges. Exercise equipt; weight machine, bicycles, whirlpool. Refrigerator, wet bar in suites. Cr cds: A, C, D, DS, MC, V.

D ⌨ ⩘ ⤢ ⚲ SC

✔ ★ ★ **DAYS INN LAKE SHORE DRIVE.** *644 N Lake Shore Dr (60611), at Ontario St, opp Lake Michigan, north of the Loop. 312/943-9200; FAX 312/649-5580.* 578 rms, 33 story. S $69-$149; D $79-$159; each addl $15; suites $165-$600; under 17 free; wkend rates. Crib free. Garage, in/out $10. TV; cable, in-rm movies avail. Pool. Restaurant 6 am-10 pm. Bar 11 am-midnight. Ck-out noon. Coin lndry. Meeting rms. Gift shop. Exercise equipt; weight machine, bicycle. Airport transportation. Some refrigerators. Panoramic view. Overlooks lake. Cr cds: A, C, D, DS, ER, JCB, MC, V.

D ⩘ ⤢ ⚲ SC

★ ★ ★ **THE DRAKE.** *140 E Walton Place (60611), at Lake Shore Dr & N Michigan Ave, north of the Loop. 312/787-2200; FAX 312/787-1431.* 535 rms, 10 story. S $195-$280; D $205-$310; suites $460-$1,500; family rates; wkend package plans. Crib free. Pet accepted, some restrictions. Valet parking $21.50/night; in-out privileges. TV; cable. Restaurant 6:30 am-midnight (also see CAPE COD ROOM). Rm serv 24 hrs. Bar 11-2 am; piano bar. Ck-out noon. Convention facilities. Concierge. Shopping arcade. Barber. Airport transportation. Tennis privileges. Exercise equipt; rower, stair machine. Health club privileges. Minibars; wet bar in suites. Complimentary newspaper. Historic building of classic design. Overlooks lake; public beach opp. **LUXURY LEVEL : VISTA FLOOR.** 312/787-2200, ext 1103. 52 rms. S $280; D $310; suites $550-$1,475. Concierge. Private lounge. Wet bars. Complimentary continental bkfst, refreshments. Cr cds: A, C, D, DS, ER, JCB, MC, V.

D ⌨ ⩘ ⤢ ⚲

★ ★ ★ **EMBASSY SUITES.** *600 N State St (60610), north of the Loop. 312/943-3800; FAX 312/943-7629.* 358 suites, 11 story. S, D $189-$229; under 12 free; wkend, wkly, monthly rates. Crib free. Garage, in/out $18. TV; cable. Indoor pool. Complimentary full bkfst.

Complimentary coffee in rms. Restaurant noon-10 pm. Bar. Ck-out noon. Meeting rms. Concierge. Gift shop. Airport, RR station, bus depot transportation. Tennis privileges. Exercise equipt; weights, bicycles, whirlpool, sauna. Health club privileges. Refrigerators, minibars, wet bars. Cr cds: A, C, D, DS, JCB, MC, V.

D ⩘ ⤢ ⚲ SC

★ ★ **EXECUTIVE PLAZA.** *71 E Wacker Dr (60601), on the south bank of the Chicago River, north of the Loop. 312/346-7100; res: 800/621-4005; FAX 312/346-1721.* 417 rms, 39 story. S $135-$175; D $155-$195; each addl $10; suites $275-$800; under 18 free; wkend rates; package plans. Garage $17. TV; cable. Coffee in rms. Restaurant 6:30 am-10 pm. Bar to 2 am. Ck-out noon. Meeting rms. Concierge. Gift shop. Airport transportation. Exercise equipt; bicycles, rowing machine. Bathrm phones, minibars. Wet bar in suites. Cr cds: A, C, D, DS, JCB, MC, V.

D ⩘ ⤢ ⚲ SC

★ ★ ★ **FAIRMONT AT ILLINOIS CENTER.** *200 N Columbus Dr (60601), north of the Loop. 312/565-8000; res: 800/527-4727; FAX 312/856-1032.* 692 rms, 42 story. S $185-$235; D $205-$255; each addl $25; suites from $500; under 18 free. Crib free. Valet parking, in/out $20. TV; cable. Pool privileges. Restaurant (see ENTRES NOUS). Rm serv 24 hrs. Bar 11-2 am; entertainment. Ck-out 1 pm. Convention facilities. Concierge. Airport transportation. Health club privileges. Bathrm phones, minibars. Contemporary & period furnishings; original artwork; antiques from around the world. Overlooks Lake Michigan; many rms with lake view. Cr cds: A, C, D, DS, ER, JCB, MC, V.

D ⤢ ⚲ SC

★ ★ ★ ★ **FOUR SEASONS.** *120 E Delaware Place (60611), at 900 N Michigan Ave Complex, north of the Loop. 312/280-8800; res: 800/332-3442; FAX 312/280-1748.* 343 rms, 66 story building, guest rms on floors 30-46, 157 suites. S $225-$300; D $250-$325; each addl $30; suites $675-$825; wkend rates; special packages. Crib free. Self-park adj, in/out $23. TV; cable, in-rm movies avail. Indoor pool. Restaurant (see SEASONS; and see SEASONS LOUNGE, Unrated Dining). Rm serv 24 hrs. Bar 11:30-1 am; entertainment. Ck-out 1 pm. Convention facilities. Concierge. Shopping access to 900 North Michigan Mall. Barber, beauty shop. Airport transportation. Extensive fitness facility. Exercise rm; instructor, weight machine, stair machine, treadmill, bicycles, whirlpool, sauna, steam rm. Masseuse. Health club privileges. Bathrm phones, minibars; some wet bars. Traditional European decor. Lake 3 blks; spectacular views of cityscape and lakefront. Cr cds: A, C, D, DS, ER, JCB, MC, V.

D ⩘ ⤢ ⤢ ⚲ SC

★ ★ ★ **GUEST QUARTERS.** *198 E Delaware Place (60611), north of the Loop. 312/664-1100; FAX 312/664-9881.* 345 suites, 30 story. S $189-$265; D $205-$285; each addl $25; under 12 free; wkend rates. Crib free. Valet parking, in/out $20. TV; cable. Indoor pool. Coffee in rms. Restaurants 6:30 am-11:30 pm. Rm serv 24 hrs. Bar 11 am-midnight, Fri-Sat to 1 am; entertainment Tues-Sat. Ck-out noon. Coin lndry. Meeting rms. Concierge. Gift shop. Airport transportation. Exercise equipt; weight machine, bicycles, whirlpool, sauna. Game rm. Refrigerators, minibars. Cr cds: A, C, D, DS, JCB, MC, V.

D ⤢ ⩘ ⤢ ⚲ SC

★ ★ ★ **HILTON & TOWERS.** *720 S Michigan Ave (60605), opp Grant Park, south of the Loop. 312/922-4400; FAX 312/922-5240.* 1,543 rms, 25 story, 95 suites. S $139-$179; D $165-$250; each addl $25; suites from $225; children free; wkend, honeymoon packages. Crib free. Garage $17; valet parking $19. TV; cable. Indoor pool. Restaurants 5:30-1:30 am (also see BUCKINGHAM'S). Rm serv 24 hrs. Bars to 2 am; entertainment, dancing. Ck-out 11 am. Convention facilities. Concierge. Shopping arcade. Barber, beauty shop. Exercise rm; instructor, weights, bicycles, 2 whirlpools, sauna. Minibars. **LUXURY LEVEL : TOWERS.** 190 rms, 45 suites, 3 floors. S $220-$245; D $245-$270. Private lounge, honor bar. Bathrm phones. Deluxe toiletry amenities. Complimentary continental bkfst, refreshments, newspaper, shoeshine. Cr cds: A, C, D, DS, ER, JCB, MC, V.

[D] [≈] [🏃] [🕴] [≥] [🔥]

★ ★ **HOLIDAY INN-CITY CENTRE.** *300 E Ohio St (60611), north of the Loop.* 312/787-6100; FAX 312/787-6238. *500 rms, 26 story.* S, D $120-$186; each addl $16; suites $350-$650; under 18 free; wkend plan. Crib free. Garage adj $14.25. TV; cable. Indoor/outdoor pool; lifeguard. Restaurant 6:30 am-11 pm. Bars 11-2 am; entertainment exc Sun. Ck-out 1 pm. Coin lndry. Meeting rms. Airport transportation. Indoor tennis privileges. Health club privileges. Some bathrm phones; sauna in suites. Cr cds: A, C, D, DS, JCB, MC, V.

[D] [🤿] [≈] [≥] [🔥] [SC]

★ ★ **HOLIDAY INN-MART PLAZA.** *350 N Orleans St (60654), atop Apparel Center, adj Merchandise Mart, River North.* 312/836-5000; FAX 312/222-9508. *524 rms, 23 story; guest rms on floors 16-23.* S $124-$144; D $140-$162; each addl $16; suites $275-$650; under 18 free; wkend plans; special package plans. Crib free. Pet accepted, some restrictions. Garage $12/day. TV. Indoor pool. Restaurant 6:30 am-2 pm 5-10:30 pm. Bars noon-2 am. Ck-out noon. Coin lndry. Convention facilities. Shopping arcade. Barber, beauty shop. Airport transportation. Exercise equipt; weights, bicycles. Refrigerator in suites. Cr cds: A, C, D, DS, JCB, MC, V.

[D] [🤿] [≈] [🕴] [≥] [🔥] [SC]

★ ★ ★ **HOTEL NIKKO CHICAGO.** *320 N Dearborn St (60610), River North.* 312/744-1900; res: 800/645-5687; FAX 312/527-2650. *421 rms, 20 story.* S $205-$225; D $230-$250; each addl $25; suites $300-$750; under 18 free; special packages. Crib free. Pet accepted, some restrictions. Valet parking $22 in/out. TV; cable. Restaurant 6:30 am-11 pm (also see BENKAY and CELEBRITY CAFE). Rm serv 24 hrs. Bar 11-1:30 am; jazz trio 6 days. Ck-out noon. Convention facilities. Concierge. Airport transportation. Tennis privileges. Racquetball privileges. Exercise rm; instructor, weights, bicycles, sauna. Masseuse. Bathrm phones, minibars. Complimentary shoeshine. Traditional Japanese suites avail. Cr cds: A, C, D, DS, ER, JCB, MC, V.

[D] [🤿] [🕴] [≥] [🔥] [SC]

★ ★ **HYATT ON PRINTERS ROW.** *500 S Dearborn St (60605), Printer's Row, south of the Loop.* 312/986-1234; FAX 312/939-2468. *161 rms, 7-12 story.* S $129-$175; D $150-$195; each addl $25; suites $350-$1,000; wkend rates. Crib free. Valet parking $18, wkends $16.50; self-park $13. TV; in-rm movies. Restaurant 6:30 am-11 pm (also see PRAIRIE). Bar 11-1 am. Ck-out noon. Meeting rms. Airport transportation. Health club privileges. Bathrm phones, minibars. Financial district nearby. Cr cds: A, C, D, DS, ER, MC, V.

[D] [≥] [🔥] [SC]

★ ★ ★ **HYATT REGENCY.** *151 E Wacker Dr (60601), opp Chicago River, north of the Loop.* 312/565-1234; FAX 312/565-2966. *2,019 rms, 34 story (East Tower), 36 story (West Tower).* S $195; D $220; each addl $25; suites $365-$2,200; under 18 free; wkend, hol package plans. Crib free. Garage, in/out $19. TV; cable. Restaurant open 6 am-midnight. Rm serv 24 hrs. Bar 11-2 am; entertainment. Ck-out noon. Convention facilities. Concierge. Shopping arcade. Barber, beauty shop. Airport transportation. Health club privileges. Minibars; some in-rm steam baths, whirlpools. Bathrm phone, refrigerator in suites. *LUXURY LEVEL : REGENCY CLUB.* 120 rms, 9 suites, 3 floors. S $220; D $245; suites $1,100. Concierge. Private lounge. Complimentary continental bkfst, refreshments, newspaper. Cr cds: A, C, D, DS, ER, JCB, MC, V.

[D] [≥] [🔥] [SC]

★ ★ ★ **INTER-CONTINENTAL CHICAGO.** *505 N Michigan Ave (60611), just north of the Chicago River, at Grand Ave, north of the Loop.* 312/944-4100; res: 800/327-0200; FAX 312/944-1320. *844 rms, 2 bldgs, 26 & 42 story, 42 suites.* S $149-$189; D $169-$289; each addl $20; under 14 free. Crib free. Covered parking $20/day. TV; cable. Indoor pool; poolside beverage and fruit. Coffee in rms. Restaurants 6:30 am-11 pm. Rm serv 24 hrs. Afternoon tea 2-5 pm. Bar 11-1 am; pianist. Ck-out noon. Convention facilities. Conci-

erge. Gift shop. Airport, RR station, bus depot transportation. Tennis privileges. Exercise rm; instructor, weight machines, bicycles, sauna. Masseuse. Minibars; some bathrm phones. Two buildings, one of which was originally constructed (1929) as the Medinah Athletic Club. Cr cds: A, C, D, DS, ER, JCB, MC, V.

[D] [🕴] [≈] [🏃] [≥] [🔥] [SC]

★ ★ **KNICKERBOCKER.** *163 E Walton Place (60611), north of the Loop.* 312/751-8100; res: 800/621-8140; FAX 312/751-9205. *254 rms, 14 story.* S $145-$195, D $165-$215; each addl $20; suites $235-$1,000; under 18 free; wkend rates. Crib free. Valet parking, in/out $20.25. TV; in-rm movies avail. Pool privileges. Restaurant 6:30 am-10:30 pm. Bar 11-2 am; entertainment Thurs-Sat 5-9 pm. Ck-out noon. Meeting rms. Concierge. Indoor tennis privileges. Health club privileges. Some refrigerators. Cr cds: A, C, D, DS, MC, V.

[🏃] [≥] [🔥] [SC]

★ ★ ★ **LE MERIDIEN CHICAGO.** *21 E Bellevue Place (60611), Gold Coast.* 312/266-2100; res: 800/543-4300 (IL); FAX 312/266-2103. *247 rms, 22 story, 41 suites.* S $210-$245; D $230-$265; each addl $20; suites $285-$625; under 12 free; wkend rates. Crib free. Pet accepted, some restrictions; $200 refundable. Valet parking $20. TV; cable, in-rm movies. Pool privileges. Restaurant (see BRASSERIE BELLEVUE). Rm serv 24 hrs. Bar 11:30-1 am, Fri, Sat to 2 am. Ck-out noon. Meeting rms. Concierge. Airport transportation. Exercise equipt; bicycle, treadmill. Health club privileges. Bathrm phones, minibars. Private patios, balconies. Penthouse suites with garden terrace. Cr cds: A, C, D, DS, JCB, MC, V.

[D] [🤿] [🕴] [≥] [🔥] [SC]

★ **LENOX HOUSE SUITES.** *616 N Rush St (60611), north of the Loop.* 312/337-1000; res: 800/445-3669; FAX 312/337-7217. *330 kit. units, 17 story, 125 suites.* S $99-$154; D $109-$164; each addl $10; under 16 free; wkend, wkly, monthly rates. Crib free. TV; cable. Complimentary coffee, tea in rms. Restaurants 6 am-11 pm. Bar 11-2 am. Ck-out 1 pm. Coin lndry. Meeting rms. Concierge. Airport transportation. Health club privileges. Cr cds: A, C, D, DS, ER, JCB, MC, V.

[D] [≥] [🔥] [SC]

★ ★ ★ **MARRIOTT.** *540 N Michigan Ave (60611), at Ohio St, north of the Loop.* 312/836-0100; FAX 312/836-6139. *1,172 rms, 46 story.* S $164-$184; D $194-$214; suites $480-$1,150; under 18 free; wkend rates. Crib free. Pet accepted. Parking $14, valet $20. TV; cable, in-rm movies avail. Indoor pool; poolside serv. Coffee in rms. Restaurant 6:30 am-midnight. Bar 11-2 am; entertainment. Ck-out noon. Convention facilities. Concierge. Shopping arcade. Barber, beauty shop. Airport transportation. Exercise equipt; weight machines, bicycles, whirlpool, sauna. Masseuse. Basketball, paddleball courts. Health club privileges. Game rm. Bathrm phone, minibar in suites. *LUXURY LEVEL : CONCIERGE LEVEL.* 99 rms, 3 floors. S $189; D $219. Private lounge, honor bar. Minibars. Bathrm phones. Complimentary continental bkfst, refreshments. Cr cds: A, C, D, DS, ER, JCB, MC, V.

[D] [🤿] [≈] [🕴] [≥] [🔥] [SC]

★ ★ **MIDLAND.** *172 W Adams St (60603), the Loop.* 312/332-1200; res: 800/621-2360; FAX 312/332-5909. *257 rms, 10 story.* S, D $160-$195; each addl $20; suites from $450; under 18 free; wkend rates. Crib free. Valet parking $18; wkends $14. TV; cable. Complimentary full bkfst, refreshments. Restaurant 6:30 am-11 pm. Bar 11 am-midnight. Ck-out noon. Convention facilities. Barber, beauty shop. Gift shop. Airport transportation. Exercise equipt; weight machine, bicycles. Some refrigerators. Cr cds: A, C, D, DS, JCB, MC, V.

[D] [🕴] [≥] [🔥] [SC]

★ ★ **OMNI AMBASSADOR EAST.** *1301 N State Parkway (60610), at Goethe St, Gold Coast.* 312/787-7200; FAX 312/787-4760. *275 rms, 17 story.* S $160-$170; D $190-$200; each addl $25; suites $190-$400; under 17 free; wkend rates. Crib free. Valet parking $20. TV; cable. Restaurant (see PUMP ROOM). Rm serv 24 hrs. Bar 11-1 am. Ck-out noon. Meeting rms. Concierge. Barber, beauty shop. Airport transportation. Indoor tennis privileges. Health club privileges. Minibars. Cr cds: A, C, D, DS, JCB, MC, V.

[D] [⚡] [🏊] [✕] [🔥] [SC]

★ ★ ★ ★ **OMNI CHICAGO HOTEL.** *676 N Michigan Ave (60611), north of the Loop.* 312/944-6664; res: 800/THE-OMNI; FAX 312/266-3015. 347 suites, 25 story. S $215; D $235; suites $260-$1,000; under 12 free. Crib free. Parking in/out $24. TV; cable. Indoor pool. Coffee in rms. Restaurant (see CIELO). Rm serv 24 hrs. Bar 11-2 am; entertainment. Ck-out noon. Meeting rms. Concierge. Airport transportation. Free area transportation. Tennis privileges. Exercise equipt; weight machine, bicycles, whirlpool, sauna. Sun deck. Minibars, wet bars. The hotel occupies 22 floors in the 40-story City Place building, an office & retail complex. The interior is reminiscent of the Art Deco period of the 1920s and 1930s. Cr cds: A, C, D, DS, JCB, MC, V.

[D] [⚡] [☀] [🏊] [✕] [🏃] [🔥] [SC]

★ ★ ★ **PALMER HOUSE HILTON.** *17 E Monroe St (60603), at State St, the Loop.* 312/726-7500; FAX 312/263-2556. 1,639 rms, 23 story. S $119-$199; D $144-$204; each addl $25; suites from $295; family, wkend rates. Crib free. Garage $13.50, valet $19.50. TV; cable. Indoor pool. Restaurants 6:30-2 am. Rm serv to midnight. Bars 11:30-2 am; entertainment. Ck-out noon. Convention facilities. Concierge. Shopping arcade. Barber, beauty shop. Airport transportation. Exercise rm; instructor, weights, bicycles, whirlpool, sauna, steam rm. Minibars. Refrigerator in suites. *LUXURY LEVEL : THE TOWERS.* 183 rms, 16 suites, 2 floors. S $139-149; D $164-$224; suites from $450. Private lounge, honor bar. Bathrm phones. Complimentary continental bkfst, refreshments, newspaper, shoeshine. Cr cds: A, C, D, DS, ER, JCB, MC, V.

[D] [⚡] [🏊] [✕] [✕] [🔥] [SC]

★ ★ ★ **PARK HYATT ON WATER TOWER SQUARE.** *800 N Michigan Ave (60611), opp Water Tower, north of the Loop.* 312/280-2222; res: 800/233-1234; FAX 312/280-1963. 255 rms, 16 story. S $220; D $245; suites $650-$1,000; under 12 free; wkend packages. Valet parking $24. TV; cable. Pool privileges. Restaurant 6:30 am-2:30 pm, 6-10:30 pm. Rm serv 24 hrs. Bar 11-2 am; entertainment. Ck-out noon. Meeting rms. Complimentary limo to business, health club, and other destinations within 5 mi of Loop. Indoor tennis privileges. Exercise equipt (delivered to rms only); bicycles, rowing machine. Bathrm phones, minibars. Suite with private patio, hot tub, sauna. Cr cds: A, C, D, DS, ER, JCB, MC, V.

[🏃] [✕] [✕] [🔥]

★ ★ **RAPHAEL.** *201 E Delaware Place (60611), north of the Loop.* 312/943-5000; res: 800/821-5343; FAX 312/943-9483. 172 rms, 17 story. S $120-$155; D $140-$175; each addl $20; under 12 free; wkend rates. Crib free. Pet accepted, some restrictions. Valet parking, in/out $19.50. TV; cable. Pool privileges. Restaurant 6:30-11 am, 11:30 am-2 pm, 5-10 pm. Rm serv 24 hrs. Bar 11-1:30 am; entertainment exc Mon. Ck-out 1 pm. Meeting rms. Indoor tennis privileges. Health club privileges. Minibars. Cr cds: A, C, D, DS, MC, V.

[D] [⚡] [🏊] [✕] [🔥]

★ ★ **RESIDENCE INN BY MARRIOTT.** *201 E Walton Place (60611), north of the Loop.* 312/943-9800; FAX 312/943-8579. 221 kit. suites, 19 story. Suites $159-$249; wkend, wkly & monthly rates. Crib free. Pet accepted, some restrictions; $50 non-refundable and $5 per day. Valet parking, in/out $18. TV; cable. Pool privileges. Complimentary continental bkfst, afternoon refreshments. Complimentary coffee in rms. Restaurant adj 6:30 am-midnight. Ck-out noon. Coin lndry. Meeting rms. Airport transportation. Exercise equipt; weight machine, bicycles. Health club privileges. Game rm. One blk from Oak St beach. Cr cds: A, C, D, DS, JCB, MC, V.

[D] [⚡] [🏃] [✕] [🔥] [SC]

✓ ★ ★ ★ ★ **THE RITZ-CARLTON.** *160 E Pearson St (60611), at Water Tower Place, north of the Loop.* 312/266-1000; res: 800/621-6906 (exc IL); FAX 312/266-1194. 429 rms, 31 story, 84 suites. S $240-$260; D $270-$315; each addl $30; suites $325-$825; under 12 free; special packages, wkend plans. Crib free. Parking in/out $20/day.

TV; cable, in-rm movies. Heated pool $8; lifeguard. Restaurant 6:30-1 am (also see RITZ-CARLTON DINING ROOM; and see THE GREEN-HOUSE, Unrated Dining). Rm serv 24 hrs. Bar 11-1 am, Fri & Sat to 2 am. Ck-out 1 pm. Convention facilities. Concierge. Shopping opp in Water Tower Mall. Tennis privileges. Exercise rm; instructor, weights, bicycles, whirlpool, sauna, steam rm. Masseuse. Bathrm phones, minibars; refrigerators avail. Kennels avail. Cr cds: A, C, D, ER, JCB, MC, V.

[D] [⚡] [🏃] [✕] [✕] [🔥]

★ ★ ★ **SHERATON CHICAGO HOTEL & TOWERS.** *301 E North Water St (60611), north of the Loop.* 312/464-1000; FAX 312/464-9140. 1,206 rms, 31-34 story, 56 suites. S $175-$225; D $200-$250; each addl $25; suites $350-$800; under 17 free. Pet accepted, some restrictions. Garage in/out $13. TV; cable. Indoor pool. Complimentary coffee in rms. Restaurant 6-1 am. Rm serv 24 hrs. Bar 11-1:30 am; pianist. Ck-out noon. Convention facilities. Concierge. Gift shop. Airport transportation. Tennis privileges. Exercise rm; instructor, weight machines, bicycles, sauna. Minibars. On Chicago River, near Navy Pier. Views of Lake Michigan and skyline. *LUXURY LEVEL : SHERATON TOWERS.* 96 rms, 12 suites, 4 floors. S $215; D $245; suites $450-$3,000. Concierge. Private lounge, honor bar. Complimentary continental bkfst, refreshments. Cr cds: A, C, D, DS, ER, JCB, MC, V.

[D] [⚡] [🏊] [🏊] [✕] [✕] [🔥] [SC]

★ ★ ★ ★ **STOUFFER RENAISSANCE.** *1 W Wacker Dr (60601), on the Chicago River, north of the Loop.* 312/372-7200; res: 800/HOTELS-1; FAX 312/372-0834. 565 units, 27 story, 40 suites. S $190-$230; D $210-$250; each addl $21; suites $450-$750; under 18 free; wkend plans. Crib free. Pet accepted, some restrictions. Garage; valet parking in/out $21. TV; cable. Indoor pool; poolside serv. Restaurants 6 am-midnight. Rm serv 24 hrs. Bar 11-2 am; pianist & jazz trio. Ck-out 1 pm. Convention facilities. Concierge. Shopping arcade. Gift shop. Airport transportation. Tennis privileges. Exercise equipt; weight machine, bicycles, whirlpool, sauna. Minibars. Bathrm phone in suites. Views of Chicago River, Lake Michigan and Wrigley Building. Lobby area has fountains, grand staircase, imported rugs, marble from around the world. *LUXURY LEVEL : CLUB LEVEL.* 62 rms, 9 suites, 4 floors. S $210; D $290; suites $750-$2,500. Concierge. Private lounge, honor bar. Complimentary continental bkfst, refreshments. Cr cds: A, C, D, DS, ER, JCB, MC, V.

[D] [⚡] [🏃] [🏊] [✕] [✕] [🔥] [SC]

★ ★ ★ **SWISSÔTEL.** *323 E Wacker Dr (60601), north of the Loop.* 312/565-0565; res: 800/644-7263; FAX 312/565-0540. 630 rms, 43 story. S $195-$220; D $215-$240; each addl $25; suites $400-$900; under 14 free. Covered parking, in/out $18. TV; cable, in-rm movies avail. Indoor pool. Restaurant 6 am-10:30 pm. Rm serv 24 hrs. Bar 11-2 am. Ck-out noon. Convention facilities. Concierge. Gift shop. Airport transportation. Exercise equipt; weights, bicycles, whirlpool, steam rm, sauna. Bathrm phones, minibars. Panoramic views of city and Lake Michigan. Cr cds: A, C, D, DS, ER, JCB, MC, V.

[D] [🏊] [✕] [🏃] [🔥] [SC]

★ ★ **TREMONT.** *(New general manager, therefore not rated)* *100 E Chestnut St (60611), north of the Loop.* 312/751-1900; res: 800/621-8133 (exc IL); FAX 312/280-2111. 118 rms, 16 story. S, D $159-$179; each addl $25; suites $375-$800; under 18 free; wkend rates. Crib free. Parking $19.50. TV; cable. Restaurant 6:30 am-11 pm (also see CAFE GORDON). Bar 11-1 am. Ck-out noon. Meeting rms. Concierge. Airport transportation. Health club privileges. Bathrm phones. Cr cds: A, C, D, DS, MC, V.

[✕] [✕] [SC]

★ ★ ★ **THE WESTIN HOTEL, CHICAGO.** *909 N Michigan Ave (60611), at Delaware Place, north of the Loop.* 312/943-7200; FAX 312/943-9347. 740 rms, 27 story. S, D $120-$195; each addl $20; suites $250-$800; under 18 free; package plans. Crib free. Pet accepted, some restrictions. Valet parking, in/out $19.25. TV; cable, in-rm movies avail. Restaurant 6:30 am-10 pm. Rm serv 24 hrs. Bar 11-1:30 am. Ck-out noon. Convention facilities. Concierge. Gift shop. Airport transportation. Exercise rm; instructor, weights, bicycles, sauna, steam

3-7 Nov '95   Badly heated.

rm, massage. Minibars; many bathrm phones. *LUXURY LEVEL : EXECUTIVE LEVEL.* 50 rms, 3 suites, 3 floors. S, D $145-$220; suites $500-$625. Private lounge, honor bar. Complimentary continental bkfst, refreshments, newspaper. Cr cds: A, C, D, DS, ER, JCB, MC, V.

[D] [✎] [✗] [⚡] [⛶] [SC]

Restaurants

★ ★ ★ **AMBRIA.** *2300 N Lincoln Park West, Lincoln Park.* 312/472-5959. Hrs: 6-9:30 pm; Fri & Sat to 10:30 pm. Closed Sun; major hols. Res accepted. French, continental menu. Serv bar. Wine list. A la carte entrees: dinner $20.50-$29.95. Prix fixe: dinner $44 & $58. Specializes in fresh seafood, seasonal offerings. Changing menu; daily specialties. Own baking. Valet parking. Art nouveau fixtures; dark woods, elegant setting. Chef-owned. Totally nonsmoking dining rm. Cr cds: A, C, D, DS, JCB, MC, V.

[D]

✔ ★ **ANN SATHER.** *929 W Belmont Ave, Lakeview.* 312/348-2378. Hrs: 7 am-10 pm. Res accepted. Swedish, Amer menu. Bar. A la carte entrees: bkfst $3.75-$6.75, lunch & dinner $4.25-$6.95. Complete meals: lunch & dinner $6.95-$10.95. Specializes in Swedish pancakes, beefsteak, fresh fish. Breakfast menu avail all day. Opened 1945. Cr cds: A, MC, V.

[D] [SC]

★ ★ ★ **ARUN'S.** *4156 N Kedzie Ave, north of the Loop.* 312/539-1909. Hrs: 5-10 pm; Sun to 9 pm. Closed Mon; major hols. Res accepted. Thai menu. Bar. A la carte entrees: dinner $10.95-$23.95. Specialties: phad Thai, three-flavored red snapper, spicy roast eggplant. Thai art display. Cr cds: A, C, D, DS, MC, V.

✔ ★ **AUSTIN KOO'S.** *318 W Adams St (60606), the Loop.* 312/853-1155. Hrs: 11:30 am-9 pm. Closed Sat & Sun; major hols. Res accepted. Mandarin menu. Bar. Semi-a la carte: lunch, dinner $7.95-$12.95. Specialties: empress duck, honey garlic chicken. Chinese decor. Cr cds: A, C, D, DS, MC, V.

[D]

★ ★ **AVANZARE.** *161 E Huron St, north of the Loop.* 312/337-8056. Hrs: 11:30 am-2 pm, 5:30-10 pm; Fri to 11 pm; Sat 5-11 pm; Sun 5-9:30 pm. Closed major hols. Res accepted. Italian menu. Bar. A la carte entrees: lunch $8.75-$14.75, dinner $15-$25. Specialties: grilled prime veal chop with natural juices, grilled salmon, spinach tortellini with four cheeses. Own pasta. Outdoor dining. Contemporary decor with Frank Lloyd Wright accents; Virginio Ferrari sculptures. Cr cds: A, C, D, DS, JCB, MC, V.

[D]

★ ★ **BELLA VISTA.** *1001 W Belmont Ave, Lakeview.* 312/404-0111. Hrs: 11:30 am-11 pm; Fri & Sat to midnight; Sun 5-10 pm. Closed Thanksgiving, Dec 25. Res accepted. Italian menu. Bar. Wine cellar. A la carte entrees: lunch $7-$10.50, dinner $9-$17.95. Specialties: penne pasta with grilled asparagus, pollo allo Spiedo, gourmet pizza. Valet parking (dinner). Contemporary, eclectic decor. In former bank building (1929). Cr cds: A, C, D, DS, MC, V.

[D]

★ ★ ★ **BENKAY.** *(See Hotel Nikko Chicago)* 312/836-5490. Hrs: 7-10 am, 11:30 am-2 pm, 5:30-10 pm. Closed Sun & Mon. Res accepted. Japanese menu. Bar. Wine list. Prix fixe: bkfst $24, kaiseki dinner $60-$100. Semi-a la carte: lunch $7.30-$18.50, dinner $22-$38.50. Specializes in variety of Japanese cooking styles. Sushi bar. Valet parking. Japanese-style tatami rms, kimono-clad waitresses. View of Chicago River. Cr cds: A, C, D, DS, ER, JCB, MC, V.

[D]

★ ★ **BERGHOFF.** *17 W Adams St, the Loop.* 312/427-3170. Hrs: 11 am-9:30 pm; Fri & Sat to 10 pm. Closed Sun; major hols. Res accepted. German, Amer menu. Semi-a la carte: lunch $5.50-$10, dinner $8-$16. Child's meals. Specialties: Wienerschnitzel, chicken Dijon, sauerbraten, fresh fish. In 1881 building. Family-owned since 1898. Cr cds: A, D, MC, V.

★ ★ **BICE.** *158 E Ontario St, north of the Loop.* 312/664-1474. Hrs: 11:30 am-2:30 pm, 5:30-10:30 pm; Fri & Sat to 11:30 pm. Closed Jan 1, Dec 25. Res accepted. Northern Italian menu. Bar. Wine list. A la carte entrees: lunch $13-$18, dinner $16-$24. Own pastries, desserts, pasta. Valet parking (dinner). Outdoor dining. Contemporary Italian decor. Cr cds: A, C, D, MC, V.

★ ★ ★ **BIGGS.** *1150 N Dearborn Pkwy (60610), Gold Coast.* 312/787-0900. Hrs: 5-10. Closed some major hols. Res accepted. Continental menu. Bar. Wine cellar. A la carte entrees: dinner $11-$23. Complete meals: dinner $20-$33. Specialties: beef Wellington, rack of lamb, roast duckling. Valet parking. Outdoor dining. Formal dining in mansion built 1874. Original oil paintings. Jacket. Cr cds: A, C, D, DS, MC, V.

★ **BINYON'S.** *327 S Plymouth Court (60604), the Loop.* 312/341-1155. Hrs: 11:30 am-9 pm; Sat from 4:30 pm. Closed Sun; major hols. Res accepted. Bar. Semi-a la carte: lunch $6.95-$12.95, dinner $8.95-$19.95. Specializes in steak, chops, fresh seafood. Valet parking. Casual atmosphere. Cr cds: A, C, D, DS, MC, V.

✔ ★ ★ **BISTRO 110.** *110 E Pearson St, north of the Loop.* 312/266-3110. Hrs: 11:30 am-10 pm; Fri & Sat to 11 pm; Sun brunch to 3 pm. Closed some major hols. French, Amer menu. Bar. A la carte entrees: lunch $6.95-$14.95, dinner $8.95-$19.95. Sun brunch $6.95-$14.95. Specializes in chicken prepared in wood-burning oven, veal, fish. Valet parking. Outdoor dining. French bistro atmosphere. Cr cds: A, C, D, DS, MC, V.

[D]

★ ★ **BLACKHAWK LODGE.** *41 E Superior St, north of the Loop.* 312/280-4080. Hrs: 11:30 am-10 pm; Fri to 11 pm; Sat 5-11 pm; Sun brunch to 3 pm. Closed some major hols. Res accepted. Bar. Semi-a la carte: lunch $7.95-$15.95, dinner $9.95-$21.95. Sun brunch $7.95-$14.95. Specializes in roasted vegetables, barbecued fish, free range chicken. Valet parking. Outdoor dining on screened porch. Lodge atmosphere; eclectic artifacts. Main dining rm totally nonsmoking. Cr cds: A, C, D, DS, MC, V.

[D]

✔ ★ **BLUE MESA.** *1729 N Halsted St, Lincoln Park.* 312/944-5990. Hrs: 11:30 am-2:30 pm, 5-11 pm; Fri to midnight; Sat 11:30 am-midnight; Sun 4-10 pm; Sun brunch 11 am-2:30 pm. Closed Thanksgiving, Dec 25. Res accepted. Southwestern menu. Bar. Semi-a la carte: lunch, dinner $6.95-$13.95. Sun brunch $6.95-$12.95. Child's meals. Specialties: blue corn chicken enchilada, stuffed sopaipilla, fajitas, grilled fresh fish. Valet parking. Outdoor dining. Cr cds: A, C, D, DS, MC, V.

[D]

★ ★ **BRASSERIE BELLEVUE.** *(See Le Meridien)* 312/266-2100. Hrs: 7 am-11 pm; Sun brunch 11 am-2:30 pm. Res accepted. Continental menu. Bar. Semi-a la carte: bkfst $6.95-$9.95, lunch $6.95-$14.95, dinner $9.25-$25.50. Sun brunch $22.95. Valet parking. Outdoor dining. Modern decor with Art Deco accent. Cr cds: A, C, D, DS, JCB, MC, V.

[D]

★ ★ ★ **BUCKINGHAM'S.** *(See Hilton & Towers Hotel)* 312/922-4400. Hrs: 5:30-10 pm; Sun brunch 10 am-2 pm. Res accepted. Bar. Wine list. A la carte entrees: dinner $14.50-$24.95. Sun brunch $26.95. Child's meals. Specialties: fresh Maine lobster, Buckingham's porterhouse, Maryland crab cakes. Own baking. Valet parking. Elegant decor; cherrywood pillars, Italian marble; artwork. Cr cds: A, C, D, DS, ER, JCB, MC, V.

[D]

★ ★ **BUKHARA.** *2 E Ontario St, north of the Loop.* 312/943-0188. Hrs: 11:30 am-2:30 pm, 5:30-10 pm. Fri to 11 pm; Sat & Sun noon-3 pm, 5:30-10 pm. Res accepted. Northwest Indian menu. Bar. A la carte entrees: lunch, dinner $6.95-$25.95. Buffet: lunch $7.95. Specialties: peshawari boti, tandoori chicken, murgh malai kabob. Own desserts. Indian artifacts. Cr cds: A, C, D, DS, MC, V.

D

★ ★ **BUTCHER SHOP.** *358 W Ontario St, River North.* 312/440-4900. Hrs: 5-10 pm; Fri & Sat to 11 pm; Sun to 9 pm. Closed major hols. Res accepted. Bar. Semi-a la carte: dinner $13-$25. Specializes in steak, prime rib. Guests may cook their own steaks on a charcoal-burning hearth grill. Cr cds: A, C, D, DS, MC, V.

CAFE GORDON. *(Too new to be rated) (See Tremont)* 312/280-2100. Hrs: 6:30 am-midnight; Sun brunch 9:30 am-2 pm. Res accepted; required Fri & Sat. Bar. Semi-a la carte: bkfst $3-$8, lunch $8-$18, dinner $10-$29. Sun brunch $9-$12. Pianist, vocalist Tues-Sat. Valet parking. Cr cds: A, C, D, DS, JCB, MC, V.

D

★ **CANTONESE CHEF.** *2342 S Wentworth Ave, Chinatown.* 312/225-3232. Hrs: 11 am-11 pm; Fri, Sat to 1 am; Sun 11:30 am-11 pm. Res accepted. Cantonese, Amer menu. Serv bar. Semi-a la carte: lunch $3.75-$4.95, dinner $8-$16. A la carte entrees: dinner $5.25-$15. Buffet: lunch $4.95 (Mon-Fri), dinner $6.95. Specialties: chi chi chicken, beef tenderloin Hong Kong style, steamed walleye pike. Chinese decor. Cr cds: A, C, D, JCB, MC, V.

★ ★ ★ **CAPE COD ROOM.** *(See The Drake Hotel)* 312/787-2200. Hrs: noon-11 pm. Closed Dec 25. Res accepted. International seafood menu. Bar. Semi-a la carte: lunch, dinner $27-$35. Specialties: Maryland crab cakes, turbot, pompano papillote, Dover sole. Own baking. Valet parking. Nautical decor. Jacket (dinner). Cr cds: A, C, D, DS, ER, JCB, MC, V.

D

★ ★ **CARLUCCI.** *2215 N Halsted St, Lincoln Park.* 312/281-1220. Hrs: 5:30-10:30 pm; Fri, Sat to 11:30 pm; Sun 5-10 pm. Closed some major hols. Res accepted. Regional Italian menu. Bar. A la carte entrees: dinner $10.50-$18.50. Specializes in homemade pasta, grilled meats and seafood, thin-crust pizza. Own pastries. Entertainment. Valet parking. Outdoor dining. Modern Italian ambiance. Cr cds: A, C, D, DS, MC, V.

D

★ ★ ★ **CELEBRITY CAFE.** *(See Hotel Nikko Chicago)* 312/836-5499. Hrs: 6:30-11 am, 11:30 am-2 pm, 5:30-10:30 pm; Fri to 11 pm; Sat 7 am-2:30 pm, 5:30-11 pm; Sun 7 am-2:30 pm, 5:30-10:30 pm; Sun brunch 9:30 am-2:30 pm. Res accepted. Bar from 11:30 am. A la carte entrees: bkfst $6-$12, lunch $6-$14, dinner $13.50-$21. Sun brunch $32. Child's meals. Specialties: sea bass wrapped in crispy potato, grilled 16-oz prime sirloin steak, grilled salmon with honey-mustard glaze, pesto pizza with tomato & cheese. Menu changes monthly & seasonally. Own pastries. Valet parking. Overlooks Chicago River. Cr cds: A, C, D, DS, ER, JCB, MC, V.

D

★ **CENTRO.** *710 N Wells St, River North.* 312/988-7775. Hrs: 11 am-3 pm, 5-10:30 pm; Fri to 11:30 pm; Sat 5-11:30 pm. Closed Sun; major hols. Res accepted. Italian menu. Bar. A la carte entrees: lunch $6-$10, dinner $7.50-$18.50. Specialties: pappardelle, chicken Vesuvio, baked cavatelli. Valet parking. Outdoor dining. Bistro atmosphere. Cr cds: A, C, D, DS, MC, V.

D

★ ★ ★ ★ **CHARLIE TROTTER'S.** *816 W Armitage Ave, Lincoln Park.* 312/248-6228. Hrs: 5:30-10 pm. Closed Sun, Mon; major hols. Res required. Americanized modern French menu. Bar. Wine cellars. A la carte entrees: dinner $28-$32. Table d'hôte (dégustation menu): dinner $55-$100. Specialties: hand-harvested sea scallop, organic beef strip loin, artichoke & goat cheese terrine. 3 dégustation menus available nightly. Own baking. Valet parking. In 1908 town house. Chef-owned. Jacket. Totally nonsmoking. Cr cds: A, C, D, JCB, MC, V.

D

★ ★ ★ **CHEZ PAUL.** *660 N Rush St, north of the Loop.* 312/944-6680. Hrs: 11:30 am-3 pm, 5:30-10:30 pm. Closed major hols. Res accepted. French menu. Bar. Wine list. A la carte entrees: lunch $8.50-$15, dinner $19-$30. Specialties: veal & lobster medallions in Cabernet & Bernaise sauce, sautéed duck breast with mango & duckling confit, crème brúlee. Own desserts. In Victorian mansion (1875). Valet parking. Jacket. Cr cds: A, C, D, DS, JCB, MC, V.

★ ★ **CHICAGO CHOP HOUSE.** *60 W Ontario St, River North.* 312/787-7100. Hrs: 11:30 am-11 pm; Fri to 11:30 pm; Sat 5-11:30 pm; Sun 5-11 pm. Closed some major hols. Res accepted. Bar. Semi-a la carte: lunch $4.95-$16.95, dinner $14.95-$28.95. Specializes in prime rib, NY strip steak, lamb chops. Valet parking. Entertainment. Turn-of-the-century Chicago decor. Cr cds: A, C, D, DS, JCB, MC, V.

★ ★ ★ **CIELO.** *(See Omni Chicago Hotel)* 312/944-7676. Hrs: 6:30 am-2:30 pm, 6-10 pm; Fri & Sat to 11 pm. Res accepted. Italian, Amer menu. Bar to midnight. Wine list. A la carte entrees: bkfst $4.95-$11.95, lunch $8.25-$12, dinner $8.50-$30. Specializes in woodburning-oven pizza, pasta, gourmet salads. Pianist, vocalist Wed-Sat. Valet parking. Elegant, stylish dining with view of city. Original art. Cr cds: A, C, D, DS, JCB, MC, V.

D

✔ ★ **CITY TAVERN.** *33 W Monroe St, opp Schubert Theater, the Loop.* 312/280-2740. Hrs: 7 am-9 pm; also Sat 4-9 pm during theater season. Closed Sun; major hols. Res accepted. Bar. Semi-a la carte: bkfst $2.95-$6.95, lunch $5.50-$16, dinner $6.95-$18.95. Specialties: grilled fresh fish, fresh salads, seafood pasta. Outdoor dining. Extensive beer selection. Cr cds: A, C, D, DS, MC, V.

D

★ ★ **CLUB GENE & GEORGETTI.** *500 N Franklin St, River North.* 312/527-3718. Hrs: 11:30-12:30 am. Closed Sun; major hols; also 1st wk July. Res accepted. Italian, Amer menu. Bar. Semi-a la carte: lunch $7-$18, dinner $12.50-$26.50. Specialties: prime strip steak, filet mignon, chicken Vesuvio. Valet parking. Chicago saloon atmosphere. Family-owned. Cr cds: A, C, D, MC, V.

★ ★ ★ **COCO PAZZO.** *300 W Hubbard St, River North.* 312/836-0900. Hrs: 11:30 am-2:30 pm, 5:30-10:30 pm; Fri to 11 pm; Sat 5:30-11 pm; Sun 5-10 pm. Closed major hols. Res accepted. Italian menu. Serv bar. Semi-a la carte: lunch $9.95-$15, dinner $13-$23. Specializes in Tuscan dishes, risotto del giorno, cous cous alla Trapanese. Own baking. Valet parking. Outdoor dining. Contemporary decor. Jacket. Cr cds: A, C, D, MC, V.

D

★ ★ **COMO INN.** *546 N Milwaukee Ave, north of the Loop.* 312/421-5222. Hrs: 11:30 am-11:30 pm; Fri, Sat to 12:30 am; Sun noon-11:30 pm. Closed Memorial Day, July 4, Labor Day, Dec 24. Res accepted. Northern Italian menu. Bar. Semi-a la carte: lunch $5.95-$12.95, dinner $12.95-$22.95. Child's meals. Specialties: chicken Vesuvio, veal al limone, veal Marsala. Pianist (dinner). Valet parking. Italian decor; antiques. Family-owned. Cr cds: A, C, D, DS, MC, V.

D

★ ★ ★ **COSTA D'ORO.** *1160 N Dearborn Pkwy (60610), Gold Coast.* 312/943-6880. Hrs: 5:30-10 pm; Fri & Sat to 11 pm. Closed Sun; Memorial Day. Res accepted. Italian, French menu. Bar. Wine list. A la carte entrees: dinner $19-$25. Specialties: risotto with saffron and sea scallops, roasted rack of lamb, smoked sturgeon with Granny Smith apple salad. Valet parking. Outdoor dining. Contemporary decor, original art. Jacket. Cr cds: A, C, D, DS, MC, V.

D

★ ★ ★ **CUISINES.** *(See Stouffer Riviere Hotel)* 312/372-4459. Hrs: 11:30 am-2 pm, 5:30-10 pm. Closed major hols. Res accepted. Mediterranean, Amer menu. Bar. Wine cellar. A la carte entrees: lunch $6.95-$14.95, dinner $6.95-$17.95. Specialities: veal medallions with wild mushrooms, roasted salmon with pepper crust, crabmeat and scallop lasagne. Valet parking. Intimate dining in Mediterranean atmosphere. Cr cds: A, C, D, DS, ER, JCB, MC, V.

[D]

★ ★ **THE ECCENTRIC.** *159 W Erie St, River North.* 312/787-8390. Hrs: 11 am-2 pm, 5:30-10 pm; Fri to 11 pm; Sat 5:30-11 pm; Sun 5-10 pm. Closed some major hols. Res accepted. Bar. A la carte entrees: lunch $6.95-$12.95, dinner $7.95-$21.95. Specialties: Oprah's potatoes, roast prime rib of beef, grilled swordfish. Valet parking. 1940's supperclub atmosphere. Eclectic decor. Cr cds: A, C, D, DS, JCB, MC, V.

[D]

✔★ **EL JARDIN.** *3335 N Clark St, Lakeview.* 312/528-6775. Hrs: 11:30 am-11 pm; Fri & Sat to midnight; Sun brunch 11 am-3 pm. Closed Thanksgiving, Dec 24, 25 & 31. Mexican menu. Bar. Semi-a la carte: lunch, dinner $5.50-$16.50. Sun brunch $8.95. Specialties: carne asada tampiqueña, carne de pollo en mole, fajitas. Outdoor dining. Festive Mexican atmosphere. Near Wrigley Field. Braille menu. Family-owned. Cr cds: A, C, D, DS, MC, V.

[D]

★ ★ **ELI'S THE PLACE FOR STEAK.** *215 E Chicago Ave, north of the Loop.* 312/642-1393. Hrs: 11 am-2:30 pm, 4-10:30 pm; Sat, Sun from 4 pm. Closed major hols. Res accepted. Bar to 12:30 am. Semi-a la carte: lunch $8.95-$12.95, dinner $19.95-$32.95. Specializes in steak, liver. Own cheesecake. Piano bar. Valet parking. Club-like atmosphere; original artwork of Chicago scenes. Jacket. Cr cds: A, C, D, DS, MC, V.

★ ★ **EMPEROR'S CHOICE.** *2238 S Wentworth Ave, Chinatown.* 312/225-8800. Hrs: noon-1 am; Sun to midnight. Cantonese seafood menu. Serv bar. A la carte entrees: lunch, dinner $6.95-$19.95. Semi-a la carte (Mon-Fri): lunch $5.95-$9.95. Prix fixe: dinner for two $38. Specialties: whole steamed oysters with black bean sauce, lobster, poached shrimp in shell with soy dip. Chinese artifacts including Ching dynasty emperor's robe; ink drawings of emperors from each dynasty. Cr cds: A, DS, MC, V.

[D]

★ ★ ★ **ENTRE NOUS.** *(See Fairmont At Illinois Center)* 312/565-7997. Hrs: 11:30 am-2:30 pm, 5:30-10:30 pm; Sat from 5:30 pm. Closed Sun; major hols. Res accepted. Continental menu. Bar. Extensive wine list. Semi-a la carte: lunch $8.50-$16.50, dinner $18-$27. Specializes in California cuisine, seasonal dishes. Valet parking. Elegant dining. Cr cds: A, C, D, DS, ER, JCB, MC, V.

[D]

★ ★ ★ **EVEREST.** *440 S La Salle St, 40th floor of Midwest Stock Exchange, the Loop.* 312/663-8920. Hrs: 5:30-9:30 pm (last sitting); Fri & Sat to 10 pm (last sitting); Closed Sun, Mon; major hols. Creative French cuisine with Alsatian influence. Res required. Serv bar. Extensive wine list; specializes in wines from Alsace. A la carte entrees: dinner $22-$32. Prix fixe: 8-course dinner $69. Pre-theater menu (5:30-6:30 pm): 3-course dinner $39. Specialties: le tournedos de cabillaud de petite pêche au Pinot Noir d'Alsace, composition of Pennsylvania farm-raised lamb, New York state foie gras roasted with suri rueve colmar style. Valet parking. Elegant contemporary decor with art deco accents. Panoramic view of city. Chef-owned. Jacket. Cr cds: A, C, D, DS, JCB, MC, V.

[D]

✔★ ★ **FRONTERA GRILL.** *445 N Clark St, River North.* 312/661-1434. Hrs: 11:30 am-2:30 pm, 5-10 pm; Fri to 11 pm; Sat 5-11 pm; Sat brunch 10:30 am-2:30 pm. Closed Sun, Mon. Mexican menu. Bar. A la carte entrees: lunch $7-$11, dinner $8-$16.95. Sat brunch $4.50-$8.95. Specialties: grilled fresh fish, duck breast adobo, carne asada. Valet parking. Outdoor dining. Regional Mexican cuisine; casual dining. Cr cds: A, C, D, DS, MC, V.

[D]

★ ★ **GEJA'S.** *340 W Armitage Ave, Lincoln Park.* 312/281-9101. Hrs: 5-10:30 pm; Fri to midnight; Sat to 12:30 am; Sun 4:30-10 pm. Closed some major hols. Res accepted Sun-Thurs. Fondue menu. Bar. Complete meals: dinner $18-$31. Specializes in cheese, meat, seafood & dessert fondues. Flamenco and classical guitarist. Variety of wines, sold by the glass. Cr cds: A, C, D, DS, JCB, MC, V.

★ **GENESEE DEPOT.** *3736 Broadway St, Lakeview.* 312/528-6990. Hrs: 11 am-3 pm, 5:30-10:30 pm; Fri, Sat to 11 pm; Sun 5-9 pm. Closed Mon; major hols. Setups. Complete meals: lunch $3.50-$6.25, dinner $9.75-$17.50. Specialties: brisket of beef, chicken Gruyere, poached Norwegian salmon with beurre blanc sauce. Own bread, desserts. Country inn decor. Cr cds: A, C, D, DS, MC, V.

★ **GOLDEN OX.** *1578 N Clybourn Ave, Lincoln Park.* 312/664-0780. Hrs: 11 am-11 pm; Sun 3-9 pm. Closed Sun July-Aug; some major hols. Res accepted. German, Amer menu. Bar. Semi-a la carte: lunch $5.95-$14.95, dinner $11.50-$21.50. Buffet: lunch (Tues-Fri) $9.95, dinner (Sat) $17.95. Specialties: Wienerschnitzel, veal shank, sauerbraten. Own strudel. Parking. Zither player Sat. Old world German decor; wood carvings, cuckoo clocks, murals of Wagner's Ring cycle. Rathskeller. Family-owned. Cr cds: A, C, D, DS, MC, V.

[D]

★ ★ ★ **GORDON.** *500 N Clark St, River North.* 312/467-9780. Hrs: 11:30 am-2 pm, 5:30-9:30 pm; Fri to 12:30 am; Sat 5:30 pm-midnight; Sun 5:30-9:30 pm. Closed major hols. Res accepted. Bar. Wine list. A la carte entrees: lunch $9-$14, dinner $20-$25. Pre-theatre menu (3 courses): $21.95. Specializes in fresh seafood, artichoke fritters, flourless chocolate cake, light American cuisine. Menu changes seasonally. Own pastries, ice cream. Pianist, jazz trio Sat. Valet parking (exc Sun). Eclectic; sophisticated elegance. Jacket. Cr cds: A, C, D, DS, MC, V.

[D]

✔★ ★ **GREEK ISLANDS.** *200 S Halsted St, Greektown.* 312/782-9855. Hrs: 11 am-midnight; Fri, Sat to 1 am. Closed Thanksgiving, Dec 25. Res accepted Sun-Thurs. Greek, Amer menu. Bar. A la carte entrees: lunch $5-$8.50, dinner $5.95-$12.95. Complete meals: lunch, dinner $9.95-$16.95. Specialties: lamb with artichoke, broiled red snapper, saganaki. Valet parking. Greek decor; 5 dining areas. Family-owned. Cr cds: A, C, D, DS, MC, V.

[D]

★ ★ **GYPSY.** *215 E Ohio St, north of the Loop.* 312/644-9779. Hrs: 11:30 am-10 pm; Fri & Sat to 11 pm; Sun to 9:30 pm; Sun brunch 11 am-2:30 pm. Closed Jan 1, Thanksgiving, Dec 25. Res accepted. Mediterranean, Amer menu. Bar. Semi-a la carte: lunch, dinner $7.95-$19.95. Sun brunch $7.95-$19.95. Specialities: linguine with Portugese clam sauce, pot roast in portobello mushroom broth, fresh fish. Outdoor dining. Casual atmosphere. Cr cds: A, C, D, DS, MC, V.

[D]

✔★ **HAMBURGER HAMLET.** *1024 Rush St, north of the Loop.* 312/649-6601. Hrs: 11 am-11 pm; Fri & Sat to midnight; Sun brunch 10 am-3 pm. Closed Thanksgiving, Dec 25. Bar. Semi-a la carte: lunch, dinner $4.25-$13.95. Sun brunch $4.25-$11.95. Specializes in gourmet hamburgers (20 varieties), chicken fajitas, chili. Outdoor dining. Eclectic 1940s saloon decor; one booth made from elevator once owned by Winston Churchill. Cr cds: A, C, D, DS, MC, V.

[D]

★ ★ **HARRY CARAY'S.** *33 W Kinzie St, at Dearborn St, River North.* 312/828-0966. Hrs: 11:30 am-3 pm, 5-10:30 pm; Fri to midnight; Sat 5 pm-midnight; Sun 4-9 pm. Closed major hols. Res accepted. Italian, Amer menu. Bar to 2 am, Sat to 3 am, Sun to midnight. A la carte entrees: lunch, dinner $8.95-$29.95. Specializes in chicken Vesuvio, lamb chop oreganato, steak. Valet parking. Outdoor dining. Baseball memorabilia. Cr cds: A, C, D, DS, MC, V.

[D]

✔★ **HAT DANCE.** *325 W Huron St, River North. 312/649-0066.* Hrs: 11:30 am-2 pm, 5:30-10 pm; Fri to 11:30 pm; Sat 11:30 am-3:30 pm, 5-11:30 pm; Sun 5-9 pm. Closed most major hols. Res accepted. Nouvelle Mexican menu. Bar. A la carte entrees: lunch $6-$10.95, dinner $7.95-$15.95. Specialties: corn pudding, marinated pork chops, wood-roasted chicken. Valet parking wkends. Outdoor snack bar. Unique decor with Aztec accents. Cr cds: A, C, D, DS, MC, V.
D

★ **HATSUHANA.** *160 E Ontario St, north of the Loop. 312/280-8287.* Hrs: 11:45 am-2 pm, 5:30-10 pm; Sat from 5 pm. Closed Sun; some major hols. Res accepted. Japanese menu. Serv bar. A la carte entrees: lunch $9-$15, dinner $9-$20. Complete meals: dinner $18-$35. Specialties: tempura, Hatsuhana and sushi specials. Sushi bar. Traditional Japanese decor. Cr cds: A, C, D, JCB, MC, V.

✔★★ **HAYLEMON.** *2201 S Wentworth Ave, Chinatown. 312/225-0891.* Hrs: 9 am-11 pm; Dim Sum to 2 pm. Cantonese, mandarin menu. Bar. A la carte entrees: lunch, dinner $5.95-$9.95. Complete meals: dinner $9-$14. Dim Sum $1.65-$2.50/item. Specialties: Cantonese fried chicken, crystal shrimp, shrimp and scallops in taro basket. Parking. Chinese decor. Family-owned. Cr cds: A, MC, V.

★ **HEIDELBERGER FASS.** *4300 N Lincoln Ave, north of the Loop. 312/478-2486.* Hrs: 11:30 am-10 pm; Sun from noon. Closed Tues. Res accepted. German, Amer menu. Bar. Semi-a la carte: lunch $5.25-$8.95, dinner $9.50-$14.50. Child's meals. Specialties: Wienerschnitzel, baked beef rouladen, venison. Parking. Authentic Old World German atmosphere. Family-owned. Cr cds: A, C, D, MC, V.

★ **HOUSE OF HUNAN.** *535 N Michigan Ave, north of the Loop. 312/329-9494.* Hrs: 11:30 am-10:30 pm. Closed Jan 1, Thanksgiving. Res accepted. Chinese menu. Bar. Semi-a la carte: lunch $6.95-$9.50, dinner $8.95-$19.95. Specialties: spicy beef & scallops, Neptune delight, empress chicken. Chinese decor. Cr cds: A, C, D, DS, JCB, MC, V.

★★★ **JACKIE'S.** *2478 N Lincoln Ave, Lincoln Park. 312/880-0003.* Hrs: 11:30 am-1:30 pm, 5:45-8:30 pm; Fri & Sat 5:30-9:30 pm. Closed Sun, Mon; major hols. Res accepted. Continental menu. Bar. Semi-a la carte: lunch $7.95-$14.95, dinner $17.95-$27.95. Specializes in rack of lamb, veal medallions, fresh fish. Own pastries. Intimate and elegant atmosphere. Valet parking (dinner only). Cr cds: A, C, D, DS, MC, V.
D

★ **JEROME'S.** *2450 N Clark St, Lincoln Park. 312/327-2207.* Hrs: 11:30 am-11 pm; Fri to midnight; Sat 9 am-midnight; Sun 9:30 am-11 pm; Sun brunch to 3 pm. Res accepted. Bar. A la carte entrees: lunch, dinner $6.50-$17.95. Sun brunch: $6-$10, buffet $12.95. Specializes in chicken, steak, fresh fish. In Victorian town house. Outdoor dining. Totally nonsmoking. Cr cds: A, C, D, DS, MC, V.

★★★★ **JIMMY'S PLACE.** *3420 N Elston Ave, north of the Loop. 312/539-2999.* Hrs: 5-9:30 pm. Closed Sun; major hols. Res accepted. Modern French menu. Bar. Wine list. Semi-a la carte: dinner $29-$32.50. Prix fixe: 4-course dinner $45. Specialties: seasonal fresh fish, saddle of lamb, veal medallions, sweetbreads. Menu changes monthly. Own baking. Operatic music. Parking. Artistic atmosphere with opera motif. Private party rm. Chef-owned. Totally nonsmoking Sat. Cr cds: C, D, MC, V.
D

★★ **KINZIE STREET CHOPHOUSE.** *400 N Wells St (60611), River North. 312/822-0191.* Hrs: 11 am-11 pm; Sun 4-10 pm. Closed major hols. Res accepted. Bar. A la carte entrees: lunch $6.95-$29.95, dinner $9.95-$39.95. Specializes in steak, chops, pasta. Valet parking. Outdoor dining. Chicago memorabilia. Cr cds: A, C, D, DS, JCB, MC, V.

★★★ **KLAY OVEN.** *414 N Orleans St, River North. 312/527-3999.* Hrs:11:30 am-2 pm, 5:30-10:30 pm; Fri & Sat to 11 pm. Closed

major hols; also Mon June-Sept. Res accepted. Indian menu. Bar. Wine list. A la carte entrees: lunch $3.95-$12.95, dinner $5.95-$24.95. Complete meals: dinner $19.95-$21.95. Specialties: sikandari champa, tandoori batera, jheenga bemisaal. Tableside preparation in elegant surroundings. Modern Indian art display. Totally nonsmoking. Cr cds: A, D, MC, V.
D

★★ **LA LLAMA.** *2666 N Halsted St, Lincoln Park. 312/327-7756.* Hrs: 5-11 pm. Closed most major hols. Res accepted. Peruvian menu. Serv bar. Semi-a la carte: dinner $9.95-$18.75. Complete meals: (exc Sat) 4-course dinner $12.95-$22.95. Specializes in Peruvian recipes for seafood, steak, chicken. Own desserts. Parking. Outdoor dining. South American art. Cr cds: A, C, D, DS, MC, V.

★★ **LA RISOTTERIA.** *2324 N Clark St (60614), Lincoln Park. 312/348-2106.* Hrs: 11 am-3 pm; Mon from 5 pm; wknd hrs vary. Closed Memorial Day. Res accepted; required wkends. Northern Italian menu. Bar to midnight. Semi-a la carte: lunch $7.95-$18.95, dinner $9.95-$21.95. Specializes in risotto, osso buco. Contemporary decor, casual atmosphere. Cr cds: A, D, MC, V.
D

★★★ **LA STRADA.** *155 N Michigan Ave, opp Grant Park, at Randolph St, the Loop. 312/565-2200.* Hrs: 11:30 am-2:30 pm, 5-10 pm; Fri, Sat 5-11 pm; early-bird dinner 5-6:30 pm. Closed Sun; some major hols. Res accepted. Northern Italian menu. Bar. Wine cellar. A la carte entrees: lunch $10-$14, dinner $15-$24. Specialties: zuppe de pesce, red snapper, veal scaloppini, broiled veal chops. Own baking, desserts. Pianist from 5 pm. Valet parking. Tableside cooking. Cr cds: A, C, D, DS, MC, V.
D

★★★ **LAWRY'S THE PRIME RIB.** *100 E Ontario St, north of the Loop. 312/787-5000.* Hrs: 11:30 am-2 pm, 5-11 pm; Fri, Sat to midnight; Sun 3-10 pm. Closed July 4, Dec 25. Res accepted. Bar. Wine list. Semi-a la carte: lunch $4.95-$6.95, dinner $18.95-$25.95. Child's meals. Specializes in prime rib, English trifle. Own baking. Prime rib only entree on dinner menu. Valet parking (dinner). In 1896 McCormick mansion. Chicago counterpart of famous California restaurant. Cr cds: A, C, D, DS, JCB, MC, V.
SC

✔★★ **LE MIKADO.** *21 W Goethe St, Gold Coast. 312/280-8611.* Hrs: 5-10 pm; Fri & Sat to 11 pm; Sun to 9 pm. Closed some major hols. Res accepted. French, Asian menu. A la carte entrees: dinner $10-$14.75. Prix fixe: dinner $16.75. Specialties: poitrine d'oie a la moutarde, cold spicy Szechwan sesame noodles, Thai-style sautéed shrimp. Seasonal menu. Cr cds: A, C, D, DS, JCB, MC, V.

★★★ **MANDAR-INN.** *2249 S Wentworth Ave, Chinatown. 312/842-4014.* Hrs: 11:30 am-9:30 pm; Fri & Sat to 11 pm. Closed Mon. Mandarin, Chinese menu. Serv bar. A la carte entrees: lunch, dinner $7.95-$12. Complete meals: lunch $5.95-$7.95, dinner $11.50-$17. Specialties: empress chicken, moo shoo pork, scallops sautéed in spicy hot sauce. Own sauces. Chinese artwork. Cr cds: A, C, D, DS, MC, V.

★★ **MARE.** *400 N Clark St (60610), north of the Loop. 312/245-9933.* Hrs: 11:30 am-2 pm, 5:30-10:30 pm; Sat 5-11:30 pm; Sun 4-9:30 pm. Closed some major hols. Res accepted. Italian menu. Bar. A la carte entrees: lunch $5.95-$11.95, dinner $5.95-$18.95. Specialties: cacciucco alla Viareggina, polenta con baccala' mantecato. Valet parking. Outdoor dining. Murals of Venice, artwork. Cr cds: A, D, MC, V.

✔★ **MIA FRANCESCA.** *3311 N Clark St, Lakeview. 312/281-3310.* Hrs: 5-10 pm; Fri & Sat to 11 pm; Sun to 9 pm. Closed major hols. Italian menu. Bar. A la carte entrees: dinner $7-$15. Child's meals. Specialities: linguine Sugo di scampi, skatewing al Balsamic, penne Siciliana. Valet parking. Marble colonnades; photographs of Rome. Cr cds: MC, V.

★ ★ ★ **MORTON'S.** *1050 N State St, north of the Loop.* *312/266-4820.* Hrs: 5:30-11 pm; Sun 5-10 pm. Closed major hols. Res accepted. Bar. Wine cellar. A la carte entrees: dinner $15.95-$29.95. Specialties: Maine lobster, prime dry-aged porterhouse steak, Sicilian veal chops. Valet parking. Menu on blackboard. English club atmosphere, decor. Cr cds: A, C, D, DS, JCB, MC, V.

D

★ ★ **NEW ROSEBUD CAFE.** *1500 W Taylor St, south of the Loop.* *312/942-1117.* Hrs: 11 am-3 pm, 5-10:30 pm; Fri to 11:30 pm; Sat 5-11:30 pm; Sun 4-9:30 pm. Closed some major hols; Dec 25. Res accepted. Italian menu. Bar. A la carte entrees: lunch $5-$12, dinner $10-$25. Complete meals: dinner for two $32-$52. Specialties: cavatelli with fresh tomato & basil, chicken Vesuvio, linguini with shrimp & broccolli, Italian antipasto salad. Valet parking. Traditional Old World decor; carved millwork, beveled glass. Cr cds: A, C, D, DS, MC, V.

D

★ ★ ★ **NICK'S FISHMARKET.** *1 First National Plaza, Dearborn & Monroe Sts, the Loop.* *312/621-0200.* Hrs: 11:30 am-3 pm, 5:30-11 pm; Fri to 11:30 pm; Sat 5:30 pm-midnight. Closed Sun; major hols. Res accepted. Bar 11-2 am. A la carte entrees: lunch $13-$25, dinner $24-$36. Specializes in fresh seafood, live Maine lobster, veal. Pianist exc Mon (dinner). Valet parking. Braille menu. Cr cds: A, C, D, DS, JCB, MC, V.

D

★ **OLD CAROLINA CRAB HOUSE.** *455 E Illinois St, at east end of North Pier, north of the Loop.* *312/321-8400.* Hrs: 11:30 am-10 pm; Fri, Sat to 11 pm. Closed Jan 1, Thanksgiving, Dec 25. Res accepted. Bar. Semi-a la carte: lunch $5.95-$14.95, dinner $8.95-$18.95. Child's meals. Specialties: crab cakes, spicy crab boil, grilled fresh seafood. Own desserts. Valet parking. Coastal Carolina decor. Glass-enclosed porch. Overlooks Chicago River; view of city. Cr cds: A, D, DS, MC, V.

D

✔ ★ ★ **PAPAGUS.** *620 N State St, in Embassy Suites Hotel, north of the Loop.* *312/642-8450.* Hrs: noon-10 pm; Fri to midnight; Sat noon-midnight; Sun noon-10 pm. Res accepted. Greek menu. Bar. A la carte entrees: lunch $3.25-$8.95, dinner $7.75-$15.50. Specializes in braised lamb with Orzo, Greek chicken, seafood. Valet parking. Outdoor dining. Rustic, country taverna atmosphere. Cr cds: A, C, D, DS, MC, V.

D

✔ ★ **PARTHENON.** *314 S Halsted St, Greektown.* *312/726-2407.* Hrs: 11-1 am; Sat to 2 am. Closed Thanksgiving, Dec 25. Greek, Amer menu. Bar. A la carte entrees: lunch $4.95-$9.95, dinner $5.95-$13. Child's meals. Specialties: broiled sea bass, red snapper, saganaki. Valet parking. Family-owned. Cr cds: A, C, D, DS, MC, V.

✔ ★ **PASTEUR CAFE.** *45 E Chicago Ave (60611), north of the Loop.* *312/587-9992.* Hrs: 11 am-10 pm; Fri, Sat to 11 pm. Closed major hols. Res accepted. Vietnamese menu. Semi-a la carte: lunch $2.95-$7.95, dinner $5.95-$10.95. Specialties: marinated beef, shrimp & calamari sate. Outdoor dining. Cr cds: A, C, D, DS, MC, V.

★ ★ **PRAIRIE.** *(See Hyatt On Printers Row Hotel)* 312/663-1143. Hrs: 6:30-10 am, 11:30 am-2 pm, 5:30-10 pm; Fri to 11 pm; Sat 7 am-2 pm, 5:30-11 pm; Sun 7-10:30 am, 5:30-10 pm; Sun brunch (winter) 10 am-2 pm. Res accepted. Bar. A la carte entrees: bkfst $4-$6, lunch, dinner $13-$25. Sun brunch $8-$15. Specialties: grilled baby Coho salmon with bacon, leeks and black walnuts, baked walleye pike stuffed with vegetables and wild rice, grilled buffalo steak. Own pastries. Seasonal menu. Valet parking. Decor in the style of Frank Lloyd Wright; oak trim, architectural photographs and drawings. Cr cds: A, C, D, DS, MC, V.

D

★ ★ ★ **PRINTER'S ROW.** *550 S Dearborn St, south of the Loop.* *312/461-0780.* Hrs: 11:30 am-2:30 pm, 5-10 pm; Fri to 11 pm;

Sat 5-11 pm. Closed Sun; major hols. Res accepted. Continental menu. Bar. Wine list. A la carte entrees: lunch $7-$11.50, dinner $13.50-$22.50. Specializes in fresh seafood, duck, seasonal game. Own pastries, desserts. In old printing building (1897). Cr cds: A, C, D, DS, MC, V.

D

★ ★ ★ **PUMP ROOM.** *(See Omni Ambassador East Hotel)* 312/266-0360. Hrs: 7 am-2:30 pm, 6-11:45 pm; Sat from 6 pm; Sun 5-9:45 pm. Sun brunch 11 am-2:30 pm. Res accepted. Bar. Wine list. Semi-a la carte: bkfst $5-$9.50. A la carte entrees: lunch $9.50-$14.95, dinner $16.50-$29.50. Sun brunch $24.95. Specializes in seared salmon, prime rib, lamb chops. Own pastries, sorbet. Pianist. Valet parking. Famous dining rm; was once haunt of stars, celebrities; celebrity photographs. Jacket (dinner). Cr cds: A, C, D, DS, MC, V.

★ ★ **RELISH.** *2044 N Halsted St, Lincoln Park.* *312/868-9034.* Hrs: 5:15-10 pm; Fri & Sat to 11 pm; Sun to 9 pm. Res accepted. Continental menu. Bar. A la carte entrees: dinner $9.50-$16.75. Specialties: wild mushroom strudel, pepper marinated tuna in olive & tomato salsa, marinated grilled venison with wild mushroom risotto. Valet parking. Outdoor dining. California atmosphere. Original paintings by local artists. Cr cds: A, C, D, MC, V.

D

★ ★ ★ **RITZ-CARLTON DINING ROOM.** *(See The Ritz-Carlton Hotel)* 312/227-5866. Hrs: 6-11 pm; Sun to 10 pm; Sun brunch 10:30 am-2:30 pm. Res accepted. French-inspired menu. Bar. A la carte entrees: dinner $24-$32. Sun brunch $31. Specialties: lobster tail and claws with corn and wild rice pancake, New Zealand venison with asparagus, poached pear and butternut squash, sautéed turbot, crab cakes. Own pastries. Pianist. Valet parking. Menu changes daily. Cr cds: A, C, D, DS, ER, JCB, MC, V.

D

★ ★ **RUSSIAN TEA CAFE.** *63 E Adams St (60604), the Loop.* *312/360-0000.* Hrs: 11 am-11 pm; Mon to 4 pm; Fri to midnight; Sat noon-midnight; Sun 1-9 pm. Closed Jan 1, Memorial Day. Res accepted. Russian, Ukrainian menu. Bar. Semi-a la carte: lunch $6-$12, dinner $17-$26. Specializes in borscht, shashlik, wild game. Traditional caviar service. Russian dolls on display. Cr cds: A, C, D, DS, JCB, MC, V.

D

★ ★ **RUTH'S CHRIS STEAK HOUSE.** *431 N Dearborn Ave (60610), north of the Loop.* *312/321-2725.* Hrs: 11:30 am-11 pm; Sat 5 pm-midnight. Closed Sun; major hols. Res accepted. Bar. Semi-a la carte: lunch $8.95-$13.95, dinner $9.95-$26.95. Specializes in steak, fresh seafood, Cajun dishes. Valet parking. Celebrity photos displayed. Cr cds: A, C, D, DS, MC, V.

★ ★ **THE SALOON.** *200 E Chestnut (60611), north of the Loop.* *312/280-5454.* Hrs: 11 am-midnight; Sun brunch to 3 pm. Closed some major hols. Res accepted. Bar. Semi-a la carte: lunch $3.95-$9.95, dinner $13.95-$22.95. Sun brunch $5.95-$9.95. Specializes in steak, prime rib, fresh seafood. Modern steakhouse atmosphere. Cr cds: A, C, D, DS, MC, V.

D

★ ★ **SANTORINI.** *800 W Adams St, Greektown.* *312/829-8820.* Hrs: 11 am-midnight; Fri & Sat to 1 am. Closed Thanksgiving, Dec 25. Res accepted. Greek menu. Bar. A la carte entrees: lunch $5.50-$13.95, dinner $6.75-$22.95. Specializes in fresh seafood, grilled lamb chops, Greek-style chicken. Valet parking. Simulated Greek town. Cr cds: A, MC, V.

D

★ **SAYAT NOVA.** *157 E Ohio St (60611), north of the Loop.* *312/644-9159.* Hrs: 11:30 am-10:30 pm; Sat noon-11 pm; Sun 3-10 pm. Closed major hols. Res accepted. Armenian menu. Bar. Semi-a la carte: lunch $5.95-$11.95, dinner $9.90-$16.95. Specializes in lamb chops, char-broiled kebab, cous cous. Family-owned. Cr cds: A, C, D, DS, MC, V.

★ **SCHULIEN'S.** *2100 W Irving Park Rd, Lakeview. 312/478-2100.* Hrs: 11:30 am-midnight; Fri to 1 am; Sat 4 pm-1 am; Sun 3-10 pm; Sun brunch (Sept-May) 11 am-2:30 pm. Closed Mon; major hols. Res accepted Tues-Fri. German, Amer menu. Bar. Semi-a la carte: lunch $5.25-$10, dinner $9.95-$19.95. Sun brunch buffet $12.95. Specialties: barbecued ribs, Wienerschnitzel, roast duck. Magician (dinner). Parking. Authentic Chicago saloon decor. Established 1886. Family-owned. Cr cds: A, C, D, DS, MC, V.

★ ★ ★ ★ **SEASONS.** *(See Four Seasons Hotel) 312/649-2349.* Hrs: 6:30 am-2:30 pm, 6-11 pm; Sun 6:30-10 am, 6-10 pm; Sun brunch 10:30 am-2 pm. Res accepted. American menu. Bar 11:30-1 am. A la carte entrees: bkfst $6-$12, lunch $9.50-$15, dinner $20-$32. Prix fixe: 3-course lunch $16.50, 5-course dinner $55. Sun brunch $37. Child's meals. Specialties: pan-roasted red snapper, rack of lamb with garlic-roasted artichoke, Nantucket stew of lobster, crab & sunchokes, vegetarian menu. Menu changes seasonally. Own baking. Pianist, jazz trio Fri-Sat. Valet parking $15; validated self-parking $5 after 5 pm. Traditional decor; walnut paneling, antique porcelains. Jacket. Cr cds: A, C, D, DS, ER, JCB, MC, V.

D

★ ★ **SHAW'S CRAB HOUSE.** *21 E Hubbard St, north of the Loop. 312/527-2722.* Hrs: 11:30 am-2 pm, 5:30-10 pm; Fri to 11 pm; Sat 5-11 pm; Sun from 5 pm. Closed Thanksgiving, Dec 25. Res accepted. A la carte entrees: lunch $7.95-$14.95, dinner $11.95-$23.95. Specializes in grilled fish, crab cakes, oysters. Valet parking. Decor re-creates look and atmosphere of 1940s seafood house. Cr cds: A, C, D, DS, MC, V.

D

★ **SHINE GARDEN.** *901 W Armitage Ave, Lincoln Park. 312/296-0101.* Hrs: 4-10:30 pm; Fri & Sat to 11 pm. Res accepted. Mandarin menu. Bar. A la carte entrees: dinner $6.95-$12.95. Specialties: dragon & phoenix, lemon chicken, kung pao shrimp & chicken. Valet parking. Contemporary decor. Cr cds: A, D, DS, MC, V.

D

★ ★ **SIGNATURE ROOM AT THE 95th.** *875 N Michigan Ave (60611), in John Hancock Center, north of the Loop. 312/787-9596.* Hrs: 7-10 am, 11 am-2:30 pm, 5:30-10 pm; Fri & Sat to 11 pm; Sun brunch 10:30 am-2 pm. Closed most major hols. Res accepted. Bar 11:30-12:30 am; Fri & Sat to 1:30 am. Semi-a la carte: bkfst $3.75-$6.25, lunch $4.95-$5.50. Lunch buffet $6.95. A la carte entrees: dinner $19-$29. Specializes in seafood, lamb, beef. Pianist, jazz Fri & Sat, Sun brunch. Magnificent views of city and lake from 95th floor. Cr cds: A, C, D, DS, MC, V.

✔ ★ **SOLE MIO.** *917 W Armitage Ave, Lincoln Park. 312/477-5858.* Hrs: 11:30 am-2 pm, 5:30-10:30 pm; Fri & Sat 5:30-11 pm; Sun 5:30-10 pm. Closed major hols. Res accepted. Italian menu. Bar. A la carte entrees: lunch, dinner $8.95-$16.95. Specialties: pappardelle verdi al prosciutto, grilled beef tenderloin, mushroom ravioli in gorgonzola sauce. Valet parking. Cr cds: A, D, MC, V.

★ ★ ★ **SPIAGGIA.** *980 N Michigan Ave, on 2nd level of One Magnificent Mile building, north of the Loop. 312/280-2750.* Hrs: 11:30 am-2 pm, 5:30-9:30 pm; Fri, Sat to 10:30 pm; Sun 5:30-9 pm. Closed major hols. Res accepted. Italian menu. Bar to 11 pm; Fri & Sat to midnight; Sun to 10 pm. Extensive wine list. A la carte entrees: lunch $8.95-$17.95, dinner $16.95-$28.95. Specialties: wood-roasted veal chops, skewered boneless quail, mussels steamed with garlic & white beans. Own pastries, pasta. Pianist (dinner). Seasonal menu. Parking. 2-story atrium; tiered tables; arches & Italian marble colonnades; display kitchen. View of Lake Michigan from 34-ft high windows. Jacket. Cr cds: A, C, D, DS, MC, V.

D

★ ★ **STEFANI'S.** *1418 W Fullerton Ave, Lincoln Park. 312/348-0111.* Hrs: 11 am-11 pm; Fri to midnight; Sat 5 pm-midnight.

Closed Sun; major hols. Res accepted. Northern Italian menu. Bar. Semi-a la carte: lunch $5-$9, dinner $8-$17. Specialties: chicken Vesuvio, calamari fritti, scaloppini di vitello a Monte Carlo. Own pasta, desserts. Valet parking. Outdoor dining. Cr cds: A, C, D, MC, V.

D

★ ★ **STREETERVILLE GRILL & BAR.** *301 E North Water St (60611), north of the Loop. 312/670-0788.* Hrs: 11:30 am-2:30 pm, 5-11 pm. Closed Jan 1, Dec 25. Res accepted. Serv bar. Semi-a la carte: lunch $7-$14. A la carte entrees: dinner $19-$26. Specializes in steak, prime rib, pasta. Valet parking. Outdoor dining. Cr cds: A, C, D, DS, ER, JCB, MC, V.

D SC

✔ ★ **SU CASA.** *49 E Ontario St, north of the Loop. 312/943-4041.* Hrs: 11:30 am-11 pm; Fri & Sat to midnight; Sun 4-9 pm. Closed Thanksgiving, Dec 25. Res accepted. Mexican menu. Bar. Semi-a la carte: lunch, dinner $4.95-$12.95. Specialties: chicken poblano, shrimp a la Veracruzana, pan-fried red snapper. Valet parking. 16th-century Mexican decor; Mexican artifacts. Cr cds: A, C, D, DS, MC, V.

★ ★ ★ **SUNTORY.** *11 E Huron St, north of the Loop. 312/664-3344.* Hrs: 11:30 am-2 pm, 5:30-9:30 pm; Sat 6-10 pm; Sun 5-9 pm. Closed Jan 1, Dec 25. Res accepted. Japanese menu. Bar. Wine list. Semi-a la carte: lunch $6.95-$16.50, dinner $15-$28. Prix fixe: kaiseki $60. Specializes in shabu-shabu and teppanyaki dining. Valet parking. Traditional Japanese decor. Cr cds: A, C, D, DS, JCB, MC, V.

D

★ ★ ★ **TOPOLOBAMPO.** *445 N Clark St, River North. 312/661-1434.* Hrs: 11:30 am-2 pm, 5:30-9:30 pm; Fri & Sat 5:30-10:30 pm. Closed Sun, Mon. Res accepted. Regional Mexican menu. Bar. Wine list. A la carte entrees: lunch $7-$13, dinner $14.50-$21. Specializes in gourmet cuisine featuring complex sauces, exotic wild game. Own pastries. Valet parking. Outdoor dining. Intimate dining. Cr cds: A, C, D, DS, MC, V.

D

★ ★ ★ **TRATTORIA NO. 10.** *10 N Dearborn St, the Loop. 312/984-1718.* Hrs: 11:30 am-2 pm, 5:30-9 pm; Fri to 10 pm; Sat 5:30-10 pm. Closed Sun; major hols. Res accepted. Italian menu. Bar. Wine list. A la carte entrees: lunch, dinner $8.95-$19.95. Specialties: ravioli, rack of lamb, veal chop. Own baking. Valet parking. Dining in grotto-style trattoria. Cr cds: A, C, D, DS, MC, V.

D

✔ ★ **TUCCI BENUCCH.** *900 N Michigan Ave, 5th floor, north of the Loop. 312/266-2500.* Hrs: 11:30 am-10 pm; Fri & Sat to 11 pm; Sun noon-9 pm. Closed Thanksgiving, Dec 25. Northern Italian menu. Bar. A la carte entrees: lunch, dinner $6.95-$10.95. Child's meals. Specializes in pasta, thin-crust pizza, salads. Own desserts. Replica of Italian country villa. Totally nonsmoking. Cr cds: A, C, D, DS, MC, V.

D

✔ ★ **TUCCI MILAN.** *6 W Hubbard St, north of the Loop. 312/222-0044.* Hrs: 11:30 am-10 pm; Fri to 11 pm; Sat noon-11 pm; Sun 5-9 pm. Closed Thanksgiving, Dec 25. Res accepted. Northern Italian menu. Bar. A la carte entrees: lunch, dinner $6.50-$15.95. Specializes in lasagne agli spinaci, rotisserie dishes. Valet parking. Original art. Cr cds: A, C, D, DS, MC, V.

D

★ ★ **TUSCANY.** *1014 W Taylor St, south of the Loop. 312/829-1990.* Hrs: 11 am-3:30 pm, 5-11 pm; Fri to midnight; Sat 5 pm-midnight; Sun 2-9:30 pm. Closed most major hols. Res accepted. Northern Italian menu. Bar. Semi-a la carte: lunch $8.50-$18, dinner $8.95-$20. Specializes in New Zealand lamb, grilled veal chops, pasta. Valet parking. Casual atmosphere; storefront windows. Cr cds: A, C, D, MC, V.

D

★ ★ **TUTTAPOSTO.** *646 N Franklin St, River North.* 312/943-6262. Hrs: 11:30 am-2 pm, 5-10 pm; Fri to 11 pm; Sat 5-11 pm; Sun 5-9 pm. Closed most major hols. Res accepted. Mediterranean, Italian menu. Bar. A la carte entrees: lunch $5-$16, dinner $9-$22. Child's meals. Specializes in wood burning oven baked pizza, Greek-style lamb chops, Portugese stew. Valet parking (dinner). Outdoor dining. Festive Mediterranean atmosphere. Original artwork. Cr cds: A, C, D, DS, MC, V.

D

★ ★ **UN GRAND CAFE.** *2300 Lincoln Park West, Lincoln Park.* 312/348-8886. Hrs: 6-10:30 pm; Fri & Sat to midnight; Sun 5-9:30 pm. Closed major hols. Res accepted. Serv bar. A la carte entrees: dinner $6.95-$21.95. Specializes in grilled fresh seafood, steak frites, salads, roast chicken. Valet parking. Outdoor dining. French bistro decor. Cr cds: A, C, D, DS, JCB, MC, V.

✔ ★ ★ **VINCI.** *1732 N Halsted St, Lincoln Park.* 312/266-1199. Hrs: 5:30-10:30 pm; Fri & Sat to 11:30 pm; Sun 4:30-9:30 pm. Closed most major hols. Res accepted. Italian menu. Bar. A la carte entrees: dinner $10.95-$14.95. Child's meals. Specialties: polenta con funghi, cuscussu' Trapanese, linguine della Nonna. Valet parking (dinner). Outdoor dining. Warm, rustic atmosphere. Cr cds: A, C, D, MC, V.

D

✔ ★ **VINNY'S.** *2901 N Sheffield Ave, Lincoln Park.* 312/871-0990. Hrs: 11:30 am-2:30 pm, 5:30-11 pm; Fri & Sat to midnight; Sun 5-11 pm. Closed most major hols. Italian, Amer menu. Bar. A la carte entrees: lunch $6-$12, dinner $8-$14. Specialties: steak Vesuvio, goombà chicken, spaghetti Napoletana. Valet parking. Outdoor dining. In converted warehouse. Dark woods; smoke-stained walls. Cr cds: A, C, D, DS, MC, V.

D

★ ★ ★ **VIVERE.** *71 W Monroe St, main floor of the Italian Village complex, the Loop.* 312/332-4040. Hrs: 11:15 am-2 pm, 5-10 pm; Fri & Sat to 11 pm. Closed Sun; major hols. Res accepted. Regional Italian menu. Bar. Extensive wine list. A la carte entrees: lunch $10-$20, dinner $15-$30. Specialties: tortelli di pecorino dolce, pesce del giorno come volete, medaglione di vitello, petto d'anatra con balsamico dolce. Valet parking. One of 3 restaurants in the Italian Village complex. Elegant dining in a contemporary Baroque setting; marble mosiac flooring. Family-owned. Cr cds: A, C, D, DS, JCB, MC, V.

D

★ **WATERFRONT.** *16 W Maple St, Gold Coast.* 312/943-7494. Hrs: 11:30 am-midnight; Fri, Sat to 1 am; Sun to 11 pm; early-bird dinner 4-6:30 pm. Res accepted. Bar. Semi-a la carte: lunch $4.50-$17, dinner $11.95-$25.95. Specialties: sole en sacque, grilled swordfish, Dungeness crab. Outdoor dining. Nautical motif, decor. Cr cds: A, C, D, DS, ER, MC, V.

Unrated Dining Spots

ARCO DE CUCHILLEROS. *3445 N Halsted St, Lakeview.* 312/296-6046. Hrs: 4 pm-11 pm; Fri to midnight; Sat noon-midnight; Sun noon-10 pm; Sun brunch to 3 pm. Closed Mon; most major hols. Res accepted. Spanish tapas menu. Bar. A la carte entrees: lunch, dinner $1.95-$5.95. Specialties: fish cheeks sauteed with garlic & white wine, mussels in white wine & cream sauce, boiled potatoes in fresh garlic mayonnaise. Patio dining. Casual atmosphere. Cr cds: A, MC, V.

BIG BOWL CAFE. *159¹/₂ W Erie St, River North.* 312/787-8297. Hrs: 11:30 am-11 pm; Fri & Sat to midnight. Closed Sun; Thanksgiving, Dec 25. Wine, beer. Semi-a la carte: lunch, dinner $1.95-$6.95. Specializes in homemade soups, stews and chowders. Casual, informal atmosphere. Cr cds: A, C, D, DS, MC, V.

D

CAFÉ BA BA REEBA. *2024 N Halsted St, Lincoln Park.* 312/935-5000. Hrs: 11:30 am-2:30 pm, 5:30-11 pm; Mon from 5:30 pm; Fri & Sat to midnight; Sun noon-10 pm. Closed some major hols. Spanish tapas menu. Bar. A la carte entrees: lunch, dinner $1.95-$7.95. Specialties: baked goat cheese, grilled squid with lemon, garlic and olive oil. Valet parking. Authentic Spanish tapas bar. Cr cds: A, C, D, DS, MC, V.

D

D.B. KAPLAN'S. *845 N Michigan Ave, in Water Tower Place, north of the Loop.* 312/280-2700. Hrs: 10 am-10 pm; Fri, Sat to midnight. Closed major hols. Bar. A la carte entrees: lunch, dinner $3.95-$7.95. Specializes in 163 sandwiches, 6-foot sandwiches, frozen fantasy desserts. Deli atmosphere. No cr cds accepted.

SC

ED DEBEVIC'S. *640 N Wells St, River North.* 312/664-1707. Hrs: 11 am-midnight; Fri to 1 am; Sun 10 am-11 pm. Closed Thanksgiving, Dec 25. Bar. Semi-a la carte: lunch, dinner $1.50-$6.25. Child's meals. Specializes in chili, hamburgers, meat loaf, salads. Own desserts. Valet parking. Replica of 1950s diner. No cr cds accepted.

D

THE GREENHOUSE. *(See The Ritz-Carlton Hotel)* 312/266-1000. Hrs: 11:30 am-2:30 pm; tea 2:30-5:30 pm; appetizers 3 pm-1 am. Buffet: lunch $9.95. Afternoon tea $7-$19.50. Child's meals. Selection of blended teas accompanied by finger sandwiches, scones with Devon cream and fruit preserves, tea bread, pastries, cookies, sherries and ports. Own desserts. Pianist. Valet parking. Cr cds: A, C, D, DS, ER, JCB, MC, V.

D

HARD ROCK CAFE. *63 W Ontario St, River North.* 312/943-2252. Hrs: 11:30 am-11 pm; Fri to midnight; Sat 11 am-midnight; Sun to 10 pm. Closed Thanksgiving, Dec 25. Bar to 12:30 am; Fri, Sat to 1:30 am; Sun to midnight. Semi-a la carte: lunch, dinner $5.95-$11.95. Specializes in lime barbecue chicken, watermelon ribs, hamburgers. Valet parking. Rock memorabilia. Cr cds: A, D, MC, V.

D

LUTZ'S CONTINENTAL CAFE & PASTRY SHOP. *2458 W Montrose Ave, north of the Loop.* 312/478-7785. Hrs: 11 am-10 pm. Closed Mon; major hols. Wine, beer. A la carte entrees: lunch, dinner $5.50-$10.50. Specializes in light lunches, whipped cream tortes, hand-dipped truffles, marzipan. Own candy, ice cream. Outdoor dining. Bakeshop. Continental café atmosphere. Family-owned. Cr cds: MC, V.

D

MICHAEL JORDAN'S. *500 N La Salle St, River North.* 312/644-3865. Hrs: 11:30 am-3 pm, 5-11 pm; Sun to 10 pm. Res accepted (lunch). Bar. Semi-a la carte: lunch $4.95-$12.95, dinner $11.95-$26.95. Specialties: Michael's "Nothin But Net" burger, Juanita's macaroni & cheese, steak, chops, seafood. Valet parking. Outdoor dining. High-ceilinged bar (1st floor) featuring video wall. Dining rm (2nd floor), Michael Jordan photos displayed; artwork; casual dining. Cr cds: A, MC, V.

D

PIZZERIA UNO. *29 E Ohio St, north of the Loop.* 312/321-1000. Hrs: 11:30-1 am; Sat to 2 am; Sun to midnight. Closed Thanksgiving, Dec 25. Bar. Limited menu. Lunch, dinner $2.95-$8. Specialty: deep-dish pizza. Family-owned. Cr cds: A, DS, MC, V.

PLANET HOLLYWOOD. *633 N Wells St, River North.* 312/266-7827. Hrs: 11 am-midnight; Fri, Sat to 2 am. Italian, Mexican, Amer menu. Bar to 1:45 am. Semi-a la carte: lunch, dinner $6.95-$17.95. Specialties: turkey burgers, vegetable pizza, grilled platters, pasta, salads, sandwiches. Faux palm trees, and searchlights evoke the glamour of Hollywood. Authentic Hollywood memorabilia displayed. Merchandise store offers shirts, hats and various signature products. Cr cds: A, C, MC, V.

POCKETS. *2618 N Clark St, Lincoln Park.* 312/404-7587. Hrs: 11 am-11 pm; Fri, Sat to midnight; Sun to 10 pm. Closed Thanksgiving, Dec 24-25. A la carte entrees: lunch, dinner $3.50-$6.25. Specialties: chipati sandwiches, calzone, pizza. No cr cds accepted.

SEASONS LOUNGE. *(See Four Seasons Hotel)* 312/280-8800. Hrs: 11:30 am-2 pm; tea 3-5 pm; Sat tea 3-5 pm. Bar to 1 am; Sun to 11 pm. Buffet: lunch $8.95. Tea $6.50-$12.75. Specializes in sandwiches. 12 teas, Italian pastries. Own baking. Pianist. Valet parking. Opulently decorated rooms off lobby; fireplace, view of Michigan Avenue. Cr cds: A, C, D, DS, ER, JCB, MC, V.

D

Chicago O'Hare Airport Area

Motels

★ ★ ★ **COURTYARD BY MARRIOTT.** *(2950 S River Rd, Des Plaines 60018)* 2 mi N of I-90 River Rd exit. 708/824-7000; FAX 708/824-4574. 180 rms, 5 story, 15 suites. S $98; D $108; suites $119; under 12 free. Crib free. TV; cable. Indoor pool. Complimentary coffee in rms. Restaurant 6:30 am-2 pm, 5-10 pm. Bar 4 pm-midnight. Ck-out 1 pm. Coin lndry. Meeting rms. Valet serv. Sundries. Free airport transportation. Exercise equipt; weight machine, bicycles, whirlpool. Refrigerator in suites. Some balconies. Cr cds: A, C, D, DS, MC, V.

D ⚊ ✈ ⚊ ♨ SC

★ **EXEL INN-O'HARE.** *(2881 Touhy Ave, Elk Grove Village 60007)* 708/803-9400. 123 rms, 3 story. S $48.99-$55.99; D $59.99-$61.99; under 18 free. Crib avail. Pet accepted, some restrictions. TV; cable. Complimentary continental bkfst. Restaurant nearby. Ck-out noon. Coin lndry. Free airport transportation. Game rm. Refrigerators avail. Cr cds: A, C, D, DS, MC, V.

D ⚊ ⚊ ♨ SC

★ **HAMPTON INN.** *(100 Busse Rd, Elk Grove Village 60007)* 1½ mi N on US 12/45 to Higgins Rd (IL 72), then 4 mi W to jct Busse Rd (IL 83). 708/593-8600; FAX 708/593-8607. 125 rms, 4 story. S $58-$63; D $61-$66; under 18 free; wkend packages. Crib free. TV; cable. Complimentary bkfst 6-10 am. Restaurant adj 6 am-10 pm. Ck-out noon. Meeting rm. Valet serv. Free airport transportation Sun-Thurs. Cr cds: A, C, D, DS, MC, V.

D ⚊ ♨ SC

✔ ★ **LA QUINTA.** *(1900 Oakton St, Elk Grove Village 60007)* 2 mi NW on I-90 to Elmhurst Rd, then N to Oakton St. 708/439-6767; FAX 708/439-5464. 142 rms, 4 story. S $56-$63; D $63-$73; each addl $7; under 18 free; wkend rates. Crib $5. TV; cable. Heated pool. Complimentary continental bkfst. Restaurant opp 7 am-11 pm. Rm serv 5-10 pm. Ck-out noon. Meeting rms. Valet serv. Free airport transportation. Health club privileges. Cr cds: A, C, D, DS, MC, V.

D ⚊ ✈ ⚊ ♨ SC

★ ★ **RESIDENCE INN BY MARRIOTT.** *(9450 W Lawrence, Schiller Park 60176)* 708/678-2210; FAX 708/678-9591. 169 kit. suites, 3-6 story. 1-bedrm $125-$195; 2-bedrm $145-$165; 3-bedrm $165-$200; wkly, monthly rates. Crib free. Pet accepted; $50. TV; cable. Complimentary continental bkfst. Coffee in rms. Restaurant adj. Ck-out noon. Coin lndry. Meeting rms. Valet serv. Free airport transportation 5 am-11 pm. Whirlpool. Health club privileges. Refrigerators. Balconies. Cr cds: A, C, D, DS, MC, V.

D ⚊ ✈ ⚊ ♨ SC

✔ ★ **TRAVELODGE-CHICAGO O'HARE.** *(3003 Mannheim Rd, Des Plaines 60018)* At Higgins Rd (IL 72), 1 mi N of O'Hare Intl Airport at jct US 12/45. 708/296-5541; FAX 708/803-1984. 93 rms, 2 story. S $49-$57; D $52-$60; each addl $3; under 17 free. Crib free. TV; cable. Pool. Ck-out noon. Meeting rms. Valet serv. Balconies. Cr cds: A, C, D, DS, ER, JCB, MC, V.

D ⚊ ⚊ ♨ SC

Motor Hotels

✔ ★ **BEST WESTERN MIDWAY.** *(1600 Oakton St, Elk Grove Village 60007)* 2 mi NW on I-90 to Elmhurst Rd, then N to Oakton St, then W. 708/981-0010; FAX 708/364-7365. 165 rms, 3 story. S $62-$66; D $68-$74; each addl $6; suites $125; under 12 free. Crib free. Pet accepted, some restrictions. Pool; whirlpool, sauna. Complimentary continental bkfst. Complimentary coffee in rms. Restaurant 6 am-2 pm, 5-10 pm. Rm serv. Bar 11-1 am; entertainment, dancing exc Sun. Ck-out noon. Symposium theater. Bellhops. Free airport transportation. Game rm. Some refrigerators. Cr cds: A, C, D, DS, JCB, MC, V.

D ⚊ ⚊ ✈ ⚊ ♨ SC

★ ★ **COMFORT INN.** *(2175 E Touhy Ave, Des Plaines 60018)* Jct Touhy Ave & River Rd. 708/635-1300; FAX 708/635-7572. 148 rms, 3 story. S $66-$75; D $70-$81; each addl $8; suites $86-$99; under 18 free; wknd rates. Crib free. TV; cable. Complimentary continental bkfst. Restaurant opp 6-2 am. Bar 11-1 am. Ck-out 1 pm. Meeting rms. Valet serv. Free airport transportation. Exercise equipt; weight machine, bicycles, whirlpool. Cr cds: A, C, D, DS, ER, JCB, MC, V.

D ⚊ ✈ ✈ ⚊ ♨ SC

Hotels

★ ★ ★ **HILTON O'HARE.** *(Box 66414, Chicago 60666)* Inside O'Hare Airport Complex, off US 45, I-294. 312/686-8000; FAX 312/601-2873. 858 rms, 10 story. S, D $165-$175; each addl $20; suites $195-$350; wknd packages. Crib free. Valet parking $16. Pet accepted; $25 deposit. TV; cable. Indoor pool. Coffee in rms. Restaurant 6-1 am. Rm serv 24 hrs. Bars 11-2 am. Ck-out 1 pm. Meeting rms. Exercise equipt; weights, bicycle, whirlpool, sauna. Minibars. Cr cds: A, C, D, DS, ER, JCB, MC, V.

D ⚊ ✈ ✈ ⚊ ♨ SC

★ ★ **HOLIDAY INN-O'HARE.** *(5440 N River Rd, Rosemont 60018)* On US 45, 1 mi E of O'Hare Intl Airport. 708/671-6350; FAX 708/671-5406. 507 rms, 14 story. S $102-$116; D $112-$126; each addl $10; suites $175-$325; under 18 free; wknd package. Crib free. Pet accepted. TV; cable. 2 pools, 1 indoor. Restaurant 6:30 am-midnight. Bars 11-2 am, wknds to 4 am; entertainment, dancing exc Sun. Ck-out noon. Coin lndry. Meeting rms. Free airport transportation. Exercise rm; weights, bicycles, whirlpool, sauna. Holidome. Game rm. Refrigerators, minibars. Cr cds: A, C, D, DS, ER, JCB, MC, V.

D ⚊ ⚊ ✈ ✈ ⚊ ♨ SC

★ ★ ★ **HOTEL SOFITEL CHICAGO AT O'HARE.** *(5550 N River Rd, Rosemont 60018)* 2 blks S of I-90, exit River Rd S. 708/678-4488; FAX 708/678-4244. 304 rms, 10 story. S $165-$195; D $185-$205; each addl $20; suites $260-$325; under 18 free. Crib free. Pet accepted. Parking $9. TV; cable. Indoor pool. Restaurants 6-2 am. Rm serv 24 hrs. Bar 11-2 am. Ck-out noon. Convention facilities. Concierge. Gift shop. Free airport transportation. Exercise equipt; weights, bicycles, sauna. Bathrm phones, minibars. Traditional European-style hotel. Cr cds: A, C, D, DS, ER, JCB, MC, V.

D ⚊ ⚊ ✈ ✈ ⚊ ♨ SC

★ ★ ★ **HYATT REGENCY O'HARE.** *(9300 W Bryn Mawr Ave, Rosemont 60018)* River Rd (US 45) at Kennedy Expy, River Rd (S) exit. 708/696-1234; FAX 708/698-0139. 1,100 rms, 10 story. S $140-$180; D $168-$207; each addl $20; suites $190-$650; studio rms $125; wknd package. Crib free. TV; cable. Indoor pool. Restaurants 6-1 am. Rm serv 24 hrs. 3 bars noon-2 am; dancing. Ck-out noon. Convention facilities. Barber, beauty shop. Free airport transportation. Exercise equipt; weights, bicycles, sauna, steam rm. Wet bar in suites. Many balconies. 12-story atrium lobby. *LUXURY LEVEL : REGENCY CLUB.* 708/696-1234, ext 2906. 2 floors. S $185-$210; D $195-$215; suites $275-$650. Concierge. Private lounge, honor bar. Complimentary continental bkfst, refreshments, newspaper, shoeshine. Cr cds: A, C, D, DS, ER, JCB, MC, V.

[D] [≈] [✗] [✈] [⊠] [♨] [SC]

★ ★ ★ **MARRIOTT SUITES.** *(6155 N River Rd, Rosemont 60018) I-190E, exit River Rd (N). 708/696-4400; FAX 708/696-2122.* 256 suites, 11 story. S $160; D $175; family, wknd rates. Crib free. Pet accepted. TV; cable. Indoor pool. Coffee in rms. Restaurant 6:30 am-10:30 pm. Bar 11:30 am-midnight. Ck-out 1 pm. Meeting rms. Gift shop. Free airport transportation. Exercise equipt; bicycles, stair machine, whirlpool, sauna. Refrigerators, wet bars. Cr cds: A, C, D, DS, ER, JCB, MC, V.

[D] [✦] [≈] [✗] [✈] [⊠] [♨] [SC]

★ ★ ★ **MARRIOTT-O'HARE.** *(8535 W Higgins Rd, Chicago 60631) On IL 72, 1¹/₂ mi E of O'Hare Intl Airport at Kennedy Expy, Cumberland Ave (N) exit. 312/693-4444; FAX 312/714-4297.* 681 rms, 12 story. S, D $133-$154; suites $185-$385; under 18 free; wkend plans. Crib free. Pet accepted. Valet parking $5. TV; cable. 2 pools, 1 indoor/outdoor; 2 wading pools, poolside serv. Restaurants 6:30 am-10 pm. Rm serv to midnight. Bars 11:30-2 am; dancing. Ck-out noon. Coin lndry. Convention facilities. Concierge. Gift shop. Barber, beauty shop. Free airport transportation. Tennis. Exercise rm; instructor, weights, bicycles, whirlpool, sauna. Game rm. Refrigerators avail. Private patios, balconies. *LUXURY LEVEL : CONCIERGE LEVEL.* 72 rms. S, D $154-$175. Private lounge. Complimentary bkfst, refreshments, newspaper. Cr cds: A, C, D, DS, ER, JCB, MC, V.

[D] [✦] [✚] [≈] [✗] [✈] [⊠] [♨] [SC]

★ ★ **RADISSON SUITE O'HARE.** *(5500 N River Rd, Rosemont 60018) 2 blks S of Kennedy Expy (I-90). 708/678-4000.* 296 suites, 8 story. S $165-$185; D $180-$200; under 17 free; wkend rates. Crib free. TV. Indoor pool. Complimentary full bkfst. Restaurant 11 am-11 pm. Rm serv 6-1 am. Bar to 1 am. Ck-out noon. Meeting rms. Gift shop. Free airport, RR station transportation. Exercise equipt; weights, bicycles, whirlpool, sauna. Refrigerators, wet bars. Opp Rosemont Convention Center. Cr cds: A, C, D, DS, ER, JCB, MC, V.

[D] [≈] [✗] [✈] [⊠] [♨] [SC]

★ ★ **RAMADA HOTEL O'HARE.** *(6600 N Mannheim Rd, Rosemont 60018) 2 mi N of O'Hare Intl Airport, just N of jct US 12/45, IL 72, N of Kennedy Expy (I-90) Mannheim exit. 708/827-5131; FAX 708/827-5659.* 723 rms, 2-9 story. S $94-$115; D $103-$125; each addl $10; suites $165-$475; studio rms $115-$135; under 18 free; wkend packages. Crib free. TV. Indoor/outdoor pool; poolside serv. Restaurants 6:30 am-midnight. Bars 11-2 am; dancing exc Sun. Ck-out 1 pm. Convention facilities. Gift shop. Free airport transportation. Tennis. Lighted 9-hole par-3 golf, putting green. Exercise equipt; weights, bicycles, whirlpool, sauna. Game rm. Lawn games. Refrigerator in some suites. Many private patios, balconies. Cr cds: A, C, D, DS, JCB, MC, V.

[D] [✗] [✚] [≈] [✗] [✈] [⊠] [♨] [SC]

★ ★ ★ **SHERATON GATEWAY SUITES.** *(6501 N Mannheim Rd, Rosemont 60018) ¹/₂ mi N of I-90, Mannheim Rd N exit. 708/699-6300; FAX 708/699-0391.* 299 suites, 11 story. S $139-$159; D $149-$169; each addl $10; under 18 free. Crib free. TV; cable, in-rm movies avail. Indoor pool. Complimentary full bkfst. Complimentary coffee in rms. Restaurant 11 am-2 pm, 5-10 pm. Rm serv 6 am-11 pm. Bar 11-1 am. Ck-out noon. Convention facilities. Gift shop. Free airport transportation. Exercise equipt; weights, bicycles, whirlpool, sauna. Refrigerators. Cr cds: A, C, D, DS, ER, JCB, MC, V.

[D] [≈] [✗] [✈] [⊠] [♨] [SC]

★ ★ ★ **THE WESTIN HOTEL, O'HARE.** *(6100 River Rd, Rosemont 60018) I-90E, exit River Rd N. 708/698-6000; FAX 708/698-4591.* 525 rms, 12 story. S $130-$175; D $150-$195; each addl $20; suites $210-$1,000; under 18 free; wknd rates. Valet parking $7. TV;

cable. Indoor pool; poolside serv. Restaurant 6 am-11 pm. Rm serv 24 hrs. Bar 2 pm to midnight, Fri, Sat 5 pm-2 am, closed Sun; dancing Fri, Sat. Ck-out 1 pm. Convention facilities. Gift shop. Free airport transportation. Exercise rm; instructor, weights, bicycles, whirlpool, sauna. Refrigerators; some bathrm phones, minibars. *LUXURY LEVEL : EXECUTIVE CLUB.* 99 rms, 2 floors. S $177; D $197; suites $225-$1,000. Concierge. Private lounge. Complimentary continental bkfst, refreshments. Cr cds: A, C, D, DS, ER, JCB, MC, V.

[D] [≈] [✗] [✈] [⊠] [♨] [SC]

Restaurants

★ ★ **BLACK RAM.** *(1414 Oakton St, Des Plaines) 1 mi N of I-90 (Kennedy Expy) River Rd (US 45) exit N. 708/824-1227.* Hrs: 11 am-midnight; Fri to 1 am; Sat from 4 pm; Sun 1-10 pm. Closed most major hols. Res accepted. Bar. Semi-a la carte: lunch $7-$13, dinner $11.95-$24.95. Specializes in steak, veal, fresh seafood. Entertainment Fri & Sat. Parking. Family-owned. Cr cds: A, C, D, DS, MC, V.

[D]

★ ★ ★ **CAFE LA CAVE.** *(2777 Mannheim Rd, Des Plaines) 1 mi N on Mannheim Rd, N of jct US 12/45, 1 blk N of jct IL 72. 708/827-7818.* Hrs: 11:30 am-11:30 pm; Sat from 5 pm; Sun 5-10:30 pm. Closed some major hols. Res accepted. French, continental menu. Bar. Wine list. Semi-a la carte: lunch $6-$13.95, dinner $16.95-$28.95. Specialties: steak Diane prepared tableside, rack of lamb à la Greque, medallions of lobster, shrimp & crab. Valet parking. Jacket (dinner). Cr cds: A, C, D, DS, JCB, MC, V.

[D]

★ ★ **CARLUCCI RIVERWAY.** *(6111 N River Rd, Rosemont) 2¹/₂ mi E off I-90 River Rd exit. 708/518-0990.* Hrs: 11 am-2:30 pm, 5-10 pm; Fri to 11 pm; Sat 5-11 pm; Sun 4:30-9 pm. Closed major hols. Res accepted. Tuscan, Italian menu. Bar to 1 am; Sat from 4:30 pm. A la carte entrees: lunch $7.95-$12.95, dinner $9.95-$23.95. Specializes in stuffed quail, fresh pasta, brick oven-baked pizza. Valet parking. Tuscan decor; traditional trattoria setting; frescos. Cr cds: A, C, D, DS, MC, V.

[D]

★ ★ ★ **MORTON'S OF CHICAGO.** *(9525 W Bryn Mawr Ave, Rosemont) I-90E, exit River Rd (S), in Columbia Center III office park. 708/678-5155.* Hrs: 11:30 am-2:30 pm, 5:30-11 pm; Sat from 5:30 pm; Sun 5-10 pm. Closed major hols. Res accepted. Bar. Wine cellar. A la carte entrees: lunch $6.95-$17.95, dinner $15.95-$29.95. Specializes in steak, fresh lobster, veal chop. Valet parking. Original Leroy Neiman prints. Cr cds: A, C, D, MC, V.

[D]

★ ★ ★ **NICK'S FISHMARKET.** *(10275 W Higgins Rd, Rosemont) Jct Mannheim & Higgins Rds. 708/298-8200.* Hrs: 6-10 pm; Fri & Sat to 11 pm. Closed most major hols. Res accepted. Continental menu. Bar to 2 am. Wine list. A la carte entrees: dinner $16-$32. Specializes in fresh seafood, steak, pasta. Jazz combo Wed-Sat evenings. Valet parking. Braille menu. 3 large saltwater aquariums. Jacket. Cr cds: A, C, D, DS, JCB, MC, V.

[D]

★ ★ **ROSEWOOD.** *(9421 W Higgins Rd, Rosemont) E of airport, at River Rd. 708/696-9494.* Hrs: 11 am-11 pm; Sat from 4 pm. Closed Sun; most major hols. Res accepted. Bar. Semi-a la carte: lunch $8-$12, dinner $20-$25. Specializes in steak, fresh seafood, lamb, veal. Pianist Wed-Sat. Valet parking. Intimate atmosphere. Rosewood millwork throughout. Cr cds: A, C, D, DS, MC, V.

[D]

★ ★ **SAYAT NOVA.** *(20 W Golf Rd, Des Plaines) On IL 58. 708/296-1776.* Hrs: 11:30 am-2 pm, 4-10:30 pm; Sat 4-11:30 pm; Sun 4-10 pm. Closed Mon; most major hols. Res accepted; required Fri, Sat. Middle Eastern menu. Serv bar. Semi-a la carte: lunch $6-$10, dinner $10-$15. Specializes in shish kebab, sautéed chicken, fresh fish. Parking. Middle Eastern decor. Cr cds: A, C, D, DS, MC, V.

D

★ ★ ★ **WALTER'S.** *(28 Main, Park Ridge) 6 mi NE of O'Hare Airport; 1¹/₂ mi N of Kennedy Expy Cumberland exit N. 708/825-2240.* Hrs: 11:30 am-2 pm, 5:30-9 pm; Sat from 5:30 pm. Closed Sun, Mon; major hols. Res accepted. Serv bar. Wine list. A la carte entrees: lunch $7.95-$12.95, dinner $9.95-$22. Specializes in grilled seafood, rack of lamb, breast of chicken with goat cheese. Own baking, pasta. Parking. In 1890s building; atrium dining; 30-ft skylight. Seasonal menu. Cr cds: A, C, D, DS, MC, V.

D

Cincinnati

Settled: 1788

Pop: 364,040

Elev: 683 feet

Time zone: Eastern

Area code: 513

The site of Cincinnati was chosen by the early settlers because it was an important river crossroads long used by Native Americans. The Miami Canal, completed in 1827, and the coming of the railroad in 1846 spurred the development of transportation and commerce.

During the 1840s and 1850s, Cincinnati prospered as a supplier of produce and goods to the cotton-rich South. Great fortunes were accumulated. It was an important station on the Underground Railroad and was generally loyal to the Union during the Civil War. Cincinnati's location on the Mason-Dixon line and its loss of trade with the South, however, caused many citizens to have mixed emotions about the outcome of the war.

After the war, continued prosperity brought art, music, a new library and a professional baseball team. A period of municipal corruption in the late 19th centruy was ended by a victory for reform elements and the establishment of a city-manager form of government, which has earned Cincinnati the title of America's best-governed city.

Business

Business people have coined the term "blue chip city" to describe business in Cincinnati; like blue chip stocks, the city has performed reliably and grown tremendously.

The economy is diverse, a factor that has helped the city weather economic downturns better than many of its neighbors. No single company employs more than three percent of the population.

Cincinnati is home to a number of national and international companies, including Procter and Gamble, G.E. Aircraft Engine Business Group, Kroger, Federated Department Stores, Cincinnati Milacron, American Financial Corp, Western-Southern Life Insurance and Great American Broadcasting.

Convention Facilities

The Cincinnati Convention Center is a first-class meeting and exposition complex, offering a 161,000-square-foot exhibit hall, which can be divided into three sections. There are 43 meeting rooms seating from 50 to 4,000 people.

A $2 million banquet kitchen is adjacent to the center's 30,000-square-foot ballroom, which seats 4,000 for meetings and 2,500 for food functions. Other features include a 30,000-square-foot lobby, enclosed loading docks with drive-in access, individual show offices, indoor landscaping, numerous lounge areas and two outdoor terraces.

Sports and Recreation

The Cincinnati Reds baseball team, the Bengals football team and the University of Cincinnati and Xavier University basketball teams have a devoted following among sports fans.

Cincinnati is home port of the only remaining overnight paddle-wheel boats traveling the nation's riverways. The owners of the *Delta Queen* introduced a new boat in 1976, the ultramodern *Mississippi Queen*, the first paddle-wheeler to be constructed in several decades. Riverboat excursions on the *Delta Queen* vary from 3 to 20 days, stopping at the ports of Pittsburgh, St Louis, Memphis, New Orleans and Minneapolis. For information and bookings, write to the *Delta Queen,* 30 Robin Street Wharf, New Orleans, LA 70130.

The Cincinnati Zoo has one of the nation's outstanding exhibits of exotic cats, including the rare white Bengal tiger. The world's first insectarium is here, along with many gorillas, a fresh and saltwater aquarium and an exhibit on birds of prey.

Within the 1,476 acres of Mt Airy Forest, there is the Mt Airy Arboretum, which contains an extensive collection of trees and woody plants. Garden of the States contains a tree, flower or shrub from each of the 50 states.

Entertainment

Cincinnati is justly proud of its symphony orchestra, which was founded in 1895. The orchestra's season is September through May, with performances at the Cincinnati Music Hall. It also offers a pop series, summer concerts in the park, young people's concerts and summer opera with Metropolitan Opera stars. The Music Hall is also home for the Cincinnati Ballet Company.

The *Majestic,* built in 1923 as a showboat, is the last of the original floating theaters still in operation today. The showboat runs a full season of drama, comedy and musical shows.

While the Cincinnati Art Museum prides itself on a world-famous collection of paintings, sculpture, prints and decorative art collectibles, the Contemporary Arts Center takes pride in being a forum for artistic ideas, rather than a museum of collected objects.

Historical Areas

The birthplace and boyhood home of William Howard Taft, maintained by the National Park Service, is now a national historic site.

The John Hauck House, an example of Italianate architecture, was once the home of a prominent brewer. It is furnished with appropriate 19th-century furniture.

In Sharon Woods County Park is Sharon Woods Village, an outdoor museum of restored 19th-century buildings transported from various parts of southwestern Ohio. It includes the Old Kemper House, a log house built in 1804 that has displays of 18th- and 19th-century utensils and furnishings.

Sightseeing

This city is an ideal headquarters from which to see much of a three-state area. It is an hour and a half away from the beautiful bluegrass country around Lexington, Kentucky. Not much farther away, directly west in Indiana, is scenic Brown County, a center for arts and crafts. Along the Ohio River are fascinating examples of old residences known by the descriptive architectural name "Steamboat Gothic."

A few minutes north of the city is the popular family theme park, Paramount's Kings Island. Another large amusement park, Americana, is located northwest of the city.

Shopping

Major hotels, stores, office complexes, restaurants, entertainment centers and the Convention Center are connected by a very extensive skywalk system, making the city easily accessible to pedestrians. The second-level pedestrian Skywalk virtually turns the downtown area into a mall, with clothing, jewelry, home furnishing stores and art galleries. Many of the suburbs offer a change of pace from the usual suburban mall with the town square concept of neighborhood shopping. Among these cities are Hyde Park, Glendale, Mt Lookout, Montgomery and O'Bryonville.

General References

Settled: 1788 **Pop:** 364,040 **Elev:** 683 feet **Time zone:** Eastern **Area code:** 513

Phone Numbers

POLICE & FIRE: 911
FBI: 421-4310
POISON CONTROL CENTER: 558-5111
TIME: 721-1700   **WEATHER:** 241-1010

Information Sources

Greater Cincinnati Convention and Visitors Bureau, 300 W 6th St, 45202; 621-2142.
Greater Cincinnati Chamber of Commerce, 300 Carew Tower, 441 Vine St, 45202; 579-3100.

Transportation

AIRLINES: American; Continental; Delta; Northwest; TWA; United; USAir; and other commuter and regional airlines. For current airline schedules and information consult the *Official Airline Guide*, published twice monthly.
AIRPORT: Cincinnati/Northern Kentucky International, 606/283-3151.
CAR RENTAL AGENCIES: (See Toll-Free Numbers) Avis 621-1479; Budget 606/283-1166; Hertz 606/283-3535.
PUBLIC TRANSPORTATION: Queen City Metro 621-4455.
RAILROAD PASSENGER SERVICE: Amtrak 800/872-7245.

Newspapers

Cincinnati Enquirer; Cincinnati Post.

Convention Facility

Dr. Albert B. Sabin Cincinnati Convention Center, 525 Elm St, 352-3750.

Sports & Recreation

Major Sports Facilities

Riverfront Coliseum, 100 Broadway, adjacent to Riverfront Stadium, 241-1818.
Riverfront Stadium, Pete Rose Way and Broadway, 352-5400 (Reds, baseball, 421-4510; Bengals, football, 621-3550).

Racetracks

River Downs, 6301 Kellogg Ave, 10 mi E on US 52, 232-8000.
Turfway Park Race Course, 7500 Turfway Rd, 10 mi SW off I-75 exit 184, in Florence, KY, 606/371-0200.

Cultural Facilities

Theaters

Cincinnati Playhouse In the Park, 962 Mount Adams Circle, 421-3888 or 800/582-3208 (OH).
Showboat *Majestic,* Public Landing, at foot of Broadway, 241-6550.

Concert Halls

Conservatory of Music, University of Cincinnati, 556-2683.
Music Hall, 1241 Elm St, 621-1919.
Riverfront Coliseum, 100 Broadway, 241-1818.

Museums

Cincinnati Art Museum, Art Museum Dr in Eden Park, 721-5204.
Cincinnati Fire Museum, 315 W Court St, 621-5553.
Contemporary Arts Center, 115 E 5th St, 721-0390.
Museum of Natural History, 1301 Western Ave, in Cincinnati Union Terminal, 287-7020.
Taft Museum, 316 Pike St, at 4th St, 241-0343.
Vent Haven (ventriloquism museum), 33 W Maple Ave, Fort Mitchell, KY, 606/341-0461.

Points of Interest

Historical

Sharon Woods Village, N on I-75, E on I-275 exit at US 42, then 1 mi S, Sharon Woods County Park, 563-9484.
Museum Center at Union Terminal, 1301 Western Ave, 287-7000.
William Henry Harrison Memorial, US 50, North Bend.
William Howard Taft National Historic Site, 2038 Auburn Ave.

Other Attractions

Americana Amusement Park, 20 mi N off I-75, Middletown, 539-7339.
Ault Park, 8 mi E, at E end of Observatory Rd in Hyde Park.
Carew Tower Observatory, 5th & Vine Sts, 241-3888.
Cincinnati Zoo and Botanical Garden, 3400 Vine St, 281-4700.
Civic Garden Center, 2715 Reading Rd, 221-0981.
Eden Park & Krohn Conservatory, Eden Park Dr, 421-4086.
Harriet Beecher Stowe Memorial, 2950 Gilbert Ave, 632-5120.
Paramount's Kings Island Theme Park, 20 mi N, I-71 & Kings Mills exit, Kings Mills, 398-5600.
Meier's Wine Cellars, 6955 Plainfield Pike, Silverton, 891-2900.
Mt Airy Forest & Arboretum, 5080 Colerain Ave, 352-4080.

Sightseeing Tours

Cities on Tour, 5658 Locust Dr, 248-0742.
Accent on Cincinnati, 105 W 4th St, 721-8687.

Annual Events

Appalachian Folk Festival, Coney Island. Mid-May.
Riverfest, riverfront. Labor Day wkend.

City Neighborhoods

Many of the restaurants, unrated dining establishments and some lodgings listed under Cincinnati include neighborhoods as well as exact street addresses. Geographic descriptions of the Downtown and Mt Adams are given, followed by a table of restaurants arranged by neighborhood.

Downtown: South of Central Pkwy, west of I-71, north of the Ohio River and east of I-75. **North of Downtown:** North of Central Pkwy. **East of Downtown:** East of I-71. **West of Downtown:** West of I-71/I-75.

Mt Adams: South of Eden Park, west of Columbia Pkwy, north of I-471 and east of I-71.

Lodgings and Food

CINCINNATI RESTAURANTS
BY NEIGHBORHOOD AREAS

(For full description, see alphabetical listings under Restaurants)

DOWNTOWN

La Normandie Grill. 118 E 6th St

Maisonette. 114 E 6th St

Orchid's (Omni Netherland Plaza). 35 W 5th St

The Palace (Cincinnatian Hotel). 601 Vine St

The Phoenix. 812 Race St

Pigalls Cafe. 127 W 4th St

NORTH OF DOWNTOWN

Aglamesis Bros. 3046 Madison Rd

Cheng-1 Cuisine. 203 W McMillan St

Chester's Road House. 9678 Montgomery Rd

China Gourmet. 3340 Erie Ave

Darci's. 7328 Kenwood Rd

Forest View Gardens. 4508 North Bend Rd

Grand Finale. 3 East Sharon Ave

House of Tam. 889 W Galbraith Rd

J's. 2444 Madison Rd

Lenhardt's. 151 W McMillan St

Montgomery Inn. 9440 Montgomery Rd

Queen City Diner. 1203 Sycamore St

Windjammer. 11330 Chester Rd

Window Garden. 3077 Harrison Ave

EAST OF DOWNTOWN

Cable House Italian Grille. 2247 Gilbert Ave

Funky's Blackstone Grille. 455 Delta Ave

Heritage. 7664 Wooster Pike (OH 50)

The Precinct. 311 Delta Ave

WEST OF DOWNTOWN

Fore & Aft. 7449 Forbes Rd

MT ADAMS

Adrica's. 934 Hatch St

Celestial. 1071 Celestial St

Cherrington's. 950 Pavilion St

Montgomery Inn Boathouse. 925 Eastern Ave

Petersen's. 1111 St Gregory

Note: *When a listing is located in a town that does not have its own city heading, it will appear under the city nearest to its location. In these cases, the address and town appear in parenthesis immediately following the name of the establishment.*

Motels

(Rates may be higher during Kool Jazz Festival)

★ ★ **BEST WESTERN MARIEMONT INN.** *6880 Wooster Pike (45227), east of downtown.* 513/271-2100; FAX 513/271-1057. 60 rms, 3 story. S $54-$56; D $59-$67; each addl $5; suites $75-$85; under 12 free. Crib free. TV; cable. Complimentary coffee. Restaurant 7 am-2 pm, 5:30-10 pm; Fri & Sat to 10:30 pm; Sun to 9 pm. Rm serv. Bar 11 am-midnight. Ck-out noon. Coin lndry. Valet serv. Cr cds: A, C, D, DS, JCB, MC, V.

🔥 SC

★ ★ **COMFORT SUITES.** *(11349 Reed Hartman Hwy, Blue Ash 45241) N on I-71, W on OH 126 to Reed Hartman Hwy.* 513/530-5999; FAX 513/530-0179. 50 suites, 3 story. Mid-June-late Aug: suites $95-$140; each addl $6; under 17 free; lower rates rest of yr. Crib free. TV; cable. Pool. Complimentary continental bkfst. Coffee in rms. Restaurant 4:30-11 pm; closed Sat, Sun. Rm serv. Bar 4:30-11 pm, closed Sat, Sun. Ck-out 11 am. Meeting rms. Valet serv. Sundries. Exercise equipt; weight machine, bicycles, sauna. Refrigerators. Cr cds: A, C, D, DS, ER, MC, V.

D ≈ 🏋 ✕ 🔥 SC

★ ★ ★ **COURTYARD BY MARRIOTT.** *(4625 Lake Forest Dr, Blue Ash 45242) I-275 exit 47.* 513/733-4334; FAX 513/733-5711. 149 rms, 2-3 story. S, D $84-$94; under 12 free; suites $94-$104; wknd rates. Crib free. TV; cable. Indoor pool. Restaurant 6:30-10:30 am; wkends 7-11:30 am. Bar 5-11 pm. Ck-out 1 pm. Coin lndry. Meeting rms. Exercise equipt; weight machines, bicycles, whirlpool. Sun deck. Cr cds: A, C, D, DS, MC, V.

D ≈ 🏋 ✕ 🔥 SC

✔ ★ **CROSS COUNTRY INN.** *(330 Glensprings Dr, Springdale 45246) N on I-75 to I-275W, exit at OH 4.* 513/671-0556; res: 800/621-1429; FAX 513/671-4953. 120 rms, 2 story. S $32.99-$39.99; D $34.99-$41.99; each addl $7; under 18 free; wkly rates. Crib free. TV; cable. Heated pool. Complimentary coffee in lobby. Restaurant adj 11 am-midnight. Ck-out noon. Meeting rm. Cr cds: A, DS, MC, V.

D ≈ ✕ 🔥 SC

✔ ★ ★ **CROSS COUNTRY INN.** *4004 Williams Dr (45255), off I-275 exit 65 at OH 125, south of downtown.* 513/528-7702; FAX 513/528-1246. 128 rms, 2 story. S $31.99-$38.99; D $33.99-$42.99; each addl $7; under 18 free. Crib free. TV; cable. Pool. Complimentary coffee in lobby. Restaurant adj 6 am-11 pm. Ck-out noon. Cr cds: A, DS, MC, V.

D ≈ ✕ 🔥 SC

★ ★ **FAIRFIELD INN BY MARRIOTT.** *(11171 Dowlin Rd, Sharonville 45241) I-75 exit 15, then 1 blk E.* 513/772-4114. 135 rms, 3 story. Late Apr-Oct: S $40.95-$48.95; D $48.95-$56.95; under 18 free; lower rates rest of yr. Crib free. TV; cable. Pool. Complimentary continental bkfst. Restaurant adj 6 am-midnight. Ck-out noon. Meeting rms. Valet serv. Cr cds: A, C, D, DS, MC, V.

D ≈ ✕ 🔥 SC

★ ★ **HAMPTON INN.** *10900 Crowne Point Dr (45241), off I-75 exit 15, north of downtown.* 513/771-6888; FAX 513/771-5768. 130 rms, 4 story. June-Aug: S $62; D $69; under 18 free; higher rates special events; lower rates rest of yr. Crib free. TV; cable. Pool. Complimentary continental bkfst. Restaurant nearby. Ck-out noon. Meeting rm. Cr cds: A, C, D, DS, MC, V.

D ≈ ✕ 🔥 SC

★ ★ **LUXBURY.** *9011 Fields Ertel Rd (45249), I-71 exit 19, north of downtown.* 513/683-9700; res: 800/252-7748; FAX 513/683-1284. 117 rms, 3 story. May-Sept: S, D $69-$95; each addl $6; under 17 free; lower rates rest of yr. Crib free. TV. Pool. Complimentary continental bkfst, coffee. Restaurant adj open 24 hrs. Ck-out 11 am. Meeting rms. Cr cds: A, C, D, DS, MC, V.

D ≈ ✕ 🔥 SC

✔★ **RED ROOF INN.** 11345 Chester Rd (45246), I-75 Sharon Rd exit 15, north of downtown. 513/771-5141; FAX 513/771-0812. 108 rms, 2 story. S $25.99-$44.99; D $31.99-$50.99; each addl $7; under 18 free; higher rates special events. Crib free. TV; cable. Restaurant adj 11-2 am. Ck-out noon. Valet serv. Health club privileges. Cr cds: A, C, D, DS, MC, V.

[icons]

★★ **RESIDENCE INN BY MARRIOTT.** 11689 Chester Rd (45246), north of downtown. 513/771-2525; FAX 513/771-3444. 144 kit. suites, 1-2 story. 1 bedrm $71-$100; 2 bedrm $92-$135. Pet accepted; $10 per night or $100 per visit. TV; cable. Pool; whirlpool. Complimentary continental bkfst. Ck-out noon. Coin lndry. Valet serv. Health club privileges. Lawn games. Some private patios. Picnic tables, grills. Cr cds: A, C, D, DS, JCB, MC, V.

[icons]

★ **SIGNATURE INN.** 8870 Governor's Hill Dr (45249), off I-71 exit 19, north of downtown. 513/683-3086; FAX 513/683-3086, ext. 500. 100 rms, 2 story. Memorial Day-Labor Day: S, D $85-$95; under 17 free; lower rates rest of yr. Crib free. TV. Pool. Complimentary continental bkfst. Ck-out noon. Meeting rms. Game rm. Cr cds: A, C, D, DS, MC, V.

[icons]

★ **SUPER 8.** 11335 Chester Rd (45246), I-75 Sharon Rd exit 15, north of downtown. 513/772-3140; FAX 513/772-1931. 144 rms, 2 story. S $46-$59; D $50-$64; each addl $6; under 18 free; higher rates: wkends, special events. Crib free. Pet accepted, some restrictions. TV; cable. Pool. Complimentary continental bkfst. Restaurant adj 11 am-11 pm. Ck-out noon. Valet serv. Cr cds: A, C, D, DS, MC, V.

[icons]

Motor Hotels

★★ **HARLEY.** 8020 Montgomery Rd (45236), I-71 exit 12, north of downtown. 513/793-4300; FAX 513/793-1413. 152 rms, 2 story. S $96; D $106; each addl $10; under 18 free. Crib free. TV; cable. 2 pools, 1 indoor. Restaurant 6:30 am-10 pm; Fri, Sat to 11 pm; Sun 7 am-9 pm. Rm serv. Bar; entertainment Fri & Sat. Ck-out 1 pm. Meeting rms. Bellhops. Lighted tennis. Putting green. Exercise equipt; weights, bicycles, whirlpool, sauna. Rec rm. Private patios, balconies. Cr cds: A, C, D, DS, MC, V.

[icons]

★★ **HOLIDAY INN NORTH.** 2235 Sharon Rd (45241), I-75 exit 15, north of downtown. 513/771-0700; FAX 513/772-0933. 409 rms, 4 story. June-Aug: S, D $95-$115; suites $135-$200; under 18 free; wkend rates; higher rates: hols (2-day min), Stadium Festival; lower rates rest of yr. Crib free. TV; cable. Indoor pool. Playground. Complimentary coffee in rms. Restaurant 5:30 am-2 pm, 5:30-10 pm. Rm serv. Bar 11-2 am; entertainment. Ck-out 11 am. Meeting rms. Bellhops. Sundries. Valet serv. Exercise equipt; weight machine, treadmill, whirlpools, sauna. Holidome. Refrigerators avail. Cr cds: A, C, D, DS, ER, JCB, MC, V.

[icons]

★★ **IMPERIAL HOUSE.** 5510 Rybolt Rd (45248), I-74 exit 11, north of downtown. 513/574-6000; FAX 513/574-6566. 198 rms, 2-5 story, 27 kits. S $48-$60; D $52-$56; each addl $5; suites $60-$75; kit. units $60; family rates. Crib free. TV; cable. Pool. Restaurant 6:30 am-10 pm. Rm serv. Bar 11-2:30 am, Sun 1 pm-1 am; entertainment, dancing Tues-Sat. Ck-out noon. Coin lndry. Meeting rms. Sundries. Exercise equipt; weights, bicycles, sauna, steam rm. Cr cds: A, C, D, DS, MC, V.

[icons]

★★ **QUALITY HOTEL CENTRAL.** 4747 Montgomery Rd (45212), north of downtown. 513/351-6000; FAX 513/351-0215. 146 rms, 8 story. S $66; D $70; each addl $5; under 18 free; wkend rates. Pet accepted. TV; cable. Pool; poolside serv. Complimentary continen-

tal bkfst. Restaurant 7 am-2:30 pm, 5-10:30 pm; Sat 7-10 am, 5-11:30 pm; Sun 7-10 am, 4-9 pm. Rm serv. Bar 11-2 am, Sat from 1 pm, Sun 4-11 pm; entertainment Tues-Sat. Ck-out noon. Meeting rms. Bellhops. Barber. Health club privileges. Some bathrm phones. Private patios, balconies. Picnic tables, grills. Cr cds: A, C, D, DS, ER, MC, V.

[icons]

↙ **RAMADA INN.** 8001 Reading Rd (45237), I-75 exit 10, north of downtown. 513/821-5111; FAX 513/821-8689. 97 rms, 6 story, 42 suites. S, D $59-$89; suites $79-$99; under 18 free; lower rates rest of yr. Crib free. TV; cable. 3 pools, 1 indoor. Playground. Restaurant 7 am-11 pm. Rm serv. Bar; entertainment Fri & Sat. Ck-out 11 am. Convention facilities. Valet serv. Barber, beauty shop. Tennis. Exercise equipt; weights, bicycles, sauna. Game rm. Lawn games. Some refrigerators. Cr cds: A, C, D, DS, JCB, MC, V.

[icons]

Hotels

CINCINNATIAN. (New owner, therefore not rated) 601 Vine St (45202), downtown. 513/381-3000; res: 800/332-2020 (OH), 800/942-9000 (exc OH); FAX 513/651-0256. 146 rms, 8 story. S, D $175-$235; each addl $25; under 12 free; wkend rates. Crib free. Covered parking $12. TV; cable. Restaurant 6:30 am-10:30 pm (also see THE PALACE). Rm serv 24 hrs. Tea Mon-Fri 3-5 pm. Bar 11:30-1 am; entertainment. Ck-out 1 pm. Meeting rms. Concierge. Airport transportation. Exercise equipt; weight machine, bicycles, sauna. Bathrm phones, minibars. Landmark hotel (1882); restored. Cr cds: A, C, D, DS, JCB, MC, V.

[icons]

★★★ **EMBASSY SUITES BLUE ASH.** 4554 Lake Forest Dr (45242), north of downtown. 513/733-8900; FAX 513/733-3720. 235 suites, 5 story. S $79-$149; D $89-$149; each addl $10; under 12 free; higher rates special events. Crib free. TV; cable. Indoor pool. Complimentary full bkfst. Complimentary coffee in rms. Restaurant 11:30 am-10 pm. Bar 5 pm-1 am; closed Sun. Ck-out 1 pm. Coin lndry. Meeting rms. Gift shop. Tennis privileges. 18-hole golf privileges. Exercise equipt; weight machine, bicycles, whirlpool, sauna. Refrigerators, wet bars. Balconies. Cr cds: A, C, D, DS, MC, V.

[icons]

★★ **GARFIELD HOUSE.** 2 Garfield Place (45202), 2 blks W of Fountain Square, downtown. 513/421-3355; res: 800/367-2155; FAX 513/421-3729. 133 kit. suites, 16 story. 1-bedrm $150-$175; 2-bedrm $165-$185; penthouse suites $325-$425; wkly, monthly rates. Crib free. Garage parking $4. TV; cable. Complimentary continental bkfst. Complimentary coffee in rms. Restaurant 11 am-10 pm; wkends from 5 pm. Rm serv 5-10 pm. Bar. Ck-out noon. Coin lndry. Meeting rms. Gift shop. Airport transportation. Exercise equipt; weight machine, stair machine. Some balconies. Cr cds: A, C, D, DS, MC, V.

[icons]

★★ **HOLIDAY INN-QUEENSGATE.** 800 W 8th St (45203), at Linn, west of downtown. 513/241-8660; FAX 513/241-9057. 244 rms, 11 story. S, D $82-$85; suites $175-$200; under 18 free. Crib free. Pet accepted. TV; cable. Pool. Coffee in rms. Restaurant 6:30 am-2 pm, 5-10 pm. Bar 4 pm-2 am, closed Sun; entertainment, dancing. Ck-out noon. Coin lndry. Meeting rms. Barber. Refrigerators avail. Cr cds: A, C, D, DS, ER, JCB, MC, V.

[icons]

★★★ **HYATT REGENCY.** 151 W 5th St (45202), downtown. 513/579-1234; FAX 513/579-0107. 485 rms, 22 story. S $180-$205; D $205-$230; each addl $25; suites $400-$750; under 18 free; wkend plans; higher rates special events. Crib free. TV; cable, in-rm movies avail. Indoor pool; poolside serv. Restaurant 6:30 am-midnight. Bar 11-2:30 am; dancing. Ck-out noon. Convention facilities. Concierge. Shopping arcade. Barber. shop. Exercise equipt; weight machines, bicycles, whirlpool, sauna. Some bathrm phones; refrigerator in suites. **LUXURY LEVEL: REGENCY CLUB.** 25 rms, 1 suite. S $210; D $235;

suite $425-$525. Private lounge. Wet bar in suite. Complimentary continental bkfst, refreshments. Cr cds: A, C, D, DS, ER, JCB, MC, V.

[D] [≈] [火] [↗] [🔥] [SC]

★ ★ ★ **OMNI NETHERLAND PLAZA.** 35 W 5th St (45202), off I-75, downtown. 513/421-9100; FAX 513/421-4291. 621 rms, 29 story. S $135-$165; D $165-$195; each addl $30; suites $175-$1,680; under 18 free; wkly, wkend rates. Crib free. Valet parking $12.50. TV. Pool. Restaurant 6 am-11 pm. Bar 11-2 am; entertainment. Ck-out noon. Concierge. Shopping arcade. Airport transportation. Exercise equipt; weight machine, treadmill, whirlpool, sauna, steam rm. Some private patios. Cr cds: A, C, D, DS, ER, JCB, MC, V.

[D] [≈] [火] [↗] [🔥] [SC]

★ ★ ★ **REGAL.** 150 W 5th St (45202), I-75 exit 5th St, downtown. 513/352-2100; FAX 513/352-2148. 887 rms, 21-32 story. S $79-$149; D $89-$159; each addl $20; suites $175-$600; under 18 free. Crib free. Garage $11. TV; cable. Heated pool. Restaurants 6:30 am-11 pm. Rm serv to 2 am. Bars 11-2:30 am; Sun from 1 pm. Ck-out 11 am. Convention facilities. Concierge. Shopping arcade. Barber. **LUXURY LEVEL : REGAL CLASS.** 50 rms, 3 suites, 4 floors. S $99; D $169; suites $275-$475. Private lounge. Cr cds: A, C, D, DS, ER, JCB, MC, V.

[D] [≈] [↗] [🔥] [SC]

★ ★ **SHERATON-SPRINGDALE.** (11911 Sheraton Lane, Springdale 45246) N on OH 4, at I-275 exit 41. 513/671-6600; FAX 513/671-0507. 267 rms, 10 story. May-Aug: S $89; D $99; each addl $10; suites $125-$150; under 18 free; Kings Island package; lower rates rest of yr. Crib free. TV; cable. Indoor pool. Coffee in rms. Restaurant 6:30 am-10 pm; Fri, Sat to 11 pm. Bar 11-2 am; entertainment, dancing. Ck-out noon. Coin lndry. Meeting rms. Gift shop. Exercise equipt; weights, bicycle, whirlpool. Game rm. Some bathrm phones. Cr cds: A, C, D, DS, ER, MC, V.

[D] [≈] [火] [↗] [🔥] [SC]

★ ★ **TERRACE.** 15 W 6th St (45202), at Vine St, downtown. 513/381-4000; FAX 513/381-5158. 270 rms, 9 story. S, D $115-$185; each addl $10; family rates. Crib free. Pet accepted, some restrictions. Valet parking (fee). TV. Restaurant 6:30 am-10 pm. Bar 11-2 am. Ck-out 1 pm. Meeting rms. Concierge. Barber, beauty shop. Airport transportation. Exercise equipt; weights, bicycles, whirlpool, sauna. Some refrigerators. Cr cds: A, C, D, DS, ER, JCB, MC, V.

[D] [🐾] [火] [↗] [🔥]

★ ★ **VERNON MANOR.** 400 Oak St (45219), north of downtown. 513/281-3300; res: 800/543-3999; FAX 513/281-8933. 173 rms, 7 story. S $79-$119; D $110-$125; each addl $10; suites $124-$430; studio rms $129-$135; under 16 free. Crib free. TV. Restaurant 7 am-10 pm; Sun from 10:30 am-2:30 pm. Bar 11-2 am; entertainment Fri & Sat. Ck-out noon. Coin lndry. Meeting rms. Barber. Valet parking. Tennis privileges. Health club privileges. Some refrigerators. Rooftop garden. Cr cds: A, C, D, DS, MC, V.

[D] [🐾] [🔥] [SC]

★ ★ ★ **WESTIN.** Fountain Sq (45202), 5th & Vine Sts, downtown. 513/621-7700; FAX 513/852-5670. 448 rms, 17 story. S $155-$185; D $175-$220; each addl $25; suites $270-$1,200; under 18 free; wkend packages. Crib free. Garage $12.95. TV; cable. Indoor pool; poolside serv. Restaurant 6:30 am-10 pm; Fri, Sat to midnight. Rm serv 24 hrs. Bar 11:30-2:30 am, Sun from 1 pm. Ck-out 1 pm. Convention facilities. Shopping arcade. Valet parking. Airport transportation. Exercise rm; instructor, weights, bicycles, whirlpool, steam rm, sauna. Massage therapy. Some bathrm phones, refrigerators. Sun deck. **LUXURY LEVEL : EXECUTIVE CLUB.** 34 rms, 1 suite. S, D $175-$200; suite $380. Concierge. Private lounge, honor bar. Complimentary continental bkfst, refreshments. Cr cds: A, C, D, DS, ER, JCB, MC, V.

[D] [≈] [火] [↗] [🔥] [SC]

Restaurants

✔★ **ADRICA'S.** 934 Hatch St, in Mt Adams. 513/721-5329. Hrs: 11 am-2 pm, 5-11 pm; Sat & Sun from 5 pm. Closed Dec 25. Res accepted. Italian menu. Bar. A la carte entrees: lunch $4.50-$6.50, dinner $7.50-$11.50. Specialties: hand-tossed fresh pizza, lasagne, eggplant Parmesan. Outdoor patio dining. Cr cds: A, C, D, DS, MC, V.

★ ★ **BLACK FOREST.** (8675 Cincinnati-Columbus Rd, West Chester) 3¹/₂ mi N of I-275, exit 46. 513/777-7600. Hrs: 11 am-2:30 pm, 4:30-10 pm; Fri to 11 pm; Sat 4:30-11 pm; Sun 4:30-10 pm. Closed some major hols. Res accepted. German menu. Bar. Semi-a la carte: lunch $4.95-$6, dinner $6.95-$17. Child's meals. Specialties: Wienerschnitzel, Oktoberfest chicken, sauerbraten. German band Fri & Sat. Parking. Old World German decor. Family-owned. Cr cds: A, C, D, DS, MC, V.

[D]

★ ★ **CABLE HOUSE ITALIAN GRILLE.** 2247 Gilbert Ave, east of downtown. 513/861-2400. Hrs: 11 am-10 pm; Fri & Sat to midnight. Closed major hols. Res accepted. Italian menu. Bar. A la carte entrees: lunch $4.95-$7.95, dinner $6.95-$18.95. Child's meals. Specializes in pasta, veal, fresh fish. Valet parking. Contemporary decor. Cr cds: A, C, D, MC, V.

★ ★ ★ **CELESTIAL.** 1071 Celestial St, in Highland Tower Apts, on Mt Adams. 513/241-4455. Hrs: 11:30 am-2:30 pm, 5:30-10 pm; Fri & Sat to 11 pm. Closed Sun; Jan 1, Dec 25. Res accepted. Continental menu. Bar. Wine list. Semi-a la carte: lunch $6.50-$11.95, dinner $16.75-$24.95. Specializes in game, fresh seafood. Own baking. Jazz Tues-Sat. Valet parking. Panoramic view of city. Jacket. Cr cds: A, C, D, MC, V.

[D]

★ **CHENG-1 CUISINE.** 203 W McMillan St, north of downtown. 513/723-1999. Hrs: 11 am-10 pm; Fri to 11 pm; Sat noon-11 pm; Sun 11:30-10 pm. Closed Thanksgiving, Dec 25. Chinese menu. Serv bar. Semi-a la carte: lunch $4.25-$5.75, dinner $5.50-$14.95. Specialties: cashew chicken, pan-fried moo-shu, sizzling shrimp & scallops. Cr cds: A, DS, MC, V.

[D]

★ ★ **CHERRINGTON'S.** 950 Pavilion St, on Mt Adams. 513/579-0131. Hrs: 7 am-3 pm, 5-9 pm; Fri to 11 pm; Sat 8-11:30 am, 5-11 pm; Sun 4-9 pm; Sun brunch 11 am-4 pm. Closed Mon; some major hols. Res accepted. Bar. Semi-a la carte: bkfst $2.95-$5.95, lunch $4.95-$8.95, dinner $8.95-$22.95. Sun brunch $3.95-$10.95. Specializes in fresh seafood. Outdoor dining. Blackboard menu. Guitarist Fri, Sat. Renovated residence (1880). Cr cds: A, C, D, JCB, MC, V.

★ ★ **CHESTER'S ROAD HOUSE.** 9678 Montgomery Rd, north of downtown. 513/793-8700. Hrs: 11:30 am-2:30 pm, 5:30-10:30 pm; Sat to 11 pm; Sun 5:30-9 pm. Closed Jan 1, July 4, Dec 25; also Super Bowl Sun. Res accepted. Bar. Semi-a la carte: lunch $6.50-$9.95, dinner $9.95-$21.50. Specializes in fresh seafood, rack of baby lamb, steak. Salad bar. Parking. Garden atmosphere; in converted brick farmhouse (1900). Family-owned. Cr cds: A, C, D, DS, MC, V.

[D]

★ ★ **CHINA GOURMET.** 3340 Erie Ave, north of downtown. 513/871-6612. Hrs: 11 am-11 pm; Fri to midnight; Sat noon-midnight. Closed Sun; major hols. Res accepted. Chinese menu. Bar. A la carte entrees: lunch $6-$9.95, dinner $9.95-$25. Specializes in fresh seafood. Parking. Cr cds: C, D, MC, V.

[D]

★ **FORE & AFT.** 7449 Forbes Rd, west of downtown. 513/941-8400. Hrs: 11 am-11 pm; Fri to midnight; Sat 4 pm-midnight. Closed Jan 1, Dec 24 & 25. Res accepted. Bar. Semi-a la carte: lunch $4.75-$14.95, dinner $7.95-$33.95. Child's meals. Specializes in steak, seafood. Parking. Outdoor dining. Floating barge on Ohio River; nautical memorabilia. Cr cds: A, MC, V.

SC

★ ★ **FOREST VIEW GARDENS.** *4508 North Bend Rd, north of downtown.* 513/661-6434. Hrs: 11 am-2 pm, 5-7:30 pm; Mon to 2 pm; Sat & Sun from 5 pm; Broadway music shows (sittings): Thurs 6 pm, Fri 7 pm, Sat 6 & 8 pm, Sun 5 pm. Closed Dec 24, 25; also 1st wk Jan. Res accepted; required for shows (Thurs-Sun). German, Amer menu. Bar. Semi-a la carte: lunch $3.95-$7.50, dinner $11.95-$18.95. Child's meals. Specializes in Wienerschnitzel, sauerbraten, prime rib, fresh fish. Parking. Outdoor dining in beer garden. Bavarian Fest atmosphere. Banquet-style seating. Family-owned. Cr cds: A, C, D, DS, MC, V.

D

★ ★ **FUNKY'S BLACKSTONE GRILLE.** *455 Delta Ave, east of downtown.* 513/321-0010. Hrs: 5-11 pm; Fri & Sat to midnight; Sun to 10 pm. Res accepted. Bar. Semi-a la carte: dinner $11.95-$20.95. Child's meals. Specializes in fresh fish, pasta. Jazz guitarist Wed. Parking. Cr cds: A, C, D, DS, MC, V.

D

★ ★ **GRAND FINALE.** *3 East Sharon Ave, north of downtown.* 513/771-5925. Hrs: 11:30 am-11 pm; Fri, Sat to 11:30 pm; Sun 5-10 pm; Sun brunch 10:30 am-3 pm. Closed Mon; Dec 25. Continental menu. Bar. Semi-a la carte: lunch $4.95-$11.95, dinner $8.95-$24.95. Sun brunch $9.95. Child's meals. Specialties: steak salad Annie, chicken Ginger, rack of lamb. Own baking, desserts. Parking. Outdoor dining. Remodeled turn-of-the-century saloon. Cr cds: A, C, D, DS, MC, V.

D

★ ★ **HERITAGE.** *7664 Wooster Pike (OH 50), east of downtown.* 513/561-9300. Hrs: 11:30 am-2:30 pm, 5-10 pm; Sat 5-11 pm; Sun 10:30 am-2:30 pm, 5-9 pm; early-bird dinner Sun-Fri 5-6:30 pm. Closed some major hols. Res accepted. Bar. Wine list. Semi-a la carte: lunch $4.95-$9.95, dinner $12.95-$20.95. Sun brunch $10.95. Child's meals. Specializes in regional American cuisine. Own baking. Valet parking. Restored 1827 farmhouse. Own herb garden. Family-owned. Cr cds: A, C, D, DS, MC, V.

✔ ★ ★ **HOUSE OF TAM.** *889 W Galbraith Rd, north of downtown.* 513/729-5566. Hrs: 11 am-9:30 pm; Fri to 10 pm; Sat 5-10:30 pm. Closed Sun; some major hols. Res accepted. Chinese menu. Bar. Semi-a la carte: lunch $3.95-$5.50, dinner $5.95-$15.95. Specialties: pine nuts chicken, sea emperor's feast, lemon walnut shrimp. Parking. Totally nonsmoking. Cr cds: A, DS, MC, V.

D

★ ★ **J'S.** *2444 Madison Rd, north of downtown.* 513/871-2888. Hrs: 11:30 am-2 pm, 5:30-10 pm; Fri to 11 pm; Sat 5-11 pm; Sun 5-9 pm. Closed Mon. Res accepted. Bar. Semi-a la carte: lunch $7.50-$12.95, dinner $11.95-$26.95. Specializes in pasta, marinated chargrilled swordfish. Antipasto table Tues-Thurs & Sun. Own baking. Valet parking. Cr cds: A, C, D, DS, MC, V.

D

★ ★ **LA NORMANDIE GRILL.** *118 E 6th St, downtown.* 513/721-2761. Hrs: 11 am-2:30 pm, 5-11 pm; Sat from 5 pm. Closed Sun; major hols. Res accepted. Bar. Semi-a la carte: lunch $5.50-$9.50, dinner $12.95-$22.75. Specializes in dry aged beef, fresh fish. Valet parking. Four-sided fireplace. Family-owned. Cr cds: A, C, D, DS, MC, V.

★ **LENHARDT'S.** *151 W McMillan St, I-71 exit 4, north of downtown.* 513/281-3600. Hrs: 11 am-9:30 pm; Sat from 4 pm. Closed Sun & Mon; July 4; also 1st 2 wks Aug, 2 wks at Christmas. Res accepted. German, Hungarian menu. Bar 7 pm-2 am, closed Sun. Semi-a la carte: lunch $3.75-$9.50, dinner $9.50-$18.95. Specialties:

Wienerschnitzel, sauerbraten, Hungarian goulash. Parking. Former Moerlin brewery mansion. Cr cds: A, DS, MC, V.

★ ★ ★ ★ **MAISONETTE.** *114 E 6th St, downtown.* 513/721-2260. Hrs: 11:30 am-2:30 pm, 6-10:30 pm; Mon from 6 pm; Sat 5:15-11 pm. Closed Sun; major hols. Res accepted. French cuisine. Bar. Wine cellar. A la carte entrees: lunch $9-$15, dinner $20.75-$32.75. Specialties: escalopes de foie gras, fresh imported French fish, seasonal offerings. Own pastries. Valet parking (dinner). Elegant dining. French decor. Family-owned. Jacket. Cr cds: A, C, D, DS, MC, V.

D

★ ★ **MONTGOMERY INN.** *9440 Montgomery Rd, north of downtown.* 513/791-3482. Hrs: 11 am-11 pm; Fri to midnight; Sat 4 pm-midnight. Closed major hols. Res accepted. Bar. A la carte entrees: lunch $3.75-$8.50, dinner $9.95-$19.95. Child's meals. Specializes in barbecued ribs, chicken. Parking. Family-owned. Cr cds: A, C, D, DS, MC, V.

D

★ ★ **MONTGOMERY INN BOATHOUSE.** *925 Eastern Ave, 1 mi E of Riverfront Stadium, on Mt Adams.* 513/721-7427. Hrs: 11 am-11 pm; Fri to midnight; Sun 3-10 pm. Closed major hols. Res accepted Sun-Fri. Bar. A la carte entrees: lunch $4.50-$15.95, dinner $9.95-$19.95. Child's meals. Specializes in barbecued ribs, seafood, chicken. Valet parking. Outdoor dining (in season). Unique circular building, located at the river; scenic view. Cr cds: A, DS, MC, V.

D

★ ★ ★ **ORCHID'S.** *(See Omni Netherland Plaza)* 513/421-1772. Hrs: 11 am-2 pm, 6-10 pm; Sat 6-11 pm; Sun 6-10 pm; Sun brunch 10 am-2 pm. Res accepted. Bar to 2 am; Sun 1 pm-midnight. Wine list. Semi-a la carte: lunch from $16.95. A la carte entree: dinner $17.95-$35.95. Sun brunch $19.95. Specializes in fresh seafood, veal, beef. Valet parking. Elegant atmosphere, art deco decor. Cr cds: A, C, D, DS, ER, JCB, MC, V.

D

★ ★ ★ ★ **THE PALACE.** *(See Cincinnatian Hotel)* 513/381-6006. Hrs: 6:30 am-2:30 pm, 6-10:30 pm; Sun to 9:30 pm; Sun brunch (Labor Day-Mother's Day) 10:30 am-2 pm. Res accepted. Bar 11-1 am; Fri, Sat to 2 am. Wine list. A la carte entrees: bkfst $5.75-$10.50, lunch $6.50-$13.95, dinner $15.50-$24.95. Sun brunch $18.95. Specializes in seafood, rack of lamb, steak, veal. Own baking. Pianist or vocalist (dinner). Valet parking. Elegant dining. Jacket. Cr cds: A, C, D, DS, JCB, MC, V.

D

★ **PETERSEN'S.** *1111 St Gregory, in Mt Adams.* 513/651-4777. Hrs: 11:30 am-11 pm; Fri & Sat to midnight; Sun brunch to 3 pm. Closed Mon; major hols. Wine. A la carte entrees: lunch $4.25-$9, dinner $5.25-$10.50. Specializes in black bean burrito, pasta, desserts. Cr cds: C, D, DS, MC, V.

D

★ ★ ★ **THE PHOENIX.** *812 Race St, downtown.* 513/721-2255. Hrs: 5-9 pm; Sat 5:30-10 pm. Closed Sun, Mon; major hols. Res required. Bar. Wine cellar. A la carte entrees: dinner $11.95-$17.95. Specializes in seafood, pasta, steak, lamb chops. Jazz trio Wed evenings. Valet parking. Formal dining. Built in 1893; white marble staircase, 12 German stained-glass windows from the 1880s, hand-carved library breakfront built on site in 1905. Cr cds: A, C, D, DS, MC, V.

D

★ ★ **PIGALLS CAFE.** *127 W 4th St, downtown.* 513/651-2233. Hrs: 11 am-2:30 pm, 5-10 pm; Fri to 11 pm; Sat 11:30 am-2:30 pm, 5-11 pm. Closed Sun; major hols. Italian, Amer menu. Semi-a la carte: lunch $6.95-$9.95, dinner $9.95-$19.95. Specialties: calypso coconut shrimp, fresh salmon croquettes, fresh seafood. Valet parking Fri, Sat. Bistro-style cafe with murals of Paris. Cr cds: A, C, D, DS, MC, V.

★ ★ ★ **THE PRECINCT.** *311 Delta Ave, east of downtown.* *513/321-5454.* Hrs: 5-10 pm; Fri, Sat to 11:30 pm. Closed some major hols. Res accepted. Bar 5 pm-2:30 am. Semi-a la carte: dinner $13.95-$24.95. Specializes in steak, fresh seafood. Own pastries. Entertainment. Valet parking. In 1890s police station. Cr cds: A, C, D, DS, MC, V.

D

✔★ **QUEEN CITY DINER.** *1203 Sycamore St, north of downtown.* *513/721-1212.* Hrs: 11:30 am-midnight; Fri, Sat to 1 am; Sun brunch 11:30 am-2:30 pm. Closed Dec 25. Bar. Semi-a la carte: lunch, dinner $4.50-$13.95. Sun brunch $4.50-$9.95. Child's meals. Specialties: Caribbean white crab chili, seafood Diablo, crab cakes. Parking. Outdoor dining. Nostalgic diner atmosphere. Cr cds: A, C, D, DS, MC, V.

D

★ ★ **WINDJAMMER.** *11330 Chester Rd (11330), north of downtown.* *513/771-3777.* Hrs: 11 am-2 pm, 5-10 pm; Fri to 11 pm; Sat 5-11 pm; Sun 5-9:30 pm. Res accepted. Bar. Semi-a la carte: lunch $3.95-$10, dinner $7.95-$21.95. Child's meals. Specializes in fresh fish, steak. Parking. Decor resembles 17th-century Spanish galleon; nautical antiques & memorabilia; aquariums. Cr cds: A, C, D, DS, MC, V.

D SC

★ **WINDOW GARDEN.** *3077 Harrison Ave, I-75 Harrison Ave exit, north of downtown.* *513/481-2743.* Hrs: 11 am-8 pm; Fri, Sat to 9 pm; Sun brunch to 2 pm. Closed Dec 25. Res accepted; required hols. Bar. Semi-a la carte: lunch $5-$7.75, dinner $7.95-$14.95. Sun brunch buffet $8.50. Child's meals. Parking. Cr cds: A, C, D, DS, MC, V.

SC

Unrated Dining Spots

AGLAMESIS BROS. *3046 Madison Rd, north of downtown.* *513/531-5196.* Hrs: 10 am-10 pm; Fri, Sat to 11 pm; Sun noon-10 pm. Closed Jan 1, Easter, Dec 25. Avg ck: $5.50. Specializes in homemade ice cream & candy. Old-time ice cream parlor; established 1908. Family-owned. Cr cds: MC, V.

DARCI'S. *7328 Kenwood Rd, north of downtown.* *513/793-2020.* Hrs: 7 am-10 pm; Fri, Sat to 11 pm. Closed Thanksgiving, Dec 25. French menu. Wine, beer. A la carte entrees: bkfst 89¢=$6.89, lunch, dinner $1.49-$12.99. Specializes in croissants, French delicatessen foods. Own baking. Cr cds: A, MC, V.

D

Cleveland

Founded: 1796	
Pop: 505,616	
Elev: 680 feet	
Time zone: Eastern	
Area code: 216	

When the Ohio Canal opened in 1832, it linked Cleveland with the Ohio and Mississippi rivers and initiated the growth of the frontier settlement into an industrial and commercial center for northern Ohio. The town prospered after becoming a thriving center for shipping and later railroads; by the mid-1800s, the new city had a population of 43,000.

By the time of the Civil War, Cleveland was in a position to take advantage of the accessibility of iron ore from the Lake Superior region and coal from Ohio and Pennsylvania. Its steel industry grew to meet the nation's needs for machinery, railroad equipment, farm implements, ships, stoves and hardware.

Just after the Civil War, Cleveland became the center of the oil industry in the United States. In 1870, Standard Oil began here, under the stewardship of John D. Rockefeller, Samuel Andrews and Henry Flagler. Corporate giants, such as industrialist Marcus Hanna, Jeptha H. Wade and the Van Sweringen brothers, also helped foster the industrial expansion and cultural growth of the city.

In the last decade, Cleveland has gone through an economic transformation after almost falling apart in the 1970s. The heavy industries slowed down after World War II, and total manufacturing in greater Cleveland declined by more than one-third between 1970 and 1985. The turnaround was led by Cleveland Tomorrow, a group of CEOs from the city's top 50 companies, who concentrated on improving such problems of the city as politics, labor relations and modernization of manufacturing technology.

The new economic progress led the way to a rebuilding of the "north coast city" centered around the $279-million Tower City Center project, an enormous retail and office complex created behind the Terminal Tower at Public Square. The once-industrial Flats in the Cuyahoga River Valley is now known as a main entertainment area, with restaurants and bars lining the river. The $65-million Nautica development on the river's west bank consists of restaurants, clubs, a boardwalk and amphitheater. North Coast Harbor will be the site of an ambitious, $900 million project that will develop several new museums, including the Rock-and-Roll Hall of Fame. The area is scheduled for completion sometime in the mid-1990s.

Business

Cleveland enjoys a strategic location for transportation and commerce. Its excellent harbors make it one of the busiest ports along the St Lawrence Seaway-Great Lakes system. It handles a significant volume of iron ore receipts for the entire Great Lakes region.

Greater Cleveland occupies less than 9 percent of Ohio's land area but has roughly one-sixth of the state's population. The Cleveland consolidated statistical area is one of the nation's largest consumer and industrial markets.

New-tech advances in manufacturing durable goods, defense hardware and aerospace and medical equipment are responsible for the new employment expansion and diversity here. The service sector is also growing, especially in the financial, legal and health care areas. The health care industry has become the number one employer in Cleveland, providing jobs for thousands of people.

People come from all over the US and many foreign countries to Cleveland Clinic, a pioneer and leader in kidney transplants and open-heart surgery. Cleveland's Case Western Reserve University School of Medicine boasts an innovative medical curriculum, and the University Hospitals complex is a world leader in medical research through direct application.

The Greater Cleveland area is one of the foremost in the country in the number and quality of educational institutions. It includes Cleveland State University, Case Western Reserve University, the Cleveland Institute of Art, Cleveland Institute of Music, Dyke, Cuyahoga Community College and Notre Dame and Ursuline colleges.

John Carroll University in University Heights (1890) and Baldwin-Wallace College in Berea (1845) are located within the county. Other nearby schools are Kent State University (1910) and Oberlin College (1833), the first coeducational institution of higher learning in the United States.

Convention Facilities

The Cleveland Convention Center is located in the heart of downtown Cleveland, within walking distance of major hotels, which have a combined room capacity of 2,300.

There are 379,000 square feet of exhibit space. The main arena can seat 10,000; the Music Hall 3,000; the Little Theater 605. There are 33 meeting rooms, each able to accommodate 100 persons or more, and a ballroom for 4,000.

The International Exposition Center (I-X Center), located next to Cleveland Hopkins International Airport, is the largest single-building exposition facility in the world. It offers 2.5 million square feet of indoor space with more than 70,000 square feet of conference area available.

In addition, Cleveland has 4 hotels capable of handling meetings of 1,000 or more: Sheraton-City Center, Holiday Inn-Lakeside, Stouffer Tower City Plaza and Marriott Society Center.

Sports and Recreation

Sports fans enjoy living in Cleveland, home of the Cleveland Indians baseball team, Cleveland Cavaliers basketball team, the Cleveland Browns football team and the Cleveland Crunch soccer team.

Within 45 minutes driving time of the city are 188 golf courses. There are two horse-racing tracks and two auto-racing tracks nearby.

Tennis is popular, and facilities are easily found. The Northeast Ohio Tennis Association has 40 member clubs. In addition, nearly every municipality in the greater Cleveland area has public courts. The Harold T. Clark Tennis Stadium, where major tournaments are held annually, is downtown.

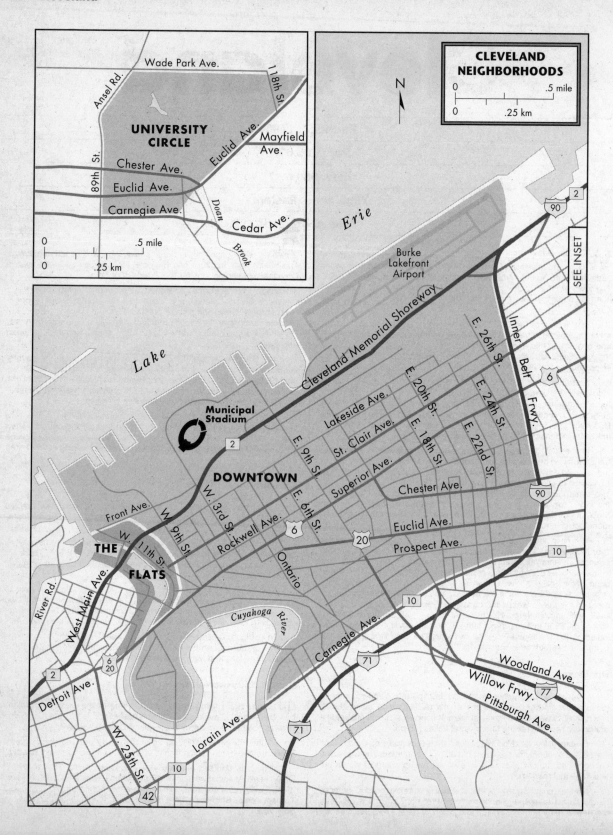

UNIVERSITY CIRCLE

Wade Park Ave.
Ansel Rd.
118th St.
Euclid Ave.
Mayfield Ave.
89th St.
Chester Ave.
Euclid Ave.
Carnegie Ave.
Cedar Ave.
Doan Brook

0   .5 mile
0   .25 km

CLEVELAND NEIGHBORHOODS

0   .5 mile
0   .25 km

N

SEE INSET

Erie
Lake

Burke Lakefront Airport

Cleveland Memorial Shoreway

Inner Belt Frwy.

E. 26th St.
E. 24th St.
E. 22nd St.
E. 20th St.
E. 18th St.

Municipal Stadium

Lakeside Ave.
St. Clair Ave.
Superior Ave.
Chester Ave.
Euclid Ave.
Prospect Ave.

DOWNTOWN

E. 9th St.
E. 6th St.

Front Ave.
W. 3rd St.
W. 9th St.
W. 11th St.
Rockwell Ave.
Ontario

THE FLATS

River Rd.
West Main Ave.
Detroit Ave.

Cuyahoga River

Carnegie Ave.

Woodland Ave.
Willow Frwy.
Pittsburgh Ave.

Lorain Ave.
W. 25th St.

Skiing is close at hand at Alpine Valley Ski Area in Chesterland. Other winter sports include tobogganing, skating and snowmobiling.

Entertainment

The Cleveland Orchestra, organized in 1918, brings outstanding guest soloists and conductors to perform at Severance Hall from mid-September to mid-May and presents summer concerts at Blossom Music Center, about 28 miles south of town.

Several theaters present varied programs of classical and contemporary drama, music and dance. One of the best-known of these is Karamu House and Theatre, also a center for arts and interracial communication. The Cleveland Play House is one of the oldest professional resident theaters in the country. The Front Row Theatre offers top-name Las Vegas-style performers year round.

Nightlife in Cleveland centers around Playhouse Square Center, three renovated motion picture palaces with a combined capacity larger than New York City's Lincoln Center. The Flats, along both sides of the Cuyahoga River, is also a favorite area for nightlife, with a variety of nightclubs and restaurants.

Historical Areas

Ohio City, west of downtown Cleveland and across the Cuyahoga River, is undergoing redevelopment. Settled shortly after Cleveland was founded, its homes are being renovated, and new shops and restaurants add to the charm of the "just like old" neighborhood.

The Dunham Tavern Museum (1830) has been preserved and houses period furnishings as well as other items from the 19th century. The tavern was originally a rest stop for the stagecoach that ran from Detroit to Buffalo.

A unique phase of history is preserved in the Dittrick Museum of Medical History, where thousands of objects relating to the history of medicine, dentistry, pharmacy and nursing are on display. There are exhibits on the development of medical concepts from ancient times to the 19th century and on the history of the X ray and microscopes; an 1880 doctor's office and a pre-Civil War pharmacy are re-created.

The Western Reserve Historical Society Museum and Library has pioneer, Native American and Shaker exhibits; it also includes the Crawford Auto-Aviation Museum, which has more than 175 classic and antique automobiles and historical exhibits. The museum also has original manuscripts dating back to the founding of Cleveland, including some of the records of the Connecticut Land Company.

Lawnfield, President John A. Garfield's house, is northeast in Mentor; his impressive tomb is in Lakeview Cemetery, along with John D. Rockefeller's monument.

Sightseeing

A good way to view the port of Cleveland and the Cuyahoga River is on a cruise aboard the *Goodtime III,* which operates from mid-June through September. Trolley Tours of Cleveland offers a 20-mile ride (1 or 2 hrs) covering 70 points of interest.

There are beautiful parks in Cleveland: Wade Park, with 88 acres, a lagoon, rose and herb gardens; Rockefeller Park with cultural gardens combining landscaping and sculpture of 22 nationalities; Gordon Park with 119 acres on the shore of Lake Erie; Brookside Park, which includes the Cleveland Metroparks Zoo; Sea World, the largest inland marine life park in the Midwest. Next door is Geauga Lake Park, with more than 50 amusement rides. Another amusement park, Cedar Point, is situated 55 miles west on the shores of Lake Erie.

For a change of pace, go back in time nearly 200 years to Hale Farm and Western Reserve Village in the heart of the beautiful Cuyahoga Valley National Recreation Area. The 19th-century village can be reached on weekends by a train pulled by an old-fashioned locomotive.

Located in University Circle are the Cleveland Museum of Art and the Cleveland Museum of Natural History. Nationally acclaimed, the Museum of Art houses extensive collections of medieval, Oriental and Renaissance art. The Museum of Natural History features exhibits of dinosaurs, mammals, birds and geological specimens.

General References

Founded: 1796 **Pop:** 505,616 **Elev:** 680 feet **Time zone:** Eastern **Area code:** 216

Phone Numbers

POLICE & FIRE: 911
FBI: 522-1400
POISON CONTROL CENTER: 231-4455
TIME & WEATHER: 931-1212

Information Sources

Convention and Visitors Bureau of Greater Cleveland, 3100 Tower City Center, 44113; 800/321-1004.
Greater Cleveland Growth Association, 200 Tower City, 44113; 621-3300.
Fun phone, 621-8860.
Department of Parks & Recreation, 664-2484.

Transportation

AIRLINES: Air Canada; American; Continental; Delta; Northwest; Southwest; TWA; United; USAir; and other commuter and regional airlines. For the most current airline schedules and information consult the *Official Airline Guide,* published twice monthly.
AIRPORTS: Cleveland Hopkins International, Cuyahoga County, 265-6000; Burke Lakefront, 781-6411.
CAR RENTAL AGENCIES: (See Toll-Free Numbers) Avis 265-3700; Budget 433-4433; Dollar 267-3133; Hertz 267-8900; National 267-0060; Thrifty 267-6811.
PUBLIC TRANSPORTATION: RTA 621-9500.

Newspaper

Cleveland Plain Dealer.

Convention Facilities

Cleveland Convention Center, 500 Lakeside Ave, 348-2200.
International Exposition Center, 6200 Riverside Dr, 676-6000.

Sports & Recreation

Major Sports Facilities
Cleveland Stadium, 1085 W 3rd St (Browns, football, 891-5000; Indians, baseball, 861-1200).
The Coliseum, 2923 Streetsboro Rd, Richfield (Cavaliers, basketball, 659-9100; Crunch, soccer, 349-2090).

Racetracks
Northfield Park Harness, 15 mi S, 10705 Northfield Rd (OH 8), Northfield, 467-4101.
Thistledown, 11 mi SE on Northfield Rd (OH 8), at Emery Rd in North Randall, 662-8600.

Cultural Facilities

Theaters
Beck Center for the Cultural Arts, 17801 Detroit Ave, Lakewood, 521-2540.
Cleveland Play House, 8500 Euclid Ave, 795-7000.

Karamu House and Theatre, 2355 E 89th St, 795-7070.
Ohio Theater, State Theater and Palace Theater, Playhouse Square Center, 1501 Euclid Ave, 771-4444.

Concert Halls

Convention Center, 500 Lakeside Ave, 348-2200.
Severance Hall, 11001 Euclid Ave, at East Blvd, 231-7300.

Museums

Cleveland Children's Museum, 10730 Euclid Ave, 791-KIDS.
Cleveland Health Education Museum, 8911 Euclid Ave, 231-5010.
Cleveland Museum of Natural History, Wade Oval Dr at University Circle, 231-4600.
Crawford Auto-Aviation Museum, 10825 East Blvd, at University Circle, 721-5722.
Dittrick Museum of Medical History, 11000 Euclid Ave, 368-3648.
Dunham Tavern Museum, 6709 Euclid Ave, 431-1060.
NASA Lewis Visitor Center, 21000 Brookpark Rd, 433-2001.
Shaker Historical Museum, 16740 S Park Blvd, Shaker Heights, 921-1201.
Western Reserve Historical Society Museum and Library, 10825 East Blvd, at University Circle, 721-5722.

Art Museums

Cleveland Museum of Art, 11150 East Blvd, 421-7340.
Temple Museum of Religious Art, 1855 Ansel Rd, 791-7755.

Points of Interest

Historical

Hale Farm and Western Reserve Village, 2686 Oak Hill, S on I-77 to Wheatley Rd in Bath, 666-3711.
Lake View Cemetery, 12316 Euclid Ave, 421-2665.
Lawnfield, 8095 Mentor Ave, 27 mi NE in Mentor, 255-8722.

Other Attractions

Alpine Valley Ski Area, 10620 Mayfield Rd, 30 mi E on US 322 in Chesterland, 285-2211.
The Arcade, 401 Euclid Ave, 621-8500.
Blossom Music Center, 1145 W Steels Corners Rd, about 28 mi S via US 422, OH 8 in Cuyahoga Falls, 566-8184 or 231-7300.
Cleveland Metroparks Zoo, 3900 Brookside Park Dr, 661-6500.
Cultural Gardens, Rockefeller Park, along East & Martin Luther King, Jr Blvds.
Cuyahoga Valley National Recreation Area, along the Cuyahoga River between Cleveland and Akron, 650-4636 or 524-1497.
Edgewater Park, West Blvd & Cleveland Memorial Shoreway, 881-8141.
Galleria, E 9th & St Clair, 621-9999.
Garden Center of Greater Cleveland, 11030 East Blvd, 721-1600.
Geauga Lake Park, 1060 Aurora Rd, in Aurora, 562-7131.
Gordon Park, E 72nd St & Cleveland Memorial Shoreway, 881-8141.

Lake Erie Nature and Science Center, 28728 Wolf Rd, 14 mi W on US 6 or I-90 to Bay Village, Metropark Huntington, 871-2900.
Public Square, Ontario St & Superior Ave.
Sea World, 1100 Sea World Dr, 23 mi SE on OH 43 in Aurora, 562-8101.
Shaker Lakes Regional Nature Center, 2600 S Park Blvd, 6 mi E on OH 87 in Shaker Heights, 321-5935.
USS COD (submarine), foot of E 9th St, 566-8770.
Wade Park, Euclid Ave near 107th St, at University Circle, 721-1600.

Sightseeing Tours

Goodtime III, pier at E 9th St, 861-5110.
North Coast Tours, 601 Rockwell Ave, 579-6160.
Trolley Tours of Cleveland, Burke Lakefront Airport, 771-4484.

Annual Events

Home and Flower Show, Cleveland Convention Center, 621-3145. Late Feb.
Greater Cleveland Auto Show, International Exposition Center. Late Feb-early Mar.
St Patrick's Day Parade, downtown. Mar 17.
Great American Rib Cook-Off, North Coast Harbor, 247-2722. May.
Boston Mills Art Festival, 467-2242. Late June-early July.
Riverfest, The Flats, 696-7700. Late July.
Cuyahoga County Fair, fairgrounds in Berea, 243-0090. Early or mid-Aug.
Cleveland Grand Prix, Burke Lakefront Airport, 781-3500. July
Slavic Village Harvest Festival, Slavic Village (Fleet Ave at E 55th St), 271-5591. Aug.
Cleveland National Air Show, Burke Lakefront Airport, 781-0747. Labor Day wkend.
Johnny Appleseed Festival, Mapleside Farms, in Brunswick, 225-5577. Sept.
Medieval Feasts & Spectacles, Trinity Cathedral, 579-9745. Dec.

City Neighborhoods

Many of the restaurants, unrated dining establishments and some lodgings listed under Cleveland include neighborhoods as well as exact street addresses. A map showing these neighborhoods can be found immediately following the city introduction. Geographic descriptions of these areas are given, followed by a table of restaurants arranged by neighborhoods.

Downtown: South of Lake Erie, west of I-90, north of Carnegie Ave and east of the Cuyahoga River. **South of Downtown:** South of OH 10. **West of Downtown:** West of Cuyahoga River.
The Flats: Area along both sides of the Cuyahoga River south of Front Ave and north of Superior Ave.
University Circle: East of Downtown; south of Wade Park Ave, west of Euclid Ave, north of Cedar Ave and east of E 89th St.

Lodgings and Food

CLEVELAND RESTAURANTS BY NEIGHBORHOOD AREAS

(For full description, see alphabetical listings under Restaurants)

DOWNTOWN

Alvie's. 2033 Ontario St

New York Spaghetti House. 2173 E 9th St

Piperade. 123 Prospect Ave NW

Sammy's. 1400 W 10th St

Sweetwater's Cafe Sausalito. 1301 E 9th St

Top of the Town. 100 Erieview Plaza

SOUTH OF DOWNTOWN

Johnny's Bar. 3164 Fulton Rd

WEST OF DOWNTOWN

Don's Lighthouse Grille. 8905 Lake Ave

Great Lakes Brewing Co. 2516 Market St

Heck's Cafe. 2927 Bridge Ave

THE FLATS

Watermark. 1250 Old River Rd

UNIVERSITY CIRCLE

Club Isabella. 2025 Abington

Guarino's. 12309 Mayfield Rd

That Place on Bellflower. 11401 Bellflower Rd

Note: *When a listing is located in a town that does not have its own city heading, it will appear under the city nearest to its location. In these cases, the address and town appear in parenthesis immediately following the name of the establishment.*

Motels

★ ★ **COMFORT INN.** *(17550 Rosbough Dr, Middleburg Heights 44130) Approx 12 mi S on I-71, exit 235. 216/234-3131; FAX 216/234-6111.* 136 rms, 3 story. S $54-$64; D $54-$69; each addl $5; under 18 free; wkend rates. Crib free. TV; cable. Pool. Complimentary continental bkfst. Restaurant nearby. Ck-out noon. Meeting rms. Valet serv. Sundries. Free airport transportation. Health club privileges. Cr cds: A, C, D, DS, ER, MC, V.

[D] [icons] SC

✔ ★ ★ **CROSS COUNTRY INN.** *(7233 Engle Rd, Middleburg Heights 44130) 15 mi S on I-71 exit 235. 216/243-2277; FAX 216/243-9852.* 112 rms, 2 story. S $35.99-$37.99; D $42.99-$46.99; each addl $7; under 18 free. Crib free. TV; cable. Heated pool. Complimentary coffee in lobby. Restaurant adj open 24 hrs. Ck-out noon. Meeting rm. Downhill ski 18 mi; x-country ski 5 mi. Cr cds: A, DS, MC, V.

[D] [icons] SC

★ ★ **FAIRFIELD INN BY MARRIOTT.** *(16644 Snow Rd, Brook Park 44142) S on I-90, W then S on I-71. 216/676-5200; FAX 216/676-5200, ext. 709.* 135 rms, 3 story. May-Aug: S $41.95-$45.95; D $48.95-$52.95; each addl $7; under 18 free; lower rates rest of yr. Crib free. TV; cable. Pool. Complimentary continental bkfst, coffee.

Ck-out noon. Meeting rms. Valet serv. Near Hopkins Intl Airport. Cr cds: A, D, DS, MC, V.

[D] [icons] SC

★ ★ **FAIRFIELD INN BY MARRIOTT-WILLOUGHBY.** *(35110 Maple Grove Rd, Willoughby 44094) 20 mi E on I-90, exit 189. 216/975-9922.* 134 rms, 3 story. June-Aug: S $60-$65; D $55-$65; each addl $10; lower rates rest of yr. Crib free. TV; cable. Heated pool. Complimentary continental bkfst. Restaurant opp 6 am-11 pm. Ck-out noon. Meeting rm. Health club privileges. Cr cds: A, C, D, DS, MC, V.

[D] [icons] SC

✔ ★ **RED ROOF INN.** *(17555 Bagley Rd, Middleburg Heights 44130) 12 mi SW via I-71 exit 235. 216/243-2441; FAX 216/243-2474.* 117 rms, 3 story. S $36.99-$42.99; D $45.99-$51.99; each addl $7; under 18 free. Crib free. Pet accepted. TV. Complimentary coffee. Restaurant nearby. Ck-out noon. Cr cds: A, C, D, DS, MC, V.

[D] [icons]

★ ★ **RESIDENCE INN BY MARRIOTT.** *(17525 Rosbough Dr, Middleburg Heights 44130) 16 mi S on I-71 exit 235. 216/234-6688; FAX 216/234-3459.* 104 kit. suites, 2 story. S, D $109-$150; wkend, wkly, monthly rates. Crib free. Pet accepted; $30 and $7 per day plus refundable deposit. TV; cable. Heated pool; whirlpool. Complimentary continental bkfst. Complimentary coffee in rms. Restaurant adj 6 am-midnight. Ck-out noon. Coin lndry. Valet serv. Sundries. Free airport transportation. Downhill ski 15 mi; x-country ski 5 mi. Lawn games. Many fireplaces. Picnic tables, grills. Cr cds: A, C, D, DS, JCB, MC, V.

[D] [icons] SC

Motor Hotels

★ ★ ★ **CLARION-EAST.** *35000 Curtis Blvd (44095), east of downtown. 216/953-8000; FAX 216/953-1706.* 115 rms, 5 story. Apr-Oct: S, D $76-$86; each addl $10; suites $95-$150; under 18 free; higher rates Dec 31; lower rates rest of yr. Crib free. TV; cable. Indoor pool; poolside serv. Restaurant 7 am-10 pm. Rm serv. Bar 2 pm-midnight; entertainment, dancing. Ck-out noon. Valet serv. Sundries. Airport transportation. Exercise equipt; weights, treadmill, sauna. Some bathrm phones; refrigerator, minibar in suites. Cr cds: A, C, D, DS, ER, JCB, MC, V.

[D] [icons] SC

★ ★ ★ **HARLEY HOTEL-EAST.** *(6051 SOM Center Rd, Willoughby 44094) At jct I-90 & OH 91. 216/944-4300; FAX 216/944-5344.* 146 rms, 2 story. S $88; D $96; each addl $8; suites $155; under 18 free; wkend plans. Crib free. TV; cable. 2 pools, 1 indoor; wading pool, poolside serv, lifeguard. Complimentary coffee. Restaurant 6:30 am-2:30 pm, 5-10 pm; Fri-Sun 7 am-11 pm. Bar 11:30-1 am, Fri & Sat to 1:30 am, Sun 1-10 pm. Ck-out 1 pm. Coin lndry. Meeting rms. Lighted tennis. Downhill ski 10 mi; x-country ski 1 mi. Exercise equipt; weights, bicycles, sauna. Lawn games. Some refrigerators. Cr cds: A, D, DS, MC, V.

[D] [icons] SC

★ ★ **HARLEY HOTEL-WEST.** *(17000 Bagley Rd, Middleburg Heights 44130) I-71 Bagley Rd exit. 216/243-5200; FAX 216/243-5240.* 220 rms, 2 story. S $82-$91; D $86-$98; each addl $10; suites $125-$195; under 18 free; wkend rates. Crib free. TV; cable. 2 pools, 1 indoor; wading pool, sauna, lifeguard. Restaurant 6:30 am-10 pm; Fri, Sat to 11 pm. Rm serv. Bar; entertainment, dancing Fri & Sat. Ck-out 1 pm. Coin lndry. Meeting rms. Bellhops. Valet serv. Sundries. Free airport transportation. Lawn games. Library. Cr cds: A, C, D, DS, MC, V.

[D] [icons] SC

★ ★ ★ **QUALITY INN EAST.** *(28600 Ridgehills Dr, Wickliffe 44092) E on I-90, exit 187 Bishop Rd. 216/585-0600; FAX 216/585-1911.* 100 rms, 3 story. S, D $58-$84; under 17 free. Crib free. TV; cable. Indoor pool. Restaurant 6:30 am-10 pm; Sat 7:30 am-10:30 pm; Sun from 8 am. Rm serv. Bar 4 pm-1 am, Sun 1 pm-midnight. Ck-out noon. Meeting rms. Valet serv. Sundries. Downhill ski 20 mi; x-country ski 5 mi. Exercise equipt; weights, bicycles, whirlpool, sauna. Cr cds: A, C, D, DS, ER, JCB, MC, V.

D ⊠ ⌖ ✕ ⊠ ⌗ SC

Hotels

★ ★ ★ **MARRIOTT AIRPORT.** *4277 W 150th St (44135), west of downtown.* 216/252-5333; FAX 216/251-1508. 375 rms, 4-9 story. S $110; D $120; each addl $10; suites $175-$350; under 18 free; wkend package. Crib free. Pet accepted; $50. TV; cable. Indoor pool; poolside serv, lifeguard. Restaurant 6 am-11 pm. Bar 11:30-2 am; dancing. Ck-out noon. Coin lndry. Convention facilities. Concierge. Gift shop. Free airport transportation. Exercise equipt; weights, bicycles, whirlpool, sauna. Rec rm. *LUXURY LEVEL:* **CONCIERGE FLOOR.** 51 rms. S, D $120. Private lounge, honor bar. Complimentary continental bkfst, refreshments. Cr cds: A, C, D, DS, ER, JCB, MC, V.

⌖ ⊠ ✕ ⊠ ⌗ SC

★ ★ ★ **MARRIOTT SOCIETY CENTER.** *127 Public Sq (44114), downtown.* 216/696-9200; FAX 216/696-0966. 400 rms, 25 story, 15 suites. S, D $129-$150; suites $250-$750; under 18 free. Crib free. Garage $12. TV; cable. Indoor pool. Restaurant 6 am-11 pm. Bar 11-2 am. Ck-out noon. Coin lndry. Convention facilities. Concierge. Gift shop. Exercise equipt; weight machine, treadmill, whirlpool, sauna. Minibars. *LUXURY LEVEL:* **CONCIERGE LEVEL.** 76 rms, 4 floors. S $140-$180; D $140-$190. Concierge. Private lounge, honor bar. Complimentary continental bkfst, refreshments, newspaper. Cr cds: A, C, D, DS, ER, JCB, MC, V.

D ⊠ ✕ ⊠ ⌗ SC

★ ★ ★ **OMNI INTERNATIONAL.** *2065 E 96th St (44106), at Carnegie, in University Circle area.* 216/791-1900; FAX 216/231-3329. 276 rms, 17 story. S $150; D $175; each addl $10; suites $225-$1,300; under 18 free. Crib free. TV; cable. Restaurant 6:30 am-11 pm. Bar 11-1 am; Sat, Sun from noon. Ck-out noon. Convention facilities. Gift shop. Entertainment in lobby. Health club privileges. *LUXURY LEVEL:* **PENTHOUSE.** 3 rms, 6 suites. S, D $400; suites $875-$1,300. Private lounges. Full wet bars. Bathrm phones. Some whirlpools. Complimentary refreshments. Cr cds: A, C, D, DS, MC, V.

D ⊠ ⌗ SC

★ ★ ★ **RADISSON PLAZA.** *1701 E 12th St (44114), downtown.* 216/523-8000; FAX 216/523-1698. 268 suites, 9 story. S, D $115-$165; under 18 free; wkend rates. Crib free. Pet accepted. Valet parking $10. TV; cable. Indoor pool. Complimentary coffee in rms. Restaurant 6:30 am-10 pm. Bar 11-1 am; entertainment. Ck-out noon. Coin lndry. Meeting rms. Concierge. Lighted tennis. Exercise rm; instructor, weights, bicycles, sauna. Minibars. Balconies. *LUXURY LEVEL:* **PLAZA CLUB.** 26 suites. S, D $150-$165. Private lounge, honor bar. Complimentary continental bkfst, refreshments. Cr cds: A, C, D, DS, ER, JCB, MC, V.

D ⌖ ⊠ ✕ ⊠ ⌗ SC

★ ★ ★ ★ **THE RITZ-CARLTON, CLEVELAND.** *1515 W Third St (44113), at Tower City Center, downtown.* 216/623-1300; FAX 216/623-0515. 208 rms, 7 story, 21 suites. S, D $135-$175; suites $350-$650; under 12 free; wkend rates. Valet parking (fee). TV; cable. Indoor pool; poolside serv, lifeguard. Restaurant 6:30-1 am. Rm serv 24 hrs. Bar 11:30-1 am; pianist. Ck-out noon. Meeting rms. Concierge. Gift shop. Airport transportation. Exercise rm; instructor, weight machine, bicycles, whirlpool, sauna. Masseuse. Bathrm phones, minibars. Overlooks Lake Erie. *LUXURY LEVEL:* **RITZ-CARLTON CLUB.** 52 rms, 8 suites. S, D $205-$270; suites $450-$2,000. Concierge. Private lounge, honor bar. In-rm whirlpool in suites. Complimentary continental bkfst, refreshments. Cr cds: A, C, D, DS, ER, JCB, MC, V.

D ⊠ ✕ ⊠ ⌗ SC

★ ★ ★ **SHERATON-CITY CENTER.** *777 St Clair Ave (44114), downtown.* 216/771-7600; FAX 216/566-0736. 475 rms, 22 story. S $129; D $139; each addl $10; suites $175-$850; under 18 free. Crib

free. Garage $9. TV; cable. Restaurant 6:30 am-11 pm. Bar 11-2:30 am, Sun from 1 pm. Ck-out noon. Convention facilities. Gift shop. Airport transportation. Exercise equipt; weight machine, bicycle. Many rms with view of lake. *LUXURY LEVEL:* **CLUB LEVEL.** 58 rms, 8 suites, 3 floors. S $149; D $169. Concierge. Private lounge. Complimentary continental bkfst, refreshments. Cr cds: A, C, D, DS, MC, V.

D ✕ ⊠ ⌗ SC

★ ★ ★ **STOUFFER RENAISSANCE.** *24 Public Square (44113), downtown.* 216/696-5600; FAX 216/696-3102. 491 rms, 14 story. S $99-$184; D $119-$204; each addl $20; suites $250-$1,500; under 18 free; wkend rates. Crib free. TV; cable. Indoor pool. Complimentary coffee. Restaurant 6:30 am-11 pm. Bar 11-2 am; entertainment. Ck-out 1 pm. Convention facilities. Concierge. Gift shop. Garage parking. Airport, RR station, bus depot transportation. Exercise equipt; weights, bicycles, sauna. Bathrm phones, refrigerators, minibars. 10 story indoor atrium. Shopping, downtown attractions nearby. *LUXURY LEVEL:* **CLUB FLOOR.** 100 rms, 8 suites, 2 floors. S $139-$184; D $139-$204; suites $400-$1,500. Private lounge. Minibar. Complimentary continental bkfst, evening refreshments. Cr cds: A, C, D, DS, ER, JCB, MC, V.

D ⊠ ✕ ⊠ ⌗ SC

Inn

★ ★ ★ **BARICELLI.** *2203 Cornell Rd (44106), at Cornell & Murray Hill, in University Circle area.* 216/791-6500; FAX 216/791-9131. 4 rms, 3 story, 3 suites. S, D $100-$130. TV; cable. Complimentary continental bkfst. Dining rm 5:30-10 pm; closed Sun. Ck-out 11 am, ck-in 2 pm. Airport, RR station, bus depot transportation. Antiques, stained glass. Brownstone (1900) with individually decorated rms. Cr cds: A, MC, V.

⊠ ⌗

Restaurants

★ **CLUB ISABELLA.** *2025 Abington, in University Circle area.* 216/229-1177. Hrs: 11:30 am-midnight; Fri to 1 am; Sat 5 pm-1 am. Res accepted; required wkends. Bar. Semi-a la carte: lunch $4.50-$7.95, dinner $5.95-$17.95. Entertainment. Valet parking (dinner). Outdoor dining. Former stagecoach house. Cr cds: A, D, MC, V.

★ ★ **DON'S LIGHTHOUSE GRILLE.** *8905 Lake Ave, west of downtown.* 216/961-6700. Hrs: 11:30 am-11 pm; Fri to midnight; Sat 5 pm-midnight; Sun 4:30-9 pm. Closed some major hols. Res accepted. Continental menu. Bar. Semi-a la carte: lunch $6.95-$9.95, dinner $10-$20. Specializes in fresh seafood, steaks. Valet parking. Outdoor dining. Contemporary bistro decor. Cr cds: A, C, D, MC, V.

D SC

✔★ ★ **GETTY'S WEST.** *(25651 Detroit Rd, Westlake) W via I-90 exit 161 to Detroit Rd.* 216/835-9332. Hrs: 11 am-2:30 pm, 5-11 pm; Fri, Sat to midnight; Sun 10 am-1 pm, 2-10 pm; early-bird dinner Sun-Thurs 4:30-6 pm. Res accepted. Continental menu. Bar noon-2:30 am. A la carte entrees: lunch $5.95-$8.95, dinner $5.95-$15.95. Child's meals. Specializes in fresh seafood, steak. Patio dining. Parking. Antique prints. Cr cds: A, D, DS, MC, V.

★ ★ **GREAT LAKES BREWING CO.** *2516 Market St, opp West Side Market, west of downtown.* 216/771-4404. Hrs: 11:30 am-midnight; Fri & Sat to 2 am; Sun 3-8 pm. Closed major hols. Res accepted. Bar. Semi-a la carte: lunch, dinner $6-$16. Child's meals. Specializes in crab cakes, fresh pasta, seafood, brew master's pie. Own beer. Outdoor dining. Located in historic 1860s brewery; turn-of-the-century pub atmosphere. Cr cds: A, C, D, MC, V.

✔★ ★ **GUARINO'S.** *12309 Mayfield Rd, in University Circle area.* 216/231-3100. Hrs: 11:30 am-10:30 pm; Thurs to 11 pm; Fri & Sat to 11:30 pm; Sun 1-8 pm. Closed major hols. Res accepted; required Fri, Sat. Italian, Amer menu. Bar. A la carte entrees: lunch $5.50-$8.50, dinner $9.50-$16. Child's meals. Specializes in Southern Italian cuisine. Valet parking. Outdoor dining. In heart of Little Italy; antiques. Cr cds: A, C, D, DS, MC, V.

★ ★ **HECK'S CAFE.** *2927 Bridge Ave, west of downtown. 216/861-5464.* Hrs: 11:30 am-11:30 pm; Fri, Sat to 12:30 am; Sun brunch 11 am-3 pm. Closed major hols. Res accepted. Semi-a la carte: lunch $3.95-$8.95, dinner $3.95-$18.95. Sun brunch $6.95-$9.95. Specializes in bouillabaisse, hamburgers. Outdoor dining. In historic 19th-century building. Cr cds: A, MC, V.

D

★ ★ **JOHNNY'S BAR.** *3164 Fulton Rd, south of downtown. 216/281-0055.* Hrs: 11 am-3 pm, 5-10 pm; Fri to 11 pm; Sat 5-11 pm. Closed Sun; most major hols. Res accepted; required Fri, Sat. Italian menu. Bar. Semi-a la carte: lunch $6-$10.50, dinner $16.95-$28.95. Specialties: "Italian Feast," veal chops. Outdoor dining. Former neighborhood grocery. Family-owned. Cr cds: A, D, MC, V.

★ **MILLER'S DINING ROOM.** *(16707 Detroit Ave, Lakewood 16707)* W on Detroit Ave. 216/221-5811. Hrs: 11 am-8 pm; Sun 11:30 am-7:30 pm. Closed Memorial Day, July 4, Labor Day. Res accepted. Bar. Complete meals: lunch $4.49-$7.25, dinner $8.50-$16.95. Child's meals. Specialties: chicken à la king in potato basket, sticky buns. Parking. Colonial decor. No cr cds accepted.

D

★ **NEW YORK SPAGHETTI HOUSE.** *2173 E 9th St, downtown. 216/696-6624.* Hrs: 11 am-10 pm; Fri, Sat to 10:30 pm; Sun 11:30 am-8 pm. Closed major hols. Res accepted. Italian, Amer menu. Bar. Semi-a la carte: lunch $6-$7, dinner $8-$18. Specializes in veal. Parking. Mural scenes of Italy. In former parsonage. Family-owned. Cr cds: A, DS, MC, V.

★ **PIER W.** *(12700 Lake Ave, Lakewood 12700)* W via Detroit Ave to Lake Ave. 216/228-2250. Hrs: 11:30 am-3 pm, 5:30-10 pm; Fri & Sat 5 pm-midnight; Sun 9:30 am-2:30 pm, 4:30-10 pm; Sun brunch to 2:30 pm. Closed Dec 25. Res accepted. Bar. Semi-a la carte: lunch $5.25-$9.95, dinner $8.95-$17.95. Sun brunch $13.95. Specializes in seafood. Own pastries. Entertainment Fri, Sat. Valet parking. Nautical decor. On water with view of Lake Erie, Cleveland skyline. Cr cds: A, C, D, DS, MC, V.

D

★ ★ **PIPERADE.** *123 Prospect Ave NW, downtown. 216/241-0010.* Hrs: 11:30 am-2:30 pm, 6-10 pm; Fri & Sat 5:30-11 pm. Closed major hols. Res accepted. Bar. Wine cellar. A la carte entrees: lunch $5.95-$11.95, dinner $15.95-$21.95. Specialties: tuna Piperade, smoked salmon with shallot vinaigrette. Valet parking. Outdoor dining. Modern European decor; ornate brass room dividers. Cr cds: A, D, MC, V.

D

★ ★ **SAMMY'S.** *1400 W 10th St, downtown. 216/523-5560.* Hrs: 11:30 am-2:30 pm, 5:30-10 pm; Fri, Sat to midnight. Closed Sun; major hols. Res accepted. Bar. Wine list. Semi-a la carte: lunch $6.95-

$13.95, dinner $19.95-$28.95. Child's meals. Specialties: boule de neige, fresh fish. Raw bar. Own baking. Entertainment exc Sun. Valet parking. In restored 1850 warehouse; view of Cuyahoga River and bridges. Jacket (dinner). Cr cds: A, C, D, DS, ER, JCB, MC, V.

D

★ ★ **SWEETWATER'S CAFE SAUSALITO.** *1301 E 9th St, in the Galleria at Erieview, downtown. 216/696-2233.* Hrs: 11:30 am-3 pm, 5-9 pm; Fri & Sat to 10 pm; Sun 11:30 am-2:30 pm. Closed Thanksgiving, Dec 25. Res accepted. Bar to midnight. Semi-a la carte: lunch $5.50-$10.95, dinner $6.95-$16.95. Sun brunch $12.95. Specialties: lobster, potato pierogi, fried okra, pasta. Pianist Fri, Sat (dinner). Valet parking. Dinner theater package. Cr cds: A, D, DS, MC, V.

D

✔ ★ **SZECHWAN GARDEN.** *(13800 Detroit Ave, Lakewood)* 6 mi W via US 20 to Detroit Ave. 216/226-1987. Hrs: 11:30 am-2:30 pm, 4:30-9:30 pm; Fri, Sat to 10:30 pm; Sun 4:30-9 pm. Closed Thanksgiving, Dec 25. Res accepted; required Fri, Sat. Chinese menu. Semi-a la carte: lunch $4.25-$5.25, dinner $6.95-$12.95. Specialties: "Happy Family" with shrimp, chicken and beef, cashew chicken. Parking. Cr cds: A, MC, V.

★ ★ **THAT PLACE ON BELLFLOWER.** *11401 Bellflower Rd, in University Circle area. 216/231-4469.* Hrs: 11:30 am-3 pm, 5:30-10 pm; Fri & Sat to 11 pm; Sun 5-8:30 pm. Closed Mon; major hols. Res accepted. Varied menu. Bar. Semi-a la carte: lunch $4.95-$6.95, dinner $10.95-$16.95. Child's meals. Specializes in beef Wellington, fresh salmon. Valet parking. Outdoor dining. Converted turn-of-the-century carriage house. Cr cds: A, D, MC, V.

★ ★ ★ **TOP OF THE TOWN.** *100 Erieview Plaza, downtown. 216/771-1600.* Hrs: 11:30 am-2:30 pm, 5:30-10 pm; Fri to 10:30 pm; Sat 5:30 pm-10:30 pm; Sun brunch 10:30 am-2:30 pm. Closed Dec 25. Res accepted. Continental menu. Bar to 11 pm; Fri, Sat to midnight. A la carte entrees: lunch $6.95-$12.50, dinner $14.95-$22.95. Sun brunch $14.95. Child's meals. Jazz duo Fri, Sat. Valet parking. View of city, Lake Erie. Jacket. Cr cds: A, C, D, DS, MC, V.

✔ ★ ★ **WATERMARK.** *1250 Old River Rd, in The Flats. 216/241-1600.* Hrs: 11:30 am-10 pm; Fri, Sat to midnight; Sun brunch 11 am-3 pm. Res accepted. Bar. Semi-a la carte: lunch, dinner $5.50-$16.95. Sun brunch $11.95. Child's meals. Specializes in marinated and mesquite-grilled seafood. Valet parking. Outdoor dining. Former ship provision warehouse on Cuyahoga River. Cr cds: A, C, D, DS, MC, V.

Unrated Dining Spot

ALVIE'S. *2033 Ontario St, downtown. 216/771-5322.* Hrs: 6:30 am-4 pm; Sat 9 am-3 pm. Closed Sun; major hols. Beer. Semi-a la carte: bkfst $2-$4, lunch $2-$5. Specializes in deli foods, salads. Own soups. Family-owned. No cr cds accepted.

D

Dallas

Founded: 1841

Pop: 1,006,887

Elev: 468 feet

Time zone: Central

Area code: 214

Fort Worth

Founded: 1849

Pop: 447,619

Elev: 670 feet

Time zone: Central

Area code: 817

While Texas is still often associated with oil, cities like Dallas and Fort Worth encourage their visitors to discover all aspects of these modern metropolises. With skyscrapers of glass and steel rising alongside oil derricks and aristocratic old houses, it is difficult to maintain an image of a Texas "cow town."

Dallas has become one of the Southwest's largest business and cultural centers. While the city houses the main offices of major oil companies, it is also one of the nation's top fashion centers and has emerged as an important location for the production of commercials and feature-length films. Dallas began as John Neely Bryan's trading post on the upper Trinity River in 1841. Two years later it acquired the name of Dallas. Bryan's customers were, for the most part, Caddo Indians. By 1890, however, Dallas was the largest city in Texas. It was eventually surpassed by Houston. In 1930 the discovery of a huge oil field southeast of the city brought great prosperity to the area.

While Dallas is sophisticated and fashionable, Fort Worth takes pride in being a warm and friendly progressive Western metropolis—a blending of cattle, oil, finance and manufacturing. Contrary to its name, Fort Worth was never a fort. Originally, it was a camp with a garrison to protect settlers from marauding Indians. After the Civil War, great herds of longhorn cattle were driven through the area en route to the Kansas railheads. Camping outside of town, cowboys came into Fort Worth at night to carouse. The citizens of the town desperately wanted a peaceful, prosperous city, which they believed could be achieved by the building of a railroad that would link the town to the East. In July of 1876, this was finally accomplished, and Fort Worth became a shipping point. It would, however, remain a part of the "wild West" for decades to come.

During World War II both Dallas and Fort Worth grew in population and wealth from defense and aircraft industries. The area also became a leading producer of electronic equipment. There has always been a friendly rivalry between the two cities, but economic and planning cooperation has resulted in benefits to both.

Business

Dallas ranks high as a business and industrial center. There are 200 planned industrial districts in Dallas. It is the home office for 250 insurance companies and many major oil companies. It is one of the major fashion markets in the United States and one of the nation's leading exporters in the cotton market.

In Fort Worth the largest segment of employment is in the defense and transportation industries, with American Airlines and General Dynamics heading the list. More than 1,500 manufacturing firms are located within the city limits.

Nearly one-fourth of all Texans live in this metropolitan area, and more than one-sixth of all nonfarm jobs are here. Thirty percent of all Texas bank deposits are in Dallas/Fort Worth.

Dallas and Fort Worth are easily accessible—with more than a dozen major highways leading to each city, two transcontinental bus lines, Amtrak service and the airport with its 13 major airlines and several commuter airlines. Flights connect with most of the principal

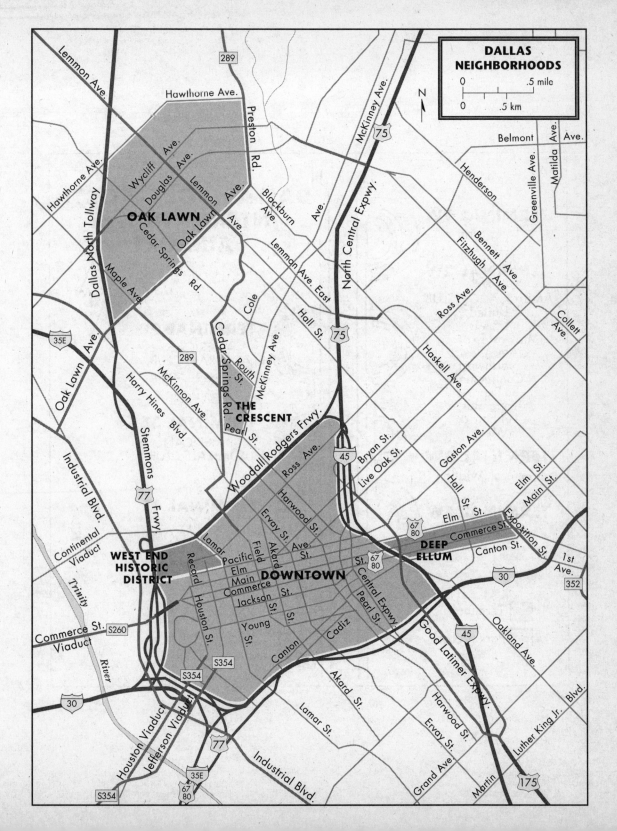

DALLAS NEIGHBORHOODS

0 .5 mile
0 .5 km

OAK LAWN

THE CRESCENT

DOWNTOWN

WEST END HISTORIC DISTRICT

DEEP ELLUM

TERMINAL 1W
Long Term
Parking

TERMINAL 2W
TWA
AMBASSADOR CLUB,
United,
US Air,
Midwest Express,
Am. West,
Northwest,
Continental,
Exec Express II,
Lone Star,
Lufthansa,
Mesa

TERMINAL 3W
General Aviation

TERMINAL 4W
Long Term
Parking

Terminals
Parking Lot

DALLAS/FORT WORTH INTERNATIONAL AIRPORT

N
W　E
S

TERMINAL 2E
AMERICAN
ADMIRALS CLUB,
American Eagle

TERMINAL 3E
AMERICAN
ADMIRALS CLUB

TERMINAL 4E
DELTA
CROWN ROOM,
British Airways,
Atlantic Southeast

TERMINAL 5E
Long Term
Parking

cities in the United States, Mexico and most major airports of the world. The Dallas-Fort Worth International Airport boasts that it is the largest in the world, covering 18,000 acres. It is bigger than JFK, O'Hare and Los Angeles airports combined; it is, in fact, bigger than the whole island of Manhattan.

Convention Facilities

There are five major centers for conventions, trade shows and exhibitions in the Dallas/Fort Worth area.

Dallas Market Center Complex, within minutes of downtown Dallas, comprises three major areas: Market Hall, with 202,000 square feet of exhibit space; Apparel Mart, with 111,000 square feet of exhibit space; and Infomart, a unique, full-service convention facility with more than 290,000 square feet of exhibit space, 35 meeting rooms, a 510-seat theater and two 500-seat conference rooms. Flexible meeting space is available. The complex has 10,000 parking spaces.

The Dallas Convention Center has more than 600,000 square feet of exhibit space total, with 306,250 square feet in one open area. Construction is underway that will expand the center to more than 800,000 square feet by 1994; a heliport—the largest elevated urban port ever built—is also being added. There are 63 meeting rooms. The main exhibit hall can seat 39,600 people; the arena can hold more than 25,000; and the theater has seating for 1,770. The Parquet Ballroom can be used for banquets of up to 3,000 people. A 1,000-seat cafeteria-dining room is located off the main lobby. Inside parking is available for 1,107 cars.

Fair Park Dallas has 330,000 square feet of exhibit space among its 7 exhibit halls. Parking is available for 9,000 cars.

In downtown Fort Worth, the Tarrant County Convention Center covers 10 city blocks. The center contains more than 200,000 square feet of exhibit space with seating for 14,000. There are 2 exhibit halls and 25 meeting rooms for groups of 22 to 1,100 people. The theater offers seating for 3,000, and there is an 800-car garage.

The Will Rogers Memorial Center in Fort Worth's Amon Carter Square has a 100,000-square-foot exhibit hall, a 2,964-seat auditorium and a 9,467-seat arena, where the "world's largest and oldest indoor rodeo" is held each year. The center has added a 10-acre equestrian center with a 2,000-seat arena and 10,000 square feet of exhibit space along with an 800-car garage. Also at the center is Casa Mañana, America's first permanent musical-arena theater.

Sports and Recreation

Dallas covers the field with professional sporting events. The season begins with baseball in April for the Texas Rangers in Arlington. The Dallas Cowboys supply the fun and excitement of football for the Texas fans, and the Dallas Mavericks take the crowds to court with basketball.

Entertainment

The countless opportunities for entertainment in these two cities range from ballet and opera to amusement parks. At the Morton H. Meyerson Symphony Center patrons listen to the Dallas Symphony Orchestra. The Dallas Theater Center, designed by Frank Lloyd Wright, is a magnificent building that houses two theaters. Works by Shakespeare as well as modern plays are enjoyed here.

Family entertainment can be found at the Dallas Zoo, the Dallas Aquarium or at the many museums in the area. Six Flags Over Texas is a theme park with more than 100 rides, shows and attractions, including musical shows, a 300-foot-high oil derrick and strolling entertainers.

There are numerous music clubs, large and small, where visitors enjoy the quiet sound of a piano or a small combo. Many of these are along McKinney Avenue, Lovers Lane, Greenville Avenue and Lemmon Avenue in Dallas. Dallas Alley, in the West End MarketPlace, and Deep Ellum also offer an eclectic mix of music in its nightclubs.

Historical Areas

The once-elegant streets, still lined with huge trees, of two areas called Old East Dallas and the Oak Cliff Historic District are currently undergoing extensive restoration. Between 1890 and 1930 many fine houses were built in these areas for the cultural, social and political elite of the city. The craftsmanship was excellent, and the architectural styles were individualistic and interesting. They will soon be the showplaces they were years ago.

The west end of downtown Dallas has been declared a historical district. The 1916 Union Station has been restored to its original beaux-arts style. Located at 400 South Houston Street in the southwest sector of downtown Dallas, the station offers Amtrak passenger service, a visitor information center and a restaurant complex. At the West End MarketPlace are more than 100 merchants in a renovated candy and cracker factory—Texas' first festival market.

The Swiss Avenue Historic District, now listed in the National Register of Historic Places, is another "museum" of early 20th-century architecture.

In Old City Park, near downtown Dallas, the Dallas County Heritage Society has established a heritage center to illustrate the development of Dallas from the 1840s to modern days. Millermore, an elegant antebellum house, has been placed there and furnished with period pieces. Two log structures are nearby. Other structures have been moved to the area to demonstrate visually how early pioneers lived. The 37 Old City Park buildings contain an impressive collection of 19th-century crafts and furniture.

The historic Fort Worth Stockyards area is now a district of renovated buildings housing retail and dining establishments; the Tarantula, a restored steam train, travels between the Stockyards District and the city's south side.

Only five minutes from Fort Worth's central business district is Ryan Place. Here too are wide, tree-shaded streets and stately Victorian houses. The residents of the area squelched plans a few years ago to raze these structures to make room for more highways to the suburbs, and they have worked together to preserve and beautify the neighborhood.

Adjacent to Forest and Trinity parks are the Log Cabin Village and the Van Zandt Cottage. This area consists of original dwellings circa 1850. Van Zandt Cottage, once used as a stopping place by both stagecoach passengers and cattlemen, is now restored and furnished with antiques in the same period.

Sightseeing

There are several lakes in the countryside surrounding metropolitan Dallas/Fort Worth with facilities for swimming, boating, fishing, camping and picnicking. An exceptionally lovely drive in Fort Worth can be taken through Trinity and Forest parks on the Clear Fork of the Trinity River.

Unusual for a city the size of Fort Worth, there is a unique museum complex within a four-square-block area. The Kimbell Art Museum features works of art from all periods in history; the Amon Carter Museum exhibits works of Remington and Russell; the Modern Art Museum of Fort Worth presents contemporary artworks; and the Fort Worth Museum of Science and History is the largest educational museum for children in the country, offering natural history displays and a planetarium.

Visitors are treated to a unique change of scenery while strolling through downtown Fort Worth. The Fort Worth Water Garden Park offers three distinct areas comprised of water falls and sprays blended with beautiful, grassy areas.

Another group of attractions is located three miles east of downtown at Fair Park Dallas, including the Age of Steam Railroad Museum, Cotton Bowl, Hall of State and the Dallas Museum of Natural History. A Shakespeare festival is held in the bandstand. There is a garden center, and the midway is open during the state fair in October.

General References
Dallas

Founded: 1841 **Pop:** 1,006,887 **Elev:** 468 feet **Time zone:** Central **Area code:** 214

Phone Numbers

POLICE & FIRE: 911
FBI: 720-2200
POISON CONTROL CENTER: 590-5000
TIME: 844-6611 **WEATHER:** 787-1111

Information Sources

Dallas Convention and Visitors Bureau, 1201 Elm St, 75270; 746-6679.
Dallas Convention Center, 650 S Griffin, 75202; 658-7000.
Park & Recreation Department, 670-8281.

Transportation

AIRLINES: American; British Airways; Continental; Delta; Lufthansa (Germany); Mexicana; Northwest; TWA; United; USAir; and other commuter and regional airlines. For the most recent airline schedules and information consult the *Official Airline Guide,* published twice monthly.
AIRPORTS: Dallas-Fort Worth, 574-8888; Love Field, 670-6080.
CAR RENTAL AGENCIES: (See Toll-Free Numbers) Avis 574-4110; Budget 574-2121; Hertz 453-0370; National 574-3400.
PUBLIC TRANSPORTATION: Dallas Area Rapid Transit (DART), 979-1111.
RAILROAD PASSENGER SERVICE: Amtrak 800/872-7245.

Newspaper

Dallas Morning News

Convention Facilities

Dallas Convention Center, 650 S Griffin St, 939-2700.
Dallas Market Center, 2100 Stemmons Frwy, 655-6100.
Fair Park Dallas, 2 mi E of downtown via I-30, 670-8400.

Sports & Recreation

Arlington Stadium, W of jct TX 360, Dallas-Ft Worth Tpke (Texas Rangers, baseball, 817/273-5100).
Cotton Bowl, Fair Park Dallas, 638-BOWL.
Dallas Convention Center, 650 S Griffin St, 939-2700.
Fair Park Dallas, Parry & 2nd Ave, 670-8400.
Reunion Arena, 777 Sports St, (Mavericks, basketball, 939-2712; Stars, hockey, GO-STARS).
Texas Stadium, TX 183 & Loop 12, 438-7676 (Cowboys, football, 579-5000).

Cultural Facilities

Theaters
Bob Hope Theatre, Southern Methodist University, 768-ARTS.
Convention Center Theater, 650 S Griffin, 939-2700.
Kalita Humphries Theater, 3636 Turtle Creek Blvd, 526-8857.
Margo Jones Theatre, Southern Methodist University, 768-ARTS.
Morton H. Meyerson Symphony Center (Dallas Symphony), Pearl & Flora Sts, 692-0203.
Music Hall, Fair Park Dallas, 565-1116.
Theatre Three, 2800 Routh St, 871-3300.

Museums
Age of Steam Railroad Museum, Fair Park Dallas, 428-0101.
Dallas Museum of Natural History, Cullum Blvd & Grand Ave, Fair Park Dallas, 421-DINO.
Hall of State, Fair Park Dallas, 421-4500.
The Science Place, 1318 2nd Ave, Fair Park Dallas, 428-5555.
Telephone Pioneer Museum of Texas, 1 Bell Plaza, Akard & Commerce Sts, 2nd floor, 464-4359.

Art Museums
Biblical Arts Center, 7500 Park Lane at Boedeker, 691-4661.
Dallas Museum of Art, 1717 Harwood St, 922-1200.
Meadows Museum, Southern Methodist University, 768-2516.

Points of Interest

Historical
John Neely Bryan Cabin, Main, Elm & Market Sts.
Old City Park (Dallas County Heritage Society), Gano & Harwood Sts, 421-5141.

Other Attractions
Dallas Aquarium, 1st Ave & M.L. King Jr Blvd, Fair Park Dallas, 670-8443.
Dallas Arboretum and Botanical Gardens, 8525 Garland Rd, 327-8263.
Dallas Civic Garden Center, 2nd Ave & M.L. King Jr Blvd, Fair Park Dallas, 428-7476.
Dallas Market Center Complex, 2100 Stemmons Frwy, 655-6100.
Dallas Zoo, 621 E Clarendon Dr, 946-5154.
Fair Park Dallas, 2 mi E of downtown via I-30, 670-8400.
J.F. Kennedy Memorial Plaza, Main, Commerce & Market Sts.
Kennedy Historical Exhibit, The Sixth Floor, 411 Elm St, 653-6666.
Mesquite Rodeo, 6½ mi E at jct I-635 & Military Pkwy, in Mesquite, 285-8777.
Observation Deck, Hyatt Regency Reunion Tower, 300 Reunion Blvd, 741-3663.
Six Flags Over Texas, 16 mi W, at jct TX 360 & I-30 in Arlington, 817/640-8900.

Sightseeing Tour

Gray Line bus tours, PO Box 1769, 75221; 824-2424.

Annual Events

Cotton Bowl Festival. New Year's Day & preceding wk.
Byron Nelson Golf Classic, Four Seasons Club Resort. May.
State Fair of Texas, Fair Park Dallas, 565-9931. Sept 30-Oct 23.

Fort Worth

Founded: 1849 **Pop:** 447,619 **Elev:** 670 feet **Time zone:** Central **Area code:** 817

Phone Numbers

POLICE & FIRE: 911
FBI: 336-7135
POISON CONTROL CENTER: 214/590-5000
TIME: 844-6611 **WEATHER:** 429-2631

Information Sources

Fort Worth Convention & Visitors Bureau, 415 Throckmorton, 76102; 336-8791 or 800/433-5747.
Dept of Parks & Recreation, 871-5700.

Transportation

AIRPORTS: Dallas-Fort Worth, 214/574-8888; Meacham Field, 871-5400. See Dallas.
CAR RENTAL AGENCIES: (See Toll-Free Numbers) Avis 214/574-4110; Budget 214/574-2121; Hertz 214/453-0370; National 214/574-3400.
PUBLIC TRANSPORTATION: Transportation Authority of Fort Worth, 871-6200.
RAILROAD PASSENGER SERVICE: Amtrak 800/872-7245.

Newspaper

Fort Worth Star-Telegram.

Convention Facilities

Fort Worth/Tarrant County Convention Center, 1111 Houston St, 884-2222.
Will Rogers Memorial Center, 3401 W Lancaster St, 871-8150.

Sports & Recreation

Arlington Stadium, I-30, near jct TX 360, Dallas-Ft Worth Tpke, Arlington (Texas Rangers, baseball, 273-5100).

Racetrack

Texas Raceway, S New Hope Rd, Kennedale, 483-0356 (car racing).

Cultural Facilities

Theaters

Casa Mañana, 3101 W Lancaster Ave, 332-CASA.
Circle Theatre, 230 W 4th St, 877-3040.
Hip Pocket Theatre, 1620 Las Vegas Trail N, 927-2833.
Omni Theater, Ft Worth Museum of Science & History, 732-1631.
Stage West Dinner Theater, 3055 S University, 784-9378.
William Edrington Scott Theater, 3505 W Lancaster Ave, 738-6509.

Concert Halls

Fort Worth/Tarrant County Convention Center Theatre, 1111 Houston St, 884-2222.
Will Rogers Auditorium, 3401 W Lancaster, 332-0909.

Museums

Cattlemen's Museum, 1301 W 7th St, 332-7064.
Fort Worth Museum of Science and History, 1501 Montgomery St, 732-1631.
Palace of Wax/Ripley's Believe It or Not, 601 E Safari Pkwy, off I-30, in Grand Prairie, 214/263-2391.
Pate Museum of Transportation, 14 mi S on US 377, near Cresson, 332-1161.

Art Museums

Amon Carter Museum, 3501 Camp Bowie Blvd, 738-1933.
Kimbell Art Museum, 3333 Camp Bowie Blvd, 332-8451.
Modern Art Museum of Fort Worth, 1309 Montgomery St, at Camp Bowie Blvd, 738-9215.
Sid Richardson Collection of Western Art, 309 Main St, 332-6554.

Points of Interest

Historical

Fort Worth Stockyards National Historic District, E Exchange & N Main Sts, 625-7245.
Log Cabin Village, Log Cabin Village Ln at South University Dr, 926-5881.
Thistle Hill, 1509 Pennsylvania Ave, 336-1212.

Other Attractions

Billy Bob's Texas (country & western bar), 2520 Rodeo Plaza, Fort Worth Stockyards, 624-7117.
Botanic Garden, 3220 Botanic Garden Blvd, 871-7686.
Fort Worth Japanese Garden, Botanic Gardens.
Fort Worth Nature Center & Refuge, 9 mi NW via TX 199 to Buffalo Rd, 237-1112.
Fort Worth Stockyards National Historic District, E Exchange & N Main Sts, 625-7245.
Fort Worth Zoo, 1989 Colonial Pkwy, in Forest Park, 871-7050.
Noble Planetarium, adj Fort Worth Museum of Science & History, 732-1631.
Six Flags Over Texas, 16 mi E on I-30, just W of jct TX 360, I-30, 640-8900.
Water Garden, downtown Fort Worth.
Will Rogers Memorial Center, 3401 W Lancaster St, 871-8150.

Annual Events

Southwestern Exposition and Livestock Show. Mid-Jan-early Feb.
Chisholm Trail Roundup, Fort Worth Stockyards. Early June.
Pioneer Days. Wkend late Sept.

City Neighborhoods

Many of the restaurants, unrated dining establishments and some lodgings listed under Dallas and Fort Worth include neighborhoods as well as exact street addresses. A map showing Dallas neighborhoods can be found immediately following the city introduction. Geographic descriptions of neighborhoods in both cities are given, followed by a table of restaurants, arranged by neighborhood.

Dallas

The Crescent: North of Downtown; bounded by Cedar Springs Rd, Maple Ave, McKinney Ave and Pearl St; also Routh St between Cedar Springs Rd and McKinney Ave.
Deep Ellum: East of Downtown; south of Elm St, west of Exposition St, north of Canton St and east of I-45.
Downtown: South of Woodall Rodgers Frwy, west of I-45, north of I-30 and east of I-35E (US 77). **North of Downtown:** North of Woodall Rodgers Frwy.
Oak Lawn: North of Downtown; along Oak Lawn Ave between Hawthorne and Maple Aves; also along Lemon Ave between Oak Lawn Ave and Dallas North Tollway.
West End Historic District: Area of Downtown south of McKinney Ave, west of Lamar St, north of Pacific Ave and east of Record St and railroad tracks.

Fort Worth

Downtown: South of Heritage Park, west of I-35W and the railroad yards, north of Lancaster Ave and east of Henderson Ave (TX 199). **North of Downtown:** North of TX 199 & US 377. **South of Downtown:** South of I-30. **West of Downtown:** West of Trinity River.
Museum/Cultural District: South of Camp Bowie Blvd, west of University Dr, north of Crestline St and east of Montgomery St; particularly along Lancaster Ave.

Lodgings and Food Dallas

DALLAS RESTAURANTS
BY NEIGHBORHOOD AREAS

(For full description, see alphabetical listings under Restaurants)

DEEP ELLUM

Osteria Da Momo. 2704 Elm St

DOWNTOWN

650 North (Plaza Of The Americas Hotel). 650 N Pearl St

Dakota's. 600 N Akard St

French Room (The Adolphus Hotel). 1321 Commerce St

Lombardi's. 311 N Market

Pyramid Room (Fairmont Hotel). 1717 N Akard St

NORTH OF DOWNTOWN

Adelmo's. 4537 Cole Ave

Alessio's. 4117 Lomo Alto

Arthur's. 1000 Campbell Center

Athenee Cafe. 5365 Spring Valley #150

Baby Routh. 2708 Routh St

Blue Mesa Grill. 5100 Belt Line Rd

Cafe Pacific. 24 Highland Park Village

Capriccio. McKinney Ave at Fairmount St

Celebration. 4503 W Lovers Lane

Chaplin's. 1928 Greenville Ave

Chez Gerard. 4444 McKinney Ave

Chimney. 9739 N Central Expy

Del Frisco's. 5251 Spring Valley Rd

The Enclave. 8325 Walnut Hill

Highland Park Cafeteria. 4611 Cole St

J Pepe's. 2800 Routh St

Javier's. 4912 Cole Ave

Jennivine. 3605 McKinney Ave

Juniper. 2917 Fairmount St

L'Ancestral. 4514 Travis #124

La Trattoria Lombardi. 2916 N Hall St

Luby's Cafeteria. 10425 N Central Expy

Mansion On Turtle Creek (Mansion On Turtle Creek Hotel). 2821 Turtle Creek Blvd

Mario's Chiquita. 4514 Travis #105

Patrizio. 25 Highland Park Village

Riviera. 7709 Inwood Rd

Royal Tokyo. 7525 Greenville Ave

Thai Taste. 4501 Cole Ave

Uncle Tai's. 13350 Dallas Pkwy

White Swan Cafe. 6334 La Vista

OAK LAWN

Old Warsaw. 2610 Maple Ave

WEST END HISTORIC DISTRICT

Morton's Of Chicago. 501 Elm St

Newport's Seafood. 703 McKinney Ave

Note: *When a listing is located in a town that does not have its own city heading, it will appear under the city nearest to its location. In these cases, the address and town appear in parenthesis immediately following the name of the establishment.*

Motels

(Rates may be higher during State Fair, Cotton Bowl, Texas/OU wkend and city-wide conventions. Most accommodations near Six Flags Over Texas have higher rates when the park is open daily.)

✔★ ★ **BEST WESTERN-OAKTREE INN.** 13333 N Stemmons Frwy (75234), north of downtown. 214/241-8521; FAX 214/243-4103. 186 rms, 2 story. S, D $46.95-$56.95; each addl $5; under 12 free; wkend, sports rates. Pet accepted; $10. TV; cable. Pool; sauna. Complimentary full bkfst. Restaurant 6:30 am-10 pm; hrs vary Sat, Sun. Rm serv. Bar noon-11 pm. Ck-out noon. Coin lndry. Meeting rms. Valet serv. Airport transportation. Health club privileges. Cr cds: A, C, D, DS, ER, MC, V.

⊘ ≈ ⊀ ⚒ SC

✔★ ★ **CLASSIC MOTOR INN.** 9229 Carpenter Frwy (75247), north of downtown. 214/631-6633; res: 800/662-7437; FAX 214/631-6616. 135 rms, 2 story. S $39-$44; D $45; each addl $5; suites $64. Crib free. TV; cable. Pool. Complimentary continental bkfst. Restaurant adj. Ck-out noon. Coin lndry. Meeting rms. Valet serv. Exercise equipt; weights, bicycles, sauna. Bathrm phones; some refrigerators. Cr cds: A, C, D, DS, MC, V.

D ≈ ⊀ ⊘ ⚒ SC

★ ★ **COURTYARD BY MARRIOTT.** 2383 Stemmons Trail (75220), 8 mi N on I-35 E, Northwest Hwy exit 436, north of downtown. 214/352-7676; FAX 214/352-4914. 146 rms, 3 story. S $74; D $84; suites $89-$99; under 12 free; wkly, wkend rates. Crib free. TV; cable. Heated pool. Complimentary coffee in rms. Bkfst avail. Bar 4-11 pm. Ck-out 1 pm. Coin lndry. Meeting rms. Valet serv. Sundries. Exercise equipt; weight machine, bicycles, whirlpool. Refrigerators avail. Cr cds: A, C, D, DS, MC, V.

D ≈ ⊀ ⊘ ⚒ SC

★ ★ **DRURY INN-NORTH.** 2421 Walnut Hill (75229), north of downtown. 214/484-3330; FAX 214/484-3330, ext. 473. 130 rms, 4 story. S $60-$65; D $70-$75; each addl $10; under 18 free. Crib free. TV; cable. Pool. Complimentary bkfst, coffee. Restaurant adj open 24 hrs. Ck-out noon. Meeting rms. Sundries. Cr cds: A, C, D, DS, MC, V.

D ⊘ ≈ ⊘ ⚒ SC

★ **HAMPTON INN.** 4154 Preferred Place (75237), south of downtown. 214/298-4747; FAX 214/283-1305. 119 rms, 2 story. June-Sept: S $57-$63; D $57-$63; family, wkly, wkend & hol rates; higher rates auto races (Oct); lower rates rest of yr. Crib free. TV; cable. Complimentary continental bkfst, coffee. Restaurant nearby. Ck-out noon. Coin lndry. Meeting rms. Valet serv. Sundries. Cr cds: A, C, D, DS, ER, JCB, MC, V.

D ≈ ⊘ ⚒ SC

✔★ ★ **HAMPTON INN-GARLAND.** 12670 E Northwest Hwy (75228), I-635 exit 11B, north of downtown. 214/613-5000; FAX 214/613-4535. 126 rms, 3 story. S $47-$49; D $49-$55; under 18 free. Crib free. Pet accepted, some restrictions. TV; cable. Pool. Complimentary continental bkfst, coffee. Restaurant opp 11-2 am. Ck-out noon. Meeting rm. Valet serv. Health club privileges. Cr cds: A, C, D, DS, ER, MC, V.

D ✆ ⩰ ⅀ 🔥 SC

★ **LA QUINTA INN.** 8303 E RL Thornton Frwy (I-30) (75228), I-30 exit Jim Miller, east of downtown. 214/324-3731; FAX 214/324-1652. 102 rms, 2 story. Mar-Oct: S $45-$59; D $52-$66; each addl $7; under 18 free; higher rates wkends; lower rates rest of yr. Crib free. Pet accepted, some restrictions. TV; cable. Pool. Complimentary continental bkfst. Restaurant adj 6 am-midnight. Ck-out noon. Sundries. Valet serv Mon-Fri. Cr cds: A, C, D, DS, MC, V.

D ✆ ⩰ ⅀ 🔥 SC

✔ ★ ★ **LA QUINTA NORTHWEST-FARMERS BRANCH.** 13235 Stemmons Frwy (75234), north of downtown. 214/620-7333; FAX 214/484-6533. 122 rms, 2 story. S $42-$50; D $48-$60; each addl $7; under 18 free. Crib free. Pet accepted, some restrictions. TV; cable. Pool. Complimentary continental bkfst in lobby, 6-10 am. Complimentary coffee. Restaurant adj 6 am-midnight. Ck-out noon. Meeting rms. Cr cds: A, C, D, DS, MC, V.

D ✆ ⩰ ⅀ 🔥 SC

✔ ★ **RED ROOF INN.** 10335 Gardner Rd (75220), I-35 E at TX L-12, north of downtown. 214/506-8100; FAX 214/556-0072. 112 rms, 2 story. S $28-$39.99; D $33-$51; each addl $6; under 18 free. Crib free. Pet accepted, some restrictions. TV; cable. Complimentary coffee. Restaurant nearby. Ck-out noon. Near Texas Stadium. Cr cds: A, C, D, DS, MC, V.

D ✆ ⩰ ⅀ 🔥 SC

★ ★ **RESIDENCE INN BY MARRIOTT.** 13636 Goldmark Dr (75240), north of downtown. 214/669-0478; FAX 214/644-2632. 70 kit. suites, 1-2 story. Suites $110-$160; wkend rates. Crib free. Pet accepted, some restrictions; $60 non-refundable and $6 per day. TV; cable. Pool; whirlpool. Complimentary continental bkfst. Ck-out noon. Coin lndry. Valet serv. Health club privileges. Refrigerators. Fireplaces. Private patios, balconies. Grills. Cr cds: A, C, D, DS, JCB, MC, V.

D ✆ ⩰ ⅀ 🔥 SC

★ **SLEEP INN.** (4801 W Plano Pkwy, Plano 75093) 20 mi N on North Tollway, Plano Parkway exit. 214/867-1111; FAX 214/612-6753. 104 rms, 2 story. S $54-$64; each addl $6; under 18 free; wkend rates. Crib free. TV; cable. Pool. Complimentary continental bkfst. Restaurant nearby. Ck-out noon. Meeting rms. Valet serv. Cr cds: A, C, D, DS, ER, JCB, MC, V.

D ⩰ ⅀ 🔥 SC

Motor Hotels

★ ★ **BEST WESTERN PRESTON SUITES HOTEL.** 6104 LBJ Frwy (75240), Preston Rd exit, north of downtown. 214/458-2626; res: 800/524-7038; FAX 214/385-8331. 91 kit. units, 2 story. Kit. units $130-$210; under 18 free; wkly rates. Crib free. Pet accepted, some restrictions; $75. TV; cable. Pool; whirlpool. Complimentary full bkfst. Restaurant nearby. Ck-out noon. Coin lndry. Meeting rm. Valet serv. Cr cds: A, C, D, DS, MC, V.

✆ ⩰ ⅀ 🔥 SC

★ ★ **COURTYARD BY MARRIOTT.** 2150 Market Center Blvd (75207), north of downtown. 214/653-1166; FAX 214/653-1892. 180 rms, 5 story. S $94-$104; D $104-$114; each addl $10; under 12 free. Crib free. TV; cable. Pool. Complimentary coffee in rms. Restaurant 6 am-2 pm, 4:30-10:30 pm. Bar. Ck-out 1 pm. Coin lndry. Meeting rms. Sundries. Valet serv. Airport transportation. Exercise equipt; weight machine, bicycles, whirlpool. Some refrigerators, balconies. Cr cds: A, C, D, DS, MC, V.

D ⩰ 🏃 ⅀ 🔥 SC

★ ★ **HARVEY HOTEL ADDISON.** 14315 Midway Rd (75244), I-635 exit Midway Rd, north of downtown. 214/980-8877; FAX 214/788-2758. 429 rms, 3 story. Feb-May: S $99-$120; D $109-$135; each addl

$10; under 12 free; wkly, wkend & hol rates; lower rates rest of yr. Crib free. Free garage parking. Pet accepted, some restrictions; $150. Exercise equipt; weight machine, treadmill, whirlpool. Health club privileges. Some refrigerators. Cr cds: A, C, D, DS, ER, MC, V.

D ✆ ⩰ 🏃 ⅀ 🔥 SC

★ ★ **HARVEY HOTEL-DALLAS.** 7815 LBJ Frwy (75240), north of downtown. 214/960-7000; res: 800/922-9222; FAX 214/788-4227. 313 rms, 3 story. S $64-$75; D $74-$79; each addl $10; suites $125-$250; under 17 free. Crib free. Pet accepted; $125 ($100 refundable). TV; cable. Pool. Restaurant 6:30 am-11 pm. Rm serv. Bar 11 am-midnight. Ck-out 1 pm. Meeting rms. Valet serv. Gift shop. Refrigerators, wet bars; bathrm phone in suites. Cr cds: A, C, D, DS, MC, V.

D ✆ ⩰ ⅀ 🔥 SC

★ ★ ★ **HARVEY HOTEL-PLANO.** (1600 N Central Expy, Plano 75074) 18 mi N on Central Expy, 15th St exit. 214/578-8555; FAX 214/578-9720. 279 rms, 3 story. S $89-$109; D $94-$114; each addl $10; suites $120-$150; under 16 free. Crib $10. Pet accepted; $100 ($25 non-refundable). TV; cable. Pool; poolside serv. Restaurants 6:30 am-10 pm. Rm serv. Private club 11 am-midnight. Ck-out 1 pm. Coin lndry. Meeting rms. Bellhops. Valet serv. Sundries. Beauty shop. Exercise equipt; weight machine, treadmill, whirlpool. Some bathrm phones; refrigerator, wet bar in suites. Cr cds: A, C, D, DS, ER, MC, V.

D ✆ ⩰ 🏃 ⅀ 🔥 SC

★ ★ **HOLIDAY INN-LBJ NORTHEAST.** 11350 LBJ Frwy (75238), at Jupiter Rd exit, downtown. 214/341-5400; FAX 214/553-9349. 244 rms, 3-5 story. S, D $62-$80; suites $80-$130; under 18 free. Crib free. TV; cable. Pool. Restaurant 6:30 am-2 pm, 5-10 pm. Rm serv. Bar 2 pm-1 am; entertainment, dancing. Ck-out noon. Coin lndry. Meeting rms. Bellhops. Valet serv. Gift shop. Exercise equipt; weight machine, treadmill, sauna. **LUXURY LEVEL : CONCIERGE FLOOR.** 66 units, 1 suite. S, D $80, suite $100-$175. Concierge. Private lounge. Complimentary continental bkfst, refreshments. Cr cds: A, C, D, DS, JCB, MC, V.

D ⩰ 🏃 ⅀ 🔥 SC

Hotels

★ ★ ★ ★ **THE ADOLPHUS.** 1321 Commerce St (75202), downtown. 214/742-8200; res: 800/221-9083; FAX 214/651-3588. 425 rms, 22 story. S $180-$295; D $200-$320; each addl $20; suites $375-$2,000; under 12 free; wkend rates. Crib free. Valet parking $10. TV; cable, in-rm movies avail. Restaurant 6:30 am-10:30 pm (also see FRENCH ROOM). Rm serv 24 hrs. Bar 11-2 am. Ck-out 1 pm. Convention facilities. Concierge. Shopping arcade. Barber, beauty shop. Complimentary downtown transportation. Tennis & golf privileges. Exercise equipt; weight machine, bicycles. Health club privileges. Bathrm phones, refrigerators, minibars. Some private patios. Grand Lobby is the setting for afternoon tea; pianist signals evening cocktails; French Renaissance decor; Flemish tapestries (ca 1660). Soundproof rooms furnished predominantly in Queen Anne and Chippendale styles. Cr cds: A, C, D, DS, ER, JCB, MC, V.

D 🏃 🦶 🏃 ⅀ 🔥

★ ★ ★ **BRISTOL SUITES.** 7800 Alpha Rd (75240), north of downtown. 214/233-7600; res: 800/922-9222; FAX 214/701-8618. 295 suites, 10 story. Suites $99-$250; each addl $15; under 17 free; wkly rates; some lower rates summer. Crib free. Pet accepted; $125 ($100 refundable). TV; cable. Indoor/outdoor pool; poolside serv. Complimentary full bkfst, coffee. Restaurant 6:30 am-10 pm. Bar 11-2 am. Ck-out 1 pm. Convention facilities. Gift shop. Exercise equipt; weights, bicycles, whirlpool. Refrigerators; some bathrm phones. Cr cds: A, C, D, DS, MC, V.

D ✆ ⩰ 🏃 ⅀ 🔥 SC

★ ★ **CLARION.** 1241 W Mockingbird Lane (75247), near Love Field Airport, north of downtown. 214/630-7000; FAX 214/638-6943. 350 rms, 13 story. S $99; D $109; each addl $10; suites $450; under 18 free; wkly, wkend, hol rates. Crib $10. Pet accepted; $20. TV; cable.

Pool; wading pool, poolside serv. Restaurant 6:30 am-2 pm, 4-10 pm. Bar. Ck-out 1 pm. Coin lndry. Convention facilities. Gift shop. Free Love Field transportation. Exercise equipt; weight machine, stair machine. Health club privileges. Cr cds: A, C, D, DS, ER, JCB, MC, V.

[D] [icons] SC

★ ★ ★ ★ **CRESCENT COURT.** *400 Crescent Court (75210), in the Crescent area, just north of downtown.* 214/871-3200; res: 800/654-6541; FAX 214/871-3272. 216 rms, 7 story. S $235-$300; D $235-$330; each addl $30; suites $400-$1,200; under 12 free; wkend rates. Crib free. Pet accepted, some restrictions; $25. Garage $10; valet $5. TV; cable. Pool; poolside serv. Restaurant 6:30 am-midnight. Afternoon tea served in LADY PRIMROSE 3-5 pm. Rm serv 24 hrs. Bar 11:30-2 am. Ck-out 1 pm. Meeting rms. Concierge. Shopping arcade. Exercise rm; instructor, weights, bicycles, whirlpool, sauna, steam rm. Massage. Fully equipped spa. Bathrm phones; some refrigerators. Suites individually decorated; some 2-story with loft & glass dormers. Cr cds: A, C, D, ER, JCB, MC, V.

[D] [icons]

★ ★ **DALLAS GRAND.** *1914 Commerce St (75201), downtown.* 214/747-7000; FAX 214/749-0231. 709 rms, 20 story. S $110-$120; D $122-$130; each addl $10; suites $250-$550; under 17 free; wkend, honeymoon packages; Dallas Cowboy wkend rates. Crib free. TV; cable. Restaurant 6:30 am-10:30 pm. Bar 11:30-2 am. Ck-out 1 pm. Coin lndry. Convention facilities. Concierge. Gift shop. Valet parking. Exercise equipt; weights, rower, rooftop whirlpools. Some refrigerators. Sun deck. Cr cds: A, C, D, DS, ER, JCB, MC, V.

[D] [icons] SC

★ ★ **DOUBLETREE AT PARK WEST.** *1590 LBJ Frwy (75234), off I-35 Luna Rd exit, north of downtown.* 214/869-4300; FAX 214/869-3295. 339 rms, 12 story. S $139-$149; D $149-$159; each addl $10; suites $160-$895; under 17 free; wkend rates. Crib free. TV; cable. Heated pool; poolside serv. Restaurant 6 am-10 pm. Bar 11-1 am. Ck-out noon. Convention facilities. Concierge. Gift shop. Exercise equipt; weight machine, bicycles, whirlpool, sauna. *LUXURY LEVEL : CONCIERGE LEVEL.* 54 rms, 6 suites, 2 floors. S $159-$169; D $169-$179; suites $180-$895. Private lounge, honor bar. Wet bar in suites. Complimentary continental bkfst, refreshments, newspaper. Cr cds: A, C, D, DS, ER, JCB, MC, V.

[D] [icons]

★ ★ ★ **EMBASSY SUITES LOVE FIELD.** *3880 W Northwest Hwy (75220), near Love Field Airport, north of downtown.* 214/357-4500; FAX 214/357-0683. 248 suites, 9 story. S $149-$159; D $159-$169; each addl $10; wkly, wkend rates. TV; cable. Indoor pool; wading pool, poolside serv. Complimentary full bkfst. Restaurant 11 am-2 pm; wkends also 5-10 pm. Bar 4 pm-1 am. Ck-out noon. Guest lndry. Meeting rms. Covered parking. Free Love Field airport transportation. Exercise equipt; weight machines, treadmill, sauna. Refrigerators; some bathrm phones. Cr cds: A, C, D, DS, MC, V.

[D] [icons] SC

★ ★ **EMBASSY SUITES PARK CENTRAL.** *13131 N Central Expwy (75243), I-635 at US 75, north of downtown.* 214/234-3300; FAX 214/437-4247. 279 suites, 9 story. S $119-$159; D $134-$174; each addl $15; under 12 free; wkend rates. Crib free. Pet accepted, some restrictions; $50. Indoor pool. Complimentary coffee in rms. Complimentary full bkfst. Restaurant 11 am-2 pm, 5-10 pm. Rm serv. Bar 4 pm-1 am. Ck-out noon. Coin lndry. Meeting rms. Gift shop. Exercise equipt; weight machine, treadmill. Game rm. Refrigerators. Cr cds: A, C, D, DS, JCB, MC, V.

[D] [icons] SC

★ ★ ★ **FAIRMONT.** *1717 N Akard St (75201), at Ross, in Dallas arts district, downtown.* 214/720-2020; FAX 214/720-5269. 550 rms, 25 story. S $140-$215; D $165-$240; each addl $25; salon suites $325; under 17 free; wkend rates. Crib free. Garage parking $12. TV; cable. Pool; wading pool, poolside serv. Restaurant 5:45 am-midnight (also see PYRAMID ROOM). Rm serv 24 hrs. Bar 11-2 am; entertainment. Ck-out 1 pm. Convention facilities. Shopping arcade. Tennis & golf

privileges. Health club privileges adj. Bathrm phones. Cr cds: A, C, D, DS, MC, V.

[D] [icons] SC

★ ★ ★ ★ **FOUR SEASONS RESORT & CLUB.** *(4150 N MacArthur Blvd, Irving 75038) NW via TX 114.* 214/717-0700; FAX 214/717-2550. 357 rms, 9 story. S, D $189-$240; suites $375-$950; under 18 free; golf, spa, wkend plans. Valet parking $5. TV; cable. 4 heated pools, 1 indoor & 1 child's; poolside serv, lifeguard (wkends in season). Supervised child's activities. Restaurant (see CAFE ON THE GREEN). Rm serv 24 hrs. Bar 11-2 am. Ck-out 1 pm. Convention facilities. Concierge. Gift shop. Barber, beauty shop. 12 tennis courts, 4 indoor, pro. 18-hole TPC golf, greens fee $90, pro, 2 putting greens, driving range. Exercise rm; instructor, weight machines, bicycles, whirlpool, sauna, steam rm. Massage. Lawn games. Minibars. Private patios, balconies. Combines full resort amenities with all the comforts of an elegant hotel; offers state-of-the-art conference facilities; superb health center and spa; comprehensive recreational activities. Cr cds: A, C, D, ER, JCB, MC, V.

[D] [icons]

★ ★ ★ **THE GRAND KEMPINSKI.** *15201 Dallas Pkwy (75248), north of downtown.* 214/386-6000; res: 800/426-3135; FAX 214/991-6937. 529 rms, 15 story. S $159; D $179; each addl $20; suites $325-$1,250; under 17 free. Crib free. Valet parking $9 overnight. TV; cable. Indoor/outdoor pool; poolside serv. 2 restaurants 6 am-11 pm. Rm serv 24 hrs. Bars 11-2 am; dancing. Ck-out noon. Convention facilities. Concierge. Shopping arcade. Barber, beauty shop. Lighted tennis. Golf privileges. Exercise rm; instructor, weight machine, bicycles, whirlpool, steam rm, sauna. Bathrm phones; some refrigerators. Private patios. *LUXURY LEVEL : CONCIERGE FLOOR.* 80 rms, 24 suites, 2 floors. S $179; D $199. Bathrm phones. Wet bars. Complimentary continental bkfst, refreshments. Cr cds: A, C, D, DS, MC, V.

[D] [icons] SC

★ ★ ★ **HILTON DALLAS PARKWAY.** *4801 LBJ Frwy (75244), jct Dallas N Tollway, north of downtown.* 214/661-3600; FAX 214/385-3156. 310 rms, 15 story. S $89-$150; D $99-$160; each addl $10; suites $250-$375; under 18 free; wkend, special rates. Crib free. TV; cable. Indoor/outdoor pool, whirlpool, sauna. Restaurant 6:30 am-10 pm. Bar 11 am-midnight. Ck-out 1 pm. Convention facilities. Gift shop. Cr cds: A, C, D, DS, ER, MC, V.

[D] [icons] SC

★ ★ ★ **HOLIDAY INN.** *2645 LBJ Frwy (75234), north of downtown.* 214/243-3363; FAX 214/243-6682. 375 rms, 6 story. S, D $99; each addl $10; suites $125-$600; under 18 free; wkend, honeymoon rates. Crib free. TV; cable. Indoor/outdoor pool; poolside serv. Complimentary morning coffee. Restaurants 6:30 am-midnight. Rm serv 7 am-10 pm. Bar 11 am; Fri, Sat to 2 am; entertainment Wed-Sat, dancing. Ck-out 1 pm. Convention facilities. Gift shop. Airport transportation. Exercise equipt; weight machine, bicycle, whirlpool. Some refrigerators. Some balconies. Cr cds: A, C, D, DS, ER, MC, V.

[D] [icons] SC

★ ★ ★ **HOLIDAY INN-ARISTOCRAT.** *1933 Main St (75201), at Harwood, downtown.* 214/741-7700; res: 800/231-4235; FAX 214/939-3639. 172 rms, 15 story. S $99-$150; D $109-$165; under 18 free; wkend rates. Crib free. TV; cable. Complimentary coffee in lobby. Restaurant 6:30 am-10:30 pm. Bar 11-1 am. Ck-out 1 pm. Meeting rms. Concierge. Business district transportation. Exercise equipt; weights, bicycles. Health club privileges. Bathrm phones, refrigerators, minibars. Historic landmark, built in 1925 by Conrad Hilton and the first to bear his name; restored to its original Sullivanesque style. Cr cds: A, C, D, DS, ER, JCB, MC, V.

[D] [icons] SC

★ ★ **HOLIDAY INN-BROOKHOLLOW.** *7050 N Stemmons Frwy (75247), near Market Center, north of downtown.* 214/630-8500; FAX 214/630-9486. 356 rms, 21 story. S $85-$105; D $95-$110; each addl $10; under 18 free; wkend rates. Crib free. TV; cable. Indoor pool. Restaurant 6 am-2 pm, 5-11 pm. Bar 1 pm-midnight, Sat & Sun to 2 am; entertainment Mon-Thurs. Ck-out 1 pm. Coin lndry. Convention facilities. Gift shop. Love Field airport transportation. Exercise equipt; weight machines, bicycles, whirlpool, sauna. *LUXURY LEVEL* **: CONCIERGE FLOOR.** 36 rms, 4 suites, 2 floors. S, D $98-$109; suites $196-$534. Concierge. Private lounge. Complimentary continental bkfst, refreshments. Cr cds: A, C, D, DS, ER, JCB, MC, V.

[D] [≈] [🏃] [†] [🔥] [SC]

★ ★ ★ **HYATT REGENCY.** *300 Reunion Blvd (75207), downtown.* 214/651-1234; FAX 214/742-8126. 943 rms, 28 story. S $165; D $190; each addl $25; suites $300-$1,100; under 18 free; wkend rates. Valet parking $12. TV; cable. Pool; poolside serv. Restaurant 6 am-midnight. Bar 11-2 am; dancing. Ck-out noon. Convention facilities. Gift shop. Lighted tennis. Golf privileges 12 mi, greens fee $50. Exercise equipt; weights, bicycles, whirlpool, sauna. Minibars; some refrigerators. *LUXURY LEVEL* **: REGENCY CLUB.** 34 rms, 2 suites. S $190; D $215; each addl $25; suites $375-$475. Concierge. Private lounge, honor bar. Complimentary continental bkfst, refreshments, newspaper. Cr cds: A, C, D, DS, ER, JCB, MC, V.

[D] [🏌] [≈] [🏃] [†] [🚣] [🔥] [SC]

★ ★ ★ **LOEWS ANATOLE HOTEL.** *2201 Stemmons Frwy (75207), opp Dallas Market Center, north of downtown.* 214/748-1200; FAX 214/761-7520. 1,620 rms, 27 story. S $135-$180; D $160-$205; each addl $15; suites $200-$1,000; under 18 free; wkend, honeymoon packages. TV. 3 pools, 2 indoor; poolside serv. Restaurants open 24 hrs. Bar 11-2 am; entertainment, dancing. Ck-out noon. Convention facilities. Concierge. Shopping arcade. Barber, beauty shop. Garage parking; valet. Lighted tennis. Exercise rm; instructor, weights, bicycles, whirlpool, steam rm, sauna. Bathrm phones, refrigerators, minibars. *LUXURY LEVEL* **: CONCIERGE FLOORS.** 79 rms, 8 suites, 2 floors. S $180-$220; D $205-$245; suites $300-$1,200. Minibars. Whirlpools in suites. Cr cds: A, C, D, DS, JCB, MC, V.

[D] [🏌] [≈] [🏃] [†] [🚣] [🔥] [SC]

★ ★ ★ ★ ★ **MANSION ON TURTLE CREEK.** *2821 Turtle Creek Blvd (75219), north of downtown.* 214/559-2100; res: 800/527-5432 (exc TX), 800/442-3408 (TX); FAX 214/528-4187. 140 rms, 9 story, 5 kits. S $270-$350; D $300-$370; each addl $40; suites, kit. units $495-$1,350; wkend packages. Crib free. Valet parking $10. TV; cable. Heated pool; poolside serv. Restaurant 7 am-10:30 pm (also see MANSION ON TURTLE CREEK). Rm serv 24 hrs. Bar 11-2 am; entertainment. Ck-out 2 pm. Meeting rms. Concierge. Downtown transportation. Lighted tennis privileges. Golf privileges. Health club. Bathrm phones; wet bar in suites. Private patios, balconies. Restored mansion (1925) situated on 4-acre site on terraced hill. Casual elegance in a residential setting. Cr cds: A, C, D, DS, ER, JCB, MC, V.

[D] [🍴] [🏌] [≈] [🚣] [🔥]

★ ★ ★ **MARRIOTT HOTEL QUORUM.** *14901 Dallas Pkwy (75240), north of downtown.* 214/661-2800; FAX 214/934-1731. 547 rms, 12 story. S, D $129-$139; suites $250-$450; under 12 free; honeymoon, wkend rates. Crib free. Pet accepted. Free covered parking. TV; cable. Heated indoor/outdoor pool; poolside serv. Restaurants 6:30 am-midnight. Bar 11-2 am; entertainment, dancing exc Sun. Ck-out 1 pm. Lndry serv. Convention facilities. Concierge. Gift shop. Tennis. Golf privileges. Exercise equipt; weights, bicycles, whirlpool, sauna. Health club privileges. *LUXURY LEVEL* **.** 99 rms, 10 suites. S $149; D $159; suites $250-$450. Private lounge, honor bar. Complimentary continental bkfst, refreshments. Cr cds: A, C, D, DS, ER, JCB, MC, V.

[D] [🔥] [🏌] [†] [≈] [🏃] [🚣] [SC]

★ ★ ★ **MELROSE.** *3015 Oak Lawn Ave (75219), in Oak Lawn.* 214/521-5151; res: 800/MEL-ROSE; FAX 214/521-2470. 184 rms, 8 story. S $130-$150; D $140-$160; each addl $10; suites $250-$400; wkend rates; honeymoon packages. Crib free. TV; cable. Pool privileges. Restaurant 6:30 am-2:30 pm, 5:30-11 pm; Sun 5:30 am-2:30 pm. Rm serv 6 am-midnight. Bar 11-2 am; entertainment. Ck-out noon. Meeting rms. Concierge. Gift shop. Valet parking. Free Love Field airport transportation. Health club privileges. Some refrigerators. Beautifully restored 1924 hotel; library. *LUXURY LEVEL* **: HERITAGE FLOORS.** 54 rms, 2 story, 6 suites. S $175-$185; D $185-$295; each

addl $10; suites $225-$450. Concierge. In-rm movies avail. Complimentary refreshments, newspaper. Cr cds: A, C, D, DS, JCB, MC, V.

[D] [🚣] [🔥] [SC]

★ ★ ★ **OMNI MANDALAY AT LAS COLINAS.** *(221 E Las Colinas Blvd, Irving 75039) W on I-35E to TX 114, O'Connor exit, right to Las Colinas Blvd.* 214/556-0800; FAX 214/556-0729. 410 rms, 28 story. S, D $130-$160; each addl $10; suites $145-$1,300; under 18 free; wkend, honeymoon rates. Crib free. Valet parking $5 overnight. TV; cable. Heated pool; poolside serv (seasonal). Restaurant (see ENJOLIE). Rm serv 6-1 am. Bar 11:30-1:30 am. Ck-out noon. Convention facilities. Concierge. Gift shop. Golf privileges. Exercise equipt; weights, bicycles, whirlpool, sauna. Bathrm phones. Some private patios, balconies. On lake; lakeside restaurant. Cr cds: A, C, D, DS, ER, JCB, MC, V.

[D] [🏃] [≈] [🏃] [🚣] [🔥] [SC]

✔ ★ **QUALITY HOTEL-MARKET CENTER.** *2015 N Market Center Blvd (75207), north of downtown.* 214/741-7481; FAX 214/747-6191. 250 rms, 11 story. S $60-$85; D $70-$95; each addl $10; suites, kit. unit $135-$200; under 18 free. Crib free. TV; cable. Pool. Restaurant 6:30-10 am, 5-10 pm. Bar 5 pm-midnight. Ck-out noon. Coin lndry. Meeting rms. Exercise equipt; weights, bicycles. Private patios, balconies. Cr cds: A, C, D, DS, ER, JCB, MC, V.

[D] [≈] [🏃] [🚣] [🔥] [SC]

★ ★ **RADISSON CENTRAL.** *6060 N Central Expy (75206), US 75 at Mockingbird Blvd exit, north of downtown.* 214/750-6060; FAX 214/750-5959. 288 rms, 9 story. S, D $99-$109; each addl $10; suites $140-$400; under 18 free; wkend rates. Crib free. Pet accepted, some restrictions. TV; cable. Indoor/outdoor pool; whirlpool, sauna, poolside serv. Restaurant 6:30 am-2 pm, 5-10 pm. Bar noon-1 am. Ck-out 1 pm. Meeting rms. Gift shop. Free Love Field airport transportation avail. Some refrigerators. Cr cds: A, C, D, DS, ER, JCB, MC, V.

[D] [🔥] [≈] [🚣] [🔥] [SC]

RADISSON NORTH. *(Remodeling incomplete when inspected, therefore not rated) 4099 Valley View Lane (75244), I-635 Midway Rd exit, north of downtown.* 214/385-900; FAX 214/788-11747881174. 292 rms, 10 story. S $119-$149; D $129-$159; each addl $10; suites $175-$425; under 18 free; wkend, hol rates. Crib $10. TV; cable. Heated pool. Restaurant 6 am-11:30 pm. Bar noon-1 am. Ck-out noon. Meeting rms. Concierge. Gift shop. Tennis privileges adj. 18-hole golf privileges adj. Exercise equipt; weight machine, stair machine, whirlpool, sauna. Health club privileges. Cr cds: A, C, D, DS, JCB, MC, V.

[D] [🍴] [🔥] [≈] [🏃] [🚣]

★ ★ **RADISSON STEMMONS.** *2330 W Northwest Hwy (75220), north of downtown.* 214/351-4477; FAX 214/351-4499. 198 rms, 8 story. S $99-$129; D $109-$139; each addl $10; suites $129-$139; under 18 free; wkly, wkend, hol rates. Crib free. Pet accepted, some restrictions; $50 refundable. TV. Pool; poolside serv. Restaurant 6:30 am-10 pm. Bar. Ck-out 1 pm. Coin lndry. Meeting rms. Concierge. Gift shop. Free Love Field transportation. Exercise equipt; weight machine, treadmill, whirlpool. Balconies. Cr cds: A, C, D, DS, ER, JCB, MC, V.

[D] [🔥] [🔥] [≈] [🏃] [🚣] [🔥] [SC]

✔ ★ ★ **RAMADA.** *1011 S Akard (75215), downtown.* 214/421-1083; FAX 214/428-6827. 238 rms, 12 story. S $55-$125; D $65-$135; each addl $10; suites $350-$450; under 13 free; wkend rates. Crib free. Pet accepted. TV; cable. Indoor pool. Restaurant 6 am-2 pm, 5-10 pm. Bar 3 pm-1 am. Ck-out noon. Meeting rms. Free garage parking. Love Field airport, downtown transportation. Exercise equipt; weights, bicycles, whirlpool. Balconies. Cr cds: A, C, D, DS, ER, JCB, MC, V.

[D] [🔥] [🔥] [≈] [🏃] [🚣] [🔥] [SC]

✔ ★ **RAMADA-MARKET CENTER.** *1055 Regal Row (75247), north of downtown.* 214/634-8550; FAX 214/634-8418. 361 units, 12 story. S $69-$89; D $69-$99; each addl $10; suites $125-$350; under 12 free. Pet accepted, some restrictions; $25 refundable. TV; cable, in-rm movies avail. Pool; poolside serv. Restaurant 6:30 am-2 pm, 5-10 pm. Bar 2 pm-midnight. Ck-out noon. Convention facilities. Gift shop. Free covered parking. Free airport transportation. Game rm. Some refrigerators. Cr cds: A, C, D, DS, MC, V.

[D] [icons] SC

★ ★ ★ **SHERATON PARK CENTRAL.** 12720 Merit Dr (75251), I-635 N at Coit Rd, north of downtown. 214/385-3000; FAX 214/991-4557. 550 rms, 20 story. S $139-$159; D $149-$169; each addl $10; under 18 free; wknd rates. Crib avail. Pet accepted, some restrictions. Valet parking $5. TV; cable. Pool; poolside serv. Restaurant 6 am-11 pm. Rm serv 24 hrs. Private club. Ck-out noon. Convention facilities. Gift shop. Concierge. Exercise equipt; weight machine, bicycles. Bathrm phones. *LUXURY LEVEL : EXECUTIVE LEVEL.* 65 rms, 22 suites, 3 story. S, D $149-$169; suites $290-$890. Full wet bar in suites. Complimentary continental bkfst, refreshments. Cr cds: A, C, D, DS, ER, JCB, MC, V.

[D] [icons] SC

★ ★ ★ **SHERATON SUITES-MARKET CENTER.** 2101 Stemmons Frwy (75207), northwest of downtown. 214/747-3000; FAX 214/742-5713. 253 suites, 11 story. S $145; D $160; each addl $10; under 18 free; wknd rates. TV; cable. Indoor/outdoor pool; poolside serv. Complimentary coffee in rms. Complimentary bkfst buffet. Restaurant 6 am-11 pm. Bar 11-1 am. Ck-out noon. Gift shop. Exercise equipt; weight machine, rowers, whirlpool. Refrigerators, wet bars. Balconies. Cr cds: A, C, D, DS, ER, JCB, MC, V.

[D] [icons] SC

★ ★ **SOUTHLAND CENTER.** 400 N Olive (75201), in Southland Center, downtown. 214/922-8000; FAX 214/969-7650. 502 rms, 29 story. S $79-$165; D $94-$180; each addl $15; suites $240-$600; under 18 free; honeymoon, wkend rates. Valet parking $8 Mon-Thurs, $3 wkends. Pet accepted; $50 refundable. TV; cable. Restaurant 6:30 am-11 pm. Bar 11-2 am. Ck-out noon. Convention facilities. Concierge. Shopping arcade. Exercise equipt; weights, bicycles. Health club privileges. Some bathrm phones. *LUXURY LEVEL : EXECUTIVE CLUB.* 46 rms, 8 suites, 3 floors. S $165; D $180; suites $240-$600. Bathrm phones; some full wet bars. Complimentary full bkfst. Cr cds: A, C, D, DS, ER, JCB, MC, V.

[D] [icons] SC

★ ★ ★ **STONELEIGH.** 2927 Maple Ave (75201), north of downtown. 214/871-7111; res: 800/255-9299; FAX 214/871-9379. 158 units, 11 story, 12 kits. S $130-$165; D $145-$180; each addl $15; suites $200-$400; kit. units from $130; family, wkend rates. Crib free. TV; cable, in-rm movies. Pool. Playground. Restaurant 6:30 am-10 pm. Bar 11-1 am. Ck-out noon. Concierge. Valet parking. Free Love Field airport transportation. Lighted tennis. Health club privileges. Refrigerator in some suites. Restored 1924 hotel. Cr cds: A, C, D, DS, MC, V.

[D] [icons] SC

★ ★ ★ **STOUFFER DALLAS.** 2222 Stemmons Frwy (I-35E) (75207), near Market Center, north of downtown. 214/631-2222; FAX 214/905-3814. 540 rms, 30 story. S $149-$169; D $169-$189; each addl $20; suites $189-$1,000; under 18 free; wknd rates. Crib free. Pet accepted, some restrictions. TV; cable. Heated pool. Complimentary coffee. Restaurant 6:30 am-10 pm. Bar 3 pm-2 am; entertainment. Ck-out 1 pm. Convention facilities. Gift shop. Love Field airport transportation. Exercise equipt; weights, bicycles, whirlpool, steam rm, sauna. Some refrigerators. Three-story chandelier; art objects. *LUXURY LEVEL : CLUB LEVEL.* 57 rms, 30 suites, 2 floors. S $169-$189; D $189-$209. Butler serv. In-rm movies avail. Some minibars, wet bars. Bathrm phones. Complimentary continental bkfst in rms, refreshments. Cr cds: A, C, D, DS, ER, JCB, MC, V.

[D] [icons] SC

★ ★ ★ **THE WESTIN.** 13340 Dallas Pkwy (75240), north of downtown. 214/934-9494; FAX 214/851-2869. 431 rms, 21 story. S $99-$169; D $99-$210; each addl $25; suites $350-$1,250; under 18 free; wkend rates. Crib free. TV; cable. Heated pool; poolside serv. Restaurants 6:30 am-10 pm. Rm serv 24 hrs. Bar 11-2 am. Ck-out 1

pm. Convention facilities. Concierge. Shopping arcade. Barber, beauty shop. Garage parking, valet $10. Health club privileges. Refrigerators. Balconies. Adj Galleria Mall complex. *LUXURY LEVEL : EXECUTIVE CLUB.* 26 rms. S, D $189-$210. Private lounge, honor bar. Minibars. Bathrm phones. Complimentary continental bkfst, refreshments. Cr cds: A, C, D, DS, ER, JCB, MC, V.

[D] [icons] SC

Inn

★ ★ ★ ★ **HOTEL ST GERMAIN.** 2516 Maple Ave (75201), Oak Lawn. 214/871-2516; res: 800/638-2516; FAX 214/871-0740. 7 suites, 3 story. EP: S, D $200-$600; wkly rates. TV; cable, in-rm movies. Complimentary refreshments. Dining rm: bkfst & dinner hrs flexible for inn guests; public by res (wkends only, dinner). Rm serv 24 hrs. Ck-out noon, ck-in 4 pm. Bellhops. Valet serv. Concierge. Victorian house (1906), refurbished to retain original character while offering modern amenities; wraparound balcony; library/sitting rm; elegant antique furnishings from New Orleans and France; canopied beds, wood-burning fireplaces. Dining rm opens onto New Orleans-style walled courtyard. Cr cds: A, C, MC, V.

[D] [icons]

Restaurants

★ ★ **650 NORTH.** (See Plaza Of The Americas Hotel) 214/855-1708. Hrs: 6:30 am-10 pm; Fri to 11 pm; Sat 7 am-11 pm. Closed Dec 24, 25. Res accepted. New American, Southwestern menu. Bar. A la carte entrees: bkfst $2.25-$7.95, lunch $6.95-$14.95, dinner $14.95-$21.95. Child's meals. Specialties: pan-seared medallions of Atlantic salmon, oven-baked gateau of beef tenderloin. Valet parking. Cr cds: A, D, DS, MC, V.

[D]

★ ★ **ADELMO'S.** 4537 Cole Ave, north of downtown. 214/559-0325. Hrs: 11:30 am-2 pm, 6-10:30 pm; Sat from 6 pm. Closed Sun; major hols. Res accepted. Mediterranean menu. Bar. Semi-a la carte: lunch $8.50-$14.50, dinner $12-$23. Specializes in Mediterranean dishes. Parking. Cr cds: A, C, D, DS, MC, V.

★ ★ **ALESSIO'S.** 4117 Lomo Alto (75219), north of downtown. 214/521-3585. Hrs: 11:30 am-2 pm, 6-10:30 pm; wkends to 11 pm. Closed some major hols. Res accepted. Italian menu. Bar. Semi-a la carte: lunch $9-$13.50, dinner $16-$19.50. Specialties: jumbo scallops Madagascar, fettuccine Genovese, scaloppine al Marsala. Valet parking. Wood paneling. Original paintings. Jacket. Cr cds: A, MC, V.

[D]

★ ★ ★ **ARTHUR'S.** 1000 Campbell Center, 8350 Central Expy, north of downtown. 214/361-8833. Hrs: 11:30 am-2:30 pm, 6-10:30 pm; Fri, Sat 6-11 pm. Closed Sun; major hols. Res accepted. Bar to 2 am; Sat from 6 pm. Semi-a la carte: lunch $7.25-$12, dinner $10-$20. Specializes in veal, steak, seafood. Entertainment. Valet parking. Cr cds: A, C, D, MC, V.

[D]

✔★ ★ **ATHENEE CAFE.** 5365 Spring Valley #150, north of downtown. 214/239-8060. Hrs: 11 am-2 pm, 5:30-11 pm; Sat from 5:30 pm. Closed Sun; Thanksgiving, Dec 25. Res accepted; required Fri, Sat. Romanian menu. Bar. A la carte entrees: lunch $5.95-$8.95, dinner $11.95-$14.95. Specialties: stuffed cabbage, eggplant moussaka, gypsy sausage, chicken dolma. Library paneling. Fountain. Cr cds: A, D, DS, MC, V.

[D]

★ ★ **BABY ROUTH.** 2708 Routh St, north of downtown. 214/871-2345. Hrs: 11:30 am-2 pm, 6-10:30 pm; Fri to 11 pm; Sat 6-11 pm; Sun 6-10:30 pm; Sun brunch 10:30 am-2:30 pm. Closed major hols. Res accepted. Bar. A la carte entrees: lunch $6.75-$12, dinner

$11.75-$19. Sun brunch $6.75-$12. Specializes in seafood, beef, chicken. Valet parking. Outdoor dining. Cr cds: A, C, D, DS, MC, V.

D

✔★★ **BLUE MESA GRILL.** 5100 Belt Line Rd, north of downtown. 214/934-0165. Hrs: 11 am-10 pm; Fri, Sat to 11 pm; Sun 10 am-10 pm; Sun brunch to 2:30 pm. Closed Thanksgiving, Dec 25. Res accepted. Southwestern menu. Bar. Semi-a la carte: lunch $5.95-$8.95, dinner $8-$13. Sun brunch $11.95. Child's meals. Specialties. "adobe pie," garlic shrimp on angel hair pasta, duck rellenos, Southwestern Caesar salad. Parking. Outdoor dining. 2 large adobe fireplaces. Cr cds: A, C, D, DS, MC, V.

D

✔★★★ **CAFE ON THE GREEN.** (See Four Seasons Resort & Club Hotel) 214/717-0700. Hrs: 6:30 am-11 pm; Sat & Sun from 7 am; Sun brunch 11 am-2 pm. Res accepted. Bar. Wine cellar. A la carte entrees: bkfst $5.75-$12, lunch $8-$14, dinner $13.95-$23. Buffet: bkfst $12.50, lunch $18.50, dinner $24. Sun brunch $24.50. Serv charge 16%. Specialties: house smoked salmon with cucumber fennel salad, roasted tenderloin of beef, roasted poblano pepper with smoked rabbit. Own baking. Valet parking. Garden-like setting; overlooks villas & pool. Cr cds: A, C, D, ER, JCB, MC, V.

D

★★★ **CAFE PACIFIC.** 24 Highland Park Village (75205), at Mockingbird & Preston Rd, north of downtown. 214/526-1170. Hrs: 11:30 am-2 pm, 6-10 pm; Fri to 11 pm; Sat 11:30 am-2:30 pm, 5:30-11 pm. Closed Sun; some major hols. Res accepted. Bar 11 am-midnight. Wine cellar. A la carte entrees: lunch $6.90-$11.90, dinner $10.90-$22.90. Specializes in seafood. Own baking. Valet parking. Outdoor terrace dining. View of kitchen behind glass. Cr cds: A, C, D, DS, MC, V.

★★★ **CAPRICCIO.** McKinney Ave at Fairmount St, north of downtown. 214/871-2004. Hrs: 11 am-3 pm, 5-10 pm; Sat 5 pm-midnight; Sun 5-11 pm. Closed Jan 1, Dec 25. Res accepted. Northern Italian menu. Bar. Semi-a la carte: lunch $9-$14, dinner $10.75-$24. Specialties: salmon Basil, duck à l'orange, veal chop Milanese, fettucine pescatore. Entertainment Thurs-Sat. Valet parking. Fireplaces. Cr cds: A, C, D, DS, ER, JCB, MC, V.

D

✔★ **CELEBRATION.** 4503 W Lovers Lane, north of downtown. 214/351-5681. Hrs: 11 am-2:30 pm, 5-10 pm; Fri, Sat to 11 pm; Sun 11 am-10 pm. Closed Thanksgiving, Dec 24-25. Bar. Semi-a la carte: lunch $4-$9, dinner $5.95-$13. Child's meals. Specializes in fresh vegetables, fish, pot roast. Own desserts. Parking. Rustic decor; copper tables. Cr cds: A, C, D, DS, MC, V.

D **SC**

★★ **CHAPLIN'S.** 1928 Greenville Ave, north of downtown. 214/823-3300. Hrs: 6-11 pm. Closed Jan 1, Thanksgiving, Dec 25. Res required wkends. Continental menu. Bar. A la carte entrees: dinner $12-$20. Child's meals. Specializes in seafood, steak, pasta. Valet parking. Cr cds: A, C, D, DS, MC, V.

D

★★ **CHEZ GERARD.** 4444 McKinney Ave, north of downtown. 214/522-6865. Hrs: 11:30 am-2:30 pm, 6-10:30 pm; Sat from 6 pm. Closed Sun; major hols. Res accepted. French menu. A la carte entrees: lunch $6.50-$9.50, dinner $13.50-$16.50. Specializes in fish, rack of lamb. Parking. Outdoor dining. Cr cds: A, C, D, DS, MC, V.

D

★★ **CHIMNEY.** 9739 N Central Expy, in Willow Creek Shopping Ctr, US 75 at Walnut Hill Lane, north of downtown. 214/369-6466. Hrs: 11:30 am-2 pm, 6-10:30 pm. Closed Mon; major hols. Res accepted. Continental menu. Bar. Semi-a la carte: lunch $7.95-$12.75, dinner $9.75-$23. Sun brunch $14.95. Specializes in seafood, veal, venison. Pianist. Parking. Colonial decor. Cr cds: A, C, D, DS, MC, V.

D

★★★ **DAKOTA'S.** 600 N Akard St, downtown. 214/740-4001. Hrs: 11 am-2:30 pm, 5-10 pm; Fri, Sat to 10:30 pm; Sun 5:30-9 pm. Closed some major hols. Res accepted. A la carte entrees: lunch $6.50-$12, dinner $9.95-$19.95. Specializes in fresh seafood, steaks. Own breads, pasta. Pianist Fri, Sat. Valet parking. Patio dining. Ceiling fans; unusual 5-tiered waterfall outside. Cr cds: A, C, D, DS, MC, V.

D

★★★ **DEL FRISCO'S.** 5251 Spring Valley Rd (75240), north of downtown. 214/490-9000. Hrs: 5-10 pm; Fri & Sat to 11 pm. Closed Sun; Thanksgiving, Dec 25. Res accepted. Bar. Wine list. A la carte entrees: dinner $15.50-$28. Specializes in steak. Valet parking. 2-story steakhouse. Native American, Western artwork. Cr cds: A, C, D, DS, MC, V.

D

★★★ **THE ENCLAVE.** 8325 Walnut Hill (75231), north of downtown. 214/363-7487. Hrs: 11 am-2:30 pm, 5:30-11 pm; Sat from 5:30 pm. Closed Sun; major hols. Res accepted. Continental menu. Bar to 2 am. Semi-a la carte: lunch $7.25-$14, dinner $14-$26. Specializes in French cuisine, veal, seafood. Pianist. Valet parking. Elegant dinner club atmosphere. Family-owned. Cr cds: A, C, D, MC, V.

D

★★★ **ENJOLIE.** (See Omni Mandalay At Las Colinas Hotel) 214/556-0800. Hrs: 6:30-10 pm. Closed Sun, Mon. Res accepted. Bar. Wine list. Semi-a la carte: dinner $19-$28. Prix fixe: dinner $45. Child's meals. Specializes in grilled fish, roast game. Own baking, smoked meats and seafood. Valet parking. Outstanding view of grounds. Cr cds: A, C, D, DS, ER, JCB, MC, V.

D **SC**

★★★★ **FRENCH ROOM.** (See The Adolphus Hotel) 214/742-8200. Hrs: 6-10:30 pm. Closed Sun. Res accepted; required Fri & Sat. Neo-classic cuisine. Bar 4 pm-1:30 am. Wine list. A la carte entrees: dinner $22-$52. Specialties: Dover sole, foie gras, roast rack of lamb, sautéed Norwegian salmon. Menu changes with season. Valet parking. Vaulted ceilings with murals; opulent decor in Louis XIV style. Jacket. Cr cds: A, C, D, DS, ER, JCB, MC, V.

D

✔★ **J PEPE'S.** 2800 Routh St (75201), north of downtown. 214/871-0366. Hrs: 11 am-10 pm; Thur-Sat to 11 pm. Closed Thanksgiving, Dec 25. Res accepted. Mexican menu. Bar. Semi-a la carte: lunch $4.75-$6.75, dinner $5.25-$10.95. Sun brunch $8.95. Child's meals. Specializes in fajitas, Margarita shrimp, chicken Mazatlan. Parking (valet wkends). Outdoor dining. Cantina decor. Cr cds: A, C, D, DS, MC, V.

D

★★ **JAVIER'S.** 4912 Cole Ave, north of downtown. 214/521-4211. Hrs: 5:30-10:30 pm; Fri, Sat to 11 pm; Sun to 10 pm. Closed major hols. Res accepted. Continental, Mexican menu. Bar. Semi-a la carte: dinner $11.50-$17.95. Specialties: filete Cantinflas, red snapper mojo de ajo. Complimentary valet parking. Eclectic decor; antiques from Mexico. Cr cds: A, C, D, DS, MC, V.

D

★★ **JENNIVINE.** 3605 McKinney Ave, north of downtown. 214/528-6010. Hrs: 11:30 am-10 pm. Closed Sun; most major hols. Res accepted. Bar. A la carte entrees: lunch $7-$8, dinner $12-$17. Specializes in rack of lamb, beef tenderloin, duck, fresh fish. Parking. Outdoor dining. British pub atmosphere. Cr cds: A, C, D, DS, MC, V.

D

★★★ **JUNIPER.** 2917 Fairmount St, north of downtown. 214/855-0700. Hrs: 6-10:30 pm; Thurs-Sat to 11 pm. Closed Sun; some major hols. Res accepted. French Provençale menu. Bar. A la carte entrees: dinner $14-$26. Specialties: fish soup, crab cakes, pheasant with linguine. Own desserts. Valet parking. Outdoor dining.

French Provincial decor in converted house. Cr cds: A, C, D, DS, MC, V.

[D]

★ ★ **L'ANCESTRAL.** *4514 Travis #124, north of downtown.* 214/528-1081. Hrs: 11:30 am-2 pm, 6-10 pm; Fri, Sat to 11 pm. Closed Sun; some major hols. Res accepted wknds. Country French menu. Bar. A la carte entrees: lunch $3.50-$12.50, dinner $12.50-$19.50. Complete meals: dinner $22.50. Specializes in pepper steak, lamb tenderloin, grilled salmon. Outdoor dining. Cr cds: A, C, D, DS, MC, V.

[D]

★ ★ ★ **LA TRATTORIA LOMBARDI.** *2916 N Hall St, north of downtown.* 214/954-0803. Hrs: 11 am-2 pm, 5:30-10:30 pm; Fri & Sat to 11 pm; Sun brunch 11 am-3 pm. Closed some major hols. Res accepted. Italian menu. Bar. Wine cellar. A la carte entrees: lunch $6-$11.95, dinner $8.95-$21. Sun brunch $19.95. Child's meals. Specializes in pasta, seafood, veal. Valet parking. Outdoor dining. Mediterranean decor. Cr cds: A, C, D, MC, V.

[D] [SC]

✔ ★ ★ **LOMBARDI'S.** *311 N Market, downtown.* 214/747-0322. Hrs: 11 am-11 pm; Fri to midnight; Sat 5 pm-midnight; Sun 5-10 pm. Italian menu. Bar. A la carte entrees: lunch, dinner $4.95-$15. Specializes in pasta, pizza. Outdoor dining. Valet parking. Cr cds: A, C, D, MC, V.

[D]

✔ ★ ★ **MANSION ON TURTLE CREEK.** *(See Mansion On Turtle Creek Hotel)* 214/559-2100. Hrs: noon-2:30 pm, 6-10:30 pm; Fri & Sat to 11 pm. Brunch: Sat noon-2:30 pm; Sun 11 am-2:30 pm. Res accepted; required Fri & Sat. Amer Southwest menu. Bar 11-2 am. Wine cellar. A la carte entrees: lunch from $15, dinner from $30. Brunch $26. Specialties: tortilla soup, lobster taco, crème brûlee, rack of lamb. Own baking. Valet parking. Restored 1925 mansion; art objects. Private dining areas. Jacket, tie. Cr cds: A, C, D, DS, ER, JCB, MC, V.

[D]

✔ ★ ★ **MARIO'S CHIQUITA.** *4514 Travis #105, north of downtown.* 214/521-0721. Hrs: 11:30 am-9:30 pm; Fri, Sat to 10 pm. Closed Jan 1, Thanksgiving, Dec 25. Mexican menu. Bar. Semi-a la carte: lunch, dinner $4.35-$10. Child's meals. Specialties: carne asada, chile rellenos, chicken a la parrilla. Colorful Mexican decor. Cr cds: A, MC, V.

[D]

★ ★ ★ **MORTON'S OF CHICAGO.** *501 Elm St, in West End Historic District.* 214/741-2277. Hrs: 5:30-11 pm; Sun 5-10 pm. Closed major hols. Res accepted. Bar. A la carte entrees: dinner $15.50-$29.95. Specializes in steak, seafood, lamb. Valet parking. Open grill; meat displayed at table for patrons to select. Cr cds: A, D, DS, MC, V.

[D]

★ ★ **NEWPORT'S SEAFOOD.** *703 McKinney Ave, in the Brewery, in West End Historic District.* 214/954-0220. Hrs: 11:30 am-2:30 pm, 5:30-10:30 pm; Fri to 11 pm; Sat 5:30-11 pm; Sun 5:30-10 pm. Closed major hols. Bar. A la carte entrees: lunch $7.95-$10.50, dinner $12.95-$16.95. Specializes in mesquite-grilled seafood, steak, chicken. Extensive seafood selection. Parking. Tri-level dining in turn-of-the-century brewery; 50-ft-deep freshwater well in dining area. Cr cds: A, C, D, DS, MC, V.

[D]

★ ★ ★ **OLD WARSAW.** *2610 Maple Ave, in Oak Lawn.* 214/528-0032. Hrs: 5:30-10:30 pm. Res required. French, continental menu. Bar. Wine cellar. A la carte entrees: dinner $21-$26. Specializes in lobster Thermidor, salmon tartare, steak au poivre. Own baking. Violinist, pianist. Valet parking. Lobster tank. Family-owned. Jacket. Cr cds: A, D, DS, MC, V.

★ ★ **OSTERIA DA MOMO.** *2704 Elm St, in Deep Ellum.* 214/748-4222. Hrs: 11 am-2 pm, 5-10:30 pm; Fri to 11:30 pm; Sat

5-11:30 pm; Sun 5-10 pm. Closed some major hols. Res accepted; required Fri, Sat. Italian menu. Bar. A la carte entrees: lunch $6.95-$12.95, dinner $9.50-$16.95. Specialties: risotto alla Milanese, filette al Barolo con polenta, ratolo verde, Gamberi alla MoMo. Totally nonsmoking. Cr cds: A, C, D, DS, JCB, MC, V.

[D]

✔ ★ ★ **PATRIZIO.** *25 Highland Park Village (75202), north of downtown.* 214/522-7878. Hrs: 11:30 am-3 pm, 5-11 pm; Mon to 10 pm; Fri to midnight; Sat 11:30 am-midnight; Sun 11:30 am-10 pm. Closed Jan 1, Thanksgiving, Dec 25. Italian menu. Bar 11 am-midnight. A la carte entrees: lunch $4.90-$8.10, dinner $5.75-$12.95. Specialties: angel hair pasta with basil & tomato, sautéed crab claws, chicken Parmesan salad. Valet parking. Outdoor dining. Oriental rugs, many large oil paintings. Cr cds: A, D, DS, MC, V.

[D]

★ ★ ★ **PYRAMID ROOM.** *(See Fairmont Hotel)* 214/720-5249. Hrs: 11:30 am-2 pm, 6-10:30 pm; Fri, Sat 6 pm-midnight; Sun from 6 pm. Res accepted. Continental menu. Bar 11:30-1:30 am. Wine list. A la carte entrees: lunch $7.50-$14, dinner $18.50-$35. Specializes in beef, veal, seafood. Own baking. Entertainment. Valet parking. Jacket. Cr cds: A, C, D, DS, MC, V.

[D]

★ ★ ★ **RIVIERA.** *7709 Inwood Rd, north of downtown.* 214/351-0094. Hrs: 6:30-10:30 pm; Fri, Sat to 11 pm. Closed most major hols. Res accepted; required Fri, Sat. Continental menu. Bar. Wine list. A la carte entrees: dinner $23.50-$32. Complete meals: dinner $45-$65. Specialties: escargots and tortilloni, glazed salmon, lobster pancake with scallops. Valet parking. Country French decor. Jacket. Cr cds: A, C, D, MC, V.

[D]

★ ★ **ROYAL TOKYO.** *7525 Greenville Ave, 2 mi S of LBJ Frwy; ³/4 mi E of US 75, Walnut Hill exit, north of downtown.* 214/368-3304. Hrs: 11:30 am-2 pm, 5:30-11 pm; Fri to 11:30 pm; Sat noon-2:30 pm, 5:30-11:30 pm; Sun 5:30-10:30 pm; Sun brunch 11:30 am-2:30 pm. Closed Jan 1, Thanksgiving, Dec 25. Res accepted. Japanese menu. Bar. Semi-a la carte: lunch $4-$15, dinner $12.95-$25. Sun brunch $16.95. Child's meals. Hibachi chefs at dinner. Specialties: tempura, shabu-shabu, hibachi steak. Sushi bar. Piano. Parking. Traditional seating avail. Japanese motif; outdoor water gardens. Cr cds: A, C, D, DS, JCB, MC, V.

[D]

✔ ★ **THAI TASTE.** *4501 Cole Ave, north of downtown.* 214/521-3513. Hrs: 11:30 am-2:30 pm, 5:30-10 pm; Fri to 11 pm; Sat 5:30-11 pm; Sun 5:30-10 pm. Closed Thanksgiving, Dec 25. Res accepted. Thai menu. Bar. A la carte entrees: lunch $4.95-$6.95, dinner $6.95-$15. Specialties: crispy catfish with red curry, chicken with peanut sauce, sizzling seafood. Parking. Outdoor dining. Housed in converted church; balcony used for seating. Cr cds: A, C, D, DS, MC, V.

★ ★ **UNCLE TAI'S.** *13350 Dallas Pkwy (13350), in the Galleria Shopping Plaza, north of downtown.* 214/934-9998. Hrs: 11 am-10 pm; Fri, Sat to 10:30 pm; Sun noon-9:30 pm. Closed some major hols. Res accepted. Chinese menu. Serv bar. A la carte entrees: lunch $7-$10.50, dinner $11-$17. Specializes in beef, chicken, seafood. Valet parking. Cr cds: A, C, D, MC, V.

[D]

★ **WHITE SWAN CAFE.** *6334 La Vista, north of downtown.* 214/824-8122. Hrs: 11 am-10 pm; Fri to 11 pm; Sat 8 am-11 pm; Sun 8 am-10 pm; Sun brunch 10 am-2 pm. Res accepted. Eclectic menu. Wine, beer. Semi-a la carte: bkfst $4.95-$6.95, lunch $4.95-$7.95, dinner $7.95-$19.95. Sun brunch $8.95. Child's meals. Specialties: paella a la Valenciana, arroz con pollo, coconut shrimp. Entertainment Thurs-Sat. Parking. Patio dining. Cr cds: C, D, MC, V.

[D]

Unrated Dining Spots

HIGHLAND PARK CAFETERIA. *4611 Cole St, north of downtown.* 214/526-3801. Hrs: 11 am-8 pm. Closed July 4, Dec 25. Buffet: lunch, dinner $10.49. Avg ck: lunch, dinner $6. Specializes in no-sugar-added desserts. Parking. Display of Meissen china. Cr cds: A, DS, MC, V.

LUBY'S CAFETERIA. *10425 N Central Expy (10425), 8¹/₂ mi N, at Meadow Rd, north of downtown.* 214/361-9024. Hrs: 10:45 am-8 pm; late spring-early fall to 8:30 pm. Closed Dec 24 eve-Dec 25. Avg ck: lunch, dinner $5.50. Specializes in prime rib, baked fish, homemade carrot cake. Parking. Cr cds: DS, MC, V.

Fort Worth

FORT WORTH RESTAURANTS
BY NEIGHBORHOOD AREAS

(For full description, see alphabetical listings under Restaurants)

DOWNTOWN

Juanita's. 115 W Second St

Reflections (Worthington Hotel). 200 Main St

SOUTH OF DOWNTOWN

Le Chardonnay. 2443 Forest Park Blvd

WEST OF DOWNTOWN

Balcony. 6100 Camp Bowie Blvd

Celebration. 4600 Dexter

Edelweiss. 3801-A Southwest Blvd

MUSEUM/CULTURAL DISTRICT

Saint-Emilion. 3617 W 7th St

Tours 7th Street Cafe. 3500 W 7th St

Note: *When a listing is located in a town that does not have its own city heading, it will appear under the city nearest to its location. In these cases, the address and town appear in parenthesis immediately following the name of the establishment.*

Motels

✔★ **BEST WESTERN-WEST BRANCH INN.** 7301 W Freeway (76116), I-30 at TX 183, west of downtown. 817/244-7444; FAX 817/244-7902. 120 rms, 2 story. S $39-$45; D $50; each addl $5; suites $60-$80; under 12 free. Crib $5. Pet accepted, some restrictions. TV; cable. Pool. Complimentary continental bkfst. Restaurant adj 3 pm-1 am; closed Sun-Tues. Ck-out noon. Coin lndry. Meeting rms. Some refrigerators. Cr cds: A, C, D, DS, JCB, MC, V.

★★★ **COURTYARD BY MARRIOTT.** (2201 Airport Frwy, Bedford 76021) 13 mi E on TX 121, Central Dr N exit, north of downtown. 817/545-2202; FAX 817/545-2319. 145 rms, 3 story, 14 suites. S $77-$80; D $87-$90; suites $97-$107; under 12 free; wkly, wkend rates. Crib free. TV; cable. Pool. Complimentary coffee in rms. Restaurant 6:30-10:30 am; wkends 7 am-noon. Bar 4-11 pm. Ck-out 1 pm. Coin lndry. Meeting rms. Valet serv. Sundries. Exercise equipt; weight ma-

chine, bicycles, whirlpool. Refrigerator in suites. Patios, balconies. Cr cds: A, C, D, DS, MC, V.

✔★ **LA QUINTA NORTHEAST.** (7920 Bedford-Euless Rd, North Richland Hills 76180) 817/485-2750. 100 rms, 2 story. S $45-$65; D $50-$65; each addl $5; under 18 free. Crib free. TV; cable. Pool. Complimentary continental bkfst. Restaurant adj. Ck-out noon. Meeting rms. Valet serv. Cr cds: A, C, D, DS, MC, V.

✔★ **LA QUINTA-WEST.** 7888 I-30W (76108), west of downtown. 817/246-5511; FAX 817/246-8870. 106 rms, 3 story. S $49-$56; D $57-$64; each addl $6; under 18 free. Crib free. Pet accepted. TV; cable. Pool. Complimentary continental bkfst. Restaurant adj open 24 hrs. Meeting rms. Cr cds: A, C, D, DS, MC, V.

★★ **RESIDENCE INN BY MARRIOTT.** 1701 S University Dr (76107), west of downtown. 817/870-1011; FAX 817/877-5500. 120 suites, 2 story. Suites: 1-bedrm $110-$120; 2-bedrm $130-$150; studio rms $95-$110; wkly, some wkend rates. Crib free. Pet accepted; $6 per day. TV; cable. Heated pool; whirlpool. Complimentary continental bkfst. Restaurant nearby. Ck-out noon. Coin lndry. Meeting rm. Valet serv. Lawn games. Refrigerators. Private patios, balconies. Picnic tables, grills. Cr cds: A, C, D, DS, ER, JCB, MC, V.

Motor Hotels

★★★ **CLARION.** 2000 Beach St (76103), off I-30, east of downtown. 817/534-4801; FAX 817/534-3761. 197 rms, 2-3 story. S, D $69-$89; each addl $10; suites $89-$225; under 18 free; some wkend rates. Crib free. TV; cable, in-rm movies. Pool. Restaurant 6 am-2 pm, 5-10:30 pm. Rm serv. Bar 2 pm-midnight. Ck-out noon. Meeting rms. Tennis. Exercise equipt; weight machine, bicycles, whirlpool. Game rm. Cr cds: A, C, D, DS, ER, MC, V.

★★★ **GREEN OAKS INN AND CONFERENCE CENTER.** 6901 W Frwy (76116), I-30 at TX 183, west of downtown. 817/738-7311; res: 800/433-2174 (exc TX), 800-772-2341 (TX); FAX 817/377-1308. 284 rms, 2-3 story. S $75; D $80; suites $95-$195; each addl $10; under 18 free; wkend, honeymoon packages. Crib free. Pet accepted, some restrictions. TV; cable. 2 pools; poolside serv. Restaurant 6 am-2 pm, 5-9:30 pm. Rm serv. Bars 4 pm-2 am; entertainment, dancing exc Sun. Ck-out noon. Convention facilities. Sundries. Lighted tennis. Exercise equipt; weights, bicycles, sauna. Adj Carswell AFB, 18-hole golf course. Cr cds: A, C, D, DS, MC, V.

★★ **HOLIDAY INN-NORTH.** 2540 Meacham Blvd (76106), I-35W at Meacham Blvd exit, north of downtown. 817/625-9911; FAX 817/625-5132. 247 rms, 6 story. S, D $79; suites $160; under 18 free; some wkend rates. Crib free. TV; cable. Indoor pool. Restaurant 6 am-11 pm; Sat, Sun from 7 am. Rm serv. Bar noon-2 am, Sun to midnight; entertainment, dancing. Ck-out noon. Coin lndry. Meeting rms. Bellhops. Valet serv. Sundries. Gift shop. Exercise equipt; bicycles, rower, whirlpool, sauna. Bathrm phone, wet bar, whirlpool in suites. Cr cds: A, C, D, DS, ER, JCB, MC, V.

Hotels

★★★ **STOCKYARDS.** 109 E Exchange St (76106), north of downtown. 817/625-6427; res: 800/423-8471 (exc TX); FAX 817/624-2571. 52 rms, 3 story. S $105; D $115; each addl $15; suites $160-$350; higher rates: Chisholm Trail Round-up, Pioneer Days, Dec 31. Valet parking $5. TV. Restaurant 6:30 am-10 pm; Fri, Sat to 11 pm. Bar

11 am-midnight, Fri, Sat to 2 am. Ck-out 1 pm. Valet serv. Restored turn of the century hotel. Western decor. Cr cds: A, C, D, DS, MC, V.

★ ★ ★ **WORTHINGTON.** *200 Main St (76102), downtown.* 817/870-1000; res: 800/433-5677; FAX 817/882-1755. 504 rms, 12 story. S, D $139-$179; each addl $10; suites $375-$800; under 18 free; wkend, honeymoon rates. Crib free. Covered parking $5.50, valet parking $8.50. TV; cable. Indoor pool; poolside serv. Restaurant 6 am-11 pm (also see REFLECTIONS). Rm serv 24 hrs. Bar 11-1:30 am; Sun from noon. Ck-out noon. Convention facilities. Concierge. Shopping arcade. Tennis. Golf privileges. Exercise rm; instructor, weights, bicycles, whirlpool, sauna. Some refrigerators. Private patios, balconies. Quiet and luxurious atmosphere. Fresh flowers in every room. Cr cds: A, C, D, DS, MC, V.

Restaurants

★ ★ **BALCONY.** *6100 Camp Bowie Blvd, in Ridglea Village, west of downtown.* 817/731-3719. Hrs: 11:30 am-2 pm, 6-10 pm; Fri to 10:30 pm; Sat 6-10:30 pm. Closed Sun; major hols. Res accepted. Continental menu. Bar. Semi-a la carte: lunch $5.25-$12.95, dinner $12-$22. Child's meals. Specializes in châteaubriand, rack of lamb. Pianist wkends. Parking. Glassed-in balcony. Cr cds: A, C, D, DS, MC, V.

★ ★ **CAFE MATTHEW.** *(8251 Bedford-Euless Rd, North Richland Hills) Northeast of downtown via S-121.* 817/577-3463. Hrs: 11:30 am-2 pm, 5:30-10 pm; Sat from 5:30 pm. Closed Sun; most major hols. Res accepted. Continental menu. Bar. A la carte entrees: lunch $9.50-$14.95, dinner $10.50-$26. Specialties: poached Norwegian salmon, angel hair pasta & chicken breast, roasted rack of lamb, grilled beef tenderloin. Parking. Contemporary decor. Cr cds: A, MC, V.

✔★ **CELEBRATION.** *4600 Dexter, west of downtown.* 817/731-6272. Hrs: 11 am-2:30 pm, 5-9 pm; Sat 11 am-10 pm; Sun 11 am-9 pm. Res accepted. Bar. Semi-a la carte: lunch $4.50-$7.25, dinner $6.50-$10.95. Child's meals. Specializes in fresh vegetables, fish, pot roast. Own desserts. Parking. Outdoor dining. Converted ice house. Cr cds: A, C, D, DS, MC, V.

★ **EDELWEISS.** *3801-A Southwest Blvd, west of downtown.* 817/738-5934. Hrs: 5-10:30 pm; Fri, Sat to 11 pm. Closed Sun, Mon; some major hols. German menu. Bar. Semi-a la carte: dinner $9.95-$17.95. Specializes in Wienerschnitzel, sauerbraten, red cabbage. Entertainment. Parking. Beer garden atmosphere. Family-owned. Cr cds: A, C, D, DS, MC, V.

✔★ ★ **JUANITA'S.** *115 W Second St, downtown.* 817/335-1777. Hrs: 11 am-midnight; Fri to 1 am; Sat noon-1 am; Sun noon-midnight. Closed some major hols. Res accepted. Mexican menu. Bar. Semi-a la carte: lunch, dinner $2.50-$12. Specialties: quail braised in tequila, chile butter chicken, fajitas. Valet parking (dinner, exc Sun). Outdoor dining. Victorian decor. Cr cds: A, D, DS, MC, V.

★ ★ **LE CHARDONNAY.** *2443 Forest Park Blvd, south of downtown.* 817/926-5622. Hrs: 11 am-10 pm; Fri & Sat to 11 pm. Closed July 4, Dec 25. Res accepted. Continental, French menu. Bar. A la carte entrees: lunch $4.95-$11.95, dinner $9.95-$23.95. Specialties: steak Parisienne, chocolate soufflé, fresh seafood. Parking. Outdoor dining. Toy train runs on overhead track. Cr cds: A, C, D, DS, MC, V.

★ ★ ★ **REFLECTIONS.** *(See Worthington Hotel)* 817/870-1000. Hrs: 6-10 pm; Sun brunch 10 am-2:30 pm. Res accepted. Continental menu. Bar 11:30-2 am; Sun noon-1 am. Wine cellar. A la carte entrees: dinner $15.95-$40. Sun brunch $22.95. Specializes in beef, seafood, veal. Own baking. Pianist. Valet parking. Multi-level dining. Cr cds: A, C, D, DS, JCB, MC, V.

★ ★ **SAINT-EMILION.** *3617 W 7th St, near Museum/Cultural District.* 817/737-2781. Hrs: 11:30 am-2 pm, 6-10 pm; Mon from 6 pm; Sat from 6 pm; Sun 5:30-10 pm. Closed most major hols. Res accepted. French menu. A la carte entrees: lunch $7.99-$14, dinner $16.75-$26.50. Specializes in roast duck, imported fish. Parking. Cr cds: A, C, D, DS, MC, V.

✔★ ★ **TOURS 7TH STREET CAFE.** *3500 W 7th St, in Museum/Cultural District.* 817/870-1672. Hrs: 11:30 am-9:30 pm; Fri, Sat to 11 pm. Closed Sun; most major hols. Res accepted. Regional menu. Bar to 11 pm. Semi-a la carte: lunch, dinner $3.95-$13.95. Specialties: pan-fried tilapia with mustard sauce, boule de Niege. Parking. Outdoor dining on patio with view of downtown. Cr cds: A, C, D, MC, V.

Dallas/Fort Worth Airport Area

Motels

✔★ ★ **COUNTRY SUITES BY CARLSON.** *(4100 W John Carpenter Frwy, Irving 75063) TX 114 exit Esters Rd.* 214/929-4008; FAX 214/929-4224. 90 kit. suites, 3 story. S $54-$109; D $64-$129; each addl $6; under 16 free. Crib free. TV; cable. Heated pool; wading pool, whirlpool. Complimentary continental bkfst. Ck-out noon. Meeting rms. Coin lndry. Free airport transportation. Health club privileges. Refrigerators. Cr cds: A, C, D, DS, JCB, MC, V.

★ ★ **DRURY INN.** *(4210 W Airport Frwy, Irving 75062) TX 183 & Esters Rd.* 214/986-1200. 129 rms, 4 story. S $57-$62; D $67-$72; each addl $10; under 18 free. Crib free. Pet accepted. TV; cable. Pool. Complimentary continental bkfst. Restaurant adj 11-2 am. Ck-out noon. Meeting rms. Sundries. Free airport transportation. Cr cds: A, C, D, DS, MC, V.

✔★ ★ **LA QUINTA DFW-IRVING.** *(4105 W Airport Frwy, Irving 75062) TX 183 & Esters Rd.* 214/252-6546; FAX 214/570-4225. 166 rms, 2 story. S $48-$52; D $52-$57; each addl $5; under 18 free. Crib free. Pet accepted, some restrictions. TV; cable, in-rm movies. Pool. Complimentary continental bkfst. Restaurant adj open 24 hrs. Ck-out noon. Meeting rms. Free airport transportation. Health club privileges. Cr cds: A, C, D, DS, MC, V.

★ ★ **WESTAR SUITES.** *(3950 W Airport Frwy, Irving 75062) W on TX 183 at Esters.* 214/790-1950; res: 800/255-1755; FAX 214/790-4750. 126 one-rm suites, 2 story. S $60; D $68; each addl $8; under 18 free; wkly, wkend rates. Crib free. TV; cable. Pool; whirlpool. Complimentary continental bkfst 6-9 am; Sat, Sun 7-10 am. Ck-out noon. Coin lndry. Meeting rms. Valet serv. Free airport transportation. Health club privileges. Refrigerators. Grills. Cr cds: A, C, D, DS, ER, MC, V.

Motor Hotels

★ ★ ★ **HARVEY SUITES.** *(4550 W John Carpenter Frwy, Irving 75063) TX 114 off Esters Blvd exit.* 214/929-4499; res: 800/922-9222; FAX 214/929-0774. 164 suites, 3 story. S $70-$130; D $135-$145; each addl $15; under 12 free; wkend rates. Crib free. Pet accepted; $25 deposit. TV; cable. Pool; poolside serv. Complimentary full bkfst. Complimentary coffee in rms. Restaurant 6:30 am-2 pm; Sat & Sun 7-11 am. Bar 4 pm-2 am. Ck-out 1 pm. Coin lndry. Meeting rms. Valet serv. Sundries. Gift shop. Free airport transportation. Exercise equipt; weights, bicycles, whirlpool. Refrigerators, wet bars. Picnic tables, grills. Cr cds: A, C, D, DS, MC, V.

★ ★ **HOLIDAY INN-AIRPORT NORTH.** *(4441 US 114, Irving 75063)* 214/929-8181. 275 rms, 8 story. S $85-$89; D $95-$99; each addl $10; suites $125-$250; under 18 free; wkend & hol rates. Crib free. Pet accepted, some restrictions; refundable deposit. TV; cable. Pool; wading pool, poolside serv. Restaurant 6:30 am-11 pm. Rm serv. Bar. Ck-out noon. Coin lndry. Meeting rms. Gift shop. Valet serv. Free airport transportation. Exercise equipt; weight machine, bicycles. Some refrigerators. Cr cds: A, C, D, DS, ER, JCB, MC, V.

★ ★ ★ **HOLIDAY INN-DFW AIRPORT SOUTH.** *(4440 W Airport Frwy, Irving 75062)* 214/399-1010; FAX 214/790-8545. 409 rms, 4 story. S $89-$109; D $99-$119; each addl $5; suites $150-$295; under 18 free; wkend rates. TV; cable. Indoor/outdoor pool; wading pool, whirlpool, sauna. Restaurant 5:30 am-midnight. Rm serv. Bar 3 pm-2 am; dancing. Ck-out noon. Coin lndry. Meeting rms. Bellhops. Valet serv. Sundries. Gift shop. Free airport transportation. Health club privileges. Holidome. Game rm. Rec rm. Cr cds: A, C, D, DS, ER, JCB, MC, V.

★ ★ **WILSON WORLD.** *(4600 W Airport Frwy, Irving 75062)* 214/513-0800; FAX 214/513-0106. 200 rms, 5 story, 100 suites. S, D $66-$98; each addl $5; suites $76-$98; under 18 free; wkend rates. Crib $5. Pet accepted, some restrictions. TV; cable. Indoor pool. Restaurant 6 am-2 pm, 5:30-10 pm. Bar 4:30 pm-midnight; entertainment Mon-Fri. Ck-out noon. Meeting rms. Gift shop. Free airport transportation. Exercise equipt; weight machine, stair machine, whirlpool. Refrigerators. Cr cds: A, C, D, DS, MC, V.

Hotels

★ ★ ★ **CROWN STERLING SUITES.** *(4650 W Airport Frwy, Irving 75062) TX 183 & Valley View Ln.* 214/790-0093; FAX 214/790-4768. 308 kit. suites, 10 story. S, D $159-$179; each addl $10; under 12 free; wkend rates. Crib free. TV; cable. Indoor pool; whirlpool, sauna, poolside serv. Complimentary full bkfst. Restaurant 11 am-11 pm. Bar 11-2 am, Sun to midnight; dancing. Ck-out noon. Coin lndry. Meeting rms. Gift shop. Free airport transportation. Health club privileges. Balconies. Atrium lobby with tropical plants. Cr cds: A, C, D, DS, ER, MC, V.

★ ★ ★ **DFW HILTON EXECUTIVE CONFERENCE CENTER.** *(1800 TX 20E, Grapevine 76051) TX 121N, Bethel Rd exit.* 817/481-8444; FAX 817/481-3160. 395 rms, 9 story. S $89-$139; D $94-$145; each addl $15; suites $225-$950; family, wkend rates. Crib free. TV; cable. 2 pools, 1 indoor; poolside serv. Restaurant 6:30 am-midnight. Bars 11-2 am; entertainment, dancing. Ck-out noon. Convention facilities. Concierge. Gift shop. Free parking, valet avail. Free airport transportation. 6 outdoor tennis courts, 2 indoor. Golf privileges, driving range. Exercise rm; instructor, weights, bicycles, whirlpool, steam rm. Minibars; some bathrm phones, refrigerators. Wooded grounds with lake. *LUXURY LEVEL : VIP/CONCIERGE LEVEL.* 22 rms. S $154; D $164. Private lounge. Honor bar. Complimentary bkfst (Mon-Fri), afternoon refreshments, shoeshine. Cr cds: A, C, D, DS, ER, JCB, MC, V.

★ ★ ★ **HYATT REGENCY-DFW.** *(PO Box 619014, DFW Airport 75261) At airport.* 214/453-1234; FAX 214/456-8668. 1,367 rms, 12 story. S $135-$175; D $160-$200; each addl $25; suites $275-$1,200; under 18 free; wkend, honeymoon rates. TV; cable. Heated pool; poolside serv. Restaurant open 24 hrs. Rm serv 6-1 am. Bar 11-2 am; entertainment, dancing. Ck-out noon. Convention facilities. Concierge. Shopping arcade. Airport transportation. Indoor & outdoor tennis, pro. 36-hole golf, greens fee $50-$60, pro, putting green, driving range. Exercise rm; instructor, weights, bicycles, steam rm, sauna. Game rm. Many refrigerators; some bathrm phones. Balconies. *LUXURY LEVEL : REGENCY CLUB.* 108 rms, 15 suites, 2 floors. S $180; D $205; suites $350-$1,200. Concierge. Private lounge. Wet bars. Complimentary bkfst, refreshments. Cr cds: A, C, D, DS, ER, JCB, MC, V.

★ ★ ★ **MARRIOTT-DFW AIRPORT.** *(8440 Freeport Pkwy, Irving 75063) TX 114 at N entrance to airport.* 214/929-8800; FAX 214/929-6501. 491 rms, 20 story. S $135-$145; D $145-$155; suites $175-$400; under 12 free; wkend plans. Crib free. Pet accepted, some restrictions. TV; cable. Indoor/outdoor pool; poolside serv. Restaurants 6 am-11 pm. Bar 11-2 am. Ck-out 1 pm. Coin lndry. Convention facilities. Sundries. Gift shop. Free airport transportation. Tennis, golf privileges. Exercise rm; instructor, weights, bicycles, whirlpool, sauna. Some bathrm phones, refrigerators. *LUXURY LEVEL : CONCIERGE LEVEL.* 80 rms, 3 floors. S $145; D $155. Private lounge. Complimentary continental bkfst, refreshments. Cr cds: A, C, D, DS, ER, JCB, MC, V.

Denver

Settled: 1858

Pop 467,610

Elev: 5,280 feet

Time zone: Mountain

Area code: 303

The state capital of Colorado had its beginnings as a small community of adventurers searching for gold. Today, Denver still attracts those with a sense of adventure, but nowadays they come in search of opportunity, excitement and recreation. The abundant scenic beauty throughout the area helps make Denver one of the most appealing cities in the US.

As a growing community rich in mineral resources, natural beauty and wild game, Denver quickly realized the need for a transportation link with the rest of the country. For several years the people of Denver actively promoted the idea of a railroad link with the Union Pacific, and a line finally was opened between Denver and Cheyenne in 1870. The ensuing rush of immigration boosted both property values and economic development, furthering the effects of the gold and silver booms of the late 1800s. Already the capital of the Colorado Territory, Denver in 1876 became the capital of the 38th state.

In the wake of its "boom town" days, Denver continues to thrive, attracting many people with its dry, mild climate and proximity to recreational activities—most notably skiing in the Rockies. A new airport 17 miles from downtown Denver is an indication of the city's vitality. Denver International Airport encompasses 53 square miles (more than Dallas/Fort Worth and Chicago's O'Hare airports combined) and was planned to be a virtual city unto itself, with hotels, shops and dining and entertainment spots. It is expected to become one of the world's busiest airports, apparently anticipating continuing prosperity for Denver in the future.

Business

Manufacturing has made great strides in Colorado due to the state's central location, diverse transportation facilities and abundant natural resources. The state is still a storehouse of mineral wealth, producing much of the nation's supply of metallic and nonmetallic minerals. Denver is an important energy center, with half of its downtown office space rented by energy-related firms.

In the Denver area there are approximately 180 major businesses with more than 250 employees. The range of industry is great—construction; electrical machinery; metal products; food, hospital and dental equipment; leather; lumber; paper; petroleum; and glass. There are also finance, insurance and real estate companies and other service industries, such as health care, education, recreation and government. Printing, publishing and allied industries add to the picture, and wholesale and retail trade areas are thriving.

Convention Facilities

There are three major convention buildings in Denver—the Denver Convention Complex, the Denver Merchandise Mart and the Colorado Convention Center. Up to 16,000 hotel rooms can be guaranteed for a convention.

The Colorado Convention Center, part of the Denver Convention Complex, contains 300,000 square feet of exhibit space and 100,000 square feet of meeting space, including a 35,000-square-foot ballroom, 46 meeting rooms and theater-style seating for 7,500.

In the Convention Complex, the Currigan Exhibition Hall has 100,000 square feet of unobstructed space. Banquets can be served here for 9,000 people, or 14,000 can be seated theater-style. The theater seats 2,240; 5 to 20 rooms can be set up in the conference area for a total capacity of 3,470 people.

At the Merchandise Mart, the Exposition Building has 100,000 square feet of space, which can hold 4,000 people; 200 individual showrooms can seat an additional 4,000 people at peak capacity. The main building has 400 permanent showrooms, plus a 65,000-square-foot hall.

Sports and Recreation

With the Rockies nearly hovering over the city, Denver has long been a mecca for skiers, climbers and hikers. Fishing, camping and snowmobiling are also popular mountain activities. Spreading out over the Rocky Mountain foothills, the Denver Mountain Park System is a spectacular recreation area. The system covers 13,448 acres in a chain beginning 15 miles west of the city and extending to Summit Lake, 60 miles west. The city parks provide picnic and playground areas, golf courses, tennis courts, lakes and swimming pools.

For sports fans, the Denver Broncos football team and the new Colorado Rockies baseball team play at Mile High Stadium, and the Nuggets basketball team plays at McNichols Arena. In addition, universities in and near Denver have active sports programs. The Colorado Rockies baseball team will have a stadium of their own, Coors Field, that is expected to be completed in time for the start of the Rockies 1995 season.

There is dog racing at the Mile High Kennel Club and auto racing at Bandimere and Lakeside speedways.

The National Western Livestock Show, Horse Show and Rodeo is held in Denver each January, attracting many of the nation's finest rodeo performers, as well as buyers and sellers of livestock from all over the world.

Entertainment

The Colorado Symphony Orchestra plays in Boettcher Hall, the first "surround" orchestra hall in the US, from September through early June. During the fall, winter and spring, the Denver Center Theatre Company performs in the Helen Bonfils Theater Complex at the Denver Performing Arts Complex. The Complex is known as one of the most innovative and comprehensive performing arts facilities in the country, offering a variety of entertainment, including musicals, classics and new plays. The addition of the 2,800-seat Temple Hoyne Buell Theatre in late 1991 made the Denver Performing Arts Complex one of the largest in the nation.

Historical Areas

Railroading was very important to the development of this part of the country, and much of its history has been preserved in such places as the Forney Transportation Museum and the Colorado Railroad Museum at Golden.

Some of the feeling of the Old West can be recaptured at the Buffalo Bill Memorial Museum on Lookout Mountain. Exhibits are centered around Buffalo Bill's Wild West Show, as well as other aspects of his exciting life.

The Molly Brown House pays homage to one of Denver's earlier and more flamboyant citizens, Margaret Tobin. A survivor of the *Titanic* disaster, she was known as the "unsinkable" Molly Brown. Molly came west to Leadville to make her fortune—and she did. Her extravagant house in Denver was built during the Victorian period, and Molly decorated the interior accordingly, particularly with purchases made during her numerous trips to Europe.

Sightseeing

The State Capitol dome, which is covered with gold leaf from Colorado mines, offers visitors a panoramic view of the city. Also downtown is the US Mint, where guided tours are conducted and a display of gold may be seen on the mezzanine. In the Civic Center complex are the Denver Public Library, the largest public library in the Rocky Mountain region, the outdoor Greek Theatre and the Denver Art Museum, with a fine collection of Native American arts.

The Denver Zoo and the Denver Museum of Natural History are located in City Park. The museum has mammals and birds from four continents displayed against natural backgrounds, geology and dinosaur exhibits, and a collection of Native American artifacts. Also in the museum is the Charles C. Gates Planetarium, which presents a variety of space science programs including star and laser light shows. The Denver Botanic Gardens and the Boettcher Memorial Conservatory have plants representative of the various climatic zones of the world.

Lakeside, Elitch Gardens and Heritage Square in Golden are amusement parks in the Denver area. Larimer Square is a restoration of Denver's oldest—and at one time wildest—streets. Where outlaws and desperados once walked, today musicians, artists and craftsmen work, and visitors enjoy restaurants, galleries and shops housed in Victorian buildings.

More than half of Colorado's land west of Denver lies within the boundaries of national forests, and two of the most popular areas of the National Park system are within the state: Rocky Mountain National Park and Mesa Verde National Park.

General References

Settled: 1858 Pop: 467,610 Elev: 5,280 feet Time zone: Mountain Area code: 303

Phone Numbers

POLICE & FIRE: 911
FBI: 629-7171
POISON CONTROL CENTER: 629-1123
TIME: 976-9999   **WEATHER:** 976-1311

Information Sources

Denver Metro Convention and Visitors Bureau, 225 W Colfax Ave, 80202; 892-1505.

Denver Chamber of Commerce, 1445 Market St, 80202; 534-8500.
Dept of Parks and Recreation, 964-2500.

Transportation

AIRLINES: American; America West; Continental; Delta; Mexicana; Northwest; TWA; United; USAir; and other commuter and regional airlines. For the most current airline schedules and information consult the *Official Airline Guide,* published twice monthly.
AIRPORT: Denver International, 342-2300 or 800/AIR-2-DEN.
CAR RENTAL AGENCIES: (See Toll-Free Numbers) Avis 398-3725; Budget 399-0444; Hertz 355-2244; National 321-7990.
PUBLIC TRANSPORTATION: Regional Transportation District 299-6000.
RAILROAD PASSENGER SERVICE: Amtrak 800/872-7245.

Newspapers

Denver Post; Rocky Mountain News.

Convention Facilities

Denver Convention Complex, 14th and Welton Sts, 640-8000.
Merchandise Mart, 451 E 58th Ave, 292-6278.

Sports & Recreation

Major Sports Facilities
McNichols Arena, W 17th Ave & Clay St (Nuggets, basketball, 893-6700).
Mile High Stadium, W 19th & Eliot Sts (Broncos, football, 433-7466; Rockies, baseball, 762-5437 or R-O-C-K-I-E-S).

Racetracks
Bandimere Speedway, 3051 S Rooney Rd, in Morrison, 697-6001 (auto racing).
Mile High Kennel Club, 7 mi NE at jct I-270 & Vasquez Blvd, at 6200 Dahlia St, 288-1591 (greyhound racing).

Cultural Facilities

Theaters
Arvada Center for the Arts & Humanities, 6901 Wadsworth Blvd, Arvada, 431-3939.
Auditorium Theater, Denver Performing Arts Complex, 14th & Curtis Sts, 893-4100 or -3272.
The Changing Scene, 1527½ Champa St, 893-5775.
Country Dinner Playhouse, 6875 S Clinton St, 799-1410.
The Helen Bonfils Theatre Complex, Denver Performing Arts Complex, 14th & Curtis Sts, 893-4100.
Temple Hoyne Buell Theatre, Denver Performing Arts Complex, 14th & Curtis Sts, 893-4100.

Concert Hall
Boettcher Concert Hall, Denver Performing Arts Complex, 14th & Curtis Sts, 640-5060.

Museums
Buffalo Bill Memorial Museum, Lookout Mountain, I-70W exit 256, 526-0747.
Children's Museum of Denver, 2121 Crescent Dr, 433-7444.
Colorado History Museum, 1300 Broadway, 866-3682.
Colorado Railroad Museum, 17155 W 44th Ave, Golden, 279-4591.
Denver Firefighters Museum, 1326 Tremont Place, 892-1436.

Denver Museum of Natural History, 2001 Colorado Blvd, City Park, 322-7009.
Forney Transportation Museum, 1416 Platte St, near I-25 exit 211, 433-3643.
Molly Brown House Museum, 1340 Pennsylvania St, 832-4092.

Art Museums

Denver Art Museum, 100 W 14th Ave Pkwy, in Civic Center, 640-2793.
Museum of Western Art, 1727 Tremont Place, 296-1880.
Turner Museum, 773 Downing St, 832-0924

Points of Interest

Denver Botanic Gardens, Boettcher Memorial Conservatory, 1005 York St, entrance off Cheesman Park, 331-4000.
Denver Public Library, 1357 Broadway, 640-8800.
Denver Zoo, E 23rd Ave, between Colorado Blvd & York St in City Park, 331-4110.
Elitch Gardens Amusement Park, 4620 W 38th Ave, at Tennyson St, 455-4771.
Grant-Humphreys Mansion, 770 Pennsylvania St, 894-2506.
Heritage Square, jct CO 40, 93, in Golden, 279-2789 or 277-0040.
Lakeside Amusement Park, W 44th Ave & Sheridan Blvd, 477-1621.
Larimer Square, Larimer St between 14th & 15th Sts.
Outdoor Greek Theater, S side of Civic Center.
Red Rocks Park, 12 mi SW, off CO 26 between I-70 & US 285.
Sakura Square, Lawrence to Larimer Sts on 19th St, 295-0305.

State Capitol, E Colfax Ave & Sherman St, 866-2604.
United States Mint, 320 W Colfax Ave, 844-3582 or -5588.

Sightseeing Tours

Gray Line bus tours, PO Box 17527, 80217-0527; 289-2841.
Historic Colorado Tours, Education Dept, 1300 Broadway, 80203; 866-4686.

Annual Events

National Western Livestock Show, Horse Show & Rodeo, National Western Complex and Coliseum. Jan.
Cherry Blossom Festival, Sakura Square. 2nd wkend June.

City Neighborhoods

Many of the restaurants, unrated dining establishments and some lodgings listed under Denver include neighborhoods as well as exact street addresses. Geographic descriptions of the Downtown and 16th St Mall are given, followed by a table of restaurants arranged by neighborhood.

Downtown: Southeast of Wynkoop St, west of Grant St, north of 14th St and east of Speer Blvd. **North of Downtown:** North of Wynkoop St. **South of Downtown:** South of 14th Ave. **East of Downtown:** East of Grant St. **West of Downtown:** West of Cherry Creek.
16th St Mall: 16th St from Market St on the NW to Broadway on the SE.

Lodgings and Food

DENVER RESTAURANTS
BY NEIGHBORHOOD AREAS

(For full description, see alphabetical listings under Restaurants)

DOWNTOWN

Al Fresco. 1515-23 Market St

The Broker. 821 17th St

European Cafe. 1515-23 Market St

Le Central. 112 E 8th Ave

McCormick's Fish House. 1659 Wazee St

Old Spaghetti Factory. 1215 18th St

Palace Arms (Brown Palace Hotel). 321 17th St

Rocky Mountain Diner. 800 18th St

Trinity Grille. 1801 Broadway

Wynkoop Brewing Company. 1634 18th St

Zenith American Grill. 1750 Lawrence St

NORTH OF DOWNTOWN

Brittany Hill. 9350 Grant

Morton's of Chicago. 900 Auraria Parkway

SOUTH OF DOWNTOWN

Buckhorn Exchange. 1000 Osage St

Chives American Bistro. 1120 E 6th Ave

Pour La France. 730 S University Blvd

Soren's. 315 Detroit St

Tuscany (Loews Giorgio Hotel). 4150 E Mississippi Ave

Wellshire Inn. 3333 S Colorado Blvd

EAST OF DOWNTOWN

Cliff Young. 700 E 17th Ave

Normandy French Restaurant. 1515 Madison

Tante Louise. 4900 E Colfax Ave

WEST OF DOWNTOWN

Baby Doe's Matchless Mine. 2520 W 23rd Ave

Furrs Cafeteria. 4900 Kipling

Note: *When a listing is located in a town that does not have its own city heading, it will appear under the city nearest to its location. In these cases, the address and town appear in parenthesis immediately following the name of the establishment.*

Motels

★ ★ **COURTYARD BY MARRIOTT.** *7415 E 41st Ave (80216), I-70 exit 278, east of downtown.* 303/333-3303; FAX 303/399-7356. 145 rms, 3 story. S, D $85-$95; each addl $10; suites $99-$109; under 18 free; wknd rates. Crib free. TV; cable. Indoor pool. Complimentary coffee in rms. Restaurant 6:30-10 am, 5-10 pm; Sat, Sun from 7 am. Bar 4-11 pm. Ck-out 1 pm. Coin lndry. Meeting rms. Valet serv. Exercise equipt; weight machine, bicycles, whirlpool. Refrigerator in suites. Balconies. Cr cds: A, C, D, DS, MC, V.

D ⊠ ⌕ ✕ ⊠ ⊠ SC

★ ★ **LA QUINTA AIRPORT.** *3975 Peoria St (80239), I-70 exit 281, east of downtown.* 303/371-5640; FAX 303/371-7015. 112 rms, 2 story. S, D $59-$79; each addl $6; under 18 free. Crib free. Pet accepted, some restrictions. TV; cable. Heated pool. Complimentary continental bkfst in lobby. Restaurant adj open 24 hrs. Ck-out noon. Coin lndry. Valet serv. Free airport transportation. Some refrigerators. Cr cds: A, C, D, DS, MC, V.

D ⌕ ⊠ ⊠ ⊠ SC

✔ ★ ★ **LA QUINTA CENTRAL.** *3500 Park Ave W (80216), I-25 exit 213, west of downtown.* 303/458-1222; FAX 303/433-2246. 106 rms, 3 story. S $48-$55; D $54-$61; under 18 free. Crib free. Pet accepted. TV; cable. Pool. Complimentary bkfst. Complimentary coffee in lobby. Restaurant adj open 24 hrs. Ck-out noon. Meeting rms. Valet serv. Cr cds: A, C, D, DS, MC, V.

D ⌕ ⊠ ⊠ ⊠ SC

★ ★ **QUALITY INN SOUTH.** *6300 E Hampden Ave (80222), I-25 exit 201, east of downtown.* 303/758-2211; FAX 303/753-0156. 185 rms, 1-2 story. S, D $55-$72; each addl $7; under 18 free; wkend rates. Crib free. Pet accepted; $5 per day. TV; cable. Pool; whirlpool, sauna, poolside serv. Complimentary coffee in rms. Restaurant 6 am-11 pm. Rm serv. Bar 4-11 pm. Ck-out noon. Coin lndry. Meeting rms. Lawn games. Some refrigerators. Private patios, balconies. Picnic tables. Cr cds: A, C, D, DS, ER, JCB, MC, V.

D ⌕ ⊠ ⊠ ⊠ SC

★ ★ **RESIDENCE INN BY MARRIOTT-DOWNTOWN.** *2777 Zuni (80211), jct Speer Blvd N, I-25 exit 212B, west of downtown.* 303/458-5318. 156 kit. suites, 2 story. S $89-$109; D $109-$139; under 16 free; wknd rates. Crib free. TV; cable. Heated pool. Complimentary continental bkfst. Restaurant nearby. Ck-out noon. Meeting rms. Valet serv. Free grocery shopping serv. Airport, RR station, bus depot transportation. Exercise equipt; weights, bicycles, whirlpool. Health club privileges. Refrigerators; many fireplaces. Private patios, balconies. Cr cds: A, C, D, DS, JCB, MC, V.

D ⊠ ✕ ⊠ ⊠ SC

Motor Hotels

✔ ★ **DAYS HOTEL-AIRPORT.** *4590 Quebec St (80216), just N of I-70 exit 278, east of downtown.* 303/320-0260; FAX 303/320-7595. 195 rms, 5 story. S $52-$69; D $57-$74; each addl $7; suite $110; under 17 free. Crib free. Pet accepted; $25. TV; cable. Pool. Restaurant 6 am-2 pm, 5:30-10 pm; Sat & Sun 6 am-1 pm, 5:30-10 pm. Rm serv. Bar 4 pm-midnight, Sat & Sun from 5 pm. Ck-out noon. Coin lndry. Meeting rms. Bellhops. Valet serv. Gift shop. Free airport transportation. Exercise equipt; weight machine, bicycles, whirlpool. Some in-rm steam baths. Cr cds: A, C, D, DS, MC, V.

⌕ ⊠ ✕ ⊠ ⊠ SC

★ ★ **MANY MANSIONS.** *1313 Steele St (80206), east of downtown.* 303/355-1313; res: 800/225-7829; FAX 303/355-1313, ext. 200. 36 kit. suites, 8 story. S $90; D $105-$145; each addl $15; under 12 free; wkly, monthly rates. Crib free. TV; cable. Free coffee in rms. Complimentary full bkfst wkdays (continental bkfst, wkends). Complimentary coffee in lobby. Restaurant nearby. Ck-out noon. Coin lndry. Meeting rms. Free garage parking. Free airport, RR station, bus depot transportation. Balconies. Picnic tables, grills. Cr cds: A, C, D, DS, ER, JCB, MC, V.

⊠ ⊠ SC

★ **RAMADA INN-AIRPORT.** *3737 Quebec St (80207), east of downtown.* 303/388-6161; FAX 303/388-0426. 148 rms, 4 story. S, D $70-$94; each addl $10; under 18 free; wkend rates. Crib free. Pet accepted. TV; cable. Heated pool. Complimentary coffee. Restaurant 6 am-11 pm. Rm serv. Bar 11-2 am, Sun to midnight. Ck-out noon. Meeting rms. Bellhops. Valet serv. Gift shop. Free airport transportation. Health club privileges. Some refrigerators. Cr cds: A, C, D, DS, ER, JCB, MC, V.

D ⌕ ⊠ ⊠ ⊠ SC

★ ★ **SHERATON-DENVER AIRPORT.** 3535 Quebec St (80207), east of downtown. 303/333-7711; FAX 303/322-2262. 196 rms, 8 story. S $75-$99; D $85-$105; each addl $15; under 17 free; wkend plans. Crib free. TV; cable. Indoor pool. Restaurant 6 am-midnight; Sun from 7 am. Rm serv. Bar 11-2 am, Sun to midnight. Ck-out noon. Coin lndry. Meeting rms. Bellhops. Valet serv. Gift shop. Free airport transportation. Exercise equipt; weight machine, stair machine, whirlpool. Lawn games. Some private patios, balconies. Cr cds: A, C, D, DS, ER, JCB, MC, V.

[D] [icons] SC

Hotels

★ ★ ★ ★ **BROWN PALACE.** 321 17th St (80202), downtown. 303/297-3111; res: 800/321-2599 (exc CO), 800/228-2917 (CO); FAX 303/293-9204. 230 rms, 9 story. S $159-$119; D $159-$214; each addl $15; suites $225-$675; under 12 free; wkend package plan. Garage in/out $12. Crib free. TV; cable, in-rm movies avail. Restaurants (see PALACE ARMS). Afternoon tea 2-4:30 pm. Rm serv 24 hrs. Bar 10:30 am-midnight; entertainment exc Sun. Ck-out 1 pm. Meeting rms. Concierge. Gift shop. Barber. Valet parking. Airport transportation. Health club privileges. Some refrigerators. A famous hotel, opened 1892. Cr cds: A, C, D, DS, JCB, MC, V.

[icons] SC

★ ★ ★ **BURNSLEY.** 1000 Grant St (80203), downtown. 303/830-1000; res: 800/231-3915 (exc CO); FAX 303/830-7676. 82 suites, 16 story. Suites $75-$135; each addl $10. Pet accepted, some restrictions; $50. TV; cable. Pool. Complimentary coffee in rms. Complimentary bkfst. Restaurant 6:30 am-2 pm, 6-9 pm. Rm serv to 11 pm. Bar from 11 am. Ck-out noon. Meeting rms. Garage parking. Refrigerators. Balconies. Converted apartment building in residential area, near State Capitol. Cr cds: A, C, D, MC, V.

[D] [icons]

✔ ★ **COMFORT INN.** 401 17th St (80202), downtown. 303/296-0400; FAX 303/297-0774. 229 rms, 22 story. S $59-$69; D $69-$79; each addl $10; suites $89-$150; under 18 free; wkend rates. Covered valet parking $8. TV; cable. Complimentary continental bkfst. Restaurant adj wkdays 6:30 am-9 pm. Rm serv 24 hrs. Bar 10:30 am-midnight. Ck-out noon. Meeting rms. Shopping arcade. Barber, beauty shop. Health club privileges. Cr cds: A, C, D, DS, ER, JCB, MC, V.

[D] [icons] SC

★ ★ **EMBASSY SUITES.** 7525 E Hampden Ave (80231), off I-25E exit 201, south of downtown. 303/696-6644; FAX 303/337-6202. 207 suites, 7 story. S $135; D $145; each addl $10; under 12 free; wkend rates. Crib free. TV; cable. Indoor pool. Coffee in rms. Complimentary bkfst. Restaurant 11:30 am-2:30 pm, 5-10 pm; Sat, Sun 11:30 am-11 pm. Bar 11:30-2 am, Sun to midnight. Ck-out 1 pm. Coin lndry. Meeting rms. Gift shop. Exercise equipt; bicycles, stair machine, whirlpool, sauna, steam rm. Refrigerators, minibars. Balconies. Cr cds: A, C, D, DS, JCB, MC, V.

[D] [icons] SC

★ ★ ★ **EMBASSY SUITES-AIRPORT.** 4444 N Havana St (80239), I-70 exit 280, east of downtown. 303/375-0400; FAX 303/371-4634. 212 suites, 7 story. Suites $105-$125; each addl $12; under 12 free; ski plans, wkend package. Crib free. Pet accepted, some restrictions. TV; cable. Indoor pool; poolside serv. Complimentary full bkfst. Coffee in rms. Restaurant 9:30 am-11 pm. Bar to 2 am; entertainment Tues-Thurs. Ck-out 1 pm. Coin lndry. Meeting rms. Gift shop. Free airport transportation. Exercise equipt; weights, bicycles, whirlpool, steam rm, sauna. Refrigerators, microwaves; some minibars. Cr cds: A, C, D, DS, JCB, MC, V.

[D] [icons] SC

★ ★ **EXECUTIVE TOWER INN.** 1405 Curtis St (80202), downtown. 303/571-0300; res: 800/525-6651; FAX 303/825-4301. 337 rms, 16 story. S $127-$154; D $137-$162; each addl $10; suites $160-$320; under 16 free; wkend rates. Crib free. Pet accepted, some restrictions. TV; cable. Indoor pool. Restaurant 6:30 am-11 pm; dining rm 11 am-2 pm, 5:30-10 pm. Bar 11-2 am, Sun to midnight. Ck-out noon. Coin lndry. Meeting rms. Garage. Tennis. Exercise rm; instructor, weights, stair machine, whirlpool, sauna, steam rm. Rec rm. Cr cds: A, C, D, ER, JCB, MC, V.

[D] [icons] SC

★ ★ ★ **HYATT REGENCY DENVER.** 1750 Welton St (80202), downtown. 303/295-1234; FAX 303/292-2472. 511 rms, 26 story. S $79-$150; D $79-$170; each addl $15; suites $350-$1,000; under 18 free. Crib free. Garage, valet parking $12. TV; cable. Pool; poolside serv. Supervised child's activities (Fri, Sat eves). Restaurant 6 am-midnight. Bar 10:30-2 am. Ck-out noon. Meeting rms. Concierge. Airport transportation. Tennis. Health club privileges. Bathrm phones, minibars; some refrigerators. **LUXURY LEVEL : REGENCY CLUB.** 20 rms. S $165; D $185. Private lounge, honor bar. Complimentary bkfst, refreshments. Cr cds: A, C, D, DS, ER, JCB, MC, V.

[D] [icons] SC

★ ★ ★ **HYATT REGENCY TECH CENTER.** 7800 Tufts Ave (80237), at jct I-25, I-225, south of downtown. 303/779-1234; FAX 303/850-7164. 448 rms, 11 story. S $115-$145; D $130-$160; each addl $15; suites $250-$800; under 18 free; wkend plans. Crib free. TV; cable. Indoor pool; poolside serv. Supervised child's activities (Fri, Sat evenings). Restaurant 6:30 am-11 pm. Bar 3 pm-2 am. Ck-out noon. Convention facilities. Concierge. Gift shop. Valet parking. Airport transportation. Lighted tennis. Exercise equipt; weights, bicycles, whirlpool, sauna. Some refrigerators, bathrm phones. **LUXURY LEVEL : REGENCY CLUB.** 45 rms, 3 suites. S $170; D $185. Private lounge, honor bar. Complimentary continental bkfst, refreshments, newspaper. Cr cds: A, C, D, DS, ER, JCB, MC, V.

[D] [icons] SC

★ ★ ★ ★ **LOEWS GIORGIO.** 4150 E Mississippi Ave (80222), south of downtown. 303/782-9300; FAX 303/758-6542. 197 rms, 11 story. S $105-$129; D $119-$140; each addl $20; suites $215-$500; under 14 free; wkend packages. Pet accepted, some restrictions. TV; cable, in-rm movies avail. Complimentary continental bkfst. Coffee in rms. Restaurant (see TUSCANY). Bar 10 am-midnight. Ck-out 11 am. Meeting rms. Concierge. Gift shop. Valet parking. Health club privileges. Bathrm phones, minibars; some refrigerators. Complimentary newspaper. Library. Italian-style hotel featuring magnificent Renaissance-style frescos. Cr cds: A, C, D, DS, JCB, MC, V.

[D] [icons] SC

★ ★ ★ **MARRIOTT-CITY CENTER.** 1701 California St (80202), downtown. 303/297-1300; FAX 303/298-7474. 612 rms, 19 story. S $150-$165; D $170-$185; each addl $10; suites $225-$500; under 12 free; wkend plans. Crib free. Valet parking; fee. Pet accepted, some restrictions. TV; cable. Indoor pool; poolside serv. Restaurant 6:30 am-10 pm. Rm serv to midnight. Bar 11-2 am. Ck-out noon. Convention facilities. Concierge. Shopping arcade. Exercise rm; instructor, weight machine, stair machines, whirlpool, sauna, steam rm. Game rm. Some bathrm phones, refrigerators. **LUXURY LEVEL : CONCIERGE LEVEL.** 68 rms, 2 floors. S $165; D $185. Private lounge, honor bar 11 am-10 pm. Complimentary continental bkfst, refreshments. Cr cds: A, C, D, DS, ER, JCB, MC, V.

[D] [icons] SC

★ ★ **MARRIOTT-SOUTHEAST.** 6363 E Hampden Ave (80222), I-25 exit 201, south of downtown. 303/758-7000; FAX 303/691-3418. 595 rms, 11 story. S, D $132; suites $150-$350; under 18 free; wkend package plan. Crib free. TV; cable. 2 pools, 1 indoor; poolside serv, lifeguard. Restaurant 6 am-11 pm. Bar 11-2 am, Sun to midnight. Ck-out 1 pm. Coin lndry. Convention facilities. Concierge. Shopping arcade. Barber, beauty shop. Covered parking. Airport transportation. Exercise rm; instructor, weight machine, bicycles, whirlpool. Game rm. Some bathrm phones, refrigerators. Balconies; some private patios. **LUXURY LEVEL .** 53 rms. S, D $139. Private lounge. Complimentary continental bkfst, refreshments, newspaper. Cr cds: A, C, D, DS, ER, JCB, MC, V.

D ✋ ≈ ✕ 🖊 🔥 SC

★ ★ **OXFORD.** *1600 17th St (80202), downtown.* 303/628-5400; res: 800/228-5838 (exc CO); FAX 303/628-5413. 81 rms, 5 story. S $125-$135; D $135-$140; each addl $10; suites from $275; under 12 free. Crib free. Valet parking $10. TV; cable. Complimentary coffee. Dining rm 6:30-10 am, 11 am-2 pm, 5-10 pm; Fri, Sat to 11 pm; Sun 7 am-10 pm. Rm serv 24 hrs. Bar. Ck-out 1 pm. Meeting rms. Concierge. Barber, beauty shop. Exercise rm; instructor, weight machine, stair machine, whirlpool, steam rm. Elegant, European-style; many antiques. First luxury hotel built in Denver (1891). Cr cds: A, C, D, DS, MC, V.

D 🖊 ✕ 🖊 🔥 SC

★ ★ **RADISSON.** *1550 Court Place (80202), on 16th St Mall.* 303/893-3333; FAX 303/623-0303. 744 rms, 22 story. S $140; D $160; each addl $10; suites $260-$850; under 18 free; wkend rates. Crib free. Garage $8 daily; in/out privileges. Pet accepted, some restrictions. TV; cable. 5th floor pool; poolside serv. Restaurant 6:30 am-11 pm. Bar 11-1 am; entertainment. Ck-out noon. Convention facilities. Concierge. Shopping arcade. Barber, beauty shops. Exercise equipt; stair machine, bicycles, steam rm, sauna. Health club privileges. Cr cds: A, C, D, DS, ER, JCB, MC, V.

D ✋ ≈ ✕ 🖊 🔥 SC

★ ★ ★ **RED LION.** *3203 Quebec St (80207), east of downtown.* 303/321-3333; FAX 303/329-5281. 576 rms, 9 story. S $109; D $119; each addl $10; under 18 free; wkend rates. Crib free. Pet accepted; $50. TV; cable. Indoor pool. Restaurant 6 am-11 pm. Rm serv 24 hrs. Bar 11-2 am, Sun to midnight. Ck-out noon. Convention facilities. Free airport transportation. Exercise equipt; weight machine, stair machine, whirlpool, sauna. Some bathrm phones, refrigerators. Balconies. Sun deck. Cr cds: A, C, D, DS, ER, MC, V.

D ✋ ≈ ✕ 🖊 🔥 SC

✔ ★ ★ **SHERATON DENVER TECH CENTER.** *4900 DTC Pkwy (80237), off I-25 exit 199, south of downtown.* 303/779-1100; FAX 303/721-0752. 625 rms, 2-10 story. S, D $87-$135; each addl $15; suites $260-$335; under 17 free; wkend plans. Crib free. TV. 2 pools, 1 indoor. Restaurant open 24 hrs. Bar 11 am-midnight; entertainment. Ck-out 1 pm. Convention facilities. Shopping arcade. Valet parking. Exercise rm; instructor, weights, bicycles, whirlpool, steam rm, sauna. Rec rm. Refrigerators. Some balconies. *LUXURY LEVEL : EMBASSY.* 26 rms. S, D $150; suites $335. Concierge. Minibar. Complimentary bkfst, refreshments. Cr cds: A, C, D, DS, JCB, MC, V.

D ≈ ✕ 🖊 🔥 SC

★ ★ **STAPLETON PLAZA.** *3333 Quebec St (80207), east of downtown.* 303/321-3500; res: 800/950-6070; FAX 303/322-7343. 300 rms, 11 story. S, D $97-$113; each addl $10; suites $205-$395; under 12 free; wkly, wkend package plans. Crib free. TV; cable. Pool; poolside serv. Complimentary coffee. Restaurant 6 am-11 pm. Rm serv 24 hrs. Bars 11-2 am; Sun to midnight. Ck-out noon. Convention facilities. Shopping arcade. Barber, beauty shop. Free garage parking. Free airport transportation. Exercise rm; instructor, weight machines, stair machine, whirlpool, sauna, steam rm. Balconies. Built around 11-story atrium; glass-enclosed elvtrs. Cr cds: A, C, D, DS, ER, JCB, MC, V.

D ≈ ✕ 🖊 🔥 SC

★ ★ ★ **STOUFFER CONCOURSE.** *3801 Quebec St (80207), east of downtown.* 303/399-7500; FAX 303/321-1783. 400 rms, 12 story. S $135-$145; D $145-$155; each addl $10; suites $250; under 18 free; wkend ski plans. Covered parking $4 overnight; valet $6. TV; cable. 2 heated pools, 1 indoor. Complimentary coffee. Restaurant 6:30 am-11 pm. Rm serv 24 hrs. Bar 11-1 am; entertainment. Ck-out 1 pm. Convention facilities. Concierge. Gift shop. Free airport transportation. Exercise equipt; weight machines, bicycles, whirlpool, steam rm. Refrigerators; minibar, some bathrm phones. Balconies. Dramatic 10-story central atrium. *LUXURY LEVEL : THE CLUB FLOOR.* 99 rms, 3 floors. S, D $160-$170, suites $400-$600. Private lounge. In-rm

movies. Complimentary continental bkfst, evening refreshments, newspaper. Cr cds: A, C, D, DS, ER, JCB, MC, V.

D ≈ ✕ 🖊 🔥 SC

★ ★ ★ **THE WARWICK.** *1776 Grant St (80203), downtown.* 303/861-2000; res: 800/525-2888; FAX 303/839-8504. 194 rms, 15 story. S, D $155-$165; each addl $16; suites $190-$000; under 18 free; wkend package plan. Crib free. Garage $5. Pet accepted. TV; cable. Rooftop pool (in season); poolside serv. Complimentary continental bkfst. Restaurant 6:30 am-2 pm, 6-10 pm. Rm serv 24 hrs. Bar 11 am-midnight. Ck-out 1 pm. Meeting rms. Concierge. Airport transportation. Free railroad station, bus depot transportation. Health club privileges. Many wet bars. Bathrm phones, refrigerators. Some balconies. Cr cds: A, C, D, DS, JCB, MC, V.

D ✋ ≈ ✕ 🖊 🔥 SC

★ ★ ★ **WESTIN HOTEL TABOR CENTER.** *1672 Lawrence St (80202), in Tabor Center, downtown.* 303/572-9100; FAX 303/572-7288. 420 rms, 19 story. S $145; D $170; each addl $15; suites $275-$410; under 18 free. Pet accepted, some restrictions. Garage $6-$12. TV; cable. Indoor/outdoor pool; poolside serv, hot tub. Restaurant 6-11 am; dining rm 11 am-2 pm, 5-10 pm, Sat to 11 pm. Rm serv 24 hrs. Bar 5 pm-1:30 am; pianist Tues-Sat. Ck-out 1 pm. Convention facilities. Shopping arcade. Exercise equipt; weight machine, stair machine, whirlpool, sauna, steam rm. Refrigerators, honor bars; some bathrm phones. Some balconies. *LUXURY LEVEL : EXECUTIVE CLUB.* 75 rms, 3 suites, 3 floors. S, D $165-$190; suites $750-$1,050. In-rm movies. Concierge. Private lounge, honor bar. Minibars. Wet bars. Bathrm phones. Complimentary continental bkfst, refreshments. Cr cds: A, C, D, DS, ER, JCB, MC, V.

D ✋ ≈ ✕ 🖊 🔥 SC

Inns

★ ★ **THE CAMBRIDGE.** *1560 Sherman St (80203), downtown.* 303/831-1252; res: 800/877-1252; FAX 303/831-4724. 27 suites, 3 story. S $145-$209; D $155-$219; each addl $10; under 12 free. Crib free. Pet accepted; $30. Valet parking $7. TV; cable. Complimentary coffee in rms. Complimentary continental bkfst. Restaurant 11 am-10 pm, Sat 5-11 pm, closed Sun. Rm serv. Ck-out noon, ck-in after 3 pm. Bellhops. Valet serv. Concierge. Airport transportation. Refrigerators. Antique furnishings, oil paintings, original prints; no two suites alike. Cr cds: A, D, DS, ER, MC, V.

✋ ✕ 🔥 SC

✔ ★ ★ ★ **CASTLE MARNE.** *1572 Race St (80206), east of downtown.* 303/331-0621; res: 800/926-2763; FAX 303/331-0623. 9 air-cooled rms, 3 story. No elvtr. S $70-$170; D $85-$170. Children over 10 yrs only. Complimentary full bkfst, coffee. Restaurant nearby. Ck-out 11 am, ck-in 4 pm. Bellhops. Valet serv. Concierge. Some street parking. Game rm. Some balconies. Antiques. Library/sitting rm. Built 1889; Romanesque mansion was residence of museum curator. Cheesman Park 3 blks. Totally nonsmoking. Cr cds: A, C, D, DS, MC, V.

✕ 🖊 🔥 SC

✔ ★ ★ **HOLIDAY CHALET.** *1820 E Colfax Ave (80218), east of downtown.* 303/321-9975; res: 800/626-4497; FAX 303/377-6556. 10 kit. suites, 3 story. S, D $49-$67.50; each addl $5; under 12 free; wkly rates. Crib free. Pet accepted; $50. Garage parking $3. Complimentary bkfst. Complimentary coffee in rms. Restaurant nearby. Ck-out noon. Concierge. Restored brownstone built in 1896. Library; 1880 salt water fish prints. Cr cds: A, C, D, DS, MC, V.

✋ ✕ 🖊 SC

★ ★ ★ **QUEEN ANNE.** *2147 Tremont Pl (80205), downtown.* 303/296-6666; res: 800/432-4667; FAX 303/296-2151. 14 rms, 3 story. No elvtr. S, D $75-$125; each addl $15; suites $135-$155. Children over 12 yrs only. Complimentary bkfst & refreshments. Ck-out noon, ck-in 3 pm. Health club privileges. Built 1879. Antiques; garden. In the

Clements Historic District. Totally nonsmoking. Cr cds: A, D, DS, MC, V.

D ⊠ 🔥

✓★ ★ **VICTORIA OAKS.** *1575 Race St (80206), east of down-town.* 303/355-1818. 9 rms, some share bath, 3 story. No elvtr. S $45-$75; D $55-$85; each addl $15. Pet accepted, some restrictions. Complimentary continental bkfst, refreshments. Ck-out noon, ck-in 3 pm. Kitchen, lndry privileges. 1897 rooming house, Victorian antiques. Cr cds: A, C, D, DS, ER, MC, V.

✹ ⊠ 🐾 SC

Restaurants

★ **AL FRESCO.** *1515-23 Market St (80202), downtown.* 303/534-0404. Hrs: 11 am-2 pm, 5-10 pm; Fri & Sat to 11 pm. Res accepted. Northern Italian menu. A la carte entrees: lunch $5.95-$10.95, dinner $5.95-$16.95. Specializes in pizza, zitti Al Fresco. Out-door dining. Casual dining on 3 levels. Cr cds: A, C, D, DS, MC, V.

D

★ ★ **BABY DOE'S MATCHLESS MINE.** *2520 W 23rd Ave, west of downtown.* 303/433-3386. Hrs: 11 am-2:30 pm, 4:30-10 pm; Fri, Sat to midnight; Sun 4-10 pm; Sun brunch 9 am-2:30 pm. Res accepted. Semi-a la carte: lunch $6.95-$8.95, dinner $12.95-$32. Buf-fet: lunch $7.95. Sun brunch $11.95. Child's meals. Specializes in seafood, steak. Parking. Replica of Matchless Mine in Leadville; memo-rabilia of era. Cr cds: A, C, D, DS, MC, V.

D

★ ★ **BRITTANY HILL.** *9350 Grant, I-25 exit 220, north of downtown.* 303/451-5151. Hrs: 11 am-10 pm; Fri, Sat to 11 pm; Sun 4-10 pm; Sun brunch 9 am-2:30 pm. Res accepted. Continental menu. Bar to midnight. Wine list. Semi-a la carte: lunch $4.95-$10.95, dinner $10.95-$26. Lunch buffet $7.95. Sun brunch $13.95. Specializes in prime rib, fresh seafood. Own pastries. Patio deck. Scenic view of city, mountains. Cr cds: A, DS, MC, V.

D

★ ★ **THE BROKER.** *821 17th St, downtown.* 303/292-5065. Hrs: 11 am-2:30 pm, 5-11 pm; Sun 4-10 pm. Closed Dec 25. Res accepted. Continental menu. Bar. Semi-a la carte: lunch $7-$15, dinner $19-$35. Specialties: prime rib, filet Wellington. In vault & board rms of converted bank (1903). Cr cds: A, D, DS, MC, V.

★ **BUCKHORN EXCHANGE.** *1000 Osage St, south of downtown.* 303/534-9505. Hrs: 11:30 am-2 pm, 5:30-9 pm; Fri & Sat 5-10 pm; Sun 4-9 pm. Closed major hols. Bar. Semi-a la carte: lunch $2.95-$12.50, dinner $17-$30. Specializes in steak, buffalo, elk. Enter-tainment Wed-Sat. Roof garden dining. Historical landmark & museum, built 1893. Cr cds: A, C, D, DS, MC, V.

D

✓★ ★ **CHIVES AMERICAN BISTRO.** *1120 E 6th Ave, south of downtown.* 303/722-3800. Hrs: 4 pm-1 am. Closed Thanksgiving, Dec 25. Res accepted. Varied menu. Bar. Semi-a la carte: dinner $5.95-$17.95. Specializes in grilled fresh seafood, pasta. New American cuisine; menu changes wkly. Parking. Cr cds: D, DS, MC, V.

★ ★ ★ **CLIFF YOUNG.** *700 E 17th Ave, east of downtown.* 303/831-8900. Hrs: 11:30 am-2 pm, 5-11 pm; Sun 5-10 pm. Closed major hols. Bar. Wine list. Semi-a la carte: lunch $7-$14, dinner $13-$33. Specialty: herb-crusted Colorado rack of lamb. Own baking. En-tertainment (evenings). Valet parking. In renovated Victorian storefront and office building (1890). Cr cds: A, C, D, DS, JCB, MC, V.

D

★ ★ **EUROPEAN CAFE.** *1515-23 Market St (80202), down-town.* 303/825-6555. Hrs: 11 am-2 pm, 5-10 pm. Fri & Sat to 11 pm. Res accepted. Continental menu. Bar. A la carte entrees: lunch $5.95-

$10.95, dinner $5.95-$26.95. Specialties: rack of lamb, spicy tuna. Valet parking. Intimate dining. Victorian decor. Cr cds: A, C, D, DS, MC, V.

D

✓★ ★ **LE CENTRAL.** *112 E 8th Ave, at Lincoln St, downtown.* 303/863-8094. Hrs: 11:30 am-2 pm, 5:30-10 pm; Sun 5-9 pm; Sun brunch 11 am-2 pm. Closed Dec 25. French menu. Serv bar. Semi-a la carte: lunch $4.99-$13.50, dinner $7.50-$13.50. Sun brunch $5-$8. Specializes in country French dishes. Cr cds: MC, V.

★ ★ **McCORMICK'S FISH HOUSE.** *1659 Wazee St, down-town.* 303/825-1107. Hrs: 6:30-10 am, 11 am-2 pm, 5-10 pm; Fri to 11 pm; Sat 7-11 am, 5-11 pm; Sun 7 am-2 pm, 5-10 pm; Sun brunch 7 am-2 pm. Closed July 4, Thanksgiving, Dec 25. Res accepted. Bar. Semi-a la carte: bkfst $4-$8, lunch, dinner $5-$22. Sun brunch $4-$12. Sterling silver chandeliers. Cr cds: A, C, D, DS, MC, V.

D

★ ★ ★ **MORTON'S OF CHICAGO.** *900 Auraria Parkway, in the Tivoli, north of downtown.* 303/825-3353. Hrs: 5:30-11 pm; Sun 5-10 pm. Closed major hols. Bar from 5 pm. Wine list. A la carte entrees: dinner $15.95-$29.95. Specializes in steak, lobster. Valet parking. Menu recited. In restored brewery (1864). Cr cds: A, D, MC, V.

D

★ ★ ★ **NORMANDY FRENCH RESTAURANT.** *1515 Madison, at E Colfax Ave, east of downtown.* 303/321-3311. Hrs: 11:30 am-2 pm, 5-10 pm; Sun 5-9 pm. Closed Mon. Res accepted; required hols. French menu. Bar. Wine cellar. A la carte entrees: lunch $7.75-$10.50, dinner $14.25-$25.50. Child's meals. Specializes in seafood, beef Wel-lington, rack of lamb. Parking. Family-owned. Cr cds: A, C, D, DS, MC, V.

✓★ **OLD SPAGHETTI FACTORY.** *1215 18th St, at Lawrence St, downtown.* 303/295-1864. Hrs: 11:30 am-2 pm, 5-10 pm; Fri to 11 pm; Sat 5-11 pm; Sun 4-10 pm. Closed Thanksgiving, Dec 24, 25. Italian menu. Bar. Semi-a la carte: lunch $3.25-$5.45, dinner $4.25-$9.25. Specialties: homemade lasagne, chicken Parmesan. Located on ground floor of Tramway Cable Bldg (1889). Trolley car, antique dis-play. Cr cds: DS, MC, V.

D

★ ★ ★ **PALACE ARMS.** *(See Brown Palace Hotel)* 303/297-3111. Hrs: 11:30 am-2 pm, 6-10 pm; Sat, Sun from 6 pm. Res required. Regional Amer menu. Bar to 1 am. Extensive wine list. Semi-a la carte: lunch $8.50-$16, dinner $19.50-$29. Specializes in rack of lamb, fresh seafood. Own baking. Valet parking. Jacket, tie. Cr cds: A, C, D, DS, JCB, MC, V.

D

✓★ **POUR LA FRANCE.** *730 S University Blvd, south of downtown.* 303/744-1888. Hrs: 7 am-10 pm; Fri, Sat to midnight. Closed Thanksgiving, Dec 25. French, Amer menu. Bar. Semi-a la carte: bkfst $2-$6.95, lunch $2.95-$6.95, dinner $6.95-$12.75. Child's meals. Specializes in desserts, pastries. Outdoor dining. Near Univ of Denver. Cr cds: A, DS, MC, V.

D SC

✓★ **ROCKY MOUNTAIN DINER.** *800 18th St, at Stout, downtown.* 303/293-8383. Hrs: 11 am-11 pm; Sun 10 am-9 pm. Closed Jan 1, July 4, Thanksgiving, Dec 25. Res accepted. Bar to midnight. Semi-a la carte: lunch, dinner $4.95-$14.95. Child's meals. Specialties: buffalo meatloaf, duck enchiladas. Outdoor dining. Saloon-style decor, western motif. Cr cds: A, D, DS, MC, V.

D

★ ★ **SOREN'S.** *315 Detroit St, 3¹/₂ blks N of Cherry Creek Shopping Center, south of downtown.* 303/322-8155. Hrs: 11 am-9:30 pm; Fri & Sat to 10 pm; Sun 10:30 am-2:30 pm. Closed Jan 1, Thanks-giving, Dec 25. Res accepted. Continental menu. Bar. Semi-a la carte: lunch $5.75-$10.50, dinner $5.75-$18. Child's meals. Specialties:

baked salmon in horseradish crust, Maryland crab cakes. Classical guitarist Fri-Sun. Outdoor dining. 3 dining areas, art deco decor. Cr cds: A, DS, MC, V.

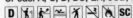

★ ★ ★ **TANTE LOUISE.** 4900 E Colfax Ave, east of downtown. 303/355-4488. Hrs: 5:30-10:30 pm; Fri 11:30 am-2 pm, 5:30-10 pm. Closed Sun. Res accepted. Continental menu. Bar. Wine cellar. Semi-a la carte: lunch $7.50-$11.50, dinner $15.95-$27.95. Child's meals. Specializes in duck, roast rack of lamb. Own pastries, dressings. Valet parking. Outdoor dining. French decor. Cr cds: A, C, D, DS, MC, V.

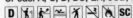

★ **TRINITY GRILLE.** 1801 Broadway, downtown. 303/293-2288. Hrs: 11 am-10:30 pm; Fri, Sat to 11 pm. Closed Sun; most major hols. Res accepted. Bar. Semi-a la carte: lunch $4.50-$9.95, dinner $5.95-$28.95. Specializes in Maryland crab cakes, fresh seafood. Casual dining. Cr cds: A, D, DS, MC, V.

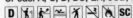

★ ★ ★ **TUSCANY.** (See Loews Giorgio Hotel) 303/782-9300. Hrs: 6 am-10 pm; Sun brunch 11 am-2 pm. Res accepted; required Sun, hols. Northern Italian menu. Bar noon-midnight. Wine cellar. Semi-a la carte: bkfst $2.50-$12.50, lunch $8.25-$15.25, dinner $12.50-$25. Sun brunch $20.95. Child's meals. Specializes in pasta, seafood. Pianist, harpist Fri-Sun. Valet parking. Quiet, elegant dining rm; fireplace, frescoes. Cr cds: A, C, D, DS, JCB, MC, V.

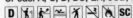

★ ★ ★ **WELLSHIRE INN.** 3333 S Colorado Blvd, south of downtown. 303/759-3333. Hrs: 7-10 am, 11:30 am-2:30 pm, 4:30-10 pm; Fri, Sat to 11 pm; Sun 10 am-2 pm, 4:30-9 pm; Sun brunch to 2 pm. Closed Memorial Day, Labor Day. Res accepted. Bar. Semi-a la carte: bkfst $4.75-$9.75, lunch $7.50-$12, dinner $14-$28. Sun brunch $5.25-$12. Specializes in salmon, rack of lamb, steak. Pianist evenings. Parking. Outdoor dining. Tudor-style inn. Totally nonsmoking. Cr cds: A, D, MC, V.

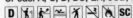

✔★ ★ **WYNKOOP BREWING COMPANY.** 1634 18th St, downtown. 303/297-2700. Hrs: 11-2 am; Sun to midnight; Sun brunch to 2 pm. Closed Super Bowl Sun, Memorial Day, Thanksgiving, Dec 25. Bar. Semi-a la carte: lunch $4.95-$7.50, dinner $4.95-$15.95. Sun brunch $8.95. Specialties: shepherd's pie, bangers & mash. Entertainment Thurs-Sat. In J.S. Brown Mercantile Bldg (1899). Brewery kettles displayed; beer brewed on premises. Cr cds: A, C, D, DS, JCB, MC, V.

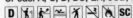

★ ★ ★ **ZENITH AMERICAN GRILL.** 1750 Lawrence St (80202), downtown. 303/820-2800. Hrs: 11 am-10 pm; Sat from 5 pm; Sun 5-9 pm. Closed some major hols. Res accepted. Bar. Wine list. Semi-a la carte: lunch $7-$12, dinner $15-$30. A la carte entrees: $5-$10.50, dinner $13-$24. Specialties: macadamla crusted sea bass, lamb loin. Valet parking. Courtyard dining. Ultra modern decor. Cr cds: A, D, MC, V.

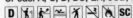

Unrated Dining Spot

FURRS CAFETERIA. 4900 Kipling, west of downtown. 303/423-4602. Hrs: 11 am-8 pm; Fri & Sat to 8:30 pm. Avg ck: lunch $4.50, dinner $5.50. Cr cds: A, MC, V.

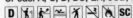

Denver International Airport Area

Motel

★ ★ **HAMPTON INN AURORA.** (1500 S Abilene St, Aurora 80012) Quebec St (CO 35) N to I-70, 4 mi E to I-225, then 5 mi S off I-225 exit 7. 303/369-8400; FAX 303/369-0324. 132 rms, 4 story. S $52-$68; D $61-$76; under 18 free. Crib free. TV; cable. Heated pool. Complimentary buffet bkfst. Ck-out noon. Coin lndry. Meeting rms. Valet serv. Health club privileges. Cr cds: A, C, D, DS, JCB, MC, V.

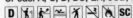

Hotel

★ ★ **DOUBLETREE.** (13696 East Iliff Place, Aurora 80014) Quebec St (CO 35) N to I-70, 4 mi E to I-225, then 7 mi S off I-225 exit 5. 303/337-2800; FAX 303/752-0296. 254 rms, 6 story. S $130; D $140; each addl $10; suites $175-$225; under 18 free; wknd rates. Crib free. TV; cable. Indoor pool; poolside serv. Restaurant 6:30 am-10 pm. Bar 11-2 am. Ck-out noon. Gift shop. Tennis & golf privileges. Exercise equipt; bicycles, stair machine. Some bathrm phones, in-rm whirlpools. Cr cds: A, C, D, DS, ER, JCB, MC, V.

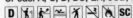

Detroit

Founded: 1701

Pop: 1,027,974

Elev: 600 feet

Time zone: Eastern

Area code: 313

The city that put the US on wheels and gave birth to Motown music is an American symbol of elbow grease and productive might; its name is synonymous with automobiles.

When the Stars and Stripes first flew over Detroit, on July 11, 1796, the settlement was already nearly a century old. It was, however, little more than a trading post and remained so until the opening of the Erie Canal and the introduction of steam navigation on the Great Lakes. With the development of better transportation, the city became a hub of industry and shipping. Population doubled every decade between 1830 and 1860.

In the 1890s the first automobile frames were made in Detroit; by the turn of the century, the auto industry dominated the city, and it changed from a quiet town that brewed beer and produced carriages and stoves to a city bursting with such industrial might that it profoundly influenced not only the rest of the nation, but the world. A century from now, historians may judge that the man who most influenced the tide of world economy in the 20th century was Henry Ford, who revolutionized industry with his production line, his understanding of mass marketing and his astonishing decision to raise wages to $5 a day when the going salary was half that amount.

Business

For a city built on the automobile industry (nearly 25 percent of the nation's automobiles are produced here), a surprising less than 10 percent of Detroit's labor force is actually employed in the industry. Detroit is a manufacturing town; it outranks many other US cities by producing a large percentage of the country's machine-tool accessories, dies, tools and jigs, internal combustion engines and metal-cutting tools. Detroit is also a major manufacturer of airplane parts, automation and military equipment, machine tools and plastics.

In addition to manufacturing, Detroit is a major world port; exports from the Michigan Customs District rank among the country's five highest in value. The Detroit River's total tonnage in an 8-month shipping season averages more than 125 million tons. Detroit is also among the largest financial centers in the United States. The city's Renaissance Center is a $430 million complex that includes 5 million square feet of office space in 6 high-rise towers, 28 restaurants and lounges, numerous shops and a magnificent lobby alive with greenery. In the middle of the complex is Michigan's tallest building, the Westin Hotel, rising 73 stories.

Convention Facilities

Cobo Conference/Exhibition Center and Arena is an innovative, modern convention center. The arena can seat 11,561 for sporting events. A movable stage can be set up for concerts, and the main ballroom can seat up to 2,000 people for banquets. If more space is needed, there are 4 exhibition areas of up to 250,000 square feet each, which can seat 10,000. Three of the exhibition areas, totaling 620,000 square feet, are interconnecting.

The facility has exhibit space totaling 720,000 square feet. In addition, 84 more meeting rooms are available with seating capacities from 50 to 5,000 people. Parking for Cobo Conference/Exhibition Center is located on the roof; public transportation is easily accessible.

Next door to Cobo is the Joe Louis Arena, which seats 21,000.

Sports and Recreation

All major professional sports are played in and around Detroit. The Tigers play baseball at the 53,000-seat Tiger Stadium; the Lions play football at the Silverdome in Pontiac; the Pistons play basketball nearby at the Palace of Auburn Hills; and the Red Wings play hockey at the Joe Louis Arena.

Belle Isle in the Detroit River offers many outdoor recreational activities, including golf, guided nature walks, swimming, fishing, boating with rentals, picnicking, baseball, softball and tennis.

More than 400 lakes and streams are within an hour's drive of the city, and the surrounding Huron-Clinton Metroparks provide numerous beaches, picnicking areas, golf courses, hiking and biking trails and winter activities.

There is horse racing in the outlying suburban areas as well as in Detroit proper; downhill skiing is available northwest near Pontiac.

Entertainment

The Detroit Symphony, one of America's major orchestras, gives concerts in Orchestra Hall. The orchestra also performs at the Meadow Brook Pavilion during the summer. The Michigan Opera Theatre performs at the Fisher Theater and Masonic Temple.

The University of Detroit Performing Arts Center and Wayne State University offer theatrical entertainment in the university theaters from October to mid-April. Numerous professional, repertory and neighborhood theaters, offering a wide variety of drama and comedy, can be found in the metropolitan area.

Historical Areas

The most famous of Michigan's historical areas is the Henry Ford Museum and Greenfield Village complex, located just west of Detroit's city limits in Dearborn. In a 254-acre setting is a re-created, full-scale panorama of American life—an unequaled collection of Americana. Built by Henry Ford as a tribute to the culture and resourcefulness of the United States, the museum and village stand as monuments to the achievements of famous Americans. The area was dedicated in 1929 to Thomas Edison.

Greenfield Village includes more than 80 historic buildings moved from all sections of the country and restored to appear exactly as they did during the 18th and 19th centuries. Here are historic houses, shops, schools, mills, stores and laboratories that figured in the lives of such

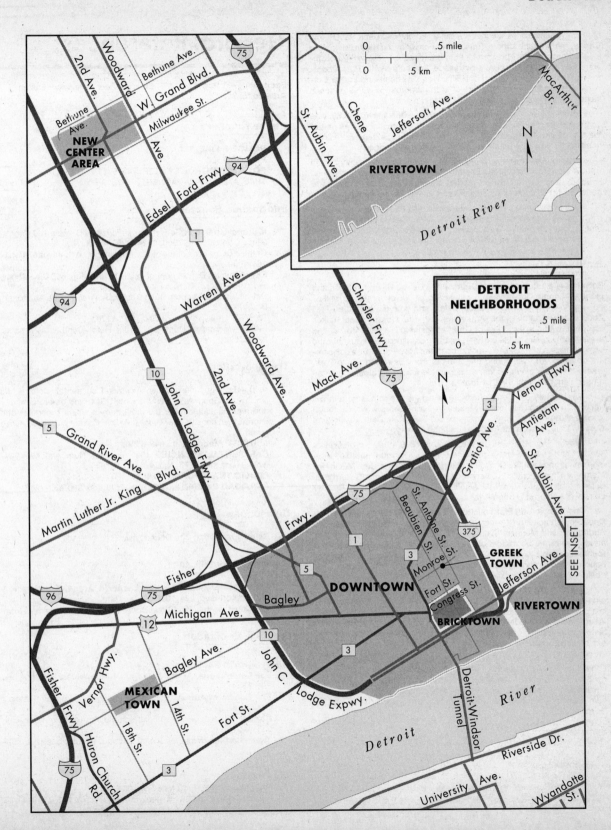

New Center Area
75
Woodward
2nd Ave.
Bethune Ave.
W. Grand Blvd.
Milwaukee St.
Bethune Ave.
Ave.
NEW CENTER AREA
94
Edsel Ford Frwy.
1

.5 mile
0
.5 km
0
St. Aubin Ave.
Chene
Jefferson Ave.
MacArthur Br.
RIVERTOWN
Detroit River
N

94
Warren Ave.
Woodward Ave.
Chrysler Frwy.
Mack Ave.
75

10
John C. Lodge Frwy.
2nd Ave.
Blvd.

DETROIT NEIGHBORHOODS
0   .5 mile
0   .5 km
N
Vernor Hwy.
3
Antietam Ave.
St. Aubin Ave.

5
Grand River Ave.
Gratiot Ave.

Martin Luther Jr. King
Frwy.
75
St. Antoine St.
Beaubien St.
3
375

1
3
Monroe St.
GREEK TOWN
DOWNTOWN
Fort St.
Congress St.
Jefferson Ave.
RIVERTOWN
SEE INSET

Fisher
5
Bagley
BRICKTOWN

96
75
Michigan Ave.
12
10
Bagley Ave.
John C.
3
Detroit-Windsor Tunnel
River

Fisher Frwy.
Vernor Hwy.
14th St.
MEXICAN TOWN
Fort St.
Lodge Expwy.
Detroit
Riverside Dr.

75
Huron Church Rd.
18th St.
3
University Ave.
Wyandotte St.

creative Americans as Lincoln, Webster, Foster, Burbank, McGuffey, Carver, the Wright brothers, Edison and Ford. Among the buildings are a courthouse where Abraham Lincoln practiced law, the Wright brothers' cycle shop, Henry Ford's birthplace, Edison's Menlo Park laboratory and the residences of H.J. Heinz, Noah Webster and Luther Burbank. Guided tours and rides are offered on horse-drawn carriages, a steam train, a riverboat and Model T Fords.

Mariners' Church, the oldest stone church building in the city, was completed in 1848. It was moved 800 feet to its present site as part of the Civic Center complex. At the time of the move, extensive restoration was done, and a bell tower with a carillon was added.

Major urban renewal projects and restoration are going on in Detroit's metropolitan area. Eastern Market, dating from 1891, was restored. It is now a farmers' market offering customers a chance to barter for fruits, vegetables, flowers and freshly baked bread.

Detroit has many fine old residential areas designated as national historic districts. Particularly worth visiting are the Boston/Edison district, Indian Village and Woodbridge. Detroit's oldest brick house, the Moross House, has been restored.

Sightseeing

Belle Isle is a 1,000-acre island-park in the Detroit River. On the island is the Whitcomb Conservatory, with seasonal flower shows, as well as continuing exhibits of ferns, cacti, palms and orchids; the Safari-Trail Zoo; a nature center; the Aquarium; and the Dossin Great Lakes Museum, with scale models of Great Lakes ships, a restored "Gothic salon" from a Great Lakes liner, marine paintings, a reconstructed ship's bridge and a full-scale racing boat, the *Miss Pepsi*. Boblo Steamers cruise down river during the summer from Detroit to Boblo Park, where there are playgrounds, picnic areas, a historic blockhouse, an amusement park and the 314-foot Sky Tower.

The century-old Detroit Institute of Arts is the fifth largest in the nation. The Detroit Historical Museum offers visitors a walk through history along reconstructed streets of Old Detroit. In Detroit's Cultural Center is the Museum of African-American History.

Wayne State University, established in 1868, has 13 professional schools and colleges and a graduate division. The most notable buildings on campus are the De Roy Auditorium, the ultramodern McGregor Memorial Community Conference Center and the Prentis Building, all designed by Minoru Yamasaki. Also on campus is the Walter P. Reuther Library of Labor and Urban Affairs, the nation's largest labor library.

The 10-acre Hart Plaza overlooks the river and connects the Cobo Conference/Exhibition Center, the Veterans Memorial Building, Ford Auditorium and Mariners' Church. The plaza also features a park and amphitheater. In the middle of the plaza is a $2 million computerized fountain capable of sending more than a million gallons of water per hour into the air through 300-plus nozzles and jets. The fountain was designed by sculptor Isamu Noguchi.

The Renaissance Center is probably the most concentrated shopping area in downtown Detroit. The revolving restaurant on the top floor is a comfortable place to relax after a day of shopping. Trappers Alley, located on Monroe in Detroit's Greektown area, is housed in a restored historic building. This five-level center features gift shops, restaurants, exhibits and entertainment.

Northwest of Detroit, in Bloomfield Hills, is Cranbrook, an internationally known cultural and educational center. An array of sculptures by Swedish sculptor Carl Milles and various buildings designed by Finnish architect Eliel Saarinen grace the complex's 300 acres. Also here are museums, galleries and gardens.

General References

Founded: 1701 **Pop:** 1,027,974 **Elev:** 600 feet **Time zone:** Eastern **Area code:** 313

Phone Numbers

POLICE & FIRE: 911
FBI: 965-2323
POISON CONTROL CENTER: 745-5711
TIME: 472-1212   **WEATHER:** 976-1212

Information Sources

Metropolitan Detroit Convention and Visitors Bureau, 100 Renaissance Center, Suite 1900, 48243; 259-4333.
Greater Detroit Chamber of Commerce, 600 W Lafayette, 48226; 964-4000.
City of Detroit, Department of Public Information, 608 City-County Bldg, 48226; 224-3755.
Detroit Visitor and Information Center, Jefferson Ave & Auditorium Dr, 567-1170.
"WHATS Line" (visitors hotline), 567-1170.
Detroit Recreation Dept, 224-1180; Huron-Clinton Metroparks, 227-2757.

Transportation

AIRLINES: American; British Airways; Continental; Delta; KLM; Northwest; Southwest; TWA; United; USAir; and other commuter and regional airlines. For the most current airline schedules and information consult the *Official Airline Guide,* published twice monthly.
AIRPORT: Metropolitan, 942-3550.
CAR RENTAL AGENCIES: (See Toll-Free Numbers) Avis 964-0494; Hertz 964-2678; National 941-7000.
PUBLIC TRANSPORTATION: SMART, 962-5515.
RAILROAD PASSENGER SERVICE: Amtrak 800/872-7245.

Newspapers

Detroit Free Press; The Detroit News.

Convention Facilities

Cobo Conference/Exhibition Center & Arena, E Jefferson & Washington Blvd, 224-1010 or 396-7600.
Joe Louis Arena, 600 Civic Center, 396-7600.

Sports & Recreation

Major Sports Facilities
Joe Louis Arena, At the Civic Center (Red Wings, NHL hockey, 396-7544).
The Palace of Auburn Hills, 3777 Lapeer Rd, Pontiac (Pistons, basketball, 377-0100).
Pontiac Silverdome, 1200 Featherstone, Pontiac (Lions, football, 335-4151).
Tiger Stadium, Michigan Ave at Trumbull (Tigers, baseball, 963-9944).

Racetracks
Hazel Park, 1650 E 10 Mile Rd, 398-1000.
Ladbroke-DRC, 28001 Schoolcraft Rd, Livonia, 525-7300.
Northville Downs, 301 S Center St, Northville, 349-1000.

Cultural Facilities

Theaters

Bonstelle Theater, 3424 Woodward Ave, Wayne State University, 577-2960.
Detroit Institute of Arts Auditorium, 5200 Woodward Ave, 833-7900.
Fisher Theater, W Grand & Second Blvds, 872-1000.
Hilberry Theatre, 4743 Cass Ave, Wayne State University, 577-2972.
Michigan Opera Theatre, 6519 Second Ave, 874-7850.
Music Hall Center for the Performing Arts, 350 Madison Ave, 963-7680.
The Theatre Company-University of Detroit, 4001 W McNichols Rd, 993-1130.

Concert Halls

Masonic Temple Theatre, 500 Temple Ave, 832-2232.
Symphony Orchestra Hall, 3711 Woodward Ave, 833-3700.

Museums

Children's Museum, 67 E Kirby Ave, 494-1210.
Detroit Fire Department Historical Museum, 2737 Gratiot, 596-2957.
Detroit Historical Museum, 5401 Woodward Ave, 833-1805.
Dossin Great Lakes Museum, Belle Isle, 267-6440.
Motown Museum, 2648 W Grand Blvd, 875-2264.
Museum of African-American History, 301 Frederick Douglass, 833-9800.

Art Galleries

Detroit Institute of Arts, 5200 Woodward Ave, between Warren Ave and Kirby St, 833-7900.
International Institute, 111 E Kirby Ave, 871-8600.

Points of Interest

Historical

Henry Ford Museum and Greenfield Village, 1/2 mi S of US 12, 11/2 mi N of Southfield Rd, on Oakwood Blvd, Dearborn, 271-1620 or -1976.
Mariners' Church, 170 E Jefferson Ave, 259-2206.

Other Attractions

Aquarium, Belle Isle, 267-7159.
Belle Isle, Island Park, reached by MacArthur Bridge, 267-7115.
Christ Church Cranbrook, Bloomfield Hills, 644-5210.
City-County Building, 2 Woodward Ave, 224-5585.
Cranbrook Academy of Art and Museum, 500 Lone Pine Rd, between MI 1 & US 24, Bloomfield Hills, 645-3312.
Cranbrook Gardens, Bloomfield Hills, 645-3149.
Cranbrook House, Bloomfield Hills, 645-3149.
Cranbrook Institute of Science, between MI 1 & US 24, Bloomfield Hills, 645-3200 or -3142.

Detroit Public Library, 5201 Woodward Ave, 833-1000.
Detroit Zoo, 8450 W 10 Mile Rd, at Woodward Ave, Royal Oak, 398-0903.
Eastern Market, 2934 Russell, via I-75 at Gratiot, 833-1560.
Fisher Building, W Grand & Second Blvds, 874-4444.
Hart Plaza & Dodge Fountain, Jefferson Ave.
Michigan Consolidated Gas Company Building, 1 Woodward Ave.
New Center One, 3031 W Grand Blvd, 874-4444.
Renaissance Center, Jefferson Ave at Beaubien, 568-5600.
Safari-Trail Zoo, Belle Isle, 267-7160.
Trappers Alley, 508 Monroe Ave at Beaubien, in Greektown, 963-5445.
Washington Boulevard Trolley Car, downtown, 933-1300.
Whitcomb Conservatory, Belle Isle, 267-7134.

Sightseeing Tours

Detroiter, foot of Joseph Campau St, 567-1400.
Gray Line bus tours, 1301 E Warren Ave, 48207; 833-5523.

Annual Events

Grand Prix, 259-5400. Mid-June.
International Freedom Festival, 259-5400. Late June-early July.
Montreux-Detroit Jazz Festival, Hart Plaza, 259-5400. Early Sept.
Michigan State Fair, Michigan Exposition & Fairgrounds, 368-1000. Late Aug-early Sept.
Christmas Carnival, Cobo Conference/Exhibition Center, 224-1184. Early Dec.

City Neighborhoods

Many of the restaurants, unrated dining establishments and some lodgings listed under Detroit include neighborhoods as well as exact street addresses. A map showing these neighborhoods can be found immediately following the city introduction. Geographic descriptions of these areas are given, followed by a table of restaurants arranged by neighborhood.

Bricktown: Area of downtown south of Fort St, west of St Antoine St, north of the Renaissance Center (Jefferson St) and east of Randolph St.
Downtown: South of Fisher Frwy (I-75), west of Walter P Chrysler Frwy (I-375), north of the Detroit River and east of John C Lodge Expy (MI 10). **East of Downtown:** East of I-375.
Greektown: Area of downtown on Monroe St between Beaubien St on the west and St Antoine St on the east.
Mexican Town: West of downtown along Bagley Ave between 14th and 18th Sts.
New Center Area: North of downtown; south of Bethune Ave, west of Woodward, north of Milwaukee and east of MI 10.
Riverton: East of downtown; south of Jefferson Ave, west of Belle Isle Bridge and north of the Detroit River.

Lodgings and Food

DETROIT RESTAURANTS
BY NEIGHBORHOOD AREAS

(For full description, see alphabetical listings under Restaurants)

DOWNTOWN

Caucus Club. 150 W Congress St

Opus One. 565 E Larned

Traffic Jam & Snug. 511 W Canfield St

Tres Vite. 2203 Woodward Ave

The Whitney. 4421 Woodward Ave

EAST OF DOWNTOWN

Van Dyke Place. 649 Van Dyke Ave

GREEKTOWN

Fishbone's Rhythm Kitchen Cafe. 400 Monroe St

Pegasus Taverna. 558 Monroe St

MEXICAN TOWN

El Zocalo. 3400 Bagley

NEW CENTER AREA

Lelli's. 7618 Woodward Ave

Pegasus In The Fisher. 3011 W Grand Blvd

RIVERTOWN

Rattlesnake Club. 300 Stroh River Place

Note: *When a listing is located in a town that does not have its own city heading, it will appear under the city nearest to its location. In these cases, the address and town appear in parenthesis immediately following the name of the establishment.*

Motels

★ ★ **COURTYARD BY MARRIOTT.** *(17200 N Laurel Park Dr, Livonia 48152)* W via I-96 to I-275, N to Six Mile Rd. 313/462-2000; FAX 313/462-5907. 149 rms, 3 story. S $82; D $92; wkend rates. Crib free. TV; cable. Indoor pool. Restaurant 6:30-10 am; Sat & Sun 7 am-1 pm. Bar 4-11 pm. Ck-out noon. Coin lndry. Meeting rms. Valet serv. Downhill/x-country ski 20 mi. Exercise equipt; weights, bicycles, whirlpool. Refrigerator in suites. Private patios, balconies. Cr cds: A, C, D, DS, MC, V.

★ ★ **PARKCREST INN.** *(20000 Harper Ave, Harper Woods 48225)* NE on I-94, exit 224B. 313/884-8800; FAX 313/884-7087. 49 rms, 2 story, 3 kits. S $57; D $65-$70; kit. units $82; family rates. Crib free. Pet accepted. TV; cable. Heated pool. Restaurant 6:30-2:30 am; Sun 7:30 am-10 pm. Rm serv. Bar to 2 am. Ck-out 11 am. Valet serv. X-country ski 15 mi. Cr cds: A, C, D, DS, MC, V.

★ ★ **QUALITY INN LIVONIA SUITES WEST.** *(16999 S Laurel Park Dr, Livonia 48154)* 20 mi W on I-96 to I-275, N on I-275 to jct Six Mile Rd. 313/464-0050; FAX 313/464-5869. 123 rms, 2 story. S $49.50-$69.50; D $57.50-$125; each addl $8. Crib free. TV; cable. Heated pool. Complimentary continental bkfst. Ck-out noon. Meeting rms. X-country

ski 5 mi. Exercise equipt; weight machine, rower. Refrigerators; some in-rm whirlpools, minibars. Cr cds: A, C, D, DS, ER, JCB, MC, V.

✔ ★ **SHORECREST MOTOR INN.** 1316 E Jefferson Ave (48207), downtown. 313/568-3000; res: 800/992-9616; FAX 313/568-3002. 54 rms, 2 story. S $48-$60; D $54-$68; family, wkly, wkend rates. Crib free. TV. Restaurant 6 am-10 pm; wkends from 7 am. Rm serv. Ck-out noon. Valet serv. Airport transportation. Refrigerators. Cr cds: A, C, D, DS, MC, V.

Motor Hotel

★ ★ ★ **HOLIDAY INN-FAIRLANE\DEARBORN.** 5801 Southfield Service Dr (48228), west of downtown. 313/336-3340; FAX 313/336-7037. 347 rms, 6 story. S, D $84; suites $165; under 18 free; wkend rates. Crib free. Pet accepted. TV; cable. 2 pools, 1 indoor; poolside serv. Coffee in rms. Restaurant 6 am-2 pm, 5-10 pm; Sat & Sun from 7 am. Rm serv. Bar 11 am-midnight. Ck-out noon. Convention facilities. Bellhops. Gift shop. Local area transportation. Exercise equipt; bicycles, stair machine, whirlpool, sauna. Game rm. Cr cds: A, C, D, DS, ER, JCB, MC, V.

Hotels

★ ★ ★ **ATHENEUM.** 1000 Brush Ave (48226), in Greektown. 313/962-2323; res: 800/772-2323; FAX 313/962-2424. 174 suites, 10 story. Suites $90-$525; each addl $20; family, wkly rates; higher rates Greektown Opaa. Crib free. Valet parking $8. TV; cable. Restaurant adj 8 am-midnight. Bar. Ck-out noon. Meeting rms. Concierge. Gift shop. Exercise equipt; bicycle, stair machine. Minibars; some bathrm phones. Neoclassical structure adj International Center. Cr cds: A, C, D, DS, ER, JCB, MC, V.

★ ★ **EMBASSY SUITES.** *(19525 Victor Pkwy, Livonia 48152)* W on I-96 to I-275N, exit Seven Mile Rd E. 313/462-6000; FAX 313/462-6003. 239 suites, 5 story. S $109-$139; D $119-$149 each addl $10; under 12 free (max 2); wkend rates; higher rates special events. Crib free. TV; cable. Indoor pool. Complimentary full bkfst, beverages. Complimentary coffee in rms. Restaurant 6-9 am, 11 am-4 pm, 5-10 pm; hrs vary Fri-Sun. Bar 5 pm-midnight, closed Sun. Ck-out noon. Coin lndry. Meeting rms. Gift shop. Exercise equipt; weight machine, rowers, whirlpool, sauna. Refrigerators. Balconies. Five-story atrium. Cr cds: A, C, D, DS, JCB, MC, V.

★ ★ **MARRIOTT-LIVONIA.** *(17100 Laurel Park Dr N, Livonia 48152)* 20 mi W on I-96 to I-275, N on I-275 to Six Mile Rd. 313/462-3100; FAX 313/462-2815. 224 rms, 6 story. S, D $99-$124; suites $225; family, wkend rates. Crib free. Pet accepted, some restrictions. TV; cable. Indoor pool; poolside serv. Restaurant 6:30 am-10 pm. Bar noon-midnight; entertainment exc Sun. Ck-out noon. Meeting rms. Gift shop. Free garage parking. Downhill/x-country ski 20 mi. Exercise equipt; weights, bicycles, whirlpool, sauna. Health club privileges. Connected to Laurel Park Mall. **LUXURY LEVEL : CONCIERGE LEVEL.** 38 rms. S, D $109-$124. Concierge. Private lounge, honor bar. Complimentary continental bkfst, refreshments, newspaper, magazines. Cr cds: A, C, D, DS, ER, JCB, MC, V.

★ ★ **OMNI INTERNATIONAL.** 333 E Jefferson Ave (48226), downtown. 313/222-7700; FAX 313/222-6509. 255 rms, 21 story. S $165-$235; D $180-$235; each addl $20; suites $250-$1,000; under 18 free; wkend, honeymoon rates. Valet parking $9. Crib free. TV; cable. Indoor pool; poolside serv. Restaurant 6:30 am-10 pm; Fri, Sat to 11 pm. Bar 11-2 am. Meeting rms. Shopping arcade. Barber, beauty shop. Tennis. Racquetball. Exercise rm; instructor, weights, bicycles, whirlpool, sauna. Bathrm phones & TVs, refrigerators in suites. Opp river. Cr cds: A, C, D, DS, MC, V.

D ☆≋✈🏃🏋≈🔥 SC

★ ★ THE RIVER PLACE. *1000 Stroh River Place (48207), in Rivertown.* 313/259-9500; res: 800/890-9505; FAX 313/259-3744. 108 rms, 5 story, 18 suites. Sept-June: S $95-$135; D $115-$155; each addl $20; suites $165-$400; under 12 free; hol rates; higher rates some special events; lower rates rest of yr. Crib free. Valet parking $6. Pet accepted, some restrictions. TV; cable. Indoor pool. Restaurant 6:30 am-10 pm; wkend hrs vary. Rm serv. Bar 11 am-10 pm; Fri & Sat to 11 pm. Ck-out noon. Meeting rms. Tennis privileges. Exercise rm; instructor, weight machine, treadmill, whirlpool, sauna. Masseur. Croquet court. On Detroit River. Cr cds: A, C, D, DS, JCB, MC, V.

D 🐾♿≈≋✈🏋🔥 SC

★ ST REGIS. *3071 W Grand Blvd (48202), in New Center Area.* 313/873-3000; FAX 313/873-2574. 221 rms, 6 story, 22 suites. S, D $69-$115; each addl $15; suites $99-$225; under 18 free; wkend rates. Valet parking $7/overnight; $4/day. TV; cable. Restaurant 6:30 am-11 pm. Bar 11-1 am, Sun from noon. Ck-out noon. Meeting rms. Exercise equipt; weight machine, bicycle. In-rm whirlpool in some suites. Refrigerators avail. Cr cds: A, C, D, DS, JCB, MC, V.

D 🏋✈≈🔥 SC

★ ★ ★ WESTIN HOTEL-RENAISSANCE CENTER DETROIT. *Renaissance Center (48243), Jefferson Ave at Brush, downtown.* 313/568-8000; FAX 313/568-8146. 1,400 rms, 73 story. S $115-$150; D $125-$165; each addl $20; suites $330-$1,200; under 18 free; wkend rates. Crib free. Pet accepted. TV; cable. Indoor pool. Restaurant 6:30 am-2:30 pm, 5:30-11 pm; dining rm 11:30 am-2:30 pm, 5:30-10:30 pm. Rm serv 24 hrs. Bar 11-2 am. Ck-out 1 pm. Convention facilities. Shopping arcade. Barber, beauty shop. Tennis privileges. Exercise rm; instructor, weights, bicycles, sauna. Many minibars. *LUXURY LEVEL :* **EXECUTIVE CLUB.** 313/568-8015. 92 rms, 4 floors. S $165; D $185. In-rm movies. Concierge. Private lounge, honor bar. Minibars. Complimentary continental bkfst, refreshments, newspaper. Cr cds: A, C, D, DS, ER, JCB, MC, V.

D 🐾♿🏃≈≋✈🔥 SC

Restaurants

★ ★ ★ CAUCUS CLUB. *150 W Congress St, in Penobscot Bldg, downtown.* 313/965-4970. Hrs: 11 am-8 pm; Fri to 11 pm; summer hrs vary. Closed Sat, Sun; major hols. Res accepted. Continental menu. Semi-a la carte: lunch $7.75-$17.25; dinner $15-$24. Child's meals. Specializes in fresh Dover sole, steak tartare, baby back ribs, Caesar salad. Entertainment Tues-Fri. Cr cds: A, C, D, DS, MC, V.

✔ ★ EL ZOCALO. *3400 Bagley, in Mexican Town.* 313/841-3700. Hrs: 11-2 am; Fri & Sat to 2:30 am. Closed Jan 1, Thanksgiving, Dec 25. Res accepted Sun-Thurs. Mexican menu. Bar. Semi-a la carte: lunch $5.95-$8.95, dinner $6.35-$9.95. Specialties: chiles rellenos, queso flameado, chimichangas. Parking. Mayan and Aztec art. Cr cds: A, C, D, DS, MC, V.

D

★ FISHBONE'S RHYTHM KITCHEN CAFE. *400 Monroe St, at Brush Ave, in Greektown.* 313/965-4600. Hrs: 6 am-midnight; Fri, Sat to 2 am; Sun brunch 10:30 am-2:30 pm. Closed Dec 25. Creole, Cajun menu. Bar. Semi-a la carte: lunch $3.95-$9.95, dinner $3.95-$18.95. Sun brunch $13.95. Specialties: smoked whiskey ribs, jambalaya, crawfish etoufee, alligator voodoo. Parking. Bourbon Street bistro atmosphere; tin ceilings, antique lamps. Cr cds: A, C, D, DS, MC, V.

D

★ ★ LELLI'S. *7618 Woodward Ave, in New Center Area.* 313/871-1590. Hrs: 11 am-10 pm; Sat to 11 pm; Sun noon-8 pm; Mon to 2 pm. Closed major hols. Res accepted. Italian, Amer menu. Bar. Semi-a la carte: lunch $8.50-$17.50, dinner $16-$30. Child's meals.

Specializes in veal, pasta, steak. Own desserts. Strolling violinists. Indoor valet parking. Family-owned. Cr cds: A, D, MC, V.

D

★ ★ ★ OPUS ONE. *565 E Larned, downtown.* 313/961-7766. Hrs: 11:30 am-10 pm; Fri to 11 pm; Sat 5-11 pm. Closed Sun; major hols. Res accepted. Bar. Wine cellar. French, Amer menu. Semi-a la carte: lunch $8.95-$17.95, dinner $19.50-$34.50. Child's meals. Specializes in seafood, aged beef. Own baking, ice cream. Pianist Tues-Sat (dinner). Valet parking. In building designed by Albert Kahn; etched glass, original artwork. Jacket. Cr cds: A, C, D, DS, MC, V.

D

✔ ★ ★ PEGASUS IN THE FISHER. *3011 W Grand Blvd, in New Center Area.* 313/875-7400. Hrs: 11 am-11 pm; Mon to 9 pm; Fri to midnight; Sat 4 pm-midnight. Closed Sun; most major hols. Res accepted. Continental menu. Bar. Semi-a la carte: lunch $5-$7, dinner $7-$16. Specializes in veal, pasta, fresh seafood. Entertainment Fri & Sat evenings. Valet parking. Art deco decor; hand-painted ceilings. Cr cds: A, C, D, DS, MC, V.

D

★ ★ PEGASUS TAVERNA. *558 Monroe St, in Greektown.* 313/964-6800. Hrs: 11-1 am; Fri & sat to 2 am; Sun to midnight. Greek, Amer menu. Bar. A la carte entrees: lunch $4.95-$7.95, dinner $5.95-$17.95. Child's meals. Specializes in lamb chops, seafood, spinach cheese pie. Parking. Lattice-worked ceiling; hanging grape vines. Cr cds: A, C, D, DS, JCB, MC, V.

D

★ ★ RATTLESNAKE CLUB. *300 Stroh River Place, in Rivertown.* 313/567-4400. Hrs: 11:30 am-10 pm; Fri to 11:30 pm; Sat 5:30-11:30 pm. Closed Sun; most major hols. Res accepted. Bar. Semi-a la carte: lunch $7-$15, dinner $12.95-$24.95. Specializes in seasonal dishes. Entertainment Fri & Sat. Valet parking. Outdoor dining. Modern decor; two dining areas overlook Detroit River. Cr cds: A, C, D, DS, MC, V.

D

✔ ★ TRES VITE. *2203 Woodward Ave, downtown.* 313/964-4144. Hrs: 11:30 am-11 pm; Fri to midnight; Sat 5 pm-midnight. Closed Sun & Mon; major hols. Res accepted. Italian menu. Bar. A la carte entrees: lunch $2.50-$8.95, dinner $3.75-$16. Specializes in pizza, pasta, steak. Valet parking. In historic Fox Theatre building. Cr cds: A, D, DS, MC, V.

D

★ ★ ★ VAN DYKE PLACE. *649 Van Dyke Ave, east of downtown.* 313/821-2620. Hrs: 6-9:30 pm; Fri, Sat from 5 pm. Closed Sun & Mon; major hols. Res accepted. Bar. Wine list. A la carte entrees: dinner $18-$30. Specializes in American fare with European accents. Own baking. Pianist Fri & Sat. Valet parking. In turn-of-the-century Louis XVI town house; crystal chandeliers, antiques, murals, many original to house. Cr cds: A, C, D, MC, V.

★ ★ ★ THE WHITNEY. *4421 Woodward Ave, downtown.* 313/832-5700. Hrs: 6-9:30 pm; Fri, Sat 5 pm-midnight; Sun 5-8 pm; Sun brunch 11 am-3 pm. Closed major hols. Res accepted. Bar 11-2 am. Wine cellar. A la carte entrees: dinner $18-$30. Sun brunch $21.95. Specializes in veal, beef, seafood, lamb. Own baking. Pianist, vocalist. Valet parking. In restored Romanesque Whitney mansion (1894); canopied stone entrance, Tiffany windows, intricate Victorian wood-lace carvings, Belgian tapestries, crystal chandeliers, antiques. Dining on two floors; bar with vaulted, skylighted ceiling on third floor. Cr cds: A, C, D, MC, V.

D

Unrated Dining Spot

TRAFFIC JAM & SNUG. *511 W Canfield St (48201), at Second St, downtown.* 313/831-9470. Hrs: 11 am-9 pm; Mon to 3 pm;

Fri to midnight; Sat 5 pm-midnight. Closed Sun; most major hols. Serv bar. Semi-a la carte: lunch $6-$10, dinner $9-$13. Child's meals. Own pastries, desserts, ice cream & cheese. Micro brewery and dairy on premises. Parking. Rustic decor, many antiques. Cr cds: DS, MC, V.

Detroit Metro Airport Area

Motels

✔★ **BUDGETEL INN.** (9000 Wickham Rd, Romulus 48174) N on Merriman Rd to Wickham Rd. 313/722-6000; FAX 313/722-4737. 102 rms, 3 story. S $37.95-$41.95; D $44.95-$52.95; each addl $7; under 18 free. Crib free. Pet accepted, some restrictions. TV; cable. Coffee in rms. Continental bkfst in rms. Restaurant opp 6 am-10 pm. Ck-out noon. Coin lndry. Meeting rms. Valet serv. Airport transportation. Cr cds: A, C, D, DS, MC, V.

★★ **COMFORT INN.** (9501 Middlebelt Rd, Romulus 48174) I-94 exit 1985. 313/946-4300; FAX 313/946-7787. 254 rms, 3 story. S $46-$49; D $54-$57; under 18 free. Crib free. Pet accepted. TV; cable. Restaurant 5 am-11 pm. Rm serv. Bar from 10:30 am. Ck-out noon. Coin lndry. Valet serv. Free airport transportation. Exercise equipt; rowing machine, bicycles, whirlpool. Cr cds: A, C, D, DS, ER, JCB, MC, V.

★★★ **COURTYARD BY MARRIOTT.** (30653 Flynn Dr, Romulus 48174) N on Merriman Rd to Flynn Dr. 313/721-3200; FAX 313/721-1304. 146 rms, 3 story. S $82; D $92; each addl $10; suites $93-$103; under 16 free; wkend rates. Crib free. TV; cable. Indoor pool. Complimentary coffee in rms. Restaurant 6:30 am-2 pm, 5-10 pm; Sat & Sun from 7 am. Bar. Ck-out 1 pm. Coin lndry. Meeting rms. Valet serv. Free airport transportation. Exercise equipt; weight machine, bicycles, whirlpool. Refrigerator in suites. Balconies. Cr cds: A, C, D, DS, MC, V.

✔★★ **FAIRFIELD INN BY MARRIOTT.** (31119 Flynn Dr, Romulus 48174) N on Merriman Rd to Flynn Dr. 313/728-2322; FAX 313/728-2322, ext. 709. 133 rms, 3 story. S $40.95-$50.95; D $48.95-$55.95; each addl (up to 3 persons) $7; under 18 free. Crib free. TV; cable. Heated pool. Complimentary continental bkfst, coffee in lobby. Restaurant adj 6 am-10 pm; Fri, Sat to 11 pm. Ck-out noon. Meeting rm. Cr cds: A, C, D, DS, MC, V.

★★ **HAMPTON INN.** (30847 Flynn Dr, Romulus 48174) N on Merriman Rd to Flynn Dr. 313/721-1100; FAX 313/721-9915. 136 rms, 3 story. S $54-$58, D $64-$68; under 17 free. Crib $5. TV; cable. Pool. Complimentary continental bkfst, coffee. Restaurant adj 6 am-10 pm; Fri, Sat to 11:30 pm. Ck-out noon. Meeting rms. Valet serv. Free airport transportation. Cr cds: A, C, D, DS, MC, V.

★★ **MERRIMAN EXECUTIVE INN.** (7600 Merriman Rd, Romulus 48174) 1/2 mi N on Merriman Rd. 313/728-2430; res: 800/937-0005; FAX 313/728-3756. 140 rms. S $49-$79; D $59-$79; each addl $7; under 17 free; wkly, monthly rates. Crib free. TV; cable. Complimentary continental bkfst. Restaurant 11-1 am. Bar. Ck-out noon. Coin lndry. Meeting rms. Valet serv. Sundries. Free airport transportation. Cr cds: A, C, D, DS, ER, JCB, MC, V.

Motor Hotels

★★ **DAYS HOTEL.** (8800 Wickham Rd, Romulus 48174) N on Merriman Rd to Wickham Rd. 313/729-9000; FAX 313/729-9000, ext. 444. 177 rms, 7 story. S, D $55; each addl $5; under 12 free. Crib free. TV; cable. Indoor pool. Restaurant 6:30 am-1 pm, 5:30-9:30 pm; wkend hrs vary. Rm serv. Ck-out noon. Bellhops. Valet serv. Free airport transportation. X-country ski 10 mi. Exercise equipt; bicycles, stair machine, whirlpool. Cr cds: A, C, D, DS, MC, V.

★★★ **HILTON SUITES.** (8600 Wickham Rd, Romulus 48174) N on Merriman Rd to Wickham Rd. 313/728-9200; FAX 313/728-9278. 151 suites, 3 story. S $99; D $109; each addl $10; family rates. Crib free. TV; cable, in-rm movies. Indoor/outdoor pool; poolside serv. Complimentary full bkfst 6-9 am. Complimentary coffee in rms. Restaurant 6 am-midnight. Bar. Ck-out noon. Coin lndry. Meeting rms. Bellhops. Valet serv. Sundries. Free airport transportation. Downhill ski 10 mi. Exercise equipt; weight machine, bicycles, whirlpool. Game rm. Refrigerators. Some balconies. Cr cds: A, C, D, DS, MC, V.

★★ **RAMADA INN.** (8270 Wickham Rd, Romulus 48174) N on Merriman Rd to Wickham Rd. 313/729-6300; FAX 313/722-8740. 243 rms, 4 story. S $59-$79; D $69-$89; each addl $10; suites from $150; family, wkend rates; package plans. Crib free. TV; cable. Indoor pool. Playground. Restaurant 6 am-10 pm. Rm serv. Bar 11-2 am, Sun from noon; entertainment, dancing Fri, Sat. Ck-out noon. Meeting rms. Bellhops. Valet serv. Gift shop. Free airport transportation. X-country ski 4 mi. Exercise equipt; weight machine, bicycle, sauna. Game rm. Cr cds: A, C, D, DS, ER, JCB, MC, V.

Hotels

★★ **HOLIDAY INN CROWNE PLAZA.** (8000 Merriman Rd, Romulus 48174) 1 mi N on Merriman Rd. 313/729-2600; FAX 313/729-9414. 365 rms, 11 story. S, D $99-$109; each addl $10; suites $179-$229; family, wkend rates. Crib free. Pet accepted, some restrictions. TV; cable. Indoor pool. Restaurant 6 am-11 pm. Bar noon-1 am. Ck-out noon. Convention facilities. Gift shop. Free airport transportation. Exercise equipt; weights, bicycles, whirlpool. Game rm. Some balconies. *LUXURY LEVEL : EXECUTIVE FLOOR.* 35 rms. S, D $119. Concierge. Private lounge, honor bar. Complimentary continental bkfst, refreshments, newspaper. Cr cds: A, C, D, DS, JCB, MC, V.

★★★ **MARRIOTT-ROMULUS.** (30559 Flynn Dr, Romulus 48174) N on Merriman Rd to Flynn Dr. 313/729-7555; FAX 313/729-8634. 245 rms, 4 story. S, D $99; suites $350; family, wkend rates. Crib free. Pet accepted, some restrictions. TV; cable. Indoor pool. Restaurant 6:30 am-midnight. Bar from 11 am. Ck-out 1 pm. Meeting rms. Gift shop. Free airport transportation. Downhill ski 15 mi. Exercise equipt; weight machine, bicycles, whirlpool. Some bathrm phones. Refrigerator, minibar in suites. *LUXURY LEVEL : CONCIERGE LEVEL.* 54 rms, 2 suites. S, D $114. Concierge. Private lounge, honor bar. Complimentary continental bkfst, refreshments. Cr cds: A, C, D, DS, ER, JCB, MC, V.

Southfield

Motels

★★★ **COURTYARD BY MARRIOTT.** 27027 Northwestern Hwy (MI 10) (48034). 810/358-1222; FAX 810/354-3820. 147 rms, 2-3 story. S $72; D $82; suites $83-$93; wkend rates; higher rates special events. Crib free. TV; cable. Indoor pool. Restaurant 6:30 am-2 pm. Serv bar. Ck-out 1 pm. Coin lndry. Meeting rms. Valet serv. Exercise equipt; weights, bicycles, whirlpool. Some refrigerators. Balconies. Cr cds: A, C, D, DS, MC, V.

[D] [icons] SC

★ ★ HAMPTON INN. 27500 Northwestern Hwy (MI 10) (48034). 810/356-5500; FAX 810/356-2083. 153 rms, 2 story. S $54-$58; D $64-$68; under 18 free; some wkly, wkend rates. Crib free. TV; cable. Indoor pool. Complimentary continental bkfst. Restaurant nearby. Ck-out noon. Coin lndry. Meeting rms. Valet serv. Downhill/x-country ski 20 mi. Exercise equipt; weights, bicycles, whirlpool. Picnic tables. Cr cds: A, C, D, DS, MC, V.

[D] [icons] SC

✔★ TRAVELODGE. 27650 Northwestern Hwy (48034). 810/353-6777; FAX 810/353-2944. 110 rms, 2 story. S, D $38-$40; family rates. Crib $6. TV; cable. Complimentary continental bkfst. Complimentary coffee in rms. Restaurant nearby. Ck-out noon. Meeting rms. Some refrigerators. Cr cds: A, C, D, DS, MC, V.

[D] [icons] SC

Motor Hotels

★ ★ ★ BERKSHIRE HOTEL. 26111 Telegraph Rd (48034). 810/356-4333; res: 800/322-2339; FAX 810/356-8544. 109 rms, 3 story. S, D $89-$99; each addl $10; suites $120-$250; under 12 free; honeymoon, wkend rates. Crib free. TV; cable, in-rm movies. Complimentary continental bkfst. Bar. Ck-out noon. Meeting rms. Bellhops. Downhill ski 20 mi; x-country ski 16 mi. Exercise equipt; weights, stair machine. Refrigerators avail. Cr cds: A, C, D, DS, ER, JCB, MC, V.

[D] [icons] SC

★ ★ ★ HOLIDAY INN. 26555 Telegraph Rd (48034). 810/353-7700; FAX 810/353-8377. 417 rms, 2-16 story. S, D $75-$81; each addl $8; suites $175-$249; under 19 free; wkend rates. Crib free. Pet accepted, some restrictions; $30 refundable. TV; cable. Indoor pool; whirlpool. Restaurant 6:30 am-2 pm, 5-10 pm; Sat, Sun from 7 am. Rm serv. Bar 11-1 am. Ck-out noon. Coin lndry. Convention facilities. Bellhops. Sundries. Gift shop. Barber, beauty shop. Downhill/x-country ski 20 mi. Game rm. Rec rm. Many rms in circular tower. Cr cds: A, C, D, DS, JCB, MC, V.

[D] [icons] SC

Hotels

★ ★ HILTON GARDEN INN. 26000 American Dr (48034). 810/357-1100; FAX 810/799-7030. 200 rms, 7 story. S, D $89; each addl $10; under 12 free; wkend rates. Crib free. Pet accepted, some restrictions; $50. TV; cable. Indoor pool. Restaurant 6-9:30 am, 11 am-2 pm, 5-10 pm; wkend hrs vary. Bar 5 pm-midnight. Ck-out 1 pm. Meeting rms. X-country ski 15 mi. Exercise equipt; weight machine, stair machine, whirlpool, sauna. Cr cds: A, C, D, ER, MC, V.

[D] [icons] SC

★ ★ MARRIOTT. 27033 Northwestern Hwy (MI 10) (48034). 810/356-7400; FAX 810/356-5501. 222 rms, 6 story. S, D $99-$109; suites $250; under 16 free; wkend rates. Crib free. TV; cable. Indoor pool. Restaurant 6:30 am-11 pm. Bar 11-1 am. Ck-out noon. Meeting rms. Concierge. Gift shop. Exercise equipt; weights, bicycles, whirlpool, sauna. Health club privileges. Refrigerator. *LUXURY LEVEL :* CONCIERGE LEVEL. 33 rms. S, D $119. Private lounge, honor bar. Complimentary continental bkfst, refreshments. Cr cds: A, C, D, DS, ER, JCB, MC, V.

[D] [icons]

★ ★ ★ RADISSON PLAZA AT TOWN CENTER. 1500 Town Center (48075). 810/827-4000; FAX 810/827-1364. 385 rms, 12 story, 42 suites. S $123-$163; D $135-$175; each addl $15; suites $180-

$425; under 17 free. Crib $15. Valet parking $7. TV; cable. Indoor pool; poolside serv. Restaurant 6:30 am-10:30 pm. Rm serv 24 hrs. Bar 11-2 am; Sun noon-midnight; entertainment, dancing Tues-Sat. Ck-out noon. Convention facilities. Concierge. Downhill/x-country ski 20 mi. Exercise equipt; weights, bicycles, whirlpool, sauna. Refrigerators avail. *LUXURY LEVEL : PLAZA FLOORS.* 75 rms, 2 floors. S, D $148-$175; each addl $10. Private lounge. Bathrm phones; some in-rm whirlpools. Complimentary bkfst, refreshments. Cr cds: A, C, D, DS, JCB, MC, V.

[D] [icons] SC

Restaurants

★ ★ ★ GOLDEN MUSHROOM. 18100 W Ten Mile Rd. 810/559-4230. Hrs: 11:30 am-4 pm, 5-11 pm; Fri to midnight; Sat 11:30 am-3 pm, 5:30 pm-midnight. Closed Sun; major hols. Res accepted. Continental menu. Bar 11:30-2 am. A la carte entrees: lunch $8.25-$19.25, dinner $15.50-$28.50. Specializes in wild game dishes. Own baking. Valet parking. Cr cds: A, C, D, DS, MC, V.

★ ★ LE METRO. 29855 Northwestern Hwy (MI 10), in Applegate Square. 810/353-2757. Hrs: 11:30 am-10 pm; Fri & Sat to 11 pm; early-bird dinner Mon-Fri 4:30-6:30 pm. Closed Sun; major hols. Res accepted. Bar. Semi-a la carte: lunch $4.25-$12.95, dinner $5.25-$20. Specialties: Norwegian salmon, stuffed medallions of provimi veal, pasta. Parking. Lively atmosphere. Cr cds: A, C, D, MC, V.

[D]

★ ★ ★ MORTON'S OF CHICAGO. One Town Square, between Civic Center Dr & Lahser. 810/354-6066. Hrs: 11:30 am-2:30 pm, 5-11 pm; Sat from 5:30 pm; Sun 5-10 pm. Closed major hols. Res accepted. Bar. A la carte entrees: lunch $7-$15, dinner $16.95-$48.95. Specializes in fresh seafood, beef. Valet parking (dinner). Menu recited. Semi-formal steak house atmosphere. Cr cds: A, C, D, MC, V.

[D]

★ ★ SWEET LORRAINE'S CAFE. 29101 Greenfield Rd. 810/559-5985. Hrs: 11 am-10:30 pm; Fri, Sat to midnight; Sun to 9 pm. Closed some hols. Bar. A la carte entrees: lunch $4.95-$9.95, dinner $9.45-$16.95. Specialties: pecan chicken, Jamaican "Jerk" steak, vegetarian entrees. Modern-style bistro. Cr cds: A, C, D, DS, MC, V.

[D]

Warren

Motels

★ ★ BEST WESTERN STERLING INN. (34911 Van Dyke Ave, Sterling Heights 48312) N on MI 53 (Van Dyke Ave), at 15 Mile Rd. 810/979-1400; FAX 810/979-0430. 160 rms, 2-3 story. S $65-$75; D $65-$80; each addl $5; suites $150-$275; under 12 free; wkend rates. Crib free. TV; cable. Indoor pool. Restaurant 6-11 pm; Fri to midnight, Sat 7 am-midnight; Sun 7 am-10 pm. Rm serv. Bar 11 am-midnight, Sun noon-10 pm. Ck-out noon. Meeting rms. Valet serv. Downhill/x-country ski 18 mi. Exercise equipt; weight machine, bicycles, whirlpool, sauna. Refrigerators; some in-rm whirlpools, bathrm phones. Cr cds: A, C, D, DS, MC, V.

[D] [icons] SC

✔★ ★ FAIRFIELD INN BY MARRIOTT. 7454 Convention Blvd (48092). 810/939-1700; FAX 810/939-1700, ext. 709. 132 rms, 3 story. S, D $37.95-$49.95; each addl $6; under 18 free. Crib free. TV; cable. Heated pool. Complimentary continental bkfst, coffee in lobby. Restaurant nearby. Ck-out noon. Meeting rm. Valet serv. Cr cds: A, C, D, DS, MC, V.

[D] [icons] SC

★ ★ **HAMPTON INN.** *7447 Convention Blvd (48092).* *810/977-7270; FAX 810/977-3889.* 124 rms, 3 story. S $62; D $65; each addl $6; suites $85; under 18 free; wkly rates. Crib free. TV; cable. Complimentary continental bkfst, coffee. Restaurant nearby. Ck-out noon. Meeting rms. Valet serv. X-country ski 20 mi. Refrigerator, wet bar in suites. Cr cds: A, C, D, DS, ER, MC, V.

★ ★ **HOLIDAY INN EXPRESS.** *11500 Eleven Mile Rd (48089), I-696 exit Hoover Rd.* 810/754-9700; FAX 810/754-0376. 125 rms, 2 story. Sept-Mar: S $57; D $62; under 17 free; wkend rates; lower rates rest of yr. Crib free. TV; cable. Pool. Complimentary continental bkfst, coffee. Restaurant adj 11 am-midnight. Ck-out noon. Meeting rms. Valet serv. Cr cds: A, C, D, DS, ER, JCB, MC, V.

★ ★ **HOMEWOOD SUITES.** *30180 N Civic Center Dr (48093).* 810/558-7870; res: 800/225-5466; FAX 810/558-8072. 76 kit. suites, 3 story. Suites $70-$130; family rates. Crib avail. Pet accepted; $50 refundable. TV; cable, in-rm movies. Pool. Complimentary continental bkfst. Complimentary coffee in rms. Restaurant nearby. Ck-out noon. Coin lndry. Meeting rms. Valet serv. Sundries. Gift shop. Downhill/x-country ski 20 mi. Exercise equipt; weight machine, bicycles, whirlpool. Health club privileges. Grills. Cr cds: A, C, D, DS, MC, V.

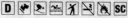

✔★ **RED ROOF INN.** *26300 Dequindre Rd (48091).* 810/573-4300; FAX 810/573-6157. 137 rms, 2 story. S $30.99-$36.99; D $37.99-$47.99; 3 or more $44.99; under 18 free; higher rates special events. Crib free. Pet accepted, some restrictions. TV; cable. Complimentary coffee. Restaurant nearby. Ck-out noon. Cr cds: A, C, D, DS, MC, V.

Restaurant

★ ★ **ANDIAMO ITALIA.** *7096 Fourteen Mile Rd.* 810/268-3200. Hrs: 11 am-11 pm; Fri to midnight; Sat 4 pm-midnight; Sun 4-10 pm. Closed some major hols. Italian menu. Bar. Semi-a la carte: lunch $8-$14, dinner $9-$22. Specializes in pasta, gnocchi, bocconcini di vitello. Valet parking. Player piano. Cr cds: A, MC, V.

District of Columbia

Founded: 1790

Pop: 606,900

Elev: 1-410 feet

Time zone: Eastern

Area code: 202 (DC); 703 (Virginia); 301 or 410 (Maryland)

Washington, DC, the first American city planned for a specific purpose, is perhaps the world's largest company town. The town's early history, like the government of the time, was inconspicuous. Washington was muddy or dusty, depending upon the season, insect-ridden and the object of savage jokes. There were few houses, still fewer public buildings, and the residents' social lives centered around the few saloons.

Not many people visited Washington prior to the Civil War. But in late May 1865, more than 100,000 people flocked to the capital city to witness the Grand Review of the victorious Union Army. For two days the throng watched 150,000 Union soldiers parade up Pennsylvania Avenue. Both tourists and soldiers stayed over the weekend to see the sights, doubling the city's normal population of 100,000. It was the beginning of Washington's biggest industry—tourism.

Washington underwent great expansion periods during the two World Wars, when new industry, new buildings and many thousands of new residents appeared almost overnight. When the wars ended, few of the migrants ever returned home.

Today, Washington is the center of a vast metropolitan area that encompasses the District of Columbia and areas of two states—Maryland and Virginia. More than 20 million tourists come to the city every year. George Washington's Federal City, once the butt of endless jokes, is indeed a thriving, vital metropolis.

Business

Washington has two major industries—government and tourism. Because government business rarely slackens, the city does not suffer from the economic fluctuations that plague many other cities. More than half a million Washingtonians work for the government. Tourism contributes approximately $4 billion in direct revenues to the local economy and accounts for nearly 60,000 jobs in the area.

Convention Facilities

The city of Washington and its immediate surroundings have a total of about 64,000 hotel and motel rooms. Conventions meet here often, and as many as 30,000 delegates have been hosted at one time. The Washington, DC Convention Center at 9th St and New York Ave NW has 3 exhibition halls, 40 meeting rooms and 381,000 square feet of exhibition space.

Sports and Entertainment

Washington has three professional sports teams—the Capitals (hockey), Bullets (basketball) and Redskins (football).

The city boasts of many good restaurants and nightclubs, as well as several dinner theaters. In the summer there are frequent outdoor concerts in various parts of town. First-class entertainment is presented at the John F. Kennedy Center for the Performing Arts, which contains a concert hall, opera house, movie theater, the Eisenhower Theatre for Drama and the innovative Terrace Theatre. The Arena Stage is popular among theater-goers, and the National Theater attracts numerous Broadway plays.

A concentration of jazz, blues and rock bars are located in Georgetown, near Georgetown University; Blues Alley is renowned for attracting the biggest names in jazz. Also in the college area is Georgetown Park, a three-level entertainment and shopping mall surrounding a Victorian garden.

On Pennsylvania Avenue on Capitol Hill are casual restaurants and many jazz bars and lounges. The restored beaux-arts Union Station on Massachusetts Avenue has a collection of shops, restaurants and movie theaters.

Sightseeing

Helpful information for tourists is easily available in Washington. The National Park Service maintains two information kiosks on the Mall: at the Washington Monument and at the Vietnam Veterans Memorial.

One of the best things about vacationing here is that the most interesting places usually have no admission charge. Following is a list of some of the more popular attractions.

—The Capitol, seat of Congress since 1800, where visitors watch the US government in action.

—The Library of Congress, ornately designed, with numerous changing exhibits.

—The Supreme Court, where court cases are open to the public and often provide an exciting show. Lectures are given when court is not in session.

—Folger Shakespeare Library, North America's foremost Shakespearean library, with an Elizabethan theater, a model of the Globe Theatre and a Shakespeare first folio edition of 1623.

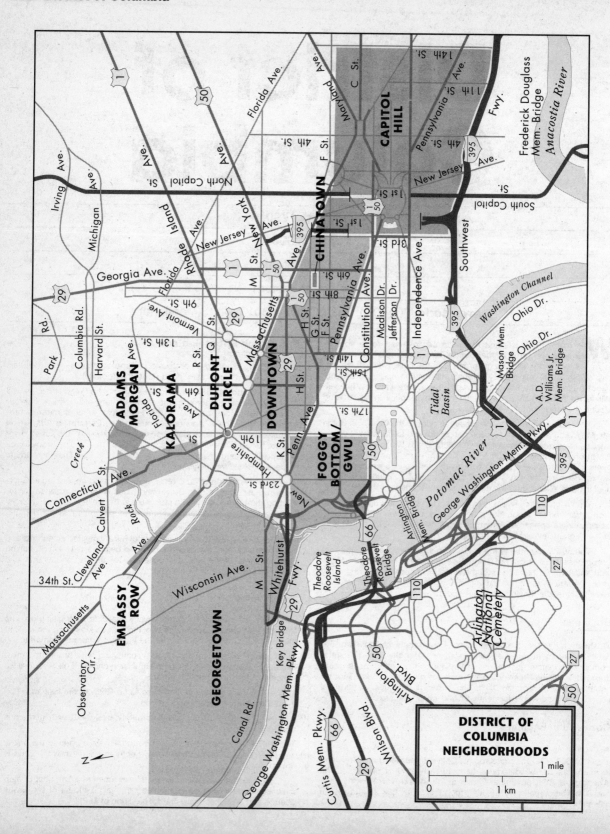

DISTRICT OF
COLUMBIA
NEIGHBORHOODS

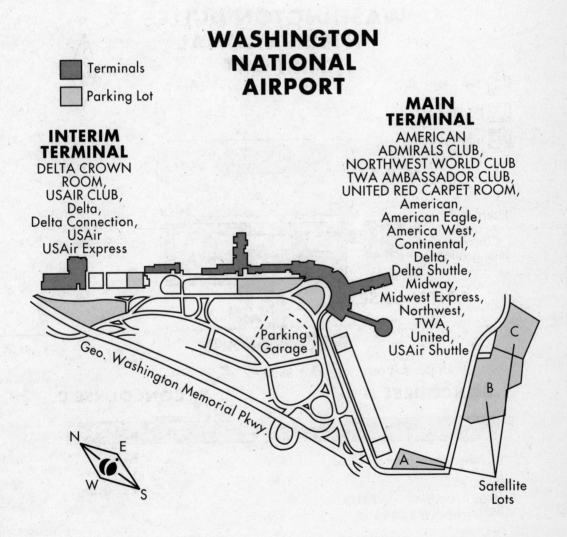

WASHINGTON NATIONAL AIRPORT

Terminals

Parking Lot

MAIN TERMINAL
AMERICAN ADMIRALS CLUB,
NORTHWEST WORLD CLUB
TWA AMBASSADOR CLUB,
UNITED RED CARPET ROOM,
American,
American Eagle,
America West,
Continental,
Delta,
Delta Shuttle,
Midway,
Midwest Express,
Northwest,
TWA,
United,
USAir Shuttle

INTERIM TERMINAL
DELTA CROWN ROOM,
USAIR CLUB,
Delta,
Delta Connection,
USAir
USAir Express

Parking Garage

Geo. Washington Memorial Pkwy.

C

B

A

Satellite Lots

N
E
W
S

WASHINGTON DULLES INTERNATIONAL AIRPORT

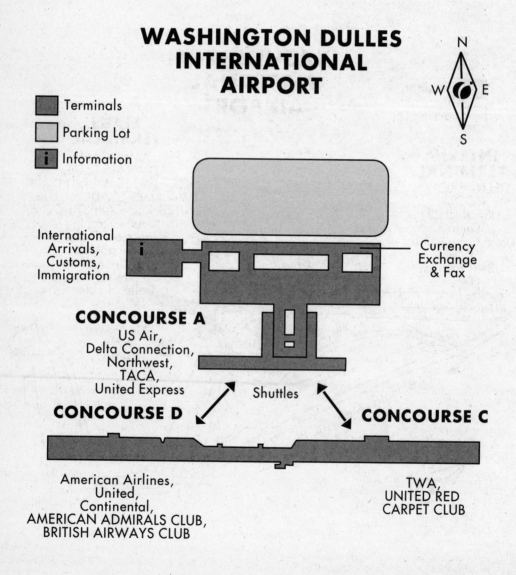

■ Terminals

■ Parking Lot

i Information

International
Arrivals,
Customs,
Immigration

Currency
Exchange
& Fax

CONCOURSE A

US Air,
Delta Connection,
Northwest,
TACA,
United Express

Shuttles

CONCOURSE D

CONCOURSE C

American Airlines,
United,
Continental,
AMERICAN ADMIRALS CLUB,
BRITISH AIRWAYS CLUB

TWA,
UNITED RED
CARPET CLUB

—US Botanic Garden Conservatory, a huge greenhouse with a waterfall and a miniature jungle.

—National Archives, where the Declaration of Independence, Bill of Rights, Constitution and other historical documents, maps and photographs are displayed.

—J. Edgar Hoover Building, FBI, fingerprint rooms and crime-detection labs.

—Interior Department, displays exhibits and dioramas depicting the history and activities of the department and its bureau.

—Smithsonian Institution Building, the "castle," an 1855 building housing the administrative offices of the institution, James Smithson's tomb and a visitors' information center.

—Arts and Industries Building, "1876: A Centennial Exhibition," also a part of the Smithsonian.

—National Air and Space Museum, houses the Wright brothers' airplane, Lindbergh's *Spirit of St Louis*, a special effects theater and Spacearium, plus hundreds of other exhibits.

—National Museum of Natural History, exhibiting the world's largest stuffed elephant, the Hope diamond and more.

—National Museum of American History, with many types of exhibits, period rooms.

—National Gallery of Art, an extensive collection of masterpieces in beautiful buildings.

—Hirshhorn Museum and Sculpture Garden, displays modern art and sculpture.

—National Museum of African Art, a branch of the Smithsonian, features traditional African sculpture and textiles.

—National Portrait Gallery, a fine building housing portraits and statues of people who have made significant contributions to the history, development and culture of the US.

—National Museum of American Art, features American art since the 18th century.

—Freer Gallery of Art, displays art of the Far East, Mid-Orient and Near East.

—Renwick Gallery, features American crafts and design.

—Anacostia Neighborhood Museum, a capsule museum with changing exhibits, designed to serve the neighborhood community.

—US Holocaust Memorial Museum, architecturally significant building houses exhibits depicting the many aspects of the Holocaust using genuine oral testimonies, photographs, documentary films and artifacts.

—Bureau of Engraving and Printing, where new money is made and old money is burned.

—Explorers Hall, at the headquarters of the National Geographic Society, exhibits show the society's explorations of land, sea and space.

—National Museum of Women in the Arts, displays of paintings, sculpture, and pottery by women from the Renaissance to the present.

—B'nai B'rith Klutznick Museum, houses Jewish ceremonial objects, history and art exhibits.

—Art Museum of the Americas, dedicated exclusively to Latin American and Caribbean contemporary art.

—US National Arboretum, exhibits floral displays year round. Also here is a Japanese garden and the National Bonsai Collection.

—Treasury Building, with a collection of rare money.

—White House, with free guided tours nearly every day.

—Washington Monument, a 555-foot obelisk, finished in 1884. (Elevator ride free.)

—Lincoln Memorial, probably the nation's most impressive and inspirational shrine.

—Jefferson Memorial, an exquisite white marble building on the Tidal Basin. The Japanese cherry trees surround the basin.

—Vietnam Veteran's Memorial, currently the capital's most popular attraction, includes the names of all who gave their lives in or are missing from the Vietnam War.

—Arlington National Cemetery, location of the Tomb of the Unknown Soldier and the grave of John F. Kennedy.

—Iwo Jima Statue, Marine Corps War Memorial.

—The Pentagon, the largest office building in the world, houses offices of the US Department of Defense.

—Emancipation Statue, bronze work by Thomas Ball, paid for by voluntary subscriptions from emancipated slaves.

—John F. Kennedy Center for the Performing Arts, a magnificent building filled with art treasures; tours.

—Theodore Roosevelt Island, a quiet wilderness area with a statuary garden, including a likeness of Teddy, nature trails and guided hikes.

—Georgetown, a section of the city built a century before the capital was located here, lovely houses, good restaurants and many shops.

—Washington National Cathedral, begun in 1907 and completed in 1990, Gothic in style, was built completely by hand and in the manner of medieval cathedrals. The tomb of Woodrow Wilson and many memorials are here.

—Rock Creek Park, 1,754 acres within the city; trails, riding, biking, picnic groves, nature center, playing fields.

—National Zoological Park, with the only pandas in this hemisphere. (The zoo parking area requires a fee.)

—Ford's Theatre, restored to its 1865 appearance; Lincoln Museum in the basement. Across the street is the house where Lincoln died (Petersen House).

—National Building Museum, exhibiting advances in architecture.

—National Shrine of the Immaculate Conception, largest Roman Catholic church in America and one of the largest in the world. Nearby is the Franciscan Monastery, with catacombs and gardens (some bloom at Christmastime).

—United States Navy Memorial, featuring *At Sea*, a high-tech, large format film.

—Navy Museum, with models, documents, weapons, displays about naval history.

—Marine Corps Museum, weapons, uniforms and artifacts describe the history of the US Marine Corps, including a display on military music.

—Organization of American States, permanent secretariat of the organization is located here. The OAS was established to maintain international peace and security and to raise the social, economic, educational and cultural standards of the people of the Americas.

—Anderson House Museum, a museum of the American Revolution, with portraits by early American artists. Books, medals, swords, silver, glass and china on display.

—Phillips Collection, one of the finest private art collections in the world.

—Frederick Douglass Home, Cedar Hill, the house where the renowned black leader lived from 1877 until his death. Another of his residences now houses the Museum of African Art. Donations.

—Old Post Office Pavilion, featuring Romanesque architecture and a 315-foot clock tower; now houses federal offices and the Pavilion, which consists of restaurants and shops around a courtyard.

—Great Falls of the Potomac, a popular attraction since Native Americans lived here.

—C & O Canal, a pleasant place for biking, hiking, canoeing, picnicking and winter ice-skating.

During the summer there are free concerts at the Capitol and at the Jefferson Memorial; during the rest of the year, concerts are performed at the National Gallery of Art and at the East Garden Court.

No visit to the Washington area would be complete without a pilgrimage to Mount Vernon and to the Alexandria landmarks that relate to George Washington's life—Gadsby's Tavern, the Stabler-Leadbeater Apothecary Shop, George Washington National Masonic Memorial and historic Christ Church.

Today's interest in restoration and preservation of historic buildings and districts would warm the heart of Ann Pamela Cunningham of South Carolina, who founded the Mount Vernon Ladies' Association in 1853. Her struggle to preserve this beautiful plantation consumed all her energies, but she won a place in history as the grandmother of the preservation movement. Mount Vernon remains for all to enjoy thanks to the dedicated efforts of Miss Cunningham, her colleagues and those who followed. It is still one of the most impressive of all historic sites.

In Georgetown the National Park Service maintains the Old Stone House, a pre-Revolutionary landmark. Craftsmen and women in colonial dress make pomander balls and bake cookies in the kitchen fireplace and demonstrate cabinet-making, quilting and candle-dipping.

Several houses of historic and architectural interest in the city charge a nominal admission fee or request donations. Among the most interesting are the 1818 Decatur House on Lafayette Square, operated by the National Trust for Historic Preservation; Octagon House, 1798-1800, the house into which James and Dollie Madison moved after the British burned the White House in the War of 1812; the Woodrow Wilson House, former residence of the 28th president; the Christian Heurich House, an ornate Victorian mansion housing the Columbia Historical Society; Hillwood Museum, former house of Marjorie Merriweather Post, heiress to the Post Toasties fortune and collector of Russian art and antiquities; the Yellow House, one of Georgetown's oldest houses; Tudor Place, residence of one of Washington's oldest families (descendants of Martha Custis Washington) and designed by Dr. William Thornton, architect of the Capitol; and Dumbarton Oaks, a Georgetown estate with Federal-style, early 19th-century mansion, elegant collections of silver and china and spectacular terraced gardens.

Four outlying attractions operated by the National Park Service are well worth special excursions. Claude Moore Colonial Farm at Turkey Run, next to the CIA complex on the outskirts of the city near McLean, Virginia, is a working farm of the revolutionary era. Oxon Hill Farm, south of the city on the Maryland shore of the Potomac, exhibits farm animals and machinery; demonstrations of farm work are given. Fort Washington National Park in Maryland is a reconstructed outpost of the earliest defense for the city. At Wolf Trap Farm Park for the Performing Arts, in Vienna, Virginia, just 15 miles from Washington, performances of all sorts are held throughout the year. This 100-acre park of lovely rolling woodland has walking paths and picnic areas.

General References

Founded: 1790 **Pop:** 606,900 **Elev:** 1-410 feet **Time zone:** Eastern
Area code: 202 (DC); 703 (Virginia); 301 or 410 (Maryland)

Phone Numbers

POLICE & FIRE: 911
FBI: 324-3000
POISON CONTROL CENTER: 625-3333
TIME: 844-1111 **WEATHER:** 936-1212

Information Sources

Washington DC Convention and Visitors Association, 1212 New York Ave NW, Suite 600, 20005; 789-7000.
Visitor Information Center, 1455 Pennsylvania Ave NW, 20004; 789-7038.
Daily recording of events, 789-7000.
Office of Recreation Info, 673-7660.

Transportation

AIRLINES: Air France; American; British Airways; Continental; Delta; Lufthansa (Germany); Northwest; Russian Intl; TWA; United; USAir; and other commuter and regional airlines. For current airline schedules and information consult the *Official Airline Guide,* published twice monthly.
AIRPORTS: National, 703/685-8000; Dulles, 703/685-8000; Baltimore-Washington Intl (BWI), 410/859-7100.
CAR RENTAL AGENCIES: (See Toll-Free Numbers) *National (703):* Avis 800/331-1212, Budget 521-0121, Hertz 979-6300; *Dulles (703):* Avis 661-3500, Budget 661-6639, Dollar 661-6630, Hertz 471-6020; *BWI (410):* Avis 859-1680, Budget 859-0850, Dollar 684-3315, Hertz 850-7400.
PUBLIC TRANSPORTATION: Metro Transit System 637-7000.
RAILROAD PASSENGER SERVICE: Amtrak 800/872-7245.

Newspapers

Washington Post; Washington Times.

Convention Facility

Washington, DC Convention Center, 900 9th St NW, 789-1600.

Sports & Recreation

Major Sports Facilities

Capital Centre, 9 mi E in Landover, MD, 301/350-3400 (Bullets, basketball; Capitals, hockey).
RFK Stadium, E Capitol St & 22nd St NE (Redskins, football, 546-2222).

Racetrack

Rosecroft Raceway, 6336 Rosecroft Dr, 8 mi SE in Ft Washington, MD, 301/567-4000 (harness racing).

Cultural Facilities

Theaters

Arena Stage, 6th St & Maine Ave SW, 488-3300.
Carter Barron Amphitheatre, 16th St & Colorado Ave NW, 260-6836.
Ford's Theatre, 511 10th St NW, 347-4833.
John F. Kennedy Center for the Performing Arts, New Hampshire Ave at F St NW, 467-4600.
National Theatre, 1321 Pennsylvania Ave NW, 628-6161.

Concert Halls

John F. Kennedy Center for the Performing Arts, New Hampshire Ave at F St NW, 467-4600.
Wolf Trap Farm Park for the Performing Arts, 14 mi NW via Washington Memorial Pkwy, VA 123, US 7, then S on Towlston Rd (Trap Rd) (VA 676) in Vienna, VA, 703/255-1900.

Museums

Anacostia Museum (Smithsonian), 1901 Fort Place SE, 357-1300.
Anderson House, 2118 Massachusetts Ave NW, 785-2040.
Arts and Industries Building (Smithsonian), 900 Jefferson Dr SW, 357-1300.
B'nai B'rith Klutznick Museum, B'nai B'rith International Center, 1640 Rhode Island Ave NW, 857-6583.
Capital Children's Museum, 800 3rd St NE, 543-8600.
Dumbarton Oaks, 1703 32nd St NW, 338-8278.
Fondo del Sol, 2112 R St NW, 483-2777.
Hillwood Museum, 4155 Linnean Ave NW, 686-5807.
Lincoln Museum, Ford's Theatre (see Theaters).
Marine Corps Museum, Bldg 58, Navy Yard, 433-3840.

National Air and Space Museum (Smithsonian), Independence Ave & 7th St SW, 357-1686.

National Building Museum, Judiciary Square NW, 272-2448.

National Museum of American History (Smithsonian), Constitution Ave & 14th St NW.

National Museum of Health and Medicine, Building #54, Walter Reed Army Medical Center, Alaska Ave and 16th St NW, 576-2348.

National Museum of Natural History (Smithsonian), Constitution Ave & 10th St NW, 357-1300.

Navy Museum, Bldg 76, Navy Yard, 9th & M Sts SE, 433-4882.

Textile Museum, 2320 S St NW, 667-0441.

US Holocaust Memorial Museum, 100 Raoul Wallenberg Pl (15th St SW), 488-0400.

Washington Dolls' House and Toy Museum, 5236 44th St NW, 363-6400.

Art Museums and Galleries

Art Museum of the Americas, 201 18th St NW, 458-6019.

Corcoran Gallery of Art, 17th St & New York Ave NW, 638-3211.

Freer Gallery of Art (Smithsonian), 12th St & Jefferson Dr SW, 357-1300.

Hirshhorn Museum and Sculpture Garden (Smithsonian), Independence Ave at 8th St SW, 357-1300.

National Gallery of Art, 4th St & Constitution Ave NW, 737-4215.

National Museum of African Art (Smithsonian), 950 Independence Ave SW, 357-1300.

National Museum of American Art (Smithsonian), 8th & G Sts NW, 357-1300.

National Museum of Women in the Arts, 1250 New York Ave NW, 783-5000.

National Portrait Gallery (Smithsonian), 8th & F Sts NW, 357-1300.

Phillips Collection, 1600 & 1612 21st St NW, 387-2151.

Renwick Gallery (Smithsonian), 17th St & Pennsylvania Ave NW, 357-1300.

Points of Interest

Historical

Antietam National Battlefield Site and Cemetery, 1 mi N of Sharpsburg on MD 65.

Arlington National Cemetery, Arlington, VA, 703/979-0690.

Blair House, 1651 Pennsylvania Ave NW.

Christ Church, 118 N Washington St, Alexandria, VA, 703/549-1450.

Christian Heurich Mansion, 1307 New Hampshire Ave NW, 785-2068.

Clara Barton National Historic Site, 5801 Oxford Rd, Glen Echo, MD, 301/492-6245.

DAR Buildings, 1776 D St NW, 628-1776.

Decatur House, 748 Jackson Pl NW, 842-0920.

Emancipation Statue, Lincoln Park, E Capitol St between 11th & 13th Sts NE.

Executive Offices, Pennsylvania Ave & 17th St NW, on White House grounds.

Fort Stevens Park, Piney Branch Rd & Quackenbos St NW, 576-6851.

Frederick Douglass National Historic Site, "Cedar Hill," 1411 W St SE, 426-5961.

Gadsby's Tavern, 134 N Royal St, Alexandria, VA, 703/838-4242.

Georgetown, W of Rock Creek Park, N of K St NW.

House where Lincoln died (Petersen House), 516 10th St NW, 426-6830.

Interior Department, C & D Sts NW, between 18th & 19th Sts NW, 208-4743.

Iwo Jima Statue, Turkey Run Park, 703/285-2598.

Judiciary Square, 2 blks bounded by F, 4th & 5th Sts NW & Indiana Ave.

Manassas (Bull Run) National Battlefield Park, 26 mi SW of Washington, at jct US 211, VA 234.

Mount Vernon, 18 mi S via George Washington Memorial Pkwy.

National Archives, Constitution Ave between 7th & 9th Sts NW, 501-5000.

National Presbyterian Church & Center, 4101 Nebraska Ave NW, 537-0800.

The Octagon, 1799 New York Ave at 18th & E Sts NW, 638-3105.

Old Stone House, 3051 M St NW, 426-6851.

Pavilion at the Old Post Office, Pennsylvania Ave & 12th St NW, 289-4224.

St John's Church, 3240 O St NW, 338-1796.

Sewall-Belmont House, 144 Constitution Ave NE, 546-3989.

Stabler-Leadbeater Apothecary Shop, 105-107 S Fairfax St, Alexandria, VA, 703/836-3713.

Treasury Building, Pennsylvania Ave & 15th St NW, 622-0896.

Tudor Place, 1644 31st St NW, in Georgetown, 965-0400.

US Court of Appeals, 5th & E Sts NW.

US District Court, Indiana Ave, between 4th & 5th Sts NW, 273-0555.

Washington Monument, Mall at 15th St NW.

White House, 1600 Pennsylvania Ave NW, 456-7041.

Woodrow Wilson House, 2340 S St NW, 387-4062.

Yellow House, 1430 33rd St NW.

Other Attractions

American Red Cross, 3 buildings bounded by 17th, 18th, D & E Sts NW, 737-8300.

American University, 4400 Massachusetts Ave NW, 885-1000.

At Sea, US Navy Memorial (see).

Bureau of Engraving and Printing, 14th & C Sts SW.

C & O Canal, W of 30th St & S of M St.

Catholic University of America, 620 Michigan Ave NE, 319-5000.

Chinatown, G and H Sts, between 6th and 8th Sts NW.

Claude Moore Colonial Farm at Turkey Run, McLean, VA, 703/442-7557.

Department of Commerce, Pennsylvania Ave between 14th & 15th Sts NW.

Department of Justice, Constitution Ave, 9th & 10th Sts NW.

Explorers Hall, 17th & M Sts NW, 857-7588.

Federal Reserve Building, C St between 20th & 21st Sts NW.

Federal Trade Commission, 6th St & Pennsylvania Ave NW, 326-2222.

Folger Shakespeare Library, 201 E Capitol St SE, 544-7077.

Fort Dupont Park, Randle Circle & Minnesota Ave S, 426-7723.

Fort Washington National Park, 4 mi S on MD 210, 3½ mi on Fort Washington Rd, in Fort Washington, MD, 301/763-4600.

Georgetown University, 37th & O Sts NW, 687-3600.

George Washington Masonic National Memorial, 101 Callahan Dr, Alexandria, VA, 703/683-2007.

George Washington University, 19th-24th Sts NW, F St-Pennsylvania Ave, 994-6460.

Government Printing Office, N Capitol between G & H Sts.

House Office Buildings, along Independence Ave, S side of Capitol grounds at Independence & New Jersey Aves.

Howard University, 2400 6th St NW between W & Harvard Sts NW, 806-6100.

Internal Revenue Building, Constitution Ave between 10th & 12th Sts NW.

Interstate Commerce Commission, Constitution Ave & 12th St NW.

Islamic Center, 2551 Massachusetts Ave NW, 332-8343.

J. Edgar Hoover Building, Pennsylvannia Ave between 9th & 10th Sts NW, 324-3447.

Jefferson Memorial, S edge of Tidal Basin.

Labor Department, 200 Constitution Ave NW, at 3rd St, 219-5000.

Lafayette Square, Pennsylvania Ave opp White House.

Library of Congress, 10 1st St SE, 707-8000.

Lincoln Memorial, W Potomac Park at 23rd St NW.

National Academy of Sciences, 2101 Constitution Ave between 21st & 22nd Sts NW, 334-2436.

National Aquarium, US Department of Commerce Building, 14th St & Constitution Ave NW, 482-2825.

National Colonial Farm, 20 mi S via I-495 exit 3A to MD 210, 10 mi right on Bryan Point Rd, 4 mi on Potomac River, 301/283-2113.
National Shrine of the Immaculate Conception, 4th St & Michigan Ave NE, 526-8300.
National Zoological Park (Smithsonian), in Rock Creek Park, 3000 blk of Connecticut Ave NW, 673-4800.
New York Ave Presbyterian Church, 1313 New York Ave at H St NW, 393-3700.
Organization of American States, Constitution Ave & 17th St NW, 458-3000.
Oxon Hill Farm, just W of jct MD 210 & I-95 in Oxon Hill, MD, 301/839-1177.
Potomac Park, N & S of Jefferson Memorial and Tidal Basin.
Rock Creek Park, NW on Beach Dr.
Senate Office Buildings, Constitution Ave, on both sides of 1st St NE.
Smithsonian Institution, The Mall and nearby, 357-2700.
Smithsonian Institution Building (the "Castle"), 900 Jefferson Dr SW, 357-2700.
State Department Building, 21st, 22nd, C & D Sts NW.
Supreme Court Building, Maryland Ave & 1st St NE, 479-3000.
Theodore Roosevelt Memorial, N end of Theodore Roosevelt Island, 703/285-2598.
US Botanic Garden Conservatory, Maryland Ave & 1st St SW, SW corner of Capitol grounds, 225-8333.
US Capitol, 1st & East Capitol Sts, 225-6827.
US National Arboretum, 3501 New York Ave NE, 475-4815.
US Naval Observatory, 3450 Massachusetts Ave NW, 653-1507.
US Navy Memorial, Pennsylvania Ave at 7th & 9th Sts NW, 737-2300.
US Postal Service, 475 L'Enfant Plaza West SW.
Vietnam Veterans Memorial, Constitution Ave between Henry Bacon Dr & 21st St NW, 619-7222.
Voice of America, 330 Independence Ave SW, between 3rd & 4th Sts SW, 619-3919.
Washington National Cathedral, Massachusetts & Wisconsin Aves, 537-6200.

Sightseeing Tours

Gray Line bus tours, 5500 Tuxedo Rd, Tuxedo, MD 20781; 301/386-8300.
Spirit of Washington and *Mt Vernon,* Pier 4, 554-8000.
Tourmobile Sightseeing, 1000 Ohio Dr SW, 20024; 554-7950.

Annual Events

Cherry Blossom Festival, The Mall. Late Mar-early Apr.

Georgetown House Tour, 338-1796. Late Apr.
Georgetown Garden Tour, 333-4953. Late Apr-early May.
Goodwill Industries Embassy Tour, 636-4225. 2nd Sat May.
Memorial Day Ceremony at Tomb of the Unknown Soldier, Arlington National Cemetery, VA.
July 4 Celebration, Washington Monument & Capitol W steps.
Pageant of Peace, Ellipse, S of White House. Dec.
New Year's Eve Celebration, Old Post Office Pavilion.

City Neighborhoods

Many of the restaurants, unrated dining establishments and some lodgings listed under Washington include neighborhoods as well as exact street addresses. A map showing these neighborhoods can be found immediately following the city introduction. Geographic descriptions of these areas are given, followed by a table of restaurants arranged by neighborhood.

Adams Morgan: North of Dupont Circle; along Columbia Rd between 18th St NW and Kalorama, NW/Kalorama Park.
Capitol Hill: Both the Hill upon which the Capitol is built (south of Constitution Ave, west of 1st St NE & SE, north of Independence Ave and east of 1st St NW & SW) and the surrounding historic neighborhood south of F St NW & NE, west of 14th St NE & SE, north of the Southwest Frwy (I-395) and east of 3rd St NW & SW.
Chinatown: Area of Downtown along G and H Sts NW between 6th and 8th Sts NW.
Downtown: South of Massachusetts Ave, west of N Capitol St, north of Pennsylvania Ave and east of 19th St. **North of Downtown:** North of Massachusetts Ave. **South of Downtown:** South of Independence Ave. **West of Downtown:** West of 19th St.
Dupont Circle: On and around the circle where Massachusetts, New Hampshire, Connecticut Aves and 19th and P Sts NW intersect.
Embassy Row: Area north of Dupont Circle; along Massachusetts Ave between Observatory Circle on the north and Sheridan Circle on the south.
Foggy Bottom: Area along the Potomac River south of K St NW (US 29), west of 19th St NW and north of Constitution Ave and I-66 interchange.
Georgetown: Northwest of Downtown; south of the Naval Observatory and W St NW, west of Rock Creek Park and north and east of the Potomac River; area around intersection of Wisconsin Ave and M St NW.
Kalorama: East and west of Connecticut Ave NW, south of Rock Creek Park and Calvert St, west of Columbia Rd and north of R St.

Lodgings and Food

DISTRICT OF COLUMBIA RESTAURANTS
BY NEIGHBORHOOD AREAS

(For full description, see alphabetical listings under Restaurants)

ADAMS MORGAN

Cafe Atlantico. 1819 Columbia Rd NW

Cities. 2424 18th St NW

I Matti Trattoria. 2436 18th St NW

Meskerem. 2434 18th St NW

Saigonnais. 2307 18th St NW

Stetson's. 1610 U Street NW

CAPITOL HILL

Head's. 400 1st St SE

La Colline. 400 N Capitol St NW

Monocle on Capitol Hill. 107 D Street NE

Sfuzzi. 50 Massachusetts Ave NE

CHINATOWN

China Inn. 631 H Street NW

Hunan Chinatown. 624 H Street NW

Mr. Yung's. 740 6th St NW

Tony Cheng's Mongolian Barbecue and Chinese Seafood Restaurant. 619 H Street NW

DOWNTOWN

701. 701 Pennsylvania Ave NW

Bice. 601 Pennsylvania Ave NW (entrance on Indiana Ave)

Bombay Club. 815 Connecticut Ave NW

Bombay Palace. 2020 K St NW

Dominique's. 1900 Pennsylvania Ave NW

Gary's. 1800 M Street NW

Gerard's Place. 915 15th St NW

German Deli-Cafe Mozart. 1331 H Street NW

I Ricchi. 1220 19th St NW

The Jefferson (Jefferson Hotel). 16th & M Sts

La Fonda. 1639 R Street NW

Le Lion d'Or. 1150 Connecticut Ave NW (entrance on 18th St)

Maison Blanche/Rive Gauche. 1725 F Street NW

Notte Luna. 809 15th St NW

Occidental Grill. 1475 Pennsylvania Ave NW

Old Ebbitt Grill. 675 15th St NW

Prime Rib. 2020 K Street NW

Primi Piatti. 2013 I Street NW

Red Sage. 605 14th St NW

Sichuan Pavilion. 1820 K Street NW

Taberna del Alabardero. 1776 I Street NW

Thai Kingdom. 2021 K Street NW

Tiberio. 1915 K Street NW

Willard Room (Willard Inter-Continental Hotel). 1401 Pennsylvania Ave NW

NORTH OF DOWNTOWN

Armand's Chicago Pizzeria. 4231 Wisconsin Ave NW

Fio's. 3636 16th St

Gaby's. 3311 Connecticut Ave NW

Guapo's. 4515 Wisconsin Ave NW

Lavandou. 3321 Connecticut Ave NW

Le Caprice. 2348 Wisconsin Ave NW

Murphy's of D.C. 2609 24th St NW,

New Heights. 2317 Calvert St NW

Old Europe Restaurant & Rathskeller. 2434 Wisconsin Ave NW

Petitto's Ristorante d'Italia. 2653 Connecticut Ave NW

Thai Taste. 2606 Connecticut Ave NW

Tucson Cantina. 2605 Connecticut Ave NW

SOUTH OF DOWNTOWN

Hogate's. 9th St & Maine Ave SW

Market Inn. 200 E Street SW

Phillips Flagship. 900 Water St SW

WEST OF DOWNTOWN

Colonnade (Ana Hotel). 2401 M Street NW

Melrose (Park Hyatt Hotel). 24th & M Street NW

DUPONT CIRCLE

Alekos. 1732 Connecticut Ave NW

Bacchus. 1827 Jefferson Place NW

Bua. 1635 P Street NW

C.F. Folks. 1225 19th St NW

Cafe Petitto. 1724 Connecticut Ave NW

Donna Adele. 2100 P Street NW

Kramerbooks & Afterwords. 1517 Connecticut Ave

Nora. 2132 Florida Ave NW

Obelisk. 2029 P Street NW

Palm. 1225 19th St NW

Pizzeria Paradiso. 2029 P Street NW

Sam & Harry's. 1200 19th St NW

Vincenzo. 1606 20th St NW

EMBASSY ROW

Jockey Club (The Ritz-Carlton Hotel). 2100 Massachusetts Ave NW

FOGGY BOTTOM

Galileo. 1110 21st St NW

Jean-Louis at The Watergate Hotel (The Watergate Hotel). 2650 Virginia Ave NW

Kinkead's. 2000 Pennsylvania Ave NW

Palladin by Jean-Louis (The Watergate Hotel). 2650 Virginia Ave NW

Roof Terrace. 2700 F Street NW

Sholl's Colonial Cafeteria. 1990 K Street NW

GEORGETOWN

1789. 1226 36th St NW

Aditi. 3299 M Street NW

Austin Grill. 2404 Wisconsin Ave NW

Billy Martin's Tavern. 1264 Wisconsin Ave NW

Bistro Francais. 3128 M Street NW

Busara. 2340 Wisconsin Ave NW

China Regency. 3000 K Street NW

El Caribe. 3288 M Street

Filomena Ristorante. 1063 Wisconsin Ave NW

Garrett's. 3003 M Street NW

Germaine's. 2400 Wisconsin Ave NW

Guards. 2915 M Street NW

J Paul's. 3218 M Street NW

Japan Inn. 1715 Wisconsin Ave NW

La Chaumière. 2813 M Street NW

Las Pampas. 3291 M Street NW

Madurai. 3316 M Street NW

Morton's of Chicago. 3251 Prospect St NW

Mr. Smith's. 3104 M Street NW

Nathans. 3150 M Street NW

Paolo's. 1303 Wisconsin Ave NW

Patisserie-Cafe Didier. 3206 Grace St NW

River Club. 3223 K Street NW

Sea Catch. 1054 31st St NW

Seasons (Four Seasons Hotel). 2800 Pennsylvania Ave NW

Sequoia. 3000 K Street NW

Tony and Joe's. 3000 K Street NW

KALORAMA

Katmandu. 2100 Connecticut Ave NW

Note: When a listing is located in a town that does not have its own city heading, it will appear under the city nearest to its location. In these cases, the address and town appear in parenthesis immediately following the name of the establishment.

Motel

★ ★ ★ **CHANNEL INN.** *650 Water St SW (20024), south of downtown.* 202/554-2400; res: 800/368-5668; FAX 202/863-1164. 100 rms, 3 story. S $100-$125; D $110-$135; each addl $10; suites $175; studio rms $125-$150; under 13 free; wkend rates. Crib free. TV; cable. Pool; poolside serv, lifeguard. Restaurant 7 am-11 pm; Sun to 10 pm. Rm serv. Bar 11:30-1 am, Fri & Sat to 2 am, Sun to 10 pm; entertainment, dancing exc Mon. Ck-out noon. Meeting rms. Bellhops. Garage parking. Balconies. At waterfront, near piers. Cr cds: A, C, D, DS, JCB, MC, V.

Motor Hotels

★ ★ **HOLIDAY INN GOVERNOR'S HOUSE.** *1615 Rhode Island Ave (20036), at 17th St NW (20036), downtown.* 202/296-2100; FAX 202/331-0227. 152 units, 9 story, 24 kits. Mar-June, Sept-Oct: S $115-$155; D $130-$170; each addl $15; suites $175-$225; kit. units $145-$155; under 19 free; wkend, monthly rates; higher rates Cherry Blossom Festival; lower rates rest of yr. Crib free. Valet parking $14. TV; cable. Pool; lifeguard. Restaurant 7 am-midnight. Rm serv. Bar from 11:30 am. Ck-out noon. Meeting rms. Bellhops. Valet serv. Health club

privileges. On original site of Governor of Pennsylvania Gifford Pinchot's house. Cr cds: A, C, D, DS, JCB, MC, V.

✔ ★ **HOWARD JOHNSON DOWNTOWN AT KENNEDY CENTER.** *2601 Virginia Ave NW (20037), in Foggy Bottom.* 202/965-2700; FAX 202/965-2700, ext. 7910. 192 rms, 8 story. Mid-Mar-Oct: S $82-$99; D $90-$99; each addl $5; under 18 free; lower rates rest of yr. Crib free. TV; in-rm movies. Rooftop pool; lifeguard (Memorial Day-Labor Day). Restaurant 6 am-11 pm. Ck-out noon. Meeting rm. Gift shop. Free covered parking. Game rm. Rec rm. Refrigerators. Some balconies. Cr cds: A, C, D, DS, ER, JCB, MC, V.

★ ★ **QUALITY HOTEL DOWNTOWN.** *1315 16th St NW (20036), downtown.* 202/232-8000; FAX 202/667-9827. 135 kit. units, 10 story. S $110-$130; D $130-$160; each addl $10; under 18 free; wkend rates. Crib free. Garage $8.50. TV; cable. Pool privileges. Restaurant 7 am-10 pm. Rm serv 7 am-2 pm, 5-9:30 pm. Bar 11:30 am-midnight. Ck-out noon. Meeting rms. Bellhops. Health club privileges. Cr cds: A, C, D, DS, ER, JCB, MC, V.

Hotels

★ ★ ★ ★ **ANA.** *2401 M Street NW (20037), west of downtown.* 202/429-2400; res: 800/228-3000; FAX 202/457-5010. 415 rms, 10 story. S $220-$255; D $250-$285; each addl $30; suites $600-$1,450; under 18 free; wkend, summer rates. Crib free. Covered parking; valet $15. Pet accepted, some restrictions. TV; cable. Indoor pool. Cafe 6:30 am-11 pm (also see COLONNADE). Rm serv 24 hrs. Bar 4 pm-midnight; entertainment. Ck-out 1 pm. Convention facilities. Concierge. Gift shop. Local shopping transportation. Exercise rm; instructor, weight machines, bicycles, whirlpool, sauna, steam rm. Massage. Squash & racquetball courts. Bathrm phones, refrigerators, minibars. Some balconies. Lobby and public areas with many antiques, old Italian statuary, 400-yr-old tapestries; distinctive decor with glass loggia creating a garden setting in lobby. *LUXURY LEVEL : EXECUTIVE CLUB FLOOR.* 202/429-2400. 50 rms, 10 suites. S $255; D $285; suites $600-$1,450. Concierge. Private lounge. Minibars. Complimentary continental bkfst, refreshments, newspaper, shoeshine. Cr cds: A, C, D, DS, ER, JCB, MC, V.

★ ★ **BARCELO-GEORGETOWN.** *2121 P Street NW (20037), in Dupont Circle area.* 202/293-3100; res: 800/257-5432; FAX 202/857-0134. 294 rms, 10 story. S $160-$190; D $180-$210; each addl $20; suites $175-$450; under 18 free; wkend rates. Crib free. Valet parking $13. TV; cable. Pool; lifeguard. Restaurant 7 am-midnight; Fri & Sat to 1 am. Bar noon-1 am. Ck-out noon. Meeting rms. Concierge. Gift shop. Exercise equipt; weights, bicycles, sauna. Bathrm phones, minibars. Cr cds: A, C, D, DS, ER, JCB, MC, V.

★ ★ **BELLEVUE.** *15 E Street NW (20001), in Capitol Hill area.* 202/638-0900; res: 800/372-6667; FAX 202/638-5132. 140 rms, 8 story. S $99.50; D $114.50; each addl $15; suites $175-$250; under 18 free; wkend rates. Crib free. TV; cable. Complimentary full bkfst. Restaurant 7 am-midnight. Bar 11:30-3 am. Ck-out noon. Meeting rms. Concierge. Free garage parking (overnight). Some refrigerators, wet bars. Old-World style hotel. Cr cds: A, C, D, DS, MC, V.

✔ ★ **BEST WESTERN SKYLINE INN.** *10 I Street SW (20024), in Capitol Hill area.* 202/488-7500; FAX 202/488-0790. 203 rms, 7 story. Apr-Oct: S $79; D $89; each addl $10; under 18 free; wkend rates; lower rates rest of yr. Crib free. TV. Pool; poolside serv, lifeguard. Restaurant 7 am-10 pm. Bar 11:30 am-midnight. Ck-out noon. Coin lndry. Meeting rms. Gift shop. Free garage parking. Refrigerators avail. Cr cds: A, C, D, DS, ER, JCB, MC, V.

★ ★ **CANTERBURY.** *1733 N Street NW (20036), downtown. 202/393-3000; res: 800/424-2950; FAX 202/785-9581.* 99 rms, 10 story. S $140-$175; D $160-$195; each addl $20; under 12 free; wkend plans. Crib free. Garage $10. TV; cable. Complimentary continental bkfst, refreshments. Restaurant 7-10 am, 11 am-2:30 pm, 5:30-10 pm. wkend hrs vary. Bar 5-11 pm; closed Sun. Ck-out noon. Meeting rms. Health club privileges. Many refrigerators. On site of "Little White Houoc," the Theodore Roosevelt house during his vice-presidency and first weeks of his presidency. Cr cds: A, C, D, DS, ER, JCB, MC, V.

🏊 🔥 SC

★ ★ ★ **THE CAPITAL HILTON.** *16th & K Streets NW (20036), downtown. 202/393-1000; FAX 202/639-5784.* 543 rms, 15 story. S $185-$295; D $210-$295; each addl $20; suites $495-$1,100; family, wkend rates; honeymoon plans. Crib free. TV; cable. Restaurants 6:30 am-midnight. Rm serv 24 hrs. Bar 11-2 am; entertainment Tues-Sat. Ck-out noon. Convention facilities. Concierge. Shopping arcade. Barber, beauty shop. Valet parking 24 hrs. Exercise equipt; weights, bicycles, sauna, steam rm. Minibars; many wet bars; some refrigerators. Tour desk. Foreign serv guide. *LUXURY LEVEL : THE TOWERS.* 71 rms, 6 suites, 4 floors. S, D $295; suites $650-$1,375. Private lounge. Some full wet bars. In-rm movies, tape library. Complimentary continental bkfst, afternoon tea, cocktails. Cr cds: A, C, D, DS, ER, JCB, MC, V.

D 🏃 🏊 🔥 SC

★ ★ ★ ★ **THE CARLTON.** *923 16th St NW (20006), downtown. 202/638-2626; FAX 202/638-4231.* 197 rms, 8 story. S $265-$280; D $265-$305; each addl $25; suites $500-$1,600; under 18 free; wkend rates. Crib free. Covered valet parking $22. Pet accepted, some restrictions. TV; cable. Pool privileges. Restaurant 6:30-1 am. Afternoon tea 2:30-5:30 pm. Rm serv 24 hrs. Bar; entertainment. Ck-out 1 pm. Meeting rms. Concierge. Gift shop. Barber, beauty shop. Tennis privileges. 18-hole golf privileges 12 mi, greens fee $36, pro, putting green, driving range. Exercise room; bicycles, treadmill, weight machine. Massage. Bathrm phones, refrigerators, minibars. Courtyard terrace. Historic Renaissance-style building (1926). 2 blks from the White House. Cr cds: A, C, D, DS, ER, JCB, MC, V.

D 🏄 ⛸ 🏃 🏊 🔥 SC

✔ ★ **CENTER CITY.** *1201 13th St NW (20005), north of downtown. 202/682-5300; FAX 202/371-9624.* 100 rms, 8 story. Apr-Sept: S $85-$115; D $95-$125; each addl $10; under 14 free; wkend rates; lower rates rest of yr. Parking $9 in/out. TV; cable. Complimentary continental bkfst. Restaurant nearby. Ck-out 11 am. Coin lndry. Exercise equipt; weight machine, bicycles, whirlpool, sauna. Cr cds: A, C, D, DS, MC, V.

D 🏃 🏊 🔥 SC

✔ ★ **COMFORT INN.** *500 H Street NW (20001), downtown. 202/289-5959; FAX 202/682-9152.* 197 rms, 10 story. Apr-May, Sept-Oct: S, D $69-$139; each addl $5; under 18 free; wkend rates; lower rates rest of yr. Crib free. Garage $10. TV; cable. Coffee in rms. Restaurant 6:30 am-9 pm. Bar from 4:30 pm. Ck-out noon. Meeting rms. Coin lndry. Exercise equipt; weight machine, bicycles, sauna. Cr cds: A, C, D, DS, ER, JCB, MC, V.

D 🏃 🏊 🔥 SC

★ ★ ★ **COURTYARD BY MARRIOTT.** *1900 Connecticut Ave NW (20009), in Kalorama. 202/332-9300; res: 800/842-4211; FAX 202/328-7039.* 147 rms, 9 story. S $59-$135; D $69-$170; each addl $15; under 18 free; wkend rates (2-night min). Crib free. Pet accepted, some restrictions. Garage parking, valet $10. TV; cable. Pool; lifeguard. Restaurant 7 am-10:30 pm. Bar 5 pm-11 pm. Ck-out 1 pm. Coin lndry. Meeting rms. Health club privileges. Some minibars. Cr cds: A, C, D, DS, MC, V.

D 🏄 ≋ 🏃 🔥 SC

✔ ★ **DAYS INN-DOWNTOWN.** *1201 K Street NW (20005), downtown. 202/842-1020; FAX 202/289-0336.* 220 rms, 9 story, 10 kit. units. Mar-May, Aug-Oct: S $75-$105; D $85-$115; each addl $10; suites $120-$150; family, wkend rates; higher rates Cherry Blossom

Festival; lower rates rest of yr. Crib free. Garage $8.50. Pet accepted, some restrictions. TV; cable. Pool; lifeguard. Restaurant 7 am-10 pm; Sat, Sun 7-10:30 am, 5-10 pm. Bar noon-midnight. Ck-out noon. Meeting rms. Exercise equipt; weight machines, treadmill. Cr cds: A, C, D, DS, JCB, MC, V.

D 🏄 ≋ 🏃 🏊 🔥 SC

★ **DUPONT PLAZA.** *1500 New Hampshire Ave NW (20036), in Dupont Circle area. 202/483-6000; res: 800/421-6662; FAX 202/328-3265.* 314 rms, 8 story. S $145-$195; D $165-$205; each addl $20; suites $195-$375; under 18 free; wkend rates. Crib free. Garage $13; valet parking. TV; cable. Restaurant 6:30 am-10:30 pm. Bar 11-1 am. Ck-out 1 pm. Meeting rms. Health club privileges. Bathrm phones, refrigerators, wet bars. Cr cds: A, C, D, ER, MC, V.

🏊 🔥 SC

★ ★ **EMBASSY SQUARE SUITES.** *2000 N Street NW (20036), in Dupont Circle area. 202/659-9000; res: 800/424-2999; FAX 202/429-9546.* 250 kit. units, 10 story, 80 suites. Mar-mid-Sept-mid-Dec: S $109-$135; D $119-$159; each addl $20; suites $139-$229; under 19 free; wkly, wkend rates; lower rates rest of yr. Crib free. Garage $10. TV; cable, in-rm movies. Pool; poolside serv, lifeguard. Complimentary continental bkfst. Rm serv noon-11 pm. Ck-out noon. Coin lndry. Meeting rms. Concierge in summer. Exercise equipt; bicycles, stair machine. Minibars. Some balconies. Cr cds: A, C, D, DS, MC, V.

D ≋ 🏃 🏊 🔥 SC

★ ★ **EMBASSY SUITES.** *1250 22nd St NW (20037), west of downtown. 202/857-3388; FAX 202/293-3173.* 318 suites, 9 story. S $189-$279; D $209-$299; each addl $20; 2-bedrm suites $600-$1,200; under 13 free; wkend rates. Crib free. Garage $14. TV; cable, in-rm movies avail. Indoor pool; lifeguard. Complimentary full bkfst 6-9:30 am; Sat, Sun & hols 7-10:30 am. Complimentary coffee in rms. Restaurant 11 am-11 pm. Bar. Ck-out noon. Meeting rms. Exercise equipt; weight machine, bicycles, whirlpool, sauna. Game rm. Refrigerators. Cr cds: A, C, D, DS, JCB, MC, V.

D ≋ 🏃 🏊 🔥 SC

★ ★ **EMBASSY SUITES CHEVY CHASE PAVILION.** *4300 Military Rd NW (20015), north of downtown. 202/362-9300; FAX 202/686-3405.* 198 suites, 9 story. S, D $145-$175; each addl $15; under 18 free; wkend rates. Crib avail. Pet accepted, some restrictions; $10 per day. Garage $10. TV; cable, in-rm movies avail. Indoor pool. Complimentary full bkfst. Complimentary coffee in rms. Restaurants 7 am-midnight. Ck-out noon. Coin lndry. Meeting rms. Exercise rm; instructor, weight machine, bicycles, whirlpool, sauna. Health club privileges. Refrigerators, wet bars. Atrium. Connected to shopping center. Cr cds: A, C, D, DS, MC, V.

D 🏄 ≋ 🏃 🏊 🔥 SC

★ ★ ★ **FOUR SEASONS.** *2800 Pennsylvania Ave NW (20007), in Georgetown. 202/342-0444; res: 800/332-3442; FAX 202/944-2076.* 196 rms, 6 story. S $265-$310; D $295-$340; each addl $30; suites $575-$975; under 18 free; wkend rates. Crib free. Valet parking $22. Pet accepted. TV; cable. Indoor pool. Afternoon tea. Restaurant 7-2 am (also see SEASONS). Rm serv 24 hrs. Bar 11-2 am. Ck-out noon. Meeting rms. Concierge. Complimentary limo serv in DC area Mon-Fri. Exercise rm; instructor, weight machine, bicycles, steam rm. Massage. Full service health club & spa. Bathrm phones, minibars. Some balconies. Tastefully appointed rooms and public areas. Luxury hotel overlooking Rock Creek Park, at entrance to historic Georgetown. Cr cds: A, C, D, ER, JCB, MC, V.

D 🏄 ≋ 🏃 🏊 🔥

★ **GEORGETOWN DUTCH INN.** *1075 Thomas Jefferson St NW (20007), in Georgetown. 202/337-0900; res: 800/388-2410; FAX 202/333-6526.* 47 kit. suites, 7 story. Feb-mid-June, Sept-mid-Nov: S $110-$140; D $120-$160; each addl $20; suites (for 4) $210-$300; under 16 free; wkly, monthly rates; higher rates Cherry Blossom season; lower rates rest of yr. Crib free. TV; cable. Complimentary continental bkfst. Ck-out noon. Limited free covered parking. Bathrm phones. Some private patios. Cr cds: A, C, D, MC, V.

⊠ 🔥 SC

★ ★ ★ **GRAND.** 2350 M Street NW (20037), west of downtown. 202/429-0100; res: 800/848-0016; FAX 202/429-9759. 262 rms, 32 suites. Sept-June: S $220-$240; D $240-$260; each addl $20; suites $450-$2,500; under 18 free; wkend packages; lower rates rest of yr. Crib free. Covered valet parking $18/day. TV; cable, in-rm movies avail. Heated pool; poolside serv, lifeguard. Restaurant 6:30 am-10:30 pm. Rm serv 24 hrs. Bar; pianist, chamber music. Ck-out 1 pm. Meeting rms. Concierge. Exercise equipt; weight machines, bicycles. Bathrm phones; some fireplaces; minibar, whirlpool in suites. Some balconies. Many rms with view of landscaped interior courtyard. Amenities package; 3 phones in each rm. Cr cds: A, C, D, JCB, MC, V.

D ≈ 🏃 🍴 ⊠ 🔥

★ ★ ★ **GRAND HYATT WASHINGTON.** 1000 H Street NW (20001), opp Washington Convention Center, downtown. 202/582-1234; FAX 202/637-4781. 889 rms, 12 story. S $224; D $249; each addl $25; suites $425-$1,500; under 18 free; wkend rates. Crib free. Garage $12. TV; cable, in-rm movies. Supervised child's activities (Fri, Sat eves). Indoor pool; poolside serv. Restaurant 6:30-1 am. Rm serv 24 hrs. Bar; entertainment, dancing. Ck-out noon. Convention facilities. Exercise equipt; weights, bicycles, whirlpool, steam rm, sauna. Minibars. 12-story atrium lobby; 3-story cascading waterfall. *LUXURY LEVEL :* REGENCY CLUB. 63 rms, 3 suites. S $245; D $270. Concierge. Private lounge. Wet bar in suites. Complimentary continental bkfst, refreshments. Cr cds: A, C, D, DS, ER, JCB, MC, V.

D ≈ 🏃 🍴 ⊠ 🔥 SC

★ **GUEST QUARTERS.** 2500 Pennsylvania Ave NW (20037), in Foggy Bottom. 202/333-8060; FAX 202/338-3818. 123 kit. suites, 10 story. S $99-$159; D $99-$174; each addl $15; under 18 free. Crib free. Pet accepted; $12 per day. Garage $13. TV; cable, in-rm movies. Restaurant adj 11 am-midnight. Ck-out noon. Health club privileges. Cr cds: A, C, D, DS, MC, V.

🏊 🔥 ⊠

★ ★ **HAMPSHIRE.** 1310 New Hampshire Ave NW (20036), in Dupont Circle area. 202/296-7600; res: 800/368-5691; FAX 202/293-2476. 82 rms, 10 story. Mid-Mar-June, early Sept-mid-Nov: S $120; D $140; each addl $15; suites, kit. units $140-$179; under 13 free; wkend, monthly rates; lower rates rest of yr. Crib free. Garage $10. TV; cable. Complimentary coffee in rms. Restaurant 7-10 am, 11:30 am-2:30 pm, 5:30-10:30 pm; wkend hrs vary. Bar 5-10:30 pm, Sat, Sun from 6 pm. Ck-out noon. Meeting rms. Health club privileges. Refrigerators, minibars. Some balconies. Cr cds: A, C, D, DS, ER, JCB, MC, V.

⊠ 🔥 SC

HAY-ADAMS. (Renovation incomplete when inspected, therefore not rated) 800 16th St NW (20006), opp White House, downtown. 202/638-6600; res: 800/424-5054; FAX 202/638-2716. 143 rms, 8 story. S, D $210-$375; each addl $30; suites $450-$1,200; under 13 free; wkend package. Pet accepted. some restrictions. TV; cable. Restaurant 6:30-1 am. Afternoon tea 3-5 pm. Rm serv 24 hrs. Bars 11-1 am. Ck-out noon. Concierge. Valet parking $18. Health club privileges. Bathrm phones, refrigerators, minibars; some fireplaces. Some balconies. English country house atmosphere. Built 1927, on site of John Hay and Henry Adams mansions. Cr cds: A, C, D, ER, JCB, MC, V.

🐾 ⊠ 🔥

★ ★ **HENLEY PARK.** 926 Massachusetts Ave NW (20001), 1 blk from Washington Convention Center, downtown. 202/638-5200; res: 800/222-8474; FAX 202/638-6740. 96 rms, 8 story. S $165-$215; D $185-$235; each addl $20; suites $295-$675; under 16 free; wkend rates. Crib free. Valet parking $15. TV; in-rm movies avail. Afternoon tea 4-6 pm. Restaurant 7-10:30 am, 11:30 am-2 pm, 6-10 pm. Rm serv 24 hrs. Bar 11-12:30 am; entertainment Fri, Sat. Ck-out noon. Meeting rms. Health club privileges. Bathrm phones, refrigerators, minibars.

Wet bar in suites. Tudor detailing; 1918 structure. Cr cds: A, C, D, DS, ER, JCB, MC, V.

⊠ 🔥 SC

★ ★ ★ **HILTON AND TOWERS.** 1919 Connecticut Ave NW (20009), in Kalorama. 202/483-3000; FAX 202/265-8221. 1,123 rms, 10 story. S $140-$236; D $160-$256; each addl $20; suites $434-$791; wkend rates. Crib free. Pet accepted, some restrictions. Garage $12. TV; cable. Heated pool; poolside serv, lifeguard (in season). Restaurants 6:30 am-11 pm. Bar 11:30-2 am; entertainment. Ck-out noon. Convention facilities. Gift shop. Drugstore. Lighted tennis, pro. Exercise rm; instructor, weight machines, bicycles, steam rm. Minibars. Some balconies. Resort atmosphere; on 6½ landscaped acres. *LUXURY LEVEL :* THE TOWERS. 95 rms, 18 suites. S $247; D $267; suites $600-$1,400. Concierge. Private lounge. Reference library. Some bathrm phones. Complimentary continental bkfst, afternoon refreshments. Cr cds: A, C, D, DS, ER, JCB, MC, V.

D 🐾 🏃 ≈ 🍴 ⊠ 🏃 🔥 SC

★ **HOLIDAY INN GEORGETOWN.** 2101 Wisconsin Ave NW (20007), in Georgetown. 202/338-4600; FAX 202/333-6113. 296 rms, 7 story. S $110-$140; D $120-$140; each addl $10; suites $200; under 19 free. Crib free. Parking in/out $10. TV; cable. Pool; lifeguard. Restaurant 6:30 am-10 pm; Sat & Sun from 7 am. Bar 11 am-midnight. Ck-out noon. Coin lndry. Meeting rms. Gift shop. Exercise equipt; weight machine, treadmill. Health club privileges. Refrigerators avail. Cr cds: A, C, D, DS, JCB, MC, V.

D 🏃 ⊠ 🔥 SC

★ ★ **HOLIDAY INN-CAPITOL.** 550 C Street SW (20024), 2 blks from Mall museums, south of downtown. 202/479-4000; FAX 202/479-4353. 529 rms, 9 story. S, D $149-$169; suites $199-$219; under 20 free; wkend packages. Crib free. Pet accepted. Garage $9. TV; cable. Pool; lifeguard. Restaurant 6 am-10 pm. Bar 11-1 am. Ck-out noon. Coin lndry. Convention facilities. Shopping arcade. Barber, beauty shop. Exercise equipt; weight machine, bicycles. Cr cds: A, C, D, DS, JCB, MC, V.

D 🐾 ≈ 🍴 ⊠ 🔥 SC

✔ ★ ★ **HOLIDAY INN-CENTRAL.** 1501 Rhode Island Ave NW (20005), north of downtown. 202/483-2000; FAX 202/797-1078. 213 rms, 10 story. Apr-May & Oct: S, D $69-$119; each addl $14; suites $150; family, wkly, wkend rates; lower rates rest of yr. Crib free. Covered parking $8.90. TV; cable. Pool; lifeguard. Restaurant 6:30 am-10 pm. Bar; entertainment. Ck-out noon. Coin lndry. Meeting rms. Gift shop. Exercise equipt; weight machine, stair machine. Game rm. Some refrigerators. Balconies. Cr cds: A, C, D, DS, JCB, MC, V.

D ≈ 🏃 ⊠ 🔥 SC

★ ★ ★ **HOTEL SOFITEL.** 1914 Connecticut Ave NW (20009), in Kalorama area. 202/797-2000; res: 800/424-2464; FAX 202/462-0944. 145 units, 9 story, 40 suites. S $175-$205; D $195-$225; each addl $20; suites $255-$550; under 18 free; wkend rates; lower rates late June-Labor Day. Crib free. Garage parking; valet $15. TV; cable. Restaurant 6:30 am-10:30 pm. Rm serv 24 hrs. Bar noon-11:30 pm; Fri, Sat to 1 am. Meeting rms. Concierge. Health club privileges. Bathrm phones, minibars. Refurbished apartment building; built 1904. Cr cds: A, C, D, JCB, MC, V.

⊠ 🔥 SC

★ ★ **HOWARD JOHNSON.** 1430 Rhode Island Ave NW (20005), downtown. 202/462-7777; FAX 202/332-3519. 186 units, 10 story, 158 kit. units. S $89-$99; D $99-$119; each addl $10; under 18 free; wkend rates. Crib free. Garage parking; valet $7. TV; cable. Pool; lifeguard. Restaurant 7-11 am; 11:30 am-2:30 pm, 5-10:30 pm. Bar 5 pm-midnight. Ck-out noon. Coin lndry. Health club privileges. Cr cds: A, C, D, DS, ER, JCB, MC, V.

D ≈ ⊠ 🔥 SC

★ ★ ★ **HYATT REGENCY WASHINGTON ON CAPITOL HILL.** 400 New Jersey Ave NW (20001), 2 blks N of Capitol, downtown. 202/737-1234; FAX 202/347-2861. 834 rms, 11 story. S $189; D $214;

each addl $25; under 18 free; wkend rates. Crib free. Garage $16. TV; cable, in-rm movies. Indoor pool. Restaurants 6:30 am-11 pm. Bar 11-2 am. Ck-out noon. Meeting rms. Concierge. Gift shop. Barber, beauty shop. Exercise rm; instructor, weight machines, bicycles, steam rm, sauna. Minibars; some refrigerators. *LUXURY LEVEL : REGENCY CLUB.* 44 rms, 4 suites. S $224; D $249; each addl $25; suites $350-$1,025. Private lounge. Wet bar in suites. Complimentary continental bkfst, evening refreshments. Cr cds: A, C, D, DS, ER, JCB, MC, V.

[D] [≈] [🏃] [🇽] [🔥] [SC]

★ ★ ★ **J.W. MARRIOTT.** *1331 Pennsylvania Ave NW (20004), at National Pl, 2 blks E of White House, downtown.* 202/393-2000; FAX 202/626-6991. 772 rms, 12 story. S, D $224-$244; each addl $20; suites $275-$1,550; family, wkend rates. Crib free. Limited valet parking $16. TV; cable, in-rm movies. Indoor pool. Restaurant 7 am-11 pm. Rm serv 24 hrs. Bars; entertainment. Ck-out noon. Convention facilities. Concierge. Shopping arcade. Exercise rm; instructor, weights, bicycles, whirlpool, sauna. Game area. Some bathrm phones. Refrigerator in suites. Private patios on 7th & 12th floors. Luxurious hotel with elegant interior detail; extensive use of marble & mirrors; a large collection of artwork is displayed throughout the lobby. *LUXURY LEVEL : CONCIERGE FLOOR.* 96 rms, 2 floors. S, D $230-$250. Private lounge, honor bar. Complimentary continental bkfst, refreshments. Cr cds: A, C, D, DS, ER, JCB, MC, V.

[D] [≈] [🏃] [🇽] [🔥] [SC]

★ ★ **JEFFERSON.** *16th & M Streets NW (20036), downtown.* 202/347-2200; res: 800/368-5966; FAX 202/331-7982. 100 rms, 8 story. Jan-June, Sept-Nov: S $220-$260; D $235-$275; each addl $25; suites $320-$1,000; under 15 free; wkend plans; lower rates rest of yr. Crib free. Garage, valet parking $20. TV; cable, in-rm movies. Pool privileges. Restaurants 6:30 am-11 pm. Rm serv 24 hrs. Afternoon tea 3-5 pm. Bar 10-2 am. Ck-out 1 pm. Concierge. Health club privileges. Some private patios. Individually decorated rms; some four-poster and canopy beds, antiques. In operation since 1923. Cr cds: A, C, D, DS, ER, JCB, MC, V.

[🇽] [🔥]

★ ★ **THE LATHAM.** *3000 M Street NW (20007), in Georgetown.* 202/726-5000; res: 800/368-5922 (exc DC), 800/LATHAM-1; FAX 202/337-4250. 143 rms, 10 story. S $155-$190; D $175-$210; each addl $20; suites $250-$450; under 16 free; wkend rates. Valet parking $15. TV; cable. Pool. Restaurant 6:30 am-10:30 pm. Bar 11 am-1 am, Fri & Sat to 2 am. Ck-out noon. Meeting rms. Health club privileges. Some minibars. Refrigerators avail. Sun deck. Overlooks historic Chesapeake & Ohio Canal. Cr cds: A, C, D, DS, ER, JCB, MC, V.

[D] [≈] [🇽] [🔥] [SC]

★ ★ ★ **LOEWS L'ENFANT PLAZA.** *480 L'Enfant Plaza SW (20024), south of downtown.* 202/484-1000; FAX 202/646-4456. 370 rms on floors 11-15. S $165-$205; D $185-$225; each addl $20; suites $370-$1,200; under 18 free; wkend rates. Crib free. Valet parking $16. TV; cable, in-rm movies. Pool; poolside serv, lifeguard. Restaurant 6:30 am-midnight. Bar 11:30-1:30 am. Ck-out 1 pm. Meeting rms. Concierge. Underground shopping arcade with Metro subway stop. Gift shop. Exercise rm; instructor, weights, bicycles. Refrigerators, minibars. Many balconies. Cr cds: A, C, D, DS, MC, V.

[D] [🤚] [≈] [🏃] [🇽] [🔥] [SC]

★ ★ **LOMBARDY.** *2019 I Street NW (20006), downtown.* 202/828-2600; res: 800/424-5486; FAX 202/872-0503. 126 units, 11 story, 106 kits. Apr-May, Sept-Oct: S $115; D $130; each addl $10; suites $150-$165; under 16 free; wkend rates; lower rates rest of yr. Crib free. TV; cable. Coffee in rms. Restaurant 7-10:30 am, 11:30 am-2:30 pm, 5-9:30 pm; Sat, Sun 8 am-1 pm, 5-9:30 pm. Ck-out noon. Coin lndry. Meeting rm. Health club privileges. Refrigerators, minibars. Cr cds: A, C, D, DS, ER, MC, V.

[🇽] [🔥] [SC]

★ ★ ★ **MADISON.** *15th & M Streets NW (20005), downtown.* 202/862-1600; res: 800/424-8577; FAX 202/785-1255. 353 rms, 14 story. S $235-$395; D $250-$395; each addl $30; suites $395-$3,000; wkend packages. Crib $25. Garage $14. TV; cable, in-rm movies avail. Restaurant 6:30 am-11 pm. Rm serv 24 hrs. Bar 11-2 am. Ck-out 1 pm. Meeting rms. Concierge. Exercise equipt; weight machine, bicycles, sauna. Bathrm phones, refrigerators, minibars. Original paintings, antiques, Oriental rugs. Cr cds: A, C, D, DS, ER, JCB, MC, V.

[D] [🏃] [🇽] [🔥]

★ ★ **MARRIOTT.** *1221 22nd St NW (20037), at M St, west of downtown.* 202/872-1500; FAX 202/872-1424. 418 rms, 9 story. S $167-$182; each addl $15; suites $250-$500; under 18 free; wkend rates. Crib free. Pet accepted, some restrictions; $50. Garage $12; valet $14. TV; cable. Heated pool; poolside serv, lifeguard. Complimentary morning coffee. Restaurant 6:30 am-10 pm; Fri, Sat to 11 pm. Rm serv to midnight. Bars 11:30 am-midnight. Ck-out noon. Meeting rms. Concierge. Gift shop. Exercise equipt; weight machines, bicycles, whirlpool, sauna. Refrigerators avail. *LUXURY LEVEL : CONCIERGE LEVEL.* 62 rms, 2 suites. S, D $185-$200; suites from $275. Private lounge, honor bar. Bathrm phones in suites. Complimentary continental bkfst, refreshments, newspaper. Cr cds: A, C, D, DS, ER, JCB, MC, V.

[D] [🤚] [≈] [🏃] [🇽] [🔥] [SC]

✔ ★ ★ **NORMANDY INN.** *2118 Wyoming Ave NW (20008), in Kalorama.* 202/483-1350; res: 800/424-3729; FAX 202/387-8241. 75 rms, 6 story. S $97; D $107; each addl $10; under 12 free. Crib free. Pet accepted, some restrictions. Garage $10. TV; cable. Continental bkfst. Complimentary coffee in rms. Restaurant nearby. Ck-out noon. Meeting rm. Refrigerators. In quiet residential neighborhood. Cr cds: A, C, D, DS, MC, V.

[🤚] [🇽] [🔥] [SC]

★ ★ **OMNI SHOREHAM.** *2500 Calvert St NW (20008), north of downtown.* 202/234-0700; FAX 202/332-1373. 770 rms, 8 story. S, D $195-$220; each addl $20; suites $275-$1,200; under 18 free; wkend, hol packages. Crib free. Pet accepted, some restrictions. Garage $12. TV; cable. Pool; wading pool, poolside serv, lifeguard. Restaurant 6:30 am-11 pm. Bar 11-2 am; entertainment. Ck-out noon. Meeting rms. Shopping arcade. Lighted tennis, pro. Exercise equipt; weight machines, bicycles, sauna. Lawn games. Cr cds: A, C, D, DS, JCB, MC, V.

[D] [🤚] [≈] [🏃] [🇽] [🔥] [SC]

★ ★ ★ **ONE WASHINGTON CIRCLE.** *One Washington Circle NW (20037), in Foggy Bottom.* 202/872-1680; res: 800/424-9671; FAX 202/887-4989. 151 kit. suites, 9 story. S $135-$275; D $145-$300; each addl $15; under 12 free; wkend plans. Pet accepted, some restrictions. Garage $15. TV; cable. Pool. Restaurant 7 am-11:30 pm; Fri & Sat to midnight. Bar; entertainment. Ck-out noon. Meeting rms. Concierge. Health club privileges. Some bathrm phones. Many balconies. Elegant furnishings; landscaped grounds in residential neighborhood. Cr cds: A, C, D, MC, V.

[🤚] [≈] [🇽] [🔥] [SC]

★ ★ ★ **PARK HYATT.** *24th & M Street NW (20037), west of downtown.* 202/789-1234; res: 800/922-PARK; FAX 202/457-8823. 224 units, 10 story, 133 suites. S $265; D $290; each addl $25; suites $295-$1,975; under 18 free; wkend rates; lower rates July, Aug. Crib free. TV; cable. Indoor pool; poolside serv. Restaurant (see MELROSE). Afternoon tea 3-5 pm. Rm serv 24 hrs. Bar 11:30-1 am, Fri & Sat to 2 am; pianist. Ck-out noon. Meeting rms. Concierge. Gift shop. Barber, beauty shop. Covered parking; valet. Tennis & golf privileges. Exercise rm; instructor, weight machines, bicycles, whirlpool, steam rm, sauna. Massage. Bathrm phones, refrigerators. Daily newspapers. Cr cds: A, C, D, DS, JCB, MC, V.

[D] [🏃] [🏊] [≈] [🏃] [🇽] [🔥] [SC]

★ ★ **PHOENIX PARK.** *520 N Capitol St (20001), opp Union Station, on Capitol Hill.* 202/638-6900; res: 800/824-5419; FAX 202/393-3236. 84 rms, 9 story. S $159-$199; D $179-$219; each addl $20; suites $300-$475; under 15 free; wkend package plans. Crib free. Valet parking $15. TV; cable. Coffee in rms. Restaurants 7-2 am. Bar from 11 am; Fri, Sat to 3 am; entertainment. Ck-out 1 pm. Meeting rms. Health club privileges. Minibars; some refrigerators. Older hotel near Capitol; traditional European, Irish decor. Cr cds: A, C, D, MC, V.

[D] [≈] [🔥] [SC]

✔★ **QUALITY HOTEL-CAPITOL HILL.** 415 New Jersey Ave NW (20001), on Capitol Hill. 202/638-1616; FAX 202/638-0707. 341 rms, 10 story. Feb-May, Sept-Nov: S, D $79-$159; each addl $20; suites $130-$375; under 18 free; wkend rates; lower rates rest of yr. Crib free. TV; cable, in-rm movies. Rooftop pool; poolside serv, lifeguard. Restaurant 6:30 am-10 pm. Bar 11-2 am. Ck-out noon. Gift shop. Free covered parking. Cr cds: A, C, D, DS, ER, JCB, MC, V.

[D] [≈] [⇥] [🔥] [SC]

★★★★ **THE RITZ-CARLTON.** 2100 Massachusetts Ave NW (20008), 1 blk NW of Dupont Circle, in Embassy Row Area. 202/293-2100; res: 800/241-3333; FAX 202/293-0641. 206 rms, 8 story. S, D $250-$340; suites $350-$2,000; under 18 free; wkend rates. Crib free. Valet parking $20. TV; cable. Restaurant 6:30 am-10:30 pm (also see JOCKEY CLUB). Bar 11:30-1 am; entertainment. Ck-out noon. Meeting rms. Concierge. Tennis, golf privileges. Health club privileges. Bathrm phones, minibars; some bathrm TVs. Complimentary newspapers. Elegant ballroom. Classic 18th-century decor, restored. Within 10 minutes of Georgetown. **LUXURY LEVEL : THE RITZ-CARLTON CLUB.** 66 rms, 12 suites, 2 floors. S, D $345; suites $350-$2,000. Concierge. Private lounge. Complimentary continental bkfst. Five complimentary food and beverage presentations daily. Cr cds: A, C, D, DS, ER, JCB, MC, V.

[D] [🧖] [🏋] [⇥] [🔥]

★★ **RIVER INN.** 924 25th St NW (20037), 2 blks from Kennedy Center, in Foggy Bottom. 202/337-7600; res: 800/424-2741; FAX 202/337-6520. 127 kit. suites. S $125-$175; D $140-$190; each addl $15; under 13 free; wkend rates. Crib free. Parking $14. TV; cable. Restaurant 7-10:30 am, 11:30 am-2:30 pm, 5-10 pm; Sat 8-10:30 am, 11 am-2:30 pm, 5:30-11:30 pm; Sun 8 am-3 pm, 5-10 pm. Bar. Ck-out noon. Meeting rms. Health club privileges. Some bathrm phones. Quiet residential area. Cr cds: A, C, D, MC, V.

[≈] [🔥] [SC]

★★ **SHERATON CITY CENTRE.** 1143 New Hampshire Ave NW (20037), at 21st & M Sts, west of downtown. 202/775-0800; FAX 202/331-9491. 351 rms, 9 story. S $165-$210; D $180-$225; each addl $15; suites $250-$600; under 18 free. Crib free. Parking $14. TV; cable. Restaurant 6 am-10 pm. Bar noon-1 am; entertainment Mon-Fri. Ck-out noon. Meeting rms. Concierge. Gift shop. Health club privileges. Some bathrm phones, refrigerators. **LUXURY LEVEL : CLUB LEVEL.** 40 rms, 2 suites. S $185-$225; D $200-$250; addl bedrm $175. Private lounge. Some wet bars. Bathrm phone in suites. Complimentary continental bkfst. Cr cds: A, C, D, DS, ER, JCB, MC, V.

[D] [⇥] [🔥] [SC]

★★ **ST. JAMES.** 950 24th St NW (20037), in Foggy Bottom. 202/457-0500; res: 800/852-8512; FAX 202/659-4492. 196 kit. suites, 12 story. Feb-June & Sept-Oct: suites $139-$169; under 16 free; wkend rates; higher rates: Cherry Blossom Festival; lower rates rest of yr. Crib free. Garage parking $15; valet. TV; cable, in-rm movies. Pool; lifeguard. Complimentary continental bkfst. Coffee in rms. Restaurant nearby. Ck-out noon. Coin lndry. Meeting rms. Concierge. Exercise equipt; weights, rower. Cr cds: A, C, D, DS, MC, V.

[≈] [🏋] [⇥] [🔥] [SC]

★★ **STATE PLAZA.** 2117 E Street NW (20037), in Foggy Bottom. 202/861-8200; res: 800/424-2859; FAX 202/659-8601. 221 kit. suites, 8 story. S $95-$140; D $115-$160; each addl $20; under 18 free; wkend rates. Crib free. Garage $12. TV; cable. Restaurant 6:30 am-10 pm. Bar from 11:30 am. Ck-out noon. Coin lndry. Meeting rms. Exercise equipt; bicycles, treadmills. Minibars. Complimentary newspaper, shoeshine. Two rooftop sun decks. Cr cds: A, C, D, DS, ER, JCB, MC, V.

[D] [🏋] [⇥] [🔥]

★★★★ **STOUFFER-MAYFLOWER.** 1127 Connecticut Ave NW (20036), 4 blks northwest of White House, downtown. 202/347-3000; FAX 202/466-9082. 659 rms, 10 story, 78 suites. S, D $250-$290; each addl $30; suites $450-$2,500; under 19 free; wkend plans. Crib free. Pet accepted, some restrictions. Garage adj $11.50. TV; cable. Complimentary coffee in rms. Restaurant 6:30 am-11:30 pm. Bar 11-1:30 am; entertainment. Ck-out 1 pm. Convention facilities. Concierge. Exercise equipt; weight machine, bicycles, sauna. Health club privileges. Bathrm phones; refrigerators avail. Foreign currency exchange. Historic grand hotel (1925) with ornate interior details; gilded moldings, stained-glass skylights, lavish use of marble. Cr cds: A, C, D, DS, ER, JCB, MC, V.

[D] [🤚] [🏋] [⇥] [🔥] [SC]

★★ **WASHINGTON.** 515 15th St NW (20004), at Pennsylvania Ave, 1 blk from White House, downtown. 202/638-5900; res: 800/424-9540; FAX 202/638-4275. 350 rms, 11 story. S $155-$209; D $170-$209; each addl $18; suites $400-$609; under 14 free; wkend rates. Crib free. TV; cable. Restaurant 7 am-10 pm. Bar 11-1 am. Ck-out 1 pm. Meeting rms. Gift shop. Exercise equipt; weight machine, bicycles, sauna. Bathrm phones. Original Jardin D'Armide murals (1854). One of the oldest continuously-operated hotels in the city. Cr cds: A, C, D, MC, V.

[D] [🤚] [🏋] [⇥] [🔥] [SC]

★★★ **THE WASHINGTON COURT ON CAPITOL HILL.** 525 New Jersey Ave NW (20001), on Capitol Hill. 202/628-2100; res: 800/321-3010; FAX 202/879-7918. 266 rms, 15 story, 11 suites. S $175-$250; D $195-$300; each addl $25; suites $360-$1,500; under 16 free; wkend rates. Crib free. Pet accepted, some restrictions. Valet parking $15. TV; cable. Restaurant 6:30 am-11 pm. Bar; pianist. Ck-out noon. Meeting rooms. Concierge. Exercise equipt; weight machines, bicycles, sauna. Bathrm phones, refrigerators. Large atrium lobby. Cr cds: A, C, D, DS, JCB, MC, V.

[D] [🤚] [🏋] [⇥] [🔥] [SC]

★★ **WASHINGTON RENAISSANCE.** 999 9th St NW (20001), across from Convention Center, downtown. 202/898-9000; FAX 202/789-4213. 800 rms, 16 story. S, D $175-$225; each addl $20; suites $260-$2,000; under 18 free; wkend rates. Crib free. Pet accepted, some restrictions. Garage $14; valet parking $14. TV; cable. Indoor pool; lifeguard. Restaurant 6:30 am-11 pm. Bar 10-1 am; entertainment. Ck-out noon. Convention facilities. Concierge. Shopping arcade. Barber, beauty shop. Exercise rm; instructor, weight machine, bicycles, whirlpool, sauna. Minibars; some bathrm phones. **LUXURY LEVEL : RENAISSANCE CLUB.** 166 rms, 26 suites, 16 floors. S, D $225-$245; suites $300-$2,000. Private lounge, honor bar. Wet bar. Bathrm phones. Complimentary continental bkfst, refreshments. Cr cds: A, C, D, DS, ER, JCB, MC, V.

[D] [🤚] [≈] [🏋] [⇥] [🔥] [SC]

★★★ **WASHINGTON VISTA.** 1400 M Street NW (20005), downtown. 202/429-1700; res: 800/VISTA-DC; FAX 202/785-0786. 399 rms, 14 story. S $165-$205; D $190-$230; each addl $25; suites $350-$975; family, wkend rates. Crib free. Pet accepted. Valet parking $14. TV; cable, in-rm movies avail. Restaurant 6:30 am-10:30 pm; Sat, Sun from 7 am. Rm serv 24 hrs. Bars 11:30-1 am. Ck-out noon. Convention facilities. Concierge. Gift shop. Exercise equipt; weights, bicycles, sauna. Refrigerators. Some balconies. **LUXURY LEVEL : EXECUTIVE FLOOR.** 60 rms, 3 suites. S, D $175-$240. Private lounge. Some wet bars, in-rm whirlpools. Complimentary continental bkfst, refreshments. Cr cds: A, C, D, DS, ER, JCB, MC, V.

[D] [🤚] [🏋] [⇥] [🔥] [SC]

★★★★ **THE WATERGATE.** 2650 Virginia Ave NW (20037), in Foggy Bottom. 202/965-2300; res: 800/424-2736; FAX 202/337-7915. 235 rms, 13 story. S $275-$410; D $300-$435; each addl $25; suites $550-$1,885; under 18 free; wkend, hol rates. Crib free. Valet parking $15. TV; cable, in-rm movies. Indoor pool; lifeguard. Restaurant 7 am-10:30 pm (also see JEAN-LOUIS AT THE WATERGATE HOTEL and PALLADIN BY JEAN-LOUIS). Rm serv 24 hrs. Bar 11:30-1 am; pianist. Ck-out noon. Meeting rms. Concierge. Shopping arcade. Barber, beauty shop. Complimentary downtown & Capitol transportation. Health club & fitness center: instructor, weight machines, bicycles, whirlpool, sauna, steam rm. Massage. Bathrm phones, minibars. Many balconies. Furnished with many fine antiques. Many extras. Landmark hotel, part of condominium complex overlooking Potomac River; most rooms overlook river. Kennedy Center adj. Cr cds: A, C, D, DS, JCB, MC, V.

D ⚏ 🏃 🏃 ⛵ ⛱ SC

★ ★ ★ ★ **WILLARD INTER-CONTINENTAL.** *1401 Pennsylvania Ave NW (20004), 2 blks E of White House, downtown.* 202/628-9100; res: 800/327-0200; FAX 202/637-7326. 340 units, 12 story, 36 suites. S $255-$350; D $285-$380; each addl $30; suites $495-$2,900; under 14 free; wkend rates. Crib free. Pet accepted, some restrictions. Covered parking, valet $16. TV; cable. Restaurant 6:30 am-11 pm (also see WILLARD ROOM). Rm serv 24 hrs. Bar 11-1 am, Sun 11:30 am-midnight; entertainment. Ck-out noon. Meeting rms. Concierge. Shopping arcade. Exercise equipt; weight machines, treadmill. Bathrm phones, minibars. Historic hotel (1847) (present building completed 1904), restored to original Edwardian elegance; turn-of-the-century decor; stately columns, mosiac floors. Famous "Peacock Alley" runs the length of the hotel, connecting Pennsylvania Ave and F St. Host to many presidents on the eves of their inaugurations. Cr cds: A, C, D, DS, ER, JCB, MC, V.

D ⛵ 🏃 ⛱ ⛱ SC

★ ★ ★ **WYNDHAM BRISTOL.** *2430 Pennsylvania Ave NW (20037), west of downtown.* 202/955-6400; FAX 202/955-5765. 240 kit. units, 8 story, 37 suites. S $179-$209; D $199-$229; each addl $20; suites $285-$850; under 17 free; monthly rates; wkend plans. Crib free. Valet garage parking $15. TV; cable. Complimentary coffee in rms. Restaurant 7 am-11 pm. Rm serv 24 hrs. Bar 11-2 am. Ck-out noon. Meeting rms. Concierge. Exercise equipt; weight machines, treadmills. Bathrm phones. Classic English furnishings, art. Cr cds: A, C, D, DS, ER, JCB, MC, V.

D 🏃 ⛱ ⛱ SC

Inns

✔ ★ **EMBASSY.** *1627 16th St NW (20009), in Dupont Circle area.* 202/234-7800; res: 800/423-9111; FAX 202/234-3309. 38 rms, 5 story. S $69-$99; D $79-$99; each addl $10; under 14 free. Crib free. TV. Complimentary continental bkfst, coffee & tea/sherry. Ck-out noon, ck-in 1 pm. Valet serv. Antiques. Originally a boarding house (1922). Cr cds: A, C, D, MC, V.

⛱ ⛱ SC

✔ ★ **KALORAMA GUEST HOUSE AT KALORAMA PARK.** *1854 Mintwood Pl NW (20009), in Kalorama.* 202/667-6369. 31 rms, some share bath, 3 story. No rm phones. S $45-$95; D $50-$100; each addl $5; suites $75-$115; wkly rates. Complimentary continental bkfst, sherry & lemonade. Ck-out 11 am, ck-in noon. Limited parking avail. Created from 4 connecting Victorian town houses (1890s); rms individually decorated, antiques. Garden. Cr cds: A, C, D, DS, MC, V.

⛱ ⛱ SC

✔ ★ **KALORAMA GUEST HOUSE AT WOODLEY PARK.** *2700 Cathedral Ave NW (20008), north of downtown.* 202/328-0860. 19 rms, 12 with bath, 4 story, 2 suites. No rm phones. Mar-mid-June, Sept-Nov: S $45-$90; D $55-$95; each addl $5; wkly rates; lower rates rest of yr. Children over 5 yrs only. Some B/W TV; TV in sitting rm. Complimentary continental bkfst, tea/sherry. Restaurant nearby. Ck-out 11 am, ck-in noon. Free lndry facilities. Limited off-street parking. Sitting rm; antiques. Early 20th-century town house (1910). Cr cds: A, C, D, DS, MC, V.

⛱ ⛱ SC

★ ★ **MORRISON CLARK.** *1015 L Street NW (20001), at Massachusetts Ave, downtown.* 202/898-1200; res: 800/332-7898; FAX 202/289-8576. 54 units, 5 story, 14 suites. Mar-June, Sept-Nov: S $125-$175; D $145-$195; each addl $20; suites $145-$185; under 12

free; wkend rates; lower rates rest of yr. Crib free. TV. Complimentary continental bkfst. Dining rm 11:30 am-2 pm, 6-10 pm; Sat from 6 pm. Rm serv. Ck-out noon, ck-in 3 pm. Bellhops. Valet serv. Exercise equipt; weight machine, treadmills. Underground parking. Restored Victorian mansion (1864); two-story veranda; period furnishings. Cr cds: A, C, D, DS, ER, JCB, MC, V.

🏃 ⛱ ⛱ SC

✔ ★ **WINDSOR.** *1842 16th St NW (20009), north of downtown.* 202/667-0300; res: 800/423-9111; FAX 202/667-4503. 46 rms, 4 story, 9 suites. No elvtr. S $69-$89; D $79-$99; each addl $10; suites $105-$150; under 15 free; wkend rates. Crib free. TV. Complimentary continental bkfst, coffee, tea & evening sherry. Restaurant nearby. Ck-out noon, ck-in 1 pm. Refrigerator in suites. Originally a boarding house (1922); bed & breakfast atmosphere. Cr cds: A, C, D, MC, V.

⛱ SC

Restaurants

★ ★ ★ **1789.** *1226 36th St NW, in Georgetown.* 202/965-1789. Hrs: 6-10 pm; Fri, Sat to 11 pm. Res accepted. Extensive wine list. Semi-a la carte: dinner $16-$26. Prix fixe: pre-theater dinner $25. Specializes in seafood, rack of lamb. Own baking. Valet parking. In restored mansion; 5 dining rms on 3 levels. Federal-period decor. Fireplace. Jacket. Cr cds: A, D, DS, MC, V.

★ ★ ★ **701.** *701 Pennsylvania Ave NW, downtown.* 202/393-0701. Hrs: 11:30 am-3 pm, 5:30-10:30 pm; Wed, Thurs to 11 pm; Fri to 11:30 pm; Sat 5:30-11:30 pm; Sun 5-9:30 pm. Closed major hols. Res accepted. Continental. Bar. Wine list. Semi-a la carte: lunch $7.50-$16.95, dinner $12.50-$22.50. Specializes in seafood, lamb chops, charred rib steak. Pianist Sun-Thurs, Jazz combo Fri-Sat. Valet parking. Outdoor dining. Overlooks fountain at Navy Memorial. Cr cds: A, C, D, MC, V.

D

✔ ★ ★ **ADITI.** *3299 M Street NW, in Georgetown.* 202/625-6825. Hrs: 11:30 am-2:30 pm, 5:30-10 pm; Fri, Sat to 10:30 pm. Closed Labor Day, Thanksgiving. Res accepted. Indian menu. Serv bar. Semi-a la carte: lunch $4.95-$7.95, dinner $4.95-$13.95. Specializes in barbecued meats, vegetarian dishes, tandoori-roasted butter chicken. Cr cds: A, C, D, DS, MC, V.

★ **ALEKOS.** *1732 Connecticut Ave NW, in Dupont Circle.* 202/667-6211. Hrs: 11:30 am-11 pm. Closed Dec 25. Res accepted. Greek menu. Bar. Semi-a la carte: lunch $6.95-$9.95, dinner $7.95-$15.95. Specializes in seafood, moussaka. Greek Islands ambience. Cr cds: A, MC, V.

✔ ★ ★ **BACCHUS.** *1827 Jefferson Place NW (20036), in Dupont Circle.* 202/785-0734. Hrs: noon-2:30 pm, 6-10 pm; Fri to 10:30 pm; Sat 6-10:30 pm. Closed Sun; most major hols. Res accepted. Lebanese menu. A la carte entrees: lunch $6.50-$10.75, dinner $11.75-$14.75. Specializes in authentic Lebanese cuisine. Valet parking. Cr cds: A, MC, V.

★ ★ ★ **BICE.** *601 Pennsylvania Ave NW (Entrance on Indiana Ave), downtown.* 202/638-2423. Hrs: 11:30 am-3 pm, 5:30-10:30 pm; Fri to 11:30 pm; Sat 5:30-11:30 pm; Sun 5:30-10 pm. Closed Jan 1, Thanksgiving, Dec 25. Res accepted. Northern Italian menu. Bar. Extensive wine list. Semi-a la carte: lunch $11-$21, dinner $12-$25. Specializes in pasta, risotto, veal. Valet parking (dinner). Outdoor dining. Bright, modern Italian decor; windows on 3 sides of dining rm. Jacket. Cr cds: A, C, D, MC, V.

D

★ **BILLY MARTIN'S TAVERN.** *1264 Wisconsin Ave NW, in Georgetown.* 202/333-7370. Hrs: 8-1 am; Fri, Sat to 2:30 am; Sat, Sun brunch to 5:30 pm. Closed Dec 25. Res accepted. Bar. Semi-a la carte: bkfst $2.95-$11.50, lunch $5.95-$8.95, dinner $5.75-$18.95. Sat, Sun brunch $5.95-$12.95. Specializes in steak, seafood, chops. Outdoor dining. Established 1933. Family-owned. Cr cds: A, C, D, DS, MC, V.

★ ★ **BISTRO FRANCAIS.** *3128 M Street NW, in Georgetown.* *202/338-3830; FAX 202/338-1421.* Hrs: 11-3 am; Fri, Sat to 4 am; early-bird dinner 5-7 pm; Sat, Sun brunch 11 am-4 pm. Closed Dec 24, 25. Res accepted. Country French menu. Semi-a la carte: lunch $6.95-$11.95, dinner $12.95-$17.95. Sat, Sun brunch $13.95. Specializes in rotisserie chicken, fresh seafood. Cr cds: A, C, D, JCB, MC, V.

★ ★ ★ **BOMBAY CLUB.** *815 Connecticut Ave NW, near White House, downtown.* *202/659-3727.* Hrs: 11:30 am-2:30 pm, 6-10:30 pm; Fri, Sat 6-11 pm; Sun 5:30-9 pm; Sun brunch 11:30 am-2:30 pm. Closed some major hols. Res accepted. Indian cuisine. Bar 11:30 am-3 pm, 5-11 pm. A la carte entrees: lunch, dinner $7-$18.50. Sun brunch $14.95. Complete meals: pre-theater dinner (6-7 pm) $21.50. Specialties: tandoori salmon, thali, lamb Roganjosh, chicken Tikka Makhani. Pianist evenings, Sun brunch. Valet parking (dinner). Outdoor dining. Extensive vegetarian menu. Elegant club-like atmosphere. Cr cds: A, C, D, MC, V.

D

✔ ★ ★ **BOMBAY PALACE.** *2020 K St NW, downtown.* *202/331-4200.* Hrs: 11:30 am-2:30 pm, 5:30-10 pm; Fri, Sat to 10:30 pm. Res accepted. Northern Indian menu. Bar. A la carte entrees: lunch, dinner $6.50-$14.95. Complete meals: lunch, dinner $13.95-$31.95. Specialties: butter chicken, gosht patiala. Indian decor and original art. Totally nonsmoking. Cr cds: A, D, MC, V.

✔ ★ **BUA.** *1635 P Street NW, in Dupont Circle.* *202/265-0828.* Hrs: 11:30 am-2:30 pm, 5-10:30 pm; Fri to 11 pm; Sat noon-4 pm, 5-11 pm; Sun brunch noon-4 pm. Closed Thanksgiving, Dec 25. Res accepted. Thai menu. Bar. A la carte entrees: lunch $4.95-$7.50, dinner $7.25-$12.95. Specializes in seafood, Thai noodles, crispy flounder. Outdoor dining on 2nd-floor balcony. In town house on quiet side street; fireplace. Cr cds: A, D, MC, V.

★ ★ **BUSARA.** *2340 Wisconsin Ave NW, in Georgetown.* *202/337-2340.* Hrs: 11:30 am-3 pm, 5-11 pm; Fri to midnight; Sat 5 pm-midnight; Sun 5-11 pm. Closed some major hols. Thai menu. Bar. Semi-a la carte: lunch $5.95-$7.95, dinner $6.95-$15.95. Specialties: panang gai, crispy whole flounder, pad Thai. Outdoor dining. Modern atmosphere. Cr cds: A, C, D, DS, MC, V.

D

★ **CAFE ATLANTICO.** *1819 Columbia Rd NW, in Adams Morgan area.* *202/328-5844.* Hrs: 5:30-10 pm; Thurs-Sat to 12:30 am; Sun 5:30-10 pm. Closed Jan 1, July 4, Dec 24-25. Caribbean menu. Bar to 1:30 am; Fri, Sat to 2:30 am. Semi-a la carte: dinner $9.25-$13.95. Specialties: jerk chicken, coconut grouper, grilled fresh fish, curried lamb. Entertainment. Valet parking Tues-Sat (dinner). Outdoor dining. Modern, bi-level dining area. Cr cds: A, D, DS, MC, V.

★ **CHINA INN.** *631 H Street NW, in Chinatown.* *202/842-0909.* Hrs: 11-1 am; Fri, Sat to 2 am. Res accepted. Chinese menu. Semi-a la carte: lunch $7.50-$20.95, dinner $9.50-$24.75. Specialties: wor hip har (butterfly shrimp), chow mai foon (fried rice noodles). Modern decor. Cr cds: A, MC, V.

★ ★ **CHINA REGENCY.** *3000 K Street NW, Suite 30, Washington Harbour complex, in Georgetown.* *202/944-4266.* Hrs: 11:30 am-11 pm; Fri, Sat to midnight; Sun noon-11 pm. Closed Thanksgiving, Dec 25. Res accepted. Chinese menu. Bar. Semi-a la carte: lunch $6-$16, dinner $8-$20. Specializes in Szechuan and Hunan dishes. Outdoor dining. Chinese artifacts. Overlooks fountains and Potomac River. Cr cds: A, C, D, MC, V.

D

★ ★ **CITIES.** *2424 18th St NW, in Adams Morgan area.* *202/328-7194.* Hrs: 6-11 pm; Fri, Sat to 11:30 pm; Sun brunch 11 am-3:30 pm. Res accepted. Bar 5 pm-2 am; Fri & Sat to 3 am. A la carte entrees: dinner $10-$19. Sun brunch $4.50-$12.50. Valet parking (dinner). Located in 1930s hardware store. Menu and decor change every

year to feature cuisine of different cities around the world. Cr cds: A, D, MC, V.

★ ★ ★ **COLONNADE.** *(See Ana Hotel) 202/457-5000.* Hrs: 11:30 am-2:30 pm, 6-10 pm; Sun brunch 10:30 am-2:30 pm. Closed Sat; Jan 1. Res accepted. Continental menu. A la carte entrees: lunch $10.75-$17.50, dinner $18-$26. Buffet: lunch (Mon-Fri) $16.50. Sun brunch $30-$35. Specializes in rack of lamb, fresh seafood, veal. Own baking, pasta. Pianist (brunch). Valet parking. Garden atmosphere; gazebo; dining rm overlooks courtyard garden. Cr cds: A, C, D, DS, ER, JCB, MC, V.

D

★ ★ ★ **DOMINIQUE'S.** *1900 Pennsylvania Ave NW, downtown.* *202/452-1126.* Hrs: 11:30 am-2:30 pm, 5:30-10:30 pm; Fri 5:30 pm-midnight; Sun 5-9:30 pm. Closed some major hols. Res accepted. French, continental menu. Bar. Semi-a la carte: lunch $9.95-$18.95, dinner $17.95-$25.95. Prix fixe: lunch $13.95, dinner (before & after theater) $18.95. Specializes in rack of lamb, seafood, seasonal game, exotic game such as rattlesnake. Own baking. Pastry chef. Valet parking (dinner). Cr cds: A, D, MC, V.

★ ★ **DONNA ADELE.** *2100 P Street NW, in Dupont Circle.* *202/296-1142.* Hrs: 11:30 am-2:30 pm, 5:30-10:30 pm; Fri to 11 pm; Sat 5:30-11 pm; Sun 5:30-9:30 pm. Closed Jan 1, Thanksgiving, Dec 25. Res accepted. Northern Italian menu. Bar. Semi-a la carte: lunch $15-$20, dinner $25-$35. Child's meals. Specializes in fresh game, fresh whole fish. Own pasta. Parking. Outdoor dining. Contemporary decor. Cr cds: A, D, ER, MC, V.

D

★ ★ **EL CARIBE.** *3288 M Street, in Georgetown.* *202/338-3121.* Hrs: 11:30 am-11 pm; Fri, Sat to 11:30 pm; Sun to 10 pm. Res accepted. South Amer, Spanish menu. Bar. Semi-a la carte: lunch $6.95-$12.95, dinner $9.95-$19.50. Specialties: fritadas con Llapingachos, paella, seafood. Spanish decor. Family-owned. Cr cds: A, C, D, DS, MC, V.

★ ★ ★ **FILOMENA RISTORANTE.** *1063 Wisconsin Ave NW, Georgetown.* *202/338-8800; FAX 202/338-8806.* Hrs: 11:30 am-11 pm. Closed Jan 1, Dec 24-25. Res accepted. Italian menu. Bar. A la carte entrees: lunch $5.95-$9.95, dinner $11.95-$29.95. Lunch buffet $6.95. Prix fixe: pre-theater dinner (exc Sun) $19.95. Specializes in pasta, seafood, regional Italian dishes. Own baking, pasta. Italian garden-like atmosphere; antiques. Overlooks Chesapeake & Ohio Canal. Cr cds: A, D, MC, V.

✔ ★ **FIO'S.** *3636 16th St, at Woodner Apts, north of downtown.* *202/667-3040.* Hrs: 5-10:45 pm. Closed Mon; some major hols; last 2 wks Aug. Italian menu. Bar. Semi-a la carte: dinner $4.50-$11. Specializes in seafood, veal, pasta. Garage parking. Informal atmosphere; building overlooks Rock Creek Park. Cr cds: A, C, D, DS, MC, V.

★ ★ ★ **GABY'S.** *3311 Connecticut Ave NW, north of downtown.* *202/364-8909.* Hrs: 11:30 am-2:30 pm, 5-10 pm; Fri, Sat to 11 pm. Res accepted. French menu. Semi-a la carte: lunch $6.50-$15, dinner $14-19. Complete meals: dinner $24.50. Specializes in fresh seafood, breast of duck. Menu changes daily. Modern French decor. Cr cds: A, C, D, DS, MC, V.

★ ★ ★ **GALILEO.** *1110 21st St NW, in Foggy Bottom.* *202/293-7191.* Hrs: 11:30 am-2 pm, 5:30-10 pm; Fri to 10:30 pm; Sat from 5:30 pm; Sun 5:30-8:30 pm. Closed some major hols. Res accepted. Northern Italian menu. Bar. Wine cellar. A la carte entrees: lunch $10.95-$17.95, dinner $16.95-$29.95. Specializes in game & seasonal dishes, pasta, seafood. Valet parking (dinner). Outdoor dining. Light Mediterranean decor; reminiscent of an Italian trattoria. Cr cds: A, C, D, DS, MC, V.

D

✔ ★ **GARRETT'S.** *3003 M Street NW, in Georgetown.* *202/333-1033.* Hrs: 11:30 am-10:30 pm; Fri, Sat to 12:30 am. Res accepted. Bars 11:30-2 am; Fri, Sat to 3 am. Semi-a la carte: lunch $3.95-$8.50, dinner $4.75-$13.95. Specializes in steaks, hamburgers, pasta. 1794 landmark bldg; originally house of MD governor T.S. Lee. Cr cds: A, C, D, DS, MC, V.

★ ★ **GARY'S.** *1800 M Street NW, at 18th St in the Courtyard, downtown.* 202/463-6470. Hrs: 11:30 am-10:30 pm; Sat 6-11 pm. Closed Sun; major hols. Res accepted. American, Italian menu. Bar. Semi-a la carte: lunch $10-$17. A la carte entrees: dinner $17-$35. Specializes in dry-aged prime beef, fresh seafood. Pianist Mon-Fri. Cr cds: A, C, D, DS, MC, V.

D

★ ★ ★ **GERARD'S PLACE.** *915 15th St NW (20005), downtown.* 202/737-4445. Hrs: 11:30 am-2:30 pm, 5:30-9:30 pm; Fri to 10:30 pm; Sat 5:30-10:30 pm. Closed Sun; most major hols. Res accepted. French menu. Wine list. A la carte entrees: lunch $13-$15.50, dinner $16-$32. Prix fixe: dinner $50. Specializes in contemporary French cooking. Valet parking (dinner). Outdoor dining. Casual atmosphere. Some modern art. Cr cds: A, C, D, MC, V.

★ ★ **GERMAINE'S.** *2400 Wisconsin Ave NW, in Georgetown.* 202/965-1185. Hrs: 11:30 am-2:30 pm, 5:30-10 pm; Fri to 11 pm; Sat 5:30-11 pm; Sun 5:30-10 pm. Closed Jan 1, Dec 25. Res accepted. Pan-Asian menu. Bar. A la carte entrees: lunch $7.25-$12.95, dinner $12.25-$25.95. Specializes in grilled Asian dishes, seafood. Skylighted atrium dining rm. Cr cds: A, C, D, MC, V.

★ **GERMAN DELI-CAFE MOZART.** *1331 H Street NW, downtown.* 202/347-5732. Hrs: 7:30 am-10 pm; Sat from 9 am; Sun from 11 am. Closed Jan 1, Thanksgiving, Dec 25. Res accepted. German, Austrian menu. Bar. Semi-a la carte: bkfst $3.10-$7.95, lunch $4.65-$18.95, dinner $8.45-$19.95. Child's meals. Specialties: Wienerschnitzel, pork roast, Kasseler rippchen. Entertainment Wed-Sat. Cr cds: A, C, D, DS, JCB, MC, V.

D

✔★ **GUAPO'S.** *4515 Wisconsin Ave NW, north of downtown.* 202/686-3588. Hrs: 11:30 am-10:30 pm; Fri, Sat to midnight. Res accepted. Latin American, Mexican menu. Bar. Semi-a la carte: lunch $3.95-$10.25, dinner $4.95-$11.95. Specializes in combination platters, fajitas, tamales. Outdoor dining. Small, colorful dining rms. Cr cds: A, DS, MC, V.

★ **GUARDS.** *2915 M Street NW, in Georgetown.* 202/965-2350. Hrs: 11:30-2 am; Fri, Sat to 3 am; Sun brunch 11:30 am-5 pm. Res accepted. Continental menu. Bar. Semi-a la carte: lunch $4.50-$10.95, dinner $8.95-$18. Sun brunch $6-$12. Specializes in rack of lamb, Angus beef, fresh seafood. Atrium dining rm; country-English decor. Cr cds: A, C, D, DS, MC, V.

✔★ **HEAD'S.** *400 1st St SE, corner of D St SE, adj to Capitol South Metro stop, on Capitol Hill.* 202/546-4545. Hrs: 11:30 am-10:30 pm. Closed Sun; Memorial Day, Dec 25. Bar. Semi-a la carte: lunch, dinner $5.75-$12.50. Specializes in barbecued beef, ribs, chicken. Eclectic decor. Cr cds: A, C, D, DS, MC, V.

★ ★ **HOGATE'S.** *9th St & Maine Ave SW, on the waterfront, south of downtown.* 202/484-6300. Hrs: 11 am-10 pm; Sat noon-11 pm; Sun 10:30 am-10 pm; Sun brunch to 2:30 pm. Closed Dec 25. Res accepted. Bar. Semi-a la carte: lunch $6-$12, dinner $13-$35. Sun brunch $16.95. Child's meals. Specialties: mariner's platter, clam bake, rum buns. Indoor parking. Outdoor dining. Overlooks Potomac River. Cr cds: A, C, D, DS, MC, V.

D

★ ★ **HUNAN CHINATOWN.** *624 H Street NW, in Chinatown.* 202/783-5858. Hrs: 11 am-11 pm; Fri, Sat to midnight. Closed Thanksgiving, Dec 25. Hunan, Szechwan menu. Serv bar. Semi-a la carte: lunch $6.50-$12, dinner $7.50-$20. Specialties: General Tso's chicken, tea-smoked half-duck, crispy prawns with walnuts. Parking (dinner). Modern, bi-level dining room. Cr cds: A, C, D, DS, MC, V.

✔★ ★ **I MATTI TRATTORIA.** *2436 18th St NW, in Adams Morgan area.* 202/462-8844. Hrs: noon-2:30 pm, 6-10:30 pm; Fri to 11 pm; Sat noon-4:30 pm, 6-11 pm; Sun 5:30-10 pm; Sun brunch 11:30 am-3 pm. Closed Jan 1, Thanksgiving, Dec 25. Res accepted. Northern Italian menu. Bar. A la carte entrees: lunch, dinner $10-$15. Sun brunch $3.95-$12. Specializes in pasta, pizza, grilled dishes. Valet parking Tues-Sat. Upscale dining; lower dining area less formal. Cr cds: A, D, MC, V.

★ ★ ★ **I RICCHI.** *1220 19th St NW, downtown.* 202/835-0459. Hrs: 11:30 am-2:30 pm, 5:30-11 pm; Sat from 5:30 pm. Closed Sun; major hols. Res accepted. Italian menu. Bar. Semi-a la carte: lunch $11.95-$19.95, dinner $13.95-$24.95. Specializes in traditional Tuscan dishes. Own baking, pasta. Valet parking (dinner). Tuscan villa decor; Italian artifacts. Cr cds: A, C, D, MC, V.

D

★ **J PAUL'S.** *3218 M Street NW, in Georgetown.* 202/333-3450. Hrs: 11:30 am-2 am; Fri, Sat to 3 am; Sun 10:30-2 am; Sun brunch to 4 pm. Bar. Semi-a la carte: lunch, dinner $4.95-$19.95. Sun brunch $4.95-$16.95. Child's meals. Specializes in ribs, crab cakes. Turn-of-the-century saloon decor; antique bar from Chicago's old Stockyard Inn. Cr cds: A, C, D, DS, MC, V.

★ ★ **JAPAN INN.** *1715 Wisconsin Ave NW, in Georgetown.* 202/337-3400. Hrs: noon-2 pm, 6-10 pm; Fri to 10:30 pm; Sat 6-10:30 pm; Sun 5:30-9:30 pm. Closed some major hols; also lunch all major hols. Res accepted. Japanese menu. Semi-a la carte: lunch $8-$12.50, dinner $12-$28. Specializes in tempura, sushi, shabu-shabu. Parking. Traditional Japanese decor. Four dining areas, each with different menu. Family-owned. Cr cds: A, C, D, JCB, MC, V.

★ ★ ★ ★ **JEAN-LOUIS AT THE WATERGATE HOTEL.** *(See The Watergate Hotel)* 202/298-4488. Hrs: 5:30-10 pm. Closed Sun. Res accepted. French menu. Serv bar. Extensive wine cellar. Table d'hôte: dinner $85-$95. Prix fixe: pre-theater dinner (5-6:30 pm) $50. Specialties: crispy Vancouver shrimp, duck foie gras, turbot with potato crust, seaweed salad. Own baking. Valet parking. Recessed lighting on mirrored ceiling; silk wall hangings; exotic flowers. Artistic food presentation. Pastry chef. Jacket. Cr cds: A, C, D, DS, JCB, MC, V.

★ ★ ★ **THE JEFFERSON.** *(See Jefferson)* 202/347-2200. Hrs: 6:30-10:30 am, 11:30 am-2:30 pm, 6-10:30 pm. Sun brunch 11 am-2 pm. Res accepted. Bar 10:30-1 am. Semi-a la carte: bkfst $4.50-$12.50, lunch $12-$24, dinner $22.50-$26. Sun brunch $21.50-$25.75. Specializes in New Virginia cuisine, seafood. Soft jazz Thurs-Sat evenings. Valet parking. Intimate club-style atmosphere. Cr cds: A, C, D, DS, ER, JCB, MC, V.

★ ★ ★ **JOCKEY CLUB.** *(See The Ritz-Carlton Hotel)* 202/659-8000. Hrs: 6:30-11 am, noon-2:30 pm, 6-10:30 pm. Res accepted. Classic French, international menu. Serv bar. Semi-a la carte: bkfst $3.75-$13.50, lunch $5.50-$25, dinner $21.50-$34. Specializes in veal, fresh seafood, Jockey Club crab cakes. Own baking. Valet parking. Tableside cooking. Club-like atmosphere in 1928 landmark building. Jacket, tie. Cr cds: A, C, D, DS, ER, JCB, MC, V.

✔★ **KATMANDU.** *2100 Connecticut Ave NW, in Kalorama.* 202/483-6470. Hrs: 11:30 am-2:30 pm, 5:30-10:30 pm; Sun 5:30-10 pm. Res accepted. Nepalese, Kashmiri menu. Bar. Semi-a la carte: lunch $5.25-$8.75, dinner $7.50-$12. Specialties: mutton biriani, Katmandu chicken. Far Eastern decor. Cr cds: A, D, DS, MC, V.

★ ★ ★ **KINKEAD'S.** *2000 Pennsylvania Ave NW (20006), in Foggy Bottom.* 202/296-7700. Hrs: 11:30 am-10:30 pm. Closed Jan 1, Thanksgiving, Dec 25. Res accepted. Bar to midnight. Semi-a la carte: lunch $10-$14, dinner $14-$19. Sun brunch $8-$12. Specialties: pepita crusted salmon, pepper-seared tuna, grilled squid. Valet parking (dinner). Outdoor dining. Three levels of dining areas. Cr cds: A, C, D, DS, JCB, MC, V.

D

★ ★ **LA CHAUMIÈRE.** *2813 M Street NW, in Georgetown.* 202/338-1784. Hrs: 11:30 am-2:30 pm, 5:30-11 pm; Sat from 5:30 pm. Closed Sun; major hols. Res accepted. Country French menu. A la carte entrees: lunch $7.75-$11.95, dinner $9.95-$17.95. Specializes in seafood, veal, duck. Intimate room with beamed ceiling, open-hearth fireplace. Cr cds: A, C, D, MC, V.

D

★ ★ ★ **LA COLLINE.** *400 N Capitol St NW, on Capitol Hill.* 202/737-0400. Hrs: 7-10 am, 11:30 am-3 pm, 6-10 pm; Sat from 6 pm. Closed Sun; major hols. Res accepted. French menu. Bar. Semi-a la carte: bkfst $2.50-$5, lunch $9-$17, dinner $14-$21. Complete meals: dinner $17.50. Specializes in seasonal foods, duck, seafood. Outdoor dining. Across from Union Station. Cr cds: A, C, D, MC, V.

D

✔★ ★ **LA FONDA.** *1639 R Street NW, downtown.* 202/232-6965. Hrs: 11:30 am-3 pm, 5-11 pm; Fri, Sat to midnight; Sun 11:30 am-10 pm. Closed Labor Day, Thanksgiving, Dec 25. Mexican, Spanish menu. Bar. Semi-a la carte: lunch $5.25-$10.50, dinner $6.95-$13.95. Specialties: enchiladas, carne asada, fajitas. Outdoor dining. Cr cds: A, D, DS, MC, V.

SC

★ **LAS PAMPAS.** *3291 M Street NW, in Georgetown.* 202/333-5151. Hrs: 11 am-11 pm; Fri, Sat to 3 am. Res accepted. Argentinean, Tex-Mex menu. Serv bar. Semi-a la carte: lunch $4.95-$8.95, dinner $6.95-$19.95. Specializes in grilled steak, boneless chicken, Argentinean empanadas, fajitas. Cr cds: A, C, D, MC, V.

✔★ ★ **LAVANDOU.** *3321 Connecticut Ave NW, north of downtown.* 202/966-3003. Hrs: 11:30 am-2:30 pm, 5-10 pm; Fri to 11 pm; Sat 5-11 pm; Sun 5-10 pm; Mon from 5 pm. Closed most major hols. Res accepted. Southern French menu. Serv bar. Semi-a la carte: lunch $9.95-$12.95, dinner $11.95-$15.95. Specialties: clam á l'ail, truite saumonée, daube Provençale. French bistro atmosphere. Cr cds: A, D, MC, V.

★ ★ **LE CAPRICE.** *2348 Wisconsin Ave NW, north of downtown.* 202/337-3394. Hrs: 6-10 pm. Res accepted. French menu. Bar. Semi-a la carte: dinner $17-$24. Prix fixe: dinner $29.50. Specialties: sliced breast of duck with glazed fruit, boneless breast of chicken in pastry crust. Own pasta, pâté. Outdoor dining. French provincial decor. Extensive wine selection. Cr cds: A, C, D, MC, V.

★ ★ ★ ★ **LE LION D'OR.** *1150 Connecticut Ave NW (Entrance on 18th St), downtown.* 202/296-7972. Hrs: noon-2 pm, 6-10 pm; Sat from 6 pm. Closed Sun; major hols; also last 3 wks Aug-Labor Day. Res accepted. Classical French menu. Bar. Wine list. A la carte entrees: lunch $15-$27, dinner $25-$36. Specialties: soufflé de homard, gateau de crab. Own baking. Gracious dining. Elegant French decor, original artwork, antiques. Chef-owned. Jacket, tie. Cr cds: A, C, D, MC, V.

★ ★ ★ ★ **MAISON BLANCHE/RIVE GAUCHE.** *1725 F Street NW, downtown.* 202/842-0070. Hrs: 11:45 am-2 pm, 6-9:30 pm; Sat from 6 pm. Closed Sun; major hols. Res accepted. French menu. Bar. Semi-a la carte: lunch $12-$25, dinner $16.50-$32.50. Prix fixe: lunch $19, dinner $24.95. Specialties: lobster with saffron pasta, Dover sole, rack of lamb. Pastry chef. Complimentary valet parking from 5 pm. European decor; four seasons tapestry. Jacket recommended. Cr cds: A, C, D, DS, MC, V.

D

★ **MARKET INN.** *200 E Street SW, south of downtown.* 202/554-2100. Hrs: 11 am-midnight; Fri to 1 am; Sat 10:30-1 am; Sun 10:30 am-midnight; major hols from 4 pm. Closed Dec 25. Res accepted. Bar. Semi-a la carte: lunch $6-$13.50, dinner $10.95-$24.95. Sat, Sun brunch $6-$13. Child's meals. Specializes in she-crab soup, Maine lobster, beef. Pianist, bass noon-midnight; jazz Sun brunch. Free valet parking. Outdoor dining. Display of drawings, photographs, newspaper headlines. Family-owned. Cr cds: A, C, D, DS, JCB, MC, V.

D

★ ★ ★ **MELROSE.** *(See Park Hyatt Hotel)* 202/955-3899. Hrs: 6:30-11 am, 11:30 am-2:30 pm, 6-10:30 pm; Fri & Sat to 11 pm; Sun brunch 11:30 am-2:30 pm. Res accepted. Contemporary Amer menu. Bar 11-1 am. Wine cellar. Semi-a la carte: bkfst $5.50-$12.75, lunch

$12-$18, dinner $19-$25. Chef's 7-course tasting dinner $48. Pre-theater dinner (5:30-7:30 pm) $22.95. Sun brunch $28; with champagne $31. Child's meals. Specializes in fresh fish, seafood, beef, veal and chicken. Own baking. Pianist. Valet parking. Outdoor dining. Sunlit atrium, fountain. Cr cds: A, C, D, DS, JCB, MC, V.

D

✔★ ★ **MESKEREM.** *2434 18th St NW, in Adams Morgan area.* 202/462-4100. Hrs: noon-midnight; Fri-Sun noon-1 am. Closed Thanksgiving, Dec 25. Res accepted. Ethiopian menu. Bar. Semi-a la carte: lunch, dinner $8.50-$11.95. Specializes in lamb, beef, chicken, seafood. Own Ethiopian breads. Ethiopian band Fri, Sat. Tri-level dining rm; traditional Ethiopian decor. Cr cds: A, C, D, MC, V.

★ ★ **MONOCLE ON CAPITOL HILL.** *107 D Street NE, adj to US Senate Office Bldg, on Capitol Hill.* 202/546-4488. Hrs: 11:30 am-midnight; Sat 6-11 pm. Closed Sun; major hols; also Sat Memorial Day-Labor Day. Res accepted. Bar. A la carte entrees: lunch $6-$15, dinner $10.50-$20. Child's meals. Specializes in seafood, aged beef. Valet parking. Located in 1865 Jenkens Hill building; fireplace. Close to Capitol; frequented by members of Congress and other politicians. Family-owned. Cr cds: A, C, D, MC, V.

★ ★ ★ **MORTON'S OF CHICAGO.** *3251 Prospect St NW, in Georgetown.* 202/342-6258. Hrs: 5:30-11 pm; Sun 5-10 pm. Closed some major hols. Res accepted. Bar. Wine list. A la carte entrees: dinner $15.95-$28.95. Specializes in steak, lobster, seafood. Valet parking. Collection of Leroy Neiman paintings. Cr cds: A, C, D, MC, V.

D

✔★ **MR. SMITH'S.** *3104 M Street NW, in Georgetown.* 202/333-3104. Hrs: 11:30-2 am; Fri, Sat to 3 am; Sat, Sun brunch 11 am-4:30 pm. Bar. Semi-a la carte: lunch, dinner $4.95-$14.95. Sat, Sun brunch $4.50-$8. Specializes in seafood, pasta, hamburgers. Pianist 9 pm-1:30 am. Old tavern atmosphere. Outdoor dining. Family-owned. Cr cds: A, C, D, MC, V.

★ **MR. YUNG'S.** *740 6th St NW, in Chinatown.* 202/628-1098. Hrs: 11 am-11 pm. Chinese, Cantonese menu. Serv bar. Semi-a la carte: lunch $5.95-$7.95, dinner $8.95-$25.95. Specialties: silver snapper with ginger, bean cake, eggplant and green pepper stuffed with shrimp in black bean sauce. Oriental decor. Cr cds: A, C, D, DS, MC, V.

✔★ **MURPHY'S OF D.C.** *2609 24th St NW, (20008), at Calvert St, north of downtown.* 202/462-7171. Hrs: 11-2 am. Closed some major hols. Irish, Amer menu. Semi-a la carte: lunch $5.95-$7.95, dinner $6.95-$11.95. Child's meals. Specialties: meat & potato pie, Irish stew, corned beef & cabbage. Traditional Irish music. Patio dining. Wood-burning fireplace. Cr cds: A, D, MC, V.

★ ★ **NATHANS.** *3150 M Street NW, in Georgetown.* 202/338-2000. Hrs: 11 am-3 pm, 6-11 pm; Thurs, Fri to midnight; Sat 6 pm-midnight; Sun 6-11 pm; Sat, Sun brunch 9 am-3 pm. Res accepted. Northern Italian, Amer menu. Bar 11-2 am; Fri & Sat to 3 am. Semi-a la carte: lunch $5.25-$11.50, dinner $14.50-$26.50. Sat, Sun brunch $5.25-$10.50. Specializes in fish, poultry, veal. Own pasta. Disc jockey Fri, Sat. Antiques. Family-owned. Cr cds: A, C, D, MC, V.

★ ★ **NEW HEIGHTS.** *2317 Calvert St NW, north of downtown.* 202/234-4110. Hrs: 5:30-10 pm; Fri, Sat to 11 pm; Sun brunch 11 am-2:30 pm. Closed major hols. Res accepted. New Amer cuisine. Bar from 5 pm. Semi-a la carte: dinner $12-$22. Sun brunch $8-$15. Specializes in calamari fritti, grilled salmon, fresh mozzarella. Menu changes seasonally; some entrees offered in half-portions. Outdoor dining. Main dining rm on 2nd floor overlooks Rock Creek Park. Cr cds: A, C, D, DS, MC, V.

★ ★ ★ **NORA.** *2132 Florida Ave NW, in Dupont Circle.* 202/462-5143. Hrs: 6-10 pm; Fri, Sat to 10:30 pm. Closed Sun; major hols; also last 2 wks Aug. Res accepted. Bar. Semi-a la carte: dinner $15.95-$23.95. Specializes in healthy dining, additive-free meats, organic produce. Menu changes daily. Own desserts. Atrium dining. In 1890 building with American folk art, Amish quilts on walls. Totally nonsmoking. Cr cds: MC, V.

★ ★ **NOTTE LUNA.** *809 15th St NW, downtown.* 202/408-9500. Hrs: 11 am-11 pm; Fri to midnight; Sat 5 pm-1 am; Sun 5-11 pm. Closed Easter, Dec 25. Res accepted. Italian menu. Bar. Semi-a la carte: lunch, dinner $8.95-$15.95. Specializes in pizza, grilled meats & fish. Own pasta. Valet parking (dinner exc Sun). Outdoor dining. Woodburning oven. Lively atmosphere. Cr cds: A, C, D, DS, MC, V.

[D]

★ ★ **OBELISK.** *2029 P Street NW, in Dupont Circle.* 202/872-1180. Hrs: 6-10 pm. Closed Sun; major hols. Res accepted; required Fri & Sat. Italian menu. Serv bar. Complete meals: dinner $35-$37. Specializes in seasonal dishes. Menu changes daily. Intimate dining rm on 2nd floor of town house. Totally nonsmoking. Cr cds: D, MC, V.

★ ★ **OCCIDENTAL GRILL.** *1475 Pennsylvania Ave NW, downtown.* 202/783-1475. Hrs: 11:30 am-11:30 pm; Sun noon-9 pm. Closed major hols. Res accepted. Bar. A la carte entrees: lunch $9.50-$16.95, dinner $11-$19. Specializes in grilled seafood, beef. Own baking. Turn-of-the-century Victorian decor with autographed photos of celebrities; originally opened 1906. Cr cds: A, C, D, MC, V.

[D]

✔ ★ ★ **OLD EBBITT GRILL.** *675 15th St NW, downtown.* 202/347-4801. Hrs: 7:30-1 am; Sat from 8 am; Sun from 9:30 am; Sun brunch to 4 pm. Res accepted. Bar to 2 am; Fri, Sat to 3 am. Semi-a la carte: bkfst $4.95-$7.95, lunch $5-$10, dinner $5-$15.95. Sun brunch $5.95-$10. Specializes in seafood, hamburgers. Own pasta. In old vaudeville theater built in early 1900s. Victorian decor, gaslights; atrium dining. Cr cds: A, D, DS, MC, V.

[D]

★ ★ **OLD EUROPE RESTAURANT & RATHSKELLER.** *2434 Wisconsin Ave NW, north of downtown.* 202/333-7600. Hrs: 11:30 am-3 pm, 5-10:30 pm; Fri, Sat to 11 pm; Sun 4-10 pm. Closed Dec 24, 25. Res accepted. German menu. Serv bar. Semi-a la carte: lunch $5-$10.50, dinner $10-$20. Child's meals. Specialties: schnitzel Old Europe, Wienerschnitzel, sauerbraten. Pianist; polka band Fri, Sat evenings. Cr cds: A, C, D, MC, V.

★ ★ ★ **PALLADIN BY JEAN-LOUIS.** *(See The Watergate Hotel)* 202/298-4455. Hrs: 7 am-2:30 pm, 5:30-10:30 pm. Sun brunch 11:30 am-2:30 pm. Res accepted; required Fri & Sat. French menu. Bar. Semi-a la carte: bkfst $4.50-$17, lunch $6.50-$26, dinner $7.50-$26. Pre-theater dinner: $35. Sun brunch $38. Specializes in southern French cooking with Italian and Spanish touches. Overlooking Potomac River. Jacket (dinner). Cr cds: A, C, D, DS, JCB, MC, V.

[D]

★ ★ **PALM.** *1225 19th St NW, in Dupont Circle.* 202/293-9091. Hrs: 11:45 am-10:30 pm; Sat from 6 pm; Sun 5:30-9:30 pm. Closed major hols. Res accepted. Bar. A la carte entrees: lunch $7.50-$17, dinner $14-$45. Specializes in steak, lobster. Valet parking (dinner). 1920s New York-style steak house. Family-owned. Cr cds: A, C, D, MC, V.

[D]

★ ★ **PAOLO'S.** *1303 Wisconsin Ave NW, in Georgetown.* 202/333-7353. Hrs: 11:30-2 am; Fri, Sat to 3 am; Sun 11 am-2 am; Sat, Sun brunch to 4 pm. Italian menu. Bar. Semi-a la carte: lunch, dinner $7.95-$18.95. Sun brunch $8.95-$10.95. Specializes in pizza, pasta, seafood. Jazz combo Sun afternoons. Patio dining; wood-burning pizza oven. Cr cds: A, C, D, DS, MC, V.

★ ★ **PETITTO'S RISTORANTE D'ITALIA.** *2653 Connecticut Ave NW, north of downtown.* 202/667-5350. Hrs: 11:30 am-2:30 pm, 6-10:30 pm; Sat from 6 pm; Sun 6-9:30 pm. Closed major hols; also Christmas wk. Res accepted. Italian menu. Bar. A la carte entrees: lunch $6.50-$11, dinner $10-$18. Specializes in pasta, fish, veal. Valet parking from 6 pm. Outdoor dining. Dessert & cappuccino rm down-

stairs. Washington town house overlooking Connecticut Ave; fireplaces. Cr cds: A, C, D, DS, MC, V.

★ **PHILLIPS FLAGSHIP.** *900 Water St SW, on waterfront, south of downtown.* 202/488-8515. Hrs: 11 am-11 pm; Fri, Sat to midnight. Closed Dec 24 & 25. Bar. Semi-a la carte: lunch, dinner $4.95-$25.95. Buffet: lunch (exc Sun) $12.95. Sun brunch $17.95. Child's meals. Specializes in crab Imperial, Eastern Shore seafood dishes. Sushi bar. Garage parking. Outdoor dining. Antiques; Tiffany lamps, stained glass. In clement weather, exterior wall is rolled up, opening dining rm to marina. Cr cds: A, C, D, DS, MC, V.

[D]

✔ ★ **PIZZERIA PARADISO.** *2029 P Street NW, in Dupont Circle.* 202/223-1245. Hrs: 11 am-11 pm; Fri to midnight; Sun noon-10 pm. Closed some major hols. Italian menu. Wine, beer. A la carte entrees: lunch, dinner $3.25-$15.75. Specializes in pizza, salads, sandwiches. Lively, colorful atmosphere; pizza-makers visible from dining area. Totally nonsmoking. Cr cds: MC, V.

★ ★ ★ **PRIME RIB.** *2020 K Street NW, downtown.* 202/466-8811. Hrs: 11:30 am-3 pm, 5-11 pm; Fri to 11:30 pm; Sat 5-11:30 pm. Closed Sun; major hols. Res accepted. Bar. Semi-a la carte: lunch $7-$17. A la carte entrees: dinner $16.50-$24. Specializes in roast prime rib, Chesapeake seafood, aged thick-cut steak. Pianist at noon, pianist & bass at night. Valet parking. Art deco decor; 1920s lithographs. Jacket & tie. Cr cds: A, D, MC, V.

✔ ★ ★ **PRIMI PIATTI.** *2013 I Street NW, downtown.* 202/223-3600. Hrs: 11:30 am-2:30 pm, 5:30-10:30 pm; Fri, Sat 5:30-11:30 pm; Sun 5-9:30 pm. Closed some major hols. Res accepted; required Fri, Sat. Italian menu. Bar. Semi-a la carte: lunch, dinner $7.95-$16.95. Specializes in grilled fish & meat. Own pasta. Outdoor dining. Cr cds: A, C, D, MC, V.

[D]

★ ★ ★ **RED SAGE.** *605 14th St NW, in Westory Bldg, downtown.* 202/638-4444. Hrs: 11:30 am-2 pm, 5:30-10:30 pm; Sun 5-10 pm. Closed Dec 25. Res accepted. Southwestern menu. Bar. Wine cellar. A la carte entrees: lunch $8.50-$15.50, dinner $16.75-$25. Specialties: herb-roasted breast of chicken, cowboy ribeye steak, grilled Atlantic salmon. Validated parking. Two-story restaurant composed of a large street-level bar and a series of dining rms below. Designed as a contemporary interpretation of the American West, each of dining level's four major spaces exhibits a particular scale and mood. Cr cds: A, D, MC, V.

[D]

★ ★ ★ **RIVER CLUB.** *3223 K Street NW, in Georgetown.* 202/333-8118. Hrs: 7 pm-2 am; Fri & Sat to 3 am. Closed Sun & Mon; major hols. Res accepted. Continental menu. Bar. Semi-a la carte: dinner $16-$26. Specialties: smoked salmon, smoked lobster, roast rack of lamb. Entertainment. Elegant supper club atmosphere with lively bar area. Jacket. Cr cds: A, C, D, DS, MC, V.

[D]

★ ★ **ROOF TERRACE.** *2700 F Street NW, within Kennedy Center, in Foggy Bottom.* 202/416-8555. Hrs: (open only on days of Kennedy Center performances) 11:30 am-3 pm, 5:30-9 pm. Sun brunch 11:30 am-3 pm. Res accepted. Semi-a la carte: lunch $10-$14, dinner $22-$24. Sun brunch 19.95. Child's meals. Specializes in regional American cooking. Pastry chef. Garage parking. Contemporary decor; floor-to-ceiling windows offer views of Lincoln Memorial, Georgetown, Potomac River and Virginia. Totally nonsmoking. Cr cds: A, C, D, MC, V.

[D]

✔ ★ ★ **SAIGONNAIS.** *2307 18th St NW, in Adams Morgan area.* 202/232-5300. Hrs: 11:30 am-3 pm, 5-11 pm; Fri to 11 pm; Sat 5:30-11 pm; Sun 5:30-10:30 pm. Closed Jan 1, Thanksgiving, Dec 25. Res accepted. Vietnamese menu. Semi-a la carte: lunch, dinner $7.95-

$14.95. Specialties: lemongrass beef, shrimp on sugar cane stick, catfish. Vietnamese artwork. Cr cds: A, C, D, DS, MC, V.

★ ★ ★ **SAM & HARRY'S.** *1200 19th St NW, in Dupont Circle.* 202/296-4333. Hrs: 11:30 am-2:30 pm, 5:30-11 pm; Sat 5:30-11 pm. Closed Sun; major hols. Res accepted. Bar. A la carte entrees: lunch $8.95-$20.95, dinner $17.95-$28.95. Specializes in dry prime aged beef, Maine lobster, grilled fresh seafood. Valet parking (dinner). Club-like atmosphere with mahogany paneling, paintings of jazz legends. Cr cds: A, C, D, DS, MC, V.

D

★ ★ ★ **SEA CATCH.** *1054 31st St NW, in Georgetown.* 202/337-8855. Hrs: noon-3 pm, 5:30-10 pm. Closed Sun. Res accepted. Bar. Wine list. Semi-a la carte: lunch $4.75-$12, dinner $14-$22. Specializes in lobster, crab cakes. Own pastries. Raw bar. Valet parking. Outdoor dining on deck overlooking historic Chesapeake & Ohio Canal. Cr cds: A, D, DS, MC, V.

D

★ ★ ★ **SEASONS.** *(See Four Seasons Hotel)* 202/342-0444. Hrs: 7-11 am, noon-2:30 pm, 6:30-10:30 pm; Sun brunch 10 am-2:30 pm. Res accepted. Bar 11-2 am. Extensive wine list. Semi-a la carte: bkfst $7-$19, lunch $14-$29, dinner $23-$32. Child's meals. Specializes in regional and seasonal dishes. Own baking. Pianist. Valet parking. Overlooks Rock Creek Park. Cr cds: A, C, D, ER, JCB, MC, V.

D

★ ★ **SEQUOIA.** *3000 K Street NW, Washington Harbour complex, in Georgetown.* 202/944-4200. Hrs: 11:30 am-midnight; Fri & Sat to 1 am; Sat, Sun brunch 11 am-4 pm. Res accepted. Bar. Semi-a la carte: lunch, dinner $6.95-$20.95. Sun brunch $6.95-$11.95. Outdoor dining. Terrace and multi-story dining rm windows overlook Kennedy Center, Potomac River and Roosevelt Bridge & Island. Cr cds: A, D, MC, V.

D

★ ★ **SFUZZI.** *50 Massachusetts Ave NE, in Union Station, on Capitol Hill.* 202/842-4141. Hrs: 11:30 am-10 pm; Fri, Sat to 11 pm; Sun to 9 pm; Sun brunch 11 am-3 pm. Closed Dec 25. Res accepted. Italian, Amer menu. Bar. Semi-a la carte: lunch $8.50-$11, dinner $12-$20. Sun brunch $14.50. Specializes in veal, pasta, seafood. Outdoor dining. Tri-level dining room in restored 1907 railroad station. Cr cds: A, C, D, MC, V.

D

★ ★ **SICHUAN PAVILION.** *1820 K Street NW, downtown.* 202/466-7790. Hrs: 11:30 am-10:30 pm. Res accepted. Chinese menu. Bar. A la carte entrees: lunch $8-$16, dinner $25-$30. Complete meals: dinner $25-$30. Specializes in Szechwan dishes. Valet parking after 6 pm. Oriental decor; original Chinese art. Artistic food preparation. Cr cds: A, C, D, DS, JCB, MC, V.

✔ ★ **STETSON'S.** *1610 U Street NW, in Adams Morgan area.* 202/667-6295. Hrs: 4 pm-2 am; Fri to 3 am; Sat 5 pm-3 am; Sun 5 pm-2 am. Tex-Mex menu. Bar. Semi-a la carte: lunch, dinner $2.95-$9.95. Specializes in chili, fajitas, chimichangas. Outdoor dining. Old West saloon-like decor and atmosphere; antique bar; Western artifacts. Cr cds: A, MC, V.

★ ★ ★ **TABERNA DEL ALABARDERO.** *1776 I Street NW, entrance on 18th St, downtown.* 202/429-2200. Hrs: 11:30 am-2:30 pm, 6-10 pm; Fri to 11 pm; Sat 6-11 pm. Closed Sun; major hols. Res accepted. Basque, Spanish menu. Bar. Semi-a la carte: lunch $6.25-$14.50, dinner $14-$24. Complete meals: dinner $24.95. Specializes in beef, fish, rice. Tapas bar. Own baking. Flamenco dancers Apr & Oct. Valet parking (dinner). Ornate, 19th-century Spanish decor. Cr cds: A, C, D, MC, V.

D

✔ ★ ★ **THAI KINGDOM.** *2021 K Street NW, downtown.* 202/835-1700. Hrs: 11:30 am-2:30 pm, 5-10:30 pm; Sat noon-11 pm; Sun noon-10 pm. Closed some major hols. Res accepted. Thai menu.

Bar. A la carte entrees: lunch $6.50-$8.95, dinner $7.25-$9.95. Specialties: crispy chili fish, scallops wrapped in minced chicken, Thai Kingdom grilled chicken. Valet parking (dinner). Outdoor dining. Bi-level dining rm with full windows overlooking K St. Cr cds: A, C, D, MC, V.

D

★ **THAI TASTE.** *2606 Connecticut Ave NW, north of downtown.* 202/387-8876. Hrs: 11:30 am-10:30 pm; Fri, Sat to 11 pm. Closed some major hols. Res accepted Sun-Thurs. Thai menu. A la carte entrees: lunch, dinner $7-$15.95. Specializes in crispy fish, chicken with basil, seafood combinations. Outdoor dining. Cr cds: A, C, D, MC, V.

★ ★ ★ **TIBERIO.** *1915 K Street NW, downtown.* 202/452-1915. Hrs: 11:45 am-2:30 pm, 6-11 pm; Sat from 5:30 pm. Closed Sun; major hols. Res accepted. Italian menu. Bar. Wine cellar. A la carte entrees: lunch $13-$15.95, dinner $16.95-$29.95. Specialties: agnolotti alla crema, osso buco alla Milanese. Own baking. Valet parking (dinner). Mediterranean decor. Jacket. Cr cds: A, C, D, MC, V.

★ ★ **TONY AND JOE'S.** *3000 K Street NW, at Washington Harbour complex, in Georgetown.* 202/944-4545. Hrs: 11 am-midnight; Sun to 10 pm; Sun brunch to 3 pm. Closed Dec 25. Res accepted. Bar. Semi-a la carte: lunch $6.95-$13.95, dinner $13.95-$25. Sun brunch $16.95. Specializes in seafood. Own desserts. Outdoor dining. Overlooks Potomac River. Cr cds: A, C, D, DS, JCB, MC, V.

D

★ ★ **TONY CHENG'S MONGOLIAN BARBECUE AND CHINESE SEAFOOD RESTAURANT.** *619 H Street NW, in Chinatown.* 202/842-8669. Hrs: 11 am-11 pm; Fri, Sat to midnight. Res accepted. Mongolian barbecue menu. Prix fixe: lunch $8.50, dinner $13.95 (serv charge 15%). Food bar surrounds Mongolian barbecue. Diners may prepare their meals in "hot pot." Oriental decor. Cr cds: A, MC, V.

★ **TUCSON CANTINA.** *2605 Connecticut Ave NW, north of downtown.* 202/462-6410. Hrs: 11:30 am-10:30 pm; Fri, Sat to 11 pm. Closed some major hols. Southwestern menu. Bar 4 pm-2 am; Fri, Sat to 3 am; Sun 6 pm-1 am. Semi-a la carte: lunch, dinner $4.25-$17.50. Child's meals. Specializes in wood-grilled meats. Patio dining. Cr cds: C, D, DS, MC, V.

★ ★ **VINCENZO.** *1606 20th St NW (20009), in Dupont Circle.* 202/667-0047. Hrs: noon-2 pm, 6-9:30 pm; Fri to 10 pm; Sat 6-10 pm. Closed Sun; major hols. Res accepted. Italian menu. Bar. Semi-a la carte: lunch, dinner $12.95-$19.95. Specializes in fresh seafood. Valet parking (dinner). Three dining rms, including atrium. Cr cds: A, C, D, MC, V.

★ ★ ★ **WILLARD ROOM.** *(See Willard Inter-Continental Hotel)* 202/637-7440. Hrs: 7:30-10 am, 11:30 am-2 pm, 6-10 pm; Sat, Sun from 6 pm; Sun brunch 11 am-2 pm; afternoon tea 3-5 pm. Res accepted. Bar 11-1 am. Extensive wine list. French, Amer regional cuisine. A la carte entrees: bkfst $7-$15.50, lunch $17-$28, dinner $18.50-$32. Afternoon tea $13. Sun brunch $28-$39. Child's meals. Specializes in seafood, lamb, veal. Seasonal specialties. Own pastries. Pianist. Valet parking. Elegant turn-of-the-century decor. Cr cds: A, C, D, DS, ER, JCB, MC, V.

D

Unrated Dining Spots

ARMAND'S CHICAGO PIZZERIA. *4231 Wisconsin Ave NW, north of downtown.* 202/686-9450. Hrs: 11:30 am-11 pm; Fri, Sat to 1 am. Closed Thanksgiving, Dec 25. Serv bar. A la carte entrees: lunch, dinner $4-$7. Buffet: lunch (pizza & salad) $4.49. Specializes in Chicago-style deep-dish pizza, sandwiches, salads, desserts. Outdoor dining. Cr cds: A, MC, V.

D

AUSTIN GRILL. *2404 Wisconsin Ave NW, in Georgetown.* 202/337-8080. Hrs: 11:30 am-11 pm; Fri, Sat 11:30 am-midnight; Sat brunch 11:30 am-3 pm, Sun brunch 11 am-3 pm. Closed Jan 1,

Thanksgiving, Dec 24, Dec 25. Tex-Mex menu. Bar. Semi-a la carte: lunch, dinner $4.95-$12.95. Sat, Sun brunch $6.25-$6.95. Specializes in enchiladas, fajitas. Southwestern decor. Cr cds: A, D, DS, MC, V.

C.F. FOLKS. *1225 19th St NW, in Dupont Circle. 202/293-0162.* Hrs: 11:45 am-3 pm. Closed Sat, Sun; major hols. Semi-a la carte: lunch $4.95-$6.35. Complete meals: lunch $7-$10. Specializes in crab cakes, daily & seasonally changing cuisines. Outdoor dining. Old-fashioned lunch counter. No cr cds accepted.

CAFE PETITTO. *1724 Connecticut Ave NW, in Dupont Circle. 202/462-8771.* Hrs: 11:30 am-10:30 pm; Fri, Sat to 11 pm; Sun to 10 pm; Sat, Sun brunch to 2:30 pm. Italian menu. Bar. A la carte entrees: lunch, dinner $6-$13. Sat, Sun brunch $8.95. Specializes in pizza, pasta, hoagies. Cr cds: A, C, D, MC, V.

KRAMERBOOKS & AFTERWORDS. *1517 Connecticut Ave, in Dupont Circle. 202/387-1462.* Hrs: 7:30-1 am; wkends open 24 hrs; Sun brunch 9:30 am-3 pm. Closed Thanksgiving, Dec 25. Bar. Semi-a la carte: bkfst $3.95-$7.50, lunch, dinner $6.75-$12.75. Sun brunch $8.25-$10.75. Specializes in pasta, fresh seafood, Thai seafood salad, smoked chichen pita. Entertainment Thurs-Sun. Oudoor dining. Lively, entertaining spot in 2-story greenhouse & terrace behind Kramerbooks bookshop. Open continuously Fri morning to Mon night. Cr cds: A, DS, MC, V.

MADURAI. *3316 M Street NW, in Georgetown. 202/333-0997.* Hrs: 11:30 am-2:30 pm, 5:30-10 pm; Fri, Sat to 11 pm; Sun noon-4 pm, 5-10 pm. Vegetarian menu. Semi-a la carte: lunch, dinner $3.50-$9.95. Sun brunch $6.95. Specializes in curry, navratan garden vegetables. Cr cds: A, MC, V.

PATISSERIE-CAFE DIDIER. *3206 Grace St NW, in Georgetown. 202/342-9083.* Hrs: 8 am-7 pm; Sun to 5 pm. Closed Mon; Jan 1, Dec 25. Semi-a la carte: bkfst $1.10-$7.95, lunch, dinner $5.95-$8.95. Specializes in European desserts, quiche, pizza. European-style cafe and pastry house. Cr cds: C, D, DS, MC, V.

SHOLL'S COLONIAL CAFETERIA. *1990 K Street NW, in Esplanade Mall, in Foggy Bottom. 202/296-3065.* Hrs: 7 am-2:30 pm, 4-8 pm. Closed Sun; major hols. Avg ck: bkfst $3, lunch, dinner $5. Specializes in spaghetti, liver & onions, homemade pie. Family-owned. No cr cds accepted.

D

Arlington County (National Airport Area), VA

Motels

✔★★ **COMFORT INN BALLSTON.** *1211 N Glebe Rd (22201), at Washington Blvd. 703/247-3399; FAX 703/524-8739.* 126 rms, 3 story. Mar-late June: S $65-$95; D $70-$100; each addl $10; suites $79-$105; under 18 free; wkend rates; lower rates rest of yr. Crib free. TV; cable. Complimentary continental bkfst. Restaurant 6:30 am-10:30 pm. Rm serv. Bar 4-11 pm. Ck-out 11 am. Meeting rms. Valet serv (Mon-Fri). Sundries. Gift shop. Garage parking. Refrigerators avail. Cr cds: A, C, D, DS, ER, JCB, MC, V.

D ⊠ ☜ SC

✔★★ **TRAVELODGE-WASHINGTON/ARLINGTON CHERRY BLOSSOM.** *3030 Columbia Pike (22204). 703/521-5570; FAX 703/271-0081.* 76 rms, 3 story, 12 kit. units. Mid-Mar-Nov: S, D $64; each addl $7; kit. units $74; under 18 free; lower rates rest of yr. Crib free. TV; cable. Pool privileges. Complimentary continental bkfst. Complimentary coffee in rms. Restaurant 11 am-midnight. Ck-out noon. Coin

Indry. Valet serv. Exercise equipt; weight machine, rowers. Refrigerators. 3 mi from downtown Washington. Cr cds: A, C, D, DS, ER, JCB, MC, V.

D ⊼ ☜ ☜ SC

Motor Hotels

★★ **DAYS INN CRYSTAL CITY.** *(2000 Jefferson Davis Hwy, Arlington 22202) 703/920-8600; FAX 703/920-2840.* 247 rms, 8 story. S $109-$150; D $119-$160; each addl $10; under 16 free; wkend, hol rates. Crib free. TV; cable. Pool; lifeguard. Complimentary coffee in rms. Restaurant 6 am-10 pm. Rm serv. Bar 4 pm-midnight. Ck-out 11 am. Meeting rms. Bellhops. Gift shop. Valet serv. Garage parking. Free airport transportation. Cr cds: A, C, D, DS, ER, JCB, MC, V.

D ☜ ⊼ ⊼ ☜ SC

✔★ **HOWARD JOHNSON NATIONAL AIRPORT.** *2650 Jefferson Davis Hwy (22202), near National Airport. 703/684-7200; FAX 703/684-3217.* 278 rms, 16 story. S $65-$135; D $73-$135; each addl $8; under 18 free; wkend rates. Crib free. TV; cable, in-rm movies avail. Pool. Complimentary coffee in rms. Restaurant 6 am-11 pm. Rm serv. Bar 6-11 pm. Ck-out noon. Coin Indry. Meeting rms. Bellhops. Valet serv. Gift shop. Free airport transportation. Exercise equipt; stair machine, bicycles. Balconies. Cr cds: A, C, D, DS, JCB, MC, V.

D ☜ ⊼ ⊼ ☜ SC

★★ **QUALITY INN-IWO JIMA.** *1501 Arlington Blvd (Fairfax Dr) (22209), 1/2 mi W of Iwo Jima Memorial. 703/524-5000; FAX 703/522-5484.* 141 rms, 1-3 story. Mar-June: S $75-$80; D $82-$87; each addl $7; suites $90-$97; family rates; higher rates Marine Corps Marathon; lower rates rest of yr. Crib free. TV; cable. Heated pool; poolside serv, lifeguard. Restaurant 6:30 am-10 pm; Sat, Sun from 7 am. Rm serv. Bar 11:30 am-2 pm, 5-11 pm. Ck-out noon. Coin Indry. Meeting rms. Bellhops. Sundries. Gift shop. Refrigerators avail. Some balconies. Cr cds: A, C, D, DS, ER, JCB, MC, V.

D ☜ ⊼ ☜ SC

Hotels

★★ **BEST WESTERN ROSSLYN WESTPARK.** *(1900 N Ft Myer Dr, Arlington 22209) 703/527-4814; FAX 703/522-8864.* 308 rms, 20 story. S, D $95-$99; suites $115-$150; under 18 free; wkly, wkend & hol rates. Crib free. Pet accepted. TV; cable. Indoor pool; whirlpool, sauna, lifeguard. Restaurant 6:30 am-11 pm. Bar 11:30 am-midnight. Ck-out noon. Coin Indry. Convention facilities. Gift shop. Garage parking. Balconies. Overlooking Potomac River. Cr cds: A, C, D, DS, ER, JCB, MC, V.

D ☜ ☜ ⊼ ☜ SC

★★ **COURTYARD BY MARRIOTT.** *2899 Jefferson Davis Hwy (22202), near National Airport. 703/549-3434; FAX 703/549-7440.* 272 rms, 14 story. S $129; D $144; each addl $15; suites $185-$215; under 12 free. Crib free. Garage parking $4. TV; cable. Indoor pool; lifeguard. Complimentary coffee in rms. Restaurant 6-10 am, 5-10 pm. Rm serv (dinner). Bar 4 pm-midnight. Ck-out 1 pm. Meeting rms. Valet serv. Sundries. Exercise equipt; weights, bicycles, whirlpool, steam rm. Some refrigerators, wet bars. Cr cds: A, C, D, DS, ER, JCB, MC, V.

D ☜ ☜ ⊼ ☜ SC

★★ **DOUBLETREE.** *300 Army/Navy Dr (22202). 703/416-4100; FAX 703/416-4126.* 632 rms, 15 story, 265 suites. S $145-$165; D $165-$185; each addl $20; suites $165-$250; under 18 free; wkend rates. Crib free. Pet accepted. Garage $9. TV; cable. Indoor pool; sauna, lifeguard. Restaurant 6:30 am-11 pm. Bar 11-2 am; entertainment, dancing. Ck-out noon. Convention facilities. Concierge. Gift shop. Free airport transportation. Health club privileges. Many bathrm phones; some refrigerators. Some balconies. *LUXURY LEVEL : PO-TOMAC CLUB.* 20 suites. Suites $185-$270. Private lounge. Bathrm phones. Complimentary continental bkfst, refreshments. Cr cds: A, C, D, DS, ER, JCB, MC, V.

[D] [☂] [≈] [⊠] [🐾] [SC]

★ ★ **EMBASSY SUITES-CRYSTAL CITY.** *1300 Jefferson Davis Hwy (22202), entrance at 1402 S Eads St, near National Airport. 703/979-9799; FAX 703/920-5947.* 267 suites, 11 story. Feb-June, Sept-Nov: S $169-$199; D $179-$209; each addl $10; under 12 free; wkend rates; lower rates rest of yr. Crib free. TV; cable. Heated pool; lifeguard. Restaurant 11:30 am-10 pm; Fri, Sat to 11 pm. Bar to 11 pm. Ck-out noon. Meeting rms. Gift shop. Free covered parking. Free airport transportation. Exercise equipt; weight machine, bicycles. Refrigerators. Atrium lobby. Cr cds: A, C, D, DS, JCB, MC, V.

[D] [≈] [⊠] [✈] [⊠] [🔥] [SC]

★ ★ **HOLIDAY INN KEY BRIDGE.** *1850 N Ft Myer Dr (22209). 703/522-0400; FAX 703/524-5275.* 177 rms, 11 story. S $106-$145; D $116-$155; each addl $10; suites $155-$165; under 18 free. Crib free. Pet accepted. TV; cable. Pool; lifeguard. Restaurant 6:30 am-10:30 pm. Ck-out noon. Meeting rms. Game rm. Refrigerator avail in suites. Cr cds: A, C, D, DS, JCB, MC, V.

[D] [☂] [≈] [⊠] [🔥] [SC]

★ ★ **HOLIDAY INN NATIONAL AIRPORT.** *(1489 Jefferson Davis Hwy, Arlington 22202) 703/416-1600; FAX 703/416-1615.* 306 rms, 11 story. S $111; D $121; each addl $10; suites $140; under 20 free; wkend, hol rates. Crib free. Garage $6. Pet accepted. TV; cable. Pool; poolside serv. Restaurant 6:30 am-10 pm; Sat & Sun from 7 am. Bar 11 am-midnight. Ck-out noon. Meeting rms. Gift shop. Free airport transportation. Health club privileges. Game rm. Cr cds: A, C, D, DS, JCB, MC, V.

[D] [☂] [≈] [✈] [⊠] [🔥] [SC]

★ ★ **HYATT ARLINGTON.** *1325 Wilson Blvd (22209), near Key Bridge at Nash St. 703/525-1234; FAX 703/875-3393.* 302 rms, 16 story. S $169; D $194; each addl $25; suites $200-$500; under 12 free; wkend rates. Crib free. Pet accepted, some restrictions. Garage $6 (Sun-Thurs). TV; cable. Restaurant 6:30 am-midnight. Bars 11:30-1:30 am. Ck-out noon. Free lndry facilities. Meeting rms. Gift shop. Exercise equipt; bicycles, treadmill. Metro adj. Cr cds: A, C, D, DS, ER, JCB, MC, V.

[D] [☂] [✈] [⊠] [🔥] [SC]

★ ★ **HYATT REGENCY-CRYSTAL CITY.** *2799 Jefferson Davis Hwy (22202), near National Airport. 703/418-1234; FAX 703/418-1289.* 685 rms, 20 story. S $160; D $185; each addl $25; suites $225-$750; under 18 free; wkend rates. Crib free. Garage; valet $8. TV; cable. Heated pool; poolside serv, lifeguard. Restaurant 6-2 am. Bar from 3 pm. Ck-out noon. Convention facilities. Concierge. Gift shop. Free airport transportation. Exercise equipt; weight machine, stair machine, whirlpool, saunas. Some refrigerators, wet bars. Some balconies. Cr cds: A, C, D, DS, ER, MC, V.

[D] [≈] [✈] [⊠] [🔥] [SC]

★ ★ **MARRIOTT CRYSTAL CITY.** *(1999 Jefferson Davis Hwy, Arlington 22202) 703/413-5500; FAX 703/413-0192.* 345 rms, 10 story. S $159; D $179; suites $250-$300; under 18 free; wkend rates. Crib free. Valet parking $15. TV; cable. Indoor pool; poolside serv, lifeguard. Restaurant 6:30 am-10:30 pm; Sat & Sun from 7 am. Bar 11:30 am-midnight. Ck-out 1 pm. Convention facilities. Concierge. Gift shop. Free airport transportation. Exercise equipt; weight machine, stair machines, whirlpool, sauna. Health club privileges. **LUXURY LEVEL : CONCIERGE LEVEL.** 33 rms. S $179; D $199. Private lounge, honor bar. Complimentary continental bkfst, refreshments, newspaper. Cr cds: A, C, D, DS, ER, JCB, MC, V.

[D] [≈] [✈] [✈] [⊠] [🔥] [SC]

★ ★ **MARRIOTT CRYSTAL GATEWAY.** *1700 Jefferson Davis Hwy (US 1) (22202), entrance on S Eads St, between 15th & 17th Sts, near National Airport. 703/920-3230; FAX 703/979-6332.* 700 units, 16 story. S, D $165-$185; each addl $20; suites $175-$600; under 18

free; wkend rates. Crib free. Pet accepted, some restrictions. Garage $10; valet parking $15. TV; cable, in-rm movies avail. Indoor/outdoor pool; lifeguard. Complimentary coffee. Restaurant 6:30 am-2:30 pm, 4:30-10 pm. Bar 4 pm-2 am, Sat from 8 pm; entertainment. Ck-out 1 pm. Convention facilities. Free airport transportation. Tennis privileges. Exercise equipt; weights, bicycles, whirlpool, sauna. Original artwork. **LUXURY LEVEL : CONCIERGE LEVEL.** 61 rms, 4 suites. S $169; D $189; suites $195-$620. Private lounge, honor bar. Complimentary continental bkfst, refreshments. Cr cds: A, C, D, DS, ER, JCB, MC, V.

[D] [☂] [✈] [≈] [✈] [⊠] [🔥] [SC]

★ ★ **MARRIOTT KEY BRIDGE.** *1401 Lee Hwy (22209). 703/524-6400; FAX 703/524-8964.* 584 rms, 4-12 story. S, D $149-$184; suites $225-$325; wkend rates. Crib free. Pet accepted; $50 refundable. Garage $6. TV; cable. Indoor/outdoor pool; poolside serv, lifeguard. Restaurant 6:30 am-10:30 pm; Fri, Sat to 11 pm (also see THE VIEW). Bar 11-2 am; entertainment, dancing exc Sun. Ck-out 1 pm. Convention facilities. Concierge. Gift shop. Barber, beauty shop. Exercise equipt; weights, bicycles, whirlpool, sauna. Refrigerators. Some balconies. Overlooks Washington across Potomac River. **LUXURY LEVEL : CONCIERGE LEVEL.** 90 rms, 4 suites, 3 floors. S $169; D $194; suites $225-$325. Concierge. Private lounge, honor bar. Complimentary continental bkfst, refreshments. Cr cds: A, C, D, DS, ER, JCB, MC, V.

[D] [☂] [≈] [✈] [⊠] [🐾] [SC]

✓ ★ ★ **QUALITY HOTEL.** *1200 N Courthouse Rd (22201). 703/524-4000; FAX 703/524-1046.* 395 rms, 1-10 story, 40 kit. suites. S $48-$101; D $54-$129; each addl $6; suites $85-$148; under 18 free; wkend rates. Crib free. TV; cable. Pool; lifeguard. Restaurant 6:30 am-2 pm, 5-10 pm. Bar 4 pm-midnight. Ck-out noon. Coin lndry. Convention facilities. Concierge. Gift shop. Exercise equipt; weight machine, rowers, sauna. Lawn games. **LUXURY LEVEL : CLUB ROYALE.** 109 rms, 11 suites, 4 floors. S, D $115-$129; each addl $14; suites $125-$152. Private lounge. Complimentary continental bkfst, refreshments, newspaper. Cr cds: A, C, D, DS, ER, JCB, MC, V.

[D] [≈] [✈] [⊠] [🔥] [SC]

★ ★ **RENAISSANCE.** *950 N Stafford St (22203), at Fairfax Dr. 703/528-6000; FAX 703/528-4386.* 209 rms, 7 story. S $135-$165; D $150-$180; suites $195; under 18 free; wkend rates. Crib free. Pet accepted, some restrictions. TV; cable. Indoor pool; whirlpool, lifeguard. Restaurant 6:30 am-11 pm. Bar 11 am-midnight. Ck-out noon. Coin lndry. Meeting rms. Concierge. Gift shop. Barber, beauty shop. Minibars. Metro stop in building. **LUXURY LEVEL .** 40 rms, 1 suite. S $165; D $180; suite $225. Concierge. Private lounge, honor bar. Complimentary continental bkfst, refreshments. Cr cds: A, C, D, DS, ER, JCB, MC, V.

[D] [☂] [≈] [⊠] [🔥] [SC]

★ ★ ★ **THE RITZ-CARLTON, PENTAGON CITY.** *1250 S Hayes St (22202), in Pentagon City Fashion Centre Mall, near National Airport. 703/415-5000; FAX 703/415-5061.* 345 rms, 18 story, 41 suites. S $160-$200; D $180-$220; each addl $20; suites $300-$1,500; under 19 free; wkend plans. Crib free. Garage, valet parking $15. TV; cable. Indoor pool; lifeguard. Restaurant (see THE GRILL). Bar; entertainment. Ck-out noon. Convention facilities. Concierge. Shopping arcade. Free airport transportation. Tennis privileges. Golf privileges. Exercise rm; instructor, weight machine, bicycles, whirlpool, sauna, steam rm. Massage. Bathrm phones, minibars. Extensive collection of fine art and antiques. Panoramic view of the Capitol and Potomac River. **LUXURY LEVEL : RITZ-CARLTON CLUB.** 40 rms, 5 suites, 2 floors. S,D $240; suites $400-$1,500. Concierge. Private lounge, honor bar. Complimentary continental bkfst, refreshments. Cr cds: A, C, D, DS, ER, JCB, MC, V.

[D] [🍽] [🏋] [≈] [✈] [✈] [⊠]

★ ★ ★ **SHERATON CRYSTAL CITY.** *1800 Jefferson Davis Hwy (22202), entrance on S Eads St; 1/2 mi S of I-395 on US 1, near National Airport. 703/486-1111; FAX 703/920-5827.* 197 rms, 15 story. S $115-$150; D $125-$165; each addl $15; suites $350; under 18 free; wkend packages. Crib free. TV; cable. Rooftop pool; lifeguard, sauna. Restaurant 6:30 am-10 pm; Sat, Sun from 7 am. Bar 11 am-midnight; entertainment, pianist. Ck-out 1 pm. Convention facilities. Concierge. Gift shop. Free airport transportation. Minibars, refrigerators; some bathrm phones. *LUXURY LEVEL :* **CLUB LEVEL.** 10 rms, 2 suites. S $170; D $185; suites $350—$850. Concierge. Private lounge, bar. Complimentary continental bkfst, refreshments, newspaper. Cr cds: A, C, D, DS, MC, V.

Restaurants

★ ★ **ALPINE.** 4770 Lee Hwy. 703/528-7600. Hrs: 11:30 am-11 pm; Sun noon-10 pm. Closed major hols. Res accepted. Italian, continental menu. Bar. Semi-a la carte: lunch $7.95-$9.50, dinner $10.50-$17.95. Child's meals. Specializes in veal, pasta dishes, seafood. Own pasta. Parking. Family-owned. Cr cds: A, C, D, MC, V.

D

★ ★ **BANGKOK GOURMET.** 523 S 23rd St, at S Eads. 703/521-1305. Hrs: 11 am-3 pm, 5:30-10 pm; Mon from 5:30 pm; Sat, Sun from 5 pm. Closed Jan 1, Thanksgiving, Dec 25. Res accepted. Thai, French menu. A la carte entrees: lunch $5.95-$8.95, dinner $8.95-$17. Outdoor dining. Cr cds: C, D, DS, MC, V.

✔★ ★ **BISTRO BISTRO.** (4021 S 28th St, Arlington 22206) 703/379-0300. Hrs: 11 am-10 pm; Fri & Sat to 11 pm; early-bird dinner Mon-Thurs 5-6:30 pm; Sun brunch 10:30 am-3 pm. Closed Thanksgiving, Dec 25. Res accepted. Bar to 2 am. A la carte entrees: lunch $5.75-$10.95, dinner $6.95-$14.95. Sun brunch $6-$11. Specializes in pasta, seafood, oyster stew. Outdoor dining. Bistro atmosphere, eclectic decor. Cr cds: A, MC, V.

D

★ **CAFÉ DALAT.** 3143 Wilson Blvd, at N Highland St. 703/276-0935. Hrs: 11 am-9:30 pm; Fri, Sat to 10:30 pm. Closed Chinese New Year, July 4, Thanksgiving, Dec 25. Vietnamese menu. Serv bar. Complete meals: lunch $3.95. Semi-a la carte: dinner $4.95-$7.95. Specialties: sugar cane shrimp, grilled lemon chicken. Own desserts. Totally nonsmoking. Cr cds: MC, V.

✔★ ★ **CARLYLE GRAND CAFE.** (4000 S 28th St, Shirlington) S on I-395, Shirlington exit. 703/931-0777. Hrs: 11:30 am-11 pm; Fri & Sat to 1 am; Sun brunch 10 am-2 pm. Closed Dec 25. Bar. Semi-a la carte: lunch $5.95-$9.95, dinner $5.95-$14.70. Sun brunch $4.95-$9.95. Specialties: Virginia trout, baby back ribs, smoked salmon filet. Outdoor dining. Totally nonsmoking. Cr cds: A, MC, V.

D

✔★ ★ **FUJI.** 77 N Glebe Rd. 703/524-3666. Hrs: 11:30 am-10:30 pm; wkends from noon. Closed Jan 1. Res accepted; required Fri, Sat. Japanese, Korean menu. A la carte entrees: lunch $4.95-$8.50, dinner $8.50-$15. Complete meals: dinner $29. Buffet: lunch $6.95. Specialties: bibimbap, fried dumplings, bulgoki. Parking. Sushi bar. Modern Oriental decor. Cr cds: A, MC, V.

D

★ ★ ★ **THE GRILL.** (See The Ritz-Carlton, Pentagon City Hotel) 703/412-2760. Hrs: 6:30 am-10:30 pm; Sat & Sun 7 am-11 pm; Sun brunch 11 am-2:30 pm. Res accepted. Bar. Wine list. Semi-a la carte: bkfst $4-$10. A la carte entrees: lunch $9.50-$18, dinner $15-$24. Buffet: bkfst $8.75-$11. Sun brunch $32. High tea (3-5 pm) $11; light tea $9. Child's meals. Specializes in beef carpaccio, rack of lamb, grilled Atlantic salmon. Pianist Fri & Sat evenings. Valet parking. English club-like decor and atmosphere. Fireplace. Cr cds: A, C, D, DS, JCB, MC, V.

D

✔★ ★ **ITALIA BELLA.** 5880 N Washington Blvd. 703/534-7474. Hrs: 11 am-2:30 pm, 4:30-10 pm; Sat 4:30-10:30 pm; Sun 5-9 pm. Closed some major hols. Res accepted. Northern Italian menu.

Serv bar. Semi-a la carte: lunch $5.50-$8.95, dinner $6.95-$11.95. Child's meals. Specialties: veal Angelica, chicken piccata, shrimp scampi. Own pasta. Parking. Outdoor dining. Italian art and ceramics. Cr cds: C, D, MC, V.

D SC

★ ★ **KABUL CARAVAN.** 1725 Wilson Blvd, in Colonial Village Shopping Ctr. 703/522-8394. Hrs: 11:30 am-2:30 pm, 5:30-11 pm; Sat, Sun from 5:30 pm. Closed Thanksgiving, Dec 25. Res accepted. Afghan menu. Bar. Semi-a la carte: lunch $7.95-$11.95, dinner $8.95-$15.95. Specialties: sautéed pumpkin with yogurt & meat sauce, eggplant & shish kebab. Walls covered with Afghan clothing, pictures, rugs, artifacts. Cr cds: A, C, D, MC, V.

D

★ ★ **L'ALOUETTE.** 2045 Wilson Blvd. 703/525-1750. Hrs: 11:30 am-2:30 pm, 6-10 pm; Fri to 10:30 pm; Sat 6-10:30 pm. Closed Sun; major hols. Res accepted. French menu. Serv bar. Semi-a la carte: lunch $7-$14.25. A la carte entrees: dinner $11.99-$20. Prix fixe: dinner $16.95. Specializes in seasonal dishes. Cr cds: A, C, D, MC, V.

✔★ ★ **LITTLE VIET GARDEN.** 3012 Wilson Blvd. 703/522-9686. Hrs: 11 am-2:30 pm, 5-10 pm; Sat & Sun 11 am-10 pm. Closed Thanksgiving, Dec 25. Res accepted. Vietnamese menu. Bar. Semi-a la carte: lunch $4.95-$6.95, dinner $5.50-$8.95. Specialties: Viet Garden steak, grilled jumbo shrimp. Parking. Outdoor dining. Cr cds: A, C, D, DS, MC, V.

D

✔★ **QUEEN BEE.** 3181 Wilson Blvd. 703/527-3444. Hrs: 11 am-10 pm. Vietnamese menu. Serv bar. Semi-a la carte: lunch $3.50-$7.50, dinner $6.50-$7.95. Specialties: spring roll, Hanoi beef noodle soup, Hanoi-style grilled pork. Totally nonsmoking. Cr cds: MC, V.

D

★ **RED HOT & BLUE.** 1600 Wilson Blvd. 703/276-7427. Hrs: 11 am-10 pm; Fri to 11 pm; Sat noon-11 pm; Sun noon-9 pm. Closed Thanksgiving, Dec 25. Bar. Semi-a la carte: lunch, dinner $4.50-$16.45. Specializes in Memphis pit barbecue dishes. Parking. Memphis blues memorabilia. Cr cds: C, D, MC, V.

D

★ ★ ★ **RISTORANTE MICHELANGELO.** 2900 Columbia Pike, at Walter Reed Dr. 703/920-2900. Hrs: 11:15 am-2:30 pm, 5-10:30 pm; Sat, Sun from 5 pm. Closed Jan 1, Thanksgiving, Dec 25. Res accepted. Bar. Northern Italian menu. Semi-a la carte: lunch $8-$11.95, dinner $11-$16. Child's meals. Specializes in veal, chicken, seafood. Own pasta. Parking. Renaissance-style dining rm; reproduction of works by Michelangelo. Cr cds: A, C, D, MC, V.

★ **TACHIBANA.** 4050 Lee Hwy. 703/528-1122. Hrs: 11:30 am-2 pm, 5-10 pm; Fri & Sat to 10:30 pm. Closed Sun; some major hols. Res accepted Mon-Thurs. Japanese menu. Serv bar. Semi-a la carte: lunch $6-$10, dinner $8.95-$16. Complete meals: dinner $14.50-$21.50. Specialties: sushi, sashimi, soft shell crab tempura (in season). Parking. Circular dining rm. Cr cds: A, C, D, MC, V.

D

★ ★ **TOM SARRIS' ORLEANS HOUSE.** 1213 Wilson Blvd. 703/524-2929. Hrs: 11 am-11 pm; Sat from 4 pm; Sun 4-10 pm. Res accepted. Bar. Semi-a la carte: lunch $3.95-$7.95, dinner $7.95-$16.95. Child's meals. Specializes in prime rib, NY steak, seafood. Salad bar. Parking. New Orleans atmosphere; fountains, iron railings, Tiffany lampshades. Family-owned. Cr cds: A, C, D, DS, MC, V.

★ ★ **THE VIEW.** (See Marriott Key Bridge Hotel) 703/243-1745. Hrs: 5-10 pm; Fri to 11 pm; Sat 6-11 pm; early-bird dinner Sun-Thurs 5-7 pm; Sun brunch 10 am-2:30 pm. Closed Jan 1. Res accepted; required July 4. Bar. Wine list. Semi-a la carte: dinner $15.95-$22.95. Sun brunch $24.95. Specializes in seafood, steak. Own pastries. Parking. Excellent view of Washington across Potomac. Cr cds: A, C, D, DS, ER, JCB, MC, V.

[D] [SC]

★ **VILLAGE BISTRO.** *(1723 Wilson Blvd, Arlington 22209) 703/522-0284.* Hrs: 11:30 am-2:30 pm, 5-10:30 pm; Fri & Sat to 11 pm; Sun 5-10 pm; early-bird dinner 5-7 pm. Closed Thanksgiving, Dec 25. Res accepted; required Fri & Sat. Continental menu. Bar. A la carte entrees: lunch $5.50-$11.95, dinner $7.95-$15.95. Specializes in seafood, pasta, vegetarian dishes. Parking. Outdoor dining. Monet prints on walls. Cr cds: A, C, D, MC, V.

[D]

★★ **WOO LAE OAK.** *1500 S Joyce St, on grounds of River House complex. 703/521-3706.* Hrs: 11:30 am-10:30 pm. Closed Jan 1. Res accepted. Korean menu. Semi-a la carte: lunch, dinner $6-$16. Specialties: barbecued dishes prepared tableside. Parking. Large, open dining rm; Korean decor. Cr cds: A, C, D, MC, V.

Dulles Intl Airport Area, VA

Motels

★★ **COMFORT INN-DULLES NORTH.** *(200 Elden St, Herndon 22070) Dulles Toll Rd exit 3 then left on Baron Cameron Ave (VA 606). 703/437-7555; FAX 703/437-7572.* 103 rms, 3 story. S $67-$80; D $73-$84; each addl $6; under 19 free; wkend plans. TV; cable. Complimentary continental bkfst. Complimentary coffee in rms. Restaurant adj 11 am-10 pm. Ck-out noon. Meeting rms. Valet serv. Free airport transportation. Tennis privileges. Golf privileges. Exercise equipt; weights, bicycles. Refrigerators. Cr cds: A, C, D, DS, ER, JCB, MC, V.

[D] [X] [symbols] [SC]

★★ **HOLIDAY INN EXPRESS.** *(485 Elden St, Herndon 22070) Dulles Toll Rd exit 2, then E on Elden St. 703/478-9777; FAX 703/471-4624.* 116 rms, 4 story. S, D $67-$79; each addl $6; under 12 free; wkly rates. Crib free. Pet accepted, some restrictions; $3 per day. TV; cable. Complimentary coffee in rms. Complimentary continental bkfst. Restaurant nearby. Ck-out 11 am. Meeting rms. Valet serv. Free airport transportation. Health club privileges. Refrigerators avail. Cr cds: A, C, D, DS, JCB, MC, V.

[D] [symbols] [SC]

★★ **HOLIDAY INN WASHINGTON DULLES.** *(1000 Sully Rd, Sterling 20166) Dulles Toll Rd exit 1 (US 28/Sully Rd), then 1 mi N. 703/471-7411; FAX 703/471-7411, ext. 515.* 297 rms, 2 story. S $75-$115; D $85-$125; each addl $10; under 18 free; wkend rates. Crib free. TV; cable. Pool; lifeguard. Restaurant 6:30 am-10:30 pm. Rm serv. Bars 11-2 am, Sun to midnight; entertainment, dancing. Ck-out noon. Coin lndry. Meeting rms. Bellhops. Valet serv. Free airport transportation. Exercise equipt; weights, bicycles, whirlpool, sauna. Rec rm. Cr cds: A, C, D, DS, JCB, MC, V.

[D] [symbols] [SC]

★★ **RESIDENCE INN BY MARRIOTT.** *(315 Elden St, Herndon 22070) Dulles Toll Rd exit Reston Pkwy N, then left on Baron Cameron Rd (VA 606). 703/435-0044; FAX 703/437-4007.* 168 kit. units, 2 story. S, D $115-$145; Wkend rates. Crib free. Pet accepted; $100 non-refundable, $6/day. TV; cable. Pool; whirlpool, lifeguard. Playground. Complimentary continental bkfst. Complimentary coffee in rms. Restaurant opp 6:30 am-10 pm. Ck-out noon. Coin lndry. Valet serv. Sundries. Health club privileges. Picnic tables. Cr cds: A, C, D, DS, JCB, MC, V.

[D] [symbols] [SC]

Motor Hotel

✔★★ **DAYS INN DULLES AIRPORT.** *(2200 Centreville Rd, Herndon 22070) 2 mi E on Dulles Toll Rd, exit 2. 703/471-6700; FAX 703/742-8965.* 205 rms, 4 story. Apr-June, Sept-Oct: S, D $49-$129; each addl $10; under 18 free; wkend, monthly rates; lower rates rest of yr. Crib free. TV; cable. Pool; whirlpool, lifeguard. Restaurant 6 am-10 pm. Rm serv. Bar. Ck-out noon. Bellhops. Sundries. Gift shop. Free airport transportation. Tennis privileges, pro. Game rm. Cr cds: A, C, D, DS, MC, V.

[D] [symbols] [SC]

Hotels

★★★ **HYATT DULLES.** *(2300 Dulles Corner Blvd, Herndon 22071) Dulles Toll Rd exit 1 (VA 28/Sully Rd), then S, left on Frying Pan Rd, left on Horsepen Rd, then left on Dulles Corner Blvd. 703/713-1234; FAX 703/713-3410.* 317 rms, 14 story. S $125-$139; D $150-$164, suites $450; wkly, wkend rates. Crib free. TV; cable. Indoor pool; lifeguard. Restaurant 6 am-12 am. Bar 11:30 am-midnight; pianist. Ck-out noon. Free airport transportation. Exercise equipt; weights, bicycles, whirlpool, sauna. Cr cds: A, C, D, DS, ER, JCB, MC, V.

[D] [symbols] [SC]

★★★ **HYATT REGENCY-RESTON TOWN CENTER.** *(1800 President's St, Reston 22090) Dulles Toll Rd Reston Ave exit, at Reston Town Center. 703/709-1234; FAX 703/709-2291.* 514 rms, 12 story. S $150-$165; D $175-$190; each addl $25; suites $250-$500; under 18 free; wkend packages. Crib free. Garage parking; valet (fee). TV; cable. Indoor pool; poolside serv, lifeguard. Restaurant 6 am-midnight. Bar 11:30-2 am; entertainment Fri-Sun. Ck-out noon. Convention facilities. Concierge. Shopping arcade. Free airport transportation. Tennis, golf privileges. Exercise rm; instructor, weights, bicycles, whirlpool, sauna. *LUXURY LEVEL : REGENCY CLUB.* 72 rms, 6 suites, 2 floors. S, D $190-$215; suites $500-$1,000. Private lounge, honor bar. Some in-rm whirlpools. Complimentary continental bkfst, refreshments. Cr cds: A, C, D, DS, ER, JCB, MC, V.

[D] [symbols] [SC]

★★★ **MARRIOTT SUITES.** *(13101 Worldgate Dr, Herndon 22070) Dulles Toll Rd exit 2, in Worldgate Center. 703/709-0400; FAX 703/709-0434.* 254 suites, 11 story. S $140; D $155; under 18 free; wkend rates. Crib free. TV; cable. Indoor/outdoor pool; lifeguard. Complimentary coffee in rms. Restaurant 6:30 am-10:30 pm. Bar to 11 pm. Ck-out 1 pm. Free lndry facilities. Meeting rms. Free garage parking. Free airport transportation. Exercise equipt; weight machine, rowers, whirlpool, sauna. Health club privileges. Refrigerators, wet bars. Cr cds: A, C, D, DS, ER, JCB, MC, V.

[D] [symbols] [SC]

★★ **MARRIOTT WASHINGTON DULLES AIRPORT.** *(333 W Service Rd, Chantilly 22021) Dulles Access Rd, at airport. 703/471-9500; FAX 703/661-8714.* 370 rms, 3 story. S $109; D $124; each addl $15; suites $275-$300; under 18 free; wkend plans. Crib free. TV; cable. 2 pools, 1 indoor; poolside serv. Complimentary continental bkfst. Restaurant 6 am-midnight; Sat, Sun from 6:30 am. Bar 11:30-1 am. Ck-out noon. Coin lndry. Convention facilities. Concierge. Gift shop. Free airport transportation. Lighted tennis. Exercise equipt; weights, bicycles, whirlpool, sauna. Picnic area. On 21 acres with small lake; attractive landscaping. *LUXURY LEVEL : CONCIERGE LEVEL.* 23 rms, S, D $129-$144. Concierge. Private lounge, honor bar. Complimentary continental bkfst, refreshments. Cr cds: A, C, D, DS, ER, JCB, MC, V.

[D] [symbols] [SC]

✔★★ **RENAISSANCE-WASHINGTON DULLES.** *(13869 Park Center Rd, Herndon 22071) On Sully Rd (VA 28), Dulles Toll Rd exit 1, then 1 mi S to McLearen Rd. 703/478-2900; FAX 703/478-9286.* 301 rms, 5 story. S, D $89-$119; each addl $10; parlor rms $126; under 18 free; wkend rates. Crib free. Pet accepted, some restrictions. TV; cable. 2 pools, 1 indoor; poolside serv, lifeguard. Restaurant 6 am-11:30 pm.

Bars 11:30-1:30 am; entertainment exc Sun, dancing. Ck-out noon. Convention facilities. Gift shop. Barber, beauty shop. Free airport transportation. Indoor tennis, pro. Exercise equipt; weight machines, bicycles. Some bathrm phones, refrigerators. 3-story atrium; glass-enclosed lobby elvtrs. *LUXURY LEVEL : RENAISSANCE CLUB.* 65 rms, 2 floors. S, D $129. Concierge. Private lounge, honor bar. Full wet bars. Complimentary continental bkfst, refreshments, newspaper. Cr cds: A, C, D, DS, ER, JCB, MC, V.

D ⚡ ≈ 🕴 ✈ 🧍 ✕ 🚭 🔥 SC

✔ ★ ★ **SHERATON RESTON.** *(11810 Sunrise Valley Dr, Reston 22091) Off Dulles Toll Rd exit 3.* 703/620-9000; FAX 703/620-0696. 302 rms, 4 & 6 story. S $88-$108; D $90-$118; each addl $15; suites $150-$250; under 17 free; wkend rates. Crib free. TV; cable. Pool; lifeguard. Coffee in rms. Restaurant 6:30 am-10:30 pm. Bar 11-1 am; entertainment. Ck-out 1 pm. Convention facilities. Free airport transportation. Lighted tennis. Exercise equipt; weight machine, rower, sauna. Some minibars. Cr cds: A, C, D, DS, ER, MC, V.

D ⚡ ≈ 🕴 🧍 🚭 🔥 SC

Restaurants

★ ★ ★ **IL CIGNO.** *(1617 Washington Plaza, Reston 22090) In Lake Anne Shopping Center.* 703/471-0121. Hrs: 11:30 am-2:30 pm, 5:30-10 pm. Closed Sun (exc summer); most major hols. Res accepted; required Fri & Sat. Northern Italian menu. Bar. Semi-a la carte: lunch $4.95-$12.95, dinner $4.95-$17.95. Specializes in fish, veal, pasta. Outdoor dining overlooking Lake Anne. Split-level dining rm with original art. Cr cds: A, C, D, MC, V.

✔ ★ **TORTILLA FACTORY.** *(648 Elden St, Herndon) Off Dulles Toll Rd exit 2, Pines Shopping Center.* 703/471-1156. Hrs: 11 am-10 pm; Mon to 9 pm; Fri & Sat to 10:30 pm; Sun noon-9 pm. Closed most major hols. Res accepted. Mexican menu. Serv bar. Semi-a la carte: lunch $4.55-$6.50 dinner $5-$11.25. Child's meals. Specialties: carne machaca, chimichangas, vegetarian dishes. Own tortillas. Folk music Tues. Cr cds: A, C, D, DS, MC, V.

D SC

Bethesda, MD

Motor Hotel

★ **AMERICAN INN OF BETHESDA.** *8130 Wisconsin Ave (20814).* 301/656-9300; res: 800/323-7081; FAX 301/656-2907. 76 rms, 5 story. S $80; D $90; each addl $5; under 18 free; wkend, wkly, monthly rates. Crib free. Pet accepted. Complimentary continental bkfst. Restaurant 6:30-9:30 am, 11:30 am-10 pm; Fri, Sat to 11 pm; Sun to 9:30 pm. Ck-out 12:30 pm. Meeting rms. Sundries. Cr cds: A, C, D, DS, MC, V.

≈ 🚭 🔥 SC

Hotels

✔ ★ ★ **HOLIDAY INN-CHEVY CHASE.** *(5520 Wisconsin Ave, Chevy Chase 20815) S on Wisconsin Ave.* 301/656-1500; FAX 301/656-5045. 216 rms, 12 story. S, D $69-$129; each addl $10; suites $99-$149; under 18 free. Crib free. Pet accepted, some restrictions. TV; cable. Pool. Restaurant 6:30 am-11 pm. Bar. Ck-out 1 pm. Free lndry facilities. Meeting rms. Health club privileges. Bathrm phones. Cr cds: A, C, D, DS, ER, JCB, MC, V.

D 🐾 ≈ 🚭 🔥 SC

★ ★ ★ **HYATT REGENCY.** *One Bethesda Metro Center (20814).* 301/657-1234; FAX 301/657-6453. 381 rms, 12 story. S $149; D $174; each addl $20; suites $175-$600; under 18 free; wkend rates.

Crib free. Covered parking $10; valet $12. TV; cable. Indoor pool; lifeguard. Restaurant 6:30 am-11:30 pm. Bar 11:30-12:30 am. Ck-out noon. Convention facilities. Exercise equipt; bicycles, rowing machine, sauna. Bathrm phones. Private patios, balconies. 12-story atrium lobby; extensive collection of artwork. *LUXURY LEVEL : GOLD PASSPORT.* 657-1234, ext 6532. 50 rms, 2 floors. S, D $165-$190. Concierge. Private lounge. Cr cds: A, C, D, DS, ER, JCB, MC, V.

D ≈ 🕴 🧍 🚭 🔥 SC

★ ★ ★ **MARRIOTT.** *5151 Pooks Hill Rd (20814), 1 blk S of I-495 exit 34.* 301/897-9400; FAX 301/897-0192. 407 rms, 4-16 story. S $95-$160; D $105-$180; each addl $10; suites $275-$700; under 18 free; wkend plan. Crib free. Pet accepted. TV; cable. 2 pools, 1 indoor; poolside serv, lifeguard. Restaurants 6:30 am-10 pm. Rm serv to 1 am. Bar 11:30 am-midnight; entertainment. Ck-out noon. Convention facilities. Gift shops. Barber. Lighted tennis. Exercise equipt; weight machines, bicycles, whirlpool, sauna. Game rm. Some balconies. On 18 landscaped acres. *LUXURY LEVEL : CONCIERGE LEVEL.* 47 rms. S $145-$165; D $175-$185. Concierge. Private lounge, honor bar. Complimentary continental bkfst, refreshments, newspaper. Cr cds: A, C, D, DS, ER, JCB, MC, V.

D ⚡ ≈ 🧍 🚭 🔥 SC

★ ★ ★ **MARRIOTT SUITES.** *6711 Democracy Blvd (20817).* 301/897-5600; FAX 301/530-1427. 274 suites, 11 story. Suites $165-$250; family rates. Crib free. Pet accepted, some restrictions. TV; cable. Indoor/outdoor pool; poolside serv, lifeguard. Complimentary continental bkfst. Complimentary coffee in rms. Restaurant 6:30 am-10:30 pm. Bar noon-midnight. Ck-out 1 pm. Meeting rms. Metro station transportation. Tennis privileges. Exercise rm: instructor, weights, bicycles, whirlpool. Refrigerators, wet bars. Balconies. Cr cds: A, C, D, DS, ER, JCB, MC, V.

D 🐾 🕴 ≈ 🧍 🧍 🚭 🔥 SC

★ ★ **RESIDENCE INN BY MARRIOTT.** *7335 Wisconsin Ave (20814).* 301/718-0200; FAX 301/718-0679. 187 kit suites, 13 story. S, D $149-$199; each addl $5; under 16 free; wkend, wkly & extended stay rates. Crib free. Pet accepted; $100 and $5 per day. Valet parking $10. TV; cable. Pool; lifeguard. Complimentary continental bkfst. Complimentary coffee in rms. Restaurant adj 6:30 am-10 pm. Ck-out noon. Coin lndry. Meeting rms. Exercise equipt; weight machine, bicycles, sauna. Rec rm. Cr cds: A, C, D, DS, JCB, MC, V.

D 🐾 ≈ 🧍 🚭 🔥 SC

Restaurants

★ ★ **BACCHUS.** *7945 Norfolk Ave.* 301/657-1722. Hrs: noon-2:30 pm, 6-10 pm; Fri to 10:30 pm; Sat 6-10:30 pm; Sun 6-10 pm. Closed Jan 1, Labor Day. Res accepted; required Fri, Sat. Lebanese menu. Serv bar. Complete meals: lunch $8. A la carte entrees: dinner $16-$25. Specializes in falafel, shish kebab. Valet parking. Cr cds: A, MC, V.

★ ★ **BUON GIORNO.** *8003 Norfolk Ave.* 301/652-1400. Hrs: 11:30 am-2:30 pm, 5:30-10 pm; Fri to 10:30 pm; Sat 5:30-10:30 pm; Sun 5:30-10 pm. Closed Mon; Jan 1, Thanksgiving, Dec 25; also mid-Aug-mid-Sept. Res accepted; required Fri, Sat. Italian menu. Serv bar. Semi-a la carte: lunch $4.50-$13.95, dinner $5.25-$19.95. Specialties: veal Marsala, trenette alla Genovese, pappardelle alla contadina, fresh fish. Own pasta. Cr cds: A, C, D, MC, V.

D

★ ★ **COTTONWOOD CAFE.** *4844 Cordell Ave.* 301/656-4844. Hrs: 11:30 am-10 pm; Fri & Sat to 11 pm; Sun 5:30-10 pm. Closed Jan 1, July 4 & Thanksgiving. Res accepted. Southwestern menu. Bar. Semi-a la carte: lunch $5.75-$11.95, dinner $12.65-$19.75. Specializes in grilled meats, seafood. Valet parking (dinner). Outdoor dining. Southwestern atmosphere. Mural of adobe village. Cr cds: A, MC, V.

✔★ **FOONG LIN.** 7710 Norfolk Ave. 301/656-3427. Hrs: 11 am-10:30 pm; Fri, Sat to 11 pm. Closed Thanksgiving. Res accepted. Chinese menu. Serv bar. Semi-a la carte: lunch $4.50-$7.50, dinner $7.25-$17.95. Specializes in fresh fish, Peking duckling, crispy beef. Cr cds: A, MC, V.

D

★★ **FRASCATI RISTORANTE ITALIANO.** 4806 Rugby Ave. 301/652-9514. Hrs: 11 am-2:30 pm, 4-10:30 pm; Sat from 5 pm; Sun 4-9:30 pm; early-bird dinner Tues-Fri & Sun 4-6:30 pm. Closed Mon; Jan 1, Easter, Dec 25. Res accepted; required Fri, Sat. Italian menu. Semi-a la carte: lunch $4.75-$8, dinner $9.75-$15.95. Child's meals. Specializes in fresh fish, veal, pasta. Cr cds: A, C, D, DS, MC, V.

D

★★ **LA MICHE.** 7905 Norfolk Ave. 301/986-0707. Hrs: 11:30 am-2:30 pm, 6-10 pm; Sat from 6 pm. Closed Sun; major hols. Res required Fri, Sat. French menu. Serv bar. A la carte entrees: lunch $6-$17, dinner $13-$24. Specialties: soufflés, fricassee of lobster, grilled breast of duck. Valet parking (dinner). Outdoor dining. Country French decor. Cr cds: A, C, D, MC, V.

★★ **LA VIEUX LOGIS.** 7925 Old Georgetown Rd. 301/652-6816. Hrs: 11:30 am-2 pm, 5:30-10 pm; Sat from 5:30 pm. Closed Sun; Jan 1, Dec 25. Res accepted; required Sat. French, Scandinavian menu. Serv bar. Wine list. A la carte entrees: lunch $8.75-$13.75, dinner $11.75-$19.95. Specialties: rack of lamb, vol au vont with lobster & Swedish meatballs. Valet parking. Rustic French inn atmosphere. Cr cds: A, C, D, MC, V.

D

★★ **O'DONNELL'S.** 8301 Wisconsin Ave. 301/656-6200. Hrs: 11:30 am-10 pm; Fri, Sat to 10:30 pm; Sun noon-9:30 pm. Closed Dec 25. Res accepted. Bar. Semi-a la carte: lunch $4.95-$9.95, dinner $11.95-$28.95. Child's meals. Specializes in seafood, rum buns. Parking. Nautical theme. Family-owned. Cr cds: A, C, D, DS, MC, V.

D

✔★ **PERSEPOLIS.** 7130 Wisconsin Ave. 301/656-9339. Hrs: noon-11 pm. Res accepted; required Fri & Sat. Persian menu. Bar. A la carte entrees: lunch, dinner $6.95-$12.95. Lunch buffet $6.95. Specializes in kebab, grilled meats, seafood. Cr cds: A, C, D, MC, V.

D

★★★ **ST ELMO'S CAFE.** 7820 Norfolk Ave. 301/657-1607. Hrs: 11:30 am-2 pm, 5:30-10 pm; Sat-Mon from 5:30 pm. Closed Jan 1, Dec 25. Res accepted. French menu. Serv bar. A la carte entrees: lunch $6-$14; dinner $12.95-$21.95. Complete meals: dinner $24.95 & $34.95. Specializes in grilled seafood, rack of lamb coated with mustard. Own desserts. Valet parking (dinner). Patio dining. Cr cds: A, C, D, DS, MC, V.

✔★ **TAKO GRILL.** 7756 Wisconsin Ave. 301/652-7030. Hrs: 11:30 am-2 pm, 5:30-9:45 pm; Fri & Sat to 10:15 pm. Closed Sun; most major hols. Japanese menu. Serv bar. Semi-a la carte: lunch $5.50-$8.75, dinner $7.95-$15.50. Specializes in seafood, sushi, robatayaki. Blend of Eastern and Western ambiance; Japanese prints. Cr cds: A, MC, V.

D

✔★ **TEQUILA SUNRISE CAFE.** 7940 Wisconsin Ave. 301/907-6536. Hrs: 11:30 am-10 pm; Fri, Sat to 11 pm. Closed Jan 1, Thanksgiving, Dec 25. Res accepted Fri, Sat. Mexican menu. Bar to 1 am; Fri, Sat to 2 am. Semi-a la carte: lunch $3.25-$13.95, dinner $3.50-$15.95. Child's meals. Specializes in fajitas, chimichangas. Entertainment. Outdoor dining. Mexican/Caribbean cantina atmosphere. Cr cds: A, C, D, MC, V.

★★★ **TERRAMAR.** 7800 Wisconsin Ave. 301/654-0888. Hrs: 11:30 am-2:30 pm, 5-10 pm; Fri to 11 pm; Sat 5-11 pm; Sun 5-9 pm. Closed Mon; some major hols. Res accepted; required Fri, Sat. Nicaraguan, Latin American menu. Bar. A la carte entrees: lunch $5.95-$7.95, dinner $10.95-$18.50. Specializes in tapas, churrasco, grilled seafood.

Entertainment Fri & Sat eves. Indoor courtyard dining. Cr cds: A, D, DS, MC, V.

D

✔★ **THAI PLACE.** 4828 Cordell Ave. 301/951-0535. Hrs: 11 am-3 pm, 5-10 pm; Fri, Sat to 10:30 pm; Sun 11 am-10 pm. Closed Thanksgiving, Dec 25. Thai menu. Serv bar. Semi-a la carte: lunch $5.75-$6.50, dinner $6.50-$11. Specializes in steamed fish, Thai curry, Pad Thai. Cr cds: A, MC, V.

D

★★★ **TRAGARA.** 4935 Cordell Ave. 301/951-4935. Hrs: 11:45 am-2:30 pm, 6-10:30 pm; Sat & Sun from 6 pm. Closed Dec 25. Res accepted; required Fri, Sat. Italian menu. Semi-a la carte: lunch $8.95-$10.95. A la carte entrees: dinner $15.95-$25. Specialties: veal scaloppini, linguine with Maine lobster, lamb chops sauteed with herbs and mustard. Own pastries. Valet parking (dinner). Italian marble, original paintings, chandelier. Cr cds: A, C, D, MC, V.

D

★★ **VAGABOND.** 7315 Wisconsin Ave. 301/654-2575. Hrs: 11:30 am-2:30 pm, 5:30-10 pm, Fri to 10:30 pm; Sat 6-10:30 pm. Closed Sun. Central European menu. Res accepted. Bar. Semi-a la carte: lunch $6.95-$9.95, dinner $9.95-$19.95. Specializes in Romanian, Austro-Hungarian & Russian dishes. Strolling musicians Fri, Sat. Parking. Old World atmosphere. Cr cds: A, C, D, DS, MC, V.

Unrated Dining Spot

BETHESDA CRAB HOUSE. 4958 Bethesda Ave. 301/652-3382. Hrs: 9 am-midnight. Closed Dec 25. Res accepted. Wine, beer. A la carte entrees: lunch, dinner $10-$30. Serves only spiced shrimp, steamed crab, crabcakes. Outdoor dining. Rustic decor; established 1961. No cr cds accepted.

College Park, MD

Motels

★★ **COURTYARD BY MARRIOTT.** (8330 Corporate Dr, Landover 20785) 1/2 mi W of I-95 exit 19B, on US 50. 301/577-3373; FAX 301/577-1780. 150 rms, 3-4 story. S $92; D $102; each addl (over 4 persons) $10; suites $105-$115; under 12 free; wkly, wkend rates. Crib free. TV; cable. Indoor pool; lifeguard. Restaurant 6:30 am-2 pm, 5-10 pm. Bar. Ck-out 1 pm. Coin lndry. Meeting rms. Valet serv. Exercise equipt; weights, bicycles, whirlpool. Many private patios, balconies. Cr cds: A, C, D, DS, MC, V.

D ≈ ✕ ⊠ 🔥 SC

✔★ **RAMADA INN-CALVERTON.** (4050 Powder Mill Rd, Beltsville 20705) Off I-95 exit 29B at MD 212. 301/572-7100; FAX 301/572-8078. 168 rms in 2 bldgs, 1-4 story, 11 kits. S $68-$79; D $75-$80; kit. units $75-$85; under 18 free; wkend plan. Crib free. Pet accepted. TV; cable. Pool; wading pool, poolside serv, lifeguard. Playground. Restaurant 6 am-11 pm; Sat from 7 am; Sun 7-11:30 am, 5-10 pm. Rm serv. Bar 11-2 am; Sun from noon. Ck-out 11 am. Meeting rms. Gift shop. Exercise equipt; weight machine, bicycles. Cr cds: A, C, D, DS, ER, JCB, MC, V.

D ✇ ≈ ✕ ⊠ 🔥 SC

Hotels

★★ **HOLIDAY INN.** 10000 Baltimore Blvd. 301/345-6700; FAX 301/441-4923. 222 rms in 2 bldgs, 4 story. S, D $74-$84; each addl $6; under 18 free. Crib free. Pet accepted, some restrictions; $50 refundable. TV; cable. Indoor pool; poolside serv, lifeguard. Restaurant 6:30 am-10 pm. Bar 11-2 am. Ck-out noon. Coin lndry. Meeting rms.

Gift shop. Exercise equipt; weights, bicycles, whirlpool, sauna. Refrigerators avail. Cr cds: A, C, D, DS, ER, JCB, MC, V.

[D] [icons] SC

✔★★ **HOLIDAY INN-CALVERTON.** *(4095 Powder Mill Rd, Beltsville 20705) I-95 exit 29B.* 301/937-4422; FAX 301/937-4455. 206 rms, 9 story. S, D $70-$85; each $6; suites $150-$175; under 18 free; wkly, wkend rates; higher rates Cherry Blossom. Crib free. TV; cable. Pool; lifeguard. Complimentary coffee in rms. Restaurant 6:30 am-11:30 pm; wkends from 7 am. No rm serv 2-5 pm. Bar. Ck-out noon. Coin lndry. Meeting rms. Gift shop. 18-hole golf privileges. Game rm. Cr cds: A, C, D, DS, JCB, MC, V.

[D] [icons] SC

★★★ **MARRIOTT GREENBELT.** *(6400 Ivy Lane, Greenbelt 20770) 2 blks N of I-95 exit 23 (Kenilworth Ave N).* 301/441-3700; FAX 301/474-9128. 283 rms, 18 story. S $80-$117; D $80-$127; family, wkend rates. Crib free. Pet accepted. TV; cable. 2 pools, 1 indoor; poolside serv, lifeguard. Restaurant 6:30 am-11 pm. Bar. Games. Ck-out noon. Convention facilities. Gift shop. Lighted tennis. Exercise equipt; weights, bicycles, whirlpool, sauna. Some bathrm phones, refrigerators. Elegantly appointed rms. *LUXURY LEVEL : CONCIERGE FLOORS.* 52 rms, 3 floors. S $114; D $129; suites $250-$350. Private lounge. Some wet bars. Complimentary continental bkfst, newspaper, refreshments. Cr cds: A, C, D, DS, ER, JCB, MC, V.

[D] [icons] SC

Restaurants

✔★ **ALAMO.** *(5508 Kenilworth Ave, Riverdale) S on US 201; 3 mi S of I-95 exit 23.* 301/927-8787. Hrs: 11 am-11 pm. Closed Thanksgiving. Res accepted. Mexican menu. Bar. Semi-a la carte: lunch $5-$7, dinner $8.30-$12.95. Child's meals. Specializes in tostadas, tacos, enchiladas. Entertainment Tues-Sat. Parking. Mexican decor. Cr cds: A, C, D, MC, V.

[D]

★★★ **CHEF'S SECRET.** *(5810 Greenbelt Rd, Greenbelt)* 301/345-6101. Hrs: 11:30 am-2:30 pm, 5-10 pm; Sat from 4:30 pm; Sun 4:30-9 pm. Closed Thanksgiving, Dec 25; also Sun in July-Aug. Res accepted. Continental menu. Serv bar. Semi-a la carte: lunch $5.95-$12.95, dinner $9.95-$24.95. Specializes in seafood, veal, steak. Own desserts. Cr cds: A, C, D, MC, V.

[D]

Fairfax, VA

Motels

★★★ **COURTYARD BY MARRIOTT-FAIR OAKS.** *11220 Lee Jackson Hwy (US 50) (22030).* 703/273-6161; FAX 703/273-3505. 144 rms, 3 story. S, D $69-$79; suites $75-$100; under 13 free; wkly, wkend rates. Crib free. TV; cable. Indoor pool; lifeguard. Complimentary coffee in rms. Restaurant 6:30-11 am. Bar 4-11 pm. Ck-out 1 pm. Coin lndry. Meeting rms. Valet serv. Sundries. Exercise equipt; weights, bicycles, whirlpool. Some refrigerators. Private patios, balconies. Cr cds: A, C, D, DS, MC, V.

[D] [icons] SC

★★ **HAMPTON INN.** *10860 Lee Hwy (22030).* 703/385-2600; FAX 703/385-2742. 86 rms, 5 story. S $68-$78; D $73-$83; under 18 free. Crib free. TV; cable. Complimentary coffee in rms. Complimentary continental bkfst. Restaurant adj 7 am-11 pm. Ck-out noon. Meeting rms. Exercise equipt; treadmill, stair machine. Some refrigerators, wet bars. Cr cds: A, C, D, DS, MC, V.

[D] [icons] SC

Motor Hotel

✔★★ **COMFORT INN-UNIVERSITY CENTER.** *11180 Main St (22030).* 703/591-5900; FAX 703/591-5900, ext. 133. 212 rms, 2-6 story, 125 kit. units. S $57-$95; D $67-$95; each addl $10; kit. units $10 addl; under 18 free; wkend rates. Crib free. Pet accepted, some restrictions; $15. TV; cable. Heated pool; poolside serv, lifeguard. Complimentary continental bkfst. Restaurant 11 am-11 pm. Rm serv. Bar. Ck-out 11 am. Coin lndry. Meeting rms. Bellhops. Valet serv. Lighted tennis. Exercise equipt; weight machine, bicycles. Game rm. Some in-rm whirlpools, wet bars. Picnic tables. Cr cds: A, C, D, DS, ER, JCB, MC, V.

[D] [icons] SC

Hotels

★★ **HOLIDAY INN FAIR OAKS MALL.** *11787 Lee Jackson Hwy (22033).* 703/352-2525; FAX 703/352-4471. 245 rms, 6 story. S $97; D $103; each addl $6; under 19 free; wkend, hol rates. Crib free. Pet accepted, some restrictions. TV; cable. Indoor pool; lifeguard. Complimentary coffee in rms. Restaurant 6:30 am-10 pm. Bar; entertainment. Ck-out noon. Coin lndry. Convention facilities. Concierge. Gift shop. Free airport transportation. Exercise equipt; weight machine, bicycles, sauna. Health club privileges. Game rm. Balconies. *LUXURY LEVEL : CONCIERGE LEVEL.* 62 rms, 5 suites. S $110; D $116; suites $150-$225. Concierge. Private lounge, honor bar. Complimentary continental bkfst, refreshments. Cr cds: A, C, D, DS, ER, JCB, MC, V.

[D] [icons] SC

★★ **HYATT FAIR LAKES.** *12777 Fair Lakes Circle (22033), at I-66 exit 55.* 703/818-1234; FAX 703/818-3140. 316 rms, 14 story. S $120; D $145; each addl $25; suites $120-$375; under 18 free; wkend rates. Crib free. Pet accepted, some restrictions. TV; cable. Indoor pool; lifeguard. Restaurant 6:30 am-11 pm. Bar 11:30-1 am; entertainment. Ck-out noon. Convention facilities. Free airport, RR station, transportation. Exercise equipt; weights, bicycles, whirlpool, sauna. Refrigerators avail. Cr cds: A, C, D, DS, ER, JCB, MC, V.

[D] [icons] SC

Inn

★★★ **BAILIWICK.** *4023 Chain Bridge Rd (VA 123) (22030).* 703/691-2266; res: 800/366-7666; FAX 703/934-2112. 14 rms, some rms with shower only, 4 story. No elvtr. Rm phones avail. S, D $130-$275. Complimentary full bkfst, tea. Ck-out 11 am, ck-in 2 pm. Some in-rm whirlpools, fireplaces. Restored private residence (1800); antiques. An early Civil War skirmish occured here (June, 1861). Totally nonsmoking. Cr cds: A, MC, V.

[D] [icons] SC

Restaurants

★★ **ARTIE'S.** *3260 Old Lee Hwy.* 703/273-7600. Hrs: 11:30-2 am; Sun from 10:30 am; Sun brunch to 3 pm. Closed Thanksgiving, Dec 25. Bar. Semi-a la carte: lunch $5.95-$8.95, dinner $5.95-$18.95. Sun brunch $5.25-$9.75. Specializes in steak, seafood, pasta. Parking. Cr cds: A, MC, V.

[D]

★★ **BAILIWICK INN.** *(See Bailiwick)* 703/691-2266. Hrs: 6-9 pm. Closed Mon & Tues. Res required. Continental menu. Wine cellar. Complete meals: dinner $45; Fri & Sat $55. Specializes in seafood, poultry, beef. Parking. Patio dining overlooking English garden. In restored inn (1800). Cr cds: A, MC, V.

★★ **HEART-IN-HAND.** *(7145 Main St, Clifton) S on VA 123 to Chapel Rd, then W.* 703/830-4111. Hrs: 11 am-2:30 pm, 6-9:30 pm; Sun 5-8 pm; Sun brunch 11 am-2:30 pm. Closed Jan 1, July 4, Dec 25.

Res accepted. Semi-a la carte: lunch $5.95-$10.95, dinner $13.95-$22.95. Sun brunch $6.95-$12.95. Child's meals. Specializes in seafood, beef Wellington, rack of lamb. Own ice cream. Parking. Outdoor dining. Converted general store (ca 1870). Antique decor; original floors, ceiling fans, antique quilts. Cr cds: A, C, D, DS, MC, V.

★ ★ ★ **HERMITAGE INN.** (7134 Main St, Clifton) W on US 29 to Clifton Rd (VA 645), then S. 703/266-1623. Hrs: 11:30 am-2:30 pm, 6-10 pm; Sun 11 am-3 pm, 5-9 pm. Closed Mon; Jan 1, Dec 25. Res accepted. French menu. Semi-a la carte: lunch $7.25-$11, dinner $14.25-$22.95. Sun brunch $17.95. Specializes in rack of lamb, Dover sole, châteaubriand. Own pastries. Parking. Outdoor dining. Located in 1869 clapboard hotel. Country French decor. Cr cds: A, C, D, DS, MC, V.

D

★ ★ **J.R.'S STEAK HOUSE.** 9401 Lee Hwy, in Circle Towers office building. 703/591-8447. Hrs: 5:30-9:30 pm; Fri, Sat to 10:30 pm; Sun 5-9:30 pm. Closed Mon; Thanksgiving, Dec 25. Res accepted. Bar. Semi-a la carte: dinner $12.95-$22.95. Child's meals. Specializes in aged steak, grilled meat and fish. Salad bar. Parking. Patio dining. Cr cds: A, C, D, DS, MC, V.

D

✔ ★ **P.J. SKIDOO'S.** 9908 Lee Hwy. 703/591-4516. Hrs: 11-2 am; Sun 10 am-9 pm. Closed Jan 1, Thanksgiving, Dec 25. Bar. Semi-a la carte: lunch, dinner $4.95-$12.95. Sun brunch $7.95. Child's meals. Specializes in salads, steak, fresh seafood, chicken. Entertainment Tues-Sat from 10 pm. Parking. 1890s saloon atmosphere. Cr cds: A, MC, V.

★ ★ **SHUN LEE.** 10195 Lee Hwy. 703/273-2800. Hrs: 11:30 am-3 pm, 5-10 pm; Fri, Sat to 11 pm; Sun brunch noon-3 pm. Closed Thanksgiving, Dec 25. Chinese menu. Bar. Semi-a la carte: lunch $4.50-$5.75, dinner $5.50-$18. Lunch buffet $5.95. Sun brunch $6.95. Specializes in seafood in a bird's nest, two season lamb, sesame chicken. Parking. Outdoor dining. Cr cds: A, MC, V.

✔ ★ **TRES AMIGOS.** 10900 Lee Hwy. 703/352-9393. Hrs: 11:30 am-11 pm. Closed Thanksgiving, Dec 25. Mexican menu. Bar to 2 am. Semi-a la carte: lunch, dinner $3.50-$11.50. Child's meals. Specializes in fajitas, enchiladas. Entertainment Thurs-Sat evenings. Outdoor dining. Parking. Cr cds: MC, V.

D SC

Unrated Dining Spot

THE ESPOSITOS/PIZZA 'N PASTA. 9917 Lee Hwy. 703/385-5912. Hrs: 11 am-11 pm; Fri to midnight; Sat noon-midnight; Sun noon-11 pm. Closed Thanksgiving, Dec 24 evening, 25. Southern Italian menu. Wine, beer. A la carte entrees: lunch, dinner $3.50-$11.50. Semi-a la carte: lunch $5.50-$12.95, dinner $6.25-$13.95. Specialties: pollo cardinale, fettucine alla Romano. Own pasta. Parking. Pizza baked in wood-burning oven imported from Italy. Italian trattoria decor. Cr cds: A, C, D, MC, V.

D

McLean, VA

Restaurants

✔ ★ **ANGKOR WAT.** 6703 Lowell Ave, at Old Dominion Dr (VA 309), in shopping center. 703/893-6077. Hrs: 11 am-2:30 pm, 5-9:30 pm; Fri, Sat to 10 pm; Sun 5-9:30 pm. Closed some major hols. Res accepted. Far Eastern menu. Wine, beer. Semi-a la carte: lunch $5.25-$6.95, dinner $6.95-$9.95. Complete meals: dinner $12.99. Specializes in Cambodian soup, char-broiled dishes, kuong. Cr cds: A, C, D, MC, V.

★ ★ **CHARLEY'S PLACE.** 6930 Old Dominion Dr, jct VA 123 & VA 309/738. 703/893-1034. Hrs: 11:15 am-10 pm; Fri, Sat to 10:30 pm; Sun 10:30 am-9 pm; early-bird dinner 4-6:30 pm. Sun brunch 10:30 am-2 pm. Closed Dec 25. Res accepted. Bar to 1 am. Semi-a la carte: lunch $5.95-$10.95, dinner $5.95-$18.95. Child's meals. Specialties: regional dishes. Outdoor dining. Parking. Fireplaces. Cr cds: A, C, D, DS, MC, V.

D

★ ★ ★ **DANTE RISTORANTE.** (1148 Walker Rd, Great Falls) 703/759-3131. Hrs: 11:30 am-2:30 pm, 5:30-10:30 pm; Sat from 5:30 pm; Sun 4-9 pm. Closed Jan 1, Thanksgiving, Dec 25. Res accepted; required Fri, Sat. Northern Italian menu. Bar. Wine list. A la carte entrees: lunch $8.25-$14.25, dinner $13.25-$21.95. Child's meals. Specialties: grilled Dover sole, grilled veal chops. Own pasta & bread. Parking. Patio dining. Converted country house. Cr cds: A, C, D, MC, V.

D

★ ★ ★ **EVANS FARM INN.** 1696 Chain Bridge Rd. 703/356-8000. Hrs: 11:30 am-2:30 pm, 5-11 pm; Sat 11:30 am-3 pm, 5-11 pm; Sun 11 am-9 pm; Sun brunch to 2 pm. Closed Dec 25. Res accepted; required Fri-Sun. Bar to 11 pm; Fri, Sat to midnight. Semi-a la carte: lunch $8.95-$10.95, dinner $12.95-$23.95. Buffet (Mon-Fri): lunch $9.95. Sun brunch $6.95-$12.25. Child's meals. Specializes in barbecued baby spare ribs, Virginia ham, fresh seafood, colonial-era cooking. Own baking. Salad bar. Parking. 18th century-style inn. Family-owned. Cr cds: A, C, D, DS, JCB, MC, V.

D

★ ★ ★ **FALLS LANDING.** (774 Walker Rd, Great Falls) I-495 exit 13A, in Village Center. 703/759-4650. Hrs: 11:30 am-2:30 pm, 5:30-10 pm; Fri to 10:30 pm; Sat 5:30-10:30 pm; Sun 4-9 pm. Closed most major hols. Res accepted. Bar. Semi-a la carte: lunch $8.95-$12.95, dinner $16.95-$24.95. Child's meals. Specializes in seafood, veal, beef. Outdoor dining. 18th-century colonial-style decor; beamed ceiling, century-old pine paneling. Cr cds: A, C, D, DS, MC, V.

D

★ ★ ★ ★ **L'AUBERGE CHEZ FRANCOIS.** (332 Springvale Rd, Great Falls) 4 mi N of jct VA 7 & 674N. 703/759-3800. Hrs: 5:30-9:30 pm; Sun 2-8 pm. Closed Mon; Jan 1, July 4, Dec 25. Res required. French menu. Serv bar. Wine cellar. Table d'hôte: dinner $30-$36. Specialties: salmon soufflé de l'Auberge, le sauté gourmandise de l'Auberge, la choucroute royale garnie comme en Alsace, Alsatian dishes. Own baking, ice cream. Outdoor dining. Chef-owned. Jacket. Cr cds: A, C, D, MC, V.

D

★ ★ ★ **LA MIRABELLE.** 6645 Old Dominion Dr, in McLean Square Shopping Ctr. 703/893-8484. Hrs: 11:30 am-2 pm, 5-9 pm; Sat from 5 pm; Sun 5-8 pm. Closed major hols; also Sun May-mid-Oct. French menu. Bar. A la carte entrees: lunch $8.95-$16.75, dinner $14.95-$22. Specialties vary with season: seafood, venison (Nov, Dec), goose (Christmas). Own desserts. Pianist Mon-Fri. Parking. Cr cds: A, C, D, DS, MC, V.

★ ★ ★ **SERBIAN CROWN.** (1141 Walker Rd, Great Falls) 5 mi W on VA 7, then 1/2 mi N on VA 743. 703/759-4150. Hrs: 11:30 am-2:30 pm, 5:30-10 pm; Mon from 5:30 pm; Sat 5:30-11 pm; Sun 4-9:30 pm; early-bird dinner Mon-Fri 5:30-6:45 pm. Res accepted; required Fri-Sun. Russian, Serbian, French menu. Bar. Wine list. A la carte entrees: lunch $9.50-$15.95, dinner $16.95-$26. Specialties: kulebiaka (Russian salmon), seasonal game. Extensive vodka selection. Gypsy music Wed-Sun. Parking. Intimate atmosphere; antique Russian paintings. Enclosed, heated terrace dining. Family-owned. Jacket. Cr cds: A, MC, V.

D

★ ★ **SITTING DUCK PUB.** 1696 Chain Bridge Rd (22102), in basement of Evans Farm Inn Restaurant. 703/356-8000. Hrs: 11:30 am-2 pm, 5-11 pm; Sat from 5 pm; Sun 11 am-2 pm. Closed Dec 25.

Res accepted. Continental menu. Bar. Semi-a la carte: lunch $7.95-$10.95, dinner $13.95-$23.95. Sun brunch $7.25-$9.95. Specializes in barbecue, beef, seafood. Pianist Fri-Sun. Parking. Large stone fireplace. Colonial-era prints. Family-owned. Cr cds: A, C, D, DS, JCB, MC, V.

Rockville, MD

Motels

★ ★ **COURTYARD BY MARRIOTT.** *2500 Research Blvd (20850). 301/670-6700; FAX 301/670-9023.* 147 rms, 3 story, 14 suites. S $89; D $99; each addl (over 4) $10; suites $108-$118; under 12 free; wkly rates. Crib free. TV; cable. Indoor pool; lifeguard. Complimentary coffee. Restaurant 6:30 am-2 pm, 5-10 pm, wknds to 2 pm. Rm serv from 5 pm. Bar 11 am-11 pm. Ck-out 1 pm. Coin lndry. Meeting rms. Valet serv. Sundries. Exercise equipt; weight machine, bicycles, whirlpool. Balconies. Refrigerators avail. Cr cds: A, C, D, DS, MC, V.

🅳 ⊠ 🏋 🏊 🔥 SC

✔★ **DAYS INN.** *16001 Shady Grove Rd (20850). 301/948-4300.* 190 rms, 2 story. S, D $45-$70; each addl $5; under 18 free; wkend rates. Crib free. Pet accepted. TV; cable. Pool. Playground. Restaurant 6:30 am-10 pm. Bar 10-12:30 am, Sun from 11 am. Ck-out 11 am. Cr cds: A, C, D, DS, MC, V.

🅳 🐾 ⊠ 🏊 🔥 SC

Motor Hotel

★ ★ **WOODFIN SUITES.** *1380 Piccard Dr (20850). 301/590-9880; res: 800/237-8811; FAX 301/590-9614.* 203 suites, 3 story. S, D $120-$151; each addl $15; 2-bedrm suites $187; under 12 free. Crib $10. TV; in-rm movies. Pool; lifeguard. Complimentary full bkfst. Restaurant 6-9 am, 11:30 am-2 pm, 5-10 pm, wknd hrs vary. Bar from 5 pm. Ck-out noon. Meeting rms. Valet serv. Sundries. Free local transportation. Exercise equipt; weight machine, treadmill, whirlpool. Refrigerators avail. Cr cds: A, C, D, DS, ER, JCB, MC, V.

🅳 ⊠ 🏊 🏋 🔥 SC

Hotel

★ ★ **HOLIDAY INN CROWNE PLAZA.** *1750 Rockville Pike (20852). 301/468-1100; FAX 301/468-0163.* 315 rms, 8 story. S $130-$135; D $145-$155; each addl $10; suites $195-$300; under 19 free; wkly, wkend rates. Crib free. TV; cable. Indoor/outdoor pool; lifeguard. Restaurant 6:30-1 am. Bar 11-1 am; Fri, Sat to 2 am. Ck-out noon. Convention facilities. Concierge. Gift shop. Beauty shop. Covered parking, valet. Exercise rm; instructor, weights, bicycles, whirlpool, sauna. Refrigerators avail. 8-story atrium; 20-ft waterfall. Gazebo. **LUXURY LEVEL : EXECUTIVE LEVEL.** 68 units. S $150-$160; D $165-$175; suites $250. Concierge. Private lounge. Free continental bkfst, refreshments. Cr cds: A, C, D, DS, ER, JCB, MC, V.

🅳 ⊠ 🏋 🏊 🔥 SC

Restaurants

★ ★ **ANDALUCIA.** *12300 Wilkins Ave (20852). 301/770-1880.* Hrs: 11:30 am-2:30 pm, 5:30-10 pm; Sat 5:30-10:30 pm; Sun 4:30-9:30 pm. Closed Mon; some major hols. Res accepted; required Fri & Sat. Spanish menu. Bar. Semi-a la carte: lunch $7.50-$10.95, dinner $11.50-$16.95. Specializes in seafood, lamb, paella zarzuela. Parking. Spanish decor, atmosphere. Cr cds: A, DS, MC, V.

🅳

★ ★ **COPELAND'S OF NEW ORLEANS.** *1584 Rockville Pike. 301/230-0968.* Hrs: 11 am-11 pm; Fri, Sat to midnight; Sun to 10 pm.

Closed Thanksgiving, Dec 25. Bar; Fri, Sat to 1 am. Semi-a la carte: lunch $5-$15.75, dinner $5.95-$15.75. Child's meals. Specializes in seafood, Creole & Cajun dishes. Parking. Art deco decor. Cr cds: A, C, D, DS, MC, V.

🅳

✔★ ★ **HOUSE OF CHINESE GOURMET.** *1485 Rockville Pike. 301/984-9440.* Hrs: 11:30 am-10 pm; Fri, Sat to 11 pm. Chinese menu. Semi-a la carte: lunch $4.75-$7.50, dinner $6.50-$14.95. Specialties: Peking duck, seafood Shanghai style, vegetarian dishes. Parking. Decorated with Chinese art. Cr cds: A, DS, MC, V.

🅳

★ ★ **NORMANDIE FARM.** *(10710 Falls Rd, Potomac) 3½ mi SW on MD 189, I-270 exit 5. 301/983-8838.* Hrs: 11:30 am-2:30 pm, 6-10 pm; Sun 5-9 pm; Sun brunch 11 am-2 pm. Closed Mon. Res accepted. French menu. Bar. Semi-a la carte: lunch $6-$12.50, dinner $12-$23. Sun brunch $16.50. Specializes in seafood, veal. Entertainment Fri, Sat. Parking. French provincial decor. Cr cds: A, C, D, MC, V.

★ ★ ★ **OLD ANGLER'S INN.** *10801 MacArthur Blvd. 301/365-2425.* Hrs: noon-2:30 pm, 6-10:30 pm. Closed Mon. Bar. Wine list. A la carte entrees: lunch $12-$16, dinner $22-$29. Specializes in seafood, rack of lamb. Parking. Patio dining overlooking wooded area. Stone inn (1860). Family-owned. Cr cds: A, C, D, MC, V.

✔★ **SILVER DINER.** *11806 Rockville Pike (MD 355) (20852), in Mid-Pike Plaza. 301/770-4166.* Hrs: 7-2 am; Fri & Sat to 3 am; early-bird dinner Mon-Fri 4-6 pm. Closed Dec 25. Serv bar. Semi-a la carte: bkfst $3.95-$5.95, lunch $5.95-$7.95, dinner $5.95-$9.95. Child's meals. Specializes in meatloaf, chicken-pot pie, turkey. 1950s-style diner with jukeboxes. Servers dressed in period clothing. Cr cds: DS, MC, V.

🅳 SC

✔★ ★ **SUNNY GARDEN.** *1302 E Gude Dr (20850), MD 28 to E Gude Dr. 301/762-7477.* Hrs: 11:30 am-10 pm; Fri & Sat to 10:30 pm. Res accepted; required Fri & Sat. Chinese, Mandarin menu. Serv bar. Semi-a la carte: lunch $4.50-$9.95, dinner $5.95-$11.95. Specialties: General Tso's chicken, steak orange peal, soft-shell crab. Parking. Tropical fish tanks. Cr cds: A, MC, V.

🅳

★ ★ **THAT'S AMORE.** *15201 Shady Grove Rd (20850). 301/670-9666.* Hrs: 11:30 am-10:30 pm; Fri to midnight; Sat 4 pm-midnight; Sun 4-9:30 pm. Italian menu. Bar. A la carte entrees: lunch $5.95-$11.95, dinner $12-$28. Specializes in pasta, veal, chicken Vesuvio. Parking. Stained-glass windows. Early 20th-century mens club atmosphere. Cr cds: A, C, D, DS, MC, V.

🅳

✔★ ★ **WÜRZBURG HAUS.** *7236 Muncaster Mill Rd, in Red Mill Shopping Center. 301/330-0402.* Hrs: 11:30 am-9 pm; Fri to 10 pm; Sat noon-10 pm. Closed Sun. German menu. Wine, beer. A la carte entrees: lunch $7.50-$10.95, dinner $8.25-$12.95. Child's meals. Specializes in schnitzel, wurst. Accordionist Fri, Sat. 2 dining areas. German, Austrian atmosphere; collection of beer steins. Cr cds: A, DS, MC, V.

Unrated Dining Spot

HARD TIMES CAFE. *1117 Nelson St (20850). 301/294-9720.* Hrs: 11:30 am-10 pm; Fri & Sat to 11 pm; Sun noon-9 pm. Closed

Thanksgiving, Dec 25. Bar. A la carte entrees: lunch, dinner $4.50-$6. Child's meals. Specializes in chili, vegetarian dishes. Cr cds: A, MC, V.

Silver Spring, MD

Motel

★ ★ ★ **COURTYARD BY MARRIOTT.** 12521 Prosperity Dr (20904), 6 mi NE on US 29, then E on Cherry Hill Rd to Prosperity Dr. 301/680-8500; FAX 301/680-9232. 146 units, 3 story. S $85-$95; D, suites $95-$105; wkly, wknd rates. Crib free. TV; cable. Indoor pool; lifeguard. Complimentary coffee in rms. Restaurant 6:30 am-2 pm, 5-10 pm; Sat, Sun from 7 am. Bar 4-11 pm. Ck-out 1 pm. Coin lndry. Meeting rms. Valet serv. Sundries. Exercise equipt; weights, bicycles, whirlpool. Refrigerator in suites. Cr cds: A, C, D, DS, ER, JCB, MC, V.

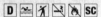

Hotel

★ ★ **HOLIDAY INN-SILVER SPRING PLAZA.** 8777 Georgia Ave (20910). 301/589-0800; FAX 301/587-4791. 226 rms, 16 story. S, D $85-$90; each addl $10; suites $125-$135; under 20 free. Crib free. Pet accepted, some restrictions. TV; cable. Pool; lifeguard. Restaurant 6 am-11 pm. Bar 11:30-1 am. Ck-out noon. Coin lndry. Meeting rms. Shopping arcade. Exercise equipt; weights, bicycles, sauna. Refrigerators avail. Cr cds: A, C, D, DS, ER, JCB, MC, V.

Restaurants

★ ★ **BLAIR MANSION INN.** 7711 Eastern Ave. 301/588-1688. Hrs: 11:30 am-9 pm; Sat from 5 pm; Sun from 2 pm. Res accepted. Italian, Amer menu. Bar. Semi-a la carte: lunch $5.95-$9.95, dinner $9.95-$19.95. Specializes in poultry, beef, crab Imperial. Parking. Murder mystery dinners. 1890s Victorian mansion; gaslight chandelier, 7 fireplaces. Family-owned. Cr cds: A, D, DS, MC, V.

✔★ **CHINA RESTAURANT.** 8411 Georgia Ave. 301/585-2275. Hrs: 11:30 am-2:30 pm, 5-9:30 pm; Sat from 5 pm; Sun 4-9 pm. Closed Mon; Thanksgiving. Chinese menu. Wine, beer. Semi-a la carte: lunch $3.75-$6.50, dinner $4.95-$10.95. Specialties: Mongolian beef, moo shu pork, Peking duck. Family-owned. No cr cds accepted.

★ ★ **CRISFIELD AT LEE PLAZA.** 8606 Colesville Rd (MD 29), ground floor of high rise building. 301/588-1572. Hrs: 11:30 am-10 pm; Fri to 11 pm; Sat 4-11 pm; Sun 4-10 pm. Closed Thanksgiving, Dec 25. Res accepted; required Fri & Sat. Bar. Semi-a la carte: lunch $4.50-$22, dinner $13-$22, Child's meals. Specializes in seafood, baked stuffed shrimp, crab Imperial. Parking (dinner). Art deco decor. Cr cds: A, D, MC, V.

[D]

★ ★ **MRS. K'S TOLL HOUSE.** 9201 Colesville Rd. 301/589-3500. Hrs: 11:30 am-2:30 pm, 5-8:30 pm; Fri, Sat to 9 pm; Sun 11 am-8:30 pm; Sun brunch to 1:45 pm. Closed Mon; Dec 25. Serv bar. Complete meals: lunch $11.40-$13.25, dinner $14.75-$22. Sun brunch $15. Specialty: roast turkey. Century-old tollhouse; antique china, glass. Gardens. Totally nonsmoking. Cr cds: A, C, D, DS, MC, V.

Tyson's Corner, VA

Motels

★ ★ **COMFORT INN.** (1587 Springhill Rd, Vienna 22182) 1½ mi W of I-495, exit 10B. 703/448-8020; FAX 703/448-0343. 250 rms, 3 story. S $55-$65; D $59-$69; each addl $6; under 18 free. Crib free. Pet accepted, some restrictions. TV; cable. Pool; lifeguard. Complimentary continental bkfst. Coffee in rms. Ck-out noon. Meeting rms. Valet serv. Free Dulles Airport, Metro transportation. Cr cds: A, C, D, DS, ER, JCB, MC, V.

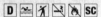

★ ★ **RESIDENCE INN BY MARRIOTT.** (8616 Westwood Center Dr, Vienna 22182) I-495 exit 10B to VA 7, then 2 mi W. 703/893-0120; FAX 703/790-8896. 96 kit. suites, 2 story. Kit. suites $132-$172; each addl $10; under 18 free; wknd rates. Crib free. Pet accepted; $85 non-refundable and $5 per day. TV; cable, in-rm movies avail. Pool; whirlpool, lifeguard. Complimentary full bkfst 6:30-9 am; Sat, Sun 7:30-10 am. Restaurant nearby. Ck-out noon. Coin lndry. Meeting rm. Valet serv. Lighted tennis. Many fireplaces. Picnic tables, grills. Cr cds: A, C, D, DS, MC, V.

Hotels

★ ★ ★ **EMBASSY SUITES.** (8517 Leesburg Pike, Vienna 22182) I-495 exit 10B to VA 7, then 2 mi W. 703/883-0707; FAX 703/883-0694. 232 suites, 8 story. S, D $164-$174; each addl $10; under 12 free; wknd rates. Crib free. TV; cable. Indoor pool. Complimentary full bkfst, coffee. Restaurant 11 am-10 pm. Bar. Ck-out noon. Gift shop. Exercise equipt; bicycles, rowers, whirlpool, sauna. Refrigerators, wet bars. Cr cds: A, C, D, DS, MC, V.

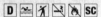

★ ★ ★ **HILTON McLEAN AT TYSONS CORNER.** (7920 Jones Branch Dr, McLean 22102) S on VA 123, turn right at Tysons Blvd, right on Galleria Dr/Westpark Dr, then right on Jones Branch Dr and continue 2 blks. 703/847-5000; FAX 703/761-5100. 456 units, 9 story. S $110-$170; D $130-$190; each addl $20; suites $275-$575; wkly, wknd rates. Crib free. TV; cable. Indoor pool; lifeguard. Restaurant 6:30 am-11 pm. Rm serv to 2 am. Bar 11-2 am; entertainment, dancing. Ck-out noon. Convention facilities. Drugstore. Exercise rm; instructor, weights, bicycles, sauna. Minibars. Atrium lobby; marble floors, fountain. *LUXURY LEVEL : TOWERS.* 38 rms, 8 suites. S $155-$200; D $170-$215; each addl $20. Concierge. Private lounge, honor bar. Bathrm phones. Complimentary continental bkfst, refreshments. Cr cds: A, C, D, DS, ER, JCB, MC, V.

✔★ ★ **HOLIDAY INN OF TYSONS CORNER.** (1960 Chain Bridge Rd, McLean 22102) 2 blks W of I-495 exit 11B. 703/893-2100; FAX 703/893-2227. 315 rms, 9 story. S $99-$132; D $109-$142; each addl $10; studio rms $103; family rates; wknd rates. Crib free. TV; cable. Indoor pool. Restaurant 6:30 am-10 pm. Bar; entertainment. Ck-out 1 pm. Meeting rms. Notary. Gift shop. Exercise equipt; weights, bicycles, whirlpool. Balconies. Cr cds: A, C, D, DS, JCB, MC, V.

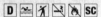

★ ★ ★ **MARRIOTT-TYSONS CORNER.** (8028 Leesburg Pike, Vienna 22182) 1 blk W of I-495 exit 10W. 703/734-3200; FAX 703/442-9301. 390 units, 15 story. S, D $134-$169; suites $250; family rates; wknd packages. Crib free. TV; cable. Indoor pool; poolside serv, lifeguard. Restaurant 6:30 am-10 pm. Bar 4:30 pm-1 am, Fri to 2 am, Sat 7 pm-2 am, closed Sun. Ck-out noon. Convention facilities. Gift shop. Some covered parking. Exercise equipt; weights, rowing machine, whirlpool, sauna. Refrigerators avail. *LUXURY LEVEL :* 26 rms,

1 suite. S $144; D $179. Concierge. Private lounge, honor bar. Complimentary refreshments. Cr cds: A, C, D, DS, ER, JCB, MC, V.

[D] [icons] SC

★ ★ ★ **RAMADA-TYSONS CORNER.** *(7801 Leesburg Pike, Falls Church 22043)* On VA 7 at I-495 exit 10E. 703/893-1340; FAX 703/847-9520. 404 rms, 11 story. 3 $99-$109; D $109-$129; each addl $20; suites $175-$250; under 18 free; wkend rates, packages. Crib free. Pet accepted, some restrictions. TV; cable. Indoor pool; lifeguard. Restaurant 6:30 am-11 pm. Bar 4 pm-2 am, Sun to 1 am; entertainment, dancing. Ck-out noon. Coin lndry. Convention facilities. Gift shop. Exercise equipt; weights, bicycles, whirlpool, sauna. Cr cds: A, C, D, DS, ER, JCB, MC, V.

[D] [icons] SC

★ ★ ★ ★ **THE RITZ-CARLTON, TYSONS CORNER.** *(1700 Tysons Blvd, McLean 22102)* N via I-495 exit 11B, adj Tysons II Mall. 703/506-4300; FAX 703/506-4305. 399 units, 24 story, 32 suites. S, D $139-$179; each addl $30; suites $325-$1,200; under 16 free; monthly rates; wkend family package; lower rates some wkends. Crib free. Pet accepted, some restrictions. Garage parking; valet $6. TV; cable. Indoor pool; lifeguard. Supervised child's activities. Restaurant (see THE RESTAURANT). Rm serv 24 hrs. Bar 11:30-1 am; entertainment. Ck-out noon. Convention facilities. Concierge. Gift shop. Airport transportation. Tennis privileges. 18-hole golf privileges, greens fee $65, pro, putting green, driving range. Exercise rm; instructor, weight machine, bicycles, whirlpool, sauna, steam rm. Masseuse. Bathrm phones, minibars. Antiques, 18th-century oil paintings in lobby. *LUXURY LEVEL :* **RITZ-CARLTON CLUB.** 24 rms, 2 floors. S, D $210. Concierge. Private lounge. Complimentary continental bkfst, lunch, afternoon tea, refreshments. Cr cds: A, C, D, DS, JCB, MC, V.

[D] [icons]

★ ★ ★ **SHERATON PREMIERE.** 8661 Leesburg Pike (22182), I-495 exit 10B, then 2¹/2 mi W on VA 7. 703/448-1234; FAX 703/893-8193. 455 rms, 24 story. S $125-$155; D $155-$175; each addl $15; suites $325-$750; under 17 free; wkly rates; lower rates wkends, hols. Crib free. TV; cable. In-rm movies avail. 2 pools, 1 indoor; poolside serv, lifeguard. Restaurant 6:30 am-midnight. Rm serv 24 hrs. Bars 11-1 am; dancing exc Sun. Ck-out noon. Convention facilities. Concierge. Gift shop. Drugstore. Free Dulles, National airport transportation. Lighted tennis privileges. 18-hole golf privileges, pro, greens fee. Exercise rm; instructor, weights, bicycles, whirlpool, sauna. Bathrm phones, minibars; some refrigerators. Cr cds: A, C, D, DS, ER, JCB, MC, V.

[D] [icons] SC

Restaurants

✓★ ★ **AMERICAN CAFE.** *(8601 Westwood Center Dr, Vienna)* I-495 exit 10B, then 2 mi W on VA 7. 703/848-9476. Hrs: 11 am-11 pm; Fri & Sat to 1 am; Sun from 10:30 am; Sun brunch to 3 pm. Res accepted. Bar. A la carte entrees: lunch, dinner $4.95-$12.95. Sun brunch $6.45-$6.95. Child's meals. Specializes in salads, sandwiches, grilled dishes. Parking. Patio dining. Take-out gourmet market. Cr cds: A, MC, V.

[D] SC

★ ★ ★ **BONAROTI.** *(428 Maple Ave E, Vienna)* 3 mi W on I-495 on VA 123, in Wolf Trappe Shopping Center. 703/281-7550. Hrs: 11:30 am-10:30 pm; Sat 5-11 pm. Closed Sun; some major hols. Res accepted. Italian menu. Bar. Wine cellar. Semi-a la carte: lunch $6.25-$9.95, dinner $11.95-$18.95. Child's meals. Specializes in veal, pasta, seafood. Own pastries. Italian art throughout. Cr cds: A, C, D, MC, V.

✓★ ★ **CLYDE'S.** *(8332 Leesburg Pike, Vienna)* 10 blks W of I-495 exit 10W on VA 7, then right. 703/734-1901. Hrs: 11-2 am; Sun brunch 10 am-4 pm. Res accepted. Bar 11-2 am. A la carte entrees: lunch $4.95-$9.95, dinner $4.95-$15.95. Child's meals. Specializes in

pasta, seafood, sandwiches. Entertainment Fri & Sat. Parking. Original art collection. Cr cds: A, C, D, DS, MC, V.

[D] SC

★ ★ **DA DOMENICO.** *1992 Chain Bridge Rd, 2 blks W of I-495 exit 11B.* 703/700-9000. Hrs: 11:30 am-11 pm; Sat from 5 pm. Closed Sun; major hols. Res accepted; required Fri, Sat. Northern Italian menu. Bar. Semi-a la carte: lunch $7-$11.95, dinner $9.95-$16.95. Specializes in veal chop, seafood, fresh pasta. Parking. Cr cds: A, C, D, MC, V.

[D]

★ ★ **FEDORA CAFE.** *(8521 Leesburg Pike, Vienna)* 703/556-0100. Hrs: 11:30 am-3 pm, 5:30-10:30 pm; Fri & Sat to 11:30 pm; Sun 10:30 am-2:30 pm, 4:30-9:30 pm. Res accepted. Bar to 12:30 am. Semi-a la carte: lunch $6.95-$9.95, dinner $8.95-$19.95. Specializes in rotisserie chicken, spit-roasted duck, fresh fish. Own desserts. Pianist Wed, Thurs & Sat (in season). Parking. Cr cds: A, C, D, DS, MC, V.

[D]

★ ★ ★ **HUNAN LION.** *(2070 Chain Bridge Rd, Vienna)* S of I-495 on VA 123. 703/734-9828. Hrs: 11:30 am-10:30 pm; Fri, Sat to 11 pm. Closed Thanksgiving. Res accepted. Chinese menu. Bar. Semi-a la carte: lunch $6-$8, dinner $12-$16. Specializes in triple delicacy prawns, orange beef, General Tso's chicken, Peking duck. Parking. Cr cds: A, D, MC, V.

[D]

★ ★ **J.R.'S STOCKYARDS INN.** *(8130 Watson St, McLean)* ¹/2 mi W of I-495 exit 10B. 703/893-3390. Hrs: 11:30 am-3 pm, 5:30-10:30 pm; Fri to 11 pm; Sat 5:30-11 pm; Sun 5-9:30 pm. Closed July 4, Thanksgiving, Dec 25. Res accepted; required Fri, Sat. Bar. Semi-a la carte: lunch $4.50-$8.95, dinner $12.95-$19.95. Child's meals. Specializes in marinated sirloin, prime aged beef, fresh seafood. Parking. Western-style chop house. Cr cds: A, C, D, DS, MC, V.

[D]

★ ★ ★ **LE CANARD.** *(132 Branch Rd, Vienna)* VA 123 at Branch Rd, in Danor Shopping Center. 703/281-0070. Hrs: 11:30 am-2:30 pm, 5:30-10:30 pm; Fri to 11 pm; Sat 6-11 pm. Closed Sun; Jan 1, Thanksgiving, Dec 25. Res accepted; required Fri, Sat. French menu. Bar to 2 am. Wine list. Semi-a la carte: lunch $4.75-$10, dinner $12.75-$21. Specializes in fresh seafood, veal, pasta. Own pastries. Piano bar Tues-Sat. Cr cds: A, C, D, DS, MC, V.

[D]

★ ★ **MARCO POLO.** *(245 Maple Ave W, Vienna)* 2¹/2 mi N of I-66 exit 62. 703/281-3922. Hrs: 11:30 am-10:30 pm; Fri, Sat to 11 pm. Closed Sun exc Mother's Day. Res accepted. French, Northern Italian menu. Serv bar. Semi-a la carte: lunch $6-$9, dinner $11-$18. Buffet: lunch (Tues-Fri) $8.25, dinner (Thurs) $14.50. Child's meals. Specializes in fresh seafood, fresh pasta. Parking. Cr cds: A, C, D, MC, V.

[D]

★ ★ ★ **MORTON'S OF CHICAGO.** *(8075 Leesburg Pike, McLean)* I-495 exit 10W, then 1/4 mi W on VA 7 (Leesburg Pike). 703/883-0800. Hrs: 11:30 am-2:30 pm, 5:30-11 pm; Sat from 5:30 pm; Sun 5-10 pm. Closed major hols. Res accepted. Bar. Wine list. Semi-a la carte: lunch $7.95-$29.95. A la carte entrees: dinner $15.95-$29.95. Specializes in steak, seafood. Valet parking. Jacket. Cr cds: A, C, D, MC, V.

[D]

★ ★ **NIZAM'S.** *(523 Maple Ave W, Vienna)* In Village Green Shopping Ctr. 703/938-8948. Hrs: 11 am-3 pm, 5-10 pm; Fri, Sat 5-11 pm; Sun 4-10 pm. Closed Mon; Thanksgiving. Res accepted. Turkish menu. Bar. Semi-a la carte: lunch $5.25-$10.50, dinner $11.95-$17.50. Specializes in lamb, chicken, fresh salmon. Turkish lanterns, artwork. Cr cds: A, DS, MC, V.

[D]

✔★ ★ **PANJSHIR II.** *(224 W Maple Ave, Vienna) 3 mi W on I-495; on VA 123. 703/281-4183.* Hrs: 11:30 am-2 pm, 5-10 pm; Sun 5-9 pm. Closed Jan 1, July 4, Thanksgiving. Res accepted. Afghan menu. Bar. Semi-a la carte: lunch $5.95-$7.25, dinner $9.95-$13.25. Specializes in kebabs, saffron rice, vegetarian dishes. Parking. Upscale atmosphere. Cr cds: A, MC, V.

D

★ ★ ★ **PIERRE ET MADELEINE.** *(246 E Maple Ave, Vienna) 2 mi N of I-66 exit 62. 703/938-4379.* Hrs: 11:30 am-2:30 pm, 5:30-10 pm; Fri to 11 pm; Sat 5:30-11 pm. Closed Sun. Res accepted. French menu. Bar. Semi-a la carte: lunch $4.75-$12.25, dinner $15-$22. Complete meals: dinner (Fri & Sat) $33.95. Specialties: fresh Maine lobster with whiskey sauce, seasonal dishes, veal with seafood. Parking. Cr cds: A, C, D, DS, MC, V.

★ ★ **PRIMI PIATTI.** *(8045 Leesburg Pike, Vienna) W of I-45 exit 10W. 703/893-0300.* Hrs: 11:30 am-2:30 pm, 5:30-10 pm; Fri to 10:30 pm; Sat 5:30-10:30 pm. Closed Sun; most major hols. Res accepted; required Fri, Sat. Italian menu. Bar. Semi-a la carte: lunch $7-$12.95, dinner $10.95-$18.95. Complete meals: lunch $12.95-

$19.95, dinner $25-$35. Specialties: agnolotti a la creme, veal involtini. Valet parking. Outdoor dining. Cr cds: A, C, D, MC, V.

D

★ ★ ★ **THE RESTAURANT.** *(See The Ritz-Carlton, Tysons Corner Hotel) 703/506-4300.* Hrs: 6:30 am-10 pm; Sun 6:30-11 am, 5-10 pm; Sun brunch 11:30 am-3 pm. Res accepted. Extensive wine list. Semi-a la carte: lunch $7.50-$18, dinner $14-$30. Sun brunch $32. Child's meals. Specializes in seafood, grilled salmon, lamb chops, prime aged beef. Pianist, harpist. Valet parking. Cr cds: A, C, D, DS, JCB, MC, V.

D

✔★ **WU'S GARDEN.** *(418 Maple Ave E, Vienna) 3 mi W off I-495 exit 11A. 703/281-4410.* Hrs: 11:30 am-10 pm; Sat noon-11 pm. Closed Thanksgiving. Res accepted. Chinese menu. Bar. Semi-a la carte: lunch $4-$7, dinner $7.95-$12. Specialties: kang pao chicken, crispy shrimp with walnuts. Parking. Oriental screens and artwork. Cr cds: A, D, DS, MC, V.

D

Hartford

Settled: 1633

Pop: 139,739

Elev: 50 feet

Time zone: Eastern

Area code: 203

Springfield

Settled: 1636

Pop: 156,983

Elev: 70 feet

Time zone: Eastern

Area code: 413

Hartford, Connecticut, and Springfield, Massachusetts, are the major cities of New England's Connecticut Valley. They are about 25 miles apart, linked by US 5, I-91 and the Connecticut River. The Hartford/Springfield area blends the subtle influences of the past with the excitement of the future.

Hartford was first settled in 1633 as a Dutch trading post. In that same year William Pynchon and seven others moved to Springfield from Roxbury and founded a tiny settlement. Both communities took their names from towns in England.

During the American Revolution, Springfield was an important city because the government chose it as the site of its armory and depot. The first US musket was made in the Springfield Armory in 1795. Guns were also important in the development of Hartford's industry. Eli Whitney devised a system of interchangeable parts for guns, which he manufactured in Connecticut in the late 18th century. Samuel Colt of Hartford refined and perfected Whitney's techniques and laid the groundwork for mass production. Eventually, Colt's guns were 80 percent machine-made.

During the 1800s, Hartford County was the center of a rum-distilling business. Molasses, spices, coffee and other imports were stored in Hartford's warehouses and shipped out by boat on the Connecticut River, as well as in the carts and stagecoaches of Yankee peddlers.

As a natural consequence of all this mercantile activity, the insurance business emerged to protect property and lives. In 1810, the Hartford Fire Insurance Company, now part of the Hartford Insurance Group, was founded. It is the oldest insurance company in the country.

Business

In the Springfield-Chicopee-Holyoke metropolitan area, there are more than 70,000 people employed by over 1,000 manufacturers and approximately 90,000 people employed by retail and wholesale firms. The chief industries of the city and surrounding areas are paper, machinery, printing, fabricated metals, apparel, primary metals, electrical machinery and chemical products.

The Greater Hartford area has several hundred manufacturing plants making small arms, foundry products, fabricated metals, machinery, aircraft parts, electrical parts and appliances, machine tools, food products, clothing and textiles, measuring and controlling devices, adhesives, precision instruments, furniture, paper products and chemicals.

Hartford is the insurance capitol of the nation. Many major insurance companies have headquarters here. Hartford is also the main marketing area for tobacco grown in the Connecticut Valley.

Convention Facilities

Hartford's Civic Center is a convention facility with theater-style seating for up to 3,200 people. An adjoining Sheraton Hotel has supplemental meeting facilities for 1,000.

The Civic Center contains an exhibition hall of 54,000 square feet and an assembly hall of 16,080 square feet. Banquet facilities can accommodate 2,000, and 9 meeting rooms can seat 30 to 900 people each. The center also features a mall with a number of specialty shops and restaurants.

Hartford's Civic Center Coliseum, where sporting events, concerts and general convention sessions are held, seats 14,500 for hockey and 16,500 for conventions.

Hotels within 2 blocks of the Civic Center have more than 2,000 rooms, and approximately 2,500 more rooms are available in nearby lodgings.

The Springfield Civic Center exhibit hall has 45,000 square feet of display area; its grand arena measures 17,000 square feet, seating 10,200. Banquet facilities can accommodate 3,000, and 6 meeting rooms seat from 60 to 600 persons. Hotels within 5 miles of downtown Springfield have more than 2,000 rooms.

Sports and Recreation

Hockey has long been popular in New England. The Springfield Indians hockey team draws enthusiastic, devoted fans to the Springfield Civic Center. The Hartford Civic Center is the home of the Hartford Whalers NHL hockey team.

Boston's professional basketball team, the Celtics, use the Hartford Civic Center as a "home away from home," playing several games there during the regular season. Located within Springfield is the Basketball Hall of Fame.

Ski areas nearby are numerous, and the season is fairly long. Runs vary from gentle slopes to some of the most rugged trails in the East.

One of the main events of the year in southern New England is the Eastern States Exposition, held each September in West Springfield. One million people attend annually to view exhibits, agricultural events, horse shows and entertainment.

Entertainment

Both cities have their own symphony orchestra; concert and lecture series bring outside performers as well. Hartford also has a ballet company, which performs at the Bushnell Memorial Hall, also the home of its symphony orchestra. Since both Boston and New York are close and easily reached, even the most avid music fans can satisfy their appetites. Both Springfield and Hartford have theater groups and supper clubs that provide live entertainment.

Historical Areas

Springfield's inner city is an area of townhouses built in the mid-1800s; most have slate mansard roofs, ornate cornices, bow fronts, large octagonal dormers and stained-glass windows. The Mattoon-Elliott Street section has been restored by individual owners with the help of various organizations.

Springfield's best-known historic building is the Springfield Armory, now a national historic site housing a collection of guns manufactured at the armory since 1795. Other gun specimens have been gathered from all over the world, making this one of the largest collections of military small arms in the world.

Hartford's Old State House, completed in 1796, is one of the architectural masterpieces of Charles Bulfinch. Two famous authors, Harriet Beecher Stowe and Samuel Clemens (Mark Twain), made Hartford their home. Both authors' houses, located within Nook Farm, are open to the public.

Sightseeing

The lower Connecticut Valley is an ideal location from which to tour all of New England. A drive up the river to Canada offers vistas of clear waters, picturesque bridges, mountains that seem almost close enough to touch, wooded side roads and postcard villages punctuated with the steeples of white frame churches. A fall foliage trip through New England is a must for many travelers.

To the east lie historic Boston, Lexington, Concord, Plymouth, Providence and Newport. The summer recreation area of Cape Cod is only two or three hours away, and the glamour and culture of New York City is also within easy driving distance.

Deerfield, 32 miles north of Springfield, has preserved a beautiful, mile-long stretch of houses from the 17th, 18th and early 19th centuries. East of Springfield, approximately 38 miles, is the incomparable Old Sturbridge Village, a re-created New England country town depicting rural life of the 1830s. Also nearby, about 50 miles southeast of Hartford, is Mystic Seaport, a maritime museum featuring ships, models, craftsmen at work, paintings and figureheads and exhibits telling the history of ships and the sea.

A scenic drive through Connecticut's Tobacco Valley, just north of Hartford, takes the visitor to Windsor and the Fyler House, the oldest house in the oldest town in Connecticut. Also along the drive are the Trolley Museum in East Windsor, the New England Air Museum in Windsor Locks and the Old New Gate Prison and copper mine in East Granby. South of Hartford is the town of Wethersfield. Several of its historic houses are open to the public.

General References Hartford

Settled: 1633 **Pop:** 139,739 **Elev:** 50 feet **Time zone:** Eastern **Area code:** 203

Phone Numbers

POLICE & FIRE: 911
FBI: 522-1201 or 777-6311
POISON CONTROL CENTER: 800/343-2722
TIME: 524-8123

Information Source

Greater Hartford Convention & Visitors Bureau, One Civic Center Plaza, Suite 301, 06103; 728-6789.
Department of Parks & Recreation, 722-6490.

Transportation

AIRLINES: Air Canada; American; Continental; Delta; Northwest; TWA; United; USAir; and other commuter and regional airlines. For the most current airline schedules and information consult the *Official Airline Guide,* published twice monthly.
AIRPORT: Bradley International, 627-3000.
CAR RENTAL AGENCIES: (See Toll-Free Numbers) Avis 627-3500; Budget 627-3660; Dollar 627-9048; Hertz 627-3850; National 627-3470; Thrifty 623-8214.
PUBLIC TRANSPORTATION: Connecticut Transit 525-9181.
RAILROAD PASSENGER SERVICE: Amtrak 800/872-7245.

Newspapers

Hartford Courant; Hartford Advocate.

Convention Facility

Hartford Civic Center, One Civic Center Plaza, 727-8080.

Sports & Recreation

Major Sports Facility

Hartford Civic Center Coliseum, One Civic Center Plaza, 727-8080 (Whalers, hockey, 728-3366).

Jai Alai
Berensons' Hartford, 89 Weston St, 525-8611.

Cultural Facilities

Theaters
Goodspeed Opera House, CT 82 at East Haddam Bridge, 873-8668.
Hartford Civic Center, One Civic Center Plaza, 727-8080.
Hartford Stage Co, 50 Church St, 527-5151.

Concert Hall
Bushnell Memorial Hall, 166 Capitol Ave, 246-6807.

Museums
Connecticut Fire Museum, 58 North Rd, East Windsor, 623-4732.
Connecticut Historical Society, 1 Elizabeth St, 236-5621.
Fyler House, 96 Palisado Ave (CT 159), Windsor, 688-3813.
Museum of American Political Life, Harry Jack Gray Center, University of Hartford, 200 Bloomfield Ave, West Hartford, 768-4090.
New England Air Museum, Adj to Bradley International Airport, Windsor Locks, 623-3305.
Noah Webster Foundation and Historical Society, 227 S Main St, West Hartford, 521-5362.
Raymond E. Baldwin Museum of Connecticut History, Connecticut State Library, 231 Capitol Ave, 566-3056.
Science Center of Connecticut, 950 Trout Brook Dr, West Hartford, 231-2824.
Trolley Museum, 58 North Rd, East Windsor, 623-7417.
Webb-Deane-Stevens Museum, 211 Main St, Wethersfield, 529-0612.

Art Museum
Wadsworth Atheneum, 600 Main St, 278-2670 or 247-9111.

Points of Interest

Historical
Butler-McCook Homestead, 396 Main St, 522-1806.
Center Church and Ancient Burying Ground, Main & Gold Sts.
Harriet Beecher Stowe House, Nook Farm, 73 Forest St, 493-6411.
Mark Twain House, Nook Farm, 351 Farmington Ave, 493-6411.
Nook Farm, Farmington Ave & Forest St, 525-9317.
Old New Gate Prison, Newgate Rd at CT 120, East Granby, 653-3563.
Old State House, 800 Main St, 522-6766.
State Capitol, 210 Capitol Ave, at Trinity St, 240-0222.

Other Attractions
Bushnell Park, downtown, between Jewell, Elm & Trinity Sts.
Charter Oak Tree Monument, Charter Oak Ave.
Connecticut Audubon Society Holland Brook Nature Center, 1361 S Main St, Glastonbury, 633-8402.
Constitution Plaza, downtown Hartford.
Elizabeth Park, Prospect & Asylum Aves.
Travelers Tower, 1 Tower Square, 277-2431.
Valley Railroad, 35 mi S in Essex, 767-0103.

Sightseeing Tour
Heritage Trails, PO Box 138, Farmington 06034, 677-8867.

Annual Events
Taste of Hartford, Constitution Plaza. Mid-June.
Riverfest. Early July.

Christmas Crafts Expo, Hartford Civic Center, 693-6335. 1st & 2nd wkends Dec.

Springfield

Settled: 1636 **Pop:** 156,983 **Elev:** 70 feet **Time zone:** Eastern **Area code:** 413

Phone Numbers
POLICE & FIRE: 911
FBI: 736-0301
POISON CONTROL CENTER: 800/682-9211
WEATHER: 499-2627

Information Sources
Greater Springfield Convention and Visitors Bureau, 34 Boland Way, 01103; 800/723-1548.
Greater Springfield Chamber of Commerce, 1350 Main St, 01103-1627; 787-1555.
Department of Parks & Recreation, 787-6434.

Transportation
AIRPORT: See Hartford.
CAR RENTAL AGENCIES: (See Toll-Free Numbers) Budget 732-5191; Thrifty 783-9181.
PUBLIC TRANSPORTATION: Pioneer Valley Transit Authority, 781-PVTA.
RAILROAD PASSENGER SERVICE: Amtrak 800/872-7245.

Newspapers
Springfield Union-News; Sunday Republican.

Convention Facilities
Eastern States Exposition, 1305 Memorial Ave, West Springfield, 737-2443.
Springfield Civic Center, 1277 Main St, 787-6610.

Sports & Recreation

Major Sports Facilities
Coliseum, Eastern States Exposition, 1305 S Memorial Ave, West Springfield, 737-2443.
Springfield Civic Center, 1277 Main St, 787-6610 (Indians, hockey, 736-4546).

Cultural Facilities

Theaters
Paramount Performing Arts Center, 1700 Main St, 734-5706.
Springfield Civic Center, 1277 Main St, 787-6610.
StageWest, One Columbus Center, 781-2340.

Concert Hall
Springfield Symphony Hall, Court St, 787-6600.

Museums
Connecticut Valley Historical Museum, 194 State St, 732-3080.
Indian Motocycle Museum, 33 Hendee St, 737-2624.
Science Museum, 236 State St, 733-1194.

Springfield Armory National Historic Site, One Armory Square Green, 734-8551.

Art Museums and Galleries

George Walter Vincent Smith Art Museum, 222 State St, 733-4214.

Museum of Fine Arts, 49 Chestnut St, 732-6092.

Zone Art Center, 395 Dwight St, 732-1995.

Points of Interest

Historical

Historic Deerfield, Deerfield, 774-5581.

Old Sturbridge Village, US 20W, Sturbridge, 508/347-3362.

Storrowton Village, Eastern States Exposition, 1305 Memorial Ave, West Springfield, 787-0136.

Other Attractions

Basketball Hall of Fame, 1150 W Columbus Ave, 781-5759.

Brimfield State Forest, 24 mi E on US 20, then SE near Brimfield, 245-9966.

Forest Park, 3 mi S, just E of US 5, I-91, 787-6440.

Granville State Forest, 22 mi W off MA 57, 357-6611.

Laughing Brook Education Center and Wildlife Sanctuary, 789 Main St, Hampden, 566-8034.

Municipal Group, NW side of Court Square.

Riverside Park, 5 mi W via MA 57 & MA 159S, Agawam, 786-9300.

Annual Events

Indian Day, Indian Motorcycle Museum. 3rd Sun July.

Glendi Greek Celebration. Early Sept.

Eastern States Exposition, 1305 S Memorial Ave, West Springfield, 737-2443. 17 days Sept.

Hall of Fame Tip-off Classic, Springfield Civic Center, 781-6500. Mid-Nov.

Parade of the Big Balloons, day after Thanksgiving.

City Neighborhoods

Many of the restaurants, unrated dining establishments and some lodgings listed under Hartford include neighborhoods as well as exact street addresses. Geographic descriptions of these areas are given, followed by a table of restaurants arranged by neighborhood.

Hartford

Civic Center District: South of Church St, west of Main St, north of Elm St and east of Union Place.

Franklin Ave Area: South of Southern Downtown; along Franklin Ave between Maple Ave on the north and Victoria Rd on the south.

Southern Downtown: Area east and south of Civic Center District; south of State St, west of Prospect St and Charter Oak Place, north of Wyllys St.

Lodgings and Food
Hartford

HARTFORD RESTAURANTS
BY NEIGHBORHOOD AREAS

(For full description, see alphabetical listings under Restaurants)

CIVIC CENTER DISTRICT

Gaetano's. 1 Civic Center Plaza

Hot Tomatoes. 1 Union Place

Que Huong. 355 New Park Ave

FRANKLIN AVE AREA

Carbone's Ristorante. 588 Franklin Ave

SOUTHERN DOWNTOWN

Max on Main. 205 Main St

Note: *When a listing is located in a town that does not have its own city heading, it will appear under the city nearest to its location. In these cases, the address and town appear in parenthesis immediately following the name of the establishment.*

Motor Hotel

★ ★ **RAMADA HOTEL DOWNTOWN.** *(100 East River Dr, East Hartford 06108) S via I-91 exit 3 to Pitkin, I-84 exit 53.* 203/528-9703; FAX 203/289-4728. 199 rms, 8 story. S $55-$99; D $65-$114; each addl $10; suites $150-$175; under 18 free; wkend rates. Crib free. Pet accepted. TV; cable. Indoor pool; sauna. Playground. Restaurant 6:30 am-2 pm, 5-10 pm. Rm serv. Bar; entertainment, dancing. Ck-out noon. Coin lndry. Meeting rms. Valet serv. Game rm. *LUXURY LEVEL : 8TH FLOOR.* 29 rms, 1 suite. S $79, D $99; suite $175. Private lounge. TV; cable, in-rm movies. Complimentary continental bkfst. Cr cds: A, C, D, DS, ER, JCB, MC, V.

D 🐾 🏊 🍸 🔥 SC

Hotels

★ ★ ★ **THE GOODWIN HOTEL.** *One Haynes St (06103), opp Hartford Civic Center at Goodwin Square.* 203/246-7500; res: 800/922-5006; FAX 203/247-4576. 124 rms, 6 story, 11 suites. D $115-$165; suites $215-$755; children free; wkend rates & packages. Crib free. Garage, valet parking $13. TV. Restaurant 6:30 am-10:30 pm. Rm serv 24 hrs. Bar 11-1 am. Ck-out noon. Meeting rms. Concierge. Exercise equipt; weight machine, bicycles. Bathrm phones; some fireplaces. Refrigerators avail. Small, European-style luxury hotel in red-brick, Queen Anne-style building (1881) built for J.P. Morgan; 19th-century paintings and replicas of sailing ships. Cr cds: A, C, D, DS, ER, JCB, MC, V.

D 🍸 🔥 🐾 SC

★ ★ **HOLIDAY INN-DOWNTOWN.** *50 Morgan St (06120), at jct I-84 exit 52 & I-91 exit 32, in Civic Center District.* 203/549-2400; FAX 203/527-2746. 343 rms, 18 story. S $79-$119; D $89-$129; each addl $10; suites $175; under 18 free; wkend rates. Crib free. Pet accepted. TV; cable. Pool; poolside serv. Restaurant 6:30 am-10 pm. Bar 4 pm-2 am. Ck-out noon. Convention facilities. Free airport transportation. Exercise equipt; weights, stair machine. Refrigerators. Cr cds: A, C, D, DS, JCB, MC, V.

D 🐾 🏊 🍸 🔥 SC

★ **RAMADA INN-CAPITOL HILL.** *440 Asylum St (06103), opp State Capitol Building, in Civic Center District.* 203/246-6591; FAX 203/728-1382. 96 rms, 9 story. S $55-$65; D $55-$65; each addl $10. Crib free. Pet accepted, some restrictions. TV; cable. Ck-out noon. Free valet parking. Cr cds: A, C, D, DS, MC, V.

D 🐾 🍸 🔥 SC

★ ★ ★ **SHERATON.** *315 Trumbull St (06103), at Civic Center Plaza.* 203/728-5151; FAX 203/522-3356. 388 rms, 22 story. S, D $120; each addl $15; suites $250-$600; under 17 free; wkend, hol packages. Crib free. Pet accepted, some restrictions. Garage parking $10. TV; cable. Indoor pool. Coffee in rms. Restaurant 6:30 am-11 pm. Bar. Ck-out noon. Convention facilities. Airport transportation. Exercise equipt; weight machines, bicycles, whirlpool, sauna. Civic Center Plaza adj; shops. Cr cds: A, C, D, DS, ER, JCB, MC, V.

D 🐾 🏊 🍸 🍸 🔥 SC

Restaurants

★ ★ ★ **BLACKSMITH'S TAVERN.** *(2300 Main St, Glastonbury) E on I-84 to CT 2, SE to exit 8; S on I-91 to exit 25, E via CT 3 to CT 2.* 203/659-0366. Hrs: 11:30 am-4 pm, 5-9 pm; Fri, Sat to 10 pm; Sun 4-9 pm; Sun brunch 11 am-2:30 pm. Closed Dec 25. Res accepted. Continental menu. Bar to 1 am. Semi-a la carte: lunch $5.95-$9.95, dinner $10.95-$21.95. Sun brunch $10.95-$11.95. Child's meals. Specializes in swordfish, prime rib, veal. Own baking. Entertainment. Parking. Outdoor dining (lunch). 18th-century bldg. Unusual shoe collection; murals. On the Town Green; fountain. Cr cds: A, D, DS, MC, V.

✔ ★ ★ **BUTTERFLY.** *(831 Farmington Ave, West Hartford) W on Farmington Ave.* 203/236-2816. Hrs: 11:30 am-10 pm; Fri & Sat to 11 pm; Sun brunch to 4 pm. Closed Thanksgiving. Res accepted. Chinese menu. Bar. A la carte entrees: lunch $5.50-$6.95, dinner $5.95-$14.95. Sun brunch $10.95. Specializes in Szechwan cuisine. Parking. Contemporary decor. Cr cds: A, D, DS, MC, V.

D

★ ★ ★ **CARBONE'S RISTORANTE.** *588 Franklin Ave, in Franklin Ave Area.* 203/296-9646. Hrs: 11:30 am-2 pm, 5-10 pm; Sat from 5 pm. Closed Sun; major hols. Res accepted. Italian menu. Bar. Semi-a la carte: lunch $8-$11, dinner $12-$20. Specialties: fettucine carbonara, vitello cuscinetto. Own baking, desserts. Parking. Tableside preparation. Family-owned. Cr cds: A, MC, V.

D

★ ★ ★ **GAETANO'S.** *1 Civic Center Plaza, in Civic Center District.* 203/249-1629. Hrs: 11:30 am-2 pm, 5-10 pm. Closed Sun; major hols. Res accepted. Northern Italian menu. Bar. Wine cellar. A la carte entrees: lunch $7.95-$11.25, dinner $12-$20. Specializes in veal, chicken, pasta, seasonal seafood. Own baking. Parking. Tableside preparation. Cr cds: A, D, MC, V.

D

★ **HOT TOMATOES.** *1 Union Place, in Civic Center District.* 203/249-5100. Hrs: 5:30-9:30 pm; Tues to 9 pm; Fri, Sat to 10 pm; Sun to 9 pm. Closed Mon; most major hols. Res accepted Tues-Fri. Italian menu. Bar. A la carte entrees: lunch $6.95-$8.95, dinner $8.95-$18.95. Specializes in pasta, veal. Outdoor dining. Cr cds: A, C, D, MC, V.

★ ★ **MAX ON MAIN.** *205 Main St, Southern Downtown.* 203/522-2530. Hrs: 11:30 am-2:30 pm, 5-10 pm; Fri to 11 pm; Sat 5-11 pm. Closed Sun; most major hols. Res accepted. Bar. A la carte entrees: lunch $6.95-$9.95, dinner $9.95-$19.50. Child's meals. Specializes in black Angus beef, stone pies. Parking. Intimate bistro atmosphere. Cr cds: A, D, MC, V.

★ ★ **PARSON'S DAUGHTER.** (2 Hopewell Rd, S Glastonbury) E on I-84, SE on CT 2 exit 8, at Main St & Hopewell Rd. 203/633-8698. Hrs: 11:30 am-2 pm, 5:30-9 pm; Sat from 5:30 pm; Sun brunch 11:30 am-2 pm. Res accepted. Continental menu. Bar. Semi-a la carte: lunch $5.95-$8.95, dinner $13.95-$18.95. Sun brunch $8.95-$11.95. Child's meals. Specializes in crab cakes, fresh vegetables, chocolate crepe with white chocolate mousse. Parking. Built 1757. Cr cds: A, D, DS, MC, V.

D SC

✔★ **QUE HUONG.** 355 New Park Ave, in Civic Center District. 203/233-7402. Hrs: 11 am-2 pm, 5-9 pm; wkends to 10 pm. Closed Jan 1, July 4, Dec 25. Res accepted wkends. Vietnamese menu. Wine, beer. Semi-a la carte: lunch $3.75-$4.50, dinner $5.55-$7.75. Specialties: spicey lemon grass chicken, marinated beef on rice noodles. Cr cds: A, D, MC, V.

D

Springfield

Motels

(Higher rates Exposition week)

★ ★ **COMFORT INN.** (450 Memorial Dr, Chicopee 01020) Off MA Tpke (I-90) exit 5. 413/739-7311. 100 rms, 3 story. S $54-$73; D $61-$80; each addl $7; under 18 free. Crib free. TV; cable. Restaurant 5-10 pm. Bar from 3 pm; entertainment Fri, Sat. Ck-out 11 am. Coin lndry. Meeting rms. Valet serv. Exercise equipt; weights, bicycles. Game rm. Cr cds: A, C, D, DS, ER, JCB, MC, V.

D X ≈ ≍ ≋ SC

✔★ **DAYS INN.** (437 Riverdale St, West Springfield 01089) Off I-91 exit 13B. 413/785-5365; FAX 413/732-7017. 84 rms. S $38-$58; D $45-$65; each addl $10; higher rates special events. Crib free. TV. Pool. Complimentary continental bkfst, coffee. Restaurant nearby. Ck-out 11 am. Meeting rms. Downhill ski 9 mi. Cr cds: A, D, DS, MC, V.

D ≈ ≈ ≍ ≋ SC

★ ★ **HAMPTON INN.** (1011 Riverdale St, West Springfield 01089) On US 5, ¼ mi S of MA Tpke (I-90) exit 4 or N of I-91 exit 13B. 413/732-1300; FAX 413/732-9883. 126 rms, 4 story. S $60; D $66; under 18 free. Crib free. TV; cable. Pool. Complimentary continental bkfst 6-10 am, coffee, tea, hot chocolate. Ck-out noon. Meeting rms. Sundries. Downhill/x-country ski 6 mi. Health club privileges. Cr cds: A, C, D, DS, MC, V.

D ≈ ≈ ≍ ≋ SC

Hotels

★ ★ **HOLIDAY INN.** 711 Dwight St (01104). 413/781-0900; FAX 413/785-1410. 252 rms, 12 story. S $85-$110; D $95-$120; suites $130-$210; under 19 free; wkend, family rates. TV; cable. Indoor pool. Restaurant 6:30 am-2 pm, 5-10 pm. Bar from 4:30 pm; Sat & Sun from noon. Ck-out noon. Meeting rm. Downhill/x-country ski 10 mi. Exercise equipt; weights, bicycle, whirlpool. Game rm. Some refrigerators. Cr cds: A, C, D, DS, ER, JCB, MC, V.

D ✦ ≈ ≈ X ≍ ≋ SC

★ ★ ★ **MARRIOTT SPRINGFIELD.** Corner Boland & Columbus Ave (01115), at I-91 Springfield Center exit. 413/781-7111; FAX 413/731-8932. 264 rms, 16 story. S $119-$129; D $139-$149; each addl $10; suites $275; under 18 free; wkend package plans. Crib free. TV. Indoor pool; poolside serv. Complimentary coffee in lobby. Restaurant 6:30 am-11 pm. Bars 11:30-2 am; entertainment, dancing. Ck-out 1 pm. Meeting rms. Bellhops. Shopping arcade. Barber, beauty shop.

Airport transportation. Downhill/x-country ski 15 mi. Exercise equipt; weights, bicycles, whirlpool, sauna. Some refrigerators. *LUXURY LEVEL.* 27 rms. S $135; D $145. Concierge. Private lounge, honor bar. TV; cable, in-rm movies. Complimentary continental bkfst, refreshments, newspapers & magazines. Cr cds: A, C, D, DS, ER, JCB, MC, V.

D ✦ ≈ ≈ X ≍ ≋ SC

★ ★ ★ **SHERATON SPRINGFIELD MONARCH PLACE.** 1 Monarch Place (01104). 413/781-1010; FAX 413/734-3249. 304 rms, 12 story. S, D $89-$155; suites $185-$225; under 18 free; wkend packages. Crib free. Garage $6. TV; cable. Indoor pool; poolside serv. Restaurant 6:30 am-midnight. Bar 11:30-2 am; entertainment Fri-Sat, dancing. Ck-out noon. Convention facilities. Shopping arcade. Bradley Field airport transportation. Exercise rm; instructor, weights, bicycles, whirlpool, sauna, steam rm. Bathrm phones. Refrigerators. Cr cds: A, C, D, DS, ER, JCB, MC, V.

D ≈ X ≍ ≋ SC

Restaurants

★ ★ **THE GATHERING.** 1068 Riverdale, 5 mi N on US 5 at jct I-91 exit 13B. 413/781-0234. Hrs: 4:30-9 pm; Fri, Sat to 10 pm. Early-bird dinner 4:30-6 pm. Sun brunch 10:30-2 pm. Closed Dec 25. Res accepted. Continental menu. Bar. Semi-a la carte: dinner $9.95-$16.95. Sun brunch $10.95. Child's meals. Specializes in fresh seafood, prime rib, steak. Salad bar. Own desserts. Parking. Cr cds: A, DS, MC, V.

★ ★ ★ **HOFBRAUHAUS.** (1105 Main St, West Springfield) Off MA Tpke (I-90) exit 4, S on US 5, then W on MA 147. 413/737-4905. Hrs: 11:30 am-midnight; Mon to 9 pm; Sat 5-midnight. Closed Sun, Dec 24, 25; also 1st 2 wks Jan, July. Res accepted. German, Amer menu. Bar 11 am-midnight. Semi-a la carte: lunch $2.75-$13, dinner $10.25-$30. Child's meals. Specialties: lobster, Wienerschnitzel, rack of lamb. Parking. Tableside cooking. Bavarian atmosphere; antiques. Cr cds: A, C, D, DS, MC, V.

✔★ **IVANHOE.** (1422 Elm St, West Springfield) I-91 exit 13 B, on US 5. 413/736-4881. Hrs: 11:30 am-10:30 pm; Mon to 9 pm; Tues to 10 pm; Sat from 4 pm; Sun 10 am-9 pm; Sun brunch to 3 pm. Closed Dec 25. Continental menu. Bar; Fri & Sat to 1 am. Semi-a la carte: lunch $3.95-$8.95, dinner $9.95-$15.95. Lunch buffet $5.75. Sun brunch $10.95. Child's meals. Specializes in prime rib, fresh seafood. Salad bar. Entertainment Fri, Sat. Parking. Contemporary decor. Casual atmosphere. Cr cds: A, C, D, DS, MC, V.

D

★ ★ **MONTE CARLO.** (1020 Memorial Ave, West Springfield) 1 mi W of I-91, opp exposition grounds. 413/734-6431. Hrs: 11:30 am-9 pm; Fri to 10 pm. Sat, Sun from 4 pm. Closed Dec 25. Res accepted. Continental menu. Bar. Semi-a la carte: lunch $3.95-$9.95, dinner $6.95-$15.95. Child's meals. Specialties: beef Marsala, veal Marsala, pasta. Family-owned. Cr cds: A, C, D, MC, V.

★ ★ ★ **OLD STORROWTON TAVERN.** (1305 Memorial Ave, West Springfield) 2 mi W on MA 147, in Eastern States Exposition. 413/732-4188. Hrs: 11:30 am-2:30 pm, 5-8:30 pm; Sat 11:30 am-4 pm, 5-9 pm. Res. Closed Sun; Jan 1, Dec 25. Continental menu. Bar. Semi-a la carte: lunch $5.75-$12, dinner $12-$22. Specializes in seafood, veal & beef dishes. Own baking. Outdoor dining. Part of restored colonial village. Cr cds: A, C, DS, MC, V.

D

★ ★ **STUDENT PRINCE AND FORT.** 8 Fort St. 413/734-7475. Hrs: 11 am-11 pm; Sun noon-10 pm. Res accepted. German, Amer menu. Bar; imported draft beer. Semi-a la carte: lunch $4.25-$7.25, dinner $8-$22. Child's meals. Specialties: jägerschnitzel, sauerbraten, fresh salmon. Large collection of German beer steins. Family-owned. Cr cds: A, C, D, DS, MC, V.

D

✔★★ **TAVERN INN.** *91 W Gardner, corner of W Columbus Ave, 2 blks S of Basketball Hall of Fame. 413/736-0456.* Hrs: 11 am-2:30 pm, 4:30-9 pm; Thurs, Fri to 10 pm; Sat noon-9 pm; Sun 4-9 pm. Closed Memorial Day, Thanksgiving, Dec 25. Res accepted. Italian, Amer menu. Bar to 1 am. Semi-a la carte: lunch $2.50-$8, dinner $5-$14. Child's meals. Specializes in seafood, pasta. Parking. Cr cds: A, DS, MC, V.

D

Houston

Founded: 1836	
Pop: 1,630,553	
Elev: 55 feet	
Time zone: Central	
Area code: 713	

Houston is a big, rich, modern city with an atmosphere of dynamic vitality. From cowboys and cotton to a major seaport and energy technology center, Houston has always been far reaching and prosperous. The space shuttle program has once again brought this city to the forefront of space exploration. All this and a strong commitment to cultural activities makes Houston a city with something for everyone.

From the beginning—when two brothers, in 1836, promoted the sale of 4,429 acres on Buffalo Bayou—Houston has been prosperous. With the discovery of oil in 1901 and again in 1904, Houston plunged headlong into a period of rapid expansion. Even during the Great Depression this city flourished.

The latest census shows Houston to be the fourth most populous city in the the nation. Ongoing development in and around the city, including a new convention center, theater center and visitor center at Johnson Space Center, shows that the same spirit and energy that raised Houston from a small pioneer settlement is still strong today.

Business

Most important to the city of Houston is its seaport—the nation's third largest and the largest in the Southwest. It handles more than 150 steamship lines providing regular service between the Port of Houston and some 250 ports throughout the world. Buffalo Bayou is part of the Houston Ship Channel, a 400-foot-wide, 40-foot-deep, 52-mile-long, man-made waterway that flows into the Gulf of Mexico.

Houston is ranked first in the nation in the manufacturing and distribution of petroleum equipment, first in pipeline transmission and first as a refinery center.

Bordering Houston's city limits is the NASA Lyndon B. Johnson Space Center, which has brought fame and another industry to this city. Space Center Houston, designed by Walt Disney Imagineering, Inc, interprets the past, present and future of American space exploration.

The Texas Medical Center, near downtown, is one of the most renowned modern medical facilities in the world. Some two million patients come here annually from around the globe. Its diversity is seen in more than 40 different medical institutions, the most famous of which specialize in the fields of heart disease and cancer treatment.

Convention Facilities

Houston has three convention centers—the George R. Brown Convention Center, the Summit and the Astrodomain Complex.

The George R. Brown Convention Center, a state-of-the-art facility, has 600,000 square feet of exhibit space, 43 meeting rooms and the largest ballroom in Texas.

The Summit contains 17,000 square feet of space, plus permanent seating for more than 17,000.

The Astrodomain Complex is an all-encompassing, 375-acre area providing year-round entertainment. Astrohall and Astroarena have a total of 750,000 square feet and 300,000 square feet of exhibition and meeting space, respectively, making it the world's largest one-floor exhibition facility. It also has 25 meeting rooms and parking for 30,000 cars.

Sports and Recreation

The world-famous Astrodome, the first all-purpose, air-conditioned, domed stadium, is the home of the Astros (baseball) and Oilers (football). The Houston Rockets (basketball) play to enthusiastic crowds in the Summit, the city's entertainment/sports complex. Professional wrestlers appear in the Sam Houston Coliseum, and Houston's international polo team plays in Memorial Park.

Located across the street from the Astrodome is AstroWorld, with its 11 different theme areas offering entertainment for the entire family with 100 rides; WaterWorld, a 15-acre water park; live entertainment; and fireworks spectaculars.

Golf courses and tennis courts abound in the Houston area. Horse and car racing are also accessible. The nearby bays and beaches on the Gulf of Mexico provide many opportunities for water sports and fishing.

Entertainment

Houston's cultural events are many and varied, with something to satisfy every taste. Among the nation's oldest permanent resident theaters, the Alley Theatre delights audiences with superb productions. Houston's many other fine repertory, campus and professional companies, including experimental stand-up comedy, Black theater and a local musical production company, round out the city's offerings for theatrical entertainment.

Since its beginning in 1913, the Houston Symphony Orchestra has been inspiring audiences. This professional body of more than 90 musicians performs some 120 concerts each year in Houston, nearby cities, around the country and abroad. During the summer there are concerts at Miller Outdoor Theater in Hermann Park. The Houston Grand Opera, Houston Ballet and many other performing companies add to Houston's cultural flavor.

Come evening, the choices of nightlife are varied. There are many restaurants that specialize in Gulf seafood. Mexican and Cajun cooking also rank high. Club music includes country and Western, contemporary jazz and popular dance.

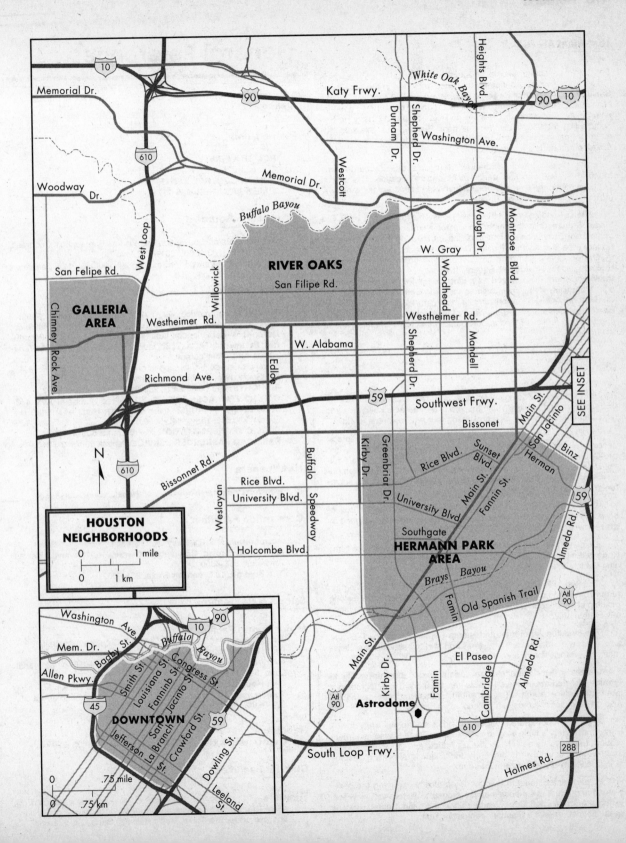

HOUSTON
NEIGHBORHOODS

0   1 mile

0   1 km

River Oaks / Galleria Area map labels

Memorial Dr.
Katy Frwy.
White Oak Bayou
Heights Blvd.
Washington Ave.
Durham Dr.
Shepherd Dr.
Westcott
Memorial Dr.
Woodway Dr.
West Loop
Buffalo Bayou
San Felipe Rd.
Chimney Rock Ave.
GALLERIA AREA
Willowick
RIVER OAKS
San Filipe Rd.
W. Gray
Woodhead
Waugh Dr.
Montrose Blvd.
Westheimer Rd.
Westheimer Rd.
W. Alabama
Edloe
Shepherd Dr.
Mandell
Richmond Ave.
Southwest Frwy.
Bissonet
Main St.
San Jacinto
Herman
Binz
SEE INSET
Rice Blvd.
Sunset Blvd.
Bissonnet Rd.
Weslayan
Rice Blvd.
University Blvd.
Buffalo Speedway
Kirby Dr.
Greenbriar Dr.
University Blvd.
Main St.
Fannin St.
Almeda Rd.
Southgate
HERMANN PARK AREA
Holcombe Blvd.
Brays Bayou
Famin
Old Spanish Trail
El Paseo
Main St.
Kirby Dr.
Famin
Cambridge
Almeda Rd.
Astrodome
South Loop Frwy.
Holmes Rd.

Downtown inset

Washington Ave.
Mem. Dr.
Bagby St.
Buffalo Bayou
Smith St.
Louisiana St.
Congress St.
Fannin St.
San Jacinto St.
Allen Pkwy.
DOWNTOWN
Jefferson St.
La Branch St.
Crawford St.
Dowling St.
Leeland St.

0   .75 mile

0   .75 km

Historical Areas

San Jacinto Battleground, a 460-acre state park, is the site where Texas won its independence from Mexico. Included in the park is the San Jacinto Museum of Regional History and the 570-foot San Jacinto Monument, one of the world's tallest monumental columns. The battleship *Texas,* presented to the state of Texas by the US Navy on San Jacinto Day in 1948, is also located here. Built in 1914, this ship saw action in major invasions of both World Wars. It is the only remaining dreadnought of its class in the US.

The Christ Church Cathedral, Houston's oldest church, was founded in 1839 and still stands at its original location. The church contains handcarved woodwork, statuary and stained-glass windows, including two designed by Tiffany.

Allen's Landing Park is the site of Houston's founding in 1836. Old Market Square, once the center of Houston's commerce near the city's original port, is now an interesting dining spot. During the 1800s Market Square was the scene of saloons, food vendors, Native American trading posts and gambling halls. The oldest commercial building in Houston faces Old Market Square; it once was a Native American trading post and also served as a stagecoach inn and slave auction site. Tranquillity Park, downtown, in the Civic Center, commemorates the historic Apollo II moon landing. Its features include a 24-level cascading fountain, with 5 stainless steel stacks resembling rockets, and an exact replica of the famous footprint that Neil Armstrong left on the moon.

Sightseeing

A visit to Houston's Zoological Gardens is a memorable experience for both children and adults. Within the zoo is a three-acre children's zoo with separate contact areas representing four regions of the world.

The Museum of Fine Arts presents sculpture, paintings, graphics, decorative arts, outstanding collections of Egyptian handiwork and pre-Columbian art, African and Native American artifacts and an outstanding collection of Remington's Western paintings. The Contemporary Arts Museum has changing exhibits of modern paintings, sculptures, films and multimedia events.

Considered one of the world's most significant private art collections, the Menil Collection is housed in a museum building designed by the renowned Italian architect Renzo Piano.

Displayed in the 24-room former residence of philanthropist Ima Hogg is the Bayou Bend Collection of American decorative arts, spanning the late 17th, 18th and early 19th centuries.

The Port of Houston maintains an observation deck for viewing the turning basin and port in action. The port also offers a free cruise along the ship channel aboard the inspection boat *Sam Houston* by advance reservation only.

The Houston Arboretum and Nature Center includes a 155-acre arboretum with a large variety of trees and shrubs, as well as a classroom, laboratory, library and greenhouse.

In Sam Houston Historical Park various guided tours are available through restored structures built between 1820 and 1905, including a late 19th-century church, a Texas plantation house and a frontier cabin. Also on premises is a museum gallery.

A good shopping area is located within a 12-block area downtown, making it relatively easy to walk around. There is also an underground tunnel system with boutiques, cafes and specialty shops. Southwest of downtown is the Houston Galleria, a shopping, restaurant, hospitality and entertainment complex.

Space Center Houston is a hands-on facility exploring the past, present and future of America's space program. Visitors can view live pictures from Mission Control and Kennedy Space Center, wear a space helmet, or pilot a manned manuvering unit.

General References

Founded: 1836 **Pop:** 1,630,553 **Elev:** 55 feet **Time zone:** Central **Area code:** 713

Phone Numbers

POLICE & FIRE: 911
FBI: 868-2266
POISON CONTROL CENTER: 654-1701
TIME & WEATHER: 976-7171

Information Source

Greater Houston Convention and Visitors Bureau, 801 Congress, 77002; 227-3100 or 800/231-7799 (exc TX).
Department of Parks & Recreation, 845-1000.

Transportation

AIRLINES: Aeromexico; Air France; American; Aviateca (Guatemala); British Airways; Cayman (British West Indies); Continental; Delta; KLM (Netherlands); Lufthansa (Germany); SAHSA (Honduras); Southwest; TACA (El Salvador); United; USAir; VIASA (Venezuela); and other commuter and regional airlines. For the most current airline schedules and information consult the *Official Airline Guide,* published twice monthly.
AIRPORTS: Intercontinental, 230-3100; Hobby, 643-4597.
CAR RENTAL AGENCIES: (See Toll-Free Numbers) Avis 443-5800; Budget 449-0145; Dollar 449-0161; Hertz 443-0800; National 654-1695; Thrifty 442-5000.
PUBLIC TRANSPORTATION: Metro Transit 635-4000.
RAILROAD PASSENGER SERVICE: Amtrak 800/872-7245.

Newspapers

Houston Chronicle; Houston Post; Houston Business Journal.

Convention Facilities

Astrodomain, I-610 & Kirby Dr, 799-9544.
George R. Brown Convention Center, 1001 Avenida de las Americas, 853-8000.
The Summit, 10 Greenway Plaza, 961-9003.

Sports & Recreation

Major Sports Facilities
Astrodome, I-610 at Kirby Dr, 799-9544. Astros (baseball), 799-9555; Oilers (football), 797-1000.
Memorial Park, west of downtown, off I-10 & I-610, on Memorial Loop, 861-3765.
Sam Houston Coliseum, 810 Bagby, at Walker, 247-2592.
The Summit, 10 Greenway Plaza, 961-9003. Rockets (basketball), 627-0600.

Racetrack
Delta Downs, Nibletts Bluff Rd, Vinton, LA, 318/433-3206.

Cultural Facilities

Theaters
Alley Theatre, 615 Texas Ave, 228-9341.
Theatre under the Stars, Music Hall, 810 Bagby St, 622-8887.

Concert Hall

Jesse H. Jones Hall for the Performing Arts, 615 Louisiana Ave, 227-ARTS.
Wortham Theater Center (Houston Symphony Orchestra, Ballet, Grand Opera and Society for the Performing Arts), 500 Texas Ave, 227-ARTS.

Museums and Art Galleries

Bayou Bend Collection, 1 Westcott, 520-2600.
Burke Baker Planetarium, Hermann Park, 639-4600.
Children's Museum of Houston, 1500 Binz, 522-1138.
Contemporary Arts Museum, 5216 Montrose Blvd, 526-3129.
Houston Museum of Natural Science, One Hermann Circle Dr, Hermann Park, 639-4600.
Menil Collection, 1515 Sul Ross, 525-9400.
Museum of Fine Arts, 1001 Bissonnet, 639-7300.
Rothko Chapel, 3900 Yupon, 524-9839.
San Jacinto Museum of History and Monument, 3800 Park Rd, San Jacinto Battleground, 479-2421.

Points of Interest

Historical

Allen's Landing Park, Main St & Buffalo Bayou.
Battleship *Texas,* San Jacinto Battleground, 479-2411.
Christ Church Cathedral, 1117 Texas Ave, 222-2593.
Old Market Square, Congress, Milam, Preston & Travis.
Sam Houston Park, 1100 Bagby, 655-1912.
San Jacinto Battleground, 20 mi E, 479-2421.
Tranquillity Park, 400 Rusk St.

Other Attractions

Arboretum & Nature Center, 4501 Woodway, Memorial Park, 681-8433.
AstroWorld & WaterWorld, Kirby Dr at South Loop I-610, 799-1234.
Port of Houston, Clinton Dr to Port area, 670-2400.

Space Center Houston, 25 mi S on I-45, exit 2351, 244-2100.
Zoological Gardens, 1513 N MacGregor, in Hermann Park, 525-3300.

Sightseeing Tours

Gray Line bus tours, 602 Sampson, 223-8800 or 800/334-4441.
Harris County Heritage Society, 1100 Bagby St, in Sam Houston Park, 655-1912.

Annual Events

Houston Livestock Show, Parade & Rodeo, Astrodome. Late Feb-early Mar.
Houston Azalea Trail. 1st 2 wkends Mar.
Houston International Festival. Apr.
Greek Festival. 1st full wkend Oct.

City Neighborhoods

Many of the restaurants, unrated dining establishments and some lodgings listed under Houston include neighborhoods as well as exact street addresses. A map showing these neighborhoods can be found immediately following the city introduction. Geographic descriptions of these areas are given, followed by a table of restaurants arranged by neighborhood.

Downtown: South of Buffalo Bayou, west of US 59, north of I-45 and east of Bagby St. **North of Downtown:** North of Buffalo Bayou. **South of Downtown:** South of I-45 & US 59. **West of Downtown:** West of I-45.
Galleria Area: South of San Felipe, west of Loop 610, north of Richmond Ave and east of Chimney Rock Ave.
Hermann Park Area: South of Bissonnet and Binz Sts, west of Almeda Rd, north of Old Spanish Trail and east of Kirby Dr.
River Oaks: South of Buffalo Bayou, west of S Shepherd Dr, north of Westheimer Rd and east of Willowick Rd.

Lodgings and Food

HOUSTON RESTAURANTS
BY NEIGHBORHOOD AREAS

(For full description, see alphabetical listings under Restaurants)

DOWNTOWN

Birraporetti's. 500 Louisiana St

Bistro Lancaster (Lancaster Hotel). 701 Texas Ave

Charley's 517. 517 Louisiana St

Damian's. 3011 Smith St

Dong Ting. 611 Stuart St

DeVille (Four Seasons Hotel-Houston Center). 1300 Lamar St

Kim Son. 2001 Jefferson St

Nino's. 2817 W Dallas St

NORTH OF DOWNTOWN

La Tour d'Argent. 2011 Ella Blvd

SOUTH OF DOWNTOWN

Brennan's. 3300 Smith St

Luby's Cafeteria. 5215 Buffalo Speedway

Maxim's. 3755 Richmond Ave

WEST OF DOWNTOWN

Anthony's. 4007 Westheimer

Bistro Vino. 819 W Alabama St

Butera's on Montrose. 4621 Montrose Blvd

Captain Benny's Half Shell. 8018 Katy Frwy

Chez Georges. 11920-J Westheimer

Churrasco's. 2055 Westheimer Rd

Confederate House. 2925 Weslayan St

The Dining Room (The Ritz-Carlton, Houston Hotel). 1919 Briar Oaks Lane

Doneraki. 7705 Westheimer Rd

Great Caruso. 10001 Westheimer Rd

Jags. 5120 Woodway Dr

La Colombe d'Or (La Colombe D'or Inn). 3410 Montrose Blvd

La Reserve (Omni Houston Hotel). 4 Riverway

Montesano Ristorante Italiano. 6009 Beverly Hill Lane

Otto's Barbecue. 5502 Memorial Dr

Pappadeaux. 6015 Westheimer Rd

Pappasito's Cantina. 6445 Richmond Ave

Rainbow Lodge. 1 Birdsall St

Rivoli. 5636 Richmond Ave

Rotisserie for Beef and Bird. 2200 Wilcrest Dr

Ruggles Grill. 903 Westheimer Rd

Ruth's Chris Steak House. 6213 Richmond Ave

Strawberry Patch. 5839 Westheimer Rd

Vargo's. 2401 Fondren Rd

GALLERIA AREA

Americas. 1800 S Post Oak Blvd

Cafe Annie. 1728 Post Oak Blvd

Chianti Cucina Rustica. 1515 S Post Oak Lane

Gugenheim's Delicatessen. 1708 Post Oak Blvd

Hunan. 1800 Post Oak Blvd

Post Oak Grill. 1415 S Post Oak Lane

HERMANN PARK AREA

Kaphan's. 7900 S Main St

Prego. 2520 Amherst St

Quilted Toque. 3939 Montrose Blvd

RIVER OAKS

Armando's. 2300 Westheimer

Brownstone. 2736 Virgina St

Carrabba's. 3115 Kirby Dr

Grotto. 3920 Westheimer Rd

La Griglia. 2002 W Gray St

River Oaks Grill. 2630 Westheimer Rd

Shanghai River. 2407 Westheimer Rd

Sierra. 4704 Montrose Blvd

Tony Mandola's Gulf Coast Kitchen. 1962 W Gray St

Note: *When a listing is located in a town that does not have its own city heading, it will appear under the city nearest to its location. In these cases, the address and town appear in parenthesis immediately following the name of the establishment.*

Motels

(Rates may be higher for sports & special events in Astrodome.)

✔★ **HAMPTON INN.** *828 Mercury Dr (77013), east of downtown. 713/673-4200; FAX 713/674-6913. 89 rms, 6 story. S $54-$60; D $57-$63; under 18 free. Crib free. Pet accepted. TV; cable. Pool. Complimentary continental bkfst. Complimentary coffee in lobby. Restaurant adj 6 am-2 pm, 5-10 pm. Ck-out noon. Coin lndry. Valet serv. Some refrigerators. Cr cds: A, C, D, DS, MC, V.*

✔★ **HOLIDAY INN EXPRESS.** *702 N Sam Houston Pkwy E (77060), north of downtown. 713/999-9942. 200 rms, 4 story. S, D $54; each addl $6; under 10 free; higher rates wkends. Crib free. TV; cable. Pool. Complimentary continental bkfst. Ck-out noon. Meeting rms. Free Intercontinental Airport transportation. Exercise equipt; weights, stair machine. Cr cds: A, C, D, DS, MC, V.*

★★ **LA QUINTA GREENWAY PLAZA.** *4015 Southwest Frwy (77027), Weslayan Rd exit, south of downtown. 713/623-4750; FAX 713/963-0599. 131 rms, 2-3 story. S, D $57-$64; each addl $8; suites $75-$83; under 18 free; family units. Crib free. Pet accepted, some restrictions. TV; cable. Pool. Complimentary continental bkfst. Ck-out noon. Coin lndry. Meeting rms. Cr cds: A, C, D, DS, MC, V.*

★ **LA QUINTA WILCREST.** *11113 Katy Freeway (77079), west of downtown. 713/932-0808; FAX 713/973-2352. 176 rms, 2 story. S $55-$65; D $61-$71; each addl $6; under 18 free. Crib free. Pet accepted. TV. Pool. Complimentary continental bkfst. Restaurant adj open 24 hrs. Ck-out noon. Meeting rms. Cr cds: A, C, D, DS, MC, V.*

✔★ **LEXINGTON HOTEL SUITES.** *16410 I-45N (77090), 25 mi N, north of downtown.* 713/821-1000; FAX 713/821-1420. 248 kit. suites, 3 story. Suites $55-$89; each addl $5; under 18 free; wkly rates. Crib free. TV; cable. Heated pool. Complimentary continental bkfst. Complimentary coffee in rms. Restaurant adj 6:30 am-10 pm. Ck-out noon. Coin lndry. Meeting rms. Valet serv. Free airport transportation. Health club privileges. Cr cds: A, C, D, DS, MC, V.

D ≈ ⅃ ⅍ SC

★ **QUALITY INN INTERCONTINENTAL AIRPORT.** *PO Box 60135 (77205), 6115 Will Clayton Pkwy, near Intercontinental Airport, north of downtown.* 713/446-9131; FAX 713/446-2251. 135 rms, 2 story. S $52-$62; D $62-$70; each addl $7; suites $75; studio rms $60-$69; under 18 free; wkend rates. Crib free. Pet accepted; $15. TV; cable. Pool; poolside serv. Restaurant 6 am-10 pm. Rm serv. Bar 4 pm-midnight; entertainment, dancing Fri. Ck-out 11 am. Meeting rms. Bellhops. Sundries. Free 24-hour airport transportation. Tennis. Balconies. Cr cds: A, C, D, DS, ER, JCB, MC, V.

D ☞ ✗ ≈ ✈ ⅃ ⅍ SC

★ **RESIDENCE INN BY MARRIOTT.** *535 Bay Area Blvd (77058), off I-45.* 713/486-2424; FAX 713/488-8179. 110 kit. units, 2 story. S, D $140-$170; under 16 free; wkend rates. Crib free. Pet accepted; $50 and $6 per day. TV; cable. Heated pool. Complimentary coffee in rms. Complimentary continental bkfst, evening refreshments. Restaurant adj 11 am-11 pm. Ck-out noon. Coin lndry. Meeting rm. Lawn games. Exercise equipt; weight machine, stair machine. Cr cds: A, C, D, DS, JCB, MC, V.

D ☞ ≈ ✗ ⅃ ⅍ SC

★ **RESIDENCE INN BY MARRIOTT-ASTRODOME.** *7710 S Main St (77030), S edge of Medical center, in Hermann Park Area.* 713/660-7993; FAX 713/660-8019. 285 kit. suites. Kit. suites $95-$125; family, medical rates. Crib free. Pet accepted; $25 and $5 per day. TV; cable. Heated pool; whirlpool. Complimentary continental bkfst. Bar. Ck-out noon. Meeting rms. Valet serv. Lawn games. Private patios, balconies. Picnic tables, grills. Cr cds: A, C, D, DS, MC, V.

D ☞ ≈ ⅃ ⅍ SC

Motor Hotels

★★★ **ALLEN PARK INN.** *2121 Allen Parkway (77019), downtown.* 713/521-9321; res: 800/231-6310; FAX 713/521-9321. 249 rms, 3 story. S, D $78-$98; each addl $8; suites $250; under 10 free; wkly, wkend rates. Crib free. TV; cable, in-rm movies avail. Pool; poolside serv. Restaurant open 24 hrs. Rm serv 24 hrs. Bar 10-2 am, Sun from noon. Ck-out noon. Coin lndry. Meeting rms. Gift shop. Barber, beauty shop. Exercise equipt; weights, bicycles, whirlpool, sauna. Bathrm phones. Some refrigerators. Private patios, balconies. Cr cds: A, C, D, DS, MC, V.

D ≈ ✗ ⅃ ⅍ SC

★★ **COURTYARD BY MARRIOTT.** *2504 N Loop West (77092), north of downtown.* 713/688-7711; FAX 713/688-3561. 202 rms, 3 story. S $77-$87; D $87-$97; each addl $10; suite $175; wkend rates. Crib free. TV; cable. Heated pool. Restaurant 6:30 am-11 pm. Rm serv. Bar 11:30 am-midnight. Ck-out 1 pm. Coin lndry. Meeting rms. Valet serv. Exercise equipt; weights, bicycles, whirlpool. Some refrigerators, wet bars. Cr cds: A, C, D, DS, ER, MC, V.

D ≈ ✗ ⅃ ⅍ SC

★★ **HOLIDAY INN-ASTRODOME.** *8111 Kirby Dr (77054), south of downtown.* 713/790-1900; FAX 713/799-8574. 235 rms, 11 story. S $75; D $85; each addl $10; suites $195-$250; under 19 free; wkend rates; higher rates Livestock Show & Rodeo. Crib free. TV; cable. Pool. Restaurant 6 am-10 pm. Rm serv. Bar 11-2 am. Ck-out noon. Meeting rms. Bellhops. Valet serv. Sundries. Gift shop. Free bus depot, Astrodomain, Medical Center, Galleria transportation. Exercise equipt; weights, treadmill, whirlpool. Some bathrm phones, refrigerators, wet bars. Cr cds: A, C, D, DS, JCB, MC, V.

D ≈ ✗ ⅃ ⅍ SC

★ **RAMADA HOTEL.** *12801 Northwest Frwy (77040), north of downtown.* 713/462-9977; FAX 713/462-9977, ext. 345. 296 rms, 10 story. S $79; D $89; each addl $10; suites $105-$210; under 12 free; wkend rates. Pet accepted, some restrictions. TV; cable. Pool; poolside serv. Restaurant 6 am-10 pm. Rm serv. Bar 11-2 am; dancing. Ck-out 1 pm. Meeting rms. Bellhops. Valet serv. Sundries. Gift shop. Free bus depot transportation. Exercise equipt; weights, stair machine, sauna. Health club privileges. Some bathrm phones; refrigerator, wet bar, in suites. Cr cds: A, C, D, DS, MC, V.

D ☞ ≈ ✗ ⅃ ⅃ ⅍ SC

★ **RAMADA HOTEL.** *2100 S Braeswood Blvd (77030), at Greenbriar, in Hermann Park Area.* 713/797-9000; FAX 713/799-8362. 339 rms, 2-3 story. S $69-$100; D $79-$109; suites $150-$275; family, medical rates. Crib free. Pet accepted. TV; cable. Pool; wading pool, poolside serv, lifeguard. Restaurants 6:30 am-2 pm, 5-10 pm. Bar. Ck-out noon. Coin lndry. Convention facilities. Valet serv. Gift shop. Barber. Free bus terminal (airport link), Medical Center transportation. Exercise equipt; weight machines, bicycles. Game rm. Private patios. Cr cds: A, C, D, DS, ER, JCB, MC, V.

D ☞ ≈ ✗ ✗ ⅃ ⅍ SC

Hotels

★★ **ADAM'S MARK.** *2900 Briar Park (77042), west of downtown.* 713/978-7400; res: 800/444-ADAM; FAX 713/235-2727, ext. 207. 604 rms, 10 story. S, D $89-$149; each addl $15; suites $175-$750; under 18 free; wkend rates. Crib free. TV; cable. Heated indoor/outdoor pool; wading pool, hot tub, poolside serv. Restaurant 6 am-midnight. Rm serv 24 hrs. Bars 11-2 am; entertainment, dancing. Ck-out noon. Meeting rms. Concierge. Gift shop. Galleria transportation. Exercise equipt; weights, bicycles, whirlpool, sauna. Game rm. Some refrigerators. Some balconies. Artwork in lobby. Cr cds: A, C, D, DS, MC, V.

D ≈ ✗ ⅃ ⅍ SC

★★★ **DOUBLETREE.** *15747 John F. Kennedy Blvd (77032), north of downtown.* 713/442-8000; FAX 713/590-8461. 309 rms, 7 story. S $103-$133; D $113-$150; each addl $10; under 18 free. Crib free. Pet accepted; $25. TV; cable. Pool; poolside serv. Restaurant 6 am-2 pm, 5-11 pm. Bar 11 am-midnight. Ck-out noon. Meeting rms. Gift shop. Free Intl Airport transportation. Exercise equipt; weight machine, treadmill, whirlpool. Cr cds: A, C, D, DS, ER, JCB, MC, V.

D ☞ ≈ ✗ ⅃ ⅍ SC

★★ **DOUBLETREE AT ALLEN CENTER.** *400 Dallas St (77002), downtown.* 713/759-0202; FAX 713/752-2734. 341 rms, 20 story. S $125-$150; D $140-$170; each addl $20; suites $225-$675; under 17 free; wkend rates. Crib free. Pet accepted, some restrictions; $100 refundable. TV; cable. Restaurants 6 am-10 pm. Bar 11-2 am; entertainment Mon-Fri. Ck-out noon. Meeting rms. Concierge. Gift shop. Free downtown area transportation. Elegant hanging tapestries. Cr cds: A, C, D, DS, ER, JCB, MC, V.

D ☞ ⅃ ⅍ SC

★★ **DOUBLETREE POST OAK.** *PO Box 22388 (77056), 2001 Post Oak Blvd, in Galleria Area.* 713/961-9300; FAX 713/623-6685. 450 rms, 14 story. S $125-$145; D $145-$165; each addl $20; suites $190-$1,200; under 18 free; wkend rates. Crib free. Valet parking $11; garage $2. TV; cable. Pool; poolside serv. Restaurant 6:30 am-11 pm. Rm serv 24 hrs. Bar 11-1 am; wkends to 2 am; Sun from noon. Ck-out noon. Convention facilities. Concierge. Shopping arcade. Barber, beauty shop. Free transportation to Galleria area. Exercise equipt; weights, stair machine, sauna. Health club privileges adj. Many bathrm phones; some refrigerators. Balconies. Cr cds: A, C, D, DS, JCB, MC, V.

D ≈ ✗ ⅃ ⅍ SC

★★ **EMBASSY SUITES.** *9090 Southwest Frwy (77074), south of downtown.* 713/995-0123; FAX 713/779-0703. 243 suites, 9 story. Suites $104-$139; each addl $10; under 12 free; wkend rates.

Crib free. TV; cable. Indoor pool. Complimentary full bkfst 6-9 am; Sat, Sun 7-10:30 am. Complimentary coffee in rms. Restaurant adj 11:30 am-11 pm. Ck-out noon. Meeting rms. Drugstore. Free bus depot transportation. Exercise equipt; weights, stair machine, whirlpool, sauna. Game rm. Refrigerators, wet bars; some bathrm phones. Balconies. Cr cds: A, C, D, DS, JCB, MC, V.

★ ★ ★ ★ **FOUR SEASONS HOTEL-HOUSTON CENTER.** *1300 Lamar St (77010), downtown.* 713/650-1300; FAX 713/650-8169. 399 rms, 30 story. S $180-$250; D $205-$275; each addl $25; suites $495-$1,175; under 18 free; wkend rates. Crib free. Pet accepted. Valet & covered parking $13/day. TV; cable, in-rm movies avail. Heated pool; poolside serv. Restaurant (see DeVILLE). Rm serv 24 hrs. Bar 11-1 am; entertainment. Ck-out 1 pm. Meeting rms. Concierge. Shopping arcade. Free transportation to downtown area. Exercise rm; instructor, bicycles, rowing machine, whirlpool, sauna. Massage. Health club privileges. Bathrm phones, minibars; some refrigerators. Cr cds: A, C, D, ER, JCB, MC, V.

★ ★ ★ **GUEST QUARTERS GALLERIA WEST.** *5353 Westheimer Rd (77056), in Galleria Area.* 713/961-9000; FAX 713/877-8835. 335 suites, 26 story. S $169; D $189; each addl $20; 2-bedrm kit. suites $229-$269; under 18 free; wkend rates. Crib free. Pet accepted; $10 per night. TV; cable. Pool; poolside serv. Restaurant 6:30 am-10 pm; Sat, Sun 7 am-10 pm. Bar 5 pm-midnight. Ck-out noon. Coin lndry. Local area, Medical Center transportation. Tennis privileges. Exercise equipt; weights, bicycles, whirlpool. Health club privileges. Game rm. Refrigerators. Some balconies. Cr cds: A, C, D, DS, MC, V.

31.11 to 3.11.95

★ ★ **HARVEY SUITES-MEDICAL CENTER.** *6800 Main St (77030), in Hermann Park Area.* 713/528-7744; res: 800/922-9222; FAX 713/528-6983. 285 rms, 12 story, 212 kit. suites. S $84; D $94; kit. suites $159; under 18 free. Crib free. TV; cable. Pool. Complimentary coffee in rms. Restaurant 6:30 am-11 pm. Rm serv. Bar from 11 am. Ck-out 1 pm. Coin lndry. Meeting rms. Bellhops. Concierge. Valet serv. Gift shop. Free medical center transportation. Health club privileges. Cr cds: A, C, D, DS, MC, V.

✔ ★ ★ **HILTON NASSAU BAY.** *3000 NASA Rd 1 (77058), south of downtown.* 713/333-9300; FAX 713/333-3750. 244 rms, 14 story. S $89-$119; D $99-$124; each addl $10; suites $250-$500; family rates; wkend packages. Crib avail. Pet accepted, some restrictions; $3 per day. TV; cable, in-rm movies. Pool; poolside serv. Restaurant 6 am-11 pm. Bar 5 pm-2 am; entertainment, dancing. Ck-out 1 pm. Meeting rms. Free airport transportation. Exercise equipt; weights, bicycles, whirlpool. Sailboating, windsurfing, waterskiing. Many bathrm phones. Marina shops. Balconies with view of lake, marina. *LUXURY LEVEL :* **PENTHOUSE LEVEL.** 18 rms. S $119-$124; D $124-$129. Concierge. Private lounge. Bathrm phones. Complimentary continental bkfst, refreshments. Cr cds: A, C, D, DS, ER, MC, V.

★ ★ ★ **HILTON PLAZA.** *6633 Travis St (77030), adj Medical Center, in Hermann Park Area.* 713/524-6633; FAX 713/529-6806. 185 units, 19 story. S $110-$145; D $120-$155; each addl $10; medical, wkend rates. Crib free. Garage $6 (wkends $3). TV; cable. Heated rooftop pool; poolside serv. Restaurant 6:30 am-11 pm. Bar 4 pm-midnight; pianist. Ck-out 1 pm. Meeting rms. Free Medical Center, Galleria transportation. Exercise rm; instructor, weights, bicycles, whirlpool, sauna. Bathrm phones, refrigerators, wet bars. Adj to museums, parks, Rice Univ. *LUXURY LEVEL :* **CONCIERGE FLOOR.** 42 units, 2 floors, 28 suites. S $120; D $130; suites $140—$150. Concierge. Private lounge, honor bar. Complimentary continental bkfst, refreshments, newspaper. Cr cds: A, C, D, DS, MC, V.

★ ★ ★ **HILTON WESTCHASE.** *9999 Westheimer Rd (77042), west of downtown.* 713/974-1000; FAX 713/974-6866. 300 rms, 13

story. S $99; $109; each addl $10; suites $114-$124; under 18 free; wkend rates. Crib free. TV; cable. Heated pool; poolside serv. Complimentary coffee in rms. Restaurant 6:30 am-10 pm. Rm serv 24 hrs. Bar 11:30 am-midnight. Ck-out 1 pm. Convention facilities. Concierge. Gift shop. Barber, beauty shop. Exercise equipt; weight machine, stair machine, whirlpool, sauna. Minibars. Cr cds: A, C, D, DS, ER, JCB, MC, V.

★ ★ **HOLIDAY INN CROWNE PLAZA-GALLERIA.** *2222 West Loop S (77027), in Galleria Area.* 713/961-7272; FAX 713/961-3327. 477 rms, 23 story. S $89-$135; D $99-$145; each addl $10; suites $150-$250; under 19 free; wkend rates. Valet parking $8. Crib free. TV; cable. Indoor pool; poolside serv, hot tub. Complimentary coffee in rms. Restaurants 6 am-10 pm. Bar 11-2 am; entertainment. Ck-out noon. Coin lndry. Convention facilities. Concierge. Gift shop. Free garage parking. Galleria area transportation. Exercise equipt; weights, bicycles, whirlpool, sauna. Some refrigerators. *LUXURY LEVEL :* **CROWNE PLAZA CLUB.** 19 rms, 2 suites. S $145; D $155; each addl $10; suites from $250. Complimentary continental bkfst, refreshments. Cr cds: A, C, D, DS, JCB, MC, V.

★ ★ **HOLIDAY INN HOBBY AIRPORT.** *9100 Gulf Freeway (I-45) (77017), near Hobby Airport, south of downtown.* 713/943-7979; FAX 713/943-2160. 288 rms, 10 story. S $98-$134; D $108-$144; each addl $10; under 18 free; wkend rates. Crib free. Pet accepted. TV; cable. Indoor pool; poolside serv. Restaurant 5:30 am-10 pm. Bar; entertainment Fri & Sat. Ck-out noon. Meeting rms. Gift shop. Free airport transportation. Exercise equipt; weight machine, stair machine, whirlpool, sauna. Cr cds: A, C, D, DS, ER, JCB, MC, V.

★ ★ **HOLIDAY INN-WEST.** *14703 Park Row (77079), west of downtown.* 713/558-5580; FAX 713/496-4150. 345 rms, 19 story. S $90-$105; D $100-$115; each addl $10; suites $250; under 18 free; wkend rates. Pet accepted; $15. TV; cable. Indoor pool; poolside serv. Restaurant 6:30 am-2 pm, 5:30-10 pm. Rm serv 6:30 am-10 pm. Bar 4 pm-midnight; Fri, Sat to 2 am; dancing exc Sun. Ck-out 1 pm. Convention facilities. Gift shop. Exercise equipt; weights, bicycles, whirlpool. Holidome. *LUXURY LEVEL :* **EXECUTIVE LEVEL.** 36 rms. S, D $115-$125. Complimentary continental bkfst, newspaper. Cr cds: A, C, D, DS, JCB, MC, V.

★ ★ **HOTEL SOFITEL.** *425 Sam Houston Pkwy E (77060), north of downtown.* 713/445-9000; FAX 713/445-9826. 337 rms, 8 story. S $115-$125; D $125-$135; each addl $20; suites $145-$300; under 18 free; wkend rates. Crib free. TV; cable, in-rm movies avail. Pool; hot tubs. Restaurant 6 am-midnight. Rm serv 5:30-2 am. Bar 11-2 am; entertainment. Ck-out noon. Convention facilities. Concierge. Shopping arcade. Airport transportation. Exercise equipt; weight machine, bicycles, whirlpool, sauna. French bakery in lobby. Cr cds: A, C, D, JCB, MC, V.

★ ★ **HOUSTON MEDALLION.** *3000 North Loop W (77092), north of downtown.* 713/688-0100; res: 800/688-3000; FAX 713/688-9224. 382 rms, 10 story. S $105-$135; D $115-$145; each addl $10; family, wkend rates. Crib free. Pet accepted, some restrictions. TV; cable. Pool; poolside serv. Restaurant 6 am-2 pm, 5-10 pm. Rm serv to 1 am. Bar 11-1 am. Ck-out noon. Meeting rms. Gift shop. Free garage parking. Exercise equipt; weight machine, bicycles, whirlpool, sauna. Refrigerators avail. *LUXURY LEVEL :* **CONCIERGE FLOORS.** 84 rms, 2 suites, 2 floors. S $120-$150; D $130-$160; suites $290-$300. Ck-out 3 pm. Concierge. Private lounge, honor bar. Complimentary continental bkfst, refreshments. Cr cds: A, C, D, DS, JCB, MC, V.

★ ★ ★ **HOUSTONIAN.** *111 N Post Oak Lane (77024), west of downtown.* 713/680-2626; res: 800/231-2759; FAX 713/680-2992. 292 rms, 4 story. S $134-$164; D $134-$164; each addl $20; suites $225;

under 18 free; wkend, hol rates, packages. Crib free. TV; cable, in-rm movies. 2 heated pools. Restaurant 6:30 am-10 pm. Bar 11-2 am; Sun from noon. Ck-out noon. Convention facilities. Concierge. Gift shop. Free garage parking; valet. Lighted tennis, pro. Golf privileges. Exercise rm; instructor, weights, bicycles, whirlpool, sauna. Game rm. Lawn games. Minibars. *LUXURY LEVEL* . 74 units. S, D $184; suites $275-$925. Complimentary continental bkfst, refreshments. Cr cds: A, C, D, DS, MC, V.

[D] [icons] SC

★ ★ ★ **HYATT REGENCY.** 1200 Louisiana St (77002), at Polk St, downtown. 713/654-1234; FAX 713/951-0934. 959 rms, 30 story. S $130-$161; D $155-$186; each addl $25; suites $300-$850; under 18 free; wkend rates. Crib free. Valet parking $11. TV; cable. Pool; poolside serv. Restaurant 6 am-11 pm. Bar 11-2 am; entertainment. Ck-out noon. Convention facilities. Concierge. Airport transportation. Exercise equipt; weights, bicycles. Bathrm phones, refrigerators. Built around spectacular 30-story atrium; glass-enclosed elvtrs. Covered passage to downtown buildings. Cr cds: A, C, D, DS, ER, JCB, MC, V.

[D] [icons] SC

★ ★ ★ **J.W. MARRIOTT-HOUSTON.** 5150 Westheimer Rd (77056), in Galleria Area. 713/961-1500; FAX 713/961-5045. 494 rms, 23 story. S $135-$155; D $145-$165; suites $175-$600; under 18 free; wkend rates. Crib free. Valet parking $11, self-park free. TV; cable. Indoor/outdoor pool; poolside serv. Restaurant 6:30 am-2 pm, 5:30-11 pm. Bar 11-1 am. Ck-out noon. Convention facilities. Concierge. Gift shop. Barber, beauty shop. Exercise rm; instructor, weights, bicycles, whirlpool, sauna, steam rm. Game rm. Bathrm phones. Refrigerator in suites. Lobby furnished with marble, rich paneling and artwork. *LUXURY LEVEL : CONCIERGE LEVEL.* 65 rms, 5 floors. S, D $145-$155; each addl $10. Private lounge, honor bar. Complimentary continental bkfst, refreshments. Cr cds: A, C, D, DS, ER, JCB, MC, V.

[D] [icons] SC

★ ★ ★ **LANCASTER.** 701 Texas Ave (77002), downtown. 713/228-9500; FAX 713/223-4528. 93 rms, 12 story. S $175-$215; D $185-$225; each addl $25; suites $325-$825; under 16 free; wkend rates. Crib free. Valet parking $12. TV; cable. Restaurant (see BISTRO LANCASTER). Rm serv 24 hrs. Bars 11 am-midnight. Ck-out 1 pm. Meeting rms. Concierge. Downtown transportation 7 am-11 pm. Health club privileges. Bathrm phones, refrigerators, minibars. Complimentary newspaper, shoe shine. Beautifully restored 1926 hotel in theater district. Cr cds: A, C, D, DS, JCB, MC, V.

[D] [icons]

★ ★ ★ **MARRIOTT AIRPORT.** 18700 Kennedy Blvd (77032), at Intercontinental Airport, north of downtown. 713/443-2310; FAX 713/443-5294. 566 rms, 3 & 7 story. S, D $110-$130; suites $250-$350; studio rms $150-$250; under 18 free; wkend rates. Crib free. Pet accepted. TV; cable. Pool; poolside serv. Restaurant 5:30 am-11:30 pm. Bar 11-2 am, Sat from 4 pm, Sun noon-midnight; dancing. Ck-out 1 pm. Free lndry facilities. Convention facilities. Shopping arcade. Barber, beauty shop. Free subway to airport terminals. Exercise equipt; stair machine, treadmill. Some bathrm phones, refrigerators. Some private patios. *LUXURY LEVEL : CONCIERGE LEVEL.* 41 units. S, D $135. Concierge. Private lounge, honor bar. Complimentary continental bkfst, refreshments. Cr cds: A, C, D, DS, ER, JCB, MC, V.

[D] [icons] SC

★ ★ ★ **MARRIOTT MEDICAL CENTER.** 6580 Fannin St (77030), at Texas Medical Center, in Hermann Park Area. 713/796-0080; FAX 713/770-8100. 389 rms, 26 story. S, D $119; suites $165-$600; under 18 free; wkend, medical rates. Crib free. Garage $7; valet parking $13. TV; cable. Indoor pool; whirlpool, sauna, poolside serv. Restaurant 6:30 am-11 pm. Ck-out noon. Coin lndry. Convention facilities. Concierge. Shopping arcade. Bus depot, medical center transportation. Health club privileges. Refrigerators. Connected to Medical Center; covered walks. *LUXURY LEVEL : CONCIERGE FLOOR.* 38 rms, 2 floors. S, D $129. Private lounge. Bathrm phones. Complimen-

tary continental bkfst, refreshments, newspaper. Cr cds: A, C, D, DS, JCB, MC, V.

[D] [icons] SC

★ ★ ★ **MARRIOTT NORTII AT GREENSPOINT.** 255 N Sam Houston Pkwy E (77060), adj Greenspoint Mall, north of downtown. 713/875-4000; FAX 713/875-6208. 391 rms, 12 story. S, D $119-$146; suites $250-$350; under 17 free; wkend rates. Crib free. Pet accepted. TV; cable. Indoor/outdoor pool; poolside serv. Restaurant 6:30 am-midnight. Bar 11-2 am. Ck-out 1 pm. Coin lndry. Convention facilities. Concierge. Gift shop. Free garage parking. Free airport, mall transportation. Exercise equipt; weights, bicycles, whirlpool, sauna. *LUXURY LEVEL : CONCIERGE LEVEL.* 713/875-4000, ext 7823. 86 rms, 2 floors. S, D $129-$146. Private lounge, honor bar. Complimentary continental bkfst, refreshments, newspaper. Cr cds: A, C, D, DS, ER, JCB, MC, V.

[D] [icons] SC

★ ★ ★ **MARRIOTT WESTSIDE.** 13210 Katy Frwy (77079), west of downtown. 713/558-8338; FAX 713/558-4028. 400 rms, 5 story. S, D $119-$130; under 10 free; wkend rates. Crib free. Valet parking $7. Pet accepted, some restrictions. TV; cable. Heated pool; poolside serv. Restaurant 6 am-3 pm, 5-11 pm. Bar; pianist Mon-Fri. Ck-out noon. Convention facilities. Gift shop. Exercise equipt; weight machine, rowers, whirlpool. Cr cds: A, C, D, DS, MC, V.

[D] [icons] SC

★ ★ ★ **OMNI HOUSTON HOTEL.** 4 Riverway (77056), west of downtown. 713/871-8181; res: 800/843-6664; FAX 713/871-0719. 381 rms, 11 story. S $145-$195; D $170-$220; each addl $25; suites $225-$650; under 17 free; wkend rates. Crib free. Garage: valet parking $11, self-park free. TV; cable, in-rm movies avail. 2 pools, 1 heated; poolside serv. Restaurant (see LA RESERVE). Rm serv 24 hrs. Bar 11:30-2 am; entertainment, dancing. Ck-out 1 pm. Meeting rms. Concierge. Transportation to Galleria area. Tennis. Exercise rm; instructor, weights, bicycles, whirlpool, sauna. Minibars. Elegant contemporary decor. Small lake, sculpture, waterfall. Cr cds: A, C, D, DS, ER, JCB, MC, V.

[D] [icons] SC

★ ★ ★ **THE RITZ-CARLTON, HOUSTON.** 1919 Briar Oaks Lane (77027), near Galleria Center, west of downtown. 713/840-7600; res: 800/241-3333; FAX 713/840-8036. 232 rms, 12 story, 3 kits. S $160-$255; D $190-$285; each addl $20; suites $475-$1,900; kit. units $1,400-$1,900; under 18 free; wkend rates. Valet parking $13.50. Crib free. TV; cable. Heated pool; poolside serv. Restaurant (see THE DINING ROOM). Bar; entertainment. Harpist at afternoon tea (3-5 pm). Ck-out noon. Meeting rms. Concierge. Gift shop. Free transportation within 3 mi radius. Exercise equipt; treadmill, bicycle. Health club privileges. Bathrm phones; whirlpool in suites. Many antiques; elegant. *LUXURY LEVEL : RITZ-CARLTON CLUB.* 66 rms, 12 suites, 3 floors. S, D $187-$255; suites $275-$525. Concierge. Private lounge. Some wet bars. Complimentary continental bkfst, refreshments, afternoon tea, newspapers. Cr cds: A, C, D, DS, ER, JCB, MC, V.

[D] [icons] SC

★ ★ **SHERATON CROWN HOTEL & CONFERENCE CENTER.** 15700 John F Kennedy Blvd (77032), north of downtown. 713/442-5100; FAX 713/987-9130. 418 rms, 10 story. S $105-$120; D $115-$130; each addl $10; suites $150-$600; under 18 free; wkend rates. Crib free. TV; cable. 2 pools, 1 indoor. Coffee in rms. Restaurants 6 am-11 pm. Bars 11 am-1 am. Ck-out noon. Convention facilities; amphitheater. Gift shop. Free airport transportation. Putting greens. Exercise equipt; treadmill, stair machine, whirlpool. Some refrigerators. *LUXURY LEVEL : CONCIERGE FLOOR.* 53 rms, 6 suites. S, D $120-$150; suites $150-$300. Concierge. Complimentary continental bkfst (Mon-Fri), refreshments. Cr cds: A, C, D, DS, ER, MC, V.

[D] [icons] SC

★ ★ **SHERATON GALLERIA.** 2525 West Loop South (77027), in Galleria area. 713/961-3000; FAX 713/961-1490. 321 rms, 14 story. S $136-$159; D $146-$169; each addl $10; suites $325-$500;

under 18 free; wkend rates. Crib free. Pet accepted; $50 deposit. Valet parking $9. Pool; poolside serv. Restaurant 6 am-10 pm. Rm serv 24 hrs. Bar 4 pm-midnight. Ck-out noon. Coin lndry. Convention facilities. Gift shop. Exercise equipt; weight machine, treadmill, whirlpool, sauna. Cr cds: A, D, DS, MC, V.

★ ★ **STOUFFER PRESIDENTE.** 6 Greenway Plaza E (77046), west of downtown. 713/629-1200; FAX 713/629-4702. 389 rms, 20 story. S $119-$159; D $129-$169; each addl $10; suites $300-$750; under 18 free; wkend rates. Crib free. Pet accepted, some restrictions. Garage parking; valet $8, self-park free. TV; cable. Pool; poolside serv, hot tub. Complimentary coffee in rms. Restaurant 6:30 am-10 pm. Rm serv 24 hrs. Bar 11:30-2 am; entertainment Mon-Sat. Ck-out 1 pm. Convention facilities. Tennis privileges. Free surrounding area transportation. Exercise equipt; weights, bicycles, sauna. Bathrm phones; some refrigerators. Complimentary newspaper in rms. Cr cds: A, C, D, DS, ER, JCB, MC, V.

★ ★ **THE WESTIN GALLERIA.** 5060 W Alabama St (77056), in Galleria Area. 713/960-8100; FAX 713/960-6553. 492 rms, 24 story. S $110-$135; D $110-$150; each addl $15; suites $180-$1,250; under 18 free; wkend rates. Crib free. Valet parking $10.25. TV; cable. Heated pool; poolside serv. Restaurant 6:30 am-11 pm. Rm serv 24 hrs. Bar 11:30-2 am; Sun from noon. Ck-out 1 pm. Convention facilities. Concierge. Gift shop. Tennis privileges. Putting green. Game deck. Health club adj. Refrigerators; some bathroom phones. Balconies. Cr cds: A, C, D, DS, ER, MC, V.

★ ★ **THE WESTIN OAKS.** 5011 Westheimer Rd (77056), in Galleria Mall. 713/960-8100; FAX 713/960-6554. 406 rms, 21 story. S $110-$145; D $125-$185; each addl $15; suites $210-$1,300; wkend rates; under 18 free. Valet parking $10.25. Crib free. TV; cable. Heated pool; poolside serv. Supervised child's activities. Restaurant 6:30 am-10 pm. Rm serv 24 hrs. Bar 11:30-2 am, Sun from noon; entertainment, dancing exc Sun. Ck-out 1 pm. Meeting rms. Gift shop. Free garage parking. Concierge. Tennis privileges. Health club privileges. Refrigerators; some bathrm phones. Balconies. Cr cds: A, C, D, DS, ER, MC, V.

★ ★ ★ **WYNDHAM GREENSPOINT.** 12400 Greenspoint Dr (77060), adj Greenspoint Mall, north of downtown. 713/875-2222; res: 800/822-4200; FAX 713/875-1652. 472 rms, 16 story. S $149-$165; D $165-$185; each addl $10; suites $175-$500; studio rms $145; under 18 free; wkend rates. TV; cable. Pool. Restaurant 6 am-11 pm. Bar 4 pm-2 am; entertainment. Ck-out noon. Coin lndry. Convention facilities. Shopping arcade. Free airport transportation. Exercise equipt; weights, bicycles, whirlpool, sauna. Some refrigerators; bathrm phone in suites. Distinctive architectural design & decor. Cr cds: A, C, D, DS, JCB, MC, V.

★ ★ ★ **WYNDHAM WARWICK.** 5701 Main St (77005), near Rice University, in Hermann Park Area. 713/526-1991; res: 800/822-4200; FAX 713/639-4545. 308 rms, 12 story, 46 suites, 5 kits. S $139-$179; D $159-$197; each addl $20; suites $175-$1,200; kits. $245-$400; under 18 free; wkend plans. Self-parking $6.50, valet parking $10. TV; cable. Pool; poolside serv. Complimentary coffee in rms. Restaurant 6 am-10 pm. Bar 3 pm-2 am; entertainment. Ck-out noon. Convention facilities. Concierge. Gift shop. Beauty shop. Free medical center, downtown transportation. Exercise equipt; weight machine, bicycles, whirlpool, sauna. Bathrm phones; some refrigerators, wet bars. Balconies. Hotel offers luxury, elegance, and personal service in the grand European manner; many antiques and objets d'art displayed. Cr cds: A, C, D, DS, ER, JCB, MC, V.

Inns

★ ★ ★ ★ **LA COLOMBE D'OR.** 3410 Montrose Blvd (77006), west of downtown. 713/524-7999; FAX 713/524-8923. 6 suites, 3 story. Suites $195-$600. TV; cable. Restaurant (see LA COLOMBE D'OR). Rm serv. Bar 11 am-midnight. Concierge. Ck-out noon, ck-in 3 pm. Whirlpool. 21-rm residence built in 1923; decorated with works of local and well-known artists. All suites have private dining room; fruit furnished daily. Cr cds: A, C, D, DS, MC, V.

✔ ★ ★ **SARA'S BED & BREAKFAST.** 941 Heights Blvd (77008), north of downtown. 713/868-1130; res: 800/593-1130. 14 rms, 12 with bath. S, D $50-$75; each addl $10; suite $120; wkly rates. TV; in-rm movies avail. Complimentary continental bkfst, coffee. Restaurant nearby. Ck-out noon, ck-in 3 pm. Victorian house (1900); antiques, collectibles. Totally nonsmoking. Cr cds: A, C, D, DS, JCB, MC, V.

Resort

★ ★ ★ **WOODLANDS.** 2301 N Millbend St (77380), north of downtown. 713/367-1100; res: 800/433-2624 (exc TX), 800/533-3052 (TX); FAX 713/298-1621. 268 rms, 2 story. S $125-$160; D $140-$180; each addl $15; suites $145-$350; kit. units $145-$225; under 12 free; AP avail; wkend rates (seasonal), golf, tennis, package plans. TV; cable. 2 pools; wading pool, poolside serv, hot tub. Restaurants 6 am-11 pm. Rm serv. 3 bars 11-2 am, Sun from noon. Ck-out noon, ck-in after 3 pm. Meeting rms. Valet serv. Airport transportation. Indoor & outdoor lighted tennis, pro. 36-hole golf, greens fee $50-$95, 3 putting greens, 3 driving ranges, pro shop. Hiking, bicycle trails. Bicycle rentals. Game rm. Exercise rm; instructor, weights, bicycles, whirlpool, steam rm, sauna. Refrigerators. Private patios, balconies. Some lake views. Cr cds: A, C, D, DS, MC, V.

Restaurants

✔ ★ ★ **AMERICAS.** 1800 S Post Oak Blvd (77056), in Galleria Area. 713/961-1492. Hrs: 11 am-10 pm; Fri to 11 pm; Sat 5-11 pm. Closed Sun; most major hols. Res accepted. South American menu. Bar. Semi-a la carte: lunch $6.95-$9.95, dinner $9.95-$16.95. Child's meals. Specialties: roasted quail breast, filet of red snapper with fresh corn, plantain chips. Rain forest, Inca decor. Suspension bridge to second level. Cr cds: A, C, D, DS, MC, V.

★ ★ ★ **ANTHONY'S.** 4007 Westheimer, west of downtown. 713/961-0552. Hrs: 11:30 am-2 pm, 5:30-11 pm; Fri to 11:30 pm; Sat 5:30-11:30 pm. Closed Sun; major hols. Res accepted. Italian, Amer menu. Bar 11:30-2 am. Wine list. Semi-a la carte: lunch $8.95-$13, dinner $11.95-$25. Specializes in seafood, veal, beef. Own baking. Valet parking. Open hearth cooking. Cr cds: A, D, MC, V.

★ ★ **ARMANDO'S.** 2300 Westheimer, in River Oaks. 713/521-9757. Hrs: 11 am-2:30 pm, 5:30-11 pm; Sun, Mon to 10 pm; Sun brunch noon-2:30 pm. Closed Thanksgiving, Dec 25. Res accepted. Mexican, Amer menu. Bar. Semi-a la carte: lunch $6.95-$16.95, dinner $8.95-$17.95. Specializes in chicken enchiladas, fajitas. Own tortillas. Valet parking. Outdoor dining. Local modern art displays. Cr cds: A, MC, V.

✔ ★ **BIRRAPORETTI'S.** 500 Louisiana St, adj to Alley Theatre, downtown. 713/224-9494. Hrs: 11 am-11 pm; Fri-Sat to midnight. Res accepted. Italian menu. Bar. Semi-a la carte: lunch, dinner $6.95-$12.95. Child's meals. Specializes in lasagne, pollo poretti, fetuccine panna e pollo. In Theater District. Cr cds: A, C, D, DS, MC, V.

★ ★ ★ **BISTRO LANCASTER.** (See Lancaster Hotel) 713/228-9502. Hrs: 6:30 am-11 pm; Fri, Sat to midnight; Sun 7:30 am-11 pm. Res accepted. Bar. A la carte entrees: bkfst $6-$9.95, lunch $6.50-$17.95, dinner $17.95-$23.95. Specializes in wild mushroom quesadillas, pecan & black pepper crusted venison, crawfish. Valet parking. Beautifully restored hotel built 1926. Cr cds: A, C, D, JCB, MC, V.

D

★ ★ **BISTRO VINO.** 819 W Alabama St, west of downtown. 713/526-5500. Hrs: 11:30 am-11 pm; Fri & Sat to midnight. Closed Sun. Closed most major hols. Res accepted. French, Italian menu. Bar. Semi-a la carte: lunch $6.95-$15, dinner $7.95-$18. Complete meals: dinner $17.95-$24.95. Specialties: veal Milanese, osso buco, filet au poivre. Entertainment. Valet parking. Outdoor dining. Romantic atmosphere. Cr cds: A, C, D, MC, V.

D

★ ★ ★ **BRENNAN'S.** 3300 Smith St, south of downtown. 713/522-9711. Hrs: 11:30 am-1:30 pm, 5:45-10 pm; Sat from 5:45 pm; Sun 5:45-9:30 pm; Sat brunch 11 am-1:30 pm, Sun brunch 10 am-2 pm. Closed Dec 24, 25. Res accepted. Creole, Amer menu. Bar. A la carte entrees: lunch $12-$22, dinner $16-$25. Complete meals: lunch $15.50-$16. Sat, Sun brunch $16-$24. Specialties: turtle soup, grilled veal chop with tchoupitoulas sauce, bananas Foster. Own baking. Jazz Sat, Sun brunch. Valet parking. Outdoor dining. Elegant decor in unique building designed by John Staub as headquarters of Junior League. Family-owned. Jacket. Cr cds: A, C, D, DS, MC, V.

D

★ ★ **BROWNSTONE.** 2736 Virgina St, at Westheimer Rd, in River Oaks. 713/520-5666. Hrs: 11:30 am-2:30 pm, 6-10:30 pm; Fri, Sat to 11 pm; Sun 11 am-2 pm. Closed Dec 25. Res accepted. Continental menu. Bar. Semi-a la carte: lunch $6.95-$11.95, dinner $14.95-$24.95. Sun brunch $17.95. Child's meals. Specializes in herb encrusted salmon, beef Wellington, veal pecan. Harpist Thurs-Sat. Valet parking. Outdoor poolside dining. Elegant, numerous antiques. Cr cds: A, D, DS, MC, V.

D

★ ★ ★ **CAFE ANNIE.** 1728 Post Oak Blvd, in Galleria Area. 713/840-1111. Hrs: 11:30 am-2 pm, 6-10 pm; Fri to 10:30 pm; Sat 6-10:30 pm. Closed Sun; most major hols. Res accepted. Bar. A la carte entrees: lunch $9-$14, dinner $18-$32. Specialties: poached shrimp with Dallas mozzarella, roast pheasant. Own pastries. Valet parking. Seasonal floral arrangements; harvest mural by local artist. Cr cds: A, D, DS, MC, V.

D

★ ★ **CARRABBA'S.** 3115 Kirby Dr, in River Oaks. 713/522-3131. Hrs: 11 am-11 pm; Fri to midnight; Sat 11:30 am-midnight; Sun noon-10 pm. Closed Thanksgiving, Dec 25. Italian menu. Semi-a la carte: lunch, dinner $7-$19.95. Specialties: pasta Carrabba, pollo Rosa Maria, veal chop. Own desserts. Valet parking. Outdoor dining. Modern decor; wood-burning pizza oven. Cr cds: A, C, D, MC, V.

D

★ ★ ★ **CHARLEY'S 517.** 517 Louisiana St, downtown. 713/224-4438. Hrs: 11:30 am-2 pm, 5:30-11 pm. Closed Sun; major hols. Res accepted. Bar. Wine cellar. A la carte entrees: lunch $8.50-$16, dinner $19-$32. Specializes in domestic and imported game, seafood. Own pastries. Valet parking. In Theater District. Jacket (dinner). Cr cds: A, C, D, MC, V.

★ ★ **CHEZ GEORGES.** 11920-J Westheimer (11920), at Kirkwood, west of downtown. 713/497-1122. Hrs: 11 am-2 pm, 6-10 pm; Fri to 10:30 pm; Sat 6-10:30 pm. Closed Sun; Dec 25. Res accepted. French menu. Wine, beer. Semi-a la carte: lunch $7-$10.95. A la carte entrees: dinner $13-$22.90. Complete meals: lunch $12.95, dinner $20-$38. Specialties: filet of red snapper with fennel & lime, french pâtes. Own pastries. Parking. Country French decor. Jacket. Cr cds: A, C, D, MC, V.

D

★ ★ ★ **CHEZ NOUS.** (217 S Ave G, Humble) Approx 22 mi NE on US 59, exit FM 1960. 713/446-6717. Hrs: 5:30-11 pm. Closed Sun. Res accepted. French menu. Bar. Wine cellar. A la carte entrees: dinner $14.95-$22.50. Specializes in filet of king salmon, mesquite-grilled tuna, rack of lamb. Own desserts. Parking. French decor. Former Pentecostal church (1928). Jacket. Cr cds: A, C, D, MC, V.

✔ ★ ★ **CHIANTI CUCINA RUSTICA.** 1515 S Post Oak Lane, in Galleria Area. 713/840-0303. Hrs: 11:30 am-2:30 pm, 5:30-10:30 pm; Fri to 11 pm; Sat 5:30-11 pm. Closed Sun; some major hols. Res accepted. Italian menu. Bar. Semi-a la carte: lunch, dinner $4.50-$13. Child's meals. Specialties: antipasti misto, grilled pork chops, tortellini. Valet parking. Open hearth cooking. View of garden from dining rm. Cr cds: A, D, MC, V.

D

★ ★ **CHURRASCO'S.** 2055 Westheimer Rd, in Shepherd Square Shopping Center, west of downtown. 713/527-8300. Hrs: 11:30 am-10 pm; Fri to 11 pm; Sat 5-11 pm; Sun brunch 11:30 am-3 pm. Closed Jan 1, July 4, Dec 25. Res accepted; required wkends. South American menu. Bar. A la carte entrees: lunch $4.95-$13.95, dinner $10.95-$21.95. Sun brunch $5.95-$12.95. Specialties: churrasco, empanadas, plantain chips. South American estancia atmosphere. Cr cds: A, C, D, DS, MC, V.

D

★ ★ ★ **CONFEDERATE HOUSE.** 2925 Weslayan St, west of downtown. 713/622-1936. Hrs: 11:30 am-2:30 pm, 6-10:30 pm; Sat from 6 pm. Closed Sun; Labor Day, Dec 25. Res accepted. Bar. Wine list. Semi-a la carte: lunch $8-$11, dinner $9.75-$21. Specialties: grilled red snapper, rib-eye steak, shrimp salad, soft shell crab. Own desserts. Valet parking. Southern colonial decor. Family-owned. Jacket (dinner). Cr cds: A, D, MC, V.

★ ★ ★ **DAMIAN'S.** 3011 Smith St, downtown. 713/522-0439. Hrs: 11 am-2 pm, 5:30-10 pm; Fri to 11:30 pm; Sat 5-11:30 pm. Closed Sun; some major hols. Res accepted. Italian menu. Bar. A la carte entrees: lunch, dinner $9.95-$24.95. Specialties: shrimp Damian, involtini di pollo, veal shoss. Valet parking. Terra cotta walls with hand-painted frescoes. Cr cds: A, C, D, MC, V.

D

★ ★ ★ **DeVILLE.** (See Four Seasons Hotel-Houston Center) 713/650-1619. Hrs: 6:30 am-1:30 pm, 6-10 pm; Sat from 6 pm; Sun 7 am-2 pm. Res accepted. Bar. Wine cellar. Complete meals: bkfst $5-$12. A la carte entrees: lunch $9-$17, dinner $16-$26. Sun brunch $27.50. Child's meals. Specializes in fresh regional cuisine. Own baking. Entertainment; pianist at Sun brunch. Valet parking. Art deco furnishings. Cr cds: A, C, D, ER, MC, V.

D

★ ★ ★ **THE DINING ROOM.** (See The Ritz-Carlton, Houston Hotel) 713/840-7600, ext. 6110. Hrs: 6:30 am-2:30 pm; Sun brunch 11 am-2:30 pm. Res accepted. Continental menu. Bar. Wine cellar. A la carte entrees: bkfst $5.50-$15, lunch $8.50-$14. Sun brunch $32. Child's meals. Specialties: tortilla soup, grilled swordfish, crême brulée, she-crab soup, pecanwood smoked salmon. Own baking. Entertainment (Sun brunch). Valet parking. Jacket. Cr cds: A, C, D, DS, ER, JCB, MC, V.

D

✔ ★ **DONERAKI.** 7705 Westheimer Rd, west of downtown. 713/975-9815. Hrs: 11 am-midnight; Fri to 3 am; Sat 8-3 am; Sun 8 am-midnight. Res accepted. Mexican menu. Bar. Semi-a la carte: bkfst $3.95-$6.95, lunch, dinner $4.95-$11.95. Child's meals. Specialties: fajitas, shrimp a la Diabla, chicken enchiladas. Mariachis (dinner). Parking. Colorful Mexican decor. Cr cds: A, DS, MC, V.

D

✔ ★ ★ **DONG TING.** 611 Stuart St, downtown. 713/527-0005. Hrs: 11 am-2 pm, 5-10 pm; wkend hrs vary. Res accepted. Chinese menu. Semi-a la carte: lunch, dinner $7.50-$12. Specialties: lamb dumplings, clay pot pork, jalapeno steak. Valet parking. Heavy wood paneling; hand-painted murals, antiques. Cr cds: A, C, D, MC, V.

★ ★ **GROTTO.** 3920 Westheimer Rd, in River Oaks. 713/622-3663. Hrs: 11:30 am-11 pm; Fri, Sat to midnight; Sun to 10 pm. Closed major hols. Southern Italian menu. Bar. Semi-a la carte: lunch $6.95-$9.95, dinner $6.95-$15.95. Specialties: pasta al Bosco, linguine alle vongole. Own pizza. Parking. Outdoor dining. Neapolitan cafe setting; large mural on wall. Cr cds: A, C, D, MC, V.

D

✔ ★ ★ **HUNAN.** 1800 Post Oak Blvd (77056), in Galleria Area. 713/965-0808. Hrs: 11:30 am-10:30 pm; Fri 10:30 am-11:30 pm; Sat noon-11:30 pm; Sun noon-10:30 pm. Closed Thanksgiving. Res accepted. Chinese, Hunan menu. Bar. Semi-a la carte: lunch $4.95-$8.75, dinner $4.95-$14.50. Specializes in Hunan-style chicken & prawn, Peking duck. Parking. Chinese decor, large oriental mural. Cr cds: A, C, D, MC, V.

★ **KAPHAN'S.** 7900 S Main St, at Kirby Dr, in Hermann Park Area. 713/668-0491. Hrs: 11:30 am-9 pm; Fri, Sat to 10 pm. Closed Wed; Jan 1, Labor Day, Dec 25. Res accepted. Bar. Semi-a la carte: lunch $8.95, dinner $9.95-$15.95. Specializes in fresh Gulf Coast seafood, beef. Parking. Garden room. Family-owned. Cr cds: A, C, D, DS, MC, V.

★ **KIM SON.** 2001 Jefferson St, downtown. 713/222-2461. Hrs: 10:30 am-midniight; Fri & Sat to 1 am. No A/C. Vietnamese, Chinese menu. Bar. A la carte entrees: lunch, dinner $6.50-$13.95. Specialties: spring rolls, beef with lemon grass, black pepper crab. Parking. Cr cds: A, C, D, DS, MC, V.

D

★ ★ ★ **LA COLOMBE D'OR.** (See La Colombe d'or Inn) 713/524-7999. Hrs: 11:30 am-2 pm, 6-10 pm; Fri to 11 pm; Sat, Sun 6-11 pm. Closed major hols. Res accepted. French menu. A la carte entrees: lunch $9.50-$18, dinner $19.50-$29. Specializes in rack of lamb, veal, fish. Own desserts. Valet parking. 21-rm residence decorated with artwork. Jacket. Cr cds: A, C, D, MC, V.

D

★ ★ ★ **LA GRIGLIA.** 2002 W Gray St, in River Oaks Shopping Center, in River Oaks. 713/526-4700. Hrs: 11:30 am-2 pm, 5:30-11 pm; Fri to midnight; Sat 5:30 pm-midnight; Sun 5:30-10 pm. Closed Dec 25. Res accepted. Italian menu. Bar. A la carte entrees: lunch $6.95-$13.95, dinner $8.95-$19.95. Specialties: shrimp & crab cheesecake, red snapper La Griglia, linguine pescatore. Valet parking. Outdoor dining. Colorful tilework and murals; lively atmosphere. Cr cds: A, C, D, MC, V.

D

★ ★ ★ ★ **LA RESERVE.** (See Omni Houston Hotel) 713/871-8181. Hrs: 11:30 am-2 pm, 6:30-10:30 pm; Sat from 6:30 pm. Closed Sun. Res accepted. Continental menu. Bar 5 pm-midnight. A la carte entrees: lunch $12-$18, dinner $19-$30. Table d'hôte: dinner $45-$65 (with wine). Specialties: morel-stuffed veal chops, charred citrus-pepper tuna, grilled double lamb chops, tian of freshwater prawns and Louisiana crab. Also dietary menu. Own baking. Menu changes daily; fresh food only. Valet parking. Unusual floral arrangements. Jacket, tie (dinner). Cr cds: A, C, D, DS, ER, JCB, MC, V.

★ ★ ★ **LA TOUR D'ARGENT.** 2011 Ella Blvd, north of downtown. 713/864-9864. Hrs: 11:30 am-2 pm, 6-11 pm. Closed Sun; major hols. Res accepted; required wkends. French menu. Bar. A la carte entrees: lunch $8.50-$12.85, dinner $16-$26. Specializes in seafood, pheasant, duck. Pastry chef. Valet parking. Antiques. Dining in 1920s hunting lodge, Houston's oldest log cabin. Overlooks bayou. Jacket. Cr cds: A, C, D, DS, MC, V.

★ ★ ★ ★ **MAXIM'S.** 3755 Richmond Ave, south of downtown. 713/877-8899. Hrs: 11:15 am-10:30 pm; Sat 5:30-11 pm; major hols. Res accepted. French menu. Bar. Extensive wine cellar. A la carte entrees: lunch, dinner $13.75-$23.75. Table d'hôte: lunch $7-$11.75, dinner $25-$28. Specialties: cream of lobster soup, Gulf sea-

food, fresh lump crabmeat, veal, lamb, flaming desserts. Own baking. Valet parking. Family-owned. Jacket. Cr cds: A, C, D, DS, MC, V.

D

★ **MONTESANO RISTORANTE ITALIANO.** 6009 Beverly Hill Lane, west of downtown. 713/977-4565. Hrs: 11 am-2:30 pm, 5:30-11 pm; Fri to midnight; Sat 5:30 pm-midnight. Closed Sun; Thanksgiving, Dec 25. Res accepted. Italian menu. Bar. A la carte entrees: lunch $7.95-$13.95, dinner $8-$18.95. Specializes in chicken, veal, seafood. Valet parking. Cr cds: A, D, DS, MC, V.

D

★ ★ **NINO'S.** 2817 W Dallas St, downtown. 713/522-5120. Hrs: 11 am-2:30 pm, 5:30-10 pm; Fri to 11 pm. Closed Sun; major hols. Res accepted. Italian menu. Bar. Semi-a la carte: lunch $8.95-$17.95, dinner $8.95-$21.95. Specializes in veal, seafood. Own pasta. Parking. Cr cds: A, C, D, MC, V.

D

★ ★ **PAPPADEAUX.** 6015 Westheimer Rd, west of downtown. 713/782-6310. Hrs: 11 am-11 pm; Fri & Sat to midnight. Closed Thanksgiving, Dec 25. Cajun menu. Bar. Semi-a la carte: lunch $5-$9, dinner $7.95-$17.95. Specialties: fried alligator, crawfish etouffée, Angus steak. Parking. Patio dining. Lively atmosphere. Cr cds: A, MC, V.

D

✔ ★ ★ **PAPPASITO'S CANTINA.** 6445 Richmond Ave, west of downtown. 713/784-5253. Hrs: 11 am-10:30 pm; Fri, Sat to midnight. Mexican menu. Bar. A la carte entrees: lunch $5.95-$8.95, dinner $5.95-$15.95. Specializes in seafood, fajitas. Own tortillas, desserts. Mexican decor. Cr cds: A, MC, V.

D

★ ★ ★ **POST OAK GRILL.** 1415 S Post Oak Lane, in Galleria Area. 713/993-9966. Hrs: 11 am-midnight; Sun 5-10 pm; Mon, Tues 11 am-11 pm; Sun brunch 11 am-3 pm. Closed some major hols. Res accepted. Bar to 2 am. Semi-a la carte: lunch $6.95-$13.95, dinner $8.25-$17.95. Sun brunch $11.95-$14.95. Specialties: tomatoes Manfred, fresh gulf trout meunière, lemon pepper chicken. Entertainment. Valet parking. Outdoor dining. Festive ambience, colorful Toulouse-Lautrec murals. Cr cds: A, D, MC, V.

D

★ **PREGO.** 2520 Amherst St, in Hermann Park Area. 713/529-2520. Hrs: 11:30 am-10 pm; Fri to 11 pm; Sat 5-11 pm; Sun 5-10 pm. Closed some major hols. Res accepted. Italian menu. Bar. A la carte entrees: lunch, dinner $5-$20. Child's meals. Specialties: veal alla pego, wild mushroom ravioli, Gulf coast crab cakes. Parking. Bistro-style dining. Cr cds: A, C, D, MC, V.

D

★ **QUILTED TOQUE.** 3939 Montrose Blvd, in Hermann Park Area. 713/942-9233. Hrs: 11 am-3 pm, 5-11 pm; Sat 10 am-11 pm; Sun 10 am-5 pm. Closed Jan 1, Dec 25. Res accepted. Eclectic Amer menu. Bar noon-11 pm. Semi-a la carte: lunch $6.95-$15.95, dinner $9-$20. Valet parking (dinner). Outdoor dining. Mexican architectural antiques;, eclectic decor. Cr cds: A, D, MC, V.

D

★ ★ **RAINBOW LODGE.** 1 Birdsall St, west of downtown. 713/861-8666. Hrs: 11:30 am-10 pm; Sat 6-10:30 pm; Sun 10:30 am-10 pm; Sun brunch 10:30 am-2 pm. Closed Mon; major hols. Res accepted. Bar. Semi-a la carte: lunch $7.25-$28, dinner $16.95-$32. Sun brunch $7.25-$15.95. Specializes in seafood, veal, wild game. Valet parking. Outdoor dining. On Buffalo Bayou; garden, gazebo. Cr cds: A, C, D, DS, MC, V.

D

★ ★ **RIVER OAKS GRILL.** 2630 Westheimer Rd, in River Oaks. 713/520-1738. Hrs: 11 am-2:30 pm, 6-10:30 pm; Fri, Sat to 11:30 pm. Closed Sun; some major hols. Res accepted; required wkends. Bar

11 am-midnight, Sat from 5 pm. Semi-a la carte: lunch $6.95-$14.50, dinner $9.95-$24.95. Specializes in steak, fresh seafood, chops. Pianist Tues-Sat. Valet parking. Club atmosphere; hunting trophies, dark paneled walls. Cr cds: A, C, D, MC, V.

D

★ ★ ★ **RIVOLI.** 5636 Richmond Ave, west of downtown. 713/780 1900. Hrs: 11:30 am-2 pm, 6-11 pm; Sat from 6 pm; Sun 6-10 pm. Closed major hols. Res accepted. Continental menu. Bar. Wine list. A la carte entrees: lunch $7.95-$13.95, dinner $16.95-$27. Specialties: Dover sole stuffed with crabmeat and shrimp, rack of lamb Diable, blackened shrimp with mustard sauce. Own pastries. Entertainment Tues-Sat. Valet parking. Jacket. Cr cds: A, D, DS, MC, V.

★ ★ **ROTISSERIE FOR BEEF AND BIRD.** 2200 Wilcrest Dr, west of downtown. 713/977-9524. Hrs: 11:30 am-2 pm, 6-10 pm; Sat from 6 pm. Closed Sun; Jan 1, Dec 25. Res accepted. Continental menu. Bar. Wine cellar. Semi-a la carte: lunch $6.95-$17.50, dinner $17.95-$27.50. Specializes in roast duckling, venison, lobster. Valet parking. New England-colonial atmosphere. Jacket (dinner). Cr cds: A, C, D, DS, MC, V.

D

★ ★ **RUGGLES GRILL.** 903 Westheimer Rd (77006), west of downtown. 713/524-3839. Hrs: 11:30 am-2 pm, 5:30-11 pm; Fri to midnight; Sat 5:30 pm-midnight; Sun 11 am-2:30 pm, 5:30-10 pm. Closed Mon; July 4, Thanksgiving, Dec 25. Res accepted. Bar. Semi-a la carte: lunch $5.95-$13.95, dinner $9.95-$16.95. Specialties: black pepper pasta, grilled beef filet, Texas goat cheese salad. Valet parking. Contemporary decor. Cr cds: A, C, D, MC, V.

★ ★ ★ **RUTH'S CHRIS STEAK HOUSE.** 6213 Richmond Ave, west of downtown. 713/789-2333. Hrs: 5-11 pm. Closed most major hols. Res accepted. Bar. A la carte entrees: dinner $17-$29. Specializes in steak, lamb chops, lobster. Valet parking. Cr cds: A, C, D, DS, MC, V.

D

✔★ ★ **SHANGHAI RIVER.** 2407 Westheimer Rd, in River Oaks. 713/528-5528. Hrs: 11 am-10:30 pm; Fri, Sat to 11:30 pm. Closed Thanksgiving. Res accepted. Chinese menu. Bar. Semi-a la carte: lunch $5.50-$6.95, dinner $6.95-$14.95. Specialties: crispy shrimp, General Tso's chicken, Peking duck. Own desserts. Parking. Chinese porcelains on display. Cr cds: A, C, D, MC, V.

D

★ ★ **SIERRA.** 4704 Montrose Blvd, in Hermann Park Area. 713/942-7757. Hrs: 11 am-2:30 pm, 5-10:30 pm; Fri to 11:30 pm; Sat 5-11:30 pm. Closed Sun; most major hols. Res accepted. Southwestern menu. Bar. Semi-a la carte: lunch $5.95-$19.95, dinner $7.50-$19.95. Specialties: filet of salmon "campfire style," filet of beef tenderloin. Valet parking. Outdoor patio dining. Southwestern decor. Cr cds: A, C, D, DS, MC, V.

D

★ **STRAWBERRY PATCH.** 5839 Westheimer Rd, west of downtown. 713/780-7352. Hrs: 11 am-10 pm; Fri, Sat to 11 pm; Sun 10:30 am-10 pm; Sun brunch to 4 pm. Closed Dec 25. Bar. Semi-a la carte: lunch $4.95-$14.95, dinner $4.95-$32.45. Sun brunch $6.30-$10. Child's meals. Specializes in Angus beef, fresh fish, chicken. Own desserts. Parking. Cr cds: A, MC, V.

D

★ ★ **TONY MANDOLA'S GULF COAST KITCHEN.** 1962 W Gray St, in River Oaks. 713/528-3474. Hrs: 11 am-10 pm; Fri & Sat to 11 pm; Sun to 9 pm. Closed some major hols. Res accepted. Italian, Amer menu. Bar. A la carte entrees: lunch, dinner $6.95-$17.95. Child's meals. Specialties: Mama's gumbo, crawfish ravioli, blackened soft shell crab. Parking. Outdoor dining. New Orleans bistro atmosphere. Cr cds: A, D, MC, V.

D

★ ★ ★ **VARGO'S.** 2401 Fondren Rd (77063), west of downtown. 713/782-3888. Hrs: 11 am-2 pm, 6-10:30 pm; Fri to 11:30 pm; Sat 5-11:30 pm; Sun 11 am-2:30 pm. Closed Jan 1, Dec 25. Res accepted. Continental menu. Bar 4 pm-midnight. Semi-a la carte: lunch $6.95-$24.95, dinner $18.95-$28. Specialties: Gulf shrimp Henry, Long Island duck, grilled snapper. Pianist. Valet parking. View of lake and gardens. Tree in center of dining rm. Family-owned. Cr cds: A, C, D, DS, MC, V.

D

Unrated Dining Spots

BUTERA'S ON MONTROSE. 4621 Montrose Blvd, on grounds of Chelsea Market, west of downtown. 713/523-0722. Hrs: 7 am-10 pm; Sat from 9 am; Sun 9 am-8 pm. Closed some major hols. Wine, beer. A la carte: bkfst $3-$5, lunch, dinner $6-$8. Specializes in chicken salad, sandwiches, pasta salad. Outdoor dining. Cafeteria-style serv. Cr cds: A, C, D, MC, V.

CAPTAIN BENNY'S HALF SHELL. 8018 Katy Frwy, I-10, Wirt exit, west of downtown. 713/683-1042. Hrs: 11 am-11:45 pm. Closed Sun; most major hols. Beer. Semi-a la carte: lunch, dinner $2.95-$7.95. Specializes in fried oysters, shrimp. Parking. Boat-shaped building; glass walls overlook freeway. No cr cds accepted.

GOODE CO. TEXAS BAR-B-Q. 5109 Kirby Dr, south of downtown. 713/522-2530. Hrs: 11 am-10 pm. Closed Jan 1, Thanksgiving, Dec 25. Wine, beer. A la carte entrees: lunch, dinner $4-$9.75. Specializes in barbecued dishes, cheese bread, pecan pie. Entertainment first Fri of month. Parking. Outdoor dining. Laid-back Western atmosphere. Cr cds: A, D, MC, V.

D

GREAT CARUSO. 10001 Westheimer Rd, west of downtown. 713/780-4900. Hrs: 6-10:30 pm; Fri, Sat to 11:30 pm. Closed Mon; Jan 1, Dec 25. Res accepted. Continental menu. Bar to 1 am. A la carte entrees: dinner $15.95-$34.95. Entertainment charge $3.50-$3.95. Specializes in veal, steak, fish. Valet parking. Unique antique decor. Broadway and light operetta performances nightly; singing waiters and dancers. Cr cds: A, C, D, DS, MC, V.

D

GUGENHEIM'S DELICATESSEN. 1708 Post Oak Blvd, in Galleria Area. 713/622-2773. Hrs: 10 am-9 pm; Fri to 10 pm; Sat 9 am-10 pm; Sun 9 am-9 pm. Closed Jan 1, Thanksgiving, Dec 25. Wine, beer. Semi-a la carte: bkfst $1-$9.95, lunch, dinner $4.95-$9.95. Specializes in deli sandwiches, cheesecake. Own desserts. Parking. Outdoor dining. NY-style deli. Cr cds: A, C, D, DS, MC, V.

D

JAGS. 5120 Woodway Dr, in Decorative Ctr, west of downtown. 713/621-4765. Hrs: 11 am-2 pm. Closed Sat, Sun; Memorial Day, Thanksgiving, Dec 25. Res accepted. Bar. A la carte entrees: lunch $8-$15. Specialties: blini Santa Fe, seared salmon with cucumber salsa. Multi-level dining area surrounded by running stream. Cr cds: A, MC, V.

LUBY'S CAFETERIA. 5215 Buffalo Speedway, south of downtown. 713/664-4852. Hrs: 10:45 am-8:30 pm. Closed Dec 25. Continental menu. Avg ck: lunch $4.75, dinner $5. Specializes in fried & baked fish, roast beef, fried chicken. Parking. Cr cds: DS, MC, V.

D

OTTO'S BARBECUE. 5502 Memorial Dr, west of downtown. 713/864-2573. Hrs: 11 am-9 pm. Closed Sun; some major hols. Beer. Semi-a la carte: lunch, dinner $4.75-$8.75. Child's meals. Specializes in barbecued meats. Parking. Outdoor dining. Rustic. Western decor; slogan-covered walls. No cr cds accepted.

Indianapolis

Founded: 1820

Pop: 731,327

Elev: 717 feet

Time zone: Eastern

Area code: 317

Indianapolis, the capital of Indiana, is truly a "city on the move." The changing downtown skyline reflects the progressive drive of this Midwestern city, which is determined never to be referred to as "India-No-Place" again.

Indianapolis became the state capital nearly four years after Indiana was admitted to the Union. Statehood became official on December 11, 1816, at the original capital, Corydon, located in the southern part of the state. The first governor of Indiana, Jonathan Jennings, decided it would be more advantageous to have the capital in the center of the state. By 1832 Indianapolis had had its first state fair. The arrival of the railroad in 1847 gave new impetus to the area. Public schools were established in 1853; a university was founded two years later. By the turn of the century, Indianapolis had become the commercial center of the rich agricultural region surrounding it and an important manufacturing center in the Midwest.

Today, Indianapolis is the largest city in the state and 12th largest in the nation. The city also is recognized as one of the nation's amateur sports capitals. It has hosted both the US Olympic Festival and the Pan American Games. The headquarters for the Amateur Athletic Union, as well as several individual sports, including track and field and gymnastics, are located here.

Business

In addition to sports, Indianapolis' economy is boosted by the health industry. Eli Lilly and Company, one of the largest pharmaceutical companies in the world, and the Indiana University Medical Center complex, one of the country's largest, are both in Indianapolis.

The city is one of the nation's leading trucking centers. Dozens of interstate carriers operate out of Indianapolis. American Trans Air, the world's largest charter carrier, is headquartered here. Indianapolis is also one of the leading US grain markets and an important livestock and meat-processing center. Among the products manufactured here are medical supply equipment, aircraft motors, automobile parts, furniture and television sets.

Indianapolis abounds in space for manufacturing, warehousing and distributing. There are virtually no barriers to expansion, since nearly 40 square miles (10 percent of the county's land) have been zoned for industrial use. More than 2,000 acres are in industrial parks, located near the interstate highway system to provide easy access to other cities or downtown Indianapolis.

Office space is plentiful and evenly distributed between downtown and suburban locations. Office space totaling more than 3 million square feet was built during the 1970s. Recently completed construction projects include the Bank One Tower, the Indianapolis Zoo in White River Park and the Eiteljorg Museum of American Indian and Western Art.

Convention Facilities

The Indiana Convention Center and Hoosier Dome feature 301,500 square feet of column-free exhibit space, including 5 halls and the stadium floor. Additionally, there are 50 meeting rooms. Maximum exhibit capacity is 1,694 booths. Meeting capacity is 10,000 in the Convention Center and 60,500 in the Dome. Banquets for up to 7,500 can be served in the same room. Indianapolis has more than 15,000 hotel and motel accommodations; 3,000 of those are within walking distance of the Indiana Convention Center and Hoosier Dome.

Sports and Recreation

The annual 500-mile automobile race at the Indianapolis Motor Speedway has brought international fame to this city. The Indianapolis 500, held each year on the Sunday before Memorial Day, is one of the most important and popular auto competitions in the world. Annual attendance is estimated at more than 350,000 people. The 2.5-mile oval track was built in 1909 as a proving ground for cars. The $7 million Speedway Museum exhibits race cars dating from 1909. The National Hot Rod Association's National Drag Races, held every Labor Day at Indianapolis Raceway Park, is the largest drag racing event of the year, with more than 150,000 fans attending.

Indianapolis has several world-class sports facilities: the Indiana University Natatorium, described by competition swimmers as the fastest pool in the nation; the IU Track and Field Stadium, an 8-lane, all-weather track; the Major Taylor Velodrome, a 333.3-meter banked bicycle track; the Indianapolis Sports Center, a tournament tennis stadium; the 60,500 seat Hoosier Dome; the 17,000-seat Market Square Arena; and the Pan American Plaza with 2 indoor skating rinks.

The NFL's Indianapolis Colts provide football excitement at the Hoosier Dome. For basketball fans, Indianapolis is the home of the Indiana Pacers, who play their home games in the Market Square Arena. Baseball fans can go to Bush Stadium to see the Indianapolis Indians, and hockey fans can watch the Indianapolis Ice take on opponents at the Indiana State Fairgrounds Event Center Coliseum.

Eighteen golf courses and more than 130 tennis courts are scattered throughout the city. The US Men's Hardcourt Championship, held annually in Indianapolis, attracts top-name tennis stars from around the world. Parks are abundant in the city and surrounding areas. Garfield Park features sunken gardens, greenhouses and an illuminated fountain; musical programs are presented in the park's amphitheater. Eagle Creek Park, a 4,900-acre park with a 1,300-acre reservoir, is one of the largest metropolitan parks in the country and features a rowing course sanctioned for international competition.

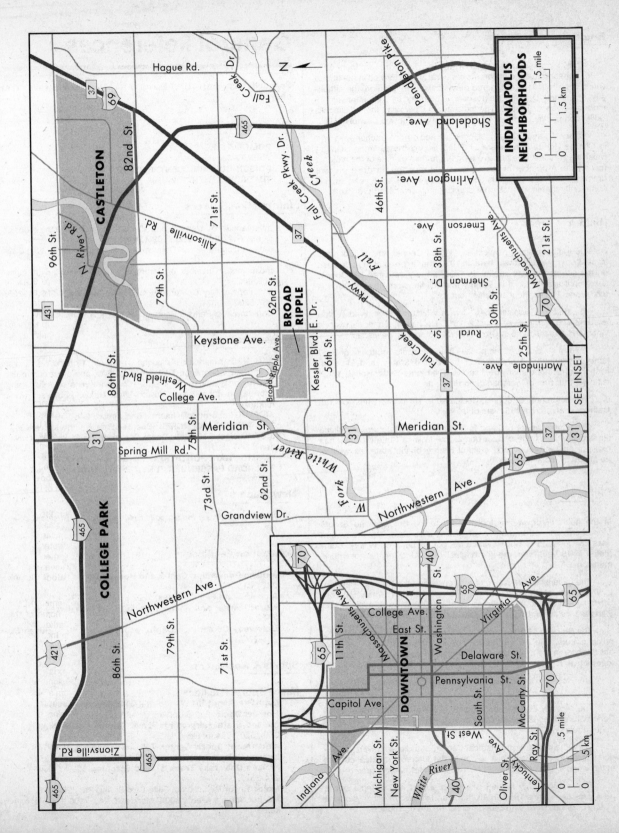

Entertainment

The highly regarded Indianapolis Symphony Orchestra was founded in 1930. Subscription and children's concerts are performed in the ornate Circle Theatre (1916), a restored movie palace. In addition, the nationally acclaimed Dance Kaleidoscope Company can be seen at the Indiana Repertory Theatre. The Indianapolis Opera and the Indianapolis Ballet companies hold their regular seasons at Clowes Memorial Hall.

Butler University's recitals, concerts and other attractions are held in Clowes Hall or in adjacent Lilly Hall. During the summer, Starlight Musicals presents an extensive program featuring some of the nation's top artists. A number of professional and repertory theaters present dramas, comedies, musicals and Broadway shows each year; several community theater groups offer dramatic and diversified programs.

Historical Areas

Outside Indianapolis in Noblesville, William Conner built a cabin and trading post in 1802. It was here, in 1820, that a group of men decided on the site of the new capital. In 1930, Eli Lilly acquired the Conner settlement and restored it. Twenty-five buildings are now included in the Conner Prairie Pioneer Settlement.

The beloved "Hoosier Poet," James Whitcomb Riley, lived in Indianapolis and died here on July 22, 1916. His house, a national historic landmark, and his tomb in Crown Hill Cemetery can be visited.

Among several restored houses in Indianapolis are those of Benjamin Harrison, 23rd president of the United States, and Meredith Nicholson, author of many best sellers. The Morris-Butler House (1862) is now a museum of Victorian decorative arts.

Two churches, St John's, dedicated in 1871, and Christ Church Cathedral, erected in 1857, are of interest.

The state capitol building is an impressive structure of Indiana limestone with a huge copper dome. The Indiana State Museum has exhibits on the natural and cultural history of the state, as well as paintings by Indiana artists.

Sightseeing

In the heart of downtown Indianapolis is the Soldiers and Sailors Monument, erected in memory of Civil War soldiers. The monument rises 284 feet and is topped with a 38-foot statue, *Miss Victory*. Completed in 1902, it is on the site originally intended for the governor's mansion.

The Indianapolis Museum of Art consists of the Krannert Pavilion, Lilly Pavilion of Decorative Arts, Mary Fendrich Hulman Pavilion, Clowes Pavilion and the sculpture court with displays of Medieval and Renaissance art and French, English and Italian decorative arts.

The Children's Museum, one of the nation's largest, offers history, social culture, science and transportation exhibits. Of particular interest to children are a planetarium, a working carousel, a wood-burning locomotive, a furnished cabin, a giant water clock and a mummy.

The Hoosier Dome houses the National Track and Field Hall of Fame.

The recently constructed Indianapolis Zoo in White River State Park features the Whale and Dolphin Pavilion, as well as Indiana's first major aquarium.

The Indiana University Medical Center, at Indiana University-Purdue University at Indianapolis, is one of the foremost medical centers in the world and a primary international center for heart research.

The restored City Market has been a part of the Indianapolis business scene since 1886. In 90 shops and stores, merchants offer a variety of goods from ethnic foods to handcrafted products.

General References

Founded: 1820 **Pop:** 731,327 **Elev:** 717 feet **Time zone:** Eastern **Area code:** 317

Phone Numbers

POLICE & FIRE: 911
FBI: 639-3301
POISON CONTROL CENTER: 929-2323
TIME & WEATHER: 222-2362

Information Sources

Indianapolis Convention and Visitors Association, One Hoosier Dome, Suite 100, 46225; 639-4282.
Indiana Department of Commerce, 1 N Capitol Ave, 46204; 232-8800.
Indianapolis Chamber of Commerce, 320 N Meridian St, Suite 200, 46204; 464-2200.
Indianapolis City Center, 201 S Capitol Ave, Suite 200, 46225; 237-5200.
Department of Parks & Recreation, 924-9151.

Transportation

AIRLINES: American; American Trans Air; Continental; Delta; Northwest; Southwest; TWA; United; USAir; and other commuter and regional airlines. For the most current airline schedules and information consult the *Official Airline Guide,* published twice monthly.
AIRPORT: Indianapolis International Airport, 248-9594.
CAR RENTAL AGENCIES: (See Toll-Free Numbers) Avis 244-3307; Budget 244-6858; Dollar 241-0829; Hertz 243-9321; National 243-7501.
PUBLIC TRANSPORTATION: Metro Transit 635-3344.
RAILROAD PASSENGER SERVICE: Amtrak 800/872-7245.

Newspapers

Indianapolis News; Indianapolis Star; Indianapolis Business Journal.

Convention Facilities

Indiana Convention Center and Hoosier Dome, 100 S Capitol, 262-3410.
Indiana State Fair Complex, 1202 E 38th St, 923-3431.
Murat Theater and Shrine Temple, 502 N New Jersey St, 635-2433.
University Conference Center at IUPUI, 850 W Michigan St, 274-2700.

Sports & Recreation

Major Sports Facilities
Bush Stadium, 1501 W 16th, 269-3545 (Indians, baseball).
Hoosier Dome, 200 S Capitol, 297-7000 (Colts, football).
Indiana State Fairgrounds Event Center Coliseum, 1202 E 38th, 630-1964 (hockey).
Indianapolis Sports Center, 755 University Blvd, 636-7719.
Indiana University Natatorium, 901 W New York, 274-3517.
Indiana University Track & Field Stadium, 900 W New York, 274-3517.
Major Taylor Velodrome, 3649 Cold Spring Rd, 926-8356.
Market Square Arena, 300 E Market St, 263-2100 (Pacers, basketball).

Racetracks

Indianapolis Motor Speedway, 4400 W 16th St, 241-2500 (auto racing).
Indianapolis Raceway Park, 10267 E US 136, 291-4090 (auto racing).
Indianapolis Speedrome, 802 S Kitley at US 52, 353-8206 (stock car racing).

Cultural Facilities

Theaters

American Cabaret Theater, 401 E Michigan St, 631-0334.
Beef 'N Boards Dinner Theatre, 9301 N Michigan Rd, 872-9664.
Christian Theological Seminary Repertory Theatre, 1000 W 42nd St, 923-1516.
Indianapolis Civic Theater, 1200 W 38th St, 923-4597.
Indiana Repertory Theatre, 140 W Washington St, 635-5252.
Madame Walker Theater, 617 Indiana Ave, 236-2099.
Phoenix Theater, 749 Park Ave, 635-PLAY.

Concert Halls

Circle Theatre, 45 Monument Circle, 639-4300.
Clowes Memorial Hall, 4600 Sunset Ave, 283-9710 (tickets); 283-9696 (info).

Museums

The Children's Museum, 3000 N Meridian St, 924-KIDS or -5431.
Hook's Historical Drugstore & Pharmacy Museum, Indiana State Fairgrounds, 1202 E 38th St, 924-1503.
Indianapolis Motor Speedway Hall of Fame Museum, 4790 W 16th St, 248-6747.
Indiana State Museum, 202 N Alabama St, at Ohio St, 232-1637.
Indiana Transportation Museum, 20 mi NW via IN 37, IN 19 in Noblesville, 773-6000 or -0300.
National Track and Field Hall of Fame, Hoosier Dome, 200 S Capitol, 237-5200.
Patrick Henry Sullivan Museum, 225 W Hawthorne, 12 mi N off US 421 in Zionsville, 873-4900.

Art Museums

Eiteljorg Museum of American Indian and Western Art, 500 W Washington St, 636-9378.
Indianapolis Museum of Art, 1200 W 38th St, 923-1331.
Morris-Butler House Museum, 1204 N Park Ave, 636-5409.

Points of Interest

Historical

Carmelite Monastery, 2500 Cold Spring Rd, 926-5654.
Christ Church Cathedral, 125 Monument Circle, 636-4577.
Conner Prairie Pioneer Settlement, 6 mi N via I-465, 13400 Allisonville Rd, Fishers, 776-6000.
Crown Hill Cemetery, 3402 Boulevard Place.
Fort Benjamin Harrison, E 56th St & Post Rd, 546-9211.
James Whitcomb Riley Home, 528 Lockerbie St, 631-5885.
President Benjamin Harrison Memorial Home, 1230 N Delaware St, 631-1898.
St John's, 7031 S East St, 881-2353.
Scottish Rite Cathedral, 650 N Meridian St, 262-3100.
Soldiers and Sailors Monument, Monument Circle, 237-2222.
State Capitol, between Washington & Ohio Sts and Capitol & Senate Aves, 933-5293.

State Library and Historical Building, 140 N Senate Ave, at Ohio St, 232-3675.

Other Attractions

City Market, 222 E Market St, 634-9266.
Eagle Creek Park, 7840 W 56th St, just W of I-465, 327-7110.
Garfield Park, 2450 S Shelby St at Raymond St & Garfield Dr, 327-7221.
Indiana University Medical Center, IUPUI campus, 550 N University Blvd, 274-5000.
Indianapolis Zoo, 1200 W Washington St, 630-2001.
J.I. Holcomb Observatory & Planetarium, Butler University campus, W 46th St & Sunset Ave, 283-9333.
Lilly Center, 893 S Delaware St, 276-2000.
Madame Walker Urban Life Center, 617 Indiana Ave, 236-2099.
Union Station, 39 Jackson Place, 267-0700.
War Memorials Plaza, 431 N Meridian St, 232-7615.

Sightseeing Tours

Gray Line bus tours, 9075 N Meridian, 573-0699.
Landmark Tours, 340 W Michigan, 639-4646.

Annual Events

"500" Festival, 636-4556. May.
Indianapolis "500," Indianapolis Motor Speedway, 241-2500. Sun before Memorial Day.
Midsummer Festival, downtown, 637-4574. June.
Strawberry Festival, downtown, 636-4577. June.
Indiana Black Expo, Convention Center, 925-2702. Late June–early July.
White River Park Games, White River Park, 634-4567. July.
Indiana State Fair, fairgrounds, 1202 E 38th St, 923-3431 or 927-7500. Aug.
RCA US Men's Hardcourt Championships, Indianapolis Sports Center, 815 W New York St, 632-4100 or 800/622-LOVE. Aug.
National Hot Rod Association Drag Races, Indianapolis Raceway Park, 293-RACE. Labor Day.
Penrod Arts Fair, Indianapolis Museum of Art, 923-1331. Sept.
Circle City Classic, Hoosier Dome, 262-3389. Oct.
International Festival, Indiana Convention Center and Hoosier Dome, 262-3410. Oct.

City Neighborhoods

Many of the restaurants, unrated dining establishments and some lodgings listed under Indianapolis include neighborhoods as well as exact street addresses. A map showing these neighborhoods can be found immediately following the city introduction. Geographic descriptions of these areas are given, followed by a table of restaurants arranged by neighborhood.

Broad Ripple: North of Downtown; south of Broad Ripple Ave, west of Keystone Ave, north of Kessler Blvd and east of College Ave.
Castleton: Northeast area of city south of 96th St, west of IN 37, north of 82nd St and east of Keystone Ave.
College Park: South of I-465, west of Meridian St, north of 86th St and east of Zionsville Rd.
Downtown: South of 11th St, west of College Ave, north of McCarty St and east of West St & Indiana Ave. **North of Downtown:** North of I-65. **South of Downtown:** South of I-70.

Lodgings and Food

INDIANAPOLIS RESTAURANTS BY NEIGHBORHOOD AREAS

(For full description, see alphabetical listings under Restaurants)

BROAD RIPPLE

Aristocrat. 5212 N College Ave

Jazz Cooker. 925 E Westfield Blvd

Jonathan's Restaurant & Pub. 9445 Threel Rd

Provincial Kitchen. 1001 Broad Ripple Ave

Renee's. 839 Westfield Blvd

COLLEGE PARK

Bombay Bicycle Club. 9111 N. Michigan Rd

DOWNTOWN

Beaulieu (Canterbury Hotel). 123 S Illinois

Benvenuti. 36 S Pennsylvania St

Key West Shrimp House. 39 W Jackson Place

King Cole. 7 N Meridian St

Mark Pi's China Gate. 135 S Illinois

Norman's. 39 W Jackson Place, suite 12

St Elmo Steak House. 127 S Illinois

NORTH OF DOWNTOWN

Hollyhock Hill. 8110 N College Ave

Iron Skillet. 2489 W 30th St

J. Ross Browne's Drydock. 7230 Pendleton Pike

La Terrace. 8250 Dean Rd

Peter's. 8505 Keystone Crossing Blvd

SOUTH OF DOWNTOWN

Laughner's Cafeteria. 4030 S East St

Note: *When a listing is located in a town that does not have its own city heading, it will appear under the city nearest to its location. In these cases, the address and town appear in parenthesis immediately following the name of the establishment.*

Motels

(Rates are usually higher during Indianapolis "500" and state fair; may be 3-day min.)

★ ★ **COMFORT INN.** *5040 S East St (46227), south of downtown.* 317/783-6711; FAX 317/787-3065. 104 rms, 3 story. S $46-$65; D $50-$82; each addl $5; under 18 free. Crib free. Pet accepted, some restrictions. TV; cable. Pool. Complimentary continental bkfst, coffee. Restaurant nearby. Ck-out noon. Refrigerator in suites. Cr cds: A, C, D, DS, ER, JCB, MC, V.

D ✦ ≈ ⊠ 🔥 SC

★ ★ **COUNTRY HEARTH INN.** *3851 Shore Dr (46254), I-465 exit 17, north of downtown.* 317/297-1848; res: 800/848-5767; FAX 317/297-1848, ext. 125. 83 rms, 2 story, 12 suites. S $45-$60; D $50-$66; each addl $6; suites, kits. $60-$66; under 18 free. Crib free. TV; cable. Pool. Complimentary continental bkfst, coffee. Restaurant

adj 6 am-10 pm. Ck-out noon. Meeting rms. Health club privileges. Cr cds: A, C, D, DS, MC, V.

D ≈ ⊠ 🔥 SC

★ ★ ★ **COURTYARD BY MARRIOTT.** *8670 Allisonville Rd (46250), in Castleton.* 317/576-9559; FAX 317/576-0695. 146 rms, 3 story. S $62; D $72; each addl $10; suites $72-$82; under 12 free; wkend rates. Crib free. TV; cable. Indoor pool. Complimentary coffee in rms. Bkfst avail. Bar. Ck-out 1 pm. Coin lndry. Meeting rms. Valet serv. Sundries. Exercise equipt; weight machine, bicycles, whirlpool. Refrigerators in suites. Balconies. Cr cds: A, C, D, DS, MC, V.

D ≈ 🏃 ⊠ 🔥

★ ★ **DRURY INN.** *9320 N Michigan Rd (46268), in College Park.* 317/876-9777; FAX 317/876-9777, ext. 473. 110 rms, 4 story. S $46-$57; D $62-$67; each addl $10; under 18 free; some wkend rates. Crib free. Pet accepted, some restrictions. TV; cable. Pool. Complimentary bkfst. Restaurant nearby. Ck-out noon. Meeting rms. Sundries. Cr cds: A, C, D, DS, MC, V.

D ✦ ≈ ⊠ 🔥 SC

✔ ★ **FAIRFIELD INN BY MARRIOTT.** *8325 Bash Rd (46250), in Castleton.* 317/577-0455. 131 rms, 3 story. S $41.95-$55.95; D $48.95-$55.95; each addl $7; under 18 free. Crib free. TV. Heated pool. Complimentary continental bkfst in lobby. Restaurant nearby. Ck-out noon. Meeting rm. Cr cds: A, C, D, DS, MC, V.

D ≈ ⊠ 🔥 SC

★ ★ **HAMPTON INN.** *7220 Woodland Dr (46278), north of downtown.* 317/290-1212. 124 rms, 4 story. S $52-$59; D $57-$62; under 18 free. Crib free. Pet accepted, some restrictions. TV. Indoor pool. Complimentary continental bkfst. Restaurant adj 11 am-midnight. Ck-out noon. Meeting rms. Valet serv. Exercise equipt; weight machine, bicycles, whirlpool. Cr cds: A, C, D, DS, MC, V.

D ✦ ≈ 🏃 ⊠ 🔥 SC

★ ★ **HAMPTON INN EAST.** *2311 N Shadeland Ave (46219), east of downtown.* 317/359-9900; FAX 317/359-9900, ext. 175. 125 rms, 4 story. S $53-$58; D $57-$61; under 18 free. Crib free. Pet accepted, some restrictions. TV; cable. Indoor pool; whirlpool. Complimentary continental bkfst, coffee. Restaurant nearby. Ck-out noon. Meeting rms. Cr cds: A, C, D, DS, MC, V.

D ✦ ≈ ⊠ 🔥 SC

★ ★ **KNIGHTS INN.** *7101 E 21st St (46219), north of downtown.* 317/353-8484. 97 rms, 10 kits. S $30.95; D $37.95; each addl $3.30; kit. units $40.95-$46.95; under 18 free. Crib free. Pet accepted; $5. TV; cable. Pool. Restaurant adj 6 am-10 pm. Ck-out noon. Meeting rm. Some refrigerators. Cr cds: A, C, D, DS, MC, V.

D ✦ ≈ ⊠ 🔥 SC

★ ★ **LA QUINTA-EAST.** *7304 E 21st St (46219), north of downtown.* 317/359-1021; FAX 317/359-0578. 122 rms, 2 story. S, D $43-$52; each addl $7; under 18 free. Crib free. TV; cable. Heated pool. Continental bkfst. Complimentary coffee in lobby. Restaurant adj open 24 hrs. Ck-out noon. Coin lndry. Valet serv. Cr cds: A, C, D, DS, MC, V.

D ✦ ≈ ⊠ 🔥 SC

★ ★ **QUALITY INN-CASTLETON SUITES.** *8275 Craig St (46250), in Castleton.* 317/841-9700; FAX 317/576-0795. 163 rms, 2 story. S $59-$79; D $65-$89; each addl $5; under 18 free. TV; cable. Complimentary full bkfst 6:30-10:30 am. Restaurant nearby. Ck-out noon. Coin lndry. Meeting rms. Health club privileges. Cr cds: A, C, D, DS, ER, JCB, MC, V.

D ≈ ⊠ 🔥 SC

★ ★ **RAMADA INN EAST.** *7701 E 42nd St (46226), north of downtown.* 317/897-4000; FAX 317/897-8100. 192 rms, 2 story. S $55-$61; D $57-$63; each addl $5; suites $110-$150; under 18 free. Crib free. TV; cable. 2 pools, 1 indoor. Restaurant 6:30 am-10 pm; Sun to 2 pm. Rm serv. Bars. Ck-out noon. Meeting rms. Bellhops. Cr cds: A, C, D, DS, ER, MC, V.

⊠ ⊠ ⊠ ⊠ SC

★ ★ **SIGNATURE INN.** 4402 E Creek View Dr (46237), I-65 & Southport Rd, south of downtown. 317/784-7006; FAX 317/784-7006, ext. 500. 101 rms, 2 story. S $55-$58; D $62-$65; under 18 free; wkend rates Nov-Apr. Crib free. TV; cable. Pool. Complimentary continental bkfst, coffee. Restaurant adj 6 am-10 pm. Ck-out noon. Meeting rms. Valet serv. Sundries. Cr cds: A, D, DS, MC, V.

D ⊠ ⊠ ⊠ SC

Motor Hotels

★ ★ ★ **COURTYARD BY MARRIOTT.** 501 W Washington St (46204), downtown. 317/635-4443; FAX 317/867-0026. 233 rms, 8 story. S $69-$89; D $79-$99; each addl $10; suites $139-$149; under 18 free; higher rates special events. Crib $10. Pet accepted. TV; cable. Heated pool. Playground. Complimentary coffee in rms. Restaurant 6:30 am-12:30 pm. Rm serv. Bar 11-12:30 am. Ck-out noon. Coin Indry. Meeting rms. Gift shop. Free airport transportation. Exercise equipt; weights, bicycles. Refrigerators, minibars in suites. Cr cds: A, C, D, DS, ER, MC, V.

D ⊠ ⊠ ⊠ ⊠ ⊠ SC

★ ★ **GUEST QUARTERS SUITE HOTEL.** (11355 N Meridian St, Carmel 46032) Approx 15 mi N on Meridian St (US 31). 317/844-7994; FAX 317/844-2118. 138 suites, 3 story. S $119; D $134; each addl $15; under 18 free. Crib free. TV; cable. Indoor/outdoor pool; poolside serv. Complimentary coffee in rms. Restaurant 6:30 am-11 pm. Rm serv. Bar 4-11 pm. Ck-out noon. Meeting rms. Exercise equipt; bicycles, stair machine, whirlpool. Refrigerators. Private patios. Cr cds: A, C, D, DS, MC, V.

D ⊠ ⊠ ⊠ ⊠ SC

★ ★ **HOLIDAY INN-NORTH.** 3850 De Pauw Blvd (46268), in College Park. 317/872-9790; FAX 317/871-5608. 351 rms, 5 story. S, D $78-$89; each addl $10; suites $130-$170; under 18 free; wkend rates. Crib free. TV; cable. Heated pool; poolside serv. Restaurant 6 am-10 pm. Rm serv. Bar 11-2 am; dancing. Ck-out 11 am. Coin Indry. Convention facilities. Bellhops. Valet serv. Sundries. Airport transportation. Putting green. Exercise equipt; weights, treadmill, whirlpool, sauna. Private patios; balconies. Cr cds: A, C, D, DS, JCB, MC, V.

D ⊠ ⊠ ⊠ ⊠ SC

★ ★ ★ **MARRIOTT.** 7202 E 21st St (46219), north of downtown. 317/352-1231; FAX 317/352-1231, ext. 7413. 252 rms, 3-5 story. S, D, studio rms $94; each addl $10; suites $250-$300; under 18 free; wkend rates; higher rates Memorial Day wkend. Crib free. Pet accepted, some restrictions. TV; cable. Indoor/outdoor pool; wading pool; poolside serv. Complimentary coffee in lobby. Restaurant 6:30 am-11 pm. Rm serv. Bar 11-1 am, Sun noon-midnight. Ck-out 1 pm. Coin Indry. Meeting rms. Bellhops. Valet serv. Sundries. Gift shop. Tennis privileges. Putting green. Exercise equipt; weights, bicycles, whirlpool. Rec rm. Some private patios. *LUXURY LEVEL* : CONCIERGE LEVEL. 36 rms, 3 suites. S, D $104. Concierge. Private lounge. Bathrm phone in some suites. Complimentary refreshments. Cr cds: A, C, D, DS, ER, JCB, MC, V.

D ⊠ ⊠ ⊠ ⊠ ⊠ ⊠ SC

★ ★ **ST VINCENT MARTEN HOUSE.** 1801 W 86th St (46260), north of downtown. 317/872-4111; res: 800/736-5634; FAX 317/875-7162. 162 rms, 2 story. S, D $70-$75; each addl $10; suites $95. Crib free. TV; cable. Indoor pool; sauna. Restaurant 6:30 am-2 pm, 5:30-9 pm; Sat, Sun 7 am-2 pm. Rm serv. Bar 4:30 pm-midnight. Ck-out noon. Coin Indry. Meeting rms. Bellhops. Valet serv. Some refrigerators. St Vincent's Hospital adj. Cr cds: A, C, D, DS, ER, MC, V.

D ⊠ ⊠ ⊠ ⊠ SC

★ ★ ★ **WYNDHAM GARDEN.** 251 E Pennsylvania Pkwy (46280), north of downtown. 317/574-4600; FAX 317/574-4633. 171 rms, 6 story, 11 suites. S, D $89-$109; suites $109-$129. Crib free. TV. Indoor pool. Complimentary coffee in rms. Restaurant 6:30 am-10 pm. Rm serv from 5 pm. Bar 11 am-midnight. Ck-out noon. Meeting rms. Sundries. Exercise equipt; weights, bicycles, whirlpool. Cr cds: A, C, D, DS, ER, JCB, MC, V.

D ⊠ ⊠ ⊠ ⊠ SC

Hotels

★ ★ ★ **ADAM'S MARK.** 2544 Executive Dr (46241), near Intl Airport, south of downtown. 317/248-2481; res: 800/444-2326; FAX 317/381-6170. 407 rms, 6 story. S $99-$119; D $114-$134; each addl $15; suites $175-$375; studio rms $99; under 18 free; some wkend rates. Crib free. TV; cable. 2 pools, 1 indoor. Restaurant 6 am-midnight. Bars 11-2 am, Sun noon-midnight; piano lounge, dancing exc Sun. Ck-out noon. Coin Indry. Convention facilities. Gift shop. Airport transportation. Exercise equipt; weights, bicycles, whirlpool, sauna. Refrigerators. Some balconies. Cr cds: A, C, D, DS, MC, V.

D ⊠ ⊠ ⊠ ⊠ ⊠ SC

★ ★ ★ **CANTERBURY.** 123 S Illinois (46225), downtown. 317/634-3000; res: 800/538-8186; FAX 317/685-2519. 99 rms, 12 story. S $145-$180; D $170-$200; each addl $25; suites $350-$1,000; lower rates wkends. Crib $15. Pet accepted. Garage $7.50/day. TV; cable. Complimentary continental bkfst. Restaurant (see BEAULIEU). Afternoon tea (Mon-Sat) 4-5:30 pm. Ck-out 1 pm. Meeting rms. Concierge. Bathrm phones, refrigerators, minibars. 2-story atrium lobby. Formal decor; 4-poster beds, Chippendale-style furniture. Historic landmark; built 1926. Cr cds: A, C, D, DS, ER, JCB, MC, V.

D ⊠ ⊠ ⊠ SC

★ ★ ★ **EMBASSY SUITES.** 110 W Washington St (46204), downtown. 317/236-1800; FAX 317/236-1816. 360 suites, 18 story. S $109-$159; D $119-$169; under 12 free. Crib free. Parking in/out $5. TV; cable. Indoor pool. Complimentary full bkfst. Complimentary coffee in rms. Restaurant noon-10 pm; Sat & Sun from 5 pm. Bar. Ck-out noon. Convention facilities. Concierge. Shopping arcade. Exercise equipt; weights, bicycles, whirlpool, sauna. Refrigerators. Cr cds: A, C, D, DS, JCB, MC, V.

D ⊠ ⊠ ⊠ ⊠ SC

★ ★ ★ **EMBASSY SUITES.** 3912 Vincennes Rd (46268-3024), north of downtown. 317/872-7700; FAX 317/872-2974. 222 suites, 8 story. S, D $99-$189; under 12 free; wkend plan. Crib avail. Pet accepted. TV; cable. Indoor pool. Complimentary coffee in rms. Complimentary full bkfst. Restaurant 11am-2 pm, 5-11 pm. Bar 5-11 pm. Ck-out noon. Meeting rms. Gift shop. Airport transportation. Exercise equipt; bicycles, weight machine, whirlpool, sauna. Game rm. Refrigerators, minibars. Cr cds: A, D, DS, MC, V.

D ⊠ ⊠ ⊠ ⊠ ⊠ SC

★ ★ ★ **HOLIDAY INN CROWNE PLAZA-UNION STATION.** Box 2186 (46206), 123 W Louisiana St, downtown. 317/631-2221; FAX 317/236-7474. 276 rms, 3 story, 33 suites. S $110-$139; D $128-$154; each addl $15; suites $169-$200; under 18 free; wkend rates; higher rates Dec 31. Crib free. Valet parking $8.50; covered self-parking free. TV; cable. Indoor pool. Restaurant 6 am-2 pm, 5-10 pm. Bar 4 pm-midnight. Ck-out noon. Convention facilities. Concierge. Shopping arcade. Free airport transportation. Exercise equipt; bicycles, rowers, whirlpool. Rec rm. First US "union" railway depot (1853); Pullman sleeper cars from the 1920s house hotel's suites. Cr cds: A, C, D, DS, JCB, MC, V.

D ⊠ ⊠ ⊠ ⊠ SC

★ ★ ★ **HYATT REGENCY.** 1 South Capitol (46204), downtown. 317/632-1234; FAX 317/231-7569. 500 rms, 21 story. S $115; D $140; each addl $25; suites $230-$700; parlor $140-$500; under 18 free; some wkend rates. Valet, garage parking $8. Crib free. TV. Indoor pool. Restaurants 6 am-midnight. Bars 11-2 am. Ck-out noon. Convention facilities. Concierge. Barber, beauty shop. Exercise equipt; weight machine, bicycles. Atrium. Revolving restaurant. Cr cds: A, C, D, DS, ER, JCB, MC, V.

D ≈ X ⋈ 🔥 SC

★ ★ ★ **OMNI NORTH.** *8181 N Shadeland Ave (46250), I-69 N exit 82nd St, north of downtown.* 317/849-6668; FAX 317/849-4936. 222 rms, 6 story. S, D $69-$126; suites $175-$250; wkend rates. Crib free. TV; cable. Indoor pool. Complimentary coffee in rms. Restaurant 7 am-10 pm; wkend hrs vary. Rm serv to midnight. Bar 11:30 am-midnight. Ck-out noon. Coin lndry. Meeting rms. Gift shop. Exercise equipt; bicycles, weight machine; sauna. Health club privileges. Game rm. Many refrigerators. Cr cds: A, D, DS, JCB, MC, V.

D ≈ X ⋈ 🔥 SC

★ ★ ★ **OMNI SEVERIN.** *40 W Jackson Place (46225), downtown.* 317/634-6664; FAX 317/687-3619. 423 rms, 13 story. S, D $100-$160; each addl $10; suites $140-$500; under 18 free. Free crib. Garage parking $5. TV; cable. Indoor pool; wading pool, poolside serv. Restaurant 6 am-11 pm. Rm serv 24 hrs. Bar 2 pm-1 am. Ck-out noon. Convention facilities. Concierge. Gift shop. Airport transportation. Exercise equipt; weight machine, bicycles, whirlpool, sauna. Game rm. Some refrigerators. Built in 1913. Across from Union Station. Cr cds: A, C, D, DS, JCB, MC, V.

D ≈ X ⋈ 🔥 SC

★ ★ ★ **RADISSON.** *8787 Keystone Crossing (46240), at 86th St & Keystone Ave, connected to Fashion Mall, north of downtown.* 317/846-2700; FAX 317/846-2700, ext. 402. 552 units, 2-12 story. S, D $110-$120; each addl $15; suites $130-$150; under 17 free; wkend rates. Crib free. Pet accepted, some restrictions. Valet parking $8. TV; cable. Indoor pool; whirlpool, sauna, poolside serv. Restaurants 6:30 am-11 pm. Rm serv to 1 am. Bar 5 pm-2 am; entertainment exc Sun; dancing. Ck-out noon. Guest lndry. Convention facilities. Concierge. Shopping arcade. Garage parking. Health club privileges. Game rm. Refrigerator in suites. Cr cds: A, C, D, DS, ER, JCB, MC, V.

D ⛷ ≈ ⋈ 🔥 SC

★ ★ ★ **RAMADA PLAZA HOTEL.** *31 W Ohio St (46204), downtown.* 317/635-2000; FAX 317/638-0782. 371 rms. S $79-$155; D $79-$160; each addl $10; suites $140-$155; under 18 free. Crib free. Garage $4. TV; cable. Pool; poolside serv. Restaurant 6:30 am-midnight. Bars 11-2 am, Sun to midnight. Ck-out noon. Convention facilities. Health club privileges. *LUXURY LEVEL : EXECUTIVE FLOOR.* 29 rms, 4 suites. S $125; D $140; each addl $15; suites $140. Concierge. Private lounge. Some full wet bars. Complimentary continental bkfst, refreshments. Cr cds: A, C, D, DS, MC, V.

D ≈ ⋈ 🔥 SC

★ ★ ★ **UNIVERSITY PLACE.** *850 W Michigan St (46206), on campus of Indiana University, downtown.* 317/269-9000; res: 800/627-2700; FAX 317/231-5179. 278 rms, 10 story. Jan-Mar & Sept-Dec: S $105-$180; D $120-$180; suites $285-$550; lower rates rest of yr. Crib avail. Pet accepted. Garage parking $4.75. TV; cable. Restaurant 6 am-midnight. Bar from 11 am. Ck-out noon. Convention facilities. Concierge. Gift shop. Barber. Airport transportation. Health club privileges. Refrigerators. Cr cds: A, C, D, DS, MC, V.

D ⛷ ⋈ 🔥

★ ★ ★ **THE WESTIN.** *50 S Capitol (46204), downtown.* 317/262-8100; FAX 317/231-3928. 572 rms, 15 story. S $140-$160; D $160; each addl $20; suites $225; under 18 free; wkend rates. Crib free. Valet, garage parking $8. TV; cable. Indoor pool. Restaurant 6:30 am-11:30 pm. Rm serv 24 hrs. Bar 11-2 am, Sun to midnight. Ck-out noon. Convention facilities. Concierge. Airport transportation. Exercise equipt; weights, bicycles, whirlpool. Health club privileges. Some bathrm phones, minibars. *LUXURY LEVEL : EXECUTIVE CLUB.* 32 rms, 3 suites. S $160; D $180; suites $600-$1,000. Ck-out noon. Concierge. Private lounge, honor bar. Minibars. Wet bars. Bathrm

phones. Complimentary continental breakfast, refreshments. Cr cds: A, C, D, DS, JCB, MC, V.

D ≈ X ⋈ 🔥 SC

Restaurants

✓ ★ **ARISTOCRAT.** *5212 N College Ave, in Broad Ripple.* 317/283-7388. Hrs: 11:30 am-midnight; Fri & Sat to 1 am; Sun 10 am-11 pm; Sun brunch to 3 pm. Closed some major hols. Bar. Semi-a la carte: lunch, dinner $4.95-$14.95. Sun brunch $4.50-$6. Child's meals. Specializes in pasta. Parking. Outdoor dining. Casual atmosphere. Cr cds: A, C, D, DS, MC, V.

D

★ ★ ★ **BEAULIEU.** *(See Canterbury Hotel)* 317/634-3000. Hrs: 7-10:30 am, 11:30 am-2 pm, 5:30-11 pm; Sun brunch 10:30 am-2 pm. Res accepted. Continental menu. Bar. Wine list. A la carte entrees: bkfst $3.50-$13.95, lunch $5.95-$13.95, dinner $16.50-$28.50. Sun brunch $5.95-$12.95. Specializes in seafood, veal. Own baking. Valet parking. International decor; artwork. Jacket (dinner). Cr cds: A, C, D, DS, MC, V.

D

★ ★ ★ **BENVENUTI.** *36 S Pennsylvania St (46225), downtown.* 317/633-4915. Hrs: 5:30-9 pm; wkends to 9:30 pm. Closed Sun; major hols. Res accepted; required wkends. Italian menu. Bar. Wine list. A la carte entrees: dinner $18.50-$27.50. Specializes in pasta, fish, veal chops. Elegant atmosphere with European flair. Jacket. Cr cds: A, D, MC, V.

✓ ★ **BOMBAY BICYCLE CLUB.** *9111 N. Michigan Rd, in College Park.* 317/872-3446. Hrs: 11 am-midnight; Sun to 10 pm. Closed Thanksgiving, Dec 25. Res accepted. Bar. Semi-a la carte: lunch, dinner $5.65-$14.20. Specializes in seafood, chicken, steak. Parking. Display of bicycle relics. Cr cds: A, C, D, DS, MC, V.

D

★ ★ **HOLLYHOCK HILL.** *8110 N College Ave, north of downtown.* 317/251-2294. Hrs: 5-8 pm; Sun noon-7:30 pm. Closed Mon; July 4, Dec 24 & 25. Res accepted. Serv bar. Complete meals: dinner $11.95-$15.95. Child's meals. Specializes in fried chicken, seafood, steak. Tea room atmosphere. Family-owned. Cr cds: A, MC, V.

D

★ ★ **IRON SKILLET.** *2489 W 30th St, at Cold Spring Rd, north of downtown.* 317/923-6353. Hrs: 5-8:30 pm; Sun noon-7:30 pm. Closed Mon, Tues; Dec 24-25; also 1st wk July. Res accepted. Serv bar. Complete meals: dinner $11.50-$15.75. Child's meals. Specializes in steak, skillet-fried chicken, fresh fish. Family-style dining. Blackboard menu. Parking. Converted homestead (1870); overlooks golf course. Family-owned. Cr cds: A, C, D, DS, MC, V.

D

★ ★ **J. ROSS BROWNE'S DRYDOCK.** *7230 Pendleton Pike, north of downtown.* 317/547-5506. Hrs: 11 am-2 pm, 5-10 pm; Fri & Sat 5-10:30 pm; early-bird dinner 5-6 pm. Res accepted. Bar. Semi-a la carte: lunch $5-$9.95, dinner $11.50-$28.95. Child's meals. Specializes in fresh fish, shellfish, prime rib. Parking. Nautical decor. Cr cds: A, D, DS, MC, V.

D

✓ ★ **JAZZ COOKER.** *925 E Westfield Blvd, in Broad Ripple.* 317/253-2883. Hrs: 5-10 pm; Sat noon-3 pm, 5-10 pm; Sun 5-9 pm; Sun brunch 11 am-3 pm. Closed most major hols. Res accepted. Bar. A la carte entrees: lunch $1.95-$6.95, dinner $2.95-$15.75. Specializes in Cajun, Creole dishes. Entertainment Thurs-Sun. Outdoor dining. New Orleans atmosphere. Cr cds: A, D, DS, MC, V.

D

★ ★ ★ **JONATHAN'S RESTAURANT & PUB.** *9445 Threel Rd, at 96th & Keystone, in Broad Ripple.* 317/844-1155. Hrs: 11 am-2:30

pm, 5-10 pm; Fri, Sat 5-11 pm; Sun 4-9 pm; Sun brunch 10:30 am-2 pm. Closed some major hols. Res accepted; required hols. Bar 11 am-midnight. Wine cellar. Semi-a la carte: lunch $4.25-$8.95, dinner $10.95-$19.95. Sun brunch $11.95. Child's meals. Specializes in prime rib, pork loin, seafood. Own baking. Parking. English country atmosphere. Cr cds: A, DS, MC, V.

D

★ ★ **KEY WEST SHRIMP HOUSE.** 39 W Jackson Place, at Union Station, downtown. 317/635-5353. Hrs: 11 am-10 pm; Fri & Sat to 11 pm; Sun to 8 pm. Closed Dec 25. Res accepted. Semi-a la carte: lunch $4.95-$7.95, dinner $8.95-$24.95. Specializes in seafood, steak. Caribbean decor; mesquite grill. Family-owned. Cr cds: A, C, D, DS, MC, V.

★ ★ **KING COLE.** 7 N Meridian St, downtown. 317/638-5588. Hrs: 11 am-2:30 pm, 5-10 pm; Sat from 5 pm. Closed Sun; major hols. Continental menu. Serv bar. Wine list. Semi-a la carte: lunch $7.55-$9.50, dinner $17.75-$24.95. Specializes in roast duckling, seafood, rack of lamb. French decor; oil paintings. Cr cds: A, C, D, DS, MC, V.

D

★ ★ **LA TERRACE.** 8250 Dean Rd, north of downtown. 317/849-3970. Hrs: 11 am-10 pm; Fri & Sat to 11 pm; Sun 10 am-10 pm. Res accepted. French, Califormia menu. Bar. Wine cellars. A la carte entrees: lunch $5-$15, dinner $12-$27. Menu changes seasonally. Specializes in prime beef, fresh fish, pasta. Outdoor dining. French Renaissance decor. Cr cds: A, C, D, DS, MC, V.

D

✔ ★ **MARK PI'S CHINA GATE.** 135 S Illinois, downtown. 317/631-6757. Hrs: 11 am-10 pm; Fri to 11 pm; Sat noon-11 pm; Sun 3:30-10 pm. Closed most major hols. Chinese menu. Bar. Semi-a la carte: lunch $3-$6.75, dinner $5.50-$15. Specialty: Peking duck. Valet parking (dinner only). Oriental decor. Cr cds: A, D, MC, V.

D

★ ★ **NORMAN'S.** 39 W Jackson Place, suite 12 (46225), at Union Station, downtown. 317/269-2545. Hrs: 11 am-10 pm; Sun 10:30 am-9 pm; Sun brunch to 1:30 pm. Closed Thanksgiving, Dec 25. Bar. Semi-a la carte: lunch, dinner $5.95-$19.95. Sun brunch $12.95. Specializes in fresh seafood, steak, pasta. Parking. Open air dining within Union Station; art deco accents. Cr cds: A, DS, MC, V.

D

★ ★ **PETER'S.** 8505 Keystone Crossing Blvd, north of downtown. 317/465-1155. Hrs: 5-10 pm; Fri & Sat to 10:30 pm. Closed Sun; major hols. Res accepted. Bar. A la carte entrees: dinner $8-$20. Specializes in Indiana duckling, fresh fish, desserts. Parking. Cr cds: A, C, D, MC, V.

D

★ **PROVINCIAL KITCHEN.** 1001 Broad Ripple Ave, in Broad Ripple. 317/255-7060. Hrs: 11:30 am-3 pm, 5:30-10 pm; wkends to 11 pm; Sun brunch 8 am-3 pm. Closed some major hols. Res accepted. Bar 4 pm-2 am. A la carte entrees: lunch $4.25-$7.50, dinner $7.95-$18. Sun brunch $3.95-$11.95. Child's meals. Specializes in various ethnic dishes. Parking. Outdoor dining. Menu changes seasonally. Informal dining. Cr cds: A, D, MC, V.

D SC

✔ ★ **RENEE'S.** 839 Westfield Blvd, in Broad Ripple. 317/251-4142. Hrs: 11 am-10 pm; Fri, Sat to 11 pm; Sun 4-9 pm. Closed major hols. Res accepted. French, Amer menu. Semi-a la carte: lunch $4.50-$8. Complete meals: dinner $11-$15. Specializes in desserts. Informal dining. Cr cds: A, D, MC, V.

★ ★ **ST ELMO STEAK HOUSE.** 127 S Illinois, downtown. 317/637-1811. Hrs: 4-10:30 pm; Sun 5-9:30 pm. Closed major hols. Res accepted. Bar. Semi-a la carte: dinner $13.95-$31.95. Specializes in steak, fresh seafood. Turn-of-the-century decor, historic photographs. Cr cds: A, C, D, DS, MC, V.

D

Unrated Dining Spot

LAUGHNER'S CAFETERIA. 4030 S East St, south of downtown. 317/787-3745. Hrs: 11 am-8 pm; Fri to 8:30 pm; Sat 11 am-8:30 pm; Sun 11 am-8 pm. Closed major hols. Avg ck: lunch $4.80, dinner $6. Specializes in beef, fried chicken, desserts. Early Amer decor. Cr cds: DS, MC, V.

Kansas City

Settled: 1838

Pop: 435,146

Elev: 800 feet

Time zone: Central

Area code: 816 (Missouri); 913 (Kansas)

Kansas City, Missouri, is the most populous city in the state and has a stable position as major distributing point for a vast agricultural region. It also has the distinction of sharing its name and economy with its neighboring city, Kansas City, Kansas.

Until the Civil War, Kansas City's economy was based on supplying and outfitting travelers along the trails to the West. Change was foreshadowed when the first railroad reached the city in 1869. By 1870 Kansas City was a railroad hub, with eight different radiating lines. Within 10 years it became the nation's most important cattle-trading center; it soon became a great grain center as well.

In the 1890s and early 1900s the city launched a program of civic improvement and beautification. These efforts can still be seen in many wide boulevards and outstanding public buildings. Considerable industrial development followed as a wide variety of new industries, including automobile assembling plants, came to Kansas City.

Business

Traditionally, Kansas City has been regarded as a major transportation, distribution and agribusiness center, but there is much diversification. The city ranks high in marketing and manufacturing. Several national manufacturers have their headquarters here. The federal government maintains many regional headquarters in Kansas City and employs more than 30,000. Eighteen major insurance companies have their home offices here. Some 50 employers maintain payrolls of 1,000 or more. Of *Fortune's* 500 largest industrial firms, almost 200 have operations in greater Kansas City.

The most dynamic growth in Kansas City's economy since 1958 has been in the nonmanufacturing sector. The wholesale and retail trade industries employ the greatest number of people, with the service industry ranking close behind.

Recently, a major building boom has taken place and given Kansas City a new look. Crown Center, developed by Hallmark Cards, Inc, is the largest private urban renewal project in the United States since Rockefeller Center. An 85-acre "city within a city" near the downtown area, Crown Center hosts festivals, fairs and exhibits. A 10-acre outdoor square is the scene of free concerts in spring and summer and provides ice-skating facilities in winter. The complex includes The Westin Hotel, the Hyatt Regency, 80 shops and restaurants, live theater and more than 50 buildings in a model business-residential-entertainment community.

Convention Facilities

Among the top convention cities, Kansas City is host to more than 400,000 annual convention delegates. The H. Roe Bartle Hall and the Municipal Auditorium are located in the heart of the downtown area. By itself the H. Roe Bartle Hall has 388,800 square feet of unobstructed, flexible exhibit space. It is a tri-level facility that offers 26 meeting rooms, seating 35 to 3,000 people, and 73,000 feet of registration area.

The H. Roe Bartle Hall is adjacent to the Municipal Auditorium; together they provide 607,800 square feet of exhibit space, 55 meeting rooms (seating from 25 to 20,000), a 600-seat theater, a 2,400-seat music hall, a 10,500-seat arena and registration and dining areas.

The American Royal Center has 627,000 square feet of indoor/outdoor exhibit space, a main arena that seats 5,000 and parking for 3,000 cars. Governors Exhibition Hall offers 96,000 square feet of clear-span, ground-level indoor space.

Sports and Recreation

Kansas City sports lovers enjoy the Royals baseball team and the Chiefs football team, which both play in the Harry S Truman Sports Complex—side-by-side professional baseball and football stadiums. The Attack soccer team and Blades ice hockey team play in the Kemper Arena. Two auto racetracks are open from March through September.

Oceans of Fun, 12 miles northeast, offers swimming, surfing, sand and sun that can be enjoyed throughout the 60-acre site.

Entertainment

Jazz survives and prospers in Kansas City. During Prohibition, a whole school of jazz musicians settled here and developed a distinctive style of music. A revival of the Kansas City jam session is again providing a stage for musicians. The spirit of Kansas City jazz is showcased each July, when thousands of devotees come to hear local and national favorites perform during the Kansas City Blues and Jazz Festival. A special service, the Jazz Hotline, is a recording of performances and jam sessions.

The Kansas City Symphony Orchestra gives regular performances from mid-October to mid-May. The Lyric Opera presents operas in English from April through May and mid-September to mid-October; advance tickets are essential. The State Ballet of Missouri has several performances a year.

The Missouri Repertory Theatre presents professional casts in performances from September through May. Each spring the William Jewell Fine Arts Series has a series of opera, symphony and ballet productions. Starlight Theater, in Swope Park, is one of the nation's finest outdoor theaters, seating nearly 8,000 people. Top stars perform here from early June through August. Plaza Dinner Playhouse has imaginative entertainment. The Theater League presents Broadway productions at the ornate Midland Theater, and the restored Folly Theater presents musical entertainment and theater productions.

Historical Areas

Westport, once a prosperous center for outfitting and Indian trade in the 1850s, has become a major restoration area. Kelly's, once a busy dry goods store during the town's heyday and now a tavern, is one of

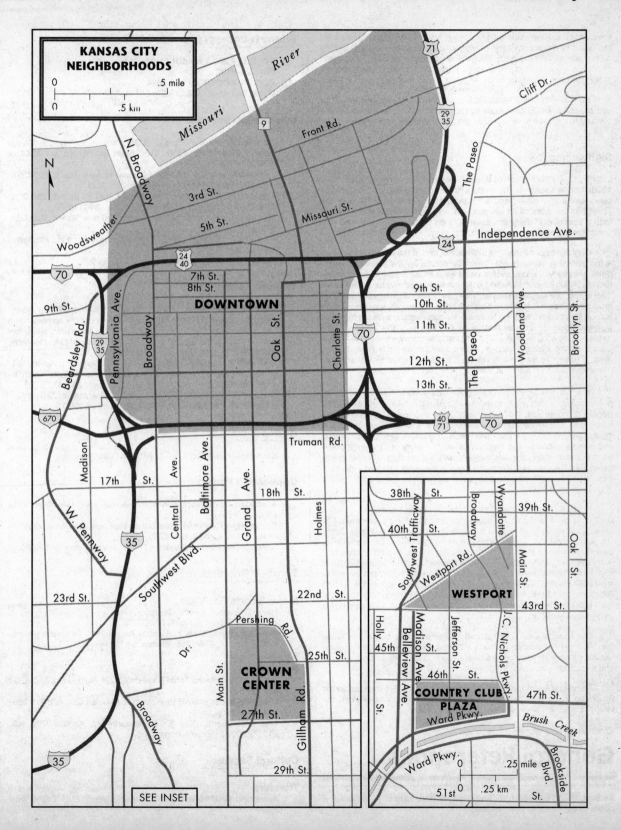

KANSAS CITY NEIGHBORHOODS

0   .5 mile
0   .5 km

N

Missouri River

Missouri

9

Front Rd.

71

29 35

Cliff Dr.

N. Broadway

3rd St.

5th St.

Missouri St.

The Paseo

Woodsweather

24

Independence Ave.

70

24 40

7th St.
8th St.

DOWNTOWN

9th St.
10th St.

11th St.

9th St.

Beardsley Rd.

29 35

Pennsylvania Ave.

Broadway

Oak St.

Charlotte St.

70

12th St.

13th St.

The Paseo

Woodland Ave.

Brooklyn St.

670

Truman Rd.

40 71

70

Madison

17th St.

Ave.

Baltimore Ave.

Grand Ave.

18th St.

Holmes

W. Pennway

35

Central Ave.

Southwest Blvd.

23rd St.

22nd St.

Pershing Rd.

Main St.

Dr.

25th St.

Broadway

CROWN CENTER

Gillham Rd.

27th St.

29th St.

35

SEE INSET

(Inset)

38th St.

Southwest Trafficway

Broadway

Wyandotte

39th St.

40th St.

Westport Rd.

Main St.

Oak St.

WESTPORT

43rd St.

J.C. Nichols Pkwy.

Holly St.

Madison Ave.

Belleview Ave.

Jefferson St.

45th St.

46th St.

47th St.

COUNTRY CLUB PLAZA

Ward Pkwy.

Brush Creek

Brookside Blvd.

Ward Pkwy.

0   .25 mile
0   .25 km

51st St.

the oldest buildings in the area. Westport Square and Manor Square are the result of the preservation of old facades of other buildings and the restoration of their interiors. They stand as contemporary, yet historic, shopping areas with many shops, art galleries, specialty and jewelry stores and fine dining spots.

Kansas City has a remarkable collection of 19th- and early 20th-century buildings. Efforts made by the city's residents at the turn of the century to improve their city have left a fine architectural legacy.

Sightseeing

Country Club Plaza, south of the downtown area, was developed in the 1920s and is known as the world's first shopping center. This area of open spaces, fountains and art treasures collected from all over the world has the aura of an elegant and venerable European city rather than a booming Midwestern town built on wealth from cattle trading, grain farming and machinery manufacturing.

Only 20 blocks away, but at the other end of the historic spectrum, is the gleaming, ultramodern Crown Center. Its central square is a focal point of activity; various events occur year round under its huge translucent roof. A large ice-skating rink in the square provides a recreation spot during the winter and an area for free concerts in the summer. Also located in Crown Center are Kaleidoscope, a participatory creative art exhibit for children, and the Hallmark Visitors Center, with exhibits and displays focusing on the history of the firm and the greeting card industry. Crown Center is also a stop on the trolley which links Crown Center to the Plaza, Westport, Town Pavilion and the River Market Area. Crown Center is home to sculptures by noted artists such as Alexander Caulder, Kenneth Snelson and Louise Nevelson.

The Harry S Truman Library and Museum is in the town of Independence, 10 miles from downtown Kansas City. As many as 30,000 people a month visit the library and Truman gravesite. Covering the lobby wall is a mural entitled *Independence and the Opening of the West*, by Kansas City's own Thomas Hart Benton. Displays of books, documents, pictures and furnishings tell the story of Truman's presidential years; there are also several exhibits relating to other presidents. The Truman residence, an excellent example of late 19th-century Victorian architecture, has been opened to the public by the National Park Service.

A family entertainment theme park is located about 15 minutes northeast of downtown Kansas City. Worlds of Fun, covering 170 acres, is open daily during the summer months, weekends only during the spring and fall. The "worlds" represent America, Europe, Africa, Scandinavia and the Orient. There are live shows and attractions and more than 100 rides, including a giant whitewater raft ride and five roller coasters. There is also a collection of Hollywood ships, purchased at the MGM auction. Visitors can climb aboard such ships as the *Cotton Blossom*, from the film *Show Boat*, and the *Victrix*, which appeared in the 1962 version of *Mutiny on the Bounty*. Adjacent is a 60-acre water park, Oceans of Fun.

The Kansas City Zoo, located in Swope Park, has a fine feline exhibit, an ape house, an African veldt area and one of the best tropical habitat exhibits in the United States. The zoo also offers pony, camel and miniature train rides.

An annual event that attracts thousands of visitors each fall is the American Royal Livestock, Horse Show and Rodeo in November, the largest combined show of its kind in the country.

General References

Settled: 1838 **Pop:** 435,146 **Elev:** 800 feet **Time zone:** Central **Area code:** 816 (Missouri); 913 (Kansas)

Phone Numbers

POLICE, FIRE & AMBULANCE: 911
FBI: 221-6100
POISON CONTROL: 234-3434
TIME: 844-4444 **WEATHER:** 531-4444

Information Sources

Convention & Visitors Bureau of Greater Kansas City, City Center Square Bldg, Suite 2550, 1100 Main St, 64105; 221-5242 or 800/767-7700.
The Chamber of Commerce of Greater Kansas City, #2600 Commerce Towers, 911 Main St, 64105; 221-2424.
Kansas City, Kansas Area Convention & Visitors Bureau, 753 State Ave, Suite 101, Kansas City, KS 66117; 913/321-5800.
Missouri Tourist Information Center, Truman Sports Complex, 889-3330.
Visitor Information Phone (24-hour information and entertainment hotline), 691-3800.
Department of Parks & Recreation, 871-5600.

Transportation

AIRLINES: American; America West; Continental; Delta; Northwest; Southwest; TWA; United; USAir; and other commuter and regional airlines. For the most current airline schedules and information consult the *Official Airline Guide*, published twice monthly.
AIRPORT: Kansas City International, 243-5237.
CAR RENTAL AGENCIES: (See Toll-Free Numbers) Alamo 464-5151; Avis 243-5760; Budget 243-5756; Dollar 243-5600; Enterprise 800/325-8007 (exc MO), 842-4700; Hertz 243-5765.
PUBLIC TRANSPORTATION: Area Transit Authority 221-0660.
RAILROAD PASSENGER SERVICE: Amtrak 800/872-7245.

Newspapers

Kansas City Star; Kansas City Business Journal.

Convention Facilities

American Royal Center, Kemper Arena, 1800 Genessee, 274-1900.
Convention Center/H. Roe Bartle Hall and Municipal Auditorium, 301 W 13th St, 871-3700.
Kansas City Market Center, 1775 N Universal Ave, 241-6200.

Sports & Recreation

Major Sports Facilities
Harry S Truman Sports Complex, I-435 & I-70 (Royals, baseball, 921-2200; Chiefs, football, 924-9300).
American Royal Center, Kemper Arena, 1800 Genessee (Attack, indoor soccer, 474-2255; Blades, ice hockey, 931-3330).

Racetracks
Kansas City International Raceway, 8201 Noland Rd, 358-6700 (car racing).
Lakeside Speedway, 5615 Wolcott Dr, Kansas City, KS, 913/299-2040 (car racing).
The Woodlands, 99th & Leavenworth Rd, Kansas City, KS, 913/299-9797 (horse & dog racing).

Cultural Facilities

Theaters
American Heartland Theatre, Crown Center, 2450 Grand Ave, 842-9999.

Coterie-Kansas City's Family Theatre, Crown Center, 2400 Pershing Ave, 474-6552.
Folly Theater, 12th & Central, 842-5500.
Granada Theatre, 1015 Minnesota Ave, Kansas City, KS, 913/621-7177 or -2232.
Lyric Theater, 11th & Central (Lyric Opera, 471-7344; Kansas City Symphony Orchestra, 471-0400).
Midland Center for the Performing Arts, 1228 Main St, 471-8600.
Missouri Repertory Theater, 50th & Cherry Sts, 276-2700.
Starlight Theater, near 63rd & Swope Pkwy in Swope Park, 363-STAR.
State Ballet of Missouri, 706 W 42nd St, 931-2232.

Concert Halls

Kemper Arena, 1800 Genessee, 274-1900.
Municipal Auditorium, 1310 Wyandotte St, adjacent to the Convention Center, 274-2900.

Museums

Arabia Steamboat Museum, 400 Grand Ave, 471-4030.
Civil War Museum, S on MO 291, 10 mi E on US 50, in Lone Jack, 566-2272.
Harry S Truman Library and Museum, US 24 & Delaware St, Independence, 833-1225.
Jesse James Bank Museum, 15 mi NE on Old Town Square, in Liberty, 781-4458.
Kansas City Museum, 3218 Gladstone Blvd, & Town Pavilion Mall, 1111 Main St, 483-8300.
Toy & Miniature Museum, 5235 Oak St at 52nd St, 333-2055.

Art Museums and Galleries

Kansas City Art Institute, 4415 Warwick Blvd, 561-4852.
Nelson-Atkins Museum of Art, 4525 Oak St at 45th St, 561-4000.
Van Ackeren Gallery, Rockhurst College campus, 5225 Troost Ave, 926-4808.

Points of Interest

Historical

Fort Osage, 14 mi E of Independence on US 24, 3 mi N, in Sibley, 881-4431.
Grinter House, 1420 S 78th St, Kansas City, KS, 913/299-0373.
Harry S Truman National Historic Site (Truman House), 219 N Delaware St, Independence, 254-9929.
Huron Indian Cemetery, Huron Park, Center City Plaza, between 6th & 7th Sts, Kansas City, KS.
John Wornall House Museum, 146 W 61st Terrace, at Wornall, 444-1858.
Liberty Memorial Museum, 100 W 26th St, near Union Station, 221-1918.
Missouri Town 1855, 20 mi SE of Kansas City off US 40, E side of Lake Jacomo, Blue Springs, 881-4431.
Thomas Hart Benton Home and Studios State Historic Site, 3616 Belleview, 931-5722.
Union Cemetery, 227 E 28th St Terrace, 472-4990.
Westport Square, Broadway at Westport Rd.

Other Attractions

Agricultural Hall of Fame and National Center, 630 N 126th St, Bonner Springs, KS, 913/721-1075.
Antiques and Art Center, 45th & State Line.
Benjamin Ranch, Old Santa Fe Trail, I-435 & E 87th, 761-5055.
Board of Trade, 4800 Main St, 753-7500.
City Market, Main to Walnut Sts, 3rd to 5th Sts, 346-0794.

Civic Center, 11th to 13th Sts, Holmes to McGee Sts.
Country Club Plaza, 47th & Main Sts, 753-0100.
Crown Center, Pershing & Grand Ave, 274-8444.
Hallmark Visitors Center, Crown Center, 274-5672.
Kaleidoscope, Crown Center, 274-8300 or -8301.
Kansas City Zoo, Swope Park, 333-7405.
Lake Jacomo, Fleming Park, in Blue Springs, 795-8200.
Lakeside Nature Center, 5600 E Gregory, 444-4656.
Lewis & Clark Point, 8th & Jefferson.
Loose Park, 51st St & Wornall Rd.
NCAA Visitors Center, 6201 College Blvd, Overland Park, KS, 913/339-0000.
Oceans of Fun, 10 mi NE of I-435 exit 54, between Parvin Rd & NE 48th St, 454-4545.
Old Shawnee Town, 12 mi SW on I-35 to Johnson Dr, then W to 5th & Cody, Shawnee, KS, 913/268-8772.
Swope Park, Meyer Blvd & Swope Pkwy.
Town Pavilion, 11th & Main Sts, 474-5909.
Worlds of Fun, 10 mi NE via I-435 exit 54, 454-4545.

Sightseeing Tours

Blue Ribbon Tours, 8901 State Line, 361-5111.
Claudette's Theatre on Wheels, 1012 Broadway, 421-1981.
Gray Line bus tours, PO Box 414475, 913/268-5252.
Heart of America Convention Services, 843 South Shore Dr, 741-3410.
Kansas City Sightseeing, PO Box 520554, 833-4083.
Kansas City Trolley, 707 E 19th St, 221-3399.
Missouri River Queen **Excursion Boat,** 1 River City Dr, Kansas City, KS, 913/281-5300.
Show-Me K.C., Box 414475, KS, 913/268-5252.
Surreys Ltd on the Plaza, PO Box 36294, 531-2673.

Annual Events

Kansas City Pro Rodeo, Benjamin Ranch, 761-5055. Wk of July 4.
Kansas City Blues and Jazz Festival. Late July.
Ethnic Enrichment Festival. 3 days Aug.
Kansas City Spirit Festival. Early Sept.
Plaza Fine Arts Fair. Mid-Sept.
American Royal Livestock, Horse Show and Rodeo, American Royal Center, 1701 American Royal Court, 221-9800. Nov.
Plaza Christmas Lights. Thanksgiving Eve-mid-Jan.

City Neighborhoods

Many of the restaurants, unrated dining establishments and some lodgings listed under Kansas City include neighborhoods as well as exact street addresses. A map showing these neighborhoods can be found immediately following the city introduction. Geographic descriptions of these areas are given, followed by a table of restaurants arranged by neighborhood.

Country Club Plaza: South of Downtown; south of 46th St, west of Nichols Pkwy, north of Ward Pkwy and east of Madison Ave.
Crown Center: South of Pershing Rd, west of Gillham Rd, north of 26th St and east of Main St.
Downtown: South of the Missouri River, west of I-70, north of Truman Rd and east of I-29/I-35. **North of Downtown:** North of Missouri River. **South of Downtown:** South of US 40. **East of Downtown:** East of US 70.
Westport: Area north of Country Club Plaza; south of Westport Rd, west of Main St, north of 43rd St and east of Southwest Trafficway.

Lodgings and Food
Kansas City, MO

KANSAS CITY RESTAURANTS
BY NEIGHBORHOOD AREAS

(For full description, see alphabetical listings under Restaurants)

COUNTRY CLUB PLAZA

Bristol Bar & Grill. 4740 Jefferson

Emile's. 302 Nichols Rd

Fedora Cafe & Bar. 210 W 47th St

Figlio. 209 W 46th Terrace

Harry Starker's. 200 Nichols Rd

K.C. Masterpiece. 4747 Wyandotte St

Parkway 600. 600 Ward Pkwy

Plaza Iii The Steakhouse. 4749 Pennsylvania

The Rooftop (The Ritz-Carlton, Kansas City Hotel). 401 Ward Pkwy

CROWN CENTER

The American Restaurant. 2450 Grand Ave

Milano. 2450 Grand Ave

DOWNTOWN

Italian Gardens. 1110 Baltimore

Jennie's. 511 Cherry St

Savoy Grill (Savoy Hotel).

NORTH OF DOWNTOWN

Cascone's. 3733 N Oak

Paradise Grill. 5225 NW 64th St

SOUTH OF DOWNTOWN

André's Confiserie Suisse. 5018 Main St

Costello's Greenhouse. 1414 W 85th St

EBT. 1310 Carondelet Dr

Golden Ox. 1600 Genessee

Grand Street Cafe. 4740 Grand Ave

Hereford House. 2 E 20th St

Jasper's. 405 W 75th St

Le Picnique. 301 E 55th St

Sensations-A Kosher Experience. 1148 W 103rd St

Stephenson's Apple Farm. 16401 E US 40

Trattoria Marco Polo. 7514 Wornall Rd

EAST OF DOWNTOWN

Smuggler's. 1650 Universal Plaza Dr

WESTPORT

Californos. 4124 Pennsylvania

Classic Cup. 4130 Pennsylvania

Metropolis American Grill. 303 Westport Rd

Note: *When a listing is located in a town that does not have its own city heading, it will appear under the city nearest to its location. In these cases, the address and town appear in parenthesis immediately following the name of the establishment.*

Motels

★ ★ **BEST WESTERN COUNTRY INN.** *7100 NE Parvin Rd (64117), northeast of downtown.* 816/453-3355; FAX 816/453-0242. 86 rms, 2 story. May-Aug: S $60-$70; D $70-$85; each addl $5; under 12 free; lower rates rest of yr. Crib free. TV; cable. Pool. Complimentary continental bkfst, coffee. Restaurant nearby. Ck-out 11 am. Cr cds: A, C, D, DS, MC, V.

[D] [symbols] SC

✔★ **BEST WESTERN COUNTRY INN.** *11900 Plaza Circle (64153), north of downtown.* 816/464-2002. 43 rms, 2 story. S $50.95-$54.95; D $55.95-$67.95; each addl $3; under 12 free; higher rates special events. Crib free. TV. Complimentary continental bkfst. Restaurant adj 6 am-11 pm. Ck-out noon. Meeting rm. Free airport transportation. Near airport. Cr cds: A, C, D, DS, MC, V.

[D] [symbols] SC

★ **BEST WESTERN SEVILLE PLAZA.** *4309 Main St (69111), in Country Club Plaza.* 816/561-9600. 77 rms, 4 story. S $61-$71; D $71-$81; each addl $5; under 18 free; higher rates hols, Plaza Lights Festival. Crib free. TV; cable, in-rm movies avail. Complimentary continental bkfst. Restaurant nearby. Ck-out noon. Meeting rms. Bellhops. Valet serv. Airport transportation. Whirlpool. Some refrigerators. Cr cds: A, C, D, DS, MC, V.

[D] [symbols] SC

✔★ **BUDGETEL INN.** *2214 Taney (64116), I-29/35 exit 6A, north of downtown.* 816/221-1200; FAX 816/471-6207. 100 rms, 3 story. S $37.95-$41.95; D $39.95-$57.95; each addl $7; under 18 free. Pet accepted, some restrictions. TV; cable. Complimentary continental bkfst, coffee. Restaurant adj 7 am-midnight. Ck-out noon. Sundries. Cr cds: A, C, D, DS, MC, V.

[D] [symbols]

★ ★ **HAMPTON INN.** *11212 N Newark Circle (64153), I-29 exit 112th St, north of downtown.* 816/464-5454; FAX 816/464-5416. 122 rms, 4 story. S $53-$57; D $61-$65. Crib free. TV; cable. Pool. Complimentary continental bkfst, coffee in lobby. Ck-out noon. Coin lndry. Meeting rms. Valet serv. Free airport transportation. Some refrigerators. Cr cds: A, C, D, DS, MC, V.

[D] [symbols] SC

★ ★ **HOLIDAY INN NORTHEAST.** *7333 NE Parvin Rd (64117), I-435 exit 54, north of downtown.* 816/455-1060; FAX 816/455-0250. 167 rms, 3 story. S, D $60-$95; under 18 free. Crib free. TV; cable. Indoor pool; whirlpool, sauna. Restaurant 6:30-11 am, 5-10 pm. Rm serv. Bar 4 pm-midnight. Ck-out noon. Coin lndry. Meeting rms. Bellhops. Valet serv. Sundries. Free airport transportation (by res). Holidome. Game rm. Near Worlds of Fun. Cr cds: A, C, D, DS, JCB, MC, V.

[D] [symbols] SC

★ ★ **RESIDENCE INN BY MARRIOTT.** *9900 NW Prairie View Rd (64153), north of downtown.* 816/891-9009; FAX 816/891-9009, ext. 3113. 110 kit. suites, 2 story. S $95-$125; D $105-$125; wkly, monthly rates. Crib free. Pet accepted, some restrictions; $100. TV; cable. Heated pool; wading pool, whirlpool. Complimentary continental bkfst. Ck-out noon. Coin lndry. Meeting rms. Valet serv. Sundries. Free airport transportation. Lawn games. Exercise equipt; stair machine, bicycles, whirlpool. Private patios, balconies. Gazebo area with grills. Cr cds: A, C, D, DS, JCB, MC, V.

[D] [symbols] SC

Motor Hotels

✔★ ★ **CLUBHOUSE INN.** 11828 NW Plaza Circle (64153), I-29 exit 13, near Intl Airport, north of downtown. 816/464-2423; res: 800/CLUB-INN; FAX 816/464-2560. 138 rms, 7 story. S $56-$64; D $66-$74; each addl $10; suites $79-$89; under 10 free. Crib free. TV; cable. Indoor pool. Complimentary full bkfst. Restaurant 6:30-9 am, Sat & Sun 7:30-10 am. Ck-out noon. Coin lndry. Meeting rms. Valet serv. Free airport transportation. Downhill ski 15 mi. Exercise equipt; treadmill, bicycles, whirlpool. Some refrigerators. Wet bar in suites. Balconies. Cr cds: A, C, D, DS, MC, V.

D ✔ ≋ ✕ ✈ ⊠ 🔥

★ ★ **DOUBLETREE AIRPORT HOTEL.** 8801 NW 112th St (64195), north of downtown. 816/891-8900; FAX 816/891-8030. 350 rms, 11 story. S, D $79-$99; each addl $10; suites $200-$325; family rates; wkend plans. Crib free. TV; cable. 2 pools, 1 indoor; poolside serv. Restaurants 6 am-11 pm, dining rm from 5 pm. Rm serv. Bar to 1 am, Sun 11 am-midnight. Ck-out 1 pm. Meeting rms. Bellhops. Valet serv. Sundries. Free airport transportation. Lighted tennis. Exercise rm; instructor, weights, bicycles, whirlpool, sauna. Some refrigerators. Picnic tables. Gazebo near pool & tennis areas. Cr cds: A, C, D, DS, ER, JCB, MC, V.

D ✔ ≋ ✕ ✕ 🔥 SC

★ ★ **HOLIDAY INN AIRPORT.** 11832 Plaza Circle (64153), I-29 exit 13, near Intl Airport. 816/464-2345; FAX 816/464-2543. 200 rms, 5 story. S, D $75-$85; family, wkend & hol rates. Crib free. Pet accepted. TV; cable. Pool. Restaurant 6 am-11 pm. Rm serv. Bar 3:30 pm-1 am. Ck-out noon. Coin lndry. Meeting rms. Bellhops. Gift shop. Valet serv. Free airport transportation. Exercise equipt; weight machine, treadmill, sauna. Game rm. Lawn games. Some refrigerators. Cr cds: A, C, D, DS, ER, JCB, MC, V.

D ✔ ≋ ✕ ✈ ✕ 🔥 SC

★ ★ **HOLIDAY INN-SPORTS COMPLEX.** 4011 Blue Ridge Cutoff (64133), east of downtown. 816/353-5300; FAX 816/353-1199. 163 rms, 6 story. S $74-$86; D $82-$94; each addl $8; under 18 free. Crib free. TV; cable. Indoor pool. Restaurant 6 am-10 pm. Rm serv. Bar 4 pm-midnight. Ck-out noon. Coin lndry. Meeting rms. Bellhops. Valet serv. Gift shop. Sundries. Underground parking. Exercise equipt; bicycles, treadmill, whirlpool, sauna. Game rm. Overlooks Harry S Truman Sports Complex. Cr cds: A, C, D, DS, JCB, MC, V.

D ≋ ✕ ✕ 🔥 SC

★ ★ **MARRIOTT KANSAS CITY AIRPORT.** 775 Brasilia (64195), 15 mi NW on I-29, at Intl Airport, north of downtown. 816/464-2200; FAX 816/464-5915. 382 rms, 9 story. S, D studio rms $69-$150; suites $250-$450; under 18 free; wkend plan. Crib free. Pet accepted. TV; cable. Indoor pool. Restaurant 6 am-11 pm. Rm serv. Bar 11:30-1 am, Sun 12:30 pm-midnight. Ck-out noon. Coin lndry. Meeting rms. Bellhops. Valet serv. Gift shop. Free airport transportation. Downhill ski 15 mi. Excercise equipt; weights, bicycles, whirlpool, sauna. Rec rm. Lawn games. Private patios, picnic tables. On lake. *LUXURY LEVEL : CONCIERGE LEVEL.* 27 rms. S, D $119. Concierge. Private lounge. Some wet bars. Complimentary continental bkfst, refreshments. Cr cds: A, C, D, DS, JCB, MC, V.

D ✔ ≋ ≋ ✕ ✈ ✕ 🔥 SC

★ ★ **QUARTERAGE HOTEL.** 560 Westport Rd (64111), in Westport. 816/931-0001; res: 800/942-4233; FAX 816/942-8891. 123 rms, 4 story. S $69-$85; D $79-$85; each addl $10; suites $80-$130; under 16 free; higher rates special events; wkend rates. Crib free. TV; cable. Complimentary bkfst buffet, coffee. Restaurant adj 11 am-11 pm. Ck-out noon. Meeting rms. Exercise equipt; weight machine, bicycles, whirlpool, sauna. Health club privileges. Some bathrm phones, wet bars. Refrigerator, whirlpool in suites. Some balconies. Cr cds: A, D, DS, MC, V.

D ✕ ✕ 🔥

✔★ ★ **RAMADA INN-SOUTHEAST.** 6101 E 87th St (64138), south of downtown. 816/765-4331; FAX 816/765-7395. 250 rms, 3-4

story. S $48-$62; D $54-$68; each addl $6; suites $100-$175; studio rms $75; under 18 free; wkend rates. Crib free. TV; cable. Heated pool. Restaurant 6:30 am-2 pm, 5-10 pm; Fri & Sat to 11 pm; Sun 7 am-2 pm, 5-10 pm. Rm serv 7 am-10 pm. Bar 1 pm-1 am, Sun 1 pm-midnight; entertainment, dancing. Ck-out noon. Convention facilities. Bellhops. Valet serv. Health club privileges. Private patios, balconies. Cr cds: A, C, D, DS, JCB, MC, V.

D ≋ ✕ ✕ 🔥 SC

Hotels

✔★ ★ ★ **ADAM'S MARK.** 9103 E 39th St (64133), south of downtown. 816/737-0200; res: 800/444-2326; FAX 816/737-4713. 374 rms, 15 story. S $59-$119; D $59-$139; each addl $20; suites $150-$565; studio rms $150; under 18 free; wkend rates. Crib free. TV; cable. 2 heated pools, 1 indoor. Restaurant 6 am-11 pm. Bars 11-3 am, Sun noon-midnight; entertainment. Ck-out noon. Coin lndry. Convention facilities. Gift shop. Tennis. Exercise rm; instructor, weights, bicycles, whirlpool, sauna. Rec rm. Some bathrm phones. Adj to Truman Sports Complex. Cr cds: A, C, D, DS, MC, V.

D ✕ ≋ ✕ ✕ 🔥 SC

★ ★ ★ **EMBASSY SUITES.** 7640 NW Tiffany Springs Pkwy (64153), I-29 Tiffany Springs exit, near Intl Airport, north of downtown. 816/891-7788; FAX 816/891-7513. 236 suites, 8 story. Suites $82-$144; under 18 free. Crib free. TV; cable. Indoor pool. Complimentary full bkfst. Complimentary coffee in rms. Restaurant 11 am-2 pm, 5-10 pm; wkends from 7 am. Bar 11-1 am, wkends to 3 am; entertainment, dancing. Ck-out noon. Coin lndry. Convention facilites. Concierge. Gift shop. Free airport transportation. Exercise equipt; rowing machine, bicycles, whirlpool, sauna. Refrigerators, wet bars. Cr cds: A, C, D, DS, JCB, MC, V.

D ✔ ✕ ✈ ✕ ⊠ 🔥 SC

★ ★ **HISTORIC SUITES.** 612 Central (64105), downtown. 816/842-6544; res: 800/733-0612; FAX 816/842-0656. 100 suites, 5 story. S, D $105-$170; under 18 free; wkly rates; lower rates hol wkends. Crib free. Pets accepted, some restrictions. TV; cable. Pool. Complimentary continental bkfst. Complimentary coffee in rms. Restaurant nearby. No rm serv. Coin lndry. Meeting rms. No bellhops. Garage parking. Exercise equipt; weight machine, bicycles, whirlpool, sauna. Turn-of-the-century design. Cr cds: A, C, D, DS, JCB, MC, V.

D ≋ ✕ ✕ 🔥 SC

★ ★ **HOLIDAY INN.** 1215 Wyandotte (64105), downtown. 816/471-1333; FAX 816/283-0541. 190 rms, 16 story. S, D $59-$79; each addl $5; suites $79-$99; under 13 free; wkend rates. Crib free. TV; cable. No rm serv. Ck-out noon. Meeting rms. Covered parking. Health club privileges. Cr cds: A, C, D, DS, MC, V.

D ⊠ 🔥 SC

★ ★ ★ **HOLIDAY INN CROWNE PLAZA.** 4445 Main St (64111), in Country Club Plaza. 816/531-3000; FAX 816/531-3007. 296 rms, 19 story. S $119-$134; D $129-$159; each addl $10; suites $350-$450; under 18 free. Crib free. Pet accepted, $50 deposit. Garage free; valet parking $5. TV; cable. Indoor pool. Restaurant 6:30 am-10 pm. Bar noon-1 am. Ck-out noon. Convention facilities. Concierge. Exercise rm; instructor, weight machines, bicycles, whirlpool. Some refrigerators. *LUXURY LEVEL : CONCIERGE LEVEL.* 17 rms, 1 suite. S $129-$159; D $159. Private lounge, honor bar. Complimentary continental bkfst. Cr cds: A, C, D, DS, JCB, MC, V.

D ✔ ≋ ✕ ✕ 🔥 SC

★ ★ ★ **HYATT REGENCY CROWN CENTER.** 2345 McGee St (64108), in Crown Center. 816/421-1234; FAX 816/435-4190. 731 rms, 42 story. S $109-$156; D $146-$180; each addl $25; suites $195-$800; under 18 free; wkend rates. Crib free. Valet parking, garage $10.75. TV; cable. Heated pool; poolside serv. Restaurants 6:30 am-midnight. Bars 11-1 am; entertainment. Ck-out noon. Convention facilities. Concierge. Gift shop. Lighted tennis. Exercise rm; instructor, weights, bicycles, whirlpool, steam rm, sauna. Minibars. *LUXURY LEVEL : REGENCY*

CLUB. 29 rms, 5 suites, 2 floors. S, D $160-$195; each addl $25; suites $275-$1,000. Private lounges. Minibars. Wet bars. Complimentary continental bkfst, refreshments. Cr cds: A, C, D, DS, JCB, MC, V.

D ⚡ ⚓ ≋ 🎿 🚫 🔥 SC

★ ★ ★ **MARRIOTT DOWNTOWN.** *200 W 12th St (64105), downtown.* 816/421-6800; FAX 816/421-6800, ext. 4418. 573 rms, 22 story. S $130; D $150; each addl $15; suites $200-$500; wkend rates. Crib free. TV; cable. Indoor pool. Restaurant 6 am-midnight. Bar 11-1:30 am; entertainment, dancing. Ck-out noon. Convention facilities. Concierge. Gift shop. Tennis. Exercise rm; instructor, weights, bicycles, sauna. Some refrigerators. *LUXURY LEVEL : EXECUTIVE FLOORS.* 55 rms, 6 suites, 2 floors. S $155; D $175; suites $200-$500. Private lounge, honor bar. Minibars. Complimentary continental bkfst, refreshments. Cr cds: A, C, D, DS, MC, V.

D ⚡ ⚓ ≋ 🎿 🚫 🔥

✔★ ★ ★ **PARK PLACE.** *1601 N Universal Ave (64120), I-435 Front St exit, north of downtown.* 816/483-9900; res: 800/821-8532; FAX 816/231-1418. 330 rms, 9 story. S, D $62-$79; each addl $10; suites $79-$99; under 18 free; wkend rates; package plans. Crib free. Pet accepted; deposit required. TV. Indoor/outdoor pool. Complimentary coffee in rms. Restaurant 6:30 am-10 pm; Fri, Sat to 11 pm. Bar 11-1:30 am; entertainment, dancing exc Sun. Ck-out noon. Meeting rms. Gift shop. Free airport transportation. Lighted tennis. Exercise equipt; weights, bicycles, sauna. Some bathrm phones, refrigerators. Private patios, some balconies. Cr cds: A, C, D, DS, ER, MC, V.

D ⚡ ⚓ ≋ 🎿 🚫 🔥

★ ★ **RADISSON SUITES.** *106 W 12th St (64105), downtown.* 816/221-7000; FAX 816/221-8902. 214 rms, 20 story, 181 suites, 16 kit. units. S, D $89-$109; each addl $10; suites, kit. units $99-$250; under 18 free; wkend rates. Crib free. Pet accepted, some restrictions. TV; cable. Complimentary buffet bkfst. Restaurants 6:30 am-11 pm. Bar 10:30 am-midnight; wkends 11-3 am. Ck-out noon. Meeting rms. Valet parking. Exercise equipt; weight machines, bicycles. Cr cds: A, C, D, DS, ER, MC, V.

D ⚡ ⚓ 🎿 🚫 🔥 SC

★ ★ ★ **RAPHAEL.** *325 Ward Pkwy (64112), in Country Club Plaza.* 816/756-3800; res: 800/821-5343; FAX 816/756-3800, ext. 2199. 123 rms, 9 story. S $95-$130; D $115-$150; each addl $20; suites $120-$150; under 18 free; hol, wkend plans. Crib free. TV; cable. Complimentary continental bkfst in rms. Restaurant 11 am-11 pm, closed Sun. Rm serv 24 hrs. Bar to 1 am, closed Sun. Ck-out 1 pm. Free garage, valet parking. Airport transportation. Refrigerators, minibars. Cr cds: A, C, D, DS, MC, V.

🚫 🔥 SC

★ ★ ★ **THE RITZ-CARLTON, KANSAS CITY.** *401 Ward Pkwy (64112), at Wornall Rd, Country Club Plaza.* 816/756-1500; res: 800/241-3333; FAX 816/756-1635. 373 rms, 12 story. S, D $149-$179; suites $225-$1,200; under 17 free; wkend rates; higher rates Thanksgiving. Crib free. Garage: free self-park, valet $9. TV; cable. Heated pool; wading pool, poolside serv. Restaurant 6 am-10 pm; wkends to midnight (also see THE ROOFTOP). Rm serv 24 hrs. Bar 5 pm-midnight; entertainment, dancing. Ck-out noon. Convention facilities. Concierge. Airport transportation. Exercise equipt; weights, bicycles, sauna, steam rm. Massage. Bathrm phones, refrigerators, minibars. Private patios, balconies. Arc-shaped hotel with a waterfall, sculptures and wrought-iron balconies reflecting a Moorish influence. *LUXURY LEVEL : RITZ-CARLTON CLUB.* 44 rms, 6 suites, 2 floors. S $199; D, suites $275. Concierge. Private lounge, complimentary bar. Complimentary continental bkfst, refreshments. Cr cds: A, C, D, DS, ER, JCB, MC, V.

D ⚓ 🎿 🚫 🔥 SC

★ ★ **SAVOY BED & BREAKFAST.** *219 W 9th St (64105), downtown.* 816/842-3575. 100 suites, 6 story. S, D $84-$125; each addl $20; under 16 free. TV; cable. Complimentary full bkfst. Complimentary coffee in rms. Restaurant (see SAVOY GRILL). Bar. Ck-out 1 pm. Coin lndry. Concierge. Wet bars. Restored 1888 landmark building

with original architectural detail; stained & leaded glass, tile floors, tin ceilings. Cr cds: A, C, D, DS, MC, V.

🚫 🔥

★ ★ ★ **SHERATON SUITES.** *770 W 47th St (64112), in Country Club Plaza.* 816/931-4400; FAX 816/516-7330. 258 suites, 18 story. S $139; D $159; each addl $20; under 16 free; wkend rates. Crib free. Valet parking $6. TV; cable. Indoor/outdoor pool; poolside serv. Complimentary buffet bkfst. Complimentary coffee in rms. Restaurant 6 am-11 pm. Bar from 11 am. Ck-out noon. Coin lndry. Meeting rms. Exercise equipt; weight machine, rower, whirlpool. Refrigerators; some wet bars. Some balconies. Cr cds: A, C, D, DS, ER, JCB, MC, V.

D ≋ 🎿 🚫 🔥 SC

★ ★ ★ **THE WESTIN CROWN CENTER.** *1 Pershing Rd (64108), at Main St, in Crown Center.* 816/474-4400; res: 800/228-3000; FAX 816/391-4438. 724 rms, 18 story. S $140-$160; D $165-$185; each addl $25; suites $300-$1,000; under 18 free; wkend package. Crib free. Pet accepted. TV; cable. Heated pool; poolside serv. Restaurants 6 am-midnight. Bars 11:30-1 am; entertainment. Ck-out noon. Convention facilities. Barber, beauty shop. Lighted tennis. Putting green. Exercise rm; instructor, weights, bicycles, whirlpool, sauna, steam rm. Rec rm. Lawn games. Refrigerators, wet bars. Private patios, balconies. Indoor tropical waterfall and garden. *LUXURY LEVEL : EXECUTIVE CLUB FLOOR.* 24 rms, 2 suites. S $160; D $185; suites $305-$495. Concierge. Private lounge, honor bar. Complimentary continental bkfst, refreshments. Cr cds: A, C, D, DS, ER, JCB, MC, V.

D ✔ ⚡ ⚓ ≋ 🎿 🚫 🔥 SC

Inns

★ **DOANLEIGH WALLAGH.** *217 E 37th St (64111), south of downtown.* 816/753-2667; FAX 816/753-2408. 5 rms, 3 story. S, D $80-$110; each addl $10. TV; cable. Complimentary full bkfst. Restaurant nearby. Ck-out 11 am, ck-in 3 pm. Private parking. Library; grand piano, organ. Built in 1907; many antiques. Cr cds: A, MC, V.

🚫 🔥

★ ★ ★ **SOUTHMORELAND.** *116 E 46th St (64112), in Country Club Plaza.* 816/531-7979; FAX 816/531-2407. 12 rms, 3 story. S $90-$135; D $100-$145. Adults preferred. TV in sitting rm; cable. Complimentary full bkfst; afternoon wine & cheese. Restaurants nearby. Ck-out 11 am, ck-in 4:30 pm. Airport transportation. Colonial-revival house (1913); solarium; antiques. Guest rms named and decorated to reflect area notables. Cr cds: A, MC, V.

D 🚫 🔥

Restaurants

★ ★ ★ **THE AMERICAN RESTAURANT.** *2450 Grand Ave, top floor of Hall's, in Crown Center.* 816/426-1133. Hrs: 11:15 am-2 pm, 6-10 pm; Fri & Sat 6-11 pm. Closed Sun; major hols. Res accepted. Bar. Wine cellar. A la carte entrees: lunch $12.50-$16.50, dinner $40-$53. Dinner tasting menu avail. Specializes in contemporary American cuisine with ethnic influences and traditional American cuisine. Own baking, ice cream. Pianist. Valet parking. Overlooks downtown and Crown Center. Original artwork from private collections. Modern decor; formal atmosphere. Jacket. Cr cds: A, C, D, DS, MC, V.

D

★ ★ **BRISTOL BAR & GRILL.** *4740 Jefferson, in Country Club Plaza.* 816/756-0606. Hrs: 11:30 am-2:30 pm, 5:30-10 pm; Fri to 11 pm; Sat 5-11 pm; Sun 5-9:30 pm; Sun brunch 10 am-2 pm. Closed Dec 25. Res accepted. Bar. Semi-a la carte: lunch $5.95-$10.95, dinner $6.95-$29.95. Sun brunch $12.95. Child's meals. Specializes in clam chowder, fresh seafood, Black Angus beef. Dixieland band Sun. Parking. English decor, domed ceiling; antiques. Cr cds: A, C, D, DS, MC, V.

D SC

★ ★ **CALIFORNOS.** *4124 Pennsylvania, in Westport.* *816/531-7878.* Hrs: 11 am-3 pm, 5-10 pm; Fri, Sat to 11 pm; Sun noon-9 pm. Closed some major hols. Res accepted. Bar to midnight. Semi-a la carte: lunch, dinner $5-$20. Specializes in California-style grilled cuisine. Pianist Fri & Sat evenings. Valet parking. Outdoor dining. Casual atmosphere. Cr cds: A, MC, V.

D

★ ★ **CASCONE'S.** *3733 N Oak, north of downtown. 816/454-7977.* Hrs: 11 am-10 pm; Fri, Sat to 11 pm; Sun 4-9 pm. Closed most major hols. Res accepted. Italian, Amer menu. Bar. Semi-a la carte: lunch $6.50-$9, dinner $12-$20. Child's meals. Specializes in chicken, steak, seafood. Parking. Cr cds: A, C, D, DS, MC, V.

D SC

✔ ★ **CHAPPELL'S.** *(323 Armour Rd, North Kansas City) N on MO 35 to Armour Rd exit. 816/421-0002.* Hrs: 11 am-10 pm; Fri, Sat to 11 pm. Closed Sun; most major hols. Bar. Semi-a la carte: lunch $4.95-$6.25, dinner $4.95-$14.95. Child's meals. Specializes in steak, prime rib, hamburgers. Extensive collection of sports memorabilia. Cr cds: A, C, D, DS, MC, V.

D

✔ ★ ★ **COSTELLO'S GREENHOUSE.** *1414 W 85th St, at Ward Parkway, south of downtown. 816/333-5470.* Hrs: 11 am-10 pm; Sat & Sun to 11 pm; Sun brunch 10 am-2:30 pm. Closed most major hols. Res accepted. Bar. Semi-a la carte: lunch $5.95-$14.95, dinner $5.95-$16.95. Sun brunch $9.95. Child's meals. Specializes in prime rib, chicken, pasta. Salad bar. Parking. Greenhouse atmosphere; many plants, flowers in bloom. Cr cds: A, C, D, DS, MC, V.

D

★ ★ ★ **EBT.** *1310 Carondelet Dr, in United Missouri Bank Building, south of downtown. 816/942-8870.* Hrs: 11 am-2:30 pm, 5-9:30 pm; Fri to 10 pm; Sat 5-10 pm. Closed Sun; major hols. Res accepted. Bar. Wine cellar. Semi-a la carte: lunch $5.50-$10, dinner $11.95-$29.95. Specializes in seafood, steak, chicken. Own baking. Jazz pianist Tues-Sat. Decorated with palm trees, fountain; antiques, gilded iron elevator. Jacket. Cr cds: A, C, D, DS, MC, V.

D SC

✔ ★ **EMILE'S.** *302 Nichols Rd, in Country Club Plaza. 816/753-2771.* Hrs: 9 am-10:30 pm; Mon to 5 pm; Fri & Sat to 11:30 pm; Sun 11 am-5 pm. Closed Jan 1, Thanksgiving, Dec 25. Res accepted. German, Amer menu. Bar. Semi-a la carte: lunch, dinner $4.95-$13.95. Specialties: beef rouladen, Wienerschnitzel, Kasseler rippchen. Accordionist Fri, Sat. Parking. Outdoor dining. Cr cds: A, MC, V.

★ ★ **FEDORA CAFE & BAR.** *210 W 47th St, in Country Club Plaza. 816/561-6565.* Hrs: 7-1 am; Sun 9 am-11 pm. Res accepted. Bar. A la carte entrees: lunch $3.95-$8.95, dinner $7.95-$18.95. Specializes in seafood, pasta, salads. Jazz & popular music. European bistro-style cafe; art deco decor. Cr cds: A, C, D, DS, MC, V.

D SC

★ ★ **FIGLIO.** *209 W 46th Terrace, in Country Club Plaza. 816/561-0505.* Hrs: 11:30 am-2:30 pm, 5-10 pm; Fri, Sat to 11 pm; Sun 11 am-10 pm. Closed Jan 1, Dec 25. Res accepted. Italian, Amer menu. Bar. Semi-a la carte: lunch $5.95-$8.95, dinner $6.95-$16.95. Child's meals. Specializes in pasta, gourmet pizza, fresh fish. Accordionist Wed-Sun. Valet parking wkends. Outdoor porch dining. Cr cds: A, C, D, DS, MC, V.

D SC

★ ★ **GOLDEN OX.** *1600 Genessee (64102), south of downtown. 816/842-2866.* Hrs: 11:20 am-10 pm; Sat 4-10:30 pm; Sun 4-9 pm. Closed Dec 25. Bar. Semi-a la carte: lunch $4.50-$7.95, dinner $7.50-$16.95. Child's meals. Specializes in steak, prime rib. Parking.

Western decor with stockyard influence. Family-owned. Cr cds: A, C, D, DS, MC, V.

D

★ ★ **GRAND STREET CAFE.** *4740 Grand Ave (64112), south of downtown. 816/561-8000.* Hrs: 11 am-10 pm; Fri & Sat to midnight; Sun from 10:30 am; Sun brunch to 3 pm. Closed Dec 25. Res accepted. Bar. Semi-a la carte: lunch $3.95-$10.95, dinner $5.95-$18.95. Sun brunch $5.95-$7.95. Child's meals. Specializes in lamb chops, pork chops, saffron chicken. Parking. Outdoor dining. Eclectic, contemporary decor. Cr cds: A, C, D, DS, MC, V.

D

★ ★ ★ **HARRY STARKER'S.** *200 Nichols Rd (64112), in Country Club Plaza. 816/753-3565.* Hrs: 11 am-3 pm, 5-10 pm; Sat to 11 pm; Sun from 5 pm. Closed major hols. Res accepted. Bar. Extensive wine list. A la carte entrees: lunch $4.95-$8.75, dinner $13-$23. Specializes in steak, fresh seafood. Entertainment, dancing. Valet parking. Country French decor; featuring 9,000 bottles of wine. Cr cds: A, C, D, DS, MC, V.

★ ★ **HEREFORD HOUSE.** *2 E 20th St, at Main St, south of downtown. 816/842-1080.* Hrs: 11 am-10 pm; Fri to 10:30 pm; Sat 4-10:30 pm; Sun 4-9 pm. Closed major hols. Res accepted. Bar. Semi-a la carte: lunch $5-$15, dinner $8.75-$22.50. Child's meals. Specializes in steak, Maine lobster tails. Parking. Casual atmosphere. Cr cds: A, C, D, DS, MC, V.

D

✔ ★ ★ **ITALIAN GARDENS.** *1110 Baltimore, downtown. 816/221-9311.* Hrs: 11 am-10 pm; Fri to 11 pm; Sat noon-11 pm. Closed Sun; major hols. Res accepted. Italian, Amer menu. Bar. Semi-a la carte: lunch $4.10-$6, dinner $7-$15. Child's meals. Specializes in pasta, veal, seafood, chicken, steak. Valet parking. Cr cds: A, C, D, DS, MC, V.

D

★ ★ ★ **JASPER'S.** *405 W 75th St, south of downtown. 816/363-3003.* Hrs: 6-10 pm. Closed Sun exc Mother's Day; major hols; also 1st wk July. Res accepted. Northern Italian menu. Bar. Wine cellar. A la carte entrees: dinner $16.95-$25.95. Child's meals. Specialties: Cappeli Angelina, Gambere a la Livornese, Vitello alla Valdostana. Own pastries, pasta. Parking. Large grappa bar. Chef-owned. Jacket (dinner). Cr cds: A, C, D, DS, MC, V.

✔ ★ **JENNIE'S.** *511 Cherry St, downtown. 816/421-3366.* Hrs: 11 am-9 pm; Fri, Sat to 10 pm; Sun noon-8 pm. Closed most major hols. Res accepted. Italian, Amer menu. Bar. Semi-a la carte: lunch $4.95-$7.95, dinner $5.25-$12.50. Child's meals. Specializes in lasagna, pizza. Parking. Family-owned. Cr cds: A, D, MC, V.

D

✔ ★ **K.C. MASTERPIECE.** *4747 Wyandotte St (64112), in Country Club Plaza. 816/531-3332.* Hrs: 11 am-10 pm; Fri & Sat to 11 pm; Sun to 9:30 pm. Closed Thanksgiving, Dec 25. Bar. Semi-a la carte: lunch $6.95-$14.25, dinner $5.95-$15.50. Child's meals. Specializes in barbecued meats, filet of pork, turkey brisket. Parking. Kansas City memorabilia. Casual atmosphere. Cr cds: A, C, D, DS, MC, V.

D

★ ★ **METROPOLIS AMERICAN GRILL.** *303 Westport Rd, in Westport. 816/753-1550.* Hrs: 11:30 am-2:30 pm, 5:30 pm-10 pm; wkends to 11 pm. Closed Sun; major hols. Res accepted. Bar. A la carte entrees: lunch $4.95-$11.95, dinner $8.50-$20.95. Specialties: stuffed Norwegian salmon, stone crab lasagna, parmesan lamb chops. Parking. Contemporary decor. Cr cds: A, D, DS, MC, V.

D

★ ★ **MILANO.** *2450 Grand Ave, in Crown Center. 816/426-1130.* Hrs: 11:30 am-9 pm; Fri & Sat to 10:30 pm; Sun noon-9 pm. Closed major hols. Res accepted. Italian menu. Bar. Semi-a la carte:

lunch $4.25-$10.50, dinner $8.95-$16.95. Child's meals. Specializes in pasta. Own ice cream. Parking. Patio dining. Casual Italian decor. Cr cds: A, D, DS, MC, V.

D SC

✔★ **PARADISE GRILL.** 5225 NW 64th St, north of downtown. 816/587-9888. Hrs; 11 am-10 pm; Fri & Sat to 11 pm; Sun from 11:30 am. Closed Thanksgiving, Dec 25. Res accepted. Bar. Semi-a la carte: lunch, dinner $4.95-$14.95. Child's meals. Specializes in chicken, fish. Bright, modern decor. Cr cds: A, DS, MC, V.

D

★ **PARKWAY 600.** 600 Ward Pkwy, in Country Club Plaza. 816/931-6600. Hrs: 7 am-11 pm; early-bird dinner Sun-Thurs 4:30-6:30 pm. Closed Jan 1, July 4, Dec 24 & 25. Res accepted. Bar to 1 am. Semi-a la carte: bkfst $3.95-$8.50, lunch $5.95-$28.95, dinner $6.95-$36.95. Child's meals. Specializes in seafood, beef, chicken. Valet parking. Outdoor dining. Brass chandelier in lobby. Casual atmosphere. Cr cds: A, D, DS, MC, V.

D SC

★ ★ ★ **PLAZA III THE STEAKHOUSE.** 4749 Pennsylvania, in Country Club Plaza. 816/753-0000. Hrs: 11:30 am-2:30 pm, 5:30-10 pm; Fri, Sat to 11 pm; Sun 5-10 pm. Res accepted. Bar 11-1 am; Sun to midnight. Extensive wine list. A la carte entrees: lunch $5.95-$8.95, dinner $14.95-$26.95. Child's meals. Specializes in veal chops, prime-aged beef, seafood. Entertainment. Valet parking. Cr cds: A, C, D, DS, MC, V.

D

★ ★ ★ **THE ROOFTOP.** (See The Ritz-Carlton, Kansas City Hotel) 816/756-1500. Hrs: 5:30-10 pm; Sun brunch 10:30 am-2 pm. Res accepted. Bar 5 pm-midnight. Wine cellar. Semi-a la carte: dinner $13.50-$28. Sun brunch $24.50. Child's meals. Specializes in steak, chicken, seafood. Own pastries. Pianist. Parking. Rooftop dining rm; panoramic view of city. Cr cds: A, C, D, DS, ER, JCB, MC, V.

D

★ ★ ★ **SAVOY GRILL.** (See Savoy Hotel) 816/842-3890. Hrs: 11 am-11 pm; Fri, Sat to midnight; Sun 4-10 pm. Closed Dec 25. Res accepted. Bar. Semi-a la carte: lunch $4.50-$12, dinner $14-$27. Specializes in fresh seafood, Maine lobster, prime dry-aged beef. Parking. 19th-century hotel dining rm; oak paneling, stained-glass windows, murals of Santa Fe Trail. ornate back bar. Cr cds: A, C, D, DS, MC, V.

D

★ ★ **SMUGGLER'S.** 1650 Universal Plaza Dr, east of downtown. 816/483-0400. Hrs: 11 am-10 pm; Fri to 11 pm; Sat 5-11 pm; Sun 4-9 pm; early-bird dinner Mon-Thurs 5-6:30 pm. Closed Jan 1, Thanksgiving, Dec 25. Res accepted. Bar to 1 am. Complete meals: lunch $4.95-$9.95, dinner $9.95-$21.95. Specializes in prime rib, fresh fish. Salad bar. Entertainment Tues-Sat. Parking. Casual atmosphere; wood-burning fireplaces. Cr cds: A, C, D, DS, MC, V.

D

★ ★ ★ **STEPHENSON'S APPLE FARM.** 16401 E US 40, south of downtown. 816/373-5400. Hrs: 11:30 am-10 pm; Sun 10 am-9 pm; Sun brunch 10 am-2 pm exc hols. Closed Dec 24 & 25. Res accepted. Bar. Semi-a la carte: lunch $6-$11.50, dinner $12.50-$21. Sun brunch $10.95. Child's meals. Specializes in hickory-smoked meats, apple fritters and dumplings. Own baking. Parking. Outdoor dining. Started as a fruit stand (1900). Early Amer decor; farm implements, cider keg in lobby. Country store. Family-owned. Cr cds: A, C, D, DS, MC, V.

D

✔★ **TRATTORIA MARCO POLO.** 7514 Wornall Rd, south of downtown. 816/361-0900. Hrs: 11:30 am-2 pm, 5:30-10 pm; Fri & Sat to 11 pm. Closed Sun; major hols. Res accepted. Italian menu. Bar. Semi-a la carte: lunch $4.95-$8.95, dinner $7.25-$15.95. Child's meals. Specialties: polenta con funghi ala Milanese, pollo alla saltimboco,

linguine Fra Diavolo, salciccia Marco Polo. Parking. Decorated to suggest outdoor trattoria. Cr cds: A, C, D, DS, MC, V.

D

Unrated Dining Spots

ANDRÉ'S CONFISERIE SUISSE. 5018 Main St, south of downtown. 816/561-3440. Hrs: 11 am-2:30 pm. Closed Sun, Mon; major hols. Swiss menu. Complete meal: lunch $7.50. Specializes in quiche, chocolate candy, pastries. Parking. Swiss chalet atmosphere. Family-owned. Founded in 1955 by Andre Bollier and continues to be operated by the Bollier family. Cr cds: A, MC, V.

D

CLASSIC CUP. 4130 Pennsylvania, in Westport. 816/756-0771. Hrs: 11:30 am-3 pm; Sat noon-3:30 pm, 6-10 pm; Sun brunch 11 am-2 pm. Closed most major hols. Continental menu. Wine, beer. Semi-a la carte: lunch $4.25-$8.75, dinner $7.95-$15. Sun brunch $8.95. Specializes in homemade soups, pastries, creative American cuisine. Parking. European bistro atmosphere. Cr cds: A, MC, V.

D SC

LE PICNIQUE. 301 E 55th St, in Sebree Galleries, south of downtown. 816/333-3387. Hrs: 11 am-2 pm. Closed Sun; most major hols. Res accepted. Country French menu. Wine, beer. Semi-a la carte: lunch $4.50-$8.50. Specialties: French herb garden sandwich, freshly grilled fish & chicken, gateau au chocolat, tarte citron. Parking. Located in European antique and gift shop; brick floor, fountain; unique courtyard atmosphere. Cr cds: A, MC, V.

D

SENSATIONS-A KOSHER EXPERIENCE. 1148 W 103rd St, south of downtown. 816/941-2299. Hrs: 7 am-8 pm; wkend hrs vary. Closed Sat (spring & summer); Thanksgiving, Dec 25; also Jewish hols. Jewish, Amer menu. Semi-a la carte: bkfst $2.35-$4.50, lunch & dinner $2.50-$8.95. Specializes in rolled cabbage, matzoball soup, falafel. Parking. A certified kosher experience. Totally nonsmoking. Cr cds: MC, V.

D

Kansas City, KS

Motels

✔★ **AMERICAN INN.** 7949 Splitlog (66112), I-70 exit 414. 913/299-2999. 158 rms, 3 story. S $29; D $34; each addl $5; under 12 free; wkly, monthly rates. Crib free. TV; cable. Pool. Complimentary coffee in lobby. Restaurant nearby. Ck-out 11 am. Coin lndry. Game rm. Cr cds: A, C, D, DS, MC, V.

D ⊠ 🛏 🔥 SC

★ ★ **BEST WESTERN INN.** 501 Southwest Blvd (66103), at jct 7th St Trafficway (US 169), 1 blk S of I-35. 913/677-3060; FAX 913/677-7065. 113 rms, 2 story. S $55-$59; D $62-$69; each addl $7; under 12 free. Crib free. TV; cable. Heated pool; whirlpool. Complimentary continental bkfst. Complimentary coffee in rms. Restaurant adj 6 am-midnight. Bar to 1:30 am. Ck-out noon. Coin lndry. Meeting rm. Valet serv. Med Center transportation. Refrigerators. Cr cds: A, C, D, DS, ER, JCB, MC, V.

D ⊠ 🛏 🔥 SC

Restaurants

✔★ **EVERGREEN.** 7648 State Ave, Wyandotte Plaza Shopping Center. 913/334-7648. Hrs: 11 am-10 pm. Closed Thanksgiving. Chinese menu. Serv bar. Complete meals: lunch $3.95-$4.95. A la carte entrees: dinner $4.95-$8.95. Specializes in seafood Szechwan style, egg rolls, sweet & sour dishes. Oriental decor. Cr cds: A, DS, MC, V.

D

✔★ **MRS. PETER'S CHICKEN DINNERS.** *4960 State Ave (US 24), 3 blks W of I-635.* 913/287-7711. Hrs: 5-9 pm; Sun noon-8 pm. Closed Mon, Tues; Jan 1, Thanksgiving, Dec 25; also 1st 2 wks Jan. Complete meals. dinner $9-$11. Specializes in fried chicken, country-fried steak, pork chops. Parking. Gift shop. Antiques. Cr cds: MC, V.

D

Overland Park, KS

Motels

★★ **BEST WESTERN HALLMARK INN EXECUTIVE CENTER.** *7000 W 108th St (66211).* 913/383-2550; FAX 913/383-2099. 181 rms, 2 story. S $62; D $67; each addl $5; suites $75-$95; under 18 free; special wkend plans. Crib free. Pet accepted, some restrictions; $25. TV; cable. Heated pool. Complimentary bkfst buffet. Restaurant 6:30 am-2 pm, 5-10 pm. Rm serv. Bar 5 pm-midnight. Ck-out 11 am. Coin Indry. Meeting rms. Valet serv. Gift shop. Refrigerators. Picnic tables, grills. Cr cds: A, C, D, DS, MC, V.

D ✔ ≈ ✗ ⚒ SC

★★ **CLUBHOUSE INN.** *10610 Marty (66212), I-435, N on Metcalf, W on 107th.* 913/648-5555; res: 800/CLUB INN; FAX 913/648-7130. 143 rms, 3 story, 22 suites. S $69-$79; D $79-$89; each addl $10; suites $79-$99; under 10 free; wkly rates. Crib free. TV; cable. Heated pool; whirlpool. Complimentary full bkfst, coffee. Restaurant nearby. Ck-out noon. Coin Indry. Meeting rms. Valet serv. Refrigerator, wet bar in suites. Balconies. Grills. Cr cds: A, C, D, DS, MC, V.

D ≈ ✗ ⚒ SC

★★ **COURTYARD BY MARRIOTT.** *11301 Metcalf Ave (66210).* 913/339-9900; FAX 913/339-6091. 149 rms, 3 story. S $85; D $95; each addl $10; suites $92-$102; under 16 free; wkly, wkend rates. Crib free. TV; cable. Indoor pool. Complimentary coffee in rms. Bkfst avail. Bar 4:30-11 pm. Ck-out 1 pm. Coin Indry. Meeting rms. Valet serv. Sundries. Exercise equipt; weights, bicycles, whirlpool. Refrigerator in suites. Balconies. Cr cds: A, C, D, DS, MC, V.

D ≈ ✗ ✗ ⚒ SC

★★ **DRURY INN.** *10951 Metcalf Ave (66210).* 913/345-1500. 155 rms, 4 story. S $59-$64; D $69-$74; each addl $10; under 18 free. Crib free. Pet accepted, some restrictions. TV; cable. Pool. Complimentary continental bkfst, coffee. Restaurant nearby. Ck-out noon. Meeting rms. Valet serv. Health club privileges. Cr cds: A, C, D, DS, MC, V.

D ✔ ≈ ✗ ⚒ SC

✔★ **FAIRFIELD INN BY MARRIOTT.** *4401 W 107th (66207), I-435 exit 77.* 913/381-5700; FAX 913/381-5700, ext. 709. 134 rms, 3 story. S $41.95-$48.95; D $48.95-$58.95; each addl $7; under 18 free. Crib free. TV; cable. Pool. Continental bkfst avail. Restaurant nearby. Ck-out noon. Meeting rm. Valet serv. Sundries. Health club privileges. Cr cds: A, C, D, DS, MC, V.

≈ ✗ ✗ ⚒ SC

★★ **HAMPTON INN.** *10591 Metcalf Frontage Rd (66212).* 913/341-1551; FAX 913/341-8668. 134 rms, 5 story. S $65-$72; D $70-$75; under 18 free. Crib free. TV; cable. Pool; whirlpool. Complimentary continental bkfst. Complimentary coffee in rms. Restaurant nearby. Ck-out noon. Meeting rms. Health club privileges. Cr cds: A, C, D, DS, MC, V.

D ≈ ✗ ⚒ SC

★★ **RESIDENCE INN BY MARRIOTT.** *6300 W 110th St (66211), I-435, S on Metcalf, E on College, N on Lamar.* 913/491-3333; FAX 913/491-1377. 112 suites, 2 story. S, D $104-$140; under 12 free; wkly, monthly rates. Crib free. Pet accepted, some restrictions. TV; cable. Pool. Complimentary continental bkfst. Ck-out noon. Coin Indry. Meeting rm. Valet serv. Exercise equipt; weights, bicycles, whirlpool, sauna. Sports court. Some fireplaces. Private patios, balconies. Picnic tables, grills. Landscaped courtyard. Cr cds: A, C, D, DS, JCB, MC, V.

D ✔ ≈ ✗ ✗ ⚒ SC

✔★ **WHITE HAVEN.** *8039 Metcalf Ave (66204).* 913/649-8200; res: 800/752-2892. 78 rms, 1-2 story, 9 kit. units. S $34-$36; D $39-$42; each addl $2; suites, kit. units $54. Crib $1. Pet accepted, some restrictions. TV; cable. Pool. Complimentary morning coffee. Restaurant adj 6:30 am-9 pm; Sun 7 am-3 pm. Ck-out noon. Meeting rm. Refrigerators. Cr cds: A, C, D, DS, MC, V.

D ✔ ≈ ✗ ⚒

Motor Hotel

★★ **RAMADA.** *8787 Reeder Rd (66214).* 913/888-8440; FAX 913/888-3438. 192 rms, 8 story. S $61-$70; D $65-$75; each addl $7; suites $99; under 18 free. Crib free. TV. Heated indoor/outdoor pool; whirlpool, sauna. Complimentary coffee in rms. Restaurant 6 am-2 pm, 5-10 pm. Rm serv. Bar; entertainment, dancing. Ck-out noon. Meeting rms. Valet serv. Kansas City Airport transportation. Cr cds: A, C, D, DS, MC, V.

D ≈ ✗ ⚒ SC

Hotels

★★★ **DOUBLETREE.** *10100 College Blvd (66210).* 913/451-6100; FAX 913/451-3873. 357 rms, 18 story. S $119-$139; D $129-$149; each addl $10; suites $175-$450; under 18 free; wkend rates. Crib free. Pet accepted, some restrictions. TV. Indoor pool; whirlpool, sauna, poolside serv. Restaurants 6 am-11 pm. Bar 4-1 am, Sun 4 pm-midnight; dancing. Ck-out noon. Convention facilities. Gift shop. Airport transportation. Some refrigerators. Cr cds: A, C, D, DS, ER, JCB, MC, V.

D ✔ ≈ ✗ ✗ ⚒ SC

★★★ **EMBASSY SUITES.** *10601 Metcalf Ave (66212).* 913/649-7060; FAX 913/649-9382. 199 suites, 7 story. S, D $114-$139; each addl $10; under 15 free; wkend rates. Crib free. TV; cable. Indoor pool. Coffee in rms. Complimentary full bkfst. Restaurant 11 am-2 pm, 5-10 pm. Bar 2 pm-1 am. Ck-out noon. Meeting rms. Gift shop. Exercise equipt; bicycles, stair machines, whirlpool, sauna. Game rm. Refrigerators. 7-story atrium with plants. Cr cds: A, C, D, DS, JCB, MC, V.

D ≈ ✗ ✗ ⚒ SC

★★★ **MARRIOTT-OVERLAND PARK.** *10800 Metcalf (66210).* 913/451-8000; FAX 913/451-5914. 397 rms, 11 story. S, D $124; suites $200-$350; under 18 free; wkly, wkend rates. Crib free. Pet accepted. TV; cable. Indoor/outdoor pool; poolside serv. Complimentary coffee. Restaurant 6-11 pm. Bar 11:30-1 am. Ck-out noon. Meeting rms. Concierge. Gift shop. Exercise equipt; weights, bicycles, whirlpool. Game rm. Traditional & Oriental decor. *LUXURY LEVEL.* 78 rms. S, D $134. Private lounge. Deluxe toiletry amenities. Complimentary continental bkfst, evening refreshments, newspaper. Cr cds: A, C, D, DS, JCB, MC, V.

D ✔ ≈ ✗ ✗ ⚒ SC

Restaurants

★★ **COYOTE GRILL.** *(4843 Johnson Dr, Mission) N on US 169, in Mission Shopping Center.* 913/362-3333. Hrs: 11 am-10 pm; wkends to 11 pm; Sun brunch to 2 pm. Bar. Semi-a la carte: lunch

$3.50-$10, dinner $3.50-$20. Sun brunch $4.50-$8. Specializes in pasta, Southwestern cuisine. Southwestern art. Cr cds: A, DS, MC, V.

✔★ **DON CHILITO'S.** *(7017 Johnson Dr, Mission) N on US 169.* 913/432-3066. Hrs: 11 am-9 pm; Fri, Sat to 10 pm. Closed Thanksgiving, Dec 25. Mexican menu. Beer. Semi-a la carte: lunch, dinner $3-$9.99. Specializes in burritos. Parking. Family-owned. No cr cds accepted.

★★ **JOHNNY CASCONE'S.** *6863 W 91st St.* 913/381-6837. Hrs: 11 am-10 pm; Sun 4-9 pm. Closed major hols. Res accepted Sun-Thurs. Italian, Amer menu. Bar. Semi-a la carte: lunch $4-$8, dinner $7-$17. Child's meals. Specializes in lasagne, seafood, steak. Parking. Country decor. Cr cds: A, C, D, DS, MC, V.

★★ **K.C. MASTERPIECE.** *10985 Metcalf.* 913/345-1199. Hrs: 11 am-10 pm; Fri, Sat to 11 pm; Sun 11 am-9:30 pm. Closed Thanksgiving, Dec 25. Bar. Semi-a la carte: lunch $5.25-$13.95, dinner $6-$15. Child's meals. Specializes in baby back ribs, filet of pork,

turkey. Parking. Authentic 1930s decor; ornamental tile floor. Display of barbecue memorabilia. Cr cds: A, C, D, DS, MC, V.

D

✔★ **LEONA YARBROUGH'S.** *(2800 W 53rd St, Fairway) W on Shawnee Mission Pkwy.* 913/722-4800. Hrs: 11 am-8 pm; Sun to 7 pm. Closed Mon; also Dec 25 and 1 wk following. Semi-a la carte: lunch $2.95-$9.50, dinner $5.25-$10.75. Child's meals. Specializes in fried chicken, liver & onions, roast pork. Parking. Full bakery on premises. Family-owned. No cr cds accepted.

Unrated Dining Spot

GATES BAR-B-QUE. *(2001 W 103rd, Leawood) E on W 103rd St, at state line.* 913/383-1752. Hrs: 10 am-11 pm; Fri, Sat to midnight. Closed Thanksgiving, Dec 25. Beer. A la carte entrees: lunch, dinner $4.50-$14. Specializes in barbecue ribs, beef, chicken. Parking. No cr cds accepted.

D

Las Vegas

Settled: 1855

Pop: 258,295

Elev: 2,020 feet

Time zone: Pacific

Area code: 702

Las Vegas is known for exceptional hotels, as well as gambling casinos and nightclubs. Entertainment facilities lines its streets, luring travelers to experience all that Las Vegas offers. Nevada's largest city, Las Vegas covers 53 square miles and is centered in a gently sloping valley ringed by mountains. To the west, the Spring Range, capped by 12,000-foot Mt Charleston, dominates the area.

Its green meadows and two natural springs made the Las Vegas valley a favorite camping place for caravans following the old Spanish Trail from Santa Fe to California. Las Vegas was first settled by Americans in 1855, when Brigham Young sent 30 men to build a fort and stockade here. The Mormons tried mining in the area but found that the ore was hard to smelt and that the metal made poor bullets. Later, this "lead" was discovered to be a silver ore.

The Mormons abandoned the settlement in 1857. From 1862 to 1899 it was operated as a ranch. Las Vegas was really born in 1905 with the advent of the railroad. A tent town sprang up, streets were laid out and permanent buildings were soon built. In the years that followed, Las Vegas developed as an agricultural area. The legalization of gambling in Nevada in 1931 paved the way for change, and after World War II a great deal of investment capital was poured into the development of Las Vegas as a resort center.

Business

Tourism is the dominant industry in Las Vegas. The combination of a pleasant year-round climate, legalized gambling and top-name entertainment lures a daily average of nearly 50,000 visitors. Prices for food, hotels and entertainment are comparatively modest, since gambling is the main diversion.

Convention Facilities

Conventions have become the second major industry in Las Vegas. The Las Vegas Convention Center has an impressive total of 1.6 million square feet, 1.3 million of which is meeting and exhibit space. The Cashman Field Center, a convention/sports complex, offers 98,100 square feet of exhibit space, a 9,300-seat stadium and a theater seating 100 to 2,000.

There are more than 70,000 first-class hotel and motel rooms, and restaurants range from very modest to gourmet. Most of the major hotels have convention facilities. The number of conventioneers coming to Las Vegas each year exceeds the permanent population of this desert city.

Sports and Recreation

The city's 21 golf courses (many championship), dotted with lakes and lined with palm trees, make Las Vegas a mecca for the nation's top professional golfers. Hotels and private clubs cater to tennis fans, offering both open play and tournament competition. There are more than 200 tennis courts within a 5-mile radius, and nearly 100 indoor handball and racquetball courts.

Las Vegas attracts a wide variety of national sporting events and top names in tennis, boxing, bowling, golfing and auto racing. Many nationally televised events originate here each year. Frequent horse shows and rodeos are a popular form of entertainment, with the National Finals Rodeo as well as the Elks Helldorado Festival and Rodeo being the best known.

The Thomas and Mack Center at the University of Nevada, Las Vegas campus serves as a center for many of the city's sports, cultural, entertainment and educational events.

In the fall, hunting in this part of the country is excellent, especially for doves, quail, geese and ducks, as well as mule deer and desert bighorn (mountain sheep).

Entertainment

The Strip, Las Vegas Boulevard south of town, and Casino Center, located on Fremont Street, are the main attractions for most visitors. They glitter with dazzling casinos, whirling roulette wheels, shiny armies of slot machines, luxurious hotels, glamorous chorus lines and brilliant stars of show business.

On a cultural level, the University of Nevada, Las Vegas, houses an art gallery, a concert hall and a theater. The Artemus W. Ham Concert Hall showcases opera, ballet, jazz and popular musical performances. The Judy Bayley Theater presents a variety of shows. The campus also has the Marjorie Barrick Museum of Natural History, with collections of historic and prehistoric Native American artifacts, mining and early pioneer materials and live desert reptiles. The university's Mineral Collection in the Geoscience Building features a display of 1,000 minerals, including specimens from southern Nevada.

Located near the natural springs at Lorenzi Park, the New Nevada State Museum has four galleries tracing the history of southern Nevada through archaeology, anthropology, biology and regional history.

Sightseeing

On a map of the United States, Las Vegas appears to be remote from other centers of population, but today's fine network of highways has placed it within a few hours, by automobile or bus, from some of the most spectacular vacation spots in the West. Mountains, lakes, desert and Utah's red-rock canyons are all there for the curious to see and enjoy.

The Grand Canyon is an ideal two-day, round-trip excursion from Las Vegas. The canyon's vastness, array of colors and beautiful sunsets defy description. The best approach is by way of US 93 and I-40 to Williams, then north on AZ 64 to the South Rim. There are many campsites and several lodges; but the facilities of this park, one of the oldest and most popular in the National Park system, are often filled to capacity, and reservations should be made in advance. Hiking into the canyon is a rugged but worthwhile experience. Other tours are available by air or by mule.

It is possible to go from Las Vegas to Zion National Park (follow I-15) and return in one day, still allowing time to appreciate the geological wonders of the park. The 12-mile Zion Canyon Scenic Drive takes the visitor past constantly changing vistas of multicolored rock formations, which thrust up above the valley floor. Several easy, self-guided nature walks and some more strenuous climbs afford a closer look at the park's natural wonders. Concessionaires provide horses and guided tours. Cabins and a lodge are available for longer stays, but reservations should be made in advance to avoid disappointment.

A little to the north and east of Zion are Cedar Breaks National Monument and Bryce Canyon National Park. Cedar Breaks is a huge natural coliseum made up of pink cliffs averaging more than 10,000 feet in elevation. Bryce Canyon boasts multicolored rock formations suggesting cathedrals, palaces and miniature cities.

Lake Mead National Recreation Area, with nearly two million acres of desert, plateaus, canyons and water playground, is in Las Vegas' backyard. Lake Mead, the country's largest man-made reservoir, was created by the construction of Hoover Dam, 726 feet high, the greatest dam construction of its day and still one of the engineering wonders of the world. Tours descend 528 feet by elevator into the heart of the power plant. The lake attracts more than six million visitors a year for swimming, boating, waterskiing and fishing. Fishing is allowed year-round.

Valley of Fire State Park, just northwest of Lake Mead, is only 55 miles from Las Vegas. Hiking trails lead past petroglyphs, beautiful desert flora, red sandstone canyons and specimens of petrified wood. Camping and picnic areas are available.

In nearby Overton is the Lost City Museum of Archaeology. Displayed here are artifacts and reconstructions of original pit dwellings and pueblos of the Moapa Valley.

Lee Canyon, about 46 miles west of Las Vegas, is southern Nevada's only ski resort. Here, in the Toiyabe National Forest, are towering mountain peaks like Mt Charleston and thick stands of pine.

Half an hour west of Las Vegas, unusual geologic formations of varied colors and shapes make up the unique Red Rock Canyon Recreation Lands. In the canyon is the Spring Mountain Ranch, a 528-acre estate that dates to the early 1900s and at one time was owned by Howard Hughes. A guided tour takes visitors to both restored and original ranch buildings.

Also within the scenic red-rock area and on the site of the Bonnie Springs Ranch is Old Nevada, a complete Old West town that has been re-created. The buildings are designed to duplicate those that stood in many of the famed gold and silver camps. A working replica of the old steam locomotive that served the Comstock takes visitors from the parking lot to the entrance. Many ghost towns also dot the area.

General References

Settled: 1855 **Pop:** 258,295 **Elev:** 2,020 feet **Time zone:** Pacific **Area code:** 702

Phone Numbers

POLICE & FIRE: 911
FBI: 385-1281
POISON INFORMATION CENTER: 732-4989
TIME: (Dial "118" locally)   **WEATHER:** 734-2010

Information Sources

Las Vegas Convention/Visitors Authority, Convention Center, 3150 Paradise Rd, 89109; 892-0711.

Greater Las Vegas Chamber of Commerce, 711 E Desert Inn Rd, 89109; 735-1616.
Department of Recreation & Leisure Activities, 229-6729.

Transportation

AIRLINES: American; America West; Continental; Delta; Northwest; Southwest; TWA; United; USAir; and other commuter and regional airlines. For current airline schedules and information consult the *Official Airline Guide,* published twice monthly.
AIRPORT: McCarran International, 261-5733.
CAR RENTAL AGENCIES: (See Toll-Free Numbers) Ajax 739-6288; Avis 739-5595; Brooks 735-3344; Budget 736-1212; Fairway 369-8533; Hertz 736-4900; National 739-5391; Thrifty 736-4706; Value 733-8886.

Newspapers

Las Vegas Review Journal; Las Vegas Sun.

Convention Facilities

Cashman Field Center, 850 Las Vegas Blvd N, 386-7100.
Las Vegas Convention Center, 3150 Paradise Rd, 892-0711.

Sports & Recreation

Thomas and Mack Center, University of Nevada, Las Vegas, 895-3900.

Cultural Facilities

Concert Halls
Artemus W. Ham Concert Hall, University of Nevada, Las Vegas, 895-3801.
Cashman Field Center, 850 N Las Vegas Blvd, 386-7100.
Convention Center, 3150 Paradise Rd, 892-0711.

Museums
Las Vegas Art Museum, 3333 W Washington, 647-4300.
Las Vegas Natural History Museum, 900 Las Vegas Blvd N, 384-3466.
Liberace Museum, 1775 E Tropicana Ave, 798-5595.
Lost City Museum of Archaeology, on NV 169, in Overton, 397-2193.
Marjorie Barrick Museum of Natural History, University of Nevada, Las Vegas, 4505 Maryland Pkwy, 895-3381.
Nevada State Museum and Historical Society, 700 Twin Lakes, in Lorenzi Park, 486-5205.

Points of Interest

Bonnie Springs Old Nevada, 20 mi W via W Charleston Blvd, 875-4191.
Casino Center, Fremont St.
Hoover Dam, 35 mi SE via US 93, 293-8321 or -8367.
Kyle Canyon, 36 mi NW via US 95, NV 39, 872-5486.
Lake Mead, 35 mi SE via US 93, 293-8907.
Lee Canyon, 46 mi NW via US 95, NV 52, 646-0008.
Mount Charleston Recreation Area, Toiyabe National Forest, 15 mi NW on US 95, then 21 mi W on NV 157, 455-8288.
Red Rock Canyon Recreation Lands, 15 mi W on W Charleston Blvd, 363-1921.
Southern Nevada Zoological Park, 1775 N Rancho Dr, 648-5955.

Sightseeing Tours

Gray Line bus tours, 1550 S Industrial Rd, 384-1234.
Scenic Airlines, Scenic Tour Center, 241 E Reno Ave, 739-1900.

Annual Events

Las Vegas LPGA International. Mar-Apr.

Las Vegas Senior Classic Golf Tournament. Apr-May.
Helldorado Festival. Mid-late May.
Las Vegas Invitational PGA Golf Tournament. Oct.
National Finals Rodeo. Dec.

Lodgings and Food

Motels

(Note on accommodations: *Rates are likely to vary upward in Las Vegas at peak occupancy and sometimes a minimum of three days occupancy is required. In addition, minimum rates quoted are generally available only from Sun through Tues, sometimes on Wed, rarely on holidays. This is not true of all accommodations but is true of many. We urge you to check the rate on any room you occupy and to make certain no other special conditions apply. Show reservations are available at most accommodations.)*

✔★ **ARIZONA CHARLIE'S.** *740 S Decatur Ave (89107), west of the Strip.* 702/258-5200; res: 800/342-2695. 100 rms, 3 story. S, D $28-$45; higher rates conventions. Crib free. TV. Pool; poolside serv, lifeguard. Restaurant open 24 hrs. Bar. Ck-out noon. Bellhops. Valet serv. Gift shop. Casino. Cr cds: A, C, D, DS, MC, V.

D ≈ ⊀ ⊠ 🔥

★★ **BEST WESTERN McCARRAN INN.** *4970 Paradise Rd (89119), near McCarran Intl Airport, east of the Strip.* 702/798-5530; FAX 702/798-7627. 98 rms, 3 story. S, D $42-$59; each addl $7; suites $65-$75; under 12 free; higher rates: national hols, major events. Crib $8. TV. Pool. Complimentary bkfst. Restaurant nearby. Coin lndry. Ck-out noon. Meeting rms. Free daytime airport transportation. Cr cds: A, C, D, DS, ER, JCB, MC, V.

D ≈ ✈ ⊠ 🔥 SC

✔★ **CENTER STRIP INN.** *3688 Las Vegas Blvd S (89109), on the Strip.* 702/739-6066; res: 800/777-7737; FAX 702/736-2521. 147 rms, 5 story, 44 suites. S, D $29.95-$89.95; each addl $6; suites $69.95-$149; under 16 free. Crib free. TV; in-rm movies. Pool. Complimentary continental bkfst. Restaurant adj open 24 hrs. Ck-out noon. Refrigerators. Whirlpool in suites. Cr cds: A, C, D, DS, ER, JCB, MC, V.

≈ ⊠ 🔥 SC

★ **COMFORT INN.** *211 E Flamingo Rd (89109), east of the Strip.* 702/733-7800; FAX 702/733-7353. 120 rms, 2 story. S, D $45-$125; under 17 free. TV; cable. Pool. Complimentary continental bkfst. Restaurant adj open 24 hrs. Ck-out 11 am. Cr cds: A, C, D, DS, MC, V.

≈ ⊠ 🔥 SC

✔★ **COMFORT INN-AIRPORT.** *5075 Koval Lane (89119), near McCarran Intl Airport, east of the Strip.* 702/736-3600; FAX 702/736-0726. 106 rms, 2 story. S, D $38-$90; under 18 free. Crib free. TV; cable. Pool. Complimentary continental bkfst, coffee. Restaurant adj open 24 hrs. Ck-out 11 am. Cr cds: A, C, D, DS, ER, JCB, MC, V.

D ≈ ✈ ⊠ 🔥 SC

★ **DAYS INN.** *707 E Fremont (89101).* 702/388-1400; FAX 702/388-9622. 146 units, 3 story, 7 suites. Feb-Nov: S $28-$120; D $32-$120; each addl $10; suites $60-$200; under 18 free; lower rates rest of yr. Crib free. TV. Pool. Restaurant 7 am-9 pm. Ck-out noon. Cr cds: A, C, D, DS, JCB, MC, V.

D ≈ ⊠ 🔥 SC

★★ **FAIRFIELD INN BY MARRIOTT.** *3850 Paradise Rd (89109), near McCarran Intl Airport, east of the Strip.* 702/791-0899. 129 rms, 4 story. S, D $44.10-$65; under 18 free. Crib free. TV; cable. Heated pool; whirlpool. Complimentary continental bkfst, coffee in lobby. Restaurant adj 7 am-10 pm. Ck-out noon. Meeting rms. Free airport transportation. Cr cds: A, C, D, DS, MC, V.

D ≈ ✈ ⊠ 🔥 SC

★ **LA QUINTA MOTOR INN.** *3782 Las Vegas Blvd S (89109), on the Strip.* 702/739-7457. 114 rms, 3 story. S $45-$62; D $53-$70; each addl $8; under 18 free. Crib free. TV; cable. Heated pool.

Restaurant nearby. Ck-out noon. Free airport transportation. Cr cds: A, C, D, DS, MC, V.

D ≈ ⊠ 🔥 SC

★★ **RESIDENCE INN BY MARRIOTT.** *3225 Paradise Rd (89109), near McCarran Intl Airport, east of the Strip.* 702/796-9300; FAX 702/796-9562. 192 kit. units, 1-2 story. S, D $95-$219. Pet accepted, some restrictions; $40-$60 deposit and $7 per day. TV. Heated pool; whirlpool. Complimentary continental bkfst. Restaurant adj 6:30 am-9 pm. Ck-out noon. Coin lndry. Meeting rms. Free airport transportation. Balconies. Picnic tables, grills. Cr cds: A, C, D, DS, JCB, MC, V.

D 🐾 ≈ 🏃 ✈ ⊠ 🔥 SC

★★ **RODEWAY INN.** *3786 Las Vegas Blvd S (89109), on the Strip.* 702/736-1434; FAX 702/736-6058. 97 rms, 2 story. S, D $59-$95; under 17 free; suites $75-$150. Crib free. Pet accepted, some restrictions; $10. TV. Heated pool. Coffee in rms. Restaurant adj open 24 hrs. Ck-out noon. Valet serv. Cr cds: A, C, D, DS, ER, JCB, MC, V.

🐾 ≈ ⊠ 🔥 SC

★★★ **ST TROPEZ.** *455 E Harmon Ave (89109), near McCarran Intl Airport, west of the strip.* 702/369-5400; res: 800/666-5400; FAX 702/369-1150. 150 suites, 2 story. Suites $93-$250; under 12 free. Crib free. TV; in-rm movies. Heated pool; poolside serv. Complimentary coffee in rms. Restaurant adj 11 am-11 pm. Bar. Ck-out noon. Meeting rms. Bellhops. Concierge. Shopping arcade. Airport transportation. Exercise equipt; weight machine, rowers. Refrigerators. Minibars. Cr cds: A, C, D, DS, ER, JCB, MC, V.

D ≈ 🏃 ✈ ⊠ 🔥 SC

✔★ **TRAVELODGE-LAS VEGAS DOWNTOWN.** *2028 E Fremont St (89101).* 702/384-7540; FAX 702/384-0408. 58 rms, 2 story. S, D $30-$70; each addl $5; family rates. Crib free. TV; cable. Heated pool. Complimentary coffee in rms. Restaurant nearby. Ck-out noon. Cr cds: A, C, D, DS, ER, JCB, MC, V.

≈ ⊠ 🔥 SC

✔★ **TRAVELODGE-LAS VEGAS INN.** *1501 W Sahara Ave (89102), west of the Strip.* 702/733-0001; FAX 702/733-1571. 223 rms, 4 story. S, D $35-$140; under 18 free. TV; cable. Pool. Restaurant 6 am-10 pm. Ck-out noon. Gift shop. Cr cds: A, C, D, ER, MC, V.

D ≈ ⊠ 🔥 SC

Motor Hotels

★★ **COURTYARD BY MARRIOTT.** *3275 Paradise Rd (89109), near McCarran Intl Airport, east of the Strip.* 702/791-3600; FAX 702/796-7981. 149 rms, 3 story, 12 suites. S $82-$110; D $92-$120; each addl $10; under 16 free; higher rates: conventions, hol wkends. Crib free. TV. Heated pool. Complimentary coffee in rms. Restaurant 6:30 am-2 pm, 5-10 pm. Bar 4-11 pm. Ck-out 1 pm. Coin lndry. Meeting rms. Valet serv. Free airport transportation. Exercise equipt; weights, bicycles, whirlpool. Some refrigerators. Balconies. Cr cds: A, C, D, DS, MC, V.

D ≈ 🏃 ✈ ⊠ 🔥 SC

★★ **HOLIDAY INN.** *325 E Flamingo Rd (89109), near McCarran Intl Airport, east of the Strip.* 702/732-9100; FAX 702/731-9784. 150 units, 3 story, 117 suites. Mid-Sept-May: S, D $69-$175; each addl $15; suites $95-$165; under 19 free; higher rates: hols, major conventions; lower rates rest of yr. Crib free. TV; cable. Heated pool; whirlpool, poolside serv. Complimentary coffee in rms. Restaurant 6:30 am-10 pm. Bar noon-2 am. Ck-out noon. Meeting rms. Concierge. Free airport, casino transportation. Health club privileges. Refrigerators. Wet bars. Cr cds: A, C, D, DS, JCB, MC, V.

D ≈ ✈ ⊠ 🔥 SC

★★ **SHEFFIELD INN.** *3970 Paradise Rd (89109), near McCarran Intl Airport, east of the Strip.* 702/796-9000. 228 units, 3 story, 171 kits. S, D $118; kits. $128-$400; under 18 free. Crib free. TV;

cable, in-rm movies. Pool. Complimentary continental bkfst. Ck-out 11 am. Coin lndry. Meeting rms. Bellhops. Free airport transportation. In-rm whirlpools. Refrigerators. Private patios, balconies. Cr cds: A, C, D, DS, ER, MC, V.

★ **WESTWARD HO HOTEL & CASINO.** 2900 Las Vegas Blvd S (09109), on the Strip. 702/731-2900; res: 800/634-6803 (exc NV); FAX 702/731-6154. 777 rms, 2-4 story. S, D $37-$67; each addl $15; 2-bedrm apt $81-$111; package plan. Crib $15. TV. 4 pools, 1 heated; whirlpools. Restaurant open 24 hrs. Rm serv. Bars open 24 hrs; entertainment. Ck-out 11 am. Free airport transportation. Some refrigerators. Casino. Cr cds: MC, V.

Hotels

★ **ALADDIN.** 3667 Las Vegas Blvd S (89193), near McCarran Intl Airport, on the Strip. 702/736-0111; res: 800/634-3424; FAX 702/734-3583. 1,100 rms, 22 story. S, D $65-$90; suites $150-$300; under 12 free. Crib free. TV. Heated pool; poolside serv, lifeguard. Restaurants, bars open 24 hrs. Ck-out noon. Convention facilities. Concierge. Shopping arcade. Barber, beauty shop. Airport transportation. Lighted tennis; pro. Casino. Cr cds: A, C, D, DS, ER, MC, V.

★ ★ **ALEXIS PARK RESORT.** Box 95698 (89109), 375 E Harmon Ave, near McCarran Intl Airport, 1 mi E of the Strip. 702/796-3300; res: 800/582-2228 (exc NV); FAX 702/796-4334. 500 suites, 2 story. 1-bedrm $85-$500; 2-bedrm $475-$1,150; each addl $15; under 12 free. Crib free. Pet accepted, some restrictions; $60. TV; cable. 3 pools, 2 heated; poolside serv. Restaurant 6 am-3 pm, 6-11 pm (also see PEGASUS). Bar 10-1 am; entertainment. Ck-out noon. Convention facilities. Concierge. Gift shop. Barber, beauty shop. Lighted tennis, pro. Golf privileges nearby. Putting green. Exercise equipt; weights, bicycles, whirlpool, sauna, steam rm. Refrigerators, minibars; some bathrm phones, in-rm whirlpools. Cr cds: A, C, D, DS, JCB, MC, V.

★ ★ **BALLY'S.** 3645 Las Vegas Blvd S (89109), on the Strip. 702/739-4111; res: 800/634-3434; FAX 702/794-2413. 2,813 rms, 26 story. S, D $87-$185; each addl $15; suites $180-$1,500; under 18 free; package plans. Crib free. TV. Heated pool; poolside serv. Restaurant, bar open 24 hrs; entertainment. Ck-out 11 am. Convention facilities. Shopping arcade. Barber, beauty shop. Lighted tennis, pro. Exercise equipt; weights, stair machine, whirlpool, sauna. Game rm. Some bathrm phones, refrigerators. Casino, wedding chapel. Cr cds: A, C, D, DS, JCB, MC, V.

★ ★ **BARBARY COAST.** 3595 Las Vegas Blvd S (89109), on the Strip. 702/737-7111; res: 800/634-6755 (exc NV); FAX 702/737-6304. 200 rms, 8 story. S, D $50-$80; each addl $5; suites $200-$300; under 12 free. TV; cable. Restaurant, bar open 24 hrs. Ck-out noon. Gift shop. Free valet, covered parking. Casino. Cr cds: A, C, D, DS, JCB, MC, V.

✔★ **BINNION'S HORSESHOE.** 128 Fremont St (89101). 702/382-1600; res: 800/622-6468; FAX 702/384-1574. 369 rms, 22 story. S $40; D $60. Crib $8. TV. Pool; lifeguard. Restaurant open 24 hrs. Bar. Ck-out noon. Gift shop. Casino. Cr cds: A, C, D, DS, ER, JCB, MC, V.

★ ★ ★ **CAESARS PALACE.** 3570 Las Vegas Blvd S (89109), 1 blk E of I-15 Dunes/Flamingo exit, on the Strip. 702/731-7110; res: 800/634-6001 (exc NV); FAX 702/731-6636. 1,509 rms, 14-22 story. S $100-$175; D $115-$190; each addl $15; suites $225-$930; under 13 free. TV; cable. 2 heated pools; lifeguard. Restaurant, bars open 24 hrs (also see PALACE COURT). Circus Maximus, star entertainment; danc-

ing. Ck-out noon. Convention facilities. Concierge. Shopping arcade. Barber, beauty shop. Parking free. Tennis, pro. Exercise rm; instructor, weight machines, bicycles, whirlpool, sauna, steam rm. Massage. Solarium. Racquetball. Handball. Game rm. Casino. Omnimax Theater: movies. Bathrm phones; many whirlpools; some refrigerators. Many bi-level suites with wet bar. Cr cds: A, C, D, DS, JCB, MC, V.

✔★ ★ **CALIFORNIA HOTEL & CASINO.** PO Box 630 (89125), 1st & Ogden Aves, I-95 Casino Center exit. 702/385-1222; res: 800/634-6255; FAX 702/388-2660. 635 rms, 9-15 story. S, D $40-$60; each addl $5; under 12 free; package plans. Crib free. TV. Pool. Restaurant, bar open 24 hrs. Ck-out noon. Gift shop. Refrigerators. Casino. Cr cds: A, D, DS, MC, V.

★ ★ **CARRIAGE HOUSE.** 105 E Harmon Ave (89109), east of the Strip. 702/798-1020; FAX 702/798-1020, ext. 112. 150 kit. suites, 9 story. S, D $85-$190; children free; wkly rates; higher rates: special events, hols. Crib free. TV; cable. Heated pool; whirlpool. Complimentary coffee in rms. Restaurant 7-10 am, 5-11 pm. Bar 5-11 pm; entertainment. Ck-out 11 am. Coin lndry. Free airport, casino transportation. Tennis. Cr cds: A, D, DS, ER, MC, V.

✔★ ★ **CIRCUS-CIRCUS HOTEL & CASINO.** Box 14967 (89114), 2880 Las Vegas Blvd S, on the Strip. 702/734-0410; res: 800/634-3450; FAX 702/734-5897. 2,800 rms, 3-29 story. S, D $19-$49; each addl $6; suites $45-$100; under 12 free. Crib $6. TV. 2 heated pools; poolside serv, lifeguard. Restaurants, bars open 24 hrs; entertainment. Ck-out 11 am. Shopping arcade. Barber, beauty shop. Casino, performing circus and midway housed together in tent-like structure. Cr cds: A, C, D, DS, MC, V.

✔★ **EL CORTEZ.** Box 680 (89125), 600 E Fremont St. 702/385-5200; res: 800/634-6703. 308 rms, 15 story. S, D $23-$40; each addl $3. Crib free. TV. Restaurant 4:30-11 pm. Rm serv 7 am-7 pm. Bar open 24 hrs. Ck-out noon. Meeting rms. Shopping arcade. Barber, beauty shop. Free valet parking. Casino. Cr cds: A, C, D, DS, JCB, MC, V.

★ ★ **EXCALIBUR.** 3850 Las Vegas Blvd S (89119), on the Strip. 702/597-7777; res: 800/937-7777; FAX 702/599-7709. 4,032 rms, 28 story. S, D $55-$89; each addl $7; suites $110; higher rates: wkends, hols. Crib $7. TV. 2 heated pools; poolside serv, lifeguard. Restaurants open 24 hrs. Dinner theater. Limited rm serv. Bar open 24 hrs; entertainment. Ck-out 11 am. Shopping arcade. Barber, beauty shop. Whirlpool in suites. Casino. Castle-like structure with medieval/old English interiors based upon legend of King Arthur and Round Table. Cr cds: A, C, D, DS, MC, V.

✔★ ★ **FITZGERALDS.** 301 Fremont St (89101), west of the Strip. 702/388-2400; res: 800/274-5825. 654 rms, 34 story. S, D $22-$80; under 12 free. Crib $5. TV. Restaurant open 24 hrs. Rm serv 24 hrs. Bar open 24 hrs. Ck-out noon. Coin lndry. Concierge. Gift shop. Casino. Cr cds: A, C, D, DS, ER, MC, V.

★ ★ **FOUR QUEENS.** Box 370 (89125), 202 Fremont, at Casino Center Blvd. 702/385-4011; res: 800/634-6045; FAX 702/383-0631. 700 rms, 19 story. S, D $47-$59; each addl $8; suites $85-$95; under 12 free. TV. Restaurant open 24 hrs; dining rm 6 pm-midnight. Bar; entertainment, jazz Mon evenings. Ck-out noon. Meeting rms. Garage parking. Wet bar in suites. Casino. Cr cds: A, C, D, DS, MC, V.

✔★ **FREMONT.** 200 E Fremont St (89125). 702/385-3232; res: 800/634-6182; FAX 702/385-6270. 452 rms, 14 story. S, D $36-

$60; package plan. TV. Restaurant, bars open 24 hrs. Ck-out noon. Gift shop. Casino. Cr cds: A, C, D, DS, JCB, MC, V.

⊠ 🔥

★ ★ **GOLD COAST.** 4000 W Flamingo Rd (89103), at Valley View Blvd, west of the Strip. 702/367-7111; res: 800/331-5334; FAX 702/367-8575. 722 rms, 10 story. S, D $35-$50; suites $100-$400; family rates; package plan. TV. Pool. Supervised child's activities. Restaurant, bar open 24 hrs; entertainment, dancing. Ck-out noon. Convention facilities. Barber, beauty shop. Free valet parking. Game rm. Bowling. Some bathrm phones. Casino. Movie theaters. Cr cds: A, C, D, DS, ER, JCB, MC, V.

D ≈ ⊠ 🔥

★ ★ ★ **GOLDEN NUGGET.** Box 610 (89125), 129 E Fremont St, at Casino Center. 702/385-7111; res: 800/634-3454 (exc NV); FAX 702/386-8362. 1,907 rms, 18-22 story. S, D $58-$150; each addl $20; under 12 free; suites $210-$750. Crib free. TV; cable. Heated pool; poolside serv, lifeguard. Restaurant open 24 hrs (also see LILY LANGTRY'S). Bar; entertainment. Ck-out noon. Meeting rms. Gift shop. Barber, beauty shop. Exercise rm; instructor, weight machines, bicycles, whirlpool, sauna, steam rm. Massage. Casino. Some bathrm phones. Cr cds: A, C, D, DS, JCB, MC, V.

D ≈ 🏃 ⊠ 🔥

✔ **HACIENDA RESORT.** Box 98506 (89119), 3950 Las Vegas Blvd S, on the Strip. 702/739-8911; res: 800/634-6713 (exc NV); FAX 702/798-8289. 1,140 rms, 2-11 story. S, D $28-$88; each addl $10; suites $125-$350; lower rates June-Aug, Dec. Crib free. TV. Pool; poolside serv, lifeguard. Restaurants, bar open 24 hrs; entertainment. Ck-out 11 am. Convention center. Shopping arcade. Beauty shop. Free valet parking. Lighted tennis, pro. Game rm. Some refrigerators. Casino. Full-serv RV park. Cr cds: A, C, D, DS, MC, V.

D 🏃 ≈ ⊠ 🔥

★ ★ ★ **HARRAH'S.** 3475 Las Vegas Blvd S (89109), on the Strip. 702/369-5000; FAX 702/369-6014. 1,725 rms, 35 story. S, D $69-$89; each addl $10; suites $190-$355; under 12 free; higher rates special events. Crib free. TV; cable. Pool; poolside serv, lifeguard. Restaurant, bar open 24 hrs; entertainment exc Sun. Ck-out noon. Coin lndry. Convention facilities. Shopping arcade. Barber, beauty shop. Valet parking; covered parking free. Exercise equipt; weights, bicycles, whirlpool, sauna. Game rm. Balconies. Casino. Wedding chapel. Cr cds: A, C, D, DS, JCB, MC, V.

D ≈ 🏃 🏃 ⊠

★ ★ ★ **HILTON.** Box 15087 (89114), 3000 Paradise Rd, east of the Strip. 702/732-5111; FAX 702/794-3611. 3,174 rms, 30 story. S, D $79-$249; each addl $20; 1-2 bedrm suites from $300; lanai suites $280-$300. Crib free. TV. Rooftop heated pool; poolside serv, lifeguard. Restaurant, bars open 24 hrs; 13 dining rms; dancing; star entertainment. Ck-out noon. Convention facilities. Shopping arcade. Barber, beauty shop. Free valet parking. 8½-acre recreation deck includes lighted tennis, pro. Golf privileges, greens fee $80, putting green. Exercise equipt; weights, whirlpool, sauna. Game rm. Some bathrm phones, refrigerators. Private patios, balconies. Casino. Cr cds: A, C, D, DS, JCB, MC, V.

D 🏃 ⊠ ≈ 🏃 ⊠ 🔥

★ ★ ★ **HILTON FLAMINGO.** 3555 Las Vegas Blvd S (89109), on the Strip. 702/733-3111; res: 800/732-2111 (exc NV); FAX 702/733-3528. 3,650 rms, 28 story. S, D $65-$139; each addl $16; suites $250-$580; family rates; package plan; lower rates Dec-Jan. Crib free. TV; cable. 2 pools; poolside serv, lifeguard. Restaurant, bar open 24 hrs; stage show, dancing. Ck-out noon. Convention center. Concierge. Shopping arcade. Barber, beauty shop. Free valet parking. Tennis privileges. Exercise equipt; weight machines, bicycles, whirlpools, sauna, steam rm. Some bathrm phones. Refrigerators avail. Casino. Cr cds: A, C, D, DS, ER, JCB, MC, V.

D 🏃 ≈ 🏃 ⊠ 🔥

★ ★ **HOLIDAY INN CROWNE PLAZA SUITES.** 4255 Paradise Rd (89109), near McCarran Intl Airport, east of the Strip. 702/369-4400; FAX 702/369-3770. 202 suites, 6 story. S, D $95-$250; each addl $15; under 18 free. Crib free. TV; cable. Heated pool; poolside serv. Complimentary coffee in rms. Restaurant 6 am-2 pm, 5-10 pm. Bar 11 am-midnight. Ck-out noon. Meeting rms. Concierge. Gift shop. Free airport transportation. Exercise equipt; weights, bicycles, whirlpool, sauna. Minibars. Cr cds: A, C, D, DS, ER, JCB, MC, V.

D ≈ 🏃 ✈ ⊠ ⊠

★ **IMPERIAL PALACE.** 3535 Las Vegas Blvd S (89109), on the Strip. 702/731-3311; res: 800/634-6441 (exc NV), 800/351-7400 (NV); FAX 702/735-8528. 2,700 rms, 19 story. S, D $45-$125; each addl $12; suites $105-$325; package plan; higher rates hols. Crib $12. TV. Heated pool; poolside serv, lifeguard. Restaurant, bar open 24 hrs; entertainment. Ck-out noon. Convention facilities. Shopping arcade. Barber, beauty shop. Free valet, covered parking. Exercise rm; instructor, weight machines, treadmills, whirlpool. Some bathrm phones, refrigerators. Private balconies. Casino. Antique auto exhibit. Cr cds: A, C, D, DS, MC, V.

D ≈ 🏃 ⊠ ⊠

★ ★ **LADY LUCK CASINO.** 206 N 3rd St (89101). 702/477-3000; res: 800/523-9582; FAX 702/477-3002. 791 rms, 17 & 25 story. Feb-Mar & Sept-Oct: S, D $45-$150; suites $60-$200; package plans; lower rates rest of yr. TV; cable. Pool. Restaurant, bar open 24 hrs. Ck-out noon. Free garage parking. Refrigerators. Casino. Cr cds: A, C, D, DS, JCB, MC, V.

D ≈ ⊠ 🔥

★ ★ ★ **LUXOR.** 3900 Las Vegas Blvd S (89193), near McCarran Intl Airport, on the Strip. 702/262-4000; res: 800/288-1000. 2,529 rms, 30 story, 298 suites. S, D $59-$159; suites $150-$500; under 12 free. Crib $10. TV. Heated pool; wading pool, poolside serv, lifeguard. Restaurant, bar open 24 hrs; entertainment. Ck-out 11 am. Concierge. Shopping arcade. Barber, beauty shop. Airport transportation. Masseur. Exercise equipt; weight machine, treadmill, sauna. Minibars. Casino. Pyramid-shaped hotel with replica of the Great Sphinx of Giza. Extensive lanscaping with Egyptian theme. Cr cds: A, C, D, DS, ER, JCB, MC, V.

D ≈ 🏃 ✈ ⊠ 🔥

MGM GRAND. (Too new to be rated) 3799 Las Vegas Blvd S (89109), near McCarran Intl Airport, on the Strip. 702/891-1111; res: 800/929-1111; FAX 702/891-1030. 5,005 rms, 30 story, 740 suites. S, D $79-$129; suites $109-$229; under 12 free; higher rates hols. Crib free. TV. Heated pool; wading pool, poolside serv, lifeguard. Supervised child's activities. Restaurants open 24 hrs (also see SIR REGINALD'S). Rm serv 24 hrs. Bars open 24 hrs; entertainment. Ck-out 11 am. Convention facilities. Concierge. Shopping arcade. Barber, beauty shop. Airport transportation. Lighted tennis; pro. Exercise rm; instructor, weight machines, treadmill, steam rm. Complete spa service with masseur, facials, body treatments. Game rm. Refrigerators, minibars. Outstanding features include a 33-acre theme park, 7-story replica of The Emerald City complete with Yellow Brick Road and two showrooms with headline entertainment. Cr cds: A, C, D, DS, ER, JCB, MC, V.

D ≈ ≈ 🏃 ✈ ⊠ 🔥

★ ★ ★ **MIRAGE.** 3400 Las Vegas Blvd S (89109), on the Strip. 702/791-7111; FAX 702/791-7446. 3,044 rms, 30 story. S, D $79-$259; each addl $15; suites $300-$3,000; under 12 free. Crib free. TV; cable. 2 heated pools. Restaurant open 24 hrs. Bar; entertainment, dancing. Ck-out noon. Convention facilities. Concierge. Shopping arcade. Barber, beauty shop. Valet parking. 18-hole golf, driving range. Exercise rm; instructor, weights, bicycles. Bathrm phone, refrigerator, wet bar in suites. Casino. Atrium features tropical rain forest; behind front desk is 20,000-gallon aquarium with sharks and tropical fish. On 100 acres with dolphin and white tiger habitats. Cr cds: A, C, D, DS, ER, MC, V.

D 🏃 ≈ 🏃 ⊠ 🔥

★ ★ ★ **PALACE STATION HOTEL & CASINO.** *2411 W Sahara (89102), at I-15, west of the Strip.* 702/367-2411; res: 800/634-3101 (exc NV). 1,030 rms, 21 story. S, D $39-$99; each addl $10; suites $150-$750; under 12 free. Crib free. TV; cable. 2 heated pools; whirlpools. Restaurants, bars open 24 hrs; entertainment. Ck-out noon. Gift shop. Garage parking. Game rm. Casino, bingo. Cr cds: A, C, D, DS, ER, MC, V.

⊡ ⊠ ⊠ SC

★ **PLAZA.** *One Main St (89125), east of the Strip.* 702/386-2110. 1,037 rms, 21 story. S, D $40-$60; under 12 free. Crib $8. TV. Heated pool; wading pool. Restaurant open 24 hrs. Rm serv 24 hrs. Bar open 24 hrs. Ck-out noon. Coin lndry. Convention facilities. Concierge. Shopping arcade. Barber. Tennis. Casino. Cr cds: A, C, D, DS, ER, MC, V.

⊡ ⊠ ⊠ ⊠ ⊠

★ ★ ★ **RIO SUITE HOTEL & CASINO.** *Box 14160 (89114), I-15 at Flamingo Rd, west of the Strip.* 702/252-7777; res: 800/PLAY-RIO; FAX 702/252-7670. 861 suites, 20 story. Suites $85-$150; under 12 free; mid-wk rates. Crib free. TV; cable. 2 heated pools. Complimentary coffee in rms. Restaurant open 24 hrs, dining rm 5-11 pm. Bar; entertainment. Ck-out noon. Convention facilities. Concierge. Shopping arcade. Barber, beauty shop. Exercise equipt; weights, bicycles. Refrigerators. Building facade of red and blue glass trimmed in neon. Casino. Cr cds: A, C, D, MC, V.

⊡ ⊠ ⊠ ⊠ SC

★ ★ **RIVIERA.** *Box 14528 (89109), 2901 Las Vegas Blvd S, on the Strip.* 702/734-5110; res: 800/634-6753 (exc NV); FAX 702/794-9663. 2,100 rms, 6-24 story. S, D $59-$95; each addl $12; suites $125-$500; under 12 free; package plan. Crib free. TV; cable. Heated pool; poolside serv, lifeguard. Restaurant, bar open 24 hrs; Versailles Room, name entertainment. Ck-out noon. Convention facilities. Shopping arcade. Barber, beauty shop. Lighted tennis. Exercise equipt; weights, bicycles, whirlpool, sauna, steam rm. Some refrigerators. Bathrm phone in some suites. Some balconies. Casino. Cr cds: A, C, D, JCB, MC, V.

⊡ ⊠ ⊠ ⊠ ⊠

★ ★ **SAHARA.** *2535 Las Vegas Blvd S (89109), on the Strip.* 702/737-2111; res: 800/634-6666; FAX 702/791-2027. 2,040 rms, 2-27 story. S, D $55-$95; each addl $10; suites $200-$300; under 12 free; package plans. Crib $10. TV. 2 pools, heated; poolside serv, lifeguard. Restaurant, bar open 24 hrs. Congo Theatre, star entertainment & revue, dancing. Ck-out noon. Convention facilities. Shopping arcade. Barber, beauty shop. Free covered parking. Many bathrm phones. Private patios, balconies. Casino. Cr cds: A, C, D, DS, MC, V.

⊡ ⊠ ⊠ ⊠ SC

★ ★ **SAN REMO.** *115 E Tropicana Ave (89109), near McCarran Intl Airport, east of the Strip.* 702/739-9000; FAX 702/736-1120. 711 rms, 19 story. 45 suites. S, D $55-$125; each addl $15; suites $75-$350; under 12 free; higher rates: hols, conventions. Crib $15. TV. Heated pool; poolside serv. Restaurant open 24 hrs, dining rm 5-11 pm. Bar; entertainment. Ck-out noon. Meeting rms. Gift shop. Free garage parking. Balconies. Casino. Cr cds: A, C, D, DS, ER, JCB, MC, V.

⊡ ⊠ ⊠ ⊠ ⊠ SC

★ ★ **SANDS.** *3355 Las Vegas Blvd (89109).* 800/634-6901; FAX 702/733-5624. 750 rms, 18 story. S, D $69-$109; suites $150-$1,500; under 12 free. Heated pool; poolside serv, lifeguard. Restaurant 10-1 am. Rm serv 24 hrs. Ck-out noon. Convention facilities. Concierge. Shopping arcade. Barber, beauty shop. Exercise rm; instructor, weights, bicycles, whirlpool. Health club privileges. Lawn games. Many refrigerators. Balconies. Cr cds: A, C, D, DS, ER, MC, V.

⊡ ⊠ ⊠ ⊠ ⊠

★ ★ **SANTA FE HOTEL & CASINO.** *4949 N Rancho Dr (89130).* 702/658-4900; res: 800/872-6823; FAX 702/658-4919. 200 rms, 5 story. S, D $36-$50; each addl $5; under 13 free; higher rates some hols. TV; cable. Free supervised child's activities. Restaurant

open 24 hrs. Bar; entertainment. Ck-out noon. Meeting rm. Gift shop. Downhill/x-country ski 20 mi. Game rm. Bowling lanes. Ice rink. Cr cds: A, C, D, DS, MC, V.

⊡ ⊠ ⊠ ⊠

★ ★ ★ **SHERATON DESERT INN.** *Box 14577 (89109), 3145 Las Vegas Blvd S, on the Strip.* 702/733-4444; res: 800/634-6906 (exc NV); FAX 702/733-4774. 821 rms, 2-14 story. S, D $135-$195; each addl $25; suites $245-$900. Crib free. TV; cable. Heated pool; poolside serv, lifeguard. Restaurant (see MONTE CARLO). Rm serv 24 hrs. Bars open 24 hrs; Crystal Room, theater, star entertainment. Ck-out noon. Convention facilities. Concierge. Shopping arcade. Barber, beauty shop. Free valet parking. Lighted tennis, pro. 18-hole golf, greens fee, putting green, driving range. Exercise rm; instructor, weights, bicycles, whirlpool, sauna, steam rm. Wet bar in suites; bathrm phones, refrigerators. Private patios, balconies, 10 whirlpools. Casino. Resort hotel on 160 acres. Cr cds: A, C, D, DS, JCB, MC, V.

⊡ ⊠ ⊠ ⊠ ⊠ ⊠ ⊠

★ ★ **SHOWBOAT.** *2800 E Fremont St (89104).* 702/385-9123; res: 800/826-2800 (exc NV); FAX 702/383-9238. 484 rms, 19 story. S, D $26-$85; each addl $5; suites $90-$255; under 12 free. Crib $5. TV. Heated pool; lifeguard. Restaurants, bar open 24 hrs. Ck-out noon. Meeting rms. Gift shop. Barber, beauty shop. Free airport, RR station, bus depot transportation. Game rm. Casino; bingo parlor. 106-lane bowling. Cr cds: A, C, D, MC, V.

⊡ ⊠ ⊠ ⊠

★ ★ **STARDUST RESORT & CASINO.** *3000 Las Vegas Blvd S (89109), on the Strip.* 702/732-6111; res: 800/634-6757; FAX 702/732-6296. 2,341 rms, 2-32 story. Jan-May, Oct-Nov: S, D $24-$150; suites $150-$500. Crib free. TV. 2 pools; lifeguard, poolside serv. Restaurants, bar open 24 hrs; entertainment. Ck-out noon. Convention facilities. Shopping arcade. Barber, beauty shop. Game rm. Some bathrm phones, refrigerators. Some private patios, balconies. Casino. Cr cds: A, C, D, DS, ER, JCB, MC, V.

⊡ ⊠ ⊠ ⊠

★ ★ **TREASURE ISLAND.** *3300 Las Vegas Blvd S (89109), on the Strip.* 702/894-7111; res: 800/944-7444; FAX 702/894-7414. 2,900 rms, 36 story. S, D $44-$229; suites $149-$400; under 12 free. Crib free. TV; cable. 3 heated pools; wading pool, poolside serv, lifeguard. Restaurants open 24 hrs. Bars; entertainment. Ck-out noon. Convention facilities. Concierge. Shopping arcade. Barber, beauty shop. Airport, RR station transportation. Health club privileges. Refrigerators. Casino. Arcade entertainment complex. Buccaneer Bay Village adventure attraction. Cr cds: A, C, D, DS, MC, V.

⊡ ⊠ SC

★ ★ **TROPICANA.** *3801 Las Vegas Blvd S (89109), near McCarran Intl Airport, on the Strip.* 702/739-2222; res: 800/634-4000 (exc NV); FAX 702/739-2469. 1,900 rms, 22 story. S, D $55-$129; each addl $15. TV. Pool; poolside serv, lifeguard. Restaurant, bar open 24 hrs; Tiffany Theatre, entertainment. Ck-out noon. Convention facilities. Concierge. Shopping arcade. Barber, beauty shop. Exercise equipt; weights, bicycles, whirlpool, sauna. Some bathrm phones, refrigerators. Private patios, balconies. Casino. Cr cds: A, C, D, DS, JCB, MC, V.

⊡ ⊠ ⊠ ⊠ ⊠ ⊠ SC

Restaurants

✓ ★ ★ **ALPINE VILLAGE INN/RATHSKELLER.** *3003 Paradise Rd, 1 blk east of the Strip.* 702/734-6888. Hrs: 5-11 pm. Res accepted. German, Swiss menu. Bar. Semi-a la carte: dinner $4.95-$16.50. Complete meals: dinner $11.25-$16.50. Child's meals. Specialties: Bavarian chicken supreme soup, sauerbraten, Wienerschnitzel, fondue Bourguignonne. Valet parking. Alpine chalet decor. Family-owned. Cr cds: A, C, D, DS, MC, V.

★ ★ ★ **ANDRE'S.** *401 S 6th St.* 702/385-5016. Hrs: 6-11 pm. Closed major hols; also 4 wks July. Res accepted. French menu. Bar. Wine cellar. A la carte entrees: dinner $19-$32. Specializes in fresh fish, duck, pastries. Own baking. Valet parking. Outdoor dining. Country French decor. Cr cds: A, C, D, JCB, MC, V.

D

★ **BATTISTA'S HOLE IN THE WALL.** *4041 Audrie St, east of the Strip.* 702/732-1424. Hrs: 4:30-11 pm. Closed Thanksgiving; also 15 days mid-Dec. Res accepted. Italian menu. Bar. Complete meals: dinner $13.95-$26.95. Specializes in fresh pasta, Battista-style cioppino. Parking. Warm, casual atmosphere. Family-owned. Cr cds: A, C, D, DS, MC, V.

D

★ **CAFE MICHELLE.** *1350 E Flamingo Rd (89109), in Mission Shopping Center, west of the Strip.* 702/735-8686. Hrs: 11 am-11 pm. Closed Dec 25. Res accepted. Continental menu. Bar. Semi-a la carte: lunch $5.95-$8.95, dinner $12.95-$19.95. Specializes in fettucini, omelets, steak. Entertainment ex Mon. Parking. Outdoor dining. Cr cds: A, C, D, DS, ER, JCB, MC, V.

D

★ **CAFE MILANO.** *3900 Paradise Rd.* 702/732-2777. Hrs: 11 am-3 pm, 5-10 pm. Closed Sun. Res accepted. Italian menu. Wine. Semi-a la carte: lunch $4.95-$12.50, dinner $9.50-$19.95. Parking. Outdoor dining. Cr cds: A, C, D, DS, ER, JCB, MC, V.

D

✔★ **CHAPALA.** *2101 S Decatur Blvd, in shopping center.* 702/871-7805. Hrs: 11 am-11 pm; Fri, Sat to midnight. Closed Jan 1, Thanksgiving, Dec 25. Res accepted. Mexican menu. Bar. Semi-a la carte: lunch, dinner $3.25-$10. Specialties: fajitas, enchilada ranchero. Cr cds: MC, V.

D

★ ★ ★ **CHIN'S.** *3200 Las Vegas Blvd S, on the Strip.* 702/733-8899. Hrs: 11 am-10 pm; Sun from noon. Closed Thanksgiving, Dec 24 & 25. Res accepted. Cantonese menu. Bar. Wine cellar. A la carte entrees: lunch $7.95-$10.95, dinner $12-$28. Complete meals: lunch $12-$15, dinner $27.50-$50. Specialties: Chin's beef, strawberry chicken, shrimp puffs, crispy pudding. Valet parking. Cr cds: A, MC, V.

D

★ ★ ★ **CIPRIANI.** *2790 E Flamingo Rd.* 702/369-6711. Hrs: 11:30 am-2:30 pm, 5:30-10:30 pm. Res accepted. Italian, Continental menu. Serv bar. Semi-a la carte: lunch $8-$15, dinner $12.95-$28. Specialties: scaloppina Monte Bianco, medallion of beef Piemontese, fresh seafood. Accordianist, vocalist. Parking. Florentine atmosphere. Cr cds: A, C, D, DS, MC, V.

✔★ **COUNTRY INN.** *1401 Rainbow Blvd.* 702/254-0520. Hrs: 7 am-10 pm; wkends to 11 pm. Closed Dec 25. Wine, beer. Semi-a la carte: bkfst $1.95-$6.50, lunch, dinner $3.25-$14.95. Child's meals. Specializes in turkey, fish, steak. Parking. Cr cds: A, C, D, DS, MC, V.

D

★ ★ ★ **EMPRESS COURT.** *(See Caesars Palace)* 702/731-7110. Hrs: 6-10 pm. Closed Tues & Wed. Res accepted. Cantonese menu. Bar. Complete meals: dinner $30-$60. Specializes in shark fin dishes. Valet parking. Elegant dining. Jacket. Cr cds: A, C, D, MC, V.

★ ★ **FERRARO'S.** *5900 W Flamingo Rd (89103).* 702/364-5300. Hrs: 6-11 pm. Closed Dec 25. Res accepted. Italian menu. Bar. Semi-a la carte: dinner $8.50-$28. Specializes in pasta, seafood, steak. Pianist. Parking. Italian decor. Cr cds: A, C, D, DS, MC, V.

★ ★ **GOLDEN STEER STEAK HOUSE.** *308 W Sahara Ave, west of the Strip.* 702/384-4470. Hrs: 5 pm-midnight. Closed Thanksgiving, Dec 25. Res accepted. Bar. Semi-a la carte: dinner $20-$34.

Specializes in steak, seafood, Italian specialties. Valet parking. 1890s Western decor. Family-owned. Cr cds: A, C, D, DS, MC, V.

D

★ ★ ★ **LILY LANGTRY'S.** *(See Golden Nugget Hotel)* 702/385-7111. Hrs: 5:30-11 pm. Res accepted. Cantonese menu. Bar. Wine cellar. A la carte entrees: dinner $9-$26.50. Specialties: lobster Cantonese, Chinese pepper steak, moo goo gai pan. Own baking. Valet parking. Oriental decor. Cr cds: A, C, D, DS, JCB, MC, V.

D

★ ★ **MARRAKECH.** *3900 Paradise Rd.* 702/737-5611. Hrs: 5:30-11 pm. Closed Dec 25. Res accepted. Moroccan menu. Bar. Complete meal: dinner $23.95. Child's meals. Specialty: shrimp scampi. Belly dancers. Valet parking. Colorful French Moroccan decor. Cr cds: A, MC, V.

D

★ ★ ★ **MONTE CARLO.** *(See Desert Inn Hotel)* 702/733-4524. Hrs: 6-11 pm. Closed Tues, Wed. Res accepted. French menu. Serv bar. Wine cellar. Semi-a la carte: dinner $25-$35. Specializes in boneless roast duckling, stuffed veal chop, quail, sea bass Kiev. Own baking. Valet parking. Elegant decor reminiscent of 18th-century France, Palace of Versailles; murals by Evans & Brown. Jacket. Cr cds: A, C, D, DS, JCB, MC, V.

D

★ ★ ★ **PALACE COURT.** *(See Caesars Palace Hotel)* 702/731-7110. Hrs: 6-11 pm. Res required. French, continental menu. Extensive wine list. A la carte entrees: dinner $28-$55. Specializes in French gourmet dishes, lobster, veal. Own baking; own smoked salmon. Valet parking. Stained-glass dome ceiling. Jacket. Cr cds: A, C, D, MC, V.

D

★ ★ **PALM RESTAURANT.** *3500 Las Vegas Blvd S, suite A7 (89109), in Forum Shops At Caesars, on the Strip.* 702/732-7256. Hrs: 11:30 am-11 pm. Res accepted. Bar. Wine list. A la carte entrees: lunch $8.50-$17, dinner $14-$28. Specializes in prime beef, seafood, chops. Valet parking. Counterpart of famous New York restaurant. Caricatures of celebrities on walls. Cr cds: A, C, D, DS, MC, V.

D

★ ★ ★ **PEGASUS.** *(See Alexis Park Resort Hotel)* 702/796-3300. Hrs: 6-11 pm. Res accepted. French, continental menu. Bar. Wine list. A la carte entrees: dinner $13.50-$75. Specialties: lobster Princess, médaillons de veau. Classical guitarist. Valet parking. Italian crystal chandelier; arched windows overlooking waterfall and garden. Jacket. Cr cds: A, C, D, DS, MC, V.

D

★ ★ **PHILIPS SUPPER HOUSE.** *4545 W Sahara.* 702/873-5222. Hrs: 5-11 pm; early-bird dinner 4:30-6:30 pm. Res accepted. Continental menu. Bar. Complete meals: dinner $14.95-$36.95. Specializes in Black Angus beef. Parking. Victorian decor. Cr cds: A, C, D, DS, ER, MC, V.

★ ★ **PIERO'S.** *355 Convention Center Dr, east of the Strip.* 702/369-2305. Hrs: 5:30-11 pm. Closed Thanksgiving, Dec 24, 25. Res accepted. Northern Italian menu. Bar. Semi-a la carte: dinner $17-$55. Specializes in veal, fettucine, linguine, fresh fish. Valet parking. Cr cds: A, C, D, MC, V.

★ ★ **PORT TACK.** *3190 W Sahara, 1¹/₄ mi west of the Strip.* 702/873-3345. Hrs: 11-5 am; early-bird dinner 4-6:30 pm. Closed major hols. Bar. Semi-a la carte: lunch $5.95-$9, dinner $10.95-$32.95. Child's meals. Specializes in steak, fresh fish. Salad bar. Valet parking. Nautical/Spanish decor. Cr cds: A, C, D, DS, MC, V.

D

✔★ **RICARDO'S.** *2380 E Tropicana (89119), east of the Strip.* 702/798-4515. Hrs: 11 am-11 pm; Fri & sat to midnight; Sun noon-10 pm. Closed Jan 1, Thanksgiving, Dec 25. Res accepted. Mexican menu. Bar. Semi-a la carte: lunch, dinner $5.95-$12.95. Buffet lunch $6.75. Specializes in fajitas, chicken Ricardo's. Guitarist, vocalist ex Mon. Parking. Old Mexican decor. Cr cds: A, C, D, DS, MC, V.

D

★ ★ ★ **RUTH'S CHRIS STEAK HOUSE.** *3900 Paradise Rd, suite 121 (89109), east of the Strip.* 702/791-7011. Hrs: 4:30-10:30 pm. Closed Thanksgiving, Dec 25. Res accepted. Bar. Wine list. A la carte entrees: dinner $18.95-$34.95. Specializes in steak. Parking. 3 dining rms, contemporary decor. Cr cds: A, C, D, DS, ER, MC, V.

D

✔★ **SHALIMAR.** *3900 Paradise Rd, in shopping mall, east of the Strip.* 702/796-0302. Hrs: 11:30 am-2 pm, 5:30-10 pm; Sat, Sun from 5:30 pm. Res accepted. Northern Indian menu. Serv bar. Buffet: lunch $5.95. A la carte entrees: dinner $7.95-$13.95. Specialties: chicken tandoori, lamb Shalimar, lamb & seafood curries. Contemporary decor. Cr cds: A, C, D, MC, V.

D

★ ★ ★ **SIR REGINALD'S.** *(See MGM Grand)* 702/891-1111. Hrs: 6-11 pm. Res accepted. Bar. Extensive wine list. Complete meals: dinner $32-$36. Specializes in prime steak. Parking. English ambience; elegant surroundings. Jacket. Cr cds: A, C, D, DS, ER, MC, V.

D

★ ★ ★ **SPAGO.** *3500 Las Vegas Blvd S, in Forum Shops at Caesars Palace Hotel.* 702/369-6300. Hrs: 11:30-12:30 am. Res accepted. Varied menu. Bar. Wine cellar. A la carte entrees: lunch $6.50-$12.50. Complete meals: dinner $30-$50. Specialties: pizza, chicken salad. Jazz pianist. Parking. Modern artwork. Art deco, wrought iron design. Counterpart of famous restaurant in West Hollywood. Cr cds: A, C, D, DS, ER, MC, V.

D

✔★ **STAGE DELI.** *3500 Las Vegas Blvd S (89109), in Forum Shops At Caesars Palace, on the Strip.* 702/893-4045. Hrs: 8 am-11 pm. Res accepted. Wine, beer. Semi-a la carte: bkfst $3.75-$7.95, lunch $5.35-$12.95, dinner $8.95-$13.95. Specializes in deli fare, potato pancakes, matzo ball soup. New York deli atmosphere; posters of Broadway shows. Cr cds: A, C, D, DS, ER, MC, V.

★ ★ ★ **TILLERMAN.** *2245 E Flamingo, east of the Strip.* 702/731-4036. Hrs: 5-11 pm. Closed major hols. Wine list. Semi-a la carte: dinner $14.95-$34.95. Specializes in fresh fish, steak, pasta. Parking. Atrium, garden, loft dining areas. Cr cds: A, C, D, DS, MC, V.

D

★ **TONY'S GRECO-ROMAN.** *220 W Sahara Ave, west of the Strip.* 702/384-5171. Hrs: 11 am-11 pm. Closed Thanksgiving. Res accepted. Greek, Italian menu. Wine, beer. Semi-a la carte: lunch $3.75-$7.95, dinner $7.50-$18.95. Parking. Cr cds: A, D, DS, MC, V.

★ **VINEYARD.** *3630 Maryland Pkwy, 1 mi east of the Strip.* 702/731-1606. Hrs: 11 am-10 pm; Fri, Sat to 11 pm. Closed major hols. Italian, Amer menu. Serv bar. Semi-a la carte: lunch $5.95-$11.95, dinner $6.95-$14.95. Complete meals: dinner for two, $25. Child's meals. Specializes in veal parmigiana, breast of chicken. Salad bar. Parking. Italian marketplace decor. Cr cds: A, D, MC, V.

SC

★ **YOLIE'S CHURRASCARIA.** *3900 Paradise Road, east of the Strip.* 702/794-0700. Hrs: 11:30 am-3 pm, 5:30-11 pm. Res required. Brazilian menu. Bar. Semi-a la carte: lunch $4.95-$10.95, dinner $12.95-$20.95. Child's meals. Specializes in steak, skewered lamb. Parking. Outdoor dining. Cr cds: A, C, D, DS, MC, V.

D

Los Angeles

Founded: 1781

Pop: 3,485,398

Elev: 330 feet

Time zone: Pacific

Area code: 213 (L.A.); 818 (San Fernando Valley); 310 (Long Beach, San Pedro, Santa Monica)

Imagine a sprawling formation made up of a thousand pieces from a thousand different jigsaw puzzles, illuminate it with klieg lights and flashing neon signs, garnish it with rhinestones, oranges and oil wells—and you have Los Angeles.

The little Spanish pueblo, begun as "the town of Our Lady the Queen of the Angels of Porciuncula," slumbered until 1846. In the treaty ending the Mexican War, the United States acquired California, and Los Angeles became a vigorous frontier community. Gold was discovered in 1848 in the foothills of the Sierra Nevada, and by 1849, the gold rush was on. For a time lawlessness became so prevalent that the city was referred to as Los Diablos—"the devils." In 1876, a rail line was completed from San Francisco to Los Angeles, and by 1885 the Santa Fe Railroad arrived from Chicago. With the introduction of the railroad, a tidal wave of immigration hit the city. A land boom developed by 1890, and the population reached 50,000. In the half century between 1890 and 1940, Los Angeles grew from 50,395 to 1,504,277—a gain of more than 2,500 percent.

Today, occupying a land area of 464 square miles, Los Angeles has spilled over from the plain into the canyons and foothills. It has spread out and around the surrounding independent cities and towns. Beyond its municipal lines, Los Angeles is hemmed in by almost 100 communities, frequently termed "suburbs in search of a city."

Business

Los Angeles is one of the nation's largest manufacturing and retail trade centers, as well as one of the top oil refining centers. Finance is big business in Los Angeles, and the city is the West Coast's leading financial center. Los Angeles is home to a large number of savings and loan associations and the headquarters for several major banks. Many insurance companies have their headquarters here as well.

A wide variety of products are manufactured here. Los Angeles is a leader in the production of machinery and equipment, electrical machinery, aerospace equipment, instruments and refined petroleum products. Other products manufactured are steel, iron, pottery, glassware, chemicals and trailers. More than 2,000 of the county's 20,000 factories are involved in industry.

Los Angeles has been called the filmmaking capital of the world. Many major movie studios are located in the area, as well as studios for the major television networks.

In addition to its manufacturing and retail might, Los Angeles is a major tourist center. In the latter half of the 1980s, almost 50 million people visited the Los Angeles area annually.

Convention Facilities

Set within a spacious, beautifully landscaped and lighted plaza, the Los Angeles Convention Center is one of the finest facilities in the world and continues to be expanded.

At plaza level, the main exhibition hall is vast. Within its immense 210,685-square-foot area is one of the largest column-free spaces to be found in any convention center. This area, 557 by 342 feet, can hold 3 football fields side by side. There are areas of the hall that can accommodate displays up to 25 feet in height. The exhibition hall's capacity is 17,000 persons for a meeting, 13,000 for a banquet or 1,150 exhibit booths. In addition, the room can be divided into 2 or 3 sections by the use of sliding, soundproof partitions. The north hall provides an additional 103,500 square feet of exhibition space.

A secondary, column-free hall is also located on the main floor. This room is large enough to accommodate 3,000 people for meetings, 2,000 for banquets or 125 exhibit booths.

The main floor also holds a 124-seat cocktail lounge, 220-seat restaurant, 450-seat cafeteria, 4 walk-in snack bars and 2 stand-up snack bars.

The mezzanine has 19 rooms of various sizes that are ideal for meetings, dinners, conferences or small exhibits. The smallest room can seat 12 people for a meeting or 20 for a meal, while the largest can seat 1,600 for a meeting and 800 for a meal.

The center is on a 31-acre site near the downtown hub of the city. Ten access ramps, adjacent to the building, connect with all six major freeways. There is parking for 4,000 cars.

There are more than 87,000 hotel rooms in the Greater Los Angeles area, 4,700 located downtown.

Sports and Recreation

For those interested in major league sports, Los Angeles is home to the Dodgers baseball team, the Lakers and Clippers basketball teams, the Raiders football team and Kings hockey team. The Rams football team and the California Angels baseball team play in nearby Anaheim.

Because of the moderate year-round temperatures, outdoor recreation is always in vogue. Parks are abundant in the Los Angeles metropolitan area. Thousands of acres of land are set aside for public enjoyment, with plenty of picnic areas, tennis courts, bridle paths, golf courses, swimming pools, nature trails, ball fields and playgrounds.

Entertainment

Performing arts events, including opera, ballet, drama and band concerts, are offered in Griffith Park at the Greek Theatre each season, from mid-June to late September.

Also during the summer, the Hollywood Bowl, one of the world's most beautiful amphitheaters, is the site of "Symphony Under the Stars," an eight-week schedule of outstanding music.

The Los Angeles Philharmonic thrills its audiences each year with superb performances and with visiting musicians at the Music Center of Los Angeles County. The Music Center is also home to the Los

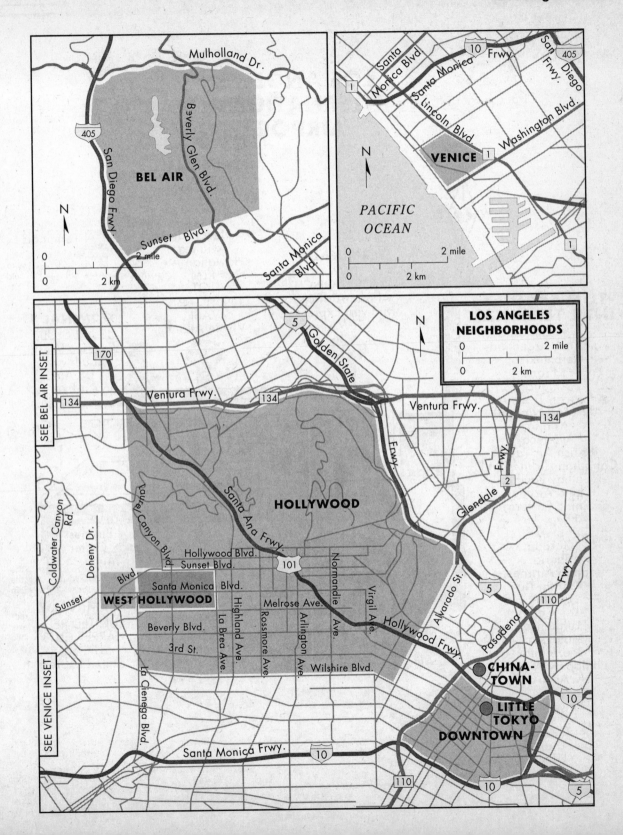

BEL AIR

Mulholland Dr.

Beverly Glen Blvd.

San Diego Frwy.

405

Sunset Blvd.

Santa Monica Blvd.

N

0
0   2 mile
     2 km

VENICE

Santa Monica Blvd.

Santa Monica Frwy.

Lincoln Blvd.

Washington Blvd.

San Diego Frwy.

10   405

1

N

PACIFIC OCEAN

0   2 mile
0   2 km

LOS ANGELES NEIGHBORHOODS

N

0   2 mile
0   2 km

SEE BEL AIR INSET

SEE VENICE INSET

5

170

134

Golden State

Ventura Frwy.

134

Ventura Frwy.

134

2

Glendale Frwy.

Coldwater Canyon Rd.

Doheny Dr.

Laurel Canyon Blvd.

Santa Ana Frwy.

HOLLYWOOD

101

Normandie Ave.

Virgil Ave.

Hollywood Frwy.

5

Pasadena Frwy.

110

Sunset

Blvd.

Hollywood Blvd.
Sunset Blvd.

Santa Monica Blvd.

WEST HOLLYWOOD

Melrose Ave.

Highland Ave.

La Brea Ave.

Rossmore Ave.

Arlington Ave.

Beverly Blvd.

3rd St.

La Cienega Blvd.

Wilshire Blvd.

Alvarado St.

CHINA-TOWN

LITTLE TOKYO

DOWNTOWN

10

Santa Monica Frwy.

10

110

10

5

LOS ANGELES INTERNATIONAL AIRPORT

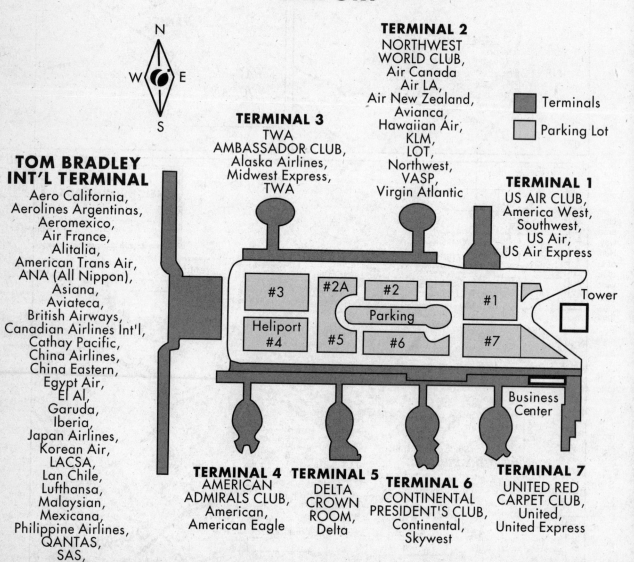

TERMINAL 2
NORTHWEST
WORLD CLUB,
Air Canada
Air LA,
Air New Zealand,
Avianca,
Hawaiian Air,
KLM,
LOT,
Northwest,
VASP,
Virgin Atlantic

Terminals
Parking Lot

TERMINAL 3
TWA
AMBASSADOR CLUB,
Alaska Airlines,
Midwest Express,
TWA

TERMINAL 1
US AIR CLUB,
America West,
Southwest,
US Air,
US Air Express

**TOM BRADLEY
INT'L TERMINAL**
Aero California,
Aerolines Argentinas,
Aeromexico,
Air France,
Alitalia,
American Trans Air,
ANA (All Nippon),
Asiana,
Aviateca,
British Airways,
Canadian Airlines Int'l,
Cathay Pacific,
China Airlines,
China Eastern,
Egypt Air,
El Al,
Garuda,
Iberia,
Japan Airlines,
Korean Air,
LACSA,
Lan Chile,
Lufthansa,
Malaysian,
Mexicana,
Philippine Airlines,
QANTAS,
SAS,
Singapore,
Swissair,
TACA,
Thai,
UTA,
VARIG

#3

#2A   #2

Parking

Heliport
#4   #5   #6

#1

Tower

#7

Business
Center

TERMINAL 4
AMERICAN
ADMIRALS CLUB,
American,
American Eagle

TERMINAL 5
DELTA
CROWN
ROOM,
Delta

TERMINAL 6
CONTINENTAL
PRESIDENT'S CLUB,
Continental,
Skywest

TERMINAL 7
UNITED RED
CARPET CLUB,
United,
United Express

Angeles Music Center Opera, which presents performances from early September to June.

In addition, there are numerous professional, repertory, neighborhood and campus theatrical productions, and all forms of drama and comedy are available.

Nightlife in the city ranges from a simple dinner or dinner theater to the most extravagant and lavish nightclub entertainment. Consult *Los Angeles Magazine*, available at newsstands, for up-to-date information.

Historical Areas

Heritage Square, a major restoration site in the Los Angeles area, is a park-like strip of land surrounded by many Victorian buildings. The first two buildings in the square were the Hale house and Valley Knudsen Garden-residence. Hale house, built in 1885, was moved to the square in 1970. Little of the beautiful ornamentation and detail of the original residence was changed. The Valley Knudsen Garden-residence was dedicated in 1971. The building is Second Empire in style, one of the last examples of a mansard-roofed house left in the Los Angeles area.

One of the oldest of Los Angeles' many missions is the Mission San Gabriel Arcángel, built in 1771. Although not open to the public due to earthquake damage, the mission possesses an exceptional collection of relics. The Mission San Fernando Rey de España, founded in 1797, has been restored and contains collections of Native American artifacts, furniture, woodcarvings and gold-leaf altars.

El Pueblo de Los Angeles Historic Park marks the area where the city was founded by settlers from Mission San Gabriel. Much of the area has already been restored, but additional restorations are underway. The Plaza, the center of the original pueblo, has been preserved. Here, too, is Nuestra Señora La Reina de Los Angeles, the first church of Los Angeles, from which the city takes its name and still the center of an active parish. The church contains old statuary and stained-glass windows. Also preserved is Olvera Street, once called "the walk of angels," an authentic and picturesque Mexican street market. There are several annual celebrations here, including the Blessing of Animals held the Saturday before Easter.

The Southwest Museum exhibits early handicrafts and displays on the history of the Native American. Near the museum is Casa de Adobe, a replica of a typical ranch home of 19th-century Spanish California.

The Natural History Museum of Los Angeles County exhibits natural history and early regional and state history; fossil remains of prehistoric animals; ethnological and archeological collections; habitat groups of North American and African mammals and birds; and mineral and marine biology collections.

The Lummis Home and Garden State Historical Monument is the picturesque home of Charles F. Lummis, author, historian, librarian and archaeologist. Just east of the city, in Pasadena, is the Gamble House, a California bungalow-style house built by Henry and Charles Greene.

Sightseeing

Los Angeles is the city of movie and television magic. Some of the most popular movies and television shows were filmed on the back lots or in the confines of the studios located here. CBS, Universal and Paramount conduct tours through their lots, studios and production areas. One of Los Angeles' most famous sites is the forecourt of Mann's Chinese Theatre, where the footprints of movie stars are set in cement.

Chinatown is a must for any visitor to this city. The tourist will find unusual shops and Chinese cafes on the "Street of the Golden Palace" and can enjoy an excellent dinner and a walking tour.

The partially excavated Rancho La Brea Tar Pits contain large numbers of prehistoric remains. Fossils and life-size statues of the giant beasts are on display at the George C. Page Museum of La Brea Discoveries Museum.

There is nothing that cannot be bought or rented in Los Angeles. For specialized shopping there is Little Santa Monica, which is lined with antique stores, Robertson Boulevard for furniture showrooms,

Sunset Plaza, and of course Rodeo Drive, synonymous with opulence, luxury and extravagance.

The city's geographic scope makes a car almost essential for sightseeing in areas other than the downtown section. Parking facilities are ample, and the freeways make travel relatively simple.

City Environs

Southern California's coastline is one long chain of beautiful beaches. No Los Angeles vacation is complete without walking along the shore, romping in the surf or at least gazing from the car window at the ocean. Malibu, Santa Monica, Ocean Park, Venice, Manhattan, Redondo and Long Beach are some of the more popular beaches.

Inland, west of the Sierra Nevadas, lies a montage of the nation's most beautiful national parks—Yosemite, Kings Canyon and Sequoia. Within them are clear lakes, giant sequoias, fields of flowers and towering cliffs.

East of the Sierras, in the high country, one can camp, explore ghost towns or fish for trout in one of the area's 2,000 lakes and streams.

In Coachella Valley, southeast of Los Angeles, is the famous Palm Springs area. The resort has a dry, sunny climate, thousands of swimming pools and more than 20 golf courses.

General References

Founded: 1781 **Pop:** 3,485,398 **Elev:** 330 feet **Time zone:** Pacific
Area code: 213 (L.A.); 818 (San Fernando Valley); 310 (Long Beach, San Pedro, Santa Monica)

Phone Numbers

POLICE, FIRE & AMBULANCE: 911
FBI: 310/477-6565
POISON CONTROL CENTER: 213/222-3212
TIME: 213/853-1212   **WEATHER:** 213/554-1212

Information Sources

Los Angeles Convention and Visitors Bureau, 633 W Fifth St, Ste. #6000, 90071; 213/624-7300.
Los Angeles Chamber of Commerce, 404 S Bixel St, 90017; 213/629-0602.
City Recreation & Parks Dept, 213/485-5555.

Transportation

AIRLINES: Aerolineas Argentinas; Aeromexico; Air Canada; Air France; Air Jamaica; Air New Zealand; Alaska; Alitalia; All Nippon Airways; American; America West; Avianca (Colombia); Aviateca (Guatamala); British Airways; CAAC (China); Canadian; China (Taiwan); Continental; Delta; El Al (Israel); Garuda (Indonesia); Hawaiian; Iberia (Spain); Japan; KLM (Netherlands); Korean; LACSA (Costa Rica); Lan Chile; LOT Polish; Lufthansa (Germany); Malaysian; Mexicana; Northwest; Philippine; QANTAS (Australia); SAS (Scandinavian); Singapore; Southwest; Swissair; TACA (El Salvador); Thai; TWA; United; USAir; UTA (France); Varig (Brazil); and other commuter and regional airlines. For the most current airline schedules and information consult the *Official Airline Guide,* published twice monthly.
AIRPORT: Los Angeles International (LAX), 310/646-5252.
CAR RENTAL AGENCIES: (See Toll-Free Numbers) Avis 310/646-5600; Budget 310/645-4500; Dollar 310/645-9333; Hertz 310/646-4861; National 310/670-4950.

PUBLIC TRANSPORTATION: Rapid Transit Department 213/626-4455.
RAILROAD PASSENGER SERVICE: Amtrak 800/872-7245.

Newspaper

Los Angeles Times.

Convention Facility

Los Angeles Convention Center, 1201 S Figueroa St, 213/741-1151.

Sports & Recreation

Major Sports Facilities
Anaheim Stadium, 2000 State College Blvd, Anaheim (Angels, baseball, 714/634-2000; Rams, football, 714/937-6767).
Dodger Stadium, 1000 Elysian Park Ave, 213/224-1491 (Dodgers, baseball).
The Great Western Forum, 3900 W Manchester Blvd, Inglewood, 310/673-1300 (Kings, hockey; Lakers, basketball).
Los Angeles Memorial Coliseum & Sports Arena, Exposition Park, 3939 S Figueroa St, 213/747-7111 (Raiders, football, 310/322-5901; Clippers, basketball, 213/748-0500; also collegiate football).

Racetracks
Hollywood Park, Century Blvd & Prairie Ave, Inglewood, 310/419-1500.
Los Alamitos Race Course, 4961 Katella Ave, Los Alamitos, 714/236-4400 or 714/995-1234.
Santa Anita Park, 285 W Huntington Dr, Arcadia, 818/574-7223.

Cultural Facilities

Theaters
Ahmanson Theatre, 135 N Grand Ave, 213/972-7211.
Dorothy Chandler Pavilion, 135 N Grand Ave, 213/972-7211.
Greek Theatre, 2700 N Vermont, Griffith Park, 213/665-1927.
Mark Taper Forum, 135 N Grand Ave, 213/972-7211.
Pantages Theatre, 6233 Hollywood Blvd, 213/468-1700.
Shubert Theatre, 2020 Avenue of the Stars, 310/201-1500.
Universal Amphitheatre, 100 Universal City Plaza, Universal City, 818/777-3931.

Concert Halls
Hollywood Bowl, 2301 N Highland Ave, Hollywood, 213/850-2000.
Music Center of Los Angeles County, 135 N Grand Ave, at 1st St, 213/972-7211.

Museums
Cabrillo Marine Museum, 3720 Stephen White Dr, San Pedro, 310/548-7562.
California Museum of Science and Industry, 700 State Dr, Exposition Park, 213/744-7400.
George C. Page Museum of La Brea Discoveries, 5801 Wilshire Blvd, Hancock Park, 213/857-6311 or 213/936-2230.
Griffith Observatory and Planetarium, Griffith Park, 2800 E Observatory Rd, 818/997-3624 (Laserium) or 213/664-1191 (planetarium).
Hollywood Wax Museum, 6767 Hollywood Blvd, Hollywood, 213/462-8860.
Los Angeles Children's Museum, 310 N Main St, 213/687-8800.
Max Factor Museum of Beauty, 1666 N Highland Ave, Hollywood, 213/463-6668.
Movieland Wax Museum, 7711 Beach Blvd, Buena Park, 714/522-1155.

Natural History Museum of Los Angeles County, 900 Exposition Blvd, Exposition Park, 213/744-3414 or -3466.
Southwest Museum, 234 Museum Dr, at Marmion Way, 213/221-2163.
Wells Fargo History Museum, 333 S Grand Ave, Plaza Level, 213/253-7166.

Art Museums and Galleries
Armand Hammer Museum of Art and Cultural Center, 10889 Wilshire Blvd, 310/443-7000.
Huntington Library, Art Collection and Botanical Gardens, 1151 Oxford Rd, San Marino, 818/405-2100.
J. Paul Getty Museum, 17985 W Pacific Coast Hwy, Malibu, 310/458-2003.
Junior Arts Center, 4814 Hollywood Blvd, in Barnsdall Art Park, 213/485-4474.
Los Angeles County Museum of Art, 5905 Wilshire Blvd, 213/857-6111 or -6000.
Museum of Contemporary Art (MOCA), 250 S Grand Ave, 213/621-2766.
Norton Simon Museum of Art, 411 W Colorado Blvd, Pasadena, 818/449-6840.
Wight Art Gallery, 405 Hilgard Ave, UCLA, 310/825-9345.

Points of Interest

Historical
Avila Adobe, El Pueblo de Los Angeles Historic Park, 213/628-1274.
El Pueblo de Los Angeles Historic Park, 622 N Main, 213/629-3101.
Lummis Home and Garden State Historical Monument, 200 E Ave 43, 213/222-0546.
Mission San Fernando Rey de España, 15151 San Fernando Mission Blvd, San Fernando, 818/361-0186.
Nuestra Señora La Reina de Los Angeles, El Pueblo de Los Angeles Historic Park, 213/629-3101.
Old Plaza Firehouse, El Pueblo de Los Angeles Historic Park, 213/628-1274.
Olvera Street, El Pueblo de Los Angeles Historic Park, 213/628-1274.
The Plaza, Sunset Blvd & Los Angeles St.
Travel Town, Forest Lawn and Zoo Drs, Griffith Park, 213/662-5874.
Will Rogers State Historic Park, 14253 Sunset Blvd, Pacific Palisades, 310/454-8212.

Other Attractions
ARCO Plaza, 515 S Flower St, 213/625-2132.
Catalina Island, approx 22 mi offshore of San Pedro, 310/510-1520.
CBS Television City, 7800 Beverly Blvd, at Fairfax Ave, 213/852-2624.
Chinatown, N Broadway near College St.
City Hall, 200 N Spring St, 213/485-4423.
Crystal Cathedral, 12141 Lewis St, Garden Grove, 714/971-4013.
Descanso Gardens, 1418 Descanso Dr, La Cañada, Flintridge, 818/952-4400.
Disneyland, 26 mi S on Harbor Blvd, off Santa Ana Frwy, Anaheim, 714/999-4565.
Elysian Park, near intersection of Pasadena & Golden State Frwys.
Exposition Park, Figueroa St & Exposition Blvd.
Fisherman's Village, 13755 Fiji Way, Marina del Rey, 310/823-5411.
Griffith Park, N end of Vermont Ave, bordered by Ventura Frwy on N, Golden State Frwy on E, Los Feliz Blvd entrances on S, 213/665-5188.
Hall of Justice, 211 W Temple St.

Knott's Berry Farm, 8039 Beach Blvd, Buena Park, 714/220-5200.

Little Tokyo, 1st St between Main & San Pedro Sts.

Los Angeles Mall, Spring St, across from city hall.

Los Angeles State and County Arboretum, 301 N Baldwin Ave, Arcadia, 818/821-3222.

Los Angeles Zoo, 5333 Zoo Dr, Griffith Park, 213/666-4090.

Mann's Chinese Theatre, 6925 Hollywood Blvd, Hollywood, 213/464-8111.

NBC Studios, 3000 W Alameda Ave, Burbank, 818/840-3537.

Paramount Film and Television Studios, 5555 Melrose Ave, 213/956-5575.

San Antonio Winery, 737 Lamar St, 213/223-1401.

Six Flags Magic Mountain, 26101 Magic Mt Pkwy, Valencia, 805/255-4111.

South Coast Botanic Garden, 26300 Crenshaw Blvd, Palos Verdes Peninsula, 310/544-6815.

Sunset Strip, Sunset Blvd.

UCLA Botanical Garden, Hilgard & Le Conte Aves, 310/825-3620.

Universal Studios Hollywood, 100 Universal City Plaza, Universal City, 818/777-1000.

Watts Towers, 1727 E 107th St, Watts, 213/847-4646.

World Trade Center, 350 S Figueroa St, 213/489-3337.

Sightseeing Tours

Gray Line bus tours, 340 N Camden, Beverly Hills 90210; 213/856-5900.

Oskar J's, 4334 Woodman Ave, Sherman Oaks 91423; 818/501-2217.

Annual Events

Tournament of Roses Parade and Rose Bowl Game, Pasadena. Jan 1.

Chinese New Year, Jan or Feb.

Easter Sunrise Services, Hollywood Bowl.

Hanamatsuri, Japanese Village Plaza. Wkend Apr.

Cinco de Mayo Celebration, El Pueblo de Los Angeles Historic Park. May 5.

Asian Cultural Festival, West Los Angeles Mall. Sat mid-July.

Nisei Week, Little Toyko. Aug.

Los Angeles County Fair, Los Angeles County Fairgrounds, Pomona. Mid-Sept-early Oct.

City Neighborhoods

Many of the restaurants, unrated dining establishments and some lodgings listed under Los Angeles include neighborhoods as well as exact street addresses. A map showing these neighborhoods can be found immediately following the city introduction. Geographic descriptions of these areas are given, followed by a table of restaurants arranged by neighborhood.

Bel Air: West of Downtown; south of Mulholland Dr, west of Beverly Hills, north of the University of California Los Angeles (UCLA) campus and east of the San Diego Frwy (I-405).

Chinatown: Directly north of Downtown; south of Bernard St, west of N Broadway, north of College St and east of Hill St.

Downtown: South of the Hollywood Frwy (US 101), west of Golden State Frwy (I-5), north of Santa Monica Frwy (I-10) and east of the Pasadena Frwy (CA 110). **North of Downtown:** North of US 101. **South of Downtown:** South of I-10. **West of Downtown:** West of CA 110.

Hollywood: Area northwest of Downtown; south of Mulholland Dr, Universal City and the Ventura Frwy (CA 134), west of the Golden State Frwy (I-5) and Alvarado St (CA 2), north of Wilshire Blvd and east of La Cienega Blvd.

Little Tokyo: Area of Downtown south of 1st St, west of Central Ave, north of 3rd St and east of San Pedro St.

Venice: Oceanfront area south of Santa Monica, west of Lincoln Blvd (CA 1) and north of Washington St.

West Hollywood: Area south and north of Santa Monica Blvd, between Doheny Dr on the west and La Brea Ave on the east.

Lodgings and Food

LOS ANGELES RESTAURANTS BY NEIGHBORHOOD AREAS

(For full description, see alphabetical listings under Restaurants; also see restaurants listed under HOLLYWOOD.)

BEL AIR

Bel-Air Dining Room (Bel-Air Hotel). 701 Stone Canyon Rd

Four Oaks. 2181 N Beverly Glen

CHINATOWN

Little Joe's. 900 N Broadway

Ocean Seafood. 747 N Broadway

DOWNTOWN

Bernard's (Biltmore Hotel). 506 S Grand Ave

Phillipe The Original. 1001 N Alameda St

Rex II Ristorante. 617 S Olive St

The Tower. 1150 S Olive St

NORTH OF DOWNTOWN

Les Freres Taix. 1911 Sunset Blvd

Tam-O-Shanter Inn. 2980 Los Feliz Blvd

WEST OF DOWNTOWN

Campanile. 624 S La Brea Ave

Cassell's. 3266 W 6th St

Gardens (Four Seasons Hotel). 300 S Doheny Dr

Hard Rock Cafe. 8600 Beverly Blvd

J.W.'s (J.W. Marriott At Century City). 2151 Avenue of the Stars

La Chaumiere (Century Plaza Hotel & Tower). 2025 Ave of the Stars

Locanda Veneta. 8638 W Third St

Madeo. 8897 Beverly Blvd

Orleans. 11705 National Blvd

Primi. 10543 W Pico Blvd

Sisley Italian Kitchen. 10800 W Pico Blvd

Note: *When a listing is located in a town that does not have its own city heading, it will appear under the city nearest to its location. In these cases, the address and town appear in parenthesis immediately following the name of the establishment.*

Motels

✔★ **BEST WESTERN EXECUTIVE MOTOR INN MID-WIL-SHIRE.** *603 S New Hampshire Ave (90005), west of downtown.* 213/385-4444. 90 rms, 5 story. July-Aug: S, D $59-$75; each addl $3; under 12 free; wkend plans; lower rates rest of yr. Crib free. TV; cable. Indoor pool. Complimentary continental bkfst 7-9 am. Ck-out noon. Coin lndry. Meeting rm. Valet serv. Sundries. Exercise equipt; treadmill, stair machine, whirlpool, sauna. Refrigerators. Cr cds: A, D, DS, JCB, MC, V.

★★ **RESIDENCE INN BY MARRIOTT.** *(1700 N Sepulveda Blvd, Manhattan Beach 90266) CA 405 to Rosecrans exit.* 310/546-

7627. 176 kit. suites, 2 story. S $115-$150; D $150-$190; each addl $10; under 12 free; wkly, monthly rates. Crib free. Pet accepted, some restrictions. TV; cable, in-rm movies. Heated pool; whirlpool. Complimentary continental bkfst. Restaurant nearby. Ck-out noon. Meeting rm. Valet serv. Free airport transportation. Balconies. Cr cds: A, C, D, DS, JCB, MC, V.

Motor Hotels

★★ **CENTURY CITY INN.** *10330 W Olympic Blvd (90064), west of downtown.* 310/553-1000; res: 800/553-1005 800/553-3253 (CAN); FAX 310/277-1633. 48 rms, 3 story, 14 suites. S $94-$109; D $94-$116; each addl $10; suites $109-$129; under 7 free; wkly rates. Crib free. Valet parking $5.50. TV; cable, in-rm movies. Complimentary continental bkfst. Ck-out noon. Bellhops. Valet serv. Lighted tennis privileges. Health club privileges. Refrigerators, bathrm phones, in-rm whirlpools. Cr cds: A, D, DS, MC, V.

★★ **COURTYARD BY MARRIOTT.** *10320 W Olympic Blvd (90064), west of downtown.* 310/556-2777; FAX 310/203-0563. 133 rms, 4 story. S $99-$119; D $109-$129; each addl $10; suites $125-$155; wkend rates. TV; cable. Coffee in rms. Restaurant 6-10:30 am, 5:30-10 pm. Bar 5 pm-midnight. Ck-out noon. Meeting rms. Bellhops. Valet serv. Free covered parking. Free shuttle to Beverly Hills, Century City. Exercise equipt; weights, bicycles, whirlpool. Minibars. Balconies. Cr cds: A, C, D, DS, JCB, MC, V.

✔★ **HOLIDAY INN DOWNTOWN.** *750 Garland Ave (90017), downtown.* 213/628-5242; FAX 213/628-1201. 205 rms, 6 story. S, D $89-$129; under 18 free. Crib free. TV; cable. Pool. Complimenatry coffee in rms. Restaurant 6 am-2 pm, 5-10 pm. Rm serv. Bar 5-11 pm. Ck-out noon. Coin lndry. Meeting rms. Bellhops. Valet serv. Airport transportation. Cr cds: A, C, D, DS, JCB, MC, V.

★★ **MIYAKO INN & SPA.** *328 E First St (90012), in Little Tokyo.* 213/617-2000; res: 800/228-6596; FAX 213/617-2700. 174 rms, 11 story. S $89-$102; D $99-$112; under 12 free. Covered parking $6.60. TV; cable. Restaurants 7 am-10 pm. Rm serv. Bar 5 pm-2 am; entertainment. Ck-out noon. Coin lndry. Meeting rms. Bellhops. Valet serv. Whirlpool, sauna, steam rm. Japanese-style massage. Some refrigerators. In heart of Little Tokyo. Cr cds: A, C, D, DS, JCB, MC, V.

Hotels

★★ **BARNABEY'S.** *(3501 Sepulveda Blvd, Manhattan Beach 90266) S via I-405, Rosecrans exit.* 310/545-8466; res: 800/552-5285 (US), 800/851-7678 (CAN); FAX 310/545-8621. 126 rms, 3 story. S $129-$144; D $144-$159; suites $149-$450; under 12 free; hol, wkend rates. Crib $15. Garage parking $4; valet. TV. Indoor/outdoor pool. Complimentary full bkfst. Complimentary coffee in rms. Restaurant 6:30 am-11 pm. Bar 11 am-midnight; entertainment Tues-Sat. Ck-out noon. Meeting rms. Gift shop. Free airport transportation. European-style decor; antiques. Cr cds: A, C, D, DS, MC, V.

★★ **BEL AGE.** *1020 N San Vicente (90069), in West Hollywood.* 310/854-1111; FAX 310/854-0926. 200 suites, 8 story. S, D $195-$500; each addl $25; under 12 free; wkend rates. Valet parking $16. TV; in-rm movies avail. Heated pool; poolside serv. Restaurants 7 am-9 pm, Thurs-Sat to 1 am. Rm serv 24 hrs. Bar 11-2 am; jazz Tues-Sat. Ck-out 1 pm. Convention facilities. Concierge. Shopping arcade. Barber, beauty shops. Exercise rm. Bathrm phones, minibars, wet bars. Private patios, balconies. Complimentary fresh fruit, mineral water upon arrival. Complimentary shoeshine. Cr cds: A, C, D, JCB, MC, V.

⬚ ⬚ ⬚ ⬚

★ ★ ★ ★ **BEL-AIR.** *701 Stone Canyon Rd (90077), in Bel Air.* 310/472-1211; FAX 310/476-5890. 92 rms, some kits. S $245-$395; D $275-$435; suites $550-$2,000. TV; cable, in-rm movies avail. Heated pool; poolside serv, lifeguard. Restaurant (see BEL-AIR DINING ROOM). Rm serv 24 hrs. Bar 10-2 am; entertainment. Ck-out 1 pm. Meeting rms. Concierge. Valet parking. Airport transportation. Fitness Center in site of former Marilyn Monroe Suite open to guests 24 hrs with private key access; stair machines, treadmills, bicycles. Bathrm phones; some wood-burning fireplaces. Private patios. Vintage resort hotel; individually decorated rms. Lush gardens, serene atmosphere. Tea service on arrival. Cr cds: A, C, D, JCB, MC, V.

⬚ ⬚ ⬚ ⬚

★ ★ ★ **BEVERLY PLAZA.** *8384 W 3rd St (90048), west of downtown.* 213/658-6600; res: 800/624-6835 (exc CA); FAX 213/653-3464. 98 rms, 5 story. S $98-$158; D $98-$168; each addl $10; under 12 free. TV; cable, in-rm movies. Valet parking. Heated pool; poolside serv. Restaurant 6:30 am-11 pm. Rm serv 24 hrs. Bar 11 am-midnight. Ck-out noon. Exercise equipt; weights, bicycles, whirlpool, sauna. Cr cds: A, C, D, DS, MC, V.

⬚ ⬚ ⬚ ⬚ ⬚ SC

★ ★ ★ ★ **BILTMORE.** *506 S Grand Ave (90071), downtown.* 213/624-1011; res: 800/245-8673; FAX 213/612-1545. 689 rms, 12 story. S $140-$230; D $160-$245; each addl $30; suites $390-$1,800; under 12 free; wknd package plan. Valet parking $17.50. Heated pool. TV; cable. Restaurants 6:30 am-11 pm (also see BERNARD'S). Rm serv 24 hrs. Bars 11-2 am. Ck-out noon. Convention facilities. Free shuttle service throughout downtown Los Angeles. Exercise equipt; weights, bicycles, sauna. Wet bar in most suites. Some bathrm phones. Historic landmark; opened 1923. Italian Renaissance architecture. *LUXURY LEVEL : CLUB FLOOR.* 65 rms, 6 suites, 2 floors. S $230; D $245. Concierge. Private lounge, honor bar. Minibars. Complimentary continental bkfst, refreshments, newspaper. Cr cds: A, C, D, ER, JCB, MC, V.

⬚ ⬚ ⬚ ⬚

★ ★ ★ ★ **CENTURY PLAZA HOTEL & TOWER.** *2025 Ave of the Stars (90067), in Century City, west of downtown.* 310/277-2000; FAX 310/551-3355. 1,072 rms, 19-30 story. S $165; D $190; each addl $25; suites $250-$1,100. Tower: S $220; D $245; suites $900-$3,000; each addl $25; under 18 free. TV. Heated pool; poolside serv in summer. Restaurant 6-1 am (also see LA CHAUMIERE). Rm serv 24 hrs. 3 bars 11-2 am; entertainment. Ck-out 1 pm. Lndry facilities 24 hrs. Convention facilities. Concierge. Barber, beauty shop. Valet parking. Airport transportation avail. Exercise equipt; weight machine, bicycles, whirlpool. Tennis & health club privileges adj. Bathrm phones. Balconies. Modern hotel on 10 landscaped acres; Japanese garden. Cr cds: A, C, D, DS, ER, JCB, MC, V.

⬚ ⬚ ⬚ ⬚ ⬚ SC

★ ★ **CHATEAU MARMONT.** *8221 Sunset Blvd (90046), in West Hollywood.* 213/656-1010; FAX 213/655-5311. 63 rms, 7 story, 54 kits. S, D $170; suites $225-$295; cottages, kits. $240; monthly rates. Pet accepted. TV; cable, in-rm movies avail. Heated pool; poolside serv. Restaurant 6-2 am. Rm serv 24 hrs. Ck-out noon. Garage, free valet parking. Refrigerators, minibars. Private patios, balconies. Neo-Gothic chateau-style building; old Hollywood landmark. Cr cds: A, C, D, MC, V.

⬚ ⬚ ⬚

★ ★ ★ ★ **FOUR SEASONS.** *300 S Doheny Dr (90048), west of downtown.* 310/273-2222; FAX 310/859-3824. 285 rms, 16 story. S $235-$315; D $260-$340; suites $350-$2,000; family, wknd rates. TV; cable. Pool; poolside serv, lifeguard. Restaurant 6:30 am-11:30 pm (also see GARDENS). Traditional afternoon tea. Rm serv 24 hrs. Bar 11-1 am; pianist. Ck-out 1 pm. Convention facilities. Concierge 24 hrs. Gift shop. Underground parking. Complimentary limo to Beverly Hills,

Century City. Tennis privileges. 18-hole golf privileges. Exercise rm; instructor, weights, bicycles, whirlpool. Massage. Bathrm phones, refrigerators. Balconies. Distinctly Californian; understated elegance. Cr cds: A, C, D, ER, JCB, MC, V.

⬚ ⬚ ⬚ ⬚ ⬚ ⬚ ⬚

★ ★ ★ **HILTON & TOWERS.** *930 Wilshire Blvd (90017), downtown.* 213/629-4321; FAX 213/488-9869. 900 rms, 16 story. S $139-$209; D $159-$229; each addl $20; suites $375-$575; family rates. Crib free. Garage $16.50. TV; cable. Heated pool; poolside serv. Restaurants 6 am-11 pm. Bar 10-2 am; pianist. Ck-out noon. Convention facilities. Concierge. Shopping arcade. Barber, beauty shop. Exercise equipt; weight machines, bicycles. Minibars. Game rm. *LUXURY LEVEL : TOWERS.* 93 rms, 4 suites, 2 floors. S $179-$229; D $199-$249; suites $425-$610. Honor bar. Complimentary bkfst, refreshments. Cr cds: A, C, D, DS, ER, JCB, MC, V.

⬚ ⬚ ⬚ ⬚ ⬚ SC

★ ★ ★ **HILTON & TOWERS, UNIVERSAL CITY.** *(555 Universal Terrace Pkwy, Universal City 91608) US 101, Lankershim Blvd.* 818/506-2500; FAX 818/509-2058. 446 units, 24 story, 26 suites. S, D $145-$175; each addl $20; suites $250-$1,395; children free with parent; monthly rates. Crib free. Garage parking $9, valet $11.50. TV; cable. Heated pool; poolside serv. Restaurant 6:30 am-11 pm. Rm serv 24 hrs. Bar 11-1:30 am; pianist. Ck-out noon. Convention facilities. Concierge. Gift shop. Barber, beauty salon. Airport transportation avail. Exercise equipt; weight machine, bicycles, whirlpool, steam rm. Bathrm phones, minibars. Wet bar in suites. Some suites with vaulted, skylit ceiling; panoramic view of city. *LUXURY LEVEL : TOWERS.* 36 rms, 8 suites, 2 floors. S, D $170-$200; suites $250-$665. Concierge. Privage lounge, honor bar. Complimentary continental bkfst, refreshments. Cr cds: A, C, D, DS, ER, JCB, MC, V.

⬚ ⬚ ⬚ ⬚ ⬚ SC

✔ ★ ★ **HOLIDAY INN BRENTWOOD-BEL AIR.** *170 N Church Lane (90049), I-405 Sunset Blvd exit, west of downtown.* 310/476-6411; FAX 310/472-1157. 211 rms, 17 story. S, D $99-$139; each addl $10; suites $210; under 19 free; hol, wkend, wkly rates; higher rates special events; some lower rates in winter. Crib free. Pet accepted, some restrictions. TV; cable. Heated pool; poolside serv. Restaurant 6 am-11 pm. Bar. Ck-out noon. Coin lndry. Meeting rms. Concierge. Exercise equipt; weight machine, bicycles, whirlpool. Refrigerators avail. Balconies. Cr cds: A, C, D, DS, JCB, MC, V.

⬚ ⬚ ⬚ ⬚ ⬚ ⬚ SC

★ ★ ★ **HOTEL NIKKO AT BEVERLY HILLS.** *465 S La Cienega Blvd (90048), N of Wilshire Blvd, La Cienega at Burton Way.* 310/247-0400; res: 800/645-5687; FAX 310/247-0315. 304 units, 7 story, 51 suites. S $250-$295; D $275-$475; each addl $25; suites $450-$1,600; under 12 free; wknd rates. Crib free. TV; cable. Complimentary coffee in rms. Restaurants 6:30 am-11 pm. Rm serv 24 hrs. Lobby bar 11:30-1 am; entertainment. Ck-out 1 pm. Concierge. Gift shop. Free garage parking. Tennis privileges. Golf privileges. Exercise rm; instructor, weight machine, bicycles. Masseuse. Complete health club. Bathrm phones. Japanese soaking tubs. Stocked minibars. Balconies. Blend of bold American architecture and traditional Japanese simplicity. Cr cds: A, C, D, DS, JCB, MC, V.

⬚ ⬚ ⬚ ⬚ ⬚

★ ★ ★ **HOTEL SOFITEL MA MAISON.** *8555 Beverly Blvd (90048), at La Cienega, west of downtown.* 310/278-5444; res: 800/221-4542; FAX 310/657-2816. 311 rms, 10 story. S, D $150-$450; each addl $20; suites $200-$450; under 18 free; wknd rates. Crib free. Valet parking $14. TV; cable. Heated pool; poolside serv. Restaurant 6 am-midnight. Rm serv 24 hrs. Bar from 11 am; entertainment. Ck-out 1 pm. Convention facilities. Concierge. Shopping arcade. Barber, beauty shop. Tennis privileges. Exercise equipt; weight machines, bicycles. Bathrm phones, refrigerators, minibars, wet bars. Balconies. Contemporary Mediterranean-style hotel features a blend of French and Californian cultures. Cr cds: A, C, D, JCB, MC, V.

⬚ ⬚ ⬚ ⬚ ⬚

★ ★ ★ **HYATT REGENCY.** *711 S Hope St (90017), downtown.* 213/683-1234; FAX 213/629-3230. 485 rms, 24 story. S $149-$195; D $174-$220; each addl $25; suites $225-$550; under 18 free; wkend, package plans. Crib free. Garage parking; valet $13.50. TV; cable. Restaurants 6:30 am-11 pm. Bar 11:30-1 am; entertainment. Ck-out noon. Convention facilities. Concierge. Shopping arcade. Barber, beauty shop. Airport transportation. Exercise equipt; weights, bicycles, whirlpool. Health club privileges. Some minibars. *LUXURY LEVEL :* **REGENCY CLUB.** 52 rms, 4 suites, 2 floors. S $214; D $239. Private lounge, honor bar. Complimentary continental bkfst, refreshments, newspaper. Cr cds: A, C, D, DS, ER, JCB, MC, V.

D ⊁ ⊠ ⊠ 🔥 SC

★ ★ ★ ★ **J.W. MARRIOTT AT CENTURY CITY.** *2151 Avenue of the Stars (90067), west of downtown.* 310/277-2777; FAX 310/785-9240. 367 rms, 17 story, 189 suites. S $205-$225; D $215-$235; suites $275-$2,500; under 18 free; wkend package plans. Valet parking $14. TV; cable. 2 heated pools, 1 indoor; poolside serv. Restaurant (see J.W.'S). Rm serv 24 hrs. Bar 11:30-1:30 am; pianist. Ck-out 1 pm. Meeting rms. Concierge. Shopping arcade. Courtesy limo 5-mi radius. Tennis & golf privileges. Exercise rm; instructor, weight machines, bicycles, whirlpool, sauna, steam rm. Massage. Bathrm phones, refrigerators, minibars. Private patios, balconies. Scenic view from all rms. French chateau decor. Cr cds: A, C, D, DS, ER, JCB, MC, V.

D ⊁ ⊁ ⊠ ⊠ ⊁ 🔥 SC

★ ★ **LE PARC.** *733 N West Knoll Dr (90069), in West Hollywood.* 310/855-8888; FAX 310/659-7812. 154 suites, 3 story. S, D $165-$215; each addl $30; under 17 free. Crib avail. TV; cable, in-rm movies. Heated pool; poolside serv. Restaurant 7 am-midnight. Bar. Ck-out noon. Coin lndry. Meeting rms. Concierge. Valet parking. Lighted tennis. Exercise equipt; weights, bicycles, whirlpool, sauna. Refrigerators, fireplaces, minibars. Balconies. Cr cds: A, C, D, JCB, MC, V.

⊁ ⊠ ⊁ ⊠ 🔥

★ ★ ★ **MONDRIAN.** *8440 Sunset Blvd (90069), at La Cienega Blvd in West Hollywood.* 213/650-8999; FAX 213/650-5215. 224 suites, 12 story. S, D $175-$475; under 12 free. TV; cable. Heated pool; poolside serv. Restaurant 7 am-11 pm. Rm serv 24 hrs. Bar 11-2 am; pianist. Ck-out noon. Concierge. Covered valet parking. Exercise equipt; weights, bicycles, whirlpool, sauna. Bathrm phones, refrigerators, minibars, wet bars. Some balconies. Contemporary decor. Cr cds: A, C, D, DS, ER, JCB, MC, V.

⊠ ⊁ ⊠ 🔥

★ ★ ★ **NEW OTANI HOTEL & GARDEN.** *120 S Los Angeles St (90012), in Little Tokyo.* 213/629-1200; res: 800/273-2294 (CA) 800/421-8795 (US); FAX 213/622-0980. 434 rms, 21 story. S $155-$275; D $180-$300; each addl $20; suites $450-$1,500; under 12 free. Crib free. Covered parking $13.20/day, valet $17.60/day. TV. Restaurants 6 am-midnight. Bar 10-1 am; pianist. Ck-out noon. Meeting rms. Concierge. Shopping arcade. Barber, beauty shop. Japanese health spa. Bathrm phones, minibars. Japanese-style decor, garden. Cr cds: A, C, D, DS, JCB, MC, V.

D ⊠ 🔥 SC

✔ ★ ★ **OXFORD PALACE.** *745 S Oxford Ave (90005), I-10 exit Western Ave, 2 mi N, west of downtown.* 213/389-8000; res: 800/532-7887; FAX 213/389-8500. 86 rms, 4 story, 9 suites. S $89-$122; D $99-$133; each addl $25; suites $100-$445; under 12 free. Crib $15. TV; cable. Restaurants 7-10 am, 11 am-3 pm, 6-11 pm. Bar 6 pm-2 am. Ck-out noon. Meeting rms. Concierge. Shopping arcade. Gift shop. Garage parking. Minibars. Some balconies. Cr cds: A, C, D, DS, MC, V.

D ⊠ 🔥 SC

★ ★ **RADISSON BEL-AIR.** *11461 Sunset Blvd (90049), in Bel Air.* 310/476-6571; FAX 310/471-6310. 162 rms, 2 story. S $129-$159; D $139-$169; each addl $10; suites $199-$499; under 18 free; wkend rates. TV; in-rm movies. Heated pool; poolside serv. Restaurant 7 am-11 pm. Bar. Ck-out noon. Meeting rms. Gift shop. Valet parking.

Free UCLA transportation. Tennis, pro. Bathrm phones, refrigerators, minibars. Private patios, balconies. Cr cds: A, C, D, MC, V.

D ⊁ ⊠ ⊠ 🔥 SC

★ ★ **RADISSON WILSHIRE PLAZA HOTEL LOS ANGELES.** *3515 Wilshire Blvd (90010), west of downtown.* 213/381-7411; FAX 213/386-7379. 393 rms, 12 story. S $109-$129; D $119-$139; each addl $10; suites $250-$500; under 18 free. Crib free. Garage parking: self-park $5.50, valet $7.70. TV; cable. Heated pool; poolside serv. Restaurants 6 am-11 pm. Bar 11-1 am; entertainment Mon-Fri. Ck-out noon. Convention facilities. Concierge. Barber, beauty shop. Putting green. Minibars. Refrigerator in some suites. Cr cds: A, C, D, DS, JCB, MC, V.

D ⊠ ⊠ 🔥 SC

★ ★ ★ **SHERATON GRANDE.** *333 S Figueroa St (90071), downtown.* 213/617-1133; FAX 213/613-0291. 469 rms, 14 story. S $180-$200; D $200-$250; each addl $25; suites $475-$1,400; studio rms $275; under 18 free. Crib free. Valet parking $16.50. TV; cable. Heated pool; poolside serv. Complimentary coffee or tea. Restaurants 6:30 am-midnight. Rm serv 24 hrs. Bars; entertainment. Meeting rms. Concierge. Butler serv (all rms). Airport transportation; free transportation to Beverly Hills Music Center. Health club privileges. Movie theaters. Bathrm phones, minibars. Cr cds: A, C, D, DS, ER, JCB, MC, V.

D ⊠ ⊠ ⊁ 🔥

★ ★ ★ **SHERATON UNIVERSAL.** *(333 Universal Terrace Pkwy, Universal City 91608)* 1/4 mi E on US 101 Lankershim Blvd exit; on lot of Universal Studios. 818/980-1212; FAX 818/985-4980. 442 rms, 20 story. S, D $160-$200; each addl $20; suites $220-$650; under 18 free. Crib free. Garage $9.50; valet parking $12.50. TV; cable. Pool; poolside serv. Coffee in rms. Restaurant 6 am-10:30 pm. Bar 11-2 am. Ck-out noon. Convention facilities. Concierge. Exercise equipt; stair machine, bicycles, whirlpool. Health club privileges. Game rm. Minibars. Some private patios, balconies. Overlooks San Fernando Valley and Hollywood Hills. Cr cds: A, C, D, DS, ER, JCB, MC, V.

D ⊠ ⊁ ⊠ ⊠ 🔥 SC

★ ★ **SUMMERFIELD SUITES.** *1000 Westmount Dr (90069), in West Hollywood.* 310/657-7400; res: 800/253-7997; FAX 310/854-6744. 109 kit. suites, 4 story. S, D $149-$179; under 12 free; monthly rates. Crib free. Covered parking $6. TV; cable. Pool; sauna. Complimentary continental bkfst. Ck-out noon. Coin lndry. Meeting rm. Bathrm phones, refrigerators, fireplaces. Balconies. Cr cds: A, C, D, JCB, MC, V.

⊠ ⊠ 🔥

★ ★ ★ ★ **SUNSET MARQUIS.** *1200 N Alta Loma Rd (90069), west of downtown.* 310/657-1333; FAX 310/652-5300. 118 suites, 19 with kit, 3 story, 12 villas, S, D suites, kit. units $215-$295; each addl $30; villas $450-$1,200. Crib free. TV; cable. 2 heated pools; poolside serv. Restaurant 7 am-midnight. Rm serv 24 hrs. Bar; entertainment. Ck-out 1 pm. Meeting rms. Concierge. Butler service avail. Free valet or self-parking. Exercise equipt; weights, bicycles, whirlpool, sauna, steam rm. Massage. Refrigerators; steam bath in some rms; wet bar in suites; bathrm phones in villas. Private patios, balconies. Cr cds: A, C, D, MC, V.

D ⊠ ⊁ ⊁ 🔥

★ ★ ★ **WESTIN BONAVENTURE.** *404 S Figueroa St (90071), downtown.* 213/624-1000; FAX 213/612-4800. 1,361 rms, 35 story. S $157-$175; D $175-$200; each addl $25; suites $190-$2,010; under 18 free. Crib free. Garage $18.15/day. TV; cable. Heated pool; poolside serv. Restaurants 6:30 am-midnight. Rm serv 24 hrs. Bars 11-2 am; entertainment Fri & Sat. Ck-out 1 pm. Convention facilities. Concierge. Shopping arcade. Barber, beauty salon. Health club privileges. Six-story atrium lobby. Cr cds: A, C, D, DS, ER, JCB, MC, V.

D ⊠ ⊠ 🔥 SC

WYNDHAM CHECKERS HOTEL LOS ANGELES. *(4-Star 1994; New management, therefore not rated)* 535 S Grand Ave

(90071), downtown. 213/624-0000; FAX 213/626-9906. 188 rms, 12 story, 15 suites. S, D $169-$205; each addl $35; suites $380-$950; under 18 free; wkend rates. Crib free. Valet parking $18. TV; cable, in-rm movies avail. Heated pool; poolside serv. Restaurant 6:30 am-10 pm. Rm serv 24 hrs. Bar 11:30-2 am; entertainment. Meeting rms. Concierge. Airport transportation. Exercise rm; instructor, weight machine, bicycles, whirlpool, sauna, steam rm. Massage. Library Bathrm phones, minibars. Residential-style luxury hotel; lobby features exquisite Oriental and contemporary works of art, antiques. Cr cds: A, C, D, DS, ER, JCB, MC, V.

Inns

✔★★ **SALISBURY HOUSE.** 2273 W 20th St (90018), I-10 exit Western Ave, 1 blk N, west of downtown. 213/737-7817; res: 800/373-1778. 5 rms, 2 share bath, 1 A/C, 3 story. Phones avail. S $70-$95, D $75-$100; each addl $10. TV; in-rm movies avail. Complimentary full bkfst. Ck-out 11 am, ck-in 3-4 pm. Refrigerators. Example of classic California Craftsman (1909), it has been used as a location for several motion picture and TV productions; antiques, original leaded and stained glass. Totally nonsmoking. Cr cds: A, DS, MC, V.

✔★★ **VENICE BEACH HOUSE.** 15 30th Ave (90291), in Venice. 310/823-1966; FAX 310/823-1842. 9 units, 5 baths, 2 share bath, 2 story. Shared bath $80-$90; private bath $110-$150. TV; cable. Complimentary continental bkfst. Afternoon refreshments. Ck-out 11 am, ck-in 3-9 pm. Some private patios, balconies. 1911 California Craftsman house. Venice beach ¼ blk. Totally nonsmoking. Cr cds: A, MC, V.

Restaurants

★★★★ **BEL-AIR DINING ROOM.** (See Bel-Air Hotel) 310/472-1211. Hrs: 7-10:30 am, 11:30 am-2:30 pm, 6:30-10:30 pm; Sat & Sun brunch 11 am-2:30 pm. Res accepted. California menu. Bar. Complete meals: bkfst $8-$13. A la carte entrees: lunch $15-$26.50, dinner $28-$40. Specializes in seasonal dishes. Own pastries. Valet parking. Outdoor dining on bougainvillea-covered terrace, overlooking Swan Lake. Intimate dining; fireplace. Cr cds: A, C, D, JCB, MC, V.

★★★ **BERNARD'S.** (See Biltmore Hotel) 213/612-1580. Hrs: 11:30 am-2:30 pm, 6-10 pm; Fri to 10:30 pm. Closed Sun; major hols. Res accepted. Continental menu. Wine cellar. A la carte entrees: lunch $13-$21, dinner $17-$30. Specializes in seafood. Own baking. Harpist. Valet parking. Cr cds: A, C, D, ER, JCB, MC, V.

★★ **CAMPANILE.** 624 S La Brea Ave, west of downtown. 213/938-1447. Hrs: 8 am-2 pm, 6-10 pm; Fri & Sat 5:30-11 pm; Sun 8 am-1:30 pm. Closed Memorial Day, Thanksgiving, Dec 25. Res accepted. California-Italian menu. Bar. Semi-a la carte: bkfst $3-$15, lunch $10-$25, dinner $30-$40. Specialties: focaccia, risotto cake, prime rib. Valet parking. Charlie Chaplin's original studio. Mexican tile fountain; skylights. Cr cds: A, DS, MC, V.

★★★ **FOUR OAKS.** 2181 N Beverly Glen, in Bel Air. 310/470-2265. Hrs: 11:30 am-2 pm, 6-10 pm; Sun & Mon from 6 pm; Sun brunch 10:30 am-2 pm. Closed some major hols. Res accepted. French, California menu. Bar. A la carte entrees: lunch $20-$25, dinner $35-$50. Sun champagne brunch $27.50. Menu changes seasonally; emphasizes natural ingredients. Own desserts. Valet parking. Patio dining. Mediterranean decor. Built 1890. Cr cds: MC, V.

★★★ **GARDENS.** (See Four Seasons Hotel) 310/273-2222. Hrs: 7 am-11 pm; Sun brunch 10 am-2:30 pm. Res accepted. Continental menu. Bar 11-1 am. Wine cellar. A la carte entrees: bkfst $5.95-$14, lunch $8.95-$18, dinner $18-$42. Sun brunch $36. Child's meals. Specializes in steak, rack of lamb, seafood. Own baking, ice cream.

Valet parking. Outdoor dining. European decor. Jacket. Cr cds: A, C, D, JCB, MC, V.

★★★ **J.W.'S.** (See J.W. Marriott At Century City) 310/277-2777. Hrs: 6:30 am-10:30 pm; Sat & Sun from 7 am; Sun brunch 10:00 am-2 pm. Res accepted. Continental, California menu. Bar 11:30-1:30 am. Wine cellar. A la carte entrees: bkfst $9.50-$15.50, dinner $13.50-$18. Sun brunch $21.95. Seasonal menu; changes monthly. Own baking. Valet parking. Outdoor dining overlooking lush garden. Cr cds: A, C, D, DS, ER, JCB, MC, V.

★★★ **LA CHAUMIERE.** (See Century Plaza Hotel & Tower) 310/277-2000. Hrs: 6-10:30 pm; Sat & Sun 6-10 pm. Res accepted. French menu. Bar; piano bar. Wine list. A la carte entrees: dinner $22-$28. Menu changes seasonally. Own baking. Valet parking. French country decor; solarium. Original artwork. Jacket. Cr cds: A, C, D, DS, MC, V.

✔★★ **LES FRERES TAIX.** 1911 Sunset Blvd, north of downtown. 213/484-1265. Hrs: 11 am-10 pm; Sun to 9 pm. Closed most major hols. Res accepted. Country French menu. Bar. Complete meals: lunch $4.95-$14.95, dinner $4.95-$16.95. Child's meals. Specialty: escargots à la Bourguignonne. Own soups. Valet parking. Family-owned. Cr cds: A, C, D, DS, MC, V.

★ **LITTLE JOE'S.** 900 N Broadway, in Chinatown. 213/489-4900. Hrs: 11 am-9 pm; Sat from 3 pm. Closed Sun; major hols. Res accepted. Italian, Amer menu. Bar. Semi-a la carte: lunch $5.95-$12.50, dinner $6.95-$18.95. Child's meals. Specializes in homemade ravioli, halibut. Near Dodger Stadium, Civic Center. Family-owned since 1910. Cr cds: A, C, D, DS, JCB, MC, V.

★★★ **LOCANDA VENETA.** 8638 W Third St, opp Cedars Sinai Hospital, west of downtown. 310/274-1893. Hrs: 11:30 am-2:30 pm, 5:30-10:30 pm; Fri to 11 pm; Sat 5:30-11 pm. Closed Sun. Res accepted. Northern Italian menu. Beer. Wine list. A la carte entrees: lunch, dinner $15-$35. Specializes in seafood, pasta. Own baking, pasta. Valet parking. Windows open to street; open kitchen. Cr cds: A, MC, V.

★★ **MADEO.** 8897 Beverly Blvd, west of downtown. 310/859-4903. Hrs: noon-3 pm, 6:30-11 pm; Sat & Sun from 6:30 pm. Closed Dec 25. Res accepted. Italian menu. Bar. Wine cellar. A la carte entrees: lunch $10-$30, dinner $30-$50. Specialties: branzino, leg of veal. Own pastries. Pianist nightly. Valet parking. Wood-burning oven. Cr cds: A, C, D, MC, V.

★★ **OCEAN SEAFOOD.** 747 N Broadway, in Chinatown. 213/687-3088. Hrs: 8 am-10 pm. Res accepted. Chinese menu. Bar. A la carte entrees: bkfst, lunch $4-$12, dinner $5-$16. Specializes in live seafood, beef, poultry. Cr cds: A, DS, MC, V.

★★ **ORLEANS.** 11705 National Blvd, at Barrington, west of downtown. 310/479-4187. Hrs: 11:30 am-2 pm, 6-9:30 pm; Fri to 10:30 pm; Sat 6-10:30 pm; Sun 5:30-9 pm. Closed some major hols. Res accepted. Cajun, Creole menu. Bar. Semi-a la carte: lunch $6-$13, dinner $9-$19. Child's meals. Specialties: blackened prime rib, Cajun "popcorn" (crawfish & alligator). Valet parking. Interior reminiscent of Louisiana antebellum home; primitive paintings; fireplace. Cr cds: A, D, MC, V.

★★ **PRIMI.** 10543 W Pico Blvd, west of downtown. 310/475-9235. Hrs: 11:30 am-2:30 pm, 5:30-11 pm. Res accepted. Italian menu. Bar. A la carte entrees: lunch $10-$19, dinner $16-$22. Specializes in homemade pasta. Own breads, desserts. Valet parking. Outdoor dining. Cr cds: A, C, D, MC, V.

★ ★ ★ **REX II RISTORANTE.** *617 S Olive St, downtown. 213/627-2300.* Hrs: 6-10 pm; Thurs & Fri also noon-2 pm. Closed Sun; hols. Res accepted. Italian menu. Bar. Wine cellar. Complete meals: lunch $35-$40 (3-course lunch $35), dinner $65-$80 (4-course dinner $55). Specializes in 6-course meals ($70). Own pastries, pasta. Pianist, dancing evenings. Valet parking. Landmark building (1928). Art deco. Jacket. Cr cds: A, C, D, MC, V.

D

✔★ **SISLEY ITALIAN KITCHEN.** *10800 W Pico Blvd, in Westside Pavilion Shopping Center, west of downtown. 310/446-3030.* Hrs: 11:30 am-10 pm; Fri & Sat to 10:30 pm; Sun noon-9 pm. Res accepted. Italian, California menu. Bar. A la carte entrees: lunch $6.25-$10, dinner $7.50-$12. Specialties: cioppino, crab cakes, pasta. Valet parking. Italian cafe decor. Cr cds: A, MC, V.

D

★ ★ **TAM-O-SHANTER INN.** *2980 Los Feliz Blvd, 5 blks east of I-5, north of downtown. 213/664-0228.* Hrs: 11 am-3 pm, 5-10 pm; Fri & Sat to 11 pm; Sun 4-10 pm; Sun brunch 10:30 am-2:30 pm. Closed July 4, Dec 25. Continental, Amer menu. Bar. Semi-a la carte: lunch $7.95-$12.95, dinner $11.95-$22.95. Sun brunch $9.50-$15.50. Child's meals. Specializes in prime rib & Yorkshire pudding, creamed spinach. Sandwich bar. Valet parking. Piano bar. Fireplace. Scottish motif. Family-owned since 1922. Cr cds: A, C, D, DS, JCB, MC, V.

SC

★ ★ **THE TOWER.** *1150 S Olive St, on top of Trans-America Center, downtown. 213/746-1554.* Hrs: 11:30 am-2 pm, 5:30-10 pm; Fri to 11 pm; Sat 5:30-11 pm; early-bird dinner 5:30-6:30 pm. Closed Sun; major hols. Res accepted. Continental menu. Bar. Wine cellar. A la carte entrees: lunch $15-$20, dinner $25-$40. Specializes in contemporary dishes. Harpist (lunch), pianist (dinner). Valet parking. 360&degrees; view of city from 32nd floor. Jacket. Cr cds: A, D, MC, V.

D

✔★ ★ **WOLFGANG PUCK CAFE.** *(1000 Universal Center Dr, Universal City 91608) N on US 101, Lankershim Blvd exit. 818/985-9653.* Hrs: 11 am-11 pm. Bar. A la carte entrees: lunch, dinner $5-$14.50. Specializes in wood-burning oven pizza, rotisserie chicken. Parking. Patio dining. Ultra modern decor; kinetic wall art. Smoking on patio only. Cr cds: MC, V.

D

Unrated Dining Spots

CASSELL'S. *3266 W 6th St, west of downtown. 213/480-8668.* Hrs: 10:30 am-4 pm. Closed Sun; major hols. A la carte entrees: lunch $4.60-$5.80. Specializes in prime beef hamburgers. Old-style hamburger diner. No cr cds accepted.

D

HARD ROCK CAFE. *8600 Beverly Blvd, west of downtown. 310/276-7605.* Hrs: 11:30-12:30 am. Closed Labor Day, Thanksgiving, Dec 25. Bar. Semi-a la carte: lunch, dinner $5.95-$15. Child's meals. Specialties: lime barbecued chicken, grilled hamburgers. Valet parking. Extensive rock 'n roll memorabilia collection. Cr cds: A, D, MC, V.

D

PHILLIPE THE ORIGINAL. *1001 N Alameda St, downtown. 213/628-3781.* Hrs: 6 am-10 pm. Closed Thanksgiving, Dec 25. Wine, beer. A la carte entrees: bkfst $1-$4.50, lunch, dinner $3.25-$5. Specializes in French dip sandwiches, salads, baked apples. Own

cinnamon rolls, muffins, donuts. Parking. Since 1908; old-style dining hall. No cr cds accepted.

D

UNCLE BILL'S PANCAKE HOUSE. *(1305 Highland Ave, Manhattan Beach) S on Pacific Coast Hwy. 310/545-5177.* Hrs: 6 am-3 pm; wkends, hols from 7 am. Closed Jan 1, Thanksgiving, Dec 25. Semi-a la carte: bkfst $3.25-$5.95, lunch $3.50-$6.50. Specializes in potatoes Stroganoff, strawberry waffles, homemade muffins. Parking. Small, cozy atmosphere. Converted 1908 house. No cr cds accepted.

Los Angeles Intl Airport Area

Motels

✔★ ★ **HAMPTON INN.** *(10300 La Cienega Blvd, Inglewood 90304) 3/4 mi E on Century Blvd, then S on La Cienega Blvd. 310/337-1000; FAX 310/645-6925.* 149 rms, 7 story. S, D $66-$70; under 18 free. Crib free. Pet accepted, some restrictions. TV. Complimentary continental bkfst, coffee. Restaurant nearby. Ck-out noon. Meeting rms. Valet serv. Free airport transportation. Exercise equipt; weight machine, bicycles, sauna. Cr cds: A, C, D, DS, MC, V.

✔★ ★ **TRAVELODGE.** *(5547 W Century Blvd, Los Angeles 90045) 1/2 mi W on I-405, at Century Blvd & Aviation Blvd. 310/649-4000; res: 800/421-3939; FAX 310/649-0311.* 147 rms, 2 story. S $62-$69; D $69-$82; each addl $8; under 18 free. Pet accepted. TV; cable, in-rm movies. Pool. Restaurant open 24 hrs. Rm serv 6 am-10 pm. Bar 10-2 am. Ck-out noon. Coin lndry. Bellhops. Valet serv. Gift shop. Free airport transportation. Some private patios, balconies. Cr cds: A, C, D, DS, ER, JCB, MC, V.

Hotels

✔★ **AIRPORT MARINA.** *(8601 Lincoln Blvd, Los Angeles 90045) Jct Lincoln Blvd and Manchester Ave, NW edge of Intl Airport. 310/670-8111; FAX 310/337-1883.* 770 rms, 12 story. S, D $75-$125; each addl $10; suites $150-$375; under 18 free. Crib free. TV; cable. Pool; poolside serv. Restaurants 5:30 am-10:30 pm. Bar 4 pm-2 am; entertainment, dancing. Ck-out 1 pm. Meeting rms. Barber, beauty shop. Free airport transportation. Some private patios, balconies. Garden patio. Golf, tennis opp. *LUXURY LEVEL : GUEST OF HONOR.* 23 rms. S, D $125. Private lounge. Some wet bars. Complimentary continental bkfst. Cr cds: A, C, D, MC, V.

★ ★ **CROWN STERLING SUITES.** *(1440 E Imperial Ave, El Segundo 90245) 1/2 mi S on Sepulveda Blvd, then 1 blk W on Imperial Ave. 310/640-3600; FAX 310/322-0954.* 350 suites, 5 story. S, D $119-$169; each addl $15; under 12 free; wkend rates. Pet accepted, some restrictions. TV; cable. Indoor pool; whirlpool. Complimentary full bkfst. Restaurant 11 am-10 pm. Bar 11-2 am. Ck-out 1 pm. Meeting rms. Gift shop. Free covered parking. Free airport transportation. Health club privileges. Refrigerators. Balconies. Sun deck. Spanish mission architecture. Near beach. Cr cds: A, C, D, DS, ER, JCB, MC, V.

★ ★ **DOUBLETREE CLUB.** *(1985 E Grand Ave, El Segundo 90245) 1 1/2 mi S of airport on Sepulveda Blvd, in business park. 310/322-0999; FAX 310/322-4758.* 215 rms, 7 story. S $99; D $109; each addl $10; suites $125; under 18 free. Crib $10. TV; cable. Heated pool. Complimentary full bkfst. Restaurant 6-10 am, 11 am-2 pm, 5-10 pm. Bar. Ck-out 1 pm. Meeting rms. Free airport transportation. Exercise equipt; weight machines, bicycles, whirlpool. Cr cds: A, C, D, DS, JCB, MC, V.

[D] [≈] [✗] [✈] [✗] [♨] [SC]

★ ★ ★ DOUBLETREE-L.A. AIRPORT. (5400 W Century Blvd, Los Angeles 90045) 1¹/4 mi E on Century Blvd. 310/216-5858; FAX 310/645-8053. 740 rms, 12 story. 3, D $119-$154; each addl $15; suites $275-$1,349; under 18 free; wkend plans. Covered parking $8. TV; cable. Heated pool. Restaurant 6 am-11 pm. Rm serv 24 hrs. Bar 10-2 am; entertainment. Ck-out noon. Convention facilities. Gift shop. Free airport transportation. Exercise rm; instructor, weights, bicycles, whirlpool, sauna. Minibars; bathrm phones in suites. Balconies. LUX- URY LEVEL : CONCIERGE LEVEL. 105 rms, 9 suites, 2 floors. S, D $134-$169. Concierge. Private lounge. Wet bar, whirlpool in suites. Complimentary continental bkfst, refreshments, newspaper, shoe shine. Cr cds: A, C, D, DS, JCB, MC, V.

[D] [≈] [✗] [✈] [✗] [♨] [SC]

★ ★ ★ HILTON & TOWERS-LOS ANGELES AIRPORT. (5711 W Century Blvd, Los Angeles 90045) ³/4 mi E on Century Blvd. 310/410-4000; FAX 310/410-6250. 1,279 rms, 17 story. S $119-$169; each addl $15; suites $280-$750; family, wkend rates. Valet parking $13.50, garage $9. TV; cable. Heated pool; poolside serv (seasonal). Restau- rants 6 am-midnight. Bar 11-2 am; entertainment, dancing. Ck-out 11 am. Convention facilities. Coin lndry. Drugstore. Airport transportation. Exercise rm; instructor, weights, bicycles, whirlpool, sauna. Game rm. Some bathrm phones; refrigerators avail. Some private patios. LUX- URY LEVEL : THE TOWERS. 108 rms, 40 suites, 2 floors. S $165; D $180; suites $380-$750. Private lounge, honor bar. Bathrm phones. Complimentary continental bkfst, refreshments. Cr cds: A, C, D, DS, ER, JCB, MC, V.

[D] [≈] [✗] [✈] [✗] [♨] [SC]

★ ★ ★ HOLIDAY INN CROWNE PLAZA-L.A. INTERNA- TIONAL AIRPORT. (5985 W Century Blvd, Los Angeles 90045) ¹/4 mi E on Century Blvd. 310/642-7500; FAX 310/417-3608. 615 rms, 16 story. S $124-$139; D $139-$154; each addl $15; suites $300-$600; under 19 free; wkend rates. Crib free. Garage $7.70. Pet accepted, some restric- tions. TV; cable. Heated pool; whirlpool, sauna. Restaurant 6 am-11 pm. Rm serv 24 hrs. Bar 11-2 am; entertainment, dancing. Ck-out noon. Concierge. Gift shop. Free airport, beach, shopping transporta- tion. Health club privileges. LUXURY LEVEL : CROWN PLAZA CLUB. 46 rms. S $139; D $154. Private lounge. Complimentary continental bkfst, refreshments. Cr cds: A, C, D, DS, MC, V.

[D] [✇] [≈] [✈] [✗] [♨] [SC]

★ ★ HYATT AT LOS ANGELES AIRPORT. (6225 W Century Blvd, Los Angeles 90045) At entrance to lntl Airport. 310/337-1234; FAX 310/641-6924. 597 rms, 12 story. S $125-$155; D $140-$170; each addl $15; suites $275-$550; under 18 free; wkend rates. TV; cable. Heated pool; poolside serv. Supervised child's activities. Res- taurant 6:30-1:30 am; dining rms 11 am-10:30 pm. Bars 11-2 am; dancing, entertainment exc Sun. Ck-out 1 pm. Convention facilities. Concierge. Barber, beauty shop. Garage. Free airport transportation. Exercise rm; instructor, weights, bicycles, whirlpool. Bathrm phones, minibars; wet bar in suites. Sun deck. LUXURY LEVEL : REGENCY CLUB. 50 rms, 14 suites. S $165; D $180. Complimentary continental bkfst, refreshments. Cr cds: A, C, D, DS, ER, JCB, MC, V.

[D] [≈] [✗] [✈] [✗] [♨] [SC]

★ ★ ★ MARRIOTT AIRPORT. (5855 W Century Blvd, Los An- geles 90045) ¹/2 mi E on Century Blvd. 310/641-5700; FAX 310/337- 5358. 1,012 rms, 18 story. S, D $144-$154; each addl $10; suites from $189; family, wkend rates. Crib free. Pet accepted, some restrictions. Valet parking $10. TV. Heated pool; poolside serv. 3 restaurants 6 am-midnight. Rm serv 24 hrs. 2 bars; entertainment, dancing. Ck-out 1 pm. Coin lndry. Convention facilities. Concierge. Shopping arcade. Barber, beauty shop. Free airport transportation. Exercise equipt; weights, bicycles, whirlpool. Game rm. Some bathrm phones, refrig- erators. Balconies. LUXURY LEVEL : CONCIERGE FLOOR. Ext 1614.

73 rms. S $149; D $159. Honor bar. Complimentary continental bkfst, refreshments. Cr cds: A, C, D, DS, JCB, MC, V.

[D] [✇] [≈] [✗] [✈] [✗] [♨] [SC]

✔★ ★ QUALITY HOTEL-LOS ANGELES AIRPORT. (5249 W Century Blvd, Los Angeles 90045) 1¹/4 mi E on Century Blvd. 310/645-2200; FAX 310/641-8214. 277 rms, 10 story. S $49-$75; D $49-$85; each addl $10; under 16 free; wkend rates. TV. Pool; poolside serv. Restaurant 6 am-10 pm. Bar 6-11 pm; pianist Mon. Ck-out 1 pm. Convention facilities. Garage parking. Free airport transportation. Exer- cise equipt; weights, bicycles. Cr cds: A, C, D, DS, ER, JCB, MC, V.

[D] [≈] [✗] [✈] [✗] [♨] [SC]

★ ★ SHERATON LOS ANGELES AIRPORT. (6101 W Cen- tury Blvd, Los Angeles 90045) ¹/4 mi E on Century Blvd. 310/642-1111; FAX 310/410-1267. 807 rms, 15 story. S $115-$175; D $120-$195; each addl $20; suites $180-$500; under 17 free; wkend rates. Crib free. TV; cable. Heated pool; poolside serv. Restaurants 6-1:30 am. Bar 11-2 am; entertainment, piano bar. Ck-out 1 pm. Convention facilities. Con- cierge. Gift shop. Valet parking. Free airport transportation. Exercise equipt; weights, bicycles, whirlpool. Minibars. LUXURY LEVEL : CLUB FLOOR. 140 rms, 8 suites, 2 floors. S, D $119; suites $195. Concierge. Private lounge, hostess. Complimentary continental bkfst; refresh- ments. Cr cds: A, C, D, DS, ER, JCB, MC, V.

[D] [≈] [✗] [✈] [✗] [♨] [SC]

Beverly Hills

Motor Hotels

✔★ ★ ★ BEVERLY HILLS RITZ HOTEL. 10300 Wilshire Blvd (90024). 310/275-5575; res: 800/800-1234; FAX 310/275-3257. 116 suites, 5 story. S, D $105-$310. Crib avail. TV; cable, in-rm movies. Heated pool; poolside serv. Restaurant 7 am-10 pm. Rm serv. Bar. Ck-out noon. Meeting rm. Bellhops. Exercise equipt; weight machine, treadmill, whirlpool. Refrigerators, minibars. Many balconies. Garden; tropical plants. Cr cds: A, C, D, DS, JCB, MC, V.

[✇] [≈] [✗] [♨]

★ ★ RADISSON BEVERLY PAVILION. 9360 Wilshire Blvd (90212). 310/273-1400; res: 800/441-5050; FAX 310/859-8551. 110 rms, 8 story. S $150-$185; D $170-$205; each addl $20; suites $275-$425. Crib free. TV. Bellhops. Rooftop pool; poolside serv. Restaurant 7 am-10 pm. Rm serv. Bar 10 am-midnight. Ck-out noon. Meeting rms. Valet serv. Gift shop. Free local transportation. Refrigerators. Cr cds: A, C, D, DS, JCB, MC, V.

[≈] [✗] [♨]

Hotels

★ ★ ★ BEVERLY HILTON. 9876 Wilshire Blvd (90210). 310/274-7777; FAX 310/285-1313. 581 rms, 8 story. S $180-$225; D $205-$250; each addl $25; suites $400-$1,200; family rates. Crib free. Garage, valet parking $15. TV; cable. Heated pool; wading pool, pool- side serv. Restaurant 6:45-10 am, 11:30 am-2:30 pm, 5:30-10 pm; dining rm 5 pm-midnight (also see L'ESCOFFIER). Rm serv 24 hrs. Bars 11:30-2 am. Ck-out noon. Meeting rms. Concierge. Shopping arcade. Barber, beauty shop. Complimentary transportation to nearby shop- ping. Exercise equipt; weight machines, bicycles. Some bathrm phones, refrigerators. Patio; balconies. Lanai rms around pool. Cr cds: A, C, D, DS, ER, JCB, MC, V.

[✇] [≈] [✗] [✗] [♨] [SC]

★ ★ ★ BEVERLY PRESCOTT. (1224 S Beverwil Dr, Los Ange- les 90035) At Pico Blvd. 310/277-2800. 140 rms, 12 story, 16 suites. S, D $99-$200; suites $250-$1,000; family & wkend rates. Crib free. Covered parking $12. TV; cable. Heated pool; poolside serv. Restaurant 7 am-10 pm. Rm serv 24 hrs. Bar 11-2 am. Ck-out noon. Meeting rms. Concierge. Exercise equipt; weight machine, treadmill. Health club privileges. Minibars. Balconies. Cr cds: A, C, D, DS, ER, JCB, MC, V.

[D] [icons]

★ ★ ★ ★ ★ THE PENINSULA, BEVERLY HILLS. *9882 Little Santa Monica Blvd (90212), at Wilshire Blvd.* 310/551-2888; res: 800/462-7899; FAX 310/858-6663. 200 units, 4 story, 32 suites, 16 villas (2 story, 1-2 bedrm). S, D $300-$450; each addl $35; suites & villas $450-$3,000; under 12 free; wknd rates. Crib free. Valet parking $17. TV; cable, in-rm movies. Heated rooftop pool; poolside serv. Complimentary tea on arrival. Restaurant 6:30 am-11 pm. Rm serv 24 hrs. Bar from 11:30 am; pianist. Ck-out noon. Meeting rms. Concierge. Gift shop. Clothing & jewelery stores. Airport transportation; Rolls-Royce limos avail. Tennis privileges. 18-hole golf privileges, pro, putting green, driving range. Exercise rm; instructor, weight machine, treadmill, whirlpool, sauna. Massage. Aerobics classes. Bathrm phones, stocked minibars; many wet bars. Balconies. Landscaped gardens with fountains. Luxurious residential setting. Cr cds: A, C, D, DS, ER, JCB, MC, V.

[icons]

★ ★ ★ ★ REGENT BEVERLY WILSHIRE. *9500 Wilshire Blvd (90212).* 310/275-2500; res: 800/545-4000; FAX 310/274-2851. 300 rms, 10 & 12 story, 36 suites. S, D $255-$395; suites $425-$4,000; under 18 free. Heated pool; poolside serv. Restaurant (see THE DINING ROOM). Rm serv 24 hrs. Bar 11-2 am; entertainment. Ck-out noon. Convention facilities. Concierge. Gift shop. Beauty shop. Golf privileges. Exercise equipt; weights, bicycles, 2 whirlpools, sauna, steam rm. Bathrm phones, refrigerators. Some balconies. Cr cds: A, C, D, DS, ER, JCB, MC, V.

[icons]

Inn

★ ★ ★ CARLYLE. *(1119 S Robertson Blvd, Los Angeles 90035) W on Wilshire Blvd to Robertson Blvd, then S; between Olympic & Pico Blvds.* 310/275-4445; res: /800-3-CA; FAX 310/859-0496. 32 rms, 5 story. S $105; D $115 each addl $10; suites $120; under 12 free; wkly rates, package plans. Crib free. TV; cable. Complimentary full bkfst, tea, sherry. Complimentary coffee in rms. Dining rm 7-10:30 am, 4-6 pm (tea). Also restaurant nearby. Ck-out 1 pm, ck-in 4 pm. Bellhops. Valet serv. Concierge. Private parking. Airport transportation avail. Exercise equipt; bicycles, treadmill, whirlpool. Health club privileges. Rms are on 4 levels of circular terraces overlooking a lush courtyard, terrace and spa. Offers European hospitality and service in a contemporary setting. Cr cds: A, C, D, DS, MC, V.

[icons] [SC]

Restaurants

★ BEVERLY HILLS R. J.'S-THE RIB JOINT. *252 N Beverly Dr.* 310/274-7427. Hrs: 11:30 am-10 pm; Fri & Sat to 11 pm; Sun from 10:30 am. Bar. Complete meals: lunch $5.95-$12.95, dinner $8.95-$29.95. Sun brunch $21.95. Child's meals. Specializes in barbecued ribs, chicken, steak, mile-high chocolate cake. Salad bar. Magician. Valet parking. Old-time atmosphere; sawdust on floor, ceiling fans, old photos. Cr cds: A, C, D, JCB, MC, V.

★ ★ BISTRO GARDEN. *176 N Canon Dr.* 310/550-3900. Hrs: 11:30 am-11:30 pm. Closed major hols. Res required. Continental menu. Bar. Semi-a la carte: lunch $15-$25, dinner $25-$40. Specialties: Swiss bratwurst, canelloni. Pianist. Valet parking. French country garden atmosphere. Outdoor dining. Cr cds: A, C, D, MC, V.

★ ★ DA PASQUALE. *9749 Little Santa Monica Blvd (90210).* 310/859-3884. Hrs: 11:30 am-3 pm, 5-10 pm; Fri to 11 pm; Sat 5-11 pm; Sun 5-10 pm. Closed major hols. Res accepted; required wkends. Italian menu. Wine, beer. A la carte entrees: lunch $7-$15, dinner

$15-$30. Specializes in pizza, pasta. Italian atmosphere. Totally non-smoking. Cr cds: A, MC, V.

[D]

★ ★ DA VINCI. *9737 Santa Monica Blvd.* 310/273-0960. Hrs: 11:30 am-2:30 pm, 5:30-10:30 pm. Res accepted. Italian menu. Bar. A la carte entrees: lunch $15-$20, dinner $30-$40. Specialties: osso buco Milanese, fresh homemade pasta, seafood. Own desserts. Valet parking. Jacket. Cr cds: A, C, D, JCB, MC, V.

[D]

★ ★ DAVID SLAY'S LA VERANDA. *225 S Beverly Dr.* 310/274-7246. Hrs: 11:30 am-2:30 pm, 5:30-10 pm; Sat 5:30-10:30 pm; Sun 5-9:30 pm. Closed most major hols. California, Italian menu. Bar. Wine list. A la carte entrees: lunch $12-$15, dinner $16-$25. Specialties: pan-roasted scallops, salmon quesadilla, fried spinach. Valet parking. Casual atmosphere; contemporary dining. Cr cds: A, D, MC, V.

★ ★ ★ THE DINING ROOM. *(See Regent Beverly Wilshire Hotel)* 310/275-5200. Hrs: 7 am-2 pm, 6-11 pm; Sun 10:30 am-2 pm, 6-11 pm; Sun brunch 10 am-2:30 pm. Res accepted. Continental menu. Bar 11-2 am; pianist. Wine cellar. A la carte entrees: bkfst $6-$20, lunch $12-$26, dinner $16-$30. Sun brunch $12-$38. Specializes in mesquite-grilled meats and fish. Own baking. Valet parking. Seasonal menu with daily specials. Display kitchen. Decor in Grand European style. Jacket. Cr cds: A, C, D, DS, ER, JCB, MC, V.

[D]

★ ★ THE GRILL. *9560 Dayton Way.* 310/276-0615. Hrs: 11:30 am-11 pm. Closed Sun; major hols. Res required. Bar. A la carte entrees: lunch $12-$20, dinner $20-$35. Specializes in fresh seafood, steak, chops. Valet parking. Turn-of-the-century decor. Cr cds: A, D, MC, V.

[D]

★ ★ ★ IL CIELO. *9018 Burton Way.* 310/276-9990. Hrs: 11:30 am-3 pm, 6-10:30 pm; Fri, Sat to 11 pm. Closed Sun; most major hols. Res accepted. Italian menu. Beer. Wine list. A la carte entrees: lunch $8-$13, dinner $13-$20. Specializes in fresh seafood, homemade pasta, veal. Own pastries. Violinist. Valet parking. Outdoor dining. Gardens, fountains. Cr cds: A, C, D, DS, JCB, MC, V.

✔ ★ ★ IL PASTAIO. *400 N Canon Dr (90210).* 310/205-5444. Hrs: 11 am-11 pm. Closed Sun; some major hols. Res accepted. Italian menu. Bar. A la carte entrees: lunch, dinner $8.50-$12. Specializes in pasta. Valet parking. Contemporary decor, artwork. Cr cds: A, D, MC, V.

[D]

★ ★ ★ JIMMY'S. *201 Moreno Dr.* 310/552-2394. Hrs: 11:30 am-3 pm, 5:30 pm-midnight. Closed Sun; major hols. French menu. Bar 11:30-2 am. Wine cellar. A la carte entrees: lunch from $15, dinner from $25. Specialties: peppered salmon, crème brulée Napoleon, Maryland crab cakes. Own pastries. Elegant French decor with a California touch. Cr cds: A, C, D, MC, V.

[D]

✔ ★ ★ KIPPAN. *260 N Beverly Dr.* 310/858-0535. Hrs: 11:30 am-2:30 pm, 5:30-10 pm; Sat to 10:30 pm; Sun from 5:30 pm. Closed major hols. Res accepted. Japanese menu. Wine, beer. A la carte entrees: lunch from $5.80, dinner from $7.80. Specialty: sushi bar. Contemporary Japanese decor. Cr cds: A, D, MC, V.

[D]

★ ★ ★ L'ESCOFFIER. *(See Beverly Hilton Hotel)* 310/274-7777. Hrs: 6:30-10:30 pm; Fri & Sat to 11:30 pm. Closed Sun, Mon. Res accepted. California, French menu. Bar. A la carte entrees: dinner $26-$32. Complete meals: dinner $47.50. Specializes in veal dishes, steak Diane flambé. Own baking. Entertainment. Valet parking. Rooftop dining. View of city. Cr cds: A, C, D, DS, ER, MC, V.

★ ★ **LA FAMIGLIA.** *453 N Canon Dr. 310/276-6208.* Hrs: 5:30 pm-closing. Closed major hols. Res accepted. Italian menu. Bar. A la carte entrees: dinner $12.75-$24. Specializes in fresh fish, homemade pasta, veal, poultry. Valet parking. Cr cds: A, C, D, MC, V,

★ ★ ★ **LA SCALA.** *410 N Canon Dr. 310/275-0579.* Hrs: 11:30 am-10:30 pm. Closed Sun; major hols. Res required. Northern Italian menu. Bar. A la carte entrees: lunch $7.50-$18, dinner $13.95-$27.95. Specializes in homemade pasta, veal. Valet parking. Family-owned. Cr cds: A, C, D, DS, JCB, MC, V.

★ ★ **LAWRY'S THE PRIME RIB.** *100 N La Cienega Blvd, at Wilshire Blvd. 310/652-2827.* Hrs: 5-10 pm; Fri to 11 pm; Sat 4:30-11 pm; Sun 4-10 pm. Closed Dec 25. Res accepted. Bar. Semi-a la carte: dinner $18.95-$25.95. Limited menu. Specializes in prime rib, fish, spinning salad bowl, Yorkshire pudding. Own desserts. Valet parking. Cr cds: A, C, D, DS, JCB, MC, V.

D

✔★ ★ ★ **THE MANDARIN.** *430 N Camden Dr. 213/272-0267.* Hrs: 11:30 am-10 pm; Fri & Sat 5-10:30 pm; Sun 5-10 pm. Closed Jan 1, July 4, Thanksgiving, Dec 25. Res accepted. Mandarin Chinese menu. Bar. A la carte entrees: lunch, dinner $15-$20. Specialties: Peking duck, beggar's chicken. 24-hr advance notice for mandarin specialties. Valet parking. Exhibition kitchen. Chinese decor. Cr cds: A, C, D, MC, V.

D

★ ★ **MAPLE DRIVE.** *345 N Maple Dr. 310/274-9800.* Hrs: 11:30 am-2:30 pm, 6-10 pm; Fri to 11 pm; Sat 6-11 pm. Closed Sun; Jan 1, Dec 25. Res required. California, Mediterranean menu. Bar. A la carte entrees: lunch $10-$17, dinner $15-$26. Specialties: fried calamari, tuna tartar, grilled swordfish, chili. Pianist. Valet parking (dinner). Exhibition kitchen. Changing display of artwork. Cr cds: A, MC, V.

★ **MATSUHISA.** *129 N La Cienega Blvd. 310/659-9639.* Hrs: 11:45 am-2:15 pm, 5:45-10:15 pm; Sat & Sun from 5:45 pm. Closed most major hols. Res accepted. Japanese menu. Wine, beer. Semi-a la carte: lunch $15-$25, dinner $40-$60. Omakase dishes from $60. Specializes in gourmet seafood, sushi. Tempura bar. Valet parking. Lobster tank. Totally nonsmoking. Cr cds: A, D, MC, V.

★ ★ **MORTON'S.** *8764 Melrose Ave (90210), at Robertson Ave. 310/276-5205.* Hrs: noon-3 pm, 6-11 pm. Closed Sun; major hols. Res accepted; required Fri & Sat. Bar to 1 am. Wine cellar. A la carte entrees: lunch $10-$15, dinner $17-$28. Specialties: Chilean seabass with mango coulis, grilled shitake mushroom sandwich. Valet parking. Modern decor. Jacket. Cr cds: A, MC, V.

★ ★ **PREGO.** *362 N Camden Dr. 310/277-7346.* Hrs: 11:30 am-midnight; Sun from 5 pm. Closed Thanksgiving, Dec 25. Res accepted. Northern Italian menu. Bar. A la carte entrees: lunch $8-$18, dinner $15-$28. Specializes in homemade pasta, fresh fish. Valet parking evenings. Oak-burning pizza oven & mesquite grill. Cr cds: A, C, D, MC, V.

D

★ ★ **ROBATA.** *250 N Robertson Blvd. 310/274-5533.* Hrs: noon-2:30 pm, 5:30-10:30 pm. Closed most major hols. Res accepted. Japanese menu. Bar. Wine list. A la carte entrees: lunch $7-$20, dinner $40-$60. Specializes in sushi, tempura, sashimi. Contemporary Japanese atmosphere; dramatic lighting, antiques, hand-painted screens. Cr cds: A, C, D, JCB, MC, V.

D

★ ★ **TATOU RESTAURANT & SUPPER CLUB.** *233 N Beverly Dr. 310/274-9955.* Hrs: 6 pm-4 am. Closed Sun; some major hols. Res required. Bar. Extensive wine list. Complete meals: dinner from $20. Specialties: roast salmon with red wine butter sauce, Szechwan stir-fried shrimp with Chinese eggplant, rack of lamb with dauphinoise

potatoes & natural jus. Entertainment. Atmosphere reminiscent of 1940s Hollywood-style supper club. Theatrical setting with ornately draped ceiling, faux palm trees; stage at one end of dining rm. Jacket. Cr cds: A, DS, MC, V.

D

★ ★ **TRIBECA.** *242 N Beverly Dr. 310/271-1595.* Hrs: noon-4 pm, 6 pm-midnight; Fri & Sat 6 pm-1 am. Closed Memorial Day, July 4, Dec 25. Res accepted. Bar to 2 am. A la carte entrees: lunch $8-$16, dinner $15-$30. Specializes in seafood, meats, pasta, salads. Valet parking (evenings). Turn-of-the-century decor. Cr cds: A, C, D, DS, MC, V.

Unrated Dining Spot

ED DEBEVIC'S. *134 N La Cienega Blvd. 310/659-1952.* Hrs: 11:30 am-11 pm; Fri & Sat to 1 am. Closed Thanksgiving, Dec 25. Res accepted. Bar. Semi-a la carte: lunch, dinner $4.50-$7.50. Child's meals. Specialties: meatloaf, hamburgers, chicken. Own desserts. Salad bar. Valet parking. 1950s-style diner; memorabilia of the era. Staff provides entertainment: singing, dancing. Cr cds: A, MC, V.

D

Hollywood

Motels

✔★ ★ **BEST WESTERN.** *6141 Franklin Ave (90028), US 101 Gower St exit to Franklin Ave, then 1 blk W. 213/464-5181; FAX 213/962-0536.* 82 units, 3-4 story, 45 kits. S $50-$55; D $65-$75; each addl $10; kit. units $10 addl; under 12 free; wkly rates; higher rates Rose Bowl. Crib $5. Pet accepted, some restrictions. Heated pool. TV; cable. Restaurant 7 am-9 pm. Rm serv. Ck-out noon. Sundries. Refrigerators. Cr cds: A, C, D, DS, ER, JCB, MC, V.

Hotels

★ ★ **HOLIDAY INN.** *1755 N Highland Ave (90028), US 101 exit Highland Ave S 1/2 mi. 213/462-7181; FAX 213/466-9072.* 470 rms, 23 story. S, D $89-$134; each addl $15; suites $119-$195; under 18 free. Crib free. Pet accepted, some restrictions. TV; cable. Heated pool. Restaurant 6 am-10 pm; revolving rooftop dining rm 6-11 pm. Bars 11-2 am; entertainment, dancing Tues-Sat. Ck-out noon. Coin lndry. Meeting rms. Concierge. Gift shop. Exercise equipt; bicycles, rower. Refrigerators avail. Cr cds: A, C, D, DS, JCB, MC, V.

D ✔ ≋ 🕇 ⊠ 🔥 SC

★ ★ ★ **LE MONTROSE SUITE HOTEL DE GRAND LUXE.** *(900 Hammond St, West Hollywood 90069) US 101 exit Sunset Blvd W to Hammond St. 310/855-1115; res: 800/776-0666; FAX 310/657-9192.* 110 suites, 5 story. Suites $155-$235; under 12 free; wknd rates. Crib free. Covered parking $10, valet. Pet accepted. TV; cable, in-rm movies. Heated pool; poolside serv. Restaurant 7 am-10:45 pm. Ck-out noon. Meeting rm. Concierge. Lighted tennis. Exercise rm; instructor, weight machine, treadmill, whirlpool, sauna. Bathrm phones, refrigerators, minibars, fireplaces; many wet bars. Balconies. Art nouveau decor. Cr cds: A, C, D, ER, JCB, MC, V.

D ✔ 🕇 ≋ 🕇 ⊠ 🔥 SC

★ ★ ★ **RADISSON HOLLYWOOD ROOSEVELT.** *7000 Hollywood Blvd (90028), US 101 exit Highland Ave, S to Hollywood Blvd. 213/466-7000; FAX 213/462-8056.* 335 rms, 2-12 story, 47 suites. S, D $109-$149; each addl $20; suites $169-$1,500; under 18 free. Crib free. Valet parking $9.50. TV; cable. Heated pool; poolside serv. Restaurant 6 am-11 pm. Bar; entertainment, dancing. Concierge. Gift shop. Exercise equipt; weight machine, bicycles, whirlpool. Game rm. Minibars; some bathrm phones. Refrigerators avail. Site of first Academy Awards presentation. Cr cds: A, C, D, DS, ER, JCB, MC, V.

★ ★ **RAMADA-WEST HOLLYWOOD.** (8585 Santa Monica Blvd, West Hollywood 90069) US 101 exit Santa Monica Blvd, then 5 mi W. 310/652-6400; FAX 310/652-2135. 175 rms, 4 story, 26 suites. S, D $105-$115; each addl $15; suites $139-$250; under 18 free. Crib free. TV; cable, in-rm movies avail. Heated pool. Restaurant 6:30 am-2 pm, 5-10 pm. Ck-out noon. Coin lndry. Shopping arcade. Airport transportation. Health club privileges. Bathrm phones; some refrigerators, minibars. Some balconies. Cr cds: A, C, D, DS, JCB, MC, V.

Restaurants

✔★ ★ **ANTONIO'S.** 7472 Melrose Ave, US 101 Melrose Ave exit, W 3 mi. 213/655-0480. Hrs: 11 am-11 pm. Closed Mon; Thanksgiving, Dec 25. Res accepted. Mexican menu. Bar. A la carte entrees: lunch $7-$10, dinner $10.75-$16.95. Specialties: pollo yucateco, chile en nogada. Strolling musicians wkend evenings. Valet parking. Outdoor dining. Family owned. Cr cds: A, MC, V.

★ ★ **CA' BREA.** 346 S La Brea Ave, I-10 La Brea Ave exit, N 2 mi. 213/938-2863. Hrs: 11:30 am-2:30 pm, 5:30-11 pm; Sat from 5:30 pm. Closed Sun. Res accepted. Northern Italian menu. Bar. A la carte entrees: lunch, dinner $8.25-$21.95. Specializes in authentic Venetian dishes. Valet parking. Italian cafe decor. Cr cds: A, C, D, DS, MC, V.

✔★ **CAIOTI.** 2100 Laurel Canyon Blvd, N of Sunset Blvd at jct Kirkwood Dr. 213/650-2988. Hrs: 11 am-11 pm. Closed some major hols. Res accepted. Italian, Amer menu. Wine, beer. Semi-a la carte: lunch $6-$10, dinner $6-$15. Specializes in pizza, pasta, salad, grilled entrees. Own breads. Outdoor dining. Rural setting. Cr cds: A, MC, V.

★ ★ **CITRUS.** 6703 Melrose Ave, US 101 Melrose Ave exit, W 2 mi. 213/857-0034. Hrs: noon-2:30 pm, 6:30-10:30 pm; Fri to 11 pm; Sat 6-11 pm. Closed Sun; major hols. Res accepted. California, French cuisine. Bar. A la carte entrees: lunch $12-$15, dinner $23.50-$29. Complete meals: dinner $50-$55 . Specializes in baby salmon, scallops. Valet parking. Open kitchen. Cr cds: A, C, D, JCB, MC, V.

★ **DAN TANA'S.** (9071 Santa Monica Blvd, West Hollywood 90069) 310/275-9888. Hrs: 5 pm-1 am. Closed Thanksgiving, Dec 25. Res required. Northern Italian menu. Bar. A la carte entrees: dinner $12-$36. Specializes in NY prime steak, white fish. Valet parking. 2 dining areas. New York-style Italian restaurant with fireplace. Family-owned. Cr cds: A, C, D, DS, MC, V.

★ ★ **EMILIO'S.** 6602 Melrose Ave, US 101 Melrose Ave exit, W 2 mi. 213/935-4922. Hrs: 5 pm-midnight; Thurs & Fri also 11:30 am-3 pm. Closed Thanksgiving, Dec 25. Res accepted. Italian menu. Bar. Wine cellar. A la carte entrees: lunch $8.50-$15, dinner $10.50-$22. Child's meals. Specialties: brodetto di mare, chitarra al pomodoro e basilico. Own pasta. Valet parking. Balcony overlooking illuminated fountain. Family-owned. Cr cds: A, C, D, ER, JCB, MC, V.

★ ★ **L'ORANGERIE.** 903 N La Cienega Blvd, US 101 Santa Monica Blvd exit, W to La Cienega Blvd then S 2 blks. 310/652-9770. Hrs: noon-2 pm, 6:30-11 pm; Sat-Mon from 6:30 pm. Res required. Classic French menu. Bar. A la carte entrees: lunch $11-$26, dinner $26-$45. Complete meals: dinner $60. Specializes in fish flown from France. Own pastries. Valet parking. Courtyard terrace & patio dining. Classic French chateau decor. Jacket. Cr cds: A, C, D, DS, JCB, MC, V.

★ ★ **LE DOME.** (8720 Sunset Blvd, West Hollywood 90069) 310/659-6919. Hrs: noon-midnight; Sat from 6 pm. Closed Sun; major hols. Res accepted. Continental, French menu. Bar. A la carte entrees: lunch $12-$20, dinner $16.50-$25. Specializes in fresh fish, prime beef. Valet parking. Circular bar. Art noveau decor. Cr cds: A, C, D, MC, V.

✔★ **LE PETIT FOUR.** 8654 Sunset Blvd. 310/652-4308. Hrs: 8 am-11 pm; Sun from 9 am; Sun brunch 9 am-6 pm. Closed Dec 25. Res accepted. French, Italian menu. Wine, beer. Semi-a la carte: bkfst $3-$10.50, lunch, dinner $4.25-$12.50. Sun brunch $3-$10.50. Specializes in fresh fish, pasta, salad. Parking. Outdoor dining. Photo collection of models who frequent the restaurant. Sidewalk dining area has bistro atmosphere; lots of "star" watching. Cr cds: A, C, D, MC, V.

★ **MUSSO & FRANK GRILL.** (6667 Hollywood Blvd, Hollywood 90028) 213/467-7788. Hrs: 11 am-11 pm. Closed Sun & Mon; major hols. Res accepted. Continental menu. Bar. A la carte entrees: lunch, dinner $7-$22.50. Specialties: grenadine of beef with Bearnaise sauce, veal scaloppini saute Marsala. Parking. Historic restaurant opened 1919. Famed "Round Table" of Saroyan, Thurber, Falkner and Fitzgerald met here. Menu changes daily. Cr cds: A, C, D, DS, MC, V.

★ ★ **THE PALM.** (9001 Santa Monica Blvd, West Hollywood) I-405 exit Santa Monica Blvd, NE 3 mi. 310/550-8811. Hrs: noon-10:30 pm; Sat from 5 pm; Sun 5-9:30 pm. Closed most major hols. Res accepted. Bar. A la carte entrees: lunch $9-$15, dinner $15-$35. Specializes in steak, lobster. Valet parking. Several dining areas. Informal, "speakeasy" atmosphere. Hollywood caricatures cover walls and ceiling. Cr cds: A, C, D, MC, V.

★ ★ ★ **PATINA.** 5955 Melrose Ave, US 101 Melrose Ave exit, W 1¹/₂ mi. 213/467-1108. Hrs: 11:30 am-2:30 pm, 6-9:30 pm; Fri to 10:30 pm; Sat 5:30-10:30 pm; Sun, Mon 6-9:30 pm. Closed some major hols. Res accepted; required wkends. French, California menu. Bar. Wine list. A la carte entrees: lunch $10-$16.50, dinner $22.95-$25.50. Complete meals: dinner $47.50-$57.50. Specialties: Santa Barbara shrimp, peppered tournedos of tuna. Valet parking. Casual elegance. Cr cds: A, D, DS, MC, V.

★ ★ ★ **RISTORANTE CHIANTI & CUCINA.** 7383 Melrose Ave, US 101 Melrose Ave exit, W 3 mi. 213/653-8333. Hrs: Cucina 11:30 am-11:30 pm, Fri, Sat to midnight; Sun 4:30-11 pm; Chianti 5:30-10:30 pm; Fri, Sat to 11 pm. Closed Thanksgiving, Dec 25. Res accepted. Northern Italian menu. Bar. A la carte entrees: lunch, dinner $6.50-$18. Specializes in fresh seafood, pasta. Valet parking. Outdoor dining. Two distinct dining areas. Cr cds: A, C, D, MC, V.

★ ★ ★ **SPAGO.** (8795 Sunset Blvd, West Hollywood) US 101 Sunset Blvd exit. 310/652-4025. Hrs: 6 pm-midnight. Closed some major hols. Res required. California menu. Bar. A la carte entrees: dinner $13-$24.50. Specializes in gourmet pizza, lobster ravioli, fresh fish. Own pasta. Valet parking. View of West Hollywood. Cr cds: C, D, DS, MC, V.

✔★ ★ **TRIGO.** (8571 Santa Monica Blvd, West Hollywood) CA 101 Santa Monica Blvd exit, W 5 mi. 310/652-9263. Hrs: 6:30-11 am, 11:30 am-2 pm, 5-10 pm; Fri, Sat to 11 pm. Res accepted. Bar. A la carte entrees: bkfst $3.95-$7.95, lunch $5.95-$8.95, dinner $7.95-$16.95. Specializes in Califorina, Mediterranean cuisine. Open grill. Cr cds: A, C, D, DS, MC, V.

★ ★ **YAMASHIRO.** 1999 N Sycamore Ave, US 101 Highland Ave exit, S to Franklin Ave then W to Sycamore, in Hollywood Hills. 213/466-5125. Hrs: 5:30-10 pm; Fri, Sat to 11 pm. Closed some major hols. Res accepted. Japanese, continental menu. Bar 4:30 pm-1 am.

Semi-a la carte: dinner $14.95-$28.95. Specialties: Yamashiro feast, tornedos Imperial. Valet parking. Outdoor garden dining. Japanese palace and garden setting. View of Hollywood. Cr cds: A, C, D, DS, JCB, MC, V.

D

Westwood Village

Motel

★★ **HOTEL DEL CAPRI.** 10587 Wilshire Blvd (90024). 310/474-3511; res: 800/44-HOTEL; FAX 310/470-9999. 80 units, 2-4 story, 46 kit. suites. S $85; D $95-$105; each addl $10; kit. suites $110-$140. Crib $10. TV; cable. Heated pool. Complimentary continental bkfst. Restaurant nearby. Ck-out noon. Guest lndry. Bellhops. Valet serv. Bathrm phones, refrigerators; some in-rm whirlpools. Cr cds: A, C, D, MC, V.

 SC

Hotels

★★ **HILGARD HOUSE, A CLARION CARRIAGE INN.** 927 Hilgard Ave (90024). 310/208-3945. 47 rms, 4 story. S $89-$99; D $99-$109; each addl $10; under 18 free. Crib free. TV; cable. Complimentary continental bkfst. Ck-out noon. Free covered parking. Refrigerators. Cr cds: A, C, D, MC, V.

D

★★ **HOLIDAY INN-WESTWOOD PLAZA.** (10740 Wilshire Blvd, Los Angeles 90024) 310/475-8711; FAX 310/475-5220. 294 rms, 19 story. S $130-$140; D $130-$145; each addl $10; suites $200-$250; under 18 free. Crib free. Pet accepted. TV; cable. Heated pool; pool-side serv. Restaurant 6:30 am-10 pm. Bar 4 pm-midnight. Ck-out noon. Meeting rms. Concierge. Gift shop. Valet parking. Free UCLA transportation. Exercise equipt; weights, bicycles, whirlpool, sauna. Game rm. Refrigerators. Cr cds: A, C, D, DS, JCB, MC, V.

 SC

WESTWOOD MARQUIS HOTEL & GARDEN. (New general manager, therefore not rated) 930 Hilgard Ave (90024), west of downtown L.A. 310/208-8765; res: 800/421-2317; FAX 310/824-0355. 258 suites (1-3 bedrm), 16 story. S, D $220-$650; wknd rates. Crib free. TV; cable, in-rm movies. 2 heated pools. 4 restaurants; dining rm 6:30 am-11 pm (also see DYNASTY ROOM). Afternoon tea. Rm serv 24 hrs. Bar 10-2 am; pianist, harpist. Ck-out noon. Meeting rms. Concierge. Maid serv 24 hrs. Barber, beauty shop. Gift shop. Garage; valet parking. Complimentary limo to Beverly Hills. Exercise rm; instructor, weights, bicycles, sauna, steam rm. Massage. Refrigerators, minibars. Butler service in penthouse suites. Individually decorated suites. European elegance. Cr cds: A, C, D, DS, JCB, MC, V.

Restaurants

★★★ **DYNASTY ROOM.** (See Westwood Marquis Hotel) 310/208-8765. Hrs: 6-10:30 pm. Res accepted. Continental menu. Bar 10-1:30 am. A la carte entrees: dinner $17.50-$25. Specialties: potato pancake with smoked salmon and cavier, rack of lamb, seafood mixed grill. Valet parking. Elegant dining; collection of Ming dynasty ceramics. Cr cds: A, C, D, JCB, MC, V.

D

★ **MONTY'S.** 1100 Glendon Ave. 310/208-8787. Hrs: 11 am-3 pm, 5 pm-1 am; Sat & Sun 5 pm-midnight. Closed Thanksgiving, Dec 25. Res accepted. Bar to 2 am, Sat & Sun from 5 pm. Semi-a la carte: lunch $6-$16, dinner $13-$50. Specializes in prime rib, steak, seafood. Entertainment Tues-Sat. Valet parking. Located on top floor of building; panoramic view. Cr cds: A, C, D, MC, V.

Louisville

Founded: 1778	
Pop: 269,063	
Elev: 462 feet	
Time zone: Eastern	
Area code: 502	

To the horse racing enthusiast, Louisville means only one thing—the famed Kentucky Derby, culmination of a 10-day festival that has been held here each spring for more than 100 years. But there is more to Louisville than the enjoyment of jockeys and juleps—it is also a major producer of bourbon and tobacco. And for fans of the great American pastime, the crack of a ball against a Louisville Slugger bat is music to the ears. There is, of course, other music in this diverse city. An opera, orchestra, theaters, ballet and other fine arts organizations are evidence of Louisville's dedication to culture.

The Spanish, French, English, Scots, Irish and Germans all had roles in the exploration and development of the area. George Rogers Clark brought settlers to the region in the winter of 1778-79. It became an informal military base and played an important role in driving the British and Native Americans out of the Midwest. Located at the falls of the Ohio River, Louisville is a city long nurtured by river traffic. In its early years, before a canal bypassed the falls, Louisville was an important portage point. With the advent of the steamboat on the Ohio in the early 19th century, the city became a vital port and its growth was rapid.

The social highlight of a very social city is the Derby, a mélange of festival, fashion show, spectacle and celebration of the horse. After the money is lost or won and the last of the mint juleps is swallowed, Louisville returns to normalcy, a city Southern in its manner, Midwestern in its pace.

Business

Known for its bourbon distilleries, Louisville is also a major distribution point for tobacco. Electrical appliances rank third in a vast array of manufactured products, from candy and clothing to synthetic rubber. Other major industries include lumber milling, meat packing, oil refining, photoengraving and publishing.

Louisville is one of the nation's leading river ports. An enormous amount of coal passes through the locks on the Ohio River each year. Louisville is also an important air and rail center.

Convention Facilities

The Kentucky Fair and Exposition Center is a single-floor, multipurpose building covering one million square feet of exhibition space under one roof. Freedom Hall, the center's main arena, seats 19,400 people. Meeting rooms can be used individually or in combination to accommodate from 350 to 1,250 people. The ballroom seats up to 850. Newmarket Hall is an air-conditioned amphitheater seating 600. There are 24 buildings in the Exposition Center Complex, with parking for 19,000 cars.

Louisville Gardens has over 36,000 square feet of multi-use space. The main arena has 5,000 permanent seats and room for 2,000 more on the arena floor. The second-floor theater seats 775. Meeting rooms have a capacity of 60 to 700 people. The Grand Arena can accommodate banquets for 2,200. Located in the heart of downtown, it is within easy walking distance of more than 2,200 hotel rooms.

A third exhibit and convention center, Commonwealth Convention Center, is situated on the 5-block 4th Avenue Mall. It is ideally suited in size, location and design for intermediate-sized conventions and trade shows. It has 150,000 square feet of exhibit space that can be divided into 3 halls of 50,000, 30,000 and 20,000 square feet, and 36 meeting rooms holding from 25 to 1,000 people. The center is the heart of a convention complex that includes 600- and 700-car garages and a 388-room hotel.

Historical Areas

Louisville is a city that reveres its past. Two beautiful historic mansions, which are open to the public, are owned and operated by the Historic Homes Foundation. Farmington, located off the intersection of I-264 and US 31E, was built in 1808-10. The design of this Federal-style mansion was based on a plan by Thomas Jefferson. The original deed to the land, signed by Governor Patrick Henry of Virginia, is displayed on a wall. Locust Grove, the last home of George Rogers Clark, is on Blankenbaker Lane near I-71. Both houses are authentically and beautifully restored and furnished and are complemented by formal gardens.

The Preservation Alliance of Louisville and Jefferson County encourages restoration efforts in the city. The West Main Street Historic District encompasses the founding site of the city and the mercantile district of the late 1800s. Old Victorian warehouses, displaying some of the best remaining cast-iron architecture in the United States, are being converted into performing arts centers and offices.

The Belgravia and St James Courts Historic District was a residential neighborhood developed on the site of the 1883 Southern Exposition. Today the fine late-Victorian houses are being privately preserved and restored.

The 19th-century German community, Butchertown, houses antique shops and the one-time residence of Thomas A. Edison.

Sports and Recreation

Louisville's biggest sporting event is, of course, Derby Week. But sports in Louisville can also mean college basketball, wrestling, ice skating, hot-air balloon racing, auto racing, harness and Thoroughbred racing.

The Redbirds, minor league farm team for the St Louis Cardinals, play baseball from April through August in the stadium at the fairgrounds.

Within and surrounding the city are 11 major urban parks. There are numerous tennis courts, golf courses and swimming pools, as well as opportunities for fishing, hiking and camping.

Entertainment

The Kentucky Center for the Arts not only houses the Kentucky Opera Association, Stage One: Louisville Children's Theatre, Louisville Ballet and the Louisville Orchestra, it also hosts bluegrass, Broadway, jazz, country & western and film series.

Actors Theatre of Louisville, designated "the state theatre of Kentucky," offers major productions, which attract large and enthusiastic audiences.

For a different kind of relaxation, the stern-wheeler steamer *Belle of Louisville,* which has been cruising the Ohio River for half a century, still sets off for pleasant afternoon or evening excursions. Each Derby season it stirs up excitement by challenging Cincinnati's *Delta Queen* to an old-time steamboat race.

Sightseeing

Two famous sights within Louisville are Riverfront Plaza and Churchill Downs. Bus and walking tours of the city begin at First and Liberty streets. An Information Center of the Visitors Bureau is also located here. Other Information Centers are located at Standiford Field Airport and in the Galleria shopping mall downtown.

Among the industrial tours of interest are Philip Morris, Inc, a major tobacco distributor, and just across the river, Hillerich and Bradsby's Slugger Park, where golf clubs and the famous Louisville Slugger baseball bats are manufactured.

The city's major shopping area is the Fourth Avenue Mall. On the Mall is the Galleria Complex, twin 26-story towers with a connecting atrium and enough shops, stores and boutiques to satisfy the most discriminating consumer.

Outside of Louisville, temptations for the sightseer include tours of horse farms in the bluegrass region to the east of the city, Fort Knox, Mammoth Cave, Abraham Lincoln's birthplace, Bardstown and a wealth of lovely lakes and mountains.

General References

Founded: 1778 **Pop:** 269,063 **Elev:** 462 feet **Time zone:** Eastern **Area code:** 502

Phone Numbers

POLICE & FIRE: 911
FBI: 583-3941
POISON CONTROL CENTER: 589-8222
TIME: 585-5961 **WEATHER:** 363-9655

Information Sources

Louisville Convention & Visitors Bureau, 400 S First St, 40202; 582-3732 or 800/626-5646.
Louisville Chamber of Commerce, 600 W Main St, 40202; 625-0000.
Metropolitan Park and Recreation Board, 456-8100.

Transportation

AIRLINES: American; Continental; Delta; Midwest Express; Northwest; Southwest; TWA; United; USAir; and other commuter and regional airlines. For the most current airline schedules and information consult the *Official Airline Guide,* published twice monthly.
AIRPORT: Standiford Field, 367-4636.
AIRPORT TRANSPORTATION: Taxi $13-$20; Limo $50-$70; Shuttle bus $5.50; Bus (TARC) 60¢.

CAR RENTAL AGENCIES: (See Toll-Free Numbers) Avis 368-5851; Budget/Sears 363-4300; Hertz 361-0181; National 361-2515; Thrifty 367-0231.
PUBLIC TRANSPORTATION: Transit Authority of River City, 10th & Broadway, 40202; 585-1234. TARC-minibuses circulate throughout the center city.

Newspaper

The Courier-Journal.

Convention Facilities

Commonwealth Convention Center, 221 4th Ave, 588-4381.
Kentucky Fair & Exposition Center, I-65 at I-264, 367-5000.
Louisville Gardens, 525 W Muhammad Ali Blvd, 587-3800.

Sports & Recreation

Kentucky Fair & Exposition Center, I-65 at I-264, 367-5000 (University of Louisville, basketball).

Racetrack
Churchill Downs, 700 Central Ave, 636-4400.

Cultural Facilities

Theaters
Actors Theatre of Louisville, 316 W Main St, 584-1265.
Bunbury Theatre, 112 S 7th St, 585-5306.
Derby Dinner Playhouse, 525 Marriott Dr, Clarksville, IN, 812/288-8281.
Kentucky Center for the Arts, 5 Riverfront Plaza, 584-7777.
Stage One: Louisville Children's Theatre, 425 W Market St, 589-5946.

Concert Hall
Memorial Auditorium, 970 S 4th St, 584-4911.

Museums
Howard Steamboat Museum, 1101 E Market St, Jeffersonville, IN, 812/283-3728.
Kentucky Derby Museum, 704 Central Ave, 637-1111.
Louisville Science Center, 727 W Main St, 561-6100.
Nicol Museum of Biblical Archaeology, Southern Baptist Theological Seminary Campus, 2825 Lexington Rd, 897-4141.

Art Museums and Galleries
Allen R. Hite Art Institute, University of Louisville, Belknap Campus, 852-6794.
J.B. Speed Art Museum, 2035 S 3rd St, 636-2893.
Kentucky Art & Craft Gallery, 609 W Main St, 589-0102.
Louisville Visual Art Association, Water Tower, 3005 Upper River Rd, 896-2146.

Points of Interest

Historical
Cave Hill Cemetery, 701 Baxter Ave, 451-5630.
Christ Church Cathedral, 421 S 2nd St, 587-1354.
Farmington, 3033 Bardstown Rd, at jct Watterson Expwy, 452-9920.
Jefferson County Courthouse, Jefferson St, between 5th & 6th Sts, 574-5700.

Locust Grove, 561 Blankenbaker Lane, 897-9845.
Thomas Edison House, 731 E Washington, 585-5247.
Zachary Taylor National Cemetery, 4701 Brownsboro Rd, 893-3852.

Other Attractions

American Printing House for the Blind, 1839 Frankfort Ave, 895-2405.
Fourth Avenue Mall, on 4th St, from Market St to Broadway.
Hadley Pottery, 1570 Story Ave, 584-2171.
Louisville Falls Fountain, Riverfront Plaza.
Louisville Zoological Gardens, 1100 Trevilian Way, 459-2181.
Philip Morris Inc, Broadway & 18th St, 566-1293.
Rauch Memorial Planetarium, 2301 S 3rd St, 852-6664.

Sightseeing Tours

Belle of Louisville, Riverfront Plaza, foot of 4th St, 574-2355.
Gray Line bus tours, 1601 S Preston St, 636-5664.

Annual Events

Kentucky Derby Festival, 584-6383. Mid-Apr-early May.
Kentucky Derby, Churchill Downs. 1st Sat May.
Kentucky State Fair, Kentucky Fair & Exposition Center, 367-5000. Late Aug.
St James Court Art Show, Old Louisville, 636-5023. Oct.
Dickens on Main St, West Main St Historic District, 583-8622. Fri after Thanksgiving.

City Neighborhoods

Many of the restaurants, unrated dining establishments and some lodgings listed under Louisville include neighborhoods as well as exact street addresses. Geographic descriptions of these areas are given, followed by a table of restaurants arranged by neighborhood.

Downtown: South of the Ohio River, west of Shelby St, north of Oak St and east of 9th St. South of Downtown: South of Oak St.
East of Downtown: East of Shelby St.
Old Louisville: South of Breckenridge St, west of I-65, north of Eastern Pkwy and east of 9th St.

Lodgings and Food

LOUISVILLE RESTAURANTS
BY NEIGHBORHOOD AREAS

(For full description, see alphabetical listings under Restaurants)

DOWNTOWN

Colonnade Cafeteria. 4th St & Muhammad Ali Blvd

The English Grill (The Brown Hotel). 335 W Broadway

Hasenour's. 1028 Barret Ave

Kunz's. 115 S 4th Ave

Old Spaghetti Factory. 235 W Market St

Timothy's. 826 E Broadway

Vincenzo's. 150 S 5th St

SOUTH OF DOWNTOWN

Fifth Quarter. 1241 Durrett Lane

Masterson's. 1830 S 3rd St

Uptown Cafe. 1624 Bardstown Rd

EAST OF DOWNTOWN

Blue Boar Cafeteria. 232 Oxmoor Shopping Center

Cafe Metro. 1700 Bardstown Rd

Darryl's 1815 Restaurant. 3110 Bardstown Rd

Ferd Grisanti's. 10212 Taylorsville Rd

Le Relais. Taylorsville Rd

Mamma Grisanti. 3938 DuPont Circle

New Orleans House East. 9424 Shelbyville Rd

Sichuan Garden. 9850 Linn Station Rd

Note: *When a listing is located in a town that does not have its own city heading, it will appear under the city nearest to its location. In these cases, the address and town appear in parenthesis immediately following the name of the establishment.*

Motels

(Rates are generally much higher during Kentucky Derby; may be 3-day min)

★ ★ **COURTYARD BY MARRIOTT.** *9608 Blairwood Rd (40222), I-64 Hurstbourne Lane exit 15, east of downtown.* 502/429-0006; FAX 502/429-5926. 151 rms, 4 story. S $82; D $92; suites $93-$99; under 18 free; wkend rates. Crib free. TV; cable. Pool. Complimentary coffee in rms. Bkfst avail. Bar 4-11 pm. Ck-out 1 pm. Coin lndry. Meeting rms. Valet serv. Exercise equipt; weights, bicycles, whirlpool. Refrigerators avail. Minibar in suites. Cr cds: A, C, D, DS, MC, V.

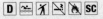

★ ★ **FAIRFIELD INN BY MARRIOTT.** *9400 Blairwood Rd (40222), I-64 exit 15, east of downtown.* 502/339-1900. 105 rms, 3 story. S $44.95-$55.95; D $53.95-$55.95; each addl $7; under 18 free. Crib free. TV; cable. Pool. Continental bkfst avail. Complimentary cof-

fee in lobby. Restaurant adj 6 am-11 pm. Ck-out noon. Meeting rms. Cr cds: A, C, D, DS, MC, V.

★ ★ **HAMPTON INN.** *1902 Embassy Square Blvd (40299), I-64 Hurstbourne Lane exit 15, east of downtown.* 502/491-2577, FAX 502/491-1325. 119 rms, 2 story. S $42-$48; D $49-$55; under 18 free. Crib free. TV; cable. Pool. Continental bkfst. Restaurant nearby. Ck-out noon. Meeting rm. Cr cds: A, C, D, DS, MC, V.

✔ ★ **RED ROOF INN.** *9330 Blairwood Rd (40222), 1 blk N of I-64 exit 15, east of downtown.* 502/426-7621; FAX 502/426-7933. 108 rms, 2 story. S $29.99; D $35.99; 3 or more, $41.99; under 18 free. Crib free. TV; cable. Complimentary coffee. Restaurant adj 6 am-11 pm. Ck-out noon. Cr cds: A, C, D, DS, MC, V.

★ ★ **RESIDENCE INN BY MARRIOTT.** *120 N Hurstbourne Pkwy (40222), east of downtown.* 502/425-1821; FAX 502/425-1821, ext. 401. 96 kit. suites, 2 story. 1-bedrm $85-$110; 2-bedrm $105-$130; family rates; some wkend rates. Crib free. TV; cable. Heated pool; whirlpool, lifeguard. Complimentary continental bkfst. Ck-out noon. Coin lndry. Valet serv. Sport court. Health club privileges. Refrigerators, fireplaces. Grills. Cr cds: A, C, D, DS, MC, V.

★ ★ **SIGNATURE INN.** *6515 Signature Dr (40213), I-65 exit 128, south of downtown.* 502/968-4100; FAX 502/968-4100. 123 rms, 2 story. S $55-$58; D $62-$65; under 18 free; wkend rates Dec-Feb. Crib free. TV; cable, in-rm movies avail. Pool. Complimentary continental bkfst, coffee. Restaurant adj 6 am-11 pm. Ck-out noon. Meeting rms. Valet serv. Sundries. Free airport transportation. Health club privileges. Cr cds: A, D, DS, MC, V.

★ ★ **STUDIO PLUS.** *9801 Bunsen Way (40299), I-64 exit 15, east of downtown.* 502/499-6215; FAX 502/495-3551. 76 kit. suites, 2-3 story. No elvtr. S, D $55-$65; wkly rates. TV. Pool. Restaurant nearby. Ck-out noon. Coin lndry. Exercise equipt; weights, bicycles, sauna. Cr cds: A, C, D, MC, V.

✔ ★ **SUPER 8.** *4800 Preston Hwy (40213), off I-65 exit 130, south of downtown.* 502/968-0088; FAX /968-0088. 100 rms, 3 story. S $39.88; D $49.88; each addl $5; under 12 free. Crib free. TV; cable. Complimentary coffee in lobby. Restaurant opp open 24 hrs. Ck-out 11 am. Airport transportation. Cr cds: A, C, D, DS, MC, V.

Motor Hotels

★ ★ **BRECKINRIDGE INN.** *2800 Breckinridge Lane (40220), I-264 exit 18A, south of downtown.* 502/456-5050; FAX 502/451-1577. 123 rms, 2 story. S, D $65; each addl $7; suites $65-$95; under 12 free. Crib $7. Pet accepted; $10. TV; cable. 2 pools, 1 indoor; lifeguard. Restaurant 7 am-1:30 pm, 5-10 pm. Rm serv. Bar. Ck-out noon. Meeting rms. Valet serv. Sundries. Gift shop. Barber shop. Free airport transportation. Lighted tennis. Exercise equipt; weights, bicycle, sauna. Cr cds: A, C, D, DS, MC, V.

★ ★ **EXECUTIVE INN.** *978 Phillips Lane (40213), Watterson Expressway at Fairgrounds, near Standiford Field Airport, south of downtown.* 502/367-6161; res: 800/626-2706; FAX 502/363-1880. 465 rms, 2-6 story. S $75; D $85; each addl $10; suites $160-$230; under 18 free. Crib free. TV; cable. 2 pools, 1 indoor; wading pool, poolside serv, lifeguard. Restaurants 6:30 am-11:45 pm. Rm serv. Bar 11-1 am, closed Sun. Ck-out 1 pm. Convention facilities. Bellhops. Sundries. Gift shop. Barber, beauty shop. Free airport transportation. Exercise rm; instructor, weights, bicycles, sauna. Lawn games. Some refrigerators. Some private patios, balconies. Tudor-inspired architecture. Cr cds: A, C, D, DS, MC, V.

`D` `≈` `⚗` `✈` `⛵` `🔥` `SC`

★ ★ ★ **EXECUTIVE WEST.** *830 Phillips Lane (40209), Freedom Way at Fairgrounds, near Standiford Field Airport, south of downtown.* 502/367-2251; res: 800/626-2708 (exc KY); FAX 502/363-2087. 611 rms, 8 story. S $72; D $82; each addl $10; suites $105-$240; under 17 free; wknd rates. Crib free. Pet accepted; $100. TV; cable. Indoor/outdoor pool; poolside serv, lifeguard. Restaurant 7 am-midnight. Rm serv. Bar; entertainment. Ck-out 1 pm. Convention facilities. Bellhops. Gift shop. Barber, beauty shop. Free airport transportation. Health club privileges. Refrigerator in suites. Kentucky Kingdom Amusement Park opp. Cr cds: A, C, D, DS, MC, V.

`D` `⚓` `≈` `✈` `⛵` `🔥` `SC`

★ ★ ★ **HOLIDAY INN.** *1325 S Hurstbourne Pkwy (40222), at I-64 exit 15, east of downtown.* 502/426-2600; FAX 502/423-1605. 267 rms, 7 story. S, D $76-$99; each addl $10; suites $89-$275; under 18 free. Crib free. TV; cable. Indoor pool; lifeguard. Coffee in rms. Restaurant 6:30 am-2 pm, 5-10 pm. Rm serv. Bar 4 pm-1 am. Ck-out noon. Meeting rms. Bellhops. Valet serv. Gift shop. Airport transportation. Exercise equipt; weight machines, bicycles, whirlpool, sauna. Game rm. Refrigerator in suites. Cr cds: A, C, D, DS, JCB, MC, V.

`D` `≈` `⚗` `⛵` `🔥` `SC`

★ ★ **HOLIDAY INN AIRPORT.** *1465 Gardiner Lane (40213).* 502/452-6361; FAX 502/451-1541. 200 rms, 3 story. S, D $67-$85; each addl $7; under 12 free; wkend rates. Crib free. Pet accepted. TV; cable. Pool; poolside serv, lifeguard. Complimentary coffee in rms. Restaurant 11 am-11 pm. Rm serv. Bar to midnight. Ck-out noon. Coin lndry. Meeting rms. Bellhops. Sundries. Valet serv. Free airport transportation. Tennis. Exercise equipt; weight machine, rowers. Game rm. Cr cds: A, D, DS, JCB, MC, V.

`D` `⚓` `⚗` `≈` `✈` `⛵` `🔥` `SC`

✔ **WILSON INN.** *9802 Bunsen Pkwy (40299), I-64 exit 15, east of downtown.* 502/499-0000; res: 800/945-7667; FAX 502/499-0000. 108 rms, 5 story, 32 suites, 50 kit. units. S $34.95-$39.95; D $41.95-$46.95; each addl $5; suites $51.95-$56.95; kit. units $41.95-$46.95; under 18 free. Crib free. Pet accepted, some restrictions. TV; cable. Complimentary continental bkfst 6-10 am, coffee. Restaurant nearby. Ck-out noon. Meeting rms. Sundries. Free airport transportation. Refrigerators. Cr cds: A, C, D, DS, MC, V.

`D` `⚓` `⛵` `🔥` `🔥` `SC`

Hotels

★ ★ ★ ★ **THE BROWN, A CAMBERLEY HOTEL.** *335 W Broadway (40202), downtown.* 502/583-1234; res: 800/866-7666; FAX 502/587-7006. 294 rms, 16 story. S $125-$145; D $140-$160; each addl $15; suites from $300; family rates; wknd package plans. Crib free. Covered parking $7/night. TV; cable. Restaurants 6:30 am-11 pm (also see THE ENGLISH GRILL). Rm serv 24 hrs. Bar 11-1 am. Ck-out 11 am. Convention facilities. Shopping arcade. Barber, beauty shop. Airport transportation. Exercise equipt; weights, stair machine. Refrigerator in suites. Elegantly restored 1923 hotel; Old English-style furnishings, artwork. *LUXURY LEVEL.* 58 rms, 2 story, 2 suites S $150-$180; D $165-$175; suite from $350. Concierge. Complimentary bkfst, refreshments, newspaper, shoe shine. Cr cds: A, C, D, DS, ER, JCB, MC, V.

`D` `⚗` `⛵` `🔥` `SC`

★ ★ **GALT HOUSE.** *140 4th St (40202), at River Rd, downtown.* 502/589-5200; res: 800/626-1814; FAX 502/589-3444. 656 rms, 25 story. S $90-$100; D $100-$125; each addl $12; suites $250; under 16 free; wkend rates. Crib free. TV; cable. Pool; poolside serv, lifeguard. Restaurants 6 am-midnight; dining rm 5:30-10:30 pm. Bar 11:30-1 am;

entertainment. Ck-out noon. Convention facilities. Shopping arcade. Garage parking. Refrigerator in suites. Overlooks Ohio River. Cr cds: A, C, D, DS, JCB, MC, V.

`D` `≈` `🔥` `SC`

★ ★ ★ **GALT HOUSE EAST.** *141 N 4th St (40202), downtown.* 502/589-3300; res: 800/843-4258; FAX 502/585-4266. 600 rms, 18 story. S $115-$130; D $130-$140; each addl $12; 2-bedrm suites $475; under 16 free. Crib free. TV; cable. Pool privileges adj. Restaurant adj 6-1 am. Bar from 11 am; entertainment. Ck-out noon. Garage parking. Refrigerators, wet bars. Private patios, balconies. Overlooks Ohio River. 18-story atrium. Cr cds: A, C, D, DS, JCB, MC, V.

`D` `⚓` `🔥` `SC`

★ ★ **HOLIDAY INN-DOWNTOWN.** *120 W Broadway (40202), downtown.* 502/582-2241; FAX 502/584-8591. 290 rms, 12 story. S $74-$95; D $84-$105; each addl $10; suites $295; under 19 free. Crib free. Pet accepted. TV; cable. Indoor pool; lifeguard. Coffee in rms. Restaurant 6 am-11 pm. Bar 11-2 am. Ck-out noon. Convention facilities. Gift shop. Barber. Free airport transportation. Health club privileges. Some refrigerators, minibars. Some balconies. *LUXURY LEVEL : EXECUTIVE LEVEL.* 29 rms. S $95; D $105. In-rm movies. Concierge. Private lounge, honor bar. Complimentary continental bkfst, refreshments, newpapers. Cr cds: A, C, D, DS, JCB, MC, V.

`D` `⚓` `≈` `⛵` `🔥` `SC`

★ ★ ★ **HYATT REGENCY.** *320 W Jefferson St (40202), downtown.* 502/587-3434; FAX 502/581-0133. 388 rms, 18 story. S, D $79-$165; each addl $25; suites $250-$550; under 18 free. Crib free. TV; cable, in-rm movies avail. Indoor pool. Restaurants 6:30 am-midnight. Bars 11-2 am, Sun to midnight. Ck-out noon. Convention facilities. Concierge. Gift shop. Tennis. Exercise equipt; weights, treadmill, whirlpool. Access to shopping center via enclosed walkway. Modern design. *LUXURY LEVEL : REGENCY CLUB LEVEL.* 24 rms, 1 suite. S $105-$165; D $105-$190; suite $500. Wet bar in suite. Complimentary continental bkfst, refreshments. Cr cds: A, C, D, DS, JCB, MC, V.

`D` `⚗` `⚓` `≈` `⛵` `🔥` `SC`

★ ★ **RADISSON.** *1903 Embassy Square Blvd (40299), E of I-264 at jct I-64, Hurstbourne Lane (exit 15), east of downtown.* 502/499-6220; FAX 502/499-2480. 255 rms, 10 story. S $82-$98; D $92-$108; each addl $10; under 18 free. Crib free. Pet accepted, some restrictions; $25. TV; cable. Indoor pool; poolside serv, lifeguard. Restaurant 6:30 am-2 pm, 5-10 pm; Fri, Sat to 11 pm. Bar 2 pm-2 am; entertainment, dancing. Ck-out noon. Convention facilities. Gift shop. Airport transportation. Exercise equipt; weights, bicycles, whirlpool. Health club privileges. Game rm. Balconies. Cr cds: A, C, D, DS, MC, V.

`D` `⚓` `≈` `⚗` `⛵` `🔥` `SC`

★ ★ ★ **SEELBACH.** *500 Fourth Ave (40202), downtown.* 502/585-3200; res: 800/333-3399; FAX 502/587-6564. 321 rms, 11 story. S $128-$160; D $148-$170; each addl $10; suites $210-$495; under 18 free; wkend package plans. Crib free. Pet accepted. Parking $7, valet $10. TV; cable. Pool privileges. Restaurants 6:30 am-midnight. Bar 4 pm-2 am; entertainment, dancing exc Sun. Ck-out 1 pm. Convention facilities. Concierge. Shopping arcade. Free airport, bus depot transportation. Health club privileges. Restored hotel, originally opened in 1905. Lobby has 8 murals by Arthur Thomas depicting Kentucky pioneers and Indians; rms have 4-poster beds, armoires and marble baths. *LUXURY LEVEL : CONCIERGE CLUB.* 39 rms. S $148-$180; D $168-$190. Concierge. Private lounge, honor bar. Complimentary continental bkfst, refreshments, newspaper. Cr cds: A, C, D, DS, JCB, MC, V.

`D` `⚓` `⛵` `🔥` `SC`

Inn

★ **OLD LOUISVILLE.** *1359 S 3rd St (40208), in Old Louisville.* 502/635-1574; FAX 502/637-5892. 11 rms, 8 with bath, 3 story. No rm phones. D $60-$90; suites $110-$195; under 12 free. Crib free. TV in sitting rm. Complimentary full bkfst. Restaurant nearby. Ck-out noon, ck-in 3 pm. Individually decorated rms in Victorian house (1901). Ceiling murals. Cr cds: MC, V.

Restaurants

A ★ CAFE METRO. 1700 Bardstown Rd, east of downtown. 502/458-4830. Hrs: 6-10 pm; Fri, Sat to 11 pm. Closed Sun; hols. Res accepted. Continental menu. Bar. A la carte entrees: dinner $16.95. Specialties: stuffed quail, swordfish, veal. Parking. Collection of pre-WW I German posters. Cr cds: A, MC, V.

D

✔★ ★ DARRYL'S 1815 RESTAURANT. 3110 Bardstown Rd, at I-264 exit 16, east of downtown. 502/458-1815. Hrs: 11 am-11 pm; Fri, Sat to 12:30 am. Bar. Semi-a la carte: lunch $4.99-$9.99, dinner $4.99-$15.99. Child's meals. Specializes in steak, chicken, ribs. Parking. Cr cds: A, C, D, DS, MC, V.

D

★ ★ ★ THE ENGLISH GRILL. (See The Brown Hotel) 502/583-1234. Hrs: 5-11 pm; Sun to 10 pm. Res accepted. Bar. Semi-a la carte: dinner $15.25-$24.95. Specializes in fresh seafood, rack of lamb, pasta, steak. Seasonal menus feature regional foods. English motif; leaded and stained-glass windows, artwork featuring English scenes and Thoroughbred horses. Jacket. Cr cds: A, C, D, DS, ER, JCB, MC, V.

D

★ ★ ★ FERD GRISANTI'S. 10212 Taylorsville Rd, east of downtown. 502/267-0050. Hrs: 5-10 pm; Fri, Sat to 11 pm. Closed Sun. Northern Italian menu. Res accepted. Bar. Wine list. Semi-a la carte: dinner $7.25-$16.50. Child's meals. Specializes in veal, pasta. Own baking. Parking. Contemporary Italian decor; artwork. In historic Jeffersontown. Cr cds: A, C, D, DS, MC, V.

D

★ ★ FIFTH QUARTER. 1241 Durrett Lane, south of downtown. 502/361-2363. Hrs: 11 am-2:30 pm, 5-10:30 pm; Fri to 11:30 pm; Sat from 4 pm; Sun from 11 am. Closed Dec 25. Bar. Semi-a la carte: lunch $4.59-$7.49, dinner $8.99-$19.99. Specializes in prime rib. Salad bar. Guitarist exc Sun. Parking. Rustic decor. Cr cds: A, DS, MC, V.

D SC

★ ★ HASENOUR'S. 1028 Barret Ave, downtown. 502/451-5210. Hrs: 11 am-midnight; Sun 5-11 pm. Closed some major hols. Res accepted. Bar. Semi-a la carte: lunch $4.25-$12.95, dinner $7.95-$24.95, after 10 pm menu $2.75-$8.25. Specializes in sauerbraten, fresh seafood, prime rib. Pianist Wed-Sat. Parking. Family-owned. Varied dining areas. Cr cds: A, C, D, MC, V.

D

★ ★ ★KUNZ'S. 115 S 4th Ave, at Market St, downtown. 502/585-5555. Hrs: 11 am-10:30 pm; Fri & Sat to 11:30 pm; Sun 4-10 pm. Closed Dec 25. Res accepted. Continental menu. Bar. Semi-a la carte: lunch $5.25-$6.95, dinner $10.95-$24.95. Specializes in seafood, steak. Raw bar. Salad bar (lunch). Own breads. Family-owned. Jacket (in formal dining rm). Cr cds: A, C, D, DS, MC, V.

D

★ ★ LE RELAIS. Taylorsville Rd, near Bownman Field, I-264 exit Taylorsville Rd, east of downtown. 502/451-9020. Hrs: 11:30 am-2:30 pm, 5:30-10 pm; Fri, Sat 5:30-11 pm; Sun 5:30-9 pm. Closed Mon; Thanksgiving, Dec 25. Res accepted. French menu. Bar. Semi-a la carte: lunch $4.25-$9.50, dinner $10-$19.95. Specializes in fish, tournedos. Parking. Outdoor dining. Jacket (dinner). View of landing strip. Cr cds: A, D, MC, V.

D

✔★ ★ MAMMA GRISANTI. 3938 DuPont Circle, east of downtown. 502/893-0141. Hrs: 11:30 am-2 pm, 5-10 pm; Fri, Sat 10 am-11 pm; Sun 10 am-9 pm. Res accepted. Italian menu. Bar. Semi-a la carte: bkfst $5.95-$7.95, lunch $4.40-$6.95, dinner $4.95-$13.50. Buffet: lunch $5.25. Child's meals. Specialties: lasagne, fettucini Alfredo, veal parmesan. Own pasta. Parking. Family-owned. Cr cds: A, D, DS, MC, V.

★ ★ MASTERSON'S. 1830 S 3rd St, south of downtown. 502/636-2511. Hrs: 11 am-11 pm; Sat from 9 am; Sun 9 am-8 pm. Closed July 4, Dec 24 & 25. Res accepted. Greek, Amer menu. Bar. Semi-a la carte: bkfst $1.95-$4.95, lunch $3.25-$9.75, dinner $9.25-$19.75. Buffet: bkfst $5.29, lunch $5.25. Sun brunch $8.43. Child's meals. Specializes in regional cooking, Greek dishes. Parking. Outdoor dining. Near Univ of Louisville. Family-owned. Cr cds: A, C, D, DS, MC, V.

D SC

★ ★ NEW ORLEANS HOUSE EAST. 9424 Shelbyville Rd, east of downtown. 502/426-1577. Hrs: 6-9 pm; Fri, Sat 5-10 pm. Closed Sun; Thanksgiving, Dec 25. Res accepted. Seafood menu. Bar. Buffet: dinner $25.95. Child's meals. Specialties: frogs' legs, oysters Rockefeller, Alaskan crab legs. Salad bar. Parking. 4 dining rms. Cr cds: A, C, D, MC, V.

D SC

✔★ OLD SPAGHETTI FACTORY. 235 W Market St, downtown. 502/581-1070. Hrs: 11:30 am-2 pm, 5-10 pm; Fri to 11 pm; Sat 4:30-11 pm; Sun 12:30-10 pm. Closed Thanksgiving, Dec 24-25. Italian menu. Bar. Semi-a la carte: lunch $2.95-$5.25. Complete meals: dinner $4.75-$9.25. Child's meals. Specializes in spaghetti. Cr cds: DS, MC, V.

D

✔★ ★ SICHUAN GARDEN. 9850 Linn Station Rd, in Plainview Shopping Center, east of downtown. 502/426-6767. Hrs: 11:30 am-10 pm; Fri to 11 pm; Sat 11:30 am-11 pm; Sun brunch noon-3:30 pm. Closed Thanksgiving, Dec 25. Res accepted. Chinese, Thai menu. Bar. Semi-a la carte: lunch $3.75-$5.95, dinner $5.55-$12.95. Sun brunch $6.95. Specializes in Sichuan orange beef, mandarin seafood-in-a-net, filet mignon. Pianist Fri & Sat evenings. Frosted-glass rm dividers. Cr cds: A, D, DS, MC, V.

D

★ ★ TIMOTHY'S. 826 E Broadway, downtown. 502/561-0880. Hrs: 11 am-2 pm, 5:30-11 pm; Fri to midnight; Sat 5:30 pm-midnight. Closed Sun, Mon; Easter, Thanksgiving, Dec 25. Res accepted. Italian, Amer menu. Bar. Semi-a la carte: lunch $5.95-$8.95, dinner $9.95-$20.95. Specializes in pasta, fresh seafood, white chili. Parking. Outdoor dining. Contemporary decor; vintage bar. Cr cds: A, D, MC, V.

D

★ ★ UPTOWN CAFE. 1624 Bardstown Rd, south of downtown. 502/458-4212. Hrs: 11:30 am-11 pm; Fri & Sat to midnight. Closed Sun; most major hols. Continental menu. Bar. Semi-a la carte: lunch $5-$9.75, dinner $5.95-$17.50. Specialities: duck ravioli, salmon croquettes, veal pockets. Parking. Converted store front. Cr cds: A, DS, MC, V.

D

★ ★ ★ VINCENZO'S. 150 S 5th St, downtown. 502/580-1350. Hrs: 11:30 am-2:30 pm, 5:30-11 pm; Fri, Sat 5:30 pm-midnight. Closed Sun; major hols. Res accepted. Continental menu. Wine list. A la carte entrees: lunch $4.95-$8.95, dinner $13.95-$22.95. Specialties: crêpes Agostino, veal Gabriele. Own baking. Pianist Fri, Sat. Valet parking. Former Federal Reserve Bank building; original artwork. Jacket. Cr cds: A, C, D, DS, MC, V.

D

Unrated Dining Spots

BLUE BOAR CAFETERIA. 232 Oxmoor Shopping Center, 1/2 mi E of I-264 Middletown exit, east of downtown. 502/426-3310.

Hrs: 11 am-8 pm; Fri to 8:30 pm; Sat 11 am-8:30 pm; Sun 11 am-7 pm. Closed Dec 25. Avg ck: lunch $4.40, dinner $5.25. Child's meals. Specializes in roast beef, fried chicken, pecan pie. Family-owned. Cr cds: MC, V.

SC

COLONNADE CAFETERIA. *4th St & Muhammad Ali Blvd, Starks Bldg, lower level, downtown.* 502/584-6846. Hrs: 7-9:30 am; continental bkfst to 10:30 am; 11 am-2 pm. Closed Sat, Sun; major hols. Avg ck: bkfst $3.50, lunch $5-$6. Large variety. No cr cds accepted.

Memphis

Settled: 1819

Pop: 610,337

Elev: 264 feet

Time zone: Central

Area code: 901

Situated on the high bluffs above the Mississippi River, on its flat, fertile alluvial delta, the city of Memphis was named after the capital of ancient Egypt, whose name meant "place of good abode." Ancient Memphis prospered primarily due to its location on the Nile River Delta, a location similar to the site upon which Andrew Jackson, General James Winchester and John Overton laid out the new Memphis. The site's natural harbor and proximity to the Mississippi promised to make the city as prosperous as its ancient namesake. River traffic rapidly developed Memphis into one of the busiest port cities in America, and the rich native soil, washed up onto the delta by the flow of the Mississippi, made the area a major cotton-producing center as well.

For a short time, Memphis was the Confederate capital of Tennessee, serving as a military supply depot and stronghold for the Southern forces during the Civil War. In 1862, however, an armada of 30 Union ships seized Memphis in a fierce river battle and the city remained in Union hands for the duration of the war. River trade suffered greatly during the war. Afterward, three separate outbreaks of yellow fever nearly wiped Memphis out entirely. But by 1892, the city had begun to emerge from its slow postwar recovery to become the busiest inland cotton market and hardwood lumber center in the world.

Much has happened in Memphis in the last few decades. A building boom brought many new factories, skyscrapers, expressways and an international airport. Memphis has four times won the Cleanest City in the Nation award and has also received many awards in safety, fire protection and noise abatement.

More than just a commercial city, Memphis has developed a cosmopolitan identity as well, as the home of ballet and opera companies, more than a dozen institutions of higher learning and one of the South's largest medical care and research centers. Still, it seems not to have lost any of its low-key, Southern charm.

Business

While much of the country's cotton crop is bought or sold in Memphis, the city's economy is highly diversified. Other agricultural products of importance are soybeans, rice, livestock and ornamental plants.

A significant percentage of the labor force works in the city's more than 800 manufacturing plants, making chemicals, food products, paper and paper products, electrical equipment, nonelectrical machinery, lumber and wood products. The city is also a large producer of hardwood flooring.

Memphis is a busy inland port on the Mississippi. Major corporations, such as Federal Express and Schering-Plough, have headquarters here. In recent years it has also become notable in the music recording field and is a major convention and distribution center.

The city is an important trade center, with retail sales topping $7.6 billion a year.

Convention Facilities

The Memphis Cook Convention Center stands on a bluff overlooking the Mississippi in downtown Memphis. The center has a total gross square footage of 1.8 million. Its 30 conference rooms can seat from 75 to 500, and the center can accommodate 25,000 persons attending several major events at the same time. Four halls have a seating capacity of 800 to 4,243; two of them can serve banquets for 800 and 1,200. The main exhibit hall has 150,000 square feet of unobstructed space.

At the Mid-South Fairgrounds is the 12,000-seat Mid-South Coliseum, with 64,000 square feet of exhibit space. Hotels and motels in Memphis have a total of 13,000 rooms.

Sports and Recreation

The lovely woods and lakes in the Memphis area are favorite spots for hunters and fishermen. Informative pamphlets on hunting and fishing facilities are available from the Memphis Convention & Visitors Bureau.

Tennessee has an extensive system of state parks; two of them are near Memphis. The T.O. Fuller State Park is the site of the Chucalissa Indian Village. Meeman-Shelby Forest State Park, on the Mississippi, has two lakes and many miles of trails, a museum, nature center, restaurant, pool, horse stable, picnic and camping areas and cabins.

Entertainment

As if to reinforce its connection with its Egyptian namesake, a 32-story, glass and steel pyramid, overlooking the Mississippi River, has been built in Memphis. The Pyramid houses a music, sports and entertainment complex.

Memphis enjoys a rich mixture of cultural activities and programs. Several art organizations belong to the Memphis Arts Council, including a ballet company, opera theater, symphony orchestra and repertory theater. A number of local theater groups are active, and more than a dozen colleges provide additional entertainment programs.

Memphis abounds in night life. Overton Square offers a variety of restaurants, bars, night spots and shops. Beale Street, birthplace of blues music in America, is another important center for nighttime fun.

Historical Areas

In the heart of the city, remnants of 19th-century Memphis have been preserved in an area known as Victorian Village. Occupying the 600 block of Adams and surrounding streets, it contains 10 early Memphis houses, from an 1840 neoclassical cottage to grand Victorian mansions. The area was designated a national historic district in 1972. The Fontaine House and the Mallory-Neely House are open to visitors. Beale Street, home of W.C. Handy, father of the blues, and a center of black culture and entertainment, has been restored.

The Magevney House, at 198 Adams, is a picturesque cottage built in 1831 and authentically furnished.

The prehistoric period of Memphis is still evident at Chucalissa Indian Village, on Mitchell Road. This was a thriving village of 1,000 to 1,500 inhabitants from about A.D. 900 to 1500. Archeological digs and the museum are administered by Memphis State University.

Sightseeing

The Mississippi River is one of Memphis' principal tourist attractions, and river sightseeing tours are an especially enjoyable bonus to a trip here. The Memphis Queen Line has several excursion boats, including the 599-passenger *Memphis Showboat*, the 308-passenger *Memphis Queen II* and the 65-passenger *Belle Carol*. Rides feature sightseeing trips into the river wilderness and short landings on the sandbar banks, with commentary on the sights, history and legends of the area.

Memphis is known throughout the world as the city where the legendary Elvis Presley's career began and where he lived until his death. The destination of thousands of visitors is Graceland, his house and the site of his grave, the Meditation Gardens. Each August, city-wide memorial celebrations are held in honor of the "King of Rock and Roll."

General References

Settled: 1819 **Pop:** 610,337 **Elev:** 264 feet **Time zone:** Central **Area code:** 901

Phone Numbers

POLICE & FIRE: 911
FBI: 525-7373
POISON CONTROL CENTER: 528-6048
TIME: 526-5261 **WEATHER:** 756-4141

Information Source

Memphis Convention & Visitors Bureau, 47 Union St, 38103; 543-5300.
Park Commission, 325-5300.

Transportation

AIRLINES: American; Delta; Delta Connection; Northwest; Northwest Airlink; TWA Express; United; USAir; and other commuter and regional airlines. For the most current airline schedules and information consult the *Official Airline Guide,* published twice monthly.
AIRPORT: Memphis International, 922-8000.
CAR RENTAL AGENCIES: (See Toll-Free Numbers) American International 345-2440; Avis 345-3514; Budget 767-1000; Hertz 345-5680; National 345-0070; Thrifty 345-0170.
PUBLIC TRANSPORTATION: Memphis Area Transit Authority, 1370 Levee Rd, 274-6282.
RAILROAD PASSENGER SERVICE: Amtrak 800/872-7245.

Newspapers

Daily News; Memphis Business Journal; Memphis Commercial Appeal; Tri-State Defender.

Convention Facilities

Agricenter International, 7777 Walnut Grove Rd, 757-7777.
Memphis Cook Convention Center, 255 Main St N, 576-1200.
Mid-South Coliseum, Mid-South Fairgrounds, 274-3982.

Shelby Farms Show Place Arena, 105 Germantown Rd S, Cordova, 756-7433.

Sports & Recreation

Major Sports Facilities

Liberty Bowl Memorial Stadium, Fairgrounds, 278-4747.
Mid-South Coliseum, Fairgrounds, 274-3982.
Tim McCarver Stadium, Fairgrounds, 272-1687.

Cultural Facilities

Theaters

Children's Theatre, 2635 Avery Ave, 452-3968.
Circuit Playhouse, 1705 Poplar Ave, 726-5523.
Germantown Community Theatre, 3037 Forest Hill Rd, Germantown, 754-2680.
Opera Memphis, Memphis State University, 678-2706.
Playhouse on the Square, 51 S Cooper, Overton Square, 725-0776 or 726-4656.
Theatre Memphis, 630 Perkins Rd, 682-8323.

Museums

Children's Museum, 2525 Central Ave, 458-2678.
Chucalissa Indian Village and Museum, 1987 Indian Village Dr, 785-3160.
Memphis Pink Palace Museum and Planetarium, 3050 Central Ave, 320-6320.
National Civil Rights Museum, 450 Mulberry St, at the Lorraine Motel, 521-9699.
National Ornamental Metal Museum, 374 W California Ave, at the river, 774-6380.

Art Museums and Galleries

Dixon Gallery & Gardens, 4339 Park Ave, 761-5250.
Kurts-Bingham Gallery, 766 S White Station Rd, 683-6200.
Memphis Brooks Museum of Art, 1934 Poplar Ave, in Overton Park, 722-3525.
Memphis College of Art, Overton Park, 726-4085.
University Gallery, Memphis State University, 678-2224.

Points of Interest

Historical

Beale Street, downtown, between Riverside Dr & Danny Thomas Blvd.
Magevney House, 198 Adams Ave, 526-4464.
Overton Square, Madison at Cooper.
Victorian Village, 600 blk of Adams Ave, 526-1469.

Other Attractions

Adventure River Water Park, 6880 Whitten Bend Cove, off I-40E, 382-9284.
Elvis Presley Plaza, Beale St at Main.
Graceland (Elvis Presley Mansion), 3764 Elvis Presley Blvd, 332-3322 or 800/238-2000 (outside TN).
Libertyland Theme Park, Mid-South Fairgrounds, on E Pkwy S, N on Airways off I-240, 274-1776.
Lichterman Nature Center, 5992 Quince Rd, 767-7322.
Meeman-Shelby Forest State Recreation Park, 13 mi N via US 51 near Millington, 876-5215.
Memphis Belle B-17 Bomber, Mud Island, 543-5333.
Memphis Botanic Garden, 750 Cherry Rd, Audubon Park, 685-1566.
Memphis Intl Motorsports Park, N on I-240, at 5500 Taylor Forge Rd, 358-7223.
Memphis Zoo & Aquarium, Overton Park, bounded by N Pkwy, E Pkwy & Poplar Ave, 726-4787.
Mud Island, riverfront, downtown Memphis, 543-5333.
Pyramid Arena, Pinch Historic District, downtown, 526-5177.

T.O. Fuller State Park, 5 mi S on US 61, then 4 mi W on Mitchell Rd, 543-7581.

Sightseeing Tours

Carriage Tours of Memphis, 393 N Main St, 527-7542.
Cottonland Tours, 2050 Elvis Presley Blvd, 774-5248.
Gray Line bus tours, 2050 Elvis Presley Blvd, 948-TOUR.
Memphis Queen Excursion Boats, foot of Monroe Ave, 527-5694.

Annual Events

Beale St Music Festival. 1st wkend May.
Memphis in May International Festival, 525-4611. May.
Carnival Memphis, Mid-South Fairgrounds, 278-0243. 10 days mid-June.
Elvis Presley International Tribute Week, 332-3322. Early-mid-Aug.
Memphis Music Festival, 526-0110. Sept.

Mid-South Fair & Exposition, Fairgrounds, E Parkway S & Southern Ave, 274-8800. Late Sept-early Oct.
National Blues Music Awards, 527-2583. Oct.
Liberty Bowl Football Classic, Liberty Bowl Memorial Stadium, 335 Hollywood S, 767-7700. Dec.

City Neighborhoods

Many of the restaurants, unrated dining establishments and some lodgings listed under Memphis include neighborhoods as well as exact street addresses. Geographic descriptions of these areas are given, followed by a table of restaurants arranged by neighborhood.

Beale Street Area: Downtown area along seven blocks of Beale St from Riverside Dr on the west to Danny Thomas Blvd on the east.
Downtown: South of I-40, west of Danny Thomas Blvd (US 51), north of Calhoun Ave and east of the Mississippi River. **East of Downtown:** East of US 51.
Overton Square: South of Poplar Ave, west of Cooper St, north of Union Ave and east of McLean Blvd.

Lodgings and Food

MEMPHIS RESTAURANTS
BY NEIGHBORHOOD AREAS

(For full description, see alphabetical listings under Restaurants)

BEALE STREET AREA

Alfred's. 197 Beale St

Beale Street BBQ. 205 Beale Street

Joyce Cobb's Dinner Club. 209 Beale St

DOWNTOWN

Butcher Shop. 101 S Front St

Dux (Peabody Hotel). 149 Union Ave

Justines. 919 Coward Place

King Cotton Cafe. 50 N Front St

Landry's Seafood House. 263 Wagner Place

Pier. 100 Wagner Place

Rendezvous. 52 S 2nd St

EAST OF DOWNTOWN

Benihana Of Tokyo. 912 Ridge Lake Blvd

Cooker Bar & Grille. 6120 Poplar Ave

Grisanti's. 1489 Airways Blvd

OVERTON SQUARE

Bourbon Street Cafe (French Quarter Suites Hotel). 2144 Madison Ave

La Tourelle. 2146 Monroe Ave

Melos Taverna. 2021 Madison Ave

Paulette's. 2110 Madison Ave

The Public Eye. 17 S Cooper

Note: *When a listing is located in a town that does not have its own city heading, it will appear under the city nearest to its location. In these cases, the address and town appear in parenthesis immediately following the name of the establishment.*

Motels

★ ★ **AIR HOST INN-MEMPHIS AIRPORT.** *2949 Airways Blvd (38131), south of downtown.* 901/345-1250; FAX 901/398-0256. 137 rms, 2 story. Apr-Oct: S $40; D $45; each addl $5; under 18 free; higher rates first two wks Nov; lower rates rest of yr. Crib $5. TV; cable. Pool. Restaurant 6:30 am-10 pm. Bar 4-10 pm, closed Sun. Ck-out noon. Free airport transportation. Cr cds: A, C, D, DS, ER, JCB, MC, V.

★ **COMFORT INN.** *2889 Austin Peay Hwy (38128), north of downtown.* 901/386-0033; FAX 901/386-0036. 69 rms, 13 kit. suites. S $49; D $54; each addl $5; kit. suites $65; under 18 free. TV; cable. Indoor pool; whirlpool. Complimentary continental bkfst. Restaurant nearby. Ck-out noon. Meeting rms. Cr cds: A, C, D, DS, ER, JCB, MC, V.

★ ★ ★ **COURTYARD BY MARRIOTT.** *6015 Park Ave (38119), east of downtown.* 901/761-0330; FAX 901/682-8422. 146 units, 3 story. S, D $68-$78; each addl $10; suites $84-$94; under 17 free; wkly rates. Crib free. TV; cable. Heated pool. Complimentary coffee in rms. Restaurant 6:30-11 am, 5-8 pm. Bar 5-11 pm. Ck-out noon. Coin lndry. Meeting rms. Valet serv. Sundries. Exercise equipt; weights, bicycles, whirlpool. Refrigerator. Cr cds: A, C, D, DS, MC, V.

✔ ★ ★ **HAMPTON INN.** *1180 Union Ave (38104), downtown.* 901/276-1175; FAX 901/276-4261. 126 rms, 4 story. S $44-$50; D $50-$57; under 18 free. Crib free. TV; cable. Pool. Complimentary continental bkfst. Restaurant nearby. Ck-out noon. Sundries. Cr cds: A, C, D, DS, MC, V.

★ ★ **LA QUINTA-MEDICAL CENTER.** *42 S Camilla St (38104), east of downtown.* 901/526-1050; FAX 901/525-3219. 130 rms, 2 story. S, D $49-$56; each addl $6; under 18 free. Crib $5. Pet accepted, some restrictions. TV; cable. Pool. Restaurant adj open 24 hrs. Ck-out noon. Meeting rms. Sundries. Cr cds: A, C, D, DS, MC, V.

✔ ★ **RED ROOF INN.** *6055 Shelby Oaks Dr (38134), I-40 exit 12, east of downtown.* 901/388-6111; FAX 901/388-6157. 108 rms, 2 story. S $33.99; D $43.99; each addl $6; under 18 free; higher rates sport events. Crib free. Pet accepted, some restrictions. TV. Complimentary coffee in lobby. Restaurant adj open 24 hrs. Ck-out noon. Cr cds: A, C, D, DS, MC, V.

✔ ★ **RED ROOF INN SOUTH.** *3875 American Way (38118), east of downtown.* 901/363-2335; FAX 901/363-2335, ext. 444. 110 rms, 3 story. S $31.99; D $40.99-$45.99; 3-4 persons $49.99; under 18 free. Pet accepted. Crib $5. TV. Complimentary coffee. Restaurant adj 6 am-10 pm. Ck-out noon. Cr cds: A, C, D, DS, MC, V.

★ ★ **RESIDENCE INN BY MARRIOTT.** *6141 Poplar Pike (38119), south of downtown.* 901/685-9595; FAX 901/685-9595, ext. 4001. 105 kit. suites, 4 story. Kit. suites $94-$119; family, monthly rates. Crib free. Pet accepted, some restrictions; $100. TV; cable. Pool; whirlpool. Complimentary continental bkfst. Restaurant nearby. Ck-out noon. Coin lndry. Meeting rms. Valet serv. Health club privileges. Private patios, balconies. Picnic tables. Free grocery shopping serv. Cr cds: A, C, D, DS, JCB, MC, V.

Motor Hotels

★ ★ **COMFORT INN-AIRPORT.** *2411 Winchester Rd (38116), near Intl Airport, south of downtown.* 901/332-2370; FAX 901/398-4085. 211 rms, 3 story. S $72; D $82; each addl $10; suites $125; under 12 free; wknd rates. Crib free. TV; cable. Pool. Complimentary continental bkfst 6-8 am. Restaurant 6 am-11 pm. Rm serv. Bar 4 pm-midnight. Ck-out noon. Meeting rms. Bellhops. Valet serv. Sundries. Free airport transportation. Lighted tennis. Cr cds: A, C, D, DS, ER, JCB, MC, V.

★ ★ **COMFORT INN-POPLAR EAST.** *5877 Poplar Ave (38119), east of downtown.* 901/767-6300; FAX 901/767-0098. 126 rms, 5 story. S, D $53-$58; each addl $5; under 18 free. Crib free. Pet accepted, some restrictions. TV; cable. Pool. Complimentary continental bkfst Mon-Fri. Restaurant 7 am-10 pm. Rm serv. Bar noon-11 pm. Ck-out noon. Meeting rms. Bellhops. Valet serv. Sundries. Airport transportation. Exercise equipt; weight machine, bicycles. Cr cds: A, C, D, DS, MC, V.

★ ★ **COUNTRY SUITES BY CARLSON.** 4300 American Way (38118), east of downtown. 901/366-9333; res: 800/456-4000; FAX 901/366-7835. 120 kit. suites, 3 story. Kit. suites $63-$90; under 16 free. Crib free. TV; cable. Pool; whirlpool. Complimentary continental bkfst. Complimentary coffee in rms. Restaurant adj open 24 hrs. Ck-out noon. Coin lndry. Meeting rms. Valet serv. Sundries. Free airport transportation. Health club privileges. Cr cds: A, C, D, DS, MC, V.

D ≋ ⊠ ⊁ SC

★ ★ **RAMADA CONVENTION CENTER HOTEL.** 160 Union Ave (38103), at 2nd St, downtown. 901/525-5491; FAX 901/525-5491, ext. 2322. 186 rms, 14 story. S $80-$95; D $85-$105; each addl $10; suites $125-$200; under 18 free. Crib free. TV; cable. Pool. Restaurant 6 am-10 pm. Rm serv. Bars 4 pm-midnight, Sat to 2 am. Ck-out noon. Meeting rms. Valet serv. Wet bar in suites. **LUXURY LEVEL: EXECUTIVE LEVEL.** 18 rms. S $95; D $105. Concierge. Complimentary continental bkfst, wine. Cr cds: A, C, D, DS, ER, JCB, MC, V.

D ≋ ⊁ ⊠ SC

★ ★ ★ **THE RIDGEWAY INN.** 5679 Poplar Ave (38119), at I-240, east of downtown. 901/766-4000; res: 800/822-3360; FAX 901/763-1857. 155 rms, 7 story. S, D $84-$109; each addl $20; suites $175-$250; under 12 free. Crib free. TV. Pool. Restaurant 6:30 am-11 pm; Fri, Sat to 1 am; Sun to 10 pm. Rm serv. Bar from 11 am, Fri, Sat to 1 am, Sun noon-10 pm. Ck-out noon. Meeting rm. Airport transportation. Exercise equipt; weight machine, bicycle. **LUXURY LEVEL: CONCIERGE LEVEL.** 21 rms, 2 suites. S from $109; D from $129; suites $200-$275. Concierge. Private lounge. Complimentary continental bkfst, refreshments. Cr cds: A, C, D, DS, ER, MC, V.

D ≋ ⊁ ⊠ ⊁ SC

★ ★ **WILSON WORLD.** 2715 Cherry Rd (38118), east of downtown. 901/366-0000; res: 800/872-8366; FAX 901/366-6361. 178 rms, 4 story, 90 suites. S $54.95; D $59.95; each addl $5; suites $59.95-$64.95; under 18 free. Crib free. TV; cable. Indoor pool. Restaurant 6 am-2 pm, 5:30-10 pm. Rm serv. Bar from 4 pm; pianist exc Sun. Ck-out noon. Meeting rms. Bellhops. Gift shop. Barber, beauty shop. Free airport transportation. Game rm. Refrigerators, wet bars. Balconies. Cr cds: A, C, D, DS, MC, V.

D ≋ ⊠ ⊁ SC

Hotels

★ ★ ★ **ADAM'S MARK.** 939 Ridge Lake Blvd (38120), south of downtown. 901/684-6664; FAX 901/762-7411. 379 rms, 27 story. S $115; D $125; each addl $10; suites $175-$425; under 18 free; wkend rates. Crib free. TV; cable. Pool. Restaurant 6:30 am-10 pm; Fri, Sat to 11 pm. Bar noon-1 am; entertainment. Ck-out noon. Convention facilities. Gift shop. Airport transportation. Exercise equipt; weight machines, bicycles. Wet bar in suites. Cr cds: A, C, D, DS, MC, V.

D ≋ ⊁ ⊠ ⊁ SC

★ ★ **BEST WESTERN.** 2240 Democrat Rd (38132), near Intl Airport, south of downtown. 901/332-1130; FAX 901/398-5206. 380 rms, 5 story. S $50-$101; D $74-$111; each addl $10; suites $175-$275; under 18 free; wkend rates. Crib free. Pet accepted, some restrictions. TV; cable. 2 pools, 1 indoor; poolside serv. Restaurant 6:30 am-11 pm. Bars 11:30 am-midnight, Fri, Sat to 1 am, Sun 3:30-11 pm. Ck-out noon. Convention facilities. Free airport transportation. 2 lighted tennis courts. Exercise equipt; weights, bicycles, sauna. Wet bar in suites. Indoor courtyard. Cr cds: A, C, D, DS, ER, MC, V.

D ⊁ ⊁ ≋ ⊁ ⊠ ⊁ SC

★ ★ **BROWNESTONE.** 300 N 2nd (38105), at Market St, downtown. 901/525-2511; res: 800/468-3515; FAX 901/525-2511, ext. 1220. 243 rms, 11 story. S $75; D $90; each addl $10; suites $125-$275; under 19 free; wkend rates. Crib free. Pet accepted, some restrictions. TV. Pool. Restaurant 6 am-10 pm. Bar 4 pm-midnight. Ck-out noon. Meeting rms. Near Pyramid Arena. **LUXURY LEVEL:**

EXECUTIVE LEVEL. 24 rms. S $80; D $90. Concierge. Private lounge. Bathrm phones. Complimentary wine. Cr cds: A, C, D, DS, ER, MC, V.

D ⊁ ≋ ⊁ ⊁ SC

★ ★ ★ **EMBASSY SUITES.** 1022 S Shady Grove Rd (38120), east of downtown. 901/684-1777; FAX 901/685-7702. 220 suites, 5 story. Suites $109-$139; under 12 free; wkend rates. Crib free. Pet accepted, some restrictions; $50. TV; cable. Indoor pool. Complimentary full bkfst. Complimentary coffee in rms. Restaurant 11 am-10 pm. Bar to 11 pm. Ck-out noon. Coin lndry. Convention facilities. Gift shop. Free airport transportation. Exercise equipt; weight machine, bicycles, whirlpool, sauna. Refrigerators, minibars. Cr cds: A, C, D, DS, MC, V.

D ≋ ⊁ ⊠ ⊁ SC

★ ★ ★ **FRENCH QUARTER SUITES.** 2144 Madison Ave (38104), in Overton Square. 901/728-4000; res: 800/843-0353 (exc TN); FAX 901/278-1262. 105 suites, 4 story. Suites $95-$150; family rates. Crib free. TV; cable. Pool; poolside serv. Complimentary full bkfst. Restaurant (see BOURBON STREET CAFE). Rm serv 24 hrs. Bar 11 am-11 pm, Fri & Sat to midnight; entertainment exc Mon. Ck-out noon. Meeting rms. Free airport transportation. Exercise equipt; weights, bicycles. Some bathrm phones, refrigerators, in-rm whirlpools. Private patios, balconies. Interior atrium; New Orleans decor. Cr cds: A, C, D, DS, ER, JCB, MC, V.

D ≋ ⊁ ⊠ ⊁ SC

★ **HOLIDAY INN MIDTOWN MEDICAL CENTER.** 1837 Union Ave (38104), in Overton Square. 901/278-4100. 174 rms, 8 story. S $66-$79; D $66-$95; suites $85-$159; under 18 free. Crib free. Pet accepted. TV; cable. Pool. Restaurant 6 am-10 pm. Bar 5-11 pm; wkends to 1 am. Ck-out 11 am. Meeting rms. Free airport transportation. Health club privileges. Cr cds: A, C, D, DS, ER, JCB, MC, V.

D ⊁ ≋ ⊁ SC

★ ★ **HOMEWOOD SUITES.** 5811 Poplar Ave (38119), east of downtown. 901/763-0500; res: 800/225-5466; FAX 901/763-0132. 140 kit. suites, 2-3 story. Suites $89-$149; family, wkly, monthly rates. Crib free. Pet accepted, some restrictions; $50. TV; cable. In-rm movies avail. Pool. Complimentary continental bkfst. Complimentary coffee in rms. Restaurant adj 11-2 am. Ck-out noon. Coin lndry. Meeting rms. Gift shop. Free airport transportation. Exercise equipt; weights, bicycles, whirlpool. Cr cds: A, D, DS, MC, V.

D ⊁ ≋ ⊁ ⊠ ⊁ SC

★ ★ ★ **MARRIOTT.** 2625 Thousand Oaks Blvd (38118), southeast of downtown. 901/362-6200; FAX 901/360-8836. 320 rms, 12 story. S $121-$131; D $140-$150; suites $165-$300; under 18 free. Crib free. TV; cable. 2 pools, 1 indoor. Restaurant 6 am-2 pm, 5-10 pm; wkends from 7 am. Bars 11-2 am, Fri & Sat to 3 am, closed Sun & Mon; entertainment, dancing. Ck-out noon. Convention facilities. Concierge. Free airport transportation. Exercise equipt; weights, bicycles, whirlpool, sauna. Some bathrm phones, refrigerators. **LUXURY LEVEL: EXECUTIVE LEVEL.** 21 rms, 1 suite. S, D $131; each addl $15; suite $275. Concierge. Private lounge, honor bar. Complimentary continental bkfst, refreshments. Cr cds: A, C, D, DS, ER, JCB, MC, V.

D ≋ ⊁ ⊠ ⊁ SC

★ ★ ★ ★ **PEABODY.** 149 Union Ave (38103), downtown. 901/529-4000; res: 800/732-2639; FAX 901/529-9600. 468 rms, 13 story. S $115-$255; D $140-$290; each addl $25; suites $350-$1,000; under 18 free. Crib free. TV; cable. Heated pool. Restaurant 6:30 am-midnight (also see DUX). Rm serv 24 hrs. Bar 11-2 am; entertainment daily; dancing Thurs-Sat. Ck-out 11 am. Meeting rms. Concierge. Shopping arcade. Barber, beauty shop. Exercise rm; instructor, weights, bicycles, whirlpool, sauna, steam rm. Extensive exercise facilities. A grand hotel, originally opened in 1869, rebuilt in 1925, and restored to former opulence. A symbol of the Peabody is the duck; guests can observe the unique sight of a daily march of these ducks across a red carpet to and from lobby fountain at 11 am & 5 pm. Cr cds: A, C, D, DS, ER, MC, V.

D ≋ ⊁ ⊠ ⊁ SC

★ ★ **RADISSON.** *185 Union Ave (38103), downtown.* 901/528-1800; FAX 901/526-3226. 283 rms, 10 story. S, D $99-$109; each addl $10; suites $120-$130; under 18 free. Crib free. Garage/valet $4. TV; cable. Pool. Restaurant 6 am-10 pm. Bar 11 am-midnight. Ck-out noon. Convention facilities. Gift shop. Free airport transportation. Exercise equipt; weight machine, bicycles, whirlpool, sauna. Atrium lobby with trees and fountain, contains reconstructed brick facade of original historic building on site. Near Beale St, Mud Island and Pyramid. Cr cds: A, C, D, DS, ER, JCB, MC, V.

D 🏊 ✈ 🏋 🔥 SC

Restaurants

★ **ALFRED'S.** *197 Beale St, in Beale St Area.* 901/525-3711. Hrs: 11-3 am; Fri & Sat to 5 am. Bar. Semi-a la carte: lunch $3.50-$6.50, dinner $6.95-$15.95. Specializes in prime rib, blackened catfish, barbecue ribs. Rock & Roll Wed-Sat; Jazz Sun. Parking. Outdoor dining. Cr cds: A, D, DS, MC, V.

D

★ **BEALE STREET BBQ.** *205 Beale Street, in Beale St Area.* 901/525-0880. Hrs: 11-1 am. Beer. Semi-a la carte: lunch $3.50-$17.50, dinner $6-$17.50. Child's meals. Specializes in barbecued ribs, red beans and rice. Parking. Cr cds: A, DS, MC, V.

D

★ ★ **BENIHANA OF TOKYO.** *912 Ridge Lake Blvd, east of downtown.* 901/683-7390. Hrs: 11:30 am-2 pm, 5-10 pm; Fri to 11 pm; Sat 5-11 pm; early-bird dinner 5-7 pm. Res accepted. Japanese menu. Bar 4:30-10 pm. Complete meals: lunch $5.95-$12, dinner $12.50-$24.25. Child's meals. Parking. Family-owned. Cr cds: A, C, D, DS, MC, V.

D

✔ ★ **BOSCOS PIZZA KITCHEN & BREWERY.** *(7615 W Farmington, Germantown) E on US 72, at Poplar Ave, in Saddle Creek Shopping Plaza.* 901/756-7312. Hrs: 11 am-10:30 pm; Fri & Sat to 12:30 am. Closed Thanksgiving, Dec 25. Bar. Semi-a la carte: lunch $3.95-$7.95, dinner $4.95-$14.95. Specializes in wood-fired oven pizza, pasta. Own beer. Parking. Outdoor dining. Mediterranean decor. Cr cds: A, C, D, DS, MC, V.

D

★ **BOURBON STREET CAFE.** *(See French Quarter Suites Hotel)* 901/728-4000. Hrs: 7 am-10 pm; wkends to 11 pm. Cajun menu. Bar. Semi-a la carte: bkfst $3.95-$12.95, lunch $3.95-$12.95, dinner $12.95-$18.95. Buffet: bkfst $5.95, lunch $6.95. Sun brunch $14.95. Specialties: catfish Louisiana, chicken Iberville, desserts. Patio dining. Jazz. Cr cds: A, C, D, DS, MC, V.

D SC

✔ ★ ★ **COOKER BAR & GRILLE.** *6120 Poplar Ave, east of downtown.* 901/685-2800. Hrs: 11 am-10:30 pm; Fri & Sat to 11:30 pm; Sun to 10 pm. Closed Thanksgiving, Dec 25. Bar. Semi-a la carte: lunch $2.95-$7.95, dinner $6.75-$14.95. Child's meals. Specializes in meat loaf, pot roast, pasta. Parking. Cr cds: A, D, DS, MC, V.

D

★ ★ ★ **DUX.** *(See Peabody Hotel)* 901/529-4199. Hrs: 6:30-10:30 am, 11:30 am-2:30 pm, 5:30-11 pm; Fri, Sat to midnight; Sun 6:30-11:30 am, 5:30-11 pm. Res accepted. Bar. Wine list. Semi-a la carte: bkfst $3.75-$8.95, lunch $5.95-$12.95, dinner $9.95-$25. Child's meals. Specializes in mesquite-grilled Black Angus steak and seafood. Own baking. Valet parking. Cr cds: A, C, D, DS, ER, MC, V.

D

★ ★ ★ **GRISANTI'S.** *1489 Airways Blvd, east of downtown.* 901/458-2648. Hrs: 11 am-2 pm, 5-10 pm; Fri, Sat to 10 pm. Closed Sun; hols. Res accepted. Northern Italian menu. Bar. Wine cellar. Semi-a la carte: lunch $3.75-$7.50, dinner $8-$23.95. Child's meals. Specialties: cannelloni alla Gusi, fettucine verde al dente, veal co-

tolétta. Own baking. Parking. Specially prepared gourmet menu on request. Family-owned. Cr cds: A, C, D, DS, MC, V.

D

✔ ★ **JOYCE COBB'S DINNER CLUB.** *209 Beale St, in Beale St Area.* 901/525-0484. Hrs: 5 pm-2 am. Bar. Semi-a la carte: dinner $5-$17. Specializes in ribs, grilled chicken, barbecued beef. Parking. Jazz club. Cr cds: A, DS, MC, V.

D

★ ★ ★ **JUSTINES.** *919 Coward Place, at East St, downtown.* 901/527-3815. Hrs: 5:30-10 pm. Closed Sun, Mon; major hols; also 2 wks Aug. Res accepted. French menu. Wine cellar. A la carte entrees: dinner $35-$40. Specializes in fresh seafood flown in daily. Own baking. Valet parking. In antebellum mansion; gardens. Family-owned. Jacket. Cr cds: A, C, D, DS, MC, V.

✔ ★ **KING COTTON CAFE.** *50 N Front St, in Morgan Keegan Tower Bldg, downtown.* 901/576-8150. Hrs: 11:30 am-2:30 pm. Closed Sat & Sun; major hols. Bar. Semi-a la carte: lunch $4.50-$10. Specializes in pasta, chicken, fish. Salad bar. Parking. Cr cds: A, D, DS, MC, V.

D

★ ★ **LA TOURELLE.** *2146 Monroe Ave (38104), in Overton Square.* 901/726-5771. Hrs: 6-10 pm; Sun brunch 11:30 am-2 pm. Closed some major hols. Res accepted. French menu. Bar. Semi-a la carte: dinner $18-$26. Sun brunch $16. Specialties: rack of lamb, tuna with thyme and pepper crust. Formal dining in restored house. Totally nonsmoking. Cr cds: MC, V.

★ ★ **LANDRY'S SEAFOOD HOUSE.** *263 Wagner Place, downtown.* 901/526-1966. Hrs: 11 am-10 pm; Fri & Sat to 11 pm. Cajun, Amer menu. Bar. Semi-a la carte: lunch $5.95-$9.95, dinner $9.95-$28.95. Child's meals. Specializes in seafood. Valet parking. Former cotton warehouse; nautical decor. Cr cds: A, C, MC, V.

D

★ **MELOS TAVERNA.** *2021 Madison Ave, in Overton Square.* 901/725-1863. Hrs: 4:30-10:30 pm. Closed Sun, Mon; July 4, Thanksgiving, Dec 25. Res accepted. Greek menu. Bar. Semi-a la carte: dinner $8.75-$21. Specializes in lamb, moussaka. Parking. Greek artwork. Cr cds: A, C, D, MC, V.

D

★ ★ ★ **PAULETTE'S.** *2110 Madison Ave, in Overton Square.* 901/726-5128. Hrs: 11 am-10 pm; Fri & Sat to 11:30 pm; Sat, Sun brunch to 4 pm. Closed major hols. Res accepted. Continental menu. Bar. Semi-a la carte: lunch $5.95-$10, dinner $8-$18.95. Sat, Sun brunch $5-$9. Child's meals. Specialties: filet Paulette, brochettes of prawn. Entertainment Fri-Sun. Parking. Cr cds: A, C, D, DS, MC, V.

D

★ ★ **PIER.** *100 Wagner Place, between Union & Beale Sts, opp Mud Island, downtown.* 901/526-7381. Hrs: 11:30 am-2 pm, 5-10 pm; Sat & Sun 5-10 pm. Bar. Semi-a la carte: lunch $5-$10, dinner $13-$20. Specializes in seafood, prime rib, steak. Located in old, riverfront warehouse. Cr cds: A, D, MC, V.

D

★ **THE PUBLIC EYE.** *17 S Cooper, in Overton Square.* 901/726-4040. Hrs: 11 am-10 pm; Fri, Sat to midnight; lunch buffet to 2 pm. Closed Jan 1, Dec 25. Bar. Semi-a la carte: lunch $4-$7, dinner $5-$15. Buffet: lunch $5.95. Child's meals. Specializes in barbecued pork, ribs. Parking. Cr cds: A, C, D, DS, MC, V.

D

Unrated Dining Spots

BUTCHER SHOP. *101 S Front St, downtown. 901/521-0856.* Hrs: 5-10 pm; Fri, Sat to 11 pm. Closed Jan 1, Thanksgiving, Dec 24, 25. Bar. Option to select and cook own steak. Served with salad, potato and bread $14-$19. Child's meals. Salad bar. Grill in dining room; 1907 building. Cr cds: A, D, MC, V.

RENDEZVOUS. *52 S 2nd St, in Gen Washburn Alley, downtown. 901/523-2746.* Hrs: 4:30 pm-midnight; Fri from 11:30 am; Sat from 12:30 pm. Closed Sun, Mon; also 2 wks late July, 2 wks late Dec. Bar (beer). Semi-a la carte: lunch, dinner $3-$10. Specializes in barbecued ribs. In 1890 downtown building; memorabilia, many antiques, collectibles; jukebox. Cr cds: A, C, D, MC, V.

Miami

Settled: 1870

Pop: 358,548

Elev: 5 feet

Time zone: Eastern

Area code: 305

Although favored by climate and geography, Miami remained a remote tropical village of frame houses until Henry Flagler brought his East Coast Railway here in 1896 and turned his hand to community development. After World War I, Florida tourism began to boom. Two enterprising businessmen, John S. Collins and Carl Fisher, almost single-handedly created Miami Beach out of a mangrove swamp. The big promotion and ballyhoo advertising for Miami Beach and other nearby communities started in 1919. Between 1920 and 1925 the population of Florida's east coast increased by 75 percent.

World War II brought thousands of military personnel to Miami, and many of them returned to the area after the war to live. Since then, the Greater Miami area has reached maturity as a vibrant, exciting major metropolis of 2 million people.

Business

Although Greater Miami, a conglomerate of 27 separate municipalities, has hundreds of hotels, motels and restaurants catering to a great number of tourists, the city is not as dependant on tourism as many other Florida cities. In addition to tourism, Miami has more than 3,000 manufacturing firms, 170 banks and a $500 million agricultural industry. It is a major gateway to and from Latin America; more than $120 million in customs fees are collected here annually. International banking is important in Miami; there are a dozen banks that engage solely in offshore operations. The Downtown Development Authority, a semi-autonomous arm of the city government, works to encourage growth and improvement in the central city. Millions of dollars have been invested in construction of new commercial buildings.

Convention Facilities

The Miami Convention Center is a $139 million conference, convention and hotel complex in the downtown area. It includes the City of Miami-Knight Convention Center, the University of Miami Conference Center and the Hyatt Regency-Miami. The center has a 5,000-seat theater-style convention hall, the 28,000-square-foot James L. Knight Center and Riverfront Exhibit Hall and 37 meeting rooms.

The Miami Beach Convention Center, site of 3 presidential nominating conventions, has doubled in size to 1.1 million square feet, including more than 500,000 square feet of contiguous exhibit floor space. The center has become one of the 10 largest facilities of its kind in the country. The Coconut Grove Convention Center, overlooking Biscayne Bay, provides a total of 150,000 square feet of contiguous space.

The Greater Miami Convention and Visitors Bureau provides several special convention services free of charge.

Sports and Recreation

The Orange Bowl Football Classic is a sports highlight in Miami. In the fall, the Miami Dolphins play professional football at Joe Robbie Stadium in Opa-locka; the University of Miami Hurricanes play college football at the Orange Bowl. The Miami Heat play professional basketball from November through April at the Miami Arena.

Miami offers a long list of activities geared to enjoyment, from deep-sea fishing to watching jai alai; from playing golf to betting on the horses; and from glamorous nightclubbing to tennis, swimming and scuba diving.

Entertainment

Many kinds of cultural events are constantly taking place. The Miami Beach Symphony and the Miami Chamber Symphony are semiprofessional orchestras that offer a series of programs. The University of Miami Symphony Orchestra and several youth symphonies give several programs a year. An International Series presents various artists and groups; the University of Miami Music Department has a number of performances by students and faculty.

The Greater Miami Opera, Miami City Ballet, Ballet Concerto, Coconut Grove Playhouse, University of Miami Ring Theater and the drama departments of Miami-Dade Community College, Florida International University and Barry College all have regular and excellent programs.

Miami evenings offer everything from nightclubs to Latin revues. It is best to consult the local newspapers and magazines for up-to-date entertainment schedules.

Sightseeing

Greater Miami's list of tourist attractions is long and varied; the city has something for everyone. Some of the more popular attractions are Vizcaya Museum and Gardens, Little Havana, Museum of Science and Space Transit Planetarium, Coconut Grove, the Art Deco District, Parrot Jungle and Gardens and Gulfstream Park.

The spectacular Metro-Dade County Cultural Plaza, a $25 million downtown complex, houses the Historical Museum of Southern Florida, the Center for the Fine Arts (an art museum of traveling exhibits) and the Miami-Dade Public Library.

Biscayne Boulevard is the prime spot for shopping, with the Omni International Mall located at 1601 Biscayne Blvd. Shopping is also excellent at the Cocowalk shopping and entertainment complex and at Mayfair in Coconut Grove, Bal Harbour Shops in Bal Harbour, downtown's Bayside Marketplace and Dadeland Mall and The Falls in southern Miami.

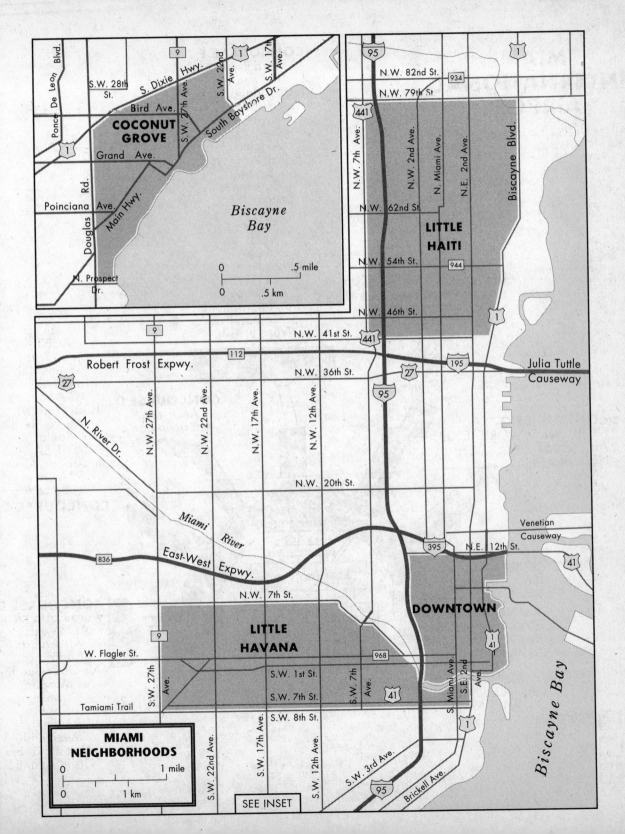

COCONUT GROVE

Ponce De Leon Blvd.

S.W. 28th St.

S. Dixie Hwy.

9

1

Bird Ave.

S.W. 22nd Ave.

S.W. 17th Ave.

S.W. 27th Ave.

South Bayshore Dr.

Grand Ave.

Poinciana Ave.

Douglas Rd.

Main Hwy.

1

N. Prospect Dr.

Biscayne Bay

0 .5 mile

0 .5 km

95

1

N.W. 82nd St.

934

N.W. 79th St.

441

N.W. 7th Ave.

N.W. 2nd Ave.

N. Miami Ave.

N.E. 2nd Ave.

Biscayne Blvd.

N.W. 62nd St.

LITTLE HAITI

N.W. 54th St.

944

N.W. 46th St.

1

N.W. 41st St.

441

9

112

Robert Frost Expwy.

N.W. 36th St.

27

195

27

Julia Tuttle Causeway

95

N.W. 27th Ave.

N.W. 22nd Ave.

N.W. 17th Ave.

N.W. 12th Ave.

N. River Dr.

N.W. 20th St.

Venetian Causeway

Miami River

836

East-West Expwy.

395

N.E. 12th St.

41

N.W. 7th St.

DOWNTOWN

LITTLE HAVANA

9

W. Flagler St.

968

S.W. 27th Ave.

1
41

S. Miami Ave.

S.E. 2nd Ave.

Tamiami Trail

S.W. 1st St.

S.W. 7th St.

S.W. 7th Ave.

41

1

S.W. 8th St.

Biscayne Bay

MIAMI NEIGHBORHOODS

0 1 mile

0 1 km

S.W. 22nd Ave.

S.W. 17th Ave.

S.W. 12th Ave.

S.W. 3rd Ave.

95

Brickell Ave.

SEE INSET

MIAMI INTERNATIONAL AIRPORT

CONCOURSE E
Aero Peru,
Air Jamaica,
Alitalia
ALM,
Avensa,
Avianca,
Aviateca,
British Airways,
BWIA,
Cayman,
Ecuatoriana,
El Al,
Faucett,
LAB,
LACSA,
Ladeco,
LAP,
Lufthansa,
Russian International,
Surinam,
Trans Brasil

CONCOURSE F
UNITED RED CARPET CLUB,
Argentina,
Dominicana,
Iberia,
Lan Chile,
LTU,
United,
VIASA,
Zuliana

CONCOURSE D
American,
American Eagle

ACES,
American Trans Air,
Continental,
Finnair,
Guyana,
Haiti Trans Air,
Air Metro North,
Saeta,
SAHSA,
South African Airway
TACA,
Turquoise Air

CONCOURSE C

CONCOURSE G
NORTHWEST WORLD CLUB,
Air Canada,
Northwest,
TWA,
Varig

Currency
Exchange

Skyride

Bank

Short Term Park

Long
Term
Park

Long
Term Park

CONCOURSE H
DELTA CROWN ROOM,
Airways International,
Bahamasair,
Delta,
Gulfstream,
Paradise Island,
US Air

CONCOURSE B
Aero Costa Rica,
AeroMexico,
Air Aruba,
Air France,
Air Guadeloupe,
Air Margarita,
Carnival,
Copa,
Laker,
Mexicana,
Midwest Express,
Virgin Atlantic

W
S N
E

Terminals

Parking Lot

i Information

City Environs

A trip into Everglades National Park is a unique sightseeing experience. From Miami, drive south on US 1 to Homestead, then take FL 9336 into the park. It is 38 miles from the Visitor Center to the end of the road, but stop along the way to truly enjoy the park. Various boardwalks lead out over the watery areas; signs and displays identify and describe the flora and fauna.

At Flamingo, there are sightseeing boat trips, and naturalists conduct nature walks along the shore. Talks, films and slide shows are given by Park Service personnel daily during the winter season.

Another beautiful drive can be taken into the Florida Keys—a long stretch of coral and sand with breathtaking views of the Atlantic and the Gulf of Mexico. The Overseas Highway (US 1) stretches from Homestead south to the tip of Key West, crossing several keys and bridges along the way. Charter fishing boats operate from most of the communities in the Keys.

General References

Settled: 1870 **Pop:** 358,548 **Elev:** 5 feet **Time zone:** Eastern **Area code:** 305

Phone Numbers

POLICE, FIRE & AMBULANCE: 911
FBI: 944-9101
POISON INFORMATION CENTER: 800/282-3171
TIME: 324-8811   **WEATHER:** 661-5065

Information Sources

Greater Miami Convention & Visitors Bureau, 701 Brickell Ave, Suite 2700, 33131; 539-3000 or 800/283-2707.
City of Miami Citizens Response Center, 300 Biscayne Blvd Way, #420, 33131; 579-2457.
Dade County Citizens Information, 140 W Flagler, 33130; 375-5656.

Transportation

AIRLINES: Aerolineas Argentinas; Aero Mexico; Aero Peru; Air Canada; Air France; Air Jamaica; Alitalia; ALM (Antillean); American; Bahamasair; British Airways; BWIA (British West Indian Airways); Cayman (British West Indies); Continental; Delta; Dominicana; Ecuatoriana (Ecuador); El Al (Israel); Faucett (Peru); Finnair (Finland); Guyana; Haiti Trans-Air; Iberia (Spain); LAB (Bolivia); LACSA (Costa Rica); Ladeco (Chile); Lan Chile; LAP (Paraguay); Lufthansa (Germany); Mexicana; Northwest; Russian Intl; SASHA (Honduras); Surinam; TACA (El Salvador); Trans Brasil; TWA; United; USAir; Varig (Brazil); VASP (Brazil); VIASA (Venezuela); Virgin Atlantic (UK); and other international, regional and commuter airlines. For the most current airline schedules and information consult the *Official Airline Guide,* published twice monthly.
AIRPORT: Miami International, 876-7000.
CAR RENTAL AGENCIES: (See Toll-Free Numbers) Avis 637-4900; Budget 871-3053; Hertz 871-0300; National 638-1026.
PUBLIC TRANSPORTATION: Metro Bus & Rail 638-6700.
RAILROAD PASSENGER SERVICE: Amtrak 800/872-7245.

Newspapers

Miami Herald; Miami Times; Diario Las Americas.

Convention Facilities

Coconut Grove Convention Center, 2700 S Bayshore Dr, Coconut Grove, 579-3310.
Miami Beach Convention Center, 1901 Convention Center Dr, Miami Beach, 673-7311.
Miami Convention Center, 400 SE 2nd Ave, 372-0277.

Sports & Recreation

Major Sports Facilities

Joe Robbie Stadium, 2269 NW 199th St, Opa-locka, 620-2578 (Dolphins, football).
Miami Arena, 721 NW First Ave, 577-4328 (Heat, basketball).
Orange Bowl Stadium, 1501 NW 3rd St, 643-7100 (Hurricanes, college football).

Racetracks

Biscayne Greyhound Track, 320 NW 115th St, Miami Shores, 754-3484 (greyhound racing).
Calder Race Course, 21001 NW 27th Ave, 625-1311 (horse racing).
Flagler Greyhound Track, NW 37th Ave & 7th St, 649-3000 (greyhound racing).
Gulfstream Park, US 1 & Hallandale Beach Blvd, Hallandale, 454-7000 (horse racing).
Hialeah Park, E 4th Ave between 22nd & 33rd Sts, Hialeah, 885-8000 (Thoroughbred racing).

Jai Alai

Miami Fronton, 3500 NW 37th Ave, 633-6400.

Cultural Facilities

Theaters

Coconut Grove Playhouse, 3500 Main Hwy, 442-4000.
Jackie Gleason Theater of Performing Arts, 1700 Washington Ave, Miami Beach, 673-7300.
University of Miami Ring Theater, 1380 Miller Dr, 284-3355.

Concert Halls

Dade County Auditorium, 2901 W Flagler St, 547-5414.
Gusman Concert Hall, 1314 Miller Dr, Coral Gables, 284-6477.

Museums

American Police Hall of Fame and Museum, 3801 Biscayne Blvd, 573-0070.
Historical Museum of Southern Florida, 101 W Flagler St, Metro-Dade County Cultural Plaza, 375-1492.
Miami Youth Museum, 5701 Sunset Dr, South Miami, 661-2787.
Museum of Science & Space Transit Planetarium, 3280 S Miami Ave, 854-4247 (museum), 854-4242 (planetarium).
Vizcaya Museum and Gardens, 3251 S Miami Ave, 579-2708.

Art Museums and Galleries

Bacardi Art Gallery, 2100 Biscayne Blvd, 573-8511.
Bass Museum of Art, 21st & Collins Ave, Miami Beach, 673-7533.
Center for the Fine Arts, 101 W Flagler St, Metro-Dade County Cultural Plaza, 375-1700.

Points of Interest

Historical

Art Deco District, from 6th to 23rd Sts, Lenox Court to Ocean Dr, Miami Beach, 672-2014.
Barnacle State Historic Site, 5 mi S, at 3485 Main Hwy, Coconut Grove, 448-9445.

Cape Florida Lighthouse, Bill Baggs Cape Florida State Park, Key Biscayne, 361-5811.

Fort Dallas, Lummus Park, NW North River Dr & NW 3rd St, 575-5240.

Peacock Inn Historic Site, McFarlane Rd at S Bayshore Dr, Coconut Grove.

South Beach. Extends south from vicinity of Dade Blvd, concentrated mainly along Ocean Dr, Miami Beach.

Tequesta Indian Village & Jesuit Mission Site, Bayfront Park, Biscayne Blvd at SE 1st St.

Other Attractions

Bayfront Park, NE 5th to SE 2nd Sts, between Biscayne Bay & Biscayne Blvd, 358-7550.

Bayside Marketplace, 401 Biscayne Blvd, on Biscayne Bay, 577-3344.

Everglades National Park, via US 1, 8 mi SW of jct SW 177th Ave, 247-6211.

Fairchild Tropical Garden, 10901 Old Cutler Rd, Coral Gables, 667-1651.

Gold Coast Railroad Museum, 12450 SW 152nd St, near Metrozoo, 253-0063.

Greynolds Park, 17530 W Dixie Hwy, 945-3425.

Lummus Park, NW N River Dr & NW 3rd St, 579-6935.

Metro-Dade County Cultural Plaza, 101 W Flagler St.

Metrozoo, 12400 SW 152nd St, 251-0400.

Miami Beach Garden Center and Conservatory, 2000 Convention Center Dr, Miami Beach, 673-7720.

Miccosukee Indian Village and Airboat Rides, 18 mi W on US 41, 223-8380.

Monkey Jungle, 14805 SW 216th St, 235-1611.

New World Center—Bicentennial Park, Biscayne Blvd, MacArthur Causeway & NE 9th St, 575-5240.

Parrot Jungle and Gardens, 11000 SW 57th Ave, 666-7834.

Seaquarium, Rickenbacker Causeway, 6 mi S on Virginia Key, 361-5705.

Watson Island, 40-acre island in Biscayne Bay.

Sightseeing Tours

All Florida Adventure Tours, 8263-B SW 107th Ave, 270-0219.

American Sightseeing Tours, Inc, 11077 NW 36th Ave, 688-7700.

Gray Line bus tours, 1642 NW 21st Terrace, 33142; 325-1000 or 800/826-6754.

Island Queen **Bay Cruise,** Bayside Marketplace, 401 Biscayne Blvd, 379-5119.

Annual Events

Orange Bowl Football Classic (preceded by festival beginning mid-Dec). Jan 1.

Art Deco Weekend, Miami Beach. 2nd wkend Jan.

Taste of the Grove, Coconut Grove. Mid-Jan.

Coconut Grove Arts Festival. Late Feb.

International Boat Show, Miami Beach Convention Center. Mid-late Feb.

Doral Ryder Open PGA Golf Tournament. Early Mar.

Toyota Grand Prix of Miami. Late Feb.

Carnaval Miami/Calle Ocho Festival. Early Mar.

Italian Renaissance Festival, Vizcaya. Mid-Mar.

South Florida Auto Show, Miami Beach Convention Center. Late Sept-early Oct.

Miccosukee Indian Arts Festival, Miccosukee Indian Villge. Late Dec-early Jan.

City Neighborhoods

Many of the restaurants, unrated dining establishments and some lodgings listed under Miami include neighborhoods as well as exact street addresses. A map showing these neighborhoods can be found immediately following the city introduction. Geographic descriptions of these areas are given, followed by a table of restaurants arranged by neighborhood.

Coconut Grove: South of S Dixie Hwy (US 1), west of SW 22nd Ave, north of Biscayne Bay and east of Douglas Rd.

Downtown: South of NE 12th St, west of Biscayne Bay, north of the Miami River and east of NW 27th St. **North of Downtown:** North of I-395. **South of Downtown:** South of US 41. **West of Downtown:** West of I-95.

Little Haiti: South of NW 79th St, west of Biscayne Blvd (US 1), north of NW 41st St and east of NW 7th Ave.

Little Havana: South of NW 7th St, west of the Miami River, north of SW 8th St and east of NW 27th St.

Lodgings and Food

MIAMI RESTAURANTS
BY NEIGHBORHOOD AREAS

(For full description, see alphabetical listings under Restaurants)

COCONUT GROVE

Brasserie Le Coze. 2901 Florida Ave

Cafe Europa. 3159 Commodore Plaza

Cafe Med. 3015 Grand Ave

Cafe Sci Sci. 3043 Grand Ave

Cafe Tu Tu Tango. 3015 Grand Ave

Grand Cafe (Grand Bay Hotel). 2669 S Bayshore Dr

Green Street Cafe. 3468 Main Hwy

Janjo's. 3131 Commodore Plaza

Kaleidoscope. 3112 Commodore Plaza

Mayfair Grill (Mayfair House Hotel). 3000 Florida Ave

Monty's Stone Crab. 2550 S Bayshore Dr

Pauloluigi's. 3324 Virginia St

Planet Hollywood. 3390 Mary St

Red Lantern. 3176 Commodore Plaza

Señor Frog's. 3008 Grand Ave

Trattoria Pampered Chef. 3145 Commodore Plaza

Tuscany Trattoria. 3484 Main Hwy

DOWNTOWN

Las Tapas. 401 Biscayne Blvd

Snappers. 401 Biscayne Blvd

NORTH OF DOWNTOWN

Crabhouse. 1551 79th St Causeway

Fish Peddler. 8699 Biscayne Blvd

Il Tulipano. 11052 Biscayne Blvd (US 1)

Mike Gordon. 1201 NE 79th St

Tony Chan's Water Club. 1717 N Bayshore Dr

SOUTH OF DOWNTOWN

Fleming. 8511 SW 136th St

Samurai. 8717 SW 136th St

Thai Orchid. 9565 SW 72nd St

Wah Shing. 9503 S Dixie Hwy (US 1)

WEST OF DOWNTOWN

East Coast Fisheries. 360 W Flagler St

El Cid. 117 NW 42nd Ave

LITTLE HAVANA

Casa Juancho. 2436 SW 8th St

Centro Vasco. 2235 SW 8th St

Note: *When a listing is located in a town that does not have its own city heading, it will appear under the city nearest to its location. In these cases, the address and town appear in parenthesis immediately following the name of the establishment.*

Motels

(Rates are usually higher during football, Bowl games)

★ ★ ★ **COURTYARD BY MARRIOTT.** *3929 NW 79th Ave (33166), west of downtown.* 305/477-8118; FAX 305/599-9363. 145 rms, 4 story. Mid-Jan-mid-Apr: S $109; D $119; each addl $10; suites $140; under 18 free; wkly rates; lower rates rest of yr. Crib free. TV; cable. Heated pool. Complimentary coffee in rms. Bkfst avail. Bar 5-10 pm. Ck-out noon. Coin lndry. Meeting rms. Valet serv. Sundries. Free airport transportation. Exercise equipt; weight machine, bicycles, whirl-pool. Refrigerator in suites. Balconies. Miami Intl Airport 5 mi SE. Cr cds: A, D, DS, MC, V.

⊡ ⩯ ✈ ⩯ 🔥 SC

✔★ ★ **FAIRFIELD INN BY MARRIOTT.** *3959 NW 79th Ave (33166), west of downtown.* 305/599-5200; FAX 305/599-5200, ext. 709. 135 rms, 3 story. Jan-mid-Apr: S $68.95; D $74.95; 1st addl $3; under 18 free; lower rates rest of yr. Crib free. TV; cable. Heated pool. Complimentary continental bkfst in lobby. Restaurant nearby. Ck-out noon. Free airport transportation. Cr cds: A, D, DS, MC, V.

⊡ ⩯ ⩯ 🔥 SC

★ **HAMPTON INN.** *2500 Brickell Ave (33129), I-95 exit 1, south of downtown.* 305/854-2070. 69 rms, 3 story. Jan-Apr & Dec: S $82.95-$89.95; D $89.95; under 18 free; lower rates rest of yr. Crib free. Pet accepted. TV; cable. Pool. Complimentary continental bkfst. Bar 3-11 pm. Ck-out noon. Meeting rms. Valet serv. Airport transportation. Ocean 4 blks. Cr cds: A, C, D, DS, MC, V.

⊡ 🐾 ⩯ ⩯ 🔥 SC

✔★ ★ **QUALITY INN SOUTH.** *14501 S Dixie Hwy (33176), south of downtown.* 305/251-2000; FAX 305/235-2225. 100 rms, 2 story, 14 kits. Dec-Apr: S $70-$87; D $76-$93; each addl $5; kit. units $93; under 18 free; varied lower rates rest of yr. Crib free. TV; cable. Heated pool. Restaurant 7 am-midnight; Fri & Sat to 1 am. Rm serv. Ck-out 11 am. Coin lndry. Cr cds: A, C, D, DS, ER, JCB, MC, V.

⩯ ⩯ ⩯ 🔥 SC

★ **WELLESLEY INN AT KENDALL.** *11750 Mills Dr (33183).* 305/270-0359; res: 800/444-8888; FAX 305/270-1334. 106 rms, 4 story. S $79.99-$89.99; D $89.99-$99.99; each addl $10; suites $150; under 12 free. Crib $10. Pet accepted, some restrictions; $10. TV; cable. Heated pool. Complimentary continental bkfst. Restaurant nearby. Ck-out 11 am. Cr cds: A, C, D, DS, MC, V.

⊡ 🐾 ⩯ ⩯ 🔥 SC

✔★ ★ **WELLESLEY INN AT MIAMI LAKES.** *7925 NW 154th St (33016), north of downtown.* 305/821-8274; FAX 305/828-2257. 100 rms, 4 story. Jan-Apr: S $54.99-$79.99; D $69.99-$99.99; each addl $10; under 18 free; higher rates special events; lower rates rest of yr. Crib free. Pet accepted, some restrictions. TV; cable. Heated pool. Complimentary continental bkfst. Restaurant adj 7-1 am. Ck-out 11 am. Coin lndry. Meeting rm. Valet serv. Refrigerator in suites. Cr cds: A, C, D, DS, MC, V.

⊡ 🐾 ⩯ ⩯ 🔥 SC

Motor Hotel

★ ★ **HOLIDAY INN-CALDER/JOE ROBBIE STADIUM.** *21485 NW 27th Ave (33056), University Dr & County Line Rd, north of downtown.* 305/621-5801; FAX 305/624-8202. 214 rms, 9 story. Jan-mid-Mar: S, D $77-$110; each addl $10; under 19 free; varied lower rates rest of yr. Crib free. TV; cable. Pool. Restaurant 6:30 am-2 pm, 5:30-10 pm. Bar 5 pm-midnight; entertainment, dancing. Ck-out noon. Coin lndry. Meeting rms. Bellhops. Valet serv. Gift shop. Private balconies. Panoramic views of Calder Racetrack and Joe Robbie Stadium. Cr cds: A, C, D, DS, JCB, MC, V.

[D] [icons] SC

Hotels

★ ★ **DOUBLETREE AT COCONUT GROVE.** 2649 S Bayshore Dr (33133), S on US 1 (S Dixie Hwy) S on SW 27th Ave, then N on S Bayshore Dr, in Coconut Grove. 305/858-2500; FAX 305/858-5776. 192 rms, 20 story, 19 suites. S $119-$229; D $129-$239; each addl $20; suites $169-$299; under 18 free. Crib free. Valet parking $8. TV; cable. Heated pool; poolside serv. Restaurant 6:30 am-11 pm. Bars from 11 am. Ck-out noon. Meeting rms. Lighted tennis. Health club privileges. Many balconies with ocean view. Fishing, sailing yachts for charter. Opp Coconut Grove Convention Center. Cr cds: A, C, D, DS, ER, JCB, MC, V.

[D] [icons] SC

★ ★ ★ ★ **GRAND BAY.** 2669 S Bayshore Dr (33133), in Coconut Grove. 305/858-9600; res: 800/327-2788; FAX 305/858-1532. 180 rms, 13 story, 49 suites. S, D $205-$275; each addl $20; suites $325-$1,100; under 18 free; wkend rates. Crib free. TV; cable. Heated pool; poolside serv. Restaurant (see GRAND CAFE). Rm serv 24 hrs. Bar 11:30-2 am; entertainment exc Sun. Ck-out noon. Meeting rms. Concierge. Hair salon. Exercise rm; instructor, weights, bicycles, whirlpool, sauna. Massage. Bathrm phones, minibars. Private patios, balconies. European-style villa, crystal chandeliers, objets d'art, commands a breathtaking view of Biscayne Bay. Cr cds: A, C, D, ER, MC, V.

[icons]

★ ★ ★ **GRAND PRIX.** 1717 N Bayshore Dr (33132), north of downtown. 305/372-0313; res: 800/872-7749; FAX 305/539-9228. 176 rms, 42 story, 24 kit. units. Dec-Apr: S, D $125-$375; suites $250-$375; kit. units $175-$375; under 18 free; higher rates Boat Show; lower rates rest of yr. Crib free. TV; cable. Heated pool; poolside serv. Complimentary coffee in rms. Restaurant 7 am-11 pm. Bar; entertainment, dancing Thurs-Sat. Ck-out noon. Coin lndry. Meeting rms. Concierge. Gift shop. Airport, RR station, bus depot transportation. Exercise rm; instructor, weights, treadmill, whirlpool, sauna. Health club privileges. Game rm. Many minibars. Refrigerator, wet bar in suites. Many balconies. On Biscayne Bay. Skywalk connects to Omni International Mall. Cr cds: A, C, D, JCB, MC, V.

[D] [icons] SC

★ ★ ★ **HOLIDAY INN CROWNE PLAZA.** 1601 Biscayne Blvd (33132), north of downtown. 305/374-0000; FAX 305/374-0020. 529 rms, 30 story. Jan-late Mar: S $150-$170; D $170-$190; each addl $20; suites $225-$975; studio rms $225; under 17 free; wkend rates; lower rates rest of yr. Crib free. Parking $8.50; self-park $4.50. TV; cable. Heated rooftop pool; poolside serv. Restaurant 6:30 am-11 pm. Rm serv to 2 am. Bar. Ck-out noon. Convention facilities. Concierge. Golf privileges. Exercise equipt; weights, treadmills. Refrigerators. Overlooks bay. 3-level shopping, dining, entertainment complex. **LUXURY LEVEL : EXECUTIVE CLUB.** 64 rms, 8 suites. S, D $180-$200; suites $225. Wet bars. Bathrm phones. Complimentary continental bkfst, newspaper. Cr cds: A, C, D, DS, ER, MC, V.

[D] [icons] SC

★ ★ ★ **HOTEL INTER-CONTINENTAL.** 100 Chopin Plaza (33131), downtown. 305/577-1000; res: 800/327-3005; FAX 305/472-4720. 644 rms, 34 story. S $199-$259; D $229-$289; each addl $30; suites $389-$2,889; under 14 free; wkly, wkend rates. Garage; valet parking $10. TV; cable. Heated pool; poolside serv. Restaurant 7 am-11 pm. Rm serv 24 hrs. Bar 11:30-2 am. Ck-out noon. Convention facilities. Concierge. Minibars. Antiques, original artwork. 5-story domed atrium in lobby. Cr cds: A, C, D, DS, ER, JCB, MC, V.

[D] [icons]

★ ★ **HOWARD JOHNSON OCCIDENTAL PLAZA.** 100 SE 4th St (33131), downtown. 305/374-5100; res: 800/521-5100 (exc FL); FAX 305/381-9826. 134 rms, 16 story, 90 suites. Mid-Dec-Easter:

suites $110-$180; under 12 free; lower rates rest of yr. Crib free. TV; cable. Pool; poolside serv. Restaurant 7 am-11 pm. Bar. Ck-out noon. Meeting rms. Concierge. Free airport transportation. Exercise equipt; weights, bicycles. Bathrm phones, minibars. On river. Cr cds: A, D, DS, MC, V.

[D] [icons]

★ ★ ★ **MARRIOTT BISCAYNE BAY HOTEL & MARINA.** 1633 N Bayshore Dr (33132), downtown. 305/374-3900; FAX 305/375-0597. 605 rms, 31 story. Mid-Dec-Apr: S, D $145; suites $400-$1,100; lower rates rest of yr. Covered parking $7; valet parking $9. TV; cable. Heated pool; poolside serv. Restaurant 6:30 am-11 pm; Fri, Sat to midnight. Bar 11-1 am. Ck-out noon. Coin lndry. Convention facilities. Shopping arcade. Barber, beauty shop. Exercise equipt; weight machines, treadmill, whirlpool. Game rm. Some bathrm phones. Minibars; refrigerators avail. Balconies. On Biscayne Bay, marina. **LUXURY LEVEL : CONCIERGE FLOOR.** 23 rms. S, D $165. Private lounge, honor bar. Complimentary continental bkfst, refreshments. Cr cds: A, C, D, DS, ER, JCB, MC, V.

[D] [icons] SC

★ ★ ★ **MARRIOTT-DADELAND.** 9090 S Dadeland Blvd (33156), south of downtown. 305/670-1035; FAX 305/670-7540. 302 rms, 24 story. S, D $164; suites $275-$450; under 18 free. Crib free. Covered parking $7.50; valet $9. TV; cable. Heated pool; poolside serv. Restaurant 6:30 am-11 pm. Bar 2 pm-midnight; entertainment Mon-Fri. Ck-out 11 am. Meeting rms. Concierge. Free airport, RR station, shopping transportation. Tennis & golf privileges. Exercise equipt; weights, bicycles, whirlpool. Game rm. **LUXURY LEVEL .** 50 rms, 2 suites, 3 floors. S, D $179; suites $275-$450. Private lounge, honor bar. Complimentary continental bkfst, refreshments, newspaper. Cr cds: A, C, D, DS, MC, V.

[D] [icons] SC

MAYFAIR HOUSE. (New general manager, therefore not rated) 3000 Florida Ave (33133), in Coconut Grove. 305/441-0000; res: 800/433-4555 (exc FL); FAX 305/447-9173. 182 suites, 5 story. Mid-Dec-Apr: S, D $230-$900; each addl $35; under 12 free; wkend, honeymoon plans; lower rates rest of yr. Crib free. Valet parking $10. TV; cable, in-rm movies. Rooftop pool. Restaurant 7 am-11 pm (also see MAYFAIR GRILL). Rm serv 24 hrs. Bars from noon. Ck-out 1 pm. Meeting rms. Concierge. Shopping arcade. Health club privileges. Bathrm phones, refrigerators, honor bars. Private patios, all with hot tub. Elegant setting in World of Mayfair Mall. Cr cds: A, C, D, DS, ER, JCB, MC, V.

[D] [icons]

★ ★ ★ **SHERATON BISCAYNE BAY BRICKELL POINT.** 495 Brickell Ave (33131), downtown. 305/373-6000; FAX 305/374-2279. 598 rms, 17 story. Jan-Mar: S $119-$149; D $129-$159; each addl $20; suites $250 & $350; under 12 free; lower rates rest of yr. Crib free. TV; cable. Heated pool; poolside serv. Restaurant 6:30 am-11:30 pm. Bar 11-2 am; entertainment, dancing. Ck-out noon. Meeting rms. Concierge. Covered parking. Exercise equipt; weight machine, treadmill. Private patios, balconies. Extensive landscaping; at bayside. Cr cds: A, C, D, DS, ER, MC, V.

[D] [icons] SC

Inn

★ ★ **MIAMI RIVER INN.** 118 SW South River Dr (33130), downtown. 305/325-0045; res: 800/HOTEL-89; FAX 305/325-9227. 40 rms in 4 bldgs, 2-3 story. S, D $60-$125; under 12 free; higher rates some special events. TV; cable. Pool; whirlpool. Complimentary continental bkfst. Restaurant nearby. Ck-out noon, ck-in 2 pm. Meeting rm. Lawn games. Opp river. Restored 1906 houses once owned by Miami's founders. Antiques. Cr cds: A, D, DS, MC, V.

[D] [icons] SC

Resorts

★ ★ ★ **DON SHULA'S HOTEL & GOLF CLUB.** *(Main St, Miami Lakes 33014) 18 mi NW; N on I-95, W on FL 826 (Palmetto Expy), 1 blk E to Main St.* 305/821-1150; res: 800/24-SHULA; FAX 305/819-8298. 301 rms, 3 story, 17 kits. Dec-Mar: S, D $169; each addl $10; suites $190-$270; golf package; varied lower rates rest of yr. Crib $10. TV; cable. 2 pools. Free supervised child's activities. Dining rms 6:30 am-11 pm. Snack bars 10 am-7 pm; Fri & Sat from 7 am. Bar 11-1 am; entertainment, dancing. Ck-out noon, ck-in 3 pm. Meeting rms. Shopping arcade. Valet parking. Lighted tennis, pro. Two 18-hole golf courses (1 lighted), pro, par 3, 2 putting greens, lighted driving range. Exercise rm; instructor, weights, bicycles, whirlpool, steam rm, sauna. Fishing trips. Wet bars; some refrigerators. Private patios, balconies. *LUXURY LEVEL : PRESS BOX.* 26 rms, 2 suites. S $179; D $189; suites from $229. Private lounge. Complimentary continental bkfst, refreshments, newspapers. Cr cds: A, C, D, DS, MC, V.

D ⚊ ⚊ ⚊ ⚊ ⚊ ⚊ ⚊ ⚊ SC

DORAL RESORT & COUNTRY CLUB. *(4-star 1994; Remodeling incomplete when inspected, therefore not rated) 4400 NW 87th Ave (33178), rated.* 305/592-2000; res: 800/22-DORAL; FAX 305/594-4682. 650 rms in 11 buildings. Dec-Apr: S, D $245-$360; each addl $40; suites $360-$1,500; under 17 free (limit 2); some lower rates rest of yr. Crib free. TV; cable. Heated pool; wading pool, poolside serv. Playground. Free supervised child's activities (hols only). Dining rm (public by res) 6:30 am-midnight; off-season to 10:30 pm; also 2 others. Rm serv 24 hrs (in season). Snack bar; box lunches. 3 bars 11-1:30 am. Ck-out 11 am, ck-in 4 pm. Convention facilities. Valet serv. 15 tennis courts (4 lighted), pro. Five 18-hole golf courses; 9-hole par 3 golf, 4 putting greens, lighted driving range, golf school, pro. Bicycle rentals. Lawn games. Soc dir; entertainment, dancing, movies. Rec rm. Game rm. Exercise rm; instructor, weights, bicycles, whirlpool, steam rm. Massage. European spa facilities. Bathrm phones, refrigerators, minibars. Private patios, balconies. Free transportation to Doral Ocean Beach Resort Hotel (see MIAMI BEACH). Luxurious resort hotel on 2,400 elaborately landscaped acres. Cr cds: A, C, D, DS, JCB, MC, V.

D ⚊ ⚊ ⚊ ⚊ ⚊ ⚊ ⚊ ⚊

★ ★ ★ ★ **FISHER ISLAND CLUB.** *(1 Fisher Island Dr, Fisher Island 33109) I-95 to MacArthur Causeway, E to ferry terminal. Accesible only by auto ferry, helicopter or seaplane.* 305/535-6020; res: 800/537-3708; FAX 305/535-6003. 60 rms, 1-5 story, 4 kit. cottages. Nov-Apr: S $350-$625; D $350-$900; each addl $25; suites $525-$1,175; cottages $575-$1,175; under 12 free; golf plan; lower rates rest of yr. Crib free. TV; cable, in-rm movies. 2 pools, 1 indoor; wading pool, poolside serv. Playground. Complimentary coffee in rms. Dining rm (see VANDERBILT MANSION). Rm serv. Bar 11-2 am; entertainment Wed-Sun. Ck-out noon, ck-in 3 pm. Gift shop. Grocery. Coin lndry. Meeting rms. Bellhops. Concierge. Valet serv. Sports dir. Lighted tennis; pro. 9-hole golf; greens fee $70, pro, putting green, driving range. Boating. Exercise rm; instructor, weight machine, treadmill, whirlpool, sauna. Health club privileges. Masseur. Lawn games. Social dir. Minibars. Balconies. Swimming beach. Mediterranean inspired architecture; cottages and guest houses circa 1925. More than 200 landscaped acres on island that was the winter estate of William Vanderbilt. Cr cds: A, C, D, MC, V.

D ⚊ ⚊ ⚊ ⚊ ⚊ ⚊ ⚊

★ ★ ★ **TURNBERRY ISLE RESORT & CLUB.** *(19999 W Country Club Dr, Aventura 33180) Approx 9 mi N via I-95, exit 20 (Ives Dairy Rd), E to US 1 (Biscayne Blvd), to Aventura Blvd.* 305/932-6200; res: 800/327-7028; FAX 305/933-6560. 340 rms in 3 bldgs, 3-7 story. Dec 20-Apr: Country Club: S, D $375-$435; each addl $30; suites $650-$2,100; Yacht Club: S, D $285; each addl $30; Marina Wing: S, D $335; each addl $30; under 12 free; golf, tennis and spa plans; lower rates rest of yr. Crib free. TV; cable, in-rm movies. 3 pools; poolside serv. Dining rm for guests 7 am-10 pm. Box lunches, snack bar, picnics. Rm serv 24 hrs. Bars 11-1 am. Ck-out noon, ck-in 4 pm. Grocery, package store 1 blk. Coin lndry. Convention facilities. Lighted tennis, pro. 36-hole golf, greens fee $75 ($40 in summer), pro, putting green. Beach, boats, diving, water sports. Entertainment, dancing. Rec rm. Exercise rm; instructor, weights, bicycles, whirlpool, sauna, steam rm. Massage.

Refrigerators; many in-rm whirlpools, hot tubs. On 300-acre secluded island with subtropical gardens; marina, private ocean club. Luxurious, gracious, comfortable. Cr cds: A, C, D, DS, ER, MC, V.

D ⚊ ⚊ ⚊ ⚊ ⚊ ⚊ ⚊ ⚊ ⚊

Restaurants

★ ★ ★ **BRASSERIE LE COZE.** *2901 Florida Ave, in Coconut Grove.* 305/444-9697. Hrs: 6-11 pm; wkends 6 pm-midnight. Closed Mon. French menu. Bar. Extensive wine list. Complete meals: dinner $29-$40. Specialties: duck confit cassoulet, snapper with portobello mushrooms/lemon emulsion. Valet parking. Outdoor dining. Casual French brasserie atmosphere. Cr cds: A, D, MC, V.

★ ★ **CAFE EUROPA.** *3159 Commodore Plaza, in Coconut Grove.* 305/448-5723. Hrs: 4 pm-midnight; Wed & Sun from noon. Res accepted. French menu. Bar. A la carte entrees: lunch $5.95-$13.95, dinner $4.95-$22. Specialties: bouillabaisse, duck á l'orange, rack of lamb. Parking. Outdoor dining. Parisian cafe atmosphere. Cr cds: A, C, D, MC, V.

D

✔★ **CAFE MED.** *3015 Grand Ave, in Coconut Grove.* 305/443-1770. Hrs: 9 am-midnight; wkends to 1 am; Sun brunch to 4 pm. Italian menu. Bar. A la carte entrees: bkfst, lunch, dinner $4.25-$14.95. Sun brunch $9.95. Child's meals. Specializes in brick oven pizza, fresh pasta dishes, Mediterranean salads. Own desserts. Outdoor dining. Cr cds: A, D, DS, MC, V.

D

★ ★ ★ **CAFE SCI SCI.** *3043 Grand Ave (33133), in Coconut Grove.* 305/446-5104. Hrs: noon-3:30 pm, 5:30 pm-1 am. Closed Jan 1, Dec 24. Res accepted. Italian menu. Wine, beer. A la carte entrees: lunch $6.95-$10.95, dinner $13.95-$23.95. Child's meals. Specializes in fresh seafood. Own pasta. Parking. Outdoor dining. Elegant dining in recreation of 18th-century Neapolitan cafe. Antique furnishings. Artwork. Cr cds: A, C, D, MC, V.

D

✔★ ★ **CAFE TU TU TANGO.** *3015 Grand Ave, in Coconut Grove.* 305/529-2222. Hrs: 11:30 am-midnight; Fri, Sat to 2 am. International menu. Bar. A la carte entrees: lunch, dinner $2.75-$7.95. Child's meals. Specialties: Barcelona stir-fry, brick oven pizza. Entertainment. Parking. Outdoor dining. On 2nd floor of Cocowalk complex. Artist loft motif; painters at work. Cr cds: A, MC, V.

D

★ ★ **CASA JUANCHO.** *2436 SW 8th St, in Little Havana.* 305/642-2452. Hrs: noon-midnight; Fri, Sat to 1 am. Res accepted. Spanish menu. A la carte entrees: lunch $8-$40, dinner $12-$40. Specializes in imported Spanish seafood, fresh seafood, tapas. Strolling musicians. Valet parking. Spanish decor. Cr cds: A, C, D, MC, V.

D

★ ★ **CENTRO VASCO.** *2235 SW 8th St, in Little Havana.* 305/643-9606. Hrs: noon-midnight. Spanish, Amer menu. Res accepted Thurs-Sat. Bar. Semi-a la carte: lunch; dinner $9.95-$27. Specialties: seafood à la Basque, filet madrilène, paella alla Valenciana. Valet parking. Entertainment Fri-Sun. Fireplace. Spanish decor. Family-owned. Cr cds: A, C, D, DS, MC, V.

D

★ ★ ★ **CHEF ALLEN'S.** *(19088 NE 29th Ave, Aventura) Approx 8 mi N on Biscayne Blvd (US 1) to NE 191st St, at jct NE 29th Ave.* 305/935-2900. Hrs: 6-10:30 pm; Sat to 11 pm. Res accepted. Bar. Wine cellar. Semi-a la carte: dinner $19-$27. Child's meals. Specializes in fresh local fish, homemade pasta, dessert soufflés. Own baking. Valet parking. Open-glass kitchen; wood-burning mesquite grill. Cr cds: A, D, MC, V.

★ **CRABHOUSE.** *1551 79th St Causeway, north of downtown.* 305/868-7085. Hrs: 11:30 am-11 pm; Fri, Sat to midnight; early-bird dinner 4:30-6:30 pm. Bar. Semi-a la carte: lunch $4.55-$10.95, dinner $9.95-$33.95. Child's meals. Specializes in crab, lobster, fresh fish. Seafood bar. Valet parking. Overlooks bay. Cr cds: A, C, D, DS, MC, V.

D

★ **EAST COAST FISHERIES.** *360 W Flagler St, west of downtown.* 305/373-5515. Hrs: 11:30 am-10 pm. Wine. A la carte entrees: lunch, dinner $9.95-$25. Specialties: roasted garlic mahi mahi, shrimp Chippewa, stone crab claws, lobster. Parking. Authentic retail fish market located at docks on Miami River. Cr cds: A, D, MC, V.

D

★ **EL CID.** *117 NW 42nd Ave, west of downtown.* 305/642-3144. Hrs: noon-midnight; wkends to 1 am. Closed Dec 24. Res accepted. Spanish, Amer menu. Bar. A la carte entrees: lunch, dinner $14.95-$23.95. Child's meals. Pianist. Valet parking. Replica of Spanish castle. Strolling minstrels. Cr cds: A, C, D, MC, V.

D

★ **FISH PEDDLER.** *8699 Biscayne Blvd (33138), on US 1, north of downtown.* 305/757-0648. Hrs: 11 am-10 pm; early-bird dinner 4-6 pm. Closed Thanksgiving, Dec 25. Bar. Semi-a la carte: lunch $5.95-$18.50, dinner $12.25-$21.50. Child's meals. Specializes in dolphin, grouper, Maine lobster. Parking. Taxidermy displays. Cr cds: A, DS, MC, V.

D

✔★ **FLEMING.** *8511 SW 136th St (33156), in shopping center, south of downtown.* 305/232-6444. Hrs: 5:30-10:30 pm. Closed Mon; July 4. Res accepted. Danish, continental menu. Bar. Semi-a la carte: dinner $8.95-$17.95. Specialties: Norwegian salmon, duck Danoise. Parking. Patio dining. Scandinavian decor. Cr cds: A, MC, V.

D

★★★★ **GRAND CAFE.** *(See Grand Bay Hotel)* 305/858-9600. Hrs: 7 am-11 pm; Fri, Sat to 11:30 pm. Res accepted. International menu. Bar 11:30-2 am; Sun & Mon to 1 am. A la carte entrees: bkfst $8.50-$17, lunch $8.50-$25, dinner $19-$30. Lunch buffet $11-$16.50. Sun brunch $24. Own baking. Valet parking. Pianist. Windows overlook garden area. Cr cds: A, D, MC, V.

D

✔★ **GREEN STREET CAFE.** *3468 Main Hwy, in Coconut Grove.* 305/444-0244. Hrs: 6-2 am. No A/C. Italian, Amer menu. A la carte entrees: bkfst $3-$6, lunch $5-$10, dinner $5-$13. Sun brunch $5-$10. Specialties: pastas, specialty salads, wood oven pizza. Parking. Outdoor sidewalk cafe on corner lot. Cr cds: A, MC, V.

D

★★★ **IL TULIPANO.** *11052 Biscayne Blvd (US 1), north of downtown.* 305/893-4811. Hrs: 6-11 pm; Fri, Sat to midnight. Closed Sun; Dec 24; also Sept. Res accepted. Northern Italian menu. Beer. Wine cellar. A la carte entrees: dinner $14-$40. Specialties: pollo scarpariello, rigatini boscaiola "bosco," lobster tail. Own baking. Cr cds: A, D, MC, V.

D

★★ **JANJO'S.** *3131 Commodore Plaza, in Coconut Grove.* 305/445-5030. Hrs: 11:30 am-midnight; wkends 10:30-2 am; Sun brunch 9 am-3 pm. Res accepted. Caribbean, Asian menu. Bar. A la carte entrees: lunch $4.95-$16.50, dinner $13.50-$24.50. Sun brunch $4.25-$7.95. Serv charge 15%. Specializes in veal chops, shrimp pasta, filet mignon. Entertainment. Parking. Outdoor dining. Designed as Caribbean island house. Cr cds: A, C, D, MC, V.

D

★★ **KALEIDOSCOPE.** *3112 Commodore Plaza, S on US 1 (S Dixie Hwy) to SW 32nd Ave, SE to Grand Ave, E to Commodore Plaza,* in Coconut Grove. 305/446-5010. Hrs: 11:30 am-3 pm, 6-11 pm; Fri, Sat to midnight; Sun 11:30 am-3 pm, 5:30-10:30 pm; Sun brunch to 3 pm. Res accepted Fri, Sat. Wine, beer. Semi-a la carte: lunch $6.95-$11.95, dinner $12.95-$19.95. Sun brunch $18.95. Specialties: red snapper with glazed bananas, pasta. Outdoor dining. On 2nd floor. Cr cds: A, C, D, DS, MC, V.

★★ **LAS TAPAS.** *401 Biscayne Blvd, downtown.* 305/372-2737. Hrs: 11:30 am-midnight; Fri, Sat to 1 am. Spanish menu. Bar. Semi-a la carte: lunch $4.95-$9.95, dinner $9.95-$19.95. Specialties: seafood, paella, tapas. Strolling minstrels. Parking. Outdoor dining. Open kitchen. Cr cds: A, C, D, DS, MC, V.

D

★★★ **MARK'S PLACE.** *(2286 NE 123rd St, N Miami) N on Biscayne Blvd (US 1) to NE 123rd St.* 305/893-6888. Hrs: noon-2:30 pm, 6-11 pm; Sat, Sun from 6 pm. Closed Dec 25. Res accepted. Serv bar. Semi-a la carte: lunch $13.95-$17.95, dinner $15.95-$34. Specializes in fresh Florida seafood, pasta. Cr cds: A, C, D, MC, V.

D

★★★ **MAYFAIR GRILL.** *(See Mayfair House Hotel)* 305/441-0000. Hrs: 7 am-11 pm; Sun brunch 11 am-3 pm. Res accepted. Bar 11 am-11 pm. Wine cellar. A la carte entrees: bkfst $6-$8, lunch $7.50-$12.95, dinner $16-$26.50. Own baking. Valet parking. Victorian setting with South Florida accents; stained-glass ceiling. Cr cds: A, C, D, DS, ER, JCB, MC, V.

D

✔★★ **MIKE GORDON.** *1201 NE 79th St, north of downtown.* 305/751-4429. Hrs: noon-10 pm; early-bird dinner 3:30-6 pm. Closed Thanksgiving, Dec 25 from 4 pm. Bar. Semi-a la carte: lunch $5.95-$16.95, dinner $13.75-$18.95. Child's meals. Specializes in fresh seafood. Valet parking; boat docking. Overlooks bay. Family-owned. Cr cds: A, D, DS, MC, V.

D

★★ **MONTY'S STONE CRAB.** *2550 S Bayshore Dr, in Coconut Grove.* 305/858-1431. Hrs: 11:30 am-4 pm, 5-11 pm; Fri, Sat to midnight. Res accepted. Bar. Complete meals: lunch $6.95-$15, dinner $22-$32. Child's meals. Specializes in Florida seafood, stone crab. Salad bar. Valet parking. Outdoor dining. Waterfront location overlooking marina. Cr cds: A, D, MC, V.

D

★ **PAULOLUIGI'S.** *3324 Virginia St (33133), in Coconut Grove.* 305/445-9000. Hrs: 11 am-midnight; Fri to 1 am; Sat 4 pm-1 am; Sun 4-11 pm. Closed some major hols. Res accepted. Italian menu. Wine, beer. Semi-a la carte: lunch $5-$7, dinner $6-$17. Child's meals. Specialties: cappellini marinara, veal Pauloluigi, linguini seafood. Outdoor dining. Cr cds: A, MC, V.

D

★ **RED LANTERN.** *3176 Commodore Plaza (33133), in Coconut Grove.* 305/529-9998. Hrs: 11:30 am-3 pm, 5-11 pm; Fri & Sat to midnight. Closed Thanksgiving. Res accepted. Chinese menu. Wine, beer. Semi-a la carte: lunch $4.95-$6.95, dinner $8.95-$21. Specializes in seafood. Tropical fish tanks. Chinese figurines. Cr cds: A, C, D, MC, V.

D

★ **SAMURAI.** *8717 SW 136th St (33176), south of downtown.* 305/238-2131. Hrs: noon-2:30 pm, 5:30-10:30 pm; Fri to 11 pm; Sat to 11:30 pm. Closed Thanksgiving. Res accepted. Japanese menu. Bar. Complete meals: lunch $5.95-$8.95, dinner $11.95-$18.95. Child's meals. Specializes in steak, chicken, seafood. Parking. Meals prepared in full view of guests. Cr cds: A, C, D, DS, ER, JCB, MC, V.

D

✔★★ **SEÑOR FROG'S.** *3008 Grand Ave, in Coconut Grove.* 305/448-0999. Hrs: 11:30-1 am; Thurs-Sat to 2 am. Res accepted. Mexican menu. Bar. A la carte entrees: lunch, dinner $7-$15. Child's meals. Specializes in enchiladas, fajitas, chiles rellenos. Parking. Outdoor dining. Mexican cantina decor. Cr cds: A, C, D, MC, V.

D

★ SNAPPERS. *401 Biscayne Blvd, at Pier #5, downtown.* 305/379-0605. Hrs: 7:30 am-midnight. Bar. A la carte entrees: lunch $7.95-$13.95, dinner $9.95-$19.95. Child's meals. Specializes in seafood, pasta. Raw bar. Parking. Outdoor dining at bayside. On pier. Cr cds: A, MC, V.

D

★ ★ THAI ORCHID. *9565 SW 72nd St, south of downtown.* 305/279-8583. Hrs: 11:30 am-3 pm, 5-10:30 pm. Closed Thanksgiving, Dec 25. Thai menu. Wine, beer. A la carte entrees: lunch $4.25-$7.95, dinner $7.25-$17.95. Specializes in beef, curry, seafood. Parking. Decorated with various types of orchids. Cr cds: A, MC, V.

D

★ ★ ★ TONY CHAN'S WATER CLUB. *1717 N Bayshore Dr, in mall area of Grand Prix Hotel, north of downtown.* 305/374-8888. Hrs: noon-3 pm, 5-11 pm; Fri to midnight; Sat 5 pm-midnight; Sun 5-11 pm. Closed Thanksgiving, Dec 25. Chinese menu. Bar. A la carte entrees: lunch $6.50-$30, dinner $9-$40. Complete meals: lunch $8-$30. Specialties: Peking duck, honey walnut shrimp, water club sea bass. Valet parking. Outdoor dining. Main dining rm has view of kitchen and of marina. Cr cds: A, D, MC, V.

D

★ ★ TRATTORIA PAMPERED CHEF. *3145 Commodore Plaza (33133), in Coconut Grove.* 305/567-0104. Hrs: 11:30 am-11:30 pm; Fri & Sat to 1:30 am; Sun to midnight. Res accepted. Northern Italian menu. Bar. A la carte entrees: lunch $4.95-$7.95, dinner $8.95-$21.95. Child's meals. Specialties: chicken Florentine, veal Marsala, pasta valverde. Sidewalk dining. Cr cds: A, D, DS, MC, V.

D

★ ★ TUSCANY TRATTORIA. *3484 Main Hwy, in Coconut Grove.* 305/445-0022. Hrs: 11:30 am-midnight. Res accepted. Italian menu. Bar. A la carte entrees: lunch $5.95-$12.95, dinner $7.95-$19.95. Complete meals: lunch $10-$15, dinner $20-$30. Child's meals. Specialties: osso buco, snapper Livornese. Parking. Outdoor dining. Cr cds: A, C, D, DS, MC, V.

D

✔★ UNICORN VILLAGE. *(3565 NE 207th St, North Miami Beach)* N on Biscayne Blvd (US 1) to NE 207th St. 305/933-8829. Hrs: 11:30 am-9:30 pm; wkends to 10 pm; Sun brunch to 3:30 pm. Serv bar. A la carte entrees: lunch $4.95-$8.95, dinner $7.95-$16.95. Sun brunch $4.95-$9.95. Child's meals. Specialties: spinach lasagne, honey mustard chicken, Jamaican-style fish. 100-seat outdoor dining. Large restaurant overlooking Waterways Yacht Harbor. Totally nonsmoking. Cr cds: A, MC, V.

D SC

★ ★ VANDERBILT MANSION. *(See Fisher Island Club)* 305/535-6020. Hrs: 7 pm-midnight; Sun brunch noon-3 pm. Closed Mon & Tues; also June-Aug. Res required. Continental menu. Bar. Wine cellar. A la carte entrees: dinner $40-$50. Complete meals: dinner $40. Specialties: pan-seared snapper with crabmeat, grilled wild salmon, rack of lamb. Harpist & bass player Wed-Sat. Valet parking. Outdoor dining. Elegant dining in mansion built for William K. Vanderbilt. Marble floor, chandeliers. Jacket. Cr cds: A, C, D, MC, V.

D

★ ★ WAH SHING. *9503 S Dixie Hwy (US 1), in Dadeland Plaza, south of downtown.* 305/666-9879. Hrs: 11:30 am-11 pm. Closed Thanksgiving. Chinese menu. Wine, beer. A la carte entrees: lunch $4.95-$6.95, dinner $7.95-$12.95. Specializes in Cantonese, mandarin & Szechwan dishes. Oriental decor. Cr cds: A, MC, V.

D

Unrated Dining Spot

PLANET HOLLYWOOD. *3390 Mary St (33133), in Coconut Grove.* 305/445-7277. Hrs: 11-2 am; Thurs-Sat to 3 am. Closed Dec 25. Bar. Semi-a la carte: lunch, dinner $4.95-$17.95. Child's meals. Specializes in fajitas, pasta, pizza. Parking. TV and movie memorabilia. Cr cds: A, D, MC, V.

D

Miami Intl Airport Area

Motel

★ ★ WELLESLEY INN. *(8436 NW 36th St, Miami 33166)* N via Le Jeune Rd (NW 42nd Ave) to NW 36th St. 305/592-4799; FAX 305/471-8461. 106 rms, 4 story, 13 suites. Jan-mid-Apr: S $74.99; D $79.99; each addl $10; suites $20 addl; under 18 free; wkly rates; lower rates rest of yr. Crib free. Pet accepted, some restrictions; $10. TV; cable. Heated pool. Complimentary continental bkfst, coffee. Ck-out 11 am. Coin lndry. Meeting rm. Valet serv. Refrigerator in suites. Cr cds: A, C, D, DS, MC, V.

D ✔ ≈ ✈ ✈ 🔥 SC

Motor Hotel

★ ★ BEST WESTERN MIAMI AIRPORT INN. *(1550 NW Le Jeune Rd, Miami 33126)* On Le Jeune Rd (NW 42nd Ave). 305/871-2345; FAX 305/871-2811. 208 rms, 6 story. S $79-$99; D $84-$104; each addl $5; suites $195; family rates. Crib $5. TV; cable. Pool. Restaurant open 24 hrs. Rm serv. Bar 11-2 am. Ck-out 1 pm. Meeting rms. Bellhops. Sundries. Free airport transportation. Game rm. Bathrm phones; some refrigerators. Cr cds: A, C, D, DS, ER, MC, V.

D ≈ ✈ ✈ 🔥 SC

Hotels

✔★ ★ AIRPORT REGENCY. *(1000 NW Le Jeune Rd, Miami 33126)* On Le Jeune Rd (NW 42nd Ave). 305/441-1600; res: 800/367-1039 (exc FL), 800/432-1192 (FL); FAX 305/443-0766. 176 rms, 6 story. S $65-$110; D $75-$125; each addl $10; suites $195. Crib free. TV. Heated pool. Restaurant 6:30 am-11 pm; Fri, Sat to midnight. Bar 11-2 am; Fri, Sat to 4 am; entertainment, dancing Fri & Sat. Ck-out noon. Meeting rms. Concierge. Gift shop. Free airport transportation. Balconies. Cr cds: A, C, D, DS, ER, MC, V.

D ≈ ✈ ✈ 🔥 SC

★ ★ CROWN STERLING SUITES. *(3974 NW South River Dr, Miami Springs 33142)* 1/2 mi N on Le Jeune Rd (NW 42nd Ave), W on NW South River Dr, just E of airport. 305/634-5000; FAX 305/635-9499. 316 suites, 10 story. Oct-mid-Apr: S $129-$189; D $139-$199; each addl $10; under 12 free; lower rates rest of yr. Crib free. Pet accepted, some restrictions; $25. TV; cable. Heated pool; whirlpool. Complimentary full bkfst. Restaurant 11 am-11 pm. Bar to 2 am; entertainment, dancing. Ck-out noon. Meeting rms. Airport transportation. Health club privileges. Cr cds: A, C, D, DS, ER, MC, V.

D ✔ ≈ ✈ ✈ 🔥 SC

★ ★ HOLIDAY INN-AIRPORT SOUTH. *(1101 NW 57th Ave, Miami 33126)* Jct FL 836 & Red Rd exit (57th Ave). 305/266-0000; FAX 305/266-9179. 264 rms, 10 story. Jan-Mar: S $95-$125; D $105-$135; each addl $10; suites $190-$215; under 18 free; higher rates Boat Show; lower rates rest of yr. Crib free. TV; cable. Pool; wading pool. Restaurant 6 am-2 pm, 5-10 pm. Bar noon-midnight. Ck-out noon.

Coin lndry. Meeting rms. Concierge. Sundries. Free airport transportation. Refrigerators avail. Cr cds: A, C, D, DS, JCB, MC, V.

D ⛷ 🚤 🏊 🏃 ✈ 🎿 🏂 🔥 SC

★ ★ ★ **HOLIDAY INN-LEJEUNE CENTRE.** *(950 NW Le Jeune Rd, Miami 33126) On Le Jeune Rd (NW 42nd Ave). 305/446-9000; FAX 305/441-0725.* 305 rms, 6 story. S $99-$119; D $109-$129; each addl $10; suites $119-$129; under 19 free; wkend rates. Crib free. TV; cable. Pool; poolside serv. Restaurant 6:30 am-2 pm, 5-11 pm. Rm serv to 1 am. Bar 4 pm-midnight. Ck-out noon. Convention facilities. Valet serv. Gift shop. Free airport transportation. Exercise equipt; weights, bicycles, whirlpool, sauna. **LUXURY LEVEL : EXECUTIVE FLOOR.** 60 units, 1 suite. S $119; D $129; suite $255. Private lounge. Complimentary continental bkfst, newspaper. Cr cds: A, C, D, DS, JCB, MC, V.

D ☇ 🏃 ✈ 🎿 🔥 SC

★ ★ ★ **MIAMI AIRPORT HILTON & TOWERS.** *(5101 Blue Lagoon Dr, Miami 33126) S of East-West Expy (Dolphin Expy, FL 836) via Red Rd (FL 959), E on Blue Lagoon Dr. 305/262-1000; FAX 305/261-6769.* 500 rms, 14 story, 83 suites. Jan-May: S $120-$195; D $140-$215; each addl $20; suites $190-$500; family rates; wkend plans; lower rates rest of yr. Crib free. TV; cable. Pool; whirlpool, poolside serv. Restaurant 6:30 am-11 pm. Rm serv 6-1 am. Bar 9-5 am, Fri-Sat to 5 am; entertainment, dancing Wed-Sun. Ck-out noon. Convention facilities. Concierge. Gift shop. Valet parking. Free airport transportation. Lighted tennis. Exercise equipt; weights, bicycles, whirlpool, sauna. Some bathrm phones, refrigerators, minibars. Private patios, balconies. On lake; marina; sailboats, jet skis; waterskiing, windsurfing. Exotic birds in cages, saltwater tanks with exotic fish. **LUXURY LEVEL : THE TOWERS.** 134 units, 16 suites, 3 floors. S $175; D $195; suites $190-$500. Private lounge. Complimentary continental bkfst, refreshments, newspaper. Cr cds: A, C, D, DS, ER, JCB, MC, V.

D 🎿 🐾 🚤 🏃 ☇ ✈ 🎿 🏂 🔥 SC

★ ★ ★ **MIAMI AIRPORT MARRIOTT HOTEL.** *(1201 NW Le Jeune Rd, Miami 33126) On Le Jeune Rd (NW 42nd Ave), SW of FL 836. 305/649-5000; FAX 305/642-3369.* 782 rms, 10 story. S $59-$149; D $59-$169; family, wkend rates. Crib free. Pet accepted, some restrictions. TV; cable. Heated pool. Restaurant 6-1 am. Bars 11-2 am; dancing. Meeting rms. Gift shop. Barber, beauty shop. Free airport transportation. Lighted tennis, pro. Exercise equipt; weights, bicycles, 2 whirlpools. Rec rm. Private patios. **LUXURY LEVEL :** 92 rms, 3 floors. S $140; D $150. Concierge. Private lounge, honor bar. Complimentary continental bkfst, newspaper, magazines. Cr cds: A, C, D, DS, ER, JCB, MC, V.

D 🎿 🐾 🏃 ☇ 🏃 ✈ 🎿 🏂 🔥 SC

★ ★ ★ **MIAMI INTERNATIONAL AIRPORT HOTEL.** *(PO Box 997510, Miami 33299) In airport terminal, Concourse E. 305/871-4100; res: 800/327-1276; FAX 305/871-0800.* 260 rms, 8 story. S $109-$149; D $119-$159; each addl $10; suites $195-$600; under 13 free; honeymoon packages. Crib free. TV; cable. Pool. Restaurant 7 am-11 pm. Bar 11-1 am. Ck-out noon. Coin lndry. Meeting rms. Drugstore. Barber, beauty shop. Exercise equipt; weights, bicycles, whirlpool, steam rm. Cr cds: A, C, D, ER, JCB, MC, V.

D ☇ 🏃 🎿 🏃 ✈ 🏂 🔥 SC

★ ★ ★ **RADISSON MART PLAZA.** *(711 NW 72nd Ave, Miami 33126) Just S of East-West Expy (Dolphin Expy/FL 836) on NW 72nd Ave. 305/261-3800; FAX 305/261-7665.* 334 rms, 12 story. S, D $129-$149; each addl $10; suites $159-$399; under 18 free; wkend package plans. Crib free. TV; cable. Pool; poolside serv. Restaurant 6 am-11 pm. Bars 11-1 am; entertainment; dancing. Ck-out noon. Convention facilities. Shopping arcade. Free airport transportation. Lighted tennis, pro. Exercise rm; instructor, weights, bicycles, whirlpool, steam rm, sauna. Balconies. **LUXURY LEVEL : PLAZA CLUB.** 30 rms. S, D $159. Concierge. Private lounge. Complimentary refreshments. Cr cds: A, C, D, DS, ER, MC, V.

D 🎿 🐾 ☇ 🏃 ✈ 🏂 🔥 SC

★ ★ ★ **SHERATON RIVER HOUSE.** *(3900 NW 21st St, Miami 33142) On NW 21st St, just E of Le Jeune Rd (NW 42nd Ave), adj to airport. 305/871-3800; FAX 305/871-0447.* 408 rms, 10 story. S, D $89-$145; each addl $10; suites $175-$500; under 18 free. Crib $10. Pet accepted, some restrictions. TV; cable. Heated pool; poolside serv. Restaurant 7 am-11 pm. Rm serv. Bar 11-2 am; dancing exc Sun. Ck-out noon. Convention facilities. Covered parking. Airport transportation. Lighted tennis. Exercise equipt; weights, bicycles, whirlpool, sauna. Bathrm phone in some suites. Golf course adj. On Miami River. Cr cds: A, C, D, DS, ER, JCB, MC, V.

D 🎿 🐾 🚤 🏃 ☇ 🎿 🏃 ✈ 🏂 SC

★ ★ ★ **SOFITEL.** *(5800 Blue Lagoon Dr, Miami 33126) S of East-West Expy (Dolphin Expy, FL 836) via Red Rd (FL 959), W on Blue Lagoon Dr. 305/264-4888; FAX 305/262-9049.* 281 rms, 15 story, 27 suites. S, D $149-$219; each addl $20; suites $219-$599; under 17 free; wkend packages. Crib free. Pet accepted, some restrictions. Valet parking $6. TV; cable. Pool. Restaurant 6 am-midnight. Bar 11-2 am; entertainment. Ck-out noon. Meeting rms. Concierge. Gift shop. Free airport transportation. Lighted tennis. Exercise equipt; weights, bicycles, whirlpool, sauna. On lagoon. Cr cds: A, C, D, MC, V.

D 🐾 🚤 🏃 ☇ 🏃 ✈ 🏂 🔥 SC

Milwaukee

Settled: 1822	
Pop: 628,088	
Elev: 634 feet	
Time zone: Central	
Area code: 414	

Thriving and progressive, Milwaukee has retained its *gemütlichkeit*—although conviviality is as likely to be expressed at a soccer game or at a symphony concert as at the beer garden. This is not to say that raising beer steins has noticeably declined as a popular local form of exercise. Milwaukee is still the beer capital of the nation. However, Milwaukee's leading single industry is not brewing but the manufacture of X-ray apparatus and tubes.

Milwaukee is on the western shore of Lake Michigan, where the Milwaukee, Menomonee and Kinnickinnic rivers meet. Long before the first settlers came to what eventually would be known as Milwaukee, the Potowatomi had a special name for their land: "Millocki," or, gathering place by the waters. The modern city was founded by Solomon Juneau, who settled on the east side of the Milwaukee River. English settlement began in significant numbers in 1833, followed by an influx of Germans, Scandinavians, Dutch, Bohemians, Irish, Austrians and large numbers of Poles. By 1846, Milwaukee was big and prosperous enough to be incorporated as a city.

By 1850, the population was 20,000, and by 1890 the population had reached 100,000. Milwaukee was a thriving metropolis and a settled community early in the development of metropolitan America. Since World War II, Milwaukee has undergone tremendous development. The skyline changed with new buildings, an expressway system was started, the St Lawrence Seaway opened new markets, new cultural activities were introduced and 44 square miles were added to the city.

Business

A city of 96.5 square miles, Milwaukee is the metropolitan center of 4 counties. Called the "machine shop of America," Milwaukee has an industrial output of $19.1 billion a year, ranks among the nation's top industrial cities and is a leader in the manufacture of diesel and gasoline engines, outboard motors, motorcycles, X-ray apparatus, mining machinery, padlocks and, of course, beer.

As a result of the opening of the St Lawrence Seaway, Milwaukee has become a major seaport on America's fourth seacoast. Docks and piers accommodate traffic of 15 marine shipping lines.

Metropolitan Milwaukee has more than 100 companies that employ 500 or more people each, producing such goods as electrical motors, electronic components, construction equipment, farming and industrial equipment, auto bodies, gears and couplings, batteries and mining equipment. Advertising and publishing are also important businesses.

Convention Facilities

Located in the heart of downtown Milwaukee is MECCA (Milwaukee Exposition Convention Center and Arena), a modern convention facility. MECCA is made up of three buildings that cover four city blocks and are connected by a walkway over Kilbourn Ave.

The 132,000-square-foot convention hall can accommodate 750 trade show booths or a banquet for 8,600 people. The center portion of the main floor, the Great Hall, has 66,000 square feet of column-free space with a 45-foot ceiling height.

Flanking the Great Hall are the East and West halls, each containing 33,000 square feet of floor space. These two halls, which may be used either in conjunction with the Great Hall or as separate meeting areas, have ceiling heights of 18 feet.

The second level of the convention hall includes 2 octagonal meeting rooms, each seating 800 people, that can be divided into 2, 3 or 4 rooms, and 27 other meeting rooms, seating 50 to 300 persons.

The Milwaukee Arena has a total floor area of 24,550 square feet, and its ceiling is 95 feet high. Its seating capacity is 12,200 people.

The Auditorium, originally constructed in 1909 and restored to its original elegance, will seat 6,000 people for a full stage production in Bruce Hall. In addition, Plankinton Theatre has stage facilities and seats 896 people. Juneau Hall, Kilbourn Hall and Walker Hall are elegant meeting rooms seating 250 to 700 people.

Sports and Recreation

Few cities can rival Milwaukee for its sporting events. Fans can watch the Brewers play baseball at County Stadium; the Green Bay Packers play a portion of their football games here also. The Bucks play basketball, the Admirals play hockey and the Wave play soccer at the Bradley Center.

Jaunt to Juneau Park by the old Coast Guard Station and see bone-crunching rugby played. There are also ample opportunities to view soccer and polo games around town.

Milwaukee winters, not known for their mildness, still fail to keep people indoors. The park department floods more than 50 sites and keeps them clear of snow for ice-skating. Cross-country skiers have numerous parks and frozen rivers from which to choose. Tobogganers will find enough hills, and for those who just enjoy a nice walk, the lakefront, in all its frozen glory, is a good place to start.

Golf courses, tennis courts and bowling alleys abound. Auto racing takes place at the Wisconsin State Fair Speedway. And of course there is Lake Michigan, haven for swimmers, sailors and fishermen.

Entertainment

Spend an evening listening to the famous Milwaukee Symphony Orchestra, or pass the time more informally in one of the many neighborhood taverns, drinking the local brew.

From September to June, the Performing Arts Center is host to the Symphony Orchestra. On warm summer afternoons, also on the grounds of the center, are the outdoor Rainbow Summer Concerts. Autumn brings Brown Bach Concerts (brown bag a lunch and listen to

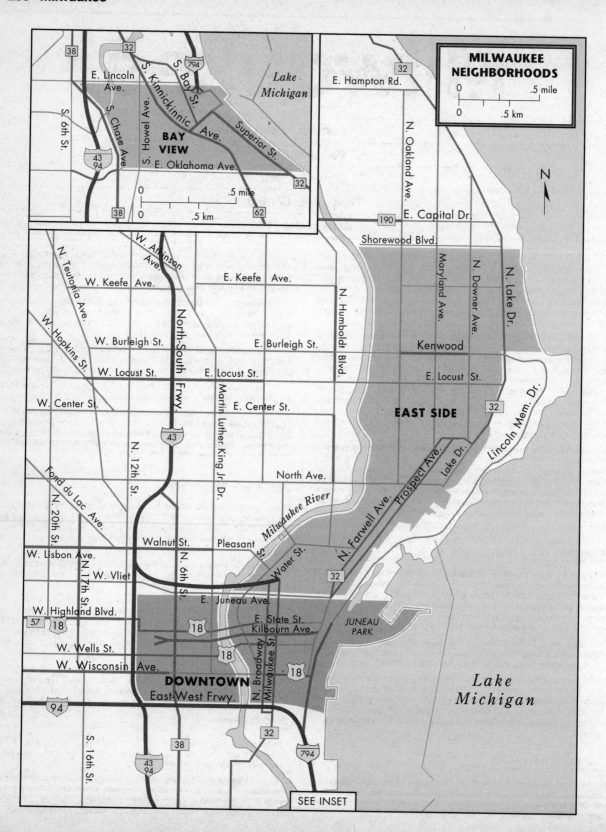

the fine music) at the Magin Lounge. Milwaukee has its own opera and ballet companies as well.

Historical Areas

The area from South Second to South Fifth and from Florida to Scott streets, known as Walker's Point, has been renovated. Originally settled by New Englanders, Germans and Scandinavians in the 1800s, Walker's Point still has an interesting blend of nationalities. Many buildings survive in nearly original form and are in excellent condition. The area reflects a typical 19th-century working-class, urban neighborhood.

Old World Third Street downtown provides a delightful walking tour for gourmets, historians and lovers of antiques and atmosphere. The tour includes the Milwaukee Journal Company's history of the newspaper. Most establishments along the way are open Monday through Saturday.

There are also several restored houses in the Milwaukee area, including Lowell Damon house, Kalvelage Schloss, Kilbourntown house and the Captain Frederick Pabst mansion.

Sightseeing

Milwaukee's lakefront is one of the most beautiful in the United States. Driving along the shore on Lincoln Memorial Drive, visitors can see many points of interest. The War Memorial Center, designed by Eero Saarinen, houses the expanded Milwaukee Art Museum. Here are spacious galleries with permanent collections of European, American and contemporary art, changing exhibits and a children's gallery.

Milwaukee's zoo is considered one of the finest in the country. The animals, birds and reptiles are arranged in geographical groupings in their native habitats, with only hidden moats separating predator from prey in natural, cageless environments. There are also rides on a miniature train.

The unique Mitchell Park Horticultural Conservatory is one of the most popular attractions in Milwaukee. Plants from around the world are displayed in three self-supporting glass domes, each of which simulates a different climate.

The Court of Honor is a three-block area in the city, bounded by Marquette University on the west and the downtown business district on the east. The area is a monument to the Civil War dead and contains several public buildings as well as sculptures of historic figures.

At the Milwaukee Public Museum are dioramas and such exhibits as the Rain Forest, a Trip through Space and Time, Native Americans, Wonders of Life, the Living Ocean, the Third Planet and the Wizard Wing. Another exhibit re-creates old Milwaukee streets.

Milwaukee is justly famous for its fine beers. A trip through one of the city's breweries is worth squeezing into even the busiest schedule. The Pabst, Miller and Sprecher brewing companies offer free tours. At the end of each tour, visitors may sample the brewery's product.

The Milwaukee County Historical Society offers many outstanding exhibits of Milwaukee history, including the Panorama Painters, Yesterday's Drug Store, a Cooper's Shop, Children's World of Toys, a mid-Victorian room, Transportation Hall and material from General Douglas MacArthur's family.

Information centers are located at Grand Avenue Shopping Center, Wisconsin St entrance, and at General Mitchell International-Lower Level. There are also small information centers in the lobby of the Pfister, the Marc Plaza and the Hyatt Regency hotels.

General References

Settled: 1822 **Pop:** 628,088 **Elev:** 634 feet **Time zone:** Central **Area code:** 414

Phone Numbers

POLICE & FIRE: 911
FBI: 276-4684
POISON CONTROL CENTER: 266-2222
TIME: 844-1414 **WEATHER:** 936-1212

Information Sources

The Greater Milwaukee Convention & Visitors Bureau, 510 W Kilbourn Ave, 53203; 273-7222 or 800/231-0903.
The Metropolitan Milwaukee Association of Commerce, 756 N Milwaukee St, 4th floor, 53202; 273-3000.
Fun Line, 799-1177 (recording).
Department of Parks, Recreation and Culture, phone 257-6100.

Transportation

AIRLINES: American; America West; Continental; Delta; Midwest Express; Northwest; TWA; United; USAir; and other commuter and regional airlines. For the most current airline schedules and information consult the *Official Airline Guide,* published twice monthly.
AIRPORT: General Mitchell International, 747-5300.
CAR RENTAL AGENCIES: (See Toll-Free Numbers) Avis 744-2266; Budget 481-2409; Dollar 747-0066; Hertz 747-5200; National 483-9800.
PUBLIC TRANSPORTATION: Milwaukee County Transit System, 4212 W Highland Blvd, 53208; 344-6711.
RAILROAD PASSENGER SERVICE: Amtrak 800/872-7245.

Newspapers

Milwaukee Journal; Milwaukee Sentinel.

Convention Facilities

MECCA, 500 W Kilbourn Ave, 271-4000.
Wisconsin State Fair Park, 84th & Greenfield, West Allis, 266-7000.

Sports & Recreation

Bradley Center, 4th & State Sts, 227-0400 (Bucks & Marquette University, basketball; Milwaukee Admirals, hockey; Wave, soccer).
MECCA, 500 W Kilbourn Ave, 271-4000; recording of events, 271-2750.
Milwaukee County Stadium, 201 S 46th St (Brewers, baseball, 933-1818; Green Bay Packers, football, 342-2717).
Pettit National Ice Center, 500 S 84th St, 266-0100.

Racetrack

Wisconsin State Fair Park, 84th & Greenfield, West Allis, 266-7000 (auto racing).

Cultural Facilities

Theaters

Milwaukee Repertory Theater, 108 E Wells, 224-1761.
Pabst Theater, 144 E Wells St, 286-3663.
Sunset Playhouse, 800 Elm Grove Rd, Elm Grove, 782-4430.

Concert Hall

Performing Arts Center, 929 N Water St, 273-7206.

Museums

Brook Stevens Automotive Museum, 10325 N Port Washington Rd, Mequon, 241-4185.
Discovery World, 818 W Wisconsin Ave, 765-9966.
Milwaukee County Historical Center, 910 N Old World Third St, Pere Marquette Park, 273-8288.
Milwaukee Public Museum, 800 W Wells St, 278-2700.

Art Museums

Charles Allis Art Museum, 1801 N Prospect Ave & 1630 E Royall Place, 278-8295.
Haggerty Museum of Art, Marquette Univ, 13th & Clybourne Sts, 288-1669.
Milwaukee Art Museum, 750 N Lincoln Memorial Dr, 224-3200.
Villa Terrace Decorative Arts Museum, 2220 N Terrace Ave, 271-3656.

Points of Interest

Historical

Captain Frederick Pabst Mansion, 2000 W Wisconsin Ave, 931-0808.
Kilbourntown House, 5 mi N on I-43, Capitol Dr E exit, in Estabrook Park, 273-8288.
Old World Third Street, W Wells St to Juneau Ave.
St Joan of Arc Chapel, Marquette University, 601 N 14th St, 288-6873.
St John's Cathedral, 802 N Jackson, 276-9814.
St Josaphat Basilica, 2333 S 6th St, 645-5623.
Walker's Point, S 2nd to S 5th Sts and Florida to Scott Sts.

Other Attractions

Annunciation Greek Orthodox Church, 9400 W Congress St, 461-9400.
Boerner Botanical Garden, 5879 S 92nd in Hales Corners, 425-1130.
City Hall, 200 E Wells St, 286-3285.
Civic Center Plaza, N of W Wells St between N 7th & 9th Sts.
Court of Honor, Wisconsin Ave bounded by Marquette University & the downtown business district.
The Grand Avenue, Wisconsin Avenue between Plankinton Ave & 5th St.
Marquette University, Wisconsin Ave & 11th-17th Sts, 288-7448.
McKinley Marina, 1750 N Lincoln Memorial Dr, 273-5224.
Miller Brewing Co, 4251 W State St, 931-BEER.

Milwaukee County Zoo, 10001 W Bluemound Rd, 771-3040.
Mitchell Park Horticultural Conservatory, 524 S Layton Blvd at W Pierce St, 649-9800.
Pabst Brewing Co, 915 W Juneau Ave, 223-3709.
Schlitz Audubon Center, 1111 E Brown Deer Rd, 352-2880.
University of Wisconsin-Milwaukee, 3203 N Downer Ave, events 229-5900.

Sightseeing Tours

Historic Milwaukee, Inc-ArchiTours, 277-7795.
Iroquois Boat Line Tours, boarding at Clybourn St Bridge, 332-4194.

Annual Events

Ethnic Festivals, (includes German, Irish, Native American and Polish). Contact Convention & Visitors Bureau. Summer-fall.
Summerfest, Lakefront, 273-FEST. Late June-early July.
Great Circus Parade, downtown. Mid-July.
Wisconsin State Fair, State Fair Park in West Allis, 266-7000. Early Aug.

City Neighborhoods

Many of the restaurants, unrated dining establishments and some lodgings listed under Milwaukee include neighborhoods as well as exact street addresses. A map showing these neighborhoods can be found immediately following the city introduction. Geographic descriptions of these areas are given, followed by a table of restaurants arranged by neighborhood.

Bay View: Area southeast of Downtown; south of E Lincoln Ave, west of Lake Michigan, north of E Oklahoma Ave and east of S Chase Ave.
Downtown: South of Juneau Ave, west of Lake Michigan, north of I-794 and east of the North-South Frwy. **North of Downtown:** North of E Juneau Ave. **South of Downtown:** South of I-794.
West of Downtown: West of I-43.
East Side: Area northeast of Downtown; south of Shorewood, west of Lake, McKinley and Juneau parks, north of Juneau Ave and east of the Milwaukee River.
Mitchell Street: Area south of Downtown; south of Lapham Ave, west of I-94, north of W Becher St and east of S 16th St.
Yankee Hill: Area of Downtown on and around Cathedral Square; south of E State St, west of N Prospect St, north of E Mason St and east of N Broadway.

Lodgings and Food

MILWAUKEE RESTAURANTS
BY NEIGHBORHOOD AREAS

(For full description, see alphabetical listings under Restaurants)

BAY VIEW
Three Brothers. 2414 S St Clair

DOWNTOWN
Boulevard Inn. 925 E Wells St

English Room (Pfister Hotel). 424 E Wisconsin Ave

Grenadier's. 747 N Broadway Ave at Mason

John Ernst's. 600 E Ogden Ave

Karl Ratzsch's. 320 E Mason St

King And I. 823 N 2nd St

Mader's. 1037 N 3rd St

Safe House. 779 N Front St

Sanford. 1547 N Jackson St

Weissgerber's Third Street Pier. 1110 N Old World Third St

NORTH OF DOWNTOWN
Bavarian Inn. 700 W Lexington Blvd

Dos Bandidos. 5932 N Green Bay Ave

Pandl's In Bayside. 8825 N Lake Dr

Yen Ching. 7630 W Good Hope Rd

SOUTH OF DOWNTOWN
Antonino's. 8412 W Morgan Ave

Mike & Anna's. 2000 S 8th St

Old Town Serbian Gourmet House. 522 W Lincoln Ave

Porter House. 800 W Layton Ave

WEST OF DOWNTOWN
O'Donoghue's. 5108 W Bluemound Rd

Saz's State House. 5539 W State St

EAST SIDE
Izumi's. 2178 N Prospect Ave

Note: *When a listing is located in a town that does not have its own city heading, it will appear under the city nearest to its location. In these cases, the address and town appear in parenthesis immediately following the name of the establishment.*

Motels

(Rates may be higher during state fair)

★ **BUDGETEL INN.** 5442 N Lovers Lane Rd (53225), just E of I-45 Silver Spring Dr exit E, north of downtown. 414/535-1300; FAX 414/535-1724. 142 rms, 3 story. S $38.95-$45.95; D $45.95-$52.95; each addl $7; suites $47.95-$56.95; under 18 free. Pet accepted, some restrictions. TV; cable. Complimentary continental bkfst. Complimentary coffee in rms. Restaurant nearby. Ck-out noon. Meeting rm. Valet serv. Cr cds: A, C, D, DS, MC, V.

D ✦ ⊠ 🔥

✔★ **EXEL INN-SOUTH.** 1201 W College Ave (53221), just E of I-94 College Ave exit E, south of downtown. 414/764-1776; FAX 414/762-8009. 110 rms, 2 story. S $32.99-$35.99; D $39.99-$43.99; each addl $4; under 18 free. Crib free. Pet accepted. TV; cable. Complimentary continental bkfst, coffee in lobby. Restaurant opp 6 am-noon. Ck-out noon. Coin lndry. Free airport transportation. Cr cds: A, C, D, DS, MC, V.

D ✦ ⊠ 🔥 SC

★ ★ **HAMPTON INN-NORTHWEST.** 5601 N Lovers Lane Rd (53225), north of downtown. 414/466-8881. 107 rms, 4 story. S, D $55-$75; under 18 free; higher rates: special events, summer wkends. Crib free. TV; cable. Indoor pool; whirlpool. Complimentary continental bkfst, coffee. Restaurant adj. Ck-out noon. Meeting rm. Valet serv. Sundries. Cr cds: A, C, D, DS, MC, V.

D ≋ ⊠ 🔥 SC

✔★ ★ **HOSPITALITY INN.** 4400 S 27th St (53221), just N of I-894 27th St exit 9N, near General Mitchell Intl Airport, south of downtown. 414/282-8800; res: 800/825-8466; FAX 414/282-7713. 167 rms in 2 bldgs, 1-5 story, 81 suites. S, D $50-$125; each addl $10; suites $80-$200. Crib free. TV; cable. 2 indoor pools. Complimentary continental bkfst. Restaurant 6 am-10 pm. Ck-out noon. Valet serv. Airport transportation. Exercise equipt; weight machine, stair machine, whirlpool. Many refrigerators. Cr cds: A, C, D, DS, MC, V.

D ≋ 🏃 ✈ ⊠ 🔥 SC

★ ★ **MANCHESTER SUITES-AIRPORT.** 200 W Grange Ave (53207), near General Mitchell Intl Airport, south of downtown. 414/744-3600; res: 800/723-8280; FAX 414/744-4188. 100 suites, 4 story. S $56-$61; D $62-$67; each addl $6; under 14 free. Crib free. TV; cable. Complimentary full bkfst 6-9 am; Sat, Sun 7:30-10:30 am. Restaurant adj 6 am-10 pm. Ck-out noon. Meeting rm. Valet serv. Sundries. Free airport transportation. Refrigerators, wet bars. Cr cds: A, C, D, DS, MC, V.

D ✈ ⊠ 🔥 SC

★ ★ **QUALITY INN-AIRPORT.** 5311 S Howell Ave (53207), opp General Mitchell Intl Airport, south of downtown. 414/481-2400; FAX 414/481-4471. 135 rms, 3 story. S, D $58-$99; each addl $5; under 18 free. Crib $5. TV; cable. Indoor pool; sauna. Complimentary continental bkfst. Restaurant 7 am-10 pm; Sun 9 am-9 pm. Rm serv. Bar 11 am-midnight. Ck-out noon. Coin lndry. Meeting rms. Bellhops. Free airport transportation. Cr cds: A, C, D, DS, ER, JCB, MC, V.

D ≋ ✈ ⊠ 🔥 SC

✔★ **RED ROOF INN.** (6360 S 13th St, Oak Creek 53154) At jct College Ave, I-94 exit 319 E. 414/764-3500; FAX 414/764-5138. 108 rms, 2 story. S $36.99-$50.99; D $41.99-$65.99; under 18 free. Crib free. Pet accepted. TV; cable. Complimentary coffee. Ck-out noon. Cr cds: A, C, D, DS, MC, V.

D ✦ ⊠ 🔥

Motor Hotels

★ ★ **HOLIDAY INN CITY CENTRE.** 611 W Wisconsin Ave (53203), downtown. 414/273-2950; FAX 414/273-7662. 246 rms, 10 story. S $66-$119; D $76-$129; each addl $10; suites $159-$199; under 18 free; higher rates special events. Crib free. TV; cable. Pool. Restaurant 6 am-11 pm. Rm serv. Bar from 4 pm. Ck-out noon. Meeting rms. Bellhops. Valet serv. Free valet parking. Cr cds: A, C, D, DS, ER, JCB, MC, V.

D ≋ ⊠ 🔥 SC

★ ★ **MANCHESTER SUITES NORTHWEST.** 11777 W Silver Spring Dr (53225), west of downtown. 414/462-3500; res: 800/723-8280; FAX 414/462-8166. 124 rms, 4 story. Suites $56-$75; under 14 free. Crib free. TV; cable. Complimentary bkfst. Restaurant nearby. Ck-out noon. Meeting rms. Valet serv. Sundries. Refrigerators, wet bars. Cr cds: A, C, D, DS, MC, V.

D ⊠ 🔥 SC

★ ★ **QUALITY INN-WEST.** *201 N Mayfair Rd (53226), just N of I-94 Mayfair Rd (WI 100) exit, west of downtown.* 414/771-4400; FAX 414/771-4517. 235 rms, 3 story. S $68-$93; D $75-$98; under 18 free. Crib free. Pet accepted, some restrictions. TV; cable. Indoor pool. Playground. Restaurant 6 am-2 pm, 5-10 pm. Rm serv. Bar 11-1 am, Fri-Sat to 2 am; entertainment, dancing Wed-Sat. Ck-out noon. Coin lndry. Meeting rms. Valet serv. Exercise equipt; weights, bicycles, whirlpool, sauna. Picnic tables. Cr cds: A, C, D, DS, ER, JCB, MC, V.

★ ★ **RAMADA INN DOWNTOWN.** *633 W Michigan St (53203), downtown.* 414/272-8410; FAX 414/272-4651. 155 rms, 7 story. S $55-$75; D $60-$85; each addl $8; suites $95-$115; under 18 free; wkend rates. Crib free. TV; cable. Heated pool. Restaurant 6 am-10 pm. Rm serv. Bar 11-2 am. Ck-out noon. Meeting rms. Valet serv. Gift shop. Downhill ski 15 mi; x-country ski 7 mi. Cr cds: A, C, D, DS, JCB, MC, V.

★ ★ ★ **SHERATON INN NORTH.** *(8900 N Kildeer Ct, Brown Deer 53209) 10 mi N via I-43, exit Brown Deer Rd W.* 414/355-8585; FAX 414/355-3566. 149 rms, 6 story. S $90-$120; D $100-$125; each addl $10; suites $125-$150; under 12 free; wkend rates. Crib free. TV; cable. Indoor/outdoor pool; whirlpool, sauna, poolside serv. Restaurant 6:30 am-10:30 pm. Rm serv. Bar 10-2 am; dancing. Ck-out noon. Meeting rms. Bellhops. Valet serv. Barber. X-country ski 3 mi. Health club privileges. Some refrigerators. Cr cds: A, C, D, DS, MC, V.

Hotels

★ ★ **ASTOR.** *924 E Juneau Ave (53202), 2 mi W of I-43, Broadway exit, downtown.* 414/271-4220; res: 800/558-0200 (exc WI), 800/242-0355 (WI); FAX 414/271-6370. 96 rms, 9 story. S $69-$79; D $77-$85; each addl $8; suites $82-$125; under 18 free; wkend rates. Crib free. TV; cable. Restaurant 7 am-11 pm. Bar 11:30-2 am. Ck-out noon. Coin lndry. Meeting rms. Beauty shop. Health club privileges. Some refrigerators. Cr cds: A, D, DS, MC, V.

★ ★ **EMBASSY SUITES-WEST.** *(PO Box 731, 1200 S Moorland Rd, Brookfield) 10 mi W via I-94, Moorland Rd S exit.* 414/782-2900; FAX 414/796-9159. 203 suites, 5 story. S, D, suites $89-$500; each addl $15; under 12 free; wkend rates; honeymoon packages. Crib free. TV; cable. Indoor pool. Complimentary full bkfst. Complimentary coffee in rms. Restaurant 11 am-11 pm. Bar to 1 am. Ck-out noon. Meeting rms. Concierge. Free airport transportation. Tennis, golf privileges. Exercise equipt; weights, bicycles, whirlpool, sauna, steam rm. Game rm. Refrigerators, wet bars. Cr cds: A, C, D, DS, ER, JCB, MC, V.

★ ★ ★ **THE GRAND MILWAUKEE HOTEL.** *4747 S Howell Ave (53207), I-94 Airport E exit, near General Mitchell Airport, south of downtown.* 414/481-8000; res: 800/558-3862; FAX 414/481-8065. 510 rms, 6 story. S, D $63-$135; each addl $10; suites $175-$275; under 17 free; wkend package plan. Crib free. TV; cable. 2 heated pools, 1 indoor. Restaurants 6 am-10 pm. Bar 11-2 am. Ck-out noon. Meeting rms. Gift shop. Barber, beauty shop. Free airport transportation. Indoor tennis. Exercise equipt; weight machines, bicycles, whirlpool, sauna. Game rm. Some refrigerators. Cr cds: A, C, D, DS, MC, V.

★ ★ ★ **HILTON INN MILWAUKEE RIVER.** *4700 N Port Washington Rd (53212), I-43 exit Hampton Ave E, north of downtown.* 414/962-6040; FAX 414/962-6166. 164 rms, 5 story. S $77-$102; D $88-$113; each addl $11; suites $160-$250; family rates. TV; cable. Indoor pool. Restaurant 6:30 am-10:30 pm; Fri, Sat to 11:30 pm; Sun to 10 pm. Bar 11-1 am. Ck-out noon. Meeting

rms. X-country ski adj. Some refrigerators. Overlooks river. Cr cds: A, C, D, DS, ER, JCB, MC, V.

★ ★ ★ **HYATT REGENCY.** *333 W Kilbourn Ave (53203), downtown.* 414/276-1234; FAX 414/276-6338. 484 rms, 22 story. S $95-$150; D $95-$165; each addl $25; parlor rms $95-$150; suites $175-$750; under 18 free; special event plans. Garage $7. TV; cable. Restaurants 6 am-midnight. Bar from 11 am, Fri, Sat to 2 am; entertainment. Ck-out noon. Convention facilities. Concierge. Gift shop. Exercise equipt; weight machine, bicycles. Cr cds: A, C, D, DS, ER, JCB, MC, V.

★ ★ **MARC PLAZA.** *509 W Wisconsin Ave (53203), I-43 Civic Center exit, downtown.* 414/271-7250; res: 800/558-7708; FAX 414/271-1039. 500 rms, 25 story. S, D $110-$130; each addl $20; suites $110-$270; under 18 free; wkend plan. Crib free. TV; cable. Indoor pool; sauna. Restaurant 6 am-11 pm. Bar 11-2 am. Ck-out noon. Convention facilities. Concierge. Shopping arcade. Barber, beauty shop. Cr cds: A, C, D, DS, MC, V.

★ ★ **PARK EAST.** *916 State St (53202), downtown.* 414/276-8800; res: 800/328-7275; FAX 414/765-1919. 159 rms, 5 story. S $81-$110; D $91-$120; each addl $10; suites $91-$200; under 18 free; wkend rates; package plans. Crib $5. TV; cable. Restaurant 6:30 am-2:30 pm, 4:30-10 pm. Bar; entertainment Fri, Sat. Ck-out noon. Meeting rms. Free downtown transportation. Some refrigerators, wet bars. Cr cds: A, C, D, DS, MC, V.

★ ★ ★ **PFISTER.** *424 E Wisconsin Ave (53202), I-794 Van Buren exit, downtown.* 414/273-8222; res: 800/558-8222. 307 rms, 23 story. S, D $165-$185; each addl $20; suites $185-$650; under 18 free; wkend rates. Crib free. Parking $8; valet avail. TV; cable. Indoor pool. Restaurant 6:30 am-11 pm (also see ENGLISH ROOM). Rm serv 24 hrs. Bars 11-2 am; entertainment, dancing exc Sun. Ck-out noon. Convention facilities. Concierge. Gift shop. Barber, beauty shop. Exercise equipt; weight machine, bicycle. Health club privileges. Bathrm phones. Restored landmark building (1893); Victorian architecture with contemporary style. Cr cds: A, C, D, DS, JCB, MC, V.

★ ★ ★ **WYNDHAM MILWAUKEE CENTER.** *139 E Kilbourn Ave (53202), downtown.* 414/271-4779; FAX 414/291-4777. 221 rms, 10 story, 77 suites. S, D $155-$185; each addl $20; suites $250-$520; under 12 free; wkend packages. Crib free. Garage $7.50. TV; cable. Complimentary coffee in rms. Restaurant 6:30 am-11 pm. Bar 11-2 am; entertainment Fri-Sat. Ck-out noon. Meeting rms. Gift shop. Airport transportation avail. Exercise equipt; weight machines, bicycles, whirlpool, sauna, steam rm. Cr cds: A, C, D, DS, ER, JCB, MC, V.

Restaurants

✔★ **ANTONINO'S.** *8412 W Morgan Ave, south of downtown.* 414/321-6365. Hrs: 4:30-10 pm; Fri & Sat to 11 pm; Sun 4-9 pm. Closed Easter, Memorial Day, Dec 24-25. Res accepted. Sicilian menu. Semi-a la carte: dinner $6.95-$12.95. Child's meals. Specializes in Sicilian veal, steak, pizza. Parking. Ornately carved and decorated pony cart on display. Cr cds: A, DS, MC, V.

★ ★ **BAVARIAN INN.** *700 W Lexington Blvd, north of downtown.* 414/964-0300. Hrs: 11:30 am-9 pm; Fri to 10 pm; Sat 5-9 pm; Sun brunch 10:30 am-2 pm. Closed Mon; Jan 1, July 4, Dec 24. Res accepted. German, Amer menu. Bar. Semi-a la carte: lunch $4.95-$9.95, dinner $7.95-$15.95. Sun brunch $11.25. Child's meals. Specializes in schnitzel, zwiebelfleisch. Trio Thurs, accordionist on Fri.

Parking. Chalet-style building; large fireplace, timbered ceilings, stein and alpine bell collections. Cr cds: A, C, D, DS, MC, V.

[D] [SC]

★ ★ ★ **BODER'S ON-THE-RIVER.** (11919 N River Rd, Mequon) 2 mi W of I-43 Mequon Rd exit W, N on Port Washington Rd, W on Highland Rd, then S on River Rd. 414/242-0335. Hrs: 11:30 am-2 pm, 5:30-8:30 pm; Fri 5-9:30 pm; Sat 5:30-9:30 pm; Sun 11:30 am-2 pm, 4-7 pm; Sun brunch to 2 pm. Closed Mon; Jan 1, July 4, Dec 24-25. Res accepted. Bar. Wine list. Complete meals: lunch $4.95-$9.95, dinner $9.95-$35.95. Sun brunch $13.25. Child's meals. Specializes in roast duck, sautéed fresh chicken livers, continental veal. Own pastries, muffins. Parking. Country inn (1840); fireplaces. At riverside, river walk. Family-owned. Cr cds: A, C, D, DS, MC, V.

[D]

★ ★ ★ **BOULEVARD INN.** 925 E Wells St, downtown. 414/765-1166. Hrs: 11:30 am-9:30 pm; Fri, Sat to 10 pm; Sun 10:30 am-9 pm; Sun brunch to 2 pm. Closed some major hols. Res accepted. Bar. Wine list. Semi-a la carte: lunch $6.50-$11.50, dinner $14.95-$35.95. Sun brunch $9.50. Child's meals. Specializes in fresh fish, veal, German dishes. Own baking. Pianist. Valet parking. Some tableside preparation. Family-owned. Cr cds: A, D, DS, MC, V.

[D]

✔★ **DOS BANDIDOS.** 5932 N Green Bay Ave, I-43 to Silver Spring exit W, north of downtown. 414/228-1911. Hrs: 11 am-2:30 pm, 4-10 pm; Fri to 11:30 pm; Sat 11 am-11:30 pm; Sun 4-10 pm. Closed major hols. Res accepted. Mexican, Amer menu. Bar. Semi-a la carte: lunch $3.50-$5.95, dinner $6.75-$11.95. Specializes in steak & chicken fajitas, spinach enchiladas, vegetarian dishes. Parking. Patio dining. Mexican cantina decor. Cr cds: A, DS, MC, V.

★ ★ ★ **ENGLISH ROOM.** (See Pfister Hotel) 414/273-8222. Hrs: 11:30 am-2 pm, 5:30-10 pm; Sat 5:30-11 pm; Sun from 5 pm. Res accepted. Bar. Extensive wine list. Semi-a la carte: lunch $5.25-$9. A la carte entrees: dinner $17-$28. Guitarist Fri & Sat. Valet parking. Established 1893; past patrons include Teddy Roosevelt, Enrico Caruso. Cr cds: A, C, D, DS, MC, V.

[D]

★ ★ ★ ★ **GRENADIER'S.** 747 N Broadway Ave at Mason, just N of I-794 Jackson-Van Buren exit, downtown. 414/276-0747. Hrs: 11:30 am-2:30 pm, 5:30-10:30 pm; Sat from 5:30 pm. Closed Sun; major hols. Res accepted. French, continental menu. Bar. Wine cellar. Semi-a la carte: lunch $6.95-$12.95. A la carte entrees: dinner $16.95-$22.95. Dégustation menu: dinner $28.95. Specialties: Dover sole, lamb curry Calcutta, sweetbreads, extensive selection of fresh seafood daily. Own pastries. Pianist. Valet parking (dinner). Four rooms, varied decor. Elegant dining. Courtesy limo serv to downtown properties. Chef-owned. Jacket. Cr cds: A, C, D, DS, MC, V.

[D]

★ **IZUMI'S.** 2178 N Prospect Ave, on the East Side. 414/271-5278. Hrs: 11:30 am-2 pm, 5-10 pm; Fri 5-10:30 pm; Sat 5-11 pm; Sun 4-9 pm. Closed major hols. Res accepted. Japanese menu. Wine, beer. Semi-a la carte: lunch $4.95-$12.95, dinner $7.50-$20.50. Specializes in sushi, sukiyaki, teriyaki dishes. Parking. Contemporary Japanese decor. Cr cds: A, D, JCB, MC, V.

[D]

★ ★ **JACK PANDL'S WHITEFISH BAY INN.** (1319 E Henry Clay St, Whitefish Bay) 6 mi N on WI 32, 2 mi NE of I-43 Hampton Ave exit E. 414/964-3800. Hrs: 11:30 am-2:30 pm, 5-9 pm; Fri, Sat to 10:30 pm; Sun 11 am-2:30 pm, 4-8 pm. Closed most major hols. Res accepted. Bar. Semi-a la carte: lunch $4.95-$9.95, dinner $6.25-$16.95. Child's meals. Specializes in whitefish, German pancakes, Schaum torte. Parking. Established in 1915; antique beer stein collection. Family-owned. Cr cds: A, C, D, DS, MC, V.

★ ★ ★ **JOHN ERNST'S.** 600 E Ogden Ave, at Jackson St, downtown. 414/273-1878. Hrs: 11:30 am-10 pm; Fri, Sat to midnight;

Sun noon-9:30 pm. Closed Mon. Res accepted. Continental, Amer menu. Bar. Semi-a la carte: lunch $6.95-$9.95, dinner $10.95-$32.95. Child's meals. Specialties: prime steak, Kasseler rippchen, jaegerschnitzel, seafood. Own pastries. Entertainment. Parking. Old World decor; stained glass, fireplace. Collection of antique mugs. Established in 1878; oldest in city. Family-owned. Cr cds: A, C, D, DS, MC, V.

[D]

★ ★ **KARL RATZSCH'S.** 320 E Mason St, I-794 Van Buren St exit, downtown. 414/276-2720. Hrs: 11:30 am-10 pm; Fri, Sat to 11 pm; Sun brunch 11 am-4 pm. Closed major hols. Res accepted. German, Amer menu. Bar. Semi-a la carte: lunch $6.50-$12.50. Complete meals: dinner $10.95-$24. Sun brunch $12.95. Child's meals. Specializes in planked whitefish, roast goose shank, aged prime steak. Pianist evenings. Valet parking. Collection of rare steins, glassware. Old World Austrian atmosphere. Family-owned. Cr cds: A, C, D, DS, MC, V.

★ ★ **KING AND I.** 823 N 2nd St, downtown. 414/276-4181. Hrs: 11:30 am-10 pm; Sat 5-11 pm; Sun 4-9 pm. Closed major hols. Res accepted. Thai menu. Bar. Semi-a la carte: lunch $5-$8, dinner $9-$18. Specialties: volcano chicken, fresh red snapper, crispy duck, pineapple rice. Southeast Asian decor; enameled wood chairs, hand-carved teakwood, native artwork. Cr cds: A, C, D, DS, MC, V.

[D]

★ ★ **MADER'S.** 1037 N 3rd St, downtown. 414/271-3377. Hrs: 11:30 am-10 pm; Fri & Sat to 11:30 pm; Mon to 9 pm; Sun 10:30 am-9 pm; Sun brunch to 2 pm. Res accepted. German, continental menu. Bar. Semi-a la carte: lunch $5.95-$10.95, dinner $12.95-$39.95. Sun Viennese brunch $12.95. Child's meals. Specialties: Rheinischer sauerbraten, Wienerschnitzel, roast pork shank. Valet parking. Old World German decor; antiques. Gift shop. Family-owned. Cr cds: A, C, D, DS, MC, V.

★ **MIKE & ANNA'S.** 2000 S 8th St, south of downtown. 414/643-0072. Hrs: 5:30-8:45 pm; Fri & Sat to 9:45 pm. Closed major hols. Res accepted. Bar. Semi-a la carte: dinner $16.50-$25.50. Specializes in salmon, rack of lamb. Menu changes daily. Restored corner tavern in residential setting; contemporary atmosphere. Cr cds: A, MC, V.

[D]

★ ★ **O'DONOGHUE'S.** 5108 W Bluemound Rd, west of downtown. 414/774-9100. Hrs: 11:30 am-2:30 pm, 5-10 pm; Fri to 11 pm; Sat 5-11 pm; Sun 11 am-2 pm, 4-9 pm; Sun brunch 11 am-2 pm. Closed Dec 24, 25. Res accepted. Bar. Semi-a la carte: lunch $4.95-$7.50, dinner $9.95-$16.95. Sun brunch $9.95. Specializes in prime rib, steak, fresh seafood. Parking. Irish theme. Extensive beer selection. Cr cds: A, D, MC, V.

[D]

✔★ ★ **OLD TOWN SERBIAN GOURMET HOUSE.** 522 W Lincoln Ave, south of downtown. 414/672-0206. Hrs: 11:30 am-2:30 pm, 5-11 pm; Sat, Sun from 5 pm. Closed Mon; some major hols. Res accepted. Serbian, Amer menu. Bar. Semi-a la carte: lunch $4-$8, dinner $10-$15. Child's meals. Entertainment (wkends). Parking. Family-owned. Cr cds: A, D, MC, V.

★ ★ ★ **PANDL'S IN BAYSIDE.** 8825 N Lake Dr, 10 mi N on WI 32, 1 mi E of I-43 Brown Deer Rd (E) exit, north of downtown. 414/352-7300. Hrs: 11:30 am-9:30 pm; Sun 4-9 pm; Sun brunch 10:30 am-2 pm. Closed Labor Day, Dec 25. Res accepted. Bar. Semi-a la carte: lunch, dinner $5-$15. Sun brunch $17.50. Child's meals. Specializes in fresh fish, prime meats. Salad bar (dinner). Own pastries. Parking. Family-owned. Cr cds: A, C, D, DS, MC, V.

[D] [SC]

★ ★ **PORTER HOUSE.** 800 W Layton Ave, south of downtown. 414/744-1750. Hrs: 11 am-2:30 pm, 5-10 pm; Fri & Sat to 11 pm; Sun 4-9 pm. Closed Mon. Res accepted. Bar. Semi-a la carte: lunch

$4.35-$9.95, dinner $8.95-$39.95. Child's meals. Specializes in char-broiled steak, ribs & seafood. Parking. Cr cds: A, C, D, DS, MC, V.

[D]

★ ★ ★ **SANFORD.** *1547 N Jackson St, downtown. 414/276-9608.* Hrs: 5:30-9 pm; Fri, Sat to 10 pm. Closed Sun; major hols. Res accepted. French, contemporary Amer menu. Serv bar. Wine cellar. Semi-a la carte: dinner $19.95-$29.95. Specialties: seared sea scallops, grilled breast of duck, cumin wafers with grilled, marinated tuna, provincial fish soup. Valet parking. Totally nonsmoking. Cr cds: A, C, D, DS, MC, V.

[D]

★ **SAZ'S STATE HOUSE.** *5539 W State St, west of downtown. 414/453-2410.* Hrs: 11 am-11 pm; Sun, Mon to 10 pm; Sun brunch 10:30 am-2:30 pm. Closed Dec 24 eve-Dec 25. Bar. Semi-a la carte: lunch $4.25-$7.95, dinner $7.50-$16.95. Specializes in barbecued ribs, fresh fish, chicken. Sing-along Thurs, band Sat. Parking. Outdoor dining. 1885 roadhouse. Cr cds: A, MC, V.

[D]

✔★ **THREE BROTHERS.** *2414 S St Clair, in Bay View. 414/481-7530.* Hrs: 5-10 pm; Fri, Sat 4-11 pm; Sun 4-10 pm. Closed Mon; some major hols. Res accepted. Serbian menu. Serv bar. Semi-a la carte: dinner $10.95-$14.95. Specialties: burek, roast pig, moussaka. Serbian artwork on display. No cr cds accepted.

★ ★ **WEISSGERBER'S THIRD STREET PIER.** *1110 N Old World Third St, downtown. 414/272-0330.* Hrs: 11:30 am-2 pm, 5-10 pm; Sat from 5 pm; Sun 4-9 pm. Res accepted. Bar 11-1 am. Semi-a la carte: lunch $6-$10, dinner $14.95-$34.95. Child's meals. Specializes in seafood & steak. Own desserts. Pianist Wed, Fri, Sat. Valet parking. Outdoor dining. Lunch & dinner cruises on Lake Michigan avail. In restored landmark building on Milwaukee River. Cr cds: A, DS, MC, V.

[D]

✔★ ★ **YEN CHING.** *7630 W Good Hope Rd, north of downtown. 414/353-6677.* Hrs: 11:30 am-2 pm, 5-10 pm; Fri to 10:30 pm; Sat 5-10:30 pm; Sun 11:30 am-2:30 pm, 5-9:30 pm. Mandarin menu. Serv bar. Semi-a la carte: lunch $4.25-$5.95, dinner $6.50-$12. Specializes in beef, chicken, seafood. Parking. Oriental decor. Cr cds: A, C, D, DS, MC, V.

[D]

Unrated Dining Spots

THE CHOCOLATE SWAN. *(890 Elm Grove Rd, Elm Grove) 2 mi W on Bluemound Rd to N Elm Grove Rd, at Elm Grove Village Court shopping center. 414/784-7926.* Hrs: 11 am-6 pm; Fri to 11 pm; Sat 10 am-11 pm. Closed Sun; most major hols. Dessert menu only. Desserts $1.75-$5.75. Specialties: Mary's chocolate interlude, yellow strawberry log. Tea room ambiance. Totally nonsmoking. Cr cds: MC, V.

SAFE HOUSE. *779 N Front St, entrance at International Exports, Ltd, downtown. 414/271-2007.* Hrs: 11:30-2 am; Fri, Sat to 2:30 am; Sun 4 pm-midnight. Res accepted. Bar. Semi-a la carte: lunch, dinner $4.25-$12.95. Specializes in sandwiches, specialty drinks. DJ Fri & Sat, magician Sun-Thurs. Spy theme decor. Cr cds: A, MC, V.

Wauwatosa

Motels

✔★ **EXEL INN-WEST.** *115 N Mayfair Rd (US 100) (53226). 414/257-0140; FAX 414/475-7875.* 123 rms, 2 story. S $33.99-$38.99; D $35.99-$48.99; each addl (up to 4) $4; under 18 free. Crib free. Pet accepted, some restrictions. TV; cable. Complimentary continental bkfst in lobby. Restaurant adj 6 am-10 pm. Ck-out noon. Cr cds: A, C, D, DS, MC, V.

[D] [symbols] [SC]

★ ★ **HOLIDAY INN EXPRESS.** *11111 W North Ave (53226), 1 blk E of I-45. 414/778-0333; FAX 414/778-0331.* 122 rms, 3 story. S $57-$67; D $60-$70; each addl $6; suites $70-$76; under 18 free. Crib free. TV; cable. Complimentary continental bkfst, coffee. Restaurant adj open 24 hrs. Ck-out noon. Meeting rms. Valet serv. Heath club privileges. Some refrigerators. Some balconies. Cr cds: A, D, DS, MC, V.

[D] [symbols] [SC]

✔★ ★ **HOWARD JOHNSON.** *2275 N Mayfair Rd (US 100) (53226). 414/771-4800; FAX 414/771-4800, ext. 113.* 80 rms, 2 story. S $39-$69; D $44-$74; each addl $5; under 18 free. Crib free. TV; cable. Heated pool. Complimentary continental bkfst. Restaurant 6 am-11 pm. Rm serv 8 am-9 pm. Bar from 11 am. Ck-out noon. Meeting rm. Valet serv. Sundries. X-country ski 2½ mi. Game rm. Private patios, balconies. Cr cds: A, C, D, DS, JCB, MC, V.

[symbols] [SC]

Motor Hotel

★ ★ ★ **SHERATON MAYFAIR.** *2303 N Mayfair Rd (US 100) (53226). 414/257-3400; FAX 414/257-0900.* 150 rms, 8 story. S $79-$110; D $91-$120; each addl $13; under 18 free; lower rates wknds. Crib free. TV; cable. Indoor pool; sauna. Restaurant 6 am-2 pm, 5-10 pm. Rm serv. Bar 11-2 am; dancing. Ck-out noon. Meeting rms. Bellhops. Sundries. X-country ski 2 mi. Health club privileges. Cr cds: A, C, D, DS, MC, V.

[D] [symbols] [SC]

Restaurants

★ ★ **ALIOTO'S.** *3041 N Mayfair Rd (US 100). 414/476-6900.* Hrs: 11:30 am-9 pm; Fri to 10 pm; Sat 4-9:30 pm. Closed Sun (exc hols); also 1st wk July. Res accepted. Italian, Amer menu. Bar. Semi-a la carte: lunch $4.25-$7.95, dinner $7-$18. Child's meals. Specializes in veal, prime rib, breaded Sicilian steak. Parking. Family-owned. Cr cds: A, C, DS, MC, V.

[D] [SC]

★ ★ **JAKE'S.** *6030 W North Ave, at N 61st St. 414/771-0550.* Hrs: 5-10 pm; Sat from 4:30 pm; Sun 4:30-9 pm. Closed some major hols; also Super Bowl Sun. Res accepted Sun-Thurs. Bar. Semi-a la carte: dinner $9.95-$18.95. Child's meals. Specializes in steak, fresh seafood, onion rings. Parking. Family-owned. Totally nonsmoking. Cr cds: A, D, MC, V.

[D]

Minneapolis

Settled: 1847

Pop: 368,383

Elev: 687-980 feet

Time zone: Central

Area code: 612

St Paul

Settled: 1840

Pop: 272,235

Elev: 874 feet

Time zone: Central

Area code: 612

Still harboring traces of frontier vigor, Minneapolis and its twin city, St Paul, form a mighty northern metropolis. In many ways they complement one another. Together they are a center for grain gathering, electronics, transportation, finance and industry. Baseball, football or basketball games at Minneapolis' Hubert H. Humphrey Metrodome Stadium and Target Center often rouse the fans of each city into a real competitive spirit.

The twin cities are perhaps best known for fine education, excellent cultural facilities and some of the best and most advanced health care in the world. Minneapolis, the largest city in Minnesota, is quite modern with its skyscrapers and skywalks; St Paul, the second largest city, is rich with the state's heritage and history.

Minneapolis began in the 1800s when two mills were built to cut lumber and grind flour for nearby Fort Snelling. Lumbermen and fur traders from New England and French Canada were its first settlers. St Paul was incorporated as a town in 1849. It was host to the first legislature of the Minnesota Territory and has been the capital ever since. Civic, cultural and industrial development was assisted by railroad magnate James Hill, who gave the city a library and the Cathedral of St Paul's.

Business

The Twin Cities area's domination by lumber and grain milling began early. Today, Minneapolis is headquarters for several of the largest milling companies in the world and has a large cash grain market. The Twin Cities area has become a center for major corporations with 3M, Northwest Airlines, Cargill, Honeywill, General Mills, Pillsbury and Control Data headquartered here. Its highly diversified industries include computer manufacturing, electronics, food processing and graphic arts. St Paul is home to the Minnesota World Trade Center, and the area is rated among the top US cities for world trade.

Also important to the local economy is the Twin Cities' placement as gateway to the vast vacationlands—the woods and lakes of northern Minnesota.

Convention Facilities

The Minneapolis Convention Center has 3 exhibit halls, 2 with 100,000 square feet of display space and a third with 80,000 square feet of space. The 3 rooms can be combined to create a 280,000-square-foot exhibit hall. The Convention Center also has a 28,000-square-foot ballroom and 54 smaller meeting rooms, which can accommodate from 70 to 2,000 people.

St Paul's Civic Center, located on the banks of the Mississippi River, has 180,000 square feet of display space. Audiences of 18,000 can be seated—7,368 in permanent theater seats and 9,800 for banquets. There is a theater with 3,684 seats, a ballroom, meeting rooms for 20 to 175 people and parking for 1,700 cars.

Sports and Recreation

Minnesotans are fiercely proud of their professional athletes. Baseball's Twins and football's Vikings bring much excitement to the Hubert H. Humphrey Metrodome in Minneapolis. The Minnesota Timberwolves play basketball at Target Center.

Minneapolis and St Paul have all the requisites of a cosmopolitan area with the recreational advantages of the nearby north woods. There is an abundance of lakes, woods, parks, beaches, golf courses and ski areas in the Twin Cities area. Contact the Greater Minneapolis Convention and Visitors Association or St Paul Convention and Visitors Bureau for further information.

Entertainment

Restaurants, theaters, museums and music in the Twin Cities rival the finest in the nation.

The Ordway Music Theatre in downtown St Paul consists of the 1,815-seat theater, which houses opera, concerts, recitals, dance, drama and pop events, and the 317-seat hall, McKinght Theatre, which is used primarily for local music, dance, theater and film presentations.

The Guthrie Theater has a national reputation for presenting fine repertory performances, which draw drama students and theater lovers from throughout the nation.

Minnesota Orchestra Hall has been acclaimed by leading music critics as an outstanding achievement in auditorium architecture. The acoustical engineering allows full appreciation of musical subtleties.

At the Met Center in Bloomington one can enjoy more extravagant events—ice shows, circuses and musicals. The University of Minnesota Theatre has summer performances on campus aboard the *Showboat,* moored on the Mississippi River.

Historical Areas

Historic Fort Snelling has been restored to its 1820s appearance. In 1960 it was designated Minnesota's first national historic landmark; the legislature established Fort Snelling State Historical Park in 1963. All 18 buildings of the original fort have been rebuilt, and staff members act as soldiers, cooks, laundresses, blacksmiths and armorers, demonstrating how frontier people lived and worked in the 1820s. The fort is open to the public from May to October.

In the heart of downtown St Paul, the Old Federal Courts Building, renamed the Landmark Center, has been refurbished and opened to the public. Also open is The William L. McKnight/3M Omnitheater in the Science Museum of Minnesota. Unlike a conventional planetarium, the Omnitheater is an amphitheater enclosed in a hemispherical dome. Its highly advanced projection equipment can show the sky from any point in the solar system and actually has the ability to simulate space travel.

The Alexander Ramsey House in St Paul, a 15-room French-Renaissance mansion built in 1872, was the home of Minnesota's first territorial governor. Many of the Victorian furnishings are original pieces. Behind the main house is the reconstructed carriage house, which serves as the visitors' center.

Across from Minnehaha Park in Minneapolis is Minnehaha Depot, an ornate railroad building, dating from the 1890s, which has been restored to its original appearance.

Sightseeing

A stroll in downtown Minneapolis is vastly different from walking about most central cities. A 12-block stretch in the center of the city, the Nicollet Mall, is a shopping promenade with a variety of shops, restaurants, museums and nightly entertainment. Private cars are banned, and people can stroll along sidewalks past landscaped plots and fountains. A system of covered skyways weaves across and along the mall at a higher level. Plans call for about 60 blocks to be connected by the skyway system. Crystal Court, made of honeycombed glass and plastic, has an "outdoor" restaurant, 130 feet above ground level, reached by the skyway system. The St Paul skyway connects 25 city blocks and is the largest publicly owned skyway system in the country.

Since the Mississippi River is the reason the Twin Cities came to be, a sightseeing jaunt on or near the river is essential for anyone who wants to know the area. An observation platform at the Upper St Anthony Falls, on Main Street and Central Avenue in Minneapolis, offers a fine view of the river, its traffic, the falls and the Army Corps of Engineers' locks and dams.

For those who would like to cruise the Mississippi on an authentic stern-wheel riverboat, the *Jonathan Padelford, Josiah Snelling* and *Anson Northrop* travel between St Paul and historic Fort Snelling during the summer months.

A drive starting from the Cathedral of St Paul and proceeding west along Summit Avenue passes dozens of beautiful 19th-century mansions, including the official residence of Minnesota's governor. Also in this area are the Alexander Ramsey House and the James J. Hill Mansion. Both are open to the public.

General References Minneapolis

Settled: 1847 **Pop:** 368,383 **Elev:** 687-980 feet **Time zone:** Central **Area code:** 612

Phone Numbers

POLICE & FIRE: 911
FBI: 376-3200
POISON INFORMATION CENTER: 347-3141
TIME & WEATHER: 452-2323

Information Sources

Greater Minneapolis Convention & Visitors Association, 4000 Multifoods Tower, 33 S 6th St 55402; 348-4313.
"The Connection," Twin Cities information line, 922-9000.
Park and Recreation Board, 661-4800.

Transportation

AIRLINES: American; America West; Continental; Delta; KLM; Northwest; TWA; United; USAir; and other commuter and regional airlines. For the most current airline schedules and information consult the *Official Airline Guide,* published twice monthly.
AIRPORT: Minneapolis/St Paul International, 726-5555.
CAR RENTAL AGENCIES: (See Toll-Free Numbers) Avis 726-5220; Budget 726-9258; Hertz 726-1600; National 726-5600.
PUBLIC TRANSPORTATION: Metropolitan Transit Commission, 3118 Nicollet, 55408; 827-7733.
RAILROAD PASSENGER SERVICE: Amtrak 800/872-7245.

Newspapers

Star & Tribune; Skyway News.

Convention Facility

Minneapolis Convention Center. 1301 S 2nd Ave, 335-6000.

Sports & Recreation

Major Sports Facilities
Hubert H. Humphrey Metrodome, 900 S 5th St, 332-0386 (Twins, baseball, 375-7444; Vikings, football, 333-8828).
Target Center, 600 First Ave, (Timberwolves, basketball), 673-1600.

Racetracks
Canterbury Downs, 1 mi S of MN 101 on County 83, Shakopee 445-0511 (horse racing).
Elko Speedway, 20 mi S via I-35W exit 76, Elko, 461-7223.
Raceway Park, MN 101 between Savage & Shakopee, Shakopee, 445-2257.

Cultural Facilities

Theaters
Children's Theater Co, 2400 3rd Ave S, 874-0400.
Dudley Riggs, 2605 Hennepin Ave, 332-6620.
Guthrie Theater, 725 Vineland Pl, 377-2224.
Hennepin Center for the Arts, 6th St & Hennepin Ave, 332-4478.
Showboat, University of Minnesota campus on Mississippi River, 625-4001.

Concert Halls
Minneapolis Convention Center, 1301 S 2nd Ave, 335-6000.
Northrop Memorial Auditorium, University of Minnesota, 625-6600.
Orchestra Hall, 1111 Nicollet Mall, 371-5656.

Museums
Bell Museum of Natural History, 17 Ave & University Ave SE, 624-7083.
Hennepin County Historical Society Museum, 2303 3rd Ave S, 870-1329.
Minneapolis Planetarium, 300 Nicollet Mall, at Public Library, 372-6644.
Minnesota Transportation Museum, W 42nd St & Queen Ave S, 228-0263.

Art Museums and Gallery
American Swedish Institute, 2600 Park Ave S, 871-4907.
Minneapolis Institute of Arts, 2400 3rd Ave S, 870-3131.
Walker Art Center, Vineland Pl, 375-7622.
Weisman Art Museum, 333 E River Rd, University of Minnesota, 625-9494.

Points of Interest

Historical
Minnehaha Depot, Minnehaha Ave near 49th St E.

Other Attractions
Buck Hill Ski Area, 14 mi S on I-35W, Burnsville, 435-7174.
Butler Square, 6th St & 1st Ave N.
Eloise Butler Wildflower Garden and Bird Sanctuary, Wirth Park, S of MN 55 (Olsen Memorial Hwy) on Theodore Wirth Pkwy, 348-4448.
Hyland Hills Ski Area, Chalet Rd, 2 mi SW off I-494, 835-4250 or -4604.
IDS Tower, 80 S 8th St.
Lyndale Park, off E Lake Harriet Pkwy & Roseway Rd, on NE shore of Lake Harriet.
Minneapolis City Hall, 5th St & 3rd Ave S, 673-2491.
Minneapolis Grain Exchange, 400 S 4th St, 338-6212.
Minneapolis Sculpture Garden, Vineland Pl, opp Walker Art Center.
Minnehaha Park, Minnehaha Pkwy & Hiawatha Ave S, 661-4806.
Minnesota Zoo, 20 mi S via I-35W to MN 77 in Apple Valley, 432-9000.
St Anthony Falls, Main St SE & Central Ave.
Valleyfair, 20 mi SW on MN 101, Shakopee, 445-6500.

Sightseeing Tour

Gray Line bus tours, 835 Decatur Ave N, 55427; 591-0999.

Annual Events

Aquatennial Festival, 377-4621. 10 days July.
Renaissance Festival, Shakopee, 445-7361. 7 wkends beginning mid-Aug.

St Paul

Settled: 1840 **Pop:** 272,235 **Elev:** 874 feet **Time zone:** Central **Area code:** 612

Phone Numbers

POLICE: 911 or 291-1111; **FIRE:** 911 or 224-7811
FBI: 291-7100
POISON TREATMENT CENTER: 221-2113
TIME & WEATHER: 452-2323

Information Sources

St Paul Convention and Visitors Bureau, 101 Norwest Center, 55 E Fifth St, 55101; 297-6985.
"The Connection," Twin Cities information line, 922-9000.
Department of Parks & Recreation, 266-6400.

Transportation

AIRPORT: See Minneapolis.
CAR RENTAL AGENCIES: (See Toll-Free Numbers) Avis 726-5220; Budget 726-9258; Hertz 726-1600; National 726-5600.
PUBLIC TRANSPORTATION: Metropolitan Transit Commission, 3118 Nicollet, Minneapolis 55807; 827-7733.
RAILROAD PASSENGER SERVICE: Amtrak 800/872-7245.

Newspapers

Pioneer Press-Dispatch; Downtowner; Skyway News.

Convention Facility

St Paul Civic Center & Roy Wilkins Auditorium, 143 W 4th St, 224-7361.

Sports & Recreation

Major Sports Facility
St Paul Civic Center & Roy Wilkins Auditorium, 143 W 4th St, 224-7361.

Racetracks
See Minneapolis.

Cultural Facilities

Theaters
Great American History Theatre, Science Museum of Minnesota, 30 E 10th St, 292-4323.
Ordway Music Theatre, 345 Washington, 224-4222 or 282-3000.
Park Square Theatre, Minnesota Museum of Art, St Peter St & Kellogg Blvd, 291-7005.
Venetian Playhouse, 2814 Rice St, 484-7215.
World Theater, 10 E Exchange St, 290-1221.

Concert Hall
St Paul Civic Center & Roy Wilkins Auditorium, 143 W 4th St, 224-7361 or -7403.

Museums
Minnesota Childrens Museum, 1217 Bandana Blvd N, 644-3818.
Gibbs Farm Museum, 2097 W Larpenteur Ave, Falcon Heights, 646-8629.

Historic Fort Snelling, MN 5 & Post Rd, 725-2390.
Minnesota History Center, 345 Kellogg Blvd W, 296-6126.
Science Museum of Minnesota & The William L. McKnight/3M Omnitheater, 30 E 10th St, 221-9444.
Sibley House Museum, 55 D St, Mendota, 452-1596.

Art Museum

Minnesota Museum of Art, Landmark Center, 75 W 5th St, 292-4355; Jemne Building, St Peter St & Kellogg Blvd, 292-4355.

Points of Interest

Historical

Alexander Ramsey House, 265 S Exchange St, 296-8760.
Cathedral of St Paul, 239 Selby Ave, 228-1766.
Chapel of St Paul Site, Kellogg Blvd between Cedar & Minnesota Sts.
City Hall and Courthouse, 15 W Kellogg Blvd.
Mounds Park, Earl St & Mounds Blvd in Dayton's Bluff section, 266-6400.
James J. Hill Mansion, 240 Summit Ave, 297-2555.
Landmark Center, 75 W 5th St, 292-3233.
Old Muskego Church, Luther Seminary Campus, 2481 W Como Ave, 641-3456.
Ramsey Mill, MN 291 on Vermillion River, Hastings.
State Capitol, 75 Constitution Ave, 296-2881.

Other Attractions

Afton Alps Ski Area, 11 mi SE on US 10/61, Hastings, 436-5245.
Alexis Bailly Vineyard, 18200 Kirby Ave, Hastings, 437-1413.
Como Park, Midway & Lexington Pkwys, 266-6400.
Norwest Center Skyway, 56 E 6th St, 291-4751.
Town Square Park, 7th & Minnesota Sts, downtown, 266-6400.

Sightseeing Tours

Gray Line bus tours, 835 Decatur Ave N, Minneapolis 55427; 591-0999.

Jonathan Padelford, Josiah Snelling and *Anson Northrup,* Harriet Island Park, W of Wabasha bridge, 227-1100.

Annual Events

Winter Carnival, throughout city, 297-6953. Last wkend Jan-1st wkend Feb.
Festival of Nations, Civic Center, 647-0191. Late Apr.
Macalester College Scottish Country Fair, Macalester College Shaw Field, Snelling & St Clair Aves, 696-6239. 1st Sat May.
Taste of Minnesota, Capitol Mall, 297-6899. Early July.
Minnesota State Fair, fairgrounds, Como & Snelling Aves, 642-2200. Aug 27-Sept 7.

City Neighborhoods

Many of the restaurants, unrated dining establishments and some lodgings listed under Minneapolis and St Paul include neighborhoods as well as exact street addresses. Geographic descriptions of these areas are given, followed by a table of restaurants arranged by neighborhood.

Minneapolis

Downtown: South of 3rd St and the Mississippi River, west of I-35W, north of 16th St and east of Spruce Place. North of Downtown: North of Mississippi River. South of Downtown: South of 16th St.
Nicollet Ave Mall Area: Downtown area from 16th St, along Nicollet Ave to Washington Ave.

St Paul

Downtown: South of 11th St, west of Jackson St, north of Kellogg Blvd and east of St Peter St. North of Downtown: North of I-94. West of Downtown: West of St Peter St.
Summit Hill: Adj to Rice Park; south of I-94, west of Kellogg Blvd, north of Summit Ave and east of Snelling Ave.
Rice Park: Area adj to Downtown; south of 11th St, west of St Peter St and north and east of Kellogg Blvd.

Lodgings and Food Minneapolis

MINNEAPOLIS RESTAURANTS
BY NEIGHBORHOOD AREAS

(For full description, see alphabetical listings under Restaurants)

DOWNTOWN

510. 510 Groveland Ave

Cafe Brenda. 300 1st Ave N

Chez Bananas. 129 N Fourth St

Ciatti's Italian Ristorante. 1346 LaSalle Ave

Coyote Cafe. 528 Hennepin Ave

D'Amico Cucina. 100 N Sixth St

J.D. Hoyt's. 301 Washington Ave N

Khan's Mongolian Barbeque. 418 13th Ave SE

Linguini & Bob. 100 N Sixth St

Loring Cafe. 1624 Harmon Place

Murray's. 26 S 6th St

Nankin Cafe. 2 S 7th St

New French Cafe & Bar. 128 N 4th St

Origami. 30 N First St

Pickled Parrot. 26 N Fifth St

Sawatdee. 607 Washington Ave S

NORTH OF DOWNTOWN

Anthony's Wharf. 201 SE Main St

Emily's Lebanese Deli. 641 University Ave NE

Jax Cafe. 1928 University Ave NE

Kikugawa. 43 SE Main St

Pracna On Main. 117 Main St

Sri Lanka Curry House. 2821 Hennepin Ave

Yvette. 65 SE Main St

SOUTH OF DOWNTOWN

Black Forest Inn. 1 E 26th St

Caravelle. 2529 Nicollet Ave S

Christos. 2632 Nicollet Ave S

Figlio. 3001 Hennepin Ave S

It's Greek To Me. 626 W Lake St

Lowry's. 1934 Hennepin Ave S

Lucia's. 1432 W 31st St

Mud Pie. 2549 Lyndale Ave S

NICOLLET AVE MALL AREA

Azur. 651 Nicollet Mall Ave

Brasserie. 1400 Nicollet Ave

Goodfellow's. 800 Nicollet Mall Ave

Ichiban Japanese Steak House. 1333 Nicollet Mall Ave

The King & I. 1034 Nicollet Ave

Manny's (Hyatt Regency). 1300 Nicollet Mall

Market Bar-B-Que. 1414 Nicollet Ave S

Ping's. 1401 Nicollet Ave S

Tejas. 9th St & Nicollet Mall Ave

Note: *When a listing is located in a town that does not have its own city heading, it will appear under the city nearest to its location. In these cases, the address and town appear in parenthesis immediately following the name of the establishment.*

Motels

★ **AMERICINN OF ROGERS.** *(Box 83, Rogers 55374) Jct I-94 & MN 101. 612/428-4346.* 30 rms, 2 story. S $34.90-$48.90; D $39.90-$48.90; each addl $5; under 12 free. Crib free. TV; cable. Complimentary continental bkfst, coffee. Restaurant adj open 24 hrs. Ck-out 11 am. Cr cds: A, C, D, DS, MC, V.

D ⊠ 🔥 SC

★ **AQUA CITY.** *5739 Lyndale Ave S (55419), south of downtown. 612/861-6061.* 37 rms, 1-2 story, 8 kit. units. S $29-$40; D $35-$48; each addl $5; under 5 free. Crib $5. Pet accepted; $2. TV; cable. Pool. Complimentary coffee. Restaurant nearby. Ck-out 11 am. X-country ski ½ mi. Game rm. Cr cds: A, C, D, DS, MC, V.

🏊 🎿 ⊠ 🔥 SC

✔ ★ **BUDGETEL INN.** *(6415 James Circle, Brooklyn Center 55430) 18 mi N on I-694, change at Shingle Creek Pkwy. 612/561-8400; FAX 612/560-3189.* 98 rms, 3 story. S $37.95-$49.95; D $44.95-$53.95; each addl $7. Crib free. TV; cable. Complimentary coffee in rms. Complimentary continental bkfst. Restaurant nearby. Ck-out noon. Meeting rm. Valet serv. X-country ski ½ mi. Cr cds: A, C, D, DS, MC, V.

D ⊠ 🎿 ⊠

★ ★ **CHANHASSEN INN.** *(531 W 79th St, Chanhassen 55317) 3 mi S on MN 101. 612/934-7373; res: 800/242-6466.* 74 rms, 2 story. S $40-$46; D $48-$55; each addl $4; under 16 free. Crib free. TV; cable. Complimentary continental bkfst. Restaurant adj 6 am-10 pm. Ck-out noon. X-country ski 1 mi. Cr cds: A, C, D, DS, MC, V.

D ⊠ 🎿 ⊠ 🔥 SC

★ **DAYS INN UNIVERSITY.** *2407 University Ave SE (55414), east of downtown. 612/623-3999; FAX 612/331-2152.* 129 rms, 6 story. S $54-$89; D $60-$89; each addl $6; under 18 free. Crib $6. TV; cable. Complimentary continental bkfst. Restaurant nearby. Ck-out 11 am. Coin lndry. Meeting rms. Downhill ski 10 mi, x-country ski 1 mi. Some refrigerators. Cr cds: A, C, D, DS, JCB, MC, V.

🎿 🔥

★ ★ **HAMPTON INN.** *10420 Wayzata Blvd (55343), west of downtown. 612/541-1094; FAX 612/541-1905.* 127 rms, 4 story. S $61-$63; D $69-$71; under 18 free; wkend rates. Crib free. TV; cable. Complimentary continental bkfst, coffee. Restaurant nearby. Ck-out noon. Meeting rms. Downhill ski 12 mi; x-country ski 1 mi. Cr cds: A, C, D, DS, ER, JCB, MC, V.

D 🎿 ⊠ 🔥 SC

✔ ★ **METRO INN.** *5637 Lyndale Ave S (55419), south of downtown. 612/861-6011.* 36 rms. Apr-Oct: S $30-$36; D $34-$45; each addl $3-$5; lower rates rest of yr. Crib $4-$5. Pet accepted, some restrictions; $2. TV; cable. Restaurant 7:30 am-2:30 pm. Ck-out 11 am. X-country ski ½ mi. Cr cds: A, C, D, DS, MC, V.

🏊 🎿 ⊠ 🔥 SC

✔ ★ ★ **MOUNDS VIEW INN.** *(2149 Program Ave, Mounds View 55112) Jct I-35W & US 10. 612/786-9151; res: 800/777-7863; FAX 612/786-2845.* 70 rms, 2 story. S $33.95-$48.95; D $41.95-$61.95; each addl $5; under 15 free; higher rates special events. Crib $3. TV; cable. Complimentary continental bkfst. Restaurant adj open 24 hrs.

Bar. Ck-out noon. Coin lndry. Meeting rms. Sundries. X-country ski 3 mi. Cr cds: A, C, D, DS, MC, V.

[D] [≈] [⊠] [≈] [🔥] [SC]

★ ★ **REGENCY PLAZA-TARGET CENTER.** *41 N 10th St (55403), 3 blks W of Nicollet Mall on 10th St, downtown.* 612/339-9311; *FAX 612/339-4765.* 192 rms, 3 story. S $68; D $74; each addl $6; suites $110-$150; under 18 free; wkend rates. Crib free. TV; cable. Indoor pool; whirlpool, poolside serv. Restaurant 6:30 am-10 pm; Sat, Sun from 7:30 am. Rm serv. Bar 4 pm-1 am; entertainment exc Sun. Ck-out noon. Coin lndry. Meeting rms. Bellhops. Valet serv. Sundries. Airport transportation. X-country ski 1 mi. Cr cds: A, C, D, DS, ER, JCB, MC, V.

[≈] [≈] [⊠] [🔥] [SC]

✔ **SUPER 8.** *(6445 James Circle, Brooklyn Center 55430) Jct I-94, I-694 & Shingle Creek Pkwy interchange exit 34.* 612/566-9810; *FAX 612/566-8680.* 103 rms, 2 story. S $35.88-$38.88; D $40.88-$46.88; each addl $5; under 12 free. Crib free. TV; cable. Complimentary continental bkfst. Restaurant adj. Ck-out 11 am. Cr cds: A, C, D, DS, MC, V.

[D] [⊠] [🔥] [SC]

Motor Hotels

✔★★★ **BEST WESTERN NORMANDY INN.** *405 S 8th St (55404), downtown.* 612/370-1400; *FAX 612/370-0351.* 160 rms, 4 story. S $75-$84; D $85-$94; each addl $10; under 16 free. Crib free. TV; cable. Indoor pool; whirlpool, sauna, poolside serv. Restaurant 6 am-10 pm. Rm serv. Bar 4:30 pm-1 am. Ck-out noon. Meeting rms. Valet serv. Sundries. Airport transportation. Cr cds: A, C, D, DS, ER, MC, V.

[D] [≈] [≈] [⊠] [🔥] [SC]

★ ★ ★ **RAMADA PLAZA HOTEL.** *(12201 Ridgedale Dr, Minnetonka 55305) W on Wayzata Blvd, behind Ridgedale Shopping Center.* 612/593-0000; *FAX 612/544-2090.* 222 rms, 4 story. S $109-$119; D $119-$129; each addl $10; suites $150; under 18 free; wkend rates. Crib free. TV. Indoor pool; poolside serv. Restaurant 6:30 am-11 pm. Bar 10:30-1 am. Ck-out noon. Meeting rms. Airport transportation. X-country ski 2 mi. Some private patios, balconies. Cr cds: A, C, D, DS, ER, JCB, MC, V.

[D] [≈] [≈] [⊠] [🔥] [SC]

Hotels

★ ★ ★ **CROWN STERLING SUITES.** *425 S 7th St (55415), downtown.* 612/333-3111; *FAX 612/333-7984.* 218 suites, 6 story. S $145-$165; D $145-$185; each addl $10; under 13 free; wkend rates. Crib free. TV; cable, in-rm movies avail. Indoor pool; whirlpool, sauna, steam rm. Complimentary bkfst. Restaurant 11 am-2:30 pm, 5-10 pm; Fri & Sat 5-11 pm. Bar 11-1 am. Ck-out noon. Meeting rms. X-country ski 1 mi. Refrigerators. Cr cds: A, C, D, DS, ER, MC, V.

[D] [≈] [≈] [⊠] [🔥] [SC]

★ ★ ★ **HOLIDAY INN CROWNE PLAZA NORTHSTAR.** *618 2nd Ave S (55402), above 6-story Northstar Parking Ramp, downtown.* 612/338-2288; *FAX 612/338-2288, ext. 318.* 226 rms, 17 story. S $132; D $147; each addl $15; suites $250-$500; under 17 free; wkend rates. Crib free. Garage parking $10, wkends $7.95. TV; cable. Restaurants 6:30 am-11:30 pm. Bar 11-1 am. Ck-out 1 pm. Meeting rms. Barber, beauty shop. Airport transportation. X-country ski 1 mi. *LUXURY LEVEL :* CONCIERGE FLOOR. 20 rms. S $150; D $165. 24-hr concierge. Private lounge. Minibars. Complimentary continental bkfst. Cr cds: A, C, D, DS, JCB, MC, V.

[D] [≈] [⊠] [🔥] [SC]

✔★ ★ ★ **HOLIDAY INN-METRODOME.** *1500 Washington Ave S (55454), south of downtown.* 612/333-4646; *FAX 612/333-7910.* 265 rms, 14 story. S $99.50-$109.50; D $109.50-$119.50; each addl $10;

suites $139.50-$149.50; under 18 free. Crib free. Garage $7. TV. Indoor pool. Restaurant 6:30 am-11 pm. Bar 11-1 am; pianist. Ck-out noon. Meeting rms. Gift shop. Exercise equipt; weights, bicycles. Cr cds: A, C, D, DS, JCB, MC, V.

[D] [≈] [⅄] [⊠] [🔥] [SC]

★ ★ ★ **HYATT REGENCY.** *1300 Nicollet Mall (55403), in Nicollet Ave Mall Area.* 612/370-1234; *FAX 612/370-1463.* 533 rms, 21 suites, 20 story. S $168-$193; D $193-$210; each addl $25; suites $290-$800; under 18 free. Crib free. Parking $9. TV. Indoor pool. Restaurant 6:30-1 am; Sun 7 am-11 pm (also see MANNY'S). Bar 11-1 am. Ck-out noon. Convention facilities. Concierge. Shopping arcade. Barber, beauty shop. Airport transportation. Indoor tennis privileges. X-country ski 1 mi. Health club privileges. *LUXURY LEVEL :* REGENCY CLUB. 29 rms. S $193; D $218. Private lounge, honor bar. Complimentary continental bkfst, refreshments. Cr cds: A, C, D, DS, ER, JCB, MC, V.

[D] [≈] [⅄] [≈] [⊠] [🔥] [SC]

★ ★ ★ **LUXEFORD.** *1101 LaSalle Ave (55403), downtown.* 612/332-6800; *res: 800/662-3232; FAX 612/332-8246.* 230 suites, 12 story. S $140; D $155; each addl $15; under 17 free; wkend rates. Covered parking $7. Crib free. TV. Restaurant 6:30 am-midnight. Bar 11-1 am. Ck-out 11 am. Meeting rms. Exercise equipt; weights, bicycles, sauna. X-country ski 1 mi. Refrigerators. Cr cds: A, C, D, DS, JCB, MC, V.

[D] [≈] [⅄] [≈] [⊠] [🔥] [SC]

★ ★ ★ **THE MARQUETTE.** *710 Marquette Ave (55402), in IDS Tower, downtown.* 612/333-4545; *FAX 612/376-7419.* 278 rms, 19 story. S $169; D $189; each addl $15; suites $330-$795; family rates; wkend package plans. Crib free. Garage parking $12; wkends $6. TV. Restaurant 6:30 am-11 pm. Bar 11:30-1 am. Ck-out noon. Convention facilities. Airport transportation. X-country ski 1 mi. Steam bath in suites. Exercise rm. *LUXURY LEVEL :* EXECUTIVE FLOORS. 38 rms, 2 floors. S $189; D $209. Private lounge. In-rm steam baths. Complimentary continental bkfst, refreshments. Cr cds: A, C, D, DS, ER, JCB, MC, V.

[D] [≈] [⅄] [≈] [⊠] [SC]

★ ★ ★ **MARRIOTT CITY CENTER.** *30 S 7th St (55402), downtown.* 612/349-4000; *FAX 612/332-7165.* 583 rms, 31 story. S $159; D $169; each addl $10; suites $250-$650; under 18 free; wkend rates. Crib free. Valet parking $16. TV; in-rm movies avail. Restaurants 6:30 am-11 pm. Bar 11-1 am. Ck-out noon. Convention facilities. Shopping arcade. X-country ski 1 mi. Whirlpool, sauna. Health club privileges. Some bathrm phones. *LUXURY LEVEL :* CONCIERGE LEVEL. 20 rms, 25 suites, 2 floors. S $169; D $179; Honor bar. Bathrm phones, minibars. Whirlpool in suites. Complimentary continental bkfst. Cr cds: A, C, D, DS, ER, JCB, MC, V.

[D] [≈] [⊠] [🔥] [SC]

★ ★ **PARK INN INTERNATIONAL.** *1313 Nicollet Ave (55403), in Nicollet Ave Mall Area.* 612/332-0371; *FAX 612/332-0970.* 325 rms, 14 story. S $135; D $155; suites $150-$250. Crib free. TV; cable. Indoor pool; sauna. Restaurant 6:30 am-10:30 pm. Bars 11-1 am. Ck-out noon. Coin lndry. Convention facilities. X-country ski 1 mi. Cr cds: A, C, D, DS, ER, JCB, MC, V.

[≈] [≈] [⊠] [🔥] [SC]

★ ★ ★ **RADISSON HOTEL & CONFERENCE CENTER.** *(3131 Campus Dr, Plymouth 55441) Jct I-494, MN 55, on Northwest Business Campus.* 612/559-6600; *FAX 612/559-1053.* 243 rms, 6 story, 6 suites. S, D $99; each addl $10; suites $150-$199; under 18 free. Crib free. TV; cable. Indoor pool; poolside serv. Restaurant 6:30 am-11 pm. Bar 11-1 am. Ck-out noon. Meeting rms. Gift shop. Lighted tennis. Downhill ski 20 mi; x-country ski 2 mi. Exercise rm; instructor, weights, bicycles, whirlpool, sauna. Racquetball. Rec rm. Refrigerators. Danish-modern design in brick, tile, glass; on wooded site. Cr cds: A, C, D, DS, ER, JCB, MC, V.

[D] [≈] [⅄] [≈] [⅄] [⅄] [⊠] [🔥] [SC]

★ ★ ★ **RADISSON PLAZA.** *35 S 7th St (55402), downtown.* 612/339-4900; FAX 612/337-9766. 357 rms, 17 story. S, D $169-$209; each addl $10; suites $209-$545; under 18 free. Crib free. Parking $10. TV; cable. Restaurant 6 am-11 pm. Bar 11-1 am; entertainment. Ck-out noon. Meeting rms. Concierge. Shopping arcade. X-country ski 1 mi. Exercise rm; instructor, weights, bicycles, whirlpool, sauna. Atrium lobby; fountain, marble columns. *LUXURY LEVEL : PLAZA CLUB.* 77 rms, 3 floors. S, D $179. Private lounge. In-rm movies. Complimentary continental bkfst, refreshments. Cr cds: A, C, D, DS, ER, JCB, MC, V.

D ⚡ 🕴 ⛷ 🏊 🏋 SC

★ ★ ★ **SHERATON METRODOME.** *1330 Industrial Blvd (55413), north of downtown.* 612/331-1900; FAX 612/331-6827. 253 rms, 8 story. S $105-$125; D, studio rms $105-$195; each addl $10; suites $150-$280; wkend packages. Crib free. TV; cable. Indoor pool; whirlpool, sauna, poolside serv. Coffee in rms. Restaurant 6:30 am-10:30 pm; Sat & Sun 7:30-11 pm. Bar 11-1 am; entertainment exc Sun. Ck-out 11 am. Meeting rms. X-country ski 1 mi. *LUXURY LEVEL : EXECUTIVE CLUB.* 25 rms, 1 suite. S $125-$145; D $135-$155; suite $280. Concierge. Private lounge. Complimentary continental bkfst, evening refreshments. Cr cds: A, C, D, DS, ER, JCB, MC, V.

D ⚡ ⛷ 🏊 🏋 🔥

★ ★ ★ **SHERATON PARK PLACE.** *1500 Park Place Blvd (55416), north of downtown.* 612/542-8600; FAX 612/542-8068. 298 rms, 15 story. S $89-$109; D $104-$124; each addl $15; suites $115-$150; under 18 free; wkend rates. Crib free. TV. Indoor pool; poolside serv. Restaurant 6:30 am-midnight. Rm serv 24 hrs. Bar 11-1 am; dancing Tues-Sat. Ck-out 11 am. Convention facilities. Airport transportation. X-country ski 2 mi. Exercise equipt; weights, bicycles, whirlpool, sauna. Game rm. Cr cds: A, C, D, DS, ER, JCB, MC, V.

D ⚡ ⛷ 🕴 ⛸ 🏊 🏋 SC

★ ★ ★ **WHITNEY.** *150 Portland Ave (55401), downtown.* 612/339-9300; res: 800/248-1879; FAX 612/339-1333. 97 rms, 8 story, 40 suites. S $150-$200; suites $190-$1,500; under 10 free. Crib free. Parking $6. TV; cable. Restaurant 6:30 am-11 pm. Rm serv 24 hrs. Bar 11:30-1 am; pianist. Ck-out noon. Meeting rms. Concierge. Bathrm phones, refrigerators. Bi-level suites with honor bar. Elegantly renovated hotel located on the banks of the Mississippi River; outdoor plaza with fountain. Cr cds: A, C, D, DS, ER, JCB, MC, V.

D ⚡ 🔥

Restaurants

★ ★ ★ **510.** *510 Groveland Ave, downtown.* 612/874-6440. Hrs: 5:30-10 pm. Closed Sun; major hols. Res accepted. French menu. Wine cellar. Semi-a la carte: dinner $12-$19. Complete meals: dinner $19. Specializes in rack of lamb, seafood. Own baking. In restored 19th-century mansion. Cr cds: A, C, D, DS, MC, V.

★ ★ **ANTHONY'S WHARF.** *201 SE Main St, under 3rd Ave Bridge on Mississippi River, north of downtown.* 612/378-7058. Hrs: 5-10 pm; Fri, Sat to 11 pm. Closed Dec 24-25. Bar. Semi-a la carte: dinner $9.50-$29.95. Specializes in lobster tail, swordfish. Historic building (1890); San Francisco wharf atmosphere. Cr cds: A, DS, MC, V.

★ ★ **AUGUST MOON.** *(5340 Watzata Blvd, Golden Valley)* Approx 3 mi W on MN 55. 612/544-7017. Hrs: 11 am-9 pm; Fri to 10 pm; Sat 4-10 pm; Sun 4-9 pm. Closed Dec 25. New Asian menu. Wine, beer. Semi-a la carte: lunch $5-$9, dinner $8-$15. Specialties: Cal-Asian crab cakes, tandoori chicken. Parking. Oriental artwork. Cr cds: MC, V.

★ ★ **AZUR.** *651 Nicollet Mall Ave, in Nicollet Ave Mall Area.* 612/342-2500. Hrs: 11:30 am-2 pm, 5:30-9 pm; Fri, Sat to 10 pm. Closed Sun; most major hols. Res accepted. French, Mediterranean menu. Bar to midnight. Semi-a la carte: lunch $10-$15, dinner $17.50-$27. Specialties: sautéed snapper with stewed artichokes, grilled Angus beef loin. Valet parking. Eclectic decor; quartz tables, mahogany walls, glass-enclosed bar. Atrium. Cr cds: A, C, D, DS, MC, V.

✔ ★ **BLACK FOREST INN.** *1 E 26th St, at Nicollet, south of downtown.* 612/872-0812. Hrs: 11-1 am; Sun noon-midnight. Res accepted. German menu. Semi-a la carte: lunch $3.50-$7.80, dinner $5.50-$14. Specialties: sauerbraten, Wienerschnitzel, bratwurst. Outdoor dining. German decor. Family-owned. Cr cds: A, C, D, DS, MC, V.

★ ★ **BRASSERIE.** *1400 Nicollet Ave, in Nicollet Ave Mall Area.* 612/874-7285. Hrs: 11 am-11 pm; Fri, Sat to midnight; Sun to 9 pm. Closed most major hols. Res accepted. French menu. Bar. Semi-a la carte: lunch $6.50-$9.25, dinner $12.95-$19.75. Specialties: coquilles St.-Jacques, beef medallions. Parking. French bistro atmosphere. Cr cds: A, MC, V.

✔ ★ **CAFE BRENDA.** *300 1st Ave N, downtown.* 612/342-9230. Hrs: 11:30 am-2 pm, 5:30-9 pm; Fri to 10 pm; Sat 5:30-10 pm. Closed Sun; most major hols. Res accepted. Vegetarian, seafood menu. Bar. Semi-a la carte: lunch $6-$8, dinner $9-$13. Specializes in fresh sautéed rainbow trout, sozai. Parking (dinner). Cr cds: A, C, D, MC, V.

✔ ★ **CARAVELLE.** *2529 Nicollet Ave S, south of downtown.* 612/871-3226. Hrs: 11 am-9 pm; Sat from noon; Sun noon-7 pm. Closed July 4, Thanksgiving, Dec 25. Res accepted. Chinese menu. Wine, beer. Semi-a la carte: lunch, dinner $5.95-$8.95. Buffet: lunch $5.50, dinner $5.95. Specializes in shrimp, scallops. Parking. Oriental decor. Cr cds: MC, V.

★ **CHEZ BANANAS.** *129 N Fourth St, downtown.* 612/340-0032. Hrs: 11:30 am-10 pm; Sat-Mon from 5 pm. Closed some major hols. Res accepted Sun-Thurs. Caribbean menu. Bar. Semi-a la carte: lunch $4.50-$8, dinner $7.50-$12. Specializes in mustard pepper chicken, Caribbean barbecue. Informal & fun atmosphere; inflatable animals hanging from ceiling, toys at tables. Cr cds: A, C, D, DS, MC, V.

✔ ★ **CHRISTOS.** *2632 Nicollet Ave S, south of downtown.* 612/871-2111. Hrs: 11 am-10 pm; Fri to 11 pm; Sat 4-11pm; Sun 4-9 pm. Closed most major hols. Res accepted. Greek menu. Wine, beer. Semi-a la carte: lunch $4.50-$7.50, dinner $6.95-$10.95. Specialities: spanakópita, moussaka, shish kebab. Cr cds: A, C, D, DS, MC, V.

★ ★ **CIATTI'S ITALIAN RISTORANTE.** *1346 LaSalle Ave, downtown.* 612/339-7747. Hrs: 11 am-10 pm; Fri & Sat to 11 pm; Sun 10 am-10 pm. Closed Thanksgiving, Dec 24, 25. Res accepted. Italian menu. Bar. Semi-a la carte: lunch $6-$9, dinner $8-$15. Specialties: fettucine Ciatti's, tortellini "straw and hay." Outdoor dining. Cr cds: A, C, D, DS, MC, V.

★ ★ **COCOLEZZONE.** *(5410 Wayzata Blvd, Golden Valley)* 5 mi W on MN 55. 612/544-4014. Hrs: 11 am-10 pm; Fri to 11 pm; Sat 5-11 pm; Sun 5-9:30 pm. Closed some major hols. Northern Italian menu. Bar. Semi-a la carte: lunch $5-$10, dinner $8-$25. Specializes in pasta, veal dishes. Parking. Cr cds: A, C, D, MC, V.

✔ ★ **COYOTE CAFE.** *528 Hennepin Ave, downtown.* 612/338-1730. Hrs: 11 am-midnight; Fri, Sat to 1 am; Sat & Sun 10 am-midnight; Sat & Sun brunch to 3 pm. Closed most major hols. Southwestern menu. Bar. Semi-a la carte: lunch $5.25-$7.95, dinner $5.25-$10.95. Sun brunch $3.85-$6.50. Specialties: Coyote chicken, jalitos. Outdoor dining. Large windows overlook Warehouse District. Cr cds: A, C, D, MC, V.

★ ★ **D'AMICO CUCINA.** *100 N Sixth St, downtown.* 612/338-2401. Hrs: 5:30-10 pm; Fri, Sat to 11 pm; Sun 5-9 pm. Closed major hols. Res accepted. Italian menu. Bar. Semi-a la carte: dinner $18.50-$25.50. Specializes in thin crust pizza, pasta. Piano, bass Fri-Sat. Restored warehouse. Cr cds: A, C, D, MC, V.

★ ★ **FIGLIO.** *3001 Hennepin Ave S, Calhoun Sq, south of downtown.* 612/822-1688. Hrs: 11:30-1 am; Fri, Sat to 2 am. Res accepted. Italian menu. Bar. Semi-a la carte: lunch, dinner $6-$15.95.

Specializes in pasta, pizza, sandwiches. Outdoor dining. Art deco decor; neon lighting. Cr cds: A, C, D, DS, MC, V.

★ ★ ★ **GOODFELLOW'S.** *800 Nicollet Mall Ave, in Nicollet Ave Mall Area.* 612/332-4800. Hrs: 11:30 am-2:30 pm, 5:30-9 pm; Fri to 10 pm; Sat 5:30-10 pm. Closed Sun; major hols. Res accepted. Bar. Wine list. Semi-a la carte: lunch $9-$12, dinner $17-$28. Specialties: grilled salmon, hickory-grilled Wisconsin veal chop. Beamed ceiling. Cr cds: A, C, D, DS, MC, V.

★ ★ **ICHIBAN JAPANESE STEAK HOUSE.** *1333 Nicollet Mall Ave, in Nicollet Ave Mall Area.* 612/339-0540. Hrs: 4:30-10 pm; Fri to 11 pm; Sat to 10:30 pm. Closed Thanksgiving, Dec 24. Res accepted. Japanese menu. Bar. Semi-a la carte: dinner $12.95-$23.95. Specializes in sushi, tempura. Tableside cooking. Japanese decor. Cr cds: A, C, D, DS, MC, V.

✔ ★ **IT'S GREEK TO ME.** *626 W Lake St, south of downtown.* 612/825-9922. Hrs: 11 am-11 pm. Closed major hols. Greek menu. Bar. Semi-a la carte: lunch, dinner $7.75-$11.95. Specialties: lamb kebab, pastitsio. Parking. Cr cds: MC, V.

★ **J.D. HOYT'S.** *301 Washington Ave N, downtown.* 612/338-1560. Hrs: 7-1 am; Sat from 7:30 am; Sun 5 pm-midnight; Sun brunch 10 am-2 pm. Closed some major hols. Res accepted. Bar. Semi-a la carte: bkfst $1.99-$7, lunch $4.99-$8.99, dinner $8-$24. Sun brunch $9.95. Specializes in pork chops, charcoal-grilled steak. Valet parking. Casual dining; roadhouse atmosphere. Cr cds: A, C, D, DS, MC, V.

★ ★ ★ **JAX CAFE.** *1928 University Ave NE, north of downtown.* 612/789-7297. Hrs: 11 am-10:30 pm; Sun to 9 pm; Sun brunch 10 am-1:30 pm. Closed Dec 24 evening. Res accepted. Wine list. Semi-a la carte: lunch $6.95-$11.95, dinner $12-$20. Sun brunch $13.95. Specializes in prime rib, seafood, rainbow trout (in season). Pianist Thurs-Sun. Parking. Overlooks trout pond; waterwheel. Fireplace. Family-owned. Cr cds: A, C, D, DS, MC, V.

★ ★ **KIKUGAWA.** *43 SE Main St, Riverplace, north of downtown.* 612/378-3006. Hrs: 11:30 am-2 pm, 5-10 pm; Sat noon-2 pm, 5-11 pm; Sun noon-2:30 pm, 4:30-9:30 pm. Closed Jan 1, Thanksgiving, Dec 25. Res accepted. Japanese menu. Bar. Semi-a la carte: lunch $4.25-$8.95, dinner $8.50-$17.50. Specialties: sukiyaki, sushi bar. Parking. Outdoor dining. Modern Japanese decor. Cr cds: A, C, D, DS, JCB, MC, V.

✔ ★ **THE KING & I.** *1034 Nicollet Ave, in Nicollet Ave Mall Area.* 612/332-6928. Hrs: 11 am-10 pm; Sat from 5 pm. Closed Sun. Res accepted. Thai menu. Wine, beer. Semi-a la carte: lunch, dinner $6.25-$15.95. Specialties: pad Thai, tom yum goong. Informal dining. Cr cds: A, C, D, DS, MC, V.

[D]

★ ★ **LINGUINI & BOB.** *100 N Sixth St, downtown.* 612/332-1600. Hrs: 11:30 am-midnight; Fri & Sat to 1 am; Sun 4-10 pm. Closed most major hols. Res accepted. Italian menu. Bar. Semi-a la carte: lunch $10-$14, dinner $18-$22. Specializes in spicy shrimp, pasta. Outdoor dining. 2nd floor overlooks Butler Square. Cr cds: A, C, D, MC, V.

★ ★ ★ **LORD FLETCHER'S OF THE LAKE.** *(Box 446, 3746 Sunset Dr, Spring Park)* 18 mi W on US 12, 6 mi S on County 15 W, then ¹/₂ mi N on County 19 to signs, on Lake Minnetonka. 612/471-8513. Hrs: 11:30 am-2:30 pm, 5-10 pm; Sun 4:30-9:30 pm; Sun brunch 11 am-2 pm. Closed Jan 1, Dec 24 evening-25. Res accepted. English, Amer menu. Bar. Wine list. Semi-a la carte: lunch $6-$11.50, dinner $9-$20.95. Sun brunch $10.95. Specializes in beef, fish, prime rib. Outdoor dining. Mesquite charcoal grill. Old English decor; fireplaces, wine kegs, antiques. Boat dockage. Cr cds: A, C, D, DS, MC, V.

★ **LOWRY'S.** *1934 Hennepin Ave S, south of downtown.* 612/871-0806. Hrs: 11 am-10 pm; Fri to 11 pm; Sat 10 am-11 pm; Sun 10 am-9 pm; Sat & Sun brunch 10 am-2 pm. Closed Thanksgiving, Dec 25. Res accepted. Wine, beer. Semi-a la carte: lunch $5-$9, dinner

$7-$15. Sat, Sun brunch $6-$12. Specializes in risotto, polenta. Parking. Local artists' work on display. Cr cds: A, C, D, MC, V.

★ **LUCIA'S.** *1432 W 31st St, south of downtown.* 612/825-1572. Hrs: 11:30 am-2:30 pm, 5:30-9:30 pm; Fri to 10 pm; Sat, Sun 5:30-9 pm; Sat, Sun brunch 10 am-2 pm. Closed Mon; most major hols. Res accepted. Italian, Amer menu. Bar. Semi-a la carte: lunch $5.50-$8.95, dinner $8.95-$16.95. Sat, Sun brunch $5.95-$8.95. Specialties: polenta, crostini. Parking. Outdoor dining. Menu changes wkly. Cr cds: MC, V.

★ ★ **MANNY'S.** *(See Hyatt Regency)* 612/339-9900. Hrs: 5:30-10 pm; Fri & Sat to 11 pm; Sun to 9 pm. Closed major hols. Res accepted. Bar. A la carte entrees: $20-$40. Specializes in steak, lobster. Contemporary decor. Cr cds: A, C, D, DS, MC, V.

★ ★ ★ **MURRAY'S.** *26 S 6th St, downtown.* 612/339-0909. Hrs: 11 am-10:30 pm; Fri to 11 pm; Sat 4-11 pm; Sun 4-10 pm. Res accepted. Bar. Wine list. Semi-a la carte: lunch $4.75-$13.75, dinner $19.50-$32.50. Specialty: silver butter knife steak for 2. Own baking. Entertainment Thurs-Sat. Extensive wine selection. Family-owned. Cr cds: A, C, D, DS, JCB, MC, V.

★ ★ **NANKIN CAFE.** *2 S 7th St, corner Hennepin Ave & 7th St, downtown.* 612/333-3303. Hrs: 11 am-10 pm; Fri & Sat to 11 pm; Sun 11 am-9 pm. Closed legal hols. Res accepted. Cantonese, Szechwan, Amer menu. Bar. Semi-a la carte: lunch $6.95-$13.50, dinner $6.95-$25. Specializes in chow mein dishes. Modern Oriental decor. Cr cds: A, C, D, DS, MC, V.

★ ★ **NEW FRENCH CAFE & BAR.** *128 N 4th St, downtown.* 612/338-3790. Hrs: 7 am-1:30 pm, 5:30-9:30 pm; Fri to 10 pm; Sat 5:30-10 pm; Sun 6-9 pm; Sat, Sun brunch 8 am-2 pm. Closed major hols. Res accepted. Country & contemporary French menu. Bar 11-1 am, Sun from 6 pm. Semi-a la carte: bkfst $3.95-$7.95, lunch $6.95-$11, dinner $20-$35. Sat, Sun brunch $3.50-$10.75. Specializes in rack of lamb, seafood. Outdoor dining (bar). Remodeled building (1900); French bistro theme. Cr cds: A, C, D, MC, V.

★ **ORIGAMI.** *30 N First St, downtown.* 612/333-8430. Hrs: 11 am-2 pm, 5-9:30 pm; Fri & Sat to 11 pm; Sun 5-9 pm. Closed major hols. Japanese menu. Bar. Semi-a la carte: lunch $5-$12, dinner $7-$25. Specialties: sushi bar, sashimi. Parking. Outdoor dining. Oriental decor; lanterns. Cr cds: A, D, DS, MC, V.

✔ ★ **PICKLED PARROT.** *26 N Fifth St, downtown.* 612/332-0673. Hrs: 11-1 am; Sun 5 pm-midnight. Closed Easter, Dec 24, 25. Res accepted. Bar. Semi-a la carte: lunch $5-$13, dinner $5-$16. Specialties: barbecued ribs, pork sandwich, Southern dishes. Colorful decor. Cr cds: A, C, D, DS, MC, V.

✔ ★ ★ **PING'S.** *1401 Nicollet Ave S, in Nicollet Ave Mall Area.* 612/874-9404. Hrs: 11 am-10 pm; Fri to midnight; Sat noon-midnight; Sun noon-9 pm. Closed Easter, Thanksgiving, Dec 24, 25. Res accepted. Chinese menu. Bar. Lunch buffet $6.95. Semi-a la carte: dinner $9-$14. Specialties: Peking duck, Ping's wings, Szechuan trio. Valet parking. Cr cds: A, C, D, DS, MC, V.

★ ★ **PRACNA ON MAIN.** *117 Main St, under 3rd Ave Bridge on Mississippi River, north of downtown.* 612/379-3200. Hrs: 11:30 am-10 pm. Bar to 1 am. Semi-a la carte: lunch $5-$10, dinner $10-$16.95. Outdoor dining. Warehouse (1890); turn-of-the-century decor. Cr cds: A, C, D, DS, MC, V.

✔ ★ **SAWATDEE.** *607 Washington Ave S, downtown.* 612/338-6451. Hrs: 11 am-10 pm; Fri, Sat to 11 pm. Res accepted. Thai menu. Bar. A la carte entrees: lunch, dinner $7-$14.95. Buffet: lunch $6.95. Specialties: Pad Thai, Bangkok seafood special. Parking. Cr cds: A, C, D, DS, MC, V.

★ **SRI LANKA CURRY HOUSE.** *2821 Hennepin Ave, north of downtown.* 612/871-2400. Hrs: 5-10 pm; Fri 11:30 am-11 pm; Sat to 11 pm. Res accepted. Sri Lankan menu. Wine, beer. Semi-a la carte:

dinner $7.95-$14.95. Specializes in curried lamb, curried fresh seafood, vegetarian dishes. Cr cds: C, D, MC, V.

★ **TEJAS.** *9th St & Nicollet Mall Ave, lowel level of Conservatory, in Nicollet Ave Mall Area.* 612/375-0800. Hrs: 11 am-2 pm; 5-9 pm; Fri to 10 pm; Sat 11 am-2 pm, 5-10 pm. Closed Sun; major hols. Res accepted. Southwestern menu. Bar. A la carte entrees: lunch $6.50-$12, dinner $7-$18. Specialties: smoked chicken nachos, grilled shrimp enchilada. Cr cds: A, C, D, DS, MC, V.

★ ★ **YVETTE.** *65 SE Main St, north of downtown.* 612/379-1111. Hrs: 11 am-11 pm; Fri, Sat to 1 am; Sun to 10 pm. Closed Jan 1, Dec 25. Res accepted. French, continental menu. Bar. Semi-a la carte: lunch $5.95-$9.95, dinner $11.95-$19.95. Specializes in Norwegian salmon, day-aged steaks. Pianist exc Sun. Outdoor dining. Many of the ingredients are provided through the restaurant's own ranch. Overlooks river. Jacket. Cr cds: A, C, D, MC, V.

[D]

Unrated Dining Spots

EMILY'S LEBANESE DELI. *641 University Ave NE, north of downtown.* 612/379-4069. Hrs: 9 am-9 pm; Fri, Sat to 10 pm. Closed Tues; Easter, Thanksgiving, Dec 25. Lebanese menu. Semi-a la carte: lunch, dinner $4.50-$7.50. Specialties: spinach pie, tabooleh salad. Parking. No cr cds accepted.

KHAN'S MONGOLIAN BARBEQUE. *418 13th Ave SE, downtown.* 612/379-3121. Hrs: 11 am-9:30 pm; Sat noon-10 pm; Sun 4-9 pm; early-bird dinner 4-6 pm. Closed Thanksgiving, Dec 25. Res accepted. Mongolian menu. Bar. Buffet: lunch $5.95, dinner $9.50. Specializes in barbecued meat, shrimp & crab. Salad bar. Oriental decor. Cr cds: A, MC, V.

LINCOLN DELI. *(4100 W Lake St, St Louis Park) Approx 3 mi S on MN 100.* 612/927-9738. Hrs: 7 am-midnight; Fri, Sat to 1 am; Sun 8 am-midnight. Closed Dec 25. Semi-a la carte: bkfst $2-$5, lunch $4-$8, dinner $6-$11. Specializes in corned beef. Parking. New York-style deli. Cr cds: D, MC, V.

LORING CAFE. *1624 Harmon Place, adj Loring Playhouse Theatre, downtown.* 612/332-1617. Hrs: 11:30 am-3:30 pm, 5:30-11 pm; Fri, Sat 11:30 am-3 pm, 4 pm-midnight; Sun 11:30 am-3 pm, 5:30-11 pm. Closed Dec 24, 25. Res accepted. Bar. Semi-a la carte: lunch $9-$15, dinner $12-$25. Specialties: shrimp with pears, manicotti with lamb & cheese. Entertainment. Outdoor dining. Restored 1918 building. Eclectic decor. Cr cds: MC, V.

MARKET BAR-B-QUE. *1414 Nicollet Ave S, in Nicollet Ave Mall Area.* 612/872-1111. Hrs: 11:30-2:30 am; Sun noon-midnight. Bar. Semi-a la carte: lunch $5-$9, dinner $9-$15.95. Specializes in barbecued chicken, ribs, pork. Valet parking. 1930s cafe atmosphere. Cr cds: A, C, D, DS, MC, V.

MUD PIE. *2549 Lyndale Ave S, south of downtown.* 612/872-9435. Hrs: 11 am-10 pm; Sat, Sun from 8 am. Closed major hols. Vegetarian menu. Wine, beer. Semi-a la carte: bkfst $2-$4.50, lunch $4-$12, dinner $7-$15. Outdoor dining. Cr cds: A, MC, V.

St Paul

ST PAUL RESTAURANTS
BY NEIGHBORHOOD AREAS

(For full description, see alphabetical listings under Restaurants)

DOWNTOWN

Gallivan's. 354 Wabasha St

Leeann Chin Chinese Cuisine. 214 E 4th St

Mancini's Char House. 531 W 7th St

NORTH OF DOWNTOWN

Dakota Bar And Grill. 1021 E Bandana

Muffuletta In The Park. 2260 Como Ave

Napoli. 1406 White Bear Ave

Toby's On The Lake. 249 Geneva Ave N

WEST OF DOWNTOWN

Caravan Serai. 2175 Ford Pkwy

Cecil's Delicatessen, Bakery & Restaurant. 651 S Cleveland

Forepaugh's. 276 S Exchange St

Khyber Pass Cafe. 1399 St Clair Ave

Old City Cafe. 1571 Grand Ave

W.A. Frost & Company. 374 Selby Ave

SUMMIT HILL

Cafe Latté Cafeteria. 850 Grand Ave

Ciatti's. 850 Grand Ave

Dixie's. 695 Grand Ave

Green Mill Inn. 57 S Hamline Ave

Lexington. 1096 Grand Ave

Note: *When a listing is located in a town that does not have its own city heading, it will appear under the city nearest to its location. In these cases, the address and town appear in parenthesis immediately following the name of the establishment.*

Motels

★ ★ **BEST WESTERN MAPLEWOOD INN.** *1780 E County Road D (55109), adj to Maplewood Mall, north of downtown.* 612/770-2811; FAX 612/770-2811, ext. 184. 118 rms, 2 story. S $54-$62; D $58-$64; each addl $4; under 18 free. Crib free. TV; cable. Indoor pool; whirlpool, sauna. Restaurant 6:30 am-2 pm, 5-10 pm. Rm serv. Bar 4 pm-1 am; entertainment Thurs-Sat. Ck-out noon. Coin lndry. Meeting rms. Valet serv. Sundries. Game rm. Cr cds: A, C, D, DS, ER, JCB, MC, V.

[D] [symbols] [SC]

✔ ★ **EXEL INN.** *1739 Old Hudson Rd (55106).* 612/771-5566; FAX 612/771-1262. 100 rms, 3 story. S $34.99-$44.99; D $39.99-$49.99; each addl $5; under 18 free; ski, wkly plans; higher rates special events. Crib free. TV; cable. Complimentary continental bkfst. Restaurant adj open 24 hrs. Ck-out noon. Coin lndry. Downhill ski 15 mi; x-country 2 mi. Game rm. Refrigerators avail. Cr cds: A, C, D, DS, MC, V.

[D] [symbols] [SC]

★ ★ **HOLIDAY INN EXPRESS.** *1010 Bandana Blvd W (55108), north of downtown.* 612/647-1637; FAX 612/647-0244. 109 rms, 2 story. S $64-$79; D $69-$87; suites $85-$125. Crib free. TV; in-rm movies avail. Indoor pool; wading pool, whirlpool, sauna. Complimentary continental bkfst. Ck-out noon. Meeting rms. Valet serv. Downhill ski 15 mi; x-country ski 1 mi. Some refrigerators. Motel built within exterior structure of old railroad repair building; old track runs through lobby. Shopping center adj; connected by skywalk. Cr cds: A, C, D, DS, ER, MC, V.

[D] [symbols] [SC]

★ ★ **HOLIDAY INN SOUTH.** *(701 S Concord St, South St Paul 55075) At jct I-494 & Concord St.* 612/455-3600. 85 rms, 4 story. S $70-$80; D $80-$90; each addl $10; under 19 free. Crib free. TV; cable. Indoor pool; whirlpool, sauna. Complimentary continental bkfst.

Restaurant 6:30 am-10 pm; Sun from 8 am. Rm serv. Bar 11-1 am. Ck-out noon. Meeting rms. Valet serv. Sundries. Airport, bus depot transportation. Cr cds: A, C, D, DS, MC, V.

✔★ **NORTHRIDGE EMERALD INN.** *(1125 Red Fox Rd, Arden Hills 55112)* N on I-35E, then W on I-694, N on I-35W. 612/484-6557. 66 rms, 3 story. S $34; D $38-$41; each addl $3; suites $59; under 16 free. Crib free. TV; cable. Complimentary coffee. Ck-out 11 am. Cr cds: A, C, D, DS, MC, V.

✔★ **RED ROOF INN.** *(1806 Wooddale Dr, Woodbury 55125)* I-494 at Valley Creek Rd. 612/738-7160; FAX 612/738-1869. 109 rms, 2 story. S $28.99-$51.99; D $38.99-$65.99; each addl $7; under 18 free. Crib free. Pet accepted. TV; cable. Complimentary coffee. Restaurant nearby. Ck-out noon. Downhill ski 15 mi; x-country ski 3 mi. Cr cds: A, C, D, DS, MC, V.

★ **SUPER 8.** *(285 N Century Ave, Maplewood 55119)* 612/738-1600; FAX 612/738-9405. 112 rms, 4 story. Late May-early Sept: S $44.88-$52.88; D $51.88-$64.88; each addl $5; suites $79.88; under 12 free; lower rates rest of yr. Crib free. Pet accepted; $50. TV; cable. Complimentary bkfst. Restaurant adj. Ck-out 11 am. Coin lndry. Sundries. Downhill ski 15 mi; x-country ski 2 mi. Picnic tables. On lake. Cr cds: A, C, D, DS, MC, V.

Motor Hotels

★★ **BEST WESTERN KELLY INN.** *161 St Anthony Blvd (55103),* I-94 exit Marion St, west of downtown. 612/227-8711; FAX 612/227-1698. 127 rms, 7 story. S $63; D $73; each addl $8; suites $110-$160; under 15 free; higher rates sports tournaments. Crib free. Pet accepted. TV. Indoor pool; wading pool, whirlpool, sauna. Restaurant 6:30 am-9 pm. Rm serv. Bar 11-1 am; Sat 4 pm-midnight; Sun 4-10 pm. Meeting rms. Sundries. Valet serv. Airport transportation. Downhill ski 20 mi; x-country ski 4 mi. Game rm. Cr cds: A, C, D, DS, MC, V.

★ **DAYS INN CIVIC CENTER.** *175 W 7th St (55102),* at Kellogg, opp St Paul Civic Center, downtown. 612/292-8929; res: 800/635-4766; FAX 612/292-1749. 203 rms, 8 story. S $58; D $66; each addl $8; suites $90-$125; under 18 free; wkend rates; higher rates state tournament wkends. Crib free. Pet accepted. TV; cable. Restaurant open 24 hrs. Bar 3 pm-1 am. Ck-out 11 am. Meeting rms. Valet serv. Airport, bus depot transportation. Downhill ski 20 mi; x-country ski 4 mi. Cr cds: A, C, D, DS, ER, MC, V.

★★★ **HOLIDAY INN-EAST.** *2201 Burns Ave (55119),* I-94 & McKnight Rd, east of downtown. 612/731-2220; FAX 612/731-0243. 192 rms, 8 story. S $76-$81; D $83-$88; each addl $7; under 19 free; wkend rates. Crib free. TV; cable, in-rm movies avail. Indoor pool. Restaurant 6 am-10 pm; Sat, Sun from 7 am. Rm serv. Bar 11-1 am; entertainment exc Sun, dancing. Ck-out noon. Coin lndry. Meeting rms. Bellhops. Valet serv. Sundries. Gift shop. Airport transportation. Downhill ski 10 mi; x-country ski 1/2 mi. Exercise equipt; weights, bicycles, whirlpool, sauna. Game rm. Some bathroom phones. *LUXURY LEVEL :* **V.I.P.** 89 rms, 3 floors. S $86; D $93. Private lounge. Complimentary bkfst, refreshments, newspaper. Cr cds: A, C, D, DS, JCB, MC, V.

★★★ **SHERATON MIDWAY.** *400 Hamline Ave N (55104),* west of downtown. 612/642-1234; FAX 612/642-1126. 197 rms, 4 story. S $83-$95; D $93-$105; each addl $10; under 18 free; wkend rates. Crib free. TV; cable. Indoor pool; poolside serv. Complimentary coffee in rms. Restaurant 6:30 am-10:30 pm. Rm serv. Bar 11-1 am,

Sun from noon; entertainment, dancing. Ck-out noon. Meeting rms. Bellhops. Downhill ski 15 mi; x-country ski 7 mi. Exercise equipt; weights, bicycles, whirlpool, sauna. Cr cds: A, C, D, DS, MC, V.

Hotels

★★★ **CROWN STERLING SUITES.** *175 E 10th St (55101), downtown.* 612/224-5400; FAX 612/224-0957. 210 kit. suites, 8 story. S, D $122; each addl $10; under 12 free; wkend, hol rates. Crib free. Pet accepted, some restrictions. TV; cable, in-rm movies avail. Indoor pool; whirlpool, sauna, steam rm. Complimentary full bkfst. Coffee in rms. Restaurant 11 am-10 pm. Bar to 1 am. Ck-out 1 pm. Meeting rms. Gift shop. Free airport transportation. Downhill ski 15 mi; x-country ski 3 mi. Refrigerators, wet bars. Atrium with pond, waterfalls, fountains, ducks; many plants and trees. Cr cds: A, C, D, DS, ER, MC, V.

★★ **HOLIDAY INN-AIRPORT.** *(2700 Pilot Knob Rd, Eagan 55121)* SW on I-494. 612/454-3434; FAX 612/454-4904. 187 rms, 6 story. S $75-$95; D $85-$105; each addl $10; suites $125-$135; under 20 free. Crib free. TV; cable. Indoor pool. Restaurant 7 am-11 pm. Bar. Ck-out noon. Coin lndry. Meeting rms. Free airport, Mall of America transportation. Exercise equipt; weight machine, bicycles, whirlpool, sauna. Cr cds: A, C, D, DS, JCB, MC, V.

★★★ **RADISSON.** *11 E Kellogg Blvd (55101), downtown.* 612/292-1900; FAX 612/224-8999. 475 rms, 22 story. S $92; D $107; each addl $10; suites $105-$200; under 18 free; package plans. Crib free. Pet accepted, some restrictions. Garage parking $7-$11. TV. Indoor pool. Restaurants 6:30 am-10 pm. Bars 11:30-1 am. Ck-out noon. Convention facilities. Airport transportation. Downhill ski 15 mi; x-country ski 4 mi. Exercise equipt; weight machine, treadmill, whirlpool. Some refrigerators. Indoor skyway to major stores, businesses. Outdoor sunning terrace. *LUXURY LEVEL :* **EXECUTIVE SUITES.** 15 suites. S $105; D $175; each addl $20. Complimentary bkfst, refreshments. Cr cds: A, C, D, DS, ER, MC, V.

★★★ **THE SAINT PAUL HOTEL.** *350 Market St (55102), downtown.* 612/292-9292; res: 800/292-9292; FAX 612/228-9506. 254 rms, 12 story. S, D $139-$154; each addl $15; suites $425-$650; under 19 free; wkend rates; package plans. Crib free. Garage $9.50. TV; cable. Restaurant 6:30 am-11 pm. Bar 11-1 am. Ck-out noon. Meeting rms. Concierge. Downhill ski 15 mi; x-country ski 4 mi. Exercise equipt; bicycles, stair machine; equipt delivered to rms on request. Health club privileges. Airport, RR station, bus depot transportation. Connected to downtown skyway system. Cr cds: A, C, D, DS, MC, V.

Restaurants

✔★★ **CARAVAN SERAI.** *2175 Ford Pkwy, west of downtown.* 612/690-1935. Hrs: 11 am-2 pm, 5-9:30 pm; Fri to 10:30 pm; Sat 5-10:30 pm; Sun 4:30-9:30 pm; early-bird dinner Sun-Thurs 5-6 pm. Closed most major hols. Res accepted. Afghani, Northern Indian menu. Wine, beer. Semi-a la carte: lunch $3.25-$5.95, dinner $7.95-$15.95. Child's meals. Specialties: tandoori chicken, vegetarian combination platter. Guitarist, Egyptian dancers, tabla drumming Tues, Thurs-Sat. Hand-crafted tapestries, floor seating. Cr cds: A, C, D, MC, V.

★★ **CIATTI'S.** *850 Grand Ave, in Summit Hill.* 612/292-9942. Hrs: 11 am-10 pm; Fri & Sat to 11 pm; Sun from 2:30 pm; Sun brunch 10 am-2 pm. Closed Thanksgiving, Dec 24, 25. Italian menu. Res accepted. Bar to 1 am. Semi-a la carte: lunch $5.79-$8.99, dinner $6.95-$14.95. Sun brunch $8.95. Child's meals. Specializes in northern Italian dishes. Own sauces. Cr cds: A, D, DS, MC, V.

★ ★ **DAKOTA BAR AND GRILL.** *1021 E Bandana, north of downtown.* 612/642-1442. Hrs: 5:30-10:30 pm; Fri, Sat to 11:30 pm; Sat, Sun to 9:30 pm; Sun brunch 10 am-2 pm. Closed most major hols. Res accepted. Bar 4 pm-midnight; Fri, Sat to 1 am. Semi-a la carte: dinner $13-$22. Sun brunch $5.50-$12.50. Child's meals. Specializes in regional and seasonal dishes. Jazz evenings. Parking. Outdoor dining. Located in restored railroad building in historic Bandana Square. Modern decor. Cr cds: A, D, DS, MC, V.

D

★ **DIXIE'S.** *695 Grand Ave, in Summit Hill.* 612/222-7345. Hrs: 11 am-midnight; Sun 2:30-11 pm; Sun brunch 10 am-2 pm. Closed Thanksgiving. Res accepted. Southern, Cajun menu. Bar to 1 am; Sun to midnight. Semi-a la carte: lunch $4.50-$12.95, dinner $4.95-$15.95. Sun brunch $9.95. Specialties; hickory-smoked ribs, Key lime pie. Parking. Informal dining. Cr cds: A, D, DS, MC, V.

D

★ ★ ★ **FOREPAUGH'S.** *276 S Exchange St, west of downtown.* 612/224-5606. Hrs: 11:30 am-2 pm, 5:30-9:30 pm; Sat from 5:30 pm; Sun 5-8:30 pm; Sun brunch 10:30 am-1:30 pm. Closed some hols. Res accepted. French menu. Bar to 1 am; Sun to 10 pm. Semi-a la carte: lunch $6.25-$8.75, dinner $11.95-$17.75. Sun brunch $11.75. Child's meals. Specialties: shrimp scampi, twin tournedos, veal calvados. Valet parking. Outdoor dining. Restored mansion (1870); 9 dining rms. Cr cds: A, MC, V.

D

★ ★ **GALLIVAN'S.** *354 Wabasha St, downtown.* 612/227-6688. Hrs: 11 am-10 pm; Fri, Sat to 11 pm. Closed Sun; major hols. Res accepted. Bar to 1 am. Semi-a la carte: lunch $3.95-$8.45, dinner $8.95-$19.95. Specializes in steak, prime rib, seafood. Entertainment Thurs-Sat. Cr cds: A, C, D, DS, MC, V.

D

✔ ★ **KHYBER PASS CAFE.** *1399 St Clair Ave (55105).* 612/698-5403. Hrs: 11 am-2 pm, 5-9 pm. Closed Sun & Mon; Thanksgiving, Dec 25. Res accepted. Afghani menu. Wine, beer. Semi-a la carte: lunch $4.95-$7.25, dinner $6.95-$11.25. Specializes in vegetarian dishes, lamb. Live entertainment Fri. Afghani decor. Totally nonsmoking. No cr cds accepted.

✔ ★ ★ **LEEANN CHIN CHINESE CUISINE.** *214 E 4th St, downtown.* 612/224-8814. Hrs: 11 am-2:30 pm, 5-9 pm; Fri, Sat to 10 pm. Closed major hols. Res accepted. Chinese menu. Serv bar. Buffet: lunch $7.95, dinner $12.95. Child's meals. Specializes in Cantonese, mandarin and Szechwan dishes. Valet parking wkend evenings. Contemporary decor. Totally nonsmoking. Cr cds: A, MC, V.

D

★ ★ **LEXINGTON.** *1096 Grand Ave, at Lexington Pkwy, in Summit Hill.* 612/222-5878. Hrs: 11 am-10 pm; Fri, Sat to midnight; Sun 4-9 pm; Sun brunch 10 am-3 pm. Closed Dec 24 eve-Dec 25. Res accepted. Bar to 1 am. Semi-a la carte: lunch $6-$11.25, dinner $8.95-$25. Sun brunch $4.95-$10.95. Child's meals. Specializes in prime rib, fresh walleyed pike. Parking. French Provincial decor. Cr cds: A, C, D, MC, V.

D

★ ★ **MANCINI'S CHAR HOUSE.** *531 W 7th St, downtown.* 612/224-7345. Hrs: 5-11 pm; Fri, Sat to 12:30 am. Closed major hols exc Easter. Bar to 1 am. Semi-a la carte: dinner $9.95-$28. Specializes in steak, lobster. Entertainment Wed-Sat. Limited menu, 9 entrees. Parking. Open charcoal hearths; 2 fireplaces. Family-owned. Cr cds: A, C, D, MC, V.

D

★ ★ **MUFFULETTA IN THE PARK.** *2260 Como Ave, north of downtown.* 612/644-9116. Hrs: 11 am-3 pm, 5-10 pm, Sat 11 am-3 pm, 5-10 pm; Sun (after Memorial Day-Labor Day) 5-9 pm; Sun brunch 10 am-2 pm. Closed some major hols. Res accepted. French, Italian, Asian, Amer menu. Wine, beer. Semi-a la carte: lunch $4.95-$8.95,

dinner $7.95-$15.95. Sun brunch $5.25-$9.95. Specializes in fettucine, fresh fish. Own pasta, soup. Parking. Outdoor dining. Cafe decor. Cr cds: A, D, DS, MC, V.

✔ ★ **NAPOLI.** *1406 White Bear Ave, north of downtown.* 612/778-0486. Hrs: 11 am-9 pm; Fri, Sat to 10 pm. Closed most major hols. Italian, Amer menu. Serv bar. Semi-a la carte: lunch $4-$9, dinner $5-$9.50. Specializes in Sicilian dishes. Cr cds: A, MC, V.

★ ★ **TOBY'S ON THE LAKE.** *249 Geneva Ave N, on Tanners Lake, north of downtown.* 612/739-1600. Hrs: 11 am-2:30 pm, 5-10 pm; Sat 11 am-11 pm; Sun 11 am-9 pm; Sun brunch to 2 pm. Closed Dec 25. Res accepted. Bar. Semi-a la carte: lunch $5.25-$9.95, dinner $8.95-$19.50. Sun brunch $5.95-$7.95. Child's meals. Specializes in prime rib, fresh seafood. Parking. Outdoor dining. English pub atmosphere. Overlooks Tanners Lake. Cr cds: A, C, D, DS, MC, V.

D

★ ★ ★ **VENETIAN INN.** *(2814 Rice St, Little Canada) S of I-694 Rice St exit.* 612/484-7215. Hrs: 11 am-10 pm; Fri & Sat to 11 pm. Closed Sun; most major hols. Res accepted. Italian, Amer menu. Bar to 1 am. Semi-a la carte: lunch $6.50-$8.50, dinner $7.95-$17.95. Complete meals: Sicilian dinner (for 2 or more) $22.50. Child's meals. Specializes in steak, barbecued ribs, lasagne. Live theatre entertainment Thurs-Sat. Parking. Family-owned. Cr cds: A, C, D, DS, MC, V.

D

★ ★ **W.A. FROST & COMPANY.** *374 Selby Ave (55102), west of downtown.* 612/224-5715. Hrs: 11-1 am; Sun 10:30 am-midnight; Sun brunch to 2 pm. Closed some major hols. Res accepted. Bar. Semi-a la carte: lunch $7-$11, dinner $6.95-$19.95. Sun brunch $5-$10. Child's meals. Specialties: Nantucket chicken, chocolate silk pie. Parking. Outdoor dining in garden area. Three dining rms; Victorian-style decor. Renovated pharmacy (1887). Totally nonsmoking. Cr cds: A, C, D, DS, MC, V.

D

Unrated Dining Spots

CAFE LATTÉ CAFETERIA. *850 Grand Ave, in Summit Hill.* 612/224-5687. Hrs: 10 am-11 pm; Fri to midnight; Sat 9 am-midnight; Sun 9 am-10 pm. Closed major hols. Continental menu. Wine, beer. Avg check: bkfst $2.50-$5.75, lunch, dinner $3.50-$8.50. Specializes in desserts, espresso. Own soup. Ultra-modern decor; chrome, neon. Cr cds: A.

D

CECIL'S DELICATESSEN, BAKERY & RESTAURANT. *651 S Cleveland, west of downtown.* 612/698-0334. Hrs: 9 am-8 pm. Semi-a la carte: bkfst $1.75-$4.50, lunch, dinner $3-$6.50. Specializes in corned beef, pastrami sandwiches, homemade desserts. Own baking, soups. Parking. Family-owned. Cr cds: MC, V.

GREEN MILL INN. *57 S Hamline Ave, in Summit Hill.* 612/698-0353. Hrs: 11 am-11 pm; Fri, Sat to midnight. Closed Dec 24 eve-Dec 25. Italian, Amer menu. Wine, beer. Semi-a la carte: lunch, dinner $2.95-$10.75. Specializes in deep dish pizza, sandwiches. Own soups, chili. Cr cds: A, D, MC, V.

D

OLD CITY CAFE. *1571 Grand Ave (55105), west of downtown.* 612/699-5347. Hrs: 7:30 am-8:30 pm; Fri to 2 pm; Sun from 10 am. Closed Sat; major Jewish hols. Wine, beer. A la carte entrees: bkfst $1.25-$4.95, lunch $1.50-$4.95, dinner $3.50-$7.50. Specializes in kosher deli fare, Middle Eastern salads, Yemenite rice. Informal neighborhood deli with Middle Eastern decor. No cr cds accepted.

D **SC**

Bloomington

Motels

★ ★ ★ **BEST WESTERN THUNDERBIRD.** *2201 E 78th St (55425).* 612/854-3411; FAX 612/854-1183. 263 rms, 2 story. S $78-$86; D $84-$92; each addl $6; suites $125-$350; under 12 free. Crib free. TV; cable. 2 pools, 1 indoor. Restaurant 6:30 am-10:30 pm. Rm serv. Bar 11:30-1 am; entertainment, dancing Fri & Sat. Ck-out 11 am. Meeting rms. Valet serv. Sundries. Gift shop. Free airport transportation. Downhill ski 10 mi; x-country ski 1 mi. Exercise equipt; weights, bicycles, whirlpool, sauna. Game rm. Refrigerators. Cr cds: A, C, D, DS, ER, JCB, MC, V.

✔ ★ **BUDGETEL INN.** *7815 Nicollet Ave S (55420).* 612/881-7311; FAX 612/881-0604. 190 rms, 2 story. S $45.95-$49.95; D $52.95-$57.95; under 18 free. Crib free. Pet accepted, some restrictions. TV; cable. Restaurant adj. Ck-out noon. Meeting rms. Free airport transportation. Downhill ski 10 mi; x-country ski 1/2 mi. Cr cds: A, C, D, DS, MC, V.

★ **EXEL INN.** *2701 E 78th St (55425), near Minneapolis/St Paul Intl Airport.* 612/854-7200; FAX 612/854-8652. 204 rms, 2 story. S $43.99-$53.99; D $50.99-$60.99; under 18 free. Crib free. TV; cable. Complimentary continental bkfst, coffee. Restaurant nearby. Ck-out noon. Sundries. Free airport transportation. Downhill ski 10 mi; x-country ski 2 mi. Cr cds: A, C, D, DS, MC, V.

★ ★ **FANTASUITE.** *(250 N River Ridge Circle, Burnsville 55337)* S on I-35. 612/890-9550; res: 800/666-7829; FAX 612/890-5161. 94 rms, 2 story, 23 suites. May-Oct: S $45; D $95; each addl $8; under 18 free; lower rates rest of yr. Crib free. TV; cable. Indoor/outdoor pool; whirlpool. Restaurant 7-10 am. Rm serv evenings. Bar. Ck-out noon. Meeting rms. Balconies. Suites decorated in different themes. Cr cds: A, C, D, DS, MC, V.

★ ★ **HAMPTON INN.** *4201 W 80th St (55437).* 612/835-6643; FAX 612/835-7217. 135 rms, 4 story. S $59-$69; D $67-$79; each addl $8; suites $69-$83; under 18 free. Crib free. TV; cable. Complimentary continental bkfst. Restaurant adj open 24 hrs. Ck-out noon. Meeting rms. Valet serv. Free airport, Mall of America transportation. Downhill/x-country ski 2 mi. Private balconies. Cr cds: A, C, D, DS, ER, JCB, MC, V.

★ ★ **HOLIDAY INN EXPRESS-AIRPORT.** *814 E 79th St (55420).* 612/854-5558; FAX 612/854-4623. 142 rms, 4 story. S $65-$69; D $73-$77; each addl $8; suites $79; under 18 free. Crib free. TV; cable. Complimentary continental bkfst. Restaurant open 24 hrs. Ck-out noon. Free airport transportation. Downhill ski 15 mi; x-country ski 2 mi. Refrigerator in suites. Cr cds: A, C, D, DS, ER, MC, V.

★ ★ **RESIDENCE INN BY MARRIOTT.** *(7780 Flying Cloud Dr, Eden Prairie 55344)* W on I-494. 612/829-0033; FAX 612/829-1935. 126 kit. suites, 1-2 story. S, D $79-$109; under 18 free. TV; cable. Heated pool; whirlpool. Complimentary buffet bkfst 6:30-9:30 am; Sat, Sun 7:30-10 am. Ck-out noon. Coin lndry. Meeting rms. Valet serv. Airport transportation. Downhill ski 10 mi; x-country ski 1 mi. Refrigerators; some bathrm phones. Private patios, balconies. Cr cds: A, C, D, DS, JCB, MC, V.

✔ ★ **SELECT INN.** *7851 Normandale Blvd (55435).* 612/835-7400; res: 800/641-1000; FAX 612/835-4124. 148 rms, 2 story. S $38.90; D $43.90; each addl $6; under 13 free. Crib $3. Pet accepted; $25. TV; cable. Indoor pool. Complimentary coffee in rms. Restaurant nearby. Ck-out 11 am. Coin lndry. Meeting rms. Downhill ski 5 mi. Cr cds: A, C, D, DS, MC, V.

✔ ★ **SUPER 8.** *(11500 W 78th St, Eden Prairie 55344)* W on I-494 to US 169. 612/829-0888; FAX 612/829-0854. 63 rms, 3 story. No elvtr. S $39.88; D $45.88-$49.88; each addl $5; under 12 free. TV; cable. Complimentary coffee in lobby. Ck-out 11 am. Coin lndry. Downhill/x-country ski 5 mi. Cr cds: A, C, D, DS, MC, V.

Motor Hotels

★ ★ **COMFORT INN.** *1321 E 78th St (55425).* 612/854-3400; FAX 612/854-2234. 276 rms, 5 story. S $58-$75; D $65-$75; each addl $7; suites $95; under 17 free. Crib free. TV. Indoor pool. Coffee in rms. Restaurant 6-11 am, 5-10 pm; Sat 7 am-midnight; Sun 8 am-10 pm. Bar 11-1 am. Ck-out 11 am. Meeting rms. Valet serv. Sundries. Free airport transportation. Downhill ski 10 mi; x-country ski 1 mi. Cr cds: A, C, D, DS, ER, JCB, MC, V.

✔ ★ ★ **HOLIDAY INN CENTRAL.** *1201 W 94th St (55431).* 612/884-8211; FAX 612/881-5574. 172 rms, 4 story. S $69-$77; D $69-$86; under 19 free. Crib avail. TV; cable. Indoor pool; poolside serv. Restaurant 6 am-10 pm. Rm serv. Bar. Ck-out 11 am. Coin lndry. Meeting rms. Sundries. Free airport, Mall of America transportation. Downhill ski 6 mi. Exercise equipt; bicycles, treadmill, sauna, whirlpool. Game rm. Refrigerators avail. Cr cds: A, C, D, DS, MC, V.

★ ★ ★ **MARRIOTT.** *2020 E 79th St (55425), at jct 24th Ave & I-494, near Minneapolis-St Paul Intl Airport.* 612/854-7441; FAX 612/854-7671. 478 rms, 2-5 story. S $115; D $125; under 18 free; wkend rates. Crib free. TV; cable. Indoor pool. Restaurant 6 am-11:30 pm; Sat, Sun 7 am-11 pm. Bar 11-1 am. Ck-out noon. Meeting rms. Gift shop. Free airport, Mall of America transportation. Exercise equipt; bicycles, stair machine, whirlpool, sauna. Game rm. **LUXURY LEVEL: CONCIERGE.** 60 rms, 12 suites. S $124; D $134; suites $145-$155. Private lounge. Complimentary continental bkfst, newspaper, refreshments. Cr cds: A, C, D, DS, ER, JCB, MC, V.

★ ★ ★ **SHERATON AIRPORT.** *2500 E 79th St (55425), near Minneapolis/St Paul Intl Airport.* 612/854-1771; FAX 612/854-5898. 236 rms, 2-4 story. S $95; D $105; suites $115-$135; each addl $5; under 18 free. Crib free. TV; cable. Indoor pool. Restaurant 6 am-10:30 pm; Sat, Sun from 7 am. Rm serv. Bar 11:30-1 am. Ck-out noon. Meeting rms. Valet serv. Sundries. Airport transportation. Exercise equipt; weights, bicycles, whirlpool. Downhill ski 10 mi; x-country ski 2 mi. Game rm. Near Mall of America. Cr cds: A, C, D, DS, ER, JCB, MC, V.

★ ★ **WYNDHAM GARDEN.** *4460 W 78th St Circle (55435).* 612/831-3131; FAX 612/831-6372. 209 rms, 8 story. S $158; D $168; each addl $10; suites $178-$350; under 19 free; wkend rates. Crib $10. TV; cable. Indoor pool. Restaurant 6:30 am-10 pm. Rm serv. Bar. Ck-out noon. Meeting rms. Valet serv. Sundries. Free airport transportation. Exercise equipt; weights, bicycles, whirlpool. Downhill ski 8 mi; x-country ski 2 mi. Wet bar in suites. Cr cds: A, C, D, DS, ER, JCB, MC, V.

Hotels

✔★ ★ **BEST WESTERN BRADBURY SUITES.** *7770 Johnson Ave (55435).* 612/893-9999; FAX 612/893-1316. 126 rms, 6 story. S $64.95-$69.95; D $69.95; each addl $5; under 16 free; wkend rates avail. Crib free. TV; cable. Complimentary buffet bkfst. Restaurant adj. Ck-out noon. Meeting rms. Downhill/x-country ski 1 mi. Exercise equipt; weights, bicycle, whirlpool. Refrigerators. Cr cds: A, C, D, DS, MC, V.

D ⚡ ✈ ⨯ ⚒ SC

✔★ ★ **BEST WESTERN HOTEL SEVILLE.** *8151 Bridge Rd (55437).* 612/830-1300; FAX 612/830-1535. 254 rms, 18 story. S $63; D $71; under 16 free; wkend rates. Crib free. TV. Indoor pool; whirlpool, sauna. Restaurant 6:30-9:30 am, 11:30 am-1:30 pm, 5:30-10 pm; wkend hrs vary. Bar. Ck-out 11 am. Convention facilities. Free airport, Mall of America transportation. Downhill ski 5 mi; x-country ski 1 mi. Game rm. Balconies. Cr cds: A, C, D, DS, MC, V.

D ⚡ ≈ ⨯ ⚒ SC

★ ★ **CROWN STERLING SUITES-AIRPORT.** *7901 34th Ave S (55425), near Minneapolis/St Paul Intl Airport.* 612/854-1000; FAX 612/854-6557. 311 rms, 10 story. S $145; D $155; each addl $10; under 13 free. Crib free. TV; cable. Indoor pool; whirlpool, sauna. Complimentary full bkfst. Restaurant 11 am-10 pm. Bar to 1 am; dancing. Ck-out 1 pm. Meeting rms. Gift shop. Airport, Mall of America transportation. Downhill ski 15 mi; x-country ski 2 mi. Private balconies. All rms open to courtyard atrium. Cr cds: A, C, D, DS, ER, MC, V.

D ⚡ ≈ ✈ ⨯ ⚒ SC

★ ★ **EMBASSY SUITES.** *2800 W 80th (55431).* 612/884-4811; FAX 612/884-8137. 219 rms, 8 story. S, D $149-$219; each addl $10; under 12 free. Crib free. TV; cable. Indoor pool; whirlpool, sauna, steam bath. Complimentary bkfst 6-9:30 am, beverages 5:30-7:30 pm. Restaurant 11:30 am-10 pm. Bar to 1 am. Ck-out noon. Coin lndry. Meeting rms. Free airport transportation. Downhill ski 8 mi; x-country ski 1 mi. Game rm. Refrigerators. Private patios, balconies. Cr cds: A, C, D, DS, JCB, MC, V.

D ⚡ ≈ ⨯ ⚒ SC

★ ★ **HAWTHORN SUITES.** *(3400 Edinborough Way, Edina 55435)* 1/2 mi E of jct MN 100 & I-494. 612/893-9300; FAX 612/893-9885. 141 kit. suites, 7 story. S, D $93-$140; under 18 free; wkend rates. Crib free. TV; cable, in-rm movies. Indoor pool. Playground. Complimentary full bkfst. Complimentary coffee in rms. Restaurant nearby. No rm serv. Ck-out noon. Coin lndry. Meeting rms. Sundries. Free airport transportation. Downhill ski 7 mi; x-country ski 1 mi. Health club privileges. Cr cds: A, C, D, DS, JCB, MC, V.

D ⚡ ≈ ⨰ ⨯ ⚒ SC

★ ★ **HOLIDAY INN-INTERNATIONAL AIRPORT.** *3 Apple Tree Square (55425), I-494 exit 34th Ave, opp river, near Minneapolis/St Paul Intl Airport.* 612/854-9000; FAX 612/854-9000, ext. 3373. 431 rms, 13 story. S $75-$85; D $85-$90; each addl $10; suites $100-$250; under 19 free; wkend plans. Crib free. TV. Indoor pool; poolside serv. Restaurant 6 am-11 pm. Bar 11-1 am. Ck-out noon. Convention facilities. Free covered parking. Free airport transportation. Exercise equipt; weights, bicycles, whirlpool, sauna. Downhill/x-country ski 10 mi. Some refrigerators. Cr cds: A, C, D, DS, ER, JCB, MC, V.

D ⚡ ≈ ⨯ ✈ ⨯ ⚒ SC

★ ★ **MALL OF AMERICA GRAND HOTEL.** *7901 24th Ave S (55425), just off I-494 exit 24th Ave, opp Mall of America, near Minneapolis/St Paul Intl Airport.* 612/854-2244; res: 800/222-8733; FAX 612/854-4421. 321 rms, 15 story. S, D $115-$129; each addl $20;

suites $200-$350; wkend rates. TV; cable. Indoor pool; poolside serv. Restaurants 6 am-11 pm. Rm serv 24 hrs. Bar from 11 am; entertainment, dancing. Ck-out noon. Gift shop. Free airport, Mall of America transportation. Downhill ski 10 mi. Exercise equipt; weights, stair machine, whirlpool, sauna. Some private patios, balconies. *LUXURY LEVEL :* CONCIERGE FLOOR. 18 rms, 1 suite. S, D $129-$145; suite $350-$450. Complimentary bkfst, refreshments. Cr cds: A, C, D, DS, ER, MC, V.

D ⚡ ≈ ⨯ ✈ ⨯ ⚒ SC

★ ★ ★ **RADISSON-SOUTH.** *7800 Normandale Blvd (55435), jct I-94 & MN 100.* 612/835-7800; FAX 612/893-8419. 575 rms, 22 story. S $109; D $119; each addl $15; suites $250-$450; under 18 free; cabañas $109-$119; wkend rates. Crib free. TV. Indoor pool. Restaurant 6:30 am-10 pm. Bar 11-1 am. Ck-out noon. Convention facilities. Shopping arcade. Airport, Mall of America transportation. Downhill/x-country ski 2 mi. Exercise equipt; weights, bicycle, whirlpool, sauna. *LUXURY LEVEL :* PLAZA CLUB. 32 rms. S $129; D $129. Private lounge, honor bar. Complimentary bkfst, refreshments. Cr cds: A, C, D, DS, ER, JCB, MC, V.

D ⚡ ≈ ⨯ ⨯ ⚒ SC

★ ★ ★ **SOFITEL.** *5601 W 78th St (55439), at jct MN 100 & I-494.* 612/835-1900; res: 800/876-6303 (exc MN); FAX 612/835-2696. 282 rms, 6 story. S $129-$139; D $144-$154; each addl $15; suites $175-$375; wkend rates. Crib free. TV. Indoor pool. Restaurant 6:30-1 am (also see LA TERRASSE). Bars 11-1 am, Sun 10 am-midnight. Ck-out noon. Convention facilities. Concierge. Valet parking. Airport, Mall of America transportation. Downhill/x-country ski 1 mi. Excercise equipt; weights, bicycles, sauna. Cr cds: A, C, D, MC, V.

D ⚡ ≈ ⨯ ⨰ ⚒ ⨯

Restaurants

★ **DA AFGHAN.** *929 W 80th St.* 612/888-5824. Hrs: 11 am-2:30 pm, 5-9:30 pm; Fri to 10:30 pm; Sat 5-10:30 pm; Sun 5-9 pm. Closed July 4. Res accepted. Middle Eastern, Greek menu. Wine, beer. Semi-a la carte: lunch $3.95-$8.95, dinner $7.95-$16. Child's meals. Specializes in lamb, chicken, vegetarian dishes. Parking. Cr cds: A, C, D, MC, V.

★ ★ ★ **KINCAID'S.** *8400 Normandale Lake Blvd.* 612/921-2255. Hrs: 11 am-2:30 pm, 5-10 pm; Fri, Sat to 11 pm; Sun 5-9 pm; Sun brunch 10 am-2 pm. Closed July 4, Thanksgiving, Dec 25. Res accepted. Bar to midnight. Semi-a la carte: lunch $5.95-$11.95, dinner $12.95-$25.95. Sun brunch $6.95-$14.95. Child's meals. Specialties: mesquite-grilled king salmon, rock salt prime rib. Own baking, desserts. Parking. Outdoor dining. In 5-story atrium; overlooks Lake Normandale. Cr cds: A, C, D, DS, MC, V.

★ ★ **TOUR CAFE.** *4924 France Ave S.* 612/929-1010. Hrs: 5-10 pm. Closed Sun; most major hols. Res accepted. Continental menu. Wine, beer. A la carte entrees: dinner $15-$25. Specialties: Szechwan salmon, red pepper meatloaf. Dining on 3 levels of remodeled house. Cr cds: A, C, D, MC, V.

Unrated Dining Spot

★ **LA TERRASSE.** *(See Sofitel Hotel)* 612/835-1900. Hrs: 11 am-midnight; Fri-Sat to 1 am; Sun 10:30 am-midnight; Sun brunch to 2:30 pm. French menu. Bar to 1 am. Semi-a la carte: lunch, dinner $5.75-$11.50. Sun brunch $8.50. Specializes in onion soup, seasonal French dishes. Valet parking. Outdoor dining. Cr cds: A, C, D, MC, V.

Nashville

Settled: 1779

Pop: 488,374

Elev: 440 feet

Time zone: Central

Area code: 615

Commercial center and capital city, Nashville is part Andrew Jackson's Hermitage and part Grand Ole Opry. It is often referred to as the "Athens of the South" because of its many colleges and universities, religious publishing houses and churches. Nashville is also known to many as "Music City USA", the home of country music and many of its stars.

Nashville, located in the heart of the rolling Tennessee hills, cherishes a rich history. Although fur traders came on the scene around 1710, the first settlers arrived in 1779, at what was then called French Lick or Big Salt Lick, along the shore of the Cumberland River. By 1796, Tennessee was part of the Union; 50 years later Nashville was named the permanent capital. In the intervening years the town went through a period of rapid growth. River traffic increased, and the city became a trading center, handling many diverse goods. Early industries included cotton mills and foundries. An early advantage in transportation facilities was later enhanced by the beginning of steamboat service in 1819 and railroad service in 1854.

During the Civil War, Nashville escaped heavy physical damage and even prospered from the Union supply activities. After a severe but short carpetbag rule, the city entered into a new era, leading as a commercial, industrial and financial center. Another surge of growth occurred in 1933 when the Tennessee Valley Authority was created.

Business

Nashville's diversified economy includes many different kinds of goods and services. As the state capital, the city employs a great number of people in federal, state and local government. With its colleges, universities and two teaching hospitals, there is also considerable employment in the educational and medical fields.

Important manufacturing operations include automobiles, printing and publishing, production of automobile and architectural glass, clothing and footwear, food products, chemicals, heating, cooling and transportation equipment. The city is the headquarters for one of the nation's largest life insurance companies and home of one of the largest hospital management companies. Nashville is also a major investment banking center in the South.

And, of course, this is the home of the "Nashville sound", which has made Nashville the premier recording center in North America. Music and its related businesses continue to play a multimillion-dollar tune for the city's economy.

Convention Facilities

Within Nashville are 7 convention halls and auditoriums, with seating capacity ranging from 1,000 to more than 9,000 people and exhibit space ranging from 33,000 square feet to 145,000 square feet. There are 20,104 motel and hotel rooms in the city and environs.

Sports and Recreation

The area's many parks and lakes are paradise for the amateur photographer and for those who simply enjoy the outdoors.

The hills of Tennessee invite nature lovers for leisurely drives and hikes. Within a short driving distance of Nashville are six large lakes and state parks offering many recreational facilities. Old Hickory Lake and J. Percy Priest Reservoir and their recreation areas are ideal spots for fishing, boating or picnicking. More than 5,500 acres of public parks plus numerous playgrounds, golf courses, swimming pools and tennis courts are provided by the city government.

Entertainment

The city provides a wide range of theatrical and concert performances. Several tourist guide publications, including the *Music City Vacation Guide* and special sections in both daily newspapers, give extensive schedules of performances. The several college campuses in town also host many events that are open to the public. Other outstanding facilities include Circle Theater, Chaffin's Barn Dinner Theater, Cheekwood Botanical Gardens and Fine Arts Center and Nashville Academy Theater. While country music is king here, Nashville is also the home of a symphony orchestra as well as professional opera, ballet and repertory companies.

The Tennessee Performing Arts Center is one of the first such facilities in the country. The center also houses the Tennessee State Museum.

For those with a variety of tastes, Printer's Alley, between 3rd and 4th avenues, and historic Market Street, 2nd Ave N, have many clubs and bars featuring live entertainment.

Historical Areas

Andrew Jackson's house, the Hermitage, was built in 1821, on a site chosen by his wife, Rachel. Certified as a national historic landmark, the fine old mansion graces a 660-acre tract of spacious and well-kept grounds near Old Hickory Lake. The grounds include a museum, log cabin, carriage house and formal gardens containing the burial place of Jackson and his wife.

Near the Hermitage is Tulip Grove, the lovely house of Andrew Donelson, who was the private secretary and nephew of President Jackson. It was Donelson who conducted the negotiations for the annexation of Texas. He later became an ambassador to Prussia. The house was built in 1836, during Jackson's presidency.

Travellers' Rest is worth a short side trip, for it was the scene of many political gatherings during the campaign days of Andrew Jackson. The house was built in 1799 by Tennessee's first supreme court judge, John Overton, Jackson's law partner, campaign manager and lifelong friend.

Another lovely mansion, Belle Meade, is also open to the public. This house was one of the most impressive showplaces in the South. Built by General William Giles Harding, it was originally part of a 5,300-acre plantation. Used as headquarters by Confederate General Chalmers during the Battle of Nashville, Belle Meade also was the breeding farm of many Thoroughbred horses, the most famous of which was Iroquois.

Also of interest is the replica of Fort Nashborough, which has been built only blocks from the original site. Within the fort are exhibits of pioneer tools and implements.

Sightseeing

During the spring, summer and fall, the paddle-wheelers *Captain Ann* and *Music City Queen* leave from Riverfront Park Dock and Music Valley Dock for two-hour narrated excursions on the Cumberland River. A guide explains the role of the river in the development of the area.

Just northeast of downtown Nashville is Opryland, a theme park for all ages. There are rides, shops, restaurants and 12 live musical performances, which range from the best of Broadway to the down-home sound of banjos and country music. The rides include a treetop sky trip with a breathtaking view of the Cumberland River, a trip on the old-time Opryland Railroad, a whitewater raft ride and a spin on roller coasters *Wabash Cannonball* and *Chaos*. *General Jackson*, a 300-foot paddle-wheeler, departs from the Opryland docks year-round for day and evening cruises and includes a stage show.

Music is everywhere in Opryland, with many live musical productions, featured bands, singing groups, strolling musicians and the Grand Ole Opry itself. The park's Grand Ole Opry House is the current broadcast site of the nation's oldest continuous radio show. Started in 1925, the show features big-name entertainers and promising newcomers providing the best in country music. The home of the show from 1943 to 1974 was the Ryman Auditorium in downtown Nashville, which is open to the public for tours daily.

General References

Settled: 1779 **Pop:** 488,374 **Elev:** 440 feet **Time zone:** Central **Area code:** 615

Phone Numbers

POLICE & FIRE: 911
FBI: 292-5159 or 901/525-7373
POISON CONTROL CENTER: 322-6435 or 800/288-9999
TIME: 259-2222   **WEATHER:** 244-9393

Information Sources

Nashville Area Chamber of Commerce, 161 4th Ave N, 37219, 259-4700.
Nashville Tourist Information Center, I-65 & James Robertson Pkwy, exit 85, 259-4747.
Department of Parks & Recreation, 862-8400.

Transportation

AIRLINES: American; American Eagle; Delta; Delta Connection; Northwest; Southwest; TWA; United; USAir; USAir Express; and other commuter and regional airlines. For the most current airline schedules and information consult the *Official Airline Guide,* published twice monthly.
AIRPORT: International Airport, 275-1675.

CAR RENTAL AGENCIES: (See Toll-Free Numbers) Alamo 275-1050; Avis 361-1212; Budget 366-0800; Dollar 366-5000; Hertz 361-3131; Thrifty 361-6050.
PUBLIC TRANSPORTATION: Metro Transit Authority, 242-4433.

Newspapers

Nashville Banner; Nashville Business Journal; The Tennessean.

Convention Facilities

The Municipal Auditorium, 417 4th Ave N, 862-6390.
Nashville Convention Center, 601 Commerce St, 742-2000.
State Fairgrounds, off I-65 S on Wedgewood, 862-8980.

Sports & Recreation

Centennial Sportsplex, 25th Ave N, 862-8480.
Herschel Greer Stadium, 534 Chestnut, 242-4371 (Sounds, baseball).
Municipal Auditorium, 417 4th Ave N, 255-PUCK (Knights, ice hockey).

Racetrack

Nashville Motor Raceway, State Fairgrounds, 726-1818.

Cultural Facilities

Theaters

Chaffin's Barn Dinner Theatre, 8204 TN 100, 646-9977.
Circle Players, 505 Deadrick St, 383-7469.
Nashville Academy Theater, 724 2nd Ave S, 254-9103.

Concert Halls

Grand Ole Opry, 2804 Opryland Dr, 6 mi E on I-40, then 4 mi N on Briley Pkwy, 889-3060.
Nashville Municipal Auditorium, 417 4th Ave N, 862-6390.
Starwood Ampitheatre, 3839 Murfreesboro Rd, 641-5800.
Tennessee Performing Arts Center, 505 Deadrick St, 741-7975.

Museums

Country Music Hall of Fame and Museum, 4 Music Square E, 255-5333.
Country Music Wax Museum, 118 16th Ave S, 256-2490.
Cumberland Science Museum, 800 Ridley Blvd, 862-5160.
Jim Reeves Museum, 1023 Joyce Ln, off Gallatin Rd, 226-2065.
Museum of Tobacco Art & History, 800 Harrison St, 271-2349.
Nashville Toy Museum, 2613 McGavock Pike, 883-8870.
Tennessee State Museum, Tennessee Performing Arts Center, 505 Deaderick, 741-2692.

Points of Interest

Historical

Belle Meade, 5025 Harding Rd, 7 mi SW, 356-0501.
Fort Nashborough, 170 1st Ave N, 255-8192.
The Hermitage and Tulip Grove, 12 mi E off I-40, The Hermitage exit, 889-2941.
The Parthenon, Centennial Park, West End Ave & 25th Ave N, 862-8431.
Ryman Auditorium, 116 5th Ave N, 254-1445.
State Capitol, On Capitol Blvd, 741-3011.
Travellers' Rest Historic House, on Farrell Pkwy, 5 mi S off US 31, 832-2962.
The Upper Room, 1908 Grand Ave, 340-7207.

Other Attractions

Car Collectors Hall of Fame, 1534 Demonbreun St, 255-6804.
Cheekwood Museum and Gardens, 1200 Forest Park Dr, 356-8000.
Grand Ole Opry, 2804 Opryland Dr, 889-3060.
J. Percy Priest Lake, 11 mi E off I-40, 889-1975.
Nashville Zoo, 17 mi NW in Joelton, 370-3333.
Opryland, 2808 Opryland Dr, 10 mi E on I-40, then 4 mi N on Briley Pkwy, 889-6611.
Twitty City, Hendersonville, 18 mi N on Gallatin Rd/US 31E, 822-6650.

Sightseeing Tours

Belle Carol Riverboats, Riverfront Park, just off Broadway near Fort Nashborough, 244-3430 or 800/342-2355.
Grand Ole Opry Tours, 2810 Opryland Dr, 889-9490.
Gray Line bus tours, 2416 Music Valley Dr, 883-5555 or 800/251-1864.

Annual Events

Heart of Country Antique Show, Opryland Hotel, 889-1000. Late Jan.

Tennessee Crafts Fair, Centennial Park, 665-0502. Early May.
Iroquois Memorial Steeplechase, Old Hickory Blvd, at entrance to Percy Warner Park, 322-7450. 2nd Sat May.
International Country Music Fan Fair, 889-7503. Early June.
Tennessee State Fair, fairgrounds, 862-8980. Mid- or late Sept.
"Trees of Christmas," Tennessee Botanical Gardens, 353-2150. Dec.

City Neighborhoods

Many of the restaurants, unrated dining establishments and some lodgings listed under Nashville include neighborhoods as well as exact street addresses. Geographic descriptions of these areas are given, followed by a table of restaurants arranged by neighborhood.

Downtown: South of Harrison St, west of I-24/65, north of McGavock St and east of 10th Ave N. **East of Downtown:** East of I-24/I-65. **West of Downtown:** West of I-40.
Music Row: Area includes 16th Ave S from West End Ave to Demonbreun St; Music Square E from South St to Demonbreun St; Music Square W from South St to Division St; and Division and Demonbreun Sts from 18th Ave S to I-40.
Opryland: Area south of McGavock Pike, west of Briley Pkwy (TN 155) and north and east of the Cumberland River.

Lodgings and Food

NASHVILLE RESTAURANTS
BY NEIGHBORHOOD AREAS

(For full description, see alphabetical listings under Restaurants)

DOWNTOWN

Arthur's (Union Station Hotel). 1001 Broadway

Captain's Table. 313½ Church St

Gerst Haus. 228 Woodland St

Jamaica. 1901 Broadway

Mario's. 2005 Broadway

The Merchants. 401 Broadway

Old Spaghetti Factory. 160 2nd Ave N

Prime Cut Steakhouse. 170 2nd Ave N

Stock-Yard. 901 2nd Ave N

Towne House Tea Room & Restaurant. 165 8th Ave N

The Wild Boar. 2014 Broadway

SOUTH OF DOWNTOWN

Belle Meade Brasserie. 101 Page Rd

Santa Fe Steak Co. 902 Murfreesboro Rd

EAST OF DOWNTOWN

101st Airborne. 1362 A Murfreesboro Rd

New Orleans Manor. 1400 Murfreesboro Rd

WEST OF DOWNTOWN

106 Club. 106 Harding Place

Applebee's. 2400 Elliston Pl

Belle Meade Buffet Cafeteria. 4534 Harding Rd

F Scott's. 2210 Crestmoor Dr

Golden Dragon. 81 White Bridge Rd

J Alexander's. 73 White Bridge Rd

Jimmy Kelly's. 217 Louise Ave

Sperry's. 5109 Harding Rd

Valentino's. 1907 West End Ave

OPRYLAND AREA

Cock Of The Walk. 2624 Music Valley Dr

Note: *When a listing is located in a town that does not have its own city heading, it will appear under the city nearest to its location. In these cases, the address and town appear in parenthesis immediately following the name of the establishment.*

Motels

(Rates may be higher during Fan Fair Week)

★ **BUDGETEL INN.** 5612 Lenox Ave (37209), I-40 exit 204, west of downtown. 615/353-0700; FAX 615/352-0361. 110 rms, 3 story. S $46.95-$66.95; D $53.95-$68.95; each addl $7; under 18 free; wkly rates; higher rates special events. Crib free. TV; cable. Pool. Complimentary continental bkfst. Complimentary coffee in rms. Res-

taurant adj 5-1 am. Ck-out noon. Meeting rms. Sundries. Cr cds: A, C, D, DS, MC, V.

D ≋ ⇗ 🔥 SC

✔★ **BUDGETEL INN GOODLETTSVILLE.** (120 Cartwright Court, Goodlettsville 37072) 14 mi N on I 65, at exit 97. 615/851-1891; FAX 615/851-4513. 102 rms, 3 story. Apr-Oct: S $39.95-$45.95; D $40.95-$46.95; each addl $6; under 18 free; lower rates rest of yr. Crib free. Pet accepted, some restrictions. TV; cable. Complimentary continental bkfst, coffee. Restaurant nearby. Ck-out noon. Meeting rm. Valet serv. Sundries. Cr cds: A, C, D, DS, MC, V.

D ✋ ≋ ⇗ 🔥 SC

★★ **CLUBHOUSE INN.** 2435 Atrium Way (37214), east of downtown. 615/883-0500; FAX 615/889-4827. 135 rms, 3 story, 17 suites. Apr-Oct: S $66, D $76; each addl $10; suites $79; under 10 free; wkend rates; lower rates rest of yr. TV; cable. Heated pool; whirlpool. Complimentary full bkfst, coffee. Ck-out noon. Coin lndry. Meeting rms. Valet serv. Free airport transportation. Refrigerator. Balconies. Cr cds: A, C, D, DS, MC.

D ≋ ✈ ⇗ 🔥 SC

★★ **COMFORT INN-NORTH.** 2306 Brick Church Pike (37207), I-65 exit 87B, north of downtown. 615/226-9560. 95 rms, 4 story. Apr-Oct: S $42.95-$48.95; D $48.95-$56.95; each addl $5; under 18 free; lower rates rest of yr. Crib free. Pet accepted. TV; cable. Pool. Complimentary continental bkfst. Restaurant adj open 24 hrs. Ck-out noon. Cr cds: A, C, D, DS, MC, V.

D ✋ ≋ ⇗ 🔥 SC

★★★ **COURTYARD BY MARRIOTT-AIRPORT.** 2508 Elm Hill Pike (37214), near International Airport, east of downtown. 615/883-9500; FAX 615/883-0172. 145 rms, 4 story. S, D $74-$84; suites $88-$98; wkend rates. Crib free. TV; cable. Pool. Complimentary coffee in rms. Restaurant 6:30 am-2 pm. Bar 4-11 pm. Ck-out noon. Coin lndry. Meeting rms. Valet serv. Sundries. Free airport transportation. Exercise equipt; weight machines, bicycles, whirlpool. Refrigerator avail. Some balconies. Cr cds: A, C, D, DS, MC, V.

D ≋ ✈ ⇗ 🔥 SC

✔★ **DAYS INN RIVERGATE.** (809 Wren Rd, Goodlettsville 37072) 12 mi N on I-65, Rivergate exit 96. 615/859-1771. 45 units, 3 story, 25 suites. No elvtr. May-Aug: S, D $35-$55; suites $39.95-$75; each addl $5; under 12 free; wkly rates; lower rates rest of yr. TV; cable. Complimentary continental bkfst, coffee. Restaurant nearby. Ck-out 11 am. Cr cds: A, C, D, DS, MC, V.

D ⇗ 🔥 SC

★★ **ECONO LODGE OPRYLAND.** 2460 Music Valley Dr (37214), in Opryland Area. 615/889-0090. 86 rms, 3 story. May-Oct: S, D $61.95; each addl $5; under 18 free; lower rates rest of yr. Crib free. Pet accepted, some restrictions. TV; cable. Pool. Complimentary coffee in lobby. Restaurant nearby. Ck-out noon. Gift shop. Cr cds: A, C, D, DS, MC, V.

D ≋ ✋ ≋ ⇗ 🔥 SC

✔★ **FIDDLERS INN-NORTH.** 2410 Music Valley Dr (37214), in Opryland Area. 615/885-1440. 202 rms, 2-3 story. Apr-Oct: S $34-$49; D $45-$65; each addl $5; varied lower rates rest of yr. Crib $5. TV. Pool. Restaurant adj 6:30 am-10 pm. Ck-out 11 am. Coin lndry. Sundries. Cr cds: A, DS, MC, V.

≋ ⇗ 🔥

★★ **HAMPTON INN-BRENTWOOD.** (5630 Franklin Pike Circle, Brentwood 37027) S on I-65, exit 74B. 615/373-2212; FAX 615/373-2212, ext. 162. 114 air-cooled rms, 5 story. S $53-$61; D $61-$71; under 18 free. Crib free. TV; cable. Complimentary continental bkfst, coffee in lobby. Restaurant adj 6 am-midnight. Ck-out noon. Meeting rms. Cr cds: A, C, D, DS, MC, V.

D ⇗ 🔥 SC

★ ★ **HoJo INN.** *323 Harding Place (37211), I-24E exit 56, south of downtown.* 615/834-0570; FAX 615/831-2831. 110 rms, 14 suites, 10 kits. May-Sept: S $39; D $45; each addl $3; suites $42-$49; kit. units $49-$55; under 12 free; lower rates rest of yr. Crib free. Pet accepted, some restrictions; $10. TV; cable. Pool. Complimentary continental bkfst, coffee. Restaurant nearby. Ck-out noon. Meeting rm. Free airport transportation. Cr cds: A, C, D, DS, MC, V.

D 🖐 ≈ ✗ 🔥 SC

★ ★ **LA QUINTA.** *2001 Metrocenter Blvd (37228), north of downtown.* 615/259-2130; FAX 615/242-2650. 121 rms, 2 story. S $47-$59; D $53-$65; each addl $7; under 18 free. Crib free. TV; cable. Pool. Complimentary continental bkfst, coffee in lobby. Restaurant adj open 24 hrs. Ck-out noon. Valet serv. Cr cds: A, D, DS, MC, V.

D ≈ ✗ ✗ 🔥 SC

★ ★ **RAMADA INN SUITES.** *2425 Atrium Way (37214), near International Airport, east of downtown.* 615/883-5201; FAX 615/883-5594. 120 suites, 3 story. S, D $58-$110; each addl $6; under 16 free. Crib free. Pet accepted, some restrictions. Pool. Coffee in rms. Complimentary continental bkfst 6:30-8:30 am. Ck-out noon. Coin lndry. Meeting rms. Valet serv. Airport transportation. Refrigerators. Cr cds: A, C, D, DS, JCB, MC, V.

D 🖐 ≈ ✈ ✗ 🔥 SC

✔ ★ **RED ROOF INN.** *510 Claridge St (37214), I-40 exit 216, near International Airport, east of downtown.* 615/872-0735; FAX 615/871-4647. 120 rms, 3 story. Mar-Sept: S $35.99-$41.99; D $41.99-$55.99; each addl $6; under 17 free; lower rates rest of yr. Crib avail. Pet accepted, some restrictions. TV. Complimentary coffee in lobby. Restaurant nearby. Ck-out 11 am. Free airport transportation. Cr cds: A, C, D, DS, MC, V.

D 🖐 ✈ ✗ 🔥

✔ ★ **RED ROOF INN-SOUTH.** *4271 Sidco Dr (37204), at jct I-65 & Harding Pl, south of downtown.* 615/832-0093; FAX 615/832-0097. 85 rms, 3 story. Mar-Sept: S $30-$36; D $38-$48; each addl $8; under 18 free; lower rates rest of yr. Crib free. Pet accepted. TV; cable. Complimentary coffee in lobby. Restaurant nearby. Ck-out 11 am. Cr cds: A, C, D, DS, MC, V.

D 🖐 ✗ 🔥

★ ★ **RESIDENCE INN BY MARRIOTT.** *2300 Elm Hill Pike (37214), near International Airport, east of downtown.* 615/889-8600; FAX 615/871-4970. 168 kit. suites, 2 story. Suites: 1-bedrm studio $86-$106; 2-bedrm penthouse $116-$136. TV; cable. Pool; whirlpool. Complimentary continental bkfst. Ck-out noon. Coin lndry. Meeting rms. Airport transportation. Refrigerators; many fireplaces. Balconies. Cr cds: A, C, D, DS, MC, V.

D ≈ ✈ ✗ 🔥 SC

★ **SHONEY'S INN.** *1521 Demonbreun St (37203), in Music Row.* 615/255-9977; res: 800/222-2222; FAX 615/242-6125. 147 rms, 3 story. S $49-$52; D $59-$66; each addl $6; suites $79-$89; under 18 free; higher rates football games. Crib free. Pet accepted, some restrictions. TV. Pool. Complimentary coffee in lobby. Restaurant adj 6 am-midnight. Ck-out noon. Meeting rms. Airport transportation. Cr cds: A, C, D, DS, ER, MC, V.

D 🖐 ≈ ✗ 🔥 SC

★ **SHONEY'S INN NORTH.** *(100 Northcreek Blvd, Goodlettsville 37072) 13 mi N on I-65, exit 97.* 615/851-1067; res: 800/222-2222; FAX 615/851-6069. 111 rms, 3 story. S $41-$47; D $45-$59; each addl $6; under 17 free. Crib free. TV; cable. Pool. Complimentary coffee in lobby. Restaurant adj 6 am-midnight; Fri & Sat to 2 am. Ck-out noon. Meeting rms. Cr cds: A, C, D, DS, ER, MC, V.

D ≈ ✗ 🔥 SC

★ **SUPER 8.** *412 Robertson Ave (37209), I-40 exit 204, west of downtown.* 615/356-0888; FAX 615/356-0888, ext. 118. 73 rms, 3 story. June-July: S $45-$57; D $59.88-$64.88; each addl $5; suites

$68.88-$70.88; under 12 free; lower rates rest of yr. Crib free. Pet accepted. TV; cable. Complimentary continental bkfst, coffee. Restaurant adj open 24 hrs. Ck-out 11 am. Meeting rm. Cr cds: A, C, D, DS, MC, V.

D 🖐 ✗ 🔥 SC

✔ ★ **TRAVELERS REST INN.** *(107 Franklin Rd, Brentwood 37027) 1 blk W of I-65 exits 74 B, Brentwood, Old Hickory Blvd.* 615/373-3033; res: 800/852-0618. 35 rms, 1-2 story, 2 kits. S $35-$42; D $47-$54; each addl $4; under 18 free. Crib $2. TV; cable. Pool; wading pool. Complimentary coffee in rms. Restaurant nearby. Ck-out noon. Coin lndry. Some refrigerators. Picnic table. Cr cds: A, C, D, DS, MC, V.

≈ ✗ 🔥 SC

Motor Hotels

★ ★ **AMERISUITES.** *220 Rudy's Circle (37214), in Opryland Area.* 615/872-0422; FAX 615/872-9283. 125 suites, 5 story. June-mid-Sept: S, D $76-$98; each addl $6; under 18 free; higher rates special events; lower rates rest of yr. Crib free. TV; cable, in-rm movies. Pool. Complimentary continental bkfst. Complimentary coffee in rms. Restaurant nearby. Ck-out 11 am. Coin lndry. Meeting rms. Bellhops. Valet serv. Free airport, Opryland Hotel transportation. Refrigerators. Cr cds: A, C, D, DS, ER, MC, V.

D ≈ ✗ 🔥 SC

★ ★ **HAMPTON INN-NORTH.** *2407 Brick Church Pike (37207), I-65 exit 87B, north of downtown.* 615/226-3300; FAX 615/226-0170. 125 rms, 5 story. S, D $47-$69; under 18 free; higher rates special events. Crib free. Pet accepted, some restrictions. TV; cable. Pool. Continental bkfst. Restaurant adj 6 am-10 pm. Ck-out noon. Meeting rms. Valet serv. Exercise equipt; weights, bicycles. Game rm. Cr cds: A, C, D, DS, MC, V.

D 🖐 ≈ ✗ ✗ 🔥 SC

★ ★ ★ **HILTON SUITES-BRENTWOOD.** *(9000 Overlook Blvd, Brentwood 37027) S on I-65, exit 74B.* 615/370-0111; FAX 615/370-0272. 203 suites, 4 story. S $104; D $114; each addl $10; family rates. Crib free. Pet accepted, some restrictions. TV; cable. Indoor pool. Coffee in rms. Complimentary full bkfst. Restaurant 6-9:30 am, 11:30 am-1:30 pm, 5-10 pm; Sat, Sun 7-11 am, 5-10 pm. Rm serv from 5 pm. Bar 4 pm-midnight. Ck-out noon. Free lndry facilities. Meeting rms. Gift shop. Exercise equipt; weight machine, bicycles, whirlpool. Rec rm. Refrigerators, wet bars. Balconies. Cr cds: A, C, D, DS, ER, JCB, MC, V.

D 🖐 ≈ ✗ ✗ 🔥

★ ★ ★ **HOLIDAY INN BRENTWOOD.** *(760 Old Hickory Blvd, Brentwood 37027) I-65 exit 74A.* 615/373-2600; FAX 615/377-3893. 248 rms, 8 story. S, D $69-$84; suites $89-$94; under 18 free; wkend rates. Crib free. TV; cable. Pool. Complimentary coffee in rms. Restaurant 6 am-10 pm. Rm serv. Bar 4 pm-midnight. Ck-out noon. Coin lndry. Meeting rms. Bellhops. Gift shop. Valet serv. Free airport transportation. 18-hole golf privileges. Exercise equipt; weight machine, stair machine, whirlpool, sauna. Minibars. Cr cds: A, C, D, DS, MC, V.

D 🏌 ≈ ✗ ✗ 🔥 SC

★ ★ **HOLIDAY INN EXPRESS.** *1111 Airport Center Dr (37214), near International Airport, east of downtown.* 615/883-1366; FAX 615/889-6867. 206 rms, 3 story. Apr-Oct: S, D $59-$68; each addl $8; under 18 free; lower rates rest of yr. Crib free. TV; cable. Pool. Complimentary continental bkfst, coffee. Restaurant nearby. Ck-out noon. Meeting rms. Bellhops. Free airport transportation. Health club privileges. Some balconies. Cr cds: A, C, D, DS, JCB, MC, V.

D ≈ ✈ ✗ 🔥 SC

★ ★ **HOLIDAY INN EXPRESS-NORTH.** *2401 Brick Church Pike (37207), I-65 exit 87B, north of downtown.* 615/226-4600; FAX 615/228-6412. 172 rms, 6 story. Apr-Oct: S $40-$58; D $52-$68; under 18 free; higher rates special events; some lower rates rest of yr. Crib free. TV; cable. Pool. Continental bkfst avail. Ck-out 11 am. Coin lndry. Meeting rms. Exercise equipt; weights, bicycles, sauna. Cr cds: A, C, D, DS, MC, V.

D ≈ ✗ ⊠ 🔥 SC

★ **MEDCENTER INN.** 1909 Hayes St (37203), downtown. 615/329-1000; res. 800/777-4904; FAX 615/329-1000, ext. 107. 107 rms, 7 story. Mar-June: S, D $55-$77; each addl $7; suites $82; under 18 free; varied lower rates rest of yr. Crib free. TV; cable. Complimentary continental bkfst, coffee. Restaurant nearby. Ck-out noon. Coin lndry. Meeting rm. Refrigerators, wet bars. Cr cds: A, C, D, DS, MC, V.

D ⊠ 🔥 SC

✔★ ★ **QUALITY INN EXECUTIVE PLAZA.** 823 Murfreesboro Rd (37217), south of downtown. 615/367-1234; FAX 615/367-7123. 150 air-cooled rms, 4 story. May-Oct: S $44-$55; D $50-$65; each addl $6; under 18 free; lower rates rest of yr. Crib avail. Complimentary continental bkfst. TV; cable. Pool. Restaurant 6 am-1 pm. Bar. Ck-out noon. Coin lndry. Meeting rms. Free airport transportation. Exercise equipt; weight machine, bicycles. Near airport. Cr cds: A, C, D, DS, ER, JCB, MC, V.

D ≈ ✗ ⊠ 🔥 SC

★ ★ **RAMADA INN.** 2401 Music Valley Dr (37214), opp Opryland Area. 615/889-0800; FAX 615/883-1230. 306 rms, 3 story. June-Oct: S, D $82-$98; each addl $8; suites $110-$140; under 18 free; lower rates rest of yr. TV; cable. Heated pool; wading pool, whirlpool, sauna. Restaurant 6 am-10 pm. Rm serv. Bar noon-1 am. Ck-out noon. Meeting rms. Bellhops. Valet serv. Sundries. Gift shop. Airport, Opryland Hotel transportation. Game rm. Cr cds: A, C, D, DS, MC, V.

D ≈ ⊠ 🔥 SC

★ **SHONEY'S INN.** 2420 Music Valley Dr (37214), in Opryland Area. 615/885-4030; res: 800/222-2222; FAX 615/391-0632. 185 rms, 5 story. June-Aug: S $82-$89; D $92-$99; each addl $6; suites $125; under 18 free; higher rates special events; varied rates rest of yr. TV; cable. Indoor pool; whirlpool. Complimentary coffee in rms. Restaurant adj 6-11 am. Bar 4-11 pm. Ck-out 11 am. Meeting rms. Valet serv. Sundries. Gift shop. Free garage parking. Free airport, Opryland Hotel transportation. Cr cds: A, C, D, DS, ER, MC, V.

D ≈ ⊠ 🔥 SC

✔★ **WILSON INN.** 600 Ermac Dr (37214), east of downtown. 615/889-4466; res: 800/333-9457. 110 rms, 5 story, 30 suites. S, D $35.95-$55.95; each addl $7; suites $48.95-$65.95; under 19 free. Crib free. TV; cable. Complimentary continental bkfst, coffee. Restaurant adj open 24 hrs. Ck-out noon. Meeting rms. Refrigerators; wet bar in suites. Cr cds: A, C, D, DS, MC, V.

D ⊠ 🔥 SC

Hotels

★ ★ **CLUBHOUSE INN CONFERENCE CENTER.** 920 Broadway (37203), downtown. 615/244-0150; FAX 615/244-0445. 285 rms, 8 story. S $70-$85; D $80-$90; each addl $10; suites $99-$129; under 12 free. Crib free. TV; cable. Pool. Complimentary full bkfst buffet. Restaurant 5:30-8:30 pm. Ck-out noon. Convention facilities. Gift shop. Free garage parking. Exercise equipt: bicycles, stair machine. Cr cds: A, C, D, DS, MC, V.

D ≈ ✗ ⊠ 🔥 SC

★ ★ **DOUBLETREE.** 315 Fourth Ave N (37219), downtown. 615/244-8200; FAX 615/747-4894. 337 rms, 9 story. S $99-$129; D $119-$149; each addl $10; suites $125-$550; under 18 free; wkend rates. Crib free. Garage $6. TV; cable. Indoor pool. Restaurant 6:30 am-10:30 pm. Bar 4 pm-1 am. Ck-out noon. Meeting rms. Gift shop. Exercise equipt; weights, bicycles, sauna. Wet bar in suites. Cr cds: A, C, D, DS, ER, MC, V.

D ≈ ✗ ⊠ 🔥 SC

★ ★ ★ **EMBASSY SUITES.** 10 Century Blvd (37214), near International Airport, east of downtown. 615/871-0033; FAX 615/883-9245. 295 suites, 9 story. Suites $109-$139; each addl $10; under 17 free; wkend plans. Crib free. Pet accepted, some restrictions. TV; cable. Indoor pool. Supervised child's activities. Complimentary full bkfst. Restaurant 6:30-9:30 am, 11 am-2:30 pm, 5-10 pm; Fri, Sat to 11 pm. Rm serv 11:30 am-11 pm. Bar 4 pm-midnight. Ck-out noon. Convention facilities. Concierge. Gift shop. Free airport transportation. Exercise equipt; weights, bicycles, whirlpool, sauna. Game rm. Refrigerators, wet bars. Atrium. Cr cds: A, C, D, DS, JCB, MC, V.

D 🚗 ≈ ✗ ✈ ⊠ 🔥 SC

★ ★ ★ **GUEST QUARTERS.** 2424 Atrium Way (37214), near International Airport, east of downtown. 615/889-8889; FAX 615/883-7779. 138 suites, 3 story. Mar-Oct: S $145-$165; D $165-$185; each addl $20; under 18 free; lower rates rest of yr. Crib free. TV; cable. Indoor/outdoor pool. Complimentary coffee in rms. Restaurant 6:30 am-10 pm. Bar 11 am-11 pm. Ck-out noon. Meeting rms. Free airport transportation. Exercise equipt; weights, bicycles. Game rm. Refrigerators. Some private patios, balconies. Cr cds: A, C, D, DS, MC, V.

D ≈ ✗ ✈ ⊠ 🔥 SC

★ ★ **THE HERMITAGE.** 231 6th Ave N (37219), downtown. 615/244-3121; res: 800/251-1908 (exc TN), 800/342-1816 (TN); FAX 615/254-6909. 112 suites, 9 story. 1-bedrm suites $95-$135; 2-bedrm suites $125-$160; each addl $10; wkend rates. Valet parking $6.50/day. Pet accepted. TV; cable. Complimentary full bkfst. Dining rm 6:30 am-9 pm. Bars 11 am-10 pm. Ck-out noon. Meeting rms. Health club privileges. Bathrm phones, refrigerators, wet bars. Hotel built in 1910 as a tribute to Beaux Arts Classicism; fully restored to original elegance. Cr cds: A, C, D, DS, ER, JCB, MC, V.

D 🚗 ⊠ 🔥

★ ★ ★ **HOLIDAY INN CROWNE PLAZA.** 623 Union St (37219), opp capitol, downtown. 615/259-2000; FAX 615/742-6056. 477 rms, 28 story. S, D $119-$139; each addl $15; under 18 free; wkend rates. Crib free. Garage $6; valet parking $8. TV; cable. Indoor pool. Restaurant 6:30 am-11 pm. Bars 4 pm-2 am. Ck-out noon. Meeting rms. Concierge. Gift shop. Airport transportation. Exercise equipt; bicycle, treadmill. *LUXURY LEVEL :* **CONCIERGE LEVEL.** 64 rms, 10 suites. S, D $139-$159; suites $250-$650. Private lounge. Complimentary continental bkfst, refreshments. Cr cds: A, C, D, DS, ER, JCB, MC, V.

D ≈ ✗ ⊠ 🔥 SC

★ ★ ★ **LOEWS VANDERBILT PLAZA.** 2100 West End Ave (37203), downtown. 615/320-1700; FAX 615/320-5019. 340 rms, 12 story. S $130-$160; D $150-$180; each addl $20; suites $325-$625; under 18 free. Crib free. Garage $6; valet parking $8. TV; cable. Restaurants 6:30 am-10 pm. Rm serv to midnight; Fri-Sun to 1 am. Bar 3 pm-1 am; entertainment exc Sun. Ck-out noon. Convention facilities. Concierge. Shopping arcade. Barber, beauty shop. Exercise equipt; weights, treadmill. Golf privileges. Minibars. *LUXURY LEVEL :* **PLAZA LEVEL.** 44 rms, 4 suites, 2 floors. S $160; D $180. Private lounge. Complimentary continental bkfst, refreshments. Cr cds: A, C, D, DS, JCB, MC, V.

D ✗ ✗ ⊠ ⊠

★ ★ ★ **MARRIOTT.** 600 Marriott Dr (37214), east of downtown. 615/889-9300; FAX 615/889-9315. 399 rms, 18 story. S $123-$130; D $145-$132; suites $175-$450; under 17 free; wkend plans. TV; cable. Indoor/outdoor pool; poolside serv, lifeguard. Restaurant 6 am-10:30 pm, snacks to midnight. Bar 11-2 am. Ck-out noon. Lndry facilities. Convention facilities. Free parking. Free airport transportation. Lighted tennis. Exercise equipt; weights, machines, bicycles, whirlpool, sauna. Picnic tables, grills. Near Percy Priest Lake. *LUXURY LEVEL :* **CONCIERGE LEVEL.** 38 rms, 2 floors. S $129; D $149. Concierge. Private lounge, honor bar. Complimentary continental bkfst, refreshments, newspapers. Cr cds: A, C, D, DS, ER, JCB, MC, V.

D 🏃 ≈ ✗ ⊠ 🔥 SC

★ ★ ★ **OPRYLAND HOTEL.** *2800 Opryland Dr (37214), 5 mi NE of jct I-40 & Briley Pkwy, in Opryland Area.* 615/889-1000; FAX 615/871-7741. 1,891 rms, 5 story. S, D $199-$239; each addl $15; suites $239-$2,000; under 12 free. Crib free. Valet parking $10. TV; cable. 3 heated pools; wading pools, poolside serv, lifeguard. Supervised child's activities. 7 restaurants 6:30-1 am. Bars 11-2 am; entertainment, dancing. Ck-out 11 am. Convention facilities. Shopping arcades. Barber, beauty shop. Airport, Opryland, Grand Ole Opry transportation. 18-hole golf course, greens fee $50. Exercise rm; instructor, weights, bicycles. Some refrigerators. Bathrm phone in suites. Some balconies overlooking garden conservatory and cascades. Showboat cruises avail. Cr cds: A, C, D, DS, MC, V.

D ⛷ 🏊 ≈ 🎿 ≋ 🔥

★ **RAMADA INN AIRPORT.** *733 Briley Pkwy (37217), I-40 exit 215, east of downtown.* 615/361-5900; FAX 615/367-0339. 200 rms, 11 story. June-Oct: S $54-$60; D $60-$70; each addl $6; suites $85-$95; under 17 free; lower rates rest of yr. Crib free. TV; cable. Pool. Playground. Restaurant 6 am-10 pm. Bars 4 pm-midnight, Fri & Sat to 2 am; entertainment. Ck-out noon. Meeting rms. Free airport transportation. Cr cds: A, C, D, DS, MC, V.

D ≈ ≋ 🔥 SC

★ ★ ★ **REGAL MAXWELL HOUSE.** *2025 Metrocenter Blvd (37228), north of downtown.* 615/259-4343; FAX 615/259-4343, ext. 7127. 289 rms, 10 story. S $98-$124; D $114-$134; each addl $10; suites $165-$395; under 17 free; wkend plans. Crib free. TV; cable. Pool. Restaurants 6:30 am-10 pm. Bar 11 am-midnight. Ck-out noon. Meeting rms. Gift shop. Lighted tennis. Exercise equipt; weight machine, bicycles, whirlpool, sauna, steam rm. **LUXURY LEVEL : REGAL CLUB.** 32 rms, 4 suites. S $114; D $124; suites $165-$395. Concierge. Private lounge. Wet bar in suites. Complimentary bkfst, refreshments, newspaper. Cr cds: A, C, D, DS, ER, JCB, MC, V.

D 🛎 ≈ 🎿 ≋ 🔥 SC

★ ★ ★ **SHERATON-MUSIC CITY.** *777 McGavock Pike (37214), near International Airport, east of downtown.* 615/885-2200; FAX 615/871-0926. 412 rms, 4 story. S $129-$139; D $144-$154; each addl $15; suites $150-$550; under 17 free; wkend rates. Pet accepted. TV; cable. Indoor/outdoor pools; wading pool, poolside serv. Restaurant 6 am-11 pm. Rm serv 24 hrs. Bar 11-3 am; entertainment, dancing. Ck-out 1 pm. Convention facilities. Concierge. Gift shop. Free airport transportation. Lighted tennis. Golf privileges. Exercise rm; instructor, weight machine, bicycles, whirlpool, sauna. Game rm. Bathrm phones; some refrigerators. Private balconies. On 23 landscaped acres on top of hill. Semiformal decor. Cr cds: A, C, D, DS, ER, JCB, MC, V.

D 🚲 ⛷ 🕴 ≈ 🎿 ✈ ≋ 🔥 SC

★ ★ **STOUFFER.** *611 Commerce St (37203), downtown.* 615/255-8400; FAX 615/255-8163. 673 rms, 25 story. S $154-$174; D $174-$194; each addl $20; suites $254-$1,000; under 18 free; wkend packages. Crib free. Garage $4; valet parking $10.54. Pet accepted, some restrictions. TV; cable, in-rm movies avail. Indoor pool; poolside serv. Restaurant 6 am-10 pm; Fri, Sat to 11 pm. Rm serv 24 hrs. Bar 11-2 am; entertainment. Ck-out noon. Convention facilities. Shopping arcade. Concierge. Airport transportation. Exercise rm; instructor, weights, bicycles, whirlpool, sauna. Some bathrm phones, refrigerators. **LUXURY LEVEL : CLUB FLOOR.** 58 rms, 5 suites, 2 floors. S $174-$194; D $194-$214; suites $294-$1,000. Private lounge. Wet bar in suites. Complimentary continental bkfst, refreshments. Cr cds: A, C, D, DS, ER, JCB, MC, V.

D 🐾 ≈ 🎿 ≋ 🔥 SC

★ ★ ★ **UNION STATION.** *1001 Broadway (37203), downtown.* 615/726-1001; res: 800/331-2123; FAX 615/248-3554. 124 rms, 7 story, 12 suites. S $85-$150; D $105-$170; each addl $10; suites $135-$400; under 13 free; wkend rates. Crib free. Valet parking $7. TV; cable. Pool privileges. Restaurant 6:30 am-11 pm (also see ARTHUR'S). Bar 11 am-11 pm; entertainment. Ck-out noon. Concierge. Gift shop. Airport transportation. Tennis, 18-hole golf privileges. Health club privileges. In renovated historic train station (1897); stained-glass roof. Cr cds: A, C, D, DS, MC, V.

D 🕴 ≈ 🎿 ≋ 🔥 SC

Restaurants

★ ★ **101ST AIRBORNE.** *1362 A Murfreesboro Rd, east of downtown.* 615/361-4212. Hrs: 11 am-2:30 pm, 5-10 pm; Fri & Sat 5-11 pm; Sun 5-10 pm; Sun brunch 10:30 am-2:30 pm. Closed Dec 25. Res accepted. Bar from 4 pm. Semi-a la carte: lunch $5.95-$8.95, dinner $13.95-$36. Sun brunch $13.95. Child's meals. Specializes in steak, seafood, prime rib. Parking. House dramatizes a headquarters operation for the 101st Airborne Division; World War II memorabilia. Cr cds: A, C, D, DS, MC, V.

D

★ ★ ★ **106 CLUB.** *106 Harding Place (37205), west of downtown.* 615/356-1300. Hrs: 5 pm-midnight. Closed most major hols. Res accepted. Bar. Semi-a la carte: dinner $14-$26. Specializes in fresh fish, wild game, veal. Pianist. Parking. Art deco decor. Cr cds: A, D, DS, MC, V.

D

★ ★ ★ ★ **ARTHUR'S.** *(See Union Station Hotel)* 615/255-1494. Hrs: 5:30-10:30 pm; Fri & Sat to 11 pm; Sun 5:30-9 pm. Closed major hols. Res accepted. Continental menu. Bar 5 pm-1 am. Wine cellar. Table d'hôte: dinner $45-$55. Specializes in seafood, lamb, flaming desserts. Own baking. Menu recited; printed menu avail on request; menu changes wkly. Valet parking. Located in historic train station (1897) that has been converted into an Old World-style hotel. Elegant dining. Jacket. Cr cds: A, C, D, DS, MC, V.

D

★ ★ **BELLE MEADE BRASSERIE.** *101 Page Rd, south of downtown.* 615/356-5450. Hrs: 5:30-10 pm; Fri & Sat to 11 pm. Closed Sun; some major hols. Res accepted. Continental menu. Bar. A la carte entrees: dinner $10-$24. Specializes in seafood, poultry, pasta. Parking. Outdoor dining. Contemporary decor; original art. Cr cds: A, MC, V.

D

★ **CAPTAIN'S TABLE.** *313¹/₂ Church St, in Printer's Alley, downtown.* 615/256-3353. Hrs: 5:30-11:30 pm. Closed Sun; Jan 1, July 4, Dec 25. Res accepted. Bar 4 pm-12:30 am. Semi-a la carte: dinner $10.95-$17.95. Specializes in steak, lobster. Country singer exc Sun. Atmosphere of ship captain's quarters. Cr cds: A, C, D, DS, MC, V.

D

✔★ **COCK OF THE WALK.** *2624 Music Valley Dr, in Opryland Area.* 615/889-1930. Hrs: 5-9:30 pm; Fri & Sat to 10 pm. Closed Thanksgiving, Dec 24, 25; also Super Bowl Sun. Res accepted. Bar. Semi-a la carte: dinner $8.50-$12.50. Child's meals. Specializes in catfish, fried dill pickles. Parking. Split level dining in rustic atmosphere. Cr cds: A, D, MC, V.

D

★ ★ ★ **F SCOTT'S.** *2210 Crestmoor Dr, west of downtown.* 615/269-5861. Hrs: 11:30 am-2 pm, 5:30-10 pm; Fri to 11 pm; Sat 5:30-11 pm; Sun brunch 11:30 am-2 pm. Closed most major hols. Res accepted. Bar. Wine list. A la carte entrees: lunch $5-$14, dinner $16-$25. Sun brunch $5-$14. Child's meals. Specializes in seafood, veal, lamb. Pianist Wed-Sat. Parking. Art deco decor. Cr cds: A, D, DS, MC, V.

D

✔★ ★ **GERST HAUS.** *228 Woodland St, downtown.* 615/256-9760. Hrs: 11 am-9 pm; Fri & Sat to 10 pm; Sun 3-9 pm. Closed Jan 1, Thanksgiving, Dec 25. Res accepted Mon-Fri. German, Amer menu. Bar. Semi-a la carte: lunch, dinner $4.95-$12.95. Specialties: Wienerschnitzel, pork loin, fresh oyster roll. German band Sat & Sun. Parking. Beer hall atmosphere. Bavarian decor; antiques. Family-owned. No cr cds accepted.

D

✔★ ★ **GOLDEN DRAGON.** 81 White Bridge Rd, west of downtown. 615/356-1110. Hrs: 11 am-10 pm. Chinese menu. Bar. Semi-a la carte: lunch $4.25-$7.50, dinner $6.25-$14.95. Child's meals. Specializes in Hunan, Szechwan and Shanghai dishes. Parking. Chinese decor; lanterns, waterfall. Cr cds: A, DS, MC, V.

D

✔★ ★ **J ALEXANDER'S.** 73 White Bridge Rd, west of downtown. 615/352-0981. Hrs: 11 am-10 pm; Fri, Sat to midnight. Closed Thanksgiving, Dec 25. Bar. Semi-a la carte: lunch, dinner $5-$15.95. Child's meals. Specializes in prime rib, fresh seafood, salads. Parking. Glass window permits diners to observe salad preparation area. Cr cds: A, D, DS, MC, V.

D

★ **JAMAICA.** 1901 Broadway, downtown. 615/321-5191. Hrs: 11 am-11 pm; Sun 5-11 pm. Closed most major hols. Res accepted. Caribbean, New Orleans menu. Bar to 1 am. Semi-a la carte: lunch, dinner $4.75-$14.75. Child's meals. Specializes in traditional Jamaican and New Orleans dishes, seafood. Parking. Relaxed West Indies atmosphere. Cr cds: A, C, D, DS, MC, V.

D

★ ★ **JIMMY KELLY'S.** 217 Louise Ave, west of downtown. 615/329-4349. Hrs: 5 pm-midnight. Closed Sun; some major hols. Res accepted. Bar. Semi-a la carte: dinner $11-$24. Child's meals. Specializes in hand-cut aged beef. Valet parking. In renovated Victorian mansion (1911). Family-owned. Cr cds: A, C, D, MC, V.

D

★ ★ ★ **MARIO'S.** 2005 Broadway, downtown. 615/327-3232. Hrs: 5:30-10:30 pm. Closed Sun; major hols. Res accepted. Northern Italian, continental menu. Bar. Two wine cellars. A la carte entrees: dinner $18-$26. Specializes in pastas, fresh seafood, veal. Theater dining rm. Parking. Wine display; memorabilia of guests and awards. Family-owned. Cr cds: A, D, DS, MC, V.

D

★ ★ ★ **THE MERCHANTS.** 401 Broadway, downtown. 615/254-1892. Hrs: 11 am-2 pm, 5-10 pm; Fri to 11 pm; Sat 5-11 pm; Sun 5-10 pm. Closed Jan 1, Thanksgiving, Dec 25. Res accepted. Bar. Wine cellar. A la carte entrees: lunch $4.95-$10.95, dinner $14.95-$19.95. Specializes in fresh grilled meats and seafood. Own baking. Pianist Mon-Sat. Valet parking. Outdoor dining. In historic building; original wood floors; dining on 3 levels. Cr cds: A, C, D, MC, V.

D

★ ★ **NEW ORLEANS MANOR.** 1400 Murfreesboro Rd, east of downtown. 615/367-2777. Hrs: 5:30-9 pm. Closed Sun, Mon; Jan 1, Thanksgiving, Dec 24, 25. Res accepted. Serv bar. Dinner buffet $27-$36. Child's meals. Specializes in seafood, lobster, prime rib. Salad bar. Parking. Scenic grounds; colonial-type mansion built in 1930. Cr cds: A, C, D, DS, MC, V.

D

✔★ **OLD SPAGHETTI FACTORY.** 160 2nd Ave N, downtown. 615/254-9010. Hrs: 11:30 am-2 pm, 5-10 pm; Fri to 11 pm; Sat 4:30-11 pm; Sun 4-10 pm. Closed Thanksgiving, Dec 24-25. Bar. Semi-a la carte: lunch $3.25-$5.25. Complete meals: dinner $4.50-$8.95. Child's meals. Specializes in spaghetti with a variety of sauces. In converted 1869 warehouse; doorway arch from the Bank of London; antiques. Cr cds: DS, MC, V.

D

★ **PRIME CUT STEAKHOUSE.** 170 2nd Ave N, downtown. 615/242-3083. Hrs: 5-10 pm; Fri, Sat to 11 pm. Closed Thanksgiving, Dec 25. Res accepted. Bar from 4 pm. Semi-a la carte: dinner $14.95-$21.95. Child's meals. Specializes in steak, marinated chicken, fresh fish. Entertainment Fri, Sat. Option of cooking own steak. Cr cds: A, C, D, DS, MC, V.

D

★ **SANTA FE STEAK CO.** 902 Murfreesboro Rd, south of downtown. 615/367-4448. Hrs: 11 am-10 pm; Fri & Sat to 11 pm. Closed Thanksgiving, Dec 25. Bar to 11 pm, Fri & Sat to midnight. Semi-a la carte: lunch $3.79-$7.99, dinner $6.95-$17.95. Child's meals. Specializes in steak, chicken. Parking. Informal dining in three areas. Cr cds: A, D, DS, MC, V.

D

★ ★ ★ **SPERRY'S.** 5109 Harding Rd, west of downtown. 615/353-0809. Hrs: 5-10 pm; Fri, Sat to 11 pm. Closed major hols. Bar to midnight. A la carte entrees: dinner $10.95-$24.95. Specializes in fresh seafood, steak. Salad bar. Own desserts, soups, sauces. Parking. Nautical and hunting decor. Cr cds: A, C, D, MC, V.

D

★ ★ **STOCK-YARD.** 901 2nd Ave N, downtown. 615/255-6464. Hrs: 11 am-2 pm, 5-11 pm; Sat & Sun from 5 pm. Closed most major hols. Bars 7:30 pm-2 am. Semi-a la carte: lunch $5.25-$8.95, dinner $14.50-$29. Child's meals. Specializes in charcoal-grilled steak, fresh seafood, grilled chicken breast. Entertainment. Parking. Cr cds: A, D, DS, MC, V.

D

★ ★ ★ **VALENTINO'S.** 1907 West End Ave, west of downtown. 615/327-0148. Hrs: 11 am-2 pm, 5-10 pm. Closed Sun; major hols. Res accepted. Northern Italian menu. Bar. Semi-a la carte: lunch $5.95-$10.95, dinner $9.95-$22.95. Specializes in chicken, seafood, pasta. Parking. Cr cds: A, C, D, DS, MC, V.

D

★ ★ ★ **THE WILD BOAR.** 2014 Broadway (37203), downtown. 615/329-1313. Hrs: 11 am-2 pm, 6-10 pm; Fri to 10:30 pm; Sat 6-10:30 pm. Closed Sun; major hols. Res accepted. Continental menu. Bar. Semi-a la carte: lunch $19.95-$32.95, dinner $60-$100. A la carte entrees: lunch $5.95-$11.95, dinner $6.95-$32.95. Specializes in fresh wild game, fresh seafood, soufflès. Pianist Wed-Sat. Valet parking. European hunting lodge decorated with fine artwork and antiques. Cr cds: A, C, D, DS, MC, V.

D

Unrated Dining Spots

APPLEBEE'S. 2400 Elliston Pl, west of downtown. 615/329-2306. Hrs: 11 am-midnight; Fri, Sat to 1 am; Sun to 10 pm; Sun brunch to 3 pm. Closed Thanksgiving, Dec 25. Bar. Semi-a la carte: lunch, dinner $3.25-$8.50. Sun brunch $3.25-$7.99. Child's meals. Specializes in chicken, steak, hamburgers. Parking. Bar & grill atmosphere; antiques, paintings. Cr cds: A, MC, V.

D

BELLE MEADE BUFFET CAFETERIA. 4534 Harding Rd, in Belle Meade Plaza, west of downtown. 615/298-5571. Hrs: 11 am-2 pm, 4:30-8 pm; Sun 10:30 am-8 pm. Closed some major hols. Avg ck: lunch $5, dinner $5.50. Child's meals. Specialties: baked squash casserole, fried chicken. No cr cds accepted.

D

MORRISON'S CAFETERIA. (1000 Two Mile Pkwy, Goodlettsville) N on I-65, in Rivergate Mall. 615/859-1359. Hrs: 10:45 am-8:30 pm; Sun to 8 pm. Avg ck: lunch $4.50, dinner $5. Child's meals. Specializes in chicken, roast beef. Cr cds: MC, V.

TOWNE HOUSE TEA ROOM & RESTAURANT. 165 8th Ave N, downtown. 615/254-1277. Hrs: 8:30 am-2:30 pm; Fri 8:30 am-2:30 pm, 5:30-10 pm; Sat 5:30-10 pm. Closed Sun; major hols. Semi-a la carte: bkfst $3.95-$7.95, lunch $3.45-$7.50, dinner $7.95-$18.95. Buffet: lunch $4.95, dinner $8.95. Salad bar. Own baking, soups. Historic 24-room mansion (1859); fireplaces, oak floors, antiques, paintings. Cr cds: A, C, D, DS, MC, V.

New Orleans

Founded: 1718

Pop: 496,938

Elev: 5 feet

Time zone: Central

Area code: 504

Few cities can compete with New Orleans' reputation for charm. Worldwide travelers come here to dine in superb restaurants, listen to incomparable jazz, browse in Royal Street's fine antique shops and dance in the streets at Mardi Gras. With top billing in food, entertainment and music, New Orleans has mastered the art of festivity.

The people of New Orleans come from a variety of backgrounds. There are Creoles, descendants of the early French and Spanish immigrants; Acadians or "Cajuns," descendants of refugees from Nova Scotia; and black descendants of the Santo Domingo slaves, who practiced a curious mix of Roman Catholicism and West African ritual known as voodoo.

Named for the Duc d'Orléans, Regent of France, New Orleans was founded by Jean Baptiste Le Moyne in 1718. Over the course of the next 85 years, the Louisiana territory changed hands three times, finally being bought by the US in 1803. The city was laid out along the lines of a late medieval French town, with a central square on the river, now called Jackson Square. The influence of its past owners, France and Spain, can be seen throughout New Orleans.

In the 1790s, great plantations were built when vast fortunes could be made from sugar cane. In 1812 (the year Louisiana became a state) steamboat transportation was begun, stimulating the trade in cotton. Before the Civil War, there was a greater concentration of millionaires in the Louisiana sugar belt than anywhere else in the country.

In the 1800s New Orleans was known as the Paris of America. Today, it is truly an international city, one of the busiest and most efficient ports in the nation. More than 35 countries maintain consular offices here, and many public places are staffed with multilingual personnel. Foreign trade is a significant part of the city's economy.

Business

Since World War II, New Orleans has experienced enormous growth and change. The constructon of new bridges, expressways, public buildings and housing developments, along with important improvements in rail traffic and handling, stimulated industrial and commercial growth.

With sources of petroleum and natural gas nearby, relatively cheap electricity and an abundance of fresh water, manufacturing has become increasingly important. Today, more than 1,000 manufacturing and processing plants employ approximately 45,000 workers.

Convention Facilities

The Ernest N. Morial Convention Center, the city's largest convention center, has 700,000 square feet of exhibit space and approximately 130,000 square feet of meeting rooms. The center is continuing to undergo expansion.

The Louisiana Superdome, located on a 52-acre site only 6 blocks from the French Quarter, seats up to 77,000 spectators for football and has a total of 270,000 square feet of convention and exhibit space on its 4 levels. The main exhibit floor has 166,000 square feet of space and can accommodate 22,500 people for meetings or 15,000 for dining. The parking lot holds 5,000 cars and an estimated 14,000 additional parking spaces are within walking distance. There are restaurants, snack bars, cafeterias and lounges throughout the building.

There are more than 25,000 guest rooms in greater New Orleans, and more than half are accessible to the central business district/French Quarter area. Many of the major downtown hotels have extensive facilities for conventions and meetings.

Sports and Recreation

The Louisiana Superdome, New Orleans' busiest sports center, is the home of the city's professional football team, the Saints. On January 1, the Sugar Bowl College Football Classic is played. The Tulane University football team also plays here.

Horse racing can be enjoyed at Fair Grounds Racetrack from Thanksgiving to late March.

No trip to New Orleans would be complete without a boat ride on a stern-wheeler. Daily narrated cruises depart from Toulouse Street Wharf at Jackson Square and from Canal Street Wharf. A Saturday night moonlight cruise with dancing is a true delight.

Entertainment

The Louisiana Philharmonic Orchestra, Orpheum Theater, Opera Guild, Opera House Association and Community Concert Association present many classical music performances. There are also several professional theater companies. In addition, the Louisiana Superdome offers visitors a rich program of major concerts and events.

On the upriver side of Canal Street is the area known as Uptown. Much of Uptown is easily accessible by the frequently run St Charles Avenue Streetcar. Numerous restaurants and lounges along St Charles Avenue offer a fascinating alternative to the French Quarter. The management at some of the more elegant restaurants frown on informal attire; be warned that New Orleans is somewhat formal.

Nightlife

New Orleans really comes to life at night. The quaint, tranquil French Quarter is transformed into a music-filled center of excitement and activity. People stroll the brightly lit streets, some of which are closed to automobile traffic in the evening, and take rides in horse-drawn buggies and carriages. They sample the exquisite fare offered by restaurants known the world over; sit on park benches and listen to the sounds coming from open doors of bistros; take cruises along the river;

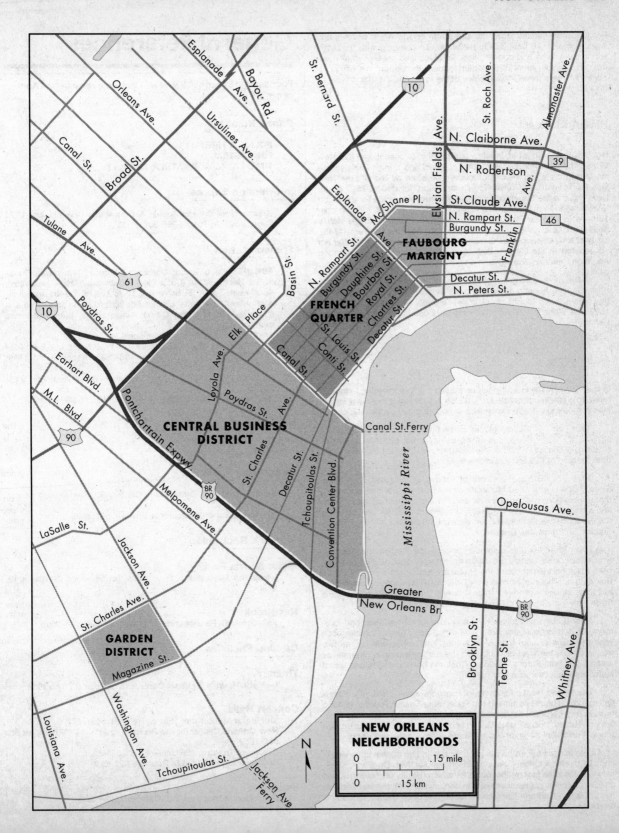

NEW ORLEANS NEIGHBORHOODS

0   .15 mile

0   .15 km

window shop for antiques, arts and crafts or souvenirs; or relax and enjoy some of the best jazz in the world. To compete with the large, well-known clubs and concert halls, hotel lounges present small combos; as a result, most of the entertainment throughout the city is far above average. New Orleans is one of the few cities left that is lively 24 hours a day.

Historical Areas

Not only is it impossible, in a few paragraphs, to describe all that New Orleans has to offer, but the visitor also will find it impossible to see everything on a first visit. A brochure published by the Greater New Orleans Tourist and Convention Commission, located at 1520 Sugar Bowl Drive in the Superdome, contains a map and guide for a walking tour of the French Quarter and lists 36 points of interest, ranging from 18th-century houses and early 19th-century apartments to the stately St Louis Cathedral (1789-94) and the Old Ursuline Convent (1745). Many of New Orleans' most beautiful houses from the pre-Civil War era are located in the Garden District in Uptown. Also see oak-shaded Audubon Park and Zoo.

A few miles from downtown is Chalmette National Historical Park. Here, General Andrew Jackson's army defeated the British in a battle that was actually fought after the peace treaty that ended the War of 1812 was signed. A beautiful plantation house in the park is open to visitors.

Sightseeing

In New Orleans the word *lagniappe* means a little something extra and refers to a small, unexpected gift. It also signifies that there is always a little something extra to experience in and near this captivating city.

There are 100 square blocks in the French Quarter. Hours spent strolling there will reveal something extra for the historian, gourmet, shopper, architecture buff or interested tourist. There is an information desk located at 529 Saint Ann Street.

New Orleans has a plethora of antique shops located on Royal Street in the Quarter and Magazine Street Uptown. For mall shopping, there is the Riverwalk, at the river and Poydras Street; Jackson Brewery, adjacent to Jackson Square; Canal Place, at Canal and N Peters Sts; New Orleans Center, at Poydras and La Salle Sts; and the Uptown Square, on Broadway, Uptown.

River Road features plantation houses and "Louisiana cottages," which have been lovingly preserved or restored. Boat trips on beautiful Lake Pontchartrain or along the bayou are further enticements. Baton Rouge, a one-hour drive from New Orleans, with its skyscraper capitol building, stately governor's mansion and the impressive Louisiana State University campus, also has special appeal.

New Orleans has a variety of annual celebrations. First and foremost, of course, is Mardi Gras. The entire city strives to make each year's fete better than the previous one. The celebration begins two weeks before the start of Lent, with the parties increasing in number and activity until Shrove Tuesday. Costume balls, parades and street festivities draw everyone into the fun.

The Spring Fiesta Association sponsors what is virtually a New Orleans open house beginning the Friday after Easter. Tours of historic houses and gardens, not open to the public at other times of the year, are conducted, and a Fiesta Queen is crowned. Candlelight courtyard tours, a historical pageant and a parade complete the festivities.

Late in April the emphasis is on jazz, with two consecutive weekends of the New Orleans Jazz and Heritage Festival. Concerts, seminars and parades feature the music for which the city is known, as well as folk, gospel and popular music. In conjunction with the jazz festival, the Louisiana Heritage Fair honors local, and often exotic, foods and crafts.

General References

Founded: 1718 **Pop:** 496,938 **Elev:** 5 feet **Time zone:** Central **Area code:** 504

Phone Numbers

POLICE & FIRE: 911
FBI: 522-4671
TIME: 976-1000   **WEATHER:** 465-9212

Information Source

Greater New Orleans Tourist & Convention Commission, 1520 Sugar Bowl Dr, 70112; 566-5011.

Transportation

AIRLINES: Aeromexico; American; Aviateca (Guatemala); Continental; Delta; LACSA (Costa Rica); Northwest; SAHSA (Honduras); Southwest; TACA (El Salvador); TWA; United; USAir; and other commuter and regional airlines. For current airline schedules and information consult the *Official Airline Guide,* published twice monthly.
AIRPORT: New Orleans International. 464-0831.
CAR RENTAL AGENCIES: (See Toll-Free Numbers) Avis 464-9511; Budget 467-2277; Hertz 468-3695; National 466-4335; Thrifty 467-8796; Value 469-2688.
PUBLIC TRANSPORTATION: Regional Transit Authority, 242-2600.
RAILROAD PASSENGER SERVICE: Amtrak 800/872-7245.

Newspaper

Times-Picayune.

Convention Facilities

Ernest N. Morial Convention Center, 900 Convention Center Blvd, 582-3000.
Louisiana Superdome, Sugar Bowl Dr, 587-3808.

Sports & Recreation

Major Sports Facility
Louisiana Superdome, Sugar Bowl Dr, 587-3808 (Saints, football).

Racetrack
Fair Grounds Racecourse, 1751 Gentilly Blvd, 944-5515.

Cultural Facilities

Theater
Le Petit Theatre du Vieux Carre, 616 St Peter St, 522-9958.

Concert Halls
Municipal Auditorium, 1201 St Peter St, 565-7470.
New Orleans Center for the Performing Arts, 143 N Rampart St, 525-1052.
Orpheum Theatre, 129 University Pl, 524-3285.
Preservation Hall, 726 St Peter St, 523-8939.

Museums
Confederate Museum, 929 Camp St, 523-4522.
Louisiana Children's Museum, 428 Julia St, 523-1357.

Louisiana Nature and Science Center, Reed Blvd, in Joe Brown Park, 246-5672.
Musée Conti-Wax Museum of Louisiana Legends, 917 Conti St, 525-2605.
Pharmacy Museum, 514 Chartres St, 565-8027.

Art Museums

Historic New Orleans Collection, 533 Royal St, 523-4662.
New Orleans Museum of Art, 1 Collins Diboll Circle, City Park, 488-2631.

Points of Interest

Historical

Adelina Patti's House & Courtyard, 631 Royal St.
Beauregard-Keyes House, 1113 Chartres St, 523-7257.
Brulatour Courtyard, 520 Royal St.
Chalmette Natl Historical Park, 6 mi E on LA 46 in Chalmette, 589-4428.
Destrehan Plantation, 17 mi W via I-10 to E 220, Destrehan, 764-9315.
Dueling Oaks, City Park.
E.H. Sothern's Home, 709 Bienville Ave.
The 1850 House, 523 St Ann St.
French Quarter, fronting on the Mississippi River and bounded by Esplanade Ave, N Rampart, Canal and Decatur Sts.
Gallier House Museum, 1118-32 Royal St, 523-6722.
Hermann-Grima Historic House, 820 St Louis St, 525-5661.
Jackson Square, Chartres, St Peter, Decatur & St Ann Sts.
Jean Lafitte Natl Historical Park and Preserve, 916 N Peter St, 589-2636.
Louis Armstrong Park (Beauregard Square), Rampart St at St Peter St.
Madame John's Legacy, 632 Dumaine St.
Maison Le Monnier, 640 Royal St.
Old Absinthe House, Bienville & Bourbon Sts.
Old U.S. Mint, Esplanade and Decatur Sts, 568-6968.
Pirate's Alley, off Jackson Square.
Pontalba Bldg, facing Jackson Square, 568-6968.
The Presbytère, 751 Chartres St, 568-6968.
St Louis Cathedral, 615 Pere Antoine Alley, 525-9585.
San Francisco Plantation, Approx 45 mi W via I-10, in Garyville, 535-2341.

Other Attractions

Aquarium of the Americas, 1 Canal, along river between Canal & Bienville Sts, 861-2537.
Audubon Park and Zoological Gardens, 6500 Magazine, 861-2537.
French Market, Decatur St, beginning at St Ann St.

Garden District, Magazine St, St Charles, Jackson & Louisiana Aves.
Jackson Brewery, 620 Decatur, 586-8015.
Levee and docks, from foot of Canal St.
Longue Vue House & Gardens, 7 Bamboo Rd, 488-5488.
Riverwalk, Mississippi River at Poydras St, 522-1555.
World Trade Center, in ITM Building, 2 Canal St, 525-2185.

Sightseeing Tours

Cajun Queen, Creole Queen, Poydras St Wharf, 529-4567 or 524-0814.
Gay 90s Carriages, Inc, 1824 N Rampart St, 943-8820.
Gray Line bus tours, 1300 World Trade Center, 70130; 587-0861 or 800/535-7786.
Riverfront Streetcar Line, riverfront between Esplanade & the Riverwalk at Poydras St, 569-7000.
St Charles Ave Streetcar, St Charles & Carrollton Aves, 861-6000.
Sternwheelers *Cotton Blossom* and *Natchez,* Toulouse St Wharf, 586-8777 or 587-0734.

Annual Events

Sugar Bowl, Superdome. Jan 1.
Mardi Gras. 2 wks preceding Shrove Tuesday.
Spring Fiesta, 581-1367. Begins 1st Fri after Easter.
Jazz & Heritage Festival, 522-4786. Last wkend Apr-1st wkend May.

City Neighborhoods

Many of the restaurants, unrated dining establishments and some lodgings listed under New Orleans include neighborhoods as well as exact street addresses. A map showing these neighborhoods can be found immediately following the city introduction. Geographic descriptions of these areas are given, followed by a table of restaurants arranged by neighborhood.

Central Business District: Fronting on the Mississippi River and bounded by Canal St, I-10 and US 90 Business. **North of Central Business District:** North of I-10. **West of Central Business District:** West of I-10/US 90 Business.
Faubourg Marigny: Adjacent to the French Quarter across Esplanade Ave; south of McShane Pl, west of Elysian Fields Ave and northeast of Esplanade Ave.
French Quarter (*Vieux Carré*): Fronting on the Mississippi River and bounded by Esplanade Ave, N Rampart, Canal and Decatur Sts.
Garden District: South of St Charles Ave, west of Jackson Ave, north of Magazine St and east of Washington Ave.

Lodgings and Food

NEW ORLEANS RESTAURANTS
BY NEIGHBORHOOD AREAS

(For full description, see alphabetical listings under Restaurants)

CENTRAL BUSINESS DISTRICT

Bon Ton Cafe. 401 Magazine St

Emeril's. 800 Tchoupitoulas St

Grill Room (Windsor Court Hotel). 300 Gravier St

Kung's Dynasty. 1912 St Charles Ave

L'Economie. 325 Girod St

Mike's on the Avenue. 628 St Charles Ave

Mother's. 401 Poydras St

Palace Cafe. 605 Canal St

Sazerac (Fairmont Hotel). 123 Baronne

The Veranda (Inter-Continental Hotel). 444 St Charles Ave

NORTH OF CENTRAL BUSINESS DISTRICT

Bart's on the Lake. 8000 Lakeshore Dr

Christian's. 3835 Iberville St

Gabrielle. 3201 Esplanade Ave

Louisiana Pizza Kitchen. 2808 Esplanade Ave

Tavern on the Park. 900 City Park Ave

WEST OF CENTRAL BUSINESS DISTRICT

Bangkok Cuisine. 4137 S Carrollton Ave

Brigtsen's. 723 Dante St

Camellia Grill. 626 S Carrollton Ave

Casamento's. 4330 Magazine

Chez Nous Charcuterie. 5701 Magazine St

Five Happiness. 3605 S Carrollton Ave

Gautreau's. 1728 Soniat St

Mosca's. 4137 US 90W

Robear's Lighthouse Bar & Grill. 7360 W Roadway

Windjammer. 8550 Pontchartrain Blvd

FAUBOURG MARIGNY

Alberto's. 611 Frenchmen St

Feelings Cafe. 2600 Chartres St

Praline Connection. 542 Frenchmen St

Santa Fe. 801 Frenchmen St

Snug Harbor Jazz Bistro. 626 Frenchmen St

FRENCH QUARTER (VIEUX CARRÉ)

Alex Patout's. 221 Royal St

Angelo Brocata's Italian Ice Cream Parlor. 537 St Ann St

Antoine's. 713 St Louis St

Arnaud's. 813 Rue Bienville

Bacco. 310 Chartres St

Bayona. 430 Rue Dauphine

Bella Luna. 914 N Peter

Bistro (Hotel Maison De Ville Inn). 727 Toulouse St

Brennan's. 417 Royal St

Broussard's. 819 Rue Conti

Cafe du Monde. 800 Decatur St

Central Grocery. 923 Decatur St

Clover Grill. 900 Bourbon St

Court of Two Sisters. 613 Royal St

Desire Oyster Bar (Royal Sonesta Hotel). 300 Bourbon St

Felix's. 739 Iberville St

G & E Courtyard Grill. 1113 Decatur St

Galatoire's. 209 Bourbon St

La Madeleine. 547 St Ann St

Maximo's Italian Grill. 1117 Rue Decatur

Mr B's Bistro. 201 Royal St

Nola. 534 St Louis St

The Original French Market. 1001 Decatur St

Port of Call. 838 Esplanade Ave

Rib Room (Omni Royal Orleans Hotel). 621 St Louis St

Tony Moran's Pasta E Vino. 240 Bourbon St

Tujague's. 823 Decatur St

GARDEN DISTRICT

Commander's Palace. 1403 Washington Ave

Versailles. 2100 St Charles Ave

Note: *When a listing is located in a town that does not have its own city heading, it will appear under the city nearest to its location. In these cases, the address and town appear in parenthesis immediately following the name of the establishment.*

Motels

(Most accommodations increase their rates greatly for the Mardi Gras Festival and the Sugar Bowl Game wkend. Reservations should be made as far ahead as possible and confirmed.)

✔★ **CHATEAU.** *1001 Rue Chartres (70116), in French Quarter.* 504/524-9636. 45 rms, 2 story, 5 suites. S $64-$84; D $74-$94; each addl $10; suites $104-$135; under 18 free; higher rates special events. Crib free. TV; cable. Pool. Restaurant 7 am-3 pm. Rm serv. Bar. Ck-out 1 pm. Bellhops. Valet serv. Valet parking. Made up of 18th-century bldgs around courtyard. Cr cds: A, C, D, ER, MC, V.

≈ 🔥 SC

✔★ **NEWCOURT INN.** *10020 I-10 Service Rd at Read Blvd (70127), I-10 exit 244, north of central business district.* 504/244-9115; res: 800/821-4009. 143 rms, 2 story. S, D $60; suites $100; family rates; higher rates special events. Crib free. TV; cable. Pool. Complimentary continental bkfst. Ck-out noon. Cr cds: A, C, D, DS, MC, V.

D ≈ 🔥 SC

★ **PRYTANIA PARK.** *1525 Prytania St (70130), in Garden District.* 504/524-0427; res: 800/862-1984; FAX 504/522-2977. 62 units, 2 story, 49 kits. S $79-$89; D $89-$99; suites $99-$150; each addl $10; under 12 free; summer packages. Crib free. TV; cable. Continental bkfst. Restaurant nearby. Ck-out noon. Refrigerators. Balconies. Cr cds: A, C, D, MC, V.

🔥 SC

✔★ **TRAVELODGE-NEW ORLEANS WEST.** *(2200 West Bank Expwy (US 90W), Harvey 70058) 3 mi S on US 90W.* 504/366-5311; FAX 504/368-2774. 211 rms, 2 story. S $42-$48; D $48-$54;

each addl $6; suites $68-$168; wkly rates; higher rates Jazz Fest. Crib free. TV; cable. Pool; wading pool. Complimentary coffee in rms. Restaurant 6 am-10 pm; Sun to 3 pm. Rm serv. Bar 4 pm-1 am. Ck-out noon. Coin lndry. Meeting rms. Free Canal Street ferry transportation. Cr cds: A, C, D, DS, ER, JCB, MC, V.

Motor Hotels

★ **BIENVILLE HOUSE.** *320 Decatur St (70130), in French Quarter.* 504/529-2345; res: 800/535-7836; FAX 504/525-6079. 83 rms, 4 story. Sept-May: S $80-$125; D $95-$150; each addl $10; suites $175-$350; under 16 free; lower rates rest of yr. Crib free. Valet parking $10-$14. TV; cable. Pool. Restaurant 7 am-10 pm. Rm serv. Bar 11 am-10 pm. Ck-out noon. Meeting rms. Bellhops. Valet serv. Health club privileges. Balconies. Courtyard surrounds pool. Cr cds: A, C, D, DS, MC, V.

★ **CLARION CARRIAGE HOUSE-FRENCH MARKET INN.** *501 Rue Decatur (70130), in French Quarter.* 504/561-5621; FAX 504/566-0160. 54 units, 4 story. Late Dec-May, Sept-Oct: S, D $129-$250; each addl $10; suites $158; higher rates special events; lower rates rest of yr. TV; cable. Complimentary continental bkfst. Restaurant nearby. Ck-out 11 am. Bellhops. Concierge. Built in 1753 for the Baron de Pontalba; served as residence for French governor. Cr cds: A, C, D, DS, ER, JCB, MC, V.

★★ **DAUPHINE ORLEANS.** *415 Dauphine St (70112), in French Quarter.* 504/586-1800; res: 800/521-7111; FAX 504/586-1409. 109 rms, 2-4 story. S $129-$175; D $149-$189; each add $15; suites $179-$359; under 12 free; higher rates special events. Crib free. Pet accepted. Garage $9. TV; cable. Pool. Complimentary continental bkfst. Bar 3:30 pm-midnight; Sat, Sun from noon. Ck-out 1 pm. Meeting rms. Bellhops. Valet parking. Exercise equipt; weights, bicycles, whirlpool. Minibars. Balconies. Also patio courtyard opp with 14 rms; varied styles, sizes. Library. Cr cds: A, C, D, DS, ER, JCB, MC, V.

★★★ **HOLIDAY INN-CHÂTEAU LE MOYNE.** *301 Dauphine St (70112), in French Quarter.* 504/581-1303; FAX 504/523-5709. 171 rms, 5 story. S $110-$195; D $125-$210; each addl $15; suites $205-$450; under 18 free. Crib free. Garage $10. TV; cable. Heated pool; poolside serv. Restaurant 6:30 am-2 pm, 5-10 pm. Rm serv. Bar 4 pm-midnight. Ck-out 11 am. Meeting rms. Bellhops. Valet serv. Concierge. Some bathrm phones in suites. Balconies. Tropical courtyard. Cr cds: A, C, D, DS, JCB, MC, V.

✔★★ **LE RICHELIEU.** *1234 Chartres St (70116), in French Quarter.* 504/529-2492; res: 800/535-9653; FAX 504/524-8179. 86 rms, 4 story. S $85-$110; D $95-$120; each addl $15; suites $145-$450; higher rates special events. Crib free. TV; cable. Pool; poolside serv. Restaurant 7 am-9 pm. Rm serv. Bar to 1 am. Ck-out 1 pm. Bellhops. Valet serv. Concierge. Refrigerators. Balconies. Landscaped courtyard. Cr cds: A, C, D, DS, ER, JCB, MC, V.

★★ **PROVINCIAL.** *1024 Rue Chartres (70116), in French Quarter.* 504/581-4995; res: 800/535-7922; FAX 504/581-1018. 106 rms, 2-4 story. S, D $115-$175; each addl $15; suites from $225; under 18 free; summer, Creole Christmas rates; higher rates special events. Crib free. TV; cable. Pool; poolside serv. Restaurant 7 am-2 pm. Rm serv. Bar. Ck-out noon. Meeting rm. Balconies. Carriageway entrance; antique furnishings. Cr cds: A, C, D, DS, MC, V.

★★ **SAINT ANN-MARIE ANTOINETTE.** *717 Rue Conti (70130), in French Quarter.* 504/581-1881. 66 rms, 5 story, 18 suites. S $99-$169; D $119-$189; each addl $15; suites $199-$499; summer

rates. Crib free. TV; cable. Pool; poolside serv. Restaurant 7-11 am; Sat, Sun to noon. Rm serv. Bar. Ck-out noon. Meeting rms. Bellhops. Valet serv. Concierge. Bathrm phones; refrigerators avail. Balconies. Cr cds: A, C, D, MC, V.

★★ **THE SAINT LOUIS.** *730 Rue Bienville (70130), in French Quarter.* 504/581-7300; res: 800/535-9111; FAX 504/524-8925. 71 rms, 5 story, 32 suites. S $129-$189; D $149-$219; each addl $15; suites $229-$639; under 12 free; summer rates. Crib free. Valet parking $10.50. TV; cable. Swimming privileges. Restaurant 7-11 am, 6-10:30 pm. Rm serv. Bar 5 pm-midnight; entertainment Fri, Sat. Ck-out noon. Meeting rms. Bellhops. Valet serv. Concierge. Bathrm phones; refrigerators avail; minibar in suites. Some balconies. French antiques. Enclosed courtyard with fountains, tropical patio. Cr cds: A, C, D, MC, V.

Hotels

★★ **BOURBON ORLEANS.** *717 Orleans St (70116), in French Quarter.* 504/523-2222; res: 800/521-5338; FAX 504/525-8166. 211 rms, 6 story, 60 suites. Mid-Sept-mid-June: S $95-$140; D $115-$160; each addl $15; suites $225-$350; under 12 free; Creole Christmas rates; higher rates special events; lower rates rest of yr. Crib free. Valet parking $12. TV. Pool; poolside serv. Coffee in rms. Restaurant 7 am-10 pm. Rm serv 24 hrs. Bar 11 am-midnight; wkends to 2 am. Ck-out noon. Meeting rms. Concierge. Bathrm phones; refrigerator, minibar in suites. Some balconies. Cr cds: A, C, D, DS, MC, V.

★★ **CLARION NEW ORLEANS.** *1500 Canal St (70112), in central business district.* 504/522-4500; FAX 504/525-2644. 759 rms, 18 story. S, D $95-$151; each addl $15; suites $150-$450; under 16 free. Crib free. Valet parking $12. TV; cable. Pool; poolside serv. Restaurant 6:30 am-2 pm, 6-11 pm; deli open 24 hrs. Bar 11 am-midnight. Ck-out noon. Coin lndry. Meeting rms. Free French Quarter transportation. Golf privileges. Exercise equipt; weights, bicycles, whirlpool. Game rm. Some refrigerators. Cr cds: A, C, D, DS, ER, JCB, MC, V.

✔★ **COMFORT INN-DOWNTOWN.** *1315 Gravier St (70112), in central business district.* 504/586-0100; FAX 504/588-9230. 172 rms, 11 story, 17 suites. S $75-$140; D $85-$150; each addl $10; suites $140-$200; under 17 free; higher rates special events; some lower rates avail. Crib free. Parking, in/out $6.75. TV; cable. Restaurant 7 am-10 pm. Bar 6 pm-1 am. Ck-out noon. Meeting rms. Some bathrm phones, refrigerators. Cr cds: A, C, D, DS, ER, JCB, MC, V.

★★ **DOUBLETREE.** *300 Canal St (70130), in central business district.* 504/581-1300; FAX 504/522-4100. 363 rms, 17 story. S $110-$150; D $120-$170; each addl $20; suites $250-$1,500; under 18 free. Crib free. Valet parking $11. TV; cable. Pool; poolside serv. Restaurant 6:30 am-10 pm; Fri, Sat to 11 pm. Rm serv. Bar from 11 am. Ck-out noon. Coin lndry. Meeting rms. Exercise equipt; weights, bicycles. Adj to French Quarter, convention center and Aquarium of the Americas. Cr cds: A, C, D, DS, ER, JCB, MC, V.

★★★ **FAIRMONT.** *123 Baronne (70140), ¹/₂ blk off Canal St between University Pl & Baronne, in central business district.* 504/529-7111; FAX 504/522-2303. 732 rms, 14 story. S $135-$180; D $160-$205; each addl $25; suites from $315; under 12 free; wkend rates, package plans avail. Crib free. Valet parking $10. TV; cable. Heated pool; poolside serv. Restaurant 6 am-midnight (also see SAZERAC). Rm serv 24 hrs. Bar. Ck-out 1 pm. Convention facilities. Concierge. Drugstore. Barber, beauty shop. Lighted tennis. Exercise equipt; weights, treadmill. Landmark turn-of-the-century hotel. Cr cds: A, C, D, DS, JCB, MC, V.

★ ★ ★ **HILTON RIVERSIDE.** *Poydras at the Mississippi River (70140), in central business district.* 504/561-0500; FAX 504/568-1721. 1,600 rms, 29 story. S $190-$210; D $215-$235; each addl $25; suites from $395; wkend packages. Crib free. Valet parking $11/24 hrs. TV; cable. 2 heated pools; poolside serv. Restaurant 6-2 am. Rm serv 24 hrs. Ck-out noon. Convention facilities. Concierge. Gift shop. Barber, beauty shop. Indoor, outdoor tennis; pro. Exercise equipt; weights, bicycles, whirlpool, sauna. Minibars. Connected to riverwalk. *LUXURY LEVEL :* **TOWERS CONCIERGE CLASS.** 138 rms, 13 suites, 4 floors. S, D $245; suites from $745. Private lounge, honor bar. Complimentary coffee, continental bkfst. Cr cds: A, C, D, DS, ER, JCB, MC, V.

D ⌨ 🏖 ⌨ ✈ ⌨ 🔥 SC

✔ ★ ★ **HOLIDAY INN DOWNTOWN-SUPERDOME.** *330 Loyola Ave (70012), in central business district.* 504/581-1600; FAX 504/586-0833. 297 rms, 18 story. S $75-$150; D $90-$165; each addl $15; under 19 free. Crib free. Garage parking $10. TV; cable, in-rm movies. Heated pool. Restaurant 6 am-10 pm. Bar. Ck-out noon. Meeting rms. Gift shop. *LUXURY LEVEL :* **CONCIERGE FLOORS.** 56 rms, 2 floors. S, D $100-$175; each addl $15. Concierge. Private lounge. Complimentary continental bkfst, refreshments. Cr cds: A, C, D, DS, JCB, MC, V.

D 🏖 ⌨ 🔥 SC

★ ★ ★ **HOLIDAY INN-CROWNE PLAZA.** *333 Poydras St (70130), in central business district.* 504/525-9444; FAX 504/581-7179. 439 units, 23 story. S, D $110-$210; each addl $15; suites $325-$645; under 18 free; higher rates special events. Crib free. Garage parking $7.50; valet $11. TV; cable. Pool. Restaurant 6:30 am-11 pm. Bar 11-2 am. Ck-out noon. Convention facilites. Concierge. Exercise equipt; weights, bicycles. Refrigerators avail. *LUXURY LEVEL :* **CONCIERGE LEVEL.** 21 rms, 1 suite. S, D $171; suite $446-$645. Private lounge, honor bar. Complimentary continental bkfst, refreshments. Cr cds: A, C, D, DS, ER, JCB, MC, V.

D 🏖 ✈ ⌨ 🔥 SC

★ ★ **HOTEL DE LA POSTE.** *316 Rue Chartres (70130), in French Quarter.* 504/581-1200; res: 800/448-4927; FAX 504/523-2910. 100 rms, 5 story. S $100-$135; D $115-$145; each addl $20; suites $145-$225; under 16 free. Crib free. TV; cable. Pool; poolside serv. Restaurant 7:30 am-10 pm. Bar. Ck-out noon. Meeting rm. Valet parking. Built around landscaped courtyard. Cr cds: A, C, D, DS, MC, V.

D 🏖 ⌨ 🔥 SC

★ ★ ★ **HYATT REGENCY.** *Poydras Plaza (70140), at Loyola, adj to Superdome in central business district.* 504/561-1234; FAX 504/587-4141. 1,184 rms, 32 story. S $165; D $190; each addl $25; suites $350-$850; under 18 free; wkend rates. Crib free. Valet parking $12. TV; cable. Heated pool; poolside serv. Restaurant 6-1 am; dining rms 10:30 am-2:30 pm, 6-10:30 pm. Bars 11-2 am; entertainment, dancing. Ck-out noon. Convention facilities. Concierge. Barber, beauty shop. Airport transportation; free local transportation. Exercise equipt; weights, treadmill. Connected to Superdome & shopping complex. *LUXURY LEVEL :* **REGENCY CLUB LEVEL.** 34 rms, 4 suites. S, D $190-$205; suites $375-$875. Private lounge, honor bar. Wet bars in suites. Complimentary continental bkfst, refreshments. Cr cds: A, C, D, DS, ER, JCB, MC, V.

D 🏖 ✈ ⌨ 🔥 SC

★ ★ ★ **INTER-CONTINENTAL.** *444 St Charles Ave (70130), in central business district.* 504/525-5566; res: 800/327-0200; FAX 504/523-7310. 482 units, 15 story, 30 suites. S $170-$210; D $190-$230; each addl $20; suites $350-$1,700; under 14 free; wkend plans. Valet parking $12. TV; cable. Heated pool; poolside serv. Restaurant 6 am-11 pm (also see THE VERANDA). Rm serv 24 hrs. Bars 11-1 am; entertainment. Convention facilities. Concierge. Gift shop. Beauty shop. Exercise equipt; weight machine, bicycles. Massage. Bathrm phones, TVs; some refrigerators, minibars. Some balconies. *LUXURY LEVEL :* **GOVERNOR'S FLOOR.** 31 rms, 8 suites. S, D $240-$260;

suites $350-$1,700. Private lounge, honor bar. Complimentary full bkfst, refreshments. Cr cds: A, C, D, DS, ER, JCB, MC, V.

D 🏖 ✈ ⌨ ⌨ 🔥 SC

★ ★ ★ **LAFAYETTE.** *600 St Charles (70130), in central business district.* 504/524-4441; res: 800/524-4754; FAX 504/523-7327. 44 rms, 5 story, 20 suites. S, D $135-$350; suites $225-$650; family rates; higher rates wkends (2-day min) & Jazz Fest. Crib free. Valet parking $10. TV. Restaurant 7 am-11 pm. Bar. Ck-out 11 am. Concierge. Airport transportation. Health club privileges. Minibars. Balconies. Renovated hotel first opened 1916. Cr cds: A, C, D, DS, ER, JCB, MC, V.

D ⌨ 🔥 SC

★ ★ ★ **LE MERIDIEN.** *614 Canal St (70130), in central business district.* 504/525-6500; res: 800/543-4300; FAX 504/525-8068. 494 rms, 30 story. S $165-$185; D $185-$205; each addl $20; suites $450-$1,500; under 16 free. Crib free. Garage $12; valet. TV; cable. Heated pool; poolside serv. Restaurant 6:30 am-10:30 pm. Rm serv 24 hrs. Bar 4 pm-1:30 am; entertainment. Ck-out noon. Convention facilities. Concierge. Shopping arcade. Exercise rm; instructor, weight machines, bicycles, whirlpool, sauna. Bathrm phones, minibars. Adj to French Quarter. Cr cds: A, C, D, DS, ER, JCB, MC, V.

D 🏖 ✈ ⌨ 🔥 SC

★ ★ ★ **LE PAVILLON.** *833 Poydras St (70140), in central business district.* 504/581-3111; res: 800/535-9095; FAX 504/522-5543. 220 rms, 10 story. S, D $99-$175; suites $295-$595; under 18 free; higher rates special events. Crib free. Valet parking $10. TV; cable. Heated pool; poolside serv. Restaurant 6:30 am-10 pm. Rm serv 24 hrs. Bar 10:30-1 am. Ck-out noon. Meeting rms. Concierge. Bathrm phones; refrigerators avail. Cr cds: A, C, D, DS, ER, MC, V.

D 🏖 ⌨ 🔥 SC

★ ★ ★ **MAISON DUPUY.** *1001 Toulouse St (70112), at Burgundy, in French Quarter.* 504/586-8000; res: 800/535-9177; FAX 504/566-7450. 198 rms, 5 story. S $130-$190; D $145-$205; each addl $25; suites $200-$800; under 12 free. Crib free. Garage $9. TV; cable. Heated pool; poolside serv. Restaurant 7 am-2 pm, 5-10 pm. Bar from 11 am. Ck-out noon. Meeting rms. Exercise equipt; weights, bicycles. Balconies. Cr cds: A, C, D, DS, MC, V.

D 🏖 ✈ ⌨ 🔥 SC

★ ★ **MARRIOTT.** *555 Canal St (70140), at Chartres St, in central business district.* 504/581-1000; FAX 504/523-6755. 1,290 units, 41 story. S, D $199; each addl $20; suites $600-$1,200; under 17 free; wkend rates. Crib free. Valet parking $12. TV; cable. Heated pool; wading pool, poolside serv. Restaurant 6:30 am-midnight. Rm serv 24 hrs. Bar 10-2 am; entertainment. Ck-out noon. Coin lndry. Convention facilities. Concierge. Gift shop. Exercise equipt; weights, bicycles, sauna. Refrigerators avail. Adj to French Quarter. *LUXURY LEVEL :* **CONCIERGE LEVEL.** 50 rms, 2 floors. S $200; D $225; each addl $20. Private lounge. Complimentary continental bkfst, refreshments. Cr cds: A, C, D, DS, ER, JCB, MC, V.

D 🏖 ✈ ⌨ 🔥 SC

★ ★ **MONTELEONE.** *214 Rue Royale (70140), in French Quarter.* 504/523-3341; res: 800/535-9595; FAX 504/528-1019. 600 rms, 16 story. S $115-$165; D $145-$210; each addl $25; suites $250-$680; under 18 free; higher rates special events. Crib free. TV; cable. Rooftop heated pool; poolside serv. Restaurant 6:30 am-11 pm. Revolving bar 11-2 am; entertainment. Ck-out noon. Meeting rms. Concierge. Shopping arcade. Barber, beauty shop. Valet parking. Exercise equipt; weights, bicycles. Some bathrm phones. Family-owned since 1886. Cr cds: A, C, D, DS, MC, V.

D 🏖 ✈ ⌨ ⌨ SC

★ ★ ★ **OMNI ROYAL ORLEANS.** *621 St Louis St (70140), in French Quarter.* 504/529-5333; res: 800/843-6664; FAX 504/529-7089. 346 rms, 7 story. S, D $140-$310; each addl $20; suites $350-$1,000; under 17 free; package plans. Crib free. Valet parking $10. TV; cable. Rooftop heated pool; poolside serv. Restaurant (see RIB ROOM). La Riviera poolside restaurant 9 am-8 pm (Apr-Oct). Rm serv 24 hrs. Bars

11-2 am; entertainment. Ck-out noon. Meeting rms. Concierge. Barber, beauty shop. Exercise equipt; weights, bicycles. Bathrm phones; some whirlpools. Some balconies. Elegantly furnished rms. Luxurious lobby with Italian marble; dramatic blend of old and modern New Orleans. Observation deck. Cr cds: A, C, D, DS, ER, JCB, MC, V.

⊡ ≈ 🏃 ⛷ 🔥 SC

★ ★ ★ **PONTCHARTRAIN.** 2031 St Charles Ave (70140), in Garden District. 504/524-0581; res: 800/777-6193; FAX 504/529-1165. 102 rms, 12 story. S, D $125-$180; each addl $25; 1-2 bedrm suites $225-$800; under 12 free. Crib free. Valet parking $9. TV; cable. Restaurants 7 am-2:30 pm, 5:30-10 pm. Rm serv 24 hrs. Bar 11-1 am; entertainment Thurs-Sat. Ck-out 1 pm. Meeting rms. Many refrigerators; some wet bars. Landmark of historic neighborhood. Cr cds: A, C, D, DS, MC, V.

⊡ ⛷ 🔥 SC

★ ★ **RADISSON SUITE HOTEL.** 315 Julia St (70130), in central business district. 504/525-1993; FAX 504/522-3044. 226 suites, 16 story. Suites $159-$275; each addl $20; under 17 free; wkend rates. Crib free. Parking privileges, $10 in/out. TV; cable. Pool; whirlpool. Complimentary full bkfst. Restaurant 6:30 am-10 pm. Bar 11 am-midnight. Ck-out noon. Meeting rms. Concierge. Bathrm phones, refrigerators. Private patios, balconies. 6-story atrium. Cr cds: A, C, D, DS, ER, JCB, MC, V.

⊡ ≈ 🏃 ⛷ 🔥 SC

✔ ★ **RAMADA.** 2203 St Charles Ave (70140), in Garden District. 504/566-1200; FAX 504/581-1352. 132 units, 9 story. S $99; D $109; each addl $10; suites $139; under 12 free; higher rates special events. Crib free. TV; cable. Restaurant 6:30 am-2 pm, 5-10 pm. Bar 4-11 pm. Ck-out noon. Meeting rms. Some refrigerators. Cr cds: A, C, D, DS, ER, JCB, MC, V.

⊡ ⛷ 🔥 SC

★ ★ **ROYAL SONESTA.** 300 Bourbon St (70140), in French Quarter. 504/586-0300; res: 800/766-3782; FAX 504/586-0335. 500 rms, 7 story. S $130-$240; D $140-$250; each addl $35; suites $260-$1,000; studio rms $260; under 17 free; travel package plans; min stay required Mardi Gras, special events. Crib free. Garage $12. TV; cable, in-rm movies. Heated pool; poolside serv. Restaurants 6:30 am-11:30 pm (also see DESIRE OYSTER BAR). Bars 9-3 am; entertainment. Ck-out noon. Meeting rms. Exercise equipt; weight machine, bicycle. Minibars. **LUXURY LEVEL : TOWER.** 26 rms, 4 suites. S, D $240; suites $525-$595. Some full wet bars, minibars. Deluxe toiletry amenities. Complimentary continental bkfst. Cr cds: A, C, D, DS, ER, JCB, MC, V.

⊡ ≈ 🏃 ⛷ 🔥 SC

★ ★ ★ **SHERATON.** 500 Canal St (70130), in central business district. 504/525-2500; FAX 504/595-5550. 1,100 rms, 49 story. S $120-$209; D $145-$229; each addl $25; suites from $250; under 18 free. Crib free. Valet parking $11. TV; cable. Pool; poolside serv. Complimentary coffee in rms. Restaurant 6:30-11 pm. Rm serv 24 hrs. Bar from 11 am; entertainment. Ck-out noon. Convention facilities. Concierge. Shopping arcade. Exercise equipt; weight machine, bicycles. Game rm. Bathrm phones. Adj to French Quarter. **LUXURY LEVEL : EXECUTIVE LEVEL.** 200 rms, 9 floors, 45 suites. S, D $185-$249; suites $350-$1,200. Concierge. Private lounge, honor bar. Minibars. Complimentary continental bkfst, refreshments, newspaper. Cr cds: A, C, D, DS, ER, JCB, MC, V.

⊡ ≈ 🏃 ⛷ 🔥 SC

★ ★ **THE WESTIN CANAL PLACE.** 100 Rue Iberville (70130), in Canal Place Shopping Ctr, in French Quarter. 504/566-7006; FAX 504/553-5120. 438 rms, 29 story. S $165-$180; D $180-$195; each addl $25; suites $245-$1,500; under 19 free; wkend, honeymoon, local attraction packages. Crib free. Garage $12; valet. TV; cable. Heated pool; poolside serv. Restaurant 6:30 am-10:30 pm. Rm serv 24 hrs. Bar 11-2 am. Ck-out 1 pm. Convention facilities. Concierge. Shopping arcade. Barber, beauty shop. Tennis privileges, pro. 18-hole golf privileges, pro, putting green, driving range. Health club privileges. Bathrm

phones, refrigerators, minibars. Outstanding views of Mississippi River. **LUXURY LEVEL : EXECUTIVE CLUB.** 55 rms, 2 floors. S, D $245-$285. Private lounge. Complimentary continental bkfst, refreshments. Cr cds: A, C, D, DS, ER, JCB, MC, V.

⊡ 🏋 ⛷ ≈ ⛷ 🔥 SC

★ ★ ★ **WINDSOR COURT.** (4-Star 1994; New general manager, therefore not rated) 300 Gravier St (70140), in central business district. 504/523-6000; res: 800/262-2662; FAX 504/596-4513. 315 units, 23 story, 275 suites. S, D $225-$275; suites $300-$500, each addl $25; under 18 free. Crib free. Valet parking $15. TV; cable. Heated pool; poolside serv. Restaurant (see GRILL ROOM). British high tea daily (2-6 pm), Sat & Sun brunch. Rm serv 24 hrs. 2 bars from 9 am; entertainment. Ck-out 1 pm. Convention facilities. Concierge. Gift shop. Indoor tennis privileges adj, pro. 18-hole golf privileges, greens fee $35, pro, putting green, driving range. Exercise rm; instructor, weights, bicycles, whirlpool, sauna, steam rm. Massage. Bathrm phones, refrigerators, minibars; wet bar in suites. Balconies. Collection of antiques and original artwork. Offers art tours Sat 4 pm. Cr cds: A, C, D, DS, MC, V.

⊡ 🏋 ⛷ ≈ 🏃 ⛷ 🔥 SC

Inns

★ **THE FRENCHMEN.** 417 Frenchmen St (70116), in Faubourg Marigny. 504/948-2166; res: 800/831-1781; FAX 504/948-2258. 25 rms, 2 story. S, D $84-$135; each addl $20; summer rates. Indoor parking $5. TV; cable. Pool; whirlpool. Complimentary continental bkfst. Serv bar 24 hrs. Ck-out 1 pm, ck-in 3 pm. Concierge serv 24 hrs. Balconies. Two town houses built 1860; individually decorated rms; antiques. Rms overlook courtyard, pool & patio. Cr cds: A, MC, V.

⊡ ≈ 🔥 SC

★ ★ **GRENOBLE HOUSE.** 329 Dauphine St (70112), in French Quarter. 504/522-1331; FAX 504/524-4968. 17 kit. suites, 3 story. S, D $145-$315; each addl $30; wkly, summer rates; higher rates special events. Crib free. TV; cable. Pool; whirlpool. Complimentary continental bkfst. Complimentary coffee in rms. Restaurant adj 7-10 pm. Ck-out noon, ck-in 3 pm. Concierge. Balconies. Restored 19th-century town house; courtyard. Antiques. Cr cds: A, MC, V.

≈ 🔥

★ ★ **HOTEL MAISON DE VILLE.** 727 Toulouse St (70130), in French Quarter. 504/561-5858; res: 800/634-1600; FAX 504/561-5858. 23 rms, 1-3 story, 5 kit. cottages. S, D $105-$415; each addl $30; suites $235; kit. cottages $325-$415. Children over 12 yrs only. Valet parking (fee). TV; cable. Pool at cottages. Complimentary continental bkfst, tea/sherry. Restaurant (see BISTRO). Rm serv. Ck-out 1 pm, ck-in 3 pm. Bellhops. Valet serv. Private patios, balconies. Overlooks courtyard with fountain and garden. Cr cds: A, C, D, DS, MC, V.

≈ 🔥 SC

★ **HOTEL ST PIERRE.** 911 Rue Burgundy (70116), in French Quarter. 504/524-4401; FAX 504/524-6800. 74 rms, 2 story. S $99; D $119; each addl $10; under 12 free; wkends (2-night min); higher rates special events; lower rates rest of yr. Crib free. Pet accepted. TV; cable. 2 pools. Complimentary continental bkfst. Restaurant nearby. Ck-out 11 am. Bellhops. Concierge. Valet serv. Refrigerators avail. Cr cds: A, C, D, DS, MC, V.

⊡ 🐾 ≈ 🔥 SC

★ ★ **LAFITTE GUEST HOUSE.** 1003 Bourbon St (70116), in French Quarter. 504/581-2678; res: 800/331-7971. 14 rms, 4 story. S, D $95-$165; each addl $20; higher rates special events. Parking $5. TV. Complimentary continental bkfst. Ck-out noon, ck-in 2 pm. Some refrigerators. Private balconies. Individually decorated rms; fine antique furnishings. Cr cds: A, DS, MC, V.

🔥

✔ ★ **LAMOTHE HOUSE.** 621 Esplanade Ave (70116), in Faubourg Marigny. 504/947-1161; res: 800/367-5858; FAX 504/943-6536.

20 rms, 3 story. S, D $75-$105; suites $140-$250. Crib free. TV; cable. Complimentary continental bkfst. Restaurant nearby. Ck-out 11 am, ck-in 2 pm. Restored town house built around patio; antique furnishings. Adj to French Quarter. Cr cds: A, MC, V.

★ ★ ★ **MELROSE MANSION.** *937 Esplanade Ave (70116), in Faubourg Marigny.* 504/944-2255. 8 rms, 2 story, 4 suites. D $225-$250; suites $325-$425. TV; cable. Heated pool. Complimentary full bkfst, coffee & tea. Restaurant nearby. Rm serv. Ck-out noon, ck-in 1 pm. Free airport, RR station, bus depot transportation. Some in-rm marble whirlpools. Balconies. Antiques. Library. Historic Victorian-Gothic mansion (1884); pillared verandas, tropical patio. Overlooks French Quarter. Cr cds: A, MC, V.

★ ★ **SONIAT HOUSE.** *1133 Chartres St (70116), in French Quarter.* 504/522-0570; res: 800/544-8808; FAX 504/522-7208. 24 rms, 3 story, 7 suites. S, D $135-$185; each addl $25; suites $225-$600. Valet parking $12. TV. Continental bkfst avail. Ck-out 1 pm, ck-in 3 pm. Bellhops. Concierge. Bathrm phones; whirlpool in suites. 1830s town house with carriage entrance and sweeping stairways. Hand-carved four-poster beds; antiques. Private courtyard with fountain and tropical plants. Cr cds: A, MC, V.

D

Restaurants

✔★ **ALBERTO'S.** *611 Frenchmen St, in Faubourg Marigny.* 504/949-5952. Hrs: 11:30 am-2:30 pm, 6-11 pm; Sat from 6 pm. Closed Sun; Dec 25; also 1 wk in summer (varies). Italian menu. Bar open 24 hrs. Semi-a la carte: lunch $6-$6.50, dinner $7.25-$16. Specialties: pane chicken & pasta, fettucine crawfish. Upstairs over bar; tables made from old-time sewing machine bases. Cr cds: DS, MC, V.

★ ★ **ALEX PATOUT'S.** *221 Royal St, in French Quarter.* 504/525-7788. Hrs: 5:30-10 pm. Closed most major hols. Res accepted. Cajun, Creole menu. Bar. Semi-a la carte: dinner $15-$32. Specializes in seasonal seafood, Cajun duck. Cr cds: A, C, D, DS, JCB, MC, V.

D

★ ★ ★ **ANTOINE'S.** *713 St Louis St, in French Quarter.* 504/581-4422. Hrs: 11:30 am-2 pm, 5:30-9:30 pm. Closed Sun; Mardi Gras; major hols. Res accepted. French, Creole menu. Serv bar. A la carte entrees: lunch $12-$24, dinner $20-$50. Specialties: oysters Rockefeller, pompano en papillote, souffléed potatoes. Many world-famous dishes have been created & served by Antoine's; one of the great wine cellars of the US. Established 1840. Family-owned. Jacket (dinner). Cr cds: A, C, D, MC, V.

D

★ ★ ★ **ARNAUD'S.** *813 Rue Bienville, in French Quarter.* 504/523-5433. Hrs: 11:30 am-2:30 pm, 6-10 pm; Fri to 10:30 pm; Sat 6-10:30 pm; Sun 6-10 pm; Sun jazz brunch 10 am-2:30 pm. Closed major hols. Res accepted. French, Creole menu. Bars. Wine cellar. A la carte entrees: lunch $9-$15, dinner $25-$50. Complete meals: lunch $9-$15. Sun brunch $16-$26. Specialties: shrimp Arnaud, pompano en croute, filet mignon Charlemond. Own desserts. Built in 1790; opened in 1918 and restored to original design. Jacket (dinner). Cr cds: A, C, D, MC, V.

★ ★ **BACCO.** *310 Chartres St, in French Quarter.* 504/522-2426. Hrs: 7-10:30 am, 11:30 am-2:30 pm, 5:30-10 pm; Sat from 5 pm; Sun from 5:30 pm; Sun brunch 10:30 am-2:30 pm. Closed Mardi Gras, Dec 24-25. Res accepted. Italian cuisine with Creole accents. Bar. Semi-a la carte: lunch $7.75-$12, dinner $10.50-$22.50. Sun brunch $7-$12. Specializes in wood-fired pizza, grilled seafood. Parking. Cr cds: A, C, D, MC, V.

D

★ **BANGKOK CUISINE.** *4137 S Carrollton Ave, west of central business district.* 504/482-3606. Hrs: 11 am-3 pm, 5-10 pm; Fri to 11 pm; Sat 5-11 pm; Sun 5-10 pm. Closed July 4, Thanksgiving, Dec 25. Res accepted. Thai menu. Semi-a la carte: lunch $4.50-$6.95, dinner $7.95-$16.95. Specializes in seafood. Parking. Candlelight dining. Cr cds: A, MC, V.

✔★ **BART'S ON THE LAKE.** *8000 Lakeshore Dr, north of central business district.* 504/282-0271. Hrs: 10:30 am-10 pm; Fri, Sat to 11 pm; Sun 10:30 am-9:30 pm; Sun brunch 10:30 am-2 pm. Closed Mon; Dec 25. Bar. Semi-a la carte: lunch $5-$10, dinner $8-$16. Sun brunch $11.95. Child's meals. Specializes in grilled fish, seafood platter. Parking. Veranda dining with view of harbor. Cr cds: A, D, DS, MC, V.

D SC

★ ★ **BAYONA.** *430 Rue Dauphine, in French Quarter.* 504/525-4455. Hrs: 11:30 am-2 pm, 6-10 pm; Fri to 11 pm; Sat 6-11 pm. Closed Sun; Mardi Gras, Easter, Dec 25. Res accepted. Mediterranean menu. Bar. Semi-a la carte: lunch $8-$12, dinner $11-$20. Specializes in grilled duck, fresh fish. Outdoor dining in courtyard with fountain. Located in a century-old Creole cottage. Cr cds: A, D, DS, MC, V.

D

★ ★ ★ **BELLA LUNA.** *914 N Peter, Decatur at Dumaine, in French Quarter.* 504/529-1583. Hrs: 6-10:30 pm; Sun 5-9:30 pm. Closed Dec 24; Mardi Gras. Res accepted. Continental menu. Bar. A la carte entrees: dinner $13-$23. Specializes in homemade fettucine, quesadillas. Own pasta. Located in French Market; exceptional view of Mississippi River. Cr cds: A, D, DS, MC, V.

D

★ ★ **BISTRO.** *(See Hotel Maison de Ville Inn)* 504/528-9206. Hrs: 11:30 am-2 pm, 6-10:30 pm; Sun from 6 pm. Res accepted. Serv bar. Wine list. Semi-a la carte: lunch $10-$13, dinner $17-$25. Specializes in pork, game, local seafood. Own desserts. Outdoor dining. Bistro setting, in 18th-century house. Cr cds: A, D, MC, V.

D

★ ★ **BON TON CAFE.** *401 Magazine St, in central business district.* 504/524-3386. Hrs: 11 am-2 pm, 5-9:30 pm. Closed Sat, Sun; major hols. Res accepted. Cajun menu. A la carte entrees: lunch $8.50-$18.50, dinner $17.50-$23.50. Child's meals. Specialties: red fish Bon Ton, crawfish dishes. Candle chandelier, shuttered windows, wildlife prints on exposed brick walls. Cr cds: A, D, MC, V.

D

★ ★ ★ **BRENNAN'S.** *417 Royal St, in French Quarter.* 504/525-9711. Hrs: 8 am-2:30 pm, 6-10 pm. Closed Dec 24 (evening), 25. Res accepted. French, Creole menu. Bar. Wine cellar. Complete meals: bkfst $18-$37, dinner $28.50-$36. Own desserts. Best known for unusual bkfsts. Cocktails served in courtyard. Located in 1795 mansion where Andrew Jackson was a frequent guest. Family-owned. Cr cds: A, C, D, DS, JCB, MC, V.

★ ★ ★ **BRIGTSEN'S.** *723 Dante St, west of central business district.* 504/861-7610. Hrs: 5:30-10 pm. Closed Sun, Mon; most major hols & Dec 24. Res accepted. Cajun, Creole menu. Serv bar. A la carte entrees: dinner $12-$20. Specializes in rabbit, duck, seafood. Parking. In restored 1900s house built from river barge timbers. French-country decor. Menu changes daily. Cr cds: A, D, MC, V.

★ ★ ★ **BROUSSARD'S.** *819 Rue Conti, in French Quarter.* 504/581-3866. Hrs: 5:30 pm-closing. Closed Dec 25. Res accepted. French, Creole menu. Bar. A la carte entrees: dinner $19-$27.50. Complete meals: dinner $27.25-$34. Specialties: veal Broussard, Pompano Napoleon, bananas Foster. Outdoor dining. Courtyard patio. Jacket. Cr cds: A, C, D, DS, MC, V.

D

✔★ **CASAMENTO'S.** *4330 Magazine, west of central business district.* 504/895-9761. Hrs: 11:30 am-1:30 pm, 5:30-9 pm. Closed

Mon; some major hols; June-Aug. Beer. Semi-a la carte: lunch, dinner $5-$15. Child's meals. Specializes in oyster loaves, seafood gumbo, soft shell crab. Family-owned. No cr cds accepted.

★ ★ ★ **CHRISTIAN'S.** *3835 Iberville St, north of central business district.* 504/482-4924. Hrs: 5:30-10 pm; Thurs-Fri also 11:30 am-2 pm. Closed Sun; Thanksgiving, Dec 25. Res accepted. French, Creole menu. Bar. Wine cellar. Complete meals: lunch $9.25-$15. A la carte entrees: dinner $12.50-$20. Specialties: oysters Roland, baby veal Christian, bouillabaisse. Homemade ices, ice cream. Parking. In renovated former church (1904). Cr cds: A, C, D, MC, V.

★ ★ ★ **COMMANDER'S PALACE.** *1403 Washington Ave, in Garden District.* 504/899-8221. Hrs: 11:30 am-2 pm, 6-10 pm; Sat brunch 11:30 am-1 pm; Sun brunch 10 am-1 pm. Closed Mardi Gras, Dec 24, 25. Res accepted. Haute Creole menu. Bar. Wine cellar. Semi-a la carte: lunch $10-$24, dinner $19-$26. Complete meals: lunch $10.50-$14, dinner $27-$35. Brunch $16-$26. Specialties: turtle soup, trout with roasted pecans, bread pudding soufflé. Dixieland band at brunch. Valet parking. Outdoor dining. Located in Queen Anne/Victorian building in residential area. Family-owned. Jacket (dinner & Sun brunch). Cr cds: A, C, D, DS, MC, V.

D

★ ★ **COURT OF TWO SISTERS.** *613 Royal St, in French Quarter.* 504/522-7261. Hrs: 5:30-11 pm; brunch 9 am-3 pm. Closed Dec 25. Res accepted. French, Creole menu. Bar. A la carte entrees: dinner $15-$25. Complete meals: dinner $35, brunch $19. Child's meals. Specialties: shrimp Toulouse, lobster étouffée. Jazz trio at brunch. Outdoor dining. Built in 1832; spacious patio; courtyard. Family-owned. Cr cds: A, D, DS, MC, V.

D

✔ ★ **DESIRE OYSTER BAR.** *(See Royal Sonesta Hotel)* 504/586-0300. Hrs: 11:30 am-11:30 pm; Fri, Sat to 12:30 am. Bar. Semi-a la carte: lunch, dinner $7-$15.25. Child's meals. Specializes in Creole cuisine. Own baking. Parking. Bistro doors & windows offer view of French Quarter streets. Family-owned. Cr cds: A, C, D, DS, ER, JCB, MC, V.

D

★ ★ ★ **EMERIL'S.** *800 Tchoupitoulas St, in central business district.* 504/528-9393. Hrs: 11:30 am-2 pm, 6-10 pm; Sat from 6 pm. Closed Sun; Mardi Gras, most major hols. Res accepted. Creole, Amer menu. Bar. A la carte entrees: lunch $7.50-$15, dinner $14-$25. Menu changes seasonally. Located in renovated warehouse. Near convention center. Cr cds: A, C, D, DS, MC, V.

D

★ ★ **FEELINGS CAFE.** *2600 Chartres St, in Faubourg Marigny.* 504/945-2222. Hrs: 6-10 pm; Fri 11 am-2 pm, 6-11 pm; Sat 6-11 pm; Sun 5-9 pm; Sun brunch 11 am-2:30 pm. Closed Thanksgiving, Dec 25; also Mardi Gras. Creole menu. Bar. Semi-a la carte: lunch $8.75-$12.50, dinner $9.75-$14.75. Sun brunch $14-$18.50. Specializes in seafood, veal, chicken. Own desserts. Pianist Fri-Sat. Outdoor dining. Located in out-building of 18th-century plantation; antiques, original artwork. Cr cds: A, C, D, DS, MC, V.

★ **FELIX'S.** *739 Iberville St, in French Quarter.* 504/522-4440. Hrs: 10:30 am-midnight; Fri, Sat to 1 am; Sun 10 am-10 pm. Closed some hols; also Mardi Gras, Mother's & Father's Day. Cajun, Creole menu. Bar. Semi-a la carte: lunch, dinner $6-$16. Child's meals. Specializes in seafood. Raw oyster bar. Cr cds: A, MC, V.

D

✔ ★ **FIVE HAPPINESS.** *3605 S Carrollton Ave, west of central business district.* 504/488-6468. Hrs: 11:30 am-10:30 pm; Fri, Sat to 11:30 pm; Sun noon-10:30 pm. Closed Thanksgiving. Chinese menu. Bar. Semi-a la carte: lunch from $5.20, dinner from $6.95. Specializes in mandarin & Szechwan dishes. Parking. Cr cds: A, C, D, DS, MC, V.

D

★ ★ **G & E COURTYARD GRILL.** *1113 Decatur St, in French Quarter.* 504/528-9376. Hrs: 11:30 am-2:30 pm, 6-10 pm; Fri, Sat to 11 pm; Sun 6-10 pm. Closed Mon; Thanksgiving, Dec 25. Res accepted. Continental menu. Bar. A la carte entrees: lunch $9-$13, dinner $11-$23. Specializing in grilled loin chops, grilled salmon filet. Patio dining in canopied courtyard. European cafe atmosphere. Cr cds: A, C, D, DS, MC, V.

★ ★ **GABRIELLE.** *3201 Esplanade Ave (70119), north of central business district.* 504/948-6233. Hrs: 5:30-10 pm. Closed Sun & Mon; major hols; also closed Mardi Gras. Res accepted. Bar. Semi-a la carte: dinner $13-$21. Specializes in contemporary Creole cuisine. Own sausage, desserts. Parking. Outdoor dining. Bistro atmosphere. Cr cds: A, C, D, DS, MC, V.

★ ★ **GALATOIRE'S.** *209 Bourbon St, in French Quarter.* 504/525-2021. Hrs: 11:30 am-9 pm; Sun from noon. Closed Mon; major hols; also Mardi Gras. French, Creole menu. Serv bar. A la carte entrees: lunch, dinner $13-$24. Specialties: trout Marguery, oysters en bronchette. Family-owned. Jacket (after 5 pm). Cr cds: A, MC, V.

D

★ ★ ★ **GAUTREAU'S.** *1728 Soniat St, west of central business district.* 504/899-7397. Hrs: 6-10 pm. Closed Sun; most major hols; also 1st 2 wks July. Res accepted. New American cuisine. Wine. A la carte entrees: dinner $14.75-$21.95. Specializes in seafood, Creole cooking. Menu changes seasonally. Valet parking. Former drug store from early 1900s; original medicine cabinets, pressed-tin ceiling. Cr cds: C, D, DS, MC, V.

★ ★ ★ ★ **GRILL ROOM.** *(See Windsor Court Hotel)* 504/522-1992. Hrs: 7-10:30 am, 11:30 am-2:30 pm, 6:30-10:30 pm; Sat, Sun brunch 11:30 am-2:30 pm. Res accepted. Continental, regional cuisine. Wine cellar. Bar 11 am-midnight. A la carte entrees: bkfst $8-$13, lunch $9.75-$19.75, dinner $19.50-$45. Sat & Sun brunch $16-$27. Specialties: oysters polo, rack of lamb, mandarin coffee glazed duck, fresh seafood. Own baking. Valet parking. View of courtyard. Traditional English decor. Jacket. Cr cds: A, C, D, MC, V.

D

★ ★ **KUNG'S DYNASTY.** *1912 St Charles Ave (70130), in central business district.* 504/525-6669. Hrs: 11:30 am-10:15 pm; wkends noon-10:30 pm. Closed Jan 1, July 4, Thanksgiving. Res accepted. Chinese menu. Serv bar. A la carte entrees: lunch $5.95-$6.95, dinner $7.95-$13.95. Specialty: Kung's chicken. Parking. In Victorian house; Chinese art. Cr cds: A, D, DS, MC, V.

D

★ ★ **L'ECONOMIE.** *325 Girod St, in central business district.* 504/524-7405. Hrs: 11 am-2 pm, 6-9:30 pm; Fri to 10:30 pm; Sat 6-10:30 pm. Closed Sun & Mon; Mardi Gras, major hols. Res accepted. French menu. Bar. A la carte entrees: lunch $6.95-$8.95, dinner $7.95-$15.50. Specialties: poached salmon with Chablis and honey, quail with dry sherry, fish with vanilla sauce. Bistro atmosphere. Cr cds: MC, V.

D

✔ ★ **LOUISIANA PIZZA KITCHEN.** *2808 Esplanade Ave, north of central business district.* 504/488-2800. Hrs: 5:30-11 pm. Closed Dec 25. Mediterranean menu. Bar. A la carte entrees: dinner $6-$10. Specializes in wood-fired gourmet pizza. Local artwork on display. Cr cds: A, C, D, DS, MC, V.

★ ★ **MAXIMO'S ITALIAN GRILL.** *1117 Rue Decatur, in French Quarter.* 504/586-8883. Hrs: 6 pm-midnight. Northern Italian menu. Bar. Semi-a la carte: dinner $5.50-$24.95. Specializes in pasta, veal, grilled fish. Own desserts, ice cream. Outdoor balcony dining. Contemporary decor with antique light fixtures. Cr cds: A, C, D, DS, MC, V.

D

★ ★ ★ **MIKE'S ON THE AVENUE.** *628 St Charles Ave, in the Lafayette Hotel, in central business district.* 504/523-1709. Hrs: 11:30

am-2 pm, 6-10 pm; Sat & Sun from 6 pm. Closed some major hols. Res accepted. Bar. Wine list. New Amer menu. Semi-a la carte: lunch $14-$22, dinner $32-$50. Specializes in Chinese dumplings, crayfish cakes, grilled lamb chops. Cr cds: A, C, D, DS, MC, V.

D

★ ★ **MOSCA'S.** 4137 US 90W, 4¹/₂ mi W of Huey Long Bridge, west of central business district. 504/436-9942. Hrs: 5:30-9:30 pm. Closed Sun, Mon; Dec 25; also Aug. Res accepted. Italian menu. Bar. A la carte entrees: dinner $24-$28. Specializes in shrimp, chicken, oysters. Own pasta. Parking. Family-owned. No cr cds accepted.

★ ★ ★ **MR B'S BISTRO.** 201 Royal St, in French Quarter. 504/523-2078. Hrs: 11:30 am-3 pm, 5-10 pm; Sun jazz brunch 10:30 am-3 pm. Closed Mardi Gras, Dec 24-25. Res accepted. Creole menu. Bar. Wine list. Complete meals: lunch $9-$13, dinner $18-$26. Semi-a la carte: lunch $9-$11, dinner $10-$22. Sun brunch $7.50-$12.75. Child's meals. Specializes in pasta, hickory-grilled food, seafood. Entertainment. Bistro decor with mahogany bar, etched-glass walls, white marble-topped tables. Cr cds: A, D, MC, V.

D

★ ★ **NOLA.** 534 St Louis St (70130), in French Quarter. 504/522-6652. Hrs: 11:30 am-2 pm, 6-10 pm; Fri & Sat to midnight; Sun from 6 pm. Closed Jan 1, Thanksgiving, Dec 25. Res accepted. Creole menu. Bar. Semi-a la carte: lunch $8-$15, dinner $10-$18. Specialties: Lafayette Boudin stewed with beer, onions, cane syrup and Creole mustard, cedar plank roasted Gulf fish. In renovated warehouse. Original artwork. Cr cds: A, C, D, DS, MC, V.

D

★ **THE ORIGINAL FRENCH MARKET.** 1001 Decatur St, in French Quarter. 504/581-9855. Hrs: 11 am-11 pm; Fri to midnight; Sat to 1 am. Closed Thanksgiving, Dec 25. Creole, Cajun menu. Bar. Semi-a la carte: lunch, dinner $6-$20. Child's meals. Specializes in fresh seafood. Entertainment; Fri, Sat evenings. Balcony dining. Beamed ceiling, gaslight sconces, brick bar. Cr cds: A, C, D, DS, MC, V.

D

★ ★ **PALACE CAFE.** 605 Canal St, in central business district. 504/523-1661. Hrs: 11:30 am-2:30 pm, 5-10 pm; Sun 10:30 am-2:30 pm. Closed Dec 24-25; also Mardi Gras. Res accepted. French brasserie menu. Bar 11:30 am-10 pm. A la carte entrees: lunch $7.25-$10.75, dinner $12-$19. Complete meals: dinner $12-$19. Specialties: catfish pecan, rotisserie pork loin, white chocolate bread pudding. Restored music store (ca 1890); murals of local jazz musicians; elaborate iron staircase leading to wrap-around mezzanine. Bi-level dining. Cr cds: A, C, D, MC, V.

D

★ **PORT OF CALL.** 838 Esplanade Ave, in French Quarter. 504/523-0120. Hrs: 11-1 am; wkends to 3 am. Bar. Semi-a la carte: lunch $3.75-$19.50. Specializes in hamburgers, steak, pizza. Casual atmosphere. Nautical decor. Cr cds: A.

✔★ **PRALINE CONNECTION.** 542 Frenchmen St, in Faubourg Marigny. 504/943-3934. Hrs: 11 am-10:30 pm; Fri, Sat to midnight. Closed Dec 25. Southern Creole menu. Bar. Semi-a la carte: lunch $3-$5.95, dinner $4-$12.95. Child's meals. Specializes in fried chicken, pork chops, bread pudding with praline sauce. Candy room features praline confections. Cr cds: A, C, D, DS, MC, V.

D

★ ★ ★ **RIB ROOM.** (See Omni Royal Orleans Hotel) 504/529-7045. Hrs: 6:30 am-3 pm, 6-11 pm; Sat & Sun brunch 11:30 am-3 pm. Res accepted. Bar. Wine cellar. Semi-a la carte: lunch $12-$17, dinner $20-$26. Sat & Sun brunch $8.50-$15.50. Specializes in rotisserie prime rib, seafood, traditional dishes with Creole flair. Own pastries. Parking. Cr cds: A, C, D, DS, MC, V.

SC

✔★ **ROBEAR'S LIGHTHOUSE BAR & GRILL.** 7360 W Roadway, West End Park, west of central business district. 504/282-3415. Hrs: 11 am-10 pm; Fri, Sat to 11 pm. Bar to 2 am. Semi-a la carte: lunch, dinner $4.95-$12.95. Child's meals. Specializes in seafood. Parking. Patio dining. Cr cds: A, MC, V.

D

✔★ ★ **SANTA FE.** 801 Frenchmen St, at Washington Sq, in Faubourg Marigny. 504/944-6854. Hrs: 5-11 pm. Closed Sun, Mon; major hols. Mexican, Southwestern menu. Bar. Wine list. Semi-a la carte: dinner from $7.25. Specializes in seafood, chicken, beef, seafood fajitas. Own pastries. Overlooks Washington Park. Cr cds: A, MC, V.

D

★ ★ ★ **SAZERAC.** (See Fairmont Hotel) 504/529-7111. Hrs: 11:30 am-2:30 pm, 6-10:30 pm; Sat, Sun from 6 pm. Res accepted. Creole menu. A la carte entrees: lunch $14-$24, dinner $16-$32. Complete meals: lunch $14.95. Specialties: roast Louisiana duckling, grilled pompano, grilled veal chops. Own pastries, desserts. Pianist 6-10 pm. Valet parking. Formal decor; original art. Family-owned. Cr cds: A, C, D, DS, JCB, MC, V.

★ **SNUG HARBOR JAZZ BISTRO.** 626 Frenchmen St (70116), in Faubourg Marigny. 504/949-0696. Hrs: 5-11:30 pm; Fri & Sat to 12:30 am. Closed Easter, Dec 25. Bar to 1:30 am. Semi-a la carte: dinner $5.50-$18. Child's meals. Specializes in hamburgers, shrimp. Modern jazz nightly. Contemporary dining. Cr cds: A, MC, V.

★ ★ **TAVERN ON THE PARK.** 900 City Park Ave, north of central business district. 504/486-3333. Hrs: 11:30 am-2:30 pm, 5-10:30 pm; Sat from 5 pm. Closed Sun; Thanksgiving, Dec 25. Res accepted. Creole menu. Bar. Semi-a la carte: lunch $7-$11, dinner $20-$25. Complete meals: lunch $10.95, dinner $24.95. Child's meals. Specialties: Australian lobster tail, stuffed soft shell crab, trout Martha. Parking. Outdoor dining. Overlooks park. Cr cds: A, C, D, JCB, MC, V.

★ **TONY MORAN'S PASTA E VINO.** 240 Bourbon St, at Old Absinthe House, in French Quarter. 504/523-3181. Hrs: 5:30 pm-12:30 am. Closed Mon; Dec 25. Res accepted. Italian menu. Bar. A la carte entrees: dinner $7-$16. Specializes in Northern Italian cuisine, fresh pasta. Family-owned. Cr cds: A, C, D, MC, V.

D

★ ★ **TUJAGUE'S.** 823 Decatur St, in French Quarter. 504/525-8676. Hrs: 11 am-3 pm, 5-10:30 pm; Sat to 11 pm. Res accepted. French, Creole menu. Bar 10 am-11 pm. Complete meals: lunch $6.95-$13.95, dinner $22.95-$28. Child's meals. Specialties: shrimp Creole, crawfish, crab & spinach bisque. Established in 1856 in old Spanish armory (1750); original tile, authentic beams. Oldest standing bar in city. Cr cds: A, C, D, DS, JCB, MC, V.

D

★ ★ ★ **THE VERANDA.** (See Inter-Continental Hotel) 504/525-5566. Hrs: 6 am-3 pm, 5:30-10:30 pm; Sun jazz brunch 11 am-3 pm. Res accepted. Continental menu. Bar 11-1 am. A la carte entrees: bkfst $10-$12, lunch $7-$14, dinner $10-$21. Buffet: bkfst $10.95, lunch $13.75. Sun brunch $24. Specializes in regional American dishes, seafood. Valet parking. Garden-like setting. Cr cds: A, C, D, DS, ER, JCB, MC, V.

D

★ ★ **VERSAILLES.** 2100 St Charles Ave, in Garden District. 504/524-2535. Hrs: 6-10 pm. Closed Sun; Mardi Gras, major hols; also 2 wks in summer. Res accepted. French, Creole menu. Bar. Wine cellar. A la carte entrees: dinner $18-$28. Specialties: bouillabaisse Marseillaise, veal Farci Versailles, chocolate pava. Own baking. Valet parking. Cr cds: A, C, D, MC, V.

D

★ ★ **WINDJAMMER.** *8550 Pontchartrain Blvd, west of central business district.* 504/283-8301. Hrs: 11 am-11 pm; Fri to midnight; Sat 5 pm-midnight; Sun 5-11 pm. Closed Mardi Gras, July 4, Labor Day, Dec 25. Res accepted. Cajun, Amer menu. Bar. Semi-a la carte: lunch $7.95-$11.95, dinner $7.95-$24.95. Specializes in seafood, steak. Family-owned. Cr cds: A, C, D, DS, MC, V.

D

Unrated Dining Spots

ANGELO BROCATA'S ITALIAN ICE CREAM PARLOR. *537 St Ann St, on Jackson Square, in French Quarter.* 504/525-9676. Hrs: 10 am-6 pm; Fri to 10 pm; Sat to 11 pm; Sun 9 am-8 pm. Closed Thanksgiving, Dec 25. Specializes in Italian ice creams, ices & baked goods. Est 1905. In Lower Portalbo Apartments on Jackson Square. No cr cds accepted.

CAFE DU MONDE. *800 Decatur St, at St Ann St in French Quarter.* 504/525-4544. Open 24 hrs. Closed Dec 25. Specializes in beignets (hot doughnuts sprinkled with powdered sugar), New Orleans chicory coffee, cafe au lait. Covered outdoor dining. In French Market. No cr cds accepted.

CAMELLIA GRILL. *626 S Carrollton Ave, west of central business district.* 504/866-9573. Hrs: 9-1 am; Fri to 3 am; Sat 8-3 am; Sun 8-1 am. Closed most hols. Semi-a la carte: bkfst, lunch, dinner $1.50-$7. Specializes in omelettes, gourmet sandwiches, pecan pie. Popular night spot; unique place. Family-owned. No cr cds accepted.

CENTRAL GROCERY. *923 Decatur St, in French Quarter.* 504/523-1620. Hrs: 8 am-5:30 pm; Sun from 9 am. A la carte entrees: bkfst, lunch, dinner $3-$5.50. Specialty: muffuletta sandwich. French, Greek & Syrian foods. Sandwich bar in Italian grocery. Near Jackson Square. Family-owned. Cr cds: MC, V.

CHEZ NOUS CHARCUTERIE. *5701 Magazine St, west of central business district.* 504/899-7303. Hrs: 11 am-6:30 pm; Sat to 5 pm. Closed Sun; most major hols. Creole menu. A la carte entrees: lunch $1.65-$6.50. Specialties: grillades, jambalaya. Outdoor dining. Gourmet delicatessen in grocery store. Cr cds: MC, V.

CLOVER GRILL. *900 Bourbon St, in French Quarter.* 504/523-0904. Open 24 hrs. A la carte entrees: bkfst $2-$5, lunch, dinner $3-$7. Specializes in hamburgers, club sandwiches. Open kitchen. Cr cds: A, MC, V.

LA MADELEINE. *547 St Ann St, in French Quarter.* 504/568-9950. Hrs: 7 am-9 pm. Closed Jan 1. French menu. Wine, beer. Avg ck: bkfst $5, lunch, dinner $7.50. Specializes in croissants, quiche, pastries. Own baking. Located in one of the famous Pontalba Bldgs (1851) on Jackson Sq. No cr cds accepted.

SC

MOTHER'S. *401 Poydras St, in central business district.* 504/523-9656. Hrs: 5 am-10 pm; Sun from 7 am. Cajun, Creole menu. A la carte entrees: bkfst $4.75-$7.50, lunch, dinner $3.75-$8. Specializes in New Orleans "po' boys" sandwiches, Mother's ferdi (mix of ham & beef). Former residence (1830); extensive collection of US Marine memorabilia. Cafeteria-style service. No cr cds accepted.

D

New York City

Settled: 1615

Pop: 7,322,564

Elev: 0-410 feet

Time zone: Eastern

Area code: 212 (Manhattan); 718 (Bronx, Brooklyn, Queens, Staten Island)

New York is the nation's most populous city and the capital of finance, business, communications and theater. It may not be the center of the universe, but it does occupy a central place in the world's imagination. In one way or another, New York affects the lives of nearly every American. Other cities may attempt to imitate, but nowhere are things done with such style and abundance as the Big Apple.

On April 30, 1789, George Washington took his oath as first president of the United States on the steps of a building on Wall Street, and for a brief time the city was the capital of the new nation. During the 1800s New York experienced tremendous growth, partially due to the opening of the Erie Canal in 1825. The New York Stock Exchange had its origin when local brokers, who had been selling securities under an old buttonwood tree, made formal agreements to do business in 1792. The NYSE opened in 1825 with most shares in canal and mining companies; no shares in industrial corportations were to appear until 1831.

After the Civil War, hardworking immigrants poured in from abroad, and their efforts produced great wealth. Hundreds of new millionaires built mansions along Fifth Avenue and Riverside Drive. In 1898, the city of New York expanded to almost 3.5 million people. Manhattan was made a borough, and four more boroughs were annexed: Bronx, Brooklyn, Queens and Richmond (now the borough of Staten Island).

The 20th century saw the city expanding upward, with the construction of dozens of skyscrapers, and underground, with the building of the world's most extensive subway system.

Business

As the largest city in the United States, New York City is growing stronger every year. Seven of the ten largest banks in the country as well as most of the nation's leading investment banking firms are located here. All three stock exchanges are headquartered in New York. The World Trade Center, with its landmark twin towers, focuses on international trade and finance.

New York City is in the geographic center of the nation's largest market for goods and services. The metropolitan area tops the list in population, personal income and retail sales. The city itself represents a consumer market totaling over $100 billion in resident buying power.

The overall figures of services offered in this city are overwhelming: over 5,000 law and legal service firms, over 3,500 public relations and management consultant companies, nearly 550 commercial photography businesses, about 1,800 computer companies, many of the nation's largest advertising agencies and so on. New York City is the communications capital of the world. All major radio and television networks, major wire services, dozens of mass circulation and specialty publications and many of the nation's leading book publishers are located here.

New York City is also one of the nation's most popular vacation destinations. Expenditures made by more than 25 million visitors annually (5.6 million from overseas) provide a substantial part of the city's total income.

Convention Facilities

Convention and meeting facilities in New York City are extensive. There are approximately 70,000 hotel rooms located in the city. Many of the large hotels have numerous meeting rooms, banquet facilities and exhibit space. There are auditoriums for large conventions with seating capacities up to 25,000, and stadiums that seat as many as 85,000. The Jacob K. Javits Convention Center boasts 900,000 square feet of exhibit space and more than 100 meeting rooms.

Sports and Recreation

Sports fans have Madison Square Garden Center, where the Knicks play basketball and the Rangers play hockey; Yankee and Shea stadiums where the Yankees and Mets play baseball; Meadowlands Stadium, East Rutherford, New Jersey, where the Jets and Giants play football; Aqueduct, Roosevelt and Belmont Park racetracks in Queens.

Many parks with ample recreation opportunities are scattered throughout the boroughs; the queen of city parks is, of course, Central Park in Manhattan. Within Central Park's 840 acres are a lake with boat rentals, skating rinks, a zoo, outdoor theater, restaurants, a castle, gardens and miles of jogging paths.

Entertainment

New York City can satisfy every taste. Cultural activities range from the traditional to the avant-garde: plays, ballet, modern dance, street theater, symphony, opera, free concerts in the parks, jazz festivals, Shakespeare in Central Park during summer, folk music, bluegrass, rock and nightclub performers.

The theater districts are known as Broadway, Off-Broadway and Off-Off-Broadway. Tickets for many shows and events are available from Ticketmaster outlets (phone 212/307-7171) or at a discount on the day of performance from the TKTS booths at 2 World Trade Center in Lower Manhattan and 47th Street and Broadway in Midtown. The Music and Dance Booth, Bryant Park, Ave of the Americas at 42nd St, offers half-price, day-of-performance tickets to music and dance events.

Times Square, the heart of entertainment, is undergoing a rebirth. New theaters, cinemas, skyscrapers and shops have been opened. Even Nathan's of Coney Island (the world-famous hot dog haven) has built a huge Times Square branch.

Historical Areas

New York has much to offer historians. Liberty Island, with the Statue of Liberty and Museum of Immigration, tells the story of the settling of America from pre-Revolutionary days to the present. The statue has

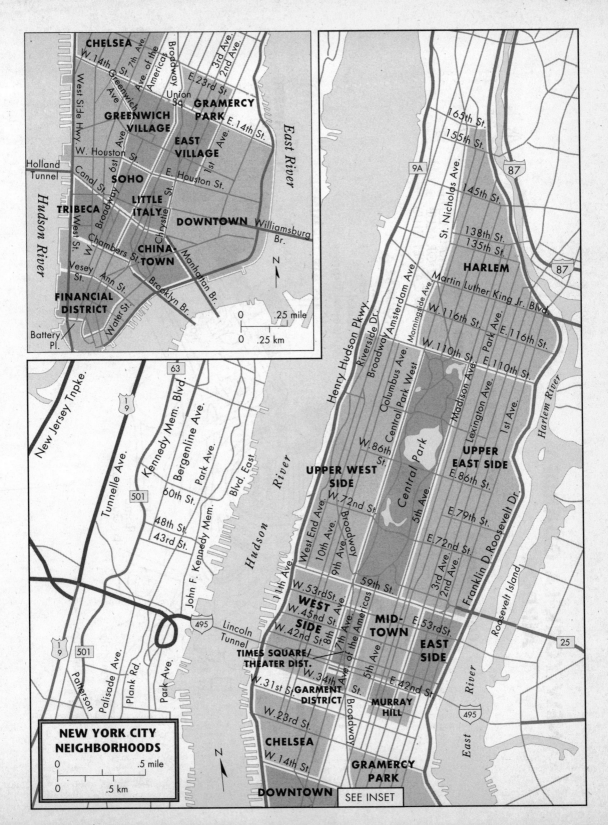

CHELSEA
W. 14th St.
W. 7th Ave.
Ave. of the Americas
Broadway
3rd Ave.
2nd Ave.
E. 23rd St.
West Side Hwy.
Greenwich Ave.
Union Sq.
GRAMERCY PARK
E. 14th St.
GREENWICH VILLAGE
W. Houston St.
6th Ave.
EAST VILLAGE
1st Ave.
Holland Tunnel
Canal St.
E. Houston St.
SOHO
Broadway
LITTLE ITALY
Chrystie St.
TRIBECA
W. Broadway
West St.
Chambers St.
DOWNTOWN
Williamsburg Br.
CHINA-TOWN
Manhattan Br.
Hudson River
Vesey St.
Ann St.
Brooklyn Br.
FINANCIAL DISTRICT
Water St.
Battery Pl.
East River
N
0   .25 mile
0   .25 km

New Jersey Tnpke.
63
1 9
Kennedy Mem. Blvd.
Bergenline Ave.
Park Ave.
Blvd. East
501
60th St.
Tunnelle Ave.
48th St.
43rd St.
John F. Kennedy Mem.
1 9
501
Palisade Ave.
Plank Rd.
Park Ave.
Patterson
495
Lincoln Tunnel
Hudson River
165th St.
155th St.
9A
87
St. Nicholas Ave.
145th St.
138th St.
135th St.
HARLEM
87
Martin Luther King Jr. Blvd.
Amsterdam Ave.
Morningside Ave.
W. 116th St.
Park Ave.
E. 116th St.
Henry Hudson Pkwy.
Riverside Dr.
Broadway
Columbus Ave.
Central Park West
W. 110th St.
Madison Ave.
Lexington Ave.
1st Ave.
E. 110th St.
Harlem River
W. 86th St.
UPPER EAST SIDE
Central Park
E. 86th St.
UPPER WEST SIDE
West End Ave.
10th Ave.
9th Ave.
Broadway
W. 72nd St.
5th Ave.
E. 79th St.
E. 72nd St.
Franklin D. Roosevelt Dr.
Roosevelt Island
59th St.
3rd Ave.
2nd Ave.
11th Ave.
W. 53rd St.
WEST SIDE
W. 45th St.
8th Ave.
7th Ave.
W. 42nd St.
MID-TOWN
E. 53rd St.
TIMES SQUARE/ THEATER DIST.
Ave. of the Americas
5th Ave.
EAST SIDE
E. 42nd St.
W. 34th St.
W. 31st St.
Broadway
GARMENT DISTRICT
MURRAY HILL
25
W. 23rd St.
East River
495
CHELSEA
W. 14th St.
GRAMERCY PARK
N
DOWNTOWN
SEE INSET

NEW YORK CITY NEIGHBORHOODS

0   .5 mile
0   .5 km

NEW YORK LA GUARDIA AIRPORT

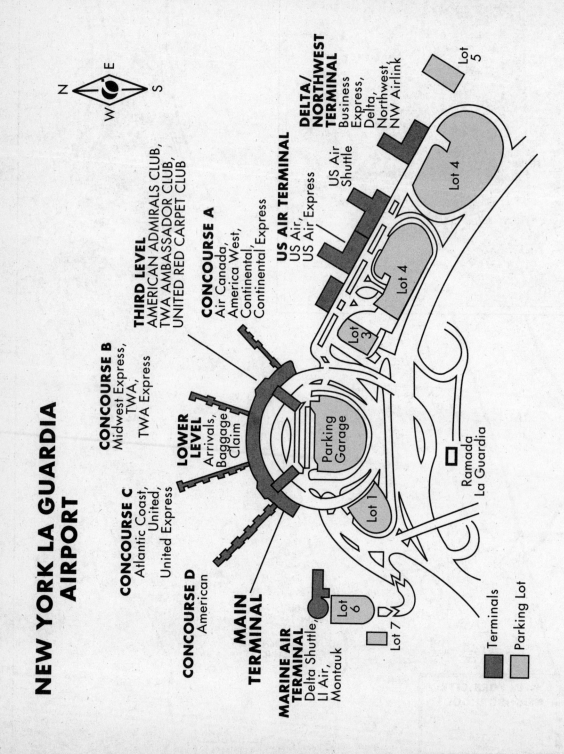

N W E S

CONCOURSE B
Midwest Express,
TWA,
TWA Express

THIRD LEVEL
AMERICAN ADMIRALS CLUB,
TWA AMBASSADOR CLUB,
UNITED RED CARPET CLUB

CONCOURSE A
Air Canada,
America West,
Continental,
Continental Express

US AIR TERMINAL
US Air,
US Air Express

**DELTA/
NORTHWEST
TERMINAL**
Business
Express,
Delta,
Northwest
NW Airlink

US Air
Shuttle

Lot 5

Lot 4

Lot 4

Lot 3

**LOWER
LEVEL**
Arrivals,
Baggage
Claim

CONCOURSE C
Atlantic Coast,
United,
United Express

Parking
Garage

Lot 1

Ramada
La Guardia

CONCOURSE D
American

**MAIN
TERMINAL**

**MARINE AIR
TERMINAL**
Delta Shuttle,
LI Air,
Montauk

Lot 6

Lot 7

Terminals

Parking Lot

New York City 299

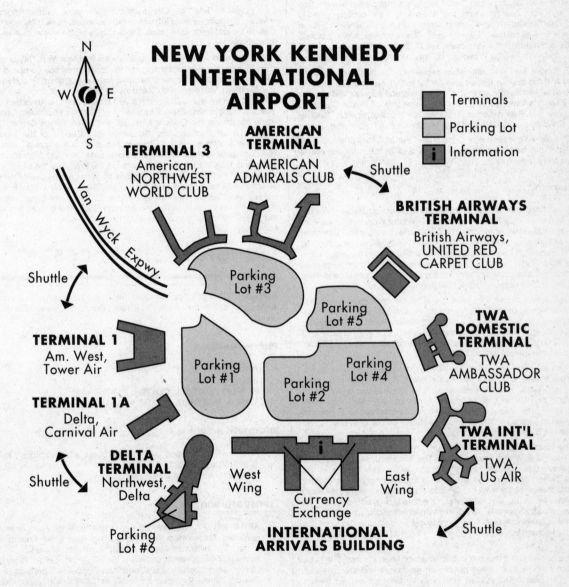

NEW YORK KENNEDY INTERNATIONAL AIRPORT

Terminals
Parking Lot
Information

TERMINAL 3
American,
NORTHWEST
WORLD CLUB

AMERICAN TERMINAL
AMERICAN
ADMIRALS CLUB

Shuttle

BRITISH AIRWAYS TERMINAL
British Airways,
UNITED RED
CARPET CLUB

Van Wyck Expwy.

Shuttle

Parking Lot #3

Parking Lot #5

TERMINAL 1
Am. West,
Tower Air

Parking Lot #1

Parking Lot #2

Parking Lot #4

TWA DOMESTIC TERMINAL
TWA
AMBASSADOR
CLUB

TERMINAL 1A
Delta,
Carnival Air

TWA INT'L TERMINAL
TWA,
US AIR

Shuttle

DELTA TERMINAL
Northwest,
Delta

Parking Lot #6

West Wing

Currency Exchange

East Wing

Shuttle

INTERNATIONAL ARRIVALS BUILDING

undergone restoration, including some reconstruction. It is open to visitors every day except December 25. Ellis Island, which has recently been restored and opened to the public, was the gateway to America for millions of immigrants; nearly one-half of all Americans have relatives who entered the US through Ellis Island.

Castle Clinton in Battery Park, completed in 1811, has been expertly restored to its original appearance. South Street Seaport, the sightseeing attraction on the East River, includes renovated 19th-century landmark buildings, the Fulton Market, a maritime museum, two piers with four historic ships and a working 19th-century printing shop. The Charlton-King-Vandam streets area in Greenwich Village features well-preserved Federal and Greek-revival town houses. Nearby is the site of the long-vanished Richmond Hill mansion, once associated with George Washington, John Adams and Aaron Burr.

Fraunces Tavern Museum has excellent exhibits of the building's history and the famous people associated with it. Federal Hall National Memorial is the site of Washington's first inaugural address and of John Peter Zenger's famous freedom-of-the-press trial. St Paul's Chapel at Broadway and Fulton Street is Manhattan's oldest church. Built in 1766, the chapel is surrounded by a picturesque old graveyard.

The New-York Historical Society and the Museum of the City of New York are both rich in art, artifacts and historic documents of 18th-century New York.

Sightseeing

The New York Convention and Visitors Bureau publishes "Visitors Guide and Map," "20 Free Things to Do," "Winter Wonders," "Summer Freebies," calendars of events, a tour package directory and pamphlet guides to shopping, hotels and restaurants in each of the five boroughs. A multilingual staff can direct foreign visitors to foreign-language tours and to attractions, restaurants and hotels with multilingual personnel. Information is also provided about many special services. The Bureau is located at 2 Columbus Circle, 10019; phone 212/397-8222.

Free tickets to live TV shows are available on a day-to-day, first come-first served basis. For information on availability of tickets, contact National Broadcasting Co, 30 Rockefeller Plaza, 10112 (phone 212/664-3055); Columbia Broadcasting System, 524 W 57th St, 10019 (phone 212/975-2476); or American Broadcasting Co, 7 Lincoln Square, 10023 (phone 212/456-7777).

The best and least expensive way to get a panoramic view of the New York skyline is to take the Staten Island Ferry across New York Harbor and back, still the least expensive sea voyage to be found anywhere. The Circle Line conducts three-hour narrated boat tours around Manhattan Island. To see the whole city from above, millions of visitors each year go to the observation decks on the 86th and 102nd floors of the Empire State Building.

The Empire State Building's rival is the observation deck on the 107th floor at 2 World Trade Center. The enclosed deck includes a fascinating exhibit on the history of trade, a souvenir shop and the world's highest escalator ride. When wind and weather permit, visitors may take the escalator from the deck to an open walkway on the roof, a quarter-mile in the sky, from which there is a dramatic and uncluttered view in all directions. The deck is open from 9:30 am to 9:30 pm seven days a week. A high-flying way to get a spectacular view of the city is by helicopter. Tours are offered by Island Helicopters Corporation.

The city has an extensive public transportation system. The subways carry nearly four million people on weekdays and are crowded during rush hours. The system covers every borough except Staten Island, which provides its own transport system. Simple maps are posted in every car and every station. Buses run on most avenues and on many cross streets. Riders must have a subway token or exact fare.

For an evening look at Manhattan's skyline, take a tour (2 hrs) with Gray Line that goes to Greenwich Village, through Chinatown to Battery Park and a ferry trip around the Statue of Liberty.

Greenwich Village, a fashionable art and literary center, is famous for such writers as Thomas Paine, Dylan Thomas, Henry James and Willa Cather. Walking tours of Greenwich Village, two new artists' neighborhoods, SoHo and Tribeca, as well as other historic and culturally significant areas of Manhattan, are conducted by various companies.

Harlem Spirituals and Harlem Your Way provide an interesting look at Harlem. A wide range of other tours, catering to many different interests, is available in New York. Contact the Convention and Visitors Bureau for further details.

A visit to New York City is not complete without an afternoon of window shopping down Fifth or Madison avenues. Absolutely anything can be bought here, for a price. But the store windows themselves are attractions.

To remind visitors and conventioneers that New York City is more than Manhattan, the Convention and Visitors Bureau has compiled this brief list of top attractions in the other four boroughs: in Brooklyn are the Brooklyn Museum, with the Botanic Garden next door, the New York Aquarium and Coney Island; in Queens are the Aqueduct and Belmont racetracks, Shea Stadium and Flushing Meadows Corona Park, containing the Queens Museum, the USTA Tennis Center, Zoo and Botanical Gardens and the American Museum of the Moving Image; in Staten Island are Richmondtown, an ongoing restoration of the borough's architectural and historic past, plus the Staten Island Ferry and Snug Harbor Cultural Center; in the Bronx are the Bronx Zoo, the Hall of Fame for Great Americans at Bronx Community College, which stands on a bluff above the Harlem River, the New York Botanical Garden, Yankee Stadium, and Wave Hill, a cultural center with 28 acres of gardens overlooking the Hudson River. The Bureau has individual pamphlets describing each of the boroughs.

General References

Settled: 1615 **Pop:** 7,322,564 **Elev:** 0-410 feet **Time zone:** Eastern
Area code: 212 (Manhattan); 718 (Bronx, Brooklyn, Queens, Staten Island)

Phone Numbers

POLICE & FIRE: 911
FBI: 212/335-2700
POISON CONTROL CENTER: 212/340-4494
TIME & WEATHER: 212/976-1616

Information Source

New York Convention and Visitors Bureau, 2 Columbus Circle, 10019; 212/397-8222.
Department of Parks, 360-8196.

Transportation

AIRLINES: *JFK International:* Aer Lingus (Ireland); Aerolineas Argentinas; Aeromexico; Air Afrique (Ivory Coast); Air France; Air India; Air Jamaica; Alitalia (Italy); American; America West; Avensa; British Airways; BWIA (British West Indian Airways); China; Delta; Dominicana (Dominican Republic); EgyptAir; El Al (Israel); Finnair (Finland); Iberia (Spain); Icelandair; Japan; KLM (Netherlands); Korean; Kuwait; LASCA; Lan Chile; LOT Polish; Lufthansa (Germany); Mexicana; Nigeria; Northwest; Pakistan; Royal Air Maroc; Russian Intl; SABENA (Belgium); Saudia; Swissair; TAP (Portugal); Tarom (Romania); TWA; United; USAir. *Newark International:* Air Canada; American; Continental; Delta; Northwest; TWA; United; USAir. *La Guardia:* Air Canada; American; Continental; Delta; Northwest; TWA; United; USAir; and other commuter and regional airlines. For the most current airline schedules and information consult the *Official Airline Guide,* published twice monthly.

AIRPORTS: John F. Kennedy International, 718/656-4444; La Guardia, 718/476-5000; Newark International, 201/961-2000.
CAR RENTAL AGENCIES: In the New York area call agencies' toll-free numbers to obtain accurate information for each airport.
PUBLIC TRANSPORTATION: Metropolitan Transportation Authority, NYC Transit Authority, 212/878-7000 or 718/330-1234.
RAILROAD PASSENGER SERVICE: Amtrak 800/872-7245.

Newspapers

Amsterdam News; Journal of Commerce; New York Daily News; New York Post; New York Times; Newsday; Village Voice; Wall Street Journal; Women's Wear Daily.

Convention Facility

Jacob K. Javits Convention Center, 34th to 39th Sts, between Eleventh & Twelfth Aves, 212/216-2000.

Sports & Recreation

Major Sports Facilities
Madison Square Garden, between Seventh & Eighth Aves & W 31st & 33rd Sts, 212/465-6000 (Knicks, basketball; Rangers, hockey).
Meadowlands Stadium, East Rutherford, NJ, 201/935-3900 (Giants, Jets, football).
Nassau Veterans Memorial Coliseum, Hempstead, L.I., 516/587-9222 (Islanders, hockey).
Shea Stadium, Flushing, Queens, 718/507-8499 (Mets, baseball).
Yankee Stadium, 161st St & River Ave, Bronx, 718/293-6000 (Yankees, baseball).

Racetracks
Aqueduct Race Track, near Cross Bay Blvd just off Belt Pkwy in Queens, 718/641-4700.
Belmont Park Race Track, Hempstead Tpke, Cross Island Pkwy & Plainfield Ave, L.I., 718/641-4700.
Yonkers Raceway, Yonkers & Central Aves, Yonkers, 914/968-4200.

Cultural Facilities

Theaters
MANHATTAN
Ambassador Theater, 215 W 49th St, 239-6200.
Belasco Theater, 111 W 44th St, 239-6200.
Booth Theatre, 222 W 45th St, 239-6200.
Broadhurst Theatre, 235 W 44th St, 239-6200.
Broadway Theater, 1681 Broadway, at 53rd St, 239-6200.
Brooks Atkinson, 256 W 47th St, 719-4099.
Circle in the Square, 1633 Broadway, 239-6200.
City Center Theater, 130 W 56th St, 581-1212.
Cort Theatre, 138 W 48th St, 239-6200.
Ethel Barrymore Theater, 243 W 47th St, 239-6200.
Eugene O'Neill Theater, 230 W 49th St, 239-6200.
Gershwin Theatre, 222 W 51st St, 586-6510.
Golden Theater, 252 W 45th St, 239-6200.
Helen Hayes Theater, 240 W 44th St, 944-9450.
Imperial Theater, 249 W 45th St, 239-6200.
Julliard School Theater, Broadway at 144 W 66th St, 799-5000.
Longacre Theater, 220 W 48th St, 239-6200.
Lunt-Fontaine Theatre, 205 W 46th St, 575-9200.
Lyceum Theatre, 149 W 45th St, 239-6200.
Majestic Theater, 245 W 44th St, 239-6200.
Martin Beck Theater, 302 W 45th St, 239-6200.
Minskoff Theatre, Broadway at 45th St, 869-0550.
Music Box, 239 W 45th St, 239-6200.
Nederlander, 208 W 41st St, 921-8000.
Neil Simon Theatre, 250 W 52nd St, 757-8646.

New York Shakespeare Festival, Delacorte Theater in Central Park, 861-PAPP, and Public Theater, at Lafayette St and Astor Place, 598-7150.
New York State Theater, Broadway at 64th St, 870-5570.
Palace Theater, Broadway at 47th St, 730-8200.
Plymouth Theater, 236 W 45th St, 239-6200.
Richard Rodgers Theater, 226 W 46th St, 221-1211.
Royale Theater, 242 W 45th St, 239-6200.
St James Theater, 246 W 44th St, 239-6200.
Shubert Theater, 225 W 44th St, 239-6200.
Virginia Theater, 245 W 52nd St, 239-6200.
Walter Kerr Theatre, 219 W 48th St, 239-6200.
Winter Garden Theater, 1634 Broadway, 239-6200.

Concert Halls
Brooklyn Academy of Music, 30 Lafayette Ave, 718/636-4100.
Brooklyn Center for the Performing Arts at Brooklyn College, Nostrand Ave & Ave H, 718/951-4500.
Carnegie Hall, 154 W 57th St at Seventh Ave, 212/247-7800.
Lincoln Center for the Performing Arts and Tour, 70 Lincoln Center Plaza, 212/875-5350.
Town Hall, 123 W 43rd St, 212/840-2824.

Museums
MANHATTAN
American Museum-Hayden Planetarium, Central Park W & 81st St, 769-5900 or -5920.
American Museum of Immigration, base of the Statue of Liberty, Liberty Island, 363-3200.
American Museum of Natural History, Central Park W at 79th St, 769-5100.
Bible House, American Bible Society, 1865 Broadway & 61st St, 408-1200.
Ellis Island Immigration Museum, Ellis Island, 363-3200.
Fraunces Tavern Museum, 54 Pearl St, 425-1778.
Hispanic Society of America, Broadway between W 155th & 156th Sts, 926-2234.
Jewish Museum, 1109 Fifth Ave at E 92nd St, 423-3200.
Museum of Television and Radio, 25 W 52nd St, 621-6600.
Museum of the American Indian (The Heye Foundation), Broadway & W 155th St, 283-2420.
Museum of the City of New York, 1220 Fifth Ave, between E 103rd & 104th Sts, 534-1672.
New York Public Library at Lincoln Center-Library & Museum of the Performing Arts, Lincoln Center, Broadway & 65th Sts, 870-1600.
Pierpont Morgan Library, 29 E 36th St, 685-0610.
South Street Seaport Museum, 207 Front St, 669-9400.
BRONX
City Island Historical Nautical Museum, 190 Fordham St, 718/885-1616.
Museum of Bronx History, 3266 Bainbridge Ave, at E 208th St, 718/881-8900.
BROOKLYN
Brooklyn Children's Museum, 145 Brooklyn Ave, 718/735-4400.
Brooklyn's History Museum: The Brooklyn Historical Society, 128 Pierrepont St, 718/624-0890.
New York Transit Museum, Boerum Place and Schermerhorn St, 718/330-3060.
QUEENS
Queens Museum, NYC Building, Flushing Meadows-Corona Park, 718/592-2405.
STATEN ISLAND
Museum of Staten Island, 75 Stuyvesant Place, 718/727-1135.
Staten Island Children's Museum, 1000 Richmond Terrace, at Snug Harbor, 718/273-2060 or 718/448-6557.

Art Museums and Galleries
MANHATTAN
American Craft Museum, 40 W 53rd St, 956-6047.
Asia Society Galleries, 725 Park Ave, at 70th St, 517-NEWS.

The Cloisters, Fort Tryon Park off Henry Hudson Pkwy, 923-3700.
Cooper-Hewitt Museum, 2 E 91st St, 860-6868.
El Museo del Barrio, 1230 Fifth Ave, 831-7272 or -7273.
The Frick Collection, 1 E 70th St, at Fifth Ave, 288-0700.
International Center of Photography, 1130 Fifth Ave, at 94th St, 860-1777.
Metropolitan Museum of Art, Fifth Ave at 82nd St, 535-7710.
Museum of Modern Art, 11 W 53rd St, 708-9480.
Solomon R. Guggenheim Museum, 1071 Fifth Ave, 423-3500.
Studio Museum in Harlem, 144 W 125th St, 864-4500.
Whitney Museum of American Art, 945 Madison Ave, 570-3676. (There are many fine art galleries along 57th St near Fifth Ave, Madison Ave, and in the downtown section known as SoHo; consult local magazines for listings.)
BRONX
Bronx Museum of the Arts, 1040 Grand Concourse, 718/681-6000.
BROOKLYN
Brooklyn Museum, 200 Eastern Pkwy at Washington Ave, 718/638-5000.
QUEENS
American Museum of the Moving Image, 35th Ave at 36th St, Astoria, 718/784-0077.
STATEN ISLAND
Jacques Marchais Center of Tibetan Art, 338 Lighthouse Ave, between New Dorp & Richmondtown, 718/987-3478 or -3500.

Points of Interest

Historical
MANHATTAN
Bowling Green, Battery Park.
Castle Clinton National Monument, Battery Park, 264-4456.
Cathedral Church of St John the Divine, Amsterdam Ave & 112th St, 316-7490.
The Church of the Ascension, 10th St & Fifth Ave, 254-8620.
City Hall Park, Broadway between Chambers and Barclay Sts.
Dyckman House Park and Museum, 4881 Broadway, at 204th St, 304-2342.
Ellis Island, 363-3200.
Federal Hall National Memorial, 26 Wall St, 264-4456.
General Grant National Memorial, Riverside Dr & W 122nd St, 666-1640.
Morris-Jumel Mansion, 65 Jummel Terrace at W 160th St, 923-8008.
St Mark's-in-the-Bouwery, Second Ave & 10th St, 674-6377.
St Patrick's Cathedral, Fifth Ave & 50th St.
St Paul's Chapel, Fulton St & Broadway.
Theodore Roosevelt Birthplace National Historic Site, 28 E 20th St, 260-1616.
Trinity Church, Broadway & Wall St, 602-0800.
US Custom House, S side of Bowling Green, Battery Park.
BRONX
Bartow-Pell Mansion, Shore Rd in Pelham Bay Park, 718/885-1461.
Hall of Fame for Great Americans, W 181st St & University Ave, 220-6003.
Poe Cottage, Grand Concourse & E Kingsbridge Rd, 718/881-8900.
Van Cortlandt Mansion, Van Cortlandt Park, N of Broadway at 246th St, 718/543-3344.
BROOKLYN
Plymouth Church of the Pilgrims, Orange St between Hicks & Henry Sts.
QUEENS
Bowne House, 37-01 Bowne St, Flushing, 718/359-0528.
STATEN ISLAND
Conference House, 7455 Hylan Blvd, Tottenville, 718/984-2086.
Richmondtown Restoration, 441 Clarke Ave, Richmond & Arthur Kill Rds, 718/351-1611.

Snug Harbor Cultural Center, 1000 Richmond Terrace, 718/448-2500.

Other Attractions
MANHATTAN
American Stock Exchange, 86 Trinity Place, 306-1000.
Brooklyn Bridge, across East River to Brooklyn.
Central Park, Fifth Ave-Central Park W (Eighth Ave) & 59th St-110th St.
Chase Manhattan Bank, 1 Chase Manhattan Plaza, Nassau and Pine Sts.
Chinatown, Pell & Mott Sts, east of Bowery.
Citicorp Center, 1 Citicorp Center, 54th St and Lexington Ave.
Cooper Union, between Third & Fourth Aves at 7th St, 353-4195.
Empire State Building, 350 Fifth Ave, at 34th St, 736-3100.
Federal Reserve Bank of New York, 33 Liberty St, 720-6130.
The Garment District, south of 42nd St, west of Sixth Ave, north of 34th St and east of Eighth Ave.
Greenwich Village, from Broadway W to the Hudson River, between 14th St & Houston St.
Guinness World of Records, 34th St & Fifth Ave, in the Empire State Building, 947-2335.
Macy's, on Herald Square, 34th St & Broadway, 695-4400.
New York Public Library, 42nd St & Fifth Ave, 869-8089.
New York Stock Exchange, 20 Broad St, 656-5167.
One Times Square, 42nd St & Broadway.
Radio City Music Hall, Rockefeller Center, 50th St and Ave of Americas, 247-4777.
Rockefeller Center, Fifth to Sixth Aves & beyond, 47th to 51st Sts.
Schomburg Center for Research in Black Culture, 515 Malcolm X Blvd, at W 135th St, 491-2200.
SoHo, W Broadway, Sixth Ave, Houston & Canal Sts, (Friends of Cast Iron Architecture walking tours), 369-6004.
Statue of Liberty, Liberty Island, 363-3200.
Temple Emanu-El, Fifth Ave & 65th St, 744-1400.
Times Square & Theater District, Sixth to Ninth Aves, 41st to 53rd Sts.
United Nations, First Ave from 42nd-48th Sts, 963-7713.
Wall Street, downtown, E from Broadway.
Washington Square, S end of Fifth Ave.
Woolworth Building, 233 Broadway.
World Trade Center, downtown off Church St, 435-7000.
BRONX
Bronx Zoo/International Wildlife Conservation Park, Bronx Park, S of Fordham Rd & Bronx River Pkwy, 718/367-1010.
New York Botanical Garden, Bronx Park, entrance on Southern Blvd, 718/817-8705.
Wave Hill, 675 W 252nd St, 549-3200.
BROOKLYN
Brooklyn Botanic Garden, Eastern Pkwy, Washington & Flatbush Aves, 718/622-4433.
Coney Island, Surf Ave, Ocean Pkwy-37th St, 718/266-1234.
New York Aquarium, Boardwalk & W 8th St, Coney Island, 718/265-FISH.
QUEENS
Flushing Meadow-Corona Park, Grand Central Pkwy-Van Wyck Expwy, Union Tpke-Northern Blvd.
Queens Botanical Garden, 43-50 Main St, 718/886-3800.
STATEN ISLAND
Staten Island Ferry, Manhattan to St George, Staten Island, 718/390-5253.
Staten Island Zoo, Barrett Park, between Broadway & Clove Rd, W New Brighton, 718/442-3100.
Verrazano-Narrows Bridge, connects Staten Island and Brooklyn.

Sightseeing Tours

Adventure on a Shoestring, 300 W 53rd St, 10019; 212/265-2663.

Circle Line Sightseeing, Inc., W 43rd St & Hudson River, Pier 83, 212/563-3200.
Discovery Tour of Brooklyn, departs from Gray Line Terminal, 212/397-2600.
Gray Line bus tours, 254 W 54th St, 10019; 212/397-2620.
Harlem Spirituals, 1697 Broadway, Suite 203, 212/757-0425.
Shortline, 166 W 46th St, 212/397-2620.

Annual Events

Chinese New Year, in Chinatown. Early-mid-Feb.
USA/Mobil Indoor Track & Field Championships, Usually last Fri in Feb.
St Patrick's Day Parade, Fifth Ave. Mar 17.
Easter Parade, Fifth Ave near St Patrick's Cathedral.
Ninth Avenue International Food Festival, mid-May.
JVC Jazz Festival-New York, 787-2020. Late June-early July.
Harbor Festival, Wkend of July 4.
San Gennaro Festival, Little Italy. Mid-late Sept.
Columbus Day Parade, upper Fifth Ave. Early Oct.
Hispanic Day Parade, Fifth Ave. Mid-Oct.
New York City Marathon. Sun, usually Nov.
Thanksgiving Day Parade, Broadway.
Lighting of Christmas tree at Rockefeller Center. Early Dec.

City Neighborhoods

Many of the restaurants, unrated dining establishments and some lodgings listed under Manhattan include neighborhoods as well as exact street addresses. A map showing these neighborhoods can be found immediately following the Manhattan introduction. Geographic descriptions of these areas are given, followed by a table of restaurants arranged by neighborhood.

Chelsea: Area of West Side south of 31st St, west of Sixth Ave, north of 14th St and east of the Hudson River.
Chinatown: Area of Downtown south of Canal St and east and west of Bowery; particularly along Bayard, Pell and Mott Sts east of Bowery.

Downtown: South of 14th St, west of the East River and east of the Hudson River; also refers specifically to the Financial District.
East Side: Area of Midtown south of 59th St, west of the East River, north of 42nd St and east of Lexington Ave.
East Village: Area of Downtown south of 14th St, west of First Ave, north of E Houston St and east of Broadway.
Financial District: Area of Downtown south of Vesey and Ann Sts, west of the East River, north of Water St and Battery Park and east of the Hudson River.
Garment District: Area of Midtown south of 42nd St, west of Sixth Ave, north of 34th St and east of Eighth Ave.
Gramercy Park: Area of Midtown on and around Gramercy Park; south of E 23rd St, west of First Ave, north of 14th St and east of Broadway.
Greenwich Village: Area of Downtown south of 14th St, west of Broadway, north of W Houston St and east of Greenwich Ave.
Harlem: South of 165th St, west of the Harlem River, north of 110th St and east of Morningside Ave and St Nicholas Ave.
Little Italy: Area of Downtown south of Houston St, west of Chrystie St and the Sara Delano Roosevelt Pkwy, north of Canal St and east of Broadway.
Midtown: Between 59th St and 34th St and the East and Hudson rivers; south of 59th St, west of Eighth Ave, north of 34th St and east of Lexington Ave.
Murray Hill: Area of Midtown south of 42nd St, west of Second Ave, north of 32nd St and east of Fifth Ave.
SoHo: Area of Downtown south of Houston St, west of Broadway, north of Canal St and east of Avenue of the Americas (Sixth Ave).
Times Square/Theater District: Area of Midtown south of 53rd St, west of Avenue of the Americas (Sixth Ave), north of 40th St and east of Eighth Ave; intersection of Broadway and Seventh Ave.
Tribeca: Area of Downtown south of Canal St, west of Broadway, north of Chambers St and east of the Hudson River.
Upper East Side: Area south of 110th St, west of the East River, north of 59th St and east of Central Park.
Upper West Side: Area south of 110th St, west of Central Park, north of 59th St and east of the Hudson River.
West Side: Area of Midtown south of 59th St, west of Eighth Ave, north of 34th St and east of the Hudson River.

Lodgings and Food

No city in the United States has as many fine restaurants serving as many different and exciting international dishes as New York. Eating here is an adventure as well as an art. With thousands of restaurants to choose from, it can also be bewildering. The list that follows is organized alphabetically under each neighborhood/area heading.

MANHATTAN RESTAURANTS
BY NEIGHBORHOOD AREAS

(For full description, see alphabetical listings under Restaurants)

CHELSEA

Chelsea Central. 227 Tenth Ave
Da Umberto. 107 W 17th St
Empire Diner. 210 Tenth Ave
Estoril Sol. 382 Eighth Ave
Gascogne. 158 Eighth Ave
Le Madri. 168 W 18th St
Man Ray. 169 Eighth Ave
Periyali. 35 W 20th St
Steak Frites. 9 E 16th St
T-Rex. 358 W 23rd St

CHINATOWN

20 Mott Street. 20 Mott St
Harmony Palace. 94-98 Mott St
Hunan Garden. 1 Mott St
Saigon House. 89-91 Bayard St

DOWNTOWN

Fraunces Tavern. 54 Pearl St
Fulton Street Cafe. 11 Fulton St
Liberty Cafe. 89 South St
Ratner's. 138 Delancey St
Sammy's Roumanian Steak House. 157 Chrystie St

EAST SIDE

Ambassador Grill (U.N Plaza-Park Hyatt Hotel). 1 UN Plaza
Charlton's. 922 Third Ave
Dawat. 210 E 58th St
Delegates Dining Room. In United Nations General Assembly Bldg
Felidia. 243 E 58th St
Girafe. 208 E 58th St
Il Nido. 251 E 53rd St
La Mangeoire. 1008 Second Ave
Le Colonial. 149 E 57th St
Matthew's. 1030 Third Ave
P.J. Clarke's. 915 Third Ave
Palm. 837 Second Ave
Rosa Mexicano. 1063 First Ave
Shun Lee Palace. 155 E 55th St
Smith & Wollensky. 201 E 49th St

Tatou. 151 E 50th St
Tre Scalini. 230 E 58th St

EAST VILLAGE

Cafe Tabac. 232 E 9th St
Second Ave Deli. 156 Second Ave

FINANCIAL DISTRICT

Edward Moran Bar And Grill. In Building 4 of World Financial Center
Harbour Lights. Fulton Pier 17
Hudson River Club. In Building 4 of World Financial Center
Le Pactole. 225 Liberty St
Yankee Clipper. 170 John St

GRAMERCY PARK

Bolo. 23 E 22nd St
C.T. 111 E 22nd St
Canastel's. 233 Park Ave S
Chefs Cusiniers Club (CCC). 36 E 22nd St
Mesa Grill. 102 Fifth Ave
Metropolis Cafe. 31 Union Square West
Moreno. 65 Irving Place
Patria. 250 Park Ave S

GREENWICH VILLAGE

Arlecchino. 192 Bleecker St
The Black Sheep. 344 W 11th St
Cuisine de Saigon. 154 W 13th St
Da Silvano. 260 Sixth Ave
Elephant & Castle. 68 Greenwich Ave
Florent. 69 Gansevoort St
Gotham Bar and Grill. 12 E 12th St
Grove Street Cafe. 53 Grove St
Il Cantinori. 32 E 10th St
La Metairie. 189 W 10th St
The Markham. 59 Fifth Ave
Marylou's. 21 W 9th St
Mi Cocina. 57 Jane St
One if by Land, Two if by Sea. 17 Barrow St
Rose Cafe. 24 Fifth Ave

LITTLE ITALY

Grotta Azzurra. 387 Broome St
Il Cortile. 125 Mulberry St
Taormina. 147 Mulberry St

MIDTOWN

'21' Club. 21 W 52nd St
Adrienne (The Peninsula New York Hotel). 700 Fifth Ave
Amarcord. 7 E 59th St
American Festival. 20 W 50th St
An American Place. 2 Park Ave
Aquavit. 13 W 54th St
Bice. 7 E 54th St

Bombay Palace. 30 W 52nd St

Box Tree (Box Tree Inn). 250 E 49th St

Bull & Bear Steakhouse (Waldorf-Astoria Hotel). 301 Park Ave

Cafe Pierre (The Pierre Hotel). 2 E 61st St

Carnegie Deli. 854 Seventh Ave

Castellano. 138 W 55th St

Chin Chin. 216 E 49th St

China Grill. In CBS Bldg

Christ Cella. 160 E 46th St

Christer's. 145 W 55th St

Cité. In Time/Life Bldg

Dawat. 210 E 58th St

Edwardian Room (The Plaza Hotel). Fifth Ave at 59th St & Central Park South

Fantino (The Ritz-Carlton Hotel). 112 Central Park South

Fifty Seven Fifty Seven (Four Seasons). 57 E 57th St

The Four Seasons. Seagram Bldg

Harley-Davidson Cafe. 1370 Ave of the Americas

Harry Cipriani. 781 Fifth Ave

Judson Grill. 152 W 52nd St

Keens Chophouse. 72 W 36th St

Kristie's. 344 Lexington Ave

La Bonne Soupe. 48 W 55th St

La Côte Basque. 5 E 55th St

La Caravelle. 33 W 55th St

La Grenouille. 3 East 52nd St

La Maison Japonaise. 125 E 39th St

La Reserve. 4 W 49th St

Le Chantilly. 106 E 57th St

Le Perigord. 405 E 52nd St

Les Célébrités (Essex House Hotel Nikko). 160 Central Park South

Lespinasse (The St Regis Hotel). 2 E 55th St

Lutèce. 249 E 50th St

Manhattan Ocean Club. 57 W 58th St

Michael's. 24 W 55th St

Mickey Mantle's Restaurant & Sports Bar. 42 Central Park South

Mitsukoshi. 461 Park Ave

Morton's Of Chicago. 551 Fifth Ave

Oceana. 55 E 54th St

Oyster Bar. At Grand Central Station

Palm Court (The Plaza Hotel). Fifth Ave at 59th St & Central Park South

Petrossian. 182 W 58th St

Planet Hollywood. 140 W 57th St

Rainbow Room. In GE Bldg

Raphael. 33 W 54th St

Remi. 145 W 53rd St

Romeo Salta. 30 W 56th St

The Rotunda (The Pierre Hotel). 2 E 61st St

Russian Tea Room. 150 W 57th St

Ruth's Chris Steak House. 148 W 51st St

San Domenico. 240 Central Park South

San Martin's. 143 E 49th St

San Pietro. 18 E 54th St

Savories. 30 Rockefeller Center

Sea Grill. 19 W 49th St

Sparks Steak House. 210 E 46th St

Stage Deli. 834 Seventh Ave

Trattoria dell'Arte. 900 7th Ave

Tre Merli Bistro. In Trump Tower

Union Square Cafe. 21 E 16th St

Vong. 200 E 54th St

Water Club. 500 E 30th St

Zarela. 953 2nd Ave

MURRAY HILL

La Colombe d'Or. 134 E 26th St

Park Bistro. 414 Park Ave S

Pigalle. 111 E 29th St

SOHO

Barolo. 398 W Broadway

Berry's. 180 Spring St

Boom. 152 Spring St

Manhattan Bistro. 129 Spring St

Mezzogiorno. 195 Spring St

Provence. 38 MacDougal St

Raoul's. 180 Prince St

Spring Street. 162 Spring St

TIMES SQUARE/THEATER DISTRICT

Cabana Carioca. 123 W 45th St

Cafe Un Deux Trois. 123 W 44th St

Gallagher's. 228 W 52nd St

Le Bernardin. In Equitable Life Tower

Palio. 151 W 51st St

Pierre au Tunnel. 250 W 47th St

René Pujol. 321 W 51st St

Sardi's. 234 W 44th St

Siam Inn. 916 8th Ave

Victor's Cafe 52. 236 W 52nd St

The View (Marriott Marquis Hotel). 1535 Broadway

TRIBECA

Arqua. 281 Church St

Barocco. 301 Church St

Bouley. 165 Duane St

Capsouto Frères. 451 Washington St

Chanterelle. In Mercantile Exchange Bldg

Duane Park Cafe. 157 Duane St

El Teddy's. 219 W Broadway

Montrachet. 239 W Broadway

The Odeon. 145 W Broadway

Tribeca Grill. 375 Greenwich St

UPPER EAST SIDE

540 Park (The Regency Hotel). 540 Park Ave

Arcadia. 21 E 62nd St

Arizona 206. 206 E 60th St

Aureole. 34 E 61st St

Boathouse Cafe. In Central Park

Cafe Metairie. 1442 Third Ave

Cafe Nosidam. 768 Madison Ave

Cafe Trevi. 1570 First Ave

Capriccio. 33 E 61st St

Carlyle Restaurant (Carlyle Hotel). Madison Ave at E 76th St

Coco Pazzo. 23 E 74th St

Coconut Grill. 1481 Second Ave

Contrapunto. 200 E 60th St

Daniel. 20 E 76th St

Divino. 1556 Second Ave

Gino. 780 Lexington Ave

Girasole. 151 E 82nd St

Il Monello. 1460 Second Ave

Jackson Hole Wyoming. 1611 Second Ave

Jim McMullen. 1341 Third Ave

Jojo. 160 E 64th St

Le Boeuf à la Mode. 539 E 81st St

Le Cirque. 58 E 65th St

Le Pistou. 134 E 61st St

Le Régence (Plaza Athénée Hotel). 37 E 64th St

Le Refuge. 166 E 82nd St

Le Veau d'Or. 129 E 60th St

Lusardi's. 1494 Second Ave

Manhattan Cafe. 1161 First Ave

March. 405 E 58th St

Mezzaluna. 1295 Third Ave

Mocca Hungarian. 1588 Second Ave

Nanni Il Valletto. 133 E 61st St

Ottomanelli's. 1370 York Ave

Our Place. 1444 Third Ave

Parioli Romanissimo. 24 E 81st St

Park Avenue Cafe. 100 E 63rd St

Parma. 1404 Third Ave

Pig Heaven. 1540 Second Ave

Pinocchio. 170 E 81st St

Polo (Westbury Hotel). 15 E 69th St

Post House. 28 E 63rd St

Primavera. 1578 First Ave

Red Tulip. 439 E 75th St

Serendipity 3. 225 E 60th St

Sign of the Dove. 1110 Third Ave

Tavola. 1481 York Ave

Vasata. 339 E 75th St

Yellowfingers. 200 E 60th St

UPPER WEST SIDE

Cafe des Artistes. 1 W 67th St

Cafe Luxembourg. 200 W 70th St

Carmine's. 2450 Broadway

Diane's Uptown. 249 Columbus Ave

Iridium. 44 W 63rd St

La Kasbah. 70 W 71st St

Panevino Ristorante/Cafe Vienna. In Avery Fisher Hall

Santa Fe. 72 W 69th St

Sarabeth's. 423 Amsterdam Ave

Shun Lee. 43 W 65th St

Tavern on the Green. Central Park at W 67th St

Terrace. 400 W 119th St

WEST SIDE

Cafe des Sports. 329 W 51st St

Chez Napoleon. 365 W 50th St

Landmark Tavern. 626 11th Ave

Orso. 322 W 46th St

Siam Grill. 586 Ninth Ave

Hotels

★ ★ **ALGONQUIN.** *59 W 44th St (10036), between Fifth Ave and Avenue of the Americas, Midtown.* 212/840-6800; res: 800/548-0345; FAX 212/944-1419. 165 rms, 12 story. S $195; D $215; each addl $25; suites $325; wkend rates. Crib free. TV; cable. Complimentary continental bkfst. Restaurant 7-1 am; Sun from noon. Bar 11-1 am. Ck-out 1 pm. Meeting rms. Health club privileges. Refrigerator in suites. 18th-century English decor; English club atmosphere. Visited by numerous literary and theatrical personalities. Cr cds: A, C, D, DS, ER, JCB, MC, V.

D ⊠ 🔥

★ **BEDFORD.** *118 E 40th St (10016), Midtown.* 212/697-4800; res: 800/221-6881; FAX 212/697-1093. 200 rms, 17 story, 137 suites. S $139-$160; D $149-$170; each addl $10; suites $180-$200; under 13 free; wkend rates; lower rates July-Aug. Crib free. TV. Restaurant noon-11 pm. Bar. Ck-out noon. Coin lndry. Cr cds: A, C, D, MC, V.

🔥 SC

★ ★ ★ **BEEKMAN TOWER.** *Three Mitchell Place (10017), at 49th St, and First Ave, near Beekman Place, on the East Side.* 212/355-7300; res: 800/637-8483; FAX 212/753-9366. 171 suites, 26 story. S, studio suites $205; D $225-$245; each addl $20; 2-bedrm suites $395-$415; under 12 free; wkend rates; lower rates June-Aug. Crib free. Garage $23. TV; cable. Complimentary coffee in rms. Restaurant 7 am-10:30 pm. Bar 5 pm-2 am; entertainment Tues-Sat. Ck-out noon. Meeting rms. Coin lndry. Exercise equipt; weights, bicycles, sauna. Refrigerators. Some private patios, balconies. Restored art-deco landmark completed in 1928. Cr cds: A, C, D, JCB, MC, V.

🏃 ⊠ 🔥 SC

★ ★ **BEST WESTERN SEAPORT INN.** *33 Peck Slip (10038), at Front St, Financial District.* 212/766-6600; FAX 212/766-6615. 65 rms, 7 story. Memorial Day wkend-Oct: S $130-$165; D $150-$205; each addl $10; under 18 free; wkend rates; higher rates July 4, special events; lower rates rest of yr. Crib free. Garage parking $25. TV; in-rm movies. Complimentary continental bkfst. Restaurant nearby. No rm serv. Ck-out 11 am. No bellhops. Airport transportation. Refrigerators. Balconies. Located in historic district in restored 19th-century building. Cr cds: A, C, D, DS, JCB, MC, V.

D ⊠ 🔥 SC

★ ★ **BEVERLY.** *125 E 50th St (10022), at Lexington Ave, Midtown.* 212/753-2700; res: 800/223-0945; FAX 212/759-7300. 187 rms, 26 story, 86 suites, 150 kits. S $129-$149; D $139-$159; studio rms $139-$169; suites $170-$255; wkend rates. Crib free. Garage $25. TV. Complimentary coffee, tea in rms. Restaurant 7 am-midnight. Bar 11:30-1 am. Ck-out noon. Meeting rms. Concierge. Drugstore. Barber, beauty shop. Airport transportation. Refrigerators. Some balconies. Cr cds: A, C, D, JCB, MC, V.

[icons] SC

★ ★ ★ ★ ★ **CARLYLE.** *Madison Ave at E 76th St (10021), Upper East Side.* 212/744-1600; FAX 212/717-4682. 196 rms, 35 story. S $260-$360; D $285-$005, suites (1-2 bedrm) $500-$2,000. Pet accepted, some restrictions. Garage $35. TV; VCR; stereo cassette and CD player. Restaurant (see CARLYLE RESTAURANT). Rm serv 24 hrs. Bar noon-1 am; Cafe Carlyle from 6 pm; entertainment: Bobby Short and other stars (cover charge). Ck-out 1 pm. Meeting rms. Business center. In-rm FAX machines. Concierge. Full facility Fitness Center: instructor, weights, bicycles, sauna, steam rm. Massages. Large rms, most with serv pantry. Bathrm phones, refrigerators, wet bars, minibars. Many in-rm whirlpools. Grand piano in many suites. Each rm individually decorated; many antiques. Some terraces. Landmark hotel, with 35-story tower; foyer boasts Aubusson carpets and Gobelins tapestries. Murals by Austrian artist Ludwig Bemelman. Truly luxurious hotel with the feel of Old World elegance. Cr cds: A, C, D, JCB, MC, V.

[icons] 7-14 Nov. '95

✔★ **COMFORT INN MURRAY HILL.** *42 W 35th St (10001), between 5th & 6th Aves, Murray Hill.* 212/947-0200. 120 rms, 12 story. S $89-$115; D $99-$130; each addl $12; under 16 free. Crib free. TV. Complimentary continental bkfst. Ck-out 1 pm. Cr cds: A, C, D, DS, MC, V.

[icons] SC

✔★ ★ **DAYS HOTEL.** *790 Eighth Ave (10019), at 49th St, Times Square/Theater District.* 212/581-7000; FAX 212/974-0291. 366 rms, 15 story. S $94-$130; D $106-$142; each addl $20; suites $170-$205; under 18 free. Crib free. TV. Pool. Restaurant 7 am-midnight. Bar noon-2 am. Ck-out 1 pm. Meeting rm. Cr cds: A, C, D, DS, JCB, MC, V.

[icons] SC

✔★ ★ **DELMONICO'S.** *502 Park Ave (10022), at 59th St, Midtown.* 212/355-2500; res: 800/821-3842; FAX 212/755-3779. 125 kit. suites, 32 story. Suites $250-$500; children free; monthly rates. Crib free. Valet parking $25. TV; cable, in-rm movies avail. Complimentary coffee in rms. Bar 11-1 am. Ck-out noon. Concierge. Health club privileges. Some balconies. Restored 1929 building. Each suite individually decorated. Cr cds: A, D, DS, MC, V.

[icons]

★ ★ ★ **DORAL COURT.** *130 E 39th St (10016), between Park & Lexington Aves, Murray Hill.* 212/685-1100; res: 800/22-DORAL; FAX 212/889-0287. 199 rms, 16 story, 53 kit. suites. S $165-$185; D $185-$205; each addl $20; kit. suites $250-$500; under 12 free; wkend packages. Crib free. Garage $25; wkends $10. TV; cable, in-rm movies avail. Restaurant 6:30 am-11 pm. Bar 11-2 am. Ck-out 1 pm. Meeting rms. Concierge. Drugstore. Exercise equipt; weights, bicycles. Health club privileges. Refrigerators. Some balconies. Restored hotel in quiet residential neighborhood. Cr cds: A, C, D, DS, ER, JCB, MC, V.

[icons] SC

★ ★ **DORAL INN.** *541 Lexington Ave (10022), between 49th & 50th Sts, Midtown.* 212/755-1200; res: 800/22-DORAL (NY); FAX 212/319-8344. 21224773008 story. S $145-$180; D $155-$190; each addl $15; 1-2 bedrm suites $200-$600. Crib free. Garage parking $23, valet. TV; cable. Restaurant open 24 hrs. Bar noon-2 am. Ck-out 1 pm. Coin lndry. Concierge. Sauna, steam room. Squash courts. Many refrigerators. Cr cds: A, C, D, DS, ER, JCB, MC, V.

[icons]

★ ★ ★ **DORAL PARK AVENUE.** *70 Park Ave (10016), at E 38th St, Murray Hill.* 212/687-7050; res: 800/22-DORAL. 188 rms, 17 story. S $185-$205; D $205-$225; each addl $20; suites $385-$650; under 12 free; wkend rates. Crib free. Parking $10-$25. TV; in-rm movies avail. Restaurant 7-10:30 am, noon-2 pm, 5-10 pm. Bar

noon-midnight. Ck-out 1 pm. Health club privileges. Minibars. Neoclassical decor. Cr cds: A, C, D, DS, ER, JCB, MC, V.

[icons] SC

★ ★ ★ **DORAL TUSCANY.** *120 E 39th St (10016), between Park & Lexington Aves, Murray Hill.* 212/686-1600; res: 800/22-DORAL; FAX 212/779-7822. 121 rms, 17 story. S $205; D $225; each addl $20; suites $400-$850; under 12 free. Crib free. Garage $25. TV; in-rm movies avail. Restaurant 7-10:30 am, noon-2:30 pm, 6-10:30 pm. Rm serv 24 hrs. Bar noon-1 am. Ck-out 1 pm. Health club privileges. Exercise bicycles avail. Bathrm phones, refrigerators, minibars. Cr cds: A, C, D, DS, ER, JCB, MC, V.

[icons]

★ ★ **DORSET.** *30 W 54th St (10019), between 5th & 6th Aves. Midtown.* 212/247-7300; res: 800/227-2348; FAX 212/581-0153. 319 rms, 20 story, 45 suites. S $175-$215; D $195-$235; suites $275-$475; wkend rates. Crib free. Garage, valet parking $26. TV; cable. Restaurant 7-3 pm. Bar 11:30-1 am. Ck-out 1 pm. Fifth Ave stores nearby. Cr cds: A, C, D, MC, V.

[icons]

★ ★ ★ **DRAKE SWISSÔTEL.** *440 Park Ave (10022), at E 56th St, Midtown.* 212/421-0900; res: 800/372-5369; FAX 212/371-4190. 550 units, 21 story. S $215-$265; D $240-$290; one addl $25; 1-2-bedrm suites $325-$1,200; under 14 free; wkend plan. Crib free. Pet accepted. Garage $24. TV; cable, in-rm movies. Restaurant 7 am-11 pm. Rm serv 24 hrs. Bar noon-2 am. Ck-out 1 pm. Meeting rms. Concierge. Free morning Wall Street transportation. Refrigerators; bathrm phones. Wet bar in suites. Cr cds: A, C, D, DS, ER, JCB, MC, V.

[icons] SC

★ ★ **DUMONT PLAZA.** *150 E 34th St (10016), near Lexington Ave, Murray Hill.* 212/481-7600; res: 800/637-8483; FAX 212/889-8856. 252 kit. suites, 37 story. S $185-$215; D $195-$420; each addl $20; under 12 free. Crib free. TV; cable. Coffee in rms. Restaurant 7 am-10 pm. Ck-out noon. Coin lndry. Meeting rms. Exercise equipt; weight machines, bicycles, sauna. Plaza with fountain. Cr cds: A, C, D, ER, JCB, MC, V.

[icons] SC

★ ★ **EASTGATE TOWER.** *222 E 39th St (10016), Murray Hill.* 212/687-8000; res: 800/637-8483 (NY); FAX 212/490-2634. 188 kit. suites, 25 story. Apr-mid-June, mid-Sept-mid-Dec: S $195-$235; D $205-$395; each addl $20; wkly rates; lower rates rest of yr. Garage; valet parking $22. TV; cable. Restaurant 8 am-11 pm. Bar to 1 am. Ck-out noon. Landscaped plaza with gazebo, fountain. Tours arranged. Cr cds: A, C, D, ER, JCB, MC, V.

[icons] SC

✔★ ★ **EDISON.** *228 W 47th St (10036), Times Square/Theater District.* 212/840-5000; res: 800/637-7070; FAX 212/596-6850. 1,000 rms, 22 story. S $92; D $99; each addl $10; suites $135-$160; family rms $115-$125. Crib free. Garage $22. TV. Restaurant 6:15 am-midnight, Sun to 7 pm; dining rm noon-1 am. Bar noon-2 am. Ck-out 1 pm. Meeting rm. Gift shop. Beauty shop. Airport transportation. Cr cds: A, C, D, DS, JCB, MC, V.

[icons] SC

★ ★ ★ **ELYSEE.** *60 E 54th St (10022), Midtown.* 212/753-1066; res: 800/535-9733; FAX 212/980-9278. 99 rms, 15 story. S, D $195; suites $325-$645; under 12 free. Crib free. TV; cable. Complimentary continental bkfst; afternoon refreshments. Restaurant 7 am-midnight. Bar 11-2 am. Ck-out 1 pm. Minibars. Bathrm phones. Health club privileges. Country French decor. Cr cds: A, C, D, JCB, MC, V.

[icons]

★ ★ **EMBASSY SUITES.** *1568 Broadway (10036), at 47th St & 7th Ave, Times Square/Theater District.* 212/719-1600; FAX 212/921-5212. 460 suites, 43 story. S $169-$355; D $169-$375; each addl $20; under 12 free; wkend rates; higher rates special events. Crib free.

Garage; valet parking $28/day. TV; cable, in-rm movies avail. Supervised child's activities. Complimentary full bkfst. Complimentary coffee in rms. Restaurant 11 am-11 pm. Bar to 1 am. Ck-out noon. Coin lndry. Meeting rms. Concierge. Gift shop. Airport, RR station, bus depot transportation. Exercise equipt; weight machine, bicycles. Game rm. Bathrm phones, refrigerators, wet bars. Cr cds: A, C, D, DS, JCB, MC, V.

D 🏃 🍽 🔥 SC

★ ★ ★ **ESSEX HOUSE HOTEL NIKKO NEW YORK.** *160 Central Park South (10019), between 6th & 7th Aves, Midtown. 212/247-0300; FAX 212/315-1839.* 595 units, 40 story, 78 suites. S $235-$275; D $255-$295; each addl $25; suites $295-$2,000; under 18 free; wkend rates. Crib free. Garage parking, valet $33. TV; cable, in-rm movies. Restaurant 7 am-11 pm (also see LES CÉLÉBRITÉS). Rm serv 24 hrs. Bar noon-1 am; pianist exc Sun. Ck-out noon. Convention facilities. Concierge. Gift shop. Airport transportation. Exercise rm; instructor, weight machine, bicycles, saunas, steam rms. Full-service health spa with massage, herbal wraps, mud packs. Stocked minibars. Children's amenity package. Renovated landmark hotel (1931) overlooking Central Park. Restoration of interiors includes original art deco in public spaces and traditional decor in enlarged guest rms. Cr cds: A, C, D, DS, ER, JCB, MC, V.

D 🐾 🏃 🍽 🔥

★ ★ **FITZPATRICK.** *687 Lexington Ave (10022), on the East Side. 212/355-0100; res: 800/367-7701; FAX 212/355-1371.* 92 rms, 17 story, 52 suites. S $190-$210; D $210-$230; each addl $20; suites $220-$240; under 12 free; wkend, hol rates. Crib free. Garage in/out $10. TV; cable. Restaurant 7 am-10:30 pm. Rm serv 24 hrs. Bar 11:30 am-midnight. Ck-out noon. Meeting rms. Concierge. Many refrigerators. Cr cds: A, D, DS, MC, V.

D 🍽 🔥

★ ★ ★ **FOUR SEASONS.** *57 E 57th St (10022), between Madison & Park Aves, on the East Side. 212/758-5700.* 367 rms, 52 story, 58 suites. S $325-$430; D $365-$470; each addl $40; suites $695-$4,000; under 12 free; wkend rates. Crib free. Pet accepted, some restrictions. Garage, valet parking $30. TV; cable, in-rm movies avail. Restaurant 7 am-10:30 pm; Fri & Sat to 11 pm (also see FIFTY SEVEN FIFTY SEVEN). Rm serv 24 hrs. Bar 11-2 am. Ck-out noon. Convention facilities. Concierge. Airport, RR station transportation. Exercise rm; instructor, weight machine, bicycles, whirlpool, sauna. Masseuse. Spa & fitness center. Bathrm phones, minibars. Some terraces. As the tallest hotel in New York City, rising 682 feet, the Four Seasons Hotel offers spectacular views of the city skyline and Central Park. Cr cds: A, C, D, ER, MC, V.

D 🐾 🏃 🍽 🔥 SC

✔★ ★ **THE FRANKLIN.** *164 E 87th St (10128), between Lexington & 3rd Aves, Upper East Side. 212/369-1000; res: 800/600-8787; FAX 212/369-8000.* 50 rms, 9 story. S, D $115-$125. Garage parking free, in/out $10. TV; cable, in-rm movies. Complimentary continental bkfst. Restaurant nearby. No rm serv. Ck-out 1 pm. Airport, RR station transportation. Health club privileges. Refrigerators avail. Renovated boutique hotel. Cr cds: A, MC, V.

🍽 🔥

★ ★ **GORHAM NEW YORK.** *136 W 55th St (10019), between 6th & 7th Aves, Midtown. 212/245-1800; res: 800/735-0710; FAX 212/582-8332.* 120 kit. units, 17 story. S $135-$260; D $145-$320; each addl $20; suites $175-$320. Crib free. Garage adj $20. TV; cable. Rm serv 7 am-11:30 pm. Ck-out noon. Cr cds: A, C, D, JCB, MC, V.

D 🍽 🔥 SC

★ ★ ★ **GRAND HYATT.** *Park Ave at Grand Central (10017), 42nd St, Midtown. 212/883-1234; FAX 212/697-3772.* 1,407 rms, 30 story. S $210-$245; D $240-$280; each addl $25; suites $350-$2,500; under 18 free; wkend rates. Crib free. Garage $34. TV. Restaurant 6:30-1 am, dining rm 11 am-11:30 pm. Rm serv 24 hrs. Bar 11-2 am; entertainment. Ck-out noon. Convention facilities. Drugstore. Tennis privileges. Health club privileges. Refrigerator in suites. *LUXURY*

LEVEL : REGENCY CLUB. 126 rms, 8 suites, 2 floors. S $245-$280; D $275-$315; suites $395-$2,535. Concierge. Private lounge, honor bar. TV; cable. Wet bar in suites. Complimentary continental bkfst, refreshments, newspaper, magazines, shoeshine. Cr cds: A, C, D, DS, ER, JCB, MC, V.

D 🏃 🍽 🔥 SC

★ ★ **HELMSLEY MIDDLETOWNE.** *148 E 48th St (10017), Midtown. 212/755-3000; res: 800/843-2157 (exc NY); FAX 212/832-0261.* 190 rms, 17 story. S $135-$175; D $145-$175; each addl $20; suites $195-$380; under 12 free; wkend rates. Crib free. TV. Complimentary coffee in lobby. Restaurant nearby. Ck-out 1 pm. Bathrm phones, refrigerators, wet bars. Convenient to UN. Cr cds: A, C, D, DS, JCB, MC, V.

D 🔥 SC

HELMSLEY PARK LANE. *(New general manager, therefore not rated) 36 Central Park South (10019), between 5th & 6th Aves, Midtown. 212/371-4000; res: 800/221-4982; FAX 212/319-9065.* 640 rms, 46 story. S $195-$265; D $215-$285; each addl $20; suites $350-$1,200; under 12 free; wkend rates. Crib free. TV; in-rm movies avail. Restaurant 7 am-midnight. Rm serv 24 hrs. Bar 11-2 am. Ck-out 1 pm. Barber, beauty shop. Garage parking. Health club privileges. Refrigerators; serv pantry in suites. View of park. Cr cds: A, C, D, DS, JCB, MC, V.

D 🍽 🔥 SC

★ ★ **HELMSLEY WINDSOR.** *100 W 58th St (10019), at Avenue of the Americas, Midtown. 212/265-2100; FAX 212/315-0371.* 300 rms, 15 story. S $135-$145; D $145-$155; each addl $20; suites $215-$325; summer, wkend rates. Crib free. Garage adj $21. TV; cable. Complimentary continental bkfst. No rm serv. Ck-out 1 pm. Health club privileges. Serv pantry in suites. Cr cds: A, C, D, DS, JCB, MC, V.

D 🔥

✔★ **HERALD SQUARE.** *19 W 31st St (10001), between 5th Ave & Broadway, near Macy's, south of Midtown. 212/279-4017; res: 800/727-1888; FAX 212/643-9208.* 114 rms, some share bath, 9 story. S $40-$90; D $55-$90; each addl $5; under 10 free. Crib free. Garage $17. TV; cable. Restaurant nearby. No rm serv. Ck-out noon. No bellhops. Airport transportation. In landmark beaux-arts building (1893) designed by Carrere and Hastings; was once lived in by Charles Dana Gibson, illustrator who created the Gibson girl; was original headquarters of Life magazine. Hotel interior decorated with Life covers & graphics. Located in shopping area; midway between Midtown & Downtown. Cr cds: A, DS, JCB, MC, V.

🍽 🔥

★ ★ ★ **HILTON MILLENIUM.** *55 Church St (10007), Dey & Fulton Sts, Financial District. 212/693-2001; res: 800/835-2220 (exc NYC); FAX 212/571-2316.* 561 rms, 55 story, 15 suites (1-3 bedrm). S $225-$295; D $265-$315; each addl $20; suites $305-$2,500; under 16 free; wkend rates; package plans. Crib free. Garage; valet parking $30. TV; cable, in-rm movies avail. Indoor pool; poolside serv, lifeguard. Restaurants 6:30 am-midnight. Rm serv 24 hrs. Bar 11:30-1:30 am. Ck-out 2 pm. Meeting rms. Concierge. Gift shop. Airport transportation. Complimentary transportation to Midtown (Mon-Fri) & theater district (evenings); shopping transportation wkends. Exercise rm; instructor, weight machine, bicycles. Fitness center. Massage. Bathrm phones, minibars. View of East River and Hudson River. Golf privileges 20 mi. Cr cds: A, D, DS, ER, JCB, MC, V.

D 🌊 🏃 🍽 🔥

★ ★ **HOLIDAY INN CROWNE PLAZA.** *1605 Broadway (10019), at 49th St, Midtown. 212/977-4000; FAX 212/333-7393.* 770 rms, 46 story. S, D $185-$210; each addl $20; under 19 free. Crib avail. Garage $29. TV; cable. Indoor pool; lifeguard. Restaurant 6:30 am-2 pm, 5 pm-2 am; Sun hrs vary. Rm serv 24 hrs. Bar from 11:30 am. Ck-out noon. Convention facilities. Concierge. Exercise rm; instructor, weight machines, bicycles, sauna, steam rm. Minibars. Refrigerator in suites. *LUXURY LEVEL :* CROWNE PLAZA CLUB. 93 rms, 3 floors. S $220; D $245; suites $350-$1,500. Private lounge. Complimentary continental bkfst, refreshments, newspapers, magazines. Cr cds: A, C, D, DS, JCB, MC, V.

D 🛎 ⚓ 🏊 🏋 🎣 🐾 SC

★ ★ **HOLIDAY INN DOWNTOWN.** *138 Lafayette St (10013), at Howard St, in Chinatown.* 212/966-8898; FAX 212/966-3933. 223 rms, 14 story. S $125-$175; D $146-$195; each addl $20; suites $160; under 12 free. Crib free. Valet parking $20. TV; cable, in-rm movies. Restaurant 7 am-11 pm. Bar noon-midnight. Ck-out noon. Meeting rms. Concierge. Airport, RR station transportation. Bathrm phones. Renovated landmark building. Cr cds: A, C, D, DS, ER, JCB, MC, V.

D 🛎 ⚓ 🐾 🔥 SC

✔ ★ **HOWARD JOHNSON PLAZA.** *851 Eighth Ave (10019), between W 51st and 52nd Sts, Midtown.* 212/581-4100; FAX 212/974-7502. 300 rms, 11 story. S $99-$142; D $105-$154; each addl $20; suites $195-$348; under 18 free; wkend packages. Crib free. Garage, in/out $7.75. TV; cable. Restaurant 6 am-midnight. Bar from 11 am. Ck-out 1 pm. Gift shop. Airport transportation. Cr cds: A, C, D, DS, JCB, MC, V.

🎣 🐾 SC

★ ★ **INTER-CONTINENTAL.** *111 E 48th St (10017), between Lexington & Park Aves, Midtown.* 212/755-5900; res: 800/327-0200; FAX 212/644-0079. 691 rms, 14 story. S $195-$255; D $225-$285 each addl $30; suites $275-$3,000; under 14 free; wkend package. Crib free. TV. Restaurant 7 am-midnight. Bar 11:30-1 am. Ck-out noon. Meeting rms. Concierge. Drugstore. Garage parking $26; valet. Airport transportation avail. Exercise equipt; bicycles, stair machine, steam rm, sauna. Massage therapy. Minibars. Cr cds: A, C, D, DS, ER, JCB, MC, V.

D 🏋 🎣 🐾 🔥 SC

★ ★ **JOLLY MADISON TOWERS.** *22 E 38th St (10016), at Madison Ave, Midtown.* 212/685-3700; res: 800/225-4340; FAX 212/447-0747. 225 rms, 18 story. S $130-$160; D $150-$180; each addl $20; suites $500; under 12 free. Crib free. TV. Restaurant 6:30 am-9:30 pm. Bar; entertainment. Ck-out noon. Meeting rms. Concierge. Airport, RR station, bus depot transportation. Cr cds: A, C, D, MC, V.

🎣 🐾 🔥 SC

★ **JOURNEY'S END.** *3 E 40th St (10016), between Fifth & Madison Aves, Murray Hill.* 212/447-1500; res: 800/221-2222; FAX 212/213-0972. 186 rms, 30 story. S $144; D $154; each addl $10; under 16 free. Crib free. Garage parking $18. TV; cable. Complimentary coffee in lobby. Ck-out noon. Health club 1 blk. Cr cds: A, D, JCB, MC, V.

D 🎣 🔥 SC

★ ★ ★ **KIMBERLY.** *145 E 50th St (10022), between Lexington & 3rd Ave, Midtown.* 212/755-0400; res: 800/683-0400; FAX 212/486-6915. 188 kit. suites, 30 story. S, D $205-$275; under 16 free; wkly, wkend & hol rates; higher rates UN events. Crib free. Garage parking $24. TV; cable. Complimentary coffee in rms. Restaurant 7 am-11 pm. Bar noon-midnight; entertainment Thurs-Sat. Ck-out noon. Coin lndry. Concierge. Health club privileges. Minibars. Balconies. Cr cds: A, C, D, DS, MC, V.

🎣 🐾

✔ ★ ★ **LEXINGTON.** *511 Lexington Ave (10017), at E 48th St, Midtown.* 212/755-4400; res: 800/448-4471; FAX 212/751-4091. 700 rms, 27 story. S, D $99-$120; each addl $25; suites $350-$500. Crib free. TV; cable. Restaurant 6:30 am-midnight. Bar 4 pm-1 am. Ck-out noon. Airport transportation. Many refrigerators. Near Grand Central Station. Cr cds: A, C, D, DS, ER, JCB, MC, V.

🎣 🐾 SC

★ ★ **LOEWS NEW YORK.** *569 Lexington Ave (10022), at E 51st St, Midtown.* 212/752-7000; FAX 212/758-6311. 726 rms, 20 story. S $185-$205; D $205-$225; each addl $25; suites $250-$850; under 16 free; wkend rates. Crib free. Pet accepted, some restrictions. Garage $20.75. TV; cable, in-rm movies. Restaurant 7 am-midnight. Bar 11-2

am. Ck-out noon. Meeting rms. Barber. Exercise rm; instructor, weight machines, bicycles, whirlpool, sauna, steam rm. Bathrm phones, refrigerators. Modern decor. *LUXURY LEVEL : CONCIERGE FLOOR.* 40 rms, 6 suites. S $205; D $225. Concierge. Private lounge, honor bar. Bathrm phones. Complimentary continental bkfst, refreshments, newspaper. Whirlpool in some suites. Cr cds: A, C, D, DS, JCB, MC, V.

D 🛎 🏋 🎣 🐾 🔥 SC

★ ★ ★ **LOWELL.** *28 E 63rd St (10021), between Madison & Park Aves, Upper East Side.* 212/838-1400; res: 800/221-4444; FAX 212/319-4230. 65 rms, 17 story, 58 kit. suites. S, D $295-$355; each addl $20; kit. suites $455-$1,500; under 12 free; wkend rates. Crib free. Valet parking $30. TV; in-rm movies. Restaurants 7 am-11 pm. Tea rm 3:30-6:30 pm. Bar noon-midnight. Ck-out 1 pm. Meeting rm. Concierge. Health club privileges. Bathrm phones, refrigerators, minibars. Many wood-burning fireplaces. Some balconies. Complimentary newspaper, shoeshine. Art deco landmark (1928) with atmosphere of a European-style hotel. Elegant accommodations; eclectic furnishings, with handsome French and Oriental period pieces. Cr cds: A, C, D, ER, JCB, MC, V.

D 🛎 🔥

★ ★ **LYDEN GARDENS.** *215 E 64th St (10021), between Second & Third Aves, Upper East Side.* 212/355-1230; res: 800/637-8483; FAX 212/758-7858. 133 kit. suites, 13 story. S $195-$215; D $215-$235; each addl $20; 1-bedrm $235-$260; 2-bedrm $395-$425; under 12 free; wkend rates. Crib free. Garage $16.50. TV; cable. Restaurant adj. No rm serv. Ck-out noon. Concierge. Balconies. Gardens. Cr cds: A, C, D, ER, JCB, MC, V.

D 🎣 🔥

★ ★ **LYDEN HOUSE.** *320 E 53rd St (10022), Midtown.* 212/888-6070; FAX 212/935-7690. 81 kit. units, 11 story. S, studio rms $180; D $200; suites $200-$220; under 12 free; wkend rates; lower rates July-Aug. Crib free. TV; cable. Coffee in rms. Ck-out noon. Coin lndry. Cr cds: A, C, D, ER, JCB, MC, V.

🔥

★ ★ ★ **MACKLOWE.** *145 W 44th St (10036), between Sixth Ave & Broadway, Times Square/Theater District.* 212/768-4400; res: 800/622-5569; FAX 212/789-7688. 629 rms, 52 story, 10 suites. S $200-$250; D $220-$270; each addl $25; suites $425-$3,500; under 18 free; wkend rates; higher rates special events. Crib free. Valet parking $30. TV; in-rm movies. Restaurant 6:30 am-11 pm. Bar 11-1 am. Ck-out noon. Convention facilities. Concierge. Airport, RR station, bus depot transportation. Exercise rm; instructor, weights, bicycles, steam rm. Minibars. Bathrm phone in suites. Post-modern skyscraper, with moderne setbacks, deco detailing, incorporates landmark, beaux-arts Hudson Theatre (1902), which has been restored. Cr cds: A, C, D, DS, ER, JCB, MC, V.

D 🏋 🎣 🐾 🔥 SC

★ ★ ★ **THE MARK.** *25 E 77th St (10021), between Madison & 5th Aves, Upper East Side.* 212/744-4300; res: 800/843-6275; FAX 212/744-2749. 120 rms, 16 story, 60 suites. S, D $285-$310; each addl $20; suites $575-$2,200; under 12 free; wkend, hols rates. Crib free. Garage $30. TV; cable, in-rm movies. Restaurant 7 am-10:30 pm. Rm serv 24 hrs. Bar. Ck-out 1 pm. Meeting rms. Concierge. Airport, RR station, bus depot transportation. Health club privileges. Bathrm phones. Cr cds: A, C, D, DS, ER, JCB, MC, V.

D 🔥

★ ★ **MARRIOTT EAST SIDE.** *525 Lexington Ave (10017), between E 48th and 49th Sts, Midtown.* 212/755-4000; FAX 212/751-3440. 664 rms, 34 story. S $139-$220; D $139-$240; suites from $300; under 18 free; wkend packages. Crib free. TV; in-rm movies. Coffee in rms. Restaurant 7 am-10 pm. Bar noon-1 am; entertainment. Ck-out noon. Concierge. Airport transportation. Exercise equipt; weight machine, stair machine. Bathrm phones, minibars. Designed by Arthur Loomis Harmon, architect of Empire State Bldg; hotel was subject of Georgia O'Keefe cityscapes. *LUXURY LEVEL : CONCIERGE LEVEL.* 64 rms, 6 floors. S $219; D $240; 1-bedrm suites $300-$600; 2-bedrm suites $450-$900. Private lounge, honor bar. Complimentary continental bkfst, refreshments. Cr cds: A, C, D, DS, ER, JCB, MC, V.

[D] [symbols] [SC]

★ ★ ★ **MARRIOTT FINANCIAL CENTER.** 85 West St (10006), at Albany St, Financial District. 212/385-4900; FAX 212/227-8136. 504 rms, 38 story, 13 suites. S, D $255-$285; each addl $25; suites $349-$1,500; under 18 free; wkend rates. Crib free. Garage parking; valet $23. TV; cable. Indoor pool; poolside serv, lifeguard. Restaurant 6:30 am-10:30 pm. Bar 11:30-2 am. Ck-out 11 am. Convention facilities. Concierge. Gift shop. Exercise equipt; weight machine, bicycles, sauna, steam rm. Walking distance to Wall St, ferry to Statue of Liberty. Cr cds: A, C, D, DS, ER, JCB, MC, V.

[D] [symbols] [SC]

★ ★ ★ **MARRIOTT MARQUIS.** 1535 Broadway (10036), between 45th & 46th Sts, Times Square/Theater District. 212/398-1900; FAX 212/704-8930. 1,874 rms, 50 story. S $206-$250; D $225-$270; each addl $25; suites $425-$3,500; under 18 free; wkend, summer packages avail. Covered parking, valet $30. TV; cable, in-rm movies. Coffee in rms. Restaurant 7 am-midnight (also see THE VIEW). Bars. Ck-out noon. Convention facilities. Concierge. Shopping arcade. Exercise equipt; weights, bicycles, whirlpool, sauna, steam rm. Minibars. Striking architecture; features city's only revolving rooftop restaurant/lounge; glass-enclosed elvtrs, 46-story atrium. **LUXURY LEVEL.** 110 rms, 2 floors. S, D $265-$290. Private lounge. Minibars. Library, billiards rm. Coffee in rms. Complimentary bkfst. Cr cds: A, C, D, DS, JCB, MC, V.

[D] [symbols] [SC]

MAYFAIR HOTEL BAGLIONI. (New owners, therefore not rated) 610 Park Ave (10021), at E 65th St, Upper East Side. 212/288-0800; res: 800/223-0542 (exc NY); FAX 212/737-0538. 201 rms, 16 story, 105 suites. S $275; D $295; suites (most with pantries) $355-$1,700; wkend plan. Crib free. Valet parking $32. TV; cable. Restaurant 7-11 am, light lunch 11 am-2:30 pm; high tea 3-5:30 pm; also dining adj. Rm serv 24 hrs. Bar 11-1 am. Ck-out 1 pm. Meeting rms. Concierge. Exercise equipt; weights, rowing machine. Complete fitness center. Exercise bicycle avail in rm on request. Bathrm phones; some refrigerators. Wood-burning fireplace in some rms. Complimentary shoeshine, newspaper. Cr cds: A, C, D, JCB, MC, V.

[D] [symbols]

★ ★ **THE MAYFLOWER.** 15 Central Park West (10023), at 61st St, Upper West Side. 212/265-0060; res: 800/223-4164; FAX 212/265-5098. 377 rms, 18 story, 200 suites. S $145-$185; D $160-$200; each addl $15; suites $195-$275; under 18 free; wkly, wkend, hol rates; lower rates July, Aug & mid-Dec-Mar. Pet accepted. Garage parking $15, valet $18. TV; cable. Restaurant 7 am-10 pm. Bar 11:30-1 am. Ck-out 1 pm. Meeting rms. Concierge. Airport transportation. Refrigerators. Some terraces. Cr cds: A, C, D, DS, ER, JCB, MC, V.

[symbols] [SC]

★ ★ ★ **THE MICHELANGELO.** 152 W 51st St (10019), between 6th & 7th Aves, Times Square/Theater District. 212/765-1900; res: 800/237-0990; FAX 212/541-6604. 178 rms, 7 story, 52 suites. S, D $255-$315; each addl $30; suites $375-$950; under 16 free; wkend rates. Crib free. Valet parking $27/day. TV; cable, in-rm movies avail. Restaurant 7 am-2:30 pm, 5:30-11:30 pm. Rm serv 24 hrs. Bar; pianist. Ck-out 1 pm. Meeting rms. Concierge. Courtesy morning limo to Wall St. Airport transportation. Exercise equipt; treadmill, stair machine. Health club privileges adj. Bathrm phones; refrigerators avail. Complimentary newspaper, shoeshine. European-style deluxe hotel; Italian marble baths, European toiletries. 18th- and 19th-century art and period furnishings in lobby. Cr cds: A, C, D, ER, JCB, MC, V.

[D] [symbols]

★ ★ ★ **MORGANS.** 237 Madison Ave (10016), between 37th & 38th Sts, Murray Hill. 212/686-0300; res: 800/334-3408; FAX 212/779-8352. 113 rms, 19 story. S $180-$210; D $205-$235; each addl $25; suites $275-$400; under 12 free; wkend rates. Garage, valet parking $27. TV; cable; in-rm movies avail. Complimentary continental bkfst.

Tea serv 4-7 pm. Rm serv 24 hrs. Ck-out 1 pm. Concierge. Health club privileges. Bathrm phones, refrigerators, minibars. Andree Putman designed interiors; combines high-tech ultra-modern look with 1930s moderne styling. Cr cds: A, C, D, ER, JCB, MC, V.

[symbols]

★ ★ ★ **NEW YORK HELMSLEY.** 212 E 42nd St (10017), between Second and Third Aves, on the East Side. 212/490-8900; FAX 212/986-4792. 800 rms, 41 story. S $190-$240; D $215-$265; each addl $30; suites $400-$800; under 12 free; wkend plan. Crib free. Garage $33. TV; cable. Restaurant 7 am-11:30 pm. Bar 11-1 am; entertainment. Ck-out 1 pm. Meeting rms. Health club privileges. Bathrm phones; some refrigerators. 2 blks E of Grand Central Station. Cr cds: A, C, D, DS, JCB, MC, V.

[D] [symbols]

★ ★ ★ **NEW YORK HILTON AND TOWERS AT ROCKEFELLER CENTER.** 1335 Avenue of the Americas (10019), between W 53rd & 54th Sts, Midtown. 212/586-7000; FAX 212/315-1374. 2,042 rms, 46 story. S $165-$260; D $190-$285; each addl $25; suites $375-$475; family rates; wkend package plan. Crib free. Garage $30. TV. Restaurant 6 am-midnight. Bar 11-2 am. Ck-out 1 pm. Convention facilities. Barber, beauty shop. Exercise rm; instructor, weights, bicycles, sauna. Minibars; refrigerators avail. **LUXURY LEVEL : EXECUTIVE TOWER.** 237 units, 6 floors. S $212; D $237; suites $375-$2,500. Bathrm phones; some full wet bars. Cr cds: A, C, D, DS, ER, JCB, MC, V.

[D] [symbols]

★ ★ ★ **THE NEW YORK PALACE.** 455 Madison Ave (10022), at 50th St, Midtown. 212/888-7000; res: 800/697-2522; FAX 212/303-6000. 963 rms, 53 story; 104 suites. S $205-$285; D $245-$310; suites $395-$3,000; under 18 free; wkend & hol rates. Crib free. Garage parking $36. TV; cable. Restaurants 6:30 am-10:30 pm. Rm serv 24 hrs. Bars 11:30-2:30 am; entertainment. Ck-out 1 am. Convention facilities. Concierge. Gift shop. Beauty shop. Health club privileges. Refrigerator in suites. Cr cds: A, C, D, DS, JCB, MC, V.

[D] [symbols]

★ ★ **NOVOTEL.** 226 W 52nd St (10019), at Broadway, Midtown. 212/315-0100; res: 800/221-3185; FAX 212/765-5369. 474 rms, 33 story. S, D $159-$169; each addl $20; under 16 free. Crib $20. Parking $10.50. TV; cable. Restaurant 6 am-midnight. Bar 3:30 pm-1 am; entertainment exc Sun. Ck-out 1 pm. Meeting rm. Cr cds: A, C, D, ER, JCB, MC, V.

[D] [symbols]

★ ★ ★ **OMNI BERKSHIRE PLACE.** 21 E 52nd St (10022), at Madison Ave, Midtown. 212/753-5800; FAX 212/308-9473. 415 rms, 16-20 story (2 wings). S $220-$255; D $240-$275; each addl $20; 2-3-rm suites $350-$1,700; under 17 free; wkend package plan. Crib free. Valet parking $28. TV; cable. 2 restaurants 6:30 am-midnight. Rm serv 24 hrs. Bar noon-1 am. Ck-out 1 pm. Meeting rms. Concierge. Drugstore. Airport, Wall St transportation. Bathrm phone in suites. Health club 2 blks. Cr cds: A, C, D, DS, JCB, MC, V.

[D] [symbols] [SC]

★ ★ ★ **PARAMOUNT.** 235 W 46th St (10036), between Broadway & Eighth Ave, Times Square/Theater District. 212/764-5500; res: 800/225-7474; FAX 212/354-5237. 600 rms, 20 story. S $99-$185; D $155-$205; each addl $20; suites $330-$430; under 16 free; monthly rates; wkend packages. Crib free. Garage $18. TV; in-rm movies. Restaurant 7 am-11 pm, Sat & Sun hrs may vary. Bar 4 pm-4 am, Sun to 2 am. Ck-out noon. Meeting rms. Concierge. Exercise equipt; weight machine, treadmill. Public areas and guest rms designed in a high-tech, futuristic style. Cr cds: A, D, DS, JCB, MC, V.

[D] [symbols]

★ ★ ★ **PARKER MERIDIEN.** 118 W 57th St (10019), between 6th & 7th Aves, Midtown. 212/245-5000; res: 800/543-4300; FAX 212/708-7477. 700 rms, 42 story. S $245-$275; D $260-$290; each addl $30; suites $325-$1,800; under 12 free; wkend plan. Crib free. Garage parking, valet $28. TV. Restaurant 7 am-10:45 pm. Rm serv 24 hrs. Bar 4 pm-midnight. Ck-out 1 pm. Whirlpool, sauna. French ambience; Italian marble flooring, French tapestries. Cr cds: A, C, D, DS, ER, JCB, MC, V.

D ⊠ ⚒

★ ★ ★ ★ **THE PENINSULA NEW YORK.** 700 Fifth Ave (10019), at 55th St, Midtown. 212/247-2200; FAX 212/903-3949. 212 rms, 23 story, 30 suites. S, D $295-$415; each addl $20; suites $550-$3,500; under 12 free. Crib free. Parking $31. TV; cable. Indoor pool; poolside serv, lifeguard. Restaurant 7 am-midnight (also see ADRIENNE). Rm serv 24 hrs. Tea served in Gotham Lounge (2:30-5:30 pm). Rooftop bar noon-midnight, closed Sun. Ck-out 1 pm. Meeting rms. Concierge. Airport transportation. Exercise rm; instructor, weight machines, bicycles, whirlpool, sauna, steam rm. Tri-level health & fitness spa. Bathrm phones, refrigerators. Beaux Arts bldg built 1905; lobby has sweeping marble staircase & original carved Gotham ceiling; rms feature Art Nouveau furnishings. Cr cds: A, C, D, DS, ER, JCB, MC, V.

≋ ✈ ⊠ ⚒

★ ★ ★ ★ **THE PIERRE.** 2 E 61st St (10021), at Fifth Ave, Midtown. 212/838-8000; res: 800/743-7734; FAX 212/940-8109. 202 rms, 42 story. S $295-$475; D $325-$505; suites $645-$2,500. Crib free. Garage $30. TV; cable. Restaurant 7-1 am (also see CAFE PIERRE; and see THE ROTUNDA, Unrated Dining). Rm serv 24 hrs. Bar 11-1 am; entertainment from 8 pm. Ck-out noon. Meeting rms. Concierge. Barber, beauty shop. Many boutiques. Exercise rm; instructor, bicycles, treadmill. Masseuse. Minibars. Serv pantry in suites. Traditional European-style hotel opp Central Park. Cr cds: A, C, D, ER, JCB, MC, V.

D ✾ ✈ ⊠ ⚒

★ ★ ★ ★ **PLAZA ATHÉNÉE.** 37 E 64th St (10021), between Madison & Park Aves, Upper East Side. 212/734-9100; res: 800/447-8800; FAX 212/772-0958. 153 rms, 17 story. S, D $275-$390; each addl $35; suites $590-$2,500. Crib free. Parking $38/24 hrs. TV; cable. Restaurant 7 am-9:30 pm (also see LE RÉGENCE). Rm serv 24 hrs. Bar 11 am-midnight. Ck-out 1 pm. Meeting rm. Concierge. Exercise equipt; weights, bicycles. Refrigerators. Deluxe toiletry amenities. In-rm movies in suites. Some suites with private dining rm. Some private patios, glassed-in balconies. Takes its name from the great Paris original; offers grandeur on an intimate scale. European elegance; twin-level lobby with fine reproduction furniture; hand-woven Oriental rugs; marble throughout. Cr cds: A, C, D, ER, JCB, MC, V.

D ✈ ⊠ ⚒

★ ★ **PLAZA FIFTY.** 155 E 50th St (10022), between Lexington & 3rd Aves, Midtown. 212/751-5710; res: 800/ME-SUITE; FAX 212/753-1468. 204 rms, 22 story, 129 suites. S $165; D $185; each addl $20; suites $195-$455; under 12 free; wkend rates; some lower rates summer & winter. Crib free. TV; cable. Coffee in rms. Ck-out noon. Exercise equipt; bicycles, stair machine. Refrigerators. Some balconies. Cr cds: A, C, D, ER, JCB, MC, V.

D ✈ ⊠ ⚒

★ ★ ★ ★ **THE PLAZA HOTEL.** Fifth Ave at 59th St & Central Park South (10019), Midtown. 212/759-3000; res: 800/759-3000; FAX 212/759-3167. 808 rms, 18 story. S, D $235-$495; each addl $40; suites $650-$1,950; under 18 free. Crib free. Garage $35. TV; cable. Restaurant (see EDWARDIAN ROOM and PALM COURT). Rm serv 24 hrs. Bar 11-2 am. Ck-out noon. Concierge. Gift shop. Barber, beauty shop. Boutiques. Exercise equipt; bicycles, treadmill. Health club privileges. Refrigerators, minibars. Elegant decor. Landmark 1907 building restored to its original opulence. Cr cds: A, C, D, DS, ER, JCB, MC, V.

D ✾ ✈ ⊠ ⚒ SC

✔★ **QUALITY INN MIDTOWN.** 157 W 47th St (10036), between Avenue of the Americas (Sixth Ave) & Seventh Ave, Times Square/Theater District. 212/768-3700; FAX 212/768-3403. 155 rms, 10 story, 33 suites. May-Sept: S, D $109-$119; each addl $20; suites $139-$159; under 18 free; wkly rates; higher rates NY City Marathon; lower rates rest of yr. Crib free. Garage $17. TV. Continental bkfst.

Restaurant nearby. No rm serv. Ck-out noon. Concierge. Airport transportation. Cr cds: A, C, D, DS, ER, JCB, MC, V.

D ⊠ ⚒ SC

★ ★ **RADISSON EMPIRE.** 44 W 63rd St (10023), at Lincoln Center, Upper West Side. 212/265-7400; FAX 212/315-0349. 375 rms, 11 story. S, D $135-$200; each addl $20; suites from $250; under 17 free. Crib free. Garage $20. TV; cable. Restaurant 7-11 am, 5 pm-midnight. Rm serv 24 hrs. Bar 4:30 pm-midnight. Ck-out noon. Health club privileges. Cr cds: A, C, D, DS, ER, JCB, MC, V.

D ⊠ ⚒

✔★ ★ **RAMADA HOTEL PENNSYLVANIA.** 401 Seventh Ave (10001), at 33rd St, opp Madison Square Garden, in Garment District. 212/736-5000; FAX 212/502-8798. 1,705 rms, 22 story. S, D $129; suites $250-$450; under 18 free. Crib free. Garage $26. TV; in-rm movies. Restaurant 6:30-1 am. Bar noon-2 am. Ck-out noon. Convention facilities. Concierge. Shopping arcade. Barber, beauty shop. Airport, RR station transportation. Health club privileges. Cr cds: A, C, D, DS, ER, JCB, MC, V.

D SC

✔★ ★ **RAMADA MILFORD PLAZA.** 270 W 45th St (10036), at Eighth Ave, Times Square/Theater District. 212/869-3600; FAX 212/944-8357. 1,300 rms, 28 story. S $95-$135; D $110-$155; each addl $15; suites $260-$500; under 14 free. Crib free. Garage $11. TV; cable. Restaurant 7 am-11 pm. Bar from noon. Ck-out noon. Convention facilities. Exercise equipt; weight machine, bicycles. Refrigerators avail. Cr cds: A, C, D, DS, ER, JCB, MC, V.

✈ ⚒ SC

★ ★ ★ ★ **THE REGENCY HOTEL.** 540 Park Ave (10021), at E 61st St, Upper East Side. 212/759-4100; res: 800/233-2356; FAX 212/826-5674. 365 rms, 21 story, 185 kit. suites. S, D $250-$300; suites $375-$1,200 under 18 free; wkend & shopping packages. Crib free. Garage $27. TV; cable, in-rm movies avail. Restaurant (see 540 PARK). Rm serv 24 hrs. Bar 11:30-2 am; pianist. Ck-out 1 pm. Meeting rms. Concierge. Barber, beauty shop. Limo service 24 hrs. Exercise rm; instructor, weights, bicycles, whirlpool, sauna. Refrigerators, bathrm TVs. Elegant period furniture; marble foyer in suites. Cr cds: A, C, D, DS, MC, V.

D ✾ ✈ ⊠ ⚒

★ ★ ★ **RENAISSANCE NEW YORK.** 714 7th Ave (10036), Times Square/Theater District. 212/765-7676; FAX 212/765-1962. 305 rms, 26 story. S, D $189-$249; each addl $15; suites $425-$475; under 12 free; wkend rates. Crib free. Garage $26; in/out $6. TV; cable, in-rm movies. Complimentary coffee in rms. Restaurant 6:30 am-11 pm. Rm serv 24 hrs. Bar; pianist. Ck-out noon. Meeting rms. Concierge. Masseur avail. Exercise equipt; weight machine, treadmill. Minibars. Cr cds: A, C, D, DS, ER, JCB, MC, V.

D ✈ ⊠ ⚒ SC

★ ★ ★ **RIHGA ROYAL.** 151 W 54th St (10019), between Sixth and Seventh Aves, Midtown. 212/307-5000; res: 800/937-5454; FAX 212/765-6530. 491 suites, 54 story. 1-bedrm $290-$420; 2-bedrm $450-$700; each addl $25; Royal suites D $900-$2,000; family, wkend, hol rates. Crib free. Garage, valet parking $28. TV; cable, in-rm movies. Restaurant 6:30-1 am. Rm serv 24 hrs. Bar 11:30-2 am; entertainment. Ck-out 1 pm. Meeting rms. Concierge. Airport, RR station, bus depot transportation. Exercise rm; instructor, weights, bicycles, sauna. Bathrm phones, refrigerators, minibars. Complimentary shoeshine. Architecturally reminiscent of the classic skyscrapers of the 1920s and 1930s. Cr cds: A, C, D, DS, ER, JCB, MC, V.

D ✈ ⊠ ⚒

★ ★ ★ **THE RITZ-CARLTON.** 112 Central Park South (10019), near 6th Ave, Midtown. 212/757-1900; FAX 212/757-9620. 214 rms, 25 story. S, D $230-$400; each addl $30; suites $495-$4,000; under 16 free. Crib free. Garage $30. TV; cable. Restaurant (see FANTINO). Rm serv 24 hrs. Bar 3 pm-2 am. Ck-out noon. Exercise equipt; bicycles, treadmill, sauna. Some refrigerators. Elegant European decor. Central Park opp. **LUXURY LEVEL : RITZ-CARLTON CLUB.** 30 rms, 20 suites, 10 floors. S, D $310-$460; suites $550-$4,000. Concierge. Private lounge, honor bar. Complimentary continental bkfst, refreshments, newspapers & magazines. Minibars. Cr cds: A, C, D, DS, ER, JCB, MC, V.

[D] [symbols] SC

★★ ROGER SMITH. 501 Lexington Ave (10017), at E 47th St, Midtown. 212/755-1400; res: 800/445-0277; FAX 212/319-9130. 136 rms, 17 story. S $160; D $180; each addl $20; suites $225-$295; under 17 free. Crib free. TV; in-rm movies avail. Complimentary continental bkfst. Restaurant noon-3 pm, 6-10 pm. Bar. Ck-out 1 pm. Meeting rms. Exercise equipt avail in rm. Health club privileges. Refrigerators; serv pantry in suites. Cr cds: A, C, D, DS, JCB, MC, V.

[symbols]

✔★ THE ROOSEVELT. 45 E 45th St (10017), Midtown. 212/661-9600; res: 800/223-1870; FAX 212/687-5064. 1,021 rms, 19 story. S, D $99-$139; each addl $15; suites $195-$1,100; under 13 free; wkend, hol rates. Crib free. Garage $24. Pet accepted, some restrictions. TV; cable. Restaurant 7 am-2 pm, 4-10 pm. Bar 4 pm-midnight. Ck-out noon. Convention facilities. Concierge. Gift shop. Drug store. Barber, beauty shop. Health club privileges. Some refrigerators. Built 1927. Cr cds: A, C, D, DS, JCB, MC, V.

[symbols] SC

★★★ ROYALTON. 44 W 44th St (10036), between Fifth Ave & Avenue of the Americas, Midtown. 212/869-4400; res: 800/635-9013; FAX 212/869-8965. 168 rms, some with shower only, 16 story. S $210-$325; D $235-$350; each addl $25; suites $370; wkend rates. Crib $25. Pet accepted, some restrictions. Valet parking $28. TV; cable, in-rm movies. Restaurant 7-1 am. Rm serv 24 hrs. Bar. Ck-out 1 pm. Meeting rm. Concierge. Exercise equipt; bicycles, treadmill. Video cassette library. Bathrm phones, refrigerators, minibars; some fireplaces. Some balconies. Ultramodern rm decor. Cr cds: A, C, D, ER, JCB, MC, V.

[D] [symbols]

★★ SALISBURY. 123 W 57th St (10019), between 6th & 7th Aves, Midtown. 212/246-1300; res: 800/223-0680 800/228-0822 (CAN); FAX 212/977-7752. 320 rms, 17 story. S $139-$149; D $149-$159; each addl $15; suites $225; under 12 free; wkend rates. Crib free. TV; cable. Complimentary continental bkfst. Ck-out noon. Meeting rms. Many refrigerators, serv pantry. Cr cds: A, C, D, JCB, MC, V.

[symbols] SC

★ SAN CARLOS. 150 E 50th St (10022), Midtown. 212/755-1800; res: 800/722-2012; FAX 212/688-9778. 200 rms, 18 story, 138 kits. S $139-$159; D $149-$169; each addl $10; suites $175-$200; under 14 free; wkend rates. Crib free. TV. Restaurant nearby. Rm serv avail 6 am-10 pm. Ck-out 11 am. Coin lndry. Airport transportation. Cr cds: A, C, D, MC, V.

[symbol]

★★★ SHELBURNE MURRAY HILL. 303 Lexington Ave (10016), between 37th & 38th Sts, Murray Hill. 212/689-5200; res: 800/637-8483; FAX 212/779-7068. 258 suites, 16 story. Suites $195-$405; under 12 free; wkend rates. Garage $23; $19 wkends. TV; cable. Complimentary coffee, tea. Restaurant 6:30 am-11 pm. Bar. Ck-out noon. Coin lndry. Convention facilities. Concierge. Exercise equipt; weights, bicycles, sauna. Private patios, balconies. Roof-top garden and terrace offer views of midtown Manhattan. Cr cds: A, C, D, JCB, MC, V.

[D] [symbols]

★★ SHERATON MANHATTAN. 790 Seventh Ave (10019), between W 51st & 52nd Sts, Midtown. 212/581-3300; FAX 212/262-4410. 650 rms, 22 story. S, D $155-$275; each addl $30; suites $350-$550; under 17 free; wkend plans. Crib free. Garage $19. TV. Indoor pool; lifeguard. Restaurant 6:30 am-11 pm. Rm serv 24 hrs. Bar 11 am-11 pm. Ck-out noon. Meeting rms. Concierge. Exercise rm; instruc-

tor, weight machine, bicycles. Refrigerators avail. Cr cds: A, C, D, DS, ER, JCB, MC, V.

[D] [symbols] SC

★★★ SHERATON NEW YORK HOTEL & TOWERS. 811 Seventh Ave (10019), between 52nd & 53rd Sts, Midtown. 212/581-1000; FAX 212/262-4410. 1,750 rms, 50 story. S, D $155-$295; each addl $30; suites $350-$1,000; under 17 free; wkend package plan. Crib free. Garage $24. TV; cable. Complimentary coffee in rms. Restaurant 6:30 am-midnight. Bar 11:30-1 am; entertainment Tues-Sat. Ck-out noon. Convention facilities. Gift shop. Exercise rm; instructor, weight machines, bicycles. LUXURY LEVEL : SHERATON TOWERS. 212/841-6464. 54 rms, 2 floors. Private lounge. Minibars. Bathrm phones. Complimentary bkfst, refreshments, shoeshine. Cr cds: A, C, D, DS, ER, JCB, MC, V.

[D] [symbols] SC

★★★ SHERATON-PARK AVENUE. 45 Park Ave (10016), between 36th & 37th Sts, Murray Hill. 212/685-7676; FAX 212/889-3193. 150 rms, 10 story. S, D $240-$285; each addl $30; suites $375-$700; under 17 free; wkend plan. Crib free. Garage $24. TV. Coffee in rms. Restaurant 6:30 am-11 pm. Rm serv 24 hrs. Bar noon-1 am. Ck-out noon. Meeting rms. Concierge. Health club privileges. Refrigerators avail; some fireplaces; serv pantry in some suites. Cr cds: A, C, D, DS, JCB, MC, V.

[D] [symbols]

★★ THE SHOREHAM. 33 W 55th St (10019), between Fifth & Sixth Aves, Midtown. 212/247-6700; res: 800/553-3347; FAX 212/765-9741. 84 rms, 11 story, 37 suites. S, D $145; each addl $15; suites $195; under 16 free; wkend & hol rates. Crib free. Garage parking $14. TV; cable, in-rm movies. Complimentary continental bkfst. Restaurant nearby. Ck-out noon. Concierge. La Guardia Airport transportation. Health club privileges. Refrigerators. Renovated hotel built 1930. Cr cds: A, C, D, MC, V.

[D] [symbols]

★★ SOUTHGATE TOWER SUITE. 371 Seventh Ave (10001), at 31st St, south of Midtown. 212/563-1800; res: 800/637-8483; FAX 212/643-8028. 522 suites (1-2 bedrms) & studio rms, 28 story. S $146-$180; D $166-$200; each addl $20; wkend, wkly, monthly rates. Crib free. TV; cable. Complimentary coffee. Restaurant 7-1 am. Ck-out noon. Meeting rms. Coin lndry. Concierge. Barber, beauty shop. Airport, RR station transportation. Exercise equipt; weight machines, bicycles. All units with full kit. Cr cds: A, C, D, DS, ER, JCB, MC, V.

[D] [symbols]

★★★★ THE ST REGIS HOTEL. 2 E 55th St (10022), at Fifth Avenue (10022), Midtown. 212/753-4500; res: 800/759-7550; FAX 212/787-3447. 322 rms, 16 story, 86 suites. S, D $350-$450; suites $575-$3,000; under 12 free; wkend packages. Crib free. Garage parking, valet, in/out $30. TV; cable, in-rm movies avail. Restaurant (see LESPINASSE). Afternoon tea 2:30-5:30 pm, harpist. Rm serv 24 hrs. Bar noon-2 am. Ck-out 1 pm. Meeting rms. Concierge. Gift shop. Barber, beauty shop. Florist. Men's designer apparel shop. Chocolatier. Business center. Airport, RR station transportation. Exercise equipt; weight machine, bicycles, sauna. Fitness center; massage by appt. Bathrm phones. Private butler (24 hrs) each floor. Some balconies. Originally built in 1904 by John Jacob Astor. Cr cds: A, C, D, DS, ER, JCB, MC, V.

[D] [symbols] SC

✔★ STANFORD. 43 W 32nd St (10001), between Fifth Ave & Broadway, near Macy's, south of Midtown. 212/563-1480; res: 800/365-1114; FAX 212/629-0043. 130 rms, 12 story, 30 suites. S $70-$80; D $80-$90; each addl $15; suites $110-$180; wkly rates. Crib free. TV; cable. Restaurant 7 am-10 pm. No rm serv. Ck-out noon. Refrigerators. Near Madison Square Garden. Cr cds: A, C, D, DS, JCB, MC, V.

[symbol] SC

★ ★ ★ ★ **THE STANHOPE.** *995 Fifth Ave (10028), at 81st St, opp Metropolitan Museum of Art, Upper East Side.* 212/288-5800; res: 800/828-1123; FAX 212/517-0088. 148 units, 17 story, 79 suites, some with kits. S, D $300; suites $425-$2,500; under 12 free; wkend rates; package plans. Crib free. Garage $35. TV; cable, in-rm movies. Restaurant 7 am-11 pm; also outdoor cafe and tea room. Rm serv 24 hrs. Bar noon-1 am. Ck-out 1 pm. Meeting rms. Concierge. Exercise rm; instructor, weight machine, bicycles, sauna. Massage. Bathrm phones, minibars; some wet bars. Fine antiques and paintings; private library. Many rms with views of Central Park and the Manhattan skyline. Landmark hotel (1926) offers old-world service and comfort in the tradition of Europe's grand hotels. Overlooks Central Park. Cr cds: A, C, D, DS, ER, JCB, MC, V.

★ ★ ★ **SURREY.** *20 E 76th St (10021), Upper East Side.* 212/288-3700; FAX 212/628-1549. 130 rms, 16 story. Apr-June & Sept-Dec: S $215-$235; D $235-$255; each addl $20; suites $310-$605; under 12 free; wkly rates; lower rates rest of yr. Crib avail. TV; cable, in-rm movies. Restaurant noon-3 pm, 5:30-11 pm. Rm serv from 7:30 am. Bar. Ck-out noon. Meeting rms. Exercise equipt; bicycles, treadmill. Cr cds: A, C, D, ER, JCB, MC, V.

★ ★ ★ **THE TUDOR.** *304 E 42nd St (10017), between 2nd and 1st Aves, Midtown.* 212/986-8800; res: 800/879-8836; FAX 212/986-1758. 300 rms in 2 towers, 17 & 20 story, 14 suites. S $195-$265; D $220-$290; each addl $25; suites $300-$600; under 12 free; wkend rates; some lower rates May-Sept. Crib free. Garage parking, valet; in/out $15-$18. TV; cable. Restaurant 6:30 am-11 pm. Rm serv 24 hrs. Bar. Ck-out 1 pm. Meeting rms. Concierge. Airport, RR station transportation. Exercise rm; instructor, weight machines, bicycles, saunas. Minibars. Some balconies. UN Bldg 1 blk. Cr cds: A, C, D, DS, ER, JCB, MC, V.

★ ★ ★ ★ **U.N. PLAZA-PARK HYATT.** *1 UN Plaza (10017), at First Ave & E 44th St, on the East Side.* 212/758-1234; res: 800/233-1234; FAX 212/702-5051. 428 rms on floors 28-38. S, D $240-$280; each addl $20; suites $460-$1,100; under 18 free; wkend rates; wkend package plan. Crib free. Garage; valet parking $26/day. TV; cable. Movies. Indoor pool; lifeguard. Restaurant (see AMBASSADOR GRILL). Bar noon-1 am; pianist from 5 pm. Ck-out noon. Meeting rms. Free morning limousine serv to Wall St, Park Ave and Garment District; evenings to theater (7:15 pm); wkends to 5th Ave shopping (mornings only). Indoor tennis $60/hr. Exercise rm; instructor, weights, bicycles, sauna, steam rm. Masseuse (fee). Minibars. Some bathrm phones, refrigerators. View from all rms. Complimentary newspaper, shoe shine. Cr cds: A, C, D, DS, ER, JCB, MC, V.

WALDORF-ASTORIA. *(4-Star 1994; New general manager, therefore not rated) 301 Park Ave (10022), between E 49th & 50th Sts, Midtown.* 212/355-3000; res: /800-HILT; FAX 212/872-7272. 1,219 rms, 42 story. S, D $215-$335; each addl $25; suites $400-$800; children free; wkend rates. Crib free. Garage $34/24 hrs. TV; cable, in-rm movies. Restaurant 7 am-11:45 pm (also see BULL & BEAR STEAKHOUSE). Rm serv 24 hrs. Bars 10:30-3 am; Sun noon-1 am. Ck-out noon. Convention facilities. Concierge. Barber, beauty shop. Great variety of shops and services. Exercise rm; instructors, weight machines, bicycles, steam rm. Massage. Complete physical fitness training center. Refrigerators, minibars. *LUXURY LEVEL : WALDORF TOWERS.* 191 rms, 109 suites, 15 floors. S, D $375-$425; suites $550-$5,500. Concierge. Butler service. Private lounge, honor bar. Full wet bar in some suites. Bathrm phones. Complimentary refreshments. Cr cds: A, C, D, DS, ER, JCB, MC, V.

★ ★ **WALES.** *1295 Madison Ave (10128), between 92nd & 93rd Sts, Upper East Side.* 212/876-6000; res: 800/428-5252 (exc NYC); FAX 212/860-7000. 95 units, 10 story, 40 suites, 10 kits. S, D $145; each addl (up to 4 persons) $20; suites, kits. $195-$215. Crib

free. Valet parking $26. TV; cable. Complimentary continental bkfst. Restaurant 8 am-11 pm. No rm serv. Ck-out 1 pm. Meeting rm. Health club privileges. Rec rm. Refrigerators avail. Restored 1902 hotel; intricate architectural details, original fireplaces. Afternoon tea & cookies in parlor. Cr cds: A, MC, V.

★ ★ **WARWICK.** *65 W 54th St (10019), at 6th Ave, Midtown.* 212/247-2700; res: 800/223-4099 (exc NY), 800/522-5634 (NY); FAX 212/957-8915. 424 rms, 33 story. S $180-$230; D $205-$245; each addl $25; suites $275-$500; under 12 free; wkend rates. Crib free. Garage $30. TV. Restaurant 6:30 am-11 pm. Bar 11-1 am. Ck-out 1 pm. Meeting rms. Cr cds: A, C, D, JCB, MC, V.

★ ★ ★ **WESTBURY.** *15 E 69th St (10021), at Madison Ave, Upper East Side.* 212/535-2000; res: 800/321-1569; FAX 212/535-5058. 232 rms, 17 story. S $245-$265; D $275-$295; each addl $30; 2-3-rm suites $325-$1,500; under 12 free; wkend rates. TV; cable, in-rm movies avail. Restaurant (see POLO). Rm serv 24 hrs. Bar noon-midnight. Ck-out 1 pm. Exercise equipt; bicycles, treadmill, sauna. Bathrm phones; serv pantry in some suites. Cr cds: A, C, D, DS, ER, JCB, MC, V.

✔ ★ **WYNDHAM.** *42 W 58th St (10019), off 5th Ave, Midtown.* 212/753-3500; FAX 212/754-5638. 204 rms, 16 story. S $115-$125; D $130-$140; suites $175-$205. Crib free. TV. Restaurant 7:30 am-10:30 pm. Bar from noon. Ck-out 1 pm. Garage adj. Refrigerator, serv pantry in suites. Cr cds: A, C, D, MC, V.

Inns

★ ★ ★ **BOX TREE.** *250 E 49th St (10017), at Second Ave, Midtown.* 212/758-8320. 13 suites in 2 town houses, 3 story. No elvtr. MAP (Fri & Sat): suites $270-$310; lower rates (AP) wkdays. TV. Complimentary continental bkfst. Restaurant (see BOX TREE). Dining credit $100 per night included MAP rates. Limited rm serv 24 hrs. Ck-out 11 am, ck-in 3 pm. Concierge. Airport, RR station transportation. Bathrm phones, fireplaces. 1840s brownstones; antique furnishings; imported French amenities; rms individually decorated. Cr cds: A.

✔ ★ **THE GRACIE INN.** *502 E 81st St (10028), Upper East Side.* 212/628-1700; FAX 212/628-6420. 12 rms, 6 story, 6 suites. S $79-$139; D $99-$159; each addl $20-$40; suites $159-$349; family rates, wkly, wkend & hol rates. Parking $20. TV; cable, in-rm movies avail. Complimentary continental bkfst. Restaurant nearby. Ck-out by arrangement. Luggage handling. Refrigerators. Some terraces. Near Gracie Mansion, East River. Rms individually decorated with country antiques. Cr cds: A, C, D, DS, MC, V.

Restaurants

✔ ★ ★ **20 MOTT STREET.** *20 Mott St, between Pell & Bowery Sts, in Chinatown.* 212/964-0380. Hrs: 8 am-midnight; Fri & Sat to 1 am. Chinese menu. A la carte entrees: dim sum from $1.90, lunch, dinner $7.95-$20. Specialties: dim sum, baked conch with curry sauce, filet mignon with black pepper sauce. Fish tank. Cr cds: A, JCB, MC, V.

★ ★ ★ **'21' CLUB.** *21 W 52nd St, between Fifth & Sixth Aves, Midtown.* 212/582-7200. Hrs: noon-midnight. Closed Sun; major hols; also Sat June-Aug. Res accepted. Bar. Wine cellar. A la carte entrees: lunch $19-$37, dinner $24-$39. Specializes in fresh seafood, Maryland crab cakes, "21" burger, chicken hash "21." Own pastries. Originally a speak-easy; famous gathering place of publishing & theater people. Jacket, tie. Cr cds: A, C, D, JCB, MC, V.

★ ★ ★ **540 PARK.** (See The Regency Hotel) 212/339-4050. Hrs: 7 am-10 pm; Sun brunch noon-2:30 pm. Res accepted. Bar 11:30-2 am. Wine cellar. A la carte entrees: bkfst $6-$20, lunch $12-$25, dinner $18-$30. Prix fixe: pre-theater dinner (6-7 pm) $27.50. Sun brunch $27.50. Child's meals. Specializes in American cuisine. Pianist 5-11 pm. Valet parking. Cr cds: A, C, D, DS, MC, V.

[D]

★ ★ ★ **ADRIENNE.** (See The Peninsula New York Hotel) 212/903-3918. Hrs: 7-10:30 am, noon-2:30 pm, 6-10 pm; Sun brunch 11 am-2:30 pm. Res accepted. Continental, Amer menu. Bar. A la carte entrees: bkfst $6-$18, lunch $18-$27, dinner $20-$32. Prix fixe: bkfst $18, lunch $28. Sun brunch $36. Specialties: grilled peppered tuna, seafood bouillabaisse, pan seared duck breast. Own baking. Harpist Sat evenings & hols. Valet parking. Dining rm overlooks Fifth Ave. Jacket. Cr cds: A, C, D, DS, ER, JCB, MC, V.

[D]

★ ★ **AMARCORD.** 7 E 59th St (10022), between Fifth & Madison Aves, Midtown. 212/935-3535. Hrs: noon-3 pm, 6 pm-midnight; Sat & Sun from 6 pm. Closed some major hols. Res accepted. Italian menu. Bar. A la carte entrees: lunch $6-$18, dinner $7-$24. Specialties: bollito misto, misto di arrosti alla Romagnola, seppioline in umido con punte verdi e patate. Own pasta. Venetian stucco; images of Ferrari race cars. Cr cds: A, D, MC, V.

[D]

★ ★ ★ **AMBASSADOR GRILL.** (See U.N Plaza-Park Hyatt Hotel) 212/702-5014. Hrs: 7 am-2:30 pm, 6-10:30 pm; Sun brunch 11:30 am-3:30 pm. Res accepted. Amer grill menu. Bar. Wine list. Complete meals: bkfst $16, lunch $19.95, dinner $24.95. Prix fixe: pre-theater dinner (6-7 pm) $19.95. Fri seafood extravaganza $35. Sun brunch $35. Child's meals. Specialties: prosciutto quesadilla, seared salmon, grilled rack of lamb, seasonal dishes. Valet parking. Modern decor. Jacket. Cr cds: A, C, D, DS, JCB, MC, V.

[D]

★ ★ **AMERICAN FESTIVAL.** 20 W 50th St, between Fifth & Sixth Aves, at Rockefeller Center, Midtown. 212/246-6699. Hrs: 7:30 am-11 pm; Fri to midnight; Sat 9 am-midnight; Sun 9 am-10 pm; Sat & Sun brunch 10 am-4 pm. Res accepted. Regional Amer menu. Bar noon-midnight. A la carte entrees: bkfst $4.75-$14, lunch, dinner $12-$24. Prix fixe: dinner $22.95 & $24.95. Seasonal dishes. Parking (after 5 pm). Outdoor dining (May-Oct). Overlooks Rockefeller Center's famous Prometheus fountain and sunken pool (summer), skating rink (winter). Cr cds: A, C, D, JCB, MC, V.

[D]

★ ★ ★ **AN AMERICAN PLACE.** 2 Park Ave (10016), at 32nd St, Midtown. 212/684-2122. Hrs: 11:45 am-3 pm, 5:30-9:30 pm; Sat from 5:30 pm. Closed Sun; major hols. Res accepted. Bar. Wine cellar. A la carte entrees: lunch $15.50-$21, dinner $22-$29.50. Specializes in seafood, game, rack of lamb. Art deco dining rm with Prairie School-style furniture. Jacket. Cr cds: A, D, MC, V.

★ ★ ★ **AQUAVIT.** 13 W 54th St, between Fifth & Sixth Aves, Midtown. 212/307-7311. Hrs: noon-3 pm, 5:30-10:30 pm; Sat from 5:30 pm. Closed Sun; major hols. Res accepted. Scandinavian menu. Bar. Wine cellar. A la carte entrees: lunch $12-$18, dinner $13-$19. Prix fixe: lunch $19.94, dinner $62. Pre-theater menu (5:30-6:30 pm): 2-course dinner $19, 3-course dinner $39. Specialties: Scandinavian shrimp, game, salmon. In town house once owned by Nelson Rockefeller; waterfall in atrium. Two dining rms; informal cafe; formal dining rm (jacket). Near Museum of Modern Art. Cr cds: A, C, D, MC, V.

★ ★ ★ **ARCADIA.** 21 E 62nd St, between Madison & Fifth Aves, Upper East Side. 212/223-2900. Hrs: noon-2:30 pm, 6-10 pm; Fri, Sat from 6-10:30 pm. Closed Sun; Jan 1, July 4, Dec 25. Res accepted. Bar. A la carte entrees: lunch $17-$23. Prix fixe: dinner $58. Specialties: chimney-smoked lobster, chocolate bread pudding with brandy custard sauce, corn cakes with caviar and creme fraiche. Own baking. Outdoor dining. Cr cds: A, D, MC, V.

[D]

✔ ★ **ARIZONA 206.** 206 E 60th St, between 2nd & 3rd Aves, Upper East Side. 212/838-0440. Hrs: Cafe: noon-midnight; Sun to 11 pm; Sun brunch 11:30 am-4 pm. Dining rm: noon-3 pm, 5:30-11 pm; Fri to 11:30 pm; Sat 5:30-11:30 pm; Sun 5:30-10:30 pm. Closed Dec 25. Res accepted. Southwestern menu. Bar. A la carte entrees: Cafe: lunch $5-$18, dinner $5-$18; Sun brunch $6-$12. Dining rm: lunch $8-$18, dinner $19-$28. Adobe Pueblo decor; Western art. Totally nonsmoking. Cr cds: A, C, D, DS, MC, V.

★ ★ **ARLECCHINO.** 192 Bleecker St, between 6th Ave and MacDougal St, in Greenwich Village. 212/475-2355. Hrs: noon-midnight; Fri & Sat to 1 am; Sun to 11 pm. Closed Dec 25. Res accepted. Northern Italian menu. Wine, beer. A la carte entrees: lunch $7.50-$12, dinner $10.50-$19.50. Specialties: fettucine verdi a modo nostro, charcoal-grilled veal chop with wild mushrooms, ravioli stuffed with mushrooms & crabmeat. Outdoor dining. Trattoria atmosphere; harlequin costumes, masks, puppets, paintings adorn walls in 2 dining areas. Cr cds: A.

★ ★ ★ **ARQUA.** 281 Church St, at White St, in Tribeca. 212/334-1888. Hrs: noon-3 pm, 5:30-11 pm; Fri & Sat to 11:30 pm. Closed Sun; major hols; also last 2 wks Aug. Res accepted. Italian menu. Bar. A la carte entrees: lunch $14-$21, dinner $14-$25. Specialties: homemade pastas, gnocchi, desserts, roasted duck. Venetian decor. Cr cds: A, D, MC, V.

★ ★ ★ **AUREOLE.** 34 E 61st St, between Madison & Park Aves, Upper East Side. 212/319-1660. Hrs: noon-2:30 pm, 5:30-10:30 pm; Fri to 11 pm; Sat 5:30-11 pm. Closed Sun; some major hols; also last wk Aug-1st wk Sept. Res required. French, Amer menu. Bar noon-1 am. A la carte entrees: lunch $16-$24. Prix fixe: lunch $32, dinner $59. Specializes in fish, game. Own baking. Outdoor dining. In town house; interior with balcony, bas-relief wildlife art; garden in rear. Jacket, tie. Cr cds: A, D, MC, V.

★ ★ **BAROCCO.** 301 Church St, between Walker & White Sts, in Tribeca. 212/431-1445. Hrs: noon-3 pm, 6-11 pm; Sat from 6 pm; Sun 6-10:30 pm. Closed major hols. Res accepted. Regional Italian menu. Bar. A la carte entrees: lunch $7-$20, dinner $12-$26. Specialties: ravioli verdi, calamari fritti, pappardelle noodles with squab, Tuscan dishes. Own gelato. Casual trattoria dining in industrial loft space. Cr cds: A, D, DS, MC, V.

★ ★ ★ **BAROLO.** 398 W Broadway (10012), between Spring & Broome Sts, in SoHo. 212/226-1102. Hrs: noon-midnight; Fri & Sat to 1 am. Res accepted. Northern Italian menu. Bar. A la carte entrees: lunch $11.50-$23, dinner $13.50-$24. Specialties: spinach flan with Piemontese cheese sauce, rissoto with porcini mushrooms, whole sea bass baked in salt. Antipasto bar. Garden dining among cherry trees and fountain. Three levels of dining. Contemporary decor. Cr cds: A, D, MC, V.

✔ ★ **BERRY'S.** 180 Spring St, at Thompson, in SoHo. 212/226-4394. Hrs: 11:30 am-11:30 pm; Fri & Sat to midnight; Sun to 10:30 pm; Sun brunch 11 am-4 pm. Closed Thanksgiving, Dec 25; also mid-Aug-early Sept. Res accepted. Bar to 1:30 am. A la carte entrees: lunch $4-$12.50, dinner $12.50-$19. Sun brunch $4.75-$12.50. Fresh herbs and vegetables from own garden. Outdoor dining. Victorian-style decor. Cr cds: A, C, D, DS, JCB, MC, V.

★ ★ **BICE.** 7 E 54th St, just off Fifth Ave, Midtown. 212/688-1999. Hrs: noon-3 pm, 6 pm-midnight. Closed Jan 1, Dec 25. Res accepted. Italian menu. Bar. A la carte entrees: lunch, dinner $20-$28. Specialties: lobster salad with raspberry vinaigrette, marinated salmon & swordfish with celery root. Own desserts. Menu changes daily. Outdoor dining. Branch of original restaurant in Milan. Cr cds: A, C, D, MC, V.

★ ★ **THE BLACK SHEEP.** 344 W 11th St, at Washington St, in Greenwich Village. 212/242-1010. Hrs: 6-11 pm; Fri & Sat to midnight; Sat & Sun brunch noon-3:30 pm. Closed Jan 1, Dec 25. Res accepted. Country French menu. Bar. A la carte entrees: dinner $16-$27. Complete meals: dinner $24-$35. Sat & Sun brunch $7.50-$12. Specialties: loin rack of young lamb Provençale, crispy confit of duck leg, shoulder of pork with red cabbage. Outdoor dining. Occupies 2 rms on ground floor of an old Victorian building; original antique tin ceiling from its days as a pool hall. Cr cds: A.

★ ★ **BOATHOUSE CAFE.** *In Central Park (10028), enter at 72nd St & 5th Ave, at lake, Upper East Side.* 212/517-2233. Hrs: 11:30 am-10 pm; Fri & Sat to 11 pm; Sun brunch to 4:30 pm. Closed Nov-Apr. Bar. Semi-a la carte: lunch $14-$20, dinner $14-$25. Sun brunch $11-$17.50. Child's meals. Specializes in pasta, herb-roasted chicken, seafood. Outdoor dining overlooking lake. View of Bethesda Fountain. Cr cds: A, MC, V.

D

★ ★ **BOLO.** *23 E 22nd St (10010), between Broadway & Park Ave S, in Gramercy Park area.* 212/228-2200. Hrs: noon-2:15 pm, 5:30 pm-midnight; Sat from 5:30 pm; Sun 11:30 am-3 pm, 5:30 pm-midnight. Closed some major hols. Res accepted. Spanish menu. Bar to 1 am. A la carte entrees: lunch $13-$16, dinner $16-$22. Specialties: curried shellfish & chicken paella for two, roasted pork loin with apricot & almond relish, tapenade-crusted salmon. Eclectic decor. Cr cds: A, D, DS, MC, V.

★ ★ **BOMBAY PALACE.** *30 W 52nd St, between Fifth & Sixth Aves, Midtown.* 212/541-7777. Hrs: noon-3 pm, 5:30-11 pm. Res accepted. Indian menu. Bar. A la carte entrees: lunch, dinner $9-$21. Buffet: lunch $11.95, dinner $19.95. Specialties: chicken keema, lamb pasanda, prawn marsala. Own pita bread. Parking. Indian art, statuary. Cr cds: A, D, MC, V.

D **SC**

★ ★ **BOOM.** *152 Spring St, between W Broadway & Wooster, in SoHo.* 212/431-3663. Hrs: noon-3 pm, 6 pm-1 am; Thurs-Sat 1 pm-3:30 am; Sat & Sun brunch noon-5 pm. Res accepted. Intl menu. Bar. A la carte entrees: lunch $5-$10, dinner $5-$24. Sat & Sun brunch $4.50-$13.50. Specialties: Vietnamese five-spiced grilled quail, avacado blinis w/grilled lobster, Chinese beggars chicken. Old World atmosphere; frescoed walls, hanging sculpture. Cr cds: A.

★ ★ ★ **BOULEY.** *165 Duane St, between Hudson & Greenwich Sts, in Tribeca.* 212/608-3852. Hrs: noon-3 pm, 5:30-11 pm; Sat from 5:30 pm. Closed Sun; major hols. Res required. Contemporary French menu. Bar. Wine list. A la carte entrees: lunch $21-$28, dinner $29-$37. Tasting menu: lunch $32, dinner $75. Specializes in seasonal dishes. Own baking. Grows own herbs, vegetables. In converted warehouse with soaring vaulted ceiling; French country decor. Jacket, tie. Cr cds: A, D, DS, MC, V.

★ ★ ★ ★ **BOX TREE.** *(See Box Tree Inn)* 212/758-8320. Hrs: noon-2 pm, 5:30-9 pm; Sat from 5:30 pm. Res required. Continental cuisine with French overtones. Bar. Wine cellar. Prix fixe: lunch $42, 5-course dinner $86. Specializes in lobster, filet of beef, rack of lamb, pheasant. Own baking. Elegant decor; antiques and art; working fireplace. Jacket, tie. Cr cds: A.

★ ★ ★ **BULL & BEAR STEAKHOUSE.** *(See Waldorf-Astoria Hotel)* 212/872-4900. Hrs: noon-11:30 pm; Sat, Sun from 5 pm. Res accepted. Semi-a la carte: lunch $13.50-$23.50, dinner $19.50-$45. Complete meals: lunch $19.75, dinner $23.75. Child's meals. Specializes in Maine lobster, prime beef, grilled fish. Own baking. Open kitchen. Club-like atmosphere. Jacket. Cr cds: A, C, D, DS, ER, JCB, MC, V.

D

★ ★ **C.T.** *111 E 22nd St, between Park & Lexington Aves, in Gramercy Park area.* 212/995-8500. Hrs: noon-2:30 pm; 5:30-10:30 pm; Fri to 11:30 pm; Sat 5:30-11:30 pm. Closed most major hols. Res accepted. French, Brazilian, Amer menu. Bar. A la carte entrees: lunch $14.50-$19, dinner $19-$26. Specialties: pan-seared duck breast, herb encrusted beef tenderloin, crispy red snapper. 2 dining rms; seating on

2 levels. Colorful decor, open kitchen. Art gallery. Cr cds: A, C, D, DS, MC, V.

D

✔ ★ **CABANA CARIOCA.** *123 W 45th St, between Sixth Ave & Broadway, Times Square/Theater District.* 212/581-8088. Hrs: noon-11 pm; Fri & Sat to midnight. Res accepted. Portuguese, Brazilian menu. Bar. A la carte entrees: lunch, dinner $9.95-$14.95. Buffet: lunch $8.95. Specialties: feijoada, paella marinheira, fried shrimp. Dining rm decorated with Angelo Romano murals. Cr cds: A, C, D, DS, MC, V.

★ ★ ★ **CAFE DES ARTISTES.** *1 W 67th St, Upper West Side.* 212/877-3500. Hrs: noon-3 pm, 5:30 pm-12:30 am; Sun 10 am-4 pm, 5-11 pm. Closed Dec 25. Res required. Country French menu. Bar. Wine list. A la carte entrees: lunch $14-$24, dinner $17-$32.50. Prix fixe: lunch $19.50, dinner $32.50. Specializes in cassoulet, grilled smoked salmon. Romantic, Old World decor; Howard Chandler Christy murals. Near Lincoln Center. Jacket (after 5 pm). Cr cds: A, C, D, JCB, MC, V.

✔ ★ ★ **CAFE DES SPORTS.** *329 W 51st St, between Eighth & Ninth Aves, on the West Side.* 212/581-1283. Hrs: noon-3 pm, 5-11:15 pm; Mon to 10 pm; Sun 5-10 pm. Res accepted. French menu. Bar. A la carte entrees: lunch $9.95-$15.95, dinner $15. Complete meals: dinner $19.95. Specialties: scaloppini in cream sauce, sea scallops Provençale, beef bourguignonne. Bistro atmosphere; display of soccer trophies. Cr cds: A, MC, V.

★ ★ **CAFE LUXEMBOURG.** *200 W 70th St, Upper West Side.* 212/873-7411. Hrs: noon-3 pm, 5:30 pm-12:30 am; Mon from 5:30 pm; Sun 6-11 pm; Sun brunch 11 am-3 pm. Closed Dec 25. Res accepted. French, Amer menu. Bar. A la carte entrees: lunch $5-$15, dinner $15.50-$25. Prix fixe: lunch $19.95, pre-theater and post-theater dinner (5:30-6:30 pm & 10:30 pm-midnight) $28.50. Specialties: country salad, sweetbreads, fresh fish. Bistro atmosphere; art deco decor. Near Lincoln Center. Cr cds: A, C, D, MC, V.

✔ ★ ★ **CAFE METAIRIE.** *1442 Third Ave, at 82nd St, Upper East Side.* 212/988-1800. Hrs: noon-3 pm, 5-11 pm; Sun brunch 11 am-4 pm. Res accepted. Continental menu. Bar. A la carte entrees: dinner $13.95-$19.95. Complete meal: pre-theater dinner (5-7 pm) $17.95. Sun brunch $9.95. Specialties: rack of lamb with herbed crust, coq au vin, roast duck with seasonal fruit sauce and wild rice, cassoulet. Warm, intimate atmosphere of a country inn; beamed ceiling, fireplace. Cr cds: A, C, MC, V.

D

★ ★ **CAFE NOSIDAM.** *768 Madison Ave (10021), between 65th & 66th Sts, Upper East Side.* 212/717-5633. Hrs: 11:30-1 am; Sun to 11 pm; Sun brunch to 3 pm. Res accepted. Italian, Amer menu. Bar. A la carte entrees: lunch, dinner $12.95-$28. Sun brunch $19.95. Specializes in pasta, fish. Outdoor dining. Contemporary decor; original art. Cr cds: A, MC, V.

★ ★ ★ **CAFE PIERRE.** *(See The Pierre Hotel)* 212/940-8185. Hrs: 7-1 am. Res required. Contemporary, continental menu. Bar. Wine list. A la carte entrees: bkfst $9-$19, lunch $18-$28, dinner $23-$39. Prix fixe: lunch $32, dinner $55. Pre-theater menu (6-7 pm) $34. Sun brunch $34. Specializes in seasonal offerings. Own pastries. Entertainment 8 pm-1 am, pianist Sun noon-3 pm. Elegant decor; intimate. Cr cds: A, C, D, ER, JCB, MC, V.

D

✔ ★ ★ **CAFE TABAC.** *232 E 9th St, between 3rd & 2nd Aves, in the East Village.* 212/674-7072. Hrs: 6 pm-12:30 am; wkends 6 pm-1:30 am. Closed Jan 1, Dec 25. Res accepted. Bar. A la carte entrees: dinner $13-$19. Specialties: steak frites, grilled filet mignon with wild mushrooms, pasta. Located in converted warehouse. Art deco-style decor. Intimate dining rm on main floor; bistro atmosphere. Unusual red-covered pool table off upstairs dining rm. Cr cds: A, MC, V.

★ ★ **CAFE TREVI.** *1570 First Ave, between 81st & 82nd Sts, in Yorkville section of Upper East Side.* 212/249-0040. Hrs: 5:30 pm-midnight. Res accepted. Northern Italian menu. Bar. A la carte entrees:

dinner $14.75-$24.75. Child's meals. Specializes in veal, pasta, chicken. Trattoria atmosphere. Cr cds: A, D, MC, V.

D

★ **CAFE UN DEUX TROIS.** *123 W 44th St, between Broadway & 6th Ave, Times Square/Theater District.* 212/354-4148. Hrs: noon-midnight; Sat from 11 am; Sun 11 am-11 pm. French menu. Bar. A la carte entrees: lunch $9.50-$19.95, dinner $10.50-$22.95. Specialties: cous-cous, stuffed duck, papillote. Bistro-like dining rm. Cr cds: A, C, D, MC, V.

★★ **CANASTEL'S.** *233 Park Ave S, at 19th St, in Gramercy Park area.* 212/677-9622. Hrs: noon-4 pm, 5:30 pm-midnight; Fri to 1 am; Sat 5:30 pm-1 am; Sun 5-11 pm. Closed Dec 25. Res accepted. Italian menu. Bar to 1 am; Fri & Sat to 2 am; Sun to midnight. A la carte entrees: lunch $9-$18.50, dinner $13-$25. Specialties: cappellini primavera, veal chop Canastel's, tortellacci Michelangelo. Family-style dinner Sun. Entertainment Fri evenings. Cr cds: A, C, D, MC, V.

★★ **CAPRICCIO.** *33 E 61st St, between Madison & Park Aves, Upper East Side.* 212/757-7795. Hrs: noon-3 pm, 5:30-11 pm; Sat 5-11:30 pm. Closed Sun; major hols. Res accepted. Italian menu. Bar. A la carte entrees: lunch $16-$25, dinner $18-$25. In town house with vaulted ceiling, stained glass, skylighted garden rm. Cr cds: A, C, D, MC, V.

★★★ **CAPSOUTO FRÈRES.** *451 Washington St, 1 blk S of Canal St, near Hudson River, in Tribeca.* 212/966-4900. Hrs: noon-3:30 pm, 6-11 pm; Fri to midnight; Sat 6 pm-midnight; Mon 6-11 pm; Sat & Sun brunch noon-3:30 pm. Res accepted. Contemporary French menu. Bar to midnight. Wine cellar. A la carte entrees: lunch $9-$22, dinner $14-$24. Prix fixe: lunch $19.95. Sat & Sun brunch $8.50-$20. Specializes in poached salmon, roast duckling, filet of beef with Madeira sauce. Own baking. Outdoor dining. In converted neo-Flemish, landmark warehouse (1891). Cr cds: A, C, D, MC, V.

★★★★ **CARLYLE RESTAURANT.** *(See Carlyle Hotel)* 212/744-1600. Hrs: 7-10:30 am, noon-2:30 pm, 6 pm-1 am; Sun from 7:30 am. Res accepted. French, continental menu. Bar noon-2 am. Wine list. A la carte entrees: bkfst $9.50-$19.50, lunch $16.50-$28.50, dinner $18.50-$36. Buffet: bkfst $19.50. Sun brunch $35. Seasonal specialties. Own baking. Valet parking. Elegant decor. Cr cds: A, C, D, JCB, MC, V.

★★ **CARMINE'S.** *2450 Broadway, between 90th & 91st Sts, Upper West Side.* 212/362-2200. Hrs: 5-11 pm; Fri & Sat to midnight; Sun 2-10 pm. Southern Italian menu. Bar. A la carte entrees: dinner $14-$36. Specialties: country-style rigatoni with sausage, cannellini beans & broccoli, chicken scarpariello. Single entrees served family-style for 2-4 people. Dining rm, originally a hotel ballroom, is re-creation of 1940s neighborhood Italian restaurant. Cr cds: A.

★★ **CASTELLANO.** *138 W 55th St, between 6th & 7th Aves, Midtown.* 212/664-1975. Hrs: noon-3 pm, 5:30-11 pm; Sat & Sun from 5:30 pm. Closed some major hols. Res accepted. Tuscan, Italian menu. Bar. A la carte entrees: lunch, dinner $18-$32. Specialties: grilled calamari, fegato Castellano, risotti. Outdoor terrace dining. 3 dining areas on 2 levels. Display of photos by Brassai. Cr cds: A, C, D, JCB, MC, V.

★★★ **CHANTERELLE.** *In Mercantile Exchange Bldg, 2 Harrison St, at Hudson St, in Tribeca.* 212/966-6960. Hrs: noon-2:30 pm, 6-10:30 pm. Closed Sun; major hols; also 2 wks Aug. Res required. French menu. Bar. Wine cellar. A la carte entrees: lunch $30-$40. Prix fixe: lunch $33, dinner $40 (Mon-Fri, 3 courses), $68 & $89. Specialty: grilled seafood sausage. Menu changes monthly. Contemporary French cuisine. Chef-owned. Cr cds: A, C, D, MC, V.

D

★★ **CHARLTON'S.** *922 Third Ave (10022), between 55th & 56th Sts, East Side.* 212/688-4646. Hrs: noon-11 pm; Sat from 5 pm; Sun 5-10 pm. Closed Dec 25. Res accepted. Bar. Semi-a la carte:

lunch $14-$26, dinner $17-$29. Specializes in steak. Gentlemens club atmosphere. Memorabilia of old New York. Cr cds: A, C, D, MC, V.

D

★★ **CHEFS CUSINIERS CLUB (CCC).** *36 E 22nd St, in Gramercy Park area.* 212/228-4399. Hrs: noon-2:30 pm, 5:30-midnight. Closed Sun; major hols; also last wk Aug. Res accepted. Amer, French, Italian menu. Bar. A la carte entrees: lunch $10-$17, dinner $15-$22. Specialties: grilled salmon, NY sirloin steak, Middle Eastern tasting plate. Own desserts. Created as place where NYC chefs can meet, converse, swap information and ideas; also open to public. Cr cds: A, D, MC, V.

D

★★ **CHELSEA CENTRAL.** *227 Tenth Ave, between 23rd & 24th Sts, in Chelsea.* 212/620-0230. Hrs: 11:30 am-3 pm, 5:30-11 pm; Sat 5:30 pm-midnight; Sun to 10 pm; Sun brunch 11:30 am-3 pm. Closed Dec 25. Res accepted. Bar. A la carte entrees: lunch $7-$12, dinner $14-$22. Sun brunch $7-$12. Specializes in grilled salmon & tuna, roast duck, seasonal dishes. An American bistro; turn-of-the-century decor. Cr cds: A, MC, V.

D

★★ **CHEZ NAPOLEON.** *365 W 50th St, between Eighth & Ninth Aves, on the West Side.* 212/265-6980. Hrs: noon-2:30 pm, 5-10 pm; Fri to 11 pm; Sat 5-11 pm. Closed Sun; major hols. Res accepted. French menu. Bar. A la carte entrees: lunch $8-$23, dinner $13-$25. Specialties: bouillabaisse, steak au poivre, duck à l'orange. Small French bistro. Cr cds: A, C, D, MC, V.

✔★★★ **CHIN CHIN.** *216 E 49th St, Midtown.* 212/888-4555. Hrs: 11:30 am-midnight; Sat from 5 pm; Sun 5-11 pm. Closed Thanksgiving. Res accepted. Chinese menu. Bar. Wine cellar. A la carte entrees: lunch $10.50-$18, dinner $13.50-$19.50. Prix fixe: lunch $17.95. Specialties: Peking duck, steamed or crispy sea bass, Grand Marnier shrimp. Sleek, contemporary decor. Cr cds: A, C, D, MC, V.

D

★★ **CHINA GRILL.** *In CBS Bldg, 52 W 53rd St, at Avenue of the Americas, Midtown.* 212/333-7788. Hrs: 11:45 am-11 pm; Fri to midnight; Sat 5 pm-midnight; Sun 5 pm-10 pm. Closed major hols. Res accepted. Bar. A la carte entrees: lunch, dinner for 2, $30-$40. Specialties: oriental antipasto, tempura shushimi, Shanghai lobster. Meals served family-style; guests encouraged to share. Cr cds: A, D, JCB, MC, V.

★★ **CHRIST CELLA.** *160 E 46th St, between Lexington & 3rd Aves, Midtown.* 212/697-2479. Hrs: noon-10:45 pm; Sat 5-10:45 pm. Closed Sun; major hols. Res accepted. Bar. A la carte entrees: lunch, dinner $60-$70; lobster higher. Daily luncheon special $29.95. Specializes in steak, seafood, Canadian lobster. Menu recited. Jacket. Cr cds: A, C, D, JCB, MC, V.

D

★★ **CHRISTER'S.** *145 W 55th St (10019), btween 6th & 7th Aves, Midtown.* 212/974-7224. Hrs: noon-2:30 pm, 5:30-11 pm; Sat from 5:30 pm. Closed Sun; Jan 1, Dec 25. Res accepted. Scandinavian, Amer menu. Bar. Semi-a la carte: lunch $11-$24, dinner $16.50-$26. Specialties: gravlax with mustard sauce, salmon chowder, braised lamb with dill sauce. Smorgasbord. Rustic fishing camp atmosphere with colorful decor. Cr cds: A, C, D, MC, V.

★★ **CITÉ.** *In Time/Life Bldg, 120 W 51st St, between Sixth & Seventh Aves, Midtown.* 212/956-7100. Hrs: 11:30 am-midnight. Closed Jan 1, July 4, Dec 25. Res accepted. French, Amer menu. Bar. Wine cellar. A la carte entrees: lunch, dinner $9.50-$28.50. Prix fixe: dinner $34.50 & $39.50. Specialties: spit-roasted chicken, grilled swordfish, steak frites. Own baking. Zinc-covered bar. One rm informal bistro. Cr cds: A, C, D, DS, JCB, MC, V.

D

★★★ **COCO PAZZO.** *23 E 74th St, between Fifth Ave & Madison Ave, Upper East Side.* 212/794-0205. Hrs: noon-3 pm, 6-11:45 pm;

Sun 5:30-11:30 pm. Closed most major hols. Res required. Italian menu. Bar. Wine cellar. A la carte entrees: lunch $12.50-$21, dinner $19-$28. Specializes in seasonal Italian cuisine. Decor features large still-life frescoes in the Morandi style. Jacket. Cr cds: A, D, MC, V.

D

✔★ **COCONUT GRILL.** *1481 Second Ave, between 77th & 78th Sts, Upper East Side.* 212/772-6262. Hrs: 11:30-12:30 am; Fri & Sat to 1 am; Sun brunch 11 am-4 pm. Res accepted. Bar. A la carte entrees: lunch $4.95-$7.50, dinner $7.95-$14.50. Sun brunch $8.95-$12.50. Specialties: baked salmon, California stir-fried shrimp & chicken. Outdoor dining. Cr cds: A, MC, V.

★★ **CONTRAPUNTO.** *200 E 60th St, at Third Ave, Upper East Side.* 212/751-8616. Hrs: noon-midnight. Closed Thanksgiving. Italian menu. Serv bar. A la carte entrees: lunch $10.50-$19, dinner $11.50-$22. Specializes in homemade pasta, cornish hen roasted with bay leaves & wine, broiled veal chop with braised escarole. Open kitchen. Totally nonsmoking. Cr cds: A, C, D, DS, MC, V.

★ **CUISINE DE SAIGON.** *154 W 13th St, between 6th St & 7th Ave, in Greenwich Village.* 212/255-6003. Hrs: 5-11 pm; Fri & Sat to 11:30 pm; Sun to 10:30 pm. Closed July 4, Thanksgiving, Dec 24, 25. Res accepted; required wkends. Vietnamese menu. Bar. A la carte entrees: dinner $7.95-$15.95. Specialties: shrimp wrapped with sugar cane, Vietnamese spring roll, Saigon famous pasta (steamed wide noodles rolled with minced pork). Cr cds: A, C, D, MC, V.

★★ **DA SILVANO.** *260 Sixth Ave, between Houston and Bleecker Sts, in Greenwich Village.* 212/982-2343. Hrs: noon-3 pm, 6-11:30 pm; Fri & Sat 6 pm-midnight; Sun 5-11 pm. Res required. Italian menu. Serv bar. A la carte entrees: lunch, dinner $11.50-$22.50. Specialties: boneless quails al radicchio, seasonal Florentine dishes. Outdoor dining. Cr cds: A, MC, V.

D

★★ **DA UMBERTO.** *107 W 17th St, between Sixth & Seventh Aves, in Chelsea.* 212/989-0303. Hrs: noon-3 pm, 5-11 pm; Fri to 11:30 pm; Sat 5:30-11:30 pm. Closed Sun; Jan 1, Dec 25; also wk of July 4. Res accepted. Northern Italian menu. Bar. A la carte entrees: lunch $11-$20, dinner $15-$28. Specializes in antipasto buffet, wild game. Florentine decor. Cr cds: A.

★★★ **DANIEL.** *20 E 76th St, between Fifth & Madison Aves, Upper East Side.* 212/288-0033. Hrs: noon-midnight; Sat & Mon from 6 pm. Closed Sun; most major hols. Res required. French menu. Bar. Wine cellar. A la carte entrees: lunch $25-$29, dinner $27-$33. Table d'hôte: lunch $31, dinner $58, $67 & $92. Specialties: black sea bass in a crispy potato shell with red wine sauce, salad of Maine crab with mango, coriander and lime dressing, seasonal cuisine. Outdoor sidewalk terrace dining offers casual, bistro-style atmosphere. Sophisticated dining in a setting reminiscent of a French country house, with changing display of paintings from local galleries; entrance is through a circular foyer paved with authentic 18th-century clay tiles. Chef-owned. Jacket. Cr cds: A, D, MC, V.

D

★★★ **DAWAT.** *210 E 58th St, between Second & Third Aves, on the East Side.* 212/355-7555. Hrs: 11:30 am-3 pm, 5:30-11 pm; Fri & Sat to 11:15 pm; Sun 5:30-11 pm. Res required. Indian menu. Bar. A la carte entrees: lunch, dinner $11.95-$22.95. Complete meals: lunch $12.95 & $13.95, dinner $23.95. Specializes in curried shrimp, salmon in coriander chutney. Parking (dinner). Contemporary East Indian decor. Cr cds: A, C, D, MC, V.

D

★★ **DELEGATES DINING ROOM.** *In United Nations General Assembly Bldg, 4th floor, at First Ave & 46th St, visitors entrance, on the East Side.* 212/963-7625. Hrs: 11:30 am-2:30 pm. Closed Sun; some major hols. Res required. International menu. Serv bar. A la carte entrees: lunch $15-$25. Buffet: lunch $19.50. Specializes in seasonal salads, fresh seafood, a daily roast, specialty desserts. Panoramic view

of East River. Open to public; identification with photograph required. Jacket. Cr cds: A, C, D, JCB, MC, V.

D

★★ **DIVINO.** *1556 Second Ave, between 80th & 81st Sts, in Yorkville section of Upper East Side.* 212/861-1096. Hrs: noon-midnight; Sat & Sun from 5 pm. Closed most major hols. Res accepted. Northern Italian menu. Bar. A la carte entrees: lunch, dinner $11.75-$22.50. Specializes in pasta, veal, seafood. Pianist (cafe). Outdoor dining. Two restaurants, ristorante & cafe, 3 doors apart; cafe less formal. Jacket (ristorante). Cr cds: A, C, D, MC, V.

D

★★ **DUANE PARK CAFE.** *157 Duane St (10013), between Hudson & W Broadway, in Tribeca.* 212/732-5555. Hrs: noon-2:30 pm, 5:30-10 pm; Fri to 10:30 pm; Sat 5:30-10:30 pm. Closed Sun; most major hols; also first wk July. Italian, Amer menu. Bar. Semi-a la carte: lunch $14-$19.95, dinner $16-$22. Specialties: grilled boneless Catskill trout, veal Milanese with arugula, grilled miso marinated duck salad. Intimate atmosphere with Italian accents. Cr cds: A, C, D, DS, MC, V.

✔★ **EDWARD MORAN BAR AND GRILL.** *In Building 4 of World Financial Center, 250 Vesey St, Financial District.* 212/945-2255. Hrs: 11:30 am-midnight. Res accepted. Bar to 1 am. Semi-a la carte: lunch, dinner $7.95-$13.50. Specializes in hamburgers, sandwiches. Salad bar. Outdoor dining. Pub-like atmosphere. Nautical decor. View of Ellis Island and Statue of Liberty. Cr cds: A, C, D, DS, MC, V.

D

★★★ **EDWARDIAN ROOM.** *(See The Plaza Hotel)* 212/759-3000. Hrs: 7-11:30 am, noon-2:30 pm, 5:30-10 pm; Fri & Sat 5:30-10:30 pm; Sun & Mon to 2:30 pm. Res accepted. Traditional European, Amer menu. Serv bar. Wine list. A la carte entrees: bkfst $12-$27, lunch $20-$30, dinner $22-$32. Complete meals: bkfst $13.50-$29. Pre-theater dinner $38, includes free transportation to theaters. Sun brunch $12-$34.50. Specialties: tuna carpaccio with lime, grilled Dover sole, roasted Muscovy duck breast. Seasonal menu. Own baking. Valet parking. 19th-century English decor; view of Central Park. Cr cds: A, C, D, DS, ER, JCB, MC, V.

D

✔★★ **EL TEDDY'S.** *219 W Broadway, between Franklin & White Sts, in Tribeca.* 212/941-7070. Hrs: noon-3 pm, 6-11:30 pm; Thurs & Fri to 1 am; Sat 6 pm-1 am; Sun 6-11 pm. Closed Jan 1, Dec 25. Res accepted. Nuevo Mexican menu. Bar. A la carte entrees: lunch $7-$13, dinner $12-$19. Specializes in grilled seafood. Outdoor dining. Wild, eccentric decor spans styles from 1920s to the present. Located in white building with replica of Statue of Liberty's spiked crown on roof. Cr cds: A, D, MC, V.

★★ **ESTORIL SOL.** *382 Eighth Ave, at 29th St, 1 blk S of Madison Square Garden, in Chelsea.* 212/947-1043. Hrs: noon-11 pm; Sat 5 pm-midnight; Sun 3-9 pm. Closed major hols; also Sun July-Sept. Res required. Italian, Portuguese menu. Bar. A la carte entrees: lunch, dinner $10.95-$26. Specialties: caldeirada, veal chop with brandy sauce, salmon with crab meat. Entertainment Tues, Fri & Sat. Rustic decor. Cr cds: A, C, D, DS, MC, V.

★★★ **FANTINO.** *(See The Ritz-Carlton Hotel)* 212/757-1900. Hrs: 6-11 pm. Closed Sun. Res accepted. Northern Italian menu. Bar from 4 pm. A la carte entrees: dinner $21-$28. Pre-theater dinner (6-7 pm). Specialties: scallops and prosciutto, tart of lobster, saddle of rabbit. Traditional European decor; fireplaces. Cr cds: A, C, D, DS, ER, JCB, MC, V.

D

★★★ **FELIDIA.** *243 E 58th St, between Second & Third Aves, on the East Side.* 212/758-1479. Hrs: noon-3 pm, 5 pm-midnight; Sat from 5 pm. Closed Sun; major hols. Res required. Italian menu. Bar. Extensive wine cellar. A la carte entrees: lunch $18-$26, dinner $18-

$29. Specializes in homemade pasta, veal, seafood. Own baking. Menu changes daily. Garden rm. Jacket. Cr cds: A, C, D, DS, MC, V.

★ ★ **FIFTY SEVEN FIFTY SEVEN.** *(See Four Seasons)* *212/758-5700.* Hrs: 7 am-2 pm, 6-10:30 pm; early-bird dinner 6-7 pm. Bar to midnight; Fri & Sat to 1 am. A la carte entrees: bkfst $15.50-$24.50, lunch $18-$25, dinner $19-$32. Pre-theater menu (6-7 pm) $45. Child's meals. Specializes in Maryland crab cakes, thyme-seared Atlantic salmon, roast rack of herb-crusted lamb. Pianist. Valet parking. Contemporary American grill with art deco accents. Jacket. Cr cds: A, D, MC, V.

D

★ ★ ★ **THE FOUR SEASONS.** *Seagram Bldg, 99 E 52nd St, Midtown.* *212/754-9494.* Hrs: Pool Dining Room: noon-2:30 pm, 5-9 pm; Sat to 11:15 pm; pre-theater dinner 5-6:15 pm, Sat also 10-11:15 pm. Grill Room: noon-2 pm, 5:30-9 pm; Sat 5-10 pm. Closed Sun; major hols. Res accepted. Bar. Wine cellar. A la carte entrees: Pool Dining Room, lunch $19-$40, dinner $30-$45. Pre-theater dinner $41.50. Grill Room: A la carte entrees: lunch $30-$38. Prix fixe: dinner $26.50-$37.50. Unusual dishes. Own baking. Grow own herbs. Menu varies with season. Picasso stage curtain; marble pool. Designed by Philip Johnson, now a historical landmark. Jacket. Cr cds: A, C, D, DS, JCB, MC, V.

★ ★ **FRAUNCES TAVERN.** *54 Pearl St, at Broad St, downtown.* *212/269-0144.* Hrs: 7-10 am, 11:30 am-4 pm, 5-9:30 pm. Closed Sat, Sun; major hols. Res accepted. Bar. Prix fixe: bkfst $12.95. A la carte entrees: lunch, dinner $15-$25. Child's meals. Specializes in fish from Fulton fishmarket. Historic landmark built 1719; George Washington bade farewell to his officers here in 1783. Museum. Family-owned since 1937. Cr cds: A, C, D, MC, V.

✔★ **FULTON STREET CAFE.** *11 Fulton St, at pier, in South Street Seaport section, downtown.* *212/227-2288.* Hrs: 11:30 am-midnight. Bar. A la carte entrees: lunch, dinner $5-$18.95. Specializes in seafood. Outdoor dining. Nautical decor. Cr cds: A, D, MC, V.

D

★ ★ **GALLAGHER'S.** *228 W 52nd St, at Broadway, Times Square/Theater District.* *212/245-5336.* Hrs: noon-midnight. Res accepted. Bar. A la carte entrees: lunch $12.75-$42, dinner $14.95-$43. Specializes in USDA prime beef, sirloin steak, seafood. Open kitchen. Photographs of sports & theater personalities. Cr cds: A, C, D, DS, JCB, MC, V.

D

✔★ ★ **GASCOGNE.** *158 Eighth Ave (10011), at 18th St, in Chelsea.* *212/675-6564.* Hrs: noon-3 pm, 6-10:30 pm; Mon from 6 pm; Fri & Sat to 11 pm; Sun noon-3 pm, 5-10 pm. Closed some major hols. Res accepted. French menu. Bar. A la carte entrees: lunch $5-$15, dinner $8-$19. Specialties: roasted quail with fresh spicy peaches, cassoulet bean stew with duck confit and sausages, warm fresh foie gras with seasonal fruit. Garden dining. French country-style decor; farmhouse ambiance. Cr cds: A, C, D, MC, V.

✔★ ★ **GINO.** *780 Lexington Ave, at E 60th St, Upper East Side.* *212/758-4466.* Hrs: noon-10:30 pm. Closed Jan 1, Thanksgiving, Dec 25. Southern Italian menu. Bar. A la carte entrees: lunch $9.50-$15.95, dinner $12.50-$19.50. Specialties: pasta e fagioli, paglia e fieno segreto, chicken Capri. Own rum cake, cheesecake. No cr cds accepted.

D

★ ★ ★ **GIRAFE.** *208 E 58th St, between Second & Third Aves, on the East Side.* *212/752-3054.* Hrs: noon-3 pm, 5:30-10:30 pm; Sat 5:30-11 pm. Closed Sun; major hols; also 1st wk July. Res accepted. Northern Italian menu. Bar. Wine list. A la carte entrees: lunch $15-$25, dinner $17-$30. Prix fixe: lunch $16.50. Pre-theater dinner $29.75. Wild animal motif. Cr cds: A, C, D, MC, V.

★ ★ **GIRASOLE.** *151 E 82nd St, between Lexington & 3rd Aves, Upper East Side.* *212/772-6690.* Hrs: noon-3 pm, 5 pm-midnight. Closed Jan 1, Dec 25. Res required. Regional Italian menu. A la carte

entrees: lunch $8.50-$15, dinner $15.50-$24.50. Specializes in game, seafood, risotto. Extensive wine selection. Trattoria atmosphere in lower level of town house. Cr cds: A.

D

★ ★ ★ **GOTHAM BAR AND GRILL.** *12 E 12th St, between Fifth Ave & University Place, in Greenwich Village.* *212/620-4020.* Hrs: noon-2 pm, 5:30-10 pm; Fri to 11 pm; Sat 5:30-11 pm; Sun from 5:30. Closed most major hols. Res required. Bar. A la carte entrees: lunch $9.25-$18, dinner $26-$31. Specializes in game, seafood, lamb, quail. Own pastries. Menu changes seasonally. In converted auction warehouse. Cr cds: A, C, D, MC, V.

✔★ ★ **GROTTA AZZURRA.** *387 Broome St, at Mulberry St, in Little Italy.* *212/925-8775.* Hrs: noon-11 pm; Fri to midnight; Sat to 12:30 am. Closed Mon; wk of Dec 25-Jan 1; also July. Neapolitan menu. Wine, beer. A la carte entrees: lunch $8.95-$13.95, dinner $9.95-$19.95. Specialties: spedini alla Romana, linguine with mussels, chicken cacciatore. Own pasta, cheesecake. Parking. Open kitchen. Family-style serv. Family-owned. No cr cds accepted.

✔★ ★ **GROVE STREET CAFE.** *53 Grove St, between Seventh Ave S & Bleecker St, in Greenwich Village.* *212/924-8299.* Hrs: 5:30 pm-midnight; Sat & Sun brunch 11:30 am-3:30 pm. Res accepted. French, Italian menu. A la carte entrees: dinner $10-$17. Specialties: Black Angus steak, crab cakes, duck a l'orange. Menu changes seasonally. Cr cds: A, D, DS, MC, V.

★ ★ **HARBOUR LIGHTS.** *Fulton Pier 17, South St Seaport, Financial District.* *212/227-2800.* Hrs: 11-1 am; Sun brunch to 3:30 pm. Closed Dec 25. Res accepted. French, continental menu. Bar. A la carte entrees: lunch $11-$24, dinner $19-$29. Specialties: pan-roasted swordfish, steamed salmon filet, grilled steak paillard. Parking. Outdoor dining. Glass greenhouse-style building; large wraparound outdoor terrace. Overlooks East River; view of Brooklyn Bridge. Cr cds: A, D, JCB, MC, V.

D

✔★ ★ **HARMONY PALACE.** *94-98 Mott St, between Canal & Hester Sts, in Chinatown.* *212/226-6603.* Hrs: 8 am-10:30 pm. Res required. Chinese menu. Bar. A la carte entrees: dim sum $1.95-$6.50, lunch & dinner from $8.50. Specializes in Cantonese banquet dishes. Original Oriental art and objets d'art. Cr cds: A, MC, V.

★ ★ ★ **HARRY CIPRIANI.** *781 Fifth Ave, at 59th St, Midtown.* *212/753-5566.* Hrs: 7-10:30 am, noon-3 pm, 6-10:45 pm. Res accepted. Northern Italian menu. Bar. Wine cellar. A la carte entrees: bkfst $15-$25, lunch $19.95-$39.45, dinner $19.95-$44.95. Complete meals: lunch $19.95. Sun buffet $27.95. Specialties: risotto alla primavera, calves liver veneziana, baked green noodles with ham. Understated decor; display of photos, posters and lithographs, reminiscent of Hemingway in Harry's Bar in Venice. Family-owned since 1931. Jacket. Cr cds: A, C, D, DS, MC, V.

★ ★ ★ **HUDSON RIVER CLUB.** *In Building 4 of World Financial Center, lobby level, 250 Vesey St, Financial District.* *212/786-1500.* Hrs: 11:30 am-midnight; Sat from 5 pm; Sun to 3:30 pm; pre-theater dinner Mon-Fri 5-6:30 pm. Closed Dec 25. Res required. Bar. Wine cellar. A la carte entrees: lunch $19-$26, dinner $23-$32. Complete meals: pre-theater dinner $24.95. Menu dégustation: 6-course dinner $60. Sun brunch $23. Child's meals. Specialties: roasted oysters with leeks, salmon in woven potatoes, Hudson River Valley dishes, seasonal dishes. Own pastries. Enterainment. Parking. Dining rm, hung with paintings of Hudson River School, overlooks NY Harbor, Statue of Liberty. Jacket. Cr cds: A, C, D, DS, MC, V.

D

✔★ **HUNAN GARDEN.** *1 Mott St, at Bowery St, in Chinatown.* *212/732-7270.* Hrs: 11 am-11 pm; Fri & Sat to midnight. Chinese menu. Bar. A la carte entrees: lunch, dinner $6-$15. Specialties: Peking duck, Kwi Yong spiced eggplant, Hong Kong stuffed scallops. Enclosed sidewalk cafe. Cr cds: A, MC, V.

★ ★ **IL CANTINORI.** 32 E 10th St, between Broadway & University Place, in Greenwich Village. 212/673-6044. Hrs: noon-2:30 pm, 6-11:15 pm; Fri to midnight; Sat 6 pm-midnight; Sun 6-11:15 pm. Closed most major hols; also last 2 wks Aug. Res accepted. Bar, Tuscan, Northern Italian menu. A la carte entrees: lunch, dinner $17.50-$29.50. Specializes in seasonal game, fresh pasta. Outdoor dining. Wkly seasonal menu. Rustic Tuscan decor. Cr cds: A, C, D, MC, V.

✔ ★ ★ **IL CORTILE.** 125 Mulberry St, between Canal & Hester Sts, in Little Italy. 212/226-6060. Hrs: noon-midnight; Fri & Sat to 1 am. Closed Thanksgiving, Dec 24-25. Res accepted. Italian menu. Bar. A la carte entrees: lunch, dinner $15-$18. Specialties: capellini piselli e prosciutto, rack of veal sautéed in wine sauce, shrimp and seppioline grilled with garlic. Own pasta. Dining in skylighted garden rm. Cr cds: A, C, D, MC, V.

★ ★ ★ **IL MONELLO.** 1460 Second Ave, between 76th & 77th Sts, Upper East Side. 212/535-9310. Hrs: noon-11 pm; Fri & Sat to midnight. Closed major hols. Res accepted. Northern Italian menu. Bar. Wine cellar. A la carte entrees: lunch $16-$26, dinner $20-$29. Specialties: combination pasta, stuffed veal chop, salmon. Own breads. Print collection by renowned 20th-century artists. Cr cds: A, C, D, MC, V.

D

★ ★ ★ **IL NIDO.** 251 E 53rd St, between Second & Third Aves, on the East Side. 212/753-8450. Hrs: noon-3 pm, 5:30-11 pm. Closed Sun; major hols. Res required. Northern Italian menu. Bar. Wine cellar. A la carte entrees: lunch $19.95-$30, dinner $20-$35. Specializes in seasonal dishes. Own pastries. Jacket. Cr cds: A, C, D, MC, V.

★ ★ ★ **IRIDIUM.** 44 W 63rd St (10023), between Broadway & Columbus Ave, Upper West Side. 212/582-2121. Hrs: 11:30-1 am; Sun to 11 pm. Res accepted. Bar. A la carte entrees: lunch $11.50-$26, dinner $16-$28. Specializes in roasted rack of lamb, seared salmon, pasta. Jazz club on lower level. Outdoor dining. Eccentric & colorful decor based on question: what would music look like if it could be seen? Unique architectual design emphasizes curves. Cr cds: A, C, D, DS, MC, V.

✔ ★ ★ **JIM McMULLEN.** 1341 Third Ave, between 76th & 77th Sts, Upper East Side. 212/861-4700. Hrs: 11:30 am-midnight. Bar. A la carte entrees: lunch $7.50-$14.95, dinner $11.95-$19.95. Specializes in fresh fish, chicken pot pie, steaks. Pub-like atmosphere. Jacket (dinner). Cr cds: A, D, MC, V.

D

★ ★ **JOJO.** 160 E 64th St, between Lexington & 3rd Aves, Upper East Side. 212/223-5656. Hrs: noon-2:30 pm, 6-11 pm; Sat 5:30-11:30 pm. Closed Sun; Jan 1, July 4, Dec 25. Res required. French menu. Serv bar. A la carte entrees: lunch $7-$20, dinner $7-$24. Complete meals: lunch $25. Specialties: codfish sautéed, roasted squab, morel and asparagus, chicken roasted in ginger, olive and coriander. 2 story townhouse; casual French bistro atmosphere. 1 dining area on main floor, 2 dining rms on 2nd floor. Jacket. Cr cds: A, MC, V.

★ ★ **JUDSON GRILL.** 152 W 52nd St (10019), between 6th & 7th Aves, Midtown. 212/582-5252. Hrs: noon-2:30 pm, 5:30-11 pm; Fri to 11:30 pm; Sat 5:30-11:30 pm. Closed Sun. Closed major hols. Res accepted. Bar. A la carte entrees: lunch $15-$25, dinner $19-$25. Specialties: seared tuna loin, grilled shell steak, grilled lamb chops. Vaulted ceiling; all glass 2-story front. Circular mahogany bar. Cr cds: A, D, MC, V.

D

★ ★ **KEENS CHOPHOUSE.** 72 W 36th St, between Fifth & Sixth Aves, Midtown. 212/947-3636. Hrs: 11:45 am-3 pm, 5:30-10 pm; Sat from 5 pm. Closed Sun; some major hols; also Sat & Sun in summer. Res accepted. Bar. A la carte entrees: lunch $7.95-$18, dinner $15-$30. Specializes in aged Porterhouse steak for 2 or 3, mutton chops. Historic restaurant, established 1885; dark oak paneling,

leaded-glass windows, famous clay pipe collection on ceiling. Famous patrons have included Teddy Roosevelt, Albert Einstein and Lillie Langtry, who sued to enter the once all-male premises. Cr cds: A, C, D, MC, V.

✔ ★ **KRISTIE'S.** 344 Lexington Ave, between 39th & 40th Sts, Midtown. 212/953-1920. Hrs: 11 am-9 pm. Closed some major hols. Res accepted. Polish, Amer menu. Wine, beer. A la carte entrees: lunch $5-$6. Complete meals: dinner $10-$12. Specializes in potato pancakes, pierogies, homemade soups. Cr cds: A, MC, V.

✔ ★ **LA BONNE SOUPE.** 48 W 55th St, Midtown. 212/586-7650. Hrs: 11:30 am-midnight; Sun to 11 pm. Closed Jan 1, Thanksgiving, Dec 25. French menu. Bar. A la carte entrees: lunch, dinner $7.50-$15.95. Sun brunch $11.75. Seasonal specialties. Guitarist Sat & Sun brunch. Limited outdoor balcony dining. Open kitchen. French bistro decor. Cr cds: A, MC, V.

★ ★ ★ ★ ★ **LA CÔTE BASQUE.** 5 E 55th St, between Fifth & Madison Aves, Midtown. 212/688-6525. Hrs: noon-2:30 pm, 6-10:30 pm; Sat to 11 pm. Closed Sun; major hols. Res required. French menu. Bar. Prix fixe: lunch $31, dinner $58. Own pastries. Elegant, luxurious atmosphere; Basque murals. Chef-owned. Jacket, tie. Cr cds: A, C, D, JCB, MC, V.

D

★ ★ ★ ★ **LA CARAVELLE.** 33 W 55th St, betw. 5th & 6th Aves. Midtown. 212/586-4252. Hrs: noon-2:30 pm, 5:30-10:30 pm. Closed Sun; major hols; also 1 wk prior to Labor Day. Res required. Classic French menu. Bar. Wine cellar. A la carte entrees avail: lunch from $25, dinner from $40. Prix fixe: 3-course lunch $35, 3-course dinner $59, 7-course tasting menu $75. Pre-theater menu 5:30-6:30 pm, $38. Child's meals. Specialties: pâte fine aux crevettes et coquilles Saint-Jacques, saumon fuméen famille au basilic, canard rôti with cranberry sauce. Own baking. Traditional French decor; outstanding murals. Cr cds: A, C, D, JCB, MC, V.

D

★ ★ ★ **LA COLOMBE D'OR.** 134 E 26th St, off Lexington Ave, in Murray Hill. 212/689-0666. Hrs: noon-2:30 pm, 6-10:30 pm; Sat 6-11 pm; Sun 5:30-9:30 pm. Closed major hols. Res accepted. French Provençale menu. Wine list. A la carte entrees: lunch, dinner $14.50-$27.50. Specialties: crisp duck legs with Turkish figs & honey, bouillabaisse, veal chops stuffed with fontina cheese. Own baking. Seasonal menu. Country French atmosphere. Cr cds: A, C, D, MC, V.

★ ★ ★ ★ **LA GRENOUILLE.** 3 East 52nd St (10022), between Fifth & Madison Aves, Midtown. 212/752-1495. Hrs: noon-2:30 pm, 6-11:15 pm; Sat (June & July) from 6 pm. Closed Sun & Mon; some major hols. Res required. Classic French menu. Bar. Wine cellar. Prix fixe: lunch $39.50, dinner $70. Specialties: le magret de canard, la poularde au Champagne, la sole grill&,ee. Elegant, romantic dining rm with extensive floral arrangements. Family-owned. Jacket. Cr cds: A, C, D, MC, V.

D

✔ ★ **LA KASBAH.** 70 W 71st St, between Central Park West & Columbus Ave, Upper West Side. 212/769-1690. Hrs: 5-11 pm; Sat & Sun from 2 pm. Closed Fri; also Sat in summer. Res accepted. Kosher Moroccan menu. Wine, beer. A la carte entrees: dinner $13.50-$20. Sun lunch $10.50-$15. Specialties: tajin of lamb, osso buco, cous-cous with vegetables. Own pita bread. Patio dining. Near Lincoln Center. Cr cds: A, D, DS, MC, V.

D

✔ ★ **LA MAISON JAPONAISE.** 125 E 39th St, at Lexington Ave, Midtown. 212/682-7375. Hrs: 11:45 am-2:30 pm, 5:30-10:30 pm; Sat from 5:30 pm. Closed Sun; major hols. Res accepted. French, Japanese menu. Bar. Semi-a la carte: lunch $10.95-$16.75, dinner $10.95-$16.95. Complete meals: lunch $14.95, dinner $15.95. Specialties: chicken flambé, shrimp & scallops tempura. Cr cds: A, C, D, MC, V.

✔ ★ **LA MANGEOIRE.** 1008 Second Ave, between 53rd and 54th Sts, on the East Side. 212/759-7086. Hrs: noon-2:30 pm, 5:30-

10:30 pm; Fri to 11 pm; Sat 5:30-11 pm; Closed Sun; major hols. Res accepted. French menu. Serv bar. A la carte entrees: lunch $10.50-$18.50, dinner $15.50-$23. Prix fixe: lunch $15, dinner $17. Daily and seasonal specialties. Country French inn atmosphere. Cr cds: A, C, D, MC, V.

D

★ ★ ★ **LA METAIRIE.** *189 W 10th St, west of 7th Ave S in Greenwich Village.* 212/989-0343. Hrs: noon-3 pm, 5 pm-1 am. Res required. French menu. A la carte entrees: lunch, dinner $11-$19. Specialties: filet mignon, rack of lamb. French country atmosphere. No cr cds accepted.

D

★ ★ ★ **LA RESERVE.** *4 W 49th St, between Fifth & Sixth Aves, Midtown.* 212/247-2993. Hrs: noon-3 pm, 5:30-10:30 pm; Fri & Sat to 11 pm. Closed Sun; major hols; also 1st wk July. Res required. French haute cuisine. Bar. Prix fixe: lunch $31, pre-theater dinner $40, dinner $49. Specialties: Dover sole with mousse of artichoke, cassolette of snails, medallions of veal. Own pastries. Wood paneled dining rm with wildlife murals, Venetian glass sconces, chandeliers. Jacket. Cr cds: A, C, D, JCB, MC, V.

D

★ **LANDMARK TAVERN.** *626 11th Ave (10036), off 46th St, on the West Side.* 212/757-8595. Hrs: noon-midnight; Sun brunch to 4 pm. Closed Dec 25. Res accepted. Irish, Amer menu. Bar. A la carte entrees: lunch $7.50-$23, dinner $8-$23. Sun brunch $10-$15. Specializes in corned beef and cabbage, prime rib, shepherds pie. Outdoor dining. 3 story tavern built 1868. Family-owned. Cr cds: A, C, D, DS, MC, V.

D

★ ★ ★ **LE BERNARDIN.** *In Equitable Life Tower, 155 W 51st St, between Sixth & Seventh Aves, Times Square/Theater District.* 212/489-1515. Hrs: noon-2:15 pm, 6-10:30 pm; Fri & Sat 5:30-11 pm. Closed Sun; major hols. Res accepted. French, seafood menu. Bar. Prix fixe: lunch $42, dinner $68. Specialty: monkfish with cabbage. Own pastries. Classic French decor. Jacket, tie. Cr cds: A, C, D, JCB, MC, V.

D

★ ★ **LE BOEUF À LA MODE.** *539 E 81st St, near East End Ave, in Yorkville section of Upper East Side.* 212/249-1473. Hrs: 5:30-11 pm. Closed major hols; also Sun in July & Aug. Res accepted. French menu. Bar. A la carte entrees: dinner $18-$26. Prix fixe: dinner $29. Specialties: duck á l'orange, rack of lamb, fish specials. Cr cds: A, D, MC, V.

D

★ ★ ★ **LE CHANTILLY.** *106 E 57th St, between Lexington and Park Aves, Midtown.* 212/751-2931. Hrs: noon-3 pm, 5:30-10:30 pm; Sun 4:30-10 pm. Closed major hols. Res required. French menu. Bar. Wine list. A la carte entrees: lunch $18-$24. Prixe fixe: dinner $49. Pre-theater dinner (5:30-6:30 pm) $29. Specialties: ravioli of crab, oven-roasted salmon, pan-seared lamb chop, roasted saddle of rabbit. Daily specials. Own baking. Murals of château of Chantilly. Cr cds: A, C, D, DS, JCB, MC, V.

D

★ ★ ★ **LE CIRQUE.** *58 E 65th St, between Madison & Park Aves, Upper East Side.* 212/794-9292. Hrs: 11:45 am-2:45 pm, 5:45-10:30 pm. Closed Sun; major hols. Res required. French menu. Bar. Wine list. A la carte entrees: lunch $22-$26, dinner $22-$32. Prix fixe: lunch $29.95. Specialties: sea bass wrapped in crisp potatoes with red wine, braised veal shank, modern and classic French cuisine. Elegant atmosphere. Jacket, tie. Cr cds: A, C, D, MC, V.

D

★ ★ **LE COLONIAL.** *149 E 57th St (10022), between Third & Lexington Aves, on the East Side.* 212/752-0808. Hrs: noon-2:30 pm, 5:30-11 pm; Fri to midnight; Sat 5:30 pm-midnight; Sun from 5:30 pm.

Closed Jan 1, Thanksgiving, Dec 25. Res accepted. Vietnamese menu. Bar. A la carte entrees: lunch $10.50-$19.50, dinner $12.50-$19.50. Specialties: whole red snapper with spicy sour sauce, roast duck with tamarind sauce, saut&,eed jumbo shrimp with curried coconut sauce. Multi-level dining. Bamboo furniture, bird cages. Cr cds: A, D, MC, V.

D

★ ★ **LE MADRI.** *168 W 18th St, at 7th Ave, in Chelsea.* 212/727-8022. Hrs: noon-3 pm, 5:30-11:30 pm; Sun 5-10:30 pm. Closed some major hols. Res accepted. Italian menu. Bar. A la carte entrees: lunch $11-$17, dinner $19-$28.50. Specializes in regional Italian cuisine, seasonal dishes. Valet parking. Outdoor dining. Vaulted ceiling supported by columns; colorfully tiled wood-burning pizza oven. Jacket. Cr cds: A, C, D, MC, V.

✔ ★ ★ ★ **LE PACTOLE.** *225 Liberty St (10281), in World Financial Center Bldg 2, Financial District.* 212/945-9444. Hrs: 7-10 am, noon-3 pm, 5:30-10 pm. Sun brunch 11:30 am-5 pm. Closed Sat; some major hols. Res required. French menu. Bar noon-1 am. Wine cellar. A la carte entrees: bkfst $7.50-$14.50, lunch $9-$17, dinner $18-$28. Sun brunch $26.50. Specialties: smoked filet of venison, grilled boneless quail, roasted filet of monkfish. Outstanding views of Hudson River and surroundings. Jacket. Cr cds: A, C, D, MC, V.

D

★ ★ ★ ★ **LE PERIGORD.** *405 E 52nd St, between First Ave & Sutton Place, Midtown.* 212/755-6244. Hrs: noon-3 pm, 5:15-10:30 pm; Sat 5:15-11 pm. Closed Sun; major hols. Res accepted. Modern French cuisine. Bar. Wine cellar. Prix fixe: lunch $32, dinner $52. Specialties: confit of duck, grilled Dover sole, boneless quails stuffed with vegetables, roast rack of lamb. Own desserts. Quiet elegance; relaxed atmosphere. Family-owned. Cr cds: A, C, D, DS, MC, V.

★ ★ **LE PISTOU.** *134 E 61st St (10021), between Lexington and Park Aves, Upper East Side.* 212/838-7987. Hrs: noon-2:30 pm, 5:30-10:30 pm. Closed Sun; some major hols; also 3 wks Aug. Res accepted. French Proven&ccale menu. A la carte entrees: lunch $15-$18, dinner $18-$25. Prix fixe: lunch $19.95, dinner $32. Specialties: grilled Dover sole with mustard sauce, rack of lamb au jus, steak au poivre. Oil paintings of French countryside. Cr cds: A, C, D, DS, MC, V.

★ ★ ★ **LE RÉGENCE.** *(See Plaza Athénée Hotel)* 212/606-4647. Hrs: 7-10 am, noon-2:30 pm, 6-9:30 pm; Sun brunch noon-2:30 pm. Res accepted. French menu. Bar 11 am-midnight. Wine cellar. A la carte entrees: bkfst $9-$16.50, lunch $21-$28, dinner $25.50-$30.50. Prix fixe: bkfst $19, lunch $25.50, dinner $49. Sun brunch $33.50. Child's meals. Specializes in seafood, steak, filet of lamb. Own pastries. Valet parking. Elegant decor. Cr cds: A, C, D, ER, JCB, MC, V.

D

★ ★ ★ **LE REFUGE.** *166 E 82nd St, between Lexington & Third Aves, Upper East Side.* 212/861-4505. Hrs: noon-3 pm, 5-11 pm; Sun noon-4 pm, 5-9:30 pm; Sat brunch to 3 pm; Sun brunch to 4 pm. Closed major hols. Res accepted. French menu. Beer. Wine cellar. A la carte entrees: lunch $10.50-$15.50, dinner $17.50-$24.50. Sat & Sun brunch $17.50. Specialties: roast duck with fresh fruit sauce, poached salmon garnished with caviar in Bordeaux sauce, rosemary roast rack of lamb. Own baking. Garden terrace dining (summer). French country inn decor. Cr cds: A.

★ ★ **LE VEAU D'OR.** *129 E 60th St, between Lexington & Park Aves, Upper East Side.* 212/838-8133. Hrs: noon-3 pm, 5:30-10:15 pm. Closed Sun; major hols. Res accepted. French Provençale menu. Bar. Complete meals: lunch $16-$22, dinner $24-$30. Specialties: navarin d'agneau, rognon de veau, cassoulet à la Toulousaine. Own desserts. Cr cds: A, D, MC, V.

★ ★ ★ **LES CÉLÉBRITÉS.** *(See Essex House Hotel Nikko)* 212/484-5113. Hrs: 6-10 pm; Sat to 10:30 pm. Closed Sun & Mon; also Aug. Res required. French menu. Bar. Wine cellar. A la carte entrees: dinner $29-$39. Dégustation menu: 6-course dinner $95. Specialties: burger of fresh duck foie gras, squab with artichokes, honey & orange lacquered duck. Valet parking. Intimate dining area; paintings by celebrities. Jacket. Cr cds: A, C, D, DS, ER, JCB, MC, V.

D

★ ★ ★ **LESPINASSE.** (See The St Regis Hotel) 212/339-6719. Hrs: 7-10:30 am, noon-2 pm, 6-10 pm; Sun to 10:30 am. Res accepted. French menu. Bar 11-2 am. Extensive wine list. A la carte entrees: bkfst $5.50-$11.50, dinner $24-$32. Complete meals: bkfst $16.50-$20.50, lunch $39, dinner $52-$66. Specialties: steamed black bass in kaffir leaf reduction, glazed veal steak and savoy cabbage with salsifys, traditional French cuisine with Far East influences. Valet parking. Louis XV style decor; quiet, elegant setting. Jacket. Cr cds: A, C, D, DS, ER, JCB, MC, V.

D

★ **LIBERTY CAFE.** 89 South St, at Pier 17, South Street Seaport, downtown. 212/406-1111. Hrs: 11:30-2 am; Sun to 1 am. Closed Dec 25. Bar to 3 am. A la carte entrees: lunch $8-$15, dinner $12-$22. Child's meals. Specializes in lobster, grilled swordfish, 21-day aged NY sirloin. Outdoor dining. Overlooks harbor and waterfront; view of downtown skyline and Statue of Liberty. Cr cds: A, C, D, DS, MC, V.

★ ★ **LUSARDI'S.** 1494 Second Ave, between 77th & 78th Sts, Upper East Side. 212/249-2020. Hrs: noon-3 pm, 5 pm-midnight. Closed most major hols. Res accepted. Northern Italian menu. Bar. A la carte entrees: lunch, dinner $13-$22. Specialties: risotto with truffles or with wild mushrooms. Italian-style trattoria. Seasonal menu. Cr cds: A, C, D, DS, MC, V.

D

★ ★ ★ ★ **LUTÈCE.** 249 E 50th St, between 2nd & 3rd Aves, Midtown. 212/752-2225. Hrs: noon-2 pm, 5:30-10 pm; Sat & Mon from 5:30 pm. Closed Sun; also Aug-Labor Day; also Sat June & July. Res required. French haute cuisine. Bar. Wine cellar. Table d'hôte: lunch $38. Prix fixe: dinner $60. Specialties: medallions of veal with morels, baby bass, pheasant. All-weather garden. Elegant, memorable dining. Chef-owned. Cr cds: A, C, D, JCB, MC, V.

D

✔ ★ **MAN RAY.** 169 Eighth Ave, between 18th & 19th Sts, in Chelsea. 212/627-4220. Hrs: noon-3 pm, 6-11 pm; Fri & Sat to midnight; Sun from 5 pm; summer 5:30-11 pm; Sun brunch 11 am-3:30 pm. Res accepted. Bar. A la carte entrees: lunch $5.50-$8.95, dinner $8-$14.95. Prix fixe: lunch $6.95. Sun brunch $4.95-$7.95. Specialties: roasted free-range chicken, grilled hanger steak, baked salmon. Own desserts. Cr cds: A, MC, V.

✔ ★ **MANHATTAN BISTRO.** 129 Spring St, between Wooster & Greene, in SoHo. 212/966-3459. Hrs: 9 am-midnight; Sat & Sun brunch 11:30 am-4:30 pm. Closed Memorial Day, Dec 25. Res accepted. French menu. Bar from 11:30 am. A la carte entrees: bkfst $3.75-$5.50, lunch, dinner $8.50-$19. Sun brunch $5.50. Specializes in pasta with pesto, steak frites. Intimate storefront bistro in area of studios & art galleries. Family-owned. Cr cds: A, MC, V.

★ ★ **MANHATTAN CAFE.** 1161 First Ave, between 63rd & 64th Sts, Upper East Side. 212/888-6556. Hrs: noon-11 pm; Sun brunch 11:30 am-4 pm. Closed Thanksgiving & Dec 25. Res accepted. Bar from 4 pm. Prix fixe: lunch $17.95-$26.95. A la carte entrees: lunch $8.50-$19, dinner $18-$29.75. Sun brunch $17.95. Specializes in steak, lobster. Club-like atmosphere; paneling, Oriental rugs, 1920s period lighting. Cr cds: A, C, D, DS, JCB, MC, V.

D

★ ★ **MANHATTAN OCEAN CLUB.** 57 W 58th St, off Sixth Ave, Midtown. 212/371-7777. Hrs: noon-11:30 pm; Sat & Sun from 5 pm. Closed Jan 1, Thanksgiving, Dec 25. Res required. All seafood menu. Bar. Wine list. A la carte entrees: lunch, dinner $19.50-$29.50. Specialties: swordfish au poivre, lobster salad with cous-cous. Own

pastries. Atmosphere of luxury ocean liner; broad sweeping staircase connects 2 floors. Cr cds: A, C, D, DS, JCB, MC, V.

★ ★ **MARCH.** 405 E 58th St (10022), between First Ave and Sutton Place, Upper East Side. 212/838-9393. Hrs: 6-10 pm; Fri & Sat to 10:30 pm. Closed Sun; Jan 1, Thanksgiving, Dec 25. Res required. Contemporary Amer menu. Bar. Complete meals: dinner $40-$55. Tasting menu $70. Specialties: five-spice salmon, grilled L.I. duck, roast rack of lamb with herbed crust. Outdoor dining. Three dining rms in romantic townhouse filled with antiques. Jacket. Cr cds: A, C, D, MC, V.

★ ★ **THE MARKHAM.** 59 Fifth Ave (10003), at 13th St, upper level, in Greenwich Village. 212/647-9391. Hrs: noon-1 am; Sun brunch 10:30 am-4 pm. Closed major hols. Res accepted. Bar. A la carte entrees: lunch $8.50-$15.50, dinner $9.50-$25. Sun brunch $7.50-$21.50. Specializes in seasonal fish, roast chicken, steak. Tin ceiling; massive antique bar. Cafe on lower level open for bkfst. Cr cds: A, D, MC, V.

★ ★ **MARYLOU'S.** 21 W 9th St, between Fifth & Sixth Aves, in Greenwich Village. 212/533-0012. Hrs: 5:30 pm-midnight; Fri & Sat to 1 am; Sun 5:30-10 pm; Sun brunch noon-4 pm. Closed some major hols. Res accepted. Continental menu. Bar. A la carte entrees: dinner $13.95-$23.95. Sun brunch $13.95. Specialties: seafood platter, mesquite-grilled fish, pan-roasted chicken. In 19th-century town house; fireplace, library, changing art exhibits. Cr cds: A, C, D, DS, MC, V.

★ ★ **MATTHEW'S.** 1030 Third Ave (10021), at 61st St, on the East Side. 212/838-4343. Hrs: noon-11 pm; Fri & Sat to midnight. Closed Dec 25. Res accepted. Bar. Semi-a la carte: lunch $12-$18.50, dinner $18-$24.50. Specialties: poached salmon, Maine crab cakes, grilled rack of lamb. Outdoor dining. Mediterranean atmosphere; white tented ceilings. Cr cds: A, C, D, DS, MC, V.

D

★ ★ **MESA GRILL.** 102 Fifth Ave, between 15th & 16th Sts, in Gramercy Park area. 212/807-7400. Hrs: noon-2:15 pm, 5:30-10:30 pm; Fri to 11 pm; Sat 5:30-11 pm; Sun 5:30-10:30 pm; Sat & Sun brunch 11:30 am-3 pm. Closed some major hols. Res accepted. Contemporary Southwestern menu. Bar. A la carte entrees: lunch $12-$16, dinner $16-$24. Specialties: shrimp and roasted garlic corn tamale, blue corn striped bass, pan-roasted venison. Cr cds: A, D, DS, MC, V.

D

★ ★ **METROPOLIS CAFE.** 31 Union Square West (10003), at E 16th St, in Gramercy Park area. 212/675-2300. Hrs: 11:30-12:30 am; Fri & Sat to 1 am; Sun brunch to 4 pm. Closed Thanksgiving, Dec 25. Res accepted. Bar. A la carte entrees: lunch $8-$17.50, dinner $14.50-$23.50. Sun brunch $19.95. Specialties: roasted Long Island Duck, grilled Kansas sirloin steak, caramelized Atlantic salmon. Jazz; flamenco on Sun. Outdoor dining. Multi-level dining in 1902 bank building; wine cellar in vault. Cr cds: A, C, D, DS, MC, V.

★ **MEZZALUNA.** 1295 Third Ave (10021), between 74th & 75th Sts, Upper East Side. 212/535-9600. Hrs: 11 am-3 pm, 6 pm-1 am. Closed Dec 25. Italian menu. Wine, beer. Semi-a la carte: lunch $15-$20, dinner $25-$30. Specializes in pizza baked in wood-burning oven, lasagne, penne alla bisanzio. Outdoor dining. Trattoria atmosphere. Antique marble top tables & bar. No cr cds accepted.

D

✔ ★ ★ **MEZZOGIORNO.** 195 Spring St, near Sullivan St, in SoHo. 212/334-2112. Hrs: noon-3 pm, 6 pm-1 am; Sat & Sun noon-1 am. Closed Dec 25. Res accepted. Northern Italian menu. Bar. A la carte entrees: lunch, dinner $12-$14. Specializes in brick-oven-baked pizza. Outdoor dining. No cr cds accepted.

✔ ★ ★ **MI COCINA.** 57 Jane St, at Hudson St, in Greenwich Village. 212/627-8273. Hrs: 5-10:45 pm; Thurs & Fri from noon; Fri & Sat to 11:45 pm; Sun brunch 11:30 am-3:30 pm. Closed most major hols & Dec 24; also 2 wks Aug. Res accepted. Mexican menu. Bar. A la carte entrees: lunch $7.95-$12.95, dinner $8.95-$17.95. Sun brunch $7.95-$12.95. Child's meals. Specialties: pechuga con rajas, camarones enchipotlados, enchiladas de mole poblano. Modern Mexican atmosphere; colorful decor with pink, green and yellow stucco walls, red tile floors. Posters of food and clusters of bright plastic peppers adorn the walls. Cr cds: A, C, D, JCB, MC, V.

★ ★ ★ **MICHAEL'S.** *24 W 55th St, between Fifth & Sixth Aves, Midtown.* 212/767-0555. Hrs: 7:30-9:30 am, noon-3 pm, 5:30-11 pm; Sat 5:30-11 pm. Closed Sun; some major hols. Res accepted. Bar. Wine cellar. A la carte entrees: bkfst $5-$15, lunch, dinner $16-$24.50. Serv charge 15%. Child's meals. Specialties: chicken with goat cheese, Atlantic swordfish, fettucine with salmon. Own baking. Original artwork throughout. Cr cds: A, D, MC, V.

🖝★ **MICKEY MANTLE'S RESTAURANT & SPORTS BAR.** *42 Central Park South, between 5th & 6th Aves, Midtown.* 212/688-7777. Hrs: noon-midnight; Sun to 11 pm. Res accepted. Bar to 1 am. A la carte entrees: lunch, dinner $10-$20. Child's meals. Specialties: chicken-fried steak, seafood, baby back ribs. Outdoor dining. Rotating collection of baseball memorabilia; original sports art. Cr cds: A, C, D, DS, JCB, MC, V.

D

★ ★ ★ **MITSUKOSHI.** *461 Park Ave, at E 57th St, Midtown.* 212/935-6444. Hrs: noon-2 pm, 5:30-10 pm. Closed Sat & Sun; major hols. Res accepted. Japanese menu. Bar. Semi-a la carte: lunch $20-$30, dinner $30-$50. Complete meal: dinner from $65. Specialties: shabu shabu, sushi & sashimi, sukiyaki. Quiet classical Japanese dining rm in office building, below street level. Jacket. Cr cds: A, C, D, JCB, MC, V.

D

🖝★ **MOCCA HUNGARIAN.** *1588 Second Ave, at 82nd St, Upper East Side.* 212/734-6470. Hrs: 11:30 am-11 pm. Closed Yom Kippur. Hungarian menu. Bar. Complete meals: lunch $5.95. Prix fixe: dinner $12.95. Specializes in goulash, duck, veal. No cr cds accepted.

D

★ ★ ★ **MONTRACHET.** *239 W Broadway, between Walker & White Sts, in Tribeca.* 212/219-2777. Hrs: 6-11 pm; Fri also noon-2:30 pm. Closed Sun; major hols. Res required. French menu. Bar. Wine list. A la carte entrees: lunch $15-$22, dinner $21-$29. Prix fixe: dinner $28, $36. Specializes in soufflé, lobster, vegetable terrine. Own pastries. Cr cds: A.

D

★ ★ **MORENO.** *65 Irving Place, at E 18th St, in Gramercy Park area.* 212/673-3939. Hrs: noon-3 pm, 5:30 pm-midnight; Sat from 5:30 pm; Sun noon-10:30 pm. Closed Thanksgiving. Res accepted. Contemporary Italian menu. Bar. A la carte entrees: lunch $12.50-$20.95, dinner $13.95-$24.95. Prix fixe: Sun $19.95. Child's meals. Specializes in seafood, pasta. Outdoor dining. Seasonal menu. Cr cds: A, D, MC, V.

D

★ ★ **MORTON'S OF CHICAGO.** *551 Fifth Ave (10017), at 45th St, Midtown.* 212/972-3315. Hrs: 11:30 am-2:30 pm, 5 pm-midnight; Sat from 5 pm; Sun 5-11 pm. Closed most major hols. Res accepted. Bar. A la carte entrees: lunch, dinner $17.95-$29.95. Specializes in steak, lobster. Counterpart of famous Chicago steak house. Cr cds: A, D, MC, V.

★ ★ **NANNI IL VALLETTO.** *133 E 61st St, Upper East Side.* 212/838-3939. Hrs: noon-3 pm, 5:30 pm-midnight; Sat from 5:30 pm. Closed Sun; major hols. Res accepted. Italian menu. Serv bar. A la carte entrees: lunch, dinner $16-$30. Specialties: capellini d'angelo primavera, chicken scarpariello. Own pasta. Cr cds: A, C, D, MC, V.

★ ★ ★ **OCEANA.** *55 E 54th St, between Park & Madison Aves, Midtown.* 212/759-5941. Hrs: noon-2:30 pm, 5:30-10:30 pm; Sat from 5:30 pm. Closed Sun; most major hols; also last wk Aug. Res accepted. Serv bar. Wine cellar. Complete meals: lunch $28-$34, dinner $38-$44. Specialties: seared Maine sea scallops, crisp Florida red snapper, grilled yellowfin tuna with foie gras. Located in 2-story townhouse; spacious, bi-level dining rm. Elegant decor; pastel-colored impressionist murals. Jacket. Cr cds: A, C, D, DS, JCB, MC, V.

★ ★ **THE ODEON.** *145 W Broadway, between Thomas & Duane Sts, in Tribeca.* 212/233-0507. Hrs: noon-2 am; Fri & Sat to 3 am; Sun brunch 11:30 am-4 pm. Closed Dec 25. Res accepted. French, Amer menu. Bar to 4 am. Complete meals: lunch $14.50. A la carte entrees: lunch, dinner $7.50-$23. Sun brunch $7.50-$18.50. Specializes in seafood, grilled dishes. Brasserie in 1930s, cafeteria-style art deco. Cr cds: A, D, MC, V.

★ ★ ★ **ONE IF BY LAND, TWO IF BY SEA.** *17 Barrow St, between Seventh Ave S & West Fourth, in Greenwich Village.* 212/228-0822. Hrs: 5:30 pm-midnight; Fri & Sat to 1 am. Closed Jan 1, July 4, Dec 24. Res required. Continental menu. Bar 4 pm-2 am. Wine cellar. A la carte entrees: dinner $26-$34. Specialties: beef Wellington, seafood. Own pastries. Pianist; vocalist from 6 pm. In restored 18th-century carriage house once owned by Aaron Burr; dining rm overlooks courtyard garden. Jacket. Cr cds: A, D, MC, V.

★ ★ **ORSO.** *322 W 46th St, between Eighth and Ninth Aves, on the West Side.* 212/489-7212. Hrs: noon-11:45 pm; Wed & Sat from 11:30 am. Res required (1 wk in advance). Regional Italian menu. Bar. A la carte entrees: lunch, dinner $13-$20. Own gelato. Italian-style trattoria with skylighted, vaulted ceiling; celebrity photo collection. Cr cds: MC, V.

★ ★ **OSTERIA AL DOGE.** *142 W 44th St (10036), between 6th Ave & Broadway, Times Square/Theater District.* 212/944-3643. Hrs: noon-3 pm, 5-11:30 pm; Fri to midnight; Sat 5 pm-midnight. Closed Sun; Jan 1, Dec 25. Res accepted. Italian menu. Bar. Semi-a la carte: lunch $10.50-$18.50, dinner $11.50-$19.50. Child's meals. Specializes in Venetian dishes, seafood, pizza. Cr cds: A, D, DS, MC, V.

D

🖝★ **OTTOMANELLI'S.** *1370 York Ave, at 73rd St, Upper East Side.* 212/794-9696. Hrs: 11:30 am-10 pm. Closed Thanksgiving, Dec 25. Wine, beer. A la carte entrees: lunch, dinner $4.95-$10.95. Specializes in pasta, pizza, burgers. Family-owned. Cr cds: A.

D

★ ★ **OUR PLACE.** *1444 Third Ave, at 82nd St, Upper East Side.* 212/288-4888. Hrs: noon-11 pm; early-bird dinner Mon-Sat 5-7 pm. Closed Thanksgiving. Res accepted. Chinese menu. Bar. A la carte entrees: lunch $6.25-$8.95, dinner $10.95-$32. Specialties: tangerine beef, Peking duck, scallops Chardonnay. Interior designed by protégé of I.M. Pei. Cr cds: A, D, MC, V.

D

★ **OYSTER BAR.** *At Grand Central Station, Vanderbilt Ave at 42nd St, Midtown.* 212/490-6650. Hrs: 11:30 am-9:30 pm. Closed Sat, Sun; major hols. Res accepted. Bars. A la carte entrees: lunch, dinner $12.95-$25.45. Extensive variety of fish, shellfish; smoke own salmon. In landmark railroad station; beaux-arts interiors, vaulted ceilings, mahogany paneling. Cr cds: A, C, D, JCB, MC, V.

D

🖝★ **P.J. CLARKE'S.** *915 Third Ave, at 55th St, on the East Side.* 212/759-1650. Hrs: noon-4 am. Res accepted. Bar. A la carte entrees: lunch, dinner $5-$17. Specializes in hamburgers, steak, veal. Juke box. Traditional, old New York-style pub (1864). Cr cds: A, C, D, MC, V.

D

★ ★ ★ **PALIO.** *151 W 51st St, at Equitable Center, Times Square/Theater District.* 212/245-4850. Hrs: noon-2:30 pm, 5:30-11 pm; Sat from 5:30 pm. Closed Sun; major hols. Res accepted. Italian menu. Bar 11:30 am-midnight; Sat from 4:30 pm. Wine cellar. A la carte entrees: lunch $25-$32, dinner $26-$39. Prix fixe: lunch $39, 3-course dinner $68. Bar lunch $20. Menu changes daily. Own baking. Large colorful murals by Chia surround bar downstairs. Palio theme. Cr cds: A, C, D, DS, JCB, MC, V.

D

★ ★ **PALM.** 837 Second Ave, near E 45th St, on the East Side. 212/687-2953. Hrs: noon-11:30 pm; Sat from 5 pm. Sun 4-10 pm. Closed major hols. Res required. Bar. A la carte entrees: lunch, dinner $14-$28. Specializes in steak, seafood, veal. Menu recited. Valet parking. Original murals; celebrity caricatures. Popular with writers and artists. Family-owned. Cr cds: A, C, D, MC, V.

★ ★ ★ **PALM COURT.** (See The Plaza Hotel) 212/546-5350. Hrs: 7 am-midnight; Sun to 11 pm; Sun brunch 10 am-2:30 pm. Res required Sun brunch. Bar from noon. Wine cellar. A la carte entrees: bkfst $10-$16.50, lunch, dinner $15-$24. Tea $9-$20. Sun brunch buffet $44.75. Specializes in seasonal dishes, fresh raspberry Napoleon, scones with Devonshire cream, Brazilian cake. Own baking. Pianist, violinist; harpist. Valet parking. Edwardian, columned court off lobby; a New York tradition. Cr cds: A, C, D, DS, ER, JCB, MC, V.

D

★ ★ ★ **PARIOLI ROMANISSIMO.** 24 E 81st St, between Madison & Fifth Aves, Upper East Side. 212/288-2391. Hrs: 6-11 pm; Fri & Sat to 11:30 pm. Closed Sun; major hols; also Aug. Res required. Northern Italian menu. Bar. Wine cellar. A la carte entrees: dinner $28-$39.50. Specialties: fettucine with white truffles, venison, roasted rack of lamb. Own baking. Neo-Renaissance architecture. Jacket, tie. Cr cds: A, D, MC, V.

★ ★ ★ **PARK AVENUE CAFE.** 100 E 63rd St, at Park Ave, Upper East Side. 212/644-1900. Hrs: 11:30 am-2:30 pm, 5:30-10:15 pm; Fri to 11:15 pm; Sat 5:30-11:15 pm; Sun 11:30 am-2:30 pm, 4:30-9 pm. Closed Jan 1, Thanksgiving, Dec 25. Res accepted. Bar. A la carte entrees: lunch $18.50-$26, dinner $24.50-$33.50. Complete meals: dinner $53. Specialties: tuna & salmon tartare with caviar, swordfish chop, Mrs. Ascher's steamed vegetable torte. Authentic American antiques, folk art, mix and match plates. Cr cds: A, D, JCB, MC, V.

★ ★ **PARK BISTRO.** 414 Park Ave S, between 28th & 29th Sts, in Murray Hill. 212/689-1360. Hrs: noon-3 pm, 6-11 pm; Sat & Sun from 6 pm. Closed major hols. Res accepted. French Provençale menu. Bar. A la carte entrees: lunch $18-$20, dinner $18-$22.50. Specialties: warm potato salad with goat cheese and herbs, fresh codfish with mashed potato and fried leeks in onion sauce, boneless lamb saddle with cumin and vegetable cous-cous. Casual dining; Parisian bistro decor and atmosphere. Cr cds: A, D, JCB, MC, V.

★ ★ **PARMA.** 1404 Third Ave, at 80th St, Upper East Side. 212/535-3520. Hrs: 5 pm-midnight. Closed July 4 & Labor Day wkends; also last 2 wks Aug. Res required. Bar. Northern Italian menu. A la carte entrees: dinner $13-$28. Specialties: green lasagne, cannelloni agnellotti, gnocchi. Own pasta. Cr cds: A.

D

★ ★ **PATRIA.** 250 Park Ave S (10003), at 20th St, in Gramercy Park area. 212/777-6211. Hrs: noon-2:45 pm, 6-10:30 pm; Fri to midnight; Sat 6 pm-midnight. Closed Sun; most major hols. Res accepted. Latin American menu. Bar to 1 am. A la carte entrees: lunch $11-$22, dinner $17-$24. Specialties: Ecuadorian ceviche, Nicaraguan skirt steak, sugar cane tuna with malanga puree. Multi-level dining with Latin American art. Cr cds: A, D, MC, V.

★ ★ **PERIYALI.** 35 W 20th St, between Fifth & Sixth Aves, in Chelsea. 212/463-7890. Hrs: noon-3 pm, 5:30-11 pm; Sat from 5:30 pm. Closed Sun. Res required. Nouvelle Greek menu. Bar. A la carte entrees: lunch $15-$19, dinner $17-$25. Specializes in charcoal-grilled fish, octopus, lamb chops. Own pastries. Outdoor dining in garden courtyard. Greek decor. Cr cds: A, C, D, MC, V.

★ ★ ★ **PETROSSIAN.** 182 W 58th St, at 7th Ave, Midtown. 212/245-2214. Hrs: 11:30-1 am; Sat & Sun brunch to 3 pm. Res accepted. French, Amer menu. Bar. A la carte entrees: lunch $16-$18, dinner $20-$31. Prix fixe: lunch $29, dinner $35. Sat & Sun brunch $22. Specialties: caviar, smoked salmon, foie gras. Own pastries. Menu changes quarterly. Art deco dining rm with Erté murals, Lalique crystal panels. Near Carnegie Hall. Jacket. Cr cds: A, C, D, MC, V.

★ ★ **PIERRE AU TUNNEL.** 250 W 47th St, between Eighth Ave & Broadway, Times Square/Theater District. 212/575-1220. Hrs: noon-3 pm, 5:30-11:30 pm; Wed & Sat noon-2:30 pm, 4:30-11:30 pm. Closed Sun; major hols. Res accepted. French menu. Bar. A la carte entrees: lunch $10-$17. Complete meals: dinner $28. French-country dining rm decor; fireplace. Family-owned. Cr cds: A, MC, V.

★ ★ **PIG HEAVEN.** 1540 Second Ave, at 80th St, Upper East Side. 212/744-4333. Hrs: noon-midnight; Sat, Sun brunch to 4:30 pm. Res required. Chinese menu. Bar. Semi-a la carte: lunch $4.95-$6.25, dinner $10.95-$19.95. Specializes in pork dishes, seafood, poultry, dumplings, pancakes. Cr cds: A, C, D, MC, V.

D

✔ ★ ★ **PIGALLE.** 111 E 29th St, between Park & Lexington Aves, in Murray Hill. 212/779-7830. Hrs: noon-3:30 pm, 5:30-11 pm; wkends to 11:30 pm; Sun brunch noon-3:30 pm. Closed Memorial Day, Dec 25. Res accepted. French, Italian menu. Bar. A la carte entrees: lunch $12.50-$15.75, dinner $13.75-$18.75. Complete meals: lunch $15.75, dinner (5:30-7 pm) $18.75. Sun brunch $12.75. Specialties: rabbit terrine, bouillabaisse (Fri & Sat), braised veal shank in mustard sauce. Jazz Mon & Thurs (dinner). Outdoor dining. French bistro atmosphere; Parisian mural; reproductions of French art. Cr cds: A, C, D, DS, JCB, MC, V.

D

✔ ★ **PINOCCHIO.** 170 E 81st St, between Lexington and Third Aves, Upper East Side. 212/650-1513. Hrs: noon-2 pm, 5:30-11 pm; Sun & Mon to 11:30 pm. Closed major hols. Res accepted. Italian menu. Wine, beer. A la carte entrees: lunch $9-$13.50, dinner $14-$18. Child's meals. Specialties: fettucine Alfredo, fegato Veneziana, veal dishes. Own pasta. Outdoor dining. Cr cds: A.

★ ★ ★ **POLO.** (See Westbury Hotel) 212/439-4835. Hrs: 7-10 am, noon-2:30 pm, 6-10 pm; Sun brunch noon-2:30 pm. Res required. Continental menu. Bar noon-midnight; Fri, Sat to 1 am. A la carte entrees: bkfst $13.50-$22, lunch, dinner $17-$26. Sun brunch $33.50. Seasonal menu. Elegant English club decor; polo motif. Jacket. Cr cds: A, C, D, ER, JCB, MC, V.

D

★ ★ **POST HOUSE.** 28 E 63rd St, Upper East Side. 212/935-2888. Hrs: noon-11 pm; Fri to midnight; Sat 5:30 pm-midnight; Sun 5:30-11 pm. Closed Jan 1, Thanksgiving, Dec 25. Res accepted. Bar. Extensive wine list. A la carte entrees: lunch $18.50-$26.50, dinner $20-$29.75. Specialties: grilled Atlantic salmon, Maryland crab cakes, Cajun rib steak. Own pastries. Club atmosphere. Cr cds: A, C, D, DS, JCB, MC, V.

★ ★ ★ **PRIMAVERA.** 1578 First Ave, Upper East Side. 212/861-8608. Hrs: 5:30 pm-midnight; Sun from 5 pm. Closed major hols. Res required. Northern Italian menu. Bar. Wine cellar. A la carte entrees: dinner $19.75-$32. Specializes in baby goat, primavera pasta, risotto ai porcini. Tuscan decor. Jacket. Cr cds: A, C, D, MC, V.

✔ ★ **PROVENCE.** 38 MacDougal St, at Avenue of the Americas (Sixth Ave), in SoHo. 212/475-7500. Hrs: noon-3 pm, 6-11:30 pm; Fri & Sat to midnight. Closed major hols. Res required. French menu. Bar. A la carte entrees: lunch $8.50-$17, dinner $16-$19. Specializes in seafood, bouillabaisse. Outdoor dining. Bistro atmosphere. Cr cds: A.

★ ★ ★ **RAINBOW ROOM.** In GE Bldg, 65th floor, 30 Rockefeller Plaza, Midtown. 212/632-5000. Hrs: 5:30 pm-1 am; Fri & Sat to 2 am; Sun to 10:30 pm; Sun brunch noon-2:30 pm. Closed Mon. Res required. Continental menu. Bar. Wine cellar. A la carte entrees: dinner $26-$42. Prix fixe: pre-theater dinner $38.50. Sun brunch $12-$16. Cover charge $15/person (exc pre-theater & brunch). Specialties: caviar, lobster Thermidor, baked Alaska. Own baking. Entertainment. Parking. At top of restored landmark skyscraper (1934); classic moderne interior with revolving dance floor under a domed ceiling; views of midtown Manhattan through two-story, floor-to-ceiling windows. Jacket, tie. Cr cds: A, C, D, MC, V.

D

★ ★ **RAOUL'S.** 180 Prince St, in SoHo. 212/966-3518. Hrs: 6-11:30 pm; Fri & Sat to 1 am; Sun brunch 11:30 am-4 pm. Closed

Thanksgiving, Dec 25. Res accepted. French menu. Bar. Wine list. A la carte entrees: dinner $17-$27. Specialty: steak au poivre. Own desserts. Bistro-inspired fare. Casual storefront dining rm; original artwork, objets d'art. Cr cds: A, MC, V.

★ ★ ★ **RAPHAEL.** *33 W 54th St, between Fifth and Sixth Aves, Midtown.* 212/582-8993. Hrs: noon-2:30 pm, 6-10 pm; Sat 6-11 pm. Closed Sun; major hols. Res accepted. French menu. Bar. A la carte entrees: lunch $17.50-$23, dinner $18.50-$26. Specializes in seafood, filet of lamb, game in winter. Own baking. Outdoor garden dining. In turn-of-the-century town house; fireplace; murals from Provence. Jacket. Cr cds: A, C, D, MC, V.

✔★ **RATNER'S.** *138 Delancey St, between Norfolk and Suffolk, downtown.* 212/677-5588. Hrs: 6 am-11:30 pm; Fri to 3 pm; Sat sundown-1:30 am. Closed Jewish hols. Res accepted. Jewish dairy menu. Serv bar. A la carte entrees: bkfst $3.75-$7.25, lunch $8-$15, dinner $8-$18. Specializes in blintzes, pirogen, broiled fish. Bakery. Parking. Cr cds: A, MC, V.

✔★ ★ **RED TULIP.** *439 E 75th St, between York & First Aves, Upper East Side.* 212/734-4893. Hrs: 6 pm-midnight. Closed Mon & Tues. Res accepted. Hungarian menu. Bar. A la carte entrees: dinner $14-$16. Specializes in seafood, chicken, veal. Strolling violinist; Gypsy music. European folk art; Hungarian antiques. Family-owned. Cr cds: A, D, MC, V.

D

★ ★ ★ **REMI.** *145 W 53rd St, between Sixth & Seventh Aves, Midtown.* 212/581-4242. Hrs: 11:45 am-2:30 pm, 5:30-11:30 pm; Sat & Sun from 5:30 pm. Closed major hols. Res required. Venetian menu. Bar. A la carte entrees: lunch $13-$24, dinner $16-$27. Specialties: rack of lamb with pistachio herb crust, seared rare tuna with black olives & shallot sauce, calf's liver in black truffle butter. Outdoor dining. Venetian-style trattoria with high, vaulted ceiling, Gothic detailing and room-length, fantasy mural of Venice. Cr cds: A, C, D, MC, V.

D

★ ★ ★ **RENÉ PUJOL.** *321 W 51st St, between 8th & 9th Aves, Times Square/Theater Distict.* 212/246-3023. Hrs: noon-3 pm, 5-10:30 pm; Fri & Sat to 11:30 pm. Closed Sun; major hols; also last 2 wks Aug. Res accepted. French menu. Bar. Extensive wine cellar. Complete meals: lunch $23, dinner $32. Specialties: roasted salmon, leeks & mushrooms in red wine sauce, sauted veal chop with braised vegetables, sliced beef tenderloin with roasted shallots. Own pastries. Informal country-French atmosphere. Cr cds: A, C, D, MC, V.

★ ★ **ROMEO SALTA.** *30 W 56th St, between 5th & 6th Aves, Midtown.* 212/246-5772. Hrs: noon-11 pm; Sat from 5 pm. Closed Sun; major hols. Res accepted. Northern Italian menu. Bar. A la carte entrees: lunch $16.95-$23.95, dinner $17.95-$24.95. Pre-theatre dinner $24.95-$27.95. Child's meals. Specializes in pasta, fish, chicken. 3 dining areas, one with fireplace and open kitchen. Family-owned since 1953. Jacket. Cr cds: A, C, D, JCB, MC, V.

★ ★ **ROSA MEXICANO.** *1063 First Ave, at 58th St, on the East Side.* 212/753-7407. Hrs: 5 pm-midnight. Closed Thanksgiving. Res accepted. Mexican menu. Bar. A la carte entrees: dinner $15-$24. Specialties: enchiladas de mole poblano, crepas camarones. Classical Mexican cuisine. Guacamole prepared tableside. Casual dining. Cr cds: A, C, D, MC, V.

D

★ **ROSE CAFE.** *24 Fifth Ave, at W 9th St, in Greenwich Village.* 212/260-4118. Hrs: 11:30 am-11 pm; Fri & Sat to midnight; Sun 5-11 pm; Sun brunch 11:30 am-3:30 pm. Closed Dec 25. Res accepted. Bar. A la carte entrees: lunch, dinner $8-$20. Sun brunch $9.95. Specialties: crisp potato pancakes with creme fraiche and 3 caviars, seven-layered vegetable torte, grilled shrimp. Atrium; window wall overlooks Fifth Ave. Cr cds: A, D, MC, V.

★ ★ ★ **RUSSIAN TEA ROOM.** *150 W 57th St, Midtown.* 212/265-0947. Hrs: 11:30 am-11:30 pm; Sat & Sun from 11 am; Sun brunch 11 am-4:15 pm. Res accepted. Russian, Amer menu. Bar;

special vodka drinks. Wine list. A la carte entrees: lunch $16.25-$26.75, dinner $22.25-$34.50, supper (from 9:30 pm) $14-$34.50. Prix fixe: lunch $25, dinner $39.75. Afternoon tea (Mon-Fri 3-5 pm). Sun brunch $14-$26.75. Specialties: beef Stroganoff, Karsky shashlik, chicken Kiev. Own desserts. Next to Carnegie Hall; pre-concert, post-concert dining. Extensive collection of paintings and Russian objets d'art. Favored by performing artists. Cr cds: A, C, D, DS, JCB, MC, V.

D

★ ★ **RUTH'S CHRIS STEAK HOUSE.** *148 W 51st St (10019), between 6th & 7th Aves, Midtown.* 212/245-9600. Hrs: noon-midnight; Sat from 4 pm; Sun 4-10 pm. Closed Thanksgiving, Dec 25. Res required. Bar. A la carte entrees: lunch $12-$26, dinner $17.50-$32. Specializes in steak, lobster. Men's club decor. Cr cds: A, C, D, MC, V.

✔★ **SAIGON HOUSE.** *89-91 Bayard St, at Mulberry St, in Chinatown.* 212/732-8988. Hrs: 11 am-10:30 pm; Fri & Sat to 11 pm. Res accepted. Vietnamese menu. Bar. A la carte entrees: lunch $5.95-$15. Specialties: jumbo shrimp fried in salt and pepper, chicken with lemon grass, Vietnamese hot & sour shrimp soup. Cr cds: A, D, DS, MC, V.

★ **SAMMY'S ROUMANIAN STEAK HOUSE.** *157 Chrystie St, just N of Delancey St, downtown.* 212/475-9131. Hrs: 3-11 pm. Closed Yom Kippur. Res required. Jewish, Roumanian menu. Bar. A la carte entrees: dinner $10.95-$23.95. Child's meals. Specialties: Roumanian steak, chopped liver, breaded veal cutlet. Entertainment. Authentic Jewish cooking. Cr cds: A, MC, V.

★ ★ **SAN DOMENICO.** *240 Central Park South (10019), Midtown.* 212/265-5959. Hrs: noon-2:30 pm, 5:30-11 pm; Sat from 5:30 pm; Sun 5:30-10 pm. Closed Jan 1, Dec 25. Res accepted. Italian menu. Bar. Wine cellar. A la carte entrees: lunch $15.50-$32, dinner $16.50-$42.50. Specialties: ravioli with truffle butter, Alaska prawns with beans, breast of duck with olive sauce. Italian marble floors, Florentine stucco walls. Overlooks Central Park. Jacket. Cr cds: A, C, D, MC, V.

★ ★ **SAN MARTIN'S.** *143 E 49th St, between 3rd & Lexington Aves, Midtown.* 212/832-9270. Hrs: noon-midnight; Sun 5-11 pm. Closed July 4, Labor Day, Dec 25. Res accepted. Continental menu. Bar. A la carte entrees: lunch, dinner $12-$28. Complete meals: dinner $19.95. Specialties: rack of baby lamb, paella Valenciana, roast suckling pig. Outdoor dining. Cr cds: A, C, D, MC, V.

★ ★ **SAN PIETRO.** *18 E 54th St, between Fifth & Madison Aves, Midtown.* 212/753-9015. Hrs: noon-midnight. Closed Sun; major hols. Res required. Southern Italian menu. Bar. A la carte entrees: lunch, dinner from $20. Specializes in fish, pasta. Outdoor dining. 2 large dining areas; massive ceramic scene of Amalfi coast. Jacket. Cr cds: A, D, MC, V.

D

✔★ ★ **SANTA FE.** *72 W 69th St, at Columbus Ave, Upper West Side.* 212/724-0822. Hrs: noon-midnight. Closed Thanksgiving, Dec 25. Res accepted. Southwestern menu. Bar. A la carte entrees: lunch $11.50-$18, dinner $12-$19. Sun brunch $11.50. Southwest Indian art, tapestries; regional paintings; 5 fireplaces. Cr cds: A, D, MC, V.

★ ★ **SARABETH'S.** *423 Amsterdam Ave, between 80th & 81st Sts, Upper West Side.* 212/496-6280. Hrs: 8 am-3:30 pm, 6-11 pm; Fri to midnight; Sat 6 pm-midnight; Sun 6-9:30 pm; Sat & Sun brunch 9 am-4 pm. Closed Labor Day, Thanksgiving, Dec 25. Serv bar. A la carte entrees: bkfst $5-$10, lunch $8-$15, dinner $13-$25. Sun brunch $8-$15. Specialties: pumpkin waffles, farmer's omelette, grilled tuna. Homey New England atmosphere. Totally nonsmoking. Cr cds: A, C, D, MC, V.

D

★ ★ **SARDI'S.** *234 W 44th St, between Broadway & 8th Ave, Times Square/Theater District.* 212/221-8440. Hrs: 11:30-12:30 am; Fri & Sat to 1 am. Res accepted. Bars. Prix fixe: lunch $24.95, dinner $35.95. Specialties: shrimp a la Sardi, veal Vincent, chicken a la Sardi. Established 1921. Famous gathering place of theatrical personalities, columnists, publishers, agents; popular for before and after-theater dinner or drinks. Family-owned. Cr cds: A, C, D, JCB, MC, V.

★ ★ ★ **SEA GRILL.** *19 W 49th St, at Rockefeller Plaza, Midtown.* 212/246-9201. Hrs: noon-3 pm, 5-10 pm; Sat from 5 pm. Closed Sun. Res required. Bar. Wine cellar. A la carte entrees: lunch $18.50-$26.50, dinner $22.50-$29.50. Complete meals: lunch $29.50, dinner $35. Specialty: Maryland crab cakes with lobster and chive sauce. Own pastries. Outdoor dining. Floral, garden displays. Overlooks Prometheus fountain and pool (summer); ice-skating rink (winter). Jacket (dinner). Cr cds: A, C, D, ER, JCB, MC, V.

D

★ ★ ★ **SHUN LEE.** *43 W 65th St, between Central Park West & Columbus Ave, Upper West Side.* 212/595-8895. Hrs: noon-midnight; Sat from 11:30 am; Sun to 10:30 pm. Closed Thanksgiving. Chinese menu. Bar. A la carte entrees: lunch $10.25-$17.95, dinner $13.95-$35. Specialties: jumbo prawns with broccoli in curry sauce, Peking duck, Norwegian salmon (Szechwan or Mandarin style). Contemporary decor. Jacket. Cr cds: A, C, D, MC, V.

D

★ ★ ★ **SHUN LEE PALACE.** *155 E 55th St, between Third & Lexington Aves, on the East Side.* 212/371-8844. Hrs: noon-11 pm; Sat to 11:30 pm; Sun to 10:30 pm. Closed Thanksgiving. Res required. Chinese menu. Bar. Wine cellar. A la carte entrees: lunch $11.95-$18.95, dinner $12.50-$37. Specializes in Cantonese, Hunan and Szechwan dishes. Parking. Cr cds: A, D, MC, V.

✔★ ★ **SIAM GRILL.** *586 Ninth Ave, between 42nd & 43rd Sts, on the West Side.* 212/307-1363. Hrs: 11:30 am-11 pm; Fri to 11:30 pm; Sat 4-11:30 pm; Sun 4-10:30 pm. Closed some major hols. Res accepted. Thai menu. Serv bar. A la carte entrees: lunch, dinner $6.25-$15.95. Specialties: sautéed chicken with cashew nuts & chili paste sauce, homemade red & green Thai curry, garlic duck. Cr cds: A, MC, V.

★ ★ **SIAM INN.** *916 8th Ave, between W 54th & 55th Sts, Times Square/Theater District.* 212/489-5237. Hrs: noon-3 pm, 5-11:30 pm; Sat from 4 pm; Sun 5-11 pm. Closed most major hols. Res accepted Mon-Thurs; required Fri & Sat. Thai menu. Bar. A la carte entrees: lunch $6.25-$9.55, dinner $6.95-$15.95. Specialties: deep-fried whole fish, duck with tamarind sauce. Thai decor; artifacts displayed, photos of Bangkok, statues, plaques. Cr cds: A, D, MC, V.

★ ★ ★ **SIGN OF THE DOVE.** *1110 Third Ave, at E 65th St, Upper East Side.* 212/861-8080. Hrs: noon-2:30 pm, 6-11 pm; Sat from 5:30 pm; Sun 6-10 pm; Sat & Sun brunch 11:30 am-2:30 pm. Res accepted. Bar. Wine cellar. A la carte entrees: lunch $12-$20, dinner $20-$32. Prix fixe: lunch $20, dinner $48. Sun brunch $14-$20. Pre-theater dinner 6 pm: $30. Specialties: pan-seared tuna with pancetta, steamed halibut with shiitakes, fava bean & Parmesan ravioli, lamb loin with braised artichokes. Own baking. Jazz combo and vocalist. Outdoor dining. Garden atmosphere. Collection of 19th-century antiques. Cr cds: A, C, D, DS, JCB, MC, V.

★ ★ ★ **SMITH & WOLLENSKY.** *201 E 49th St, at Third Ave, on the East Side.* 212/753-1530. Hrs: noon-midnight; Sat & Sun from 5 pm. Closed Jan 1, Dec 25. Res accepted. Bar. Extensive wine cellar. A la carte entrees: lunch $12-$26, dinner $18-$42. Specializes in steak, seafood. Built 1897; turn-of-the-century decor; old New York steakhouse atmosphere. Also Wollensky's Grill, entrance at 205 E 49th St, open 11:30-2 am. Outdoor dining. Cr cds: A, C, D, DS, JCB, MC, V.

D

★ ★ ★ **SPARKS STEAK HOUSE.** *210 E 46th St, Midtown.* 212/687-4855. Hrs: noon-3 pm, 5-11 pm; Fri to 11:30 pm; Sat 5-11:30 pm. Closed Sun; major hols. Res required. Bar. Extensive wine list. A la carte entrees: lunch, dinner $19.95-$29.95. Specializes in steak, lobster, seafood. Early Amer decor; etched glass, wood paneling. Jacket. Cr cds: A, C, D, MC, V.

D

★ ★ **SPRING STREET.** *162 Spring St, at W Broadway, in SoHo.* 212/219-0157. Hrs: 11:45 am-midnight; Sat & Sun 11:30-4 am.

Closed Dec 25. Res accepted. Bar. A la carte entrees: lunch $8.50-$16, dinner $8.50-$18.50. Sun brunch $4-$17.50. Specialties: T-bone of pork, grilled salmon with asparagus rissotto, Porterhouse steak. Cr cds: A, C, D, DS, MC, V.

★ ★ **STEAK FRITES.** *9 E 16th St, between Fifth Ave & Broadway, in Chelsea.* 212/463-7101. Hrs: noon-4:30 pm, 5-midnight; Sun to 10 pm; Sun brunch noon-5 pm. Closed Jan 1, Dec 25. Res accepted. French menu. Bar. A la carte entrees: lunch $7-$17.50, dinner $12.50-$19. Sun brunch $7-$17.50. Specializes in Black Angus steak. Outdoor dining. French bistro-style atmosphere; murals of Paris scenes. Cr cds: A, D, MC, V.

D

✔★ ★ **T-REX.** *358 W 23rd St, between 8th & 9th Aves, in Chelsea.* 212/620-4620. Hrs: 11:30 am-11 pm; Wed-Sat to midnight. Res accepted. Bar. A la carte entrees: lunch $7.95-$12.95, dinner $9.95-$18.95. Specialties: grilled rare tuna tostada, apricot-glazed rock Cornish game hen, grilled aged sirloin. Jurassic era cave; glass-enclosed garden; casual dining. Cr cds: A, D, DS, JCB, MC, V.

D

✔★ ★ **TAORMINA.** *147 Mulberry St, between Grand & Hester Sts, in Little Italy.* 212/219-1007. Hrs: 11 am-11:30 pm; Sat to 1 am; Sun to 11 pm. Closed Thanksgiving, Dec 25, 31. Res required. Italian menu. Bar. A la carte entrees: lunch, dinner $9.90-$17.50. Specializes in seafood, pasta, penne al cognac. Valet parking. Modern Italian decor. Cr cds: A, C, D, MC, V.

★ ★ **TATOU.** *151 E 50th St, between Lexington Ave & 3rd Ave, on the East Side.* 212/753-1144. Hrs: noon-3 pm, 5:30-10:45 pm; Sat 5:30 pm-4 am. Closed Sun; some major hols. Res required. Bar to 4 am. A la carte entrees: lunch $9-$19, dinner $15-$25. Pre-theater dinner (before 7 pm) $19.95. Specialties: honey-mustard roasted salmon, broiled chicken with mushroom dressing, sweet potato and collard green crisps. Entertainment. Terrace dining. Old theater setting; former nightclub from the 1940s. Jacket. Cr cds: A, C, D, MC, V.

★ ★ ★ **TAVERN ON THE GREEN.** *Central Park at W 67th St, Upper West Side.* 212/873-3200. Hrs: 11:30 am-midnight; Fri & Sat 5 pm-12:45 am; Sun 5-11 pm; Sat & Sun brunch 10 am-3:30 pm. Res accepted. Continental menu. Bar. A la carte entrees: lunch $10.75-$24.95, dinner $12.75-$32.50. Table d'hôte: lunch $15.50-$23.50, pre-theater dinner (5:30-6:45 pm) $21.50-$24.95, post-theater supper $16.50-$24.50. Sat & Sun brunch $9.85-$26.50. Varied, extensive menu. Own baking. Entertainment (exc Mon) in Chestnut Room: show times 8:30 pm & 10:30 pm, Fri & Sat 9 & 11 pm; $17-$25. Valet parking. Garden terrace dining & dancing. Gourmet shop. Elaborate decor; in 1874 building within Central Park. Cr cds: A, C, D, JCB, MC, V.

D

★ **TAVOLA.** *1481 York Ave, at 78th St, Upper East Side.* 212/570-9810. Hrs: 6-11 pm; Sat & Sun to 11:30 pm; Sun brunch 11:30 am-3 pm. Closed Jan 1, July 4. Res accepted. Bar. A la carte entrees: dinner $10-$20. Sun brunch $14. Specializes in fresh seafood, antipasta, homemade pastas. Outdoor dining. Cr cds: A, MC, V.

D

★ ★ ★ **TERRACE.** *400 W 119th St, between Amsterdam & Morningside Dr, on rooftop of Butler Hall, Columbia University, Upper West Side.* 212/666-9490. Hrs: noon-2:30 pm, 6-10 pm; Sat from 6 pm. Closed Sun & Mon; Dec 25. Res accepted. French cuisine, with a light touch. Bar to 11 pm. Wine cellar. A la carte entrees: lunch $8.50-$18.50, dinner $21-$29. Prix fixe: lunch $25, dinner $36. Specializes in seafood, game. Own pastries. Classical harpist evenings. Valet parking (dinner). Outdoor terrace. Panoramic view of Hudson River, George Washington Bridge and Manhattan skyline. Cr cds: A, C, D, MC, V.

★ ★ **TRATTORIA DELL'ARTE.** *900 7th Ave, at 57th St, Midtown.* 212/245-9800. Hrs: 11:30 am-2:45 pm, 5-11:30 pm; Fri & Sat to 12:30 am; Sun to 10:30 pm; Sat & Sun brunch to 3:45 pm. Closed Dec 25. Res accepted. Italian menu. Bar. A la carte entrees: lunch, dinner $12-$29. Sat & Sun brunch $16-$17. Specializes in pizza, handmade pastas, veal chops, seafood. Authentic Italian antipasto bar. Modern Italian atmosphere. Opp Carnegie Hall; frequented by celebrities. Cr cds: A, JCB, MC, V.

★ ★ **TRE MERLI BISTRO.** *In Trump Tower, 725 Fifth Ave, between 56th & 57th Sts, Midtown.* 212/832-1555. Hrs: 11:30 am-4 pm; Sun from noon. Closed some major hols. Res accepted. Northern Italian menu. Bar. A la carte entrees: lunch $15-$22. Child's meals. Specializes in pasta, risotto, fish. Contemporary decor with prints & oils on display; overlooks wall with cascading water. Cr cds: A, D, MC, V.

[D]

★ ★ ★ **TRE SCALINI.** *230 E 58th St, between Second & Third Aves, on the East Side.* 212/688-6888. Hrs: noon-midnight. Closed Mon. Res accepted. Italian menu. Bar. Wine cellar. A la carte entrees: lunch $14.50-$29, dinner $16-$34. Prix fixe: pre-theater dinner (5-7 pm) $32. Specializes in seafood, chicken, pasta. Cr cds: A, C, D, DS, MC, V.

★ ★ **TRIBECA GRILL.** *375 Greenwich St, at Franklin St, in Tribeca.* 212/941-3900. Hrs: noon-3 pm, 5:30-11 pm; Fri to 11:30 pm; Sat 5:30-11:30 pm; Sun 5-10 pm; Sun brunch 11:30 am-3 pm. Res accepted. Bar. A la carte entrees: lunch $12-$17, dinner $17-$26. Prix fixe: lunch $19.95. Specializes in fish, ravioli, duck. Casual dining in converted warehouse. Cr cds: A, D, MC, V.

[D]

★ ★ ★ **UNION SQUARE CAFE.** *21 E 16th St, between 5th Ave & Union Square W, Midtown.* 212/243-4020. Hrs: noon-2:30 pm, 6-10:30 pm; Fri & Sat to 11:30 pm; Sun 5:30-10 pm. Closed major hols. Res accepted. French, Italian menu. Bar. Extensive wine list. A la carte entrees: lunch $11-$17.50, dinner $17.50-$26. Specialties: grilled marinated fillet mignon of tuna, fried calamari with spicy anchovy mustard, seasonal vegetables. Own pastries. Contemporary American bistro. Cr cds: A, D, MC, V.

✔ ★ **VASATA.** *339 E 75th St, between First & Second Aves, Upper East Side.* 212/650-1686. Hrs: 5-11 pm; Sun noon-10 pm. Closed Mon; also 1st 3 wks July. Res accepted. Czechoslovakian menu. Serv bar. A la carte entrees: dinner $13.95-$18. Child's meals. Specialties: roast duckling, game in season, boiled beef with dill sauce. Family-owned. Established 1890. Cr cds: A, MC, V.

★ ★ **VICTOR'S CAFE 52.** *236 W 52nd St, Times Square/Theater District.* 212/586-7714. Hrs: noon-midnight. Res accepted. Cuban, Caribbean menu. Bar. A la carte entrees: lunch $5.95-$18.95, dinner $7.95-$26.95. Specialties: paella, stone crab creole, suckling roast pig. Entertainment. Skylight; garden. Cr cds: A, C, D, MC, V.

★ ★ ★ **THE VIEW.** *(See Marriott Marquis Hotel)* 212/704-8900. Hrs: 5:30-11 pm; Fri & Sat 5 pm-midnight; Sun brunch 10:30 am-2 pm. Res required. Continental menu. Bar. Wine cellar. A la carte entrees: dinner $24.50-$33. Prix fixe: pre-theater dinner $39.95. Brunch $29.95. Child's meals. Specializes in American, French and Italian dishes. Own baking. Valet parking. Revolving rooftop restaurant, lounge and ballroom. Braille menu. Jacket. Cr cds: A, C, D, DS, ER, JCB, MC, V.

[D]

★ ★ ★ **VONG.** *200 E 54th St, between 2nd & 3rd Aves, Midtown.* 212/486-9592. Hrs: noon-2:30 pm, 6-11 pm; Sat 5:30-11:30 pm; Sun 5:30-10 pm. Closed major hols. Res required. Thai, French menu. Bar. Wine cellar. A la carte entrees: lunch, dinner $16-$22. Specialties: sautéed foie gras with ginger and mango, black bass with wok-fried Napa cabbage, lobster with Thai herbs. Outdoor dining. Exotic decor of Southeast Asia; ceiling and walls covered with gold leaf collage; Thai-style seating (sunken seating) in one area of dining rm. Cr cds: A, D, MC, V.

[D]

★ ★ **WATER CLUB.** *500 E 30th St, at the East River, Midtown.* 212/683-3333. Hrs: noon-2:30 pm, 5:30-11 pm; Sun 5:45-10 pm; Sun brunch 11:30 am-2:30 pm. Res required. Bar. A la carte entrees: lunch $14-$24, dinner $16-$28. Sun brunch $29. Specializes in lobster,

oysters, swordfish. Piano bar. Valet parking. Outdoor dining (Memorial Day-Labor Day). Overlooks the East River. Jacket. Cr cds: A, C, D, JCB, MC, V.

[D]

★ ★ **YANKEE CLIPPER.** *170 John St, Financial District.* 212/344-5959. Hrs: 11:30 am-10 pm; Sun noon-9 pm. Closed Thanksgiving, Dec 25. Res accepted. Bar. A la carte entrees: lunch, dinner $11-$24. Prix fixe: dinner $23. Specializes in jumbo shrimp, Norwegian salmon, grilled swordfish steak. Three dining areas; main dining rm resembles dining salon on a luxury liner; display of ship models and prints of ships. Cr cds: A, C, D, DS, MC, V.

✔ ★ **YELLOWFINGERS.** *200 E 60th St, at Third Ave, Upper East Side.* 212/751-8615. Hrs: 11:30-1 am; Fri, Sat to 2 am; Sun to 11:45 pm. Italian, regional California menu. Bar. A la carte entrees: lunch, dinner $4.50-$16.50. Specialties: focaccia, salads, gourmet individual pizza. Own desserts. Outdoor dining. Cr cds: A, C, D, DS, MC, V.

★ ★ **ZARELA.** *953 2nd Ave, between 50th & 51st Sts, Midtown.* 212/644-6740. Hrs: noon-3 pm, 5-11 pm; Fri to 11:30 pm; Sat 5-11:30 pm; Sun 5-10 pm. Closed major hols. Res accepted. Mexican menu. Bar. A la carte entrees: lunch $12-$20, dinner $25-$35. Specializes in roasted duck, snapper hash, regional cuisine. Entertainment Tues-Sat. Colorful Mexican decor; paper lanterns, masks, toys, piñatas. Cr cds: A, D.

Unrated Dining Spots

CARNEGIE DELI. *854 Seventh Ave, off 55th St, Midtown.* 212/757-2245. Hrs: 6:30-3:45 am. Kosher deli menu. Semi-a la carte: bkfst $5-$7, lunch $7-$12, dinner $8-$15. Specializes in sandwiches, corned beef, cheesecake. Traditional Jewish-style New York deli. No cr cds accepted.

[D]

DIANE'S UPTOWN. *249 Columbus Ave, between 71st & 72nd Sts, Upper West Side.* 212/799-6750. Hrs: 11-2 am. Closed Thanksgiving eve, Dec 24-25. Wine, beer. A la carte entrees: bkfst from $3.90, lunch, dinner $4.50-$7.65. Specializes in hamburgers, omelettes, sodas, ice cream sundaes. No cr cds accepted.

[D]

ELEPHANT & CASTLE. *68 Greenwich Ave, Seventh Ave & 11th St, in Greenwich Village.* 212/243-1400. Hrs: 8:30 am-midnight; Fri to 1 am; Sat 10-1 am; Sun 10 am-midnight. Wine, beer, setups. A la carte entrees: bkfst $2.75-$7, lunch, dinner $2.75-$11.50. Specializes in omelettes, hamburgers. Daily specials. Village coffee shop. Cr cds: A, C, D, MC, V.

EMPIRE DINER. *210 Tenth Ave, between 22nd & 23rd Sts, in Chelsea.* 212/243-2736. Open 24 hrs; Sun brunch noon-4 pm. Bar. A la carte entrees: bkfst $1.50-$8.50, lunch, dinner $4.25-$14.95. Sun brunch $9.50. Specializes in sandwiches, omelettes. Own muffins, scones. Pianist. Outdoor dining. Authentic chrome and stainless steel art-deco diner. Cr cds: A, D, DS, MC, V.

FLORENT. *69 Gansevoort St, between Washington & Greenwich Sts, in Greenwich Village.* 212/989-5779. Open 24 hrs. Closed Dec 25. Res accepted. Bar. French, Amer menu. A la carte entrees: bkfst $3.50-$10, lunch $3.95-$11, dinner $8.50-$13.50. Specialties: boudin noir, fresh fish. Chrome- & aluminum-trimmed diner attached to meat market in warehouse area of the Village. No cr cds accepted.

[D]

HARLEY-DAVIDSON CAFE. *1370 Ave of the Americas (10019), at 56th St, Midtown.* 212/245-6000. Hrs: 11:30 am-midnight; Fri & Sat to 1 am. Closed Dec 25. Semi-a la carte: lunch, dinner $7.50-$19.95. Child's meals. Specializes in seafood, barbecue chicken, Harley Hog sandwich. Outdoor dining on wrap-around terrace. Extensive Harley-Davidson motorcycle memorabilia; multi-media displays. Cr cds: A, D, MC, V.

JACKSON HOLE WYOMING. *1611 Second Ave, between 83rd & 84th Sts, Upper East Side.* 212/737-8788. Hrs: 10-1 am; Fri, Sat to 4 am. Closed Thanksgiving, Dec 25. Bar. A la carte entrees: bkfst $4-$6, lunch, dinner $6-$10. Specializes in sandwiches, hamburgers. Outdoor dining. Chrome and stainless steel art deco diner; juke box. Cr cds: A, MC, V.

PANEVINO RISTORANTE/CAFE VIENNA. *In Avery Fisher Hall, Lincoln Center, Broadway & 64th St, Upper West Side.* 212/874-7000. Hrs: Panevino Ristorante 11:30 am-8 pm; Cafe Vienna 11:30 am-11 pm. Italian menu at Panevino Ristorante; Viennese dessert & coffee menu at Cafe Vienna. Bar. A la carte entrees at Panevino: lunch $10-$14, dinner $13-$21. A la carte desserts at Cafe Vienna: $5-$7. Outdoor dining. Cafe is authentic Viennese coffee house. Both establishments overlook Lincoln Center plaza. Cr cds: A, D, MC, V.

PLANET HOLLYWOOD. *140 W 57th St, Midtown.* 212/333-7827. Hrs: 11-1 am. Closed Dec 25. Bar to 1:45 am. Semi-a la carte: lunch, dinner $6.95-$16.95. Specializes in pizza, hamburgers, pasta, homemade bread pudding with homemade whiskey sauce. Music videos and movie clips are shown daily. Authentic Hollywood memorabilia displayed. Cr cds: A, MC, V.

THE ROTUNDA. *(See The Pierre Hotel)* 212/940-8185. Hrs: 10:30 am-3 pm, 5:30-8:30 pm; tea 3-5:30 pm. A la carte entrees: bkfst, lunch, dinner $5-$15. Prix fixe: tea $19.50. Beaux-arts architecture with marble columns & pilasters. Murals by Edward Melcarth. Cr cds: A, C, D, ER, JCB, MC, V.

SAVORIES. *30 Rockefeller Center, downstairs, Midtown.* 212/246-6457. Hrs: 7 am-6 pm; Sat 9 am-5 pm. Closed Sun May-Nov. Wine, beer. A la carte entrees: bkfst $2.50-$3.95, lunch $5-$13. Specializes in hot and cold pasta, desserts. Outdoor garden dining. Afternoon tea after 3 pm. Parking. Bistro atmosphere. Cr cds: A, C, D, JCB, MC, V.

SECOND AVE DELI. *156 Second Ave, at 10th St, in the East Village.* 212/677-0606. Hrs: 8 am-midnight; Fri, Sat to 2 am. Closed Rosh Hashanah, Yom Kippur, Passover. Kosher menu. Semi-a la carte: bkfst, lunch, dinner $7.95-$15. Complete meals: dinner $13.40-$20.45. Specializes in pastrami, corned beef, chopped liver. Kosher deli; full menu served all day. Family-owned. Cr cds: A.

SERENDIPITY 3. *225 E 60th St, Upper East Side.* 212/838-3531. Hrs: 11:30-12:30 am; Fri to 1 am; Sat to 2 am; Sun to midnight. Closed Dec 25. Res accepted. A la carte entrees: lunch, dinner $4.50-$15. Specializes in burgers, pizza, frozen hot chocolate. Art nouveau decor; Tiffany lamps; marble-top tables. Famous for ice cream specialties, pastries, chocolate blackout cake. Enter restaurant through gift shop. Favorite of celebrities. Cr cds: A, C, D, DS, ER, MC, V.

STAGE DELI. *834 Seventh Ave, at 53rd St, Midtown.* 212/245-7850. Hrs: 6-2 am. Kosher deli menu. Bar. A la carte entrees: bkfst $2.95-$7.50, lunch $4.50-$13.95, dinner $5.50-$20. Specializes in corned beef, pastrami, brisket. Deli counter. Well-known New York deli; pickles own meats. Enclosed sidewalk dining. Celebrity photos. Cr cds: A, MC, V.

Bronx

Restaurants

★ ★ ★ **AMERIGO'S.** *3587 E Tremont Ave.* 718/792-3600. Hrs: noon-11 pm; Fri & Sat to midnight. Closed Mon; Thanksgiving, Dec 25; also 3 wks July. Res accepted; required wkends. Italian menu. Bar. Wine cellar. A la carte entrees: lunch, dinner $7.95-$25.95. Child's meals. Specialties: osso buco with risotto, veal chops, seafood. Valet parking wkends. Cr cds: A, C, D, DS, MC, V.

★ **ANNA'S HARBOR INN.** *565 City Island Ave, on City Island.* 718/885-1373. Hrs: noon-midnight; Sat to 1 am. Res accepted. Italian, seafood menu. Complete meals: lunch $8.95-$11.95. A la carte entrees: dinner $11.95-$29.95. Child's meals. Specialties: seafood, clams Posillipo, fried calamari, twin lobsters, combo marinara. Valet parking. Signed Norman Rockwell prints; functioning gaslights original to building; terrace overlooks marina, Long Island Sound. Family-owned. Cr cds: A, C, D, MC, V.

✔ ★ **DOMINICK'S.** *2335 Arthur Ave.* 718/733-2807. Hrs: noon-10 pm; Sun 1-9 pm. Closed Tues; major hols; also first 3 wks Aug. Italian menu. Bar. A la carte entrees: lunch, dinner $6-$15. Child's meals. Informal, family-style dining. No cr cds accepted.

★ ★ **JOE NINAS.** *3019 Westchester Ave.* 718/892-8282. Hrs: noon-3 pm, 5:30-10:30 pm; Sat 2-11 pm; Sun 2-8:30 pm. Closed Dec 25. Res required. Northern Italian menu. Bar. A la carte entrees: lunch $8.50-$18.50, dinner $10.50-$22.50. Child's meals. Specializes in veal, fish. Valet parking. Jacket. Cr cds: A, D, MC, V.

★ ★ **LOBSTER BOX.** *34 City Island Ave, on City Island.* 718/885-1952. Hrs: noon-11 pm. Closed Nov-late Mar. Bar. Semi-a la carte: lunch $7.95-$14.95, dinner $12.95-$33.50. Complete meals: dinner $12.50-$34.50. Child's meals. Specializes in seafood, lobster cooked 19 ways, shrimp cooked 15 ways, steamed clams. Valet parking. Terrace dining overlooks L.I. Sound. Family-owned. Cr cds: A, C, D, DS, MC, V.

★ ★ **MARIO'S.** *2342 Arthur Ave, between 184th & 187th Sts.* 718/584-1188. Hrs: noon-11 pm; Fri, Sat to midnight. Closed Mon; Dec 25; also last 2 wks Aug, 1 wk Sept. Res accepted. Italian menu. Semi-a la carte: lunch, dinner $13-$28. Child's meals. Specializes in pasta, veal, seafood. Valet parking. Family-owned. Cr cds: A, C, D, DS, MC, V.

✔ ★ **RIVERDALE DINER.** *3657 Kingsbridge Ave, W 238th St & Broadway.* 718/884-6050. Hrs: 6-2 am; Fri & Sat to 3 am. Res accepted. Serv bar. Semi-a la carte: bkfst $1.50-$6.95, lunch $5.95-$6.45. Complete meals: lunch $4.95-$9.50. A la carte entrees: dinner $5.95-$19.95. Child's meals. Specializes in fresh seafood, steak, chicken, pasta. Parking. Family-owned. Cr cds: A, D, MC, V.

★ ★ **SEA SHORE.** *591 City Island Ave, on City Island.* 718/885-0300. Hrs: 11 am-midnight; Fri & Sat to 2 am. Res accepted. Bar. A la carte entrees: lunch $9.95-$16.95, dinner $15.95-$38.95. Child's meals. Specializes in fresh seafood, jumbo lobster. Valet parking. Outdoor dining. Greenhouse dining rm & dock area overlooking L.I. Sound; marina. Family-owned. Cr cds: A, C, D, DS, MC, V.

Brooklyn

Restaurants

★ ★ **ABBRACCIAMENTO ON THE PIER.** 2200 Rockaway Pkwy, at Canarsie Pier, in Canarsie area. 718/251-5517. Hrs: 11:30 am-midnight; Fri & Sat to 1 am; Sun brunch 11:30 am-3 pm. Closed Jan 1, Dec 25. Res required. Northern Italian, Amer menu. Bar. A la carte entrees: lunch $9-$15, dinner $12-$25. Complete meals: dinner $22.50. Specialties: veal scaloppini with artichoke champagne sauce, chicken breast stuffed with fontina cheese, pasta seafood bianco. Entertainment. Outdoor dining. On Canarsie Pier; overlooks Jamaica Bay; docking facilites. Cr cds: A, C, D, MC, V.

D

★ ★ **BAY RIDGE SCHOONER SEA FOOD.** 8618 4th Ave, in Bayridge area. 718/921-6100. Hrs: 11:30 am-10 pm; Fri & Sat to 11 pm; Sun brunch to 3:30 pm. Closed Mon; Dec 25. Res accepted. Bar. Complete meals: lunch $8.95-$12.95. A la carte entrees: dinner $8.95-$29.95. Sun brunch $8.95-$12.95. Child's meals. Specialties: clam chowder, lobster bisque, red snapper gumbo, steak. Own desserts & breads. Valet parking. Nautical decor. Family-owned. Cr cds: A, D, MC, V.

D SC

★ ★ **CUCINA.** 256 5th Ave, between Carrol & Garfield Place, Park Slope area. 718/230-0711. Hrs: 5:30-10:30 pm; Fri & Sat to 11 pm; Sun 5-10 pm. Closed Thanksgiving, Dec 25. Res accepted. Italian menu. Bar. A la carte entrees: dinner $7-$22. Child's meals. Specialties: roast rack of lamb, cappelli vongole, osso buco & pappardelle. Antipasto bar. Two dining rms; gold leaf wall montage by New York artist. Cr cds: A, MC, V.

D

★ **EMBERS.** 9519 Third Ave, between 95th & 96th Sts, in Bayridge area. 718/745-3700. Hrs: noon-2:45 pm, 5-10:30 pm; Sat noon-1:45 pm, 4:30-10 pm; Sun 2-9:45 pm. Closed Thanksgiving, Dec 24 & 25. Bar. A la carte entrees: lunch $3.75-$6.95, dinner $6.95-$26.95. Specializes in pasta, T-bone steak. Adj to meat market. Cr cds: A.

D

★ ★ **GAGE & TOLLNER.** 372 Fulton St (Mall), between Adams & Jay Sts, near Borough Hall. 718/875-5181. Hrs: noon-3 pm, 5-10 pm; Fri & Sat 4-11 pm; Sun 4-9 pm; Sun brunch noon-3 pm. Res accepted. Bar. A la carte entrees: lunch, dinner $9-$22. Complete meals: lunch $18.95, dinner $21.95. Sun brunch $15.95. Child's meals. Specialties: Charleston she-crab soup, crab cakes Freetown, soft clam bellies, steak. Valet parking (dinner). Established 1879; mahogany paneling and furnishings, tin ceiling, working bronze gaslight fixtures. Cr cds: A, C, D, DS, MC, V.

D

★ ★ **GIANDO ON THE WATER.** 400 Kent Ave, under Williamsburg Bridge. 718/387-7000. Hrs: noon-4 pm, 5-11 pm; Sun 3-9 pm; early-bird dinner 5-7 pm. Res accepted. Italian menu. Bar. Prix fixe: lunch $17.95, dinner $29.95. A la carte entrees: dinner $12-$27. Specializes in pasta, seafood, fish, penne a la vodka. Pianist Fri, Sat. Valet parking. On East River overlooking Williamsburg & Brooklyn bridges and Manhattan skyline from Empire State Bldg to Statue of Liberty. Cr cds: A, C, D, DS, MC, V.

D

✔ ★ ★ **GREENHOUSE CAFE.** 7717 Third Ave, between 77th & 78th Sts, in Bayridge area. 718/833-8200. Hrs: 11:30 am-11 pm; Fri & Sat to midnight; Sun 4-10 pm; Sun brunch noon-3 pm. Closed Dec 25. Res accepted. Bar. A la carte entrees: lunch $5.25-$13. Semi-a la carte: dinner $10-$17.95. Child's meals. Specialties: roast Long Island

duckling, aged steak, seafood festival platter. Garden atrium. Cr cds: A, C, D, DS, MC, V.

D

★ ★ **PETER LUGER'S.** 178 Broadway, at foot of Williamsburg Bridge. 718/387-7400. Hrs: 11:30 am-9:45 pm; Fri to 10:45 pm; Sat to 11:15 pm; Sun 1-9:45 pm. Res accepted. Bar. Semi-a la carte: lunch $6.95-$11.95. A la carte entrees: dinner $18.95-$26.95. Specializes in steak, lamb chops. Established in 1887; in 19th-century riverfront building. No cr cds accepted.

D

★ ★ **PONTE VECCHIO.** [B10 Fourth Ave, between 88th & 89th Sts, in Bayridge area. 718/238-6449. Hrs: noon-10:30 pm; Fri & Sat to 11:30 pm. Closed July 4, Thanksgiving, Dec 25. Res accepted. Italian menu. Serv bar. A la carte entrees: lunch $14-$22, dinner $27-$32. Specializes in pasta, veal, seafood. Valet parking. Cr cds: A, MC, V.

D

★ ★ ★ **RASPUTIN.** 2670 Coney Island Ave, in Sheepshead Bay area. 718/332-8111. Hrs: noon-midnight; Fri-Sun to 3 am. Closed Yom Kippur & Rosh Hashana. Res required. Russian & French menus. Serv bar. Wine cellar. A la carte entrees (served Mon-Thurs only): French menu, lunch & dinner $17-$21. Complete meals: Russian menu, lunch $14.95, dinner $45-$55; French menu, dinner $20 addl. Serv charge 10%. Specialties: grilled sturgeon on skewer, pork shish kebab, stuffed loin of rabbit, blini with red or black caviar. Entertainment: Mon-Thurs 6-piece band; Fri-Sun 12-piece band and 6-person ballet, laser-light show. Valet parking. Unique Russian dinner-theater with seating for 300 on 2 levels; 3-tiered bandstand, vaulted ceiling with domed skylight, faux marble columns, mural of St Petersburg. Jacket. Cr cds: A, C, D, DS, MC, V.

★ ★ ★ **RIVER CAFE.** 1 Water St, on East River at foot of Brooklyn Bridge, in Brooklyn Heights area. 718/522-5200. Hrs: noon-2:30 pm, 6-11 pm; Sun brunch 11:30 am-2:30 pm. Res required. A la carte entrees: lunch $17-$24. Prix fixe: dinner $58, tasting menu $78. Sun brunch $15-$24. Specialties: rack of lamb, homemade chocolate desserts. Own baking. Pianist. Valet parking. Contemporary dining rm on barge moored on East River; views of Brooklyn Bridge, river and Manhattan skyline. Jacket. Cr cds: A, C, D, MC, V.

★ ★ **ROSSINI.** 8712 4th Ave, between 87th & 88th Sts, in Bayridge area. 718/748-4545. Hrs: noon-11 pm. Closed Mon; Dec 25. Northern Italian, continental menu. Bar. A la carte entrees: lunch, dinner $10-$23. Specializes in pasta, seafood, veal, chicken. Own desserts. Strolling musician Fri. Valet parking. Cr cds: A, C, D, MC, V.

D

★ ★ **TOMMASO.** 1464 86th St, in Bayridge area. 718/236-9883. Hrs: noon-10 pm; Sat to midnight; Sun 1-10 pm. Closed Dec 25. Res accepted. Italian menu. Bar. A la carte entrees: lunch, dinner $8-$20. Complete meals: lunch $8.95, dinner $19.95. Specializes in regional Italian dishes. Opera Thurs-Sun evenings. Family-owned. Cr cds: A, C, D, MC, V.

D

Queens (La Guardia & JFK Intl Airport Areas)

Hotels

★ ★ **HILTON JFK AIRPORT.** *138-10 135th Ave (11436), at Kennedy Intl Airport.* 718/322-8700; FAX 718/529-0749. 333 rms, 9 story. S $139-$179; D $139-$189; each addl $10; suites $250-$380; under 21 free. Crib free. TV. Restaurant 6 am-11:30 pm. Bar noon-2 am. Ck-out 1 pm. Convention facilities. Free airport transportation. Exercise equipt; weights, bicycles. *LUXURY LEVEL : CONCIERGE FLOOR.* 32 rms, 2 suites. S $179; D $189; suites $350-$525. Concierge. Private lounge, honor bar. In-rm movies. Cr cds: A, C, D, DS, ER, JCB, MC, V.

D ✗ ✈ 〰 🔥 SC

★ ★ **HOLIDAY INN-JFK.** *144-02 135th Ave (11436), near Kennedy Intl Airport.* 718/659-0200; FAX 718/322-2533. 360 rms, 12 story. S $135-$150; D $145-$160; each addl $10; suites from $235; under 19 free. Crib free. TV; cable. Indoor/outdoor pool; lifeguard. Restaurant 6 am-10:30 pm. Bar 11:30-1 am. Ck-out noon. Coin lndry. Convention facilities. Free airport transportation. Exercise equipt; bicycles, stair machine, whirlpool, sauna. Cr cds: A, C, D, DS, JCB, MC, V.

D ≈ ✗ ✈ 〰 🔥 SC

★ ★ **MARRIOTT LA GUARDIA.** *102-05 Ditmars Blvd (11369), opp La Guardia Airport, in East Elmhurst area.* 718/565-8900; FAX 718/898-4995. 436 rms, 9 story. S $165; D $175; each addl $15; suites $350-$650; under 18 free; wkly rates; wkend plans. Crib free. Covered parking $4. TV; cable, in-rm movies avail. Indoor pool; lifeguard. Restaurants 6:30 am-11 pm. Bar 11-2 am; entertainment. Ck-out 1 pm. Convention facilities. Gift shop. Free airport transportation. Exercise rm; instructor, weight machines, bicycles, whirlpool, sauna. *LUXURY LEVEL : CONCIERGE LEVEL.* 60 rms. S, D $185; each addl $15. Concierge. Private lounge, honor bar. Complimentary continental bkfst, refreshments. Cr cds: A, C, D, DS, ER, JCB, MC, V.

D ≈ ✗ ✈ 〰 🔥 SC

✔ ★ ★ **TRAVELODGE.** *Van Wyck Expy (11430), on I-678 (Van Wyck Expy), just S of jct Belt Pkwy (NY 27A), near Kennedy Intl Airport.* 718/995-9000; FAX 718/995-9075. 475 rms, 6 story. S, D $99-$140; each addl $10; suites $200-$300; under 18 free. Crib free. Pet accepted; $30. TV. Restaurant 5:30-11 am, noon-3 pm, 6-11:45 pm. Bar noon-2 am. Ck-out 11 am. Convention facilities. Gift shop. Free airport transportation. Cr cds: A, C, D, DS, MC, V.

D ✔ ✈ 〰 🔥 SC

Restaurants

★ ★ **IL TOSCANO.** *42-05 235th St, in Douglaston area.* 718/631-0300. Hrs: 5-10 pm. Closed Sun. Res required. Italian menu. Bar. A la carte entrees: dinner $14-$24. Specialties: sweetbreads sautéed with fresh thyme, green peppercorn and sherry, grilled brook trout with rasberry lemon, grilled radiccio de Traviso, grilled veal chop with mushrooms. Casual, trattoria atmosphere. Cr cds: A, C, D, MC, V.

★ ★ **KARYATIS.** *35-03 Broadway, in Astoria area.* 718/204-0666. Hrs: noon-midnight. Res accepted; required wkends. Greek menu. Serv bar. A la carte entrees: lunch $10-$15, dinner $20-$25. Specialties: Greek spicy sausage stuffed with kefalograviera cheese, moussaka, beef casserole in red wine, fresh tomato sauce and herbs, baked shredded chicken in red wine, onions, green peppers, fresh tomatoes, garlic, mild spices and Greek sausages. Valet parking

wkends. Named for Acropolis caryatides. Decorated with antique casts of ancient Greek statuary. Cr cds: A, MC, V.

D

★ ★ ★ **WATER'S EDGE.** *44th Drive, at East River, in Long Island City area.* 718/482-0033. Hrs: noon-3 pm, 5:30-11 pm; Fri & Sat 5:30-11:30 pm. Closed Sun. Res required. Bar. Wine cellar. A la carte entrees: lunch $7.50-$25, dinner $21-$30. Specializes in seafood, lobster. Own baking. Pianist. Valet parking. Complimentary transportation to and from Manhattan ferry. Outdoor dining. European decor. On riverfront opp United Nations complex; views of New York City midtown skyline. Cr cds: A, C, D, JCB, MC, V.

D

Newark Intl Airport Area

Motels

✔ ★ ★ **BEST WESTERN-NEWARK AIRPORT.** *(450 US 1S, Newark 07114)* Off NJ Tpke exit 14, S on US 1/9. 201/242-0900; FAX 201/242-8480. 191 rms, 8 story. S, D $55.95-$89.95; each addl $5; suites $99-$120; under 18 free; wkend rates. Crib free. TV; cable. Restaurant 6:30 am-midnight. Rm serv. Bar from noon. Ck-out noon. Coin lndry. Meeting rms. Sundries. Free airport transportation. Cr cds: A, C, D, DS, MC, V.

D ✗ 〰 🔥 SC

★ ★ ★ **COURTYARD BY MARRIOTT.** *(600 US 1/9, Newark 07114)* NJ Tpke exit 14, S on US 1/9. 201/643-8500; FAX 201/648-0662. 146 rms, 3 story. S $104; D $114; suites $125-$135; children free; wkly, wkend rates. Crib free. TV; cable. Indoor pool. Complimentary coffee in rms. Restaurant 6:30 am-11 pm. Bar from 4 pm. Ck-out noon. Coin lndry. Meeting rms. Valet serv. Sundries. Free airport, RR station transportation. Exercise equipt; weight machine, bicycles, whirlpool. Some balconies. Cr cds: A, C, D, DS, MC, V.

D ≈ ✗ ✈ 〰 🔥 SC

✔ ★ **HOWARD JOHNSON.** *(50 Port St, Newark 07114)* Off NJ Tpke exit 14, Frontage Rd. 201/344-1500; FAX 201/344-3311. 170 rms, 3 story. S, D $49.99-$99.99; children free; wkend rates. Crib free. TV; cable. Restaurant 6-1 am. Ck-out noon. Coin lndry. Meeting rms. Gift shop. Free airport transportation. Cr cds: A, C, D, DS, MC, V.

D ✗ 〰 🔥 SC

Motor Hotel

★ ★ **HOLIDAY INN INTL AIRPORT-NORTH.** *(160 Holiday Plaza, Newark 07114)* Off NJ Tpke exit 14, opp N terminal; use Service Rd. 201/589-1000; FAX 201/589-2799. 234 rms, 10 story. S $69-$93; D $79-$123; each addl $5; under 18 free; wkend rates by res. Crib free. Pet accepted, some restrictions. TV; cable. Pool; lifeguard. Restaurant 6:30 am-11 pm; Sat, Sun 7 am-10:30 pm. Rm serv. Bar 11-2 am; Sun from 1 pm; entertainment, dancing Wed-Sat. Ck-out noon. Meeting rms. Bellhops. Sundries. Gift shop. Free airport transportation. Tennis. Lawn games. Some in-rm steam baths. Cr cds: A, C, D, DS, JCB, MC, V.

D ✔ 🏌 ≈ ✗ 〰 🔥 SC

Hotels

★ ★ **HILTON-NEWARK AIRPORT.** *(1170 Spring St, Elizabeth 07201)* Off NJ Tpke exit 13 A. 908/351-3900; FAX 908/351-9556. 374 rms, 12 story. S, D $125-$175; each addl $10; suites $225-$700;

children free; wkend rates. Crib free. TV; cable. Indoor pool. Restaurant 6:30 am-11 pm. Bar 4 pm-2 am. Ck-out noon. Convention facilities. Gift shop. Free airport, RR station transportation. Exercise equipt; weight machines, bicycles, whirlpool, sauna. Cr cds: A, C, D, DS, ER, JCB, MC, V.

D ⊠ 🏋 ✈ ⅀ 🔥 SC

★ ★ ★ **MARRIOTT-AIRPORT.** (Newark Intl Airport, Newark 07114) On airport grounds; follow signs from main terminal. 201/623-0006; FAX 201/623-7618. 590 rms, 10 story. S, D $125-$150; suites $400-$500; under 18 free; wkend rates. Crib free. Pet accepted, some restrictions. TV; cable. Indoor/outdoor pool; poolside serv. Restaurants 6 am-11 pm. Rm serv 24 hrs. Bars 11:30-1:30 am. Ck-out noon. Convention facilities. Concierge. Free airport transportation. Exercise equipt; weights, bicycles, whirlpool, sauna. Some refrigerators. Oriental carpets in lobby. *LUXURY LEVEL : CONCIERGE FLOOR.* 60 rms,

3 suites. S, D $175. Private lounge, honor bar. Complimentary continental bkfst, refreshments. Cr cds: A, C, D, DS, ER, JCB, MC, V.

D ⚓ ⊠ 🏋 ✈ ⅀ 🔥 SC

★ ★ ★ **RADISSON-NEWARK AIRPORT.** (128 Frontage Rd, Newark 07114) Off NJ Tpke exit 14; use Service Rd. 201/690-5500; FAX 201/465-7195. 502 rms, 12 story. S, D $99-$125; each addl $10; suites $325-$495; under 18 free; wkend rates. Crib free. TV; cable. Indoor pool; poolside serv, lifeguard. Restaurants 6:30 am-11 pm. Bar 2 pm-2 am; entertainment Mon-Fri. Ck-out noon. Convention facilities. Concierge. Gift shop. Free airport transportation. Exercise equipt; weights, bicycles, whirlpool. Game rm. Refrigerators avail. Balconies. Atrium. *LUXURY LEVEL) PLAZA CLUB LEVEL.* 45 rms. S $129; D $144. Private lounge. Complimentary continental bkfst, refreshments. Cr cds: A, C, D, DS, MC, V.

D ⊠ 🏋 ✈ ⅀ 🔥 SC

Norfolk

Founded: 1682

Pop: 261,229

Elev: 12 feet

Time zone: Eastern

Area code: 804

Surrounded on three sides by the historic waters that have been its lifeline for more than three centuries, Norfolk is a vivid, colorful city. Sightseers will delight in the clean salt air, the world-famous seafood and the proud nautical history. The hub of a cluster of communities surrounding the Port of Hampton Roads, Norfolk offers both peaceful shorelines and urban excitement. The metropolitan area, formed by Norfolk, Newport News, Hampton, Virginia Beach, Portsmouth and Chesapeake, is the most populous and most important commercial and industrial center in Virginia.

In 1682, Virginia's General Assembly bought 50 acres on the Elizabeth River from Nicholas Wise, a pioneer settler. By 1736, the town had become the largest in Virginia. Norfolk was an important colonial tobacco and naval supply port, carrying on trade with England and the West Indies. Many of the residents, who were chiefly Scots, became wealthy merchants.

Norfolk's value as a port facility also made it an important military objective. The city was shelled by the British in 1776 and later burned by the colonials to prevent a British takeover. After Virginia's secession from the Union in 1861, the federal command evacuated and burned the navy yard. On March 9, 1862, one of the few naval battles of the Civil War was fought in Hampton Roads channel, between the Union *Monitor* and the Confederate *Merrimac*. The battle was inconclusive, but Union forces recaptured Norfolk two months later and held it for the remainder of the war.

Today Norfolk houses the largest naval facility in the world and is the location of headquarters for the Atlantic Fleet. Several shore-based naval commands are located here. It is a bustling commercial center and has many historic and resort areas nearby to attract the tourist.

Business

Greater Norfolk has several manufacturing companies employing more than 1,000 people and many with 100 or more employees. It is also headquarters for Norfolk Southern, a billion-dollar railway corporation.

Shipping and shipbuilding are still major industries in the area, as are fishing, seafood processing, the production of consumer and industrial equipment, the military and tourism.

Norfolk International Airport is the world's only air facility located in a botanical garden.

Convention Facilities

Norfolk Scope is the name of the city's convention and cultural center. The complex houses four major structures: Convention Hall, with 8,900 permanent seats and 2,600 portable seats; Chrysler Hall, a 2,500-seat theater; Exhibit Hall, with 58,400 square feet of floor space (83,600 when combined with Convention Hall); and underground parking facilities for 600 vehicles. More than 3,700 additional parking spaces are within the immediate area. Scope also houses 24 smaller meeting rooms ranging in size from 154 to 1,369 square feet. Kitchen and

banquet facilities can cater to 5,100 persons, while a restaurant and lounge, with a capacity of 150, are also on the premises.

Sports and Recreation

Excellent beaches along the Chesapeake Bay are Norfolk's greatest recreational asset. A 7.5-mile stretch of sand and surf along East Ocean View Avenue offers opportunities for swimming, sunning, hiking, fishing and crabbing. The waters are gentle and perfect for children. There are several hotels, motels, apartments and cottages in the area.

Ocean beaches are within a 25-minute drive. Deep-sea fishing, sailing, swimming and boat cruises of one of the world's foremost harbors make this a magnificent water playground.

There are two public golf courses and a yacht and country club in the city.

Recreation and entertainment opportunities are also available in nearby Virginia Beach.

Entertainment

In Norfolk are the excellent Virginia Opera, the Virginia Symphony and the Virginia Stage Company, as well as other visual and performing arts groups. The Chrysler Museum has one of the most comprehensive art collections in the Southeast.

The International Azalea Festival is presented each April as a salute to the North Atlantic Treaty Organization, which is headquartered in Norfolk. Each June, Norfolk also pays tribute to the city's maritime past and present at its Harborfest celebration. The event takes place on the downtown waterfront and includes air shows, boat races, a parade of ships and many other events.

For year-round entertainment and activities there is The Waterside, Norfolk's multimillion-dollar festival marketplace. It contains more than 120 shops and eateries. The adjacent Town Point Park hosts after-work gatherings, outdoor concerts and lively ethnic festivals.

Historical Areas

The history of Norfolk is ever present. The Moses Myers House is a vintage town house built after the American Revolution and has a collection of the original family's silver, china and glass, especially interesting because President James Monroe was once a guest here and used these appointments. St Paul's Episcopal Church, built in 1739, was the lone structure spared by the British bombardment and fiery destruction of Norfolk on the eve of the American Revolution. A cannonball fired by the British remains embedded in the outer wall of the church. Outside, four centuries of graves fill the churchyard, which is shaded by giant oaks.

The Willoughby-Baylor House, a brick town house constructed in 1794, has been restored and furnished with authentic 18th-century articles, collected according to an inventory made after the owner's death in 1800. Virginia Beach has the Adam Thoroughgood House, built in the late 1600s and believed to be one of America's oldest brick houses.

More recent history is commemorated in the General Douglas MacArthur Memorial, burial place of the famous commander of Allied forces in the southwest Pacific. Four buildings house galleries of exhibits relating to his life.

Norfolk and its sister city, Portsmouth, make up one of the oldest naval facilities in the US. Norfolk is now the site of the Norfolk Naval Base. The largest naval installation in the world is home port for approximately 100 ships of the Atlantic Fleet, more than 20 aircraft squadrons and several shore-based commands. Naval facilities may also be seen from one of Norfolk's harbor tour boats.

Nauticus, The National Maritime Center, provides travelers with further insight into man's relationship with the oceans. Visitors can navigate a simulated ocean voyage, design a model ship or view actual researchers at work.

Sightseeing

Visitors to Norfolk will certainly want to take advantage of the historical sights to be seen in the famous triangle of the Virginia Peninsula, which includes Williamsburg, Jamestown and Yorktown.

Jamestown, established in 1607, was the first permanent English settlement in the New World. There are ruins of early houses, taverns and shops and reconstructions of the three ships that brought the colonists from England.

Williamsburg, capital of Virginia after it was moved from Jamestown, is the most extensive and well-executed restoration in the world. More than 400 buildings look as they did in colonial days. Over half of these are original structures; the rest are authentic reproductions. Costumed guides explain many fascinating details about colonial life in Williamsburg.

Stop first at the Colonial Williamsburg Visitor Center at Colonial Parkway and Virginia 132. It is open from 8 am to 9 pm in the summer and 8 am to 6 pm in the winter; it offers information, guidebooks, food and souvenirs. Buses leave continuously from here for the center of town. A 35-minute film, *Williamsburg: The Story of a Patriot,* is a good introduction to the entire restoration. A one-day general admission ticket includes the film, bus service and admission to several of the exhibition buildings.

Near Williamsburg is Busch Gardens, a family theme park with rides, shows and entertainment. The areas are arranged according to Old World countries.

At Yorktown, site of the final battle of the Revolution and the surrender by Lord Cornwallis, a self-guided motor drive circles the battlefield, encampment areas and the old town.

Nearby Virginia Beach offers resort facilities and nightlife, but also has the Virginia Marine Science Museum, with over 100,000 gallons of live aquaria and many hands-on educational exhibits.

General References

Founded: 1682 **Pop:** 261,229 **Elev:** 12 feet **Time zone:** Eastern **Area code:** 804

Phone Numbers

POLICE & FIRE: 911
FBI: 623-3111
POISON CONTROL CENTER: 800/552-6337
TIME: 622-9311 **WEATHER:** 666-1212

Information Sources

Norfolk Convention and Visitors Bureau, 236 E Plume St, 23510; 800/368-3097.
Festevents, 627-7809.

Transportation

AIRLINES: American; Continental; Delta; Northwest; TWA; United; USAir; and other commuter and regional airlines. For the most current airline schedules and information consult the *Official Airline Guide,* published twice monthly.
AIRPORT: Norfolk International Airport, 857-3351.
CAR RENTAL AGENCIES: (See Toll-Free Numbers) Avis 855-1944; Budget 855-8035; Hertz 857-1261; National 857-5385; Thrifty 855-5900.
PUBLIC TRANSPORTATION: Tidewater Regional Transit, 1500 Monticello Ave, 623-3222.
RAILROAD PASSENGER SERVICE: Amtrak 800/872-7245.

Newspaper

Virginian-Pilot/Ledger-Star.

Convention Facilities

Norfolk Scope, Scope Plaza, 441-2161.
Waterside Convention Center, 235 E Main St, 628-6501.

Recreation

Fishing

Harrison's Fishing Pier, 414 W Ocean View Ave, 587-9630.
Lynnhaven Inlet Fishing Pier, 2350 Starfish Rd, Virginia Beach, 481-7071.
Willoughby Bay Marina, 1651 Bayville St, 588-2663.

Cultural Facilities

Theaters & Concert Halls

Chrysler Hall, Scope Plaza, 441-2764; Virginia Symphony, 623-2310.
Harrison Opera House, Virginia Opera, 160 Virginia Beach Blvd, 623-1223.
Wells Theatre, Virginia Stage Company, 110 E Tazwell, 627-1234.

Museums

Fort Monroe Casemate Museum, 4 mi NE on I-64, near Hampton, 727-3973.
General Douglas MacArthur Memorial, MacArthur Square, City Hall Ave & Bank St, 441-2965.
Hampton Roads Naval Museum, in Nauticus, The National Maritime Center, 444-8971.
Hunter House Victorian Museum, 240 W Freemason St, 623-9814.
Mariners' Museum, at jct US 60 & J. Clyde Morris Blvd, Newport News, 595-0368.
Portsmouth Naval Shipyard Museum, 2 High St, Portsmouth, 393-8591.
US Army Transportation Museum, Bldg 300, Besson Hall, Fort Eustis, Newport News, 878-1182.
Virginia Marine Science Museum, 717 General Booth Blvd, Virginia Beach, E via I-64 & VA 44 to Pacific Ave, then N, 425-FISH.
War Memorial Museum of Virginia, 9285 Warwick Blvd in Huntington Park, on US 60, 247-8523.

Art Museums

Chrysler Museum, Olney Rd at Mowbray Arch, 664-6200.
Hermitage Foundation Museum, 7637 North Shore Rd, 423-2052.

Points of Interest

Historical

Adam Thoroughgood House, 1636 Parish Rd, Virginia Beach, 460-0007.
Cape Henry Memorial & Lighthouse, 10 mi E on US 60.
Colonial National Historical Park and Jamestown Settlement, Jamestown, SW of Williamsburg, 229-1607.
Colonial Williamsburg Visitors Center, about 45 mi NE off I-64, 800/447-8679.
Fort Norfolk, 810 Front St, 625-1720.
Lynnhaven House, Wishart Rd, Virginia Beach, 460-1688.
Moses Myers House, 323 E Freemason, at Bank St, 622-1211.
St Paul's Episcopal Church, 201 St Paul's Blvd, 627-4353.
Willoughby-Baylor House, 601 E Freemason St, 664-6200.
Yorktown Battlefield, surrounds village of Yorktown, about 30 mi NW via I-64 and US 17, 898-3400.

Other Attractions

Busch Gardens, on US 60, Williamsburg, 253-3350.
D'Art Center, 125 College Place, 625-4211.
Great Dismal Swamp National Wildlife Refuge, 31.00 Desert Rd, 986-3705.

Nauticus, The National Maritime Center, One Waterside Dr, 664-1000.
Norfolk Botanical Garden, Azalea Garden Rd, adj Norfolk Intl Airport, 441-5830.
Norfolk Naval Base, Hampton Blvd & I-564, 444-7955.
Ocean View Beach, foot of Granby St at N city limits.
Virginia Zoological Park, 3500 Granby St, 441-2706.
The Waterside, 333 Waterside Dr.

Sightseeing Tours

American Rover, docks behind The Waterside, 627-SAIL.
Gray Line bus tours, PO Box KE, Williamsburg, 23187; 853-6480.
Spirit of Norfolk, docks beside The Waterside, 627-7771.
Norfolk Naval Base Tour, Hampton Blvd & I-564, 444-7955.
Norfolk-Portsmouth Harbor Ferry, departs from The Waterside, 640-6300.
Norfolk Trolley Tours, 640-6300.

Annual Events

International Azalea Festival, Norfolk Botanical Gardens & downtown. Mid-Apr.
Ghent Arts Festival, Town Point Park, 627-7809. Mother's Day wkend.
Harborfest, downtown. 1st full wkend June.
Town Point Jazz Festival, Town Point Park, 627-7809. Early Aug.
(For further information contact the Convention & Visitors Bureau.)

Lodgings and Food

Motels

★ **COMFORT INN.** 8051 Hampton Blvd (23505), adj to Naval Base. 804/451-0000; FAX 804/451-8394. 120 rms, 2 story. S $56-$60; D $60; each addl $5; under 18 free. Crib free. TV; cable. Indoor pool; whirlpool. Complimentary continental bkfst, coffee. Restaurant nearby. Ck-out 11 am. Coin lndry. Refrigerators. Cr cds: A, D, DS, JCB, MC, V.

✔★ **ECONO LODGE-WEST OCEAN VIEW BEACH.** 9601 4th View St (23503). 804/480-9611; FAX 804/480-1307. 70 units, 3 story, 22 kits. Mid-May-Labor Day: S $49.95; D $59.95; each addl $5; kit. units $63.95; under 18 free; wkly rates; higher rates: some hols, special events; lower rates rest of yr. Pet accepted, some restrictions; $50 refundable. TV; cable, in-rm movies avail. Complimentary continental bkfst. Restaurant nearby. Ck-out 11 am. Coin lndry. Sauna, hot tub. Ocean; fishing pier. Beach nearby. Cr cds: A, C, D, DS, ER, JCB, MC, V.

★★ **HAMPTON INN-AIRPORT.** 1450 N Military Hwy (23502). 804/466-7474; FAX 804/466-7474, ext. 309. 130 units, 2 story. Late May-early Sept: S $51; D $61; under 18 free; lower rates rest of yr. Crib free. TV; cable. Pool. Continental bkfst. Restaurant opp 7 am-11 pm. Ck-out noon. Valet serv. Free airport transportation. Health club privileges. Cr cds: A, C, D, DS, MC, V.

★ **HOLIDAY SANDS.** 1330 E Ocean View Ave (23503). 804/583-2621; res: 800/525-5156; FAX 804/587-7540. 102 units, 2-5 story, 77 kits. Memorial Day-Labor Day: S, D $45-$90; each addl $5; suites $75-$95; kit. units $65-$95; 1 child under 12 free; lower rates rest of yr. Crib free. TV; cable. Pool. Complimentary coffee. Restaurant nearby. Ck-out 11 am. Coin lndry. Airport transportation avail. Refrigerators. Private patios, balconies. On beach. Cr cds: A, C, D, MC, V.

✔★ **SUPER 8.** 7940 Shore Dr (23518). 804/588-7888; FAX 804/588-7888, ext. 400. 74 units, 3 story, 10 kit. units. June-Labor Day: S, D $46.95-$51.33; suites, kit. units $72.88-$87.47; higher rates: July 4, Labor Day; lower rates rest of yr. Crib free. TV; cable. Complimentary continental bkfst. Restaurant nearby. Ck-out 11 am. Some refrigerators. Cr cds: A, D, DS, MC, V.

Hotels

★★★ **HILTON-NORFOLK AIRPORT.** 1500 N Military Hwy (23502), at Northampton Blvd, near Norfolk Intl Airport. 804/466-8000; FAX 804/466-8000, ext. 639. 250 rms, 6 story. S $89-$129; D $99-$134; each addl $15; suites $170-$360; under 12 free; wkly rates; some wkend rates. Crib $12. TV; cable. Pool; poolside serv. Coffee in rms. Restaurant 6:30 am-midnight. Bars noon-1 am; entertainment, dancing. Ck-out 1 pm. Convention facilities. Gift shop. Free valet parking. Free airport transportation. Lighted tennis. Exercise equipt; weights, bicycles, whirlpool, sauna. Minibars. *LUXURY LEVEL :* **CONCIERGE TOWER.** 27 rms. S $129; D $134; suites $270-$360. Concierge. Private lounge. Complimentary continental bkfst, refreshments. Cr cds: A, C, D, DS, ER, JCB, MC, V.

★★★ **MARRIOTT-WATERSIDE.** 235 E Main St (23510). 804/627-4200; FAX 804/628-6452. 405 rms, 24 story. S, D $104-$119; suites $250-$600. Crib free. Garage parking $8; valet $10. TV; cable. Indoor pool; poolside serv. Restaurant 6 am-2:30 pm, 5:30-11 pm. Bar 11-1 am; entertainment Tues-Thurs. Ck-out noon. Coin lndry. Convention facilities. Concierge. Gift shop. Exercise equipt; weight machine, treadmill, whirlpool, sauna. Game rm. Refrigerator, wet bar in suites. *LUXURY LEVEL :* 60 units, 1 suite, 3 floors. S, D $125; suite $600. In-rm movies. Private lounge, honor bar. Complimentary continental bkfst, refreshments. Cr cds: A, C, D, DS, ER, JCB, MC, V.

★★★ **OMNI WATERSIDE.** 777 Waterside Dr (23510), at St Paul's Blvd and I-264. 804/622-6664; FAX 804/625-8271. 446 rms, 10 story. S, D $128-$138; each addl $15; suites $150-$350; under 17 free; wkend packages. Crib free. Valet parking $8.50. TV. Pool; poolside serv. Restaurant 6:30 am-11 pm. Bars 11-2 am; entertainment, dancing. Ck-out noon. Convention facilities. Gift shop. Health club privileges. Dockage. Some refrigerators. Balconies. Atrium-like lobby. On harbor. *LUXURY LEVEL :* **OMNI CLUB.** 52 rms, 5 suites. S, D $138-$148; suites $250-$650. Concierge. Private lounge. Bathrm phones, refrigerators. Full wet bar in suites. Continental bkfst. Cr cds: A, C, D, DS, JCB, MC, V.

✔★★ **RAMADA-NORFOLK.** Box 1218 (23501), Granby & Freemason Sts. 804/622-6682; FAX 804/623-5949. 124 units, 8 story. S $55-$85; D $65-$95; each addl $10; suites $85-$150; under 12 free; wkend rates Nov-Feb. Crib free. Pet accepted, some restrictions; $15 non-refundable. TV; cable. Restaurant 6:30 am-2:30 pm, 5-10 pm. Bar from 5 pm. Ck-out noon. Meeting rms. Health club privileges. Cr cds: A, C, D, DS, MC, V.

★★ **SHERATON MILITARY CIRCLE.** 880 N Military Hwy (23502). 804/461-9192; FAX 804/461-8290. 208 rms, 14 story. S $64-$115; D $74-$123; each addl $10; suites $175; under 18 free; wkend rates. Crib free. TV. Pool. Restaurant 6:30 am-10:30 pm. Bar 11-1 am. Ck-out noon. Meeting rms. Barber, beauty shop. Free airport transportation. Private balconies. Shopping mall adj. Cr cds: A, C, D, DS, ER, JCB, MC, V.

Inn

★★★ **PAGE HOUSE.** 323 Fairfax Ave (23507). 804/625-5033; FAX 804/623-9451. 6 rms, 1 with shower only, 3 story, 2 suites. S $70-$115; D $75-$120; suites $125-$145. Children under 12 yrs only by arrangement. TV avail; cable. Complimentary continental bkfst, tea & coffee. Restaurant nearby. Rm serv. Ck-out 11 am, ck-in 4-6 pm. Refrigerator in suites. Totally restored Georgian-revival residence (1898) in historic district. Totally nonsmoking. Cr cds: A, MC, V.

Restaurants

★ **BIENVILLE GRILL.** 723 W 21st St. 804/625-5427. Hrs: 11:30 am-2:30 pm, 5:30-10 pm; Fri to 1 am; Sat 5:30 pm-1 am; Sun 5:30-9 pm. Closed Mon; some major hols. Bar. A la carte entrees: lunch, dinner $4.95-$17. Specializes in grilled seafood, steak, chicken. Jazz Thurs-Sat. Parking. Cr cds: A, D, DS, MC, V.

✔★★ **BISTRO 210.** 210 W York St. 804/622-3210. Hrs: 11:30 am-2:30 pm, 5:30-11 pm; Sat & Sun from 5:30 pm. Closed major hols. Bar. Semi-a la carte: lunch $5-$10, dinner $8.95-$15. Specializes in fresh local fish, vegetables. Own pastries, pasta. Totally nonsmoking. Cr cds: MC, V.

★ **ELLIOT'S.** 1421 Colley Ave. 804/625-0259. Hrs: 11 am-11 pm; Fri, Sat to midnight; Sun, Mon to 10 pm; Sun Brunch 11 am-2:30 pm. Closed Thanksgiving. Bar. Semi-a la carte: lunch $2.95-$6.95, dinner $2.95-$16.95. Sun brunch $5-$6.95. Child's meals. Specializes in pasta, fresh vegetables, veal. Parking. Outdoor dining. Cr cds: A, C, D, DS, MC, V.

★ ★ **FREEMASON ABBEY.** 209 W Freemason St. 804/622-3966. Hrs: 11:30 am-10 pm; Wed & Thurs to 11 pm; Fri & Sat to midnight; Sat & Sun brunch 11:30 am-2 pm. Closed Jan 1, Thanksgiving, Dec 25. Bar. Semi-a la carte: lunch $3.95-$7.95, dinner $9.95-$17.95. Sun brunch $4.95-$7.95. Child's meals. Specializes in whole Maine lobster, prime rib. Parking. Renovated church (1873); many antiques. Cr cds: A, MC, V.

✔★ **IL PORTO.** 333 Waterside Dr, at the Waterside complex. 804/625-5483. Hrs: 11 am-11 pm; Fri & Sat to midnight. Closed Thanksgiving, Dec 25. Res accepted. Italian menu. Bar to 1:30 am. A la carte entrees: lunch $3.25-$8, dinner $6.50-$15. Child's meals. Specializes in nautical pasta, veal. Own pasta. Entertainment (evenings). Outdoor dining. Overlooks river. Mediterranean cantina atmosphere; antiques, original artwork. Cr cds: A, DS, MC, V.

★ ★ **LA GALLERIA.** 120 College Place. 804/623-3939. Hrs: 5:30-11:30 pm; Mon to 11 pm; Fri 11:30 am-2:30 pm, 5:30 pm-midnight; Sat 5:30 pm-midnight. Closed Sun; Easter, Thanksgiving, Dec 25. Res accepted. Italian menu. Bar 4:30 pm-2 am. Semi-a la carte: Fri lunch $3.95-$7.95, dinner $11.95-$21.95. Child's meals. Specialty: salmon La Galleria. Own pasta, desserts. Valet parking. Outdoor dining. Modern decor. Cr cds: A, D, MC, V.

★ **MONASTERY.** 443 Granby St. 804/625-8193. Hrs: 11:30 am-2:30 pm, 5-10 pm; May-Labor Day from 5 pm. Closed Mon; Easter, Thanksgiving, Dec 25. Res accepted; required Fri, Sat. Czech, eastern European menu. Bar. Semi-a la carte: lunch $2.75-$8.50, dinner $4.75-$21. Specializes in roast duck, Wienerschnitzel, goulash. Antique mirrors, original works by local artists. Cr cds: A, MC, V.

★ **PHILLIPS WATERSIDE.** Waterside Dr, at the Waterside. 804/627-6600. Hrs: 11 am-10 pm; Sun brunch to 2 pm. Closed Thanksgiving, Dec 25. Bar. Semi-a la carte: lunch $4.95-$9, dinner $10-$24. Sun brunch $4.95-$8.95. Specialties: blackened alligator, crab cakes, herb-crusted tuna. Guitarist Fri & Sat evenings. Some antiques. Cr cds: A, D, DS, MC, V.

★ ★ **PIRANHA-AN EATING FRENZY.** 8180 Shore Dr, at Taylor's Landing Marina. 804/588-0100. Hrs: 11 am-10 pm; Fri & Sat to 11 pm; Sun brunch to 3 pm. Closed Jan 1, Dec 24 & 25. Res accepted; required wkends. Continental menu. Bar. A la carte entrees: lunch $3.95-$8.95, dinner $4.95-$16.95. Sun brunch $9.95. Child's meals. Specialties: paella for two, Trinidadian shrimp curry, cajun crawfish ettouffe. Own desserts. Parking. Outdoor dining. Overlooks marina. Cr cds: A, MC, V.

★ **REGGIE'S BRITISH PUB.** 333 Waterside Dr, at the Waterside. 804/627-3575. Hrs: 11:30 am-11 pm; Sun brunch noon-3 pm. Closed Thanksgiving, Dec 25. British menu. Bar. Semi-a la carte: lunch $5.95-$7.95, dinner $7.95-$17.95. Sun brunch $5.95-$6.95. Specializes in fish & chips, mixed grill, shepherd's pie. Outdoor dining. Overlooks Elizabeth River. Cr cds: A, C, D, MC, V.

★ ★ ★ **SHIP'S CABIN.** 4110 E Ocean View Ave. 804/362-2526. Hrs: 5:30-10 pm; Sun 5-9 pm. Res accepted. Bar. Wine list. Semi-a la carte: dinner $12.95-$21.95. Specializes in grilled fish & meat, live Maine lobster, local seafood. Own baking. Parking. View of bay. Fireplaces. Cr cds: A, C, D, MC, V.

✔★ **UNCLE LOUIE'S.** 132 E Little Creek Rd. 804/480-1225. Hrs: 8 am-11 pm; Fri & Sat to 2 am. Sun 10 am-10 pm. Closed Thanksgiving, Dec 25. Res accepted. Bar. Semi-a la carte: bkfst $3.50-$6.95, lunch, dinner $3.50-$15.95. Child's meals. Specializes in angus beef, fresh fish, specialty coffees. Parking. Cr cds: A, C, D, DS, MC, V.

Unrated Dining Spots

DOUMAR'S. 1919 Monticello Ave. 804/627-4163. Hrs: 8 am-11 pm. Closed Sun; major hols. A la carte entrees: bkfst, lunch, dinner 60¢-$4. Ice cream 90¢-$2.90. Specializes in sandwiches, ice cream. Hand-rolled cones. Parking. 1950s-style drive-in with addl seating inside. Abe Doumar invented the ice cream cone in 1904; his original cone making machine is on display here. Family-owned. No cr cds accepted.

GREEN GROCER TOO. 122 Bank St. 804/625-2455. Hrs: 7:30 am-3 pm. Closed Sat, Sun; major hols. Wine, beer. A la carte entrees: bkfst 75¢-$2.50. Semi-a la carte: lunch $3.50-$6.95. Specializes in white meat chicken salad, soups. Own baking, desserts. Cafe, wine bar and bakery. Sandwich kiosk with take-out serv, small dining area. Cr cds: MC, V.

Oklahoma City

Founded: 1889

Pop: 444,719

Elev: 1,207 feet

Time zone: Central

Area code: 405

On the morning of April 22, 1889, with the sound of a gunshot, a thunder of hooves and a billowing cloud of dust, what had been a barren prairie became a metropolis of 10,000. Oklahoma City was born in one morning when the federal government opened to settlement land that had previously been granted to five Native American tribes. Today, while continuing its commitment to development, the community is holding on to its heritage, as a wealth of museums and monuments attest.

Oklahoma City was incorporated in 1890. By 1910, the population had grown to more than 64,000, making Oklahoma City the largest city in the state. In December, 1928, oil was discovered here. In fact, the city stands in the middle of an oil field—there are even oil wells on the lawn of the capitol. Oklahoma City now produces large quantities of high-gravity oil and manufactures oil-well equipment as well.

Business

The city's industries produce fabricated iron and steel, furniture, tires, electrical equipment, electronics, aircraft and automobiles. Research into aeronautical development and space medicine also takes place here. Tinker Air Force Base is one of the city's major employers.

Oklahoma City's stockyard and meat-packing plants are the largest in the state; in fact, the city claims to be the nation's leading cattle market. Oklahoma City is also a grain-milling and cotton-processing center.

Convention Facilities

For conventions, sports, meetings, exhibits, entertainment, social gatherings and religious presentations, the Myriad Convention Center provides a variety of accommodations.

The Great Hall has nearly 17,000 square feet of space, which can be divided into halves by electrically operated soundproof walls. There is also an 80-by-40-foot stage with offstage dressing room facilities. When used as an auditorium, the hall's capacity is 2,200; as a dining room, 1,500; as a ballroom, 1,200.

The center's exhibition hall has 140,000 square feet of space and can be divided into as many as 8 smaller areas, each with its own utility, light and sound services. A stage area and arena floor are also available.

On the upper concourse level, 24 meeting rooms are designed to accommodate between 50 and 400 people. These rooms are also suited for club luncheons or dinners, parties, convention committee sessions, lectures or seminars.

Sports and Recreation

Oklahoma City offers a wide variety of sporting events to both spectators and players alike. The 89ers, AAA farm team for the Texas Rangers, start swinging their bats here every spring. Throughout the year, Oklahoma City is host to many world class, state and regional horse shows, thus earning the title "horse show capital of the world."

The Myriad Convention Center Arena, with a permanent hockey rink, a basketball floor and a portable indoor track, can host just about any indoor sport, including rodeos. The total seating capacity is 15,600, of which 12,000 are permanent seats. The arena seats 13,800 for basketball and 13,400 for hockey.

Many challenging golf courses, most of which are open year-round, dot the metro area. Tennis players also will find an abundance of both indoor and outdoor courts. Water lovers will be pleased to know that Oklahoma has more man-made shoreline than the entire Atlantic coast of the US; Oklahoma City has a good share of that shoreline. There are several lakes and recreation areas within the metropolitan district that offer facilities for fishermen, sailors, swimmers, horseback riders and campers.

Entertainment

The city's many professional theaters provide audiences with everything from the traditional to the avant-garde. The Lyric Theatre, a professional summer stock company, presents musicals from mid-June through August. Ballet Oklahoma, the city's professional ballet company, dances from October through April.

On Friday and Saturday nights, the doors of the Oklahoma Opry swing open for live country and western music. There are also taverns and clubs throughout the city that cater to a variety of musical tastes.

Historical Areas

The Oklahoma Heritage Center is concerned with the preservation of the state's past and the direction of its future. The center is located in the mansion of Judge R.A. Hefner, who in 1970 gave his house to the Oklahoma Heritage Association for its permanent headquarters and for the public's enjoyment.

The Heritage Center includes Oklahoma Hall of Fame Galleries, exhibiting portraits, bronzes and photographs of prominent Oklahomans; Oklahoma Heritage Galleria, exhibiting art and displays pertaining to the state's history; Shepherd Oklahoma Heritage Library, housing 10,000 volumes of Oklahoma-oriented books and periodicals; and the Oklahoma Heritage Archives, containing historical documents, letters and papers. Also included are the Hefner Memorial Chapel and Chapel Garden, Anthony Oklahoma Heritage Gardens and the Robert A. Hefner, Jr. Conservatory.

The National Cowboy Hall of Fame and Western Heritage Center contains statuary and paintings by Remington and Russell, a Rodeo Hall of Fame and the West of Yesterday Gallery, featuring life-size re-creations of early Native American and pioneer life. This museum, sponsored by 17 Western states, also contains exhibits explaining the development of the West, with sight and sound, and an animated relief map depicting the nation's westward expansion.

Sightseeing

Oklahoma City is the home of several art museums and galleries. Exhibits include modern paintings and sculpture and collections of art and artifacts from Egypt, Mesopotamia, the Orient and pre-Columbian America.

Other sights to see in Oklahoma City are the Kirkpatrick Center, which houses the Kirkpatrick Planetarium; the Airspace Museum; the International Photography Hall of Fame and Museum; OMNIPLEX, featuring both art and hands-on exhibits; and the Harn Homestead and 1889er Museum. Not to be missed are the Myriad Botanical Gardens, a beautiful landscaped lake retreat in the heart of downtown Oklahoma City.

Also of interest are the neoclassical State Capitol Building, with working oil wells on its grounds; the Oklahoma Historical Society Building, which contains an extensive collection of Native American material, as well as exhibits on the history of the state; the Civic Center, which houses the Music Hall; the National Softball Hall of Fame and Museum; the Oklahoma Firefighters Museum, which displays the state's first fire station and antique firefighting equipment; and the Oklahoma City Zoo, which features a dolphin and sea lion show.

Sightseers who are interested in shopping will find an interesting variety here—from authentic Western wear and Native American art and jewelry at Stockyards City, to designer jeans, dinner jackets and diamonds at the posh 50 Penn Place. Shopping malls, department stores, boutiques and antique shops throughout the city cater to a whole range of needs, wants and whims.

General References

Founded: 1889 Pop: 444,719 Elev: 1,207 feet Time zone: Central
Area code: 405

Phone Numbers

POLICE & FIRE: 911
FBI: 842-7471
POISON CONTROL CENTER: 271-5454
TIME: 599-1234 **WEATHER:** 478-3377

Information Sources

Oklahoma City Convention and Visitors Bureau, 123 Park Ave, 73102; 297-8912 or 800/225-5652.
Oklahoma Tourism and Recreation Department, 500 Will Rogers Bldg, 73105; 521-2409.
Oklahoma City Chamber of Commerce, 123 Park Ave, 73102; 278-8900.
Department of Parks & Recreation, 297-3882.

Transportation

AIRLINES: American; Continental; Delta; Northwest; Southwest; TWA; United; and other commuter and regional airlines. For the most current airline schedules and information consult the *Official Airline Guide*, published twice monthly.
AIRPORT: Will Rogers World, 681-5311.
CAR RENTAL AGENCIES: (See Toll-Free Numbers) Avis 685-7781; Budget 681-4977; Dollar 681-0151; Hertz 681-2341; National 685-7726; Thrifty 682-5433.
PUBLIC TRANSPORTATION: Central Oklahoma Transportation & Parking Authority, 300 SW 7th St, 235-7433.

Newspapers

Daily Oklahoman; The Journal-Record.

Convention Facilities

Myriad Convention Center, 1 Myriad Gardens, 232-8871.
State Fair Park, Fair Park, 500 Land Rush St, 948-6700.

Sports & Recreation

Major Sports Facilities
All Sports Stadium, state fairgrounds, 946-8989.
Myriad Convention Center Arena, Sheridan & Robinson Aves, 232-8871.

Racetrack
Remington Park, off I-35 at NE 50th St & Martin Luther King, Jr Blvd, 424-9000 or 800/456-9000 (horse racing).

Cultural Facilities

Theaters
Carpenter Square Theatre, 400 W Main St, 232-6500.
Jewel Box Theatre, 3700 N Walker Ave, 521-1786.
Lyric Theatre, 2501 N Blackwelder Ave, 524-7111.

Concert Hall
Civic Center Music Hall, 201 Channing Square, 297-2584.

Museums
Enterprise Square, USA, 2501 E Memorial Rd, 425-5030.
45th Infantry Division Museum, 2145 NE 36th St, 424-5313.
Harn Homestead & 1889er Museum, 313 NE 16th St, 235-4058.
International Photography Hall of Fame & Museum, Kirkpatrick Center, 424-4055.
Kirkpatrick Center, 2100 NE 52nd St, 427-5461.
Museum of Natural History, 1335 Asp Ave, Oklahoma University campus, Norman, 325-4711.
National Cowboy Hall of Fame & Western Heritage Center, 1700 NE 63rd St, 478-2250.
National Softball Hall of Fame and Museum, 2801 NE 50th St, 424-5266.
Oklahoma Air Space Museum, Kirkpatrick Center, 427-5461.
Oklahoma Firefighters Museum, 2716 NE 50th St, 424-3440.
Oklahoma Heritage Center, 201 NW 14th St, 235-4458.
OMNIPLEX, NE 52nd St & Martin Luther King, Jr Blvd, 424-5545.
Red Earth Indian Center, Kirkpatrick Center, 427-5228.
State Museum of History, 2100 N Lincoln Blvd, 521-2491.

Art Museums and Galleries
ArtsPlace, 20 W Main, downtown, 232-1787.
Oklahoma City Art Museum, 3113 Pershing Blvd, 946-4477.
Oklahoma Indian Art Gallery, 2335 SW 44th St, 685-6162.

Points of Interest

Historical
Governor's Mansion, 820 NE 23rd St, 521-2342.
Overholser Mansion, 405 NW 15th St, 528-8485.

Other Attractions
Enterprise Square, 2501 E Memorial Rd, 425-5030.
Frontier City, 11501 NE Expy (I-35), 478-2412.
Garden Exhibition Building and Horticulture Gardens, 3400 NW 36th St, 943-0827.
Heritage Place (Horse Sale Pavilion), 2829 S MacArthur Blvd, 682-4551.
Kirkpatrick Planetarium, Kirkpatrick Center, 424-5545.

Myriad Botanical Gardens, Reno & Robinson Sts, downtown, 297-3995.
Oklahoma City Zoo, 2101 NE 50th St, 424-3344.
Oklahoma National Stockyards, 2500 Exchange Ave, 235-8675.
State Capitol Building, NE 23rd St & Lincoln Blvd, 521-2011.
State Fair Park, NW 10th St & N May Ave, 948-6700.
White Water Bay, 3908 W Reno, 943-9687.

Sightseeing Tour

Territorial Tours, 1636 SW 79th Terrace, 681-6432.

Annual Events

International Finals Rodeo, Myriad Convention Center, 297-3000. Dec.
Festival of the Arts, downtown. Mid-Apr.
State Fair of Oklahoma, Fair Park, NW 10th St & N May Ave, 948-6700. Late Sept-early Oct.

World Championship Quarter Horse Show, state fairgrounds, NW 10th St & N May Ave. Mid-Nov.
(For further information contact the Chamber of Commerce or Department of Parks & Recreation, 297-3882.)

City Neighborhoods

Many of the restaurants, unrated dining establishments and some lodgings listed under Oklahoma City include neighborhoods as well as exact street addresses. Geographic descriptions of Downtown and Bricktown are given, followed by a table of restaurants arranged by neighborhood.

Bricktown: South of Sheridan Ave, west of Oklahoma Ave, east of the railroad tracks and along California St from Oklahoma Ave.
Downtown: South of 10th St, west of Walnut St, north of I-40/US 270 and east of Classen Blvd. **North of Downtown** North of 10th St. **South of Downtown** South of I-40/US 270.

Lodgings and Food

OKLAHOMA CITY RESTAURANTS
BY NEIGHBORHOOD AREAS

(For full description, see alphabetical listings under Restaurants)

NORTH OF DOWNTOWN

Classen Grill. 5124 N Classen Blvd

Coach House. 6437 Avondale Dr

Eagle's Nest. 5900 Mosteller Dr

Eddy's of Oklahoma City. 4227 N Meridian Ave

Furrs Cafeteria. 2842 NW 63rd St

Harry's American Grill & Bar. 4540 NW 23rd St

Jamil's. 4910 N Lincoln

La Baguette. 7408 N May Ave

Lady Classen Cafeteria. 6903 N May Ave (OK 74)

Michael's Supper Club. 1601 Northwest Expy (OK 3)

Sleepy Hollow. 1101 NE 50th St

Waterford (The Waterford Hotel). 6300 Waterford Blvd

SOUTH OF DOWNTOWN

Aloha Garden. 2219 SW 74th St

WEST OF DOWNTOWN

Applewoods. 4301 SW 3rd St

Molly Murphy's House of Fine Repute. 1100 S Meridian Ave

Shorty Small's. 4500 W Reno

Texanna Red's. 4600 W Reno

Note: *When a listing is located in a town that does not have its own city heading, it will appear under the city nearest to its location. In these cases, the address and town appear in parenthesis immediately following the name of the establishment.*

Motels

★ ★ ★ **BEST WESTERN-SADDLEBACK INN.** *4300 SW 3rd St (73108), 1/2 blk NE of I-40 Meridian Ave exit, west of downtown. 405/947-7000; FAX 405/948-7636.* 220 rms, 2-3 story. S $53-$60; D $60-$67; each addl $7; suites $68-$75; under 17 free; wkend rates. Crib free. TV; cable. Heated pool; poolside serv. Restaurant 6 am-2 pm, 5-10 pm; Sat, Sun to 9 pm. Rm serv. Bar 4 pm-midnight. Ck-out noon. Coin lndry. Meeting rms. Bellhops. Valet serv. Gift shop. Sundries. Free airport transportation. Exercise equipt; weights, bicycles, whirlpool, sauna. Southwestern decor. Cr cds: A, C, D, DS, MC, V.

[D] [≈] [✗] [⊠] [🔥] [SC]

✔★ **COMFORT INN.** *4017 NW 39th St Expy (US 66/270) (73112), north of downtown. 405/947-0038; FAX 405/946-7450.* 112 rms, 2 story, 15 kit. units. S, D $42-$55; each addl $6; kit. units $52-$62; under 18 free. Crib free. Pet accepted, some restrictions. TV; cable. Pool. Complimentary continental bkfst, coffee in rms. Restaurant adj open 24 hrs. Ck-out noon. Coin lndry. Meeting rms. Valet serv. Sundries. Some refrigerators. Cr cds: A, C, D, DS, ER, JCB, MC, V.

[D] [👆] [≈] [⊠] [🔥] [SC]

★ ★ ★ **COURTYARD BY MARRIOTT.** *4301 Highline Blvd (73108), near Will Rogers World Airport, west of downtown. 405/946-6500; FAX 405/946-7638.* 149 rms, 3 story. S $75; D $85; suites $97-$107; under 12 free; wkend rates. TV; cable. Heated pool. Complimentary coffee in rms. Restaurant 6:30-11 am; wkends 7-11 am. Bar 4-11 pm. Ck-out 1 pm. Coin lndry. Meeting rms. Valet serv. Sundries. Free airport transportation. Exercise equipt; weight machine, bicycles, whirlpool. Refrigerator in suites. Balconies. Cr cds: A, C, D, DS, MC, V.

[D] [≈] [✗] [✈] [⊠] [🔥] [SC]

✔★ **DAYS INN-NORTHWEST.** *2801 NW 39th St (73112), north of downtown. 405/946-0741; FAX 405/942-0181.* 191 rms, 2 story. S $39-$44; D $44-$49; each addl $5; suites $75; under 16 free; wkend rates. Crib free. TV; cable. Pool. Restaurant 6:30 am-1:30 pm, 5-10 pm. Rm serv. Bar 4 pm-midnight. Ck-out 11 am. Coin lndry. Meeting rms. Valet serv. Sundries. Airport transportation avail. Some bathrm phones, refrigerators. Cr cds: A, C, D, DS, MC, V.

[D] [≈] [⊠] [🔥] [SC]

✔★ **ECONO LODGE.** *820 S MacArthur Blvd (73128), near Will Rogers World Airport, west of downtown. 405/947-8651; FAX 405/942-6792.* 100 rms. S $27.95-$30.95; D $34.95-$38.95; each addl $5; under 18 free; wkly rates. Crib free. Pet accepted, some restrictions; $20. TV; cable. Pool. Complimentary coffee in lobby. Restaurant adj open 24 hrs. Bar 11-2 am; Sat, Sun from 6 pm. Ck-out 11 am. Coin lndry. Free airport, bus depot transportation. Cr cds: A, C, D, DS, JCB, MC, V.

[D] [👆] [≈] [✗] [⊠] [🔥] [SC]

★ ★ **HAMPTON INN.** *1905 S Meridian Ave (73108), 1 mi S of I-40, near Will Rogers World Airport, west of downtown. 405/682-2080; FAX 405/682-3662.* 134 rms, 3 story. S $56-$60; D $63-$67; each addl $7; suites $73; under 18 free; wkend rates. Crib free. Pet accepted, some restrictions. TV; cable. Pool. Complimentary continental bkfst. Ck-out noon. Meeting rms. Valet serv. Free airport transportation. Some refrigerators. Some private patios, balconies. Cr cds: A, C, D, DS, ER, JCB, MC, V.

[D] [👆] [≈] [≈] [⊠] [🔥] [SC]

★ **HOLIDAY INN NORTH.** *12001 NE Expressway (73131), I-35 exit 137. 405/478-0400; FAX 405/478-2774.* 210 rms, 2 story. June-Aug: S $55-$60; D $60-$65; each addl $5; suites $75-$125; under 19 free; higher rates special events; lower rates rest of yr. Crib free. Pet accepted. TV. Pool; sauna. Playground. Restaurant 6 am-2 pm, 5-10 pm. Rm serv. Bar 5 pm-midnight. Ck-out noon. Coin lndry. Meeting rms. Bellhops. Game rm. Lawn games. Cr cds: A, C, D, DS, JCB, MC, V.

[D] [👆] [≈] [⊠] [🔥] [SC]

★ ★ **LA QUINTA.** *8315 S I-35 (73149), 7 mi SE on I-35, exit 121A, south of downtown. 405/631-8661; FAX 405/631-1892.* 121 rms, 2 story. S, D $46-$58; each addl $8; under 18 free. Crib free. TV; cable. Pool. Complimentary bkfst in lobby. Restaurant opp open 24 hrs. Ck-out noon. Meeting rms. Valet serv. Cr cds: A, C, D, DS, MC, V.

[D] [≈] [⊠] [🔥] [SC]

★ ★ **RAMADA INN-AIRPORT WEST.** *800 S Meridian Ave (73108), west of downtown. 405/942-0040; FAX 405/942-0638.* 171 rms, 2 story. S $44-$48; D $50-$58; suites $75; each addl $8; under 18 free. Pet accepted, some restrictions. TV; cable. Pool; wading pool, poolside serv. Restaurant 6:30 am-midnight. Rm serv. Bar from 10 am. Ck-out noon. Meeting rms. Free airport, bus depot transportation. Cr cds: A, C, D, DS, MC, V.

[D] [👆] [≈] [⊠] [🔥] [SC]

★ ★ **RESIDENCE INN BY MARRIOTT.** *4361 W Reno Ave (73107), 2 blks NE of I-40 Meridian exit, west of downtown. 405/942-4500; FAX 405/942-7777.* 135 kit. suites, 1-2 story. 1-bedrm suites

$95; 2-bedrm suites $115. Crib free. Pet accepted, some restrictions; $25 and $6 per day. TV; cable. Heated pool; whirlpool. Complimentary continental bkfst. Complimentary coffee in rms. Ck-out noon. Coin lndry. Meeting rms. Valet serv. Airport transportation. Health club privileges. Refrigerators, fireplaces. Private patios, balconies. Picnic tables, grills. Cr cds: A, C, D, DS, JCB, MC, V.

[D] [icons] SC

★ ★ **RICHMOND SUITES HOTEL.** 1600 Richmond Square (73118), north of downtown. 405/840-1440; res: 800/843-1440; FAX 405/843-4272. 50 suites, 2 story. S, D $80-$125; under 18 free; wkend, hol rates. Crib $5. Pet accepted, some restrictions; $50. TV; cable. Pool. Complimentary continental bkfst. Complimentary coffee in rms. Restaurant 11:30 am-2 pm, 6-10 pm; Sat from 6 pm; closed Sun. Rm serv. Bar, closed Sun; pianist. Meeting rms. Free airport transportation. Refrigerators, minibars. Cr cds: A, C, D, DS, MC, V.

[D] [icons] SC

✔ ★ **RODEWAY INN.** 4601 SW 3rd (73128), west of downtown. 405/947-2400; FAX 405/947-2931. 184 rms, 2 story. S $38; D $42; each addl $4; suites $65-$125; under 17 free. Crib free. Pet accepted. TV; cable. Pool. Complimentary continental bkfst. Restaurant adj open 24 hrs. Ck-out noon. Coin lndry. Valet serv. Free airport transportation. Cr cds: A, C, D, DS, JCB, MC, V.

[D] [icons] SC

Motor Hotels

★ ★ **BEST WESTERN SANTA FE INN.** 6101 N Santa Fe (73118), I-44 exit 127. 405/848-1919; FAX 405/840-1581. 96 rms, 3 story. S $49-$54; D $56-$61; each addl $7; suites $65-$85; under 12 free. Crib free. Pet accepted, some restrictions; $50 deposit. TV; cable. Pool; whirlpool. Complimentary coffee in rms. Complimentary full bkfst. Restaurant 6 am-1:30 pm, 5-9 pm. Rm serv. Bar 5 pm-midnight. Ck-out 11 am. Meeting rms. Valet serv. Health club privileges. Refrigerator in suites. Cr cds: A, C, D, DS, JCB, MC, V.

[D] [icons] SC

★ ★ ★ **CLARION.** 4345 N Lincoln Blvd (73105). 405/528-2741; FAX 405/525-8185. 68 rms, 3 story. S $88; D $98; under 18 free; wkend rates. Crib $10. TV; cable. Pool; wading pool, poolside serv. Complimentary continental bkfst. Restaurant 6:30 am-9 pm. Rm serv to 10 pm. Bar 11-2 am. Ck-out noon. Meeting rms. Bellhops. Concierge. Gift shop. Valet serv. Lighted tennis. Exercise equipt; weight machine, stair machine, sauna. Minibars. Cr cds: A, C, D, DS, JCB, MC, V.

[icons] SC

★ **COMFORT INN.** 4445 N Lincoln Blvd (73105), off I-44. 405/528-6511; FAX 405/528-8185. 240 rms, 7 story. S $49-$69; D $55-$75; each addl $6; suites $125-$175; under 18 free; wkend rates. Crib free. TV; cable. Pool; wading pool, poolside serv. Complimentary continental bkfst. Restaurant 6:30 am-9 pm. Rm serv. Bar 11-2 am. Ck-out noon. Meeting rms. Bellhops. Gift shop. Valet serv. Lighted tennis. Exercise equipt; weight machine, stair machine, sauna. Cr cds: A, C, D, DS, MC, V.

[D] [icons] SC

★ ★ ★ **RADISSON.** 401 S Meridian Ave (73108), at I-40, Meridian Ave exit, west of downtown. 405/947-7681; FAX 405/947-4253. 509 rms, 2 story. S $59-$79; D $69-$89; each addl $10; suites $175-$190; family, wkend rates. Crib free. Pet accepted, some restrictions. TV; cable. 4 pools, 1 indoor; poolside serv. Restaurants 6 am-11 pm. Rm serv. Bars 11:30-2 am; entertainment, dancing. Ck-out noon. Meeting rms. Bellhops. Sundries. Gift shop. Barber shop. Free airport transportation. Tennis. Paddle tennis. Exercise equipt; weights, bicycles, whirlpool, sauna. Bathrm phone, wet bar in townhouse suites; whirlpool in some suites. Cr cds: A, C, D, DS, ER, JCB, MC, V.

[D] [icons] SC

Hotels

★ ★ **CENTURY CENTER.** One N Broadway (73102), downtown. 405/235-2780; FAX 405/272-0369. 399 rms, 15 story. S, D $89; each addl $10; suites $150-$350; wkend rates. Crib free. Garage $3.75. TV; cable. Pool. Bar 11-2 am. Ck-out noon. Convention facilities. Valet parking. **LUXURY LEVEL** . 55 rms, 7 suites, 2 floors. S, D $109; suites $175-$350. Concierge. Private lounge. Complimentary bkfst, refreshments, newspaper. Cr cds: A, C, D, DS, ER, MC, V.

[D] [icons] SC

★ ★ ★ **EMBASSY SUITES.** 1815 S Meridian Ave (73108), west of downtown. 405/682-6000; FAX 405/682-9835. 236 suites, 6 story. S, D $115-$125; each addl $10; under 12 free; wkend rates. Crib free. Pet accepted. TV; cable. Indoor pool. Complimentary bkfst. Complimentary coffee in rms. Restaurant 6 am-10 pm; Sat, Sun from 6:30 am. Bar 4 pm-2 am. Ck-out noon. Meeting rms. Gift shop. Airport transportation. Exercise equipt; weights, bicycles, whirlpool, steam rm, sauna. Refrigerators, wet bars. Some balconies. Atrium. Cr cds: A, C, D, DS, MC, V.

[D] [icons] SC

★ ★ **FIFTH SEASON.** 6200 N Robinson Ave (73118), north of downtown. 405/843-5558; res: 800/682-0049 (exc OK), 800/522-9458 (OK); FAX 405/840-3410. 202 rms, 3 story, 27 suites. S, D $65-$85; each addl $10; suites $79-$150; under 12 free; wkend rates; race track plans. Crib free. Pet accepted, some restrictions. TV; cable. Indoor pool; poolside serv. Complimentary full bkfst. Restaurant 6:30 am-2 pm, 5-10 pm. Bar 3 pm-2 am. Ck-out noon. Coin lndry. Meeting rms. Gift shop. Free airport transportation. Health club privileges. Refrigerator, minibar in suites. Cr cds: A, C, D, DS, JCB, MC, V.

[D] [icons] SC

★ ★ ★ **HILTON-NORTHWEST.** 2945 Northwest Expy (OK 3) (73112), west of downtown. 405/848-4811; FAX 405/843-4829. 212 rms, 9 story. S $80-$105; D $90-$115; each addl $10; suites $175-$299; under 18 free; wkend rates. Crib free. TV; cable Heated pool; poolside serv. Complimentary coffee in rms. Restaurant 6 am-10 pm. Bar 4 pm-midnight; Fri, Sat to 1 am; Sun to 10 pm; pianist exc Sun. Ck-out noon. Meeting rms. Free airport transportation. Exercise equipt; weights, bicycles. Refrigerator in suites. Cr cds: A, C, D, DS, ER, MC, V.

[D] [icons] SC

★ ★ ★ **MARRIOTT.** 3233 Northwest Expy (OK 3) (73112), northwest of downtown. 405/842-6633; FAX 405/842-3152. 354 rms, 15 story. S, D $129-$139; suites $175-$350; studio rms $89; under 18 free; wkend rates. Crib free. Pet accepted, some restrictions. TV; cable. Indoor/outdoor pool. Restaurant 6:30 am-11 pm. Bar 4 pm-2 am, Sun to midnight; entertainment Sat; dancing. Ck-out noon. Coin lndry. Convention facilities. Concierge. Gift shop. Exercise equipt; weights, bicycles. Health club privileges. Some balconies. **LUXURY LEVEL :** 23 rms. S $139; D $149. Private lounge. Complimentary continental bkfst, refreshments. Cr cds: A, C, D, DS, ER, JCB, MC, V.

[D] [icons] SC

★ ★ **RAMADA EDMOND.** (930 E 2nd St, Edmond 73034) 10 mi N, 1¹/₂ mi W of I-35 exit Edmond-2nd St, opp University of Central OK. 405/341-3577; res: 800/322-4686; FAX 405/341-9279. 145 rms, 8 story. S $55-$65; D $60-$75; each addl $10; suites $85-$150; under 18 free; wkend rates. Crib free. Pet accepted, some restrictions. TV; cable. Pool; whirlpool. Complimentary continental bkfst. Restaurant 6 am-2 pm, 5-9:30 pm. Bar 4 pm-midnight, Sat to 1:30 am, Sun 4-10 pm; entertainment Fri & Sat, dancing. Ck-out 11 am. Meeting rms. 18-hole golf privileges, greens fee $12, pro. Cr cds: A, C, D, DS, MC, V.

[D] [icons] SC

THE WATERFORD HOTEL. (New general manager, therefore not rated) 6300 Waterford Blvd (73118), north of downtown. 405/848-4782; res: 800/992-2009; FAX 405/843-9161. 197 rms, 9 story. S $118-$128; D $128-$142; each addl $10; suites $145-$750;

under 18 free; honeymoon, wkend packages. Crib free. TV; cable. Heated pool; poolside serv. Restaurant (see WATERFORD). Bar 11-2 am; entertainment, dancing. Ck-out noon. Concierge. Airport transportation; free transportation to Remington Park race track. Lighted tennis. Exercise rm; instructor, weights, bicycles, whirlpool, sauna, steam rm. Massage. Squash. Bathrm phones; some refrigerators. Some balconies. **LUXURY LEVEL : V.I.P. FLOOR.** 18 rms, 4 suites. S $145; D $155; suites $165 $750. Deluxe toiletry amenities. Complimentary bkfst, refreshments, newspaper, shoeshine. Cr cds: A, C, D, DS, MC, V.

Restaurants

✔★★ **ALOHA GARDEN.** 2219 SW 74th St, in Walnut Square Shopping Center, I-240 exit Pennsylvania Ave S, south of downtown. 405/686-0288. Hrs: 11 am-9:30 pm; Fri, Sat to 10:30 pm; Sun brunch 11 am-2:30 pm. Closed major hols. Res accepted. Chinese, Amer menu. Bar. Semi-a la carte: lunch $3.95-$5.50, dinner $4.25-$13.95. Sun brunch $6.25. Buffet: lunch $4.95, dinner (Fri, Sat) $6.95. Child's meals. Specializes in seafood combinations, willow beef. Own sauces. Oriental decor. Cr cds: A, C, D, DS, MC, V.

D

★★ **APPLEWOODS.** 4301 SW 3rd St, west of downtown. 405/947-8484. Hrs: 11 am-2 pm, 5-10 pm; Fri to 11 pm; Sat 4-11 pm; Sun 11 am-3 pm, 4:30-10 pm. Closed major hols. Bar. Semi-a la carte: lunch $3.95-$8.95, dinner $8.95-$17. Buffet: lunch (Sun) $6.50. Child's meals. Specializes in pot roast, pork chops, hot apple dumplings. Magician on wkends. Cr cds: A, C, D, DS, MC, V.

D

★★★ **COACH HOUSE.** 6437 Avondale Dr, north of downtown. 405/842-1000. Hrs: 11:30 am-2 pm, 6-10 pm. Closed Sun; major hols. Res accepted. French, Amer menu. Serv bar. A la carte entrees: lunch $6-$12, dinner $18-$24. Specializes in rack of lamb, Dover sole, Grand Marnier souffle. Parking. Formal dining. Cr cds: A, C, D, DS, MC, V.

D

★★★ **EAGLE'S NEST.** 5900 Mosteller Dr, top of United Founder's Tower, north of downtown. 405/840-5655. Hrs: 11 am-2 pm, 6-10 pm; Fri to 10:30 pm; Sat 6-10:30 pm; Sun 6-9 pm. Closed major hols. Res accepted. Bar to midnight. Semi-a la carte: lunch $4.95-$9.75, dinner $14.95-$25.95. Child's meals. Specializes in steak, fresh seafood. Classical pianist Wed, Thurs & Sun; trio Fri & Sat. Parking. Scenic view of city; revolving room. Family-owned. Cr cds: A, C, D, DS, MC, V.

D

★★★ **EDDY'S OF OKLAHOMA CITY.** 4227 N Meridian Ave, north of downtown. 405/787-2944. Hrs: 5-10:30 pm; Fri, Sat to 11 pm; Easter, Mother's Day & Father's Day 11 am-8:30 pm. Closed Sun; Thanksgiving, Dec 25. Semi-a la carte: dinner $9.95-$18.95. Child's meals. Specialties: Lebanese hors d'oeuvres, steak, seafood. Own pastries. Parking. Display of Jack Riley bronze Western sculpture. Family-owned. Cr cds: A, C, D, DS, MC, V.

D

★★ **GREYSTONE.** (1 N Sooner Rd, Edmond) 10 mi N on I-35 to exit 141, west to Sooner Rd, turn right. 405/340-4400. Hrs: 11 am-2 pm, 4:45-9 pm; Fri, Sat to 10 pm; early-bird dinner Tues-Fri 4:45-6:30 pm; Sun brunch 10 am-2:30 pm. Closed Mon; July 4, Dec 25. Res accepted. Continental menu. Bar. Semi-a la carte: lunch $5.75-$9.95, dinner $10.75-$42.50. Sun brunch $11.95. Child's meals. Specializes in steak, lobster. Valet parking. Elegant dining in quiet atmosphere. Cr cds: A, C, D, DS, MC, V.

D

★★ **JAMIL'S.** 4910 N Lincoln, north of downtown. 405/525-8352. Hrs: 11 am-2 pm, 5-10 pm; Fri, Sat to 11 pm; Sun 5-10 pm. Closed most major hols. Res accepted. Bar. Complete meals: lunch

$3.95-$7.95, dinner $9.95-$26.95. Child's meals. Specializes in steak. Parking. Antiques from frontier period; Tiffany-style lamps, etched-glass doors. Family-owned. Cr cds: A, MC, V.

D SC

★ **LA BAGUETTE.** 7408 N May Ave, north of downtown. 405/840-3047. Hrs: 8 am-10 pm; Mon to 5 pm; Sun 10 am-2 pm. Closed some major hols. Res accepted. French menu. Bar. Semi-a la carte: bkfst $1.25-$6.95, lunch $3.75-$7.95, dinner $6.95-$20.95. Sun brunch $4.95-$8.95. Specializes in lamb chops, North Carolina duck. Parking. Bistro atmosphere. Cr cds: A, D, DS, MC, V.

D

★★★ **MICHAEL'S SUPPER CLUB.** 1601 Northwest Expy (OK 3), in Bank IV Tower, north of downtown. 405/842-5464. Hrs: 11 am-2 pm, 5:30-11 pm. Closed Sun; most major hols. Res accepted. Bar to 2 am. Wine list. Semi-a la carte: lunch $6-$8, dinner $11.95-$31.95. Specializes in steak, seafood, veal. Own baking. Pianist evenings. Parking. Skylight, Italian chandelier. Cr cds: A, C, D, MC, V.

D

★★ **MOLLY MURPHY'S HOUSE OF FINE REPUTE.** 1100 S Meridian Ave, west of downtown. 405/942-8589. Hrs: 5-11 pm; Fri to midnight; Sat 4 pm-midnight; Sun 4-10 pm. Closed Jan 1, Dec 25. Bar. A la carte entrees: dinner $11.95-$16.95. Child's meals. Specialties: prime rib, Bacchus Feast. Salad bar. Parking. The salad bar is set within a 1962 Jaquar XKE convertible. A unique dining experience featuring costumed servers portraying various characters and an eclectic atmosphere replete with antiques and varied design motifs. Cr cds: A, MC, V.

D

✔★★ **SHORTY SMALL'S.** 4500 W Reno, west of downtown. 405/947-0779. Hrs: 11 am-10 pm; Fri, Sat to 11 pm. Closed Thanksgiving, Dec 25. Bar. Semi-a la carte: lunch, dinner $2.99-$14.99. Child's meals. Specializes in St Louis-style ribs, barbecued brisket, steak. Parking. Rustic decor. Cr cds: A, C, D, DS, MC, V.

D

★★ **SLEEPY HOLLOW.** 1101 NE 50th St, north of downtown. 405/424-1614. Hrs: 11 am-2 pm, 5-10 pm; Sat, Sun 10:30 am-3 pm. Closed Dec 25. Res accepted. Bar. Semi-a la carte: lunch $4.25-$10.95. Complete meals: dinner $10.95-$24.95. Specializes in pan-fried chicken, steak, seafood. Own biscuits. Valet parking. Cr cds: A, DS, MC, V.

D

✔★ **TEXANNA RED'S.** 4600 W Reno, west of downtown. 405/947-8665. Hrs: 11 am-10:30 pm; Fri, Sat to 11 pm; Sun to 10 pm. Closed major hols. Res accepted exc Fri & Sat. Mexican menu. Bar to midnight; Fri, Sat to 2 am. Semi-a la carte: lunch, dinner $4.95-$15.95. Child's meals. Specializes in fajitas, mesquite-broiled dishes. Parking. Southwestern decor. Game rm in bar. Cr cds: A, C, D, DS, MC, V.

D

★★★ **WATERFORD.** (See The Waterford Hotel) 405/848-4782. Hrs: 6-10:30 pm; Fri & Sat to 11 pm. Closed Sun. Res accepted. Continental menu. Bar. Wine list. A la carte entrees: dinner $9.75-$32. Specializes in Black Angus beef. Own baking, sauces. Valet parking. English country decor. Cr cds: A, C, D, DS, MC, V.

Unrated Dining Spots

CLASSEN GRILL. 5124 N Classen Blvd, north of downtown. 405/842-0428. Hrs: 7 am-10 pm; Sat from 8 am; Sun 8 am-2 pm. Closed Mon; some major hols. Bar from 10 am. Semi-a la carte: bkfst $2.50-$5.95, lunch $4-$6, dinner $5-$9. Child's meals. Specializes in chicken-fried steak, fresh seafood. Parking. Local artwork. Cr cds: C, D, DS, MC, V.

FURRS CAFETERIA. *2842 NW 63rd St, in French Market Mall, north of downtown.* 405/848-5656. Hrs: 10:45 am-2:30 pm, 4-8 pm; Sat, Sun 11 am-8 pm. Closed Dec 24 eve, 25. Avg ck: lunch, dinner $5. Specializes in chicken-fried steak, millionaire pie. Cr cds: MC, V.

HARRY'S AMERICAN GRILL & BAR. *4540 NW 23rd St, north of downtown.* 405/946-1421. Hrs: 11 am-10:30 pm; Fri, Sat to midnight. Closed Thanksgiving, Dec 25. Mexican, Amer menu. Bar. Semi-a la carte: lunch, dinner $2.99-$12.99. Child's meals. Specializes in gourmet hamburgers, chicken, fried peaches. Parking. Outdoor dining. Antique sports equipment on walls. Cr cds: A, C, D, MC, V.

LADY CLASSEN CAFETERIA. *6903 N May Ave (OK 74), in Lakewood Shopping Center, north of downtown.* 405/843-6459. Hrs: 11 am-2 pm, 5-8 pm; Sun 11 am-8 pm. Closed major hols; also 2 wks after Christmas. Avg ck: lunch, dinner $4.95-$5.95. Specializes in fried chicken, rhubarb pie. Own desserts. Colonial decor. Family-owned. No cr cds accepted.

Orlando/Walt Disney World

Founded: 1837

Pop: 169,675

Elev: 106 feet

Time zone: Eastern

Area code: 407

Orlando has always enjoyed the advantage of being a city with unusually lush gardens and beautiful scenic areas for walking and biking. Today, as the host to Walt Disney World, it is also a growing metropolitan area with the greater Orlando population reaching more than one million.

It has been said that one of the best things about Orlando is its location: it is within a short day's drive from many of Florida's major attractions and less than 400 miles from either of the two most remote Florida cities—Pensacola and Key West. Orlando is an ideal headquarters for the business traveler or vacationer interested in covering much of the state.

Orlando lies in the heart of the citrus and lake country of central Florida, just north of the cattle-growing region. It is only about 100 miles from the Gulf coast and half that distance from the Atlantic.

Business

As recently as the early 1970s, Orlando was a sleepy little community that depended largely on the citrus industry. Today it is a major transportation hub, as well as a center for high technology industries, film/TV production, manufacturing, warehousing, insurance and support services for tourism. Orlando is also an important service center for the Kennedy Space Center.

More than 850 manufacturers in the area employ in excess of 43,000 workers. The principal industries are the manufacturing of electronic supplies and laser systems, the processing of food and food products and printing and publishing. Orlando is a shipping center for citrus and vegetable crops. Agricultural products include oranges, grapefruit, cabbage, celery, beans, sweet corn, lettuce, spinach, escarole, endive, radishes, beef, dairy products, poultry and ornamental plants.

The opening of Walt Disney World gave an enormous boost to the neighboring economies. Motels, hotels and shopping centers were constructed with unprecedented speed as everyone rushed to accommodate the expected influx of tourists. Overnight, Walt Disney World became one of the most popular tourist attractions in the world and a favorite honeymoon destination.

Convention Facilities

There are more than 78,000 rooms at 360 hotels and motels in the greater Orlando area, with 30 major hotels providing meeting rooms and exhibit space for conventions. There are more than 150 meeting rooms in all, with capacities ranging from 25 to 2,500 people. Exhibit areas range from approximately 300 to more than 350,000 square feet.

The Orange County Convention/Civic Center provides 350,000 square feet of exhibit space with 7 connecting halls ranging from 5,100 to 18,000 square feet and 55 meeting rooms with a seating capacity of 50 to 2,500.

Expo Center in downtown Orlando offers 71,000 square feet of convention/exhibition space and 7 connecting halls seating up to 2,500.

The Tupperware Convention Center is also available for conferences, meetings, musicals, theatricals, exhibits and seminars. The facility includes a 2,000-seat theater/auditorium, a 2,000-seat dining area and a 23,600-square-foot conference/exhibit hall.

Walt Disney World

Every company produces its own product; the Walt Disney Company manufactures fantasy. From the Magic Kingdom to the *Empress Lilly* riverboat restaurants, everything is run with a touch of make-believe. It takes approximately 35,000 people to keep the "Vacation Kingdom" moving, and every facet of operation is devoted to keeping visitors happy and content. Since its opening in 1971, more than 400 million people have passed through the gates of Walt Disney World, making it one of the most visited tourist attractions in history.

The Magic Kingdom, the first of the theme parks constructed, offers more than 45 attractions as well as shows, shops, exhibits, refreshment areas and special experiences divided into seven "lands": Adventureland, Frontierland, Liberty Square, Fantasyland, Tomorrowland, Mickey's Starland and Main Street, U.S.A.

While the Magic Kingdom is the heart of Walt Disney World, it takes up only a fraction of the thousands of acres that make up the total vacation complex. Linked to the Kingdom by monorail is Epcot Center (Experimental Prototype Community of Tomorrow). This park, situated on 260 acres of land, is a sprawling two-part entertainment and educational complex. Future World, sponsored by several American corporations, is a futuristic look at technology and its possible directions. World Showcase is an architectural and cultural appreciation of 11 celebrated nations, including the United Kingdom, France, Norway, Canada, Mexico, Italy, Germany, Japan, China, Morocco and the United States. Disney-MGM Studios, southwest of Epcot Center, houses production and administration facilities of the Walt Disney

Company, as well as movie and television-related attractions. A tour of the area includes an animation studio, backlots, TV theaters and sound effects theaters.

In addition to the three major theme parks, the Walt Disney World complex includes several other interesting and imaginative areas. Typhoon Lagoon, a 56-acre water park between Epcot Center and Disney Village Marketplace, features the world's largest wave pool, 9 waterslides, saltwater snorkeling, inner-tube rides, restaurants and picnic sites.

Fort Wilderness Campground has 785 campsites and 407 "wilderness homes" with complete utilities, shopping and recreation facilities, a restaurant featuring Western menus and entertainment and a ranch with trail rides. Within Fort Wilderness are River Country, a water recreation complex with waterfalls, slides and rapids reminiscent of the old swimming hole and Discovery Island, housing exotic birds and animals, a flower garden and nature trails.

Walt Disney World Village in Lake Buena Vista, five miles east of the Magic Kingdom, is a vacation community of town houses, a European-style shopping center, conference center, eight major hotels and tennis and boating facilities. Also here is Pleasure Island, a nighttime entertainment center, featuring a ten-screen theater complex, six night clubs, restaurant and snack facilities and the *Empress Lilly,* an authentically reconstructed riverboat that boasts three dining salons. The *Empress Lilly* is permanently anchored at Walt Disney World Village. Other types of recreation available in Walt Disney World include horseback riding, fishing, swimming, sailing, motorboating, waterskiing, tennis, steamboat excursions, picnicking and nature hikes. Five championship golf courses are here as well as miles of beaches.

The Disney-owned hotels are a form of entertainment unto themselves, with imaginatively decorated interiors, bars and restaurants and swimming pool fantasies. They include the Disney Inn Resort, Disney's Yacht Club and Beach Club resorts, Disney's Caribbean Beach Resort, Disney's Contemporary Resort, Disney's Grand Floridian Beach Resort, Disney's Polynesian Resort, Disney's Village Resort, Disney's Port Orleans and Dixie Landings resorts and the Disney Vacation Club. Other hotels on Disney property but run by private companies include the Walt Disney World Dolphin and Walt Disney World Swan.

A conservation/wilderness area of 7,500 acres is at the southern end of the park. The area retains virgin stands of pine, cypress and bay trees and maintains a buffer zone for ecological protection.

Walt Disney World is open every day of the year, with extended hours during the summer and holiday periods. Various ticket combinations are available. For further information phone 824-4321; for hotel reservations phone W-DISNEY.

Sports and Recreation

Orlando itself has much to offer the visitor. The Orlando Magic play professional basketball at the 16,000-seat Orlando Arena. Top sports events occur frequently at the Eddie Graham Sports Stadium. There are also football games and concerts at the Florida Citrus Bowl, dog racing at the Sanford-Orlando Kennel Club and Seminole Greyhound Park and jai alai at nearby Orlando-Seminole Jai Alai Fronton.

Entertainment

The Florida Symphony Orchestra performs in Bob Carr Performing Arts Center from September to May with a series of classical, pops, chamber and outdoor concerts.

Food and entertainment also can be found at Church Street Station in downtown Orlando and at the dinner theaters southeast of town in the Kissimmee/St Cloud area.

Sightseeing

The John F. Kennedy Space Center, one of the most historic sites in the world, is located 47 miles east of Orlando. It was from here that Apollo astronauts left earth for man's first voyages to the moon. Today,

Kennedy Space Center is the launch and landing site of the Space Shuttle, the world's first reusable, manned space vehicle.

Millions of tourists visit the Space Center each year, coming from across the country and around the world. The visitors center and two-hour bus tours focus on the Apollo, Skylab and Space Shuttle programs based here. Tours of Cape Canaveral Air Force Station, which is near the Space Center, include the launch sites of the Mercury and Gemini missions and the Air Force Space Museum.

Universal Studios Florida, southwest of Orlando, is one of central Florida's newest attractions. Universal's 444-acre lot accommodates more than 40 rides, shows and attractions, 35 full-scale movie sets and 6 working sound stages.

Other attractions less than 100 miles from Orlando include Sea World of Florida, Busch Gardens Tampa, Adventure Island, Cypress Gardens, Silver Springs-Source of the Silver River, Gatorland, Mystery Fun House, Xanadu and Wet 'N Wild.

General References Orlando

Founded: 1837 **Pop:** 164,693 **Elev:** 106 feet **Time zone:** Eastern **Area code:** 407

Phone Numbers

POLICE, FIRE & PARAMEDICS: 911
FBI: 875-9976
POISON CONTROL CENTER: 813/253-4444
TIME & WEATHER: 976-1611

Information Sources

Orlando Convention & Visitors Bureau, 7208 Sand Lake Rd, Suite 300, 32819; 363-5800.
Orlando Official Visitor Information Center, 8445 International Dr, 32819; 363-5871.
Parks & Special Facilities, 246-2283.

Transportation

AIRLINES: American; Bahamasair; British Airways; Continental; Delta; KLM (Netherlands); Northwest; Trans Brasil; TWA; United; USAir; Virgin Atlantic; and other commuter and regional airlines. For the most current airline schedules and information consult the *Official Airline Guide,* published twice monthly.
AIRPORT: Orlando International Airport, 825-2001
CAR RENTAL AGENCIES: (See Toll-Free Numbers) Avis 851-7600; Budget 850-6749; Hertz 859-8400; Thrifty 380-1002.
PUBLIC TRANSPORTATION: Orlando Transit Authority 841-8240.
RAILROAD PASSENGER SERVICE: Amtrak 800/872-7245.

Newspaper

Orlando Sentinel.

Convention Facilities

Expo Center, 500 W Livingston St, 849-2562.
Orange County Convention/Civic Center, 9800 International Dr, 345-9800.
Tupperware Convention Center, 5 mi S of FL Tpke, 847-1809.

Sports & Recreation

Major Sports Facilities
Florida Citrus Bowl, 1610 W Church St, 849-2020.
Orlando Arena, 600 W Amelia St, 896-2442 (Orlando Magic, basketball).

Racetracks
Sanford-Orlando Kennel Club, Longwood, 831-1600 (greyhound racing).
Seminole Greyhound Park, US 17/92, N of FL 436, Casselberry, 699-4510 (greyhound racing).

Jai Alai
Orlando-Seminole Jai Alai, US 17/92, Fern Park, 339-6221.

Cultural Facilities

Theaters & Concert Halls
Bob Carr Performing Arts Center 401 W Livingston Ave, 849-2577 (Florida Symphony Orchestra).
Central Florida Civic Theatre, 1001 E Princeton, 896-7365.
Mark Two Dinner Theater, 3376 Edgewater Dr, 843-6275.
Tupperware Convention Center, S on US 441, 847-1802.

Museums & Art Museums
Charles Hosmer Morse Museum of American Art, 133 E Welbourne Ave, Winter Park, 644-3686.
Orange County Historical Museum, 812 E Rollins St, Loch Haven Park, 897-6350.
Orlando Museum of Art, 2416 N Mills Ave, Loch Haven Park, 896-4231.
Orlando Science Center, 810 E Rollins St, Loch Haven Park, 896-7151.

Points of Interest
Bok Tower Gardens, off US 27A, Lake Wales, 813/676-1408.
Busch Gardens Tampa, 3000 E Busch Blvd, Tampa, 813/987-5082.
Church Street Station, 129 W Church St, 422-2434.
Cypress Gardens, FL 540 near Winter Haven, 813/324-2111.
Flying Tigers Warbird Air Museum, 231 N Hoagland Blvd, Kissimmee, 933-1942.
Kennedy Space Center, 47 mi E, entrance at visitors center; N or S via US 1, I-95 to NASA Pkwy then E, 452-2121.

Leu Botanical Gardens, 1730 N Forest Ave, 246-2620.
Marineland, on FL A1A, S of St Augustine, 904/471-1111.
Mystery Fun House, 5767 Major Blvd, off Kirkman Rd, 351-3355.
Sea World of Florida, 7007 Sea World Dr, 351-3600.
Silver Springs-Source of the Silver River, on FL 40 near Ocala, 904/236-2121.
Universal Studios Florida, 10 mi SW on I 4, exits 29 & 30B, at jct FL Tpke, 363-8000.
Walt Disney World, 22 mi SW of Orlando via I-4, at FL 535, 824-4321; res, W-DISNEY.
Wet 'N Wild, 6200 International Dr, 10 mi SW via I-4, at FL 435, 351-3200.
Xanadu, W of Kissimmee, at jct US 192 & FL 535, 396-1992.

Sightseeing Tours

Gray Line bus tours, PO Box 1671, Orlando 32802, 422-0744.
Rivership *Grand Romance,* 15 mi NE on US 17/92, Sanford, 321-5091, 800/225-7999 (exc FL).
St Johns River Cruises & Tours, 15 mi NE on US 17/92, Sanford, 330-1612.

Annual Events

Florida Citrus Sports. Jan 1.
Orlando Scottish Highland Games. Last wkend Jan.
Central Florida Fair. Phone 295-3247. Late Feb-early Mar.
Walt Disney World-Golf Classic. At the "Magic Linkdom". Late Oct.

City Neighborhoods

Many of the restaurants, unrated dining establishments and some lodgings listed under Orlando include neighborhoods as well as exact street addresses. Geographic descriptions of Downtown and the International Drive Area are given, followed by a table of restaurants arranged by neighborhood.

Downtown: South of Colonial Dr (FL 50), west of Magnolia Ave (FL 527), north of Holland East-West Expy and east of Parramore Ave.
North of Downtown: North of FL 50. **South of Downtown:** South of FL 408. **East of Downtown:** East of Magnolia Ave. **West of Downtown:** West of Parramore Ave.
International Drive Area: On and around International Drive between the FL Turnpike on the north and I-4 (exit 27A) on the south.

Lodgings and Food
Orlando

ORLANDO RESTAURANTS
BY NEIGHBORHOOD AREAS

(For full description, see alphabetical listings under Restaurants)

DOWNTOWN

Crackers. 129 W Church St

Lee's Lakeside. 431 E Central Blvd

Lili Marlene's Aviators Restaurant & Pub. 129 W Church St

Vivaldi. 107 Pine St

NORTH OF DOWNTOWN

Del Frisco's. 729 Lee Rd

SOUTH OF DOWNTOWN

Charley's Steak House. 6107 S Orange Blossom Trail

Chatham's Place. 7575 Dr Phillips Blvd

China Garden. 1303 S Semoran Blvd

Gary's Duck Inn. 3974 S Orange Blossom Trail

Hard Rock Cafe. 5800 Kirkman Rd

Le Coq Au Vin. 4800 S Orange Ave

Ming Court. 9188 International Dr

EAST OF DOWNTOWN

4th Fighter Group. 494 Rickenbacker Dr

La Normandie. 2021 E Colonial Dr (FL 50)

Ronnie's. 2702 E Colonial Dr (FL 50)

INTERNATIONAL DRIVE AREA

Blazing Pianos. 8445 International Dr

Caruso's Palace. 8986 International Dr

Charlie's Lobster House. 8445 International Dr

China Coast. 7500 International Dr

King Henry's Feast. 8984 International Dr

Passage To India. 5532 International Dr

Siam Orchid. 7575 Republic Dr

Note: *When a listing is located in a town that does not have its own city heading, it will appear under the city nearest to its location. In these cases, the address and town appear in parenthesis immediately following the name of the establishment.*

Motels

✔★★ **COMFORT INN-SOUTH.** *8421 S Orange Blossom Trail (32809), at Florida Mall, south of downtown.* 407/855-6060; FAX 407/859-5132. 204 rms, 2 story. S, D $40-$99; each addl $6; suites $59-$145; under 18 free. TV; cable. Heated pool. Playground. Bkfst buffet 7-11 am. Ck-out 11 am. Coin lndry. Meeting rms. Sundries. Gift shop. Free transportation to area attractions. Game rm. Florida Mall adj. Cr cds: A, C, D, DS, ER, JCB, MC, V.

D ≈ ⊠ 🕷 SC

★★ **COMFORT SUITES.** *9350 Turkey Lake Rd (32819), off I-4 exit 29, south of downtown.* 407/351-5050; FAX 407/363-7953. 215 rms, 3 story. Late Dec-early Jan, mid-Feb-mid-Apr, mid-June-Aug: S, D $89-$109; under 12 free; lower rates rest of yr. Crib free. TV; cable. Heated pool; wading pool, whirlpool, poolside serv. Playground. Complimentary continental bkfst. Bar. Ck-out 11 am. Coin lndry. Sundries. Airport transportation. Game rm. Refrigerators. Cr cds: A, C, D, DS, ER, JCB, MC, V.

D 🕴 ≈ ⊠ 🕷 SC

★★★ **COURTYARD BY MARRIOTT.** *7155 Frontage Rd (32812), near Intl Airport, south of downtown.* 407/240-7200; FAX 407/240-8962. 149 rms, 3 story. S, D $89-$120; suites $109-$130; under 18 free; wkend rates. Crib free. TV; cable. Heated pool; poolside serv. Complimentary coffee in rms. Restaurant 6-11 am. Ck-out 1 pm. Coin lndry. Meeting rms. Free airport transportation. Exercise equipt; weights, bicycles, whirlpool. Some refrigerators. Balconies. Cr cds: A, C, D, DS, MC, V.

D ≈ 🕴 ✈ ⊠ 🕷 SC

★ **ECONO LODGE-CENTRAL.** *3300 W Colonial Dr (32808), west of downtown.* 407/293-7221; FAX 407/293-1166. 103 rms, 1-2 story. Feb-Apr, mid-June-mid-Aug: S $46; D $52; each addl $6; under 17 free; lower rates rest of yr. Crib free. TV; cable. Pool. Complimentary coffee in lobby. Restaurant adj open 24 hrs. Bar 11-2 am. Ck-out 11 am. Coin lndry. Meeting rm. Lawn games. Picnic tables. Cr cds: A, C, D, DS, MC, V.

≈ ⊠ 🕷 SC

✔★ **ECONOMY INNS OF AMERICA.** *8222 Jamaican Ct (32819), south of downtown.* 407/345-1172. 121 rms, 3 story. Mid-Jan-mid-Apr: S, D $39.90-$59.90; lower rates rest of yr. TV; cable. Heated pool. Complimentary continental bkfst. Ck-out 11 am. Cr cds: A, MC, V.

D ≈ ⊠ 🕷 SC

★ **FAIRFIELD INN BY MARRIOTT.** *8342 Jamaican Ct (32819), south of downtown.* 407/363-1944. 135 rms, 3 story. Mid-Dec-Aug: S, D $59-$64; under 18 free; lower rates rest of yr. Crib free. TV; cable. Pool. Complimentary continental bkfst. Complimentary coffee in lobby. Ck-out noon. Game rm. Cr cds: A, C, D, DS, MC, V.

D ≈ ⊠ 🕷 SC

★★ **GATEWAY INN.** *7050 Kirkman Rd (32819), east of I-4, in International Drive Area.* 407/351-2000; res: 800/327-3808 (exc FL), 800/432-1179 (FL), 800/62; FAX 407/363-1835. 354 rms, 2 story. Feb-mid-Apr, early June-early Sept, mid-Dec-early Jan: S, D $78-$92; each addl $6; under 18 free; lower rates rest of yr. Crib $6. Pet accepted, some restrictions. TV; cable. 2 pools, heated; wading pool, poolside serv. Playground. Continental bkfst in rms. Restaurant 7 am-10 pm. Bar 11:30-2 am; entertainment, dancing. Ck-out 11 am. Coin lndry. Meeting rm. Bellhops. Valet serv. Sundries. Gift shop. Airport transportation. Free transportation to area attractions. Miniature golf. Game rm. Lawn games. Picnic tables. Cr cds: A, C, D, ER, MC, V.

🐾 ≈ ⊠ 🕷 SC

★★ **HAMPTON INN.** *7110 S Kirkman (32819), International Drive Area.* 407/345-1112; FAX 407/352-6591. 170 rms, 8 story. Feb-late Apr, early June-early Sept & late Dec-early Jan: S $59-$79; D $69-$84; suites $119; under 17 free; lower rates rest of yr. Crib free. TV; cable. Heated pool; wading pool. Complimentary continental bkfst, coffee. Restaurant adj open 24 hrs. Ck-out 11 am. Coin lndry. Meeting rms. Gift shop. Exercise equipt; weight machine, stair machine. Game rm. Cr cds: A, C, D, DS, MC, V.

D ≈ 🕴 ⊠ 🕷 SC

★★ **HAWTHORN SUITES.** *6435 Westwood Blvd (32821), International Drive Area.* 407/351-6600; FAX 407/351-1977. 150 suites, 5 story. Mid-Feb-Easter & late Dec: suites $135-$185; under 18 free; lower rates rest of yr. Crib free. TV; cable, in-rm movies. Heated pool; wading pool, poolside serv. Playground. Complimentary bkfst. Complimentary coffee in rms. Restaurant adj 7 am-11 pm. Ck-out 11 am. Coin

Indry. Meeting rms. Bellhops. Concierge. Sundries. Airport transportation. Exercise equipt; weights, stair machine, whirlpool. Game rm. Refrigerators, wet bars. Grills. Cr cds: A, C, D, DS, ER, JCB, MC, V.

[D] [≈] [🏃] [⌧] [🔥] [SC]

★ ★ **HERITAGE INN.** 9861 International Dr (32819), in International Drive Area. 407/352-0008; res: 800/447-1890; FAX 407/352-5440. 150 rms, 2 story. Late Dec-early Jan, Feb-Aug: S, D $79-$109; each addl $10; under 18 free; lower rates rest of yr. Crib free. TV; cable. Heated pool. Restaurant 6:30 am-2 pm, 4-10 pm. Rm serv. Bar. Ck-out noon. Coin Indry. Meeting rms. Valet serv. Sundries. Refrigerators. Turn-of-the-century architecture; Victorian decor. Cr cds: A, C, D, DS, ER, MC, V.

[D] [≈] [⌧] [🔥]

★ ★ **HOLIDAY INN-CENTRAL PARK.** 7900 S Orange Blossom Trail (32809), south of downtown. 407/859-7900; FAX 407/859-7442. 266 rms, 2 story. S, D $65-$117; each addl $7; under 18 free. Crib free. TV. Pool; wading pool. Restaurant 6:30 am-2 pm, 5:30-10 pm. Rm serv. Bar 5 pm-midnight. Ck-out 11 am. Coin Indry. Meeting rms. Bellhops. Free airport transportation. Exercise equipt; weight machine, bicycles. Cr cds: A, C, D, DS, JCB, MC, V.

[D] [≈] [🏃] [⌧] [🔥] [SC]

★ **INTERNATIONAL GATEWAY INN.** 5859 American Way (32819), in International Drive Area. 407/345-8800; res: 800/327-0750; FAX 407/363-9366. 192 rms, 4 story. June-early Sept, late Dec: S, D $66-$82; each addl $6; under 18 free. Crib $6. Pet accepted, some restrictions. TV; cable. Heated pool. Restaurant adj open 24 hrs. Ck-out 11 am. Coin Indry. Game rm. Cr cds: A, C, D, ER, MC, V.

[D] [🖐] [≈] [⌧] [🔥]

✔★ **RAMADA LIMITED.** 8296 S Orange Blossom Trail (32809), 10 mi S on FL 441, near Florida Mall, south of downtown. 407/240-0570; FAX 407/856-5507. 75 rms, 2 story. Mid-Dec-mid-Apr: S $45-$75; D $49-$75; each addl $6; under 9 free; higher rates: some hols, Daytona 500; lower rates rest of yr. Crib free. TV; cable. Pool. Complimentary coffee in lobby. Restaurant nearby. Ck-out 11 am. Coin Indry. Meeting rm. Bellhops. Airport, RR station, bus depot, Walt Disney World transportation. Golf privileges. Cr cds: A, C, D, DS, ER, JCB, MC, V.

[D] [🏃] [≈] [⌧] [🔥] [SC]

★ ★ **RESIDENCE INN BY MARRIOTT.** 7975 Canada Ave (32819), south of downtown. 407/345-0117; FAX 407/352-2689. 176 kit. suites (1-2 bedrm). S, D $94-$144; wkly, monthly rates. Crib free. TV; cable. Heated pool; whirlpools. Complimentary continental bkfst. Restaurant nearby. Ck-out 11 am. Coin Indry. Meeting rms. Valet serv. Airport, RR station, bus depot transportation. Many fireplaces. Balconies. Grills. Lighted sports court. Cr cds: A, C, D, DS, JCB, MC, V.

[D] [≈] [⌧] [🔥] [SC]

★ ★ **TANGO BAY LEXINGTON SUITES.** 6800 Villa DeCosta Dr (32821). 407/293-0707; res: 800/633-1405; FAX 407/239-8243. 260 kit. suites, 2-3 story. S $139; D $149; each addl $7; under 18 free; wkend rates; higher rates special events. Crib free. TV; cable. Pool. Playground. Complimentary continental bkfst. Ck-out noon. Coin Indry. Sundries. Valet serv. 18-hole golf privileges; greens fee $55-$75. Exercise equipt; weights, stair machine, whirlpool. Game rm. Balconies. Cr cds: A, C, D, DS, MC, V.

[🏃] [≈] [🏃] [⌧] [🔥]

✔★ **TRAVELODGE CENTROPLEX.** 409 N Magnolia Ave (32081), downtown. 407/423-1671; FAX 407/423-1523. 75 rms, shower only, 2 story. Feb-Apr & June-Aug: S $45; D $55; each addl $5; under 18 free; higher rates Citrus Bowl; lower rates rest of yr. TV; cable. Pool. Complimentary coffee in rms. Restaurant nearby. Ck-out noon. Coin Indry. Airport transportation. Cr cds: A, C, D, DS, ER, JCB, MC, V.

[≈] [⌧] [🔥] [SC]

✔★ ★ **WYNFIELD INN.** 6263 Westwood Blvd (32821), in International Drive Area. 407/345-8000; FAX 407/345-1508. 299 rms, 3 story. Feb-late Apr, early June-late Aug: S, D $60-$74; each addl $5; under 18 free; lower rates rest of yr. Crib free. TV. 2 pools, 1 heated; 2 wading pools, poolside serv. Complimentary coffee, fruit. Restaurant adj 6:30 am-midnight. Ck-out 11 am. Coin Indry. Airport, area attraction transportation. Game rm. Cr cds: A, C, D, DS, MC, V

[D] [≈] [⌧] [🔥] [SC]

Motor Hotels

★ ★ **BEST WESTERN PLAZA INTERNATIONAL.** 8738 International Dr (32819), in International Drive Area. 407/345-8195; FAX 407/352-8196. 673 rms, 4 story, 176 kits. Feb-Apr, mid-June-Aug, mid-Dec-early Jan, hols: S, D $80-$85; each addl $6; suites $100-$105; kit. units $90-$95; under 19 free; lower rates rest of yr. Crib free. TV; cable, in-rm movies. Heated pool; wading pool, whirlpool, poolside serv. Ck-out 11 am. Coin Indry. Bellhops. Sundries. Gift shop. Game rm. Some in-rm whirlpools. Cr cds: A, C, D, DS, MC, V.

[D] [≈] [⌧] [🔥] [SC]

★ ★ **COLONY PLAZA.** (11100 W Colonial Dr, Ocoee 34761) 10 mi W on FL 50. 407/656-3333; res: 800/821-0136; FAX 407/656-2232. 300 rms, 7 story. Feb-Apr, July-Aug: S $70; D $85; each addl $5; under 18 free; lower rates rest of yr. Crib free. TV. Pool; wading pool, poolside serv. Playground. Restaurant 6:30 am-10 pm. Bar noon-night; entertainment, dancing Tues-Sat. Ck-out noon. Coin Indry. Meeting rm. Concierge. Gift shop. Airport, RR station, bus depot transportation. Lighted tennis. Game rm. Lawn games. Private patios, balconies. Cr cds: A, C, D, DS, ER, MC, V.

[D] [🏃] [≈] [⌧] [🔥] [SC]

★ ★ ★ **DELTA ORLANDO RESORT.** 5715 Major Blvd (32819), jct FL 435 & I-4 exit 30B at entrance of Universal Studios, south of downtown. 407/351-3340; FAX 407/351-5117. 800 units, 4 story. Mid-Feb-Apr, mid-June-Aug, late Dec: S, D $110-$150; suites $175-$475; under 18 free; lower rates rest of yr. Crib free. Pet accepted, some restrictions; $25. TV; cable. 3 pools, heated; wading pools, whirlpools, sauna, poolside serv. Playground. Free supervised child's activities. Restaurants 6:30 am-midnight. Rm serv. Bar 11:30-2 am; entertainment exc Sun. Ck-out 11 am. Coin Indry. Convention facilities. Bellhops. Valet serv. Concierge. Sundries. Gift shop. Lighted tennis. Golf privileges. Miniature golf. Game rm. Lawn games. Private balconies. Cr cds: A, C, D, DS, ER, JCB, MC, V.

[D] [🖐] [🏃] [🏃] [≈] [⌧] [🔥] [SC]

★ ★ **FLORIDIAN.** 7299 Republic Dr (32819), in International Drive Area. 407/351-5009; res: 800/445-7299; FAX 407/363-7807. 300 rms, 8 story. Feb-Aug, late Dec: S, D $75-$110; lower rates rest of yr. Crib free. TV; cable, in-rm movies. Heated pool; poolside serv. Restaurant 7-11 am, 5-11 pm. Rm serv. Bar 5 pm-2 am. Ck-out 11 am. Coin Indry. Meeting rms. Bellhops. Valet serv. Concierge. Sundries. Gift shop. Airport transportation. Game rm. Cr cds: A, C, D, DS, MC, V.

[D] [≈] [⌧] [🔥] [SC]

✔★ ★ **HAMPTON INN AT UNIVERSAL.** 5621 Windhover Dr (32819), in International Drive Area. 407/351-6716; FAX 407/363-1711. 120 rms, 5 story. Late May-mid-Aug & late Dec-late Mar: S $69; D $79; under 18 free; golf plan; lower rates rest of yr. Crib free. TV; cable. Heated pool. Complimentary continental bkfst, coffee. Restaurant opp 7 am-midnight. Ck-out noon. Meeting rms. Airport transportation. Game rm. Cr cds: A, C, D, DS, MC, V.

[D] [≈] [⌧] [🔥] [SC]

★ ★ **HOLIDAY INN.** 626 Lee Rd (32810), north of downtown. 407/645-5600; FAX 407/740-7912. 201 rms, 5 story. S, D $59-$69; each addl $10; under 18 free; MAP avail. Crib free. TV; cable. Pool. Restaurant 6 am-10 pm. Rm serv. Bar 4 pm-midnight; entertainment Thurs-Sat. Ck-out 11 am. Coin Indry. Meeting rms. Bellhops. Valet serv. Airport, RR station, bus depot transportation. Tennis privileges. Golf privileges, greens fee $18-$30, driving range. Exercise equipt; weight machine, bicycle. Health club privileges. Game rm. Cr cds: A, C, D, DS, JCB, MC, V.

D ⬛ ⬛ ⬛ ⬛ ⬛ ⬛ ⬛ **SC**

★ ★ ★ **HOLIDAY INN-UNIVERSITY OF CENTRAL FLORIDA.** 12125 High Tech Ave (32817), off University Blvd, north of downtown. 407/275-9000; FAX 407/381-0019. 250 units, 6 story. S $85; D $95; each addl $10; suites $135; under 18 free. Crib free. TV; cable. Pool. Restaurant 6:30 am-2 pm, 5-10 pm. Rm serv. Bar 11 am-midnight. Ck-out 11 am. Meeting rms. Bellhops. Tennis privileges. Golf privileges. Exercise equipt; weights, bicycles, whirlpool, sauna. Lawn games. Some refrigerators. On lake. *LUXURY LEVEL*. 42 units. S $100; D $110; suites $125-$200. Concierge. Private lounge. Minibars. Complimentary bkfst, refreshments. Cr cds: A, C, D, DS, JCB, MC, V.

D ⬛ ⬛ ⬛ ⬛ ⬛ ⬛ ⬛ ⬛ **SC**

✔ ★ **INTERNATIONAL INN.** 6327 International Drive (32819), in International Drive Area. 407/351-4444; res: 800/999-6327; FAX 407/352-5806. 315 rms, 4-9 story. Mid-Mar-mid-Aug: S, D $55; each addl (after 4th person) $6; suites $100; lower rates rest of yr. Crib free. Pet accepted, some restrictions. TV; cable, in-rm movies. Heated pool. Restaurant 6:30-10:30 am, 5:30-10 pm. Bar 6 pm-midnight. Ck-out 11 am. Coin lndry. Meeting rms. Bellhops. Sundries. Gift shop. Valet serv. Walt Disney World transportation. Game rm. Refrigerators avail. Cr cds: A, C, D, DS, ER, JCB, MC, V.

⬛ ⬛ ⬛ ⬛

★ ★ **MARRIOTT.** 8001 International Dr (32819), off I-4 exit 29, in International Drive Area. 407/351-2420; FAX 407/345-5611. 1,054 units in 16 bldgs, 2 story, 191 kits. S, D $125-$130; suites $210-$450; kit. units $10 addl; under 18 free. Crib free. TV; cable, in-rm movies. 3 pools, heated; 2 wading pools, poolside serv. Playground. Restaurant open 24 hrs. Rm serv. Bar 11-2 am; entertainment, dancing. Ck-out 11 am. Coin lndry. Convention facilities. Bellhops. Sundries. Gift shop. Lighted tennis. Exercise equipt; weight machine, rowers, whirlpool. Game rm. Balconies. Cr cds: A, C, D, DS, ER, JCB, MC, V.

D ⬛ ⬛ ⬛ ⬛ ⬛ ⬛ ⬛ **SC**

✔ ★ **QUALITY INN-PLAZA.** 9000 International Dr (32819), in International Drive Area. 407/345-8585; FAX 407/352-6839. 1,020 rms, 4-10 story. Late Dec-early Jan, mid-Feb-late Apr, mid-June-mid-Aug: S, D $53; lower rates rest of yr. Crib free. Pet accepted, some restrictions; $5. TV; cable. 3 pools, heated; poolside serv in season. Restaurant 6:30-10:30 am, 5:30-9 pm. Bar 5:30 pm-2 am. Ck-out 11 am. Coin lndry. Gift shop. Game rm. Cr cds: A, C, D, DS, ER, JCB, MC, V.

D ⬛ ⬛ ⬛ ⬛ **SC**

★ ★ **RADISSON INN.** 8444 International Dr (32819), in International Drive Area. 407/345-0505; FAX 407/352-5894. 299 rms, 5 story. Mid-Dec-Apr: S, D $69-$99; each addl $10; lower rates rest of yr. Crib free. TV; cable. Pool; poolside serv. Restaurant 6:30 am-10 pm. Bar. Ck-out noon. Meeting rms. Sundries. Gift shop. Airport, RR station, bus transportation. Lighted tennis. Health club privileges. Game rm. Bathrm phones; refrigerators. Shopping center opp. Cr cds: A, C, D, DS, ER, MC, V.

D ⬛ ⬛ ⬛ ⬛ ⬛ **SC**

★ ★ ★ **SHERATON WORLD RESORT.** 10100 International Dr (32821), in International Drive Area. 407/352-1100; res: 800/327-0363 (exc FL), 800/341-4292 (FL); FAX 407/352-3679. 800 units, 2-3 story. Jan-mid-May: S $90-$120; D $105-$135; each addl $15; suites $225-$465; under 18 free; lower rates rest of yr. Crib $5. TV; cable. 3 pools, heated; 2 wading pools, poolside serv. Playground. Restaurants 6:30 am-11 pm. Rm serv. Bar; entertainment. Ck-out 11 am. Coin lndry. Meeting rms. Bellhops. Sundries. Gift shop. Airport transportation. Lighted tennis. Golf privileges. Miniature golf. Exercise equipt; weights, bicycles, whirlpool. Game rm. Cr cds: A, C, D, DS, ER, JCB, MC, V.

D ⬛ ⬛ ⬛ ⬛ ⬛ ⬛ ⬛ **SC**

★ ★ ★ **SONESTA VILLA RESORT.** 10000 Turkey Lake Rd (32819), I-4 exit 29, south of downtown. 407/352-8051; res: 800/424-0708; FAX 407/345-5384. 370 villas, 2 story. 1-bedrm $98-$149; 2-

bedrm $135-$235. TV; cable. Heated pool; wading pool, poolside serv. Free supervised child's activities. Restaurant 6:30 am-11 pm. Bar 11 am-midnight. Ck-out noon. Meeting rms. Bellhops. Valet serv. Gift shop. Lighted tennis. Exercise equipt; weights, bicycles, 11 whirlpools, sauna. Game rm. Lawn games. Refrigerators. Private patios, balconies. Bicycle rentals. Mediterranean architecture. On lake; paddle boats, jet skis, water-skiing. Cr cds: A, C, D, DS, ER, JCB, MC, V.

D ⬛ ⬛ ⬛ ⬛ ⬛ ⬛ ⬛ **SC**

★ **SUPER 8 HAWAIIAN.** 9956 Hawaiian Court (32819), in International Drive Area. 407/351-5100; FAX 407/352-7188. 222 rms, 2 story, 49 kit. suites. S $61; D $67; suites $87; under 18 free. Crib free. TV; cable. Pool; whirlpool. Playground. Complimentary coffee in lobby. Restaurant nearby. Bar 5:30 pm-1 am. Ck-out noon. Coin lndry. Meeting rms. Valet serv. Airport, Walt Disney World transportation. Game rm. Refrigerator in suites. Cr cds: A, C, D, DS, ER, MC, V.

D ⬛ ⬛ ⬛ ⬛ **SC**

Hotels

★ ★ **CLARION PLAZA.** 9700 International Dr (32819), in International Drive Area. 407/352-9700; FAX 407/351-9111. 810 rms, 14 story. S, D $125-$145; suites $200-$660; under 18 free. Crib free. Valet parking $5. TV; cable. Heated pool; whirlpool. Restaurant 6:30 am-midnight. Bar 11-2 am; entertainment. Ck-out noon. Coin lndry. Convention facilities. Shopping arcade. Airport transportation. Golf privileges, pro, putting green, driving range. Game rm. Some refrigerators, bathrm phones. Cr cds: A, C, D, DS, ER, MC, V.

D ⬛ ⬛ ⬛ ⬛ ⬛ **SC**

★ ★ ★ **EMBASSY SUITES.** 8978 International Dr (32819), in International Drive Area. 407/352-1400; FAX 407/363-1120. 245 kit. suites, 8 story. Suites $125-$175; each addl $15; under 17 free. Crib free. TV; cable. 2 pools, 1 indoor; whirlpool, steam rm, sauna. Complimentary bkfst. Restaurant 6 am-11 pm. Bar. Ck-out noon. Coin lndry. Meeting rms. Gift shop. Free Disney World transportation; airport transportation. Game rm. Refrigerators. Sun deck. Mediterranean-style atrium. Cr cds: A, C, D, DS, MC, V.

D ⬛ ⬛ ⬛ **SC**

★ ★ **EMBASSY SUITES AT PLAZA INTERNATIONAL.** 8250 Jamaican Ct (32819), south of downtown. 407/345-8250; res: 800/327-9797; FAX 407/352-1463. 246 suites, 8 story. Suites $159; under 18 free; package plans. Crib free. TV; cable. Indoor/outdoor pool; poolside serv. Complimentary full bkfst buffet 6-10 am. Bar 5-11 pm. Ck-out noon. Gift shop. Tennis & golf privileges. Exercise equipt; weights, rower, whirlpool, sauna. Game rm. Refrigerators. Cr cds: A, C, D, DS, JCB, MC, V.

D ⬛ ⬛ ⬛ ⬛ ⬛ ⬛ **SC**

★ ★ **THE ENCLAVE.** 6165 Carrier Dr (32819), south of downtown. 407/351-1155; res: 800/457-0077; FAX 407/351-2001. 321 kit. suites, 10 story. Mid-Dec-mid-Apr & mid-June-mid-Aug: studio & 2-bedrm suites (to 6 persons) $99-$160; golf, Walt Disney World packages; lower rates rest of yr. Crib $5. TV; cable. 3 pools, 2 heated, 1 indoor; wading pool, poolside serv. Complimentary continental bkfst. Restaurant 11 am-10 pm. Bar. Ck-out 11 am. Coin lndry. Meeting rm. Airport, attractions transportation. Lighted tennis. Golf privileges. Exercise equipt; weights, bicycles, whirlpool. Game rm. Private patios, balconies. On lake. Cr cds: A, C, D, JCB, MC, V.

D ⬛ ⬛ ⬛ ⬛ ⬛ ⬛ **SC**

★ ★ **HARLEY.** 151 E Washington St (32801), downtown. 407/841-3220; FAX 407/849-1839. 281 units, 6 story. Mid-Jan-mid-Apr: S, D $75-$85; 2-bedrm suites $105-$200; under 18 free; wkend rates; lower rates rest of yr. Crib free. TV; cable. Heated pool; poolside serv. Restaurant 6:30 am-10:30 pm. Bar 3 pm-midnight; entertainment, dancing Fri-Sat. Ck-out noon. Meeting rms. Garage parking. Airport, Walt Disney World transportation. Golf privileges. Exercise equipt;

weights, bicycles. Refrigerators avail. Some balconies. Cr cds: A, C, D, DS, MC, V.

D 🛏 🧍 ≈ ✈ ⊠ 🔥 SC

★ ★ HOLIDAY INN. 5905 Kirkman Rd (32819), just W of jct FL 435 & I-4 exit 30B, south of downtown. 407/351-3333; FAX 407/351-3333, ext. 1000. 256 units, 10 story. Mid-Feb-mid-Apr, mid-June-mid-Aug, last 2 wks Dec: S, D $79-$129; each addl $10; under 18 free; lower rates rest of yr. Crib free. TV; cable. Pool; wading pool. Restaurant 6:30-2 am. Rm serv 7 am-10 pm. Bar. Ck-out noon. Coin Indry. Meeting rms. Gift shop. Airport, RR station, bus depot transportation. Game rm. Some refrigerators. Private patios, balconies. Near main entrance to Universal Studios Florida. Cr cds: A, C, D, DS, ER, JCB, MC, V.

D ≈ ⊠ 🔥 SC

✔★ ★ HOWARD JOHNSON UNIVERSAL TOWER. 5905 International Dr (32819), at jct FL 435 & I-4, in International Drive Area. 407/351-2100; FAX 407/352-2991. 302 units, 21 story. Feb-Aug, late Dec-early Jan: S, D $69-$89; suites $125-$225; under 18 free; lower rates rest of yr. Crib free. TV; cable. Heated pool; poolside serv. Restaurant 6:30-11:30 am, 5:30-10 pm. Bar 4:30 pm-2 am; entertainment, dancing. Ck-out noon. Coin Indry. Meeting rms. Concierge. Gift shop. Barber, beauty shop. Airport, RR station, bus depot transportation. Game rm. Rec rm. Refrigerators avail. Cylindrical building. Cr cds: A, C, D, DS, ER, JCB, MC, V.

≈ ⊠ 🔥 SC

★ ★ ★ HYATT REGENCY ORLANDO INTL AIRPORT. 9300 Airport Blvd (32827), atop main terminal of Intl Airport, south of downtown. 407/825-1234; FAX 407/856-1672. 446 rms, 10 story, 23 suites. S, D $139-$180; suites $200-$400; under 18 free. Crib avail. Garage parking $8; valet parking $11. TV; cable. Heated pool. Restaurant 6 am-11 pm. Rm serv 24 hrs. Bar. Ck-out noon. Convention facilities. Concierge. Shopping arcade. Golf privileges. Exercise equipt; weights, bicycles, whirlpool. Bathrm phones. Balconies. Dramatic 7-story atrium lobby; airport's main terminal is located 1 level below. Cr cds: A, C, D, DS, ER, JCB, MC, V.

D 🛏 🧍 ≈ ✈ ✈ ⊠ 🔥 SC

★ ★ ★ MARRIOTT DOWNTOWN. 400 W Livingston St (32801), at Orlando Centroplex Center, downtown. 407/843-6664; FAX 407/648-5414. 290 rms, 15 story. S $79-$160; D $114-$175; each addl $15; suites $220-$415; under 18 free; wkend, special package plans. Crib free. Valet parking $5.50/night. TV; cable. Pool; poolside serv. Restaurant 6:30 am-10 pm. Bar; dancing exc Sun. Ck-out noon. Convention facilities. Gift shop. Airport transportation. Exercise equipt; weights, bicycles, whirlpool. Bathrm phones. Refrigerators avail. Landscaped garden terrace. LUXURY LEVEL : OMNI CLUB SERVICE. 39 rms, 8 suites, 2 floors. S $125; D $140; each addl $10; suites $200-$395. Private lounge, honor bar. Complimentary continental bkfst, refreshments. Cr cds: A, C, D, DS, ER, MC, V.

D ≈ ✈ 🔥 SC

★ ★ MARRIOTT ORLANDO AIRPORT. 7499 Augusta National Dr (32822), near Intl Airport, south of downtown. 407/851-9000; FAX 407/857-6211. 484 units, 9 story. S, D $59-$169; suites $175-$500; under 18 free; wkend rates. Crib free. TV; cable. Indoor/outdoor pool; wading pool, poolside serv. Restaurant 6 am-11 pm. Bar 11-2 am. Ck-out noon. Convention facilities. Gift shop. Free airport transportation. Lighted tennis. Exercise equipt; weights, bicycles, whirlpool, steam rm, sauna. Game rm. Rec rm. LUXURY LEVEL : CONCIERGE LEVEL. 62 rms. S, D $155-$199; suites $175-$500. Private lounge, honor bar. Full wet bar in suites. Bathrm phones. Complimentary coffee. Cr cds: A, C, D, DS, ER, MC, V.

D 🛏 🧍 ≈ ✈ 🧍 ✈ ⊠ 🔥 SC

★ ★ ★ PEABODY ORLANDO. 9801 International Dr (32819), near Convention & Civic Center, in International Drive Area. 407/352-4000; res: 800/PEABODY; FAX 407/351-9177. 891 units, 27 story, 56 suites. S, D $190-$240; each addl $15; suites $375-$1,200; under 18 free; some lower rates May-Sept. Crib free. Valet parking $7. TV. Heated pool; wading pool, poolside serv. Supervised child's activities.

Restaurant open 24 hrs. Bar 11-2 am; entertainment exc Sun. Ck-out noon. Convention facilities. Shopping arcade. Beauty shop. Airport transportation. Lighted tennis, pro shop. 18-hole golf privileges, greens fee. Exercise rm; instructor, weight machines, bicycles, whirlpool, sauna, steam rm. Massage therapy. Game rm. Refrigerators avail. Extensive grounds; fountains at entrance. Guests delight in watching as ducks march to the fountain each morning at 11 am and back to their duck palace at 5 pm. LUXURY LEVEL : PEABODY CLUB. 49 rms, 6 suites, 3 story. S, D from $240; suites $375-$1,200. Concierge. Private lounge, honor bar. Full wet bar in suites. Complimentary continental bkfst, refreshments. Cr cds: A, C, D, DS, ER, JCB, MC, V.

D 🛏 🧍 ✈ ≈ ✈ ⊠ 🔥 SC

★ ★ ★ RADISSON PLAZA. 60 S Ivanhoe Blvd (32804), I-4 exit 42, north of downtown. 407/425-4455; FAX 407/843-0262. 336 rms, 15 story. Jan-Apr: S $124; D $134; each addl $15; under 17 free; wkend rates; lower rates rest of yr. TV; cable. Heated pool; poolside serv. Restaurant 6:30 am-10:30 pm. Bar. Ck-out noon. Meeting rms. Concierge. Gift shop. Lighted tennis. Exercise equipt; weights, bicycles, whirlpool, sauna. Minibars; some refrigerators. LUXURY LEVEL : PLAZA CLUB. 46 suites, 2 floors. S $134; D $144; suites $195-$275. Concierge. Private lounge, honor bar. Complimentary continental bkfst, refreshments. Cr cds: A, C, D, DS, ER, MC, V.

D 🧍 ≈ ✈ 🧍 ⊠ 🔥 SC

★ ★ ★ RENAISSANCE HOTEL. 5445 Forbes Place (32812), near Orlando Intl Airport, south of downtown. 407/240-1000; FAX 407/240-1005. 300 rms, 9 story. S, D $110-$145; each addl $15; suites $290-$435; under 17 free. Crib free. TV; cable, in-rm movies. Heated pool; poolside serv. Restaurant 6 am-11 pm. Bar; entertainment exc Sun. Ck-out noon. Convention facilities. Concierge. Gift shop. Free airport transportation. 36-hole golf privileges. Exercise equipt; weight machines, bicycles, whirlpool, sauna, steam rm. Game rm. Bathrm phones, minibars. LUXURY LEVEL : CLUB FLOOR. 33 rms, 3 suites, 1 floor. S, D $145; suites $290-$435. Private lounge, honor bar. Complimentary continental bkfst, refreshments. Cr cds: A, C, D, DS, ER, JCB, MC, V.

D 🛏 🧍 ≈ ✈ ✈ ⊠ 🔥 SC

★ ★ ★ STOUFFER ORLANDO RESORT. 6677 Sea Harbor Dr (32821), in International Drive Area. 407/351-5555; FAX 407/351-9991. 780 rms, 10 story. Late Dec-mid-May: S, D $169-$259; each addl $10; suites $339-$519; under 18 free; lower rates rest of yr. Crib free. TV; cable, in-rm movies avail. Heated pool; wading pool, poolside serv. Supervised child's activities. Restaurant open 24 hrs. Bar; entertainment. Ck-out noon. Convention facilities. Shopping arcade. Barber, beauty shop. Airport, area attractions transportation avail. Lighted tennis, pro. Golf privileges. Exercise rm; instructor, weights, bicycles, whirlpool, steam rm, sauna. Massage therapy. Game rm. Bathrm phones, minibars. Balconies. Atrium lobby; extensive art collection. LUXURY LEVEL : CLUB FLOOR. 94 rms, 8 suites. S, D $209-$249; suites $400-$1,000. Private lounge, honor bar. Full wet bar in suites. Complimentary continental bkfst, refreshments, shoeshine. Cr cds: A, C, D, DS, ER, JCB, MC, V.

D 🧍 🛏 ≈ ✈ 🧍 ⊠ 🔥 SC

★ ★ ★ TWIN TOWERS. 5780 Major Blvd (32819), in International Drive Area. 407/351-1000; res: 800/327-2110; FAX 407/363-0106. 760 rms, 18-19 story. Mid-Feb-mid-Apr: S, D $95-$165; suites $250-$750; under 18 free; lower rates rest of yr. Crib free. TV; cable. Heated pool; wading pool, poolside serv. Playground. Restaurant open 24 hrs. Rm serv 24 hrs. Bar 4:30 pm-2 am; entertainment, dancing Tues-Sat. Ck-out noon. Coin Indry. Convention facilities. Concierge. Shopping arcade. Beauty shop. Airport transportation. Exercise equipt; weight machine, rowers, whirlpool, sauna. Game rm. Refrigerator, wet bar in suites. Located directly in front of Universal Studios entrance. Cr cds: A, C, D, DS, ER, JCB, MC, V.

≈ ✈ ⊠ 🔥 SC

Inn

★ ★ ★ **COURTYARD AT LAKE LUCERNE.** *211 N Lucerne Circle E (32801), near Church St Station, downtown.* 407/648-5188; res: 800/444-5289; FAX 407/246-1368. 22 units in 3 bldgs, 2 story. S, D $65-$150; kit. unit $85. Crib free. TV; cable. Complimentary continental bkfst. Restaurant nearby. Ck-out 11 am, ck-in 3 pm. Airport, RR station, bus depot transportation. Consists of 3 houses-Victorian, antebellum and art deco-located in historic downtown neighborhood; Victorian Norment-Parry is city's oldest structure (1883). Each guest rm uniquely designed by different artist; large collection of English and American antiques and objets d'art. Gardens. Overlooks lake. Cr cds: A, MC, V.

⊠ ⚞ 🐾 SC

Restaurants

★ ★ **4TH FIGHTER GROUP.** *494 Rickenbacker Dr, east of downtown.* 407/898-4251. Hrs: 4-10 pm; Fri, Sat 4-11 pm; Sun 4-10 pm; early-bird dinner 4-6:30 pm; Sun brunch 9 am-2:30 pm. Res accepted. Bar. Semi-a la carte: dinner $14.95-$19.95. Sun brunch $14.95. Child's meals. Specializes in prime rib, steak, fresh seafood. Entertainment. Parking. Modeled after WWII English farmhouse; artifacts. Overlooks Orlando Executive Airport. Cr cds: A, C, D, DS, MC, V.

D

★ ★ ★ **CARUSO'S PALACE.** *8986 International Dr, in International Drive Area.* 407/363-7110. Hrs: 5-10 pm. Res accepted. Italian menu. Bar. Wine list. A la carte entrees: dinner $14-$20. Child's meals. Specializes in pasta, veal, seafood. Interior replica of European opera house; marble furnishing, frescoes, central garden with sculpture and fountains. Cr cds: A, C, D, DS, MC, V.

D

★ ★ **CHARLEY'S STEAK HOUSE.** *6107 S Orange Blossom Trail, at Oakridge Rd, south of downtown.* 407/851-7130. Hrs: 4:30-10 pm; Fri & Sat to 10:30 pm; Sun 4-9:30 pm. Closed Thanksgiving, Dec 25. Res accepted. Bar. Semi-a la carte: dinner $9.95-$19.95. Child's meals. Specializes in flame-broiled aged steak, fresh seafood. Salad bar. Parking. Antiques. Cr cds: A, MC, V.

D SC

★ ★ **CHARLIE'S LOBSTER HOUSE.** *8445 International Dr, at Mercado Shopping Village, in International Drive Area.* 407/352-6929. Hrs: 11 am-10 pm; Fri, Sat to 11 pm. Res accepted. Bar. Semi-a la carte: lunch $4.95-$25.95, dinner $12.95-$36.95. Child's meals. Specializes in seafood, crab cakes. Nautical decor with wood and brass fixtures. Cr cds: A, C, D, DS, ER, MC, V.

D

★ ★ **CHATHAM'S PLACE.** *7575 Dr Phillips Blvd, in Phillips Place, south of downtown.* 407/345-2992. Hrs: 6-9 pm; Fri, Sat to 10 pm. Closed most major hols. Res accepted. Beer. Semi-a la carte: dinner $18.50-$28. Specialties: filet mignon, grouper with pecan butter, rack of lamb. Own specialty desserts. Parking. Intricate wrought-iron grillwork on windows. Totally nonsmoking. Cr cds: A, D, DS, MC, V.

D

✔★ **CHINA COAST.** *7500 International Dr, in International Drive Area.* 407/351-9776. Hrs: 11 am-10 pm; Fri, Sat to 11 pm; Sun brunch to 3 pm. Closed Thanksgiving, Dec 25. Chinese menu. Bar. Semi-a la carte: lunch $4.95-$5.95, dinner $4.95-$12.95. Lunch buffet $5.99. Sun brunch $5.99. Child's meals. Parking. Cr cds: A, C, D, DS, MC, V.

D

★ **CHINA GARDEN.** *1303 S Semoran Blvd, south of downtown.* 407/273-3330. Hrs: 4-10 pm; Fri, Sat to 11 pm; Sun 4-10 pm. Closed Thanksgiving. Res accepted. Chinese menu. Wine, beer. Semi-a la carte: dinner $5.50-$15.95. Complete meals: dinner $10-$16.

Specialty: honey garlic ribs. Parking. Modern decor; Chinese artwork. Cr cds: A, MC, V.

D

★ ★ **CRACKERS.** *129 W Church St, at Church Street Station, downtown.* 407/422-2434. Hrs: 11 am-midnight. Bar. Semi-a la carte: lunch $5.50-$7.95, dinner $9.75-$19.95. Child's meals. Specialties: seafood gumbo, clam chowder, live Maine lobster. Turn-of-the-century carved and paneled bar. Cr cds: A, D, DS, MC, V.

D

★ ★ **DEL FRISCO'S.** *729 Lee Rd (32810), north of downtown.* 407/645-4443. Hrs: 5-10 pm; wkends to 11 pm. Closed Sun; Jan 1, Memorial Day, Dec 25. Res accepted. Bar from 4 pm. A la carte entrees: dinner $14.95-$27.95. Specializes in prime beef, lobster tails. Parking. Steak house atmosphere. Cr cds: A, C, D, MC, V.

D

✔★ ★ **GARY'S DUCK INN.** *3974 S Orange Blossom Trail, south of downtown.* 407/843-0270. Hrs: 11:30 am-10 pm; Sat 5-10 pm; Sun 11:30 am-9 pm. Closed Thanksgiving, Dec 25. Res accepted. Bar. Semi-a la carte: lunch $3.95-$8.95, dinner $8.95-$17.95. Child's meals. Specializes in seafood, steak. Parking. Nautical decor. Family-owned. Cr cds: A, MC, V.

D

★ ★ ★ **LA NORMANDIE.** *2021 E Colonial Dr (FL 50), east of downtown.* 407/896-9976. Hrs: 11:30 am-2 pm, 5-10 pm; Sun to 8 pm; early-bird dinner Mon-Sat 5-6:30 pm. Closed Dec 25. Res accepted. French, continental menu. Bar. Wine list. Semi-a la carte: lunch $7-$11, dinner $10-$19. Specialties: veal fishermen, salmon with lobster sauce, soufflé Grand Marnier. Own baking. Parking. Country French decor. Cr cds: A, C, D, DS, ER, MC, V.

D

★ ★ **LE COQ AU VIN.** *4800 S Orange Ave, south of downtown.* 407/851-6980. Hrs: 11:30 am-2 pm, 5:30-10 pm; Sat from 5:30 pm; Sun 5-9 pm. Closed Mon; Jan 1, Easter, Dec 25. Res accepted. French, Amer menu. Wine, beer. Semi-a la carte: lunch $6.50-$12, dinner $13-$18. Child's meals. Parking. Cr cds: A, C, D, MC, V.

D

★ ★ **LEE'S LAKESIDE.** *431 E Central Blvd, downtown.* 407/841-1565. Hrs: 11 am-11 pm; Sat from 5 pm; Sun to 9 pm; early-bird dinner 4-6 pm. Res accepted. Continental menu. Bar. Semi-a la carte: lunch $7.95-$8.95, dinner $16.95-$22.95. Child's meals. Specializes in fresh seafood, prime rib, veal. Entertainment. Parking. View of skyline across Lake Eola. Cr cds: A, D, DS, MC, V.

D SC

★ ★ **LILI MARLENE'S AVIATORS RESTAURANT & PUB.** *129 W Church St, at Church Street Station, downtown.* 407/422-2434. Hrs: 11 am-4 pm, 5:30 pm-midnight; Sun brunch 10:30 am-3 pm. Bar 11-1 am. Semi-a la carte: lunch $4.95-$9.95, dinner $15.95-$23.95. Sun brunch $9.95. Child's meals. Specializes in aged beef, fresh grilled Florida seafood. Entertainment. Valet parking. In historic district; antiques, WWI aviation artifacts. Cr cds: A, C, D, DS, MC, V.

D

★ ★ ★ **MING COURT.** *9188 International Dr, south of downtown.* 407/351-9988. Hrs: 11 am-2:30 pm, 4:30 pm-midnight. Res accepted. Chinese menu. Bar. Semi-a la carte: lunch $5-$9, dinner $7-$20. Specialties: Peking duck, dim sum. Own sorbets. Chinese performers. Parking. Chinese-style architecture with undulating "Great Wall" enclosing gardens and waterways. Cr cds: A, C, D, DS, JCB, MC, V.

D SC

✔★ ★ **PASSAGE TO INDIA.** *5532 International Dr, in International Drive Area.* 407/351-3456. Hrs: 5-11 pm. Res accepted. Indian menu. Wine, beer. A la carte entrees: dinner $8.95-$15.95. Child's meals. Specializes in clay oven preparations, vegetarian dishes. Parking. Richly carved wooden screens, brass. Cr cds: A, DS, MC, V.

D SC

✔★ **RONNIE'S.** 2702 E Colonial Dr (FL 50), in Colonial Plaza Shopping Ctr, east of downtown. 407/894-2943. Hrs: 7 am-11 pm; Fri, Sat to 1 am. Res accepted. Jewish, Amer menu. Semi-a la carte: bkfst $2.55-$7.95, lunch $3.95-$8.95, dinner $4.75-$9.95. Child's meals. Specializes in corned beef, cheesecake. Own baking. Parking. Bakery and deli; large selection of pastries and ice cream specials. Family-owned. No cr cds accepted.

D

★★★ **SIAM ORCHID.** 7575 Republic Dr, in International Drive Area. 407/351-0821. Hrs: 5-11 pm. Closed July 4, Dec 25. Res accepted. Thai menu. Bar. Semi-a la carte: dinner $12-$22.95. Specialties: Siam Orchid roast duck, fresh seafood. Parking. Thai decor and artifacts. On lake. Cr cds: A, D, MC, V.

D

★★ **VIVALDI.** 107 Pine St, downtown. 407/423-2335. Hrs: 11 am-11 pm; Sat & Sun from 4 pm. Closed Thanksgiving, Dec 25. Res accepted. Italian menu. Bar. A la carte entrees: lunch $6.95-$9.95, dinner $9.90-$22.95. Specialty: Vivaldi's Pride (veal & chicken dish). Parking. Own bread, pasta. Outdoor dining. Intimate gourmet dining. Cr cds: A, D, DS, MC, V.

D SC

Unrated Dining Spots

BLAZING PIANOS. 8445 International Dr, at Mercado Mediterranean Village, in International Drive Area. 407/351-5151; res: 800/347-8181. Dinner show hrs vary each season. Res accepted. Bar. Complete meals: adult $28.95, children $19.95. Dinner show featuring cabaret-style songs and dances of the world's carnival capitals. Parking. Cr cds: A, C, D, DS, MC, V.

D

HARD ROCK CAFE. 5800 Kirkman Rd, at Universal Studios Florida, south of downtown. 407/351-7625. Hrs: 11-2 am. Bar. Semi-a la carte: lunch, dinner $6.95-$15.95. Child's meals. Specializes in hamburgers, "pig sandwich," barbecue dishes. Parking. Outdoor dining. Building shaped like an electric guitar; stained-glass windows depict Elvis Presley, Jerry Lee Lewis and Chuck Berry. Rock & roll and entertainment memorabilia throughout. Cr cds: A, MC, V.

D

KING HENRY'S FEAST. 8984 International Dr, in International Drive Area. 407/351-5151. Dinner show hrs vary each season. Res required. Bar. Complete meals: adult $25.95; children $17.95. Specializes in baked chicken, barbecued ribs. Entertainment includes dueling knights, magicians, jesters. Parking. Medieval palace decor; costumed servers. Cr cds: A, DS, MC, V.

Walt Disney World

Motor Hotels

✔★ **COMFORT INN.** (Box 22776, Lake Buena Vista 32830) 8442 Palm Pkwy, at Vista Ctr. 407/239-7300; res: 800/999-7300; FAX 407/239-7740. 640 rms, 5 story. Feb-mid-Apr, June-Aug: S, D up to 4, $69; family rates; lower rates rest of yr. Crib free. Pet accepted. TV. 2 pools, 1 heated. Restaurant 6:30-10:30 am, 6-9 pm. Bar 5:30 pm-2 am. Ck-out 11 am. Coin lndry. Valet serv. Sundries. Gift shop. Free Walt

Disney World transportation. Game rm. Cr cds: A, C, D, DS, ER, JCB, MC, V.

D 🏊 🎿 🏸 🔥 SC

★★★ **HOLIDAY INN LAKE SUN SPREE RESORT-LAKE BUENA VISTA.** (Box 22184, 13351 FL 535, Lake Buena Vista 32830) I-4 exit 27, S on FL 535. 407/239-4500; FAX 407/239-7713, 507 rms. 6 story. Mid-Feb-mid-Apr, mid-June-mid-Aug, late Dec: S, D $106-$140; under 18 free; lower rates rest of yr. Crib free. TV; cable, in-rm movies. Heated pool; wading pool, poolside serv. Playground. Supervised child's activities. Restaurant 7 am-10:30 pm. Rm serv. Bar from 4:30 pm; entertainment. Ck-out 11 am. Coin lndry. Bellhops. Valet serv. Concierge. Sundries. Airport transportation. Free Walt Disney World transportation. 36-hole golf privileges, pro, putting green, driving range. Exercise equipt; weight machine, stair machine, whirlpools. Game rm. Refrigerators. Pink and white stone structure with blue-tiled roofs. Cr cds: A, C, D, DS, ER, JCB, MC, V.

D 🏃 🎿 🏊 🏸 🔥 SC

★★ **HOWARD JOHNSON PARK SQUARE INN AND SUITES.** (PO Box 22818, Lake Buena Vista 32830) 8501 Palm Pkwy. I-4 exit 27 to FL 535, N to Vista Center. 407/239-6900; FAX 407/239-1287. 222 rms, 3 story, 86 suites. Feb-mid-Apr, June-Aug, late Dec: S, D $80-$115; each addl $10; suites $90-$140; under 18 free; lower rates rest of yr. Crib free. TV; in-rm movies. 2 pools, heated; wading pool, whirlpool. Playground. Restaurant 7-11 am, 5-10 pm. Bar 4:30 pm-midnight. Ck-out 11 am. Coin lndry. Meeting rms. Bellhops. Sundries. Gift shop. Airport transportation. Free Walt Disney World transportation. Game rm. Lawn games. Refrigerator in suites. Balconies. Landscaped courtyard. Cr cds: A, C, D, DS, ER, JCB, MC, V.

D 🏊 🏸 🔥 SC

Hotels

★★★ **BUENA VISTA PALACE.** (1900 Buena Vista Dr, Lake Buena Vista 32830) In Walt Disney World Village. 407/827-2727; res: 800/327-2990; FAX 407/827-6034. 1,028 rms, 27 story, 128 suites. Feb-Apr, late Dec: S, D $145-$240; suites $230-$850; under 18 free; lower rates rest of yr. Crib free. TV; cable. 3 pools, 2 heated; wading pool, poolside serv. Playground. Supervised child's activities (June-Labor Day; also wk of Christmas & Easter). Restaurant open 24 hrs (also see ARTHUR'S 27). Bar 11-2 am; entertainment, dancing. Ck-out 11 am. Coin lndry. Convention facilities. Shopping arcade. Barber, beauty shop. Valet parking. Airport transportation. Free Walt Disney World transportation. Lighted tennis. 18-hole golf privileges, pro, pro shop, putting green, driving range. Exercise equipt; weights, bicycles, whirlpool, sauna. Game rm. Minibars. Some in-rm whirlpools, refrigerators. Many balconies. **LUXURY LEVEL : CROWN LEVEL.** 36 rms, 2 suites. S, D (to 5 persons) $240; 1-bedrm suites $385-$615. Concierge. Private lounge. Bathrm phones. Some in-rm steam baths. Complimentary continental bkfst, refreshments. Cr cds: A, C, D, DS, MC, V.

D 🏃 🎿 🏊 🏸 🔥

✔★★ **DOUBLETREE CLUB.** (8688 Palm Pkwy, Lake Buena Vista 32836) I-4 exit 27 to FL 535, N to Vista Center. 407/239-8500; FAX 407/239-8591. 167 rms, 6 story. S, D $85; each addl $10; under 12 free. Crib free. TV; cable, in-rm movies. Heated pool; poolside serv. Restaurant 5-10 pm. Bar to 11 pm. Ck-out 11 am. Coin lndry. Meeting rms. Concierge. Airport, area attractions transportation. Free Walt Disney World transportation. Exercise equipt; weights, rowing machine, whirlpool. Game rm. Rec rm. Refrigerators avail. Cr cds: A, C, D, DS, ER, JCB, MC, V.

D 🏊 🏸 🎿 🔥 SC

★★★ **EMBASSY SUITES RESORT.** (8100 Lake Ave, Orlando 32836) Near jct I-4, FL 535. 407/239-1144; res: 800/257-8483; FAX 407/239-1718. 280 suites, 6 story. Feb-Apr & mid-Dec-Jan 1: S, D (up to 4 adults) $135-$250; family rates; golf, Disney plans; lower rates rest of yr. Crib free. TV; cable, in-rm movies. 2 heated pools, 1 indoor; wading pool, poolside serv. Playground. Supervised child's activities. Complimentary full bkfst. Complimentary coffee in rms. Restaurant 11 am-11 pm. Bar 5 pm-midnight. Ck-out 11:30 am. Coin lndry. Meeting rms. Gift shop. Airport transportation; free scheduled shuttle to all Disney theme parks. Lighted tennis. 18-hole golf privileges, pro, putting green, driving range. Exercise equipt; weight machines, bicycles, whirlpool, sauna. Game rm. Rec rm. Refrigerators, minibars. Cr cds: A, C, D, DS, ER, JCB, MC, V.

🅳 ♨ SC

★ ★ ★ **GROSVENOR RESORT.** *(Box 22202, 1850 Hotel Plaza Blvd, Lake Buena Vista 32830) In Walt Disney World Village. 407/828-4444; res: 800/624-4109; FAX 407/828-8192.* 630 rms, 19 story. Feb-late Apr: S, D $79-$170; suites $175-$520; under 18 free; lower rates rest of yr. Crib free. TV; cable, in-rm movies. 2 heated pools; wading pool, whirlpool, poolside serv. Playground. Coffee, tea in rms. Restaurant open 24 hrs. Bar 11-2 am; entertainment in season. Ck-out 11 am. Coin lndry. Convention facilities. Concierge. Shopping arcade. Free Walt Disney World transportation. Lighted tennis. Golf privileges, pro, putting green, driving range. Game rm. Lawn games. Activities dir (summer). Sherlock Holmes Museum on grounds. Cr cds: A, C, D, DS, ER, JCB, MC, V.

🅳 ♨ SC

★ ★ ★ **GUEST QUARTERS SUITE RESORT.** *(2305 Hotel Plaza Blvd, Lake Buena Vista 32830) In Walt Disney World Village. 407/934-1000; FAX 407/934-1008.* 229 suites (1-2 bedrm), 7 story. Late Dec-Apr: S, D $139-$280; each addl $20; lower rates rest of yr. Crib free. TV; cable. Heated pool; wading pool, poolside serv. Playground. Restaurant 7 am-midnight. Bar 2 pm-midnight. Ck-out 11 am. Coin lndry. Meeting rms. Concierge. Gift shop. Airport transportation. Free Walt Disney World transportation. Lighted tennis. 18-hole golf privileges, pro, putting green, driving range. Exercise equipt; weights, bicycles, whirlpool. Game rm. Lawn games. Refrigerators. Some private patios. Cr cds: A, C, D, DS, ER, MC, V.

🅳 ♨ SC

★ ★ ★ **HILTON AT WALT DISNEY WORLD VILLAGE.** *(1751 Hotel Plaza Blvd, Lake Buena Vista 32830) In Walt Disney World Village. 407/827-4000; FAX 407/827-6370.* 814 rms, 10 story, 26 suites. Feb-mid-Apr, late Dec: S, D $220-$250; each addl $20; suites $459-$1,500; family rates; lower rates rest of yr. Crib free. TV; cable. 2 heated pools; wading pool, poolside serv. Playground. Free supervised child's activities. Restaurant 6:30 am-midnight. Bar 11-2 am; dancing (seasonal). Ck-out 11 am. Coin lndry. Convention facilities. Barber, beauty shop. Valet parking. Airport transportation. Free Walt Disney World transportation. Lighted tennis, pro. Golf privileges, pro, pro shop, putting green, driving range. Exercise equipt; weight machine, bicycles, whirlpool, sauna. Game rm. Minibars; some bathrm phones, refrigerators. Some private patios, balconies. *LUXURY LEVEL : TOWERS.* 80 rms, 4 suites, 2 floors. S, D $260-$290; suites $509-$1,500. Private lounge, honor bar. Concierge. Wet bar in suites. Complimentary continental bkfst, refreshments, newspaper. Cr cds: A, C, D, DS, ER, JCB, MC, V.

🅳 ♨

✔★ ★ **HOWARD JOHNSON RESORT.** *(Box 22204, 1805 Hotel Plaza Blvd, Lake Buena Vista 32830) In Walt Disney World Village. 407/828-8888; FAX 407/827-4623.* 323 rms, 14 story. Feb-Apr, wk of Dec 25: S, D $65-$155; each addl $15; suites $250-$395; under 18 free; lower rates rest of yr. Crib free. TV; in-rm movies. 2 pools, heated; wading pool, poolside serv. Playground. Restaurant 6 am-midnight. Rm serv 7 am-10 pm. Bar 4 pm-midnight. Ck-out 11 am. Coin lndry. Convention facilities. Gift shop. Airport transportation. Free Walt Disney World transportation. Tennis & golf privileges. Exercise equipt; weights, bicycles, whirlpool. Game rm. Many private patios, balconies. Cr cds: A, C, D, DS, ER, JCB, MC, V.

🅳 ♨ SC

★ ★ **ROYAL PLAZA.** *(1905 Hotel Plaza Blvd, Lake Buena Vista 32830) In Walt Disney World Village. 407/828-2828; res: 800/248-7890; FAX 407/827-6338.* 396 rms, 2-17 story. Feb-Apr: S, D $147-$157; suites $404-$550; family rates; lower rates rest of yr. Crib free. TV; cable; in-rm movies. Heated pool; whirlpool, sauna, poolside serv. Playground. Restaurant 6:30 am-midnight. Pizza & beer noon-mid-

night. Bar 11-2:30 am; entertainment, dancing. Ck-out 11 am. Coin lndry. Convention facilities. Gift shop. Barber, beauty shop. Free valet parking. Airport transportation. Free Walt Disney World transportation. Lighted tennis. 18-hole golf privileges, driving range. Game rm. Lawn games. Some bathrm phones. Refrigerators avail. Balconies. Cr cds: A, C, D, DS, ER, JCB, MC, V.

🅳 ♨ SC

★ ★ **TRAVELODGE.** *(Box 22205, 2000 Hotel Plaza Blvd, Lake Buena Vista 32830) In Walt Disney World Village. 407/828-2424; FAX 407/828-8933.* 325 rms, 18 story. S, D $109-$169; suites $199-$299. Crib free. TV. Heated pool; wading pool, poolside serv. Playground. Coffee in rms. Restaurant 7 am-midnight. Bar 11:30-1:30 am; entertainment, dancing. Ck-out 11 am. Coin lndry. Meeting rms. Concierge. Gift shop. Airport transportation. Free Walt Disney World transportation. Lighted tennis privileges, pro. 18-hole golf privileges, pro, putting green, driving range. Game rm. Lawn games. Minibars; some refrigerators. Balconies. On lake. Cr cds: A, C, D, DS, ER, JCB, MC, V.

🅳 ♨ SC

Inn

✔★ ★ **PERRI HOUSE BED & BREAKFAST.** *(PO Box 22005, 10417 FL 535, Orlando 32836) N of I-4 exit 27 on FL 535. 407/876-4830; res: 800/780-4830; FAX 407/876-0241.* 6 rms. S $65; D $75-$85; higher rates special events, major hols. Crib free. TV; cable. Pool; whirlpool. Complimentary continental bkfst. Ck-out 11:30 am, ck-in 3 pm. Airport, RR station transportation. Secluded on 20 acres; bird sanctuary. Adj Walt Disney World property. Cr cds: A, DS, MC, V.

♨ SC

Resorts

★ ★ ★ **DISNEY'S BEACH CLUB RESORT.** *(1800 Epcot Resorts Blvd, Lake Buena Vista 32830) In Walt Disney World Village; 5 minute walk to Epcot Center. 407/934-8000; FAX 407/934-3850.* 584 rms, 5 story. Mid-Feb-Apr, mid-June-late Aug, major hols: S, D $230-$290; each addl $15; suites $410-$800; under 18 free; Disney packages; lower rates rest of yr. Crib free. TV; cable. 2 pools; poolside serv. Dining rm 7 am-10 pm. Rm serv 24 hrs. Bar 11-1 am. Ck-out 11 am, ck-in 3 pm. Coin lndry. Convention facilities. Valet serv. Sundries. Gift shop. Barber, beauty shop. Free valet parking. Airport transportation. Free Disney transportation, water transportation to Disney-MGM Studios Theme Park. Lighted tennis, pro. Golf privileges. Mini waterpark; boating, marina. Lawn games. Game rm. Exercise rm; instructor, weight machine, bicycles, sauna, steam rm. Bathrm phones, minibars; wet bar in suites. Balconies. Located on the shores of a 25-acre man-made lake. Architect Robert A.M. Stern has re-created a New England Village with a turn-of-the-century theme. DISNEY'S BEACH CLUB RESORT meets with DISNEY'S YACHT CLUB RESORT (see) in a central courtyard and shares a Fantasy Lagoon. Cr cds: A, MC, V.

♨

★ ★ **DISNEY'S CARIBBEAN BEACH RESORT.** *(PO Box 10000, Lake Buena Vista 32830) 900 Cayman Way, off I-4 exit 36B. 407/934-3400; FAX 407/934-3288.* 2,112 rms in several village groups, 2 story. S, D $89-$121; each addl $12; under 18 free. Crib free. TV; cable. 7 heated pools; wading pool, whirlpool, poolside serv, lifeguard. 4 playgrounds. Coffee in rms. Dining rm 5:30 am-midnight; several dining areas. Pizza delivery. Bar noon-1:30 am. Ck-out 11 am, ck-in 3 pm. Coin lndry. Shopping arcade. Free bus transportation within Disney complex & to all Disney attractions. Tennis privileges. Golf privileges, greens fee. Marina; boat rentals. Game rm. Minibars. Picnic tables. 1½-acre island-like resort with lake. Each village has a pool and beach area, lndry facilities and bus stop. 1¼-mi promenade around lake; island play area for children in middle of lake. Cr cds: A, MC, V.

🅳 ♨

★ ★ **DISNEY'S CONTEMPORARY RESORT.** *Box 10000 (32830), Off US 192, I-4 in Walt Disney World. 407/824-1000; FAX*

407/824-3539. 1,041 rms, 14 story tower, 2 3-story bldgs. Mid-Dec-Jan 1, mid-Feb-late Apr, early June-mid-Aug: S, D $215-$270; each addl $15; 1-bedrm suites $450-$470; under 18 free; lower rates rest of yr. Crib free. TV; cable. 2 heated pools; wading pool, lifeguard. Playground. Restaurant (see TOP OF THE WORLD). Rm serv 24 hrs. Snack bar 24 hrs. Bars noon-1 am; entertainment, dancing. Ck-out 11 am, ck-in 3 pm. Convention facilities. Shopping arcade. Barber, beauty shop. Airport transportation. Valet parking. Lighted tennis. 99-hole golf privileges. Exercise rm; instructor, weights, bicycles, sauna. Massage therapy. Lawn games. Refrigerator in suites. Balconies. Monorail runs through 12-story atrium lobby. On lake. *LUXURY LEVEL : SUITE FLOOR.* 33 rms, 11 suites. S, D $350-$365; suites $750-$1,100. Concierge. Private lounge. Bathrm phones. Complimentary bkfst, refreshments. Cr cds: A, MC, V.

★ ★ ★ ★ **DISNEY'S GRAND FLORIDIAN BEACH RESORT.** *Box 10,000, 4001 Grand Floridian Way (32830), in Walt Disney World. 407/824-3000; FAX 407/824-3186.* 900 rms: 65 rms in main bldg, 9 suites, 817 rms, 17 suites in 5 lodge bldgs, 4 & 5 story. Mid-Dec-Jan 1, mid-Feb-late Apr, early June-mid-Aug: S, D $265-$440; each addl $15; suites (see LUXURY LEVEL); under 18 free; special package plans; lower rates rest of yr. Crib free. TV; cable. Heated pool; wading pool, poolside serv, lifeguard. Dining rm 7 am-11 pm; five addl dining rms (also see VICTORIA & ALBERT'S); afternoon high tea. Rm serv 24 hrs. Bar 11-1 am. Ck-out 11 am, ck-in 3 pm. Coin lndry. Convention facilities. Valet parking. Barber, beauty shop. Airport transportation; also monorail to Magic Kingdom, Epcot Center & Disney/MGM Studios. Tennis, clay courts, pro. 99-hole golf privileges, greens fee, pro. Private beach; waterskiing, sailing, marina, boat rentals. Lawn games. Game rm. Exercise rm; instructor, weight machines, bicycles, whirlpool, steam rm. Massage. Fishing guides. Bathrm phones, minibars; wet bar in suites. Balconies. Kennels avail. Complimentary newspaper daily. Striking Victorian-style hotel with broad verandas, cupolas and gingerbread porches, palatial vaulted lobby, open-cage elevator, an aviary, palms and ferns; creates a luxurious, turn-of-the-century atmosphere. On 40 acres, overlooking lagoon. Bldgs #7 and #9 (335 rms) are totally nonsmoking. *LUXURY LEVEL : CONCIERGE.* 83 rms, 9 suites, 5 story (entire main bldg). S, D $430-$440; suites $805-$1,475. Concierge. Private lounge. Deluxe toiletry amenities. Complimentary continental bkfst, refreshments. Cr cds: A, MC, V.

★ ★ ★ **DISNEY'S POLYNESIAN RESORT.** *Box 10000 (32830), off US 192, I-4 in Walt Disney World. 407/824-2000; FAX 407/824-3174.* 853 rms, 2-3 story. Mid-Dec-Jan 1, mid-Feb-late Apr, early June-mid-Aug: S, D $190-$325; each addl $15; suites $350-$750; under 18 free; lower rates rest of yr. Crib free. TV; cable. 2 heated pools; wading pool, poolside serv, lifeguard. Playground. Restaurant open 24 hrs; dining rm 7 am-11 pm (also see PAPEETE BAY VERANDAH). Children's dinner theater. Rm serv 6:30-1 am. Bar 1 pm-1:30 am; entertainment. Ck-out 11 am, ck-in 3 pm. Coin lndry. Sundries. Shopping arcade. Barber, beauty shop. Airport, RR station, bus depot transportation. Lighted tennis, pro. 99-hole golf privileges, greens fee, pro. Health club privileges. Fishing (guides avail). Game rm. Balconies. Kennels. On lake; 2 swimming beaches, boat rentals, waterskiing, marina. *LUXURY LEVEL : KING KAMEHAMEHA SERVICE.* 102 rms, 3 floors. S, D $325. Concierge. Private lounge. Valet parking. Cr cds: A, MC, V.

★ ★ **DISNEY'S PORT ORLEANS.** *(PO Box 10000, Lake Buena Vista 32830) 1662 Old South Rd, off I-4 exit 26B. 407/934-5000; FAX 407/934-5353.* 1,008 rms in 7 bldgs, 3 story. S, D $89-$121; each addl $12; under 18 free. Crib free. TV; cable. Pool; wading pool, whirlpool, sauna. Dining rms 6:30 am-10 pm. Bar 11 am-midnight. Ck-out 11 am, ck-in after 3 pm. Grocery. Coin lndry. Bellhops. Valet serv. Gift shop. Airport transportation. Lighted tennis privileges, pro. Golf privileges, pro, putting green, driving range. Boats. Bicycle rentals. Game rm. Located on a canal, ornate row-house buildings with courtyards and intricate railings are reminiscent of the French Quarter in New Orleans; cobblestone streets, trips by flat-bottom boats down river to shops and showplaces. Cr cds: A, MC, V.

★ ★ **DISNEY'S VILLAGE RESORT.** *(PO Box 10150, Lake Buena Vista 32830) 1901 Buena Vista Dr, in Walt Disney World Village. 407/827-1100; FAX 407/934-2741.* 324 suites, 261 1-3-bedrm villas, 4 townhouses, 1-3 story, 261 kits. No elvtr. Mid-Dec-Jan 1, mid-Feb-late Apr, early June-mid-Aug: suites $200-$290; villas, townhouses $270-$375; homes $750-$825; lower rates rest of yr. Crib free. TV; cable. 6 heated pools; wading pool. 6 playgrounds. Ck-out 11 am, ck-in 4 pm. Free lndry facilities. Convention facilities. Valet serv. Concierge. Shopping arcade. Lighted tennis. 99-hole golf, greens fee, pro, putting green, driving range. Exercise equipt; weights, bicycles. Electric cart, bicycle and boat rentals. Game rm. Refrigerators; some bathrm phones. Private patios, balconies. Picnic tables, grills. Located on 450 wooded acres. Cr cds: A, MC, V.

★ ★ ★ **DISNEY'S YACHT CLUB RESORT.** *(1700 Epcot Resort Blvd, Lake Buena Vista 32830) In Walt Disney World Village; 5 minute walk to Epcot Center. 407/934-7000; FAX 407/934-3450.* 635 rms, 5 story, 60 suites. Mid-Feb-mid-Apr, mid-June-late Aug, major hols: S, D $230-$295; each addl $15; suites from $435; under 18 free; Disney packages; lower rates rest of yr. Crib free. TV; cable. Pool. Dining rm 7 am-10 pm. Rm serv 24 hrs. Bar 11-1 am. Ck-out 11 am, ck-in 3 pm. Coin lndry. Convention facilities. Bellhops. Valet serv. Concierge. Sundries. Gift shop. Barber, beauty shop. Free valet parking. Airport transportation. Free Disney transportation, including water taxi, to Disney-MGM Studios Theme Park. Lighted tennis, pro. Golf privileges. Mini waterpark; boating, marina. Lawn games. Game rm. Exercise rm; instructor, weight machine, bicycles, whirlpool, sauna, steam rm. Massage. Bathrm phones, minibars; wet bar in suites. Located on the shores of a 25-acre man-made lake. Architect Robert A.M. Stern's design echoes New England seaside summer residences of the 1890s. DISNEY'S YACHT CLUB RESORT meets with DISNEY'S BEACH CLUB RESORT (see) in a central courtyard with a "quiet pool" and shares a Fantasy Lagoon with poolside serv. *LUXURY LEVEL : CONCIERGE LEVEL.* 75 rms, 18 suites. S, D $380-$395 suites from $475. Concierge. Private lounge, honor bar. Whirlpool in suites. Complimentary continental bkfst, refreshments. Cr cds: A, MC, V.

★ ★ **DIXIE LANDINGS.** *(PO Box 10000, 1251 Dixie Dr, Lake Buena Vista 32830) I-4 exit 26B. 407/934-6000; FAX 407/934-5024.* 2,048 rms in 15 bldgs, 2-3 story. S, D $89-$121; each addl $12; family rates; golf plans. Crib free. TV; cable. 6 pools, some heated; wading pool, whirlpool, poolside serv, lifeguards. Playground. Restaurant 6:30 am-midnight. Bar; entertainment. Ck-out 11 am, ck-in 3 pm. Grocery, coin lndry, package store. Bellhops. Valet serv. Gift shop. Airport transportation. Lighted tennis, pro. 99-hole golf, greens fee, pro, putting green, driving range. Boat, bicycle rentals. Game rm. Old South plantation-style project located "on the Sassagoula River." Alligator Bayou region is reminiscent of old Cajun country, while Magnolia Bend showcases stately mansions typical of the upriver South. Cr cds: A, MC, V.

★ ★ ★ **HYATT REGENCY GRAND CYPRESS.** *(1 Grand Cypress Blvd, Orlando 32836) 2 mi E of I-4 exit 27, Lake Buena Vista exit. 407/239-1234; FAX 407/239-3800.* 750 units, 18 story, 75 suites. Feb-May: S, D $250-$330; suites $600-$1,200; golf plans; lower rates rest of yr. Crib free. Valet parking $8. TV; cable, in-rm movies. Heated pool; poolside serv. Supervised child's activities. Dining rm (see HEMINGWAY'S). 5 restaurants. Rm serv 24 hrs. Bar; entertainment. Ck-out noon, ck-in 4 pm. Convention facilities. Valet serv. Concierge. Shopping arcade. Personal care salon. Walt Disney World transportation. 12 tennis courts, 6 lighted, pro, instruction avail. 45-hole golf, Academy of Golf, pro, putting green, driving range, pitch & putt. Sailing, canoes, paddleboats, windsurfing, scuba diving; rentals avail. Lake with white sand beach. Nature area, Audubon walk; jogging trails. Bicycle rentals. Lawn games. Game rm. Equestrian center; Western and English trails.

Exercise rm; instructor, weights, bicycles, whirlpool, sauna, steam rm. Massage therapy. Minibars. Bathrm phone, refrigerator in some suites. Some private patios. Balconies. Elegant decor. Extensive art collection and artifacts; hotel tours avail. On 1,500 landscaped acres. Trolley and van transport throughout property. *LUXURY LEVEL : REGENCY CLUB.* 68 units, 14 suites. S, D $420; each addl $25; suites $800-$4,000. Concierge. Private lounge. Wet bar in suites. Complimentary continental bkfst, refreshments, newspaper. Cr cds: A, C, D, DS, ER, JCB, MC, V.

★ ★ **MARRIOTT'S ORLANDO WORLD CENTER.** *(8701 World Center Dr, Orlando 32821)* I-4 exit 26A, jct FL 536. 407/239-4200; FAX 407/238-8777. 1,503 rms, 28 story, 101 suites. S, D $149-$229; suites from $250; under 18 free. Crib free. Valet parking $5, overnight $8. TV; cable. 3 heated pools, 1 indoor; wading pool, poolside serv. Free supervised child's activities. Dining rms 6 am-11 pm (also see TUSCANY'S). Rm serv 24 hrs. Bar; pianist, dancing. Ck-out 11 am, ck-in 4 pm. Convention facilities. Coin lndry. Concierge. Shopping arcade. Barber, beauty shop. Airport, area attractions transportation. Lighted tennis, pro. 18-hole golf, greens fee $95 (incl half-cart), pro, putting green, driving range. 5-acre activity court with pools, lagoon, waterfalls, sun deck. Lawn games. Game rm. Exercise rm; instructor, weights, bicycles, whirlpool, sauna. Massage therapy. Some refrigerators, minibars. Private patios, balconies. On 200 landscaped acres; view of many lakes. Cr cds: A, C, D, DS, ER, JCB, MC, V.

★ ★ **RESIDENCE INN BY MARRIOTT.** *(8800 Meadow Creek Dr, Orlando 32821)* , 4 mi S, I-4 exit 27. 407/239-7700; FAX 407/239-7605. 688 kit. villas (1-2 bedrm, 8 villas to unit), 2 story. Mid-Dec-early Jan, mid-Feb-Apr, mid-June-mid Aug: S $125-$175; D $149-$199; wkly, monthly rates; lower rates rest of yr. Crib free. TV; cable, in-rm movies. 3 heated pools; poolside serv. Complimentary coffee in rms. Rm serv. Ck-out 11 am, ck-in 4 pm. Grocery, coin lndry. Meeting rms. Bellhops. Gift shop. Airport, Walt Disney World transportation. Lighted tennis. Balconies. Cr cds: A, C, D, DS, JCB, MC, V.

★ ★ ★ **VISTANA.** *(PO Box 22051, Lake Buena Vista 32830)* 8800 Visitana Center Dr; I-4 exit 27, then 1 mi S on FL 535. 407/239-3100; res: 800/877-8787; FAX 407/239-3062. 916 kit. villas (2-bedrm) 1, 2 & 3 story. Feb-mid-Apr, late Dec: villas $225-$275; family rates; package plans; lower rates rest of yr. Crib $10. TV; in-rm movies. 6 pools, heated; wading pools, poolside serv. Playgrounds. Supervised child's activities. Dining rm 7 am-11 pm. Snack bar. Ck-out 10 am, ck-in 4 pm. Grocery. Package stores. Sports dir. 13 lighted tennis courts, pro, pro shop. Bicycle rentals. Lawn games. Soc dir. Movies, planned activities. Game rm. Exercise equipt; weights, bicycles, whirlpool, steam rm, sauna. Refrigerators, washers & dryers. Private patios, balconies. Grills. On 110 acres. Cr cds: A, C, D, DS, MC, V.

★ ★ ★ **WALT DISNEY WORLD DOLPHIN.** *(Box 22653, 1500 Epcot Resorts Blvd, Lake Buena Vista 32830)* In Walt Disney World Village, adj to Epcot Center. 407/934-4000; res: 800/227-1500; FAX 407/934-4099. 1,509 rms, 27 story, 140 suites. Mid-Feb-mid-Apr, late Dec: S, D $255-$335; suites from $450; under 18 free; Disney packages; lower rates rest of yr. Crib free. TV; cable. 4 pools, 3 heated; wading pool, poolside serv, lifeguard. Playground. Supervised child's activities. Dining rm open 24 hrs. Rm serv 24 hrs. Bars noon-2 am; pianist. Ck-out 11 am, ck-in 3 pm. Coin lndry. Convention facilities. Concierge. Shopping arcade. Barber, beauty shop. Airport transportation. Free Walt Disney World transportation, by both land and water. Lighted tennis, pro. Golf privileges. Exercise rm; instructor, weight machine, bicycles, whirlpool. Game rm. Rec rm. Minibars; many bathrm phones; wet bar in suites. Designed by architect Michael Graves as "entertainment architecture," the hotel features a waterfall cascading down the front of the building into a pool supported by two dolphin statues. *LUXURY LEVEL : DOLPHIN TOWERS.* 172 rms, 35 suites, 8 floors. S, D $365; suites $550-$2,400. Concierge. Private

lounge, honor bar. In-rm whirlpool in suites. Complimentary continental bkfst, refreshments. Cr cds: A, C, D, DS, ER, JCB, MC, V.

★ ★ ★ **WALT DISNEY WORLD SWAN.** *(1200 Epcot Resort Blvd, Lake Buena Vista 32830)* In Walt Disney World Village, adj to Epcot Center. 407/934-3000; res: 800/248-SWAN; FAX 407/934-4499. 758 rms, 12 story, 64 suites. S, D $260-$350; each addl $20; suites $350-$1,300; under 18 free; Disney packages. Crib free. Valet parking $7 overnight. TV; cable. 2 pools, 1 rock-sculptured grotto; wading pool, poolside serv, lifeguard (grotto). Playground. Supervised child's activities. Dining rm 6:30 am-11 pm. Rm serv 24 hrs. Bar 3 pm-midnight. Ck-out 11 am, ck-in 3 pm. Convention facilities. Concierge. Gift shop. Beauty shop. Airport transportation. Free transportation, including water taxi, to Epcot Center, Disney-MGM Studios Theme Park and other Kingdom areas. 8 lighted tennis courts, pro. Golf privileges. Exercise equipt; weight machine, bicycles, whirlpool, sauna. Game rm. Minibars; many bathrm phones; some wet bars. Balconies. Situated on 150-acre resort site. Dramatic style of "entertainment architecture," created by Michael Graves; two 28-ton, 47.3-ft high swan statues grace the roofline. *LUXURY LEVEL : ROYAL BEACH CLUB.* 45 rms, 6 suites, 2 floors. S, D $350; suites $1,100-$1,300. Concierge. Private lounge, honor bar. Complimentary continental bkfst, refreshments. Cr cds: A, C, D, DS, ER, JCB, MC, V.

Restaurants

★ ★ ★ **ARTHUR'S 27.** *(See Buena Vista Palace Hotel)* 407/827-3450. Hrs: 6-10:30 pm. Res accepted. International menu. Bar. Wine cellar. Semi-a la carte: dinner $23-$35. Complete meals: dinner $45-$60. Specializes in gourmet dishes, some custom-prepared. Pianist. Valet parking. On 27th floor; view of Walt Disney World. Cr cds: A, C, D, DS, MC, V.

★ ★ **CHEF MICKEY'S.** *In Walt Disney World Village.* 407/828-3830. Hrs: 8 am-2 pm, 5-10 pm. Res accepted. Family dining with character dinner. Semi-a la carte: bkfst $4.75-$9, lunch $5-$9, dinner $10.75-$22. Child's meals. Specializes in beef, seafood. Parking. Chef Mickey appears at dinner. View of lake. Totally nonsmoking. Cr cds: A, MC, V.

★ ★ **CRAB HOUSE.** *(8496 Palm Pkwy, Lake Buena Vista)* I-4 exit 27 to FL 535, N to Vista Center. 407/239-1888. Hrs: 11:30 am-11 pm. Bar. Semi-a la carte: lunch $4.95-$10.95, dinner $10.95-$29.95. Child's meals. Specializes in prime rib, fresh seafood, Maryland crab. Salad bar. Parking. Patio dining. Rustic, New England-style decor. Cr cds: A, C, D, DS, MC, V.

★ ★ ★ ★ **EMPRESS ROOM.** *Aboard the Empress Lilly in Walt Disney World Village.* 407/828-3900. Hrs: 6-9:30 pm. Res accepted. Continental menu. Wine list. A la carte entrees: dinner $30-$40. Serv charge 20%. Specialty: Empress Room Trio. Own baking. Valet parking. Gourmet dining aboard 1890s Mississippi riverboat overlooking lake. Louis XV decor. Jacket. Totally nonsmoking. Cr cds: A, MC, V.

★ ★ ★ **FISHERMAN'S DECK.** *Aboard the Empress Lilly in Walt Disney World Village.* 407/828-3900. Hrs: Disney character bkfst, sittings 8:30 & 10 am (res required); 11:30 am-2 pm, 5:30-10 pm. Res accepted. Continental menu. Bar. Complete meals: bkfst $11.50, children $7.95. A la carte entrees: lunch $6.25-$10.95, dinner $15.75-$25. Child's meals. Valet parking. Aboard 1890s Mississippi riverboat overlooking lake. Totally nonsmoking. Cr cds: A, MC, V.

★ ★ ★ **HEMINGWAY'S.** *(See Hyatt Regency Grand Cypress Resort)* 407/239-1234. Hrs: 11:30 am-2:30 pm, 6-10:30 pm; Sun & Mon 6-10:30 pm. Res accepted. Bar to 1 am. Extensive wine list. A la carte entrees: lunch $7-$14, dinner $14-$30. Child's meals. Specializes in live Maine lobster, Floridita seafood salad, seafood, steak. Valet parking. Outdoor dining. Atmosphere of old Key West with ceiling fans, wicker furnishings, tropical palms. Perched atop a rock precipice, overlooking lagoon-like pool. Cr cds: A, C, D, DS, ER, JCB, MC, V.

D

★ ★ **KOBÉ JAPANESE STEAK HOUSE.** *(8460 Palm Pkwy, Lake Buena Vista)* I-4 exit 27 to FL 535, N to Vista Center. 407/239-1119. Hrs: 5-10:30 pm. Res accepted. Japanese menu. Bar. Semi-a la carte: dinner $9.95-$23.95. Child's meals. Specializes in fresh seafood, beef, sushi. Parking. Tableside preparation. Cr cds: A, C, D, DS, MC, V.

D

✔★ ★ ★ **PAPEETE BAY VERANDAH.** *(See Disney's Polynesian Resort)* 407/824-1391. Hrs: 7:30-10:30 am, 5:30-10 pm. Res accepted. Polynesian menu. Bar. Character bkfst buffet: $12.95, children 3-11, $7.95. A la carte entrees: dinner $8.95-$16.50; under 3 free. Own baking. Entertainment. Overlooks lagoon. Cr cds: A, MC, V.

D

★ ★ **PEBBLES.** *(12551 SR 535, Lake Buena Vista 12551)* I-4 to FL 535, right to Crossroads Shopping Center. 407/827-1111. Hrs: 11 am-midnight. Closed Thanksgiving, Dec 25. Bar. Semi-a la carte: lunch, dinner $5.25-$19.25. Child's meals. Specialties: Mediterranean salad, chicken with avocado and sour orange sauce, fresh fish and daily specials. Parking. Outdoor dining. Vaulted ceilings. Cr cds: A, D, DS, MC, V.

D

★ ★ ★ **STEERMAN'S QUARTERS.** *Aboard the Empress Lilly in Walt Disney World Village.* 407/828-3900. Hrs: Disney character bkfst, sittings 8:30 & 10 am (res required); 5:30-10 pm. Res accepted. Continental menu. Bar. Complete meals: bkfst $11.50. A la carte entrees: dinner $18-$27. Child's meals. Valet parking. Aboard 1890s Mississippi riverboat; view of giant paddle wheel. Totally nonsmoking. Cr cds: A, MC, V.

D

★ ★ **TOP OF THE WORLD.** *(See Disney's Contemporary Resort)* 407/824-3611. Hrs: 8 am-10 pm. Res accepted. Continental menu. Wine list. A la carte entrees: bkfst $1.75-$9.50, lunch $6-$9.25, dinner $10.95-$19.95. Own pastries. Valet parking. Rooftop dining; view of the Magic Kingdom. Totally nonsmoking. Cr cds: A, MC, V.

D

★ ★ ★ **TUSCANY'S.** *(See Marriott's Orlando World Center Resort)* 407/239-4200. Hrs: 6-10 pm. Res accepted. Bar to 10 pm. Wine list. Semi-a la carte: dinner $19-$30. Child's meals. Specialties: seafood, pasta combo, tiramisu. Own baking, desserts. Valet parking. Aquarium. European decor. Cr cds: A, C, D, DS, ER, JCB, MC, V.

D **SC**

★ ★ ★ **VICTORIA & ALBERT'S.** *(See Disney's Grand Floridian Beach Resort)* 407/824-2383. 2 Sittings: 6 & 9 pm. Res required. Continental menu. Wine cellar. Complete meals: dinner $80. Child's meals. Own baking. Harpist nightly. Valet parking. Gourmet menu changes daily. Victorian decor. Jacket. Totally nonsmoking. Cr cds: A, D, MC, V.

D

Philadelphia

Founded: 1682	
Pop: 1,585,577	
Elev: 45 feet	
Time zone: Eastern	
Area code: 215	

The Quakers, Philadelphia's first settlers, arrived in 1681 and prospered in trade and commerce, making the city the leading port in the colonies. The first and second Continental Congresses convened here, and Philadelphia became the headquarters of the Revolution. The city continued to be, for the most part, the main seat of the new federal government until 1800.

The Cradle of the Nation, as Philadelphia is often called, is now enjoying the advantages of a much deserved face lift. Restoration of old houses and historic landmarks is matched only by the redevelopment of previously barren areas of the city—all of which has given Philadelphia a rebirth of tourist interest. The city-wide improvement program has brought Philadelphia's historic sites to the forefront. Entire neighborhoods have been restored; vast highway systems have been superimposed on the city; blocks of warehouses that impinged on Independence Hall have been torn down; and Fairmount Park, one of the world's largest municipal parks, has been developed further. By the waterfront, a major redevelopment program has given new life to Penn's Landing, offering maritime lovers a commercial and recreational paradise.

Business

Philadelphia has a prosperous and diversified economy. One important factor that adds to the success of the city's industries is the Port of Philadelphia, with its ample facilities for international shipping.

About 20 percent of the city's work force is engaged in manufacturing such items as communications equipment, electrical and nonelectrical machinery, appliances, automobile and truck bodies, carpets, periodicals, cigars, scientific instruments, food products, chemicals and apparel.

Many small businesses are opening regularly, particularly retail shops, restuarants and entertainment spots. With a number of medical schools, dental schools and a host of research institutions located here, the health care industry continues to expand.

Convention Facilities

The Philadelphia Civic Center is one of the largest and most versatile convention centers in the nation. The complex consists of the museum, the convention hall, the center hall, Pennsylvania Hall and three exhibition halls.

The convention hall has an arena and an exhibit area that can accommodate between 9,000 and 12,000 people. The exhibit hall, on the lower level, has 36,000 square feet of space; movable walls make possible almost any division of this area. There is also a cafeteria that can accommodate 600 people.

The center hall has 2 levels, each containing 25,000 square feet of floor space. This hall can be used for exhibits or divided into meeting rooms. Pennsylvania Hall contains 78,000 square feet of space.

Exhibition halls A and C each have 40,000 square feet of space, and exhibition hall B has 140,000 square feet of space. There is also an auditorium with 10,000 square feet of space. All of these areas can be used in almost any combination and can be divided easily into meeting rooms or exhibit rooms.

There is one restaurant accessible from exhibition hall A, and another restaurant accessible from exhibition halls B and C. In addition, a catering service provides food throughout the buildings for 6,000 or more people. There is also parking for 1,500 cars, and an additional 2,000 cars can be accommodated in adjacent areas.

More than a dozen major hotels serve downtown Philadelphia, with more on the drawing board. A rail line connects Philadelphia International Airport with downtown.

Sports and Recreation

For the professional sports fan, the Phillies play baseball and the Eagles play football in Veterans Stadium. The 76ers play basketball and the Flyers play hockey at the Spectrum.

There are four major racetracks in the area: Philadelphia Park in nearby Bensalem, Atlantic City and Garden State in New Jersey and Brandywine in Delaware.

Entertainment

Free concerts are performed at Temple University, Community College of Philadelphia, the University of Pennsylvania, Robin Hood Dell East, the Mann Music Center and the Free Library. The Philadelphia Orchestra, the Philly Pops, the Opera Company of Philadelphia and the Pennsylvania Ballet hold their regular seasons at the Academy of Music. Other musical series include All-Star Forum Concerts, Coffee Concerts, Concerto Soloists of Philadelphia, Philadelphia Classical Guitar Society and the Philadelphia Folk Festival. For repertory theater, there are the Philadelphia Drama Guild, the Philadelphia Company (four contemporary American plays per season) and the Walnut Street Theatre.

Nightlife also thrives in Philadelphia. When the sun sets, entertainment establishments come alive, offering an exciting array of places from which to choose. For those seeking rock or jazz, South Street by the Delaware River is a hot spot. Many of the downtown hotels have live music and dinner theaters.

Historical Areas

Few places in the world have as many spots of historic significance concentrated within a small area as does the vicinity of Independence National Historical Park.

Two areas are especially important to see early in any visit to Philadelphia—the Benjamin Franklin Parkway, the city's cultural espla-

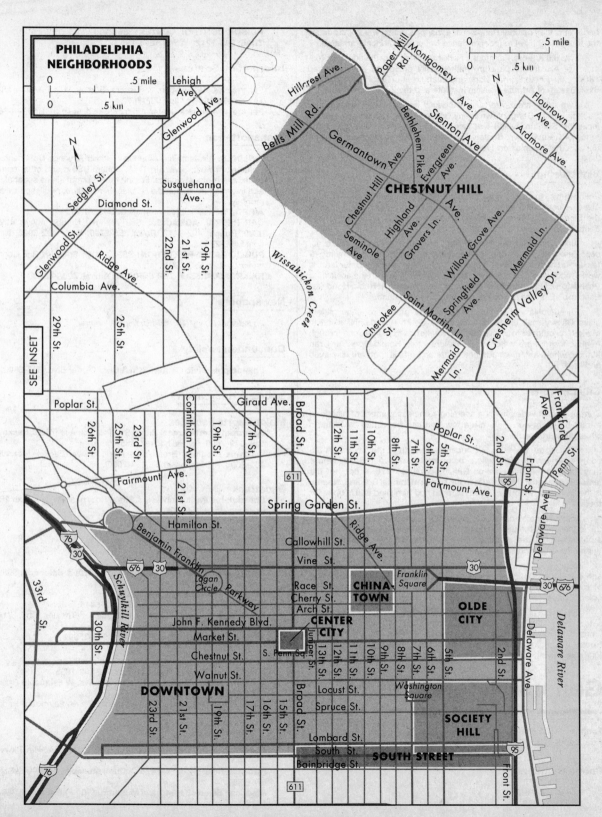

nade, and the National Park Service Visitor Center, which introduces the tourist to the entire Independence National Historical Park area.

The 8,000-acre Fairmount Park begins at the Philadelphia Museum of Art. In the park are authentically preserved and furnished 18th-century colonial mansions and such great cultural institutions as the Museum of Art, the Franklin Institute and the Zoological Garden.

Two other areas are also of special interest: Germantown and Society Hill. In Germantown many houses date from the Revolution, including Stenton, which was used by Sir William Howe during the battle of Germantown. Society Hill, another revolutionary-era residential area, has been extensively restored.

Sightseeing

Philadelphia, the city where the most significant events of 1776 took place, is continuing many of the projects and programs begun during the Bicentennial. Many buildings and areas that have been restored continue to be open to the public.

Along the Schuylkill River in May, the nation's leading scholastic, collegiate and club rowing and sculling crews compete in many regattas, including the Dad Vail. Concerts at the Mann Music Center feature world-renowned musicians and singers performing with the acclaimed Philadelphia Orchestra from late June through July. At Robin Hood Dell East, top stars in jazz and popular music set the pace.

Philadelphia's shopping areas run the gamut from the glittery glass Gallery mall on Market Street to South Philadelphia's Italian Market, an outdoor food mall. During weekends from late June through August, visitors are welcome to explore Head House Open Air Craft Market, where antiques, arts and crafts and ethnic food are displayed and sold.

City Environs

Surrounding Philadelphia is a seemingly endless number of places to attract the sightseer. Here are a few that can be visited by taking a circle drive around the city.

Washington Crossing Historical Park, north of the city on PA 32, commemorates the place where the general and his men stayed before they crossed the Delaware on Christmas night, 1776. A copy of the famous painting of this event is in the park's Memorial Building. Nearby is the Old Ferry, which has been restored and furnished and is open for tours.

Valley Forge National Historical Park, west of Philadelphia on PA 23, is the site of the turning point of the American Revolution. Bus and auto tape-tours are available. This is a dramatically beautiful spot during the dogwood season.

New Hope, on PA 32, is proud of its art galleries, unusual shops and the Bucks County Playhouse. In Doylestown, on US 202, is the Mercer Museum, housing more than 30,000 objects dating back to colonial days.

Southwest of the city, on the Delaware River, is Chester, the oldest settlement in the state. It was established in 1643 by Swedes and Finns. This is where William Penn landed in 1682. The Caleb Pusey House, at Landingford Plantation, west of town near Upland, was built for Penn's agent. It has been restored and furnished with period pieces.

General References

Founded: 1682 **Pop:** 1,585,577 **Elev:** 45 feet **Time zone:** Eastern **Area code:** 215

Phone Numbers

POLICE & FIRE: 911
FBI: 629-0800

POISON CONTROL CENTER: 386-2100
TIME: 846-1212 **WEATHER:** 936-1212

Information Sources

Philadelphia Convention & Visitors Bureau, 1515 Market St, 19102; 636-1666 or 800/537-7676.
Philadelphia Visitors Center, 1525 JFK Blvd, at 16th St, 636-1666.

Transportation

AIRLINES: Air Jamaica; American; British Airways; Continental; Delta; Northwest; Swissair; TWA; United; USAir; and other commuter and regional airlines. For the most current airline schedules and information consult the *Official Airline Guide*, published twice monthly.
AIRPORT: Philadelphia International, 492-3181.
CAR RENTAL AGENCIES: (See Toll-Free Numbers) Avis 492-0900; Budget 492-9447; Dollar 365-2700; Hertz 492-2925; National 492-2750.
PUBLIC TRANSPORTATION: SEPTA High Speed & Rail Commuter System 580-7800.
RAILROAD PASSENGER SERVICE: Amtrak 800/872-7245.

Newspapers

Philadelphia Daily News; Philadelphia Inquirer.

Convention Facility

Philadelphia Civic Center, 34th & Civic Center Blvd, 823-5600.

Sports & Recreation

Major Sports Facilities
Spectrum Sports Arena, Broad St & Pattison Ave (76ers, basketball, 339-7600; Flyers, hockey, 465-4500).
Veterans Stadium, Broad St & Pattison Ave (Eagles, football, 463-2500; Phillies, baseball, 463-1000).

Racetrack
Philadelphia Park, Richelieu & Street Rds, near PA Tpke exit 28, in Bensalem, 639-9000.

Cultural Facilities

Theaters
Annenberg Center for Communication Arts & Sciences, 3680 Walnut St, 898-6791.
Forrest, 1114 Walnut St, 923-1515.
Merriam Theater, 250 S Broad St, 732-5446.
Plays and Players Theatre, Philadelphia Theater Co, 1714 Delancey St, 735-0631.
Walnut St Theatre, 9th & Walnut Sts, 574-3550.

Concert Halls
Academy of Music, Broad & Locust Sts, 893-1935.
Mann Music Center, 52nd St & Parkside Ave, W Fairmount Park, 567-0707.
Robin Hood Dell East, 33rd & Dauphin Sts, in Fairmount Park, 477-8810.

Museums
Academy of Natural Sciences, 19th St & Ben Franklin Pkwy, 299-1000.
Afro-American Historical and Cultural Museum, 7th & Arch Sts, 574-0380.
American Swedish Historical Museum, 1900 Pattison Ave, 389-1776.

Athenaeum of Philadelphia, 219 S 6th St, 925-2688.
Atwater Kent Museum—The History Museum of Philadelphia. 15 S 7th St, 922-3031.
Balch Institute for Ethnic Studies, 18 S 7th St, 925-8090.
Civil War Library & Museum, 1805 Pine St, 735-8196.
Fireman's Hall Museum, 149 N 2nd St, 923-1438.
Franklin Institute Science Museum, 20th St & Ben Franklin Pkwy, 448-1200.
Historical Society of Pennsylvania, 1300 Locust St, 732-6201.
Mütter Museum, 19 S 22nd St, 563-3737.
National Museum of American Jewish History, 55 N 5th St, 923-3811.
New Hall (Marine Corps Memorial Museum), 4th & Chestnut Sts.
New Year Shooters and Mummer's Museum, 2nd St & Washington Ave, 336-3050.
Pearl S. Buck's House, Green Hills Farm, 520 Dublin Rd, in Perkasie, 249-0100.
Philadelphia Maritime Museum, 321 Chestnut St, 925-5439. *Scheduled to relocate to Port of History Museum in spring of 1995.*
Please Touch Museum for Children, 210 N 21st St, 963-0667.
Port of History Museum, Penn's Landing, Columbus Blvd & Walnut St, 823-7280.
Rosenbach Museum, 2010 DeLancey Pl, 732-1600.
University Museum of Archaeology and Anthropology, University of Pennsylvania, 33rd & Spruce Sts, 898-4000.
Wagner Free Institute of Science, 17th & Montgomery Sts, 763-6529.

Art Museums & Galleries

Brandywine River Museum, 25 mi SW via US 1 at Brandywine River, Chadd's Ford, 388-7601.
Institute of Contemporary Art, 36th & Sansom Sts, University of Pennsylvania, 898-7108.
Norman Rockwell Museum, 601 Walnut St, 922-4345.
Pennsylvania Academy of the Fine Arts, 118 N Broad St, 972-7600.
Philadelphia Art Alliance, 251 S 18th St, 545-4302.
Philadelphia Museum of Art, 26th St & Ben Franklin Pkwy, 763-8100.
Rodin Museum, 22nd St & Ben Franklin Pkwy, 684-7788.

Points of Interest

Historical

Arch St Friends Meeting House, 4th & Arch Sts, 627-2667.
Bartram's Garden, 54th St & Lindbergh Blvd, 729-5281.
Betsy Ross House, 239 Arch St, 627-5343.
Bishop White House, 309 Walnut St, 597-8974.
Carpenters' Hall, 320 Chestnut St, 925-0167.
Christ Church, 2nd St between Market & Arch Sts, 922-1695.
Christ Church Burial Ground, 5th & Arch Sts, 922-1695.
City Tavern, 2nd & Walnut Sts, 923-6059.
Cliveden, 6401 Germantown Ave (US 422) between Johnson & Cliveden Sts, 848-1777.
Colonial Mansions, Fairmount Park, 684-7924.
Congress Hall, 6th & Chestnut Sts, 597-8974.
Deshler-Morris House, 5442 Germantown Ave, 596-1748.
Edgar Allan Poe National Historic Site, 532 N 7th St, 597-8780.
Elfreth's Alley, off 2nd St between Arch & Race Sts, 574-0560.
First Bank of the United States, 3rd St between Walnut & Chestnut Sts, 597-8974.
Franklin Court, between Market & Chestnut Sts, in block bounded by 3rd & 4th Sts.
Gloria Dei Church National Historic Site, Columbus Blvd & Christian St, 389-1513.
Hill-Physick-Keith House, 321 S 4th St, 925-7866.
Independence Hall, Chestnut betweeen 5th & 6th Sts, 597-8974.
Independence National Historical Park, visitor center located at 3rd & Chestnut Sts, 597-8974.
Independence Square, Chestnut, Walnut, 5th & 6th Sts.

Jacob Graff House, 701 Market St.
Liberty Bell Pavilion, Market St between 5th & 6th Sts.
Library Hall, 5th & Library Sts.
Longwood Gardens, 30 mi SW via US 1 near Kennett Square, 388-6741.
Memorial Hall, 42nd St & Parkside Ave, Fairmount Park.
Mikveh Israel Cemetery, 8th & Spruce Sts.
New Hall, 4th & Chestnut Sts, in Carpenters' Court.
Old City Hall, Chestnut & 5th Sts.
Old Pine St Presbyterian Church, 412 Pine St, 925-8051.
Old St Mary's Church, 252 S 4th St between Locust & Spruce Sts, 923-7930.
Pennsylvania Hospital, 8th & Spruce Sts.
Powel House, 244 S 3rd St, 627-0364.
St George's United Methodist Church, 235 N 4th St, 925-7788.
St Peter's Church, 3rd & Pine Sts, 925-5968.
Second Bank of the United States, 420 Chestnut St between 4th & 5th Sts.
Society Hill Area, bounded by Front, Walnut, 7th & Lombard Sts.
Stenton House, 18th St & Windrim Ave, 329-7312.
Todd House, 4th & Walnut Sts.
USS *Olympia,* Penn's Landing, Columbus Blvd & Spruce St, 922-1898.
Valley Forge National Historical Park, 22 mi NW via I-76 & PA 23, 783-1077.
Washington Square, Walnut St from 6th St.

Other Attractions

Boat House Row, on E bank of Schuylkill River, 546-9000.
The Bourse, 21 S 5th St, Independence Mall East, 625-0300.
City Hall, Broad & Market Sts.
Fairmount Park, NW on both sides of Wissahickon Creek & Schuylkill River, 685-0000.
Free Library, Logan Sq, 19th & Vine Sts, 686-5322.
Head House Open Air Craft Market, Pine & 2nd, in Society Hill.
Japanese Exhibition House, Horticulture Center, Fairmount Park, 878-5097.
Morris Arboretum, Northwestern & Germantown Aves, in Chestnut Hill, 247-5777.
Pennypack Environmental Center, 8600 Verree Rd, 671-0440.
Philadelphia Zoological Garden, 3400 Girard Ave, Fairmount Park, 243-1100.
Schuylkill Center for Environmental Education, 8480 Hagy's Mill Rd, 482-7300.
Sesame Place, 20 mi NE via I-95, near Bristol, 757-1100.
Tinicum National Environmental Center, 86th St & Lindbergh Blvd, 365-3118 or 610/521-0662.
US Mint, 5th & Arch Sts, 597-7350.

Sightseeing Tours

AudioWalk and Tour, 6th & Sansom Sts, 922-4345.
Centipede Tours, 1315 Walnut St, 735-3123.
Gray Line bus tours, 3101 E Orthodox St, 569-3666 or 800/220-3133.
Philadelphia Carriage Co, 500 N 13th St, 922-6840.
Spirit of Philadelphia, Columbus Blvd & Market St, Pier 3, 923-1419.

Annual Events

Mummers' Parade, Broad St. Jan 1.
Philadelphia Flower Show, Convention Hall, Civic Center, 33rd St. Early-mid-Mar.
Penn Relays, Franklin Field. Late Apr.
Philadelphia Open House, write 313 Walnut St, 19106; 928-1188. Late Apr-early May.
Devon Horse Show, 20 mi NW via US 30 at Horse Show Grounds, in Devon, 610/964-0550. 9 days beginning Memorial Day wkend.
Elfreth's Alley Fete Day. 1st wkend June.
Freedom Festival. Early July.

Cliveden Battle of Germantown Re-enactment and the Upsala Country Fair, 6401 Germantown Ave. 1st Sat Oct.
Thanksgiving Day Parade.
Army-Navy Football Game, Veterans Stadium. Early Dec.
Historical Christmas Tours, Fairmount Park, 684-7922. Early Dec.

City Neighborhoods

Many of the restaurants, unrated dining establishments and some lodgings listed under Philadelphia include neighborhoods as well as exact street addresses. A map showing these neighborhoods can be found immediately following the city introduction. Geographic descriptions of these areas are given, followed by a table of restaurants arranged by neighborhood.

Center City: Area of Downtown around city hall; south of Kennedy Blvd, west of Juniper St, north of S Penn Square and east of 15th St.

Chestnut Hill: South of Stenton Ave, west and north of Cresheim Valley Dr and east of Fairmount Park; commercial area along Germantown Ave.

Chinatown: North central area of Downtown; south of Vine St, west of 8th St, north of Arch St and east of 11th St.

Downtown: South of Spring Garden St, west of I-95, north of South St and east of the Schuylkill River. **North of Downtown** North of Spring Garden St. **South of Downtown** South of South St. **West of Downtown** West of Schuylkill River.

Olde City: Area of Downtown south of I-696, west of the Delaware River, north of Chestnut St and east of Independence Mall.

Society Hill: Southeast side of Downtown; south of Walnut St, west of Front St, north of Lombard St and east of 7th St.

South Street: Downtown area of South St between Broad St on the west and the Delaware River on the east; also north to Pine St and south to Bainbridge St.

Lodgings and Food

PHILADELPHIA RESTAURANTS
BY NEIGHBORHOOD AREAS

(For full description, see alphabetical listings under Restaurants)

CENTER CITY

Bookbinder's Seafood House. 215 S 15th St

Di Lullo Centro. 1407 Locust St

CHESTNUT HILL

Flying Fish. 8142 Germantown Ave

Roller's. 8705 Germantown Ave

Under The Blue Moon. 8042 Germantown Ave

CHINATOWN

Ho Sai Gai. 1000 Race St

Van's Garden. 121 N 11th St

DOWNTOWN

Baci Bistro. 211 S Broad St

Ciboulette. 200 S Broad St

Cutters Grand Cafe. 2005 Market St

Deux Cheminées. 1221 Locust St

The Dining Room (The Ritz-Carlton, Philadelphia Hotel). 17th and Chestnut Sts

Dock Street Brewery & Restaurant. 2 Logan Square

Fountain (Four Seasons Hotel Philadelphia). 1 Logan Square

The Garden. 1617 Spruce St

Harry's Bar & Grill. 22 S 18th St

Jack's Firehouse. 2130 Fairmount Ave

Le Bar Lyonnais. 1523 Walnut St

Le Bec-Fin. 1523 Walnut St

London Grill. 2301 Fairmount Ave

Mango Bay. 264 S 16th St

Marabella's. 1420 Locust St

The Palm. 200 S Broad St

Restaurant 210 (The Rittenhouse Hotel). 210 W Rittenhouse Square

Sfuzzi. 1650 Market St

Suzanna Foo. 1512 Walnut St

Swann Lounge (Four Seasons Hotel Philadelphia). 1 Logan Square

White Dog Cafe. 3420 Sansom St

NORTH OF DOWNTOWN

Dilullo Oggi. 7955 Oxford Ave

Fisher's Seafood. 7312 Castor Ave

Napoleon Cafe. 2652 E Somerset St

SOUTH OF DOWNTOWN

D'Medici. 824 S 8th St

Famous 4th St Delicatessen. 700 S 4th St

Felicia's. 1148 S 11th St

Osteria Romana. 935 Ellsworth St

WEST OF DOWNTOWN

The Restaurant School. 4207 Walnut St

Zocalo. 3600 Lancaster Ave

OLDE CITY

Cafe Einstein. 208 Race St

Dinardo's. 312 Race St

La Famiglia. 8 S Front St

La Truffe. 10 S Front St

Los Amigos. 50 S 2nd St

Meiji-En. Pier 19 North

Middle East. 126 Chestnut St

Sassafras. 48 S 2nd St

Serrano. 20 S 2nd St

Spirit Of Philadelphia. Pier 3

SOCIETY HILL

Dickens Inn. Head House Square

Old Original Bookbinder's. 125 Walnut St

SOUTH STREET AREA

Alouette. 334 Bainbridge St

Bridget Foy's South Street Grill. 200 South St

Cafe Nola. 328 South St

Knave Of Hearts. 230 South St

Monte Carlo Living Room. 2nd & South Sts

South Street Diner. 140 South St

Note: *When a listing is located in a town that does not have its own city heading, it will appear under the city nearest to its location. In these cases, the address and town appear in parenthesis immediately following the name of the establishment.*

Motels

★ ★ **BEST WESTERN HOTEL PHILADELPHIA NORTH-EAST.** *11580 Roosevelt Blvd (19116), north of downtown.* 215/464-9500; FAX 215/464-8511. 100 rms, 2 story. S, D $80-$125; under 18 free; wkly, wkend rates. Crib free. TV. Pool; lifeguard. Complimentary continental bkfst. Bar from 4 pm. Ck-out 11 am. Coin lndry. Meeting rms. Exercise equipt; weight machine, bicycles. Lawn games. Some bathrm phones, refrigerators, minibars. Many balconies. Picnic tables. Cr cds: A, C, D, DS, ER, JCB, MC, V.

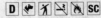

✔ ★ **COMFORT INN.** *(3660 Street Rd, Bensalem 19020) N on I-95 to Street Rd W exit, 3 mi W.* 215/245-0100; FAX 215/245-0100, ext. 451. 141 units, 3 story. S $60-$95; D $70-$95; each addl $10; suites $99-$109; family rates. Crib free. Pet accepted, some restrictions. TV; cable, in-rm movies avail. Complimentary continental bkfst. Restaurant nearby. Bar 4 pm-1 am; entertainment. Ck-out noon. Meeting rms. Gift shop. Exercise equipt; weights, bicycles. Game rm. Some in-rm whirlpools. Cr cds: A, C, D, DS, ER, JCB, MC, V.

Motor Hotels

✔ ★ ★ **DAYS INN-AIRPORT.** *4101 Island Ave (19153), near Intl Airport, south of downtown.* 215/492-0400; FAX 215/365-6035. 177 rms, 5 story. S $99; D $109; each addl $15; under 18 free. Crib free. TV.

Pool; lifeguard. Restaurant 6 am-2 pm, 5-11 pm; Sat, Sun to noon. Rm serv. Bar 4 pm-midnight. Ck-out noon. Coin lndry. Meeting rms. Valet serv. Free airport transportation. Cr cds: A, C, D, DS, MC, V.

Ⓓ ≈ 🏃 ✈ 🦮 🔥 SC

★ **HOLIDAY INN EXPRESS MIDTOWN.** *1305 Walnut St (19107).* 215/735-9300; FAX 215/732-2682. 164 rms, 20 story. S $105-$125; D $115-$135; each addl $10; under 19 free. Crib free. Garage $9.75. TV; cable. Pool; lifeguard. Restaurant nearby. Ck-out 1 pm. Meeting rms. Bellhops. Concierge. Airport transportation. Cr cds: A, C, D, DS, JCB, MC, V.

Ⓓ ≈ 🦮 🔥 SC

★ ★ **HOLIDAY INN-INDEPENDENCE MALL.** *400 Arch St (19106), downtown.* 215/923-8660; FAX 215/923-4633. 364 rms, 8 story. S, D $85-$150; each addl $10; suites $250-$300; under 19 free; wkend rates. Garage $12. Crib free. TV; cable. Rooftop pool; lifeguard. Restaurant 6:30 am-10:30 pm; dining rm 11:30 am-2 pm, 5:30-10:30 pm. Rm serv. Bar 11-1 am, Sun from noon. Ck-out 11 am. Coin lndry. Meeting rms. Bellhops. Valet serv. Sundries. Gift shop. Cr cds: A, C, D, DS, JCB, MC, V.

Ⓓ ≈ 🦮 🔥 SC

★ ★ ★ **MARRIOTT-PHILADELPHIA AIRPORT.** *4509 Island Ave (19153), at lntl Airport, south of downtown.* 215/365-4150; FAX 215/365-3875. 331 rms, 9 story. S $132; D $145; suites $350; studio rms $150; under 18 free; wkend rates. Crib free. Pet accepted, some restrictions. TV; cable. Indoor pool. Restaurant 6 am-11 pm. Rm serv. Bar 11-2 am; dancing. Ck-out 1 pm. Meeting rms. Bellhops. Valet serv. Gift shop. Free airport transportation. Exercise equipt; weights, bicycles, whirlpool, sauna. Game rm. *LUXURY LEVEL :* 38 rms, 2 suites. S $139; D $155. Concierge. Private lounge, honor bar. Complimentary continental bkfst, refreshments, newspaper. Cr cds: A, C, D, DS, ER, MC, V.

Ⓓ 🏊 ≈ 🏃 ✈ 🦮 🔥 SC

★ ★ **SHERATON INN-PHILADELPHIA, NORTHEAST.** *9461 Roosevelt Blvd (19114), north of downtown.* 215/671-9600; FAX 215/464-7759. 188 rms, 6 story. S $99; D $109; each addl $10; suites $175; under 17 free; wkend rates. Crib free. TV; cable. Indoor/outdoor pool; poolside serv. Restaurant 6:30 am-10 pm. Rm serv. Bar 2 pm-midnight. Ck-out 11 am. Coin lndry. Meeting rms. Valet serv. Sundries. Gift shop. Exercise equipt; weights, bicycles. Health club privileges. Some refrigerators. Cr cds: A, C, D, DS, MC, V.

Ⓓ ≈ 🏃 🦮 🔥 SC

Hotels

★ ★ ★ **ADAM'S MARK.** *City Ave & Monument Rd (19131), west of downtown.* 215/581-5000; res: 800/444-2326; FAX 215/581-5069. 515 rms, 23 story. S $145-$157; D $144-$164; each addl $12; suites $150-$600; under 18 free; wkend, wkly rates. Crib free. TV; cable. Indoor/outdoor pool; poolside serv, lifeguard. Restaurant 6 am-11 pm. 3 bars; entertainment, dancing. Ck-out noon. Convention facilities. Concierge. Shopping arcade. Barber, beauty shop. Airport, RR station, bus depot transportation. Exercise rm; instructor, weights, bicycles, whirlpool, sauna, steam rm. Refrigerators. Cr cds: A, C, D, DS, MC, V.

Ⓓ ≈ 🏃 🦮 🔥 SC

★ ★ **BARCLAY.** *237 S 18th St (19103), on Rittenhouse Square, downtown.* 215/545-0300; res: 800/421-6662; FAX 215/545-2896. 240 rms, 22 story. S $145-$185; D $155-$195; each addl $10; suites, kit. suites $200-$400; under 18 free; wkend rates. Crib free. Pet accepted; $50. Valet parking $15.75. TV; cable. Complimentary continental bkfst. Restaurant 7 am-11 pm. Bar to 2 am; entertainment Fri & Sat. Ck-out 1 pm. Meeting rms. Concierge. Airport, RR station, bus depot transportation. Bathrm phones. Cr cds: A, C, D, DS, ER, MC, V.

🐾 🦮 🔥 SC

★ ★ ★ **BEST WESTERN INDEPENDENCE PARK INN.** *235 Chestnut St (19106), in Society Hill.* 215/922-4443; FAX 215/922-4487.

36 rms, 5 story. S, D $99-$155; each addl $10. Crib free. TV; cable. Complimentary continental bkfst, afternoon tea. Ck-out noon. Meeting rms. Restored historic building (1856); ornate furnishings. Cr cds: A, C, D, DS, ER, JCB, MC, V.

Ⓓ 🦮 🔥 SC

✔ ★ ★ **BEST WESTERN RADNOR.** *(591 E Lancaster, St Davids 19087)* 17 mi W on US 30, ¼ mi W of Blue Rte (I-476) exit 5. 610/688-5800; res: 800/537-3000; FAX 610/341-3299. 168 rms, 4 story. S $69-$110; D $79-$120; each addl $10; suites $162-$180; under 16 free. Crib free. TV; cable. Pool; wading pool, lifeguard. Restaurant 6:30 am-10 pm. Rm serv 24 hrs. Bar 11-2 am; entertainment. Ck-out noon. Meeting rms. Airport transportation. Exercise equipt; weight machine, rowing machine. Game rm. *LUXURY LEVEL :* 45 rms, 7 suites. S, D $99-$120. Private lounge. Complimentary continental bkfst, refreshments, newspaper. Cr cds: A, C, D, DS, ER, JCB, MC, V.

Ⓓ ≈ 🏃 ✈ 🦮 🔥 SC

★ ★ **CHESTNUT HILL.** *8229 Germantown Ave (19118), I-76 exit Lincoln Dr to Allen's Lane, in Chestnut Hill.* 215/242-5905; res: 800/628-9744; FAX 215/242-8778. 28 rms, 4 story, 3 bldgs, 3 suites. S, D $80-$120; each addl $10; suites $120; under 12 free; package plans. Crib free. TV. Complimentary continental bkfst. Restaurants 11:30 am-10 pm. Bar to midnight. Ck-out 11 am. Meeting rms. Airport transportation. Cr cds: A, C, D, MC, V.

Ⓓ 🦮 SC

✔ ★ **COMFORT INN.** *100 N Christopher Columbus Blvd (19106), downtown.* 215/627-7900; FAX 215/238-0809. 185 rms, 10 story. S, D $75-$125; each addl $10; suites $160; under 18 free; higher rates some hols. Crib free. TV; cable. Complimentary continental bkfst, coffee. Coffee in rms. Restaurant nearby. Bar 5 pm-2 am. Ck-out noon. Meeting rms. Valet serv. Airport, RR station, bus depot transportation. Overlooking Delaware River. Cr cds: A, C, D, DS, ER, JCB, MC, V.

Ⓓ 🦮 🔥 SC

★ ★ ★ **DOUBLETREE.** *Broad St at Locust (19107), downtown.* 215/893-1600; FAX 215/893-1663. 428 rms, 25 story. S $155-$170; D $165-$180; each addl $15; suites $250-$500; under 18 free; wkend rates; higher rates New Year's hols. Crib free. Garage $13, valet $17. TV; cable. Indoor pool; poolside serv, lifeguard. Restaurant 6:30 am-11 pm; Fri, Sat to midnight. Bar to midnight, Fri, Sat to 1:30 am. Ck-out noon. Convention facilities. Concierge. Gift shop. Airport transportation. Exercise rm; instructor, weights, bicycles, whirlpool, sauna, steam rm. *LUXURY LEVEL :* 40 rms. S, D $190-$225. Private lounge. Cr cds: A, C, D, DS, ER, MC, V.

Ⓓ ≈ 🏃 🏃 🦮 🔥 SC

★ ★ ★ ★ **FOUR SEASONS HOTEL PHILADELPHIA.** *1 Logan Square (19103), on Logan Circle, downtown.* 215/963-1500; FAX 215/963-9506. 371 rms, 8 story. S $220-$295; D $250-$325; each addl $30; suites $525-$1,275; under 18 free; wkend rates. Garage $12-$21. Pet accepted. TV; cable. Indoor pool; poolside serv, lifeguard. Restaurant 6:30-1 am; Sat, Sun from 7 am (also see FOUNTAIN; and see SWANN LOUNGE, Unrated Dining). Rm serv 24 hrs. Bar 11-2 am; pianist. Ck-out 1 pm. Convention facilities. Concierge. Beauty shop. Complimentary downtown transportation (as available). Exercise rm; instructor, weights, bicycles, whirlpool, sauna. Massage. Minibars. Some balconies. Cr cds: A, C, D, ER, JCB, MC, V.

Ⓓ 🐾 ≈ 🏃 🦮 🔥 SC

★ ★ ★ **GUEST QUARTERS.** *4101 Island Rd (19153), at I-95 Island Ave exit, near lntl Airport, south of downtown.* 215/365-6600; FAX 215/492-8421. 251 suites, 8 story. S, D $119-$155; each addl $15; under 18 free; wkend rates. Crib free. TV; cable. Indoor pool; lifeguard. Complimentary continental bkfst (wkends). Restaurant 6 am-11 pm. Bar noon-2 am. Ck-out noon. Meeting rms. Gift shop. Free airport transportation. Exercise equipt; weights, bicycles, whirlpool, sauna, steam rm. Bathrm phones, refrigerators, minibars. Cr cds: A, C, D, DS, JCB, MC, V.

Ⓓ ≈ 🏃 🏃 ✈ 🦮 🔥 SC

★ ★ ★ **GUEST QUARTERS.** *(640 W Germantown Pike, Plymouth Meeting 19462) W on I-76, exit I-476N to Germantown Pike West exit, right on Hickory Rd.* 610/834-8300; FAX 610/834-7813. 252 suites, 7 story. S, D $150-$170; family, wkend rates. Crib free. TV; cable. Indoor pool; wading pool, poolside serv, lifeguard. Restaurant 6:30 am-10 pm. Bar. Ck-out noon. Coin lndry. Meeting rms. Shopping arcade. Airport, RR station, bus depot transportation. Exercise equipt; weights, bicycles, whirlpool, sauna. Bathrm phones, refrigerators, minibars. Some private patios, balconies. Cr cds: A, C, D, DS, MC, V.

⬜ 🏊 🏃 🚭 🔥 SC

★ ★ ★ **HOLIDAY INN-CITY CENTRE.** *1800 Market St (19103), in Center City.* 215/561-7500; FAX 215/561-4484. 445 rms, 25 story. S, D $118-$140; each addl $10; suites $200-$350; under 18 free; wkend rates. Crib free. Garage fee. TV; cable. Pool; lifeguard. Restaurant 6:30 am-11 pm. Bar 11 am-midnight. Ck-out noon. Coin lndry. Convention facilities. Gift shop. Airport transportation. Exercise equipt; weights, bicycles. **LUXURY LEVEL :** 53 rms, 6 suites, 2 floors. S $140; D $150. Private lounge. Complimentary continental bkfst. Cr cds: A, C, D, DS, JCB, MC, V.

⬜ 🏊 🏃 🚭 🔥 SC

★ ★ ★ **HOTEL ATOP THE BELLEVUE.** *1415 Chancellor Court (19102), downtown.* 215/893-1776; res: 800/221-0833; FAX 215/893-9868. 170 rms, 7 story. S $210-$260; D $230-$290; suites $350-$1,300; under 18 free; special packages. Crib free. Garage $13, valet $18.50. TV; cable, in-rm movies. Indoor pool privileges; whirlpool, sauna, lifeguard. Restaurants 7 am-11 pm. Dinner/dancing Fri & Sat. Rm serv 24 hrs. Bar 11-1 am. Ck-out 1 pm. Meeting rms. Concierge. Shopping arcade. Barber, beauty shop. Airport, RR station, bus depot transportation. Health club privileges. Bathrm phones, minibars. Some balconies. Turn-of-the-century decor. European-style service and amenities. Hotel is located atop French Renaissance-style, restored landmark building and features a sunlit 7-story atrium. State-of-the-art athletic club is connected by skywalk. Cr cds: A, C, D, DS, ER, JCB, MC, V.

⬜ 🏊 🏃 🚭 🔥

✔ ★ ★ ★ **KORMAN SUITES.** *2001 Hamilton St (19130), just off the Pkwy, downtown.* 215/569-7000. 99 suites, 27 story. Suites $109-$159; under 18 free; wkend rates. Crib free. TV; cable, in-rm movies. Pool; poolside serv, lifeguard. Complimentary continental bkfst. Restaurant 6:30 am-2:30 pm, 5:30-9:30 pm. Bar; entertainment. Ck-out 11 am. Convention facilities. Gift shop. Barber, beauty shop. Lighted tennis. Exercise rm; instructor, weight machine, bicycles, whirlpool. Complete fitness center. Three original art installations: Neon for Buttonwood," a roofline neon sculpture; Spirit Dance,"a glass wall with carved, etched and painted designs; and a landscaped Japanese sculpture garden. Cr cds: A, D, MC, V.

⬜ 🏌 🏊 🏃 🚭 🔥 SC

★ ★ ★ **MARRIOTT PHILADELPHIA WEST.** *(111 Crawford Ave, West Conshohocken 19428) 11 W on I-76, exit 29.* 215/482-5600. 288 rms, 17 story. S $134-$154; D $149-$169; each addl $15; suites $295-$375; under 18 free; wkend, hol rates. Crib free. Valet parking $8. TV; cable. Indoor pool; poolside serv, lifeguard. Restaurant 6 am-11 pm. Bar. Ck-out 3 pm. Convention facilities. Concierge. Shopping arcade. Free airport, RR station transportation. Exercise equipt; weight machine, stair machine, whirlpool, sauna. 1 blk from Schuylkill River. **LUXURY LEVEL :** 52 rms, 3 story, 1 suite. S $139-$159; D $154-$174; suite $295-$350. Concierge. Private lounge. Honor bar. Complimentary newspaper. Cr cds: A, C, D, DS, MC, V.

⬜ 🏊 🏃 🚭 🔥 SC

★ ★ ★ ★ **OMNI HOTEL AT INDEPENDENCE PARK.** *4th & Chestnut Sts (19106), on Independence Park, adj to Independence Hall, in Olde City.* 215/925-0000; FAX 215/925-1263. 150 rms, 14 story, 10 suites. S $195; D $225; each addl $25; suites from $350; under 18 free; wkend rates. Crib free. Garage (fee). TV; cable, in-rm movies. Indoor pool. Restaurant 7 am-3 pm, 5:30-10 pm. Rm serv 24 hrs. Bar 3-11 pm; entertainment Tues-Sat. Ck-out noon. Meeting rms. Concierge. Airport transportation. Exercise equipt; weight machine,

bicycles, whirlpool, sauna. Bathrm phones, minibars. Complimentary newspaper. Every room has a view of Independence Park. Cr cds: A, C, D, DS, ER, JCB, MC, V.

⬜ 🏊 🏃 🚭 🔥 SC

★ ★ ★ **RADISSON.** *500 Stevens Dr (19113), near Intl Airport, south of downtown.* 610/521-5900; FAX 610/521-4362. 353 rms, 12 story. S $119; D $129; each addl $10; suites $275; under 18 free; wkend packages. Crib free. TV; cable. Indoor pool; poolside serv. Restaurant 6:30 am-2:30 pm, 5-11 pm. Bars 2 pm-midnight. Ck-out noon. Meeting rms. Gift shop. Free airport transportation. Exercise equipt; weight machine, bicycle, whirlpool. Game rm. Wet bars. Balconies. Cr cds: A, C, D, DS, ER, MC, V.

⬜ 🏊 🏃 🚭 🔥 SC

★ ★ ★ ★ **THE RITTENHOUSE.** *210 W Rittenhouse Square (19103), downtown.* 215/546-9000; res: 800/635-1042; FAX 215/732-3364. 133 rms, 9 story, 11 suites. S $225-$250; D $250-$275; suites $350-$1,000; wkend rates. Crib free. Garage; valet parking $21. Pet accepted. TV; cable, in-rm movies. Indoor pool; poolside serv. Restaurant 6:30 am-10:30 pm (also see RESTAURANT 210). Rm serv 24 hrs. Bar; entertainment. Ck-out 1 pm. Meeting rms. Concierge. Shopping arcade. Barber, beauty shop. Airport transportation. Exercise rm; instructor, weight machine, bicycles, sauna, steam rm. Massage. Health club privileges. Bathrm phones, minibars. Complimentary newspaper. Luxury hotel with expansive views of Rittenhouse Square and the city panorama. Cr cds: A, C, D, DS, MC, V.

⬜ ✔ 🏊 🏃 🚭 🔥

★ ★ ★ ★ **THE RITZ-CARLTON, PHILADELPHIA.** *17th and Chestnut Sts (19103), at Liberty Place, downtown.* 215/563-1600; FAX 215/567-2822. 290 rms, 15 story, 17 suites. S, D $175-$245; suites $350-$950; wkend rates. Crib free. Garage fee. TV; cable. Swimming privileges. Restaurant (see THE DINING ROOM). Rm serv 24 hrs. Bar 11-1 am; pianist. Ck-out noon. Meeting rms. Concierge. Gift shop. Airport, RR station transportation. Town car transportation within city. Exercise rm; instructor, weight machine, bicycles, Masseuse. Bathrm phones, minibars. **LUXURY LEVEL :** THE RITZ-CARLTON CLUB. 30 rms, 8 suites, 2 floors. S, D $245; suites $410-$950. Concierge. Private lounge. Complimentary continental bkfst, refreshments. Cr cds: A, C, D, DS, ER, JCB, MC, V.

⬜ 🏃 🚭 🔥

★ ★ ★ **SHERATON SOCIETY HILL.** *1 Dock St (19106), in Society Hill.* 215/238-6000; FAX 215/922-2709. 365 units, 4 story. S, D $145-$215; suites $300-$1,000; under 17 free; wkend rates. Crib free. Covered parking fee. TV; cable. Indoor pool; wading pool, poolside serv, lifeguard. Coffee in rms. Restaurant 6:30 am-2 pm, 5-10 pm. Rm serv 24 hrs. Bar noon-2 am. Ck-out noon. Convention facilities. Concierge. Shopping arcade. Transportation to business district (Mon-Fri). Exercise rm; instructor, weights, bicycles, whirlpool, sauna. Minibars; some refrigerators. Complimentary newspaper. Cr cds: A, C, D, DS, ER, JCB, MC, V.

⬜ 🏊 🏃 🚭 🔥 SC

★ ★ ★ **THE WARWICK.** *1701 Locust St (19103), downtown.* 215/735-6000; res: 800/523-4210 (exc PA); FAX 215/790-7766. 180 rms, 20 story, 20 kits. S $145-$185; D $195-$200; each addl $15; suites $180-$380; studio rms $185; apt $195; under 12 free; wkend plans. Crib free. Garage (fee). TV; cable. Restaurant 6:30 am-midnight. Bar 11-2 am. Ck-out noon. Meeting rms. Concierge. Barber, beauty shop. Health club privileges. Complimentary newspaper. Cr cds: A, C, D, DS, MC, V.

⬜ ✔ 🚭 🔥 SC

★ ★ ★ **WYNDHAM FRANKLIN PLAZA.** *2 Franklin Plaza (19103), jct 17th & Vine Sts, downtown.* 215/448-2000; FAX 215/448-2864. 758 rms, 26 story. S $145-$185; D $165-$195; each addl $20; suites $300-$1,000; under 18 free; wkend rates. Crib free. Garage $13. TV; cable. Indoor pool; poolside serv. Complimentary coffee in rms. Restaurant 6:30 am-11:30 pm. Bars 11-1 am. Ck-out noon. Convention facilities. Drugstore. Barber, beauty shop. Airport transportation avail.

Tennis. Exercise rm; instructor, weights, bicycles, whirlpool, sauna, steam rm. Masseuse. Refrigerators. Cr cds: A, C, D, DS, ER, JCB, MC, V.

D 🏃 ≈ 🏋 🏃 ⚲ 🔥 SC

Inns

★ ★ ★ **PENN'S VIEW.** *14 N Front St (19106), in Olde City.* 215/922-7600; *res:* 800/331-7634; FAX 215/922-7642. 27 rms, 5 story. S, D $100-$150; under 12 free; wkend rates. Crib free. TV; cable. Complimentary continental bkfst. Dining rm noon-2:30 pm, 5:30-10 pm; Fri, Sat 5:30-11 pm. Ck-out noon, ck-in 3 pm. Bellhops. Concierge. Airport, RR station, bus depot transportation. Overlooks Delaware River. Built 1828; Old World elegance, antiques, some fireplaces in rms. Cr cds: A, D, MC, V.

⚲ 🔥 SC

✔★ **SOCIETY HILL HOTEL.** *301 Chestnut St (19106), in Society Hill.* 215/925-1919. 12 rms, 4 story. S, D $95-$135. TV. Complimentary continental bkfst in rms. Restaurant 11 am-11 pm. Bar; jazz pianist Tues-Sat. Ck-out noon, ck-in 3 pm. Historic building (1832); pension ambience. Cr cds: A, C, D, MC, V.

🔥

✔★ ★ **THE THOMAS BOND HOUSE.** *129 S 2nd St (19106), in Olde City.* 215/923-8523; *res:* 800/845-2663. 12 rms, 4 story, 2 suites. No elvtr. S, D $80-$150; each addl $15; suites $150. Parking $9. TV. Complimentary continental bkfst (full bkfst wkends), tea/sherry. Restaurant nearby. Ck-out noon, ck-in 3-9 pm. Valet serv. Airport transportation. Library/sitting rm; antiques. Restored guest house (1769) built by Dr Thomas Bond, founder of the country's first public hospital. Individually decorated rms. Cr cds: A, D, MC, V.

🔥

Restaurants

★ ★ **ALOUETTE.** *334 Bainbridge St, in South Street Area.* 215/629-1126. Hrs: 11:30 am-2:30 pm, 5:30-9:30 pm; Fri to 10:30 pm; Sat 5:30-10:30 pm; Sun brunch 11:30 am-2:30 pm. Closed Tues; Dec 25. Res accepted wkends. French, Asian menu. Bar. Semi-a la carte: lunch $10-$15, dinner $17-$24. Sun brunch $8.95-$15.75. Specialties: escargot in puff pastry, Thai chicken curry. Courtyard dining. 1890s decor includes brass railings, tin ceiling, etched glass. Cr cds: A, D, MC, V.

D

★ ★ **BACI BISTRO.** *211 S Broad St, downtown.* 215/731-0700. Hrs: 11:30 am-11 pm; wkends 12:30 pm-midnight. Closed Dec 25. Res accepted. Italian menu. Bar. A la carte entrees: lunch $5-$12, dinner $9-$25. Specialties: capellini brivido, pollo al girarrosto, mezze lune con mascarpone. Own pasta, desserts. Cr cds: A, C, D, MC, V.

D

★ ★ **BOOKBINDER'S SEAFOOD HOUSE.** *215 S 15th St, in Center City.* 215/545-1137. Hrs: 11:30 am-10 pm; Sat 4-11 pm; Sun 3-10 pm. Closed Thanksgiving, Dec 25. Res accepted. Bar. Semi-a la carte: lunch $6-$13.50, dinner $14.95-$23.95. Child's meals. Specializes in seafood, steak. Own pastries. Family-owned since 1893. Cr cds: A, C, D, MC, V.

D

✔★ ★ **BRIDGET FOY'S SOUTH STREET GRILL.** *200 South St, near Head House Square, in South Street Area.* 215/922-1813. Hrs: 11:30 am-10:30 pm; Fri & Sat to midnight. Closed Thanksgiving, Dec 25. Res accepted. Bar to 2 am. A la carte entrees: lunch $5.95-$8.95, dinner $10.95-$15.95. Specializes in grilled fish & meat. Outdoor dining. Cr cds: A, C, D, DS, MC, V.

✔★ **CAFE EINSTEIN.** *208 Race St, in Olde City.* 215/625-0904. Hrs: 5-11 pm; Fri, Sat to midnight; Sun brunch 11:30 am-2:30 pm. Closed most major hols. Res accepted. Bar to 1 am. Semi-a la carte: dinner $9.95-$18.95. Sun brunch $3.95-$9.95. Specializes in crab cakes, Caesar salad. Jazz Sun. Parking. Informal bistro-type cafe. Cr cds: A, MC, V.

★ ★ **CAFE NOLA.** *328 South St, in South Street Area.* 215/627-2590. Hrs: noon-2:45 pm, 5-11 pm; Mon from 5 pm; Fri & Sat to 10:45 pm; Sun brunch 10:30 am-2:45 pm. Res required Fri, Sat. Bar. A la carte entrees: lunch $8-$12, dinner $15-$26. Sun brunch $11.95-$16.95. Specializes in Creole and Cajun dishes. Parking. Colorful New Orleans decor. Cr cds: A, C, D, DS, MC, V.

D

★ ★ ★ **CIBOULETTE.** *200 S Broad St, downtown.* 215/790-1210. Hrs: noon-2 pm, 5:30-10:30 pm; Mon & Sat from 5:30 pm. Closed Sun; most major hols. Res accepted; required Sat. French Provençal menu. Bar. Wine cellar. Complete meals: lunch $21-$29, dinner $45 (4-course) & $60 (5-course). A la carte entrees: dinner $18-$35. Specialties: roasted Maine lobster, black sea bass, loin of veal. Own desserts. Valet parking. French Renaissance-style architecture; tapestry wall hangings, many paintings; original mosaic tile floor; one rm with ceiling mural. Cr cds: A, MC, V.

D

★ ★ **CUTTERS GRAND CAFE.** *2005 Market St, at Commerce Square, downtown.* 215/851-6262. Hrs: 11:30 am-midnight; Fri to 1 am; Sat 5 pm-1 am; Sun 5-11 pm. Closed July 4, Dec 25. Res accepted. Bar. A la carte entrees: lunch $3.95-$13.95, dinner $9.95-$23.95. Specializes in fresh seafood, pasta, salads. Parking (evenings). Outdoor dining. Contemporary decor, murals. Cr cds: A, C, D, DS, MC, V.

D

★ ★ **D'MEDICI.** *824 S 8th St (19147), south of downtown.* 215/922-3986. Hrs: 5-11 pm; Sun 3-10 pm. Closed Mon; some major hols. Res accepted. Italian menu. Bar. A la carte entrees: dinner $7.95-$32.95. Child's meals. Specialties: veal Luisa, shrimp d'Medici, stuffed sirloin. Valet parking. Exposed brick & stucco walls; statuary in alcoves. Bronze & glass chandeliers. Cr cds: A, MC, V.

D

★ ★ ★ ★ **DEUX CHEMINÉES.** *1221 Locust St, downtown.* 215/790-0200. Hrs: 5:30-8:30 pm; Sat to 9 pm. Closed Sun & Mon; major hols. Res accepted. French menu. Serv bar. Wine cellar. Prix fixe: dinner $65. Specializes in rack of lamb, crab soup. Menu changes daily. Own baking, desserts. 3 dining areas in Frank Furness-designed mansion (1880); antique furnishings; 5 fireplaces. Chef-owned. Cr cds: A, C, D, DS, MC, V.

★ ★ ★ **DI LULLO CENTRO.** *1407 Locust St, opp Academy of Music, in Center City.* 215/546-2000. Hrs: 5:30-9 pm; Fri also 11:45 am-2 pm; Sat 5:30-10 pm; Sun 4-8 pm. Closed most major hols. Res accepted. Northern Italian menu. Bar. Wine cellar. A la carte entrees: lunch $8-$13, dinner $8-$27. Prix fixe: dinner $27. Specializes in seafood, homemade pasta, rack of lamb. Own pastries. In Old Locust St Theatre; elegant decor, hand-painted murals. Cr cds: A, C, D, MC, V.

D

★ ★ ★ **DICKENS INN.** *Head House Square, on 2nd St, in Society Hill.* 215/928-9307. Hrs: 11:30 am-3 pm, 5:30-10 pm; Sat to 10:30 pm; Sun 4:30-9 pm; Sun brunch 11:30 am-3 pm. Closed Dec 25. Res accepted. Continental menu. Bar. A la carte entrees: lunch $4.75-$10.75, dinner $7.50-$21.50. Sun brunch $14.75. Child's meals. Specializes in roast beef with Yorkshire pudding, beef Wellington, seafood. In historic Harper House (1788); Victorian decor; artwork imported from England. Cr cds: A, D, DS, MC, V.

D

✔★ ★ **DILULLO OGGI.** *7955 Oxford Ave, north of downtown.* 215/725-6000. Hrs: 5:30-9 pm; Sat to 10 pm; Sun 5-8 pm. Closed Dec 25. Italian menu. Wine cellar. Semi-a la carte: dinner $12-$19. Specializes in homemade pasta, veal dishes, fish. Own pastries. Parking. Cr cds: A, C, D, MC, V.

D

★ ★ **DINARDO'S.** 312 Race St, in Olde City. 215/925-5115. Hrs: 11 am-10 pm; Fri & Sat to 11 pm; Sun 3-9 pm. Closed major hols. Bar. Semi-a la carte: lunch $4-$9, dinner $7-$20. Specializes in steamed hard shell crab, seafood. Family-owned. Cr cds: A, C, D, MC, V.

D

★ ★ ★ **THE DINING ROOM.** (See The Ritz-Carlton, Philadelphia Hotel) 215/563-1600. Hrs: 6:30 am-2:30 pm, 6-10 pm; Mon to 11:30 am; Sun brunch 10:30 am-2:30 pm. Res accepted. Bar 11-1 am. Wine list. A la carte entrees: bkfst $7-$15, lunch $15-$21, dinner $22-$50. Sun brunch $32. Child's meals. Specialities: fresh Maine scallops with seaweed salad, baby rack of lamb with eggplant. Pianist. Valet parking. Formal dining; antique china displayed, chandeliers. Jacket. Cr cds: A, C, D, DS, ER, JCB, MC, V.

D

✔★ ★ **DOCK STREET BREWERY & RESTAURANT.** 2 Logan Square, at 18th & Cherry Sts, downtown. 215/496-0413. Hrs: 11:30 am-midnight; Fri to 2 am; Sat noon-2 am; Sun noon-11 pm. Closed Labor Day, Dec 25. Res accepted. Bar (beer). Setups. A la carte entrees: lunch $5-$9.95, dinner $5-$14.95. Specializes in freshly brewed beer, homemade breads, desserts. Entertainment Fri & Sat. Brewery tanks; beer brewed on premises, tours avail Sat. Billiard tables and English dart board. Cr cds: A, C, D, DS, MC, V.

D

★ ★ **FELICIA'S.** 1148 S 11th St, south of downtown. 215/755-9656. Hrs: 11:30 am-2:30 pm, 5-10:30 pm; Fri to 11 pm; Sat 5-11 pm; Sun 4-9:30 pm. Closed Mon; most major hols. Res accepted; required Sat, Sun. Italian menu. Bar. Semi-a la carte: lunch $6.95-$12.50, dinner $10.95-$18.50. Specialties: ricotta gnocci, ricotta cheesecake, veal chop. Own desserts. Valet parking. Cr cds: A, C, D, MC, V.

D

✔★ **FISHER'S SEAFOOD.** 7312 Castor Ave, north of downtown. 215/725-6201. Hrs: 11 am-9 pm; Fri & Sat to 10 pm; Sun noon-9 pm. Closed Mon; Labor Day, Dec 25. Bar. Semi-a la carte: lunch $3.25-$6.95, dinner $6.25-$12.95. Complete meals: lunch $6-$9.20, dinner $9.25-$15.95. Child's meals. Specializes in seafood, stir-fried dishes. Parking. Six large dining areas, individually decorated. Family-owned. Cr cds: A, MC, V.

D

★ ★ **FLYING FISH.** 8142 Germantown Ave, in Chestnut Hill. 215/247-0707. Hrs: 11:30 am-2:30 pm, 5:30-9 pm; Mon from 5:30 pm; Sat noon-2:30 pm, 5:30-10 pm. Closed Sun; some major hols. Bar. A la carte entrees: lunch $6.50-$8, dinner $12-$18. Child's meals. Specializes in seafood, clam bake (summer). Own pasta, pastries, ice cream. Totally nonsmoking. No cr cds accepted.

D

★ ★ ★ **FOUNTAIN.** (See Four Seasons Hotel Philadelphia) 215/963-1500. Hrs: 6:30 am-2:30 pm, 6-10:30 pm; Fri, Sat to 11 pm; Sun brunch 11 am-2:30 pm. Res accepted. Continental menu. Bar to 2 am. Wine cellar. A la carte entrees: bkfst $10-$15, lunch $22-$25, dinner $29-$38. Prix fixe: dinner $49. Sun brunch $16-$32. Child's meals. Specialties: vegetable lasagne, whole-roasted snapper, sautéed venison medallion. Own baking, desserts. Entertainment exc Sun. Valet parking. Overlooks Logan Square and fountain. Jacket (dinner). Cr cds: A, C, D, ER, JCB, MC, V.

D

★ ★ ★ **THE GARDEN.** 1617 Spruce St, downtown. 215/546-4455. Hrs: 11:30 am-1:45 pm, 5:30-9:30 pm; Sat 5:30-10 pm. Closed Sun; major hols. Res accepted. Continental menu. Bar. Extensive wine list. A la carte entrees: lunch $9.95-$24.95, dinner $15.95-$24.95.

Specializes in fresh seafood, aged prime beef. Valet parking. Spacious outdoor dining. Cr cds: A, C, D, MC, V.

★ ★ **GENERAL WAYNE INN.** (625 Montgomery Ave, Merion) 7 mi W on I-76, exit City Line Ave. 610/667-3330. Hrs: 11:30 am-11 pm; Sun 11:30 am-10 pm. Closed Mon. Res accepted. Continental menu. Bar. Semi-a la carte: lunch $4.95-$10.95, dinner $11.50-$19.95. Sun brunch $15.95. Specializes in prime beef, seafood. Own desserts. Valet parking. Established as inn in 1704. Family-owned. Cr cds: A, D, MC, V.

D

★ ★ ★ **HARRY'S BAR & GRILL.** 22 S 18th St, downtown. 215/561-5757. Hrs: 11:30 am-1:45 pm, 5:30-9 pm. Closed Sat, Sun; major hols. Res accepted. Italian, Amer menu. Bar 11:30 am-9:30 pm. Wine cellar. A la carte entrees: lunch $9.95-$23.95, dinner $14.95-$23.95. Specializes in fresh seafood, homemade pasta, aged prime steak. Own pastries. Parking. English club atmosphere. Jacket. Cr cds: A, C, D, MC, V.

D

✔★ **HO SAI GAI.** 1000 Race St, in Chinatown. 215/922-5883. Hrs: 11:30-4 am; Fri & Sat to 5 am. Closed Thanksgiving. Res accepted. Chinese menu. Serv bar. Semi-a la carte: lunch $4.95-$8.95, dinner $9-$15.95. Specializes in Mandarin & Hunan cuisine. Cr cds: A, C, D, MC, V.

★ ★ **JACK'S FIREHOUSE.** 2130 Fairmount Ave, downtown. 215/232-9000. Hrs: 11 am-2:30 pm, 5-10:30 pm; Sat & Sun from 5 pm; Sun brunch 11 am-3 pm. Closed some major hols. Res accepted. Bar 4:30 pm-1 am. A la carte entrees: lunch $5-$13, dinner $15-$22.95. Sun brunch $14.95. Specialties: bison with Jack Daniel's sauce, venison with beech nut sauce. Guitarist Thur-Sat; jazz trio Sun brunch. Outdoor dining. Red brick firehouse (ca 1860); original wood-paneled walls and brass pole, local artwork. Cr cds: A, C, D, MC, V.

D

★ **KNAVE OF HEARTS.** 230 South St, in South Street Area. 215/922-3956. Hrs: noon-4 pm, 5:30-11 pm; Fri, Sat to 11:30 pm; Sun 5-10 pm; Sun brunch 11 am-4 pm. Closed Dec 25. Res accepted. Bar. A la carte entrees: lunch $5-$9, dinner $12-$20. Sun brunch $12.50-$13.50. Specialties: rack of lamb, roast duckling, cajun salmon. Intimate dining. Cr cds: A, C, D, MC, V.

★ ★ ★ **LA COLLINA.** (37-41 Ashland Ave, Bala Cynwyd) W on I-76, exit 31, left at exit, right on Jefferson St, 1st bldg on the right. 610/668-1780. Hrs: 11:30 am-2:30 pm, 5:30-10 pm; Fri & Sat to 11 pm. Closed Sun; major hols. Res accepted. Italian menu. Bar. Wine cellar. A la carte entrees: lunch $8.95-$13.95, dinner $13.95-$24.95. Specializes in grilled fish, rack of veal, soft shell crab in season. Entertainment Wed, Fri & Sat. Valet parking. Atop a hill overlooking the city; brick fireplace; intimate atmosphere. Cr cds: A, C, D, MC, V.

D

★ ★ ★ **LA FAMIGLIA.** 8 S Front St, in Olde City. 215/922-2803. Hrs: noon-2 pm, 5:30-9:30 pm; Sat 5:30-10 pm; Sun 4:30-9 pm. Closed Mon; major hols; also last wk Aug. Res accepted. Italian menu. Bar. Wine cellar. A la carte entrees: lunch $12.95-$19.95, dinner $19.95-$32. Specializes in veal, fresh fish. Own desserts, pasta. Built in 1878 in one of city's first blocks of buildings. Jacket. Cr cds: A, C, D, MC, V.

D

★ ★ ★ **LA TRUFFE.** 10 S Front St, in Olde City. 215/925-5062. Hrs: noon-2 pm, 5:30-11 pm; Mon, Sat from 5:30 pm. Closed Sun; major hols. Res accepted. Bar. Wine list. A la carte entrees: lunch $9.50-$14.95, dinner $22-$35. Specialties: rack of lamb with thyme, Dover sole meunière, sea bass with white pepper corn sauce. Own pastries. Singer Fri. Elegant French Provincial decor; former coffeehouse built in 1783. Cr cds: A, MC, V.

★ ★ ★ **LE BAR LYONNAIS.** 1523 Walnut St (19102), downstairs at Le Bec Fin, downtown. 215/567-1000. Hrs: 11:30-1 am; Sat from 6 pm. Closed Sun; major hols. French bistro menu. Bar. A la carte entrees: lunch, dinner $6-$18. Specialties: escargots au champagne, galette de crabe, thon au poivres. Valet parking (dinner). Elegant bistro atmosphere; original art. Cr cds: A, C, D, DS, MC, V.

★ ★ ★ ★ ★ **LE BEC-FIN.** 1523 Walnut St, downtown. 215/567-1000. Sittings: lunch 11:30 am & 1:30 pm, dinner 6 pm & 9 pm, Fri & Sat 9:30 pm. Closed Sun; major hols. Res required. French menu. Bar to 1 am. Wine cellar. Prix fixe: lunch $32, dinner $94. Specializes in seasonal dishes. Own baking. Valet parking. Elegant dining. Louis XVI furnishings and decor. Chef-owned. Jacket. Cr cds: A, C, D, DS, MC, V.

D

★ ★ **LONDON GRILL.** 2301 Fairmount Ave (19130), downtown. 215/978-4545. Hrs: 11:30 am-3 pm, 5:30-10:30 pm; Sat 5:30 pm-midnight; Sun 11:30 am-9 pm. Closed Jan 1, Thanksgiving, Dec 25. Res accepted; required Sun brunch. Continental menu. Bar to 2 am. A la carte entrees: lunch $5.95-$9, dinner $14-$20. Sun brunch $4-$10. Child's meals. Specialties: Szechuan duck, salmon with horseradish crust, rack of lamb. Parking. Eclectic decor. Atrium. Cr cds: A, D, DS, MC, V.

✔ **LOS AMIGOS.** 50 S 2nd St, in Olde City. 215/922-7061. Hrs: 11:30 am-11:30 pm; Fri & Sat to 1:30 am; Sun 11 am-11:30 pm; Sun brunch to 2 pm. Closed some major hols. Mexican menu. Bar. Semi-a la carte: lunch $3.95-$11.95, dinner $6.75-$12.95. Sun brunch $9.95. Own desserts. Cr cds: A, C, D, MC, V.

D

✔★ **MARABELLA'S.** 1420 Locust St, downtown. 215/545-1845. Hrs: 11:30 am-11 pm; Fri & Sat to midnight; Sun 3-10 pm. Closed Dec 25. Italian menu. Bar. Semi-a la carte: lunch $5.50-$9.75, dinner $7-$14.50. Child's meals. Specializes in pizza, pasta with fresh seafood, oven-baked manicotti. Cr cds: A, D, DS, MC, V.

★ ★ **MEIJI-EN.** Pier 19 North, Delaware Ave at Callowhill St, Penn's Landing, in Olde City. 215/592-7100. Hrs: 5-9 pm; Fri & Sat to 11 pm; Sun brunch 10:30 am-2:30 pm. Closed Thanksgiving, Dec 24, 25. Res accepted; required Sun. Japanese menu. Bar; wkends to 1 am. A la carte entrees: dinner $13-$30. Sun brunch $18.95. Specialties: sukiyaki, sushi, tempura, teppanyaki-grilled items. Jazz trio Fri-Sun. Valet parking. Exotic bird display. Overlooks Delaware River. Cr cds: A, C, D, DS, MC, V.

D

★ ★ **MIDDLE EAST.** 126 Chestnut St, in Olde City. 215/922-1003. Hrs: 5 pm-midnight; Fri, Sat to 2 am; Sun from 3 pm. Closed Thanksgiving, Dec 24 & 25. Res accepted. Middle Eastern, Amer menu. Bar. Semi-a la carte: dinner $14.50-$21.50. Specializes in shish kebab, moussaka, seafood. Middle Eastern band Fri-Sun, belly dancing. Middle Eastern decor. Cr cds: A, C, D, DS, MC, V.

D

★ ★ ★ **MONTE CARLO LIVING ROOM.** 2nd & South Sts, in South Street Area. 215/925-2220. Hrs: 6-10:30 pm; Fri, Sat 5:30-11 pm; Sun 5-9 pm. Closed major hols. Res accepted. Northern Italian menu. Bar; closed Sun, Mon. Wine cellar. A la carte entrees: dinner $24-$30. Degustation dinner $65. Specializes in fresh imported & domestic fish, veal, beef. Own pastries. Mediterranean decor. Jacket. Cr cds: A, C, D, MC, V.

★ ★ **NAPOLEON CAFE.** 2652 E Somerset St, Port Richmond area, north of downtown. 215/739-6979. Hrs: 11:30 am-2:30 pm, 5-8:30 pm; Fri & Sat to 10:30 pm; Sun 5-8 pm. Closed Mon & Tues; major hols. Res accepted; required Sat. Continental menu. Serv bar. A la carte entrees: lunch $6-$9.50, dinner $12.50-$18.50. Specialties: tagliolini vongole, rosemary & lemon roasted chicken. Outdoor dining. 4 dining rms on 2nd floor; 2 rms on 1st floor lunch/coffee house. Each dining area individually decorated. Totally nonsmoking. Cr cds: A, D, DS, MC, V.

★ ★ **OLD ORIGINAL BOOKBINDER'S.** 125 Walnut St, in Society Hill. 215/925-7027. Hrs: 11:45 am-10 pm; Sun 3-9 pm; Sat, Sun hrs vary July-Aug. Closed Thanksgiving, Dec 25. Res accepted. Bars. A la carte entrees: lunch $7.95-$14.95, dinner $16.95-$35. Child's

meals. Specializes in seafood, steak. Own pastries. Valet parking. Established 1865; in historic bldg. Family-owned. Cr cds: A, C, D, DS, MC, V.

D

★ ★ **OSTERIA ROMANA.** 935 Ellsworth St, south of downtown. 215/271-9191. Hrs: 5:30-10:30 pm. Closed Mon; most major hols. Res accepted wkends. Italian menu. Bar. A la carte entrees: dinner $14.50-$26.50. Specialties: pappardelle verdi ai porcini, angel hair pasta with salmon caviar, pescatora capricciosa. Parking. Intimate dining. Cr cds: A, D, MC, V.

★ ★ **THE PALM.** 200 S Broad St (19102), downtown. 215/546-7256. Hrs: 11:30 am-11 pm; Sat from 5 pm; Sun 4:30-9:30 pm. Closed most major hols. Res accepted. Continental menu. Bar. A la carte entrees: lunch $7.50-$25, dinner $12.50-$40. Specializes in fresh seafood, prime aged beef, lamb chops. Valet parking. Counterpart of famous New York restaurant. Caricatures of celebrities. Cr cds: A, C, D, MC, V.

D

★ ★ ★ **RESTAURANT 210.** (See The Rittenhouse Hotel) 215/790-2534. Hrs: 11:30 am-2:30 pm, 6-10 pm; Sat 6-10:30 pm. Closed Sun. Res accepted. Continental cuisine with regional American influences. Bar 11:30-2 am. Wine list. Semi-a la carte: lunch, $23-$30, dinner $21.50-$35. Specializes in seafood, steak, veal. Seasonal menu. Own pastries. Valet parking. Formal decor. Overlooks park. Cr cds: A, C, D, DS, MC, V.

D

★ ★ **RISTORANTE ALBERTO.** (1415 City Line Ave, Wynnewood) I-76 W to City Line Ave. 215/896-0275. Hrs: 5-10 pm; Fri, Sat 5-11 pm; Sun 4-10 pm. Closed Jan 1, Thanksgiving, Dec 25; also month of Aug. Res accepted; required Fri & Sat. Italian menu. A la carte entrees: dinner $12.95-$24.95. Specializes in grilled Dover sole, double veal chop, fresh fish. Guitarist wkends. Valet parking. Display of wine bottles; original art. Cr cds: A, D, MC, V.

D

✔★ **SERRANO.** 20 S 2nd St, in Olde City. 215/928-0770. Hrs: 11:30 am-2:30 pm, 5:30-10 pm; Fri & Sat to 11 pm. Closed Sun; major hols. Res accepted. International menu. Bar. Semi-a la carte: lunch $5.50-$7.50, dinner $6.95-$15.95. Child's meals. Specialties: chicken Hungarian, Malaysian pork chops, filet mignon. Own desserts. Entertainment Wed-Sat. Cr cds: A, D, DS, MC, V.

D

★ **SFUZZI.** 1650 Market St, downtown. 215/851-8888. Hrs: 11:30 am-3 pm, 5:30-10 pm; Thurs-Sat to 11 pm; Sun 5-9 pm; Sun brunch 11:30 am-3 pm. Closed Thanksgiving, Dec 25. Res accepted. Italian menu. Bar. A la carte entrees: lunch $10.50-$17.50, dinner $11.50-$17.50. Sun brunch $14.50. Specializes in calamari, pasta, vegetable lasagne. Outdoor dining. Cr cds: A, D, MC, V.

D

✔★ **SOUTH STREET DINER.** 140 South St, in South Street Area. 215/627-5258. Open 24 hrs. Semi-a la carte: bkfst $1.95-$7.95, lunch, dinner $1.50-$13.95. Specializes in seafood, Greek and Italian specialties. Cr cds: A, C, D, DS, MC, V.

★ ★ ★ **SUZANNA FOO.** 1512 Walnut St (19102), downtown. 215/545-2666. Hrs: 11:30 am-2:30 pm, 5:30-10 pm; Fri & Sat to 11 pm; Sun to 9 pm. Closed some major hols. Res accepted. Chinese, French menu. Bar. Wine cellar. A la carte entrees: lunch $9-$16, dinner $11-$24. Specialties: crispy duck, soft-shell crabs, hundred corner crab cake. Valet parking. Chinese art and artifacts. Dim Sum bar on second level. Jacket. Cr cds: A, C, D, MC, V.

D

★ ★ **UNDER THE BLUE MOON.** 8042 Germantown Ave, in Chestnut Hill. 215/247-1100. Hrs: 6-9 pm; Fri, Sat to 10 pm. Closed Sun, Mon, major hols. Continental menu. Bar. A la carte entrees: dinner

$10-$18. Specializes in seafood, chicken, duck. Unique modern decor. Cr cds: MC, V.

✔★ **VAN'S GARDEN.** *121 N 11th St, in Chinatown. 215/923-2438.* Hrs: 10 am-10 pm. Closed Thanksgiving. Vietnamese menu. Semi-a la carte: lunch, dinner $2.95-$6.95. Specialties: lobster salad, barbecued beef on rice noodles, sautéed chicken with lemon grass. Adj to convention center. No cr cds accepted.

★★ **WHITE DOG CAFE.** *3420 Sansom St, downtown. 215/386-9224.* Hrs: 11:30 am-2:30 pm, 5:30-10 pm; Fri-Sat 5:30-11 pm; Sun 5-10 pm; Sat, Sun brunch 11 am-2:30 pm. Closed Thanksgiving & Dec 25. Res accepted. Bar. Semi-a la carte: lunch $6.50-$10, dinner $14-$19. Sat, Sun brunch $6-$10. Child's meals. Specializes in seafood, roasted quail, spring trout. Own desserts. Former house (ca 1870) of author Madame Blavatsky, founder of the Theosophical Society. Cr cds: A, D, DS, MC, V.

✔★★ **ZOCALO.** *3600 Lancaster Ave, west of downtown. 215/895-0139.* Hrs: noon-2:30 pm, 5:30-10 pm; Fri & Sat 5:30-11 pm; Sun 5-9:30 pm. Closed major hols. Res accepted. Mexican menu. Bar. Semi-a la carte: lunch $6-$10, dinner $10-$18. Prix fixe: dinner $13.95 & $15. Specializes in spicy shrimp, swordfish tacos. Parking. Outdoor dining. Cr cds: A, D, DS, MC, V.

Unrated Dining Spots

FAMOUS 4TH ST DELICATESSEN. *700 S 4th St, south of downtown. 215/922-3274.* Hrs: 7 am-6 pm; Sun to 4 pm. Closed Rosh Hashana, Yom Kippur. Delicatessen fare. Beer. A la carte: bkfst $2-$6, lunch $3.50-$10. Specializes in chocolate chip cookies, fresh roasted turkey, corned beef. Antique telephones. Family-owned more than 70 yrs. Cr cds: A.

MANGO BAY. *264 S 16th St, downtown. 215/735-3316.* Hrs: noon-midnight; Mon to 11 pm; Sun noon-3 pm, 4:30-11 pm. Closed Dec 25; also lunch most major hols. Res accepted. Bar to 2 am. A la carte entrees: lunch, dinner $6.50-$15. Specializes in Caribbean cuisine, seafood, pasta. Island atmosphere. Cr cds: A, D, MC, V.

THE RESTAURANT SCHOOL. *4207 Walnut St, near University of Pennsylvania, west of downtown. 215/222-4200.* Hrs: 5:30-10 pm. Closed Sun, Mon; also during student breaks. Res accepted. Bar. Complete meals: dinner $13.50. Seasonal menu; occasionally an extraordinary and elaborate theme dinner is offered. Own baking. Valet parking. Bakery shop on premises. Unique dining experience in a "restaurant school." Consists of 2 buildings; a restored 1856 mansion is linked by a large atrium dining area to a new building housing the kitchen and classrooms. Cr cds: A, C, D, DS, MC, V.

Ⅾ

ROLLER'S. *8705 Germantown Ave, in Top-of-the-Hill Plaza, in Chestnut Hill. 215/242-1771.* Hrs: 11:30 am-2:30 pm, 5:30-9 pm; Fri to 10 pm; Sat noon-2:30 pm, 5:30-10 pm; Sun 5-9 pm; Sun brunch 11 am-2:30 pm. Closed Mon. Bar. Semi-a la carte: lunch $6-$11, dinner $16-$24. Sun brunch $6-$10. Specializes in fresh fish, veal, duck. Parking. Outdoor dining. Modern cafe atmosphere. No cr cds accepted.

SASSAFRAS. *48 S 2nd St, in Olde City. 215/925-2317.* Hrs: noon-midnight; Fri, Sat to 1 am. Closed Sun; major hols. Bar. A la carte entrees: dinner $4-$15. Specializes in salads, omelettes, Béarnaise burgers, grilled fish. Cr cds: A, D, MC, V.

SPIRIT OF PHILADELPHIA. *Pier 3, on Delaware Ave, in Olde City. 215/923-1419.* Hrs: lunch cruise noon-2 pm, dinner cruise 7-10 pm; Sun brunch cruise 1-3 pm. Closed Dec 25. Res required. Bar. Buffet: lunch $16.95 (adults), $9.50 (children), dinner $28.95-$32.95 (adults), $15.95 (children). Sun brunch $18.95 (adults), $9.50 (children). Musical revue, bands, dancing. Parking. Dining and sightseeing aboard Spirit cruise liner. Cr cds: A, MC, V.

Ⅾ

SWANN LOUNGE. *(See Four Seasons Hotel Philadelphia)* 215/963-1500. Hrs: 7-10 am, 11:30 am-2:30 pm; tea 3-5 pm; Sun brunch 11 am-2:30 pm; Viennese buffet Fri, Sat 9 pm-1 am. Closed Mon. Res accepted. Bar 11:30-1 am; Fri, Sat to 2 am. Buffet: bkfst $9.75-$14, lunch $12-$21. Afternoon tea $12. Sun brunch $24. Viennese buffet $11. Specializes in English tea service with sandwiches & cakes. Valet parking. Outdoor dining (lunch). Elegant atmosphere. Cr cds: A, C, D, ER, JCB, MC, V.

Ⅾ

Phoenix

Settled: 1864

Pop: 983,403

Elev: 1,090 feet

Time zone: Mountain

Area code: 602

The capital of Arizona lies on a flat desert surrounded by mountains and green fields. The climate, with its warm temperatures and low humidity, makes Phoenix one of the most desirable vacation spots in the United States. In the Valley of the Sun there is just enough rainfall to sustain the summer desert plants, which makes Phoenix ideal for sun-loving visitors.

Phoenix's known history began about 300 B.C. when the Hohokam started irrigation farming in the area. When the present city was founded in 1871, the settlers decided to name their city after the mythological phoenix bird. According to legend, the bird lived 500 years, then burned itself alive, and from its ashes came forth another phoenix.

By 1873, the cultivation of cotton had begun. Phoenix was incorporated in 1881. Six years later, the first railroad was brought to the city, and industrial expansion followed. Within two years Phoenix was chosen as the capital of the territory, and when Arizona attained statehood in 1912, Phoenix was named state capital.

The industrial growth of the city was boosted by the two world wars. After World War II, manufacturing became the chief industry in Phoenix, and the city's population began to increase dramatically. Today, the Phoenix-Scottsdale area continues to prosper as a popular resort and retirement center. As a vacation spot, it combines sophistication with informality.

Business

Phoenix relies on manufacturing for its economic stability. Among the products made here are fertilizers, computers, electronic equipment, chemicals, processed foods and weapons for the military. Almost one-fifth of Phoenix's working population is employed in manufacturing. Honeywell Information Systems, Motorola, Sperry Flight Systems and Western Electric are among the city's larger employers.

Tourism is the city's number two industry and contributes greatly to the local economy.

Convention Facilities

The Phoenix Civic Plaza Convention Center provides 300,000 square feet of exhibit space, part of which can be divided into a 72,000-square-foot exhibit area and a 36,000-square-foot assembly area. The center features 5 exhibit halls and a 28,000-square-foot ballroom.

The lobby contains 18,000 square feet of space. Symphony Hall, adjacent to the Convention Center, has permanent seating for 2,557 people. The center also has 5 large meeting rooms that can be divided into 43 smaller rooms, accommodating between 25 and 1,500 people.

A cocktail lounge, which seats 90 people, is just off the lobby. The Executive Conference Room, VIP Lounge, press, TV and broadcasting facilities are on the mezzanine level, which overlooks the exhibit floor.

There is parking for 1,100 cars under the plaza. An additional 550 cars can be parked east of the exhibit hall.

The Arizona Veterans Memorial Coliseum and Exposition Center features a 25,500-square-foot arena with 14,000 permanent seats and space for 1,000 additional seats. It also has 2 exhibition halls, each with 20,000 square feet of space.

America West Arena, opened in 1992, has 25,000-square-feet of exhibition space and parking garages for 2,500 automobiles.

The Phoenix/Scottsdale and Valley of the Sun area has 35,000 hotel and motel rooms.

Recreation and Entertainment

The Phoenix area offers a wide variety of professional and collegiate sports entertainment. For fans of professional basketball, the Phoenix Suns play from October through March at the America West Arena, downtown. The Phoenix Cardinals play professional football at Sun Devil Stadium. This stadium also plays host to the nationally televised collegiate Fiesta Bowl football game every New Year's Day. Major League Baseball's Angels, Cubs, Giants, Mariners, A's and Brewers all have spring training facilities in the Phoenix area.

More than 100 golf courses in Phoenix range from 9-hole "pitch-and-putt" to championship courses. The Phoenix Tennis Center provides 16 lighted courts for tennis buffs; public courts are located throughout the metropolitan area. There are also many places to enjoy horseback riding, swimming, boating and fishing. Horse, dog, boat and auto racing are popular here as well.

Metropolitan Phoenix features a continuous schedule of music and plays. Concert programs, ranging from pop and semi-classical to the works of the masters, are performed by top musicians, including visiting stars of national and international fame. The Phoenix Symphony's season runs from September through June.

Community theater groups and touring companies of Broadway shows are joined by stars of stage, screen and television. The Scottsdale Center for the Arts has a seating capacity of 1,700 people. It is the home of the Scottsdale Symphony Orchestra and offers year-round performances of symphony, pops, chorale and youth orchestra.

Historical Areas

Phoenix has many fine museums with extensive exhibits. The Arizona Museum exhibits include a post office, a flour mill and pioneer and Native American artifacts; the Pueblo Grande Museum includes a Hohokam ruin, thought to have been occupied from 300 B.C. to A.D. 1400; the Arizona History Room has changing exhibits depicting life in early Arizona; the Heard Museum houses fascinating exhibits detailing the culture of the Southwest; and the Phoenix Art Museum features 15th-20th-century paintings, sculpture and decorative arts.

A gem of Victorian architecture, the 1894 Rosson House is part of Heritage Square, a unique area that includes museums, shops, restaurants and an open-air lath house.

Prehistoric Indian ruins can be found in many nearby sections of the state. Casa Grande Ruins National Monument, located between Phoenix and Tucson at the edge of the Gila River Indian Reservation, consists of a four-story, castle-like building of classic Indian construction. There is a museum with exhibits explaining Arizona archaeology and ethnology. Montezuma Castle, north of the city on the highway to Flagstaff, is another "apartment house" in remarkable condition. It is tucked into the side of a cliff and dates back to the 13th century. Tonto National Monument, east of Phoenix near Theodore Roosevelt Lake, preserves prehistoric cliff dwellings built during the 14th century by tribesmen drifting southward from the Little Colorado River valley.

Other excavated ruins are at Tuzigoot National Monument, west of Montezuma Castle; Walnut Canyon and Wupatki national monuments, near Flagstaff; and Canyon de Chelly and Navajo national monuments, on the Navajo Reservation in the northeastern part of the state.

Sightseeing

Various attractions in Phoenix are worth a visit. One such place is the Hall of Flame Firefighting Museum, which houses a collection of antique firefighting equipment. The Phoenix Zoo contains more than 1,300 mammals, birds and reptiles. A safari train tour and a 45-minute trained animal show are popular with visitors.

Parks are plentiful in the Phoenix area, offering an enormous selection of activities on land and water. There are also thousands of acres of wilderness nearby.

No visit to this part of the country would be complete without seeing Scottsdale, a resort town at the foot of Camelback Mountain. This town is famous for its antiques, crafts, jewelry and Western clothing shops. There are numerous art galleries, resorts and golf courses. Many rodeos and horse shows are held at various times of the year.

Scottsdale is the location of Taliesin West, the architectural school and winter residence of Frank Lloyd Wright. On Scottsdale Road, four miles north of Bell Road, is Rawhide 1880s Western Town, a re-creation of an 1880 pioneer village.

The Arizona scenery is tremendously varied—deserts, mountains, canyons, forests—and easily accessible from Phoenix. Two of the nation's most popular and spectacular national parks, Grand Canyon and Petrified Forest, can be reached within a few hours.

General References

Settled: 1864 **Pop:** 983,403 **Elev:** 1,090 feet **Time zone:** Mountain **Area code:** 602

Phone Numbers

POLICE, FIRE & PARAMEDICS: 911
FBI: 279-5511
POISON CONTROL CENTER: 800/362-0101
TIME: 260-9111 **WEATHER:** 265-5550

Information Sources

Phoenix & Valley of the Sun Convention & Visitors Bureau, 400 E Van Buren St, Suite 600, 85004; 254-6500.
Visitor Information, activities hotline, 252-5588.
Parks and Recreation Department, 262-6861.

Transportation

AIRLINES: Alaska; American; America West; Continental; Delta; Northwest; Southwest; TWA; United; USAir; and other commuter and regional airlines. For the most current airline schedules and information consult the *Official Airline Guide*, published twice monthly.
AIRPORT: Sky Harbor International, 273-3300.
CAR RENTAL AGENCIES: (See Toll-Free Numbers) Avis 273-3222; Budget 267-4000; Dollar 275-7588; Hertz 944-5225; National 275-4771.
PUBLIC TRANSPORTATION: City of Phoenix Transit System, 253-5000.
RAILROAD PASSENGER SERVICE: Amtrak 800/872-7245.

Newspapers

The Arizona Republic; Phoenix Gazette.

Convention Facilities

America West Arena, 1st and Jefferson, 379-2000.
Arizona Veterans Memorial Coliseum & Exposition Center, 1826 W McDowell Rd, 252-6771.
Phoenix Civic Plaza Convention Center, 225 E Adams, 262-6225.

Sports & Recreation

Major Sports Facilities
America West Arena, 1st and Jefferson, 379-7800 (Suns, basketball, 379-2000).
Arizona Veterans Memorial Coliseum & Exposition Center, 1826 W McDowell Rd, 258-6711.
Sun Devil Stadium, Arizona State University, Tempe, 965-3933 (Cardinals, football, 967-1402).

Racetracks
Greyhound Park, 40th & E Washington Sts, 273-7181.
Phoenix International Raceway, Baseline Rd & S 115th Ave, access via I-10W, 252-3833 (auto racing).
Turf Paradise, 19th Ave & Bell Rd, 942-1101 (horse racing).

Cultural Facilities

Theater
Phoenix Little Theater, 25 E Coronado Rd, in Civic Center, 254-2151.

Concert Halls
Grady Gammage Memorial Auditorium, Arizona State University, Tempe, 965-3434.
Scottsdale Center for the Arts, 7383 Scottsdale Mall, Scottsdale, 994-2301.
Symphony Hall, Phoenix Civic Plaza, 225 E Adams St, 262-7272.

Museums
Arizona Historical Society Museum, 1300 N College Ave, Tempe, 929-0292.
Arizona Mining & Mineral Museum, 1502 W Washington St, 255-3791.
Arizona Museum of Science and Technology, 147 E Adams St, 256-9388.
Hall of Flame Firefighting Museum, 6101 E Van Buren, opposite zoo, 275-3473.
Heard Museum, 22 E Monte Vista Rd, 252-8848.
Phoenix Museum of History, 1002 W Van Buren St, at 10th Ave, 253-2734.

Art Museum

Phoenix Art Museum, 1625 N Central Ave, 257-1222.

Points of Interest

Historical

Heritage Square, Rosson House, 7th St & Monroe, 262-5029.
Pueblo Grande Museum, 4619 E Washington St, 4 mi S off US 60/89, on AZ 143, 495-0900.
Rawhide 1880s Western Town, 23023 N Scottsdale Rd, Scottsdale, 563-1880 or 563-5600.
State Capitol, 1700 W Washington St, 542-4581 or -4675.

Other Attractions

Arcosanti, 65 mi N via I-17 at Cordes Junction, 632-7135.
Big Surf, 1500 N McClintock Dr, Tempe, 947-7873.
Camelback Mountain, Scottsdale.
Canyon de Chelly National Monument, NE corner of state near Chinle, on Navajo Indian Reservation, 674-5436.
Casa Grande Ruins National Monument, near Coolidge, at edge of Gila River Indian Reservation, 723-3172.
Cosanti Foundation, 6433 Doubletree Ranch Rd, Scottsdale, 948-6145.
Desert Botanical Garden, Galvin Pkwy, in Papago Park, 941-1217.
Fifth Avenue Shops, from Scottsdale Rd W to Indian School Rd, Scottsdale.
Gila Indian Center, 25 mi S of Phoenix, on I-10, at Casa Blanca exit 175, near Chandler, on Gila River Indian Reservation, 963-3981.
McCormick Railroad Park, 7301 E Indian Bend Rd, Scottsdale, 994-2312.
Montezuma Castle National Monument, 90 mi N via I-17 exit 289, 567-3322.

Mystery Castle, 800 E Mineral Rd at S 7th Street at foot of South Mountain, 268-1581.
Navajo National Monument, 20 mi SW of Kayenta on US 160, then 9 mi N on AZ 564, on Navajo Indian Reservation, 672-2366.
Phoenix Zoo, 455 N Galvin Pkwy, in Papago Park, 273-1341.
South Mountain Park, 7 mi S at end of Central Ave, 495-0222.
Superstition Mountain & Tonto National Forest, 20 mi NE on AZ 87.
Taliesin West, Frank Lloyd Wright Blvd & Cactus Rd, Scottsdale, 860-2700.
Tonto National Monument, 3 mi E on US 60/89, then 30 mi NE on AZ 88, 467-2241.
Valley Garden Center, 1809 N 15th Ave, 252-2120.
Walnut Canyon National Monument, 9 mi E of Flagstaff, on I-40, 526-3367.
Wupatki National Monument, 15 mi N of Flagstaff on US 89, then 18 mi N on Forest Service Rd 545, 556-7040.

Sightseeing Tour

Gray Line bus tours, PO Box 21126, 85036, 495-9100 or 800/732-0327.

Annual Events

Indian Fair, Heard Museum, 22 E Monte Vista Rd. 1st wkend Mar.
Jaycees Rodeo of Rodeos, Veterans Memorial Coliseum, 19th Ave & McDowell Rd, 263-8671. Mid-Mar.
Yaqui Indian Holy Week Ceremonials. 883-2838, Friday evenings leading to Easter.
Arizona State Fair, state fairgrounds, 252-6771. Mid-Oct.
Cowboy Artists of America, Phoenix Art Museum, 257-1880. Late Oct-late Nov.

Lodgings and Food

Motels

✔★ COMFORT INN-NORTH. *1711 W Bell Rd (85023). 602/866-2089; FAX 602/789-7669.* 155 rms, 3 story, 24 suites. Jan-Apr: S $59-$69; D $64-$74; each addl $5; suites $79-$89; under 18 free; lower rates rest of yr. Crib free. Pet accepted, some restrictions; $5. TV; cable. Heated pool; whirlpool. Complimentary continental bkfst, coffee. Restaurant nearby. Ck-out noon. Coin lndry. Valet serv. Refrigerator, wet bar in suites. Suites have balconies. Cr cds: A, C, D, DS, ER, JCB, MC, V.

★★ COURTYARD BY MARRIOTT. *9631 N Black Canyon (85021). 602/944-7373; FAX 602/944-0079.* 146 rms, 3 story. Jan-mid-Apr: S, D $98-$130; under 18 free; wkend, hol rates; lower rates rest of yr. Crib free. TV; cable. Restaurant 6:30-10 am, 6-9 pm. Ck-out 1 pm. Coin lndry. Valet serv. Exercise equipt; weights, stair machine, whirlpool. Some refrigerators. Balconies. Cr cds: A, C, D, DS, MC, V.

★★ COURTYARD BY MARRIOTT. *2101 E Camelback Rd (85016). 602/955-5200; FAX 602/955-1101.* 155 rms, 4 story. Jan-Apr: S $115-$125; D $125-$135; suites $135-$155; wkend, wkly, hol rates; lower rates rest of yr. Crib free. TV; cable. Heated pool. Complimentary coffee in rms. Restaurant 6:30-11 am; wkends 7 am-1 pm. Rm serv. Bar 4-11 pm. Ck-out 1 pm. Coin lndry. Meeting rms. Valet serv. Exercise equipt; weight machine, bicycles, whirlpool. Refrigerator in suites. Balconies. Cr cds: A, C, D, DS, MC, V.

★★ COURTYARD BY MARRIOTT- AIRPORT. *2621 S 47th St (85034), near Sky Harbor Intl Airport. 602/966-4300; FAX 602/966-0198.* 145 units, 4 story. Jan-late Apr: S $116-$120; D $126-$130; each addl $10; suites $130-$145; wkend, wkly rates; some lower rates of yr. Crib free. TV; cable. Heated pool. Complimentary coffee in rms. Restaurant 6-10 am, 5-10 pm; wkends from 7-11 am, 5-11 pm. Bar 4-11 pm. Ck-out 1 pm. Coin lndry. Meeting rms. Valet serv. Free airport transportation. Exercise equipt; weight machine, bicycles, whirlpool. Refrigerator in suites. Many balconies. Cr cds: A, C, D, DS, MC, V.

★★ HAMPTON INN. *8101 N Black Canyon Hwy (85021), I-17 exit Northern Ave. 602/864-6233; FAX 602/995-7503.* 149 rms, 3 story. Jan-mid-Apr: S $75; D $80 under 18 free; lower rates rest of yr. Crib free. Pet accepted, some restrictions. TV; cable. Heated pool; whirlpool. Complimentary continental bkfst. Ck-out noon. Meeting rm. Cr cds: A, C, D, DS, MC, V.

★★ LA QUINTA-COLISEUM WEST. *2725 N Black Canyon Hwy (85009), I-17 exit Thomas Rd. 602/258-6271; FAX 602/340-9255.* 139 rms, 2 story. Jan-Apr: S, D $73; each addl $10; under 18 free; lower rates rest of yr. Crib free. Pet accepted, some restrictions. TV; cable. Heated pool. Complimentary continental bkfst in lobby. Restaurant adj open 24 hrs. Ck-out noon. Coin lndry. Valet serv. Cr cds: A, C, D, DS, MC, V.

✔★ PREMIER INN. *10402 N Black Canyon Hwy (85051), at I-17 Peoria Ave exit. 602/943-2371; res: 800/786-6835; FAX 602/943-5847.* 253 rms, 2 story. Jan-Apr: S $56.95-$74.95; D $58.95-$74.95; suites $99.95; lower rates rest of yr. Crib $3. Pet accepted, some restrictions. TV; cable. 2 pools, 1 heated; wading pool. Bar 11-2 am.

Ck-out noon. Coin lndry. Meeting rms. Tennis. Bathrm phone in suites. Some private patios. Cr cds: A, D, DS, MC, V.

Motor Hotels

★★★ BEST WESTERN GRACE INN AHWATUKEE. *10831 S 51st St (85044), just S of I-10 Elliott Rd exit. 602/893-3000; FAX 602/496-8303.* 160 rms, 6 story. Jan-May: S, D $100-$145; each addl $10; suites $125-$145; under 17 free; lower rates rest of yr. Crib free. TV; cable. Heated pool; poolside serv. Restaurant 6 am-9 pm. Rm serv. Bar 11:30-1 am, Sun from noon; entertainment, dancing exc Sun. Ck-out noon. Meeting rms. Bellhops. Valet serv. Sundries. Barber, beauty shop. Free airport transportation. Lighted tennis. 18-hole golf privileges. Exercise rm; instructor, weights, bicycles, whirlpool. Lawn games. Refrigerators. Balconies. *LUXURY LEVEL : CONCIERGE LEVEL.* 26 rms. S $125-$155. Private lounge. Complimentary full bkfst 6:30-8:30 am, refreshments. Cr cds: A, C, D, DS, MC, V.

★★ BEST WESTERN INNSUITES AT SQUAW PEAK. *1615 E Northern Ave (85020). 602/997-6285; FAX 602/943-1407.* 123 rms, 2 story, 4 kits. Jan-mid-Apr: S $75-$85; D $80-$90; kit. suites $99-$149; under 19 free; wkend rates; lower rates rest of yr. Crib free. Pet accepted; $25 refundable. TV; cable. Heated pool. Complimentary continental bkfst. Complimentary coffee & juice in rms. Ck-out noon. Meeting rms. Exercise equipt; stair machine, bicycle, whirlpool. Refrigerators. Picnic tables, grills. Cr cds: A, C, D, DS, MC, V.

✔★★ DAYS INN CAMELBACK. *502 W Camelback Rd (85013). 602/264-9290; FAX 602/264-3068.* 166 rms, 4 story. Jan-Apr: S $65-$85; D $72-$89; each addl $10; suites $130-$160; lower rates rest of yr. Crib free. Pet accepted; $10 per day. TV; cable. Heated pool; whirlpool, poolside serv. Restaurant 6:30 am-2 pm, 5-9:30 pm. Rm serv. Bar 5 pm-1 am. Ck-out noon. Meeting rms. Valet serv. Some refrigerators. Cr cds: A, C, D, DS, MC, V.

★★★ FOUNTAIN SUITES. *2577 W Greenway Rd (85023). 602/375-1777; res: 800/527-7715 (exc AZ); FAX 602/375-1777, ext. 5555.* 314 suites, 2-3 story. Jan-mid-May: S, D $99-$170; under 18 free; lower rates rest of yr. Pet accepted, some restrictions; $100 non-refundable. TV; cable. Heated pool; whirlpool, sauna. Restaurant 6 am-10 pm. Rm serv. Bar 11-1 am; entertainment. Ck-out noon. Coin lndry. Meeting rms. Bellhops. Valet serv. Lighted tennis. Golf privileges. Refrigerators, minibars. Stucco and red-tile roofed building reminiscent of traditional resort hotels. Cr cds: A, C, D, DS, ER, JCB, MC, V.

★★ LOS OLIVOS EXECUTIVE HOTEL. *202 E McDowell Rd (85004). 602/258-6911; res: 800/669-5858; FAX 602/257-0776.* 48 rms, 3 story, 15 suites. Jan-Apr: S, D $79; each addl $3; suites $99; under 15 free; lower rates rest of yr. TV; cable. Heated pool; whirlpool. Complimentary coffee in rms. Complimentary continental bkfst. Restaurant 6:30 am-2 pm. Rm serv. Ck-out noon. Coin lndry. Meeting rms. Sundries. Valet serv. Tennis. Health club privileges. Refrigerator in suites. Balconies. Picnic tables. Cr cds: A, C, D, MC, V.

★★★ PHOENIX AIRPORT HILTON. *2435 S 47th St (85034), near Sky Harbor Intl Airport. 602/894-1600; FAX 602/894-0326.* 255 units, 4 story. Jan-Apr: S $124-$189; D $139-$204; each addl $15; suites $185-$275; under 18 free; lower rates rest of yr. Crib avail. TV; cable. Pool; poolside serv. Restaurant 6 am-10 pm. Rm serv to midnight. Bar 11 am-midnight. Ck-out noon. Convention facilities. Bellhops. Valet serv. Concierge. Sundries. Gift shop. Free airport transportation. Exercise equipt; weight machines, bicycles, whirlpool. Minibars. Many balconies. *LUXURY LEVEL : TOWERS.* 62 rms, 4 suites. S $144-$209; D $159-$224. Private lounge. Complimentary continental bkfst, refreshments. Cr cds: A, C, D, DS, ER, JCB, MC, V.

D ⊠ ✕ ✈ ⊠ ⊠

✔★ QUALITY INN SOUTHMOUNTAIN. 5121 E La Puente Ave (85044). 602/893-3900; FAX 602/496-0815. 193 rms, 4 story. Jan-Apr: S $69-$79; D $79-$89; suites $105-$125; under 17 free; lower rates rest of yr. Crib free. Pet accepted; $25 refundable. TV; cable. Heated pool; whirlpool. Restaurant 6:30-11 am, 5-9 pm. Rm serv. Ck-out 11 am. Coin lndry. Meeting rms. Valet serv. Cr cds: A, C, D, DS, ER, JCB, MC, V.

D ⊠ ⊠ ⊠ ⊠ SC

★★ RAMADA INN METROCENTER. 12027 N 28th Dr (85029). 602/866-7000; FAX 602/942-7512. 167 rms, 4 story. Jan-Apr: S $75-$90; D $85-$100; each addl $10; suites $105-$150; under 18 free; lower rates rest of yr. Crib free. Pet accepted, some restrictions; $20 refundable. TV; cable. Heated pool; whirlpool, poolside serv. Restaurant 6 am-10 pm. Rm serv. Bar 4 pm-midnight. Ck-out noon. Meeting rms. Valet serv. Gift shop. Cr cds: A, C, D, DS, ER, JCB, MC, V.

D ⊠ ⊠ ⊠ ⊠ SC

★★ WYNDHAM GARDEN HOTEL. 2641 W Union Hills Dr (85027), at I-17. 602/978-2222; FAX 602/978-9139. 166 rms, 2 story. Jan-May: S $108; D $118; each addl $10; under 18 free; lower rates rest of yr. Pet accepted, some restrictions; $25 non-refundable. TV; cable. Heated pool; whirlpool, poolside serv. Restaurant 6:30 am-10 pm. Rm serv 5-10 pm. Bar 4:30-11 pm. Ck-out noon. Coin lndry. Meeting rms. Valet serv. Sundries. Some private patios. Cr cds: A, C, D, DS, ER, JCB, MC, V.

D ⊠ ⊠ ⊠ ⊠

★★ WYNDHAM GARDEN HOTEL-AIRPORT. 427 N 44th St (85008), near Sky Harbor Intl Airport. 602/220-4400; FAX 602/231-8703. 210 rms, 7 story, 24 suites. Jan-Apr: S $149-$159; D $159-$169; each addl $10; suites $169-$179; under 18 free; lower rates rest of yr. Crib free. TV; cable. Heated pool; poolside serv. Coffee in rms. Restaurant 6:30 am-2 pm, 5-10 pm. Rm serv. Bar 3-11 pm. Ck-out noon. Meeting rms. Valet serv. Sundries. Free airport transportation. Exercise equipt; weight machine, bicycles, whirlpool. Some bathrm phones. Cr cds: A, C, D, DS, ER, JCB, MC, V.

D ⊠ ✕ ✈ ⊠ ⊠ SC

Hotels

★★★ BEST WESTERN EXECUTIVE PARK. 1100 N Central Ave (85004). 602/252-2100; FAX 602/340-1989. 107 rms, 8 story. Jan-Apr: S $95-$105; D $105-$115; each addl $10; suites $150; under 13 free; wkend rates; lower rates rest of yr. Crib free. TV; cable. Heated pool; poolside serv. Coffee in rms. Restaurant 6:30 am-10 pm. Bar 11 am-11 pm, Sun from noon. Ck-out noon. Meeting rms. Free airport transportation. Exercise equipt; weight machine, bicycles, whirlpool, sauna. Some bathrm phones, refrigerators, wet bars. Balconies. Panoramic mountain views. Cr cds: A, C, D, DS, ER, MC, V.

⊠ ✕ ⊠ ⊠ SC

★★★ CROWN STERLING SUITES-BILTMORE. 2630 E Camelback Rd (85016). 602/955-3992; res: 800/433-4600; FAX 602/955-6479. 232 kit. suites, 5 story. Jan-Apr: S $205-$226; D $215-$236; each addl $10; under 13 free; lower rates rest of yr. Crib free. TV; cable. Heated pool; whirlpool, poolside serv. Complimentary coffee in rms. Complimentary full bkfst. Restaurant 11 am-10 pm. Bar to midnight; entertainment Tues-Sat. Ck-out 1 pm. Meeting rms. Coin lndry. Gift shop. Tennis, golf privileges. Private patios, balconies. Atrium with lush garden & fish pond. Cr cds: A, C, D, DS, ER, JCB, MC, V.

D ⊠ ✕ ⊠ ⊠ ⊠ SC

★★★ DOUBLETREE SUITES-PHOENIX GATEWAY CENTER. 320 N 44th St (85008), near Sky Harbor Intl Airport. 602/225-0500; FAX 602/225-0957. 242 suites, 6 story. Jan-Apr: S $145-$245, D $155-$255; each addl $10; under 17 free; wkend rates; lower rates rest of yr.

Crib free. Pet accepted, some restrictions. TV; cable. Heated pool; poolside serv. Complimentary coffee in rooms. Complimentary full bkfst. Restaurant 6:30 am-10 pm. Bar 11-1 am. Ck-out noon. Meeting rms. Gift shop. Free airport transportation. Tennis. Exercise equipt; bicycle, stair machine, whirlpool, sauna. Refrigerators, minibars. Atrium with 2 banks of glass elevators. Cr cds: A, C, D, DS, MC, V.

D ⊠ ⊠ ✕ ✈ ⊠ ⊠

★★ EMBASSY SUITES-CAMELHEAD. 1515 N 44th St (85008), near Sky Harbor Intl Airport. 602/244-8800; FAX 602/244-8800, ext. 7534. 229 suites, 4 story. Jan-Apr: S, D $165-$175; each addl $10; under 12 free; lower rates rest of yr. Crib free. TV; cable. Heated pool; whirlpool, poolside serv. Complimentary coffee in rms. Complimentary full bkfst. Restaurant 11:30 am-10 pm. Bar. Ck-out noon. Coin lndry. Meeting rms. Gift shop. Free airport transportation. Health club privileges. Balconies. Grills. Glass-enclosed elvtr overlooks courtyard. Cr cds: A, C, D, DS, JCB, MC, V.

D ⊠ ⊠ ✈ ⊠ ⊠

★ HOLIDAY INN AIRPORT. 4300 E Washington St (85034), near Sky Harbor Intl Airport. 602/273-7778; FAX 602/275-5616. 301 rms, 10 story. Jan-mid-May: S $99-$149; D $109-$159; each addl $10; suites $198-$298; under 18 free; higher rates hols (3-day min), spring training; lower rates rest of yr. Crib $10. Garage parking. TV; cable. Heated pool; whirlpool, poolside serv. Restaurant 6 am-11 pm. Bar 11-1 am; entertainment exc Sun. Ck-out noon. Coin lndry. Meeting rms. Gift shop. Free airport transportation. 18-hole golf privileges; greens fee $35-$120, pro. Health club privileges. Cr cds: A, C, D, DS, JCB, MC, V.

D ⊠ ✕ ⊠ ✈ ⊠ ⊠ SC

★★★ HOTEL WESTCOURT. 10220 N Metro Pkwy E (85051), at Metrocenter Shopping Ctr, I-17 Peoria exit. 602/997-5900; res: 800/858-1033; FAX 602/943-6156. 284 rms, 5 story. Jan-May: S $95-$152; D $105-$162; each addl $10; suites $150-$250; under 12 free; wkend rates; lower rates rest of yr. Crib free. TV; cable. Heated pool; poolside serv. Restaurant 6:30 am-11 pm. Bar, Sun from 10 am; entertainment. Ck-out noon. Concierge. Shopping arcade. Lighted tennis. Golf privileges. Exercise equipt; weights, bicycles, whirlpool, sauna. Refrigerators. Heliport. *LUXURY LEVEL : PLAZA COURT.* 38 rms. S $115-$152; D $125-$152. Private lounge, honor bar. Library, meeting rms. Complimentary continental bkfst, refreshments. Cr cds: A, C, D, DS, ER, JCB, MC, V.

D ✕ ✕ ⊠ ✕ ⊠ ⊠ SC

★★★ HYATT REGENCY PHOENIX AT CIVIC PLAZA. 122 N 2nd St (85004). 602/252-1234; FAX 602/254-9472. 712 rms, 24 story. Jan-May: S, D $175-$225; suites $275-$700; under 18 free; wkend rates; lower rates rest of yr. Crib free. Valet, garage $8/day. TV; cable. Heated pool; poolside serv. Restaurant 6 am-midnight (also see COMPASS). Bar 11-1 am. Ck-out noon. Meeting rms. Concierge. Shopping arcade. Tennis privileges. Golf privileges. Exercise equipt; weight machine, bicycles, whirlpool. Wet bar in some suites. Some balconies. Cr cds: A, C, D, DS, ER, JCB, MC, V.

D ✕ ✕ ⊠ ✕ ⊠ ⊠

★★ LEXINGTON HOTEL & CITY SQUARE SPORTS CLUB. 100 W Clarendon Ave (85013). 602/279-9811; FAX 602/631-9358. 167 rms, 7 story. Dec-Apr: S, D $79-$119; under 18 free; wkend rates; lower rates rest of yr. Crib free. Pet accepted, some restrictions. TV; cable. Heated pool; poolside serv. Restaurant 6:30 am-10 pm. Bar 11 am-10 pm, Sun from noon. Ck-out noon. Shopping arcade. Valet parking. Free transportation from airport. Exercise rm; instructor, weights, bicycles, whirlpool, steam rm, sauna. Many refrigerators. Some balconies. Cr cds: A, C, D, DS, ER, MC, V.

D ⊠ ⊠ ✕ ⊠ ⊠

★★ RADISSON-MIDTOWN. 401 W Clarendon Ave (85013), between Indian School Rd & Osborn Ave. 602/234-2464; FAX 602/277-2602. 106 rms, 4 story, 88 kits. Jan-May: S, D $112-$138; each addl $10; suites $105-$135; under 18 free; lower rates rest of yr. Crib free. TV; cable. Heated pool; whirlpool, poolside serv. Complimentary continental bkfst. Restaurant 6 am-10 pm. Bar 11:30-1 am. Ck-out noon. Meeting rms. Free airport transportation. Some refrigerators. Courtyard. Cr cds: A, C, D, DS, ER, JCB, MC, V.

≋ ⊠ 🔥 SC

★ ★ ★ ★ **THE RITZ-CARLTON, PHOENIX.** *2401 E Camelback Rd (85016), in the Camelback Esplanade.* 602/468-0700; res: 800/241-3333; FAX 602/957-6076. 281 rms, 11 story, 14 suites. Jan-May: S, D $170-$225; suites $275-$375; under 12 free; lower rates rest of yr. Crib avail. TV; cable. Heated pool; poolside serv. Restaurant (see THE GRILL). Rm serv 24 hrs. Bar 11-1 am; entertainment Tues-Sat. Ck-out noon. Convention facilities. Concierge. Gift shop. Covered parking. Airport, RR station, bus depot transportation; free transportation to golf courses. Lighted tennis. Golf privileges. Exercise rm; instructor, weight machines, treadmill, whirlpool, sauna. Massage. Bicycle rentals. Bathrm phones, minibars. Old World elegance in a cosmopolitan setting. ***LUXURY LEVEL : RITZ-CARLTON CLUB.*** 16 rms, 5 suites. S, D $225; suites $350-$550. Concierge. Private lounge, honor bar. Complimentary continental bkfst, refreshments. Cr cds: A, C, D, DS, ER, JCB, MC, V.

D ⚓ 🏊 ≋ 🏃 ⊠ 🔥

✔ ★ ★ **SAN CARLOS.** *202 N Central Ave (85004).* 602/253-4121; res: 800/528-5446; FAX 602/253-4121, ext. 209. 120 rms, 7 story. Jan-Apr: S, D $89; each addl $10; suites $129-$159; under 12 free. Crib free. TV; cable. Heated pool. Restaurant 6:30 am-10 pm. Ck-out noon. Meeting rms. Exercise equipt; weights, stair machine. Refrigerators avail. Cr cds: A, C, D, DS, MC, V.

≋ 🏃 ⊠ 🔥

★ ★ ★ **SHERATON CRESCENT.** *2620 W Dunlap Ave (85021), at I-17.* 602/943-8200; res: 800/423-4126; FAX 602/371-2857. 342 rms, 8 story. Early Jan-mid-May: S $131-$175; D $143-$197; each addl $15; suites $250-$500; some wkend rates; lower rates rest of yr. Crib free. Pet accepted, some restrictions; $100 ($75 refundable). TV; cable. Heated pool; poolside serv. Restaurant 6 am-11 pm. Bar 11-1 am; entertainment. Ck-out noon. Convention facilities. Gift shop. Free covered parking. Lighted tennis. Exercise rm; instructor, weights, bicycles, whirlpool, sauna, steam rm. Lawn games. Refrigerators, minibars. Balconies. Some fireplaces. Some suites with panoramic view of north mountain range. Elaborate information & business center just off lobby. ***LUXURY LEVEL : CONCIERGE LEVEL.*** 78 rms, 2 floors, 12 suites. S $153-$197; D $164-$208; suites $250-$500. Concierge. Private lounge. Complimentary continental bkfst, refreshments. Cr cds: A, C, D, DS, ER, JCB, MC, V.

D ⚓ 🏃 ≋ 🏃 ⊠ 🔥 SC

Inn

★ ★ ★ **MARICOPA MANOR.** *15 W Pasadena Ave (85013).* 602/274-6302; FAX 602/266-3904. 5 rms, 1 kit. Sept-May: S, D, kit. unit $129; each addl $15; under 6 free; lower rates rest of yr. TV; cable. Complimentary continental bkfst in rms. Restaurant nearby. Ck-out 11 am, ck-in 4-6 pm. Picnic tables. Totally nonsmoking. Restored Spanish mission-style mansion (1928); antiques, library/sitting rm. Cr cds: A, DS, MC, V.

⊠ 🔥

Resorts

★ ★ ★ **POINTE HILTON ON SOUTH MOUNTAIN.** *7777 South Pointe Pkwy (85044).* 602/438-9000; FAX 602/431-6535. 638 suites, 2-4 story. Jan-mid-May: S, D $219-$249; each addl $10; suites $299-$475; under 18 free; lower rates rest of yr. TV; cable. 6 heated pools; wading pool, poolside serv. Supervised child's activities. Dining rm (public by res) 6 am-midnight. Rm serv. Bar 11-1 am. Ck-out noon, ck-in 4 pm. Coin lndry. Convention facilities. Airport, RR station, bus depot transportation. Sports dir. Lighted tennis, pro. 18-hole golf, greens fee $85 (incl cart), pro, putting green. Bicycles. Game rm. Rec rm. Exercise rm; instructor, weights, bicycles, whirlpool, sauna, steam

rm. Minibars; some fireplaces. Private patios, balconies. Cr cds: A, C, D, DS, ER, MC, V.

D ⚓ 🏃 🏃 ≋ 🏃 ⊠ 🔥 SC

★ ★ **ROYAL PALMS INN.** *5200 E Camelback Rd (85018).* 602/840-3610; res: 800/672-6011 (exc AZ), 800/548-1202 (CAN); FAX 602/840-0233. 120 rms, 1-2 story, 34 kits. Mid-Jan-late Apr: S $100-$150; D $140-$220; each addl $10; suites, kit. units $165-$220; under 5 free; some wkend rates; lower rates rest of yr. Crib $10. Pet accepted. TV; cable. 2 heated pools; poolside serv. Dining rm 7 am-2 pm, 6-10 pm. Box lunches. Bar 11 am-midnight. Ck-out noon. Coin lndry. Meeting rms. Valet serv. Airport, RR station, bus depot transportation. Tennis, pro. 9- & 36-hole golf, putting green. Entertainment, dancing. Some balconies. Spanish architecture; antiques; tile walks in date & citrus orchard. Cr cds: A, C, D, DS, ER, MC, V.

D ⚓ 🏃 🏃 ≋ 🏃 ⊠ 🔥 SC

Restaurants

★ ★ ★ **AVANTI'S OF PHOENIX.** *2728 E Thomas Rd.* 602/956-0900. Hrs: 11:30 am-3 pm, 5:30-11 pm; Sat, Sun from 5:30 pm. Closed Dec 25. Res accepted. Continental, Northern Italian menu. Bar. Wine list. Semi-a la carte: lunch $4.75-$15.50, dinner $8.75-$25.50. Specializes in veal, fresh pasta, fresh mussels. Own pastries, pasta. Entertainment Tues-Sat. Valet parking. Cr cds: A, C, D, MC, V.

D

★ **BAXTER'S.** *4514 E Cactus Rd.* 602/953-9200. Hrs: 4-10 pm; Sat & Sun 8 am-10 pm. Closed Dec 25. Res accepted. Bar. Semi-a la carte: bkfst, lunch $4.95-$8.95, dinner $4.95-$15.95. Child's meals. Specializes in barbecued ribs, chicken, steak. DJ (evenings). Parking. Western ranch atmosphere. Cr cds: A, C, D, DS, MC, V.

D

★ **CHIANTI RISTORANTE.** *3943 E Camelback Rd.* 602/957-9840. Hrs: 11:30 am-10 pm; Sat, Sun from 5 pm. Closed Thanksgiving, Dec 25. Res accepted. Italian menu. Serv bar. Semi-a la carte: lunch $5.95-$8.95, dinner $6.95-$12.95. Child's meals. Specializes in pasta, pizza, chicken. Parking. Cr cds: A, MC, V.

D

★ ★ ★ **CHRISTOPHER'S.** *2398 E Camelback Rd (85016), in Biltmore Financial Center.* 602/957-3214. Hrs: 6-10 pm; Fri & Sat to 11 pm. Closed Jan 1, Memorial Day, Labor Day; also Mon & Tues in summer. Res accepted. Contemporary French cuisine. Bar. Extensive wine cellar, one of the largest in the state. Semi-a la carte: dinner $22-$32. Prix fixe: dinner $70, with wine $110. Child's meals. Specialties: crêpe foie gras, house-smoked salmon, chocolate mousse tower. Own baking. Valet parking. Glass-encased wine cellar focal point of well-appointed, cherrywood-trimmed dining room. Antiques. Chef-owned. Jacket. Cr cds: A, C, D, MC, V.

D

★ ★ ★ **CHRISTOPHER'S BISTRO.** *2398 E Camelback Rd, in Biltmore Financial Center.* 602/957-3214. Hrs: 11 am-midnight; Sun from 5 pm. Closed some major hols. Res accepted. Bar. Wine cellar. A la carte entrees: lunch $6-$16, dinner $8-$21. Specializes in seafood, grilled veal chop, rack of lamb. Valet parking. Outdoor dining. Bistro-style dining room. Cr cds: A, C, D, MC, V.

D

★ ★ **COMPASS.** *(See Hyatt Regency Phoenix at Civic Plaza Hotel)* 602/440-3166. Hrs: 11:30 am-2:30 pm, 5:30-10 pm; Sun brunch 10 am-2:30 pm. Res accepted. Southwestern menu. Bar 11-12:30 am. Semi-a la carte: lunch $6.50-$9, dinner $16-$21. Sun brunch $21.50. Child's meals. Specializes in prime rib, stuffed chicken with jalapeño cornbread. Own baking. Valet parking. Revolving dining area on 24th floor; panoramic view of city. Cr cds: A, C, D, DS, ER, JCB, MC, V.

D

★ ★ **COPPER CREEK STEAKHOUSE & GRILLE.** *455 N 3rd St, at the Arizona Center.* 602/253-7100. Hrs: 11 am-10 pm; Fri & Sat to 11 pm. Closed Easter, Thanksgiving, Dec 25. Res accepted. Bar. Semi-a la carte: lunch $5-$10, dinner $10-$18. Specializes in steak, fire-roasted chicken, ribs. Parking. Blue sky mural. Overlooks Arizona Center gardens. Cr cds: A, D, MC, V.

D

★ ★ ★ **DIFFERENT POINTE OF VIEW.** *11111 N 7th St, at The Pointe Hilton at Tapatio Cliffs Resort.* 602/863-0912. Hrs: 6-10 pm. Res accepted. International American fusion cuisine. Bar 5 pm-1 am. Award-winning wine cellar. A la carte entrees: dinner $19-$30. Prix fixe: dinner (June-Sept) $18.95. Sun brunch (Oct-Father's Day) $18.95. Child's meals. Specializes in seafood, regional dishes, vegetarian dishes, wild game. Own baking. Entertainment Tues-Sat. Valet parking. On mountaintop, beautiful view. Cr cds: A, C, D, DS, JCB, MC, V.

D

✔★ ★ **EVITA'S.** *1906 E Camelback Rd (85016).* 602/263-8482. Hrs: 5-10 pm; Fri & Sat to 11 pm; Sun 4:30-9 pm. Closed Easter, Thanksgiving. Res accepted. South American menu. Bar. Semi-a la carte: dinner $9.95-$16.90. Child's meals. Specializes in steak, lamb, Brazilian feijoada. Pianist Wed-Sun. Parking. Casual atmosphere with art deco flair. Cr cds: A, C, D, DS, ER, JCB, MC, V.

D

★ ★ **FISH MARKET.** *1720 E Camelback Rd.* 602/277-3474. Hrs: 11 am-9:30 pm; Fri & Sat to 10 pm; Sun noon-9:30 pm. Closed Thanksgiving, Dec 25. Res accepted. Bar. Semi-a la carte: lunch $8-$20, dinner $9-$20. Child's meals. Specializes in fresh fish, live shellfish, smoked fish. Oyster bar. Parking. Outdoor dining. Nautical decor. Retail fish market. Cr cds: A, D, DS, MC, V.

D

★ ★ **GREEKFEST.** *1940 E Camelback Rd.* 602/265-2990. Hrs: 11 am-2:30 pm, 5-10 pm; Fri, Sat to 11 pm; Sun 5-9 pm. Closed some major hols. Res accepted. Greek menu. Bar. Semi-a la carte: lunch $4.95-$12, dinner $6.95-$18. Child's meals. Specializes in lamb exohiko, fresh fish "chios," souvlaki. Parking. Greek taverna-style decor; festive atmosphere. Cr cds: A, D, MC, V.

D

★ ★ ★ **THE GRILL.** *(See The Ritz-Carlton, Phoenix Hotel)* 602/468-0700. Hrs: 5-10:30 pm; Sept-mid-May also 11:30 am-2:30 pm (Mon-Fri). Res accepted. Bar 11:30-1 am. Wine cellar. Semi-a la carte: lunch $7-$12.50, dinner $19-$25. Child's meals. Specialties: sautéed veal medallions, free range chicken breast, seafood mixed grill. Own baking. Pianist and saxophonist. Valet parking. Dining rm features brass chandeliers. Cr cds: A, C, D, DS, ER, JCB, MC, V.

D

★ ★ **HAVANA CAFE.** *4225 E Camelback Rd (85018).* 602/952-1991. Hrs: 11:30 am-10 pm; Sun hrs vary off-season. Closed some major hols. Res accepted. Cuban, Spanish menu. Bar. A la carte entrees: lunch $3.95-$10.95, dinner $7.95-$15.95. Specialties: pollo Cubano, masas de puerco fritas, paella. Parking. Patio dining. Totally nonsmoking. Cr cds: A, C, D, MC, V.

D

✔★ **HOUSTON'S.** *2425 E Camelback Rd, #110.* 602/957-9700. Hrs: 11 am-11 pm; Fri, Sat to midnight; Sun to 10 pm. Closed Thanksgiving, Dec 25. Bar. Semi-a la carte: lunch, dinner $6.25-$15. Specializes in baby back ribs, fresh grilled fish, thin-crust pizza. Parking. Outdoor dining. Cr cds: A, MC, V.

D

★ ★ ★ **LA FONTANELLA.** *4231 E Indian School Rd.* 602/955-1213. Hrs: 11 am-2 pm, 4:30-9:30 pm; Sat, Sun from 4:30 pm. Closed Dec 25; also Mon May-Sept. Res accepted. Italian menu. Bar. Semi-a la carte: lunch $4.50-$7.50, dinner $6.50-$17.75. Child's meals. Specialties: rack of lamb, osso buco, pasta with seafood. Own desserts. Parking. Cr cds: A, MC, V.

D

★ ★ **LE RHONE.** *(9401 W Thunderbird Rd, Peoria) US 101 exit Thunderbird Rd.* 602/933-0151. Hrs: 5:30-8:30 pm. Closed Mon; Jan 1; also 1st 3 wks in Aug. Res accepted. Swiss, continental menu. Bar. Semi-a la carte: dinner $16.90-$23.75. Specialties: châteaubriand, jumbo gulf shrimp provençale, rack of lamb. Pianist. Parking. Smoking in bar only. Cr cds: A, C, D, DS, MC, V.

D

✔★ ★ **LOMBARDI'S AT THE ARIZONA CENTER.** *455 N 3rd St, at the Arizona Center.* 602/257-8323. Hrs: 11 am-11 pm; Fri & Sat to midnight; Sun to 10 pm. Closed Dec 25. Res accepted. Italian menu. Bar. A la carte entrees: lunch $6-$12, dinner $8-$15. Specialties: risotto del giorno, tagliolini al frutti di mare, capelli d'angelo al pomodoro e basilico. Valet parking. Patio dining. Open kitchen. Cr cds: A, C, D, MC, V.

D

✔★ **LONG LIFE.** *7575 N 16th St.* 602/997-8785. Hrs: 11:30 am-2:30 pm, 4:30-9:30 pm; Sat & Sun from 4:30 pm. Closed most major hols. Res accepted. Chinese menu. Bar. Semi-a la carte: lunch $3.95-$4.95, dinner $6.75-$10.95. Specialties: Yui-shan spicy shrimp, Hunan beef. Parking. Cr cds: A, D, DS, MC, V.

D

✔★ **MARILYN'S.** *12631 N Tatum Blvd.* 602/953-2121. Hrs: 11 am-10 pm; Sun & Mon to 9 pm; Fri & Sat to 10:30 pm. Closed Thanksgiving, Dec 25. Mexican menu. Bar. Semi-a la carte: lunch $4.50-$7.50, dinner $7-$12.95. Child's meals. Specialties: fajitas, chimichangas, pollo fundido. Parking. Southwestern decor; fiesta atmosphere. Totally nonsmoking. Cr cds: A, MC, V.

D

★ **MR. LOUIE'S MILANO'S.** *1044 E Camelback Rd.* 602/241-1044. Hrs: 11 am-3 pm, 5-10 pm; Sat from 5 pm. Closed Sun; some major hols. Res accepted. Italian menu. Bar. Semi-a la carte: lunch $5.95-$8.95, dinner $7.95-$14.95. Child's meals. Specializes in lamb shanks, eggplant Parmesan, fresh seafood. Parking. Italian country cottage decor. Fireplace. Cr cds: A, C, D, MC, V.

D

★ ★ **OSCAR TAYLOR.** *2420 E Camelback Rd, at 24th St, in Biltmore Fashion Park.* 602/956-5705. Hrs: 11 am-10 pm; early-bird dinner 4-6:30 pm. Closed Dec 25. Res accepted. Bar 11 am-midnight, Sun to 10 pm. Semi-a la carte: lunch $7-$12, dinner $8-$24. Child's meals. Specializes in barbecued ribs, prime steak, desserts. Parking. Outdoor dining. Bakery, deli on premises. Cr cds: A, D, DS, MC, V.

D

✔★ **PASTA SEGIO'S.** *1904 E Camelback Rd.* 602/277-2782. Hrs: 11:30 am-2:30 pm, 5-10 pm; Mon from 5 pm; Fri to 11 pm; Sat 5-11 pm; Sun 4:30-9 pm. Closed Easter, Thanksgiving. Res accepted. Italian menu. Serv bar. Semi-a la carte: lunch $5.80-$7.80, dinner $7.95-$15. Child's meals. Specialties: pastas, osso buco, chocolate mousse. Parking. Cr cds: A, C, D, DS, ER, JCB, MC, V.

D

★ ★ **PRONTO.** *3950 E Campbell Ave (85018).* 602/956-4049. Hrs: 11:30 am-2:30 pm, 5:30-10 pm; Fri & Sat to 10:30 pm. Closed Sun; Thanksgiving, Dec 25. Res accepted. Italian menu. Bar. Semi-a la carte: lunch $5.95-$10.95, dinner $8.95-$15.95. Specialties: capellini alla pescarese, veal Marsala, gnocchi di patate. Parking. 3 dining areas. Stained-glass; antique instruments. Dinner theater Fri & Sat evenings. Cr cds: A, D, DS, MC, V.

D

★ ★ **RAFFAELE'S.** *2999 N 44th St.* 602/952-0063. Hrs: 11:30 am-3 pm, 5-10 pm; Fri to 11 pm; Sat 5-11 pm; Sun 5-10 pm. Closed

Thanksgiving, Dec 25. Res accepted. Italian menu. Bar. Semi-a la carte: lunch $5.95-$8.95, dinner $6.95-$21.95. Specialties: spaghetti al cartoccio, vitello saltimbocca. Valet parking (Mon-Sat). Outdoor dining. Contemporary decor; view of fountain, courtyard. Cr cds: A, D, MC, V.

🅳

★ ★ **ROXSAND.** *2594 E Camelback Rd, Biltmore Fashion Park.* 602/381-0444. Hrs: 11 am-10 pm; 11-10:30 Fri & Sat; Sun noon-9:30 pm. Closed most major hols. Res accepted. Contemporary continental cuisine. Bar. Semi-a la carte: lunch $6.95-$9.95, dinner $10.95-$23. Specializes in air-dried duck, roasted rack of lamb, seafood. Valet parking. Outdoor dining. Offers over 15 daily selections of pastries/desserts. Cr cds: A, C, D, MC, V.

🅳

★ ★ **RUSTY PELICAN.** *9801 N Black Canyon Hwy (85021).* 602/944-9646. Hrs: 11 am-10 pm; Sun from 4:30 pm; early-bird dinner 4:30-6 pm. Res accepted. Bar. Semi-a la carte: lunch $4.95-$9.95, dinner $11.95-$17.95. Specializes in fresh seafood, steak, pasta. Parking. Outdoor dining. Nautical decor. Cr cds: A, C, D, DS, MC, V.

🅳 🆂🅲

★ ★ **STEAMERS GENUINE SEAFOOD.** *2576 E Camelback Rd.* 602/956-3631. Hrs: 11:30 am-11 pm; Sun 5-10 pm; early-bird dinner 5-6:30 pm. Closed Thanksgiving, Dec 25. Bar to midnight. Semi-a la carte: lunch $4.25-$12.95, dinner $13.95-$21.95. Child's meals. Specialties: Maryland crab cakes, live Maine lobster. Oyster bar. Valet parking. Outdoor dining. Bright and colorful, spacious dining area. Cr cds: A, C, D, DS, MC, V.

🅳

★ ★ **STOCKYARDS.** *5001 E Washington St.* 602/273-7378. Hrs: 11 am-10 pm; Sat from 5 pm; Sun 4:30-9 pm. Closed Memorial Day, July 4, Thanksgiving, Dec 25. Res accepted. Bar. Semi-a la carte: lunch $3.95-$12, dinner $9-$27.95. Specializes in prime rib, steak, fresh fish. Parking. Located in landmark Stock Exchange Bldg. Restored dining rm; fireplace. Old West cattlemen's club atmosphere. Cr cds: A, C, D, MC, V.

🅳

★ **T-BONE STEAKHOUSE.** *10037 S 19th Ave, 11 mi S in South Mountain area.* 602/276-0945. Hrs: 5-10 pm; Fri & Sat to 11 pm. Closed Thanksgiving, Dec 24 & 25. Bar. Semi-a la carte: dinner $7.95-$19.95. Child's meals. Specializes in steak. Salad bar. Vocalist Fri, Sat. Parking. Outdoor dining. Rustic, old Western steakhouse in foothills of the mountains; scenic view of valley and downtown Phoenix. All cooking is done over mesquite coals and much of it is done outside. Cr cds: A, MC, V.

★ ★ **TAPAS PAPA FRITA.** *3213 E Camelback Rd.* 602/381-0474. Hrs: 11:30 am-11 pm; Fri to midnight; Sat 5:30 pm-midnight; Sun 5:30 pm-10 pm. Closed most major hols. Res accepted. Spanish menu. Bar. Semi-a la carte: lunch $4.95-$6.95, dinner $10.95-$16.95. Specialties: grouper with clams, asparagus and egg, fresh seafood. Flamenco guitarist nightly; flamenco dancers Thurs-Sat. Parking. Spanish atmosphere; colorful decor. Cr cds: A, C, D, MC, V.

🅳

★ ★ **TIMOTHY'S.** *6335 N 16th St.* 602/277-7634. Hrs: 5 pm-1 am. Closed Labor Day, Dec 24-25. Res accepted. Bar. Semi-a la carte: dinner $17.95-$21.95. Jazz musicians. Valet parking. Art deco, jazz theme. Cr cds: A, C, D, DS, MC, V.

🅳

★ ★ **TOMASO'S.** *3225 E Camelback Rd (85016).* 602/956-0836. Hrs: 11:30 am-2:30 pm, 5-10:30 pm. Closed Easter, Thanksgiving, Dec 25. Res accepted. Italian menu. Bar. A la carte entrees: lunch $6-$10, dinner $9-$21. Child's meals. Specializes in pasta, veal, chicken. Parking. Cr cds: A, C, D, DS, MC, V.

🅳

★ ★ **TOP OF THE MARKET.** *1720 E Camelback Rd (85016), top floor of Fish Market.* 602/277-3474. Hrs: 5-9:30 pm; Fri & Sat to 10 pm. Closed Thanksgiving, Dec 24 & 25. Res accepted. Bar. A la carte entrees: dinner $12.25-$33. Child's meals. Specializes in seafood, pasta, pizza. Parking. Nautical decor. View of Camelback Mountain. Cr cds: A, C, D, DS, MC, V.

🅳

✔ ★ **TUCCHETTI.** *2135 E Camelback Rd (85016), in Town & Country Shopping Center.* 602/957-0222. Hrs: 11:15 am-10 pm; Fri to 11 pm; Sat noon-11 pm; Sun 4:30-9 pm. Closed some major hols. Res accepted. Italian menu. Bar. A la carte entrees: lunch, dinner $5.95-$12.95. Child's meals. Specializes in pasta, thin crust pizza. Outdoor dining. Italian atmosphere. Smoking at bar only. Cr cds: A, C, D, DS, MC, V.

🅳

★ ★ ★ **VINCENT GUERITHAULT ON CAMELBACK.** *3930 E Camelback Rd.* 602/224-0225. Hrs: 11:30 am-2:30 pm, 6-10:30 pm; Sat from 5:30 pm. Closed major hols; also Sun June-Sept. Res accepted. Southwestern menu. Bar. Wine list. A la carte entrees: lunch $5.50-$8.95, dinner $18.50-$22. Specializes in mesquite-grilled lamb, chicken & seafood, homemade ice cream. Own baking. Valet parking. Country French decor. Cr cds: A, D, MC, V.

🅳

Unrated Dining Spots

CHOMPIE'S. *3202 E Greenway Rd, Greenway Park Plaza.* 602/971-8010. Hrs: 6 am-9 pm; Mon to 3 pm; Fri to 9:30 pm; Sun 7 am-8 pm. Kosher style deli menu. Wine, beer. Semi-a la carte: bkfst $2.50-$6, lunch $3.50-$7, dinner $5.95-$10.95. Child's meals. Own baking. Parking. Family-owned New York kosher style deli, bakery & bagel factory. Cr cds: MC, V.

🅳 🆂🅲

DUCK AND DECANTER. *1651 E Camelback Rd.* 602/274-5429. Hrs: 9 am-7 pm; Thurs, Fri to 9 pm; Sun from 10 am. Closed some major hols. A la carte entrees: lunch, dinner $2.50-$5.50. Child's meals. Specializes in albacore tuna sandwich. Guitarist Thurs-Sun evenings. Parking. Outdoor dining. Gourmet, wine shop. Totally nonsmoking. Cr cds: A, MC, V.

🅳

ED DEBEVIC'S. *2102 E Highland Ave, in Town & Country Shopping Ctr.* 602/956-2760. Hrs: 11 am-10 pm; Fri, Sat to 11 pm. Closed Thanksgiving, Dec 25. Bar. A la carte entrees: lunch, dinner $2.75-$5.95. Child's meals. Specializes in hamburgers, malts, french fries. Salad bar. 50s-style diner; jukebox. Cr cds: A, D, MC, V.

🅳

EDDIE'S GRILLE. *4747 N 7th St.* 602/241-1188. Hrs: 11:30 am-2:30 pm. Contemporary Amer menu. Bar. Semi-a la carte: lunch $5-$12.95. Specializes in steak, seafood, lamb. Outdoor dining. Patio with pool and fountain. Cr cds: A, MC, V.

🅳

FURRS CAFETERIA. *8114 N Black Canyon Hwy.* 602/995-1588. Hrs: 11 am-8 pm. Closed Dec 25. Avg ck: lunch, dinner $5-$5.50. Specialties: chicken-fried steak, millionaire pie. Parking. Cr cds: A, MC, V.

🅳

Pittsburgh

Settled: 1758

Pop: 369,879

Elev: 760 feet

Time zone: Eastern

Area code: 412

With dazzling modern buildings, clean parks and community pride, Pittsburgh today has had a remarkable renaissance and has achieved one of the most spectacular civic redevelopments in America.

Industry in Pittsburgh grew out of the West's needs for manufactured goods; foundries and rolling mills began producing nails, axes, frying pans and shovels. The Civil War added tremendous impetus to industry, and by the end of the war, Pittsburgh was producing half of the steel and one-third of the glass made in the country.

By the end of World War II, Pittsburgh was financially prosperous from its war effort but aesthetically bankrupt. Financier Richard King Mellon and Mayor Lawrence were the spiritual architects of the revival. A merciless antismoke campaign swept clean the smog-polluted air, and under the spur of a civic group called the Allegheny Conference on Community Development, great new skyscrapers of steel, aluminum and glass arose. Entire areas of the city were erased and rebuilt. Pittsburgh accomplished this $3 billion civic revitalization without surrendering an ounce of its industrial might. On the contrary, many new companies have located in the area since World War II. They deal in everything from atomic energy to plate glass. Within a 30-mile radius of the city more than 150 research and testing laboratories have opened.

Business

Pittsburgh's economy experienced a successful transformation in the 1980s following the decline of the domestic steel industry. Substantial growth in education, health care, high technology and service industries have helped bridge the gap.

Although Pittsburgh is not one of the largest metropolitan areas in the nation, it is the fourth largest headquarters city for *Fortune 500* corporations. It also ranks near the top in the number of industrial plants, the number of industrial workers and in value added by manufacturing. Research and development is also an important industry, employing more than 15,000 in the 4-county metropolitan area, and more than 20,000 technical and support people in the 9-county economic area.

Convention Facilities

The David L. Lawrence Convention Center has 131,000 square feet of exhibition space and 25 meeting rooms accommodating between 50 and 2,100 people. A glass-enclosed walkway spans the exhibition floor. The center is within walking distance of major hotels.

To the east, in nearby Monroeville, the Greater Pittsburgh Expo Mart caters to retailers in a three-state area. It has two floors of exhibition space, as well as office space. Total exhibition space is 106,000 square feet. Twenty-four meeting rooms hold between 40 and 2,000 people.

Closer to the airport, The Charles L. Sewall Center for Leadership Development in Coraopolis has 40,000 square feet of display and exhibit space, as well as 4 meeting rooms, which can accommodate between 20 and 300 people.

The Civic Arena and Exhibit Hall is one of the city's unique structures. Its primary feature is a vast, 148-foot-high retractable stainless steel roof. The roof is divided into eight leaves, six of which rotate around a pin at the top as they roll back for performances under the stars.

Sports and Recreation

Any resident will attest to the fact that Pittsburgh is a sports town. The Steelers football team has enough Super Bowl rings to grace the fingers of one hand. The Pirates baseball team also has had their share of winning seasons. Both play at Three Rivers Stadium. The Pittsburgh Penguins hockey team plays at the Civic Arena. There is also harness racing at the Meadows, south of the city, and Thoroughbred racing in nearby Chester, West Virginia.

Golfers and tennis players will find many courses and courts on which to test their skills. For outdoor enthusiasts, western Pennsylvania is a paradise of mountain wilderness, lakes, rivers, parks and resorts. Within a two-hour drive of the city one can find hiking, camping, whitewater rafting, fishing, hunting and skiing.

Entertainment

The internationally acclaimed Pittsburgh Symphony performs at Heinz Hall. The American Waterways Wind Orchestra performs at Point State Park during May and June. At the Benedum Center, the Civic Light Opera presents a series of Broadway musicals during July and August. The Pittsburgh Ballet and Pittsburgh Opera also give performances. Other quality entertainment is available at the Pittsburgh Folk Festival in late May, as well as at many theaters in the city offering professional performances.

For nightlife on a more informal level, Pittsburgh is a city with an abundance of neighborhood taverns. They range from tiny corner rooms, where patrons sip glasses of Iron City, the local beer, and talk about the chances for a local pennant winner, to high-energy rock-and-roll bars, and all categories in between.

Historical Areas

The Fort Pitt Block House, built in 1764, is the last remaining building of the original fortress. The Fort Pitt Museum, built on part of the original fort, houses exhibits and displays on Native American and frontier life and the military struggles for the Ohio Valley. Also displayed are unusual war artifacts. The museum and blockhouse are located in Point State Park.

On the campus of the University of Pittsburgh is the Stephen Foster Memorial, said to be the most elaborate memorial ever built to a

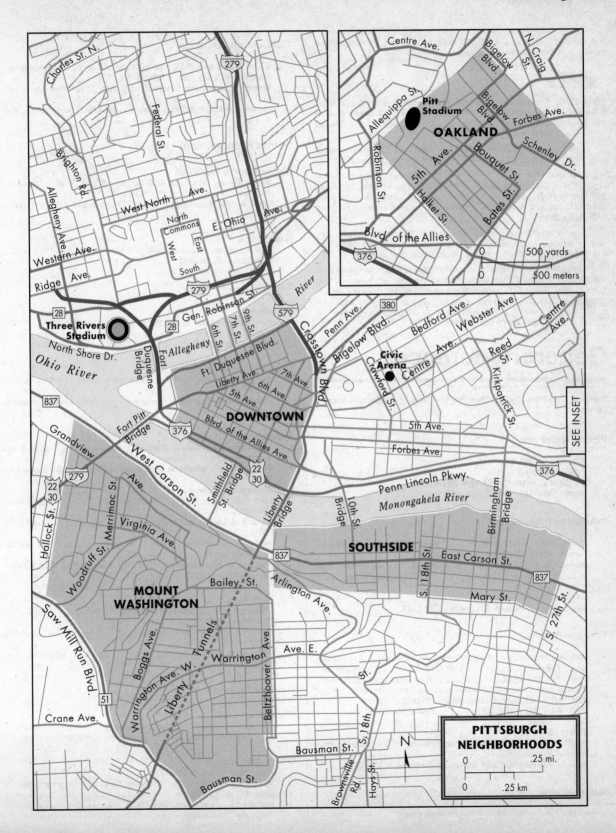

Charles St. N.

279

Federal St.

Brighton Rd.

Allegheny Ave.

West North   Ave.

North Commons
West
East
South

E Ohio   Ave.

Western Ave.

Ridge   Ave.

279

28

Three Rivers Stadium

North Shore Dr.

Ohio River

Duquesne Bridge

Fort

Allegheny   River

Gen. Robinson St.

6th St.
7th St.
9th St.

Ft. Duquesne Blvd.

Liberty Ave.

7th Ave.

6th Ave.

5th Ave.

DOWNTOWN

Blvd. of the Allies Ave.

837

Grandview

Fort Pitt Bridge

West Carson St.

Smithfield St. Bridge

376

Liberty Bridge

22
30

837

579

Crosstown Blvd.

Penn Ave.

Bigelow Blvd.

380

Bedford Ave.

Webster Ave.

Centre Ave.

Civic Arena

Crawford St.

Centre

Reed St.

Kirkpatrick St.

5th Ave.

Forbes Ave.

Penn Lincoln Pkwy.

Monongahela River

10th St. Bridge

Birmingham Bridge

376

SOUTHSIDE

East Carson St.

837

S. 18th St.

Mary St.

S. 27th St.

SEE INSET

Inset — OAKLAND

Centre Ave.

Bigelow Blvd.

N. Craig St.

Allequippa St.

Pitt Stadium

Bigelow Blvd.

Forbes Ave.

OAKLAND

Robinson St.

5th Ave.

Bouquet St.

Schenley Dr.

Halket St.

Bates St.

Blvd. of the Allies

376

0   500 yards

0   500 meters

Mount Washington area

22
30

279

Hallock St.

Merrimac St.

Woodruff St.

Virginia Ave.

MOUNT WASHINGTON

Bailey St.

Arlington Ave.

Saw Mill Run Blvd.

Boggs Ave.

Warrington Ave. W. Tunnels

Liberty

Warrington Ave.

Ave. E.

Belzhoover Ave.

St.

S. 18th

Bausman St.

Brownsville Rd.

Hays St.

51

Crane Ave.

Bausman St.

N

PITTSBURGH NEIGHBORHOODS

0   .25 mi.

0   .25 km

musician. It contains a $250,000 collection of the Pittsburgh-born composer's music and memorabilia.

Sightseeing

For a thrilling and delightful experience, take a ride on the inclines (hill-climbing trolleys). Travelers ascend from the city's South Side to the top of Mount Washington for an excellent view of the Golden Triangle, where two rivers meet to form a third.

Trips aboard the Gateway Clipper Fleet offer the tourist scenic cruises on the three rivers. All the ships have cruises daily year round.

A unique structure on the University of Pittsburgh campus is the Cathedral of Learning, a Gothic skyscraper of classrooms, 42 floors, 542 feet high; an observation point is on the 36th floor. Bordering the 3-story Commons Room are 23 rooms, each furnished by a different nationality group.

The Pittsburgh Zoo houses more than 6,000 animals on a 70-acre site. In addition to the Main Habitat Zoo, there is also the Children's Farm, Aqua Zoo, Twilight Zoo and Tropical Forest complex.

Shoppers will find no lack of retail outlets at which to spend their money. The Golden Triangle area has major department stores. Oxford Centre, PPG Place, Fifth Avenue Place and Station Square are unique complexes with shops, restaurants and interesting architectural features. East of the city, in Shadyside and Squirrel Hill, is a variety of boutiques, specialty shops and studios.

General References

Settled: 1758 **Pop:** 369,879 **Elev:** 760 feet **Time zone:** Eastern **Area code:** 412

Phone Numbers

POLICE & FIRE: 911
FBI: 471-2000
POISON CONTROL CENTER: 681-6669
TIME: 391-9500 **WEATHER:** 936-1212

Information Sources

Greater Pittsburgh Convention & Visitors Bureau, Inc, 4 Gateway Center, 15222; 281-7711, 800/366-0093.
Visitor Information Centers, Liberty Ave, adj Gateway Center, 281-9222; University of Pittsburgh, Oakland, 624-4660; Mount Washington, 381-5134.
24-hour Activities Line, 391-6840.
Department of Parks & Recreation, 255-2365.

Transportation

AIRLINES: American; British Airways; Continental; Delta; Northwest; TWA; United; USAir; and other commuter and regional airlines. For the most current airline schedules and information consult the *Official Airline Guide*, published twice monthly.
AIRPORT: Pittsburgh International, 472-3525.
CAR RENTAL AGENCIES: (See Toll-Free Numbers) Avis 472-5204; Budget 262-1500; Hertz 472-5955; National 472-5094; Thrifty 264-1775.
PUBLIC TRANSPORTATION: Port Authority of Allegheny County 442-2000.
RAILROAD PASSENGER SERVICE: Amtrak 800/872-7245.

Newspapers

Pittsburgh Post-Gazette; The Pittsburgh Press.

Convention Facilities

Charles L. Seawall Center for Leadership Development, Narrows Run Rd, Coraopolis, 262-8436.
David L. Lawrence Convention Center, 1001 Penn Ave, 565-6000.
Greater Pittsburgh Expo Mart, 105 Mall Blvd, Monroeville, 856-8100.

Sports & Recreation

Major Sports Facilities
Three Rivers Stadium, 600 Stadium Circle (Pirates, baseball, 323-5000; Steelers, football, 323-1200).
Civic Arena, downtown in Golden Triangle, 642-1800 (Penguins, hockey).

Racetrack
The Meadows, Meadowlands, I-79 S of exit 8, 563-1224 or 225-9300 (harness racing).

Cultural Facilities

Theaters
City Theatre Company, 57 S 13th St, 431-4900.
Pittsburgh Public Theatre, Allegheny Square, 321-9800.
Pittsburgh Playhouse, 222 Craft Ave, Oakland, 621-4445.

Concert Halls
Benedum Center for the Performing Arts, 719 Liberty Ave, 456-6666.
Heinz Hall for the Performing Arts, 600 Penn Ave, 392-4800 or -4900.

Museums
The Carnegie Science Center, 1 Allegheny Ave, adj to Three Rivers Stadium, 237-3400.
The Carnegie: Museum of Natural History, 4400 Forbes Ave, 622-3131.
Children's Museum, 1 Landmarks Square, 322-5058.
Fort Pitt Museum, 101 Commonwealth Pl, Point State Park, 281-9284.
Historical Society of Western Pennsylvania, 4338 Bigelow Blvd, 681-5533.
James L. Kelso Bible Lands Museum, Pittsburgh Theological Seminary, 616 N Highland Ave, 362-5610.
Stephen Foster Memorial, Forbes Ave at Bigelow Blvd, University of Pittsburgh, 624-4100.

Art Museums
The Carnegie: Museum of Art, 4400 Forbes Ave, 622-3131.
The Frick Art Museum, 7227 Reynolds St, 371-0600.
Henry Clay Frick Fine Arts Building, Schenley Plaza, University of Pittsburgh, 648-2400.
Pittsburgh Center for the Arts, Mellon Park, 6300 5th Ave, 361-0873.

Points of Interest

Historical
Allegheny County Courthouse, Grant St & 5th Ave, 355-5313.
Fort Pitt Block House, Point State Park, 471-1764.

Other Attractions
Alcoa Building, 425 6th Ave.
Allegheny Observatory, Riverview Park, 159 Riverview Ave, N Side, 321-2400.
Cathedral of Learning, 5th Ave & Bigelow Blvd, University of Pittsburgh, 624-6000.

Duquesne Incline, lower station, 1220 Grandview Ave, SW of Fort Pitt Bridge, 381-1665.
Equitable Plaza, Gateway Center.
Frick Park, Beechwood Blvd & English Lane.
Fallingwater, approx 60 mi E via PA Tpke to Donegal, then approx 15 mi S on PA 381, near Mill Run, 329-8501.
Gateway Center, adj to Point State Park, 392-6000.
Heinz Chapel, University of Pittsburgh, 624-4157.
Kennywood Park, 4800 Kennywood Blvd, in West Mifflin, 461-0500.
Mellon Bank Building, 5th Ave & Grant St.
Mellon Square Park, 6th Ave between Smithfield St & William Penn Place.
Monongahela Incline, W Carson St near Smithfield St Bridge, 231-5707.
One Oxford Centre, Grant St at 4th Ave, 391-5300.
Phipps Conservatory, Schenley Park, 622-6914.
Pittsburgh Aviary, West Park, West Ohio & Arch St, 323-7234.
Pittsburgh Zoo, NE on Highland Ave in Highland Park area, 665-3640.
Point State Park, foot of Fort Duquesne & Fort Pitt Blvds, 471-0235.
PPG Place, 1 PPG Place, Market Square.
Rodef Shalom Biblical Botanical Garden, 4905 5th Ave, 621-6566.
Soldiers and Sailors Memorial Hall, 5th Ave & Bigelow Blvd, 621-4253.
Station Square, foot of Smithfield St Bridge, S Side, 471-5808.

Sightseeing Tours

Gray Line bus tours, 110 Lenzer Court, Sewickley 15143; 761-7000 or 741-2720.
River Cruises, Gateway Clipper Fleet, at Station Square Dock, 355-7980.

Annual Events

Allegheny West Springfest, Galveston & Beech Aves. May.
Pittsburgh Folk Festival, Greater Pittsburgh Expo Mart, 105 Mall Blvd, Monroeville. Memorial Day wkend.
Three Rivers Shakespeare Festival, University of Pittsburgh campus. Late May-Aug.
Three Rivers Arts Festival, Gateway Center Plaza, PPG Place and Point State Park, 481-7040. June.
Fourth of July Celebration, Point State Park.
Shadyside Summer Art Festival, Shadyside. 1st wkend Aug.
Regatta, Point State Park. 1st wkend Aug.
Christmas Tree Display, The Carnegie. Dec.

City Neighborhoods

Many of the restaurants, unrated dining establishments and some lodgings listed under Pittsburgh include neighborhoods as well as exact street addresses. A map showing these neighborhoods can be found immediately following the city introduction. Geographic descriptions of these areas are given, followed by a table of restaurants arranged by neighborhood.

Downtown: South of the Allegheny River, west of I-579, north of the Monongahela River and east of Point State Park. **North of Downtown** North of Allegheny River. **South of Downtown** North of Monongahela River. **East of Downtown** East of US 579.
Mount Washington: Across the Monongahela River south of Downtown; north of Saw Mill Run Blvd, south of West Carson St, east of Hallock and west of Beltzhoover.
Oakland: East of Downtown; centered on and around 5th Ave between Bellefield St on the north and Halket St on the south.
South Side: Across the Monongahela River south of Downtown; Station Square area east and west of the Smithfield St Bridge.

Lodgings and Food

PITTSBURGH RESTAURANTS BY NEIGHBORHOOD AREAS

(For full description, see alphabetical listings under Restaurants)

DOWNTOWN

1902 Landmark Tavern. 24 Market St

British Bicycle Club. 923 Penn Ave

Carlton. 1 Mellon Bank Center

Common Plea. 308 Ross St

Jake's Above The Square. 430 Market St

Palm Court (Westin William Penn Hotel). 530 Wm Penn Place

NORTH OF DOWNTOWN

Max's Allegheny Tavern. Middle & Suisman Sts

Rico's. 1 Rico Lane

SOUTH OF DOWNTOWN

Colony. Greentree & Cochran Rds

Piccolo Mondo. 661 Anderson Dr

Samurai Japanese Steak House. 2100 Greentree Rd

Tambellini's. PA 51

EAST OF DOWNTOWN

Bentley's. 5608 Wilkens Ave

D'Imperio's. 3412 Wm Penn Hwy

Jimmy Tsang's. 5700 Centre Ave

Pasta Piatto. 738 Bellefonte St

Poli's. 2607 Murray Ave

Thai Place. 809 Bellefonte St

MOUNT WASHINGTON

Christopher's. 1411 Grandview Ave

Cliffside. 1208 Grandview Ave

Le Mont. 1114 Grandview Ave

OAKLAND

Dave And Andy's Ice Cream Parlor. 207 Atwood St

Per Favore. 3955 Bigelow Blvd

SOUTH SIDE

Cafe Allegro. 51 S 12th St

Grand Concourse. 1 Station Square

Le Pommier. 2104 E Carson St

Station Square Cheese Cellar. #25 Freight House Shops

Note: *When a listing is located in a town that does not have its own city heading, it will appear under the city nearest to its location. In these cases, the address and town appear in parenthesis immediately following the name of the establishment.*

Motels

★ ★ **CLUBHOUSE INN.** *5311 Campbells Run Rd (15205), jct I-279 & PA 60, west of downtown.* 412/788-8400; FAX 412/788-2577. 150 rms, 3 story, 26 suites. S $73-$86; D $83-$96; each addl $10; suites $86-$96; under 10 free; lower rates Fri, Sat. Crib free. TV; cable. Heated pool. Complimentary full buffet bkfst, coffee. Restaurant adj 11 am-11 pm. Ck-out noon. Coin lndry. Meeting rms. Free airport transportation. Exercise equipt; treadmill, stair machine, whirlpool. Refrigerator in suites. Cr cds: A, D, DS, MC, V.

★ ★ **HAMPTON INN.** *555 Trumbull Dr (15205), across river, west of downtown.* 412/922-0100; FAX 412/922-0100, ext. 109. 135 rms, 6 story. June-Nov: S $65-$70; D $68-$73; under 18 free; wkend rates; lower rates rest of yr. Crib free. Pet accepted. TV; cable. Complimentary continental bkfst, coffee. Restaurant nearby. Ck-out noon. Meeting rms. Valet serv. Free airport transportation. Picnic tables. Cr cds: A, C, D, DS, ER, MC, V.

★ ★ **HAWTHORN SUITES.** *700 Mansfield Ave (15205), at Noblestown Rd, south of downtown.* 412/279-6300; FAX 412/279-4993. 152 suites, 2 story. S $82-$116; D $103-$146; wkly, monthly rates. Crib free. Pet accepted, some restrictions; $50 and $6 per day. TV; cable. Pool; whirlpool, lifeguard. Complimentary continental bkfst. Ck-out noon. Meeting rms. Airport, RR station, bus depot transportation. Health club privileges. Sport court. Refrigerators, fireplaces. Private patios, balconies. Picnic tables, grills. Chalet-style buildings. Cr cds: A, C, D, DS, MC, V.

★ ★ **HOLIDAY INN ALLEGHENY VALLEY.** *180 Gamma Dr (15238), PA 28 exit 10.* 412/963-0600; FAX 412/963-7852. 225 rms, 2 story. S $90; D $100; each addl $10; suites $150-$175; under 18 free. TV; cable. Heated pool; pooside serv, lifeguard. Restaurant 6 am-10 pm; Sat, Sun from 7 am. Rm serv. Bar 11-2 am; Sun 1 pm-1 am. Ck-out 11 am. Meeting rms. Bellhops. Valet serv. Free airport transportation. Refrigerators in suites. Cr cds: A, C, D, DS, MC.

★ ★ **HOLIDAY INN GREENTREE-CENTRAL.** *401 Holiday Dr (15220), south of downtown.* 412/922-8100; FAX 412/922-6511. 201 rms, 4 story. S $99-$107; D $99-$124; each addl $10; under 18 free. Crib free. Pet accepted. TV; cable. Heated pool; poolside serv, lifeguard. Restaurant 6:30 am-10 pm; Fri, Sat to 11 pm. Rm serv. Bar 11-2 am, Sun from 1 pm; entertainment. Ck-out noon. Meeting rms. Valet serv. Sundries. Free airport transportation. Tennis privileges. Exercise equipt; weight machine, bicycles. Private patios. Cr cds: A, C, D, DS, ER, JCB, MC, V.

★ ★ **HOWARD JOHNSON-SOUTH.** *5300 Clairton Blvd (PA 51) (15236), south of downtown.* 412/884-6000; FAX 412/884-6009. 95 rms, 3 story. No elvtr. S $67-$79; D $77-$89; each addl $10; under 18 free. Crib free. TV. Pool; lifeguard. Complimentary bkfst. Restaurant nearby. Ck-out noon. Meeting rms. Valet serv. Near Allegheny County Airport. Cr cds: A, C, D, DS, ER, JCB, MC, V.

✔ ★ **RED ROOF INN.** *6404 Steubenville Pike (PA 60) (15205), south of downtown.* 412/787-7870; FAX 412/787-8392. 120 rms, 2 story. S $38-$43; D $45-$53; under 18 free. Crib free. Pet accepted, some restrictions. TV; cable. Complimentary morning coffee. Restaurant adj open 24 hrs. Ck-out noon. Cr cds: A, C, D, DS, MC, V.

✔ ★ ★ **REDWOOD INN.** *2898 Banksville Rd (US 19) (15216), south of downtown.* 412/343-3000; res: 800/334-0060; FAX 412/341-4611. 95 rms, 4 story. S $55-$62; D $61-$66; each addl $5; under 12 free; some wkend rates. Crib free. Pet accepted, some restrictions. TV; cable. Pool; lifeguard. Restaurant 6:30-10:30 am, 5-9 pm; Sat 6 am-noon; Sun 6:30 am-1 pm. Rm serv. Bar 3 pm-2 am. Ck-out 11 am. Meeting rms. Bellhops. Cr cds: A, C, D, DS, MC, V.

Motor Hotels

✔ ★ ★ ★ **BEST WESTERN-PARKWAY CENTER INN.** *875 Greentree Rd (15220), adj Parkway Center Mall, west of downtown.* 412/922-7070; FAX 412/922-4949. 138 rms, 6 story, 44 kits. S $55-$101; D $61-$107; each addl $9; kit. units $93-$107; under 12 free; wkly (14-day min), wkend rates. Crib free. Pet accepted; $25. TV; cable. Indoor pool; sauna, lifeguard. Complimentary bkfst. Ck-out noon. Coin lndry. Meeting rms. Bellhops. Valet serv. Sundries. Barber, beauty shop. Free airport transportation. Rec rm. Cr cds: A, C, D, DS, ER, MC, V.

★ ★ ★ **HARLEY.** *699 Rodi Rd (15235), at jct PA 791 & I-376, east of downtown.* 412/244-1600; FAX 412/829-2334. 152 rms, 3 story. No elvtr. S $92-$99; D $100-$109; each addl $8; under 18 free; wkend plan. Crib free. TV; cable. 2 heated pools, 1 indoor; whirlpool, sauna, poolside serv, lifeguard. Restaurant 6:30 am-10 pm; Fri, Sat 7 am-11 pm. Rm serv 7 am-11 pm. Bar 4:30 pm-midnight, Fri to 1:30 am, Sat noon-1:30 am, Sun 4:30-11 pm; entertainment, dancing Fri & Sat. Ck-out 1 pm. Meeting rms. Bellhops. Valet serv. Sundries. Airport transportation. Lighted tennis. Private patios, balconies. Cr cds: A, C, D, DS, MC, V.

★ ★ ★ **HOLIDAY INN.** *164 Fort Couch Rd (15241), south of downtown.* 412/343-4600; FAX 412/831-8539. 210 rms, 8 story. S $64; D $74; each addl $10; suites $120-$130; under 18 free; wkend rates. Crib free. Pet accepted, some restrictions. TV; in-rm movies avail. Pool; poolside serv, lifeguard. Restaurant 6:30 am-11 pm; Sat, Sun from 7 am. Rm serv. Bar 11-2 am; entertainment, dancing Tues-Sat. Ck-out noon. Meeting rms. Bellhops. Valet serv. Shopping arcade. Airport transportation. Health club privileges. Game rm. Balconies. Cr cds: A, C, D, DS, ER, JCB, MC, V.

★ ★ ★ **MARRIOTT GREENTREE.** *101 Marriott Dr (15205), across river, west of downtown.* 412/922-8400; FAX 412/922-8981. 467 rms, 7 story. S $99-$125; D $115-$135; each addl $15; suites $175-185; studio rms $99; under 18 free; wkend, honeymoon rates. Crib free. Pet accepted. TV; cable. 3 pools, 1 indoor; poolside serv, lifeguard. Restaurant 6:30 am-midnight. Rm serv. Bar 11-2 am; entertainment, dancing. Ck-out noon. Meeting rms. Bellhops. Valet serv. Sundries. Gift shop. Barber, beauty shop. Free airport transportation. Lighted tennis. Indoor tennis privileges. Exercise equipt; weight machines, bicycles, whirlpool, sauna, steam rm. Rec rm. Many minibars. *LUXURY LEVEL : CONCIERGE LEVEL.* 41 rms, 2 suites. S $135; D $150. Private lounge, honor bar. Complimentary continental bkfst, refreshments. Cr cds: A, C, D, DS, ER, MC, V.

Hotels

★ ★ ★ **HILTON.** *Gateway Center (15222), at Point State Park, downtown.* 412/391-4600; FAX 412/391-0927 or 594-5161. 712 rms, 24 story. S $129-$189; D $149-$199; each addl $20; suites $325; studio rms $100; children free; wkend plans. Crib free. Pet accepted, some restrictions. TV; cable. Restaurant 6:30 am-11:30 pm. 2 bars 11-2 am; entertainment. Ck-out noon. Meeting rms. Concierge. Drugstore. Barber, beauty shop. Garage avail; valet parking. Airport transportation. Exercise equipt; weights, treadmill. Minibars; some bathrm phones, refrigerators. *LUXURY LEVEL : TOWERS.* 118 rms, 4 floors. S $165-$185; D $185-205; suites $350-$1,200. Private lounge, honor bar. In-rm movies. Full wet bar & kitchen area in suites. Bathrm phones.

Complimentary continental bkfst, refreshments, newspaper. Cr cds: A, C, D, DS, ER, JCB, MC, V.

★ ★ ★ **HYATT REGENCY-CHATHAM CENTER.** *112 Washington Place (15219), downtown.* 412/471-1234; FAX 412/355-0315. 400 rms, 21 story. S $115-$145; D $131-$170; each addl $15; suites $220-$500; under 18 free; wkend rates. Crib free. Garage $5-$10. TV; cable. Pool. Restaurants 6:30 am-11 pm. Bars 11-1 am; entertainment. Ck-out noon. Meeting rms. Airport, RR station, bus depot transportation. Exercise equipt; weights, bicycles, whirlpool, sauna, steam rm. Cr cds: A, C, D, DS, ER, JCB, MC, V.

★ ★ ★ **SHERATON.** *7 Station Square (15219), on South Side.* 412/261-2000; FAX 412/261-2932. 293 rms, 15 story. S $141-$156; D $156-$181; each addl $15; suites $210-$600; under 18 free; wkend rates. Crib free. TV; cable, in-rm movies avail. Indoor pool; lifeguard. Coffee in rms. Restaurant 6 am-midnight. Bar 11-2 am; entertainment. Ck-out noon. Meeting rms. Shopping arcade. RR station, bus depot transportation. Exercise equipt; weights, bicycles, whirlpool. Game rm. On riverfront. *LUXURY LEVEL : EXECUTIVE FLOOR.* 18 rms, 3 suites. Private lounge. Complimentary continental bkfst, refreshments. Cr cds: A, C, D, DS, ER, JCB, MC, V.

★ ★ ★ **VISTA INTERNATIONAL.** *1000 Penn Ave (15222), downtown.* 412/281-3700; FAX 412/227-4500. 616 rms, 26 story. S $160-$200; D $180-$215; each addl $20; suites $245-$1,550; family rates; wkend packages. Crib free. TV; cable. Indoor pool. Restaurants 6:30 am-10:30 pm. Rm serv 24 hrs. Bar 11-2 am. Ck-out noon. Lndry facilities. Convention facilities. Concierge. Shopping arcade. Courtesy limo downtown. Exercise rm; instructor, weights, bicycles, whirlpool, sauna, steam rm. Refrigerators; many bathrm phones. Private patios. Cr cds: A, C, D, DS, ER, JCB, MC, V.

★ ★ ★ **WESTIN WILLIAM PENN.** *530 Wm Penn Place (15219), on Mellon Square, downtown.* 412/281-7100; FAX 412/553-5252. 595 rms, 24 story. S $99-$140; D $120-$150; each addl $20; suites $275-$1,115; under 18 free; wkend rates. Crib free. Pet accepted. Valet parking $15.75. TV; cable. Restaurant 6:30 am-11 pm (also see PALM COURT, Unrated Dining). Rm serv 24 hrs. Bar 11-2 am; entertainment. Ck-out 1 pm. Convention facilities. Gift shop. Barber shop. Airport, RR station, bus depot transportation. Exercise equipt; bicycles, treadmill. Bathrm phones. Historic, landmark hotel. Cr cds: A, C, D, DS, ER, JCB, MC, V.

Inn

★ ★ ★ **THE PRIORY.** *614 Pressley St (15212), north of downtown.* 412/231-3338; FAX 412/231-4838. 24 rms, 3 story. S $68-$98; D $103-$120; each addl $10; suites $110-$143; under 7 free; lower rates wkends. TV; cable. Complimentary continental bkfst, evening refreshments. Ck-out 11 am, wkends noon, ck-in 3 pm. Meeting rms. Previously a haven for Benedictine monks (1888); European-style inn with fountain and floral arrangements in courtyard. Cr cds: A, C, D, DS, MC, V.

Restaurants

★ ★ **1902 LANDMARK TAVERN.** *24 Market St, downtown.* 412/471-1902. Hrs: 11:30 am-11 pm; Fri & Sat to midnight. Closed Sun; major hols. Res accepted. Continental menu. Bar to 1 am. Semi-a la carte: lunch $5.25-$11.50, dinner $10.95-$22. Specialties: veal

Marengo, prime rib, pasta. Restored tavern (1902); ornate tin ceiling, original tiles. Cr cds: A, D, DS, MC, V.

✔★ ★ **BENTLEY'S.** *5608 Wilkens Ave, east of downtown.* *412/421-4880.* Hrs: 11:30 am-10 pm; Fri & Sat to 11 pm; extended hrs summer; early-bird dinner Mon-Sat 4-6 pm. Closed Thanksgiving, Dec 25. Res accepted. Continental menu. Bar. Complete meals: lunch $5.95-$6.95, dinner $8.95-$14.95. Child's meals. Specializes in seafood, veal, pasta. Parking. Outdoor dining. Cr cds: A, D, DS, MC, V.

✔★ **BRITISH BICYCLE CLUB.** *923 Penn Ave, downtown.* *412/391-9623.* Hrs: 10 am-10 pm. Closed Sat & Sun; major hols. Res accepted. Bar. Semi-a la carte: lunch $3.25-$8.75, dinner $3.25-$14.95. Specializes in prime rib, sandwiches, steak salad. English pub atmosphere. Cr cds: A, C, D, DS, MC, V.

★ ★ **CAFE ALLEGRO.** *51 S 12th St, on South Side.* *412/481-7788.* Hrs: 5-11 pm. Closed major hols. Res accepted. Bar. Semi-a la carte: dinner $17-$23. Child's meals. Specialties: pasta del sole, grilled seafood, seafood arrabbiata, grilled veal chop. Parking. Ambience of Riviera cafe; artwork. Cr cds: D, MC, V.

D

★ ★ ★ **CARLTON.** *1 Mellon Bank Center, on grounds of Mellon Bank Center Commercial Bldg, at Grant St, downtown.* *412/391-4099.* Hrs: 11:30 am-2:30 pm, 5-10 pm; Fri to 11 pm; Sat 5-11 pm. Closed Sun; major hols. Res accepted. Continental menu. Bar. Semi-a la carte: lunch $7.95-$13.95, dinner $13.95-$24.95. Child's meals. Specializes in charcoal-grilled seafood, prime steak, veal. Own pastries. Parking. Cr cds: A, C, D, DS, MC, V.

D

★ ★ ★ **CHRISTOPHER'S.** *1411 Grandview Ave, on Mount Washington.* *412/381-4500.* Hrs: 5-10 pm; Fri & Sat to 11 pm. Closed Sun; major hols. Res accepted. American menu. Bar 5 pm-midnight. Wine list. Semi-a la carte: dinner $15-$33. Child's meals. Specializes in seafood, lamb, flaming desserts. Own baking. Pianist (dinner). Valet parking. View of the Golden Triangle. Braille menu. Jacket. Cr cds: A, C, D, DS, MC, V.

D

★ ★ ★ **CLIFFSIDE.** *1208 Grandview Ave, on Mount Washington.* *412/431-6996.* Hrs: 5-10 pm; Fri & Sat to 11 pm. Closed major hols. Res accepted. Continental menu. Bar. Semi-a la carte: dinner $15.25-$24. Child's meals. Specializes in fresh seafood, chicken, veal. Pianist. Contemporary decor in older building (1897). Cr cds: A, C, D, DS, MC, V.

★ ★ ★ **COLONY.** *Greentree & Cochran Rds, south of downtown.* *412/561-2060.* Hrs: 5-10:30 pm; Sun 4-9 pm. Res accepted. Continental menu. Bar 4 pm-1 am. Wine list. Complete meals: dinner $20.50-$29.95. Specializes in swordfish, sirloin, grilled veal steak. Own baking. Pianist exc Mon, vocalist Fri, Sat. Valet parking. Family-owned. Jacket. Cr cds: A, C, D, DS, MC, V.

★ ★ ★ **COMMON PLEA.** *308 Ross St, downtown.* *412/281-5140.* Hrs: 11:30 am-2:30 pm, 5-10:30 pm; Sat 5-10 pm. Closed Sun; major hols. Res accepted. Bar. Complete meals: lunch $6.50-$10.75, dinner $15.50-$26.95. Child's meals. Specializes in seafood, veal, chicken. Own baking. Valet parking (dinner). Family-owned. Cr cds: A, D, MC, V.

★ ★ ★ **D'IMPERIO'S.** *3412 Wm Penn Hwy, east of downtown.* *412/823-4800.* Hrs: noon-3 pm, 5-11 pm; Sat & Sun from 5 pm. Closed major hols. Res accepted; required wkends. Italian, Amer menu. Bar. Semi-a la carte: dinner $13.50-$28. Child's meals. Specialties: shrimp Sorrento, lobster sausage, veal Genovese. Own bread. Pianist. Parking. Cr cds: A, C, D, DS, MC, V.

D

★ ★ ★ **GRAND CONCOURSE.** *1 Station Square, jct Carson & Smithfield Sts, on South Side.* *412/261-1717.* Hrs: 11:30 am-2:30 pm, 4:30-10 pm; Fri to 11 pm; Sat 4:30-11 pm; Sun 4:30-9 pm; early-bird dinner 4:30-6 pm; Sun brunch 10 am-2:30 pm. Closed Dec 25. Res

accepted. Continental menu. Bar 11:30-2 am; Sun 11 am-10 pm. Wine list. Semi-a la carte: lunch $6-$12, dinner $10-$20. Sun brunch $15.95. Child's meals. Specializes in seafood, steak, pasta. Own baking, pasta. Pianist. Parking. Converted railroad station. Braille menu. Cr cds: A, C, D, DS, MC, V.

D

★ ★ ★ **JAKE'S ABOVE THE SQUARE.** *430 Market St, downtown.* *412/338-0900.* Hrs: 11 am-11 pm; Fri to midnight; Sat 5 pm-midnight; Sun 4-10 pm. Closed most major hols. Res accepted. Continental menu. Bar. Wine cellar. Semi-a la carte: lunch $4.50-$11.50, dinner $17.50-$29.50. Child's meals. Specialties: Dover sole, soft shell crabs, homemade dessert and pastries. Valet parking. Casual elegance in atrium setting. View of historic Market Square. Cr cds: A, C, D, DS, MC, V.

✔★ ★ **JIMMY TSANG'S.** *5700 Centre Ave, at Negley, in Kennilworth Bldg, east of downtown.* *412/661-4226.* Hrs: 11:30 am-10 pm; Fri & Sat to 11 pm; Sun 3:30-9 pm; early-bird dinner Mon-Sat 3-6 pm. Closed July 4, Thanksgiving. Chinese menu. Bar. A la carte: lunch $4.95-$5.75, dinner $7.95-$9.95. Specializes in Peking duck, honey chicken, Mongolian Beef. Parking. Oriental decor, artwork. Cr cds: A, C, D, MC, V.

D

★ ★ ★ **LE MONT.** *1114 Grandview Ave, on Mount Washington.* *412/431-3100.* Hrs: 5-11:30 pm; Sun 4-10 pm. Closed major hols. Res accepted. American menu. Bar to midnight. Wine list. Semi-a la carte: dinner $11-$35. Specialties: rack of lamb Persille, variety of wild game dishes, flaming desserts. Own baking. Pianist Fri & Sat. Valet parking. Atop Mt Washington; panoramic view of city. Cr cds: A, C, D, DS, MC, V.

D

★ ★ ★ **LE POMMIER.** *2104 E Carson St, on South Side.* *412/431-1901.* Hrs: 5:30-9 pm; Sat to 10:30 pm. Closed Sun; some major hols. Res accepted. French menu. Bar. Wine cellar. A la carte entrees: dinner $18-$30. Specialties: couscous, veal chops with fresh herbs, bouillabaisse. Own baking. Located in oldest storefront in area (1863). Country French decor. Cr cds: A, C, D, DS, MC, V.

D

✔★ **MAX'S ALLEGHENY TAVERN.** *Middle & Suisman Sts, north of downtown.* *412/231-1899.* Hrs: 11 am-11 pm; Fri & Sat to midnight; Sun to 8:30 pm. Closed most major hols. German menu. Bar. A la carte entrees: lunch $4.25-$7.95, dinner $5.95-$13.95. Specialties: jägerschnitzel, käse spätzle, sauerbraten. Entertainment Fri, Sat. Tavern with German memorabilia and collection of photographs. Cr cds: A, D, DS, MC, V.

★ ★ **PASTA PIATTO.** *738 Bellefonte St, in Shadyside, east of downtown.* *412/621-5547.* Hrs: 11:30 am-3 pm, 4:30-10 pm; Wed & Thurs to 10:30 pm; Fri & Sat to 11 pm; Sun 3-9 pm. Closed major hols. Northern Italian menu. Bar. Semi-a la carte: lunch $3.50-$8.95, dinner $8.50-$19.95. Child's meals. Specializes in homemade pasta, veal, seafood. Cr cds: A, MC, V.

★ ★ **PER FAVORE.** *3955 Bigelow Blvd, in Oakland.* *412/681-9080.* Hrs: 11 am-10 pm; Fri to 11 pm; Sat 4-11 pm. Closed Sun; major hols. Res accepted. Continental menu. Bar. Semi-a la carte: lunch $6.95-$8.95, dinner $12.95-$21.95. Child's meals. Specialties: veal piccata, angel hair Favore, salmon with lump crab meat. Entertainment Fri, Sat. Valet parking. Roman garden setting. Italian paintings. Cr cds: A, C, D, DS, MC, V.

D

★ ★ **PICCOLO MONDO.** *661 Anderson Dr, Bldg 7, Foster Plaza, Green Tree, south of downtown.* *412/922-0920.* Hrs: 11:30 am-4 pm, 5-10 pm; Sat 5-11 pm. Closed Sun exc Mother's Day; some hols. Res accepted. Northern Italian menu. Bar. Wine list. Semi-a la carte:

lunch $5.50-$13, dinner $13-$23. Child's meals. Specializes in fresh fish, veal. Own desserts. Parking. Jacket. Cr cds: A, C, D, DS, MC, V.

D

★ ★ **POLI'S.** *2607 Murray Ave, east of downtown.* 412/521-6400. Hrs: 11:30 am-11 pm; Sun 11 am-9:30 pm; early-bird dinner Tues-Fri 3-5 pm. Closed Mon; Thanksgiving, Dec 25. Italian menu. Bar. Semi-a la carte: lunch $5.95-$9.95, dinner $10.25-$21.95. Child's meals. Specializes in fresh seafood, veal, pasta. Own baking. Valet parking. Family-owned. Cr cds: A, C, D, MC, V.

D

★ ★ **RICO'S.** *1 Rico Lane, off of Evergreen Rd in North Hills, north of downtown.* 412/931-0556. Hrs: 11:30 am-3 pm, 4-10:30 pm; Fri & Sat 4-11:30 pm. Closed Sun; major hols. Italian, Amer menu. Bar to midnight. Wine cellar. Semi-a la carte: lunch $6.50-$11.50, dinner $14-$30. Specializes in fresh seafood, veal. Valet parking. Old World atmosphere; Italian lithographs. Jacket. Cr cds: A, D, DS, MC, V.

D

★ ★ **SAMURAI JAPANESE STEAK HOUSE.** *2100 Greentree Rd, south of downtown.* 412/276-2100. Hrs: 11:30 am-2 pm, 5:30-10 pm; Fri to 11 pm; Sat 5-11:30 pm; Sun 4:30-9 pm. Closed Thanksgiving, Dec 25. Res accepted. Japanese menu. Bar. Semi-a la carte: lunch $5.50-$8.50, dinner $10.50-$28. Child's meals. Specializes in steak, seafood. Parking. Japanese garden. Cr cds: A, C, D, DS, MC, V.

D

✔★ ★ **STATION SQUARE CHEESE CELLAR.** *#25 Freight House Shops, Station Square (Smithfield & Carson Sts), on South Side.* 412/471-3355. Hrs: 11:30-1 am; Sun 10:30 am-11 pm. Closed Dec 25. Res accepted Sun-Thurs. Continental menu. Bar to 2 am. Semi-a la carte: bkfst $5.95-$6.50, lunch, dinner $4.95-$9.95. Child's meals. Specializes in fondues, imported cheese, pasta. Outdoor dining. Rustic decor. Cr cds: A, C, D, DS, MC, V.

D

★ ★ **TAMBELLINI'S.** *PA 51, 2 mi south of downtown.* 412/481-1118. Hrs: 11:30 am-10 pm. Closed Sun; Jan 1, Thanksgiving, Dec 25. Res accepted. Continental menu. Bar. Semi-a la carte: lunch $7.50-$7.95, dinner $11.95-$27.50. Complete meals: dinner $21.95. Child's meals. Specializes in seafood, pasta, steak. Valet parking. Modern decor. Cr cds: A, D, MC, V.

D

✔★ ★ **THAI PLACE.** *809 Bellefonte St, in Shadyside, east of downtown.* 412/687-8586. Hrs: 11:30 am-10 pm; Fri to 11 pm; Sat noon-11 pm; Sun noon-9:30 pm; Mon from 4:30 pm. Thai menu. Bar. A la carte entrees: lunch $5.50-$7.50, dinner $7.50-$14.95. Specializes in authentic Thai cuisine. Outdoor dining. Oriental art. Cr cds: A, D, DS, MC, V.

Unrated Dining Spots

DAVE AND ANDY'S ICE CREAM PARLOR. *207 Atwood St, in Oakland.* 412/681-9906. Hrs: 11:30 am-10 pm; Fri to 11 pm; Sat 1 pm-11 pm; Sun 1-11 pm. Closed major hols. Specialties: homemade ice cream (fresh daily), homemade cones. 1930s look; no tables, some counters. No cr cds accepted.

PALM COURT. *(See Westin William Penn Hotel)* 412/281-7100. Hrs: tea time 2:30-4:30 pm. English custom tea serv. Bar. Complete tea: $7.25. A la carte items also avail. Specializes in tea, finger sandwiches, pastries. Pianist. Parking avail opp. Lobby room; Georgian decor; elaborate floral arrangements. Cr cds: A, C, D, DS, ER, JCB, MC, V.

D

PIZZERIA UNO. *(333 Penn Center Blvd, Monroeville 15146) 15 mi E on US 376, Penn Center Blvd exit.* 412/824-8667. Hrs: 11 am-11 pm; Fri & Sat to 12:30 am; Sun noon-10 pm. Closed Thanksgiving, Dec 25. Italian, Amer menu. Bar. Semi-a la carte: lunch $3.95-

$8.95, dinner $4.95-$10.95. Specialties: deep-dish pizza, pasta, salad. Parking. Casual dining. Cr cds: A, DS, MC, V.

D

SEASON'S HARVEST. *(Box 115, Valencia 16059) 15 mi N of PA Turnpike exit 4, on PA 8.* 412/898-3030. Hrs: 4:30-8:30 pm; Sun from 11:30 am. Closed Mon; Dec 24 evening, Dec 25. Buffet: dinner $7.95-$9.95. Specializes in roast beef, baked chicken, french fried mushrooms. Salad bar. Own soups. Parking. Two dining levels. Art exhibits. Cr cds: MC, V.

SC

Pittsburgh Intl Airport Area

Motels

★ ★ **HAMPTON INN-NORTHWEST.** *(1420 Beers School Rd, Coraopolis 15108) N on PA 60.* 412/264-0020; FAX 412/264-0020, ext. 185. 128 rms, 5 story. S $57-$63; D $62-$68; under 18 free. Crib free. Pet accepted, some restrictions. TV. Complimentary continental bkfst. Restaurant adj 6 am-10 pm. Ck-out noon. Meeting rms. Valet serv. Airport transportation. Cr cds: A, C, D, DS, ER, MC, V.

D ✔ ✈ ⛶ 🔥 SC

★ ★ **LA QUINTA.** *(1433 Beers School Rd, Coraopolis 15108) N on PA 60.* 412/269-0400; FAX 412/269-9258. 129 rms, 3 story. S $56-$61; D $63-$71; each addl $7; under 18 free. Crib free. Pet accepted. TV; cable. Heated pool; lifeguard. Complimentary continental bkfst, coffee. Restaurant adj 6 am-11 pm. Ck-out noon. Meeting rms. Valet serv. Sundries. Free airport transportation. Cr cds: A, C, D, DS, MC, V.

D ✔ ≈ ✈ ⛶ 🔥 SC

✔★ ★ **PITTSBURGH PLAZA.** *(1500 Beers School Rd, Coraopolis 15108) I-79 Bus 60 exit.* 412/264-7900; res: 800/542-8111; FAX 412/262-3229. 185 rms, 2 story. S, D $39.99; suites $59.99; under 18 free. Crib free. Pet accepted; $50 refundable. TV; cable. Complimentary continental bkfst 5-9 am in lobby. Restaurant adj open 24 hrs. Ck-out noon. Meeting rms. Valet serv. Sundries. Free airport transportation. Exercise equipt; weights, bicycles, sauna. Some refrigerators. Some balconies. Cr cds: A, C, D, DS, MC, V.

✔ 🏋 ✈ ⛶ 🔥 SC

✔★ **RED ROOF INN.** *(1454 Beers School Rd, Coraopolis 15108) N on PA 60.* 412/264-5678; FAX 412/264-8034. 119 rms, 3 story. S $39.99-$45.95; D $46.99-$52.99; each addl $4; under 18 free. Crib free. TV. Coffee in lobby 6-10 am. Restaurant opp 6 am-10 pm. Ck-out noon. Coin lndry. Meeting rm. Valet serv. Free airport transportation. Cr cds: A, C, D, DS, MC, V.

D ✈ ⛶ 🔥

Motor Hotels

★ ★ **BEST WESTERN AIRPORT INN.** *(PA 60 at Montaur Run Rd, Pittsburgh 15231)* 412/262-3800; FAX 412/695-1068. 140 rms, 4 story. S $75-$90; D $85-$100; each addl $10; suites $175-$215; studio rms $85-$100; family rates; wkend plan. Crib free. Pet accepted. TV. Heated pool; lifeguard. Restaurant 6:30 am-10 pm; Sat, Sun from 7 am. Rm serv. Bar 11-2 am; entertainment exc Sun. Ck-out noon. Meeting rms. Bellhops. Valet serv. Gift shop. Free airport transportation. Exercise equipt; weights, bicycles. Cr cds: A, C, D, DS, ER, MC, V.

★ ★ **RAMADA INN AIRPORT.** *(1412 Beers School Rd, Coraopolis 15108) N on PA 60.* 412/264-8950; FAX 412/262-5598. 135 rms, 6 story. S $65-$75; D $75-$80; each addl $10; suites $125; under 18 free; wkend rates. Crib free. Pet accepted, some restrictions; $10. TV. Pool; poolside serv, lifeguard. Restaurant 6 am-2 pm, 5-11 pm; Sun to 3 pm, 5-11 pm. Rm serv. Bar 4 pm-2 am; entertainment Wed, Fri-Sat, dancing exc Sun. Ck-out noon. Meeting rms. Free airport transportation. Cr cds: A, C, D, DS, JCB, MC, V.

Hotels

★ ★ **MARRIOTT.** *(100 Aten Rd, Coraopolis 15108) S on PA 60, exit Montaur Run Rd.* 412/788-8800; FAX 412/788-6299. 314 rms, 14 story. S, D $99-$159; each addl $15; suites $175-$425; family, wkly rates. Crib free. Pet accepted. TV; cable, in-rm movies avail. 2 pools, 1 indoor; poolside serv, lifeguard. Restaurant 6:30 am-11 pm. Bar 11-2 am; entertainment, dancing. Ck-out noon. Convention facilities. Concierge. Shopping arcade. Free airport, bus depot transportation. Exercise equipt; weights, bicycles, whirlpool, sauna. Some refrigerators. *LUXURY LEVEL :* **CONCIERGE LEVEL.** 21 rms, 1 floor, 1 suite. S, D $137-$180. Private lounge, honor bar. Complimentary continental bkfst, refreshments. Cr cds: A, C, D, DS, ER, JCB, MC, V.

★ ★ ★ **ROYCE.** *(1160 Thorn Run Rd Extension, Coraopolis 15108) S on PA 60, exit Thorn Run Rd.* 412/262-2400; FAX 412/264-9373. 198 rms, 9 story. S $59-$119; D $59-$129; each addl $10; suites $79-$139; under 18 free; wkend rates. Crib free. TV; cable. Pool; lifeguard. Restaurant 6 am-2 pm, 5-11 pm; Sat, Sun 7 am-11 pm. Bar 11-2 am; entertainment, dancing Thurs-Sat. Ck-out noon. Meeting rms. Free airport transportation. Exercise equipt; weight machines, bicycles. Cr cds: A, C, D, DS, MC, V.

Restaurant

★ ★ ★ **HYEHOLDE.** *(190 Hyeholde Dr, Coraopolis) PA 60 to Beers School Rd, right on Beaver Grade Rd, left on Coraopolis Heights Rd.* 412/264-3116. Hrs: 11:30 am-2 pm, 5-10 pm; Sat from 5 pm. Closed Sun exc Mother's Day; major hols. Res accepted. Continental menu. Serv bar. Wine list. Complete meals: lunch $8.50-$13.50, dinner $19-$32. Specialties: rack of lamb, baked Virginia spots fish (in season). Own baking, desserts. Valet parking. Patio dining. Herb garden. English Tudor decor; fireplaces; estate grounds. Cr cds: A, C, D, DS, MC, V.

D SC

Portland

Founded: 1851	
Pop: 437,319	
Elev: 77 feet	
Time zone: Pacific	
Area code: 503	

Portland, Oregon's largest city, sprawls across both banks of the northward-flowing Willamette River, just south of its confluence with the Columbia. The lush and fertile Willamette Valley brings the city both beauty and riches. Through its leadership in rose culture, Portland has earned the title "city of roses." The International Rose Test Garden is a showpiece with 10,000 bushes and more than 400 varieties, and the 24-day Rose Festival is Portland's biggest event of the year.

Portland was established in 1844, named after Portland, Maine, the hometown of one of its early settlers. In 1851, Portland was incorporated as a town. The city grew steadily during its first 10 years, with the major growth taking place on the west side of the Willamette River. Eventually, small towns and cities were incorporated on the east side as well. A devastating fire burned 22 blocks of the west side of Portland in 1873, but the city was rebuilt and continued to grow. In 1889, the world's first long-distance transmission of electricity brought light to the streets of Portland. The electricity's power came from a plant on the Willamette Falls at Oregon City, southwest of Portland.

During the Depression Portland's population declined; however, during World War II the population began to increase when people from all parts of the country came to Portland looking for work. Since that time there has been a steady influx of people.

Business

Portland's economy is not dominated by any one firm or industry; there are many small and medium-sized firms representing diverse industries. This diversity has resulted in stable economic growth. Some of the items produced here are oscilloscopes, electronic equipment, silicon wafers, pulp, paper, ships, boats, barges, plywood, trucks, railroad cars, power tools, aircraft, furniture, lumber, alloy steel, glass containers, sportswear, footwear, canned fruits and vegetables and chocolate candy.

Portland's harbor strengthens the area's economic base. It is one of the more active harbors in the United States; more than 1,400 ships call on the city annually.

The distribution of commodities and merchandise to the Pacific Northwest is another major factor in Portland's economy.

Convention Facilities

The Oregon Convention Center, a state-of-the-art facility, has 150,000 square feet of column-free exhibition space that can accommodate 870 exhibit booths. Theater-style seating is available for up to 10,000. In addition, there are 28 meeting rooms and a 25,000 square foot ballroom. The convention facility also features a fully staffed visitor center.

The Memorial Coliseum Complex is a fully equipped convention center able to accommodate most functions. The complex itself has a total exhibit area of 108,000 square feet. The arena is equipped with 9,231 permanent theater seats; portable seating can be arranged to increase the capacity to 14,000. There is also a large movable stage and an 85-by-185-foot ice floor.

The exhibit hall has 55,800 square feet of space that can accommodate up to 320 exhibit booths. The convention hall provides an additional 25,200 square feet of exhibit space. The assembly hall, which covers 19,800 square feet, can be used as a single large area or divided into 6 smaller meeting rooms. In addition to the major rooms, there are 5 meeting rooms with seating for 30 to 300 persons.

The Portland Exposition Center is also available for most functions. The center has a total exhibit space of 117,315 square feet. The exhibit hall has 82,348 square feet, which can be divided into 2 sections. The exhibit hall has a seating capacity for 2,000. The arena floor has 23,067 square feet for exhibits. In addition, the west hall can seat 250 individuals within an 11,900 square foot room.

For exhibits, meetings or banquets there is also the Georgia-Pacific Room. It can accommodate 32 standard-size exhibit booths or seat up to 1,000 people for meetings, 800 for banquets.

Sports and Recreation

Portland's professional basketball team, the Trail Blazers, provides exciting sports enjoyment. Both the Trail Blazers and the city's hockey team, the Winter Hawks, play at the Memorial Coliseum. The Beavers, Portland's minor league baseball team, play at the Civic Stadium.

Portland has more than 30 challenging golf courses, all located within 45 minutes of the downtown area. There are approximately 115 tennis courts in the city operated by the Portland Park Bureau and more than 100 additional courts in the suburbs.

In the western hills of Portland, overlooking downtown, is Washington Park, which forms part of a 5,000-acre nature preserve. Within the park is the International Rose Test Garden, the Japanese Gardens and the Metro Washington Park Zoo.

Within 30 miles of the city are 7 state parks, including Crown Point, with a view of the Columbia River Gorge National Scenic Area and its 2,000-foot-high rock walls.

Approximately 50 miles east of Portland is Mt Hood National Forest, with one of the best slopes in the Northwest for skiing. The surrounding area is used for camping, climbing, fishing, tobogganing and horseback riding.

Entertainment

Touring Broadway companies present performances at the Portland Civic Auditorium. This is also the stage for each season's presentations by the Oregon Ballet, the Portland Opera Society and other local and traveling artists. Portland has a Youth Philharmonic Orchestra, a Pops Symphony, Symphonic Choir, an active civic theater and numerous small theater groups. During the summer, Washington Park is the scene

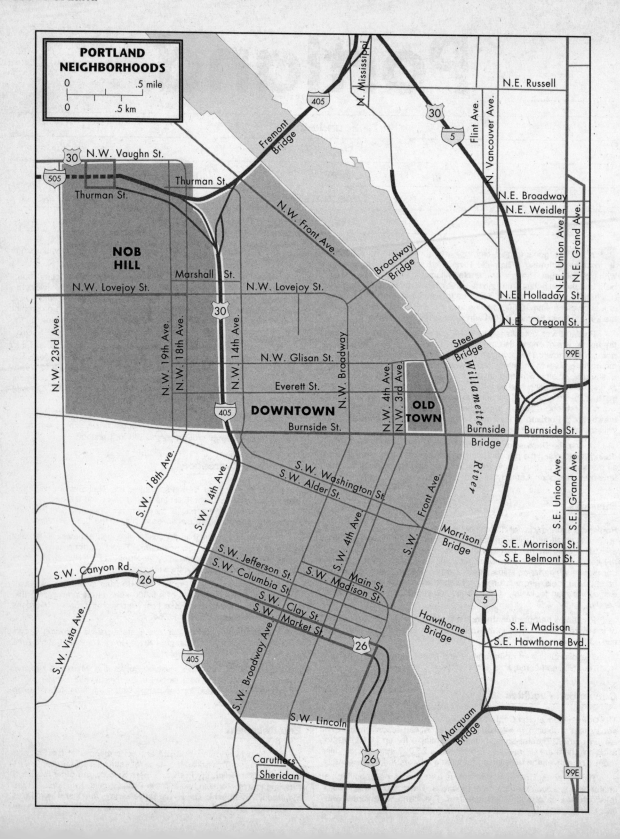

PORTLAND NEIGHBORHOODS

0   .5 mile

0   .5 km

of outdoor entertainment, including folk dancing, opera, free concerts and theater.

The Portland Center for the Performing Arts houses the 2,750-seat Arlene Schnitzer Concert Hall, the home of the Oregon Symphony Orchestra. Also in the center are the Intermediate Theater and the Winningstad Theater.

Historical Areas

Johns Landing, a major urban development project begun in 1969, has carefully preserved the rambling charm of an old factory. The Water Tower was the first portion of Johns Landing to open. Today, the building houses some 40 apparel, art, gift and import shops, delis, cafes and restaurants.

The Oregon Historical Society's museum contains a history of the Northwest with permanent and special exhibits and a regional reference library.

Pittock Mansion, a restored French-Renaissance structure, is surrounded by 46 forested and landscaped acres with a view of mountains, rivers and the city.

The Howell Park-Bybee House, built in 1856, has also been restored. The dwelling is located in a 120-acre park; a children's agricultural museum is on the grounds.

Sightseeing

St Johns Bridge is an architectural masterpiece, with a beautiful scenic setting in the city. The structural steel is planned for beauty of lines, proportion, light and shadows.

Within the city itself, there is a 22-block transit mall consisting of 11 blocks on both SW Fifth and SW Sixth avenues downtown. Broad red-brick sidewalks with flower-bedecked planters, trees, fountains, statuary and kiosks have transformed once ordinary streets into a park-like setting.

Old Town, located between SW Fifth and Front avenues on both sides of W Burnside Street, has many excellent examples of early Portland architecture. Here visitors can find ethnic restaurants and many unusual shops. The Tri-Met buses provide free service within Fareless Square, which includes Old Town. A small Chinatown is also located here.

One of the more recent additions to Portland is quite magnificent. Spectacular *Portlandia* is a hammered-copper statue throned above 5th Avenue on the Portland Building, a structure by Michael Graves that triggered the post-modern movement in American architecture.

Every weekend between early March and Christmas, an open air market is held beneath the west end of the Burnside Bridge between SW First and Front Avenues. Crafts, gourmet foods, locally grown produce and many forms of live entertainment abound at Portland Saturday Market.

The Yamhill Historic District has a marketplace housing produce and meat markets, restaurants and retail shops.

One of the most scenic routes east of Portland is a drive on I-84. Waterfalls, parks, forests and a breathtaking view of the Columbia River Gorge lie along the road.

Spectacular Multnomah Falls, about 30 miles east of the city, is one of a series of 11 lovely waterfalls that adorn this stretch of highway.

Across the Columbia River, in Washington, is Beacon Rock, which has been called the world's second largest monolith. Trails lead to the top of the rock.

Camping and picnic areas are numerous along the entire drive to The Dalles, a busy city that was a Native American trading area during the time of Lewis and Clark. Located in town is the site of Old Fort Dalles, built around 1850. Only one of the fort's original buildings remains; it is now an historical museum.

Lost Lake, with Mount Hood in the background, is one of the most exquisite sights in Oregon. It lies southwest of Hood River in an area reached by county and forest roads.

General References

Founded: 1851 **Pop:** 437,319 **Elev:** 77 feet **Time zone:** Pacific **Area code:** 503

Phone Numbers

POLICE & FIRE: 911
FBI: 224-4181
POISON CONTROL CENTER: 279-8968
TIME: 976-1616   **WEATHER:** 236-7575

Information Sources

Portland/Oregon Visitors Association, 26 SW Salmon, 97204; 222-2223 or 800/962-3700.
Portland Event Line, 233-3333.
Bureau of Parks & Recreation, 823-2223.

Transportation

AIRLINES: Alaska; American; America West; Continental; Delta; Horizon Air; Northwest; TWA; United; and other commuter and regional airlines. For the most current airline schedules and information consult the *Official Airline Guide,* published twice monthly.
AIRPORT: Portland International, 335-1234.
CAR RENTAL AGENCIES: (See Toll-Free Numbers) Budget 249-4556; Dollar 249-4792; Hertz 249-8216; National 249-4900; Thrifty 254-6565.
PUBLIC TRANSPORTATION: Tri-County Metropolitan Transportation District (Tri-Met), 701 SW 6th Ave, 233-3511.
RAILROAD PASSENGER SERVICE: Amtrak 800/872-7245.

Newspapers

The Oregonian; Daily Journal of Commerce.

Convention Facilities

Memorial Coliseum Complex, 1401 N Wheeler Ave, 248-4496.
Oregon Convention Center, 777 NE Martin Luther King Blvd, 235-7575.
Portland Exposition Center, 2060 N Marine Dr, 285-7756.

Sports & Recreation

Major Sports Facilities
Civic Stadium, 1844 SW Morrison, 248-4345 (Beavers, baseball).
Memorial Coliseum, 1401 N Wheeler Ave, 248-4496 (Trail Blazers, basketball; Winter Hawks, hockey).
Portland Exposition Center, 2060 N Marine Dr, 285-7756.

Racetracks
Multnomah Greyhound Park, NE 223rd Ave, between NE Halsey & Glisan Sts, 667-7700 (dog racing).
Portland International Raceway, Delta Park, 1940 N Victory Blvd, 285-6635 (auto racing).
Portland Meadows, 1001 N Schmeer Rd, 285-9144 (thoroughbred & quarter horse racing).
Portland Speedway, 9727 N Union Ave, 285-2883 (auto racing).

Cultural Facilities

Theaters
Ladybug Theater, Oaks Park, SE Spokane St at Sellwood Bridge, 232-2346.

Lakewood Theatre Company, 368 S State St, Lakewood Center for the Arts, Lake Oswego, 635-3901.
Oregon One-Act Festival, 1436 SW Montgomery St, 274-1717.
Portland Repertory Theatre, 25 SW Salmon, 224-4491.

Concert Halls

Arlene Schnitzer Concert Hall, 1057 SW Broadway, 248-4496.
Memorial Coliseum, 1401 N Wheeler, 248-4496.
Portland Center for the Performing Arts, 1111 SW Broadway, 248-4496.
Portland Civic Auditorium, 222 SW Clay St, 248-4496.

Museums

American Advertising Museum, 9 NW 2nd Ave, 226-0000.
Children's Museum, 3037 SW 2nd Ave, 823-2227.
Oregon Historical Center, 1200 SW Park Ave, 222-1741.
Oregon Museum of Science and Industry, 1945 SE Water Ave, 797-4000.
Police Historical Museum, 1111 SW 2nd Ave, 823-0019.
World Forestry Center, 4033 SW Canyon Rd, 228-1367.

Art Museums

Oregon Society of Artists, 2185 SW Park Pl, 228-0706.
Portland Art Musuem, 1219 SW Park Ave, 226-2811.

Points of Interest

Historical

Howell Park-Bybee House, 12 mi N via US 30, on Howell Park Rd, Sauvie Island, 621-3344 or 222-1741.
Old Church, 1422 SW 11th Ave, 222-2031.
Pittock Mansion, Pittock Acres Park, 3229 NW Pittock Dr, 823-3624.

Other Attractions

Council Crest Park, S on SW Greenway Ave, 823-2223.
Crown Point State Park, 25 mi E off I-84 on US 30 Scenic Rte, 695-2230.
Crystal Springs Rhododendron Garden, SE 28th Ave, N of SE Woodstock Blvd, 796-5193.
Forest Park, off US 30, NW of Fremont Bridge, 823-2223.
Grotto—Sanctuary of Our Sorrowful Mother, NE 85th Ave at Sandy Blvd, 254-7371.
Hoyt Arboretum, 4000 SW Fairview Blvd, 228-8733.
International Rose Test Garden, Washington Park, 823-2223.
Jantzen Beach Center, I-5 at Jantzen Beach on Hayden Island, 289-5555.
Japanese Garden, Washington Park, 223-4070.
Johns Landing, 5331 SW Macadam Ave, 228-9431.
Leach Botanical Gardens, S of Foster on SE 122nd St, 761-9503.
Lloyd Center, NE 9th Ave & NE Multnomah, 282-2511.

Metro Washington Park Zoo, 4001 SW Canyon Rd, 226-1561.
Mt Hood National Forest, SE on US 26.
Multnomah Falls, 32 mi E on I-84.
Oaks Amusement Park, SE Oaks Park Way, E end of Sellwood Bridge, 233-5777.
Pendleton Woolen Mills, 10505 SE 17th St, Milwaukie, 654-0444.
Pioneer Courthouse Square, 701 SW 6th Ave, 223-1613.
Shakespeare Garden, Washington Park, 823-2223.
Washington Park, accessible via W Burnside St or Canyon Rd, 823-2223.
Washington Square, off OR 217 near Scholls Ferry & Greenburg Rds, 639-8860.
Willamette Stone State Park, 4 mi W off NW Skyline Blvd.

Sightseeing Tours

Gray Line bus tours, 4320 N Suttle Rd, 285-9845 or 800/442-7042.
Hillsboro Helicopters, Inc, 3565 NE Cornell, Hillsboro 97124; 648-2831.
Sternwheeler *Columbia Gorge,* 1200 NW Front Ave, Suite 110, 223-3928.

Annual Events

Portland Rose Festival, 227-2681. Early-mid-June.
Scottish Highland Games & Clan Gathering, Mt Hood Community College, Gresham, 636-3553. Mid-July.
Multnomah County Fair, Portland Exposition Center. Late July.
Mt Hood Festival of Jazz, Gresham, 666-3810. 1st wkend Aug.
Portland Marathon. Early Oct.
Pacific International Livestock Show, Washington County Fairplex, Hillsboro, 684-1416. Early Oct.
Christmas Boat Parade, along Willamette & Columbia rivers. Early-mid-Dec.

City Neighborhoods

Many of the restaurants, unrated dining establishments and some lodgings listed under Portland include neighborhoods as well as exact street addresses. A map showing these neighborhoods can be found immediately following the city introduction. Geographic descriptions of these areas are given, followed by a table of restaurants arranged by neighborhood.

Downtown: Southeast of I-405, west of the Willamette River, north of SW Lincoln and east of I-30. East of Downtown East of Willamette River. West of Downtown West of I-30.
Nob Hill: West of Downtown; south of Vaughn St, west of I-405, north of Burnside St and east of NW 23rd St.
Old Town: Area of Downtown south of Glisan St, west of Front St and the river, north of Burnside St and east of NW 3rd St.

Lodgings and Food

PORTLAND RESTAURANTS
BY NEIGHBORHOOD AREAS

(For full description, see alphabetical listings under Restaurants)

DOWNTOWN

Alessandro's. 301 SW Morrison

Bush Garden. 900 SW Morrison

Esplanade at Riverplace (Riverplace Hotel). 1510 SW Harbor Way

Heathman (Heathman Hotel). 1009 SW Broadway

Huber's. 411 SW 3rd Ave

Jake's Famous Crawfish. 401 SW 12th Ave

London Grill (The Benson). 309 SW Broadway

Mandarin Cove. 111 SW Columbia

Pazzo Ristorante (Vintage Plaza Hotel). 422 SW Broadway

Rafati's. 25 SW Salmon

River Queen. 1300 NW Front Ave

EAST OF DOWNTOWN

Genoa. 2832 SE Belmont St

Holland Gateway. 10805 NE Halsey

Korgan's Restaurant & Strudel House. 1605 SE Bybee

Matterhorn. 3 NE 82nd Ave

Papa Haydn. 5829 SE Milwaukie

Perry's on Fremont. 2401 NE Fremont

Poor Richard's. 3907 NE Broadway

Rheinlander. 5035 NE Sandy Blvd

Ringside East. 14021 NE Glisan

Salty's on the Columbia. 3839 NE Marine Dr

Sayler's Old Country Kitchen. 10519 SE Stark

Sylvia's. 5115 NE Sandy Blvd

WEST OF DOWNTOWN

Cafe des Amis. 1987 NW Kearney

Chart House. 5700 SW Terwilliger Blvd

Delfina's. 2112 NW Kearney St

L'auberge. 2601 NW Vaughn

Old Spaghetti Factory. 0715 SW Bancroft

Original Pancake House. 8601 SW 24th Ave

Plainfield's Mayur. 852 SW 21st Ave

Ringside. 2165 W Burnside St

Yankee Pot Roast. 2839 NW St Helen's Rd

NOB HILL

Cody's Cafe. 115 NW 22nd Ave

OLD TOWN

Alexis. 215 W Burnside

Couch Street Fish House. 105 NW 3rd Ave

Dan & Louis Oyster Bar. 208 SW Ankeny St

Note: *When a listing is located in a town that does not have its own city heading, it will appear under the city nearest to its location. In these cases, the address and town appear in parenthesis immediately following the name of the establishment.*

Motels

★ ★ ★ **BEST WESTERN PONY SOLDIER.** *9901 NE Sandy Blvd (97220), near Intl Airport, east of downtown.* 503/256-1504; FAX 503/256-5928. 104 rms, 2 story, 15 suites. S $70-$80; D $83-$93; each addl $5; suites, kit. units $105-$140; under 12 free. Crib $3. TV; cable. Heated pool. Complimentary continental bkfst, coffee. Restaurant adj 6 am-10 pm. Ck-out noon. Free lndry facilities. Meeting rms. Valet serv. Sundries. Free airport transportation. Exercise equipt; weight machine, bicycle, whirlpool, sauna. Refrigerators. Balconies. Cr cds: A, C, D, DS, ER, MC, V.

D ≈ ⚡ ✈ ⤢ ⚐ SC

✔★ **CARAVAN.** *2401 SW 4th Ave (97201), south of downtown.* 503/226-1121; res: 800/248-0506; FAX 503/274-2681. 40 rms in 2 buildings, 2 story. S, D $48-$55; each addl $6. Crib $6. TV; cable. Heated pool. Complimentary coffee in lobby. Restaurant 7 am-10 pm. Bar 11-2 am. Ck-out noon. Balconies. Cr cds: A, C, D, DS, JCB, MC, V.

≈ ⤢ ⚐ SC

✔★ **CHESTNUT TREE INN.** *9699 SE Stark St (97216), east of downtown.* 503/255-4444. 58 rms, 2 story. S $35; D $40; each addl $2. Crib free. TV; cable. Complimentary coffee, tea. Restaurant adj 6 am-11 pm. Ck-out noon. Refrigerators. Cr cds: A, D, MC, V.

D ⤢ ⚐

✔★ **CYPRESS INN-DOWNTOWN.** *809 SW King Ave (97205), west of downtown.* 503/226-6288; res: 800/225-4205; FAX 503/274-0038. 83 rms, 2-5 story, 41 kit. suites. S $45-$95; D $52-$100; each addl $7; kit. suites $65-95; under 12 free; wkly rates. Crib free. Pet accepted; $15-$30 non-refundable. TV. Complimentary continental bkfst, coffee. Restaurant nearby. Ck-out noon. Coin lndry. Meeting rms. Valet serv. Free airport, RR station, bus depot transportation. Refrigerators. Cr cds: A, C, D, DS, MC, V.

D 🐾 ⤢ ⚐ SC

★ **DAYS INN.** *(9717 SE Sunnyside Rd, Clackamas 97015) I-205 Sunnyside exit.* 503/654-1699; FAX 503/659-2702. 110 rms, 3 story. S $49-$70; D $55-$80; each addl $7; studio rms $65-$120; under 12 free. Crib free. TV; cable. Heated pool. Complimentary continental bkfst. Ck-out noon. Free airport transportation. Exercise equipt; weights, bicycles, whirlpool, sauna. Some refrigerators. Cr cds: A, C, D, DS, JCB, MC, V.

D ≈ ⚡ ⤢ ⚐ SC

★ ★ **HOLIDAY INN EXPRESS.** *(2323 NE 181st Ave, Gresham 97230) I-84 exit 13.* 503/492-4000; FAX 503/492-3271. 71 rms, 3 story, 23 suites. May-Sept: S $61; D $68; each addl $7; suites $80-$101; under 12 free; lower rates rest of yr. Crib free. Pet accepted, some restrictions. TV; cable. Indoor pool; whirlpool, sauna. Complimentary continental bkfst. Restaurant adj 7 am-10 pm. Ck-out 1 pm. Coin lndry. Meeting rms. Gift shop. Valet serv. Cr cds: A, D, DS, MC, V.

D 🐾 ≈ ⤢ ⚐ SC

★ ★ **McMENAMINS EDGEFIELD.** *(2126 SW Halsey St, Troutdale 97060) E on I-84, Wood Village exit 16A.* 503/669-8610; res: 800/669-8610; FAX 503/665-4209. 105 rms (102 share bath), 3 story. No rm phones. S $35-$105; D $65-$180; each addl $15; under 6 free; wkly rates. Crib free. Complimentary full bkfst. Restaurant (see BLACK RABBIT). Bar 11-1 am. Ck-out 11 am. Concierge. Bellhops. Game rm. Built 1911 as county poor farm; was converted to nursing home in 1960s. Renovated in style of European village complete with theater, winery and brewery. Formal and herb gardens. Totally nonsmoking. Cr cds: A, DS, MC, V.

D ⚡ ⤢ ⚐ SC

★ ★ **RAMADA INN-AIRPORT.** *6221 NE 82nd Ave (97220), east of downtown.* 503/255-6511; FAX 503/255-8417. 202 rms, 2 story. S,D $85-$120; each addl $10; suites $95-$250; under 18 free; wkend rates. Crib free. TV. Heated pool. Restaurant 6:30 am-11 pm. Rm serv. Bar. Ck-out noon. Coin lndry. Meeting rms. Bellhops. Valet serv. Free airport transportation. Exercise equipt; weights, bicycles, whirlpool, sauna. Some private patios, balconies. Cr cds: A, C, D, DS, ER, JCB, MC, V.

D ≈ ✕ ⊠ 🔥 SC

★ ★ **RESIDENCE INN BY MARRIOTT-SOUTH.** *(PO Box 1110, 15200 SW Bangy Rd, Lake Oswego 97035) S on I-5, exit 292.* 503/684-2603; FAX 503/620-6712. 112 kit. units, 2 story. 1 & 2-bedrm suites $114-$149. Crib $5. Pet accepted; $10. TV; cable, in-rm movies avail. Heated pool. Complimentary continental bkfst, coffee. Restaurant adj. Ck-out noon. Coin lndry. Valet serv. Health club privileges. Refrigerators. Fireplace in suites. Private patios, balconies. Picnic tables, grills. Cr cds: A, C, D, DS, JCB, MC, V.

D ☞ ≈ ⊠ 🔥 SC

★ ★ **SHILO INN-WASHINGTON SQUARE.** *(10830 SW Greenburg Rd, Tigard 97223) S on OR 217, Greenburg Rd exit.* 503/620-4320; FAX 503/620-8277. 77 rms, 4 story, 6 kits. S, D $59-$85; each addl $8; kit. units $85; under 12 free; wkly, monthly rates. Crib free. Pet accepted; $7. TV; cable. Complimentary continental bkfst, coffee. Restaurant nearby. Ck-out noon. Coin lndry. Meeting rm. Valet serv. Free airport transportation. Exercise equipt; weight machines, bicycles, sauna, steam rm. Cr cds: A, C, D, DS, ER, JCB, MC, V.

D ☞ ✕ ≈ ⊠ SC

✔ ★ **SUPER 8.** *(25438 SW Parkway Ave, Wilsonville 97070) I-5 exit 286.* 503/682-2088; FAX 503/682-0453. 72 rms, 4 story. S $42.67; D $46.95-$51.88; each addl $4. Crib free. Pet accepted; $25 refundable. TV; cable. Complimentary coffee in lobby. Restaurant opp open 24 hrs. Ck-out noon. Coin lndry. Meeting rm. Cr cds: A, D, MC, V.

D ☞ ⊠ 🔥

★ **TRAVELODGE SUITES.** *7740 SE Powell Blvd (97206), east of downtown.* 503/788-9394; FAX 503/788-9378. 39 suites, 2 story. S $57; D $65; each addl $6; under 17 free. Crib free. Pet accepted, some restrictions; $25. TV; cable. Complimentary continental bkfst. Ck-out noon. Coin lndry. Whirlpool, sauna. Refrigerators. Cr cds: A, C, D, DS, MC, V.

D ☞ ⊠ 🔥 SC

✔ ★ **WAYSIDE MOTOR INN.** *(11460 SW Pacific Hwy, Tigard 97223) S on I-5, exit 294.* 503/245-6421; res: 800/547-8828; FAX 503/245-6425. 117 rms, 4 story. S $50-$56; D $56-$58; each addl $6. Crib $5. TV; cable, in-rm movies avail. Heated pool; sauna. Complimentary continental bkfst. Restaurant adj open 24 hrs. Ck-out 11 am. Meeting rms. Valet serv. Airport transportation. Cr cds: A, C, D, DS, MC, V.

D ≈ ⊠ 🔥 SC

Motor Hotels

★ **BEST WESTERN-INN AT THE COLISEUM.** *10 N Weidler (97227), east of downtown.* 503/287-9900; FAX 503/287-3500. 181 rms, 5 story. S $60-$65; D $70-$80; each addl $5; suites $125; under 12 free. TV; cable. Indoor pool. Restaurant 6:30 am-9 pm. Rm serv 6:30 am-9:30 pm. Bar 11-2 am. Ck-out noon. Meeting rms. Covered parking. Free airport, RR station, bus depot transportation. Cr cds: A, C, D, DS, MC, V.

D ≈ ⊠ 🔥 SC

✔ ★ **DELTA INN.** *9930 N Whitaker Rd (97217), I-5 exit 306B, north of downtown.* 503/289-1800; res: 800/833-1800; FAX 503/289-3778. 212 rms, 4 story. S $46; D $51-$61; each addl $5; under 12 free; wkly rates. Crib free. Pet accepted; $10 non-refundable. TV. Complimentary coffee. Restaurant adj open 24 hrs. Ck-out noon. Coin lndry.

Meeting rm. Sundries. Free airport, RR station, bus depot transportation. Park adj. Cr cds: A, C, D, DS, MC, V.

D ☞ ≈ ⊠ 🔥 SC

★ ★ **HOLIDAY INN-AIRPORT.** *8439 NE Columbia Blvd (97220), 2½ mi N of I-84, on I-205, exit 23B/Columbia Blvd, near Intl Aiport, east of downtown.* 503/256-5000; FAX 503/257-4742. 286 rms, 8 story. S $89-$110; D $95-$120; each addl $6; suites $125-$250. Crib free. TV; cable. Indoor pool. Restaurant 6 am-10 pm. Rm serv. Bar. Ck-out noon. Coin lndry. Convention facilities. Bellhops. Valet serv Mon-Fri. Sundries. Free airport transportation. Exercise equipt; weights, bicycles, whirlpool, sauna. Game rm. Cr cds: A, C, D, DS, ER, JCB, MC, V.

D ≈ ✕ ✈ ⊠ 🔥 SC

★ ★ **PORTLAND INN.** *1414 SW 6th Ave (97201), at Columbia, downtown.* 503/221-1611; res: 800/648-6440; FAX 503/226-0447. 173 rms, 5 story. S $72; D $75-$80; each addl $10; under 12 free. Crib free. TV; cable. Heated pool. Restaurant 6:30 am-10 pm; Sat, Sun from 7 am. Rm serv. Bar 11 am-midnight. Ck-out noon. Meeting rms. Valet serv. Health club privileges. Cr cds: A, C, D, MC, V.

≈ ⊠ 🐾 SC

★ ★ **QUALITY INN-AIRPORT.** *8247 NE Sandy Blvd (97220), east of downtown.* 503/256-4111; FAX 503/254-1507. 120 rms, 2-3 story. No elvtr. S $65-$75; D $70-$80; each addl $5; suites $100; under 18 free. Crib free. Pet accepted; $10 non-refundable. TV. Heated pool. Restaurant 7 am-11 pm; Sun 5-9 pm. Bar noon-11 pm; entertainment, dancing. Ck-out noon. Coin lndry. Meeting rms. Valet serv. Free airport transportation. Some in-rm whirlpools. Some balconies. Cr cds: A, C, D, DS, MC, V.

D ☞ ≈ ⊠ 🔥 SC

★ ★ ★ **RED LION-COLUMBIA RIVER.** *1401 N Hayden Island Dr (97217), just W of I-5, Jantzen Beach exit, north of downtown.* 503/283-2111; FAX 503/283-4718. 351 rms, 3 story. S $99-$125; D $114-$140; each addl $15; suites $195-$300; under 18 free. Crib free. Pet accepted; $15 non-refundable. TV; cable, in-rm movies. Heated pool. Restaurants 6 am-10 pm. Rm serv. Bars 11-2 am; entertainment, dancing Tues-Sat. Ck-out noon. Convention facilities. Bellhops. Valet serv. Gift shop. Barber, beauty shop. Free airport, RR station, bus depot transportation. Tennis adj. Putting green. Some refrigerators, bathrm phones. Whirlpool in some suites. Private patios, balconies. Spacious, attractive grounds. On Columbia River. Cr cds: A, C, D, DS, ER, JCB, MC, V.

D ☞ ≈ ⊠ 🔥 SC

★ ★ ★ **RED LION-JANTZEN BEACH.** *909 N Hayden Island Dr (97217), just E of I-5 exit Jantzen Beach, north of downtown.* 503/283-4466; FAX 503/283-4743. 320 rms, 4 story. S $105-$125; D $120-$140; each addl $15; suites $175-$450; under 18 free; special package plans; wkend rates. Crib free. Pet accepted. TV; cable. Heated pool. Restaurant 6 am-10 pm; wkends to 11 pm. Rm serv. Bar 10-2:30 am; entertainment, dancing. Ck-out noon. Convention facilities. Bellhops. Valet serv. Sundries. Free airport transportation. Tennis. Health club privileges. Some bathrm phones, in-rm whirlpools. Private patios, balconies. On river; boat dock. Cr cds: A, C, D, DS, ER, JCB, MC, V.

D ☞ 🚴 ≈ ✕ 🔥 SC

★ ★ **RIVERSIDE INN.** *50 SW Morrison St (97204), downtown.* 503/221-0711; res: 800/648-6440; FAX 503/274-0312. 138 rms, 5 story. S $73-$78; D $83-$88; each addl $10; under 17 free. Crib free. TV. Restaurant 6:30 am-10 pm; Sat & Sun 7 am-9 pm. Rm serv. Bar 11 am-midnight. Ck-out noon. Meeting rm. Health club privileges. Balconies. Cr cds: A, C, D, DS, ER, MC, V.

⊠ ⊠ SC

★ ★ **SHILO HOTEL.** *9900 SW Canyon Rd (97225), west of downtown.* 503/297-2551; res: 800/222-2244; FAX 503/297-7708. 141 rms, 2-3 story. S, D $65-$89; each addl $10; suites $95-$175; under 12 free. Crib free. TV; cable. Heated pool. Restaurant 6 am-10 pm. Rm serv. Bar 11-2 am; entertainment exc Sun. Ck-out noon. Meeting rms.

Valet serv. Sundries. Airport transportation. Exercise equipt; weights, bicycles. Refrigerators. Private patios, balconies. Cr cds: A, C, D, DS, ER, JCB, MC, V.

Hotels

★ ★ ★ ★ **THE BENSON.** *309 SW Broadway (97205), at Oak St, downtown.* 503/228-2000; res: 800/426-0670; FAX 503/226-4603. 287 units, 13 story, 44 suites. S $145-$190; D $170-$205; each addl $25; suites $325-$600; under 18 free; wkend rates. Crib $25. Garage, valet $10/day. TV; cable. Restaurant (see LONDON GRILL). Rm serv 24 hrs. Bar 11-1 am; entertainment. Ck-out noon. Convention facilities. Concierge. Gift shop. Health club privileges. Minibars. Bathrm phone in suites. Historical landmark (1913); restored. Hotel's public areas feature classically ornamented pillars, plaster coffered ceilings and surfaces of marble, rare Circassian walnut and mahogany. Originally built by Simon Benson, Oregon lumberman. Cr cds: A, C, D, DS, ER, JCB, MC, V.

★ ★ **COURTYARD BY MARRIOTT-AIRPORT.** *11550 NE Airport Way (97220), near Intl Airport, east of downtown.* 503/252-3200; FAX 503/252-8921. 150 rms, 6 story. June-Aug: S,D $73-$83; each addl $10; suites $110; under 18 free; wkly rates; higher rates Rose Festival; lower rates rest of yr. Crib $10. TV; cable, in-rm movies. Heated pool; whirlpool, poolside serv. Restaurant 6 am-11 pm. Rm serv 5-10 pm. Bar 4 pm-midnight. Ck-out noon. Free airport transportation. Refrigerator, minibar in suites. Cr cds: A, C, D, DS, MC, V.

★ ★ ★ **EMBASSY SUITES.** *(9000 SW Washington Square Rd, Tigard 97223) S on OR 217, Progress exit.* 503/644-4000; FAX 503/641-4654. 354 suites, 9 story. S $137; D $147; each addl $10; under 18 free. Crib free. TV; cable. Indoor pool; whirlpool, sauna. Complimentary bkfst. Restaurant 11:30 am-2 pm, 5-10 pm; Fri to 11 pm. Bar to midnight, Fri & Sat to 1 am; entertainment, dancing Fri-Sat. Ck-out 1 pm. Convention facilities. Gift shop. Airport transportation. Refrigerators. Health club privileges. Cr cds: A, C, D, DS, JCB, MC, V.

★ ★ ★ **THE GOVERNOR.** *611 SW 10th (97205), at SW Alder Ave, downtown.* 503/224-3400; res: 800/554-3456; FAX 503/241-2122. 100 rms, 6 story, 32 suites. S $145-$165; D $165-$185; each addl $20; suites $175-$500; under 12 free; wkend rates. Crib free. Garage parking $10. TV; cable. Indoor pool. Restaurant 6:30 am-11 pm. Rm serv 24 hrs. Bar 11 am-11 pm. Ck-out noon. Meeting rms. Concierge. Barber, beauty shop. Exercise rm; instructor, weights, treadmill, whirlpool, sauna. Refrigerators, minibars. Some balconies. Cr cds: A, C, D, DS, MC, V.

★ ★ ★ **HEATHMAN.** *1009 SW Broadway (97205), downtown.* 503/241-4100; res: 800/551-0011; FAX 503/790-7110. 151 rms, 10 story. S $140-$185; D $160-$205; each addl $20; suites $225-$295; under 6 free; wkend rates. Crib $7. Garage in/out $10. TV; cable. Restaurant (see HEATHMAN). Rm serv 24 hrs. Afternoon tea. Bars 11-2 am; entertainment. Ck-out 2 pm. Meeting rms. Concierge. Gift shop. Exercise equipt; bicycles, rowers. Health club privileges. Minibars. Landmark hotel listed on National Register of Historic Places. Cr cds: A, C, D, DS, ER, JCB, MC, V.

★ ★ ★ **HILTON.** *921 SW 6th Ave (97204), downtown.* 503/226-1611; FAX 503/220-2565. 455 rms, 23 story. S $145; D $165; each addl $20; suites $400-$950; family, wkend rates. Garage in/out $12; valet $3 addl. Crib free. TV; cable. Pool; poolside serv. Restaurant 6:30 am-11:30 pm. Bar 11-1 am; entertainment Tues-Sat. Ck-out noon. Convention facilities. Gift shop. Barber, beauty shop. Airport transportation.

Exercise equipt; weights, treadmills. Cr cds: A, C, D, DS, ER, JCB, MC, V.

★ **IMPERIAL.** *400 SW Broadway (97205), at Stark St, downtown.* 503/228-7221; res: 800/452-2323; FAX 503/223-4551. 136 rms, 9 story. S $60-$70; D $65-$85; each addl $5; under 12 free. Crib free. TV; cable. Restaurants 6:30 am-8 pm. Bar 11 am-midnight, Sat & Sun 1-9 pm. Ck-out 2 pm. Meeting rms. Airport transportation. Cr cds: A, C, D, DS, MC, V.

✔ **MALLORY.** *729 SW 15th Ave (97205), just W of I-405, downtown.* 503/223-6311; res: 800/228-8657; FAX 503/223-0522. 143 rms, 8 story. S $50-$80; D $55-$90; each addl $5; suites $80. Crib free. TV; cable. Restaurant 6:30 am-9 pm; Sun from 7 am. Bar 11:30-1 am, Sun 1-9 pm. Ck-out 2 pm. Some refrigerators. Cr cds: A, C, D, DS, MC, V.

★ **MARK SPENCER.** *409 SW 11th Ave (97205), downtown.* 503/224-3293; res: 800/548-3934; FAX 503/223-7848. 101 kit. units, 6 story. S, D $57-$88; each addl $10; suites $86-$88; studio rms $57; under 12 free; monthly rates. Crib free. Parking lot 1 blk $7. TV. Complimentary coffee in lobby. Restaurant nearby. Ck-out noon. Coin lndry. Health club privileges. Refrigerators. Rooftop garden. Cr cds: A, C, D, DS, MC, V.

★ ★ **MARRIOTT.** *1401 SW Front Ave (97201), downtown.* 503/226-7600; FAX 503/221-1789. 503 rms, 15 story. S $145; D $155; each addl $15; suites $350-$500; under 18 free. Crib free. Pet accepted. Valet parking in/out $14/day. TV; cable, in-rm movies. Indoor pool; poolside serv. Restaurant 6 am-11 pm; Fri, Sat to midnight. Bar 11:30-2 am; entertainment, dancing. Ck-out noon. Coin lndry. Convention facilities. Concierge. Gift shops. Barber, beauty shop. Airport transportation. Exercise equipt; bicycles, rowing machine, whirlpool, sauna. Game rm. Some bathrm phones, refrigerators; wet bar in suites. Some private patios, balconies. Japanese garden at entrance. **LUXURY LEVEL : CONCIERGE LEVEL.** 79 rms. S $155; D $165. Private lounge. Complimentary continental bkfst, refreshments. Cr cds: A, C, D, DS, ER, JCB, MC, V.

★ ★ ★ **RED LION-LLOYD CENTER.** *1000 NE Multnomah St (97232), I-84 exit 1 (Lloyd Blvd), east of downtown.* 503/281-6111; FAX 503/284-8553. 476 rms, 15 story. S $120-$145; D $125-$160; each addl $15; suites $199-$545; under 18 free. Crib free. TV; cable, in-rm movies. Pool; poolside serv. Restaurant 6 am-11 pm. Rm serv 6 am-11 pm. Bar; entertainment. Ck-out noon. Convention facilities. Valet parking. Free airport transportation. Exercise equipt; weights, bicycles. Some bathrm phones, in-rm whirlpools, refrigerators. Many private patios, balconies. Cr cds: A, C, D, DS, ER, JCB, MC, V.

★ ★ ★ **RIVERPLACE.** *1510 SW Harbor Way (97201), downtown.* 503/228-3233; res: 800/227-1333; FAX 503/295-6161. 84 rms, 4 story. S $145; D $165; each addl $20; suites $180-$500; under 18 free. Valet, garage parking in/out $10. Crib free. Pet accepted, some restrictions. TV; cable. Complimentary continental bkfst, newspaper. Restaurant (see ESPLANADE AT RIVERPLACE). Rm serv 24 hrs. Bar 11-1 am; entertainment Wed-Sun evenings. Ck-out 1 pm. Meeting rms. Concierge. Shopping arcade. Whirlpool, sauna. Health club privileges. Minibars. Some bathrm phones. Refrigerator, fireplace in suites. Balconies. On river. Cr cds: A, C, D, DS, JCB, MC, V.

★ ★ ★ **SHERATON-PORTLAND AIRPORT.** *8235 NE Airport Way (97220), near Intl Airport, east of downtown.* 503/281-2500; FAX 503/249-7602. 215 rms, 5 story. S $108-$118; D $120-$130; each addl $10; suites $140-$395; under 18 free; wkend rates. Crib $5. TV; cable, in-rm movies. Indoor pool. Restaurant 5:30 am-10:30 pm; Sat & Sun 6 am-10 pm. Rm serv 24 hrs. Bar. Ck-out noon. Meeting rms. Concierge. Free airport transportation. Exercise equipt; weights, bicycles, whirlpool, sauna. Minibars. Cr cds: A, C, D, DS, JCB, MC, V.

⬛D ≈ 🏋 ✈ ⛱ 🔥 SC

★ ★ ★ **SHILO INN SUITES-AIRPORT.** 11707 NE Airport Way (97220), near Intl Airport, east of downtown. 503/252-7500; FAX 503/254-0794. 200 suites, 4 story. S, D $112-$129; each addl $15; under 13 free; higher rates Rose Festival. Crib free. TV; cable, in-rm movies. Indoor pool. Complimentary continental bkfst. Complimentary coffee in rms. Restaurant 6 am-11 pm. Rm serv to 10 pm. Bar 8-2 am; entertainment. Ck-out noon. Coin lndry. Meeting rms. Concierge. Free airport, RR station, bus depot transportation. Exercise equipt; weight machine, bicycles, whirlpool, sauna. Bathrm phones, refrigerators, wet bars. Cr cds: A, C, D, DS, ER, JCB, MC, V.

⬛D ≈ 🏋 ✈ ⛱ 🔥 SC

★ ★ ★ **TRAVELODGE.** 1441 NE 2nd Ave (97232), east of downtown. 503/233-2401; FAX 503/238-7016. 240 rms, 10 story. S $88; D $98; each addl $5; suites $175; under 18 free. Crib free. TV; cable. Pool. Complimentary coffee in rms. Restaurant 6:30 am-2 pm, 5:30-10 pm. Bar. Ck-out noon. Meeting rms. Free airport transportation. Cr cds: A, C, D, DS, ER, JCB, MC, V.

⬛D ≈ ⛱ 🔥 SC

★ ★ ★ **VINTAGE PLAZA.** 422 SW Broadway (97205), downtown. 503/228-1212; res: 800/243-0555; FAX 503/228-3598. 107 rms, 10 story, 23 suites. S $145-$160; D $160; each addl $15; suites $190-$205; under 18 free; wkend packages. Crib free. Valet parking $12. TV; in-rm movies avail. Restaurant (see PAZZO RISTORANTE). Rm serv 24 hrs. Bar 11-1 am. Ck-out noon. Meeting rms. Concierge. Gift shop. Airport transportation. Exercise equipt; bicycles, rowers. Minibars. Complimentary wine tasting. Historic building; dramatic decor inspired by Oregon vineyards; winery theme throughout atrium lobby. Cr cds: A, C, D, DS, JCB, MC, V.

⬛D 🏋 ⛱ 🔥 SC

Inns

★ ★ **HERON HAUS.** 2545 NW Westover Rd (97210), in Nob Hill. 503/274-1846; FAX 503/243-1075. 5 rms, 3 story. S $85; D $125-$250; each addl $65. TV rm; cable. Pool. Complimentary continental bkfst, coffee, tea. Restaurant nearby. Ck-out noon, ck-in 4-6 pm. Restored house (1904) in NW hills overlooking city; library, morning rm. Totally nonsmoking. Cr cds: MC, V.

≈ ⛱ 🔥

★ ★ **JOHN PALMER HOUSE.** 4314 N Mississippi Ave (97217), north of downtown. 503/284-5893. 7 rms, 2 story, 2 suites. Some rm phones. May-Oct: S $30-$125; D, suites $85-$125; each addl $10; under 3 free; wkly rates; lower rates rest of yr. Crib free. Complimentary full bkfst. Dining rm 6-10 pm (Fri & Sat evenings). Ck-out 11 am, ck-in 2 pm. Bellhops. RR station, bus depot transportation. Whirlpool. Picnic tables. Built in 1890; completely furnished with antiques. Totally nonsmoking. Cr cds: A, DS, MC, V.

⛱ 🔥

★ ★ ★ **PORTLAND'S WHITE HOUSE.** 1914 NE 22nd Ave (97212), east of downtown. 503/287-7131; FAX 503/287-1152. 6 rms, 2 story. S $87-$103; D $96-$112; each addl $20; under 6 free. Crib free. TV avail. Complimentary full bkfst, tea/sherry. Complimentary coffee in rms. Restaurant nearby. Rm serv (bkfst). Ck-out 11 am, ck-in 2 pm. Bellhops. Street parking. Free airport, RR station, bus depot transportation. Game rm. Some balconies. White Federal-style mansion with Greek columns and fountain at entrance. Ballroom; antique stained-glass windows. Totally nonsmoking. Cr cds: MC, V.

⛱ 🔥

Restaurants

★ ★ **ALESSANDRO'S.** 301 SW Morrison, downtown. 503/222-3900. Hrs: 11:30 am-10 pm; Sat to 5 pm. Closed major hols. Res required. Italian menu. Bar. Semi-a la carte: lunch $5.50-$9.95, dinner $8.50-$19.95. Complete meals: dinner $27.50. Specializes in Roman-style Italian seafood, poultry, veal. Entertainment. Parking. Cr cds: A, MC, V.

⬛D

✔ ★ **ALEXIS.** 215 W Burnside, in Old Town. 503/224-8577. Hrs: 11:30 am-2 pm, 5-10 pm; Fri to 11 pm; Sat 5-11 pm; Sun 4:30-9 pm. Closed major hols. Greek menu. Bar. Semi-a la carte: lunch $5.95-$8.95, dinner $8.95-$13.95. Specialties: deep fried squid, eggplant casserole, grape leaves stuffed with ground lamb, lamb dishes. Belly dancers Fri, Sat. Greek decor. Cr cds: A, D, DS, MC, V.

★ **BLACK RABBIT.** (See McMenamins Edgefield) 503/492-3086. Hrs: 7 am-10 pm. Res accepted. Bar 11-1 am. Semi-a la carte: bkfst $3.75-$6.25, lunch $5.75-$9, dinner $9.50-$20. Child's meals. Specializes in fresh Northwestern cuisine. Parking. Outdoor dining. Totally nonsmoking. Cr cds: A, DS, MC, V.

⬛D

★ ★ **BUSH GARDEN.** 900 SW Morrison, downtown. 503/226-7181. Hrs: 11:30 am-1:45 pm, 5-9:45 pm; Sat to 1:45 pm; Sun 5-8:45 pm. Closed most major hols. Res accepted. Japanese menu. Bar to 12:45 am; Fri, Sat to l:45 am. Semi-a la carte: lunch $5.75-$11.95, dinner $10.50-$24.95. Specializes in sashimi, sukiyaki. Sushi bar. Karaoke singing. Parking. Dining in tatami rms. Cr cds: A, D, DS, JCB, MC, V.

⬛D

★ ★ **CAFE DES AMIS.** 1987 NW Kearney, west of downtown. 503/295-6487. Hrs: 5:30-10 pm. Closed Sun; major hols. Res accepted. Country French menu. Serv bar. Semi-a la carte: dinner $8-$24. Specializes in filet of beef with garlic & port sauce, fresh fish. Parking. Country French decor. Totally nonsmoking. Cr cds: A, MC, V.

⬛D

★ ★ **CHART HOUSE.** 5700 SW Terwilliger Blvd, west of downtown. 503/246-6963. Hrs: 11:30 am-2 pm, 5-10 pm; Sat from 5 pm; Sun 5-9 pm. Res accepted. Bar to midnight. Semi-a la carte: lunch $5-$13, dinner $15-$35. Child's meals. Specializes in prime rib, steak, fresh seafood. Valet parking. Fireplaces. 1,000 ft above Willamette River; panoramic view of Portland, Mt Hood and Mt St Helens. Cr cds: A, D, DS, MC, V.

⬛D

★ ★ **CODY'S CAFE.** 115 NW 22nd Ave, in Nob Hill. 503/248-9311. Hrs: 11 am-2:30 pm, 5:30-10 pm; Fri & Sat to 11 pm; Sun 5-10 pm. Closed Dec 24, 25. Res accepted. Mediterranean, Northwest menu. Bar. Semi-a la carte: lunch $5-$12, dinner $6-$17. Child's meals. Specialties: rotisserie chicken, turkey piccata. Parking. Show kitchen. Cr cds: A, MC, V.

⬛D

★ ★ ★ **COUCH STREET FISH HOUSE.** 105 NW 3rd Ave, just N of OR 30, in Old Town. 503/223-6173. Hrs: 5-10 pm; Fri to 11 pm; early-bird dinner 5-6:30 pm. Closed Sun; some major hols. Res accepted. Bar. Wine list. Semi-a la carte: dinner $12.95-$29.95. Specializes in Chinook salmon, live Maine lobster, Dungeness crab. Valet parking. Old San Francisco decor. Totally nonsmoking. Cr cds: A, C, D, DS, MC, V.

⬛D

✔ ★ **DAN & LOUIS OYSTER BAR.** 208 SW Ankeny St, in Old Town. 503/227-5906. Hrs: 11 am-11 pm; Nov-May to 10 pm. Closed some major hols. Semi-a la carte: lunch $2.50-$6.50, dinner $5.95-$11. Child's meals. Specializes in stewed, fried, pan-fried & raw oysters, variety of fresh seafood. Antique seafaring decor. Ship models. 19th-century bldg (1907). Family-owned. Cr cds: A, C, D, DS, MC, V.

SC

★★ **DELFINA'S.** *2112 NW Kearney St (97210).* 503/221-1195. Hrs: 11:30 am-2:30 pm, 5-11 pm; Sat & Sun from 5 pm. Closed July 4, Thanksgiving, Dec 25. Res accepted. Italian menu. Bar. Semi-a la carte: lunch $5-$10, dinner $10-$20. Specializes in seafood, pasta. Valet parking. Outdoor dining. Original artwork. Totally nonsmoking. Cr cds: A, D, DS, MC, V.

D

★★★ **ESPLANADE AT RIVERPLACE.** *(See Riverplace Hotel)* 503/228-3233. Hrs: 6:30 am-10:30 pm; Sat 6:30-11 am, 5:30-10:30 pm; Sun 6:30-10 am, 5:30-10 pm; Sun brunch 11 am-2:30 pm. Res accepted. Continental menu. Bar 11-1 am. Wine cellar. Semi-a la carte: bkfst $3.50-$10.50, lunch $5.75-$15, dinner $9-$22.50. Sun brunch $16.50. Child's meals. Specializes in salmon. Own pastries, desserts. Outdoor dining. Split-level dining; view of Willamette River & marina. Totally nonsmoking. Cr cds: A, C, D, DS, JCB, MC, V.

D

★★★ **GENOA.** *2832 SE Belmont St, east of downtown.* 503/238-1464. Hrs: 5:30-9:30 pm. Closed Sun; major hols. Res accepted. Northern Italian menu. Prix fixe: seven-course dinner $48. Specializes in foods of Northern Italy. Own baking. Menu changes every 2 wks. 200-yr-old Persian tapestry. Totally nonsmoking. Cr cds: A, C, D, DS, MC, V.

★★★ **HEATHMAN.** *(See Heathman Hotel)* 503/790-7752. Hrs: 6:30 am-11 pm. Res accepted. Bar 11-2 am. Wine cellar. Semi-a la carte: bkfst $4-$14, lunch $6-$15, dinner $13-$35. Specializes in Chinook salmon, Oregon lamb. Own baking. Entertainment. Valet parking. Outdoor dining. Built 1927. Formal decor. Cr cds: A, C, D, DS, ER, JCB, MC, V.

D

✔★ **HOLLAND GATEWAY.** *10805 NE Halsey, east of downtown.* 503/253-0079. Hrs: 6:30 am-9 pm; Sat from 7 am; Sun from 8 am. Closed most major hols. Wine, beer. Semi-a la carte: bkfst $2.50-$5.99, lunch, dinner $2.50-$9. Child's meals. Specializes in chicken pot pie, fish & chips, roast turkey, vegetable stir fry. Soup & salad bar. Parking. Family-owned. Totally nonsmoking. Cr cds: MC, V.

D **SC**

★ **HUBER'S.** *411 SW 3rd Ave, downtown.* 503/228-5686. Hrs: 11 am-midnight; Fri to 1 am. Closed Sun; major hols. Res accepted. Bar. Semi-a la carte: lunch $3.95-$9, dinner $6.50-$16. Specializes in turkey, seafood. Originally a saloon established in 1879 that became a restaurant during Prohibition. Arched stained-glass skylight, mahogany paneling and terrazzo floor. Cr cds: A, D, DS, MC, V.

★★ **JAKE'S FAMOUS CRAWFISH.** *401 SW 12th Ave, downtown.* 503/226-1419. Hrs: 11:30 am-11 pm; Fri to midnight; Sat 5 pm-midnight; Sun 5-10 pm. Closed July 4, Thanksgiving, Dec 25. Res accepted. Bar. Wine list. A la carte entrees: lunch $4.95-$10, dinner $8.95-$24.95. Specializes in fresh regional seafood. Own baking. Turn-of-the-century decor. Cr cds: A, C, D, DS, MC, V.

D

★★★ **L'AUBERGE.** *2601 NW Vaughn, west of downtown.* 503/223-3302. Hrs: 5 pm-midnight; Fri, Sat to 1 am. Closed most major hols. Res accepted. Bar. Wine list. Complete meals: dinner $20-$44. Specializes in seafood, steak, lamb. Own baking. Parking. Tri-level dining; wall hangings, 2 fireplaces. Family-owned. Cr cds: A, C, D, DS, MC, V.

★★★ **LONDON GRILL.** *(See The Benson)* 503/295-4110. Hrs: 6:30 am-2 pm, 5-10 pm; Sat & Sun to 11 pm; early-bird dinner Mon-Fri 5-7 pm; Sun brunch from 9:30 am. Res accepted. German, Amer menu. Bar 11-2 am. Wine cellar. Semi-a la carte: bkfst $7.95-$8.95, lunch $12-$13, dinner $19.95-$25. Sun brunch $17.50. Specializes in North-west salmon, Caesar salad. Harpist, pianist Tues-Sat. Valet parking. Elegant dining in historic hotel. Jacket (dinner). Cr cds: A, C, D, DS, ER, JCB, MC, V.

D

★★ **MANDARIN COVE.** *111 SW Columbia, downtown.* 503/222-0006. Hrs: 11 am-2 pm, 4:30-10 pm; Sat noon-11 pm; Sun 4-10 pm. Res accepted. Mandarin, Chinese menu. Bar. Semi-a la carte: lunch $4.95-$6.50, dinner $6.50-$19. Specializes in Hunan and Szechwan meats and seafood. Valet parking. Cr cds: A, D, MC, V.

D

★★ **MATTERHORN.** *3 NE 82nd Ave, at E Burnside, east of downtown.* 503/255-4218. Hrs: 11:30 am-10 pm; Fri, Sat to 11 pm; Sun & hols noon-9 pm. Res accepted. Swiss, German, Amer menu. Bar. Semi-a la carte: lunch $5.50-$8.25, dinner $9.95-$14.95. Child's meals. Specializes in Swiss & German dishes, fresh seafood, steak. Entertainment Wed-Sun; dancing Sat. Parking. Alpine decor. Family-owned. Cr cds: A, DS, MC, V.

✔★★ **MAZZI'S ITALIAN-SICILIAN FOOD.** *5833 SW Macadam Ave, west of downtown.* 503/227-3382. Hrs: 11:30 am-11 pm; Fri to midnight; Sat 5 pm-midnight; Sun 5-11 pm. Closed Thanksgiving, Dec 24, 25. Italian menu. Bar. Semi-a la carte: lunch $2.50-$7.50, dinner $5.50-$14.50. Specializes in fresh seafood, calzone, homemade pasta, pizza. Salad bar (lunch). Parking. Mediterranean decor; fireplaces. Cr cds: A, MC, V.

✔★ **OLD SPAGHETTI FACTORY.** *0715 SW Bancroft, west of downtown.* 503/222-5375. Hrs: 11:30 am-2 pm, 5-10 pm; Fri to 11 pm; Sat 1-11 pm; Sun noon-10 pm. Closed Thanksgiving, Dec 24-25. Italian menu. Bar. Semi-a la carte: lunch $3.25-$5.45, dinner $4.25-$8.10. Child's meals. Specializes in pasta. Own sauces. Parking. 1890s decor; dining in trolley car. Family-owned. Cr cds: DS, MC, V.

D

★★★ **PAZZO RISTORANTE.** *(See Vintage Plaza Hotel)* 503/228-1515. Hrs: 7 am-10 pm; Fri, Sat 8 am-11 pm; Sun 8 am-10 pm. Closed Dec 25. Res accepted. Italian menu. Bar noon-1 am. Wine cellar. A la carte entrees: bkfst $3.50-$6.25, lunch $8-$14, dinner $9-$16. Specializes in hardwood-grilled seafood, meat, fowl, gourmet pizza. Own bread, pasta. Outdoor dining. Italian marble floors, mahogany bar; also dining in wine cellar. Cr cds: A, C, D, DS, ER, JCB, MC, V.

D

★★★ **PLAINFIELD'S MAYUR.** *852 SW 21st Ave, west of downtown.* 503/223-2995. Hrs: 5:30-10 pm. Closed Thanksgiving, Dec 25. Res accepted. East Indian menu. Serv bar. A la carte entrees: dinner $5.50-$15.95. Specialties: spiced lamb, lobster & spices, prawns, hot & sour pork loin. Own baking. Parking. Patio dining. In 1901, shingle-style mansion; centerpiece of dining room is functioning Indian clay oven (tandoor). Cr cds: A, DS, MC, V.

★ **POOR RICHARD'S.** *3907 NE Broadway, at Sandy Blvd, east of downtown.* 503/288-5285. Hrs: 11:30 am-10 pm; Fri to 11 pm; Sat 4-11 pm; Sun noon-9 pm. Closed most major hols. Res accepted. Bar. Semi-a la carte: lunch $4.75-$7.50, dinner $8.25-$19.95. Child's meals. Specializes in steak, seafood. Parking. Colonial decor; fireplace. Family-owned. Cr cds: A, DS, MC, V.

★★ **RAFATI'S.** *25 SW Salmon, downtown.* 503/248-9305. Hrs: 11:30 am-2 pm, 5:30-9 pm; Fri, Sat to 10:30 pm. Closed Sun; major hols. Res accepted. Bar. Northwestern cuisine. Semi-a la carte: lunch $5.75-$9.95, dinner $13.75-$18.75. Child's meals. Specializes in steak, seafood broiled over mesquite charcoal. Pianist Wed-Sat. Parking. Outdoor dining Fri, Sat in summer. View of river. Cr cds: A, D, JCB, MC, V.

★ ★ **RHEINLANDER.** *5035 NE Sandy Blvd, east of downtown. 503/288-5503.* Hrs: 11:30 am-10 pm; Sat to 11 pm; Sun 10 am-9 pm; early-bird dinner 4-6 pm; Sun brunch to 2 pm. Closed Labor Day, Dec 24, 25. Res accepted. German menu. Bar. Semi-a la carte: dinner $3.95-$16. Sun brunch $8.95. Child's meals. Specialties: hasenpfeffer, schnitzel, sauerbraten. Strolling accordionist; group singing. Parking. Family-owned. Cr cds: A, MC, V.

[D]

★ ★ **RINGSIDE.** *2165 W Burnside St, west of downtown. 503/223-1513.* Hrs: 5 pm-midnight; Sun 4-11 pm. Closed major hols. Res accepted. Bar. Semi-a la carte: dinner $11.50-$34. Specializes in steak, prime rib, seafood. Valet parking. Fireplace. Prizefight pictures; sports decor. Family-owned. Cr cds: A, D, DS, MC, V.

★ ★ **RINGSIDE EAST.** *14021 NE Glisan, east of downtown. 503/255-0750.* Hrs: 11:30 am-2:30 pm, 5 pm-midnight; Sat, Sun from 5 pm. Closed most major hols. Res accepted. Bar. Semi-a la carte: lunch $4.50-$10.50, dinner $10.50-$36.75. Specializes in prime rib, steak, seafood. Parking. Cr cds: A, C, D, DS, MC, V.

[D]

★ ★ ★ **RIVER QUEEN.** *1300 NW Front Ave, between Broadway & Fremont bridges, just off W end of Broadway Bridge, downtown. 503/228-8633.* Hrs: 11 am-9:30 pm; Fri & Sat to 11 pm; Sun 4-9:30 pm. Closed major hols. Res accepted. Bar; Fri, Sat to midnight. Semi-a la carte: lunch $4.50-$11.50, dinner $6.50-$18. Child's meals. Specializes in steak, seafood. Parking. Converted ferryboat on Willamette River. Family-owned. Cr cds: A, C, D, MC, V.

[D]

★ ★ **SALTY'S ON THE COLUMBIA.** *3839 NE Marine Dr, east of downtown. 503/288-4444; FAX 503/288-3426.* Hrs: 11 am-midnight; Fri & Sat 5-10 pm; Sun 4:30-9 pm; Sun brunch 9:30 am-2 pm. Closed Dec 25. Res accepted. Bar. Semi-a la carte: lunch $6.95-$14.95, dinner $14-$30. Sun brunch buffet $8.95-$13.95. Child's meals. Specializes in seafood, halibut supreme, blackened salmon. Parking. Outdoor dining. Overlooks Columbia River. Cr cds: A, D, DS, MC, V.

[D]

★ ★ **SAYLER'S OLD COUNTRY KITCHEN.** *10519 SE Stark, just E of I-205 Washington exit, east of downtown. 503/252-4171.* Hrs: 4-11 pm; Fri to midnight; Sat 3 pm-midnight; Sun noon-11 pm. Closed some major hols. Bar. Complete meals: dinner $8.95-$35. Child's meals. Specializes in steak, seafood, chicken. Parking. Family-owned. Cr cds: A, DS, MC, V.

[D] [SC]

✔ ★ ★ **SYLVIA'S.** *5115 NE Sandy Blvd, east of downtown. 503/288-6828.* Hrs: 4-10 pm; Fri & Sat to 11 pm. Closed Thanksgiving, Dec 24, 25. Res accepted; required for theater. Italian menu. Bar. Semi-a la carte: dinner $7.75-$14.50. Child's meals. Specializes in lasagne, fettucine Alfredo. Parking. Dinner theater adj. Family-owned. Cr cds: A, DS, MC, V.

[D]

✔ ★ **YANKEE POT ROAST.** *2839 NW St Helen's Rd, west of downtown. 503/223-1331.* Hrs: 11 am-8 pm; Fri to 9:30 pm; Sat 4-9 pm; Sun noon-8 pm. Closed Dec 25. Res accepted; required hols. Wine, beer. Semi-a la carte: lunch $2.95-$5.95. Complete meals: dinner $8.95. Child's meals. Specializes in Yankee pot roast, baked ham, chicken, whitefish. Parking. Cr cds: MC, V.

[D]

Unrated Dining Spots

KORGAN'S RESTAURANT & STRUDEL HOUSE. *1605 SE Bybee, east of downtown. 503/232-7711.* Hrs: 11 am-11 pm; Fri to midnight; Sat 9 am-midnight; Sun 9 am-11 pm; Sat, Sun brunch 9 am-4 pm. Closed Tues, Wed; July 4, Thanksgiving, Dec 24, 25. Res accepted. Continental menu. Wine, beer. A la carte entrees: lunch $3.65-$6.50. Semi-a la carte: dinner $7.95-$18.95. Sat, Sun brunch $3.25-$9.95. Specializes in European pastries, creamed soups, sandwiches. Parking. Outdoor dining. Cr cds: A, MC, V.

ORIGINAL PANCAKE HOUSE. *8601 SW 24th Ave, west of downtown. 503/246-9007.* Hrs: 7 am-3 pm. Closed Mon, Tues. Semi-a la carte: bkfst, lunch $5-$10. Serv charge $1.50. Specializes in omelettes, apple pancakes, cherry crêpes. Parking. Colonial decor. No cr cds accepted.

PAPA HAYDN. *5829 SE Milwaukie, east of downtown. 503/232-9440.* Hrs: 11:30 am-11 pm; Fri, Sat to midnight. Closed Sun, Mon; major hols. Continental menu. Wine, beer. Semi-a la carte: lunch $4.95-$6.95, dinner $6.95-$13.95. Specializes in European pastries, desserts. Outdoor dining. Cr cds: A, MC, V.

[D]

PERRY'S ON FREMONT. *2401 NE Fremont, east of downtown. 503/287-3655.* Hrs: 11 am-9 pm; Fri, Sat to 10 pm; Sun from noon. Closed most major hols. Beer. Semi-a la carte: lunch, dinner $4.50-$7.50. Child's meals. Specializes in desserts, fish & chips, soups. Outdoor dining. Murals. Totally nonsmoking. Cr cds: A, MC, V.

[D]

Rochester

Founded: 1803

Pop: 231,636

Elev: 515 feet

Time zone: Eastern

Area code: 716

Rochester is a thriving industrial and cultural center and the third largest city in New York State. Located on the Genesee River, near its outlet to Lake Ontario, the city is in the midst of rich fruit and truck-gardening country.

The completion of Rochester's section of the Erie Canal in 1823 marked the beginning of economic growth for the city. The flour milling business, based on the grain yield of the fertile Genesee River valley, blossomed with the coming of new means of transportation. Another important link with the rest of the United States was completed in 1837 with the arrival of the Tonawanda Railroad.

During the 1840s, with its newfound prosperity and accessibility, Rochester became a leading cultural center. Also during this time, many businesses were attracted to Rochester's growing economy. While flour milling continued as a major industry, such business enterprises as machine shops, boat yards, breweries, shoe and clothing manufacturing and carriage making developed rapidly. At the same time, the seed business began to flourish. By 1850, about 2,000 acres were in use as nurseries. Rochester was known as the Flower City, and its fine parks show the influence of this early industry. In 1866, the Vacuum Oil Company, a predecessor of Mobil Oil Corporation, was founded here.

Bausch & Lomb began as a small Rochester optical shop in 1853; in 1888, young George Eastman began the manufacture of photographic equipment; in 1906, the Haloid Company, renamed Xerox in 1961, was born in a loft above a shoe factory. Other important industries, including the production of optical equipment and precision instruments, also originated in Rochester.

Business

Rochester is a world leader in the manufacture of photographic, optical, dental, check-protecting, industrial fluid-mixing and gear-cutting equipment. The city also ranks high in the manufacture of office copiers, communications and electronics equipment, precision machinery, automotive products, and printing and lithography supplies. Perhaps the most famous, internationally known companies based in Rochester are Eastman Kodak and Bausch and Lomb.

The city is also in the center of a productive agricultural region. Rochester and Monroe County are a part of the Lake Ontario fruit belt, one of the largest apple and apple-processing areas in the nation.

Convention Facilities

The Riverside Convention Center has a main exhibit hall of 50,000 square feet. This area can be divided in half and has easy access for exhibit and equipment transport. The main exhibit hall can accommodate meetings of up to 6,500 people or food functions for more than 4,000. In addition, the center has 27,000 square feet of meeting and banquet space on its lower level, which can be subdivided into 22 different meeting rooms.

Rochester's War Memorial is a multipurpose facility, with an auditorium seating 10,000 for conventions or concerts, nearly 8,000 for hockey and 7,600 for basketball. The auditorium, also used for ice shows, circuses, exhibits and civic and promotional ventures, can seat up to 1,000 for banquets. A staff decorator is available to help with convention arrangements.

In the basement of the War Memorial is the Exhibit Hall, with 50,000 square feet of space. Meeting rooms can accommodate a total of 500 people and are flexible in size. Parking is convenient, with a connected 1,300-car covered garage, an 1,800-car parking ramp and nearly 3,000 spaces within a 2-block area in public and private lots.

The Dome Center also offers 50,000 square feet of meeting space in 2 buildings. Seating capacity is 5,600 persons, and banquet capacity is 2,000 persons.

Sports and Recreation

Sports fans will enjoy the Rochester Red Wings baseball team and the Rochester Americans hockey team.

Batavia Downs, 33 miles west of Rochester, has harness racing in March, April and August through December. For Thoroughbred racing, the Finger Lakes Racetrack season extends from April to November.

Rochester is the gateway to 7,000 square miles of lovely wooded land in the Finger Lakes region. The lakes—Canandaigua, Keuka, Seneca, Cayuga, Owasco and Skaneateles—offer boating, swimming and fishing.

Yacht races are held on Lake Ontario, Irondequoit Bay and Canandaigua Lake on summer weekends.

Bristol Mountain Ski Area, near Naples, is 45 minutes from Rochester. With one of the longest vertical drops of any ski area between the Adirondack and the Rocky mountains, the area has two triple and two double chairlifts, one rope tow and slopes for beginners through experts. Powder Mill Park has one rope tow, machine-made snow and a ski lodge. Other ski areas within one hour's drive are Brantling Hill, Frost Ridge and Swain.

Many lovely parks, such as Cobbs Hill, Durand-Eastman, Genesee Valley, Highland and Ellison, are within or near the city.

Rochester claims to have more bowlers per capita than any other city in the United States. Visiting bowlers will easily find excellent facilities.

An indoor ice skating rink in the Frank Ritter Memorial Arena is open from mid-June through late March. Skates can be rented.

Entertainment

Rochester also has a full complement of music and theater entertainment. The Rochester Philharmonic Orchestra presents concerts in various locations, including the Eastman Theatre and in summer at the Finger Lakes Perfoming Arts Center in Canandaigua.

Other musical groups include Rochester Chamber Orchestra, Eastman School of Music instrumental, choral and operatic groups, Rochester Oratorio Society, Opera Theater of Rochester and Rochester Theater Organ Society.

Dramas, musicals and comedies are performed by a number of theater companies including GeVa Theatre, Rochester's resident professional theater group.

Historical Areas

In 1872, Susan B. Anthony led 50 women to vote as a test of the 4th and 15th amendments. Today her house is open to the public.

Other historical sites are the Campbell-Whittlesey House and the Stone-Tolan House. The former, a Greek-revival house, was built in 1835 and has been authentically restored. The Stone-Tolan House (ca 1792) is a restored farmstead furnished with period artifacts, featuring craft exhibits in the barn.

At the Rochester Historical Society, exhibits of 18th- and 19th-century furniture, glass, china, musical instruments and early 19th-century portraits are on display.

Sightseeing

Highland Park houses a conservatory and the world's largest display of lilacs, with more than 1,200 bushes of over 500 varieties. The Lilac Festival occurs over 10 days in mid-May.

The Seneca Park Zoo has wildlife from all parts of the world. The zoo also has a free-flight bird room, a nocturnal animal display, reptile house and polar bear area.

Children will enjoy nearby Lollypop Farm, where they can get acquainted with the animals in a petting area.

The Rochester Museum and Science Center has exhibits on early civilization and American Indian life. There are life-size period rooms and shops of the 1790-1890 era. There are also geology, plant, bird and animal life displays. Also on the grounds are the Garden of Fragrance and the Strasenburgh Planetarium.

The George Eastman House, a 50-room mansion where Eastman lived from 1905 to 1932, houses the International Museum of Photography. The museum contains one of the largest collections of photographs, motion pictures and photographic equipment in the world. The exhibits span 150 years, from the earliest days of photography to the space programs. The museum's Dryden and Curtis theaters feature a wide variety of classic movies, silent films and special interest subjects.

Another interesting stop in nearby Mumford is the Genesee Country Village. The village is a restored 19th-century settlement consisting of over 50 buildings. All the buildings were moved from their original locations and range from simple log structures to a Greek-revival mansion. Many of the stores and village smith shops are operational, demonstrating various facets of pioneer life. Also here are the Gallery of Sporting Art and the Carriage Museum.

General References

Founded: 1803 Pop: 231,636 Elev: 515 feet Time zone: Eastern Area code: 716

Phone Numbers

POLICE & FIRE: 911
FBI: 546-2220
POISON CONTROL CENTER: 275-5151
TIME: 974-1616 WEATHER: 235-0240

Information Sources

Greater Rochester Visitors Association, 126 Andrews St, 14604; 546-3070.
Rochester Area Chamber of Commerce, 55 St Paul St, 14604; 454-2220.
Department of Parks and Recreation, 428-6755.

Transportation

AIRLINES: American; Continental; Delta; Mohawk; Northwest; United; USAir; and other commuter and regional airlines. For the most current airline schedules and information consult the *Official Airline Guide,* published twice monthly.
AIRPORT: Greater Rochester International Airport, 464-6000.
CAR RENTAL AGENCIES: (See Toll-Free Numbers) Avis 328-8800; Budget 436-9310; Dollar 235-0772; Hertz 328-3700; National 235-5400.
RAILROAD PASSENGER SERVICE: Amtrak 800/872-7245.

Newspapers

Democrat & Chronicle; Times-Union; Daily Record.

Convention Facilities

Dome Center, E Henrietta Rd, 334-4000.
Rochester Riverside Convention Center, 123 Main St E, 232-7200.
Rochester Community War Memorial, 100 Exchange St at Broad St, 546-2030.

Sports & Recreation

Major Sports Facilities

Rochester Community War Memorial, 100 Exchange St, 546-2030 (Rochester Americans, hockey, 454-5335).
Silver Stadium, 500 Norton (Rochester Red Wings, baseball, 467-3000).

Racetracks

Batavia Downs, Park Rd, on NY 5, 63, Batavia, 343-3750 (harness racing).
Finger Lakes Racetrack, at NY 96 & NY 332, Farmington, 924-3232.

Cultural Facilities

Theaters

Auditorium Theatre, 875 Main St E, 454-7743.
GeVa Theatre, 75 Woodbury Blvd, 232-1363.

Concert Hall

Eastman Theatre, 26 Gibbs St, 222-5000.

Museums

Memorial Art Gallery of the University of Rochester, 500 University Ave, 473-7720.
Rochester Museum and Science Center, 657 East Ave at Goodman St, 271-4320.
Strong Museum, One Manhattan Square, 263-2700.
Victorian Doll Museum, 4332 Buffalo Rd, North Chili, 247-0130.

Points of Interest

Historical

Campbell-Whittlesey House, 123 S Fitzhugh St at Troup St, 546-7029.

George Eastman House, 900 East Ave, 271-3361.
Rochester Historical Society, 485 East Ave, 271-2705.
Stone-Tolan House, 2370 East Ave, 4 mi SE off I-490 in Brighton, 442-4606.
Susan B. Anthony House, 17 Madison St, 235-6124.

Other Attractions

Bristol Mountain Ski Area, South Bristol, 374-6000.
Genesee Country Village, 20 mi SW via NY 36, Flint Hill Rd in Mumford, 538-6822.
Highland Park, Highland Ave, 244-8079.

Lollypop Farm Petting Zoo, NY 31E at Victor Rd in Fairport, 223-1330.
Seabreeze Amusement Park, 4600 Culver Rd at Irondeqoit Bay, 323-1900.
Seneca Park Zoo, 2222 St Paul St at jct NY 104, 266-6846.
Strasenburgh Planetarium, 657 East Ave, 442-7171.

Annual Events

Lilac Festival, Highland Park, Highland Ave. Mid-May.
Monroe County Fair, fairgrounds, E Henrietta & Calkins Rds, 334-4000. Late July-early Aug.

Lodgings and Food

Motels

★ ★ **COMFORT INN-WEST.** *1501 Ridge Rd W (14615).* 716/621-5700; FAX 716/621-8446. 83 rms, 5 story. S $51.95-$82.95; D $57.95-$82.95; each addl $5; under 18 free. Crib free. Pet accepted, some restrictions. TV. Continental bkfst. Restaurant nearby. Ck-out noon. Valet serv. Some in-rm whirlpools. Cr cds: A, C, D, DS, ER, JCB, MC, V.

D 🐾 🏊 🛜 🔥 SC

★ ★ **COURTYARD BY MARRIOTT.** *33 Corporate Woods (14623).* 716/292-1000; FAX 716/292-0905. 149 rms, 2 story. S $86; D $96; each addl $10; suites $99-$119; under 18 free; wkend rates. Crib free. TV; cable. Indoor pool; lifeguard. Complimentary coffee in rms. Restaurant 7 am-10 pm. Rm serv. Bar. Ck-out 1 pm. Coin lndry. Meeting rms. Sundries. Free airport transportation. Exercise equipt; weight machine, bicycles, whirlpool. Balconies. Cr cds: A, C, D, DS, MC, V.

D 🏊 ✈ 🛜 🔥 SC

★ ★ ★ **DEPOT INN.** *(31 N Main St, Pittsford 14534) Approx 10 mi S on NY 96.* 716/381-9900; res: 800/836-3376; FAX 716/381-2907. 101 rms, 3 story. S $61-$68; D $64-$75; each addl $7; under 12 free; wkend package avail. Crib free. TV; cable. Indoor pool. Restaurant 6:30-10 am, 11:30 am-2:30 pm, 5-10 pm; Sun 8 am-2:30 pm, 4:30-9:30 pm. Rm serv. Bar 4 pm-12:30 am; Fri & Sat to 2 am. Ck-out noon. Meeting rms. Guest lndry. Bellhops. Airport transportation. Exercise equipt; bicycle, treadmill. Some refrigerators. Cr cds: A, C, D, DS, MC, V.

🏊 🧍 🛜 🔥 SC

✔★ **DORKAT.** *3990 W Henrietta Rd (14623), I-90 exit 46.* 716/334-7000. 52 rms, 2 story. S $28.95-$35.95; D $35.95-$42.95; each addl $5. Pet accepted, some restrictions. TV; cable. Restaurant adj 6 am-7 pm. Ck-out 11 am. Cr cds: A, D, MC, V.

D 🐾 🛜 🔥

✔★ **ECONO LODGE.** *940 Jefferson Rd (14623).* 716/427-2700; FAX 716/427-8504. 102 rms, 3 story. S $37.95-$48.95; D $44.95-$57.95; each addl $5; suites $85-$95; under 18 free. Crib free. Pet accepted, some restrictions. TV; cable. Continental bkfst. Restaurant opp open 24 hrs. Ck-out 11 am. Coin lndry. Valet serv. Free airport transportation. Some in-rm whirlpools. Cr cds: A, C, D, MC, V.

D 🐾 🛜 🔥 SC

★ **ECONO LODGE-BROCKPORT.** *(Jct NY 19 & 31, Brockport 14420)* 716/637-3157; FAX 716/637-0434. 40 rms, 2 story. S $44-$48; D $53; each addl $5; kit. units $55; under 13 free. Crib $5. TV; cable. Heated pool. Playground. Complimentary continental bkfst. Restaurant nearby. Ck-out 11 am. Coin lndry. Cr cds: A, D, DS, MC, V.

D 🐾 🛜 🔥 SC

★ ★ **HAMPTON INN.** *717 E Henrietta Rd (14623).* 716/272-7800; FAX 716/272-1211. 113 rms, 5 story. S $66-$74; D $73-$78; under 18 free. Crib free. Pet accepted, some restrictions. TV; cable. Complimentary continental bkfst. Restaurant adj 7 am-midnight. Ck-out noon. Meeting rms. Valet serv. Cr cds: A, C, D, DS, ER, MC, V.

D 🐾 🛜 🔥 SC

★ ★ **HOWARD JOHNSON LODGE.** *3350 W Henrietta Rd (14623), I-90 exit 46.* 716/475-1661; FAX 716/475-1667. 96 rms, 2 story. S, D $50-$69; each addl $8; under 18 free; some wkend rates. Crib free. TV; cable. Pool; lifeguard. Complimentary coffee in lobby. Restaurant nearby. Ck-out 11 am. Meeting rms. Valet serv. Downhill ski 20 mi. Health club privileges. Private patios, balconies. Cr cds: A, C, D, DS, ER, JCB, MC, V.

D 🏊 🏊 🛜 🔥 SC

★ ★ **MARKETPLACE INN.** *800 Jefferson Rd (14623), I-390 exit 15.* 716/475-9190; res: 800/888-8102; FAX 716/424-2138. 144 rms, 3 story. S $59-$69; D $65-$75; each addl $6; under 18 free. Crib free. Pet accepted, some restrictions. TV; cable. Pool; poolside serv, lifeguard. Restaurants 6:30 am-midnight. Rm serv. Bar. Ck-out noon. Meeting rms. Free airport transportation. Health club privileges. Game rm. Cr cds: A, C, D, DS, JCB, MC, V.

🐾 🏊 🛜 🔥 SC

✔★ **MICROTEL.** *905 Lehigh Station Rd (14467), I-390 exit 12A.* 716/334-3400; res: 800/999-2005; FAX 716/334-5042. 99 rms, 2 story. S $36.95; D $40.95; under 18 free. Crib free. Pet accepted, some restrictions. TV; cable. Restaurant nearby. Ck-out noon. Cr cds: A, D, DS, MC, V.

D 🐾 🛜 🔥

★ ★ **RAMADA INN.** *1273 Chili Ave (14624), I-390 exit 19, near Greater Rochester Intl Airport.* 716/464-8800. 155 rms, 2 story. S $80; D $90; each addl $10; under 18 free; wkend rates. Crib free. TV. Pool; lifeguard. Playground. Restaurant 6 am-10 pm; Sat & Sun from 8 am. Rm serv. Bar. Ck-out noon. Meeting rms. Bellhops. Valet serv. Free airport transportation. Cr cds: A, C, D, DS, ER, JCB, MC, V.

D 🏊 ✈ 🛜 🔥 SC

✔★ **RED ROOF INN.** *4820 W Henrietta Rd (14467), I-90 exit 46.* 716/359-1100; FAX 716/359-1121. 108 rms, 2 story. S $39.99-$49.99; D $41.99-$65.99; each addl $8; under 18 free. Crib free. Pet accepted. TV; cable. Restaurant nearby. Ck-out noon. Cr cds: A, C, D, DS, MC, V.

D 🐾 🛜 🔥

★ ★ **RESIDENCE INN BY MARRIOTT.** *1300 Jefferson Rd (14623).* 716/272-8850; FAX 716/272-7822. 112 kit. suites, 2 story. S $108-$118; D $138-$158; under 12 free; wkly, monthly rates. Crib free. Pet accepted, some restrictions; $8 per day. TV; cable. Pool; whirlpool, lifeguard. Complimentary continental bkfst. Complimentary coffee in rms. Restaurant nearby. Ck-out noon. Coin lndry. Meeting rms. Sundries. Free airport transportation. Downhill ski 20 mi; x-country ski 1 mi. Health club privileges. Picnic tables, grills. Cr cds: A, C, D, DS, ER, JCB, MC, V.

D 🐾 🏊 🏊 🛜 🔥

★ **WELLESLEY INN NORTH.** *1635 W Ridge Rd (14615).* 716/621-2060; res: 800/444-8888; FAX 716/621-7102. 99 rms (2 with shower only), 4 story. Apr-Nov: S $44.95-$50.95; D $49.95-$59.95; each addl $5; under 18 free; higher rates some special events; lower rates rest of yr. Crib free. Pet accepted, some restrictions; $3. TV; cable. Complimentary coffee in rms. Complimentary continental bkfst. Restaurant adj 11 am-10 pm. Ck-out 11 am. Health club privileges. Some refrigerators. Cr cds: A, C, D, DS, MC, V.

D 🐾 🛜 🔥 SC

★ **WELLESLEY INN SOUTH.** *797 E Henrietta Rd (NY 15A) (14623).* 716/427-0130; FAX 716/427-0903. 98 rms, 4 story. S $43-$50; D $50-$60; each addl $5; suites $60-$85; under 18 free. Crib free. Pet accepted, some restrictions; $3. TV; cable, in-rm movies avail. Complimentary continental bkfst. Complimentary coffee in rms. Ck-out 11 am. Meeting rm. Sundries. Cr cds: A, C, D, DS, JCB, MC, V.

D 🐾 🛜 🔥 SC

Motor Hotels

★ ★ ★ **BROOKWOOD INN.** *(800 Pittsford-Victor Rd, Pittsford 14534) 11 mi E on I-490, Bushnell's Basin exit.* 716/248-9000; res: 800/426-9995; FAX 716/248-8569. 108 rms, 4 story. S $86; D $94; each addl $8; suites $135-$215; under 18 free; wkend rates. Crib free. TV; cable. Indoor pool; poolside serv, lifeguard. Restaurant 8 am-10 pm. Rm serv 6:30 am-midnight. Bar. Ck-out noon. Meeting rms. Bell-hops. Valet serv. Sundries. Downhill ski 20 mi. Exercise equipt; weights, bicycles, whirlpool, sauna. Bicycle path along Erie Canal; bike rentals. Cr cds: A, C, D, DS, MC, V.

⊡ ⛟ ≋ ✈ ⊠ 🔥 SC

★ ★ ★ **HOLIDAY INN AIRPORT.** *911 Brooks Ave (14624).* 716/328-6000; FAX 716/328-1012. 281 rms, 2 story. S $99-$119; D $109-$129; each addl $10; suites $150-$250; under 19 free. Crib free. Pet accepted, some restrictions. TV. Indoor pool; wading pool, life-guard. Restaurant 6 am-2 pm, 5-10 pm. Rm serv. Bar 11-2 am; enter-tainment. Ck-out noon. Coin lndry. Meeting rms. Bellhops. Concierge. Gift shop. Valet serv. Free airport, RR station, bus depot transportation. Exercise equipt; weight machine, treadmill, whirlpool, sauna. Cr cds: A, C, D, DS, JCB, MC, V.

⊡ ⛟ ≋ ✈ ✈ ⊠ 🔥 SC

★ ★ ★ **HOLIDAY INN-SOUTH.** *1111 Jefferson Rd (14623), at NY 15A;* I-390 exit 14. 716/475-1510; FAX 716/427-8673. 250 rms, 6 story. S $97-$107; D $107-$115; each addl $10; suites $190; under 19 free; package plans; wkend rates. Crib free. TV; cable. Indoor pool. Indoor playground. Restaurant 6:30 am-10 pm. Rm serv. Bar; entertain-ment. Ck-out noon. Meeting rms. Bellhops. Free airport transportation. Exercise equipt; weights, bicycles, whirlpool. Holidome. Game rm. Balconies. Cr cds: A, C, D, DS, MC, V.

⊡ ≋ ✈ ⊠ 🔥 SC

★ ★ ★ **MARRIOTT AIRPORT.** *1890 W Ridge Rd (14615).* 716/225-6880; FAX 716/225-8188. 210 rms, 7 story. S, D $79-$99; each addl $15; suites $185-$310; under 18 free; wkend rates. Crib free. Pet accepted, some restrictions. TV; cable. Indoor pool; poolside serv. Restaurant 6:30 am-11 pm. Rm serv. Bar 11-2 am, Sun from noon; dancing. Ck-out noon. Meeting rms. Bellhops. Valet serv. Concierge. Sundries. Free airport transportation. Exercise equipt; weight machine, bicycles, whirlpool, sauna. Cr cds: A, C, D, DS, ER, JCB, MC, V.

⊡ ⛟ ≋ ✈ ⊠ 🔥 SC

★ ★ ★ **MARRIOTT THRUWAY.** *Box 20551 (14602), 5257 W Henrietta Rd, 8 mi S on NY 15;* I-90 exit 46. 716/359-1800; FAX 716/359-1349. 307 rms, 5 story. S, D $95-$105; each addl $15; suites $275-$425; under 18 free; wkend rates. Crib free. TV; cable. 2 pools, 1 indoor; whirlpool, sauna, poolside serv, lifeguard. Complimentary cof-fee. Cafe 6:30 am-11 pm; Sun to 10 pm. Rm serv. Bar 11-2 am; entertainment, dancing. Ck-out noon. Convention facilities. Bellhops. Valet serv Mon-Fri. Sundries. Gift shop. Free airport transportation. Putting green. Tennis, golf privileges. Game rm. Some refrigerators. Some private patios. *LUXURY LEVEL.* 26 rms. S, D $105. Honor bar. Complimentary bkfst, refreshments, wine at ck-in. Cr cds: A, C, D, DS, ER, JCB, MC, V.

⊡ 🎾 ⛟ ≋ ✈ ⊠ 🔥 SC

★ ★ ★ **RADISSON.** *175 Jefferson Rd (14623), I-90 exit 46, adj Rochester Institute of Technology.* 716/475-1910; FAX 716/475-1910, ext. 199. 171 rms, 4 story. S $79-$109; D $89-$119; each addl $10; family, wkend rates. Crib free. Pet accepted, some restrictions. TV; cable. Indoor pool; sauna, poolside serv, lifeguard. Restaurant 6 am-10 pm. Rm serv. Bar 11-2 am; entertainment, dancing Fri, Sat. Ck-out noon. Meeting rms. Bellhops. Valet serv. Sundries. Free airport trans-portation. Game rm. Lawn games. Cr cds: A, C, D, DS, ER, JCB, MC, V.

⊡ ⛟ ≋ ✈ 🔥 SC

Hotels

★ ★ **HOLIDAY INN-GENESEE PLAZA.** *120 E Main St (14604).* 716/546-6400; FAX 716/546-3908. 466 rms, 15 story. S, D $93-$109; suites $125-$450; under 19 free. Crib free. Pet accepted, some restrictions. TV; cable. Heated pool; poolside serv. Restaurant 6:30 am-10 pm. Bar 11-2 am. Ck-out noon. Coin lndry. Convention facilities. Shopping arcade. Free airport, RR station, bus depot trans-portation. Some balconies. On river. Cr cds: A, C, D, DS, JCB, MC, V.

⊡ ⛟ ≋ ✈ 🔥 SC

★ ★ ★ **HYATT REGENCY.** *125 E Main St (14604).* 716/546-1234; FAX 716/546-6777. 337 rms, 25 story. S $89-$150; D $89-$165; each addl $25; suites $190-$390; under 18 free; wkly rates. Crib free. Parking garage $3. TV; cable. Indoor pool; poolside serv, lifeguard. Restaurant 6:30 am-10 pm. Rm serv 24 hrs. Bar 11:30-1:30 am; enter-tainment Tues-Sat. Ck-out noon. Convention facilities. Gift shop. Free airport transportation. Exercise rm; instructor, weights, bicycles, whirl-pool. Bathrm phones. Refrigerator, wet bar in suites. *LUXURY LEVEL : REGENCY CLUB.* 34 rms, 7 suites, 3 floors. S $175; D $190; suites $390-$1,000. Concierge. Private lounge, honor bar. Complimentary continental bkfst, refreshments, newspaper. Cr cds: A, C, D, DS, ER, JCB, MC, V.

⊡ ≋ ✈ ⊠ 🔥

★ ★ ★ **STRATHALLAN.** *550 East Ave (14607), I-490 Goodman St exit.* 716/461-5010; res: 800/678-7284; FAX 716/461-3387. 150 rms, 8-9 story. S, D, suites, kit. units $125-$165; under 18 free; wkend plans. Crib free. TV; cable. Complimentary coffee in rms. Restaurant 6:30 am-9:30 pm. Rm serv to midnight. Rooftop bar 5 pm-2 am; entertain-ment Tues-Sat. Ck-out 1 pm. Meeting rms. Concierge. Beauty shop. Free valet parking; underground for overnight guests. Free airport transportation. Exercise equipt; bicycles, rowing machine, sauna. So-larium. Game rm. Refrigerators. Many balconies. In sedate residential area. *LUXURY LEVEL :* 43 rms, 21 suites, 2 floors. Apr-mid-Nov: S $145; D $155; each addl $10; suites $295; lower rates rest of yr. Concierge. Private lounge, honor bar. Complimentary full bkfst. Com-plimentary refreshments, newspaper. Cr cds: A, C, D, DS, MC, V.

⊡ ✈ ⊠ 🔥 SC

Inns

★ ★ ★ **DARTMOUTH HOUSE.** *215 Dartmouth St (14607).* 716/271-7872. 4 rms, 2 story, 1 suite. S $45-$65; D $65-$85. Children over 12 yrs only. TV; also in sitting rm. Complimentary full bkfst. Complimentary coffee in rms. Rm serv. Ck-out 11 am, ck-in 3-6 pm. Free airport, RR station, bus depot transportation. Library/sitting rm. English Tudor house (1905); antiques, fireplace. Totally nonsmoking. Cr cds: A.

⊠

★ ★ ★ **GENESEE COUNTRY INN.** *(Box 340, 948 George St, Mumford 14511) 12 mi S via NY 383.* 716/538-2500; FAX 716/538-4565. 9 air-cooled rms, 2 story. S $80-$110; D $80-$125; each addl $10; 2-night min wkends. Closed Sun-Tues from Nov-May exc by arrangement. TV. Complimentary full bkfst, afternoon tea. Restaurant nearby; dinner pkgs avail. Ck-out noon, ck-in 3 pm. Meeting rm. Lawn games. Picnic table, grill. Restored inn (1830) on 8 wooded acres; spring-fed trout stream; waterfall. Antiques; fireplaces. Totally non-smoking. Cr cds: D, MC, V.

⊡ ⛟ ⊠ 🔥

★ ★ ★ **OLIVER LOUD'S.** *(1474 Marsh Rd, Pittsford 14534) I-490 E to Bushnell's Basin exit.* 716/248-5200; FAX 716/248-9970. 8 rms, 2 story. S $125; D $135-$145. Children over 12 yrs only. TV avail; cable. Complimentary continental bkfst in rms. Complimentary tea. Restaurant (see RICHARDSON'S CANAL HOUSE). Ck-out 11 am, ck-in 3 pm. On Erie Canal. Built 1812; stagecoach inn. Cr cds: A, C, D, MC, V.

⊡ ⊠ 🔥

Restaurants

★ ★ **ALFIE'S.** *5157 W Ridge Rd (14615).* 716/225-6880. Hrs: 6 am-2 pm, 4:30-10 pm; Fri & Sat to 11 pm; Sun brunch 11:30 am-2 pm. Res accepted Fri-Sun. Bar 11-2 am. Semi-a la carte: bkfst $1.95-$7.95, lunch $5.50-$7.95, dinner $8.95-$16.95. Sun brunch $11.95. Child's meals. Specialties: seafood Delamar, veal French. Salad bar. Parking. Split-level dining. Impressionist prints. Cr cds: A, C, D, DS, ER, MC, V.

⊡ SC

✔★ **BANGKOK.** *163 State St.* 716/325-3517. Hrs: 11 am-10 pm; Fri & Sat to 11 pm; Sun 4-9:30 pm. Closed Easter, Thanksgiving.

Res accepted Fri & Sat. Thai, Chinese menu. Wine, beer. Semi-a la carte: lunch $4.95-$5.25, dinner $6.50-$12.95. Specializes in vegetarian dishes, seafood, salt & pepper squid. Parking (dinner). Thai decor. Cr cds: A, MC, V.

D

★ ★ ★ **BRASSERIE.** *387 E Main St, at Eastman Place.* 716/232-3350. Hrs: 11:30 am-4:30 pm, 5:30-10:30 pm; Sat from 5:30 pm. Closed Sun; most major hols. Res accepted. Bar. Wine list. A la carte entrees: lunch $6-$10, dinner $16-$22. Specializes in fresh fish, Black Angus steak. Seasonal menu. Valet parking. Outdoor dining. 2 dining rms. Country French atmosphere. Cr cds: A, C, D, DS, MC, V.

D

✔★ **CAFE SAUSALITO.** *289 Alexander St.* 716/546-2095. Hrs: 11:30 am-2 pm, 4-10:30 pm; Fri to midnight; Sat 5-10 pm; Sun 5-9 pm. Res accepted. California menu. Bar. A la carte entrees: lunch, dinner $4-$13. Specializes in Cajun cuisine. Parking. Outdoor dining. Restored 1850s landmark building. Cr cds: A, MC, V.

★ ★ **CARTWRIGHT INN.** *(5691 W Henrietta Rd, W Henrietta)* I-90 exit 46. 716/334-4444. Hrs: 11:30 am-10 pm; Sun from 12:30 pm; early-bird dinner 4:30-6:30 pm. Res accepted. Bar to 2 am. Semi-a la carte: lunch $3.50-$5.95, dinner $6.95-$18.95. Child's meals. Specializes in New England clam chowder, prime rib, lobster. Parking. In former stagecoach stop; built 1831. Cr cds: A, C, D, DS, MC, V.

★ ★ ★ **CHAPEL'S.** *30 W Broad St.* 716/232-2300. Hrs: 11:30 am-2 pm, 5:30-9 pm; Fri, Sat 5:30-9:30 pm. Closed Sun, Mon; wk of July 4. Res accepted. French, Amer menu. Bar. Wine list. Semi-a la carte: lunch $1.95-$9.50, dinner $14.75-$24. Specializes in seasonal dishes. Own baking, ice creams, sorbets. Valet parking. In old city hall and jail (1873); historic artifacts. Cr cds: A, C, D, DS, MC, V.

D

✔★ **CREME DE LA CREME.** *295 Alexander St (14607).* 716/263-3580. Hrs: 11 am-midnight; Fri & Sat to 1 am. Closed Thanksgiving, Dec 25. Continental menu. Bar. Semi-a la carte: lunch, dinner $3.95-$7.95. Specializes in light bistro fare, European pastries, chicken Santa Fe. Outdoor dining. Continental tea room atmosphere. Cr cds: D, DS, MC, V.

★ ★ ★ **EDWARDS.** *13 S Fitzhugh.* 716/423-0140. Hrs: 11:30 am-2 pm, 5-9 pm; Fri & Sat 11:30 am-2 pm, 5-10 pm. Closed Sun; major hols. Res accepted. Continental menu. Bar. Wine cellar. Complete meals: lunch $3.50-$11.50, dinner $12.50-$23.50. Specializes in seafood, beef, wild game. Own baking. Pianist. Valet parking. Gourmet store on premises. Built 1873 as school; Edwardian decor. Cr cds: A, C, D, DS, MC, V.

D

★ ★ ★ **GLEN EDITH.** *(1078 Glen Edith Dr, Webster)* E on NY 104. 716/671-6200. Hrs: 5-10 pm; Sun from 4 pm. Closed Mon; also Nov-Mar. Semi-a la carte: dinner $9.95-$18.95. Child's meals. Specializes in prime rib, roast duckling, seafood. Own pastries. Parking. Overlooks Irondequoit Bay; boat dockage, outdoor patio. Family-owned. Cr cds: MC, V.

✔★ **GRISANTI'S.** *749 E Henrietta Rd.* 716/427-0744. Hrs: 11 am-10 pm; Fri, Sat to 11 pm; Sat and Sun 10 am-9 pm; Italian menu. Bar. Semi-a la carte: lunch, dinner $3.95-$13.95. Child's meals. Specializes in ravioli, seafood, pasta. Parking. Braille menu. Cr cds: A, D, DS, MC, V.

D

★ **HONG KONG.** *291 Alexander St.* 716/325-6121. Hrs: 11:30 am-11 pm; Fri, Sat to midnight; early-bird dinner Mon-Fri 4-6 pm. Closed Thanksgiving. Res accepted. Chinese, Amer menu. Bar. Semi-a la carte: lunch $3.95-$5.95, dinner $4.25-$15.95. Specialties: Szechwan beef with scallops, lemon chicken, seafood plate. Parking. Chinese decor. Cr cds: A, C, D, DS, MC, V.

★ ★ **OLIVE TREE.** *165 Monroe Ave.* 716/454-3510. Hrs: 11:30 am-2 pm, 5-9 pm; Sat from 5 pm. Closed Sun; Jan 1, Thanksgiv-

ing, Dec 25. Res accepted. Greek menu. Bar. Semi-a la carte: lunch $4-$7.50, dinner $11.50-$17.50. Specialties: seafood in filo, lamb, baklava. Parking. Outdoor dining. Restored dry goods store (1864). Cr cds: A, MC, V.

✔★ **RAJ MAHAL.** *324 Monroe Ave.* 716/546-2315. Hrs: 11:30 am-2:30 pm, 5-10 pm. Closed some major hols. Res accepted wkends. Indian menu. Bar. Buffet lunch $6.95. Semi-a la carte: dinner $6.95-$13.95. Specializes in tandoori and vegetarian dishes. Parking. Traditional Indian decor. Cr cds: A, C, D, MC, V.

D SC

★ ★ ★ **RICHARDSON'S CANAL HOUSE.** *(See Oliver Loud's Inn)* 716/248-5000. Hrs: 6-9 pm. Closed Sun; Jan 1, Dec 25. Res accepted. French, Amer menu. Bar 5-11 pm; Fri, Sat to midnight. Wine list. Complete meals: dinner $25-$32. Specializes in duckling, seafood, beef tenderloin. Own baking. Parking. Historic inn. Terrace overlooks Erie Canal. Cr cds: A, C, D, MC, V.

D

★ ★ ★ **THE RIO.** *282 Alexander St.* 716/473-2806. Hrs: 5-10 pm; early-bird dinner Mon-Fri 5-6:30 pm. Closed Sun; most major hols. Res accepted. Continental menu. Bar to midnight. Wine cellar. A la carte entrees: dinner $14.95-$24.95. Specialties: steak au poivre, veal di Medici, rack of lamb. Valet parking. Intimate dining. Curved stairway in entry hall; antiques. Cr cds: A, C, D, DS, MC, V.

★ ★ ★ **ROONEY'S.** *90 Henrietta St.* 716/442-0444. Hrs: 5-10 pm. Closed Thanksgiving, Dec 25. Res accepted. Continental menu. Bar from 5 pm. Wine list. Semi-a la carte: dinner $14-$21. Specializes in wood-grilled fish & game. Own baking. Parking. In tavern built 1860. Cr cds: D, DS, MC, V.

D

★ **SCOTCH 'N SIRLOIN.** *3450 Winton Place (14623).* 716/427-0808. Hrs: 5-10 pm; Fri & Sat to 11 pm. Closed Mon; most major hols. Res accepted. Bar. Semi-a la carte: dinner $9-$18. Child's meals. Specializes in steak, seafood. Salad bar. Parking. Old West decor; antiques. Cr cds: A, C, D, MC, V.

D SC

★ ★ ★ **SPRING HOUSE.** *3001 Monroe Ave.* 716/586-2300. Hrs: 11:30 am-3 pm, 5-9 pm; Fri, Sat to 10 pm; Sun noon-9 pm. Closed Mon; Labor Day, Dec 25. Res accepted. Bar to 2 am. Semi-a la carte: lunch $4.95-$7.95, dinner $11.50-$16.95. Child's meals. Specialties: chicken Ketchikan, veal moutard, lobster thermidore. Own baking. Parking. Outdoor dining. Colonial landmark, Erie Canal inn. Family-owned since 1959. Cr cds: A, D, MC, V.

D

★ **TOKYO JAPANESE.** *2930 W Henrietta Rd.* 716/424-4166. Hrs: 11:30 am-10 pm; Fri & Sat to 11 pm; Sun 4-10 pm; early-bird dinner Sun-Thurs 4-6 pm. Closed Thanksgiving. Res accepted. Japanese menu. Bar. Semi-a la carte: lunch $4.95-$9.95, dinner $7.95-$21.95. Child's meals. Specializes in sushi and hibachi dishes. Parking. Traditional decor. Cr cds: A, MC, V.

D SC

✔★ **VILLAGE COAL TOWER.** *(9 Schoen Place, Pittsford 14534)* Approx 10 mi S on NY 96. 716/381-7866. Hrs: 7 am-8 pm; wkends from 8 am. Closed some major hols. Semi-a la carte: bkfst $2-$4, lunch $2-$5, dinner $4-$6. Child's meals. Specializes in hamburgers, chicken. Parking. Outdoor dining. In turn-of-the-century coal storage structure used to service boats on Erie canal. No cr cds accepted.

D SC

★ ★ **WATER STREET GRILL.** *175 N Water St.* 716/546-4980. Hrs: 11:30 am-3 pm, 5-11 pm. Closed Sun; major hols. Res accepted. Bar. Semi-a la carte: lunch $2.50-$9, dinner $12.50-$23.95.

Specializes in steak, pasta, fresh fish. Pianist Fri & Sat. Valet parking. Outdoor dining. Casually chic atmosphere. Cr cds: A, C, D, MC, V.

D

Unrated Dining Spots

CAPTAIN TONY'S PIZZA. *721 Monroe Ave. 716/442-8540.* Hrs: 11 am-midnight; Fri, Sat to 1 am. Closed Easter, Thanksgiving, Dec 25. Italian menu. A la carte entrees: lunch, dinner $3.25-$14.95. Specializes in pizza, sub sandwiches, chicken wings. Pizza parlor with bench seating. Family-owned. Totally nonsmoking. Cr cds: MC, V.

TIVOLI PASTRY SHOP. *688 Park Ave. 716/461-4502.* Hrs: 11 am-11 pm; Fri to midnight; Sat 10 am-midnight; Sun 10 am-11 pm. Closed Dec 25. A la carte entrees: $1-$3.25. Specializes in frozen yogurt, ice cream, bakery items. Outdoor dining. Some antiques. Murals of Venice. No cr cds accepted.

St Louis

Settled: 1764

Pop: 396,685

Elev: 470 feet

Time zone: Central

Area code: 314

One of the oldest settlements in the Mississippi Valley, St Louis was founded as a fur-trading post and named for Louis IX of France. In 1804 the United States annexed the area as part of the Louisiana Purchase, and in 1820 Missouri's first constitutional convention was held in the city.

St Louis played an important role in the westward expansion of the United States. Lewis and Clark set off on their expeditions from this area, and many traders, adventurers, scouts and pioneers passed through on their way west. Steamboats docked here on their way up and down the Mississippi; railroads helped to stimulate trade between the Southwest and the East. The arrival of many German immigrants swelled the population, which had reached more than 160,000 by 1860. During the Civil War, though its residents were divided in sympathy, the city was a base of Union operations. Growth continued after the war, and by 1870 the city was the third largest in the nation.

For more than 200 years St Louis has been the dominant city in the state. It is distinguished by wealth, grace and culture, as well as solid and diversified industry. The huge, gleaming stainless-steel Gateway Arch, the symbol of the westward expansion, today casts its shadow over St Louis and provides a landmark for this Midwestern metropolis.

Business

Some 2,000 plants in St Louis produce more than $4 billion worth of goods annually. Approximately half of the area's labor force is employed in industry.

St Louis is one of the world's largest markets for wool, lumber and pharmaceuticals and is an important producer of beer, chemicals and transportation equipment. Other major products of the area include food and food products, aircraft, barges and towboats. Anheuser-Busch, one of the world's largest beer producers, has its headquarters here, as do Ralston Purina, Monsanto, General Dynamics and other major companies. McDonnell Douglas, one of the area's largest employers, continues to play an important role in the city's economy.

A principal grain and hog center, St Louis is also the only industrial area in the country producing six basic metals: iron, lead, zinc, copper, aluminum and magnesium. The city is the financial center of the central Mississippi Valley, and its location has helped it become prominent as a railroad and trucking transportation center.

Convention Facilities

The A.J. Cervantes Convention and Exhibition Center covers 4 city blocks within the 16-block Convention Plaza area. The exhibit area contains 240,000 square feet of space, which is convertible to 3 smaller, self-contained, soundproof units of approximately 80,000 square feet each. An additional 85,000 square feet can be converted into 52 separate meeting rooms. A permanent full-service kitchen can serve banquets for 5,000 people. In the heart of the downtown area, the center is within walking distance of 6,000 hotel rooms and within a 3-mile drive of 2,100 more. Lambert-St Louis International Airport is a 20-minute drive away, and 4 interstate highways leading into St Louis are just blocks from the center.

Sports and Recreation

St Louis' Busch Stadium, home of the Cardinals, seats 54,000 for baseball. The Arena hosts the Blues hockey team as well as Ambush home soccer games and college basketball games.

Six Flags Over Mid-America, southwest of the city, is a 200-acre entertainment park with more than 100 different rides, shows and attractions, including the Screamin' Eagle roller coaster.

Grant's Farm, operated by Anheuser-Busch Company, preserves a 281-acre tract once owned by Ulysses S. Grant. A section of the farm is an open range where buffalo, deer and elk roam. A train carries visitors through the game preserve to the miniature zoo and bird show. Also on the property is the cabin where Ulysses S. Grant, the 18th president, once lived.

Entertainment

The St Louis Symphony Orchestra is the second-oldest symphony in the nation. Its regular season runs from mid-September to June; in the summer, the symphony performs pop concerts at Edgar M. Queeny Park.

Also during the summer months, the Muny Opera performs light opera and musical comedy nightly in a 12,000-seat outdoor theater in Forest Park.

Broadway plays are presented frequently at the Fox Theatre and the Westport Playhouse, and first-rate productions can be seen on local college campuses. The Repertory Theatre of St Louis presents dramas, children's theater, mime artists, touring programs and a theater fun fair.

Bars and bistros along St Louis' riverfront are alive with the sound of authentic Dixieland jazz.

Historical Areas

The Old Courthouse at Fourth and Market streets contains exhibits on the Louisiana Purchase and St Louis. This 19th-century building was the scene of slave auctions and of the historic Dred Scott trial. Murals on St Louis history decorate the walls and interior of the cast-iron dome. The Old Cathedral at Second and Walnut streets, St Louis' earliest church, was completed in 1831.

Laclede's Landing, nine blocks along the north edge of the riverfront, is a renovated 1850s commercial district with specialty shops and restaurants. In addition, several 19th-century houses in the city have been preserved and furnished with period pieces or historical

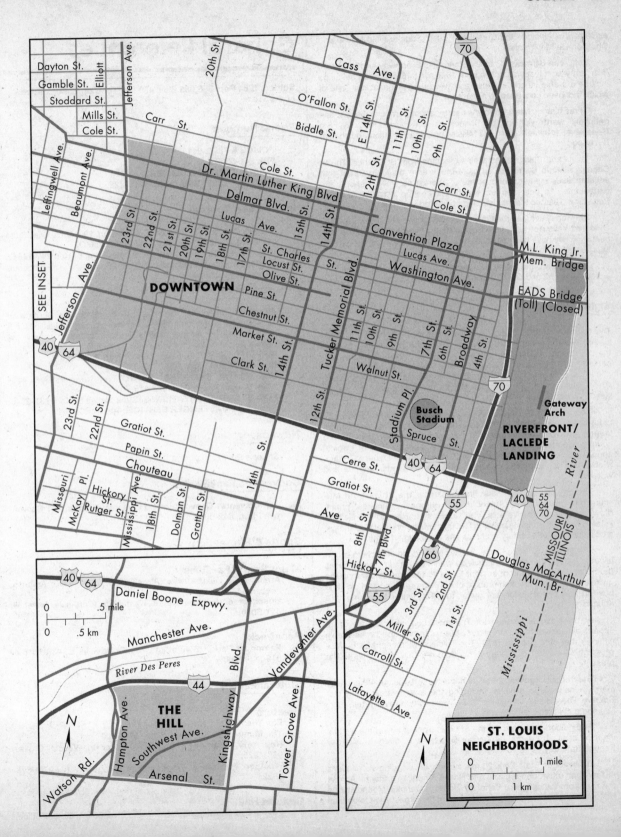

Dayton St.
Gamble St.
Stoddard St.
Mills St.
Cole St.
Jefferson Ave.
Elliott
Leffingwell Ave.
Beaumont Ave.

Cass   Ave.
O'Fallon St.
Biddle St.
Carr   St.
Cole St.
Dr. Martin Luther King Blvd.
Delmar Blvd.

20th St.
E 14th St.
12th St.
11th St.
10th St.
9th St.

Carr St.
Cole St.

Convention Plaza

Lucas Ave.
Washington Ave.

DOWNTOWN

23rd St.
22nd St.
21st St.
20th St.
19th St.
18th St.
17th St.

Lucas   Ave.
St. Charles
Locust St.
Olive St.
Pine St.
Chestnut St.
Market St.
Clark St.

15th St.
14th St.

St.
Tucker Memorial Blvd.
11th St.
10th St.
9th St.
7th St.
6th St.
Broadway
4th St.

14th St.
12th St.
St.

Walnut St.
Stadium Pl.

Spruce
St.

**Busch
Stadium**

M.L. King Jr.
Mem. Bridge

EADS Bridge
(Toll) (Closed)

**Gateway
Arch**

**RIVERFRONT/
LACLEDE
LANDING**

River

Jefferson Ave.

SEE INSET

Jefferson

23rd St.
22nd St.

Gratiot St.
Papin St.
Chouteau

Missouri
Pl.
Hickory
St.
Rutger St.
McKay

Mississippi Ave.
18th St.
Dolman St.
Grattan St.
14th
St.

Cerre St.
Gratiot St.

Ave.
St.

8th
St.
Hickory St.
7th Blvd.

3rd St.
2nd St.
1st St.
Miller St.
Carroll St.
Lafayette   Ave.

Douglas MacArthur
Mun.l Br.

MISSOURI
ILLINOIS

Mississippi

Daniel Boone Expwy.

Manchester Ave.

River Des Peres

**THE
HILL**

Watson Rd.
Hampton Ave.
Southwest Ave.
Arsenal   St.
Kingshighway   Blvd.
Vandeventer Ave.
Tower Grove Ave.

0   .5 mile
0   .5 km

N

**ST. LOUIS
NEIGHBORHOODS**

0   1 mile
0   1 km

N

exhibits. They include the Campbell House, Eugene Field House and Chatillon-De Menil House.

Jefferson Barracks Historical Park, at S Broadway and Kingston, is an army post that was active from 1826 to 1946. Restored buildings include a stable laborer's house and two powder magazines, one of which has been converted to a museum.

Three historic Missouri towns nearby are of particular interest and definitely worth visiting: St Charles, northwest of the city, Ste Genevieve, southeast along the Mississippi, and Florissant, north near the airport.

Lewis and Clark started their expedition from St Charles. The St Charles Historic District is an eight-block area on Main Street that encompasses many historic points of interest as well as shops and restaurants. An entire street, which has been put on the National Register of Historic Places, is being converted to a mall.

Ste Genevieve was the first permanent settlement in Missouri. The Guibourd-Valle House and the Bolduc House were built in the late 18th century. They have been carefully restored and contain period furnishings.

In Florissant are many restored Victorian buildings, as well as antique and arts and crafts shops housed in 19th-century structures.

Sightseeing

The Gateway Arch (Jefferson National Expansion Memorial), a stainless-steel structure that soars 630 feet above the St Louis riverfront, is the city's most recognized landmark. The arch honors westward expansion, and the museum located beneath the arch illustrates St Louis' role in the movement to the West. Excursion boats on the Mississippi, which operate during the summer months, provide a pleasant way to view St Louis and its environs.

The Missouri Botanical Garden contains more than 75 acres of nature trails and botanical exhibits. The Climatron, a two-level, transparent, geodesic dome, was the first geodesic greenhouse in the country. Complete climate control allows a great number of tropical and subtropical plants to be exhibited. The garden's Japanese Garden, "Seiwa-En," is complete with teahouse, lake, islands, bridges and waterfall.

The city also boasts many fine museums. The St Louis Art Museum has collections of American and European paintings, prints, drawings and decorative arts. The Cupples House and Art Gallery, located in a Romanesque building (1890), contains original furnishings, a collection of 20th-century graphics and changing art exhibits.

The St Louis Science Center houses a multitude of exciting exhibits and displays. The National Bowling Hall of Fame and Museum traces the history of bowling from ancient Egypt to the present. Among the museum's features are memorabilia of bowling greats and an old-time bowling alley where visitors are invited to roll 90-year-old bowling balls at hand-set pins.

At the National Museum of Transportation, visitors may climb aboard old locomotives, streetcars, buses, trucks and horse-drawn vehicles that date back to 1870. The Soldiers' Memorial Military Museum offers exhibits of military items from pre-Civil War times to the present.

The St Louis Zoological Park is home to more than 3,400 animals, many in naturalistic exhibits, including the award-winning Big Cat Country. There is also an aquatic house, walk-through aviary, herpetarium and a children's petting zoo.

Free guided tours through the St Louis plant of one of the world's largest beer breweries—Anheuser-Busch—are offered Monday through Saturday.

At Mastodon State Park, 20 miles south, are ongoing excavations of American mastodon remains and Native American artifacts. Across the river from the city, near Cahokia, Illinois, is Cahokia Mounds State Historic Site. Preserved here are the ruins of the largest pre-Columbian community in the Mississippi River valley.

General References

Settled: 1764 **Pop:** 396,685 **Elev:** 470 feet **Time zone:** Central **Area code:** 314

Phone Numbers

POLICE & FIRE: 911
FBI: 241-5357
POISON CONTROL CENTER: 772-5200
TIME: 321-2522   **WEATHER:** 321-2222

Information Sources

St Louis Convention & Visitors Commission, 10 S Broadway, Suite 1000, 63102; 421-1023, 800/325-7962 (exc MO).
St Louis Visitors Center, 308 Washington Ave, 63102; 241-1764.
Tourist Information, (recording) 421-2100.

Transportation

AIRLINES: American; Continental; Delta; Northwest; Southwest; TWA; United; USAir; and other commuter and regional airlines. For the most current airlines schedules and information consult the *Official Airline Guide,* published twice monthly.
AIRPORT: Lambert-St Louis International, 426-8000.
BUS TERMINAL: 231-7800.
CAR RENTAL AGENCIES: (See Toll-Free Numbers) Avis 426-7766; Budget 423-3000; Hertz 426-7555.
PUBLIC TRANSPORTATION: Bi-State Transit System 231-2345.
RAILROAD PASSENGER SERVICE: Amtrak 800/872-7245.

Newspaper

St Louis Post-Dispatch.

Convention Facility

A.J. Cervantes Convention and Exhibition Center, 801 Convention Plaza, 342-5036.

Sports & Recreation

Major Sports Facilities
Arena, 5700 Oakland Ave (Blues, hockey, 781-5300; Ambush, soccer, 647-1001).
Busch Stadium, Broadway & Walnut Sts (Cardinals, baseball, 421-3060).

Racetrack
Fairmount Park, US 40 at jct I-255, Collinsville, IL, 436-1516 or 618/345-4300.

Cultural Facilities

Theaters
Fox Theatre, 527 N Grand, 534-1678.
The Muny (outdoor), Forest Park, 361-1900.
Repertory Theatre of St Louis, 130 Edgar Rd, Webster Groves, 968-4925.
Westport Playhouse, Westport Plaza, Page Ave & I-270, 878-3322.

Concert Hall
Powell Symphony Hall, 718 N Grand Blvd, 534-1700 (box office).

Museums

History Musuem-Missouri Historical Society, Forest Park, Lindell Blvd & DeBaliviere Ave, 746-4599.
The Magic House, 516 S Kirkwood Rd, Kirkwood, 822-8900.
Museum of Westward Expansion, Gateway Arch, 425-4465.
National Bowling Hall of Fame, 111 Stadium Plaza, 231-6340.
National Museum of Transportation, 16 mi SW via I-44, N on I-270 to Big Bend & Dougherty Ferry Rd exits, 965-7998.
St Louis Science Center, 5050 Oakland Ave, 289-4444.
Soldiers Memorial Military Museum, 1315 Chestnut St, 622-4550.

Art Museum and Galleries

Cupples House and Art Gallery, On campus of St Louis University, 658-3025.
Gallery of Art, Steinberg Hall, Washington University, 935-5490.
St Louis Art Museum, Forest Park, 721-0072.

Points of Interest

Historical

American Institute of Architects, 911 Washington, 621-3484.
Campbell House Museum, 1508 Locust St, 421-0325.
Cathedral of St Louis, 4431 Lindell Blvd at Newstead Ave, 533-2824.
Chatillon-De Menil House, 3352 De Menil Pl, 771-5828.
Christ Church Cathedral, 1210 Locust St, 231-3454.
Eads Bridge, foot of Washington Ave.
Eugene Field House and Toy Museum, 634 S Broadway, 421-4689.
Grant's Farm, 10501 Gravois Rd, 843-1700.
Jefferson Barracks Historical Park, S Broadway at Kingston, 10 mi S on I-55, 544-5714.
Laclede's Landing, N edge of Riverfront.
Lafayette Square, bounded by Jefferson, I-44, 18th St & Couteau.
Mastadon State Park, 20 mi S off US 67, near US 67 Imperial exit, 464-2976.
Old Cathedral, 209 Walnut St at Memorial Dr, 231-3250.
Old Courthouse, 11 N 4th St at Market St, 425-4465.
Tower Grove House, Missouri Botanical Garden, 577-5150.
Union Station, 1820 Market St, 421-6655 or -4314.

Other Attractions

Admiral Riverboat Casino, at Gateway Arch, 621-4040.
Aloe Plaza, Market St between 18th & 20th Sts.
Anheuser-Busch, 13th & Lynch, 577-2626.
Cahokia Mounds State Historic Site, E on Collinsville Rd, in Collinsville, IL, 618/346-5160.

Forest Park, Skinker & Kingshighway Blvds & Oakland Ave, 535-0100.
Gateway Arch, 11 N 4th St, 425-4465.
Jewel Box Floral Conservatory, Wells & McKinley Drs, Forest Park.
Laumeier Sculpture Garden, Geyer Rd & Rott St, 821-1209.
Missouri Botanical Garden, 4344 Shaw Blvd, 577-9400.
Purina Farms, 35 mi W via I-44, Grays Summit exit to County MM, 982-3232.
St Louis Sports Hall of Fame, Busch Stadium, 100 Stadium Plaza, 421-3263.
St Louis Zoological Park, Forest Park, 781-0900.
Six Flags Over Mid-America, 30 mi SW off I-44, Allenton Rd exit, Eureka, 938-4800.

Sightseeing Tours

Excursion boats *Huck Finn, Tom Sawyer* and *Becky Thatcher,* dock below Gateway Arch, 621-4040.
Fostaire Heliport, 400 N Leonor K Sullivan Blvd, on river at N end of Gateway Arch, 421-5440 or -3388.
Gray Line bus tours, 312 W Morris, Caseyville, IL, 618/334-1272.

Annual Events

Japanese Festival, Missouri Botanical Garden. Labor Day wkend.
Hot-air Balloon Race, Jefferson Barracks Historical Park. Sept.

City Neighborhoods

Many of the restaurants, unrated dining establishments and some lodgings listed under St Louis include neighborhoods as well as exact street addresses. A map showing these neighborhoods can be found immediately following the city introduction. Geographic descriptions of these areas are given, followed by a table of restaurants arranged by neighborhood.

Downtown: South of Martin Luther King Blvd, west of I-70, north of I-64 (US 40) and east of Jefferson Ave. **North of Downtown:** North of Martin Luther King Blvd. **West of Downtown:** West of Jefferson Ave.
The Hill: South of I-44, west of Kingshighway Blvd, north of Arsenal St and east of Hampton Ave.
Riverfront/Laclede Landing: On Mississippi River south of Eads Bridge, east of I-70 and north of I-40; Laclede Landing on riverfront directly north of Eads Bridge and south of M.L. King Jr Memorial Bridge.

Lodgings and Food

ST LOUIS RESTAURANTS
BY NEIGHBORHOOD AREAS

(For full description, see alphabetical listings under Restaurants)

DOWNTOWN

Cafe De France. 410 Olive St

Charlie Gitto's. 207 N 6th St

Faust's (Adam's Mark Hotel). 4th & Chestnut

J.F. Sanfilippo's. 705 N Broadway

Kemoll's. 1 Metropolitan Square

Premio. 7th & Market Sts

Tony's. 410 Market St

NORTH OF DOWNTOWN

Crown Candy Kitchen. 1401 St Louis Ave

SOUTH OF DOWNTOWN

Bevo Mill. 4749 Gravois Ave

Patty Long's 9th Street Abbey. 1808 S 9th St

Sidney Street Cafe. 2000 Sidney St

WEST OF DOWNTOWN

Blueberry Hill. 6504 Delmar Blvd

Dierdorf & Hart's. 323 West Port Plaza

THE HILL

Bruno's Little Italy. 5901 Southwest Ave

Cunetto. 5453 Magnolia Ave

Dominic's. 5101 Wilson Ave

Gian Peppe's. 2126 Marconi Ave

Gino's. 4502 Hampton Ave

Giovanni's. 5201 Shaw Ave

Lorusso's Cucina. 3121 Watson Rd

O'Connells. 4652 Shaw Ave

RIVERFRONT/LACLEDE LANDING

Lt Robert E. Lee. 100 S Leonor K Sullivan Blvd

Note: *When a listing is located in a town that does not have its own city heading, it will appear under the city nearest to its location. In these cases, the address and town appear in parenthesis immediately following the name of the establishment.*

Motels

✔★★ **COMFORT INN SOUTHWEST.** *(3730 S Lindbergh Blvd, Sunset Hills 63127) SW via I-44 to S Lindbergh Blvd, south of down-town.* 314/842-1200; FAX 314/849-7220. 100 rms, 2 story. S $48-$52; D $48-$65; each addl $4; under 18 free. Crib $3. Pet accepted, some restrictions; $25 deposit. TV; cable. Pool. Complimentary continental bkfst. Restaurant 11 am-10 pm; Sat to 11 pm. Bar. Ck-out noon. Exercise equipt: weight machine, bicycle, whirlpool. Some in-rm steam baths. Cr cds: A, C, D, DS, ER, JCB, MC, V.

★★ **COURTYARD BY MARRIOTT.** *2340 Market St (63103), near Union Station, west of downtown.* 314/241-9111; FAX 314/241-8113. 151 units, 4 story, 12 suites. S, D $72-$115; suites $85-$135; under 18 free; wkly, monthly rates. Crib free. TV; cable, in-rm movies. Indoor pool; poolside serv. Complimentary coffee in rms. Bkfst avail. Rm serv. Ck-out noon. Valet serv. Exercise equipt: weight benches, bicycles, whirlpool. Some balconies. Cr cds: A, C, D, DS, ER, MC, V.

✔★ **KNIGHTS INN BRIDGETON.** *(12433 St Charles Rock Rd, Bridgeton 63044) NW via I-70, N on I-270, then E at St Charles Rock Rd exit 20B.* 314/291-8545; res: 800/843-5644. 104 rms. S $31.95-$37.95; D $32.95-$44.95; each addl $6; kits. $41.95-$53.95; under 18 free. Crib free. Pet accepted, some restrictions; $35 deposit. TV; cable. Pool. Complimentary coffee. Restaurant adj 6 am-10:30 pm. Ck-out noon. Some refrigerators. Cr cds: A, C, D, DS, MC, V.

★★ **RESIDENCE INN BY MARRIOTT.** *1881 Craigshire Rd (63146), north of downtown.* 314/469-0060. 128 kit. suites, 2 story. Suites $109-$159; wkly, monthly rates; wkend plans. Crib free. Pet accepted; $25. TV; cable, in-rm movies avail. Heated pool; whirlpool. Complimentary continental bkfst. Restaurant adj 6 am-10:30 pm. Ck-out noon. Coin lndry. Meeting rm. Airport transportation. Health club privileges. Lawn games. Refrigerators; many fireplaces. Private patios, balconies. Picnic tables, grills. Library. Cr cds: A, C, D, DS, ER, JCB, MC, V.

★★ **SUMMERFIELD SUITES.** *1855 Craigshire Rd (63146), I-270, Page Ave exit E to Craigshire Rd, north of downtown.* 314/878-1555; res: 800/833-4353; FAX 314/878-9203. 106 kit. suites, 2 story. 1-bedrm $138; 2-bedrm $158; wkend rates. Crib free. Pet accepted, some restrictions; $75. TV; cable, in-rm movies. Heated pool. Complimentary continental bkfst. Complimentary coffee in rms. Restaurant nearby. Ck-out noon. Coin lndry. Meeting rms. Valet serv. Sundries. Free airport transportation. Exercise equipt; weight machine, bicycles, whirlpool. Picnic tables, grills. Cr cds: A, C, D, DS, ER, MC, V.

Motor Hotels

★★★ **HILTON FRONTENAC.** *(1335 S Lindbergh Blvd, Des Peres 63131) W via I-64 (US 40), at S Lindbergh Blvd.* 314/993-1100; FAX 314/993-8546. 266 rms, 3 story. S, D $80-$180; each addl $10; suites $120-$500; under 14 free; wkend, wkly rates. Crib free. TV; cable. Pool; poolside serv, lifeguard. Restaurant 6:30 am-10 pm. Rm serv. Bar 11-1 am; entertainment, dancing Wed-Sat. Ck-out noon. Convention facilities. Bellhops. Valet serv. Sundries. Gift shop. Free airport transportation. Exercise equipt; weights, bicycles, whirlpool, sauna. *LUXURY LEVEL : CONCIERGE FLOOR.* 23 rms, 4 suites. S $120; D $130. Concierge. Private lounge. Complimentary continental bkfst, refreshments. Cr cds: A, C, D, DS, ER, MC, V.

✔★★★ **HOLIDAY INN-SOUTHWEST.** *10709 Watson Rd (63127), SW via I-44 exit 277B, Lindbergh Blvd to Watson Rd, south of downtown.* 314/821-6600. 144 rms, 4 story. May-Sept: S $74-$99; D $77-$99; each addl $10; suites $90-$120; under 12 free; lower rates rest of yr. Crib free. TV; cable. Pool. Complimentary coffee in rms. Restaurant 6:30 am-2 pm, 5-10 pm. Rm serv. Bar 11-1 am; entertainment, dancing. Ck-out noon. Meeting rms. Bellhops. Valet serv. Health club privileges. Game rm. Some bathrm phones, refrigerators. Cr cds: A, C, D, DS, ER, JCB, MC, V.

Hotels

ADAM'S MARK. *(New general manager, therefore not rated) 4th & Chestnut (63102), opp Gateway Arch, downtown.* 314/241-7400; res: 800/444-2326; FAX 314/241-9839. 910 rms, 18 story. S

$149; D $169-$179; each addl $15; suites $185-$1,200; under 18 free; wkend packages. Crib free. Garage parking $1/hr, in/out $10 unlimited; valet $3. TV; cable. 2 heated pools, 1 indoor; poolside serv. Afternoon tea. Restaurant 6 am-midnight (also see FAUST'S). Rm serv 24 hrs. Bar 11-2 am; entertainment, dancing exc Sun. Ck-out noon. Convention facilities. Concierge. Shopping arcade. Barber, beauty shop. Exercise rm; instructor, weight machines, bicycles, whirlpool, sauna. Bathrm phones; some refrigerators. Three-story atrium lobby decorated with bronze equestrian sculpture by De Luigi. View of Gateway Arch & riverfront from many rms; near Laclede's Landing & riverfront showboats. *LUXURY LEVEL : CONCORDE LEVEL.* 110 rms, 2 floors. S $179; D $199. Private lounge. Private dining rm. Complimentary full bkfst, refreshments, newspaper. Cr cds: A, C, D, DS, MC, V.

D ⊠ ≈ ✗ ⊠ 🔥 SC

★ ★ ★ **DOUBLETREE HOTEL & CONFERENCE CENTER.** (16625 Swingley Ridge Rd, Chesterfield 63017) Approx 20 mi W on I-64 (US 40), exit 19A, N to Swingley Ridge Rd. 314/532-5000; FAX 314/532-9984. 223 rms, 12 story. S $140; D $150; under 18 free; wkend rates. Crib free. Pet accepted, some restrictions. TV; cable. 2 pools, 1 indoor; wading pool, poolside serv, lifeguard. Supervised child's activities. Restaurant 6:30-10 pm. Bar 11-1 am. Ck-out noon. Meeting rms. Gift shop. Free airport, local transportation. Lighted tennis. Exercise rm; instructor, weights, bicycles, whirlpool, steam rm, sauna. Game rm. Rec rm. Refrigerators avail. *LUXURY LEVEL : EXECUTIVE REGISTRY.* 12 rms, 5 suites. S, D $160-$170; suites $200-$450. Concierge. Private lounge. Wet bar. Bathrm phones. Complimentary continental bkfst, refreshments, newspaper. Cr cds: A, C, D, DS, ER, JCB, MC, V.

D ⊠ ⚴ ≈ ✗ 🐾 ⊠ 🔥 SC

★ ★ ★ **DOUBLETREE SUITES.** 806 St Charles St (63101), downtown. 314/421-2500; FAX 314/421-6254. 184 suites, 18 story. S $125-$145; D $135-$155; each addl $10; under 18 free. Crib free. Parking $9. Pet accepted, some restrictions; $50 deposit. TV; cable, in-rm movies avail. Rooftop pool; poolside serv, lifeguard. Restaurants 6:30 am-10:30 pm. Bar 11 am-midnight. Ck-out noon. Meeting rms. Exercise equipt; weight machine, bicycles. Bathrm phones, refrigerators, minibars; some wet bars, fireplaces. Renovated 1925 hotel; Georgian-style interior, preserved millwork. Cr cds: A, C, D, DS, ER, JCB, MC, V.

D ⊠ ≈ ✗ ⊠ 🔥 SC

★ ★ **EMBASSY SUITES.** 901 N 1st St (63102), downtown. 314/241-4200; FAX 314/241-6513. 297 suites, 8 story. S, D $140-$150; each addl $15; under 18 free; higher rates hols; wkend rates. Crib free. Pet accepted, some restrictions; $200 deposit. TV; cable. Indoor pool; wading pool, lifeguard. Complimentary bkfst served in atrium. Restaurant 11 am-11 pm. Bar to 1 am. Ck-out noon. Lndry facilities. Meeting rms. Exercise equipt; treadmill, bicycles, whirlpool. Game rm. Rec rm. Refrigerators, wet bars. Balconies. 8-story atrium courtyard. Cr cds: A, C, D, DS, ER, JCB, MC, V.

D ⊠ ≈ ✗ ⊠ 🔥 SC

★ ★ **HAMPTON INN.** 2211 Market St (63103), opp Union Station, west of downtown. 314/241-3200. 240 rms, 11 story, 9 suites. S $79-$89; D $85-$94; suites $110-$125; under 18 free; wkend rates. Crib free. Pet accepted, some restrictions. TV; cable. Indoor pool. Complimentary continental bkfst. Restaurant 11-3 am. Bar. Ck-out noon. Coin lndry. No bellhops. Free garage parking. Exercise equipt; weights, bicycles, whirlpool. Cr cds: A, C, D, DS, ER, MC, V.

D ⊠ ≈ ✗ ⊠ 🔥 SC

✔ ★ ★ **HOLIDAY INN-DOWNTOWN RIVERFRONT.** 200 N 4th St (63102), downtown. 314/621-8200; FAX 314/621-8073. 458 rms, 29 story, 167 kits. S $49-$89; D $59-$99; each addl $10; suites $69-$175; under 17 free; wkend rates; higher rates: July 4th. Pet accepted, some restrictions. TV. Pool; lifeguard. Restaurant 6:30 am-2 pm, 4:30-10 pm; 24-hr deli. Bar 11-3 am; Sun 1 pm-midnight. Ck-out

noon. Meeting rms. Gift shop. Garage. Game rm. Some balconies. Cr cds: A, C, D, DS, ER, JCB, MC, V.

D ⊠ ≈ ✗ ⊠ 🔥 SC

★ ★ ★ **HOTEL MAJESTIC.** 1019 Pine St (63101), downtown. 314/436-2355; res: 800/451-2355; FAX 314/436-0223. 91 units, 9 story. S, D $155; each addl $15; suites $290-$850; studio rms $290; under 12 free; wkend rates. Crib free. Valet, in/out parking $8. TV; cable. Coffee in rms. Complimentary continental bkfst. Restaurant. Rm serv 24 hrs. Bar 11-1 am; in season to 3 am; entertainment 8 pm-midnight. Ck-out noon. Meeting rms. Concierge. Bathrm phones, minibars. European elegance in 1914 building; marble floors, Oriental rugs. Individually decorated rms. Complimentary newspaper. Cr cds: A, C, D, DS, ER, MC, V.

D ⊠ 🔥 SC

★ ★ ★ **HYATT REGENCY AT UNION STATION.** One Union Station (63103), west of downtown. 314/231-1234; FAX 314/923-3971. 538 rms, 3-6 story. S, D $114-$160; each addl $25; under 12 free; wkend rates. Crib free. Pet accepted, some restrictions. TV; cable. Pool; lifeguard. Restaurant 6:30 am-10:30 pm. Bar 11-1:30 am. Ck-out noon. Convention facilities. Shopping arcade. Exercise equipt; weight machine, bicycles. Refrigerators avail. Bathrm phones. In renovated Union Station railroad terminal (1894); main lobby and lounge occupy Grand Hall, which features rare marble, barrel-vaulted frescoed ceilings, elaborate gold-leafed plasterwork and stained-glass window depicting St Louis as "Crossroads of America." *LUXURY LEVEL : REGENCY CLUB.* 68 rms, 3 floors. S, D $177-$202; suites $190-$900. Concierge. Private lounge. Complimentary continental bkfst, refreshments, newspaper. Cr cds: A, C, D, DS, ER, JCB, MC, V.

D ⊠ ≈ ✗ ⊠ 🔥 SC

★ ★ ★ **MARRIOTT PAVILION.** 1 Broadway (63102), downtown. 314/421-1776; FAX 314/331-9269. 672 rms, 22-25 story. S $115; D $130; each addl $15; under 18 free; wkend rates. Garage, in/out $9, valet $12. Pet accepted, some restrictions. TV; cable. Pool; poolside serv. Restaurant 6:30 am-11 pm. Bar 11-1 am. Ck-out noon. Coin lndry. Convention facilities. Concierge. Gift shop. Exercise equipt; weights, bicycles, whirlpool, sauna. Some bathrm phones, refrigerators. Cr cds: A, C, D, DS, ER, JCB, MC, V.

D ⊠ ≈ ✗ ⊠ 🔥 SC

★ ★ ★ **REGAL RIVERFRONT.** 200 S 4th St, downtown. 314/241-9500; res: 800/222-8888; FAX 314/241-9977. 796 rms, 27 story. S $160; D $175; each addl $15; suites $500-$1,000; under 18 free; weekly, wkend rates; higher rates: baseball games, some hols. Crib free. Garage parking $9.50. TV; cable. 2 pools, 1 indoor; wading pool, poolside serv, lifeguard. Restaurant 6:30 am-10 pm. Bar. Ck-out noon. Coin lndry. Convention facilities. Gift shop. Barber, beauty shop. Exercise equipt; weight machine, bicycles. Game rm. Refrigerators. Renovated hotel near river. Cr cds: A, C, D, DS, ER, JCB, MC, V.

D ✗ ⊠ 🔥 SC

★ ★ ★ ★ **THE RITZ-CARLTON, ST LOUIS.** 100 Carondelet Plaza (63105), 7 mi W on I-64, Hanley exit, in downtown Clayton. 314/863-6300; res: 800/241-3333; FAX 314/863-7486. 301 rms, 18 story, 34 suites. S, D $150-$205; suites $295-$1,500; under 12 free; wkend, package plans. Crib free. Garage, valet parking in/out $10/day. TV; cable. Indoor pool; poolside serv. Restaurant (see THE GRILL). Rm serv 24 hrs. Bar 11-1 am; entertainment. Ck-out noon. Convention facilities. Concierge. Gift shop. Airport transportation. Exercise equipt; weight machine, bicycles, whirlpool, sauna, steam rm. Massage. Bathrm phones, refrigerators, minibars. Complimentary newspaper. 18th- and 19th-century antiques and fine art featured in public areas throughout hotel. *LUXURY LEVEL : RITZ-CARLTON CLUB.* 28 rms, 6 suites, 2 floors. S, D $205; suites $395-$1,500; wkend packages. Concierge. Private lounge. Complimentary continental bkfst, refreshments. Cr cds: A, C, D, DS, ER, MC, V.

D ≈ ✗ ⊠ 🔥 SC

★ ★ ★ **SHERATON PLAZA.** 900 West Port Plaza (63146), W via I-64 (US 40), N on I-270 to Page Ave exit, west of downtown. 314/434-

5010; FAX 314/434-0140. 209 rms, 12 story. S $110-$117; D $119-$129; each addl $10; suites $210; under 18 free; wkend rates. Crib free. TV; cable. Indoor pool; whirlpool, sauna. Complimentary coffee in rms. Restaurant 6:30 am-10:30 pm. Bar 11-1 am. Ck-out 1 pm. Meeting rms. Concierge. Shopping arcade. Free covered parking. Free airport transportation. Tennis & health club privileges. Some refrigerators. Private balconies. Fully landscaped pool area. Cr cds: A, C, D, DS, ER, JCB, MC, V.

★ ★ ★ **SHERATON-WEST PORT INN.** 191 West Port Plaza (63146), W via I-64 (US 40), N on I-270 to Page Ave exit, west of downtown. 314/878-1500; FAX 314/878-2837. 300 rms, 4-6 story. S, D $115-$135; each addl $10; suites $160-$265; under 18 free; wkend rates. Pet accepted, some restrictions. TV; cable. Pool; poolside serv, lifeguard. Complimentary coffee in rms. Restaurant 6:30 am-10:30 pm. Bar 11-1 am; pianist Tues-Sat. Ck-out 1 pm. Convention facilities. Concierge. Free covered parking. Free airport transportation. Health club privileges. Some refrigerators. Balconies. In shopping plaza. Cr cds: A, C, D, DS, JCB, MC, V.

Restaurants

★ ★ ★ **AGOSTINO'S COLOSSEUM.** (12949 Olive Blvd, Creve Coeur) 14 mi W on I-64 (US 40) to I-270, N on I-270 to Olive Blvd, 2 mi W. 314/434-2959. Hrs: 5 pm-midnight. Closed major hols. Res accepted. Italian menu. Bar. Wine cellar. A la carte entrees: dinner $10.95-$15.95. Child's meals. Specialties: salmone al Siciliana, costoletta di vitello alla Sicilia, maccheroni del Vesuvio. Own baking. Jacket. Cr cds: A, C, D, DS, ER, MC, V.

★ ★ **BEVO MILL.** 4749 Gravois Ave, south of downtown. 314/481-2626. Hrs: 11 am-9 pm; Sat to 10 pm; early-bird dinner Mon-Fri 3-5 pm; Sun brunch 10 am-2 pm. Closed Dec 25. Res accepted. German menu. Bar. Semi-a-la carte: lunch $4.95-$7.95, dinner $10.95-$17.95. Sun brunch $8.95. Child's meals. Specializes in sauerbraten, Wienerschnitzel, fresh seafood. Own baking. Parking. Large stone fireplace. Bavarian exterior; operable windmill. Cr cds: A, C, D, ER, MC, V.

✔★ ★ **BIG SKY CAFE.** (47 S Old Orchard, Webster Groves) 8 mi W on I-44, Shrewsbury West exit, S on Big Bend. 314/962-5757. Hrs: 5:30-10 pm; Fri & Sat 4:30-11 pm; Sun to 9:30 pm. Closed some major hols. Res accepted. Bar. A la carte entrees: dinner $7.95-$12.50. Specialties: pecan encrusted catfish, barbecued salmon, roasted garlic mashed potatoes. Parking. Outdoor dining. Micro-brewery. Contemporary decor. Cr cds: MC, V.

★ ★ **BRISTOL BAR & GRILL.** (11801 Olive Blvd, Creve Coeur) 14 mi W on I-64 to I-270, N to Olive Blvd, turn E. 314/567-0272. Hrs: 11:30 am-2:30 pm, 5:30-10 pm; Fri & Sat 5-10:30 pm; Sun 10 am-2:30 pm, 5-9 pm. Closed Memorial Day, July 4, Dec 25. Res accepted. Bar to 1 am. Semi-a-la carte: lunch $5.95-$10.95, dinner $7.95-$19.95. Sun brunch $12.95. Child's meals. Specializes in mesquite-grilled seafood, steak, fresh fish. Own pastries. Stained-glass windows. Cr cds: A, C, D, DS, ER, MC, V.

★ ★ **BRUNO'S LITTLE ITALY.** 5901 Southwest Ave, on The Hill. 314/781-5988. Hrs: 5 pm-midnight. Closed Mon; major hols. Res accepted Fri-Sun. Italian menu. Bar. Wine cellar. Semi-a-la carte: dinner $12-$18. Specialties: papardelle alla Genovese, veal Vesuvio, fresh salmon. Own pastries. Located in old Italian neighborhood. Antiques, stained glass, original art. Jacket. Cr cds: A, C, D, DS, ER, MC, V.

★ ★ ★ **CAFE DE FRANCE.** 410 Olive St, downtown. 314/231-2204. Hrs: 11:30 am-2 pm, 5:30-10:30 pm; Fri to 11:30 pm; Sat 5:30-11:30 pm. Closed Sun; most major hols. Res accepted. French menu. Bar. Wine cellar. A la carte entrees: lunch $5-$12, dinner $15-$22.

Complete meals: dinner (3, 4 & 5 courses) $19.50, $23.50 & $27.50. Specializes in fresh seafood, breast of duck, game. Own baking. Valet parking. European ambience. Jacket. Cr cds: A, C, D, DS, ER, MC, V.

✔★ ★ **CHARLIE GITTO'S.** 207 N 6th St, downtown. 314/436-2828. Hrs: 11 am-11 pm. Closed Sun; some major hols. Italian, Amer menu. Bar. A la carte entrees: lunch $5-$8, dinner $7.95-$12.95. Child's meals. Specializes in veal, seafood, pasta. Sports bar atmosphere. Cr cds: A, C, D, DS, ER, MC, V.

✔★ ★ **CUNETTO.** 5453 Magnolia Ave, on The Hill. 314/781-1135. Hrs: 11 am-2 pm, 5-10:30 pm; Fri to 11:30 pm; Sat 5-11:30 pm. Closed Sun; major hols. Italian menu. Bar 11 am-11:30 pm. Semi-a-la carte: lunch $4-$9, dinner $6.75-$12. Child's meals. Specialties: linguine tutto mare, veal with crabmeat, Sicilian steak. Parking. In old Italian neighborhood. Cr cds: A, C, D, ER, MC, V.

★ ★ **DIERDORF & HART'S.** 323 West Port Plaza, W via I-64 (US 40) to I-270, N on I-270 to Page Ave exit, west of downtown. 314/878-1801. Hrs: 11 am-10 pm; Fri to 11 pm; Sat 4:30-11 pm; Sun 4:30-10 pm. Closed July 4, Thanksgiving. Res accepted. Bar to 12:30 am; Fri & Sat to 1:30 am. Semi-a-la carte: lunch $5.95-$11.95, dinner $13.50-$39.50. Specializes in steak, broiled seafood. Pianist Tues-Sat. 1940s steakhouse atmosphere. Jacket. Cr cds: A, C, D, DS, MC, V.

★ ★ ★ **DOMINIC'S.** 5101 Wilson Ave, on The Hill. 314/771-1632. Hrs: 5-11 pm; Fri & Sat to midnight. Closed Sun; major hols; also 1st wk of July. Res accepted. Italian menu. Bar. Wine cellar. Semi-a-la carte: dinner $14.50-$23. Specialties: osso buco, shrimp elegante, artichoke stuffed with shrimp, fresh seafood, pasta dishes. Own pastries, pasta. Valet parking. Family-owned. Jacket. Cr cds: A, C, D, DS, ER, MC, V.

★ ★ ★ **FAUST'S.** (See Adam's Mark Hotel) 314/342-4690. Hrs: 11:30 am-2 pm, 5:30-10 pm; wkends to 10:30 pm. Res accepted. French, Amer menu. Bar. Extensive wine list. Semi-a-la carte: lunch $6.25-$13.95, dinner $18-$27.25. Complete meals: dinner $19.95-$38. Child's meals. Specializes in rack of lamb, halibut Chardonnay, crispy duck. Own bread, pastries. Valet parking. Two-tiered dining rm with beamed ceilings; upper tier with view of Gateway Arch. Jacket (dinner). Cr cds: A, C, D, DS, ER, MC, V.

★ ★ ★ **G P AGOSTINO'S.** (15846 Manchester Rd, Ellisville) 22 mi W on I-64 (US 40) to Clarkson Rd, 4 mi S to Manchester Rd. 314/391-5480. Hrs: 11 am-2:30 pm, 5 pm-midnight. Closed Jan 1, Thanksgiving, Dec 25. Res accepted. Italian menu. Bar. Wine cellar. Semi-a-la carte: lunch $3.95-$9.95, dinner $8.95-$19.95. Sun brunch $11.95 Specialties: veal salto in bocca Romano, ossobuco Milanese, salmon con pappardelle. Parking. Chef-owned. Jacket (dinner). Cr cds: A, C, D, DS, ER, MC, V.

★ ★ ★ **GIAN PEPPE'S.** 2126 Marconi Ave, on The Hill. 314/772-3303. Hrs: 11 am-2 pm, 5-11 pm; Sat from 5 pm. Closed Sun; major hols; also Mon Jan-Sept. Res accepted. Italian menu. Bar. Wine list. Semi-a-la carte: lunch $5.25-$13.95, dinner $12.50-$24.50. Specializes in veal, fresh seafood. Own pastries. Valet parking. Jacket. Cr cds: A, C, D, ER, MC, V.

✔★ **GINO'S.** 4502 Hampton Ave, on The Hill. 314/351-4187. Hrs: 11 am-2 pm, 5-10 pm; Fri to 11 pm; Sat 5-11 pm; Sun 5-9 pm. Closed Mon; major hols. Italian menu. Bar. Semi-a-la carte: lunch $3.95-$9, dinner $6.95-$15.95. Child's meals. Specialties: veal Spedine, linguine Pescatore, veal chops. Cafe atmosphere. Cr cds: A, MC, V.

★ ★ ★ **GIOVANNI'S.** 5201 Shaw Ave, on The Hill. 314/772-5958. Hrs: 5-11 pm; Fri & Sat to midnight. Closed Sun; major hols. Res accepted. Italian menu. Wine cellar. A la carte entrees: dinner $14.50-$24. Specialties: tuna San Martino, maltagliati al funchetto, vitello con porcini, "presidential bow tie" al salmone (created for former President Reagan). Own pastries. Most pasta homemade. Valet parking. European decor. Cr cds: A, C, D, DS, ER, MC, V.

★ ★ GIOVANNI'S LITTLE PLACE. (14560 Manchester Rd, Ballwin) 14 mi W on I-64 (US 40) to I-270, S on I-270 to Manchester Rd, in shopping center. 314/227-7230. Hrs: 5-10 pm. Closed hols. Res accepted. Italian menu. Bar. Wine cellar. Semi-a la carte: dinner $10.95-$24. Specialties: fusilli ai quattro formaggi, involtini di vitello alla villa Igea, vitello alla Maria. Own pastries. Cr cds: A, C, D, DS, ER, MC, V.

★ ★ THE GRILL. (See The Ritz-Carlton, St Louis Hotel) 314/863-6300. Hrs: 5-11 pm. Res accepted. Continental menu. Bar. Wine cellar. A la carte entrees: dinner $9.50-$25. Child's meals. Specialties: Dover sole, double-cut lamb chops, Norwegian salmon. Own baking. Valet parking. Marble fireplace in main rm; English pub atmosphere. Cr cds: A, C, D, DS, ER, JCB, MC, V.

D

✔★ ★ HACIENDA. (9748 Manchester Rd, Rock Hill) W of downtown via Manchester Rd (MO 100). 314/962-7100. Hrs: 11 am-11 pm; Fri, Sat to midnight; Sun noon-9 pm. Closed some major hols. Res accepted. Mexican menu. Bar. Semi-a la carte: lunch, dinner $4.95-$10.95. Specialties: chicken mole, fajitas. Parking. Built as residence for steamboat captain (1861). Cr cds: A, C, DS, MC, V.

D

★ ★ J.F. SANFILIPPO'S. 705 N Broadway, downtown. 314/621-7213. Hrs: 11 am-2 pm, 4:30-11 pm; Sat from 4:30 pm. Closed Sun; some major hols. Res accepted. Italian menu. Bar. Semi-a la carte: lunch $4.50-$10.25, dinner $4.75-$16.95. Child's meals. Specializes in pasta, fresh seafood, veal Franco. Garage parking. Low slatted ceiling of metal and wood. Casual, trattoria atmosphere. Cr cds: A, C, D, DS, ER, MC, V.

D

★ ★ JOHN MINEO'S. (13490 Clayton Rd, Town & Country) 15 mi W of downtown via I-64 (US 40), exit Mason Rd, 1 mi S to Clayton Rd. 314/434-5244. Hrs: 5 pm-midnight. Closed Sun. Res accepted. Italian menu. Bar. Wine list. A la carte entrees: dinner $8.95-$16.95. Specialties: veal alla panna, Dover sole, fresh fish. Parking. Chef-owned. Jacket. Cr cds: A, C, D, DS, ER, MC, V.

★ ★ KEMOLL'S. 1 Metropolitan Square, downtown. 314/421-0555. Hrs: 11 am-2 pm, 5-9 pm; Fri & Sat to 10 pm; early-bird dinner 5-6:30 pm. Closed major hols. Res accepted. Italian menu. Bar. Semi-a la carte: lunch $11-$15.75, dinner $15-$27. Specializes in fresh seafood, veal Francesco, carciofi fritti. 3 dining rms. Family-owned. Cr cds: A, C, D, DS, ER, MC, V.

D

★ ★ LORUSSO'S CUCINA. 3121 Watson Rd, on The Hill. 314/647-6222. Hrs: 11:30 am-2 pm, 5-10 pm; Fri & Sat 5-11 pm; early-bird dinner Mon-Fri 5-6 pm. Closed Sun; major hols. Italian menu. Bar. Semi-a la carte: lunch $5.50-$8, dinner $8.50-$17.95. Child's meals. Specialties: linguine Granno, chicken Teresa, tenderloin Mudega. Cr cds: A, C, D, ER, MC, V.

D

★ ★ LT RODERT E. LEE. 100 S Leonor K Sullivan Blvd, Riverfront/Laclede Landing. 314/241-1282. Hrs: 11 am-11 pm. Closed Dec 25. Res accepted. Bar to 1:30 am. Semi-a la carte: dinner $9.95-$22.95. Dinner buffet $18.95. Specializes in fresh seafood, prime rib. Salad bar. Dixieland jazz Fri-Sat. Parking. Replica of riverboat; moored on Mississippi riverfront. Cr cds: A, DS, MC, V.

SC

✔★ PASTA HOUSE COMPANY. (295 Plaza Frontenac, Frontenac 63131) 10 mi NW on I-40, exit Lindbergh. 314/569-3040. Hrs: 11 am-10:30 pm; Sun noon-8 pm. Closed Easter, Dec 25. Italian menu. Bar. Semi-a la carte: lunch $4.50-$9.50, dinner $6-$15.99. Specializes in pasta. Salad bar. Contemporary decor, casual atmosphere. Cr cds: A, DS, MC, V.

D SC

★ ★ PATTY LONG'S 9TH STREET ABBEY. 1808 S 9th St, south of downtown. 314/621-9598. Hrs: 11 am-2 pm; Wed-Fri also 5-10 pm; Sun 10 am-2 pm. Closed most major hols. Res accepted. Bar. Semi-a la carte: lunch $6.95-$11, dinner $13.95-$18.95. Specialties: almond chicken salad, beef tenderloin with gorgonzola, shitake mushrooms & caramelized onion. Valet parking. In former church (ca 1895); stained-glass windows and paneling. Cr cds: A, D, MC, V.

D SC

★ ★ PREMIO. 7th & Market Sts, downtown. 314/231-0911. Hrs: 11 am-10 pm; Fri to 11 pm; Sat 5-11 pm. Closed Sun; major hols. Res accepted. Italian menu. Bar. Semi-a la carte: lunch $6.25-$11.95, dinner $7.95-$21.95. Specializes in fresh seafood, veal, creative pasta. Garage parking. Outdoor dining. Modern decor. Cr cds: A, C, D, DS, ER, MC, V.

D

★ ★ SCHNEITHORST'S HOFAMBERG INN. (1600 S Lindbergh Blvd, Ladue) W of downtown, via I-64 (US 40), exit Lindbergh Blvd, S to Clayton Rd. 314/993-5600. Hrs: 11 am-10 pm; Fri, Sat to 11 pm; Sun 10 am-8 pm; early-bird dinner Mon-Fri 4-6:30 pm (exc hols); Sun brunch to 1:30 pm. Closed Dec 25. Res accepted. German, Amer menu. Bar. Semi-a la carte: lunch $5.95-$16.95, dinner $8.95-$24.50. Sun brunch $9.95. Child's meals. Specializes in steak, prime rib, fresh seafood. Parking. Outdoor dining. Antique clocks, stein display. Cr cds: A, C, D, DS, ER, MC, V.

D

★ ★ SIDNEY STREET CAFE. 2000 Sidney St, south of downtown. 314/771-5777. Hrs: 11 am-3 pm, 5-9:45 pm; Sat 5-10:45 pm. Closed Sun & Mon. Res accepted. Bar. Semi-a la carte: lunch $5.25-$8, dinner $15-$20. Specializes in grilled seafood, lamb, steak au poivre. In restored building (ca 1885); antiques. Dinner menu recited. Cr cds: A, C, D, DS, ER, MC, V.

D

★ ★ ★ ★ TONY'S. 410 Market St, downtown. 314/231-7007. Hrs: 5-11 pm; Fri & Sat to 11:30 pm. Closed Sun; major hols; also 1st wk July. Res accepted. Italian menu. Bar. Extensive wine cellar. Semi-a la carte: dinner $18.75-$28.75. Child's meals. Specializes in prime veal and beef, fresh seafood, homemade pasta. Own baking. Valet parking. Artwork, statuary. Family-owned. Jacket. Cr cds: A, C, D, DS, ER, MC, V.

D

Unrated Dining Spots

BARN DELI. (180 Dunn Rd, Florissant) N on I-70 to I-270. 314/838-3670. Hrs: 11 am-4 pm. Closed Sun; major hols. Wine, beer. Semi-a la carte: lunch $3.50-$4.95. Specializes in deli sandwiches, salads. Own soups, desserts. Parking. In late 1800s barn. Cr cds: MC, V.

D

BLUEBERRY HILL. 6504 Delmar Blvd, west of downtown. 314/727-0880. Hrs: 11 am-midnight; Sun to 11 pm. Closed Jan 1. Res accepted Sun-Thurs. Bar to 1:30 am; Sun to midnight. Semi-a la carte: lunch, dinner $3.25-$7. Specializes in hamburgers, vegetarian platters, soups. Own beer. Entertainment Thurs, Fri & Sat evenings. Large display of pop culture memorabilia including Chuck Berry and Elvis. Vintage jukeboxes. Sidewalk has "stars" for celebrities from St Louis. Cr cds: A, C, D, DS, MC, V.

CROWN CANDY KITCHEN. 1401 St Louis Ave, north of downtown. 314/621-9713. Hrs: 10:30 am-10 pm; Sun from noon. Closed some major hols. Specialty: ice cream. Also sandwiches, chili

$2-$4. Homemade candy. Old neighborhood building (1889) with old-fashioned soda fountain (1930s), antique juke box and Coca-Cola memorabilia. No cr cds accepted.

O'CONNELLS. *4652 Shaw Ave, on The Hill. 314/773-6600.* Hrs: 11 am-midnight. Closed Sun; major hols. Bar. Semi-a la carte: lunch, dinner $3.50-$6.50. Specializes in hamburgers, roast beef sandwiches, soup. Parking. Pub atmosphere; antique bar, blackboard menu. Cr cds: A, D, MC, V.

St Louis Lambert Airport Area

Motels

✓★ ★ **BEST WESTERN AIRPORT INN.** *(10232 Natural Bridge Rd, Woodson Terrace 63134)* I-70 exit 236. 314/427-5955. 135 rms, 2 story. May-Sept: S $54.95-$70; D $59.95-$70; under 18 free; lower rates rest of yr. Crib free. Pet accepted, some restrictions; $5. TV; cable. Pool. Restaurant adj open 24 hrs. Ck-out noon. Coin lndry. Meeting rms. Free airport transportation. Cr cds: A, C, D, DS, JCB, MC, V.

D 🚷 ✈ 🛬 🔥 SC

★ ★ **DRURY INN.** *(490 Natural Bridge Rd, St Louis 63134)* W via I-70, 1 blk N of exit 236. 314/423-7700; FAX 314/423-7700. 172 rms, 6 story. S $67-$87; D $77-$97; under 18 free; some wkend rates. Crib free. TV; cable. Heated pool. Complimentary continental bkfst. Restaurant adj noon-10 pm. Ck-out noon. Meeting rms. Free airport transportation 24 hrs. Cr cds: A, C, D, DS, MC, V.

D 🏊 ✈ 🛬 🔥 SC

✓★ **FAIRFIELD INN BY MARRIOTT.** *(9079 Dunn Rd, Hazelwood 63042)* 6 mi NW on I-270, exit 25. 314/731-7700. 135 rms, 3 story. May-Sept: S $35.95-$62.95; each addl $7; under 18 free; wkend rates; higher rates VP Fair. Crib free. TV; cable. Pool. Complimentary continental bkfst, coffee in lobby. Restaurant adj 7 am-10pm. Ck-out noon. Cr cds: A, C, D, DS, MC, V.

D 🏊 🛬 🔥 SC

Motor Hotels

★ ★ ★ **HOLIDAY INN AIRPORT OAKLAND PARK.** *(4505 Woodson Rd, Berkely 63134)* E on Natural Bridge Rd to Woodson Rd, S on Woodson. 314/427-4700; FAX 314/427-6086. 154 rms, 5 story. S $79.50; D $84.50; each addl $10; suites $100-$230; under 17 free; wkend rates. Crib free. TV; cable. Pool. Restaurant 6:30 am-2 pm, 5-10 pm. Rm serv. Bar 11:30 am-midnight. Ck-out 1 pm. Coin lndry. Meeting rms. Bellhops. Valet serv. Free airport transportation. Exercise equipt; weights, bicycles, whirlpool, sauna. Cr cds: A, C, D, DS, ER, JCB, MC, V.

D 🏊 🏃 ✈ 🛬 🔥 SC

✓★ ★ **RAMADA-HENRY VIII.** *(4690 N Lindbergh, St Louis 63044)* W via I-70 N Lindbergh exit. 314/731-3040; FAX 314/731-4210. 384 units, 2-5 story, 190 suites, 35 kit. units. May-Oct: S $65-$85; D $75-$95; suites $85-$115; kit. units $95-$105; under 18 free; wkly, monthly rates; lower rates rest of yr. Crib free. TV; cable. 2 pools, 1 indoor. Restaurant 7 am-midnight; Sun to 11 pm. Rm serv. Bar from 11 am. Ck-out 11 am. Coin lndry. Convention facilities. Bellhops. Gift Shop. Free airport transportation. Lighted tennis. Exercise equipt; weights, weight machine, whirlpool, sauna. Game rm. Refrigerators, wet bars. Some bathrm phones. Some balconies. English Tudor architecture. Cr cds: A, C, D, DS, ER, MC, V.

D 🏖 🏊 🏃 ✈ 🛬 🔥 SC

Hotels

★ ★ ★ **HILTON.** *(10330 Natural Bridge Rd, Berkeley 63134)* 2 mi E on Natural Bridge Rd. 314/426-5500; FAX 314/426-3429. 220 rms, 9 story. S $95-$145; D $96-$154; each addl $15; suites $200-$350; under 18 free; wkend package plan. Crib free. TV; cable, in-rm movies. Indoor pool; poolside serv. Complimentary coffee in rms. Restaurant 6 am-10 pm. Bars 11-1:30 am, Sun to midnight; entertainment. Coin lndry. Ck-out 1 pm. Meeting rms. Gift shop. Free airport transportation. Exercise equipt; weights, bicycles, whirlpool, sauna. Game rm. Some refrigerators. *LUXURY LEVEL : CONCIERGE FLOOR.* 36 rms, 3 suites, 2 floors. S $129; D $154. Concierge. Private lounge. Complimentary continental bkfst, refreshments, newspaper. Cr cds: A, C, D, DS, ER, MC, V.

D 🏊 🏃 ✈ 🛬 🔥 SC

★ ★ ★ **MARRIOTT.** *(I-70 at Lambert St Louis Intl Airport, St Louis 63134)* S on Airflight Dr to Pear Tree Ln. 314/423-9700; FAX 314/423-0213. 601 rms, 8-9 story. S $110-$130; D $125-$155; suites $200-$375; studio rms $115; wkend rates; some lower rates. Crib free. Pet accepted. TV; cable. 2 pools, 1 indoor/outdoor; poolside serv. Restaurant 6 am-midnight. Bars 11:30-1 am; dancing. Ck-out 1 pm. Coin lndry. Convention facilities. Free airport transportation. 2 lighted tennis courts. Exercise rm; instructor, weights, bicycles, whirlpool, sauna. *LUXURY LEVEL : CONCIERGE LEVEL.* 72 rms. S $125; D $150. Private lounge, honor bar. Complimentary continental bkfst, refreshments, newspaper. Cr cds: A, C, D, DS, ER, JCB, MC, V.

D 🏊 🏃 ✈ 🛬 🔥 SC

✓★ ★ **QUALITY HOTEL.** *(9600 Natural Bridge Rd, Berkeley 63134)* 2 mi E on Natural Bridge Rd. 314/427-7600; res: 800/221-2222; FAX 314/427-4972. 197 rms, 7 story. S, D $62-$74; each addl $7; under 18 free; wkend, extended stay rates. Crib free. Pet accepted, some restrictions. TV; cable. Pool. Complimentary continental bkfst. Restaurant 6 am-2 pm, 5:30-9:30 pm; Fri & Sat to 10 pm. Bar 4 pm-1:30 am. Ck-out noon. Meeting rms. Free airport transportation.Exercise equipt; weight machine, stair machine, whirlpool, sauna. Some bathrm phones, refrigerators, minibars. Balconies. Cr cds: A, C, D, DS, MC, V.

🏖 🏊 🏃 ✈ 🛬 🔥 SC

★ ★ ★ **RADISSON ST LOUIS AIRPORT.** *(11228 Lone Eagle Dr, Bridgeton 63044)* I-70 exit 235, S on Lindberg Dr. 314/291-6700; FAX 314/770-1205. 353 rms, 8 story. S $109-$119; D $119-$129; each addl $10; suites $379; under 17 free; wkend rates. Crib $10. TV. Indoor pool. Restaurant 6:30 am-midnight. Bar from 11 am. Ck-out noon. Convention facilities. Gift shop. Free airport transportation. Exercise equipt; weight machine, bicycles, whirlpool. Game rm. Some balconies. Wet bar in suites. Atrium with waterfall. Cr cds: A, C, D, DS, ER, JCB, MC, V.

D 🏊 🏃 ✈ 🛬 SC

★ ★ ★ **STOUFFER CONCOURSE.** *(9801 Natural Bridge Rd, Berkeley 63134)* 2 mi E on Natural Bridge Rd, adj to airport. 314/429-1100; FAX 314/429-3466. 393 rms, 12 story. S $140-$150; D $150-$160; each addl $10; suites $175-$700; under 18 free; wkend rates. Crib free. TV; cable. 2 pools, 1 indoor; poolside serv. Restaurant 6:30 am-11 pm. Rm serv 24 hrs. Bar 3 pm-1 am. Ck-out 1 pm. Convention facilities. Gift shop. Concierge. Airport transportation. Exercise equipt; weights, bicycles, whirlpool, sauna. Bathrm phones, minibars. *LUXURY LEVEL : CLUB LEVEL.* 33 rms. S, D $165-$185. Private lounge. Some wet bars, refrigerators. Complimentary continental bkfst, refreshments, newspaper. Cr cds: A, C, D, DS, ER, MC, V.

D 🏊 🏃 ✈ 🛬 🔥 SC

Restaurants

★ **CHINA ROYAL.** *(5911 N Lindbergh, St Louis)* I-70 exit Lindbergh Blvd S. 314/731-1313. Hrs: 11 am-9:30 pm; wkends to 10:30 pm. Chinese menu. Bar. Semi-a la carte: lunch $4.75-$4.95, dinner

$6.75-$24.95. Specializes in dim sum, seafood. Parking. Chinese decor. Cr cds: A, D, MC, V.

★ ★ **TORNATORE'S.** *(12315 Natural Bridge Rd, Bridgeton) 3 mi E on Natural Bridge Rd.* 314/739-6644. Hrs: 11 am-3 pm, 5-10 pm; Sat from 5 pm; early-bird dinner Mon-Fri 5-6:30 pm. Closed Sun; major hols. Res accepted. Continental Italian menu. Bar. Extensive wine list. Semi-a la carte: lunch $7.95-$15.95, dinner $12.95-$30.95. Specializes in fresh seafood, Sicilian veal chops. Own pastries. Parking. Modern art; etched glass-paneled room divider. Cr cds: A, C, D, DS, MC, V.

Clayton

Motor Hotel

★ ★ ★ **CHESHIRE INN & LODGE.** *(6300 Clayton Rd, Richmond Heights 63117) S on Brentwood Blvd to Clayton Rd.* 314/647-7300; res: 800/325-7378; FAX 314/647-0442. 107 rms, 4 story. S $95-$112; D $109-$119; each addl $6; suites $125-$250; under 12 free; wkend rates. Crib free. TV; cable. Indoor pool; poolside serv. Complimentary continental bkfst Mon-Fri. Restaurant (see CHESHIRE INN). Rm serv. Bar 11-1:30 am; entertainment exc Sun. Ck-out 2 pm. Meeting rms. Bellhops. Valet serv Mon-Fri. Sundries. Free garage. Exercise rm; instructor, weights, bicycles, whirlpool, steam rm, sauna. Some refrigerators. Some balconies. Elegant Tudor decor. English garden. Cr cds: A, C, D, DS, ER, MC, V.

Hotels

★ ★ ★ **DANIELE.** *216 N Meramac.* 314/721-0101; FAX 314/721-0609. 90 rms, 3 story. S, D $99; suites $150-$450; under 18 free; wkly, wkend rates. Pet accepted, some restrictions. TV; cable. Pool. Restaurant 6:30 am-10 pm. Bar. Ck-out noon. Meeting rms. Free covered parking. Airport transportation. Health club privileges. Some refrigerators, wet bars. Cr cds: A, C, D, DS, ER, MC, V.

★ ★ ★ **RADISSON.** *7750 Carondelet Ave.* 314/726-5400; FAX 314/726-6105. 189 rms, 2-8 story. S $75-$99; D $85-$109; each addl $10; suites $109.95-$170; under 18 free; wkly rates, wkend package plan. Crib $10. TV; cable. 2 pools, 1 indoor; poolside serv. Complimentary continental bkfst 6-9 am. Restaurant 6 am-11 pm. Bar 11-1 am. Ck-out noon. Meeting rms. Barber. Free garage parking; valet. Airport transportation. Exercise equipt; weights, bicycles, whirlpool, sauna. Game rm. Refrigerators; some wet bars. Cr cds: A, C, D, DS, ER, JCB, MC, V.

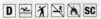

Inn

★ ★ ★ **SEVEN GABLES.** *26 N Meramec.* 314/863-8400; FAX 314/863-8846. 32 rms, 3 story. No elvtr. S, D $95-$130; suites $159-$260; each addl $20; wkend rates. Pet accepted, some restrictions; $20. Valet parking $6. TV; cable. Restaurant 6:30 am-11 pm. Rm serv. Bar 11-12:30 am. Ck-out 1 pm, ck-in 3 pm. Meeting rm. Bellhops. Valet serv. Health club privileges. Balconies. Designed in early 1900s; inspired by sketches in Hawthorne's novel House of Seven Gables. Renovated inn; European country-style furnishings. Cr cds: A, C, D, DS, ER, MC, V.

Restaurants

★ ★ **CANDICCI'S.** *7910 Bonhomme.* 314/725-3350. Hrs: 11:30 am-11 pm; Fri, Sat to midnight; Sun 4:30-9:30 pm. Closed major hols. Res accepted. Italian menu. Bar. Semi-a la carte: lunch $3-$7, dinner $7.25-$18.50. Parking. Outdoor dining. In restored apartment building. Cr cds: A, C, D, DS, ER, MC, V.

★ ★ **CHESHIRE INN.** *(See Cheshire Inn & Lodge Motor Hotel)* 314/647-7300. Hrs: 6:30 am-10 pm; Sat 7:30 am-11 pm; Sun 9 am-2 pm, 5-9:30 pm; Sun brunch to 2 pm. Res accepted. Bar 11-1:30 am; Sun to midnight. Semi-a la carte: lunch $4.95-$8.95, dinner $9.95-$21.95. Sun brunch $10.95. Child's meals. Specializes in prime rib, steak, fresh seafood. Pianist. Valet parking. Spit roasting in view. Old English architecture, decor. Carriage ride with dinner Fri, Sat (weather permitting; res one wk in advance suggested; fee). Transportation to Muni Opera. Cr cds: A, C, D, DS, ER, MC, V.

✔ ★ ★ **FIO'S LA FOURCHETTE.** *7515 Forsyth Ave, S on Brentwood Blvd to Clayton Rd.* 314/863-6866. Hrs: 6-11 pm. Closed Sun & Mon; major hols. Res accepted. French menu. Bar. Semi-a la carte: dinner $7.75-$39.75. Complete meals: dinner $39.75 & $44.75. Specializes in fresh seasonal dishes, soufflé. Valet parking. Intimate dining in two dining rms. Cr cds: A, C, D, MC, V.

★ ★ ★ **L'AUBERGE BRETONNE.** *200 S Brentwood Blvd.* 314/721-0100. Hrs: 11:30 am-3 pm, 5:30-10:30 pm; Sat from 5:30 pm. Closed Sun; major hols. Res accepted. Continental menu. Bar. Semi-a la carte: lunch $5.95-$11.95, dinner $11.95-$24.95. Specializes in magret de canard, pheasant, venison, Dover sole. Own baking. Pianist. Valet parking. Jacket. Cr cds: A, C, D, ER, MC, V.

D

Unrated Dining Spot

ANDRÉ'S SWISS CONFISERIE. *(1026 S Brentwood Blvd, Richmond Heights) S on Brentwood Blvd.* 314/727-9928. Hrs: 7:30 am-5:30 pm; Fri to 9 pm. Closed Sun; major hols. Res accepted. Swiss menu. Wine, beer. Semi-a la carte: bkfst $2.95-$5.25, lunch, dinner $6-$12.50. Specialties: cheese fondue, vol au vent, quiche Lorraine. Parking. Tea rm/candy/pastry shop. Swiss decor. Family-owned. Cr cds: DS, MC, V.

D

Salt Lake City

Founded: 1847

Pop: 159,936

Elev: 4,330 feet

Time zone: Mountain

Area code: 801

Salt Lake City has been called a living monument to the invincibility of the human spirit. Once a desert wilderness, it was built by settlers who sought refuge from religious persecution. Neither the barrenness of the land, drought, a plague of crickets nor the surge of empire to the west that passed through and engulfed their Zion swerved the Mormons from their purpose.

Brigham Young brought the first group of Mormons over the Wasatch Mountains to central Utah in 1847. The city these people built was planned and laid out on a spacious scale, with 132-foot-wide streets and 10-acre blocks. Trees were planted, and despite many obstacles, these industrious and dedicated people succeeded in making their dream come true. In 1869, the completion of the transcontinental railroad helped boost the economy of the Salt Lake City area. During the late 1800s and early 1900s, copper, lead and silver mining in several nearby canyons created great wealth for the city. Between 1900 and 1930 the population of Salt Lake City almost tripled, growing from 53,531 to 140,267. World War II intensified the importance of mining and refining.

In the 1960s, to help counteract the movement away from the city to the suburbs, the Mormon Church invested $40 million in the development of a downtown shopping mall—the ZCMI (Zion's Cooperative Mercantile Institution) Shopping Center. Encouraged by the success of ZCMI, the downtown area expanded rapidly. New business, several shopping malls, the renovation of historic buildings and city-wide beautification projects revitalized the downtown community.

Business

More than 350,000 persons are employed in Salt Lake County. Trade is the largest sector, followed by service industries and government jobs.

Approximately 1,300 manufacturing plants employ some 50,000 people in the production of chemicals, electronics, food and metal products, petroleum and steel.

Salt Lake City is the major banking center for the surrounding geographic area.

An important natural resource is the nearby mountains, where ski areas, an important part of the tourism industry, have been developed.

Convention Facilities

The Salt Palace has 200,832 square feet of exhibit space and banquet facilities for 4,500 people. It can seat 13,000 people for meetings, and it is within walking distance of more than 10,000 hotel rooms.

The assembly hall, with 18,288 square feet of floor space, has a seating capacity of 2,400 or a dining capacity of 1,100. Flexible meeting areas can be arranged into 30 rooms accommodating from 15 to 500. The theater has 734 permanent seats.

Sports and Recreation

Sports fans can watch semi-professional hockey (Salt Lake Golden Eagles) and professional basketball (Utah Jazz) in the Delta Center, downtown, as well as college football and basketball.

The area around Salt Lake City offers unlimited opportunities for the sports activist—superb hunting and fishing, camping, picnicking and hiking in nearby mountains and canyons.

Some skiers call the snow that covers the Wasatch Mountains "the greatest snow on Earth." It is deep and powdery and lasts from November to May. In winter this scenery forms a breathtaking backdrop for unparalleled skiing. Within a 30-mile drive east and southeast of Salt Lake City are 7 major ski resorts; Park City, ParkWest and Deer Valley up Parley's Canyon, Solitude and Brighton up Big Cottonwood Canyon and Snowbird and Alta ski resorts in Little Cottonwood Canyon are destinations for thousands of skiers each year.

The Great Salt Lake, which is twice as salty as any ocean, is 16 miles west of the city and offers sailing and swimming. Its white beaches, marshes and bays are inhabited by countless species of waterfowl and upland game birds.

Entertainment

Music has been an important element in Utah life since the first Mormon settlers arrived, bringing their musical instruments with them. The Utah Symphony Orchestra, which has made lengthy and successful tours of Europe and Latin America, regularly performs from September to April in Symphony Hall. The orchestra tours the western states annually.

The Mormon Tabernacle Choir, one of the best-known choral groups in the world, admits the public free of charge to its Sunday morning radio performances and Thursday evening rehearsals. Both the Salt Lake Oratorio Society and the Utah Opera Company present additional concerts.

Ballet West and the Utah Repertory Dance Theatre (RDT), made up of artists-in-residence at the University of Utah, both present dance performances at the restored Capitol Theatre (1913). The University of Utah is one of the nation's few institutions of higher learning to grant a degree in ballet. The Ririe-Woodbury Dance Company, a nationally acclaimed modern dance group that weds multimedia with the choreographic arts, is also showcased in the Capitol Theatre.

Historical Areas

Trolley Square, a registered state historic site, is a renovation of the site used for a territorial fairgrounds at the turn of the century, and later for trolley barns and repair shops. More than 100 shops, markets, restaurants and entertainment spots are busily operating in the remodeled trolley barn. The square is complete with converted trolleys, brick-paved streets, wrought-iron balconies, and stained-glass and ornamental staircases rescued from old Salt Lake mansions.

Another restoration area is Arrow Press Square, where three vintage buildings—the Arrow Press Building (1890), the Upland Hotel (1910) and the Midwest Office Building (1910)—have been gutted, stripped, scrubbed and reshaped into a complex of retail establishments.

For an introduction to the history of the Mormons, the Visitor Centers on Temple Square have information and exhibits. Free daily guided tours of Temple Square are conducted every 15 minutes. The Temple, built in 1867, is open only to Mormons, but other buildings and sites on the square are open to the public. The famous Tabernacle, built in 1867, has an elongated dome roof with a simple exterior design; its great organ is fitted with 11,000 pipes. The 1882 Assembly Hall and the Lion House and Beehive House are included in the tour. The two houses were residences and offices for Brigham Young, 19 of his wives and 56 children. Also on the square is the Sea Gull Monument, erected in 1913 to commemorate the saving of crops in 1848 from a plague of crickets.

Sightseeing

Few cities can rival Salt Lake City for surrounding natural beauty and variety. The Salt Lake Convention and Visitors Bureau provides many pamphlets and brochures that introduce visitors to the city and the state. Information may also be obtained at Visitor Information Centers, located in Trolley Square, the Delta Terminal building at Salt Lake International Airport and the Utah Travel Council in Council Hall (Old City Hall).

Within the city proper are Hansen Planetarium, with its space science library; Hogle Zoological Garden, with wildlife exhibits; the "This is the Place" monument, opposite the zoo; Lagoon Amusement Park, Pioneer Village and Water Park, with a 19th-century re-creation of a Utah town; and Salt Lake Art Center, with changing exhibitions of Utah art. Pioneer history is memorialized at the state capitol and the Pioneer Memorial Museum.

The Great Salt Lake is 48 miles wide and 92 miles long. Between the lake and the Nevada border are the Bonneville Salt Flats, an incomparable expanse covering more than 200 square miles. The flats were formed when the ancient and gigantic Lake Bonneville receded to the present Great Salt Lake, leaving behind salt beds in its lowest area. Early in this century racers discovered the salt flats to be an ideal place to race automobiles. From late August through September, races between world-speed-record jet cars are held on 12- to 14-mile tracks. During the Bonneville National Speed Trials, the tracks are used by hot rods, motorcycles, drag racers and all types of powerful automobiles attempting to set new records in their class.

Six canyons slice through the Wasatch range of the Rocky Mountains, which rims the city limits. In addition to providing unparalleled skiing, the canyons promenade some of the most spectacular scenery in the West. Aerial trams and gondolas offer summertime rides to the 11,000-foot Hidden Peak, providing riders with a view of mountain peaks including Timpanogos, Lone Peak and the Pfeifferhorn.

Many of Utah's national parks and monuments are located in the southern portion of the state and are approximately a day's drive from Salt Lake City. Timpanogos Cave National Monument, perhaps the most colorful and least developed area, is the closest to the city. Timpanogos is approximately 35 miles southeast between Salt Lake City and Provo. The national parks include Arches, approximately 235 miles southeast, near Moab; Canyonlands, approximately 245 miles southeast, near Moab; Capitol Reef, approximately 230 miles south, near Loa; Bryce Canyon, about 270 miles south, near Panguitch; and Zion, approximately 320 miles south, near St George.

Utah's national monuments include Dinosaur, approximately 195 miles east, near Vernal; Hovenweep, approximately 250 miles southeast, near Blanding; Cedar Breaks, roughly 260 miles south, near Cedar City; Natural Bridges, approximately 330 miles southeast, near Blanding; and Rainbow Bridge, about 435 miles southeast, near Page, Arizona. The national parks and monuments are filled with natural stone arches, columnns, bridges, spires and precipices.

The national recreation areas in Utah are Flaming Gorge, approximately 220 miles east, on the Utah-Wyoming border, and Glen Canyon, approximately 430 miles southeast, at the Utah-Arizona border. Flaming Gorge forms a 91-mile lake surrounded by vertical cliffs, forested mountains and clear streams.

General References

Founded: 1847 **Pop:** 159,936 **Elev:** 4,330 feet **Time zone:** Mountain **Area code:** 801

Phone Numbers

POLICE & FIRE: 911
FBI: 579-1400
POISON CONTROL CENTER: 581-2151
TIME & WEATHER: 976-1212

Information Sources

Salt Lake Convention & Visitors Bureau, 180 S West Temple St, 84101-1493; 521-2822 or -2868.
Utah Travel Council and Visitor Information Center, Council Hall, 300 N State St, 84114; 538-1030.
Visitor Information Center, Terminal 2, Salt Lake City International Airport, 84116; 575-2800.
Parks Department, 972-7800.

Transportation

AIRLINES: Alaska Air; Alpine Air; American; America West; Continental; Delta; Horizon; Northwest; TWA; United; and other commuter and regional airlines. For the most current airline schedules and information consult the *Official Airline Guide*, published twice monthly.
AIRPORT: Salt Lake City International, 575-2460.
CAR RENTAL AGENCIES: (See Toll-Free Numbers) Agency 534-1622; Alamo 575-2211; Avis 575-2847; Budget 363-1500; Hertz 575-2683.
PUBLIC TRANSPORTATION: Utah Transit Authority 287-4636.
RAILROAD PASSENGER SERVICE: Amtrak 800/872-7245.

Newspapers

Salt Lake City Deseret News; Salt Lake City Tribune.

Convention Facility

Salt Palace, 100 S West Temple, 534-4777.

Sports & Recreation

Major Sports Facility
Delta Center, 301 S West Temple, 325-SEAT (Utah Jazz, basketball, 355-3865; Golden Eagles, hockey, 532-4653).

Cultural Facilities

Theaters
Capitol Theatre, 50 W 200 South St, 355-2787.
Hale Center Theatre, 2801 S Main St, 484-9257.
Kingsbury Hall, University of Utah, 581-7100.
Pioneer Memorial Theatre, 300 South St at University, 581-6270.
Promised Valley Playhouse, 132 S State St, 364-5696.
Salt Lake Acting Company, 168 W 500 North St, 363-7522.

Concert Hall

Symphony Hall, 123 W South Temple St, 533-6408.

Museums

Fort Douglas Military Museum, 3 mi NE, Bldg 32, Potter St, 588-5188.
Hansen Planetarium, 15 S State St, 538-2098.
Museum of Church History and Art, 45 N West Temple St, 240-3310.
Pioneer Memorial Museum, 300 N Main St, 538-1050.
Utah Museum of Natural History, University of Utah, 581-4303.

Art Museums

Salt Lake Art Center, 20 S West Temple St, 328-4201.
Utah Museum of Fine Arts, University of Utah, 581-7332.

Points of Interest

Historical

Assembly Hall, SW corner of Temple Square.
Brigham Young Monument, Main & South Temple Sts.
Council Hall, Capitol Hill, 538-1030.
Lion House & Beehive House, 67 & 63 E South Temple Sts, 240-2977 (Lion) or -2672 (Beehive).
Tabernacle, Temple Square.
Temple Square, bounded by North, South & West Temple Sts & Main St, 240-2534.

Other Attractions

Arrow Press Square, 165 S West Temple St.
Hogle Zoological Garden, 2600 Sunnyside Ave, 582-1631.
Lagoon Amusement Park, Pioneer Village and Water Park, 17 mi N on I-15, 451-8000.
Marriott Library, University of Utah, 581-8558.
Old Deseret Pioneer Village, Pioneer Trail State Park, 584-8392.
Pioneer Trail State Park, 2601 Sunnyside Ave, 584-8392.
Raging Waters, 1200 West 1700 S, 973-4020.
Seagull Monument, Temple Square.

State Capitol, head of State St, 538-3000.
"This Is the Place" Monument, In Pioneer Trail State Park.
Timpanogos Cave National Monument, 26 mi S on I-15, then 10 mi E on UT 92, 756-5238 or -5239.
Trolley Square, bounded by 500 & 600 South Sts and 600 & 700 East Sts, 521-9877.
Wasatch-Cache National Forest, E & N of city, 524-5030.
ZCMI (Zion's Cooperative Mercantile Institution) Shopping Center, Main & South Temple Sts, 321-8743.

Sightseeing Tours

Gray Line bus tours, 553 W 100 South St, 84101; 521-7060.
Scenic West Tours, PO Box 369, Draper 84020; 572-2717 or 800/723-6429.

Annual Events

Utah Arts Festival, downtown. Last wk June.
"Days of '47" Celebration. Mid-July.
Utah State Fair, State Fairgrounds. 11 days beginning Thurs after Labor Day.
Temple Square Christmas, 240-2534. Early Dec.

City Neighborhoods

Many of the restaurants, unrated dining establishments and some lodgings listed under Salt Lake City include neighborhoods as well as exact street addresses. Geographic descriptions of Downtown and Trolley Square are given, followed by a table of restaurants arranged by neighborhood.

Downtown: South of 9th Ave, west of A St and 300 East St, north of 700 South St and east of 400 West St. **East of Downtown:** East of 9th East St.
Trolley Square: South of 500 South St, west of 700 East St, north of 600 South St and east of 600 East St.

Lodgings and Food

SALT LAKE CITY RESTAURANTS BY NEIGHBORHOOD AREAS

(For full description, see alphabetical listings under Restaurants)

DOWNTOWN

Baci Trattoria. 134 W Pierpont Ave

Benihana of Tokyo. 165 S West Temple St

Litza's for Pizza. 716 E 400 South St

Market Street Grill. 48 Market St

Mikado. 67 W 100 South St

Ristorante della Fontana. 336 S 400 East St

EAST OF DOWNTOWN

Cowboy Grub. 2350½ Foothill Blvd

Market Street Broiler. 258 S 1300 East St

Old Salt City Jail. 460 S 1000 East St

Rino's Italian Ristorante. 2302 Parleys Way

Note: *When a listing is located in a town that does not have its own city heading, it will appear under the city nearest to its location. In these cases, the address and town appear in parenthesis immediately following the name of the establishment.*

Motels

(Rates may be higher during state fair)

★ ★ **BEST WESTERN EXECUTIVE INN.** *(280 W 7200 South St, Midvale 84047) 8 mi S on I-15, exit 301.* 801/566-4141; FAX 801/566-5142. 92 rms, 2 story. Late Dec-Mar: S $59-$69; D $69-$84; each addl $5; suites $69-$149; under 18 free; lower rates rest of yr. Crib $6. TV; cable. Heated pool; whirlpool. Complimentary coffee in lobby. Restaurant adj 6 am-midnight. Ck-out noon. Meeting rms. Downhill ski 15 mi; x-country ski 20 mi. Balconies. Cr cds: A, C, D, DS, ER, JCB, MC, V.

★ **BRIGHTON LODGE.** *(Big Cottonwood Canyon, Brighton 84121) Approx 15 mi W via UT 190.* 801/532-4731; res: 800/873-5512 (exc UT); FAX 801/649-1787. 22 rms, 2 story. Mid-Nov-mid-Apr: S, D $90-$120; lower rates rest of yr. TV in game rm; cable. Heated pool; whirlpool. Restaurant adj 8 am-10 pm; Sun to 4:30 pm. Bar. Ck-out 11 am. Shopping arcade. Downhill/x-country ski on site. Game rm. Refrigerators. Picnic tables, grills. On creek. Cr cds: A, DS, MC, V.

★ ★ **COMFORT INN.** *8955 S 255 West St (84070), south of downtown.* 801/255-4919; FAX 801/255-4998. 98 rms, 2 story. S $55-$65; D $65-$75; each addl $5; under 18 free. Crib free. TV; cable, in-rm movies. Indoor pool; whirlpool. Complimentary continental bkfst. Ck-out noon. Meeting rm. Valet serv. Game rm. Cr cds: A, C, D, DS, ER, JCB, MC, V.

✔★ **DAYS INN AIRPORT.** *1900 W North Temple St (84116), west of downtown.* 801/539-8538; FAX 801/539-8538, ext. 122. 110 rms, 2 story. S, D $47-$61; each addl $7; suites $70-$75; under 18 free. Crib free. Pet accepted. TV; cable, in-rm movies. Complimentary continental bkfst. Restaurant nearby. Ck-out 11 am. Valet serv. Free airport, RR station, bus depot transportation. Cr cds: A, C, D, DS, MC, V.

★ ★ **HAMPTON INN.** *(10690 S Holiday Park Dr, Sandy 84070) S via I-15, exit 10600 South St, then ½ blk E.* 801/571-0800. 131 rms, 4 story. S $59-$69; D $65-$75; under 18 free; wkly rates, ski plans. Crib free. TV; cable. Indoor pool; whirlpool. Complimentary continental bkfst. Restaurant adj 6 am-11 pm. Ck-out noon. Coin lndry. Meeting rms. Sundries. Free bus depot transportation. Downhill ski 20 mi. Shopping center opp. Cr cds: A, C, D, DS, MC, V.

✔★ ★ **LA QUINTA.** *(530 Catalpa Rd, Midvale 84047) 8 mi S on I-15, 72nd South St exit, E to Catalpa Rd.* 801/566-3291; FAX 801/562-5943. 122 rms, 2 story. S $49; D $57; each addl $8; under 18 free. Crib free. Pet accepted. TV; cable. Heated pool. Continental bkfst. Complimentary coffee in lobby. Restaurant adj open 24 hrs. Ck-out noon. Meeting rms. Downhill ski 15 mi; x-country ski 20 mi. Cr cds: A, C, D, DS, MC, V.

★ ★ **QUALITY INN-MIDVALLEY.** *4465 Century Dr (84123), south of downtown.* 801/268-2533; FAX 801/266-6206. 131 rms, 2 story, 17 kits. Feb-Mar & July-Sept: S $53-$69; D $62-$79; kit. units $69-$79; under 18 free; ski plan; lower rates rest of yr. Crib free. Pet accepted; $5-$7. TV; cable. Pool; whirlpool. Complimentary continental bkfst. Restaurant adj open 24 hrs. Ck-out noon. Coin lndry. Game rm. Balconies. Cr cds: A, C, D, DS, ER, JCB, MC, V.

★ ★ **RAMADA INN-DOWNTOWN.** *230 W 600 South St (84101), downtown.* 801/364-5200; FAX 801/364-0974. 160 rms, 2 story. S, D $56-$86; each addl $10; under 19 free. Crib free. TV; cable. Indoor pool. Restaurant 6:30 am-2 pm, 5-10 pm. Rm serv. Private club from 5 pm, closed Sun. Ck-out noon. Coin lndry. Meeting rms. Valet serv exc Sun. Free airport, RR station, bus depot transportation. Exercise equipt; weight machine, bicycles, whirlpool, sauna. Rec rm. Cr cds: A, C, D, DS, JCB, MC, V.

★ ★ **RESIDENCE INN BY MARRIOTT.** *765 E 400 South St (84102), east of downtown.* 801/532-5511; FAX 801/531-0416. 128 kit. suites (1-2-bedrm), 2 story. Suites $130-$176; wkly, monthly rates; ski packages. Pet accepted, some restrictions; $10-$100. TV; cable, in-rm movies avail. Heated pool. Complimentary continental bkfst. Ck-out noon. Coin lndry. Bellhops. Valet serv. Airport, RR station, bus depot transportation. Many fireplaces. Cr cds: A, C, D, DS, JCB, MC, V.

★ **SLEEP INN.** *(10676 S 300 West St, South Jordan 84095) S on I-15, exit 10600 South St, then ½ blk W.* 801/572-2020; res: 800/221-2222; FAX 801/572-2459. 68 rms, shower only, 2 story. S $50-$60; D $55-$65; each addl $5; family rates. Crib free. TV; cable, in-rm movies. Complimentary continental bkfst. Restaurant nearby. Ck-out noon. Downhill ski 20 mi. Cr cds: A, C, D, DS, ER, JCB, MC, V.

✔★ **SUPER 8.** *616 S 200 West St (84101), downtown.* 801/534-0808; FAX 801/355-7735. 123 rms, 4 story. S, D $47.88-$69.88; each addl $3-$4; under 12 free; wkend rates; higher rates special events. Crib free. TV; cable. Complimentary coffee. Restaurant opp open 24 hrs. Ck-out 11 am. Cr cds: A, C, D, DS, MC, V.

Motor Hotels

★ ★ **COMFORT INN.** *200 N Admiral Byrd Rd (84116), in Salt Lake Intl Center, near Intl Airport, west of downtown.* 801/537-7444; FAX 801/532-4721. 154 rms, 4 story. S $72; D $82; each addl $10; under 18 free. Crib free. TV. Heated pool; whirlpool. Restaurant 6:30

am-midnight. Rm serv. Ck-out 11 am. Meeting rms. Valet serv. Free airport transportation. Some refrigerators. Balconies. Cr cds: A, C, D, DS, MC, V.

D ⊠ ⌔ ≋ ✈ ⊠ 🔥 SC

★ ★ ★ **HOLIDAY INN-DOWNTOWN.** *999 S Main St (84111), south of downtown.* 801/359-8600; FAX 801/359-7816. 263 rms, 3 story, 50 suites. S $85-$135; D $95-$135; each addl $10; under 18 free; ski plans. Crib free. Pet accepted, some restrictions; $100 refundable. TV; cable. Indoor/outdoor pool. Playground. Restaurants 6 am-10 pm. Rm serv. Bar. Ck-out noon. Coin lndry. Convention facilities. Bellhops. Gift shop. Barber, beauty shop. Free airport, RR station, bus depot transportation. Tennis. Putting green. Exercise equipt; weight machine, bicycles, whirlpool, sauna. Lawn games. Some refrigerators. Wet bar in suites. Cr cds: A, C, D, DS, ER, JCB, MC, V.

D ⊠ ⌔ ✦ ≋ ✈ ⊠ 🔥 SC

★ ★ **HOWARD JOHNSON.** *122 W South Temple St (84101), downtown.* 801/521-0130; FAX 801/322-5057. 226 rms, 13 story. S $63-$95; D $69-$99; each addl $7; suites $165; under 18 free. Crib free. Pet accepted; $10. TV; cable. Heated pool; whirlpool. Restaurant 6 am-11 pm; Fri-Sun to 2 am. Rm serv. Ck-out noon. Lndry facilities. Meeting rms. Bellhops. Valet serv. Gift shop. Free airport, RR station, bus depot transportation. Some refrigerators. Cr cds: A, C, D, DS, JCB, MC, V.

⊠ ≋ ⊠ 🔥 SC

★ ★ ★ **RADISSON AIRPORT.** *2177 W N Temple St (84116), near Intl Airport, west of downtown.* 801/364-5800; FAX 801/364-5823. 127 rms, 3 story, 46 suites. S $69-$139; D $79-$149; each addl $10; suites $99-$149; under 18 free; ski, golf plans. Crib free. TV; cable, in-rm movies. Heated pool. Complimentary continental bkfst. Complimentary coffee in rms. Restaurant 6:30-11 am, 5-10 pm. Rm serv. Ck-out noon. Meeting rms. Bellhops. Free garage parking. Free airport, RR station, bus depot transportation. Exercise equipt; bicycles, stair machine. Bathrm phones, refrigerators, wet bars. Balconies. Cr cds: A, C, D, DS, ER, JCB, MC, V.

D ≋ ✈ ✈ ⊠ 🔥 SC

Hotels

★ ★ **BEST WESTERN OLYMPUS.** *161 W 600 South St (84101), downtown.* 801/521-7373; FAX 801/524-0354. 393 rms, 13 story. S, D $75-$95; suites $125; under 18 free; wkend rates; ski plan. Crib free. TV; cable. Pool. Restaurant open 24 hrs. Ck-out noon. Convention facilities. Barber, beauty shop. Airport transportation. Exercise equipt; bicycles, stair machine, whirlpool. Refrigerators. Balconies. Cr cds: A, C, D, DS, ER, MC, V.

D ≋ ✈ ⊠ 🔥 SC

★ ★ ★ **DOUBLETREE.** *215 W South Temple St (84101), downtown.* 801/531-7500; FAX 801/328-1289. 381 rms, 15 story. S, D $69-$149; each addl $10; suites $179-$550; under 18 free; wkend, hol rates; ski packages. Crib free. TV; cable. Indoor pool. Restaurant 6 am-11:30 pm. Bar noon-midnight. Ck-out noon. Coin lndry. Convention facilities. Concierge. Gift shop. Free airport, RR station transportation. Exercise equipt; stair machines, bicycles, whirlpool, sauna. Adj to Delta Center. Cr cds: A, C, D, DS, MC, V.

D ≋ ✈ ⊠ 🔥 SC

★ ★ ★ **EMBASSY SUITES.** *600 S West Temple St (84101), downtown.* 801/359-7800; FAX 801/359-3753. 241 suites, 9 story. S $99-$119; D $119-$139; each addl $10; under 12 free; wkend, ski rates. Crib free. TV; cable, in-rm movies. Indoor pool. Complimentary full bkfst. Complimentary coffee in rms. Restaurant 11 am-11 pm. Private club to 1 am. Ck-out noon. Coin lndry. Meeting rms. Concierge. Gift shop. Covered parking. Free airport, RR station, bus depot transportation. Exercise equipt; bicycles, stair machine, whirlpool, sauna. Refrigerators, wet bars. Atrium lobby. Cr cds: A, C, D, DS, MC, V.

D ≋ ✈ ⊠ 🔥 SC

★ ★ ★ **HILTON.** *150 W 500 South St (84101), downtown.* 801/532-3344; FAX 801/532-3344, ext. 1029. 351 rms, 10 story. S, D $105-$120; each addl $15; suites $120-$350; family rates; ski plans. Crib free. Pet accepted. TV; cable. Pool; poolside serv. Restaurant 6 am-midnight. Private clubs 11:30-1 am, Sun 11 am-10 pm; entertainment. Ck-out noon. Convention facilities. Barber, beauty shop. Airport transportation. Exercise equipt; weight machine, bicycles, whirlpool, sauna. Ski rentals avail. Balconies. *LUXURY LEVEL : EXECUTIVE QUARTERS.* 39 rms, 2 floors. S, D $125-$140. Private lounge. Bathrm phones. Complimentary continental bkfst, refreshments. Cr cds: A, C, D, DS, ER, JCB, MC, V.

D ⌔ ≋ ✈ ⊠ 🔥

✔ ★ ★ ★ **LITTLE AMERICA.** *Box 206 (84101), 500 S Main St, downtown.* 801/363-6781; res: 800/453-9450 (exc UT), 800/662-5888 (UT); FAX 801/322-1610. 850 rms, 17 story. S $63-$118; D $73-$128; suites $450; under 13 free; wkend, ski rates. Crib free. TV. 2 pools, 1 indoor; wading pool. Restaurant 5 am-midnight; dining rm 7-10 am, 11 am-2 pm, 5-11 pm. Bar 11 am-midnight; entertainment. Ck-out 1 pm. Convention facilities. Shopping arcade. Barber, beauty shop. Free covered parking. Free airport, RR station, bus depot transportation. Exercise equipt; weights, bicycles, whirlpool, sauna. Bathrm phones, refrigerators. Domed, stained-glass ceiling in lobby. Garden setting on 10 acres. Cr cds: A, C, D, DS, MC, V.

≋ ✈ ⊠ 🔥 SC

★ ★ ★ **MARRIOTT.** *75 S West Temple St (84101), downtown.* 801/531-0800; FAX 801/532-4127. 515 rms, 15 story. S, D $134-$154; suites $250-$759; family rates; wkend, honeymoon, ski plans. Crib free. TV; cable. Heated indoor/outdoor pool; poolside serv. Restaurant 6:30 am-11 pm; Fri, Sat to midnight. Private club; entertainment. Ck-out noon. Convention facilities. Concierge. Covered valet parking. Free airport, RR station, bus depot transportation. Exercise equipt; weights, bicycles, whirlpool, sauna. Balconies. Inside access to shopping mall. *LUXURY LEVEL : CONCIERGE LEVEL.* 54 rms. S, D $152-$166. Complimentary continental bkfst, refreshments, newspaper. Cr cds: A, C, D, DS, ER, JCB, MC, V.

D ⌔ ≋ ✈ ⊠ 🔥 SC

✔ ★ ★ ★ **PEERY.** *110 W 300 South St (84101), downtown.* 801/521-4300; res: 800/331-0073; FAX 801/575-5014. 77 rms, 3 story. S, D $69-$115; under 16 free; wkend rates. Crib free. TV; cable. Complimentary continental bkfst. Restaurant 11:30 am-10:30 pm. Bar. Ck-out noon. Meeting rms. Concierge. Gift shop. Free airport transportation. Exercise equipt; weight machine, bicycles, whirlpool. Historic building (1910). Cr cds: A, C, D, DS, MC, V.

✈ ⊠ 🔥 SC

★ ★ ★ **RED LION.** *255 S West Temple St (84101), downtown.* 801/328-2000; FAX 801/532-1953. 501 rms, 18 story. S, D $125-$160; each addl $15; suites $200-$1,000; under 18 free; wkend rates; ski package. Crib free. Pet accepted, some restrictions. TV. Indoor pool; poolside serv. Restaurant 6 am-11 pm. Private club; entertainment. Ck-out 1 pm. Convention facilities. Concierge. Gift shop. Free covered parking; valet. Free airport, RR station, bus depot transportation. Exercise equipt; weights, bicycles, whirlpool, sauna. Game rm. Some refrigerators. *LUXURY LEVEL : EXECUTIVE LEVEL.* 28 rms, 2 suites. S, D $145-$160; suites $250-$1,000. Private lounge. Full wet bars. Bathrm phones. Complimentary continental bkfst, refreshments. Cr cds: A, C, D, DS, ER, JCB, MC, V.

D ⌔ ≋ ✈ ⊠ 🔥 SC

★ ★ **SHILO INN.** *206 S West Temple St (84101), downtown.* 801/521-9500; FAX 801/359-6527. 200 rms, 12 story. S, D $95-$105; each addl $10; suites $250-$300; kit. units $200-$250; under 12 free. Crib free. TV; cable. Heated pool; whirlpool, sauna. Complimentary continental bkfst. Restaurant 6 am-10 pm. Bar. Ck-out noon. Coin lndry. Meeting rms. Shopping arcade. Free airport transportation. Wet bars, refrigerators; some bathrm phones. Balconies. Cr cds: A, C, D, DS, ER, JCB, MC, V.

≋ ✈ 🔥 SC

★ ★ ★ **UNIVERSITY PARK.** *480 Wakara Way (84108), east of downtown.* 801/581-1000; res: 800/637-4390; FAX 801/583-7641. 220 rms, 7 story, 29 suites. S, D $99-$140; suites $119-$160; under 12 free. Crib free. TV; cable. Indoor pool. Restaurant 5:30 am-10 pm. Bar 4 pm-midnight; entertainment, dancing Thurs-Sat. Ck-out noon. Meeting rms. Concierge. Gift shop. Free airport, RR station, bus depot transportation. Downhill/x-country ski 15 mi. Exercise equipt; weight machine, bicycles, whirlpool. Rec rm. Refrigerators; wet bar in suites. Cr cds: A, C, D, DS, MC, V.

Inns

★ ★ ★ **BRIGHAM STREET INN.** *1135 E South Temple St (84102), 2 mi east of Main St, east of downtown.* 801/364-4461; FAX 801/521-3201. 9 rms, 3 story. S, D $75-$175; each addl $10. Crib free. TV. Complimentary continental bkfst, coffee. Setups. Ck-out noon, ck-in 3 pm. X-country ski 15 mi. Fireplace in 5 rms. Historic Victorian mansion; restored. Award-winning, individually decorated rms. Cr cds: A, D, DS, MC, V.

★ ★ ★ **INN AT TEMPLE SQUARE.** *71 W S Temple St (84101), downtown.* 801/531-1000; res: 800/843-4668; FAX 801/536-7272. 90 rms, 7 story, 10 suites. S, D $85-$125; each addl $10; suites $150-$220; under 18 free. Crib free. TV; cable. Pool privileges. Complimentary full bkfst. Dining rm 6:30-9:30 am, 11:30 am-2:30 pm, 5-10 pm. Rm serv. Ck-out noon, ck-in 3 pm. Bellhops. Valet serv. Concierge. Free airport, RR station, bus depot transportation. Health club privileges. Bathrm phones, refrigerators. Elegant inn built in 1929; antiques from old Hotel Utah. Antique horsedrawn carriage rides. Opp Temple Square. Totally nonsmoking. Cr cds: A, C, D, DS, MC, V.

★ ★ **SPRUCES BED & BREAKFAST.** *6151 S 900 East St (84121), 15 mi S on I-15, exit 72S, south of downtown.* 801/268-8762. 4 rms, 1 air-cooled, 2 story, 2 kit. units. Mid-Nov-mid-Apr: S, D $55-$100; kit. units $75-$135; under 12 free; lower rates rest of yr. Crib free. TV. Complimentary continental bkfst. Restaurant nearby. Ck-out 11 am, ck-in 2 pm. Downhill/x-country ski 15 mi. Health club privileges. Balconies. Picnic tables. Surrounded by spruce trees. Built in 1902 by a Norwegian carpenter; folk art and Southwestern decor. Totally nonsmoking. Cr cds: A, MC, V.

Restaurants

★ ★ **BACI TRATTORIA.** *134 W Pierpont Ave, downtown.* 801/328-1500. Hrs: 11:30 am-2:30 pm, 5-10 pm; wkends to 11 pm; early-bird dinner 5-7 pm. Closed Sun; major hols; also July 24. Italian menu. Bar. A la carte entrees: lunch $4.99-$11.99, dinner $7.99-$21.99. Child's meals. Specializes in fresh pasta, rotisserie meats, fresh seafood. Parking. Large stained-glass partitions, murals. Cr cds: A, D, DS, MC, V.

★ **BAHIA GRILL.** *(1114 E Ft Union Blvd, Midvale 84047) 3 mi E of I-15, 7200 South St exit.* 801/566-3985. Hrs: 11:30 am-10 pm; Fri, Sat to 11 pm; Sun 4-9 pm. Res accepted. Mexican menu. Bar. Semi-a la carte: lunch, dinner $1.95-$9.95. Child's meals. Salsa bar. Parking. Cr cds: A, D, DS, MC, V.

★ ★ **BENIHANA OF TOKYO.** *165 S West Temple St, opp Salt Palace, on Arrow Press Square, downtown.* 801/322-2421. Hrs: 11:30 am-2, 5:30-10 pm; Fri to 11 pm; Sat 5:30-11 pm; Sun & hols 4-9 pm. Res accepted. Japanese menu. Bar. Semi-a la carte: lunch $4.75-$12, dinner $12.50-$24.25. Child's meals. Specializes in sea-food, steak, chicken. Tableside cooking. Japanese decor. Cr cds: A, C, D, DS, MC, V.

★ **COWBOY GRUB.** *2350½ Foothill Blvd, east of downtown.* 801/466-8334. Hrs: 11 am-10 pm; Fri, Sat to 11 pm. Closed Sun; major hols & July 24. Res accepted. Semi-a la carte: lunch, dinner $4-$11. Child's meals. Specializes in barbecued ribs, Mexican dishes. Salad bar. Parking. Western decor. Cr cds: A, DS, MC, V.

★ ★ **MARKET STREET BROILER.** *258 S 1300 East St, east of downtown.* 801/583-8808. Hrs: 11:30 am-10 pm; Sun 4-9 pm; early-bird dinner 4-6 pm. Bar from noon. Semi-a la carte: lunch $4.99-$14.99, dinner $7.99-$24.99. Child's meals. Specializes in fresh fish, barbecued ribs. Parking. Outdoor dining. Modern decor in historic former fire station. Cr cds: A, D, DS, MC, V.

★ ★ **MARKET STREET GRILL.** *48 Market St, downtown.* 801/322-4668. Hrs: 6:30 am-3 pm, 5-10:30 pm; Fri to 11:30 pm; Sat 7 am-11:30 pm; Sun 4-9:30 pm; early-bird dinner 5-7 pm; Sun brunch 9:30 am-3 pm. Closed Labor Day, Thanksgiving, Dec 25. Bar noon-11:30 pm. Semi-a la carte: bkfst $2.99-$7.99, lunch $5.99-$12.99, dinner $10.99-$21. Sun brunch $4.99-$10.99. Child's meals. Specializes in steak, seafood. Parking. In renovated 1906 hotel. Cr cds: A, D, DS, MC, V.

★ ★ **MIKADO.** *67 W 100 South St, downtown.* 801/328-0929. Hrs: 5:30-9:30 pm; Fri, Sat to 10:30 pm; summer: 6-10 pm; Fri, Sat to 11 pm. Closed Sun; major hols. Res accepted. Japanese menu. Semi-a la carte: dinner $11-$21. Child's meals. Specialties: shrimp tempura, chicken teriyaki, beef sukiyaki. Sushi bar. Zashiki rms. Cr cds: A, C, D, DS, JCB, MC, V.

★ ★ **OLD SALT CITY JAIL.** *460 S 1000 East St, east of downtown.* 801/355-2422. Hrs: 5-10 pm; Fri & Sat 4:30-11 pm; Sun 4-9 pm; early-bird dinner 4:30-7 pm. Res accepted. Bar. Semi-a la carte: dinner $8.95-$17.95. Child's meals. Specializes in prime rib, steak, seafood. Salad bar. Cowboy singer Thurs-Sat. Parking. Early brewery re-created as an old country jail. Cr cds: A, D, DS, MC, V.

★ **RAFAEL'S.** *(889 E 9400 South St, Sandy) S on I-15, exit 9000 South St, then 2 mi E, in Aspen Plaza.* 801/561-4545. Hrs: 11:30 am-9 pm; Fri, Sat to 10 pm. Closed Sun; Memorial Day, Labor Day, Dec 25. Mexican menu. Semi-a la carte: lunch, dinner $3.75-$8.50. Specializes in enchiladas, fajitas. Parking. Mexican, Indian and Aztec artwork. Cr cds: DS, MC, V.

★ ★ **RINO'S ITALIAN RISTORANTE.** *2302 Parleys Way, east of downtown.* 801/484-0901. Hrs: 6-10 pm; Fri, Sat 5:30-10:30 pm; Sun 5-9 pm. Closed major hols. Res accepted. Italian, continental menu. Serv bar. Semi-a la carte: dinner $7.95-$19.95. Parking. Patio dining. Bistro-style cafe. Cr cds: A, MC, V.

★ ★ **RISTORANTE DELLA FONTANA.** *336 S 400 East St, downtown.* 801/328-4243. Hrs: 11 am-10 pm. Closed Sun; some major hols; also July 24th. Res accepted. Italian, Amer menu. Semi-a la carte: lunch $6.39-$13.99, dinner (6-course) $9.95-$17.95. Child's meals. Specializes in pasta, veal, chicken. Parking. Historic converted church, stained-glass windows, antique chandeliers. Waterfall in dining rm; decor changed seasonally. Cr cds: A, C, D, DS, MC, V.

Unrated Dining Spot

LITZA'S FOR PIZZA. *716 E 400 South St, downtown.* 801/359-5352. Hrs: 11 am-11 pm; Fri, Sat to 12:30 am. Closed Sun; Thanksgiving, Dec 25. Italian menu. Semi-a la carte: lunch $5.15-$11, dinner $8-$15. Specializes in pizza. Parking. No cr cds accepted.

San Antonio

Founded: 1718

Pop: 935,933

Elev: 701 feet

Time zone: Central

Area code: 210

San Antonio has a charm and grace common to many Texas cities. Part of this charm stems from its Spanish beginnings, signs of which can still be found almost everywhere. In the course of its history, San Antonio has been under six flags: France, Spain, Mexico, Republic of Texas, Confederate States of America and United States of America. Although the Spanish influence predominates, traces of each remain today.

The Mission San Antonio de Valero (the Alamo) was founded by Friar Antonio de San Buenaventura Olivares in May 1718, near the San Antonio River. Four more missions were built along the river during the next 13 years, and all continued to operate until about 1794. It was at the Alamo that, from February 23 to March 6, 1836, Davy Crockett, Colonel James Bowie, Colonel William B. Travis and 186 other Texans unsuccessfully resisted Santa Anna and his force of 5,000 troops. Every defender died, their bravery giving rise to the battle cry "Remember the Alamo!" Three months after the tragedy, the city was almost deserted, but within a few years it became a great Western outpost.

The arrival of adventurers and cowboys in the 1870s earned San Antonio a reputation as a tough, hard-drinking, hard-fighting gambling town. Now the state's third largest city, tenth largest in the country, San Antonio has become a prosperous, modern city that still retains much of the flavor of its colorful past.

Business

About 25 percent of the working population of San Antonio is employed in the retail and wholesale industry. Some 1,300 manufacturing firms in the city employ roughly 8.5 percent of the work force. San Antonio's 5 military installations also employ more than 32,000 civilians. San Antonio is one of the Southwest's leading science centers, particularly in the field of medical research.

Some of the products manufactured in San Antonio are fertilizer, oil field equipment, clothing, airplane parts, food products and medical supplies.

Convention Facilities

The San Antonio Convention Center is a multipurpose facility available for business meetings, conventions, entertainment, trade shows and other events. The expanded convention center has 2 exhibit halls measuring 120,000 square feet each; 2 banquet halls at 29,600 square feet and 22,000 square feet; and an additional 25,000 square feet of meeting rooms on 3 levels. The center's theater for the performing arts has a seating capacity of 2,733 people, while the arena in the convention center seats 15,342 people. The total convention center complex has 793,506 square feet.

The Alamodome provides 160,000 gross square feet of exhibit space and 30,000 square feet of conference space and can be configured to host various sports events, major concerts, conventions and trade shows (maximum seating 73,200).

The San Antonio Municipal Auditorium seats 4,982 people in the main hall, with 24,000 square feet of meeting and exhibit space on the lower level. The Joe and Harry Freeman Coliseum has 155,964 square feet of exhibit space, meeting rooms and parking for 10,000 cars.

Recreation and Entertainment

The almost subtropical climate of San Antonio (average annual temperature of 68°F) allows year-round recreation. Championship golf courses with beautiful greens and tree-lined fairways offer a challenge to golfers. San Antonio has 8 public and 6 private courses. The city also has numerous public tennis facilities. There is sailing, fishing, waterskiing, sail boarding, canoeing and whitewater rafting within a half-hour drive from the city.

Fiesta Texas is a 200-acre amusement park featuring rides and entertainment in four themed areas. Featured is the Rattler, said to be the world's tallest and fastest wooden roller coaster.

Sea World of Texas, located on a 250-acre site in northwest San Antonio, is the world's largest marine-life park.

San Antonio is the home of the San Antonio Spurs (National Basketball Association), the San Antonio Missions (Texas Baseball League) and the San Antonio Racquets (Team Tennis League).

The city has many fine repertory and neighborhood theaters offering diverse entertainment.

Historical Areas

The most famous of all historic sites in the city is the Alamo, built in 1718. The Long Barrack, once the mission rectory, has been restored and contains a museum of fascinating Texas relics.

Within walking distance of the Alamo are many historic areas. The Spanish Governor's Palace, completed in 1749, was the residence and office of Spanish administrators. The José Antonio Navarro Residence, home of a Texas patriot, is a complex of three adobe houses built about 1850. The Articles of Capitulation were signed in Cos House by General Perfecto de Cos on December 10, 1835, after Texans had taken the town. The Menger Hotel is a famous hostelry in which Robert E. Lee, Theodore Roosevelt and William Jennings Bryan stayed. Located in the hotel is a bar, still in use, where Roosevelt recruited "Rough Riders."

Part of the Rosa Verde Urban Renewal Project is the restoration of Market Square (El Mercado). Since 1830, there has been a market square in San Antonio, at various locations. The reconstructed market has been on its present site for more than 40 years.

La Villita, the original civil settlement area, is a neighborhood of old adobe buildings, vine-covered stone walls, flagstone walks and fountains. The area is the setting for various traditional fiestas during the year.

There are several restored missions in the San Antonio area, which, like the Alamo, were founded in the early 1700s by Franciscan friars. Mission Concepción, established in 1731 and constructed of porous limestone, is the oldest unrestored mission in Texas. The San José Mission (1720), one of the most successful missions in the Southwest, includes a restored church, Indian quarters, granary and old mill. Built of limestone and tufa, the church is famous for its carvings, including Pedro Huizar's sacristy window, sometimes referred to as "Rosa's window." These missions plus San Juan Capistrano, San Francisco de la Espada and the Espada Dam and Aqueduct form the San Antonio Missions National Historical Park. The missions are active Roman Catholic parishes and are open for public touring and worship. Sunday Mariachi Mass at Mission San José is memorable.

Sightseeing

The heart of San Antonio is the Paseo del Rio. Only a few steps away from the business activities of the city is a tranquil, landscaped path reached from the street level by winding stone stairways. Along its route are sidewalk restaurants and cafes, botanical gardens, shops and an outdoor theater. It is a place to relax, to enjoy a glass of wine or a Mexican beer, a Texas steak or a plate heaped with tacos, enchiladas and refried beans. It is ideal for an evening stroll along the cobblestone walkways or a riverboat ride along the 45-minute, round-trip course.

Several great modern buildings were built for the city's HemisFair '68. One of the most interesting is the Institute of Texan Cultures, which honors the contribution to Texas history of 26 ethnic and cultural groups through an unusual audiovisual program and various exhibits. From the imposing 750-foot Tower of the Americas, the city and surrounding hills are spread before the visitor.

San Antonio has a variety of parks to enjoy. Brackenridge Park, covering 340 acres, houses the Witte Museum, Pioneer Hall, Zoological Gardens and Aquarium, the Japanese Tea Gardens and the Brackenridge *Eagle* miniature train.

Just north of the city is the San Antonio Museum of Art, located in a restored Lone Star brewery. Its collection is built around the art of the Americas—Spanish colonial, Mexican folk, contemporary and modern American Indian.

North of San Antonio is the Texans' beloved "hill country," a land of gentle hills and rushing rivers; waterfalls, caverns and springs; wild growths of mesquite and neat ranches. Lyndon Johnson was born and grew up here, and it is the location of the LBJ State Park.

The city of New Braunfels attracts more than 160,000 visitors each fall to its 10-day Wurstfest. North of New Braunfels is San Marcos, where a beautiful subtropical resort and park, Aquarena Springs, presents a lush contrast to the rugged country to the west.

General References

Founded: 1718 **Pop:** 935,933 **Elev:** 701 feet **Time zone:** Central **Area code:** 210

Phone Numbers

POLICE & FIRE: 911
FBI: 225-6741
POISON CONTROL CENTER: 911
TIME: 226-3232   WEATHER: 828-0683

Information Sources

San Antonio Convention and Visitors Bureau, 121 Alamo Plaza, PO Box 2277, 78298; 270-8700 or 800/447-3372.
Visitor Information Center, 317 Alamo Plaza, 78205; 270-8748.

Transportation

AIRLINES: Aeromexico; American; Continental; Delta; Mexicana; Northwest; Southwest; TWA; United; USAir; and other commuter and regional airlines. For the most current airline schedules and information consult the *Official Airline Guide,* published twice monthly.
AIRPORT: San Antonio International, 821-3411.
CAR RENTAL AGENCIES: (See Toll-Free Numbers) Avis 826-6332; Budget 828-5693; Hertz 841-8800; National 824-7544.
PUBLIC TRANSPORTATION: VIA Metropolitan Transit Service 227-2020.
RAILROAD PASSENGER SERVICE: Amtrak 800/872-7245.

Newspaper

San Antonio Express News.

Convention Facilities

Alamodome, 100 Montana, 223-3663.
Convention Center, HemisFair Park, 200 E Market St, 299-8500.
Municipal Auditorium, 100 Auditorium Circle, 299-8511.

Sports & Recreation

Alamodome, 100 Montana, 223-3663.
Convention Center Arena, HemisFair Park, 200 E Market St, 299-8500 (Spurs, basketball, 554-7787).

Cultural Facilities

Concert Halls
Convention Center Arena, HemisFair Park, 200 E Market St, 299-8500.
Joe & Harry Freeman Coliseum, 3201 E Houston St, 224-6080.

Museums
Buckhorn Hall of Horns & Hall of Texas History, 600 Lone Star Blvd, 270-9467.
Fort Sam Houston Museum, off I-35, N New Braunfels Ave exit, 221-1886.
Hertzberg Circus Museum, 210 W Market St, 299-7819.
Institute of Texan Cultures, 801 S Bowie St, 558-2300.
McNay Art Museum, 6000 N New Braunfels Ave at US 81, 824-5368.
Pioneer Hall, Brackenridge Park, 3805 Broadway, 824-2537.
San Antonio Museum of Art, 200 W Jones Ave, 829-7262.

Points of Interest

Historical
The Alamo, 300 Alamo Plaza, 225-1391.
Cos House, 418 La Villita, 299-8610.
El Mercado, 514 W Commerce, 299-8600.
José Antonio Navarro State Historical Park, 228 S Laredo St, 226-4801.
La Villita, S of Paseo de la Villita, W at S Alamo St, 299-8610.
Menger Hotel, 204 Alamo Plaza, 223-4361.
Mission Concepción, 807 Mission Rd, 229-5701.
Mission San Francisco de la Espada, 10040 Espada Rd, 627-2021.
Mission San Juan Capistrano, 9102 Graf Rd, 229-5734.
The Quadrangle, Fort Sam Houston, Grayson St, 221-1886.
San Antonio Missions National Historic Park, 229-5701.
San Fernando Cathedral, 115 Main Plaza, 227-1297.
San José Mission, 6539 San Jose Dr, 229-4770.
Spanish Governor's Palace, 105 Military Plaza, 224-0601.
Steves Homestead, 509 King William St, 225-5924.

Other Attractions

Cascade Caverns Park, 14 mi NW on I-10, exit 543, W to Boerne, 755-8080.
Fiesta Texas, 17000 I-10W, 697-5443.
HemisFair Park, 200 S Alamo, 299-8572.
Paseo del Rio, 21-blk River Walk along the San Antonio River.
Botanical Gardens, 555 Funston Pl, 821-5115.
Sea World of Texas, 10500 Sea World Dr, 16 mi NW on TX 151, 523-3611.
Splashtown, I-35 exit 160, 227-1400.
Tower of the Americas, HemisFair Park, 299-8615.
Zoological Gardens and Aquarium, 3903 N St Mary's St, 734-7183.

Sightseeing Tour

Gray Line bus tours, 1430 E Houston St, 78202; 226-1706.

Annual Events

San Antonio Livestock Show and Rodeo, Joe and Harry Freeman Coliseum, 3201 E Houston St, 225-5851. Mid Feb.
Fiesta San Antonio, 227-5191. Apr 21-30.
Texas Folklife Festival, HemisFair Park, 226-7651. Early Aug.
Fiestas Navidenas, Market Square, 299-8600. Mid-Dec.
Las Posadas, Paseo del Rio, 224-6163. Dec.

City Neighborhoods

Many of the restaurants, unrated dining establishments and some lodgings listed under San Antonio include neighborhoods as well as exact street addresses. Geographic descriptions of these areas are given, followed by a table of restaurants arranged by neighborhood.

Downtown: South of I-35, west of I-35/37, north of Durango St and east of I-10. **North of Downtown:** North of I-35. **South of Downtown:** South of Durango St. **West of Downtown:** West of I-10.
La Villita: Downtown area south of Paseo de la Villita, west of S Alamo St, north of Nueva St and east of S Presa St.
Riverwalk (Paseo Del Rio): Downtown area along San Antonio River and along canal extending east from the river between E Commerce and Market Sts.

Lodgings and Food

SAN ANTONIO RESTAURANTS
BY NEIGHBORHOOD AREAS

(For a full description, see alphabetical listings under Restaurants)

DOWNTOWN

Guenther House. 205 E Guenther St
Mi Tierra. 218 Produce Row
Paesano's. 1715 McCullough Ave
Tower Of The Americas. 222 HemisFair Plaza

NORTH OF DOWNTOWN

410 Diner. 8315 Broadway St
5050 Diner. 5050 Broadway St
Aldo's Ristorante. 8539 Fredericksburg Rd
Biga. 206 E Locust St

Billy Blues. 330 E Grayson St
Brazier At Los Patios. 2015 NE Loop I-410
Cappy's. 5011 Broadway St
Chez Ardid. 1919 San Pedro Ave
Crumpet's. 5800 Broadway St
Fujiya Japanese Garden. 4315 Fredericksburg Rd
Gazebo At Los Patios. 2015 NE Loop I-410
L'Etoile. 6106 Broadway St
La Calesa. 2103 E Hildebrand Ave
La Fogata. 2427 Vance Jackson Rd
La Hacienda. 2015 NE Loop I-410
La Louisiane. 2632 Broadway St
Los Barrios. 4223 Blanco Rd
Luby's Cafeteria. 9919 Colonial Dr
Mencius' Gourmet Hunan. 7959 Fredericksburg Rd
Old San Francisco Steak House. 10223 Sahara St
Romano's Macaroni Grill. 24116 I-10 West
Ruffino's. 9802 Colonnade Blvd
Ruth's Chris Steakhouse. 7720 Jones Maltsberger Rd

SOUTH OF DOWNTOWN

Carranza Meat Market. 701 Austin St
El Mirador. 722 S St Mary's St

WEST OF DOWNTOWN

La Margarita. 120 Produce Row

LA VILLITA

Anaqua Grill (Plaza San Antonio Hotel). 555 S Alamo St
Fig Tree. 515 Villita St
Little Rhein Steak House. 231 S Alamo St
Polo's At The Fairmount (Fairmount Hotel). 401 S Alamo St

RIVERWALK

The Bayous. 517 N Presa St
Boudro's, A Texas Bistro. 421 E Commerce St
Casa Rio. 430 E Commerce St
Dick's Last Resort. 406 Navarro St
Lone Star. 521 Riverwalk
Michelino's. Commerce St
Rio Rio Cantina. 421 E Commerce St

Note: *When a listing is located in a town that does not have its own city heading, it will appear under the city nearest to its location. In these cases, the address and town appear in parenthesis immediately following the name of the establishment.*

Motels

✔★★★ **BEST WESTERN CONTINENTAL INN.** *9735 I-35N (78233), north of downtown.* 210/655-3510; FAX 210/655-0778. 161 rms, 2 story. S $46-$56; D $58-$68; each addl $4. Crib $3. TV; cable. 2 pools; wading pool, whirlpools. Playground. Restaurant 6 am-10 pm. Rm serv. Bar. Ck-out noon. Coin lndry. Meeting rms. Sundries. Some refrigerators. Cr cds: A, C, D, DS, MC, V.

★★ **COURTYARD BY MARRIOTT.** *8585 Marriott Dr (78229), at Fredericksburg Rd, north of downtown.* 210/614-7100; FAX 210/614-

7110. 146 rms, 3 story. S $73-$79; D $82; each addl (after 4th person) $10; wkend rates. Crib avail. TV; cable. Heated pool. Complimentary coffee in rms. Restaurant 6:30-10:30 am; Sat, Sun 7 am-noon. Bar 5-10 pm. Ck-out 1 pm. Coin lndry. Meeting rms. Valet serv. Exercise equipt; weights, bicycles, whirlpool. Game rm. Refrigerator in suites. Balconies. Cr cds: A, C, D, DS, MC, V.

[D] [≈] [🏃] [⊠] [🔥] [SC]

★ ★ **HAWTHORN SUITES.** 4041 Bluemel Rd (78240), at I-10, north of downtown. 210/561-9660; FAX 210/561-9663. 128 kit. suites, 2 story. S, D $89-$129; under 12 free; wkly, wkend rates. Crib free. Pet accepted, some restrictions; $25. TV; cable, in-rm movies avail. Heated pool; whirlpool. Complimentary bkfst; evening refreshments. Ck-out noon. Coin lndry. Meeting rm. Valet serv. Health club privileges. Private patios, balconies. Picnic table. Fireplace in some suites. Cr cds: A, C, D, DS, MC, V.

[D] [🐾] [≈] [⊠] [🔥] [SC]

★ **LA QUINTA INGRAM PARK.** 7134 NW Loop I-410 (78238). 210/680-8883; FAX 210/681-3877. 195 rms, 3 story. S $56-$78; D $67-$78; suites $74-$132; under 18 free. Crib free. Pet accepted, some restrictions. TV; cable. Pool. Complimentary continental bkfst. Restaurant adj open 24 hrs. Ck-out noon. Meeting rms. Refrigerators in suites. Cr cds: A, C, D, DS, MC, V.

[D] [🐾] [≈] [⊠] [🔥] [SC]

★ ★ **LA QUINTA-MARKET SQUARE.** 900 Dolorosa St (78207), downtown. 210/271-0001; FAX 210/228-0663. 124 rms, 2 story. S, D $84-$91; each addl $10; suites $126; under 18 free; higher rates Fiesta wk. Crib free. Pet accepted, some restrictions. TV; cable, in-rm movies. Pool. Continental bkfst. Complimentary coffee. Restaurant opp open 24 hrs. Ck-out noon. Valet serv. Cr cds: A, C, D, DS, MC, V.

[D] [🐾] [≈] [⊠] [🔥] [SC]

★ ★ **SIERRA ROYALE HOTEL.** 6300 Rue Marielyne (78238), north of downtown. 210/647-0041; res: 800/289-2444; FAX 210/647-4442. 78 kit. suites, 1-2 story. May-Sept: S $89-$99; D $129; each addl $10; monthly rates; lower rates rest of yr. Crib free. TV; cable, in-rm movies avail. Pool; whirlpool. Complimentary continental bkfst; refreshments. Complimentary coffee in rms. Restaurant nearby. Bar. Ck-out noon. Lndry facilities. Meeting rm. Valet serv. Balconies. Picnic tables. Cr cds: A, C, D, DS, MC, V.

[D] [≈] [⊠] [🔥] [SC]

Motor Hotels

✓★ **COMFORT INN AIRPORT.** 2635 NE Loop 410 (78217). 210/653-9110; FAX 210/653-8615. 203 rms, 6 story. S, D $47-$85. Crib free. Pet accepted. TV; cable. Pool. Complimentary continental bkfst. Restaurant adj open 24 hrs. Ck-out noon. Meeting rms. Bellhops. Free airport transportation. Health club privileges. Near airport. Cr cds: A, C, D, DS, MC, V.

[≈] [⊠] [🔥] [SC]

★ ★ **DRURY INN.** 143 NE Loop 410 (78216), at I-410 & Airport Blvd, near Intl Airport, north of downtown. 210/366-4300. 125 rms, 4 story. S $69-$79; D $79-$89; each addl $10; under 18 free. Crib free. Pet accepted, some restrictions. TV; cable. Pool. Complimentary bkfst; evening refreshments. Restaurant adj open 24 hrs. Serv bar. Ck-out noon. Coin lndry. Meeting rms. Free airport transportation. Some refrigerators. Cr cds: A, C, D, DS, MC, V.

[D] [🐾] [≈] [✈] [⊠] [🔥] [SC]

★ ★ **DRURY SUITES.** 8811 Jones Maltzberger Rd (78216), near Intl Airport, north of downtown. 210/308-8100. 139 suites, 6 story. S $95-$105; D $105-$115; each addl $10; under 18 free. Crib free. TV; cable. Pool; whirlpool. Complimentary continental bkfst; evening refreshments. Restaurant opp 6 am-midnight. Ck-out noon. Meeting rm. Free airport transportation. Refrigerators. Cr cds: A, C, D, DS, MC, V.

[D] [≈] [✈] [⊠] [🔥] [SC]

✓★ ★ **HAMPTON INN.** 11010 I-10W (78230), north of downtown. 210/561-9058; FAX 210/690-5566. 122 rms, 6 story. S $51-$82; D $61-$92; each addl $10; suites $89-$129; under 18 free. Crib free. TV; cable. Pool. Complimentary continental bkfst. Complimentary coffee in lobby. Restaurant adj open 24 hrs. Ck-out noon. Meeting rms. Valet serv. Health club privileges. Many refrigerators. Cr cds: A, C, D, DS, MC, V.

[D] [≈] [⊠] [🔥] [SC]

★ **HOLIDAY INN RIVERWALK NORTH.** 110 Lexington Ave (78205), downtown. 210/223-9461; FAX 210/223-9267. 324 rms, 9 story. S, D $69-$129; suites $150-$450; under 18 free. Crib free. Pool. Restaurant 6 am-2 pm, 5-10 pm. Rm serv. Bar 2 pm-midnight. Ck-out noon. Coin lndry. Meeting rms. Bellhops. Gift shop. Exercise equipt; weights, bicycles. Game rm. Refrigerators in suites. On river. Cr cds: A, C, D, DS, MC, V.

[D] [≈] [🏃] [⊠] [🔥] [SC]

Hotels

★ ★ ★ **EMBASSY SUITES.** 10110 US 281N (78216), near Intl Airport, north of downtown. 210/525-9999; FAX 210/525-0626. 261 suites, 9 story. S $109; D $119; each addl $10; under 12 free; wkend rates. Crib free. TV; cable. Indoor pool. Complimentary full bkfst. Restaurant 11:30 am-2:30 pm, 5:30-10 pm. Bar 11-1 am. Ck-out 1 pm. Meeting rms. Gift shop. Free airport transportation. Exercise equipt; weights, treadmill, whirlpool, sauna. Refrigerators. Cr cds: A, C, D, DS, MC, V.

[D] [≈] [🏃] [✈] [⊠] [🔥] [SC]

★ **EXECUTIVE GUESTHOUSE.** 12828 US 281N (78216), 12 mi N on US 281, exit Bitters, north of downtown. 210/494-7600; res: 800/362-8700; FAX 210/545-4314. 124 rms, 4 story. S $89-$170; D $99-$170; each addl $10; under 12 free; wkend rates. Crib free. Pet accepted, some restrictions; $100 ($50 refundable). TV; cable. Indoor pool. Complimentary full bkfst; evening refreshments. Complimentary coffee in rms. Ck-out noon. Meeting rms. Free airport transportation. Exercise equipt; weights, bicycles, sauna. Bathrm phones, refrigerators; some in-rm whirlpools. Atrium. Cr cds: A, C, D, DS, MC, V.

[D] [🐾] [≈] [🏃] [✈] [⊠] [🔥] [SC]

★ ★ ★ **FAIRMOUNT.** 401 S Alamo St (78205), at La Villita. 210/224-8800; res: 800/642-3363; FAX 210/224-2767. 37 rms, 3 story, 17 suites. S $165-$185; D $175-$185; suites $225-$550; under 12 free. Crib free. Valet parking $6. TV; cable. Restaurant (see POLO'S AT THE FAIRMOUNT). Bar 11:30-1 am; entertainment Wed-Sat. Ck-out noon. Meeting rms. Concierge. Bathrm phones. Balconies. Garden courtyard. Offers casual elegance and Southwestern comfort. Near the Riverwalk. Cr cds: A, C, D, MC, V.

[D] [⊠] [🔥] [SC]

★ ★ ★ **HILTON PALACIO DEL RIO.** Box 2711 (78205), 200 S Alamo St, on Riverwalk. 210/222-1400; FAX 210/270-0761. 481 rms, 22 story. S $155-$185; D $175-$205; each addl $20; suites $325-$550; package plans. Crib free. Pet accepted, some restrictions. Garage $7, valet $17. TV; cable. Pool; poolside serv. Complimentary coffee in rms. Restaurant 6:30-1 am. Bars 11:30-1:30 am, wkends to 2 am; entertainment, dancing. Ck-out 11 am. Convention facilities. Concierge. Gift shop. Tennis, golf privileges. Exercise equipt; weights, bicycles, whirlpool. Some bathrm phones, refrigerators. Balconies. ***LUXURY LEVEL :*** **TOWERS.** 70 rms, 3 floors, 5 suites. S $180-$210; D $200-$230. Wet bars. Complimentary bkfst, refreshments. Cr cds: A, C, D, DS, ER, JCB, MC, V.

[D] [🐾] [🏃] [⛷] [≈] [🏃] [⊠] [🔥] [SC]

★ ★ **HOLIDAY INN-RIVER WALK.** 217 N St Mary's St (78205), on Riverwalk. 210/224-2500; FAX 210/223-1302. 313 rms, 23 story. S, D $125-$145; suites $225-$350; under 18 free. Crib free. Pet accepted, some restrictions. Valet parking $7; in/out $5. TV; cable. Heated pool; poolside serv. Restaurant 6:30 am-2 pm, 5:30-10 pm. Rm serv 6 am-midnight. Bar noon-12:30 am; Fri, Sat to 2 am; entertainment, dancing exc Sun & Mon. Ck-out noon. Convention facilities. Exercise equipt; bicycles, treadmill, whirlpool. Refrigerator in suites. Balconies. View of river. Cr cds: A, C, D, DS, JCB, MC, V.

[D] [⚡] [≈] [✗] [✗] [⚡] [SC]

★ **HOWARD JOHNSON RIVERWALK PLAZA.** *100 Villita St (78205), near La Villita.* 210/226-2271; FAX 210/226-9453. 133 rms, 6 story. S $89; D $95; each addl $10; under 18 free; higher rates Fiesta Wk, special events. Crib free. Garage parking $4.75 in/out. TV; cable. Pool. Complimentary coffee in rms. Restaurant 6:30 am-2 pm, 4-11 pm. Bar 4-11 pm; entertainment Fri & Sat. Ck-out 11 am. Meeting rms. Gift shop. Some balconies. Overlooks river. Cr cds: A, C, D, DS, MC, V.

[D] [≈] [✗] [⚡] [SC]

★ ★ ★ **HYATT REGENCY.** *123 Losoya St (7 (82050), on Riverwalk.* 210/222-1234; FAX 210/227-4925. 631 rms, 11 story. S $125-$185; D $135-$210; each addl $20; suites $200-$665; under 18 free; wkend packages. Garage parking $7, valet $11. TV. Pool; poolside serv. Restaurants 6:30 am-11 pm. Bar 11-2 am; entertainment, dancing. Meeting rms. Concierge. Shopping arcade. Exercise equipt; weights, bicycles, whirlpool. Minibars; some refrigerators. Balconies. River flows through lobby; waterfalls, atrium. Cr cds: A, C, D, DS, JCB, MC, V.

[D] [≈] [✗] [✗] [⚡] [SC]

LA MANSION DEL RIO. *(New general manager, therefore not rated) 112 College St (78205), on River Walk.* 210/225-2581; FAX 210/226-0389. 337 rms, 7 story. S $120-$245; D $145-$270; each addl $25; suites $375-$1,500; under 18 free; wkend rates; Sea World packages. Crib free. Garage $7, valet parking. TV; cable. Pool; poolside serv. Restaurants 6:30 am-10 pm. Rm serv 24 hrs. Bar 11-2 am; entertainment. Ck-out noon. Convention facilities. Concierge. Gift shop. Minibars. Private patios, balconies. Beamed ceilings; rms overlook courtyard or river. Property built around restored historic 19th-century law school building; on San Antonio River. Cr cds: A, C, D, DS, JCB, MC, V.

[D] [≈] [✗] [⚡] [SC]

★ ★ **MARRIOTT RIVERCENTER.** *101 Bowie St (78205), opp convention Center, on Riverwalk.* 210/223-1000; FAX 210/223-6239. 1,000 units, 38 story, 82 suites. S $165; D $185; each addl $20; suites $225-$950; under 18 free; honeymoon plan. Crib free. Pet accepted. Garage $7, valet $10. TV; cable. Indoor/outdoor pool; poolside serv. Coffee in rms. Restaurant 6 am-midnight. Rm serv 24 hrs. Bar. Ck-out noon. Free lndry facilities. Convention facilities. Concierge. Shopping arcade. Barber, beauty shop. 18-hole golf privileges, greens fee $55, pro, putting green, driving range. Exercise equipt; weight machine, bicycles, whirlpool, sauna. Some refrigerators, wet bars. Balconies. Located on the banks of the San Antonio River and adj to spectacular Rivercenter shopping complex. *LUXURY LEVEL :* **CONCIERGE LEVEL.** 48 rms, 2 suites, 2 floors. S $179; D $199; suites $350. Concierge. Privage lounge, honor bar. Complimentary continental bkfst, refreshments. Cr cds: A, C, D, DS, MC, V.

[D] [⚡] [✗] [≈] [✗] [✗] [⚡] [SC]

★ ★ ★ **MARRIOTT RIVERWALK.** *711 E River Walk (78205), on Riverwalk.* 210/224-4555; FAX 210/224-2754. 500 rms, 30 story. S $144-$160; D $164-$180; each addl $20; suites $395; under 17 free; wkend rates. Crib free. Pet accepted. Garage parking $7, valet $10. TV; cable. Indoor/outdoor pool. Restaurant 6:30 am-11 pm. Rm serv 24 hrs. Bar 11:30-2 am; entertainment Tues-Sat, dancing. Ck-out noon. Meeting rms. Gift shop. Golf privileges. Exercise equipt; weights, bicycles, whirlpool, sauna. Some bathrm phones, refrigerators. Balconies. Many rms overlook San Antonio River. *LUXURY LEVEL :* **CONCIERGE.** 20 rms. S $170-$179; D $180-$190. Concierge. Private lounge, honor bar. In-rm movies avail. Bathrm phones. Complimentary continental bkfst, refreshments. Cr cds: A, C, D, DS, ER, JCB, MC, V.

[D] [⚡] [✗] [≈] [✗] [✗] [⚡] [SC]

★ ★ ★ **MENGER.** *204 Alamo Plaza (78205), downtown.* 210/223-4361; res: 800/345-9285; FAX 210/228-0022. 350 rms, 5 story. S $102-$122; D $122-$142; each addl $10; suites $182-$456;

under 18 free; package plans. Crib free. Garage $4.95, valet $9.95. TV; in-rm movies. Pool. Restaurant 6:30 am-10 pm; wkends to 11 pm. Rm serv 24 hrs. Bar 11 am-midnight; piano bar. Ck-out noon. Convention facilities. Concierge. Shopping arcade. Exercise equipt; bicycle, stair machine, whirlpool, sauna. Balconies. Historic atmosphere. Alamo opp. Cr cds: A, C, D, DS, ER, MC, V.

[D] [≈] [✗] [✗] [⚡] [SC]

★ ★ ★ **PLAZA SAN ANTONIO.** *555 S Alamo St (78205), in La Villita.* 210/229-1000; res: 800/421-1172; FAX 210/229-1418. 252 rms, 5-7 story. S $160-$230; D $180-$250; each addl $20; suites $320-$700; under 18 free; wkend rates. Crib free. Pet accepted, some restrictions. Valet parking $7. TV; cable. Pool; poolside serv. Restaurant (see ANAQUA GRILL). Rm serv 24 hrs. Bar noon-1 am; entertainment Thurs-Sat. Ck-out noon. Meeting rms. Concierge. Free downtown area transportation (Mon-Fri, 7:30-9:30 am). Lighted tennis. Golf privileges. Exercise equipt; weights, bicycles, whirlpool, sauna. Massage. Complimentary bicycles. Private patios. Balconies. Complimentary newspaper. Cr cds: A, C, D, DS, ER, MC, V.

[D] [⚡] [✗] [✗] [≈] [✗] [✗] [⚡] [SC]

★ ★ **RADISSON DOWNTOWN MARKET SQUARE.** *52 W Durango (78207), downtown.* 210/224-7155; FAX 210/224-9130. 250 rms, 6 story. S $69-$89; D $79-$109; each addl $10; suites $125-$175; under 12 free. Crib free. Pet accepted; $50 deposit. TV; cable. Pool. Complimentary coffee in rms. Restaurant 6:30 am-11 pm. Bar noon-midnight. Ck-out noon. Coin lndry. Meeting rms. Garage parking. Gift shop. Exercise equipt; weights, bicycles, whirlpool. Game rm. Refrigerator in suites. Balconies. Cr cds: A, C, D, DS, MC, V.

[D] [≈] [✗] [✗] [⚡] [SC]

★ **RAMADA EMILY MORGAN.** *705 E Houston St (78205), adj to the Alamo, downtown.* 210/225-8486; res: 800/824-6674; FAX 210/225-7227. 177 rms, 14 story. S $89-$135; D $94-$149; each addl $10; package plans. Crib free. Parking $6.50. TV; cable. Pool. Complimentary coffee in rms. Restaurant 6:30 am-2 pm, 5-10 pm. Bar 4-11 pm. Ck-out noon. Meeting rms. Exercise equipt; weights, bicycles, whirlpool, sauna. In-rm whirlpools; many refrigerators. Former medical arts bldg (1925); renovated; contemporary decor. unusually-shaped rms. Cr cds: A, C, D, DS, JCB, MC, V.

[D] [≈] [✗] [✗] [✗] [⚡] [SC]

★ ★ **SHERATON FIESTA.** *37 NE Loop 410 (78216), near Intl Airport, north of downtown.* 210/366-2424; FAX 210/341-0410. 290 rms, 5 story. S $120-$140; D $130-$150; each addl $15; suites $220-$290; under 17 free; wkend rates. Crib free. TV; cable. Pool. Restaurants 6:30 am-10 pm; dining rm 6-10:30 pm. Rm serv 24 hrs. Bar 11-2 am; pianist Mon-Fri. Ck-out noon. Convention facilities. Airport transportation. Exercise equipt; weight machine, bicycles, whirlpool, sauna. Some refrigerators. Private patios, balconies. *LUXURY LEVEL :* **CONCIERGE.** 69 rms. S $150; D $160. Concierge. Private lounge, honor bar. Complimentary continental bkfst, refreshments, newspapers. Cr cds: A, C, D, DS, ER, JCB, MC, V.

[D] [≈] [✗] [✗] [✗] [⚡] [SC]

★ ★ ★ **SHERATON GUNTER.** *205 E Houston St (78205), downtown.* 210/227-3241; FAX 210/227-3299. 322 rms, 12 story. S $85-$125; D $95-$135; each addl $10; suites $195-$390; under 18 free. Crib free. Garage $9. TV; cable. Heated pool. Coffee in rms. Restaurant 6 am-10 pm; Fri, Sat to 11 pm. Bar 4 pm-2 am; Fri, Sat noon-2 am; Sun to midnight. Ck-out noon. Convention facilities. Barber. Exercise equipt; weights, bicycles, whirlpool. Refrigerators avail. Built 1909. Cr cds: A, C, D, DS, ER, JCB, MC, V.

[D] [≈] [✗] [✗] [✗] [⚡] [SC]

★ ★ ★ **WYNDHAM.** *9821 Colonnade Blvd (78230), north of downtown.* 210/691-8888; res: 800/822-4200; FAX 210/691-1128. 326 rms, 20 story. S $119-$150; D $129-$160; each addl $10; suites $275-$535; under 18 free; wkend rates. Crib free. TV; cable. 2 pools, 1 indoor; poolside serv. Restaurant 6:30 am-11 pm. Bar 3 pm-1 am, Sun noon-1 am; entertainment. Ck-out noon. Meeting rms. Gift shop. Airport transportation. Exercise equipt; weights, bicycles, whirlpools, sauna. Some refrigerators. Garden with fountain. Crystal chandelier, marble in lobby. Cr cds: A, C, D, DS, ER, JCB, MC, V.

[D] [icons]

Inns

★ **ADAM'S HOUSE.** 231 Adams St (78210), downtown. 210/224-4791; FAX 210/223-5125. 5 rms (3 with shower only), 2 story. S, D $60-$120. Children over 12 yrs only. Complimentary full bkfst, afternoon tea/sherry. Ck-out 11 am, ck-in 3 pm. Luggage handling. Built 1902; many antiques. Library; piano in sitting rm. Totally non-smoking. Cr cds: A, DS, MC, V.

[icons]

★ **B & B ON THE RIVER.** 129 Woodward Place (78204), Riverwalk. 210/225-6337; FAX 210/225-2632. 7 rms (4 with shower only), 2 story. Some rm phones. S, D $79.50-$119; each addl $20; under 6 free. Some TV. Complimentary full bkfst. Ck-out 11 am, ck-in noon. Balconies. Victorian decor; antiques. Totally nonsmoking. Cr cds: A, C, D, DS, MC, V.

[icons]

★★ **BEAUREGARD HOUSE.** 215 Beauregard St (78204), downtown. 210/222-1198; res: 800/841-9377. 3 rms, 2 with shower only, 2 story. S $75; D $85; each addl $11; under 8 free; package plans. Crib avail. TV in sitting rm; cable. Complimentary full bkfst 7-9 am. Complimentary tea. Restaurant nearby. Ck-out 1 pm, ck-in 4 pm. Lndry facilities. Restored Victorian house (1902) in King William District; Riverwalk 1 blk. Totally nonsmoking. Cr cds: MC, V.

[icons] SC

★★ **BECKMANN.** 222 E Guenther St (78204), downtown. 210/229-1449. 5 rms (4 with shower only), 3 story, 2 suites. No rm phones. S, D $80-$100; suites $120-$130. Children over 12 yrs only. TV; cable. Complimentary full bkfst. Restaurant opp 7 am-3 pm. Ck-out 11 am, ck-in 4-6 pm. Luggage handling. Victorian house (1886) with wrap-around porch. Many antiques. Totally nonsmoking. Cr cds: A, D, MC, V.

[icons] SC

★★★ **OGE HOUSE.** 209 Washington (78204), Riverwalk. 210/223-2353; res: 800/242-2770; FAX 210/226-5812. 9 rms (1 with shower only), 3 story. S, D $110-$175; higher rates wkends. Children over 16 only. TV; cable. Complimentary continental bkfst. Ck-out 11 am, ck-in 3 pm. Luggage handling. Refrigerators, many fireplaces. Mansion built 1857 for prominent rancher; antiques. Smoking on veranda only. Cr cds: A, C, D, DS, MC, V.

[icons]

Resort

★★★★ **HYATT REGENCY HILL COUNTRY.** 9800 Hyatt Resort Dr (78251), north of downtown. 210/647-1234; FAX 210/681-9681. 500 units, 4 story. Late Feb-May & mid-Sept-Nov: S, D $220-$240; each addl $25; suites $405-$1,450; under 18 free; holiday, golf plans; lower rates rest of yr. Parking; valet $4. TV; cable. 4 heated pools; poolside serv. Supervised child's activities. Coffee in rms. Restaurants 6:30 am-10 pm. Rm serv 6 am-midnight. Bar 4 pm-1 am; entertainment. Ck-out noon. Coin lndry. Convention facilities. Bellhops. Valet serv. Concierge. Sundries. Shopping arcade. Airport transportation. Lighted tennis, pro. 18-hole golf, pro, greens fee $70-$85. Bicycle rentals. Exercise rm; instructor, weights, treadmill, whirlpool. Masseuse. Lawn games. Rec rm. Game rm. Refrigerators. Balconies. **LUXURY LEVEL : REGENCY.** 86 rms, 6 suites. Late Feb-May & mid-Sept-Nov: S, D $280; each addl $35. Concierge. Private lounge, honor bar. Complimentary continental bkfst, refreshments, newspaper. Cr cds: A, C, D, DS, JCB, MC, V.

[D] [icons] SC

Restaurants

✔★ **410 DINER.** 8315 Broadway St, north of downtown. 210/822-6246. Hrs: 11 am-10 pm; Fri, Sat to 10:30 pm. Bar. Semi-a la carte: lunch, dinner $3.95-$7.95. Specializes in chicken-fried steak, snapper, vegetable platters. Parking. 1950s-style diner; counter service avail. Cr cds: A, C, D, DS, MC, V.

[D]

★★ **ALDO'S RISTORANTE.** 8539 Fredericksburg Rd (78229), north of downtown. 210/690-2536. Hrs: 11 am-10 pm; Fri to 11 pm; Sat 5-11 pm; Sun from 5 pm. Closed most major hols. Res accepted. Italian menu. Bar. Semi-a la carte: lunch $6-$10, dinner $9-$18. Specialty: salmone alla Pavarotti. Valet parking. Outdoor dining. Intimate dining in early 1900s house. Cr cds: A, C, D, DS, MC, V.

★★★ **ANAQUA GRILL.** (See Plaza San Antonio Hotel) 210/229-1000. Hrs: 7 am-2 pm, 6-10 pm; Fri & Sat to 11 pm; Sun brunch 10 am-2 pm. Res accepted. Bar. A la carte entrees: bkfst $4.25-$9.25, dinner $6.95-$17.95. Semi-a la carte: lunch $7.50-$12. Tapas $3.50-$9.95. Sun brunch $12.50-$17.95. Child's meals. Specializes in fresh seafood, Southwestern and Eurasian cuisine. Also dietary menu. Own baking. Valet parking. Outdoor dining. View of garden, courtyard, fountains. Cr cds: A, C, D, DS, ER, MC, V.

[D]

★ **THE BAYOUS.** 517 N Presa St, on Riverwalk. 210/223-6403. Hrs: 11:30 am-11 pm; Fri, Sat to midnight; Sun brunch 11:30 am-3 pm. Res accepted. Cajun, Amer menu. Bar. Semi-a la carte: lunch $4.95-$9.95, dinner $7.95-$19.95. Buffet: lunch $4.95-$7.50. Sun brunch $10.95. Child's meals. Specialties: red snapper Valerie, shrimp Barataria, marinated crab claws. Oyster bar. Entertainment. Parking. Outdoor dining. Dining rm overlooks river. Cr cds: A, C, D, DS, MC, V.

[D]

★★ **BIGA.** 206 E Locust St, north of downtown. 210/225-0722. Hrs: 11 am-2 pm, 6-10:30 pm; Mon from 6 pm; Fri 11 am-2 pm, 5:30-11 pm; Sat 5:30-11 pm. Closed Sun; some major hols. Wine, beer. Semi-a la carte: lunch $4.95-$8, dinner $11-$25. Specializes in Gulf seafood, breads, wild game. Parking. In converted old mansion. Extensive wine selection. Cr cds: A, C, D, DS, MC, V.

★★ **BOUDRO'S, A TEXAS BISTRO.** 421 E Commerce St, on Riverwalk. 210/224-8484. Hrs: 11 am-11 pm; Fri, Sat to midnight. Res accepted. Southwestern menu. A la carte entrees: lunch $4-$9, dinner $12-$22. Specialties: blackened prime rib, smoked shrimp enchiladas, fresh Gulf red snapper. Outdoor dining. Historic building; pictographs on walls, original artwork. Cr cds: A, C, D, DS, MC, V.

[D]

★★ **CAPPY'S.** 5011 Broadway St, north of downtown. 210/828-9669. Hrs: 11 am-10 pm; Fri, Sat to 11 pm; Sun 10:30 am-10 pm; Sun brunch to 3 pm. Closed July 4, Thanksgiving, Dec 25. Res accepted. Bar. Semi-a la carte: lunch $5.95-$7.95, dinner $9.95-$16.50. Sat, Sun brunch $7.50-$9.95. Child's meals. Specialties: chicken with artichoke hearts, blackened snapper. Parking. Outdoor dining. Local artworks on display. Totally nonsmoking. Cr cds: A, C, D, MC, V.

★ **CARRANZA MEAT MARKET.** 701 Austin St, south of downtown. 210/223-0903. Hrs: 11 am-2 pm, 5-10 pm; Fri to 11 pm; Sat 5-11 pm. Closed Sun; Thanksgiving, Dec 25. Mexican, Amer menu. Wine, beer. Semi-a la carte: lunch $5.95-$28.95, dinner $7.95-$28.95. Specializes in steak, seafood. Parking. Originally a saloon and nightclub (1870). Family-owned. Cr cds: A.

✔★ **CASA RIO.** 430 E Commerce St, on Riverwalk. 210/225-6718. Hrs: 11:30 am-10:30 pm; Sun noon-10 pm. Closed Jan 1, Dec 25. Mexican menu. Serv bar. Semi-a la carte: lunch, dinner $3.95-$8.95. Child's meals. Specialties: green chicken enchiladas, fajitas, pollo asado. Strolling musicians Sat. Parking. Outdoor dining. Riverboat dining by res, $22 per person. On San Antonio River. Family-owned. Cr cds: A, C, D, DS, MC, V.

D

★ ★ ★ **CHEZ ARDID.** *1919 San Pedro Ave, north of downtown.* 210/732-3203. Hrs: 11:30 am-2 pm, 6-10:30 pm; Sat from 6 pm. Closed Sun; Jan 1, Thanksgiving, Dec 25. Res accepted. French menu. Bar. Wine cellar. Semi-a la carte: dinner $12.50-$25. Specialties: grilled quail salad, crab meat Chez Ardid, rack of lamb. Valet parking. Pianist Fri & Sat. Located in stone mansion (ca 1900); fine dining in formal setting; main dining rm located in what was once the mansion's ballroom; also dining in the wine cellar. Chef-owned. Jacket. Cr cds: A, C, D, MC, V.

D

★ ★ **CRUMPET'S.** *5800 Broadway St, north of downtown.* 210/821-5454. Hrs: 11 am-2:30 pm, 5:30-10 pm; Fri to 11 pm; Sat 11 am-3 pm, 5:30-11 pm; Sun 11 am-3 pm, 5-9 pm. Closed Jan 1, Dec 25. Res accepted. Bar. Wine list. Complete meals: lunch $6.95-$7.95, dinner $8.95-$16.50. Brunch $14.95. Specializes in beef, pasta, seafood. Own pasta, pastries. Classical musicians. Cr cds: A, C, D, DS, MC, V.

D

★ ★ **FIG TREE.** *515 Villita St, in La Villita.* 210/224-1976. Hrs: 6-11 pm. Closed Jan 1, Thanksgiving, Dec 24, 25. Res accepted. Continental menu. Serv bar. Complete meal: dinner $45. Specializes in seafood, châteaubriand, rack of lamb. Outdoor dining. Elegant decor. Overlooks Riverwalk. Cr cds: A, C, D, DS, MC, V.

★ **FUJIYA JAPANESE GARDEN.** *4315 Fredericksburg Rd (78201), north of downtown.* 210/734-3551. Hrs: 11 am-2:30 pm, 5-10 pm; wkend hrs vary. Closed Thanksgiving, Dec 25. Res accepted. Japanese menu. Bar. Semi-a la carte: lunch $3.95-$7.25, dinner $7.95-$18.50. Child's meals. Specializes in sukiyaki, teriyaki. tempura. Sushi bar. Parking. Traditional dining (tatami) avail. Waterfall in dining rm. Family-owned. Cr cds: A, C, D, DS, MC, V.

D

★ ★ **L'ETOILE.** *6106 Broadway St, at Albany St, north of downtown.* 210/826-4551. Hrs: 11 am-2:30 pm, 5:30-10 pm; Fri, Sat to 11 pm; Sun 5-9:30 pm; early-bird dinner 5:30-6:30 pm. Res accepted. French menu. Bar. Wine list. Semi-a la carte: lunch $5.95-$14.95, dinner $9.95-$21.95. Specializes in pasta, fresh seafood, veal. Salad bar (lunch). Own baking, pasta. Valet parking. Outdoor dining. French Provincial, garden-style dining rm. Cr cds: A, C, D, MC, V.

✔★ **LA CALESA.** *2103 E Hildebrand Ave, at Broadway St, north of downtown.* 210/822-4475. Hrs: 11 am-9:30 pm; Fri to 10:30 pm; Sat 9 am-10:30 pm; Sun 9 am-9 pm. Closed Easter, Thanksgiving, Dec 25. Mexican menu. Serv bar. Semi-a la carte: lunch, dinner $4.15-$11.95. Child's meals. Specialties: cochinita pibil, pollo en Escabeche. Parking. Outdoor dining. Authentic Mexican cuisine. Totally nonsmoking. Cr cds: A, C, D, DS, MC, V.

D

✔★ **LA FOGATA.** *2427 Vance Jackson Rd, 6 mi N on I-10, Vance Jackson exit, north of downtown.* 210/340-1337. Hrs: 7:30 am-11 pm; Fri, Sat to midnight. Closed Jan 1, Dec 25. Mexican menu. Bar. Semi-a la carte: bkfst $3.25-$4.25, lunch, dinner $5.25-$14.95. Child's meals. Specializes in enchilada verdes, Mexican bkfst. Own tortillas. Parking. Outdoor dining. Mexican decor. Cr cds: A, C, D, DS, MC, V.

D

★ **LA HACIENDA.** *2015 NE Loop I-410, Starcrest exit, north of downtown.* 210/655-6225. Hrs: 11:30 am-2:30 pm. Closed Mon; also Jan 1, Thanksgiving, Dec 25. Southwestern menu. Bar. Semi-a la carte: lunch $5.95-$9.95. Specializes in quesadillas, chiles rellenos, margaritas. Parking. Outdoor dining. Cr cds: A, D, MC, V.

★ ★ **LA LOUISIANE.** *2632 Broadway St, north of downtown.* 210/225-7984. Hrs: 11:30 am-2 pm, 6-10:30 pm; Fri to 11 pm; Sat 6-11 pm; Sun 11 am-2 pm. Closed Jan 1, Dec 25. Res accepted. French,

Creole menu. Bar. Wine list. A la carte entrees: lunch $9-$19, dinner $18-$48. Complete meals: gourmet dinner (for 2) $160. Sun brunch $11-$25. Specialties: lobster Louisiane, red snapper à la George, lamb, veal chops. Entertainment Fri & Sat. Parking. Formal dining; elegant. Family-owned. Cr cds: A, C, D, DS, MC, V.

D

✔★ **LA MARGARITA.** *120 Produce Row, west of downtown.* 210/227-7140. Hrs: 11 am-10 pm; Fri, Sat to midnight. Closed Thanksgiving. Mexican menu. Bar. Semi-a la carte: lunch, dinner $4.95-$9.50. Child's meals. Specializes in fajitas, shrimp cocktail, oyster cocktail. Entertainment. Parking. Outdoor dining. Restored farmers market building (1910). Cr cds: A, C, D, DS, MC, V.

D

★ ★ **LITTLE RHEIN STEAK HOUSE.** *231 S Alamo St, in La Villita.* 210/225-2111. Hrs: 5-11 pm. Closed Jan 1, Thanksgiving, Dec 24-25. Res accepted. Bar. Semi-a la carte: dinner $16.95-$29.95. Child's meals. Specializes in steak, seafood, lamb chops. Terrace dining. Overlooks San Antonio River and Outdoor theater. First 2-story structure in San Antonio (1847). Cr cds: A, C, D, DS, MC, V.

D

★ **LONE STAR.** *521 Riverwalk, on Riverwalk.* 210/223-9374. Hrs: 11 am-10:30 pm; Fri, Sat to 11:30 pm. Closed Thanksgiving, Dec 24 & 25. Bar. Semi-a la carte: lunch $4.75-$16.95, dinner $6.95-$16.95. Child's meals. Specializes in chicken-fried steak, rib-eye steak, filet mignon. Outdoor dining. Cr cds: A, DS, MC, V.

D

✔★ **LOS BARRIOS.** *4223 Blanco Rd (78212), north of downtown.* 210/732-6017. Hrs: 10 am-10 pm; Fri & Sat to midnight; Sun from 9 am. Closed Easter, Thanksgiving, Dec 25. Mexican menu. Bar. Semi-a la carte: lunch, dinner $5-$14. Child's meals. Specialties: enchilada verdes, cabrito, churrasco. Parking. Traditional Mexican dining. Cr cds: A, C, D, DS, MC, V.

★ **MENCIUS' GOURMET HUNAN.** *7959 Fredericksburg Rd, north of downtown.* 210/690-1848. Hrs: 11 am-2:15 pm, 5-10 pm; Sun-Tues to 9:30 pm. Closed Jan 1, Thanksgiving, Dec 25. Res accepted. Chinese menu. Bar. Semi-a la carte: lunch $4.50-$4.95, dinner $5.95-$14.95. Specialties: Mencius beef, shrimp & scallops, General Tso's chicken. Parking. Large aquarium in waiting area. Cr cds: A, C, D, MC, V.

D

✔★ **MI TIERRA.** *218 Produce Row, at Market Square, downtown.* 210/225-1262. Open 24 hrs. Mexican menu. Bar 5 pm-2 am; Sat, Sun from noon. Semi-a la carte: bkfst $2.50-$6.75, lunch, dinner $2.98-$9.95. Specializes in fajitas, cabrito, Mexican dinner combinations. Entertainment. Outdoor dining. Located in old farmers market building; built 1910. Family-owned. Cr cds: A, C, D, DS, MC, V.

D

★ **MICHELINO'S.** *Commerce St, on Riverwalk.* 210/223-2939. Hrs: 11 am-11 pm; Fri, Sat to 11:30 pm. Northern Italian menu. Bar. Semi-a la carte: lunch $4.25-$12.25, dinner $5.95-$14.95. Child's meals. Specializes in fettucine verde, chicken Florentine, veal Messicani. Outdoor dining. Cr cds: A, DS, MC, V.

★ ★ **OLD SAN FRANCISCO STEAK HOUSE.** *10223 Sahara St (10223), north of downtown.* 210/342-2321. Hrs: 5-11 pm; Fri, Sat to midnight; Sun 4-10 pm. Res accepted. Bar. Complete meals: dinner $10.95-$29.95. Child's meals. Specializes in steak, poultry, prime rib, seafood. Pianist; girl on red velvet swing. Valet parking. Victorian decor. Cr cds: A, C, D, DS, MC, V.

D

★ ★ **PAESANO'S.** *1715 McCullough Ave, downtown.* 210/226-9541. Hrs: 11 am-2 pm, 5-11 pm; Sat 5-11:30 pm; Sun 5-10 pm. Closed Mon; some major hols. Northern Italian menu. Bar. A la carte entrees: lunch $6.50-$7.95, dinner $6.95-$18.50. Specialties:

shrimp Paesano, penne all'arrabbiata, veal Christina. Parking. Cr cds: A, C, D, MC, V.

[D]

★ ★ ★ **POLO'S AT THE FAIRMOUNT.** *(See Fairmount Hotel)* *210/224-8800.* Hrs: 7-10:30 am, 11:30 am-2 pm, 6-10 pm; Fri to 10:30 pm; Sat 7-10:30 am, 6-10:30 pm; Sun 7 am-noon. Res accepted. Bar 11:30-1 am. A la carte entrees: bkfst $5-$8, lunch $5-$11.95, dinner $17-$29. Child's meals. Specialties: grilled duck, Norwegian salmon, spinach salad with grilled quail. Valet parking. Outdoor dining. Cr cds: A, C, D, MC, V.

[D]

✔★ **RIO RIO CANTINA.** *421 E Commerce St, on Riverwalk.* *210/226-8462.* Hrs: 11 am-11 pm; Fri & Sat to midnight. Tex-Mex, California menu. Bar. Semi-a la carte: lunch $3.95-$9, dinner $6.95-$13. Child's meals. Specialties: botano grande, carmones al mojo de ajo, enchiladas Rio Rio. Outdoor riverside dining. Mexican murals. Cr cds: A, C, D, DS, MC, V.

[D]

★ ★ **ROMANO'S MACARONI GRILL.** *24116 I-10 West* *(78257), 13 N on I-10W at Leon Springs exit, north of downtown.* *210/698-0003.* Hrs: 11 am-2:30 pm, 5-10 pm; Sat 5-11 pm; Sun 5-10 pm. Closed Thanksgiving, Dec 25. Italian menu. Wine, beer. Semi-a la carte: lunch $5.95-$10.95, dinner $6.95-$16.50. Specializes in pasta, calamari fritti. Parking. No cr cds accepted.

✔★ **RUFFINO'S.** *9802 Colonnade Blvd, north of downtown.* *210/641-6100.* Hrs: 11 am-midnight. Res accepted. Northern Italian menu. Bar to 2 am. Semi-a la carte: lunch $3.95-$9.75, dinner $5.25-$11.95. Child's meals. Specializes in veal in wine sauce, fresh snapper with basil. Entertainment. Parking. Outdoor dining. Italian atmosphere. Cr cds: A, C, D, DS, MC, V.

★ ★ **RUTH'S CHRIS STEAKHOUSE.** *7720 Jones Maltsberger Rd, at Concord Plaza, north of downtown.* *210/821-5051.* Hrs: 5-11 pm; Sun 4-10 pm. Closed Thanksgiving, Dec 25. Res accepted. Bar. A la carte entrees: dinner $17.95-$29.95. Child's meals. Specializes in steak, live Maine lobster, lamb. Parking. Upscale Southwestern decor. Cr cds: A, C, D, MC, V.

[D]

★ ★ **TOWER OF THE AMERICAS.** *222 HemisFair Plaza,* *downtown.* *210/223-3101.* Hrs: 11 am-2 pm, 5:30-10 pm; Fri to 10:30 pm; Sat 11 am-2:30 pm, 5:30-10:30 pm; Sun 11 am-2:30 pm. Closed Dec 25. Res accepted. Bar 5-11 pm; Fri, Sat 11-12:30 am. Complete meals: lunch $5.95-$11.95, dinner $10.95-$19.95. Child's meals. Specializes in lobster, steak, prime rib. Parking. Revolving tower; view of city. Elvtr fee is added to bill. Cr cds: A, C, D, DS, MC, V.

[D] [SC]

Unrated Dining Spots

5050 DINER. *5050 Broadway St, north of downtown.* *210/828-4386.* Hrs: 11-2 am. Res accepted. Mexican, Amer menu. Bar.

Semi-a la carte: lunch, dinner $3.50-$7.50. Child's meals. Specialties: chicken-fried steak, Tex-Mex dishes. Parking. Neighborhood bistro atmosphere; art deco decor. Cr cds: A, D, DS, MC, V.

[D]

BILLY BLUES. *330 E Grayson St, north of downtown.* *210/225-7409.* Hrs: 11-1 am; wkends to 2 am. Closed some major hols. Res accepted. Bar. Semi-a la carte: lunch, dinner $4.25-$11.95. Child's meals. Specialties: smoked sausage, barbecued ribs, barbecued brisket. Own desserts. Entertainment. Parking. Outdoor dining. Features rock bands and dining in the "Billy Dome." Cr cds: A, D, DS, MC, V.

[D]

BRAZIER AT LOS PATIOS. *2015 NE Loop I-410, Starcrest exit, north of downtown.* *210/655-9270.* Hrs: 11:30 am-10 pm. Closed Mon; Jan 1, Thanksgiving, Dec 25. Southwestern menu. Bar. Semi-a la carte: lunch, dinner $5.95-$14.95. Specializes in mesquite-grilled steak, fish, chicken. Salad bar. Parking. Outdoor dining. On Salado Creek. Cr cds: A, D, MC, V.

DICK'S LAST RESORT. *406 Navarro St, on Riverwalk.* *210/224-0026.* Hrs: 11-2 am. Bar. Semi-a la carte: lunch $3.75-$8.95, dinner $8.95-$16.95. Specializes in barbecued ribs, fried catfish, honey-roasted chicken. Entertainment. Outdoor dining. Honky-tonk decor. Cr cds: A, C, D, DS, MC, V.

[D]

EL MIRADOR. *722 S St Mary's St, south of downtown.* *210/225-9444.* Hrs: 6:30 am-3 pm; Wed-Sat also 5:30-10 pm; Sun 9 am-3 pm. Closed some major hols. Mexican menu. Wine, beer. Semi-a la carte: bkfst $1.50-$4, lunch $2.50-$5.50, dinner $4.95-$11. Specialties: xochitl soup, Azteca soup. Parking. Cr cds: MC, V.

[D]

GAZEBO AT LOS PATIOS. *2015 NE Loop I-410, Starcrest exit, north of downtown.* *210/655-6190.* Hrs: 11:30 am-2:30 pm; Sat to 3 pm; Sun 11 am-3 pm. Closed Jan 1, Thanksgiving, Dec 25. Continental menu. Bar 11:30 am-2:30 pm. Semi-a la carte: lunch $7.50-$9.95. Sun brunch $13.95. Specializes in crepes, salads, quiche. Parking. Outdoor dining. Cr cds: A, DS, MC, V.

GUENTHER HOUSE. *205 E Guenther St (78204), downtown.* *210/227-1061.* Hrs: 7 am-3 pm; Sun 8 am-2 pm. Closed Jan 1, Thanksgiving, Dec 25. Semi-a la carte: bkfst $2.50-$5.95, lunch $4.50-$6.25. Specializes in Belgian waffles, chicken salad, pastries. Parking. Outdoor dining. House built by founder of Pioneer Flour Mills (1860). Museum and gift shop on grounds. Cr cds: A, DS, MC, V.

LUBY'S CAFETERIA. *9919 Colonial Dr, north of downtown.* *210/696-2741.* Hrs: 10:45 am-8:30 pm; winter to 8:15. Closed Dec 25. Avg ck: lunch $4.20, dinner $4.75. Specializes in fish, chicken-fried steak, fresh vegetables. Parking. Cr cds: DS, MC, V.

[SC]

San Diego

Founded: 1769

Pop: 1,110,549

Elev: 42 feet

Time zone: Pacific

Area code: 619

The southernmost city in California, San Diego has a distinct Mexican flavor because of its proximity to Mexico's border city of Tijuana. San Diego is built around the water, with 70 miles of beaches at its western edge. Extending from the Pacific Ocean eastward over rolling hills of 1,591 feet, San Diego is a warm city where the sun almost always shines, summer and winter. This balmy year-round climate encourages outdoor living. Within San Diego County are mountains as high as 6,500 feet, a desert area, resorts, flowers, palm trees and a flourishing cultural program.

San Diego was "the place where California began" when explorer Juan Rodriguez Cabrillo, hired by Spain, landed here in 1542. In 1769, the Franciscan priest Fray Junipero Serra built his first mission here, San Diego de Alcala. In 1821, control of San Diego passed from Spain to the new Mexican government. By 1841, however, enough Americans had settled in the area to warrant interest by the United States in what was undoubtedly good real estate. The Mexican government's loose control over California, combined with the United States' new-found theory of Manifest Destiny, led to the acquisition of San Diego by the United States after the short-lived Mexican War.

For many years San Diego has been an important naval base. Its natural harbor is home to several Coast Guard, Marine Corps and Navy installations, including the largest naval air station on the West Coast. Today, San Diego is a growing oceanography center as well.

Business

Nearly one-third of San Diego County's work force is employed by government agencies; the majority of these workers are employed at the various military bases. Half of these people are in some way involved in the manufacture of aircraft products. Second in importance to government is the production of aerospace equipment and missiles.

There are approximately 3,000 manufacturing firms in San Diego County, employing nearly 15 percent of the work force. Biomedical research and manufacturing, as well as other high-technology fields, are becoming increasingly important to the city's economy. Tourism is the third largest industry.

San Diego County is the world's largest avocado producer and one of the leading agricultural counties in the United States.

Convention Facilities

The San Diego Convention Center, located on San Diego Bay, has 254,000 square feet of space in the main exhibit hall and 100,000 square feet of column-free space in the upper-level special events pavilion. The facility also includes 100,000 square feet of meeting space on the upper and mezzanine levels, 32 meeting rooms and a 40,000-square-foot ballroom. The center is less than 10 minutes away from the airport and has underground parking available for 2,000 vehicles.

The San Diego Concourse is a self-contained complex with facilities for theatrical performances, conventions, conferences, meetings, trade shows, workshops, exhibits, banquets, dances, luncheons, recitals, ceremonies, lectures and receptions. There are 64,000 square feet of exhibit space and 25 meeting rooms with capacities ranging from 35 to 4,300 persons. Parking for 1,100 cars is available.

The Civic Theatre, the showplace of the concourse, incorporates the most modern architectural techniques. Its seating capacity is 2,992.

Golden Hall is the most versatile of the halls in the convention complex. It can be used for conventions, trade shows, exhibits, theatrical presentations, concerts and sport shows. Seating capacity is 4,337.

The Plaza Hall, the Copper Room, the Silver Room and the Terrace Room can accommodate many types of events. The Silver and Terrace rooms have dividers that can be used to reduce or enlarge room size.

Sports and Recreation

Day or night, something is going on in San Diego. The city provides a tremendous variety of spectator and participant sports. Major league sports events include football (Chargers), baseball (Padres), ice hockey (Gulls) and indoor soccer (Sockers). Racing enthusiasts can enjoy Thoroughbred racing at Del Mar Thoroughbred Club in Del Mar.

There are more than 80 municipal and public golf courses and more than 1,200 tennis courts. In addition, visitors can choose hiking, biking, horseback riding, boating in San Diego's protected bays and lagoons, waterskiing, surfing, windsurfing, swimming or sunbathing. A favorite diving spot is San Diego's La Jolla Cove, which has the clearest waters on the California coast. The offshore waters are famous for exceptional, year-round ocean fishing.

Entertainment

At night the city offers an array of nightclub entertainment as well as Broadway theater productions and performances by local professional and repertory theater groups. The 581-seat Old Globe Theatre, a locally treasured landmark, is one of three different theaters of the Simon Edison Centre for the Performing Arts. The others are the 225-seat Cassius Carter Centre Stage and the 612-seat outdoor Lowell Davies Festival Theater.

The San Diego Concourse's Civic Theatre is home to the opera and two ballet companies and also hosts popular performers throughout the year. The San Diego Symphony, the only orchestra in California to own its own location, plays in the refurbished Fox Theater, now called Copley Symphony Hall; in summer, the symphony plays under the stars at Embarcadero Marina Park South, on San Diego Bay. Popular musicals are staged at the Starlight Bowl in Balboa Park.

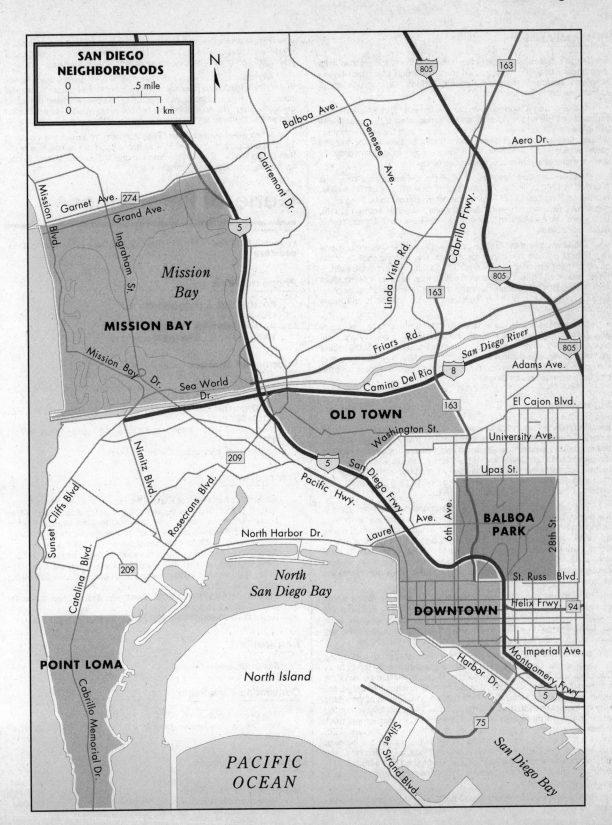

SAN DIEGO
NEIGHBORHOODS

N

0   .5 mile

0   1 km

Mission
Bay

MISSION BAY

POINT LOMA

North
San Diego Bay

North Island

PACIFIC
OCEAN

OLD TOWN

DOWNTOWN

BALBOA
PARK

San Diego Bay

Mission Blvd.

Garnet Ave.   274

Grand Ave.

Ingraham St.

Mission Bay Dr.

Sea World Dr.

Nimitz Blvd.

Rosecrans Blvd.

Sunset Cliffs Blvd

Catalina Blvd.

Cabrillo Memorial Dr.

209

209

North Harbor Dr.

Silver Strand Blvd.

Harbor Dr.

75

Balboa Ave.

Clairemont Dr.

Genesee Ave.

Linda Vista Rd.

Friars Rd.

San Diego River

Camino Del Rio

Washington St.

Pacific Hwy.

San Diego Frwy.

5

5

Laurel

6th Ave.

Ave.

St. Russ Blvd.

Helix Frwy   94

Imperial Ave.

Montgomery Frwy

5

28th St.

Upas St.

University Ave.

El Cajon Blvd.

Adams Ave.

8

163

163

163

Cabrillo Frwy.

805

805

805

163

Aero Dr.

Historical Areas

San Diego's Spanish heritage is nowhere more firmly rooted than in its dramatically beautiful missions. Of the 21-mission chain that began here and stretched northward through California, 2 missions and 2 *asistencias* are within the county.

Mission San Diego de Alcala, California's first mission, was founded in 1769 on Presidio Hill and was relocated to its present site along the San Diego River in 1774. Services are held daily in the mission chapel. Cassette tape players allow visitors to take self-conducted tours. A museum contains some of the mission's original records, as well as many liturgical robes, books and relics.

Mission San Luis Rey, largest of all the California missions, was founded in 1798 by Father Fermin Lasuen, near the city of Oceanside. Named for King Louis IX of France, it is often referred to as "king of the missions." Also worth visiting are Asistencia de San Antonio (1816), better known as Mission San Antonio de Pala, and Santa Ysabel Asistencia (1818).

Old Town, site of the first European settlement in California, is one of the most popular attractions for visitors. This historic section of the city has many restored and reconstructed buildings, old adobe structures, museums, quaint shops and restaurants. Guided walking tours are offered daily by the state park and the Old Town Historical Society. Also, a green line painted on the street directs visitors to the many interesting landmarks.

Other points of interest include the Villa Montezuma, a fine example of Victorian Byzantine-style architecture housing displays of local history; the *Star of India*, a century-old windjammer, which is the oldest iron sailing vessel still afloat and is part of the Maritime Museum; and the famous Hotel del Coronado (1888), located in Coronado, across the bay from downtown San Diego.

Sightseeing

Beautiful Balboa Park, a 1,200-acre site in the center of the city, has art galleries, museums, theaters, restaurants and many recreational facilities in addition to garden walks, subtropical plants and ponds. Most of the park's activities take place in buildings of Spanish-Moorish architecture left from the Panama-California Exposition of 1915 and the California Pacific International Exposition of 1936. This oasis in the middle of the city is best experienced on foot.

The San Diego Zoo, one of the largest and most famous zoos in the world, has some of the rarest specimens in captivity in its vast collection of animals. The exhibits are contained in open areas, where the public is separated from the animals only by moats. The Skyfari aerial tramway gives zoo-goers a panoramic view of the zoo. In addition, a 40-minute guided tour on double-deck buses takes visitors through miles of winding roads as driver/guides point out interesting facts.

Sea World, the 150-acre oceanarium on Mission Bay's south shore, is one of California's most popular attractions. Featured are aquariums, marine exhibits and shows with performing animals, such as "Baby Shamu" in a killer whale show. Pilot and beluga whales, sea lions, playful dolphins and walruses are included in the shows.

Seaport Village, an elaborate $14 million shopping and dining complex on San Diego Bay, re-creates the atmosphere of 19th-century California with authentic architectural styles and furnishings, including a turn-of-the-century carousel. Just south of downtown San Diego, the sights and sounds of a bustling California waterfront town of the 1890s may be experienced in the Gaslamp Quarter. The most fully renovated street in this 16-block area is Fifth Avenue, with its gas lamps, brick sidewalks and spectacular examples of Victorian architecture. Fifth Avenue formed the city's business center at the turn of the century. Just west of the Gaslamp Quarter is Horton Plaza, a 7-block retail and entertainment district in the heart of downtown; the 11½-acre complex includes 4 major department stores, 150 small shops and restaurants and a 7-screen theater.

Whale-watching cruises are available during the migration season (mid-December-mid-February), when herds of gray whales make their way from Alaska's Bering Sea to the warm bays and lagoons of Baja. A whale-watching station at Cabrillo National Monument on Point Loma has a glassed-in observatory from which to spot the whales.

A ride along San Diego's 59-mile scenic drive gives a quick lesson in the city's fascinating history, scenery, people and places. The drive takes about three hours, but a week could be spent enjoying the sights along the way. The route is marked about every quarter-mile with blue and yellow highway signs illustrated with a white seagull.

A few miles south of San Diego and directly across the border is Tijuana, a popular tourist destination and a short trip by car, bus or the San Diego Trolley. Contact the International Visitor Information Center for border-crossing regulations.

General References

Founded: 1769 **Pop:** 1,110,549 **Elev:** 42 feet **Time zone:** Pacific **Area code:** 619

Phone Numbers

POLICE, FIRE & PARAMEDICS: 911
FBI: 231-1122
POISON CONTROL CENTER: 543-6000
TIME: 853-1212 **WEATHER:** 289-1212

Information Sources

San Diego Convention and Visitors Bureau, 401 B Street, Suite 1400, 92101; 232-3101.
San Diego Chamber of Commerce, 402 W Broadway, Suite 1000, 92101; 232-0124.
International Visitor Information Center, 11 Horton Plaza, 92101; 236-1212.
Balboa Park Information Center, 239-0512.

Transportation

AIRLINES: Aeromexico; Alaska; American; America West; Continental; Delta; Midwest Express; Northwest; Southwest; TWA; United; USAir; and other commuter and regional airlines. For the most current airline schedules and information consult the *Official Airline Guide,* published twice monthly.
AIRPORTS: San Diego International Lindbergh Field, 231-2100.
CAR RENTAL AGENCIES: (See Toll-Free Numbers) Avis 231-7171; Budget 438-4030; Hertz 231-7000; National 231-7100; Thrifty 239-2281.
PUBLIC TRANSPORTATION: San Diego Transit, San Diego-Tijuana Trolley 233-3004.
RAILROAD PASSENGER SERVICE: Amtrak 800/872-7245.

Newspaper

San Diego Union-Tribune.

Convention Facilities

San Diego Concourse, 202 C St, 236-6500 or -6510.
San Diego Convention Center, 111 W Harbor Dr, at 5th Ave, 525-5000.

Sports & Recreation

Major Sports Facilities
Jack Murphy Stadium, I-8, Murphy Canyon Rd exit (Padres, baseball, 283-4494; Chargers, football, 280-2111).

San Diego Sports Arena, 3942 Hancock St (Sockers, indoor soccer, 224-4625; Gulls, ice hockey, 688-1800).

Racetrack
Del Mar Thoroughbred Club, County Fairgrounds, Del Mar, 755-1141.

Jai Alai
Fronton Palacio, Revolucion Ave & 7th St, Tijuana, Mexico, 298-4105.

Cultural Facilities

Theaters
Cassius Carter Centre Stage, Balboa Park, 239-2255.
Coronado Playhouse, 1775 Strand Way, Coronado, 435-4856.
Hahn Cosmopolitan Theatre, 444 4th Ave, 234-9583.
La Jolla Playhouse, 2910 La Jolla Village Dr, La Jolla, 534-6760.
Lawrence Welk Resort Theatre-Museum, 8860 Lawrence Welk Dr, Escondido, 749-3448 or -3000.
Lowell Davies Festival Theater, Balboa Park, 239-2255.
Marquis Public Theater, 3717 India St, 295-5654.
Old Globe Theatre, Balboa Park, 239-2255.
Old Town Theatre, 4040 Twiggs St, 688-2494.
San Diego Repertory Theatre, Lyceum Theatre, 79 Horton Plaza, 231-3586.
Spreckels Theatre, 121 Broadway, 235-9500.
Starlight Musical Theatre, Starlight Bowl, Balboa Park, 544-7827.

Concert Halls
Civic Theatre, San Diego Concourse, 202 C St, 236-6510.
Symphony Hall, 750 B St, 699-4200.

Museums
International Aerospace Museum Hall of Fame, Aerospace Historical Center, Balboa Park, 232-8322.
Junipero Serra Museum, Presidio Park, 2727 Presidio Dr, 297-3258.
Maritime Museum Association, 1306 N Harbor Dr, 234-9153.
Mingei International Museum, 4405 La Jolla Village Dr, La Jolla, 453-5300.
Museum of Man, Balboa Park, 239-2001.
Natural History Museum, Balboa Park, 232-3821.
Reuben H. Fleet Space Theater and Science Center, 1875 El Prado, Balboa Park, 238-1168 or -1233.
San Diego Aerospace Museum, Aerospace Historical Center, Balboa Park, 234-8291.
San Diego Hall of Champions, 1649 El Prado, Balboa Park, 234-2544.
Stephen Birch Aquarium-Museum, 2300 Expedition Way (entrance on N Torrey Pines), at Scripps Institution of Oceanography, University of California at San Diego, La Jolla, 534-6933, -3474 or -4109.
Villa Montezuma/Jesse Shepard House, 1925 K St, 239-2211.

Art Museums and Galleries
Museum of Art, Balboa Park, 232-7931.
Museum of Contemporary Art, 1001 Kettner Blvd, 234-1001.
Museum of Photographic Arts, 1649 El Prado, Casa de Balboa, 239-5262.
Spanish Village Arts and Crafts Center, 1770 Village Place, Balboa Park, 233-9050.
Timken Museum of Art, 1500 El Prado, Balboa Park, 239-5548.

Points of Interest

Historical
Cabrillo National Monument, 10 mi W of I-8 on Catalina Blvd (CA 209), at tip of Point Loma, 557-5450.

Gaslamp Quarter, bordered by 4th, 6th & Broadway Aves & K St, 233-5227.
Heritage Park, Juan & Harney Sts, near Old Town.
Hotel del Coronado, 1500 Orange Ave, Coronado, 435-6611.
Mission Basilica San Diego De Alcala, 10818 San Diego Mission Rd, 281-8449 or 283-7319.
Mission San Antonio de Pala, 44 mi N via I-15, then 7 mi E on CA 76 in Pala, 742-3317.
Mission San Luis Rey de Francia, N on I-5 to Oceanside, then 4½ mi E on CA 76, 757-3651.
Old Town, around the plaza at Mason St & San Diego Ave.
Presidio Park, Presidio Dr off Taylor St, in Old Town.
Star of India, Maritime Museum Association, 234-9153.

Other Attractions
Balboa Park, center of city; visitor center 239-0512.
House of Pacific Relations, Balboa Park, 234-0739.
Mission Bay Park, N of San Diego River via I-5, 276-8200.
Navy Installation, Broadway Pier, 532-1430 or -1431.
San Diego Trolley, Santa Fe Depot, at Kettner Blvd & C St, 595-4949.
San Diego Wild Animal Park, 30 mi NE via I-15 (US 395/CA 163) to Via Rancho Pkwy exit, follow signs, 234-6541.
San Diego Zoo and Children's Zoo, Balboa Park, 234-3153.
Seaport Village, W Harbor Drive at Kettner Blvd, 235-4014.
Sea World, Mission Bay Park, Sea World Dr, exit W off I-5, 226-3901, 800/325-3150 (CA) or 800/SEA-WRLD (exc CA).
Spreckels Outdoor Organ Pavilion, Balboa Park.

Sightseeing Tours
Gray Line bus tours, 3855 Rosencrans St, 491-0011.
San Diego Harbor Excursion, 1050 Harbor Dr, 234-4111.
Southwest Coaches, 1601 Newton Ave, 232-7579.

Whale-Watching Trips
Fisherman's Landing, 2838 Garrison St, 222-0391.
H & M Landing, 2803 Emerson St, 222-1144.
Invader Cruises, 1066 N Harbor Dr, 234-8687.
San Diego Natural History Museum, Balboa Park, 232-3821.

Annual Events
Cinco de Mayo, Old Town San Diego State Historic Park, 237-6770. Wkend closest to May 5.
Corpus Christi Fiesta, Mission San Antonio de Pala. 1st Sun June.
Del Mar Fair, Del Mar Fairgrounds, 755-1161 or 793-5555. 16 days late June-early July.
Festival of Bells, Mission Basilica San Diego de Alcala, 283-7319. Wkend mid-July.
Admission Day, phone 297-1183. Early Sept.
Cabrillo Festival, Cabrillo National Monument. Last wkend Sept-early Oct.
Christmas on the Prado, Spreckels Outdoor Organ Pavilion, Balboa Park. First wkend Dec.
Christmas-Light Boat Parade, San Diego Harbor, Shelter Island Yacht Basin, 222-4081. Late Dec.

City Neighborhoods

Many of the restaurants, unrated dining establishments and some lodgings listed under San Diego include neighborhoods as well as exact street addresses. A map showing these neighborhoods can be found immediately following the city introduction. Geographic descriptions of these areas are given, followed by a table of restaurants arranged by neighborhood.

Balboa Park: Northeast of Downtown; south of Upas St, west of 28th St, north of St Russ Blvd and east of 6th Ave.

Downtown: South and west of I-5 and north and east of the San Diego Bay. **North of Downtown:** North of US 5.
Mission Bay: South of Garnet Ave, west of I-5, north of I-8 and Mission Bay Channel and east of the Pacific Ocean.

Old Town: South of I-8, west of CA 163, north of I-5 and Washington St and east of I-5.
Point Loma: Peninsula west of San Diego Bay and east of the Pacific Ocean.

Lodgings and Food

SAN DIEGO RESTAURANTS BY NEIGHBORHOOD AREAS

(For full description, see alphabetical listings under Restaurants)

BALBOA PARK

Hob Nob Hill. 2271 1st Ave

DOWNTOWN

Anthony's Star of the Sea Room. 1360 Harbor Dr
Athens Market Taverna. 109 W F Street
Bella Luna. 748 Fifth Ave
Bice Ristorante. 777 Front St
Corvette Diner Bar & Grill. 3946 5th Ave
Dakota. 901 Fifth Ave
Dick's Last Resort. 345 5th Ave
Dobson's. 956 Broadway Circle
Fio's. 801 5th Ave
Harbor House. 831 W Harbor Dr
Karl Strauss' Old Columbia Brewery & Grill. 1157 Columbia St
Kenny's Steak House. 939 Fourth Ave
Le Fontainebleau (The Westgate Hotel). 1055 Second Ave
Luigi Al Mare. 861 W Harbor Dr
Panda Inn. 506 Horton Plaza
Rainwater's. 1202 Kettner Blvd
Särö. 926 Broadway Circle
Salvatore's. 750 Front St
San Diego Pier Cafe. 885 W Harbor Dr
Sfuzzi. 340 5th Ave
Top of the Market. 750 N Harbor Dr

NORTH OF DOWNTOWN

Aesop's Tables. 8650 Genesee Ave
Afghanistan Khyber Pass. 4647 Convoy St
Anthony's Fish Grotto. 11666 Avena Place
Benihana of Tokyo. 477 Camino del Rio South
Busalacchi's. 3683 5th Ave
California Cuisine. 1027 University Ave
Calliope's Greek Cafe. 3958 5th Ave
Celadon. 3628 5th Ave
City Delicatessen. 535 University Ave
D.Z. Akin's. 6930 Alvarado Rd
El Bizcocho (Rancho Bernardo Inn Resort). 17550 Bernardo Oaks Dr
El Indio Shop. 3695 India St
El Tecolote. 6110 Friars Rd
Greek Corner. 5841 El Cajon Blvd
Imperial House. 505 Kalmia St
Jasmine. 4609 Convoy St
Kelly's. 500 Hotel Circle N
Liaison. 2202 Fourth Ave

Mister A's. 2550 5th Ave
Nati's. 1852 Bacon St
Saffron. 3731-B India St
Thee Bungalow. 4996 W Point Loma Blvd
Tom Ham's Lighthouse. 2150 Harbor Island Dr
Winesellar & Brasserie. 9550 Waples St

MISSION BAY

Baci Ristorante. 1955 W Morena Blvd
Belgian Lion. 2265 Bacon St

OLD TOWN

Cafe Coyote. 2461 San Diego Ave
Cafe Pacifica. 2414 San Diego Ave
Casa de Bandini. 2754 Calhoun St
Lino's. 2754 Calhoun St
Old Town Mexican Cafe & Cantina. 2489 San Diego Ave

POINT LOMA

Fairouz. 3166 Midway Dr

Note: *When a listing is located in a town that does not have its own city heading, it will appear under the city nearest to its location. In these cases, the address and town appear in parenthesis immediately following the name of the establishment.*

Motels

★★ **BALBOA PARK INN.** *3402 Park Blvd (92103), in Balboa Park.* 619/298-0823; res: 800/938-8181; FAX 619/294-8070. 26 rms, 2 story, 17 kit. suites. S, D $80; kit. suites $85-$190; under 12 free. Crib $5. TV; cable. Complimentary continental bkfst. Complimentary coffee in rms. Ck-out noon. Free lndry facilities. Refrigerators; some in-rm whirlpools. Many patios, balconies. Sun deck. Each rm is a "theme" rm, with individual decor. Cr cds: A, C, D, DS, MC, V.

✔★★ **BEST WESTERN SEVEN SEAS.** *411 Hotel Circle S (92108), in Old Town.* 619/291-1300; FAX 619/291-6933. 309 rms, 2 story, 9 kit. units. S, D $49-$89; kit. units $59-$99; under 12 free. Crib free. Pet accepted, some restrictions; $10. TV; cable. Heated pool; whirlpool, poolside serv. Playground. Complimentary coffee in rms. Restaurant 6 am-midnight. Rm serv. Bar 10-2 am. Ck-out noon. Coin lndry. Meeting rms. Bellhops. Valet serv. Sundries. Gift shop. Free airport, RR station, bus depot transportation. Lawn games. Game rm. Some balconies. Cr cds: A, C, D, DS, ER, JCB, MC, V.

★ **BEST WESTERN SHELTER ISLAND MARINA INN.** *2051 Shelter Island Dr (92106), in Point Loma.* 619/222-0561; FAX 619/222-9760. 97 rms (83 with shower only), 2 story, 29 kit. units. Mid-June-mid-Sept: S $80-$90; D $85-$95; each addl $10; kits. $125-$135; under 12 free; wkly rates; lower rates rest of yr. Crib $10. TV; cable. Pool; whirlpool, poolside serv. Complimentary coffee in rms. Restaurant 6 am-10 pm. Bar 11-2 am; entertainment wkends. Ck-out noon. Coin lndry. Meeting rms. Valet serv. Many balconies. On ocean. Near airport. Cr cds: A, C, D, DS, ER, JCB, MC, V.

★★ **COMFORT SUITES-MISSION VALLEY.** *631 Camino del Rio S (92108), north of downtown.* 619/294-3444; FAX 619/260-0746. 122 suites, 3 story. Suites $68-$90; under 17 free. Crib free. TV; cable. Heated pool. Complimentary continental bkfst, coffee. Restaurant adj 10 am-10 pm. Ck-out 11 am. Meeting rms. Coin lndry. Free airport transportation. Exercise equipt; weight machine, bicycles, whirlpool. Refrigerators. Cr cds: A, C, D, DS, ER, JCB, MC, V.

[D] [≈] [✈] [⊠] [🔥] [SC]

★ **DANA INN & MARINA.** *1710 W Mission Bay Dr (92109), in Mission Bay.* 619/222-6440; res: 800/345-9995; FAX 619/222-5916. 196 rms, 2 story. Late May-mid-Sept: S $69-$119; D $79-$129; each addl $10; under 18 free; lower rates rest of yr. Crib free. TV; cable. Heated pool; whirlpool, poolside serv. Coffee in rms. Restaurant 7 am-10 pm. Rm serv. Bar. Ck-out noon. Coin lndry. Bellhops. Valet serv. Free airport, RR station, bus depot transportation. Tennis. Marina. Boat launch adj. Cr cds: A, C, D, DS, MC, V.

[🏃] [≈] [⊠] [🔥] [SC]

✔★ **DAYS INN-HOTEL CIRCLE.** *543 Hotel Circle S (92108), in Old Town.* 619/297-8800; FAX 619/298-6029. 280 rms, 3 story, 49 kit. units. S $49-$62; D $55-$73; each addl $10; kit. units $57-$79; under 18 free; wkly rates (kit. units); higher rates special events. Crib free. TV; cable. Heated pool; whirlpool. Restaurant 6:30 am-9 pm. Ck-out noon. Coin lndry. Bellhops. Valet serv. Sundries. Barber, beauty shop. Free airport, RR station, bus depot transportation. Refrigerators. Cr cds: A, C, D, DS, JCB, MC, V.

[D] [≈] [⊠] [🔥] [SC]

★★ **FABULOUS INN.** *2485 Hotel Circle Place (92108), north of downtown.* 619/291-7700; res: 800/824-0950; FAX 619/297-6179. 175 rms, 4 story. July-early Sept: S $56-$70; D $65-$75; suites $109; under 18 free; lower rates rest of yr. Crib $10. TV; cable. Heated pool; whirlpool. Complimentary continental bkfst. Restaurant nearby. Ck-out noon. Coin lndry. Meeting rms. Free covered parking. Some refrigerators, in-rm whirlpools. Many balconies. Cr cds: A, C, D, DS, ER, MC, V.

[D] [≈] [⊠] [SC]

✔★ **GOOD NITE INN.** *4545 Waring Rd (92120), north of downtown.* 619/286-7000; res: 800/648-3466; FAX 619/286-8403. 96 rms, 2 story. S, D $35-$45; each addl $6; under 18 free. Pet accepted. TV; cable. Heated pool. Restaurant 8 am-10 pm. Ck-out 11 am. Coin lndry. Meeting rm. Refrigerators avail. Private patios, balconies. Cr cds: A, C, D, DS, MC, V.

[D] [🐾] [≈] [⊠] [🔥] [SC]

★★ **GROSVENOR INN.** *3145 Sports Arena Blvd (92110), near Lindbergh Field Intl Airport, in Point Loma.* 619/225-9999; res: 800/232-1212; FAX 619/225-0958. 206 rms, 2 story. S, D $64-$82; suites $165-$250. Crib free. TV; cable. Heated pool; whirlpool. Coffee in rms. Restaurant 11 am-10 pm. Ck-out noon. Coin lndry. Meeting rms. Bellhops. Valet serv. Sundries. Free airport, RR station, bus depot transportation. Refrigerators. Shopping arcade adj. Cr cds: A, C, D, DS, MC, V.

[D] [≈] [✈] [⊠] [🔥] [SC]

★★ **HAMPTON INN.** *5434 Kearny Mesa Rd (92111), north of downtown.* 619/292-1482; FAX 619/292-4410. 150 rms, 5 story. June-Aug: S, D $72-$83; under 18 free; lower rates rest of yr. Crib free. TV; cable, in-rm movies avail. Heated pool. Complimentary continental bkfst, coffee. Restaurant adj 7 am-11 pm. Ck-out 11 am. Coin lndry. Meeting rms. Valet serv. Some refrigerators. Cr cds: A, C, D, DS, MC, V.

[D] [≈] [⊠] [🔥] [SC]

★★ **HUMPHREY'S HALF MOON INN & SUITES.** *2303 Shelter Island Dr (92106), in Point Loma.* 619/224-3411; res: 800/542-7400; FAX 619/224-3478. 182 rms, 2 story. 30 kit. units. Late May-early Sept: S $89-$149; D $99-$159; each addl $10; kit. suites $119-$225; under 18 free; lower rates rest of yr. Crib free. TV; cable. Heated pool; whirlpool, poolside serv. Complimentary coffee in rms. Restaurant 6:30 am-10 pm. Rm serv. Bar 11-2 am; entertainment. Ck-out noon. Coin lndry. Meeting rms. Bellhops. Sundries. Free airport, RR station transportation. Bicycles. Lawn games. Refrigerators. Many private patios,

balconies. South Sea island decor. Garden. On marina; 3 slips. C cds: A, C, D, DS, ER, JCB, MC, V.

[D] [≈] [⊠] [🔥] [SC]

★ **LA QUINTA.** *10185 Paseo Montril (92129), north of downtown.* 619/484-8800; FAX 619/538-0476. 120 rms, 3 story. S $53-$66; D $59-$75; each addl $5; under 18 free. Crib free. Pet accepted. TV; cable. Heated pool. Complimentary continental bkfst in lobby. Restaurant adj open 24 hrs. Ck-out noon. Meeting rms. Cr cds: A, C, D, DS, JCB, MC, V.

[D] [🐾] [≈] [⊠] [🔥] [SC]

★ **OLD TOWN INN.** *4444 Pacific Coast Hwy (92110), near Lindbergh Field Intl Airport, north of downtown.* 619/260-8024; res: 800/643-3025; FAX 619/296-0524. 84 rms (41 with shower only), 1-3 story, 69 with A/C. June-Sept: S $34-$51; D $38-$56; each addl $5; suites $80-$105; kit units $49-$69; under 12 free; wkly rates; higher rates hols (3-day min); lower rates rest of yr. Crib $5. Pet accepted; $5. TV; cable. Complimentary coffee in lobby. Restaurant nearby. Ck-out 11 am. Coin lndry. Airport, RR station, bus depot transportation. Refrigerators avail. Cr cds: A, C, D, DS, MC, V.

[D] [🐾] [✈] [⊠] [🔥] [SC]

★★ **TRAVELODGE SEA WORLD-SPORTS ARENA.** *3737 Sports Arena Blvd (92110), opp Sports Arena, in Point Loma.* 619/226-3711; FAX 619/224-9248. 307 rms, 3 story. May-Sept: S, D $64-$69; suites $75-$150; under 17 free; lower rates rest of yr. TV. Heated pool; whirlpool. Complimentary continental bkfst. Restaurant adj 6 am-11 pm. Rm serv. Ck-out noon. Coin lndry. Meeting rms. Bellhops. Some covered parking. Health club privileges adj. Some refrigerators. Cr cds: A, C, D, DS, ER, JCB, MC, V.

[≈] [⊠] [🔥] [SC]

★★ **VACATION INN.** *3900 Old Town Ave (92110), in Old Town.* 619/299-7400; res: 800/451-9846; FAX 619/299-1619. 125 rms, 3 story. Mid-May-mid-Sept: S $85-$119; D $95-$119; each addl $10; suites $105-$160; under 17 free; lower rates rest of yr. Crib free. TV; cable. Heated pool; whirlpool. Complimentary continental bkfst. Complimentary coffee in rms. Restaurant opp 10 am-10 pm. Ck-out noon. Coin lndry. Meeting rms. Covered parking. Free airport, RR station transportation. Refrigerators; some wet bars. Some balconies. Cr cds: A, C, D, DS, ER, MC, V.

[D] [≈] [⊠] [🔥] [SC]

✔★ **VAGABOND INN.** *625 Hotel Circle S (92108), north of downtown.* 619/297-1691; FAX 619/692-9009. 87 rms, 2 story. Mid-May-mid-Sept: S $60-$72; D $65-$77; each addl $5; under 18 free; lower rates rest of yr. Crib free. Pet accepted; $5. TV; cable. 2 heated pools; whirlpool. Complimentary continental bkfst, coffee. Restaurant adj open 24 hrs. Ck-out noon. Cr cds: A, C, D, DS, MC, V.

[🐾] [≈] [⊠] [🔥] [SC]

Motor Hotels

★★★ **BAY CLUB HOTEL & MARINA.** *2131 Shelter Island Dr (92106), in Point Loma.* 619/224-8888; res: 800/672-0800; FAX 619/225-1604. 105 rms, 2 story. S $115-$175; D $130-$200; each addl $10; suites $195-$295; under 12 free; honeymoon, island getaway packages. Crib $10. TV; cable. Heated pool; poolside serv. Complimentary bkfst. Restaurant 6:30 am-10 pm. Rm serv. Bar 10 am-midnight. Ck-out noon. Meeting rms. Bellhops. Valet serv. Concierge. Sundries. Covered parking. Free airport, RR station, bus depot transportation. Exercise equipt; weight machine, bicycles, whirlpool. Refrigerators. Private patios, balconies. On bay; marina. Fishing from nearby pier. Cr cds: A, C, D, DS, ER, MC, V.

[D] [≈] [✈] [⊠] [🔥] [SC]

★★★ **BEST WESTERN HACIENDA HOTEL.** *4041 Harney St (92110), in Old Town.* 619/298-4707; FAX 619/298-4707, ext. 2460. 149 suites, 2-3 story. June-Aug: S $109-$119; D $119-$129; each addl $10; under 16 free; lower rates rest of yr. Crib free. TV; cable, in-rm movies.

Heated pool; poolside serv. Complimentary coffee in rms. Restaurants 6 am-10 pm. Rm serv. Bar 11-1:30 am. Ck-out noon. Meeting rms. Bellhops. Valet serv. Concierge. Covered parking. Free airport, RR station, bus depot transportation. Exercise equipt; weights, bicycles, whirlpool. Refrigerators. Some private patios, balconies. Grills. Spanish architecture. Cr cds: A, C, D, DS, MC, V.

D ⌘ ✗ ⊠ ▨ SC

★ ★ **BEST WESTERN SAN DIEGO CENTRAL.** 3805 Murphy Canyon Rd (92123), north of downtown. 619/277-1199; FAX 619/277-3442. 176 rms, 4 story, 19 suites. S $75-$95; D $81-$100; each addl $6; suites $100-$120; under 12 free; higher rates: Memorial Day, July 4, Labor Day. Crib free. Pool. Complimentary continental bkfst. Restaurant 6:30 am-8 pm. Rm serv. Bar. Ck-out noon. Coin lndry. Meeting rms. Free garage parking. Exercise equipt; weight machine, bicycles, whirlpool. Refrigerators. Wet bar in suites. Most suites with balcony. Cr cds: A, C, D, DS, ER, JCB, MC, V.

D ⌘ ✗ ⊠ ▨ SC

★ ★ **DOUBLETREE-RANCHO BERNARDO.** 11611 Bernardo Plaza Court (92128), north of downtown. 619/485-9250; FAX 619/451-7948. 209 rms, 4 story. S $129; D $149; each addl $10; suites $300; under 10 free; wkend rates. Crib free. TV; cable. Heated pool. Restaurant 6-9 am, 5-10 pm; Sat & Sun from 7 am. Bar from 5 pm. Ck-out 1 pm. Meeting rms. Exercise equipt; weight machine, bicycles, whirlpool. Cr cds: A, C, D, DS, ER, JCB, MC, V.

D ⌘ ✗ ⊠ ▨ SC

★ ★ ★ **HANDLERY HOTEL & COUNTRY CLUB.** 950 Hotel Circle N (92108), I-8 Hotel Circle exit, north of downtown. 619/298-0511; res: 800/676-6567; FAX 619/298-9793. 217 rms, 2 story. S $75; D $85; each addl $10; suites $150-$190; under 12 free. Crib free. TV; cable, in-rm movies. 2 pools (1 lap pool); poolside serv. Coffee in rms. Restaurant 6 am-11 pm. Rm serv 7 am-10 pm. Bars 11-1 am; entertainment Tues- Sat. Ck-out noon. Lndry facilities. Meeting rms. Bellhops. Valet serv. Sundries. Gift shop. Barber, beauty shop. Tennis. Putting green, driving range. Exercise equipt; weight machines, treadmill, whirlpool. Some balconies. Cr cds: A, C, D, DS, ER, JCB, MC, V.

D ⚐ ⌘ ✗ ⊠ ⊠ ▨ SC

★ ★ ★ **HOLIDAY INN RANCHO BERNARDO.** 17065 W Bernardo Dr (92127), north of downtown. 619/485-6530; FAX 619/485-6530, ext. 324. 178 rms, 2-3 story, 13 kits. S, D $58-$76; each addl $10; suites $76-$125; under 18 free. Crib free. Pet accepted, some restrictions; $10. TV; cable, in-rm movies. Heated pool. Complimentary bkfst. Coffee in rms. Restaurant opp 11 am-10 pm. Ck-out noon. Coin lndry. Meeting rms. Valet serv. Some covered parking. Exercise equipt; weights, bicycles, whirlpool, sauna. Some refrigerators, in-rm whirlpools. Many private patios, balconies. Cr cds: A, C, D, DS, JCB, MC, V.

D ⚐ ⌘ ✗ ⊠ ▨ SC

✔ ★ ★ **HOWARD JOHNSON HARBORVIEW.** 1430 7th Ave (92101), near Lindbergh Field Intl Airport, north of downtown. 619/696-0911; FAX 619/234-9416. 136 rms, 3 story. June-Sept: S $55-$75; D $65-$95; each addl $5; suites $90-$150; under 12 free; wkly rates; lower rates rest of yr. Crib free. Covered parking $3. TV; cable. Heated pool. Complimentary continental bkfst. Restaurant adj 6 am-10 pm. Ck-out noon. Free airport, RR station, bus depot transportation. Exercise equipt; weight machine, bicycles. Some refrigerators. Many balconies. Cr cds: A, C, D, DS, ER, JCB, MC, V.

⌘ ✗ ✈ ⊠ ▨ SC

★ ★ **QUALITY SUITES.** 9880 Mira Mesa Blvd (92131), at jct I-15, north of downtown. 619/530-2000; FAX 619/530-2000, ext. 145. 130 suites, 4 story. Early July-Labor Day: suites $79-$159; each addl $10; under 18 free; lower rates rest of yr. TV; cable, in-rm movies. Heated pool. Complimentary continental bkfst. Ck-out noon. Meeting rms. Gift shop. Exercise equipt; weights, bicycles, whirlpool. Refrigerators. Cr cds: A, C, D, DS, ER, JCB, MC, V.

D ⌘ ✗ ⊠ ▨ SC

✔ ★ ★ **RAMADA INN-HOTEL CIRCLE.** 2151 Hotel Circle S (92108), north of downtown. 619/291-6500; FAX 619/294-7531. 183 rms, 4 story. July-Aug: S $52-$99; D $59-$119; each addl $10; under 18 free. Crib free. TV; cable. Heated pool; whirlpool. Complimentary coffee, newspaper in rms. Restaurant 6:30-11 am, 5-10 pm. Rm serv. Bar 5-11 pm. Ck-out noon. Meeting rms. Bellhops. Valet serv. Some covered parking. Free airport, RR station, bus depot transportation. Refrigerators avail. Cr cds: A, C, D, DS, JCB, MC, V.

D ⌘ ⊠ ▨ SC

✔ ★ ★ **RODEWAY INN.** 833 Ash St (92101), downtown. 619/239-2285; FAX 619/235-6951. 45 rms, 4 story. July-Aug: S $59-$69; D $64-$79; each addl $5; studio rms $50-$70; under 18 free; lower rates rest of yr. Crib free. TV; cable. Complimentary continental bkfst. Restaurant opp open 6-3 am. Ck-out noon. Meeting rm. Valet serv. Whirlpool, saunas. Some refrigerators. Some balconies. Cr cds: A, C, D, DS, ER, JCB, MC, V.

⊠ ▨ SC

✔ ★ ★ **SEAPOINT.** 4875 N Harbor Dr (92106), near Lindbergh Field Intl Airport, north of downtown. 619/224-3621; res: 800/345-9995; FAX 619/224-3629. 237 rms, 2-5 story. July-mid-Sept: S $59.50-$109.50; D $69.50-$119.50; each addl $10; suites $125-$145; under 18 free; lower rates rest of yr. Crib free. TV; cable. Heated pool. Complimentary coffee in rms. Restaurant adj 6 am-10 pm. Ck-out noon. Coin lndry. Meeting rms. Bellhops. Valet serv. Sundries. Free airport, RR station, bus depot transportation. Exercise equipt; weights, bicycles. Lawn games. Some refrigerators. Some private patios, balconies. Opp marina. Cr cds: A, C, D, DS, JCB, MC, V.

⌘ ✗ ✈ ⊠ ▨ SC

★ ★ ★ **TOWN & COUNTRY.** 500 Hotel Circle N (92108), north of downtown. 619/291-7131; res: 800/854-2608; FAX 619/291-3584. 953 rms, 1-10 story. S $80-$120; D $90-$130; each addl $10; suites $250-$450; under 18 free. Crib free. Parking $5. TV; cable. 4 pools, 1 heated; whirlpool, poolside serv. Restaurant 6:30 am-9:30 pm. Rm serv. Bar 11-2 am; entertainment, dancing. Ck-out noon. Convention facilities. Bellhops. Valet serv. Barber. Lighted tennis privileges, pro. Golf privileges; driving range adj. Health club privileges. Some refrigerators. Some private patios, balconies. On 32 acres. Cr cds: A, C, D, DS, MC, V.

D ⚐ ⚐ ⚐ ⌘ ✗ ⊠ ▨ SC

Hotels

★ ★ **CLARION BAYVIEW.** 660 K Street (92101), downtown. 619/696-0234; FAX 619/231-8199. 312 rms, 21 story, 48 suites. Late May-early Sept: S $89-$139; D $99-$149; each addl $10; suites $140-$165; under 18 free; lower rates rest of yr. Crib free. Covered parking $7/night. TV; cable. Restaurant 6:30 am-10 pm. Bar 11-2 am; entertainment Fri, Sat. Ck-out noon. Coin lndry. Meeting rms. Gift shop. Free airport, RR station, bus depot transportation. Exercise equipt; weight machine, bicycles, whirlpool, sauna. Some bathrm phones. Balconies. View of San Diego Bay. Cr cds: A, C, D, DS, JCB, MC, V.

D ✗ ⊠ ▨ SC

★ ★ **DOUBLETREE-HORTON PLAZA.** 910 Broadway Circle (92101), downtown. 619/239-2200; FAX 619/239-0509. 450 rms, 16 story. S, D $139-$174; each addl $10; suites $250-$975; under 18 free; wkend & wkday packages. Crib free. Covered parking $8; valet $10. TV; cable. Heated pool; poolside serv. Restaurant 6:30 am-10 pm. Rm serv 24 hrs. Bar to 2 am; entertainment (exc Sun). Ck-out noon. Convention facilities. Concierge. Lighted tennis. Exercise rm; instructor, weight machines, bicycles, whirlpool, sauna. Bathrm phones, refrigerators, minibars. Some balconies. Connected to Horton Plaza. *LUXURY LEVEL : EXECUTIVE LEVEL.* 55 units, 8 suites. Private lounge. Some wet bars. Cr cds: A, C, D, DS, ER, JCB, MC, V.

D ⚐ ⌘ ✗ ⊠ ▨ SC

★ ★ ★ **EMBASSY SUITES.** 601 Pacific Hwy (92101), near Seaport Village, west of downtown. 619/239-2400; FAX 619/239-1520. 337 suites, 12 story. Mid-June-mid-Sept: suites $145-$165; under 12 free; lower rates rest of yr. Crib free. Covered parking $8. TV; cable. Indoor pool. Complimentary full bkfst. Complimentary coffee in rms. Restaurant 10 am-10 pm. Bar to midnight. Ck-out noon. Coin lndry. Meeting rms. Gift shop. Barber, beauty shop. Exercise equipt; weight machine, bicycles, whirlpool, sauna. Refrigerators. Some balconies. San Diego Bay 1 blk. Cr cds: A, C, D, DS, JCB, MC, V.

D ≈ 🏃 ⚓ 🔥

★ ★ ★ **HILTON BEACH AND TENNIS RESORT.** 1775 E Mission Bay Dr (92109), in Mission Bay. 619/276-4010; FAX 619/275-7991. 357 rms, 8 story. S $125-$225; D $145-$225; each addl $20; suites $325-$575; family, wkend rates. Crib free. Pet accepted. TV; cable. Heated pool; wading pool, poolside serv. Playground. Restaurant 6:30 am-11 pm. Bars 10:30 am-midnight & 5 pm-1:30 am; entertainment, dancing Fri-Sun. Ck-out noon. Coin lndry. Convention facilities. Gift shop. Beauty shop. Free airport transportation. Lighted tennis, pro. Putting greens. Exercise equipt; weights, bicycles, whirlpool, sauna. Rec rm. Lawn games. Many bathrm phones, refrigerators, minibars. Private patios, balconies. Dock; boats. On beach. Cr cds: A, C, D, DS, ER, JCB, MC, V.

D 🐾 🎣 ≈ 🏃 ⚓ 🔥 SC

★ ★ ★ **HILTON-MISSION VALLEY.** 901 Camino del Rio S (92108), off I-8 Mission Center Rd exit, north of downtown. 619/543-9000; FAX 619/543-9358. 350 rms, 14 story. S $99-$149; each addl $10; suites $200-$400; under 18 free. Crib free. Pet accepted, some restrictions; $250 ($200 refundable). TV; cable. Heated pool; poolside serv. Coffee in rms. Restaurant 6:30 am-10:30 pm. Bar 11-2 am. Ck-out noon. Convention facilities. Some covered parking. Free Mission Valley shopping transportation. Exercise equipt; weights, bicycles, whirlpool, sauna. Refrigerators. Large entrance foyer. Cr cds: A, C, D, DS, ER, MC, V.

D 🐾 ≈ 🏃 ⚓ 🔥 SC

★ ★ **HOLIDAY INN HARBOR VIEW.** 1617 1st Ave (92101), downtown. 619/239-6171; FAX 619/233-6228. 203 rms, 16 story. S $85; D $95; each addl $10; under 19 free. Crib free. TV; cable. Heated pool. Coffee in rms. Restaurant 6 am-2 pm, 5-10 pm. Bar 11 am-midnight. Ck-out noon. Coin lndry. Meeting rms. Gift shop. Exercise equipt; stair machine, weight machine. Circular building. Cr cds: A, C, D, DS, ER, JCB, MC, V.

D ≈ 🏃 ⚓ 🔥 SC

★ ★ **HOLIDAY INN ON THE BAY.** 1355 N Harbor Dr (92101), downtown. 619/232-3861; FAX 619/232-4924. 600 rms, 14 story. July-Aug: S $95-$135; D $105-$145; each addl $10; suites $250-$800; under 19 free; lower rates rest of yr. Crib free. Pet accepted, some restrictions. Parking $10/day. TV; cable. Heated pool. Restaurant 6 am-10 pm. Bar 11-1 am. Ck-out noon. Convention facilities. Shopping arcade. Airport, RR station transportation. Exercise equipt; bicycle, treadmill. Some bathrm phones, refrigerators. Balconies. Sun deck. Many bay view rms. Outside glass-enclosed elvtr. Cruise ship terminal opp. Cr cds: A, C, D, DS, JCB, MC, V.

D 🐾 ≈ 🏃 ⚓ 🔥 SC

★ ★ ★ **THE HORTON GRAND.** 311 Island Ave (92101), downtown. 619/544-1886; res: 800/542-1886; FAX 619/239-3823. 132 rms, 4 story. S $99-$109; D $119-$129; each addl $20; suites $139-$189; under 12 free. Crib free. Some covered parking, valet $8. TV; cable. Restaurant 7 am-10 pm. Tea 2:30-5:30 pm. Bar noon-midnight. Ck-out noon. Meeting rms. Concierge. Fireplaces; refrigerator in suites. Some balconies. Victorian building; built 1886. Antiques, oak staircase. Chinese Museum & Tea Room. Skylight in lobby; bird cages. Oldest building in San Diego. Cr cds: A, C, D, DS, MC, V.

D ⚓ 🔥 SC

HOTEL SAN DIEGO. (New owners, therefore not rated) 339 W Broadway (92101), downtown. 619/234-0221; res: 800/621-5380; FAX 619/232-1305. 219 rms, 6 story. S, D $59-$79; suites $99-

$109; under 18 free; wkly rates. TV; cable. Restaurant adj 7 am-9 pm. Ck-out noon. Coin lndry. Meeting rms. Gift shop. Free airport, RR station, transportation. Some refrigerators. Cr cds: A, C, D, DS, JCB, MC, V.

⚓ 🔥 SC

★ ★ ★ **HYATT ISLANDIA.** 1441 Quivira Rd (92109), in Mission Bay. 619/224-1234; FAX 619/224-0348. 422 rms, 17 story. S, D $109-$174; suites $159-$2,000; under 18 free. Crib free. TV; cable. Heated pool; whirlpool, poolside serv. Supervised child's activities (June-Sept). Restaurant 6 am-11 pm. Bar 11:30-2 am; entertainment Thurs-Sat. Ck-out noon. Convention facilities. Concierge. Airport transportation avail. Some refrigerators. Many private patios, balconies. Most rms with view of ocean or bay. Bicycle rentals. Marina; sport fishing; sailboat charters. Whale watching (Dec-Mar). Cr cds: A, C, D, DS, ER, JCB, MC, V.

D 🐾 ≈ 🏃 🔥 SC

★ ★ ★ **HYATT REGENCY.** One Market Place (92101), adj to Convention Center and Seaport Village, downtown. 619/232-1234; FAX 619/233-6464. 875 units, 40 story, 56 suites. S, D $145-$255; under 18 free. Crib free. Garage parking $8-$11. TV; cable. Pool; poolside serv. Restaurant 6 am-10 pm. Rm serv 24 hrs. Bar noon-1:30 am. Ck-out noon. Convention facilities. Concierge. Shopping arcade. 4 tennis courts. Exercise equipt; weight machine, bicycles, whirlpool, sauna, steam rm. Some refrigerators, minibars. Located on San Diego Bay; panoramic view of harbor and marina. **LUXURY LEVEL : REGENCY CLUB.** 52 rms, 9 suites, 5 floors. S $230; D $250. Concierge. Private lounge, honor bar. Complimentary continental bkfst, refreshments. Cr cds: A, C, D, DS, ER, JCB, MC, V.

D 🐾 🎣 ≈ 🏃 ⚓ 🔥 SC

★ ★ ★ **MARRIOTT HOTEL & MARINA.** 333 W Harbor Dr (92101), adj to Seaport Village & Convention Center, downtown. 619/234-1500; FAX 619/234-8678. 1,355 rms, 26 story. S, D $180-$205; each addl $20; suites from $310; under 18 free; wkend rates. Crib free. Pet accepted. TV; cable. Pool; poolside serv. Restaurant 6:30 am-11 pm. Rm serv 24 hrs. Bar 11-2 am; entertainment. Ck-out noon. Coin lndry. Meeting rms. Concierge. Shopping arcade. Barber, beauty shops. 6 lighted tennis courts, pro. Exercise equipt; weight machines, treadmill, whirlpool, sauna. Game rm. Bathrm phones, minibars; some refrigerators. Some balconies. Luxurious; large chandeliers in lobby. Bayside; marina. **LUXURY LEVEL .** 62 rms, 4 suites, 2 floors. S, D $180-$205; suites $325-$2,200. Private lounge. In-rm steam bath in some suites. Deluxe toiletry amenities. Complimentary continental bkfst, refreshments, newspaper. Cr cds: A, C, D, DS, ER, JCB, MC, V.

D 🐾 🎣 ≈ 🏃 ⚓ 🔥 SC

★ ★ ★ **MARRIOTT SUITES-DOWNTOWN.** 701 A Street (92101), downtown. 619/696-9800; FAX 619/696-1555. 264 suites, 27 story. S, D $99-$174; under 18 free. Crib free. Pet accepted, some restrictions; $50. Garage $10, valet parking $15. TV; cable. Indoor pool. Coffee in rms. Restaurant 6:30 am-10 pm. Bar 10 am-midnight. Ck-out noon. Meeting rms. Gift shop. Free airport, RR station, bus depot transportation. Exercise equipt; weight machine, bicycles, whirlpool, sauna. Health club privileges. Refrigerators, minibars. Cr cds: A, C, D, DS, ER, JCB, MC, V.

D 🐾 ≈ 🏃 ⚓ 🔥 SC

★ ★ ★ **PAN PACIFIC.** 400 W Broadway (92101), near Lindbergh Field Intl Airport, downtown. 619/239-4500; res: 800/626-3988; FAX 619/239-3274. 436 rms, 25 story. S, D $150-$190; each addl $15; suites $300-$2,000; under 16 free. Crib free. Garage $8. TV; cable. Heated pool; poolside serv. Restaurant 6 am-10 pm. Bar 11-1 am; entertainment Tues-Fri. Ck-out noon. Convention facilities. Concierge. Shopping arcade. Free airport, convention center transportation. Exercise rm; instructor, weight machine, bicycle, whirlpool, steam rm. Bathrm phones, minibars. Cr cds: A, C, D, DS, ER, JCB, MC, V.

D ≈ 🏃 ✈ ⚓ 🔥

★ ★ ★ **RADISSON.** 1433 Camino del Rio S (92108), north of downtown. 619/260-0111; FAX 619/260-0853. 260 rms, 13 story. S, D

$139; each addl $10; under 17 free; wkend packages. Crib free. Pet accepted, some restrictions. TV; cable. Heated pool. Restaurant 6:30 am-10 pm. Bar 2 pm-1:30 am; entertainment Fri & Sat. Ck-out noon. Convention facilities. Free airport transportation. Exercise equipt; weight machine, bicycles, whirlpool. Some balconies. *LUXURY LEVEL : EXECUTIVE LEVELS.* 24 rms, 11 suites, 2 floors. S, D $179; suites $195-$1,350. Concierge. Private lounge. Full wet bar in some suites. Complimentary continental bkfst, refreshments. Cr cds: A, C, D, DS, ER, JCB, MC, V.

D ⚐ 🏊 🏃 🎿 🐾 SC

★ ★ ★ **RADISSON SUITE.** *11520 W Bernardo Court (92127), north of downtown.* 619/451-6600; FAX 619/592-0253. 175 suites, 3 story. S, D $79-$150; each addl $10; under 12 free; golf plans. Crib $10. Pet accepted, some restrictions. TV; cable, in-rm movies. Heated pool. Complimentary full bkfst. Complimentary coffee in rms. Restaurant 6-9:30 am, 5-11 pm. Bar 5-11 pm. Ck-out noon. Coin lndry. Meeting rms. Tennis, golf privileges. Exercise equipt; weight machine, bicycles, whirlpool. Refrigerators, minibars. Cr cds: A, C, D, DS, ER, JCB, MC, V.

D ⚐ 🏃 🏌 🏊 🏃 🎿 🐾 SC

★ ★ ★ **RED LION.** *7450 Hazard Center Dr (92108), north of downtown.* 619/297-5466; FAX 619/297-5499. 300 rms, 11 story. S, D $130-$165; each addl $20; under 18 free. Crib free. Pet accepted. TV; cable. 2 pools, 1 indoor; poolside serv. Restaurant 6 am-11 pm. Bar 5 pm-2 am; entertainment, dancing Tues-Sat. Ck-out noon. Convention facilities. Gift shop. Garage parking; valet. Free airport, RR station, bus depot transportation. Lighted tennis, pro. Exercise equipt; weight machine, stair machine, whirlpool, sauna. Some balconies. *LUXURY LEVEL : EXECUTIVE LEVEL.* 21 rms, 4 suites. S, D $145-$180; suites $395-$495. Private lounge, honor bar. Complimentary continental bkfst, refreshments, newspaper. Cr cds: A, C, D, DS, ER, JCB, MC, V.

D ⚐ 🏃 🏊 🏃 🎿 🐾 SC

★ ★ ★ **SHERATON HARBOR ISLAND.** *1380 Harbor Island Dr (92101), near Lindbergh Field Intl Airport, north of downtown.* 619/291-2900; FAX 619/296-5297. 1,048 rms, 12 story. S, D $180-$200; each addl $20; suites $375-$1,100; under 18 free. Crib free. TV; cable. 3 pools, heated; 2 wading pools, poolside serv. Playground. Complimentary coffee in rms. Restaurant 6 am-10 pm. Rm serv 24 hrs. Bar 11-1 am. Ck-out noon. Coin lndry. Convention facilities. Concierge. Shopping arcade. Free airport transportation. Lighted tennis, pro. Exercise rm; instructor, weights, bicycles, whirlpool, sauna. Bicycle rentals. Minibars. Bathrm phone in suites. Balconies. All rms with view of marina, city or bay. Elaborate landscaping. Boat dock, beach; bicycles. Cr cds: A, C, D, DS, ER, JCB, MC, V.

D ⚐ 🏃 🏊 🏃 🏃 ✈ 🐾 SC

✔ ★ ★ **TRAVELODGE HOTEL-HARBOR ISLAND.** *1960 Harbor Island Dr (92101), near Lindbergh Field Intl Airport, north of downtown.* 619/291-6700; FAX 619/293-0694. 208 rms, 9 story. S, D $69-$139; each addl $10; suites $175-$350; under 17 free. Crib free. TV. Heated pool. Complimentary coffee in rms. Restaurant 6:30 am-2 pm, 5:30-10 pm. Bar 11-1 am. Ck-out noon. Meeting rms. Gift shop. Free airport transportation. Exercise equipt; weights, bicycles, whirlpool, sauna. Some refrigerators. Balconies. Cr cds: A, C, D, DS, ER, JCB, MC, V.

D 🏊 🏃 🏃 ✈ 🐾 SC

★ ★ ★ **U. S. GRANT.** *326 Broadway (92101), downtown.* 619/232-3121; res: 800/237-5029 (exc CA), 800/334-6957 (CA); FAX 619/232-3626. 280 rms, 11 story, 68 suites. S, D $99-$160; each addl $20; suites $245-$1,000. Crib $15. Valet parking $10. TV; cable. Cafe 6:30-10:30 am, 11:30 am-2:30 pm, 5:30-11 pm. Bar 11-2 am; entertainment Fri-Sat. Ck-out noon. Concierge. Gift shop. Exercise equipt; weights, bicycles. Masseuse. Bathrm phones, minibars. Antiques, artwork, period chandeliers and fixtures. 1910 landmark has been restored to its original elegance. Cr cds: A, C, D, DS, MC, V.

D 🏃 🐾 🔥 SC

★ ★ ★ ★ **THE WESTGATE HOTEL.** *1055 Second Ave (92101), downtown.* 619/238-1818; res: 800/221-3802; FAX 619/557-3737. 223 units, 19 story, some kits. S, D from $154; each addl $10; suites from $315; under 18 free; wkend rates. Valet parking $8.50/day. Crib free. TV; cable. Complimentary coffee 6-9 am. Restaurant 6 am-11 pm (also see LE FONTAINEBLEAU). Afternoon tea. Rm serv 24 hrs. Bar 11-2 am; entertainment. Ck-out noon. Meeting rms. Concierge. Shopping arcade. Free airport, RR station, bus depot transportation; downtown transportation on request. Exercise equipt; weight machine, bicycles. Bathrm phones, minibars. Cr cds: A, C, D, DS, ER, MC, V.

🏃 🏃 🔥 🐾

Resorts

★ ★ ★ **DOUBLETREE CARMEL HIGHLAND GOLF & TENNIS RESORT.** *14455 Penasquitos Dr (92129), north of downtown.* 619/672-9100; FAX 619/672-9166. 172 rms, 3 story, 14 suites. S, D $109-$169; each addl $10; suites $129-$179; under 12 free; golf, tennis, fitness plans. Crib free. Pet accepted, some restrictions; $150. TV; cable. 2 pools; poolside serv, lifeguard (summer). Supervised child's activities (June-early Sept). Dining rms 6:30 am-10:30 pm. Rm serv. Bar 11-1 am; entertainment Thurs-Sat, dancing. Ck-out noon, ck-in 3 pm. Convention facilities. Bellhops. Concierge. Gift shop. 6 lighted tennis courts, pro. 18-hole golf, greens fee $44-$54, pro, putting green. Exercise rm; instructor, weights, bicycles, whirlpool, 2 saunas, steam rm. Private patios, balconies. On 130 acres. Cr cds: A, C, D, DS, ER, JCB, MC, V.

D ⚐ 🏃 🏊 🏃 🎿 🔥 SC

★ ★ ★ **RANCHO BERNARDO INN.** *17550 Bernardo Oaks Dr (92128), north of downtown.* 619/487-1611; res: 800/542-6096; FAX 619/673-0311. 287 rms, 3 story. Oct-Mar: S, D $190-$225; suites $275-$620; under 12 free; golf, tennis plans; lower rates rest of yr. TV; cable. 2 pools, heated; poolside serv. Supervised child's activities (Aug; also Easter, Memorial Day wkend, July 4 wkend, Labor Day wkend, Thanksgiving hols & Christmas hols). Dining rm 6:30 am-10 pm (also see EL BIZCOCHO). Snack bar. Rm serv 6:30 am-midnight. Bars 11-1 am; entertainment, dancing Tues-Sat. Ck-out 1 pm. Convention facilities. Concierge. Gift shop. Drugstore. Airport transportation. Complimentary shuttle service to shopping mall. Lighted tennis, pro. Three 18-hole and one 27-hole golf courses, pro, putting green, driving range. Volleyball. Bicycles. Exercise rm; instructor, weight machine, bicycles, 7 whirlpools, sauna, steam rm. Masseuse. Many honor bars; some bathrm phones. Private patios, balconies. Beautifully appointed rms in mission-style building. Extensive grounds. Noted tennis and golf colleges. Complimentary tea, sherry, finger sandwiches 4-5 pm. Cr cds: A, C, DS, ER, JCB, MC, V.

D 🏃 🏌 🏊 🏃 🎿 🔥 SC

★ ★ ★ **SAN DIEGO PRINCESS.** *1404 W Vacation Rd (92109), in Mission Bay.* 619/274-4630; res: 800/542-6275; FAX 619/581-5929. 462 cottage rms, 153 kits. May-Aug: S, D $130-$150; each addl $15; suites $225-$345; kit. units $170-$180; lower rates rest of yr. Crib free. TV; cable. 5 pools, 2 heated; wading pool, poolside serv. Complimentary coffee in rms. Dining rms 7 am-10 pm. Rm serv. Bars 11-2 am; entertainment, dancing Tues-Sat. Ck-out noon, ck-in 4 pm. Coin lndry. Convention facilities. Valet serv. Concierge. Gift shop. Lighted tennis, pro. Putting green. Exercise rm; instructor, weights, stair machine, whirlpool, sauna, steam rm. Bicycles. Game rm. Lawn games. Boats; windsurfing. Some bathrm phones, refrigerators, minibars. Private patios. On beach. Botanical walk. Cr cds: A, DS, ER, MC, V.

D ⚐ 🏌 🏊 🏃 🏃 🎿 🔥 SC

Restaurants

✔ ★ **AFGHANISTAN KHYBER PASS.** *4647 Convoy St, north of downtown.* 619/571-3749. Hrs: 11 am-2:30 pm, 5-10 pm; Sun from 5 pm. Res accepted. Afghan menu. Wine, beer. Semi-a la carte: lunch $5.25-$8.25, dinner $10.95-$14.95. Buffet lunch (Mon-Fri): $6.95. Spe-

cializes in shish kebab, curries. Parking. Interior designed as an Afghan cave. Cr cds: A, DS, MC, V.
[SC]

★ ★ ANTHONY'S FISH GROTTO. 11666 Avena Place, off Bernardo Center Dr in Rancho Bernardo, north of downtown. 619/451-2070. Hrs: 11:30 am-8:30 pm. Closed major hols. Res accepted. Bar. Semi-a la carte: lunch $4-$13, dinner $7-$26. Child's meals. Specializes in fresh seafood. Parking. Overlooks Webb Lake Park. Family-owned. Cr cds: A, C, D, DS, MC, V.
[D]

★ ★ ★ ANTHONY'S STAR OF THE SEA ROOM. 1360 Harbor Dr, downtown. 619/232-7408. Hrs: 5:30-10:30 pm. Closed major hols. A la carte entrees: dinner $25-$44. Specialties: planked fish, stuffed fish, loin of swordfish. Valet parking. Harbor view. Family-owned. Totally nonsmoking. Cr cds: A, C, D, DS, MC, V.
[D]

★ ★ ATHENS MARKET TAVERNA. 109 W F Street, downtown. 619/234-1955. Hrs: 11:30 am-11 pm; Fri & Sat to midnight. Closed Jan 1, Thanksgiving, Dec 25. Res accepted. Greek menu. Bar to 2 am. Semi-a la carte: lunch $4.75-$12.50, dinner $9.95-$19.95. Specializes in lamb, fish. Belly dancers Fri, Sat evenings. Cr cds: A, C, D, DS, MC, V.

★ ★ ★ BACI RISTORANTE. 1955 W Morena Blvd, Mission Bay. 619/275-2094. Hrs: 11:30 am-2:30 pm, 5:30-10 pm; Sat from 5:30 pm. Closed Sun; major hols. Res required Fri, Sat. Northern Italian menu. Bar. Wine list. A la carte entrees: lunch $6.95-$11.95, dinner $10.95-$17.95. Specializes in seafood, veal, pasta. Own baking, pasta. Parking. Intimate atmosphere; many art pieces, prints. Cr cds: A, C, D, DS, MC, V.
[D]

★ ★ BELGIAN LION. 2265 Bacon St, Mission Bay. 619/223-2700. Hrs: 5-10 pm. Closed Sun-Wed; major hols. Res accepted. French, Belgian menu. Beer. Wine list. A la carte entrees: dinner $15-$18.50. Specialties: fresh fish, classic duck confit. Own pastries. Parking. Outdoor dining. Country Belgian decor. Cr cds: A, C, D, DS, MC, V.

★ ★ BELLA LUNA. 748 Fifth Ave (92101), downtown. 619/239-3222. Hrs: 11:30 am-2:30 pm, 5-11 pm; Fri & Sat to midnight. Closed Thanksgiving, Dec 25. Res accepted. Italian menu. Bar. A la carte entrees: lunch $8.95-$11.95, dinner $10.95-$16.95. Specializes in pasta, rack of lamb. Valet parking. Patio dining. Original artwork with moon motif; ceiling painted to look like sky. Totally nonsmoking. Cr cds: A, MC, V.
[D] [SC]

★ ★ BENIHANA OF TOKYO. 477 Camino del Rio South, north of downtown. 619/298-4666. Hrs: 11:30 am-2 pm, 5-10 pm; Fri to 11 pm; Sat 5-11 pm; Sun 5-10 pm. Res accepted. Japanese menu. Bar. Semi-a la carte: lunch $6.50-$12.50, dinner $13.50-$26.25. Child's meals. Specializes in Japanese steak & seafood. Sushi bar. Valet parking. Japanese village settings. Cr cds: A, C, D, DS, JCB, MC, V.
[D]

★ ★ ★ BICE RISTORANTE. 777 Front St, on top floor of Palladium, downtown. 619/239-2423. Hrs: 11:30 am-2:30 pm, 6-10 pm; Fri to 11 pm; Sat noon-3 pm, 6 pm-11 pm. Closed Sun. Res accepted. Milanese-style Italian menu. Bar. Wine list. A la carte entrees: lunch $9-$15, dinner $9-$20. Specializes in homemade pasta. Valet parking. Cr cds: A, C, D, MC, V.
[D]

★ ★ ★ BUSALACCHI'S. 3683 5th Ave, north of downtown. 619/298-0119. Hrs: 11:30 am-2:15 pm, 5-10 pm; Fri & Sat to 11 pm. Closed most major hols. Res accepted. Italian menu. Bar. A la carte entrees: lunch $7.75-$15, dinner $8.95-$21.95. Specializes in Sicilian

dishes. Pianist Fri & Sat. Valet parking. Outdoor dining. Victorian-style house. Cr cds: A, C, D, DS, MC, V.

✔★ CAFE COYOTE. 2461 San Diego Ave, in Old Town Esplanade, in Old Town. 619/291-4695. Hrs: 7:30 am-10 pm; Fri & Sat to 11 pm; Sun to 9 pm. Closed Dec 25. Res accepted. Mexican, Amer menu. Bar. Semi-a la carte: bkfst $2.95-$5.95, lunch $3.95-$8.95, dinner $4.95-$9.95. Child's meals. Specialties: blue corn pancakes, carnitas, carne asada. Own tortillas. Entertainment Fri-Sun on patio. Parking. Outdoor dining. Pictures, statues of Southwestern wildlife. Cr cds: A, D, DS, MC, V.
[D]

★ ★ ★ CAFE PACIFICA. 2414 San Diego Ave, in Old Town. 619/291-6666. Hrs: 11:30 am-2 pm, 5:30-10 pm; Sat & Sun from 5:30 pm; early-bird dinner 5:30-6:45 pm. Closed Thanksgiving, Dec 25. Res accepted. Bar. Semi-a la carte: lunch $6-$9, dinner $12-$18. Specializes in seafood. Valet parking. Near Old Spanish Cemetery. Cr cds: A, C, D, DS, MC, V.
[D]

★ ★ CALIFORNIA CUISINE. 1027 University Ave, north of downtown. 619/543-0790. Hrs: 11 am-10 pm; Sat & Sun from 5 pm. Closed Mon; Jan 1, Thanksgiving, Dec 25. Res accepted. French, California menu. Wine, beer. Semi-a la carte: lunch $5.50-$12, dinner $7-$18. Specializes in fresh seafood, game, salad. Outdoor dining. Menu changes daily. Original paintings change monthly. Cr cds: A, C, D, DS, MC, V.

★ ★ CALLIOPE'S GREEK CAFE. 3958 5th Ave, north of downtown. 619/291-5588. Hrs: 11:30 am-2:30 pm, 5-10 pm; Sat to 11 pm. Closed some hols. Res accepted. Greek menu. Wine, beer. Semi-a la carte: lunch $5.95-$9.95, dinner $10.95-$16.95. Specializes in fresh seafood, vegetarian dishes, traditional Greek dishes. Valet parking. Totally nonsmoking. Cr cds: A, C, D, DS, MC, V.
[D]

★ ★ CASA DE BANDINI. 2754 Calhoun St, in Old Town. 619/297-8211. Hrs: 11 am-10 pm; Sun from 10 am; winter to 9 pm. Closed Thanksgiving, Dec 25. Mexican menu. Bar. Semi-a la carte: lunch, dinner $5.50-$15.50. Child's meals. Specializes in seafood. Mariachi band. Parking. Outdoor dining. Early California atmosphere, garden patio with fountain. Adobe bldg (1827) once served as headquarters for Commodore Stockton. Cr cds: A, C, D, DS, MC, V.

★ ★ CELADON. 3628 5th Ave, north of downtown. 619/295-8800. Hrs: 11:30 am-2 pm, 5-10 pm. Closed Sun; Jan 1, July 4, Thanksgiving, Dec 25. Res accepted. Thai menu. Wine, beer. A la carte entrees: lunch $6.25-$12, dinner $8.25-$17. Specializes in shrimp, chicken, beef. Cr cds: A, MC, V.

✔★ ★ DAKOTA. 901 Fifth Ave (92101), downtown. 619/234-5554. Hrs: 11:30 am-3 pm, 5-10 pm; Sat & Sun from 5 pm. Closed Dec 25. Res accepted. Bar. Semi-a la carte: lunch $5.95-$8.95, dinner $7.95-$16.95. Specializes in barbecue ribs, mesquite-broiled meat & seafood. Pianist Fri & Sat. Valet parking (dinner). Balcony dining. Original artwork. Totally nonsmoking. Cr cds: A, C, D, DS, MC, V.
[D]

★ ★ DOBSON'S. 956 Broadway Circle, downtown. 619/231-6771. Hrs: 11:30 am-3 pm, 5:30-10 pm; Thur-Sat to 11 pm. Closed major hols. Res accepted. Continental menu. Bar to 1:30 am. Semi-a la carte: lunch $5.50-$12.50, dinner $10-$27. Specializes in fresh seafood, veal. Own sourdough bread. Covered parking. Cr cds: A, MC, V.

★ ★ ★ EL BIZCOCHO. (See Rancho Bernardo Inn Resort) 619/487-1611. Hrs: 6-10 pm; Fri & Sat to 10:30 pm; Sun brunch 10 am-2 pm. Res accepted. French menu. Bar. Extensive wine list. A la carte entrees: dinner $19-$28. Sun brunch $19.50. Specializes in roast duckling, rack of lamb, fresh salmon. Pianist. Valet parking. View of grounds with waterfall. Jacket (exc brunch). Cr cds: A, C, D, DS, MC, V.

✔★ **EL TECOLOTE.** 6110 Friars Rd, north of downtown. 619/295-2087. Hrs: 11 am-10 pm; Sun 4-9 pm. Closed Jan 1, Thanksgiving, Dec 25. Mexican menu. Serv bar. Semi-a la carte: lunch $1.95-$9.95, dinner $4.95-$10.95. Child's meals. Specialties: cheese-filled zucchinis, beef tongue Veracruz, mole poblano. Parking. Outdoor dining. Mexican artifacts, photographs, original art. Totally nonsmoking. Cr cds: A, D, DS, MC, V.

D

✔★ **FAIROUZ.** 3166 Midway Dr, in Point Loma. 619/225-0308. Hrs 11 am-10 pm. Closed Jan 1. Res required Fri & Sat. Greek, Lebanese menu. Bar. Semi-a la carte: lunch $3.95-$12.95, dinner $5-$13.95. Buffet: lunch $5.25, dinner $10.95. Specialties: hommos taboleh, kabobs. Parking. Paintings, prints available for purchase. Cr cds: A, D, DS, MC, V.

D

★★★ **FIO'S.** 801 5th Ave, downtown. 619/234-3467. Hrs: 11:30 am-3 pm, 5-11 pm; Fri & Sat 5 pm-midnight; Sun 5-10 pm. Closed Dec 25. Res accepted. Italian menu. Bar. Wine cellar. A la carte entrees: lunch, dinner $3.75-$17.95. Specializes in pasta, wood-fired pizza. European decor; original artwork depicting Palio of Siena. Cr cds: A, C, D, DS, MC, V.

D

★★ **HARBOR HOUSE.** 831 W Harbor Dr, in Seaport Village, downtown. 619/232-1141. Hrs: 11:30 am-10 pm; Fri & Sat to 11 pm; Sun brunch 10:30 am-2:30 pm. Res accepted. Bar from 11 am. A la carte entrees: lunch $6.95-$9.95, dinner $13.95-$20.95. Sun brunch $7.95-$11.95. Child's meals. Specializes in fresh seafood broiled over mesquite. Parking. View of harbor, boat docks, Coronado Bay Bridge. Cr cds: A, DS, MC, V.

D

✔★★ **HOB NOB HILL.** 2271 1st Ave, adj to Balboa Park. 619/239-8176. Hrs: 7 am-9 pm. Closed Dec 25. Res accepted. Wine, beer. Semi-a la carte entrees: bkfst $2.35-$10.95. Complete meals: lunch $5.45-$9.95, dinner $5.45-$13.45. Child's meals. Specializes in eastern fried scallops, lamb shanks, roast turkey. Family-owned. Cr cds: A, DS, MC, V.

D

★★ **IMPERIAL HOUSE.** 505 Kalmia St, north of downtown. 619/234-3525. Hrs: 11 am-4 pm, 5-9 pm; Mon to 2 pm; Fri & Sat to 11 pm; early-bird dinner Mon-Fri 5-6:30 pm. Closed Sun; most major hols. Res accepted. Continental menu. Bar to 11 pm; Fri & Sat to 12:30 am. A la carte entrees: lunch $6-$11, dinner $9-$19. Specializes in rack of lamb, pepper steak, seafood. Pianist Wed-Sat. Valet parking. Old world decor. Family-owned. Cr cds: A, C, D, MC, V.

★★ **JASMINE.** 4609 Convoy St (92111), north of downtown. 619/268-0888. Hrs: 10 am-11 pm. Res accepted. Chinese menu. Bar. Semi-a la carte: lunch $5.95-$17, dinner $6-$17. Specializes in dim sum, fresh seafood. Parking. Large dining rm with movable walls. Cr cds: A, MC, V.

★★ **KARL STRAUSS' OLD COLUMBIA BREWERY & GRILL.** 1157 Columbia St, downtown. 619/234-2739. Hrs: 11:30 am-10 pm; Thurs, Fri & Sat to midnight. Closed most major hols. Res accepted. Bar. Semi-a la carte: lunch $7-$9, dinner $8-$12. Specialties: hamburgers, fresh fish, German-style sausage. Brew own beer; some seasonal varieties. View of microbrewery from restaurant. Cr cds: MC, V.

D

★★ **KELLY'S.** 500 Hotel Circle N, north of downtown. 619/291-7131. Hrs: 11 am-11 pm; Sat, Sun & hols from 4 pm; early-bird dinner 4-6 pm. Closed Easter, Thanksgiving, Dec 25. Bar to 2 am; Sat & Sun from 4 pm. Semi-a la carte: lunch $3.50-$7.50, dinner $5.75-

$23.95. Specializes in barbecued ribs, steak. Entertainment. Parking. Waterfalls. Cr cds: A, C, D, DS, MC, V.

★★ **KENNY'S STEAK HOUSE.** 939 Fourth Ave (92101), downtown. 619/238-9891. Hrs: 11:30 am-9:30 pm; Fri & Sat 5-11 pm. Closed Sun; Memorial Day, Thanksgiving, Dec 25. Res accepted. Bar. Semi-a la carte: lunch $4.50-$12.95, dinner $9.50-$24.95. Specializes in prime steak. Pianist Fri & Sat. Classic steakhouse atmosphere. Memorabilia from John Wayne movie "The Quiet Man" on display. Cr cds: A, DS, MC, V.

D

★★★ **LE FONTAINEBLEAU.** (See The Westgate Hotel) 619/238-1818. Hrs: 11:45 am-2 pm, 6-10 pm; Sun brunch 10 am-2 pm. Res accepted. Continental menu. Bar. Wine cellar. Semi-a la carte: lunch $7.95-$16.75, dinner $19.50-$30. Complete meals: dinner $24.95. Sun brunch $26.95. Child's meals. Specializes in seafood, veal. Pianist, harpist. Valet parking. Lavish French period setting. Original 17th-century oils; antiques. Cr cds: A, C, D, DS, ER, MC, V.

D

★★ **LIAISON.** 2202 Fourth Ave (92101), north of downtown. 619/234-5540. Hrs: 11:30 am-2 pm, 5-9:30 pm; Fri to 10:30 pm; Sat 5-10:30 pm; Sun & Mon 5-9:30 pm. Closed most major hols. Res accepted. French menu. Beer, setups. Semi-a la carte: lunch $5.95-$12.95. Prix fixe: dinner $17.50-$26.50. Specialties: saumon au beure d'&'ecrevisse, soufflé Grand Marnier. Patio dining with fountain. French farmhouse decor. Cr cds: A, C, D, DS, MC, V.

D

✔★★ **LINO'S.** 2754 Calhoun St, in Old Town. 619/299-7124. Hrs: 11 am-10 pm; winter to 9 pm. Closed Thanksgiving, Dec 25. Res accepted. Italian menu. Bar. Semi-a la carte: lunch $4.50-$8.25, dinner $5.75-$14.95. Specializes in veal, chicken, shrimp. Own pasta. Parking. Outdoor dining. Cr cds: A, C, D, DS, ER, JCB, MC, V.

★★ **LUIGI AL MARE.** 861 W Harbor Dr, in Seaport Village, downtown. 619/232-7581. Hrs: 11 am-10 pm. Res accepted. Italian menu. Bar. A la carte entrees: lunch $7.95-$13.95, dinner $10.95-$19.95. Child's meals. Specializes in seafood, fresh pasta. Outdoor dining. View of San Diego Harbor. Cr cds: A, DS, MC, V.

D

★★★ **MISTER A'S.** 2550 5th Ave, on 12th floor of Financial Center, north of downtown. 619/239-1377. Hrs: 11 am-2:30 pm, 6-10:30 pm. Closed some major hols. Res accepted. Continental menu. Bar 11-2 am; Sat, Sun from 5 pm. Wine list. Semi-a la carte: lunch $6.50-$12.95, dinner $16.95-$28.95. Specialties: beef Wellington, rack of lamb, fresh fish. Entertainment Wed-Sat. Valet parking. Rococo decor; oil paintings. Rooftop dining; panoramic view. Family-owned. Jacket (dinner). Cr cds: A, C, D, DS, MC, V.

✔★ **NATI'S.** 1852 Bacon St, north of downtown. 619/224-3369. Hrs: 11 am-9 pm; winter to 8 pm, Sat 9 am-9 pm, Sun 9 am-8 pm. Closed some major hols. Mexican menu. Bar. Semi-a la carte: bkfst $3-$6.50, lunch, dinner $4.35-$8.50. Specializes in chiles rellenos, sour cream tostadas, carne asada. Parking. Outdoor dining. Cr cds: MC, V.

✔★ **OLD TOWN MEXICAN CAFE & CANTINA.** 2489 San Diego Ave, in Old Town. 619/297-4330. Hrs: 7 am-11 pm. Closed Thanksgiving, Dec 25. Mexican menu. Bar to 1 am. A la carte entrees: bkfst $2.95-$5.95, lunch, dinner $2.25-$11. Specialties: carnitas, Old Town pollo, Mexican-style ribs, homemade tortillas. Child's meals. Parking. Patio dining. Cr cds: A, DS, MC, V.

D

★★ **PANDA INN.** 506 Horton Plaza, on top floor, downtown. 619/233-7800. Hrs: 11 am-10 pm; Fri & Sat to 11 pm. Closed Thanksgiving. Res accepted. Mandarin menu. Bar. Semi-a la carte: lunch $6-$9, dinner $8-$14. Specialties: sweet & pungent shrimp, orange-flavored beef. Parking. Outdoor dining. Several dining areas, all with

Chinese art pieces, 1 with entire ceiling skylight; pandas depicted in stained-glass windows. Cr cds: A, D, DS, MC, V.

D

★ ★ ★ **RAINWATER'S.** 1202 Kettner Blvd, near train depot, downtown. 619/233-5757. Hrs: 11:30 am-midnight; Sat 5 pm-midnight; Sun 5-11 pm. Closed Thanksgiving, Dec 24, 25. Res accepted. Bar. Wine list. Semi-a la carte: lunch $8-$19, dinner $15-$40. Specializes in fresh seafood, prime steaks. Own pastries. Valet parking. Outdoor dining. Cr cds: A, D, MC, V.

D

★ ★ ★ **SALVATORE'S.** 750 Front St (92101), downtown. 619/544-1865. Hrs: 11 am-3:30 pm, 5-10 pm; Sat & Sun from 5 pm. Res accepted. Italian menu. Bar. Wine list. A la carte entrees: lunch $7-$13, dinner $11-$22. Specializes in Northern Italian dishes. Pianist Tues-Sat. Parking. Italian villa atmosphere; original artwork. Cr cds: A, C, D, DS, MC, V.

D

★ ★ **SAN DIEGO PIER CAFE.** 885 W Harbor Dr, in Seaport Village, downtown. 619/239-3968. Hrs: 7 am-9 pm; Fri & Sat to 10 pm. Serv bar. Semi-a la carte: bkfst $4-$7.95, lunch $6.95-$13.95, dinner $7.95-$27.95. Child's meals. Specializes in fresh fish broiled. Outdoor dining. On harbor pier. Cr cds: A, DS, MC, V.

★ ★ **SÄRÖ.** 926 Broadway Circle, downtown. 619/232-7173. Hrs: 11 am-10 pm; Sat 5-10:30 pm. Closed Sun; some major hols. Res accepted Sat & Sun. Swedish, International menu. Bar. Semi-a la carte: lunch $6-$15, dinner $7-$22. Outdoor dining. 2-story dining rm; main floor & balcony dining areas. Cr cds: A, D, MC, V.

D

★ ★ **SFUZZI.** 340 5th Ave (92101), downtown. 619/231-2323. Hrs: 11:30 am-10 pm; Sat & Sun to 11:30 pm; Sun brunch 11 am-3 pm. Closed Thanksgiving, Dec 25. Res accepted. Bar. Semi-a la carte: lunch $6-$9, dinner $9-$16. Sun brunch $14.50. Child's meals. Specializes in Northern Italian cuisine. Valet parking (wknds). Outdoor dining. Frescoes. Cr cds: A, D, MC, V.

D

★ ★ **THEE BUNGALOW.** 4996 W Point Loma Blvd, north of downtown. 619/224-2884. Hrs: 5:30-9:30 pm; Fri & Sat 5-10 pm; Sun from 5 pm. Closed July 4. Res accepted. Extensive wine list. Continental menu. Semi-a la carte: dinner $9-$22. Specializes in roast duck, rack of lamb, fresh seafood. Parking. In converted house. Many special wine dinners planned throughout the year. Totally nonsmoking. Cr cds: A, C, D, DS, MC, V.

★ ★ **TOM HAM'S LIGHTHOUSE.** 2150 Harbor Island Dr, north of downtown. 619/291-9110. Hrs: 11:15 am-3:30 pm, 5-10:30 pm; Sat 4:30-11 pm; Sun 4-10 pm; early-bird dinner Mon-Fri 5-6 pm, Sun 4-6 pm; Sun brunch 10 am-2 pm. Closed Dec 25. Res accepted. Bar 11-2 am. Semi-a la carte: lunch $4.95-$13.95, dinner $9.95-$30. Sun brunch $10.50. Child's meals. Specializes in steak, seafood. Salad bar (lunch). Entertainment Wed-Sat. Parking. Early California, Spanish decor. View of bay, San Diego skyline. Official Coast Guard No. 9 beacon. Family-owned. Cr cds: A, C, D, DS, MC, V.

SC

★ ★ **TOP OF THE MARKET.** 750 N Harbor Dr, downtown. 619/234-4867. Hrs: 11 am-9:45 pm; Fri & Sat to 10 pm; Sun brunch 10 am-3 pm. Closed Thanksgiving, Dec 25. Res accepted. Bar to 11 pm. Semi-a la carte: lunch $5.75-$23, dinner $10.50-$34. Sun brunch $12-$15. Child's meals. Specializes in seafood. Oyster, sushi bar. Parking.

Outdoor dining. Pictures of turn-of-the-century fishing scenes. Retail fish market lower floor. Cr cds: A, D, DS, MC, V.

D

★ ★ ★ **WINESELLAR & BRASSERIE.** 9550 Waples St, Suite 115, 2nd fl, north of downtown. 619/450-9576. Hrs: 5:30-10 pm; Sun to 9 pm. Closed Mon; Jan 1, Easter, Thanksgiving, Dec 25. Res accepted; required Fri-Sun. Contemporary French menu. Bar. Extensive wine list. A la carte entrees: dinner $17-$25. Complete meals (Tues-Thurs): 3-course dinner with 3 glasses of specially selected wine $29. Prix fixe: dinner (Sun only) $17.95. Menu changes seasonally. Parking. Intimate, formal dining. Cr cds: A, C, D, DS, MC, V.

D

Unrated Dining Spots

AESOP'S TABLES. 8650 Genesee Ave, in Costa Verde Center, north of downtown. 619/455-1535. Hrs: 11 am-10 pm; Sun from 4 pm. Closed major hols. Greek, Middle Eastern menu. Bar. Semi-a la carte: lunch $4-$9.95, dinner $5-$12.95. Patio dining. Cr cds: A, C, D, DS, MC, V.

D

CITY DELICATESSEN. 535 University Ave, north of downtown. 619/295-2747. Hrs: 7 am-midnight; Fri, Sat to 2 am. Closed Dec 25; Yom Kippur. Jewish-style delicatessen. Wine, beer. A la carte entrees: bkfst, lunch $4.50-$8.50, dinner $4.50-$9.95. Child's meals. Own baking. Delicatessen and bakery. Cr cds: MC, V.

CORVETTE DINER BAR & GRILL. 3946 5th Ave, downtown. 619/542-1001. Hrs: 11 am-midnight. Closed Jan 1, Easter, Dec 24 eve, 25. Bar. Semi-a la carte: lunch $4.85-$7.95, dinner $5.50-$9.95. Specializes in hamburgers, chicken-fried steak. DJ. 1950s-style diner with soda fountains. Corvette in center of room. Cr cds: A, DS, JCB, MC, V.

D.Z. AKIN'S. 6930 Alvarado Rd, north of downtown. 619/265-0218. Hrs: 7 am-9 pm; Fri, Sat to 11 pm. Closed July 4, Thanksgiving, Dec 25; some Jewish hols. Semi-a la carte: bkfst $3.50-$6, lunch $6-$8, dinner $8-$12. Specializes in delicatessen items. Own pastries. Parking. Cr cds: MC, V.

DICK'S LAST RESORT. 345 5th Ave (92101), downtown. 619/231-9100. Hrs: 11-1 am. Closed Dec 25. Res accepted. Bar to 2 am. Semi-a la carte: lunch $3.25-$8.95, dinner $6.95-$14.95. Child's meals. Specialties: beef & pork ribs, crab, chicken. Entertainment. Valet parking Fri & Sat. Outdoor dining. Large warehouse setting. Casual dining. Cr cds: A, DS, MC, V.

D

EL INDIO SHOP. 3695 India St, north of downtown. 619/299-0333. Hrs: 8 am-9 pm. Mexican menu. Semi-a la carte: bkfst $3-$4, lunch, dinner $5-$7. Outdoor dining. Cafeteria-style. Tortilla factory in kitchen. Family-owned. Cr cds: DS, MC, V.

D SC

GREEK CORNER. 5841 El Cajon Blvd, north of downtown. 619/287-3303. Hrs: 11 am-10 pm. Greek, Middle Eastern menu. Wine, beer. Semi-a la carte: lunch, dinner $6-$10. Specializes in Greek dishes, Middle Eastern vegetarian dishes. Parking. Outdoor dining. Greek cafe-style dining. Cr cds: MC, V.

SAFFRON. 3731-B India St, north of downtown. 619/574-0177. Hrs: 11 am-9 pm. Closed Sun; Jan 1, Thanksgiving, Dec 25. Thai menu. A la carte entrees: lunch, dinner $3.75-$12. Specializes in Thai grilled chicken. Take-out with outdoor dining. Picnic baskets avail. Cr cds: MC, V.

San Francisco

Founded: 1776

Pop: 723,959

Elev: 63 feet

Time zone: Pacific

Area code: 415

When the fog rolls in off the Pacific and the foghorns bellow from the bay, when the city's lights are muted and the cable cars clatter up and down the hills, San Francisco's many charms become evident. The city's setting is part of its allure. Houses of infinite variety and imagination are perched on hills overlooking the San Francisco Bay, the Golden Gate Bridge and the Pacific Ocean. The town's many cultures coexist peacefully, yet each retains its identity and adds to the city's character. It is an international city—ships from all parts of the world come and go. Even San Francisco's sinful past is an asset, titillating the visitor with reminders of its Barbary Coast beginnings.

San Francisco's lusty story began with early Portuguese, English and Spanish explorers who sailed into the bay in the 1700s. In 1848, gold was discovered in California, and as the news spread around the world, a torrent of people and ships descended on the city. By the next year, San Francisco was a wild boom town of 20,000 transients living in tents. Farsighted businessmen realized that fortunes could be made in San Francisco as well as in the gold camps. Mercantile establishments, small industries and the shipping of goods to the Orient prospered.

On April 18, 1906, the great earthquake and fire struck San Francisco. Raging unchecked for 3 days, the fire destroyed the entire business area and burned 497 blocks in the heart of the city. Although losses amounted to some 2,500 lives and $350 million, rebuilding started before the ashes cooled, and San Francisco was soon well on its way to becoming the city it is today.

Business

Tourism is the most important industry in San Francisco, but the economy has many other strong bases. San Francisco is a leading seaport, and many people are employed in occupations related directly or indirectly to shipping. Exports, many of which are sent to the Far East, include cotton, grain, lumber, machinery, paper and petroleum products. This is a world communications center—most telephone calls and cables that cross the Pacific are relayed through San Francisco.

Food processing, petroleum refining, printing and publishing and the manufacture of metal products are major industrial pursuits. San Francisco is also a leader in insurance, banking and investment. Government and education are important sectors of employment.

Convention Facilities

The Moscone Center is situated on an 11-acre site at 4th and Howard streets. The columnless main exhibit hall contains 261,000 square feet of exhibit space, seats 20,000 people and can be divided into 3 sections. The hall is wired for closed-circuit TV and simultaneous translation. There are also 37 additional meeting rooms, with seating capacities from 10 to 3,000, a 3,200-seat ballroom and a 43,000 square foot addition. Parking for 4,000 cars is adjacent.

The Civic Auditorium has theater seating for 7,000; 2 adjoining halls seat 825 each. The main arena can accommodate 186 exhibit booths, each 10 by 10 feet. The auditorium occupies the entire south side of Civic Center Plaza. Adjoining it is Brooks Hall, where 478 exhibit booths, each 10 by 10 feet, can be set up. An underground garage accommodates 840 cars.

The California Masonic Memorial Temple has theater seating for 3,165 and a 16,500-square-foot exhibit hall. A completely equipped catering kitchen can serve banquets of 1,200 people.

The Cow Palace, on the southern edge of the city, is divided into 4 exhibit areas; 2 with 49,000 square feet of space and 2 with 62,380 square feet of space. The main arena has 30,000 square feet of floor space, seating for 14,700, 3 restaurants, 12 food stands, 4 cocktail bars and catering service. There are 6 meeting rooms for 50 to 600 persons. A lighted parking area accommodates 4,000 cars.

Sports and Recreation

Sports fans can choose from such teams as baseball's San Francisco Giants or football's 49ers; both play in Candlestick Park. The Bay Area also hosts baseball's Athletics, basketball's Golden State Warriors and amateur soccer competitions.

Riding the cable cars, a national historic landmark and a vital part of the city's public transportation system, is a form of recreation unique to San Francisco.

Federally protected Golden Gate National Recreation Area takes in much of San Francisco's shoreline, as well as the bay islands of Angel and Alcatraz and a good portion of the Marin County coast. The area boasts numerous beaches, historic fortifications, hiking trails, a bridle path and much more. The Golden Gate Promenade, a 3½-mile footpath, provides access to previously restricted areas of the Presidio and Fort Mason. Park headquarters is at Fort Mason.

Entertainment

The performing arts are represented by the San Francisco Symphony, the San Francisco Opera, American Conservatory Theatre and the San Francisco Ballet. Various touring concert artists, orchestras and dance companies perform at the War Memorial/Opera House, Louise M. Davies Symphony Hall and Masonic Memorial Auditorium.

Numerous small theaters, nonequity companies, cabaret theater and university groups present dramatic performances. The San Francisco International Film Festival is held each spring.

Nightlife

Nightlife in San Francisco varies from posh clubs in the best hotels to cozy comedy clubs to bars featuring various entertainers. Most popular are the small, elegant piano bars, where prices are comparatively

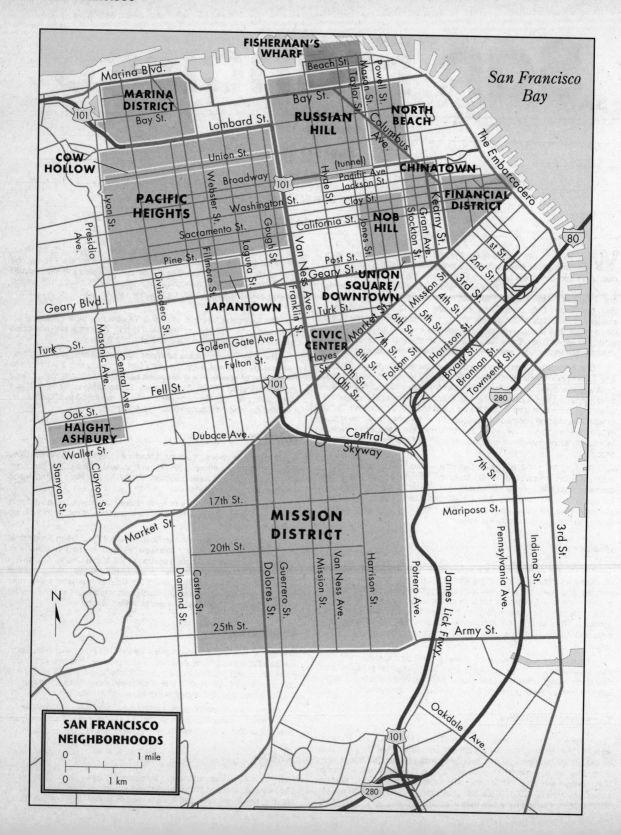

FISHERMAN'S WHARF

San Francisco Bay

Marina Blvd.

MARINA DISTRICT
Bay St.

Beach St.

Bay St.

RUSSIAN HILL

NORTH BEACH

Lombard St.

COW HOLLOW

Union St.

(tunnel)

Broadway

Pacific Ave
Jackson St

CHINATOWN

PACIFIC HEIGHTS

Washington St.

Clay St.

FINANCIAL DISTRICT

The Embarcadero

Sacramento St.

California St.

NOB HILL

Pine St.

Post St.

UNION SQUARE/ DOWNTOWN

Geary Blvd.

Geary St.

JAPANTOWN

Turk St.

Turk St.

Golden Gate Ave.

CIVIC CENTER

Market St.

Fulton St.

Hayes St.

Fell St.

Oak St.

HAIGHT-ASHBURY

Waller St.

Duboce Ave.

Central Skyway

17th St.

MISSION DISTRICT

Mariposa St.

20th St.

Market St.

25th St.

Army St.

Oakdale Ave.

Lyon St.
Presidio Ave.
Webster St.
Fillmore St.
Laguna St.
Gough St.
Van Ness Ave.
Franklin St.
Divisadero St.
Masonic Ave.
Central Ave.
Stanyan St.
Clayton St.
Diamond St.
Castro St.
Guerrero St.
Dolores St.
Mission St.
Van Ness Ave.
Harrison St.
Potrero Ave.
James Lick Fwy.
Pennsylvania Ave.
Indiana St.
3rd St.

Powell St.
Mason St.
Taylor St.
Columbus Ave.
Hyde St.
Jones St.
Grant Ave.
Stockton St.
Kearny St.
Mission St.
4th St.
5th St.
6th St.
7th St.
8th St.
9th St.
10th St.
Folsom St.
Harrison St.
Bryant St.
Brannan St.
Townsend St.
1st St.
2nd St.
3rd St.
7th St.

SAN FRANCISCO NEIGHBORHOODS

0   1 mile

0   1 km

SAN FRANCISCO INTERNATIONAL AIRPORT

INTERNATIONAL TERMINAL

Concourse D

Air China,
Air France,
Alaska,
British Airways,
China Airlines,
Hawaiian,
Japan Airlines,
Lufthansa,
Mexicana,
Northwest,
Philippine Airlines,
QANTAS,
Russian International,
Singapore,
TACA,
United,
UTA

Concourse C

DELTA CROWN ROOM,
NORTHWEST
WORLD CLUB,
America West,
Delta,
Northwest

Concourse E

AMERICAN
ADMIRALS CLUB,
American,
Canadian,
Midwest Express

SOUTH TERMINAL

NORTH TERMINAL

Concourse B

CONTINENTAL
PRESIDENT'S CLUB,
Alaska,
American Trans Air,
Continental,
TWA,
Southwest,

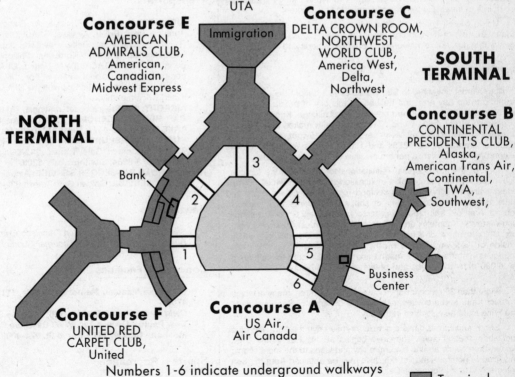

Concourse F

UNITED RED
CARPET CLUB,
United

Concourse A

US Air,
Air Canada

Numbers 1-6 indicate underground walkways

Immigration
Bank
Business Center

Terminals
Parking Lot

moderate. One of the most famous cocktail lounges in the world is "The Top of the Mark" in the Mark Hopkins Inter-Continental Hotel. The principal club areas are North Beach, downtown to some extent, Union Street and south of Market Street.

The gold of the mining camps attracted some of the finest chefs in the world to San Francisco. This heritage remains today. Chinatown features the cuisine of the Orient; Fisherman's Wharf is famous for seafood dinners; exotic cuisine from around the world is available.

Historical Areas

Alcatraz, the old fortification in San Francisco Bay, used as a penitentiary from 1934 to 1962, is now part of the Golden Gate National Recreation Area. Alcatraz is accessible only by boat; public boats depart frequently from docks, and reservations can be made for a combined boat trip and walking tour of the island.

Jackson Square, the city's oldest pocket of the past, is a designated historic district. Mission Dolores, originally the Mission San Francisco de Asis, was the fountainhead from which the city grew. Cornerstone of the present building was laid in 1782. Many pioneers are buried in the ancient cemetery beside the church.

The Old Mint, a restored classical-revival building used as the US Mint from 1873 to the 1950s, boasts a collection of money, special coins, medals, Old West artifacts and other exhibits. Several rooms, particularly the director's office, are worth a visit. The Presidio, a wooded tract of 1,450 acres, has been fortified since 1776 and is now a US Army Reservation. The Golden Gate Promenade allows visitors to see points of interest in the Presidio indicated by markers.

Union Street, known as Cow Hollow, is an area of restored or renovated turn-of-the-century dwellings, cow barns and carriage houses that now house restaurants, boutiques, shops and art galleries.

Sightseeing

Strolling almost anywhere in San Francisco is a delight, as are drives throughout the Bay Area and beyond. In this city of precipitous hills, Lombard Street at Hyde Street offers a real challenge. Known as "the crookedest street in the world," Lombard Street makes nine hairpin turns in a single block. Coit Memorial Tower, a 210-foot monument to volunteer firemen of the 1850s and 1860s, is located at the top of Telegraph Hill and offers a panoramic view of San Francisco Bay.

One of the most popular destinations for visitors is the famous Fisherman's Wharf, center of a multimillion-dollar commercial fishing industry and location of many seafood restaurants. Other musts include the Cannery, a complex of shops, restaurants and markets housed in an old fruit-processing factory; Ghirardelli Square, a shopping-restaurant complex on the site of the Ghirardelli Chocolate Factory; Chinatown, which is believed to be the largest Oriental community outside of Asia; and Pier 39 on the Northern Waterfront, which has boutiques, entertainment, a marina and a park. Be sure to walk amid the 6,000 different shrubs and plants in the 1,017-acre Golden Gate Park.

More than 200 wineries are located in the Bay Area, many of which conduct tours and are within easy driving distance of San Francisco. The Wine Institute is located in the city.

San Francisco also has a scenic 49-mile drive marked with blue and white seagull signs. The drive begins at City Hall in the Civic Center, then twists around the entire city and leads to the most scenic and historic points. A map of the drive may be obtained from the San Francisco Visitor Information Center.

General References

Founded: 1776 **Pop:** 723,959 **Elev:** 63 feet **Time zone:** Pacific **Area code:** 415

Phone Numbers

POLICE & FIRE: 911
FBI: 553-7400
POISON CONTROL CENTER: 800/523-2222
TIME: 767-8900 **WEATHER:** 936-1212

Information Sources

San Francisco Convention & Visitors Bureau, 201 3rd St, PO Box 6977, 94101; 391-2000.
San Francisco Chamber of Commerce, 465 California St, 94104; 392-4511.
Daily Events (recorded), 391-2001.
Visitor Information Center, Swig Pavilion, Hallidie Plaza, Powell and Market Sts, lower plaza level.
Parks Department, 666-7107.

Transportation

AIRLINES: Aeroflot; Air Canada; Air France; Alaska; American; America West; British Airways; CAAC (China); Canadian; China (Taiwan); Continental; Delta; Hawaiian; Japan; Lufthansa; Midwest Express; Mexicana; Northwest; Philippine; QANTAS; Singapore; Southwest; TACA; TWA; United; USAir; VASP; and other commuter and regional airlines. For the most current airline schedules and information consult the *Official Airline Guide*, published twice monthly.
AIRPORT: San Francisco International, 761-0800.
CAR RENTAL AGENCIES: (See Toll-Free Numbers) Avis 877-6780; Budget 877-4477; Hertz 877-1600; National 877-4745.
PUBLIC TRANSPORTATION: Bay Area Rapid Transit (BART), 788-2278; Golden Gate Transit, 332-6600; Municipal Railway (MUNI), 673-6864; Samtrans, 508-6200.
RAILROAD PASSENGER SERVICE: Amtrak 800/872-7245.
FERRY SERVICE: Golden Gate Transit 332-6600.

Newspapers

San Francisco Chronicle; San Francisco Examiner; San Francisco Business Times; Wall Street Journal (San Francisco edition).

Convention Facilities

California Masonic Memorial Temple, 1111 California St, 776-4702.
Civic Auditorium & Brooks Hall, 99 Grove St, 974-4058.
Cow Palace, Geneva Ave, W off Bayshore Blvd, 469-6000.
Moscone Center, 747 Howard St, 974-4000.

Sports & Recreation

Major Sports Facility
Candlestick Park, Gilman Ave, E of Bayshore Frwy (Giants, baseball, 467-8000; 49ers, football, 468-2249).

Racetracks
Bay Meadows Racecourse, Bayshore Frwy (US 101) & Hillsdale Blvd, SE of CA 92, San Mateo, 574-7223.
Golden Gate Fields, 1100 Eastshore Hwy, Albany, 510/526-3020.

Cultural Facilities

Theaters

American Conservatory Theatre, Box office at Geary Theatre, 415 Geary St, at Mason St, 749-2200.
Curran, 445 Geary St, at Mason St, 474-3800.
Golden Gate Theatre, Golden Gate, Taylor & Market Sts, 474-3800.
Marines' Memorial, 749-2228.
Orpheum Theatre, 1192 Market St at 8th St, 474-3800.
Theatre On The Square, 450 Post St, 2nd floor, 433-9500.

Concert Halls

California Masonic Memorial Temple, 1111 California St, 776-4702.
Herbst Theatre, 401 Van Ness Ave, 621-6600 or 392-4400.
Louise M. Davies Symphony Hall, Van Ness Ave & Grove St, Civic Center, 431-5400 (symphony, concerts).
Palace of Fine Arts, 3601 Lyon St, 561-0360.
War Memorial/Opera House, Van Ness Ave & Grove St, Civic Center, 864-3330 (opera), 621-3838 (ballet).

Museums

California Academy of Sciences, Natural History Museum & Aquarium, Golden Gate Park, 750-7145.
Chinese Culture Center, 750 Kearny St, 3rd floor, 986-1822.
Exploratorium, Palace of Fine Arts, 3601 Lyon St, 561-0360.
The Mexican Museum, Fort Mason Center, Bldg D, Laguna St & Marina Blvd, 441-0445.
National Maritime Museum, foot of Polk St, 556-3002.
Old Mint, 5th & Mission Sts, 744-6830.
Presidio Army Museum, Lincoln Blvd & Funston, the Presidio, 561-3660.
Randall Museum, 199 Museum Way, 554-9600.
Ripley's Believe It or Not Museum, 175 Jefferson St, at Fisherman's Wharf, 771-6188.
San Francisco African-American Historical and Cultural Society, Bldg C, Fort Mason Center, Laguna St & Marina Blvd, 441-0640.
Treasure Island Museum, Bldg #1 on Treasure Island, 395-5067.
Wells Fargo Bank History Museum, 420 Montgomery St, 396-2619.

Art Museums

Asian Art Museum, M.H. deYoung Memorial Museum, Golden Gate Park, 668-8921.
M.H. deYoung Memorial Museum, Golden Gate Park, 863-3330.
San Francisco Museum of Modern Art, 151 3rd St, 252-4000.

Points of Interest

Historical

The *Balclutha*, Hyde St Pier, Aquatic Park, 556-3002.
Fort Point National Historic Site, Long Ave & Marine Dr, the Presidio, 556-1693.
Haas-Lilienthal House, 2007 Franklin St, 441-3004.
Hyde St Pier Historic Ships, Aquatic Park, 556-3002.
Mission Dolores, 16th & Dolores Sts, 621-8203.
The Presidio, Richardson Ave & Lombard St, NW corner of city, 561-3660 or -3843.
SS *Jeremiah O'Brien*, Pier 3 East, in Fort Mason Center, 441-3101.
USS *Pampanito*, Pier 45, Fisherman's Wharf, 441-5819.

Other Attractions

Acres of Orchids (Rod McLellan Co), 1450 El Camino Real (CA 82), South San Francisco, 871-5655.
Alcatraz Island, San Francisco Bay, 1¼ mi from shore; tours from Pier 41, Fisherman's Wharf, 546-2805 or 392-7469 (Ticketron).

Aquatic Park, foot of Polk St at Beach St.
"A World of Oil" (Chevron USA), 555 Market St, 894-4086.
The Cannery, 2801 Leavenworth St, at Beach St.
Chinatown, Grant Ave, gateway at Bush St.
Civic Center, bounded by Franklin, Hyde, Golden Gate & Hayes Sts.
Coit Tower (Telegraph Hill), Lombard St & Telegraph Blvd.
The Embarcadero, China Basin to Fisherman's Wharf.
Embarcadero Center, between Montgomery St & the Ferry Bldg.
Fisherman's Wharf, foot of Taylor St.
Fort Mason Center, Buchanan St & Marina Blvd, 441-5706.
Ghirardelli Square, North Point, Beach & Larkin Sts.
Golden Gate Bridge, N on CA 1/101.
Golden Gate National Recreation Area, headquarters at Fort Mason, Bldg 201, 556-0560.
Golden Gate Park, bounded by Lincoln Way, Stanyan & Fulton Sts & Great Hwy.
Jackson Square, Washington, Jackson & Pacific Sts from Montgomery St to Battery St.
Japan Center, Post & Geary Sts, between Fillmore & Laguna Sts, 922-6776.
Japanese Tea Garden, Golden Gate Park.
Marine World, Marine World Pkwy, jct I-80 & CA 37, Vallejo, 707/643-ORCA.
Muir Woods National Monument, 17 mi N, off CA 1 in Marin County, 388-2595.
Performing Arts Center, Van Ness Ave & Grove St, Civic Center.
Pier 39, 2 blks E of Fisherman's Wharf, 981-7437.
San Francisco Maritime National Historical Park, in Golden Gate National Recreation Area.
San Francisco-Oakland Bay Bridge, E on CA 80.
San Francisco Public Library, Larkin & McAllister Sts, 557-4400.
San Francisco Zoo, Sloat Blvd at 45th Ave, 753-7083 or -7080.
Sigmund Stern Memorial Grove, Sloat Blvd & 19th Ave.
Twin Peaks, near center of city.

Sightseeing Tours

Blue & Gold Fleet, Pier 39, adj to Fisherman's Wharf, 705-5444.
Gray Line bus tours, 350 8th St, 558-7373 or 800/826-0202.
Hornblower Dining Yachts, Pier 33, along Embarcadero, 394-8900 ext 7 or 788-8866, ext 7.
Near Escape, PO Box 193005-G, 94119; 386-8687.

Annual Events

Chinese New Year Festival, Chinatown. Feb.
Cherry Blossom Festival, Japan Center. 2 wkends Apr.
Carnaval, Mission District. May.
Grand National Rodeo, Horse & Stock Show, Cow Palace. Late Oct-early Nov.

City Neighborhoods

Many of the restaurants, unratred dining establishments and some lodgings listed under San Francisco include neighborhoods as well as exact street addresses. A map showing these neighborhoods can be found immediately following the city introduction. Geographic descriptions of these areas are given, followed by a table of restaurants arranged by neighborhood.

Chinatown: South of Broadway, west of Kearny St, north of California St and east of Stockton St; along Grant Ave.
Civic Center: South of Golden Gate Ave, west of 7th St, north of Hayes St and east of Franklin St.
Cow Hollow: Area along Union St between Van Ness Ave on the east and Lyon St on the west.
Downtown: Area on and around Union Square; south of Post St, west of Stockton St, north of Geary St and east of Powell St.
Financial District: South of Jackson St, west of San Francisco Bay, north of Market St and east of Chinatown (Kearny St).

Fisherman's Wharf: On San Francisco Bay, west of Powell St, north of Bay St and east of Hyde St; at foot of Taylor St.

Haight-Ashbury: Between University of San Francisco and University of California San Francisco; south of Oak St (Panhandle of Golden Gate Park), west of Buena Vista Park, north of Waller St and east of Golden Gate Park.

Japantown: South of Pine St, west of Laguna St, north of Geary Blvd and east of Fillmore St.

Marina District: South of Marina Blvd, west of Webster St, north of Lombard St and east of the Palace of Fine Arts and Lyon St.

Mission District: Area around Mission Dolores; south of Market St and I-101, west of Potrero Ave, north of Army St and east of Castro St.

Nob Hill: Area on and around crest at Sacramento and Jones Sts.

North Beach: South of Fisherman's Wharf, west of Telegraph Hill, north of Chinatown and east of Russian Hill.

Pacific Heights: South of Lombard St, east of Van Ness Ave, north of Pine St and west of Lyon St.

Russian Hill: South of Jefferson St, west of Mason St, north of Pacific Ave and west of Van Ness Ave.

Union Square: South of Post St, west of Stockton St, north of Geary St and east of Powell St. **North of Union Square:** North of Post St. **South of Union Square:** South of Geary St. **West of Union Square:** West of Powell St.

Lodgings and Food

SAN FRANCISCO RESTAURANTS BY NEIGHBORHOOD AREAS

(For full description, see alphabetical listings under Restaurants)

CHINATOWN

Empress Of China. Top floor of China Trade Center Bldg
The Pot Sticker. 150 Waverly Place
Yamato. 717 California St

CIVIC CENTER

Eleven. 374 11th St
Hayes Street Grill. 320 Hayes St
Stars. 150 Redwood Alley
Zuni Cafe. 1658 Market St

COW HOLLOW

Bontà. 2223 Union St
Prego. 2000 Union St
Yoshida-Ya. 2909 Webster St

FINANCIAL DISTRICT

Agua. 252 California St
Ariana's. 659 Merchant St
Bix. 56 Gold St
Carnelian Room. 52nd floor of Bank of America Center
Ciao. 230 Jackson St
Circolo. 161 Sutter St
Cypress Club. 500 Jackson St
Eric. 121 Spear St
Ernie's. 847 Montgomery St
Fog City Diner. 1300 Battery St
Gabbianos. 1 Ferry Plaza
Harbor Village. 4 Embarcadero Center
Harry Denton's. 161 Steuart St
Hunan. 924 Sansome St
Just Desserts. 3 Embarcadero Center
Mac Arthur Park. 607 Front St
Palio d'Asti. 640 Sacramento St
Park Grill (Park Hyatt Hotel). 333 Battery St
Schroeder's. 240 Front St
Silks (Mandarin Oriental Hotel). 222 Sansome
Splendido. Embarcadero Center Four
Tadich Grill. 240 California St
Tommy Toy's. 655 Montgomery St
Waterfront. Pier 7
Yank Sing. 427 Battery St

FISHERMAN'S WHARF

A. Sabella's. 2766 Taylor St

Bobby Rubino's. 245 Jefferson St
Cafe Pescatore. 2455 Mason St
Chic's Place. Pier 39
Franciscan. Pier 43$^{1}/_2$
Gaylord India. 900 North Point St
Ghirardelli Chocolate Manufactory. 900 North Point St
Lolli's Castagnola. 286 Jefferson St
Mandarin. 900 North Point St
Scoma's. Pier 47
Swiss Louis. Pier 39

JAPANTOWN

Elka (Miyako Hotel). 1625 Post St
Isobune. 1737 Post St
Mifune. 1737 Post St

MARINA DISTRICT

Angkor Palace. 1769 Lombard St
Balboa Cafe. 3199 Fillmore St
Greens. Building A at Fort Mason
La Pergola. 2060 Chestnut St
North India. 3131 Webster St
Scott's Seafood Grill And Bar. 2400 Lombard St

MISSION DISTRICT

Ramis Cafe. 1361 Church St

NOB HILL

The Big 4 (Huntington Hotel). 1075 California St
The Dining Room (The Ritz-Carlton, San Francisco Hotel). 600 Stockton St
Fournou's Ovens (Stouffer Renaissance Stanford Court). Nob Hill
Le Club. 1250 Jones St
Legends (Mark Hopkins Inter-Continental Hotel). 1 Nob Hill
Rue Lepic. 900 Pine St

NORTH BEACH

Amelio's. 1630 Powell St
Basta Pasta. 1268 Grant St
Caffe Roma. 414 Columbus Ave
Enrico's Sidewalk Cafe. 504 Broadway
Fior d'Italia. 601 Union St
Julius Castle. 1541 Montgomery St
Mo's Gourmet Hamburgers. 1322 Grant Ave
Moose's. 1652 Stockton St
North Beach. 1512 Stockton St
The Shadows. 1349 Montgomery St

PACIFIC HEIGHTS

Harris'. 2100 Van Ness Ave
La Fiammetta. 1701 Octavia St
Pacific Heights Bar & Grill. 2001 Fillmore St
Trio Cafe. 1870 Fillmore St
Tuba Garden. 3634 Sacramento Ave

RICHMOND DISTRICT

Alejandro's. 1840 Clement

Cafe Riggio. 4112 Geary Blvd

Dynasty Fantasy. 6139 Geary Blvd

Flower Lounge. 5322 Geary Blvd

Fountain Court. 354 Clement St

Khan Toke Thai House. 5937 Geary Blvd

RUSSIAN HILL

Acquerello. 1722 Sacramento St

Frascati. 1901 Hyde St

Golden Turtle. 2211 Van Ness Ave

House Of Prime Rib. 1906 Van Ness Ave

I Fratelli. 1896 Hyde St at Green

UNION SQUARE

Campton Place (Campton Place Kempinski Hotel). 340 Stockton St

NORTH OF UNION SQUARE

Anjou. 44 Campton Pl

Café Latté. 100 Bush St

Fleur de Lys. 777 Sutter St

Liberté. 248 Sutter St

Masa's (Vintage Court). 648 Bush St

SOUTH OF UNION SQUARE

Abiquiu. 129 Ellis St

The Acorn. 1256 Folsom St

Fino. 1 Cosmo Place

Fringale. 570 Fourth St

Kuleto's. 221 Powell St

Marrakech Moroccan. 419 O'Farrell St

Wu Kong. 101 Spear St

WEST OF UNION SQUARE

China Moon Cafe. 639 Post St

David's. 474 Geary St

Dottie's True Blue Cafe. 522 Jones St

French Room (Four Seasons Clift Hotel). 495 Geary St

New Joe's. 347 Geary St

Pacific Grill (Pan Pacific Hotel). 500 Post St

Postrio (The Prescott Hotel). 545 Post St

Salmagundi. 442 Geary St

Note: *When a listing is located in a town that does not have its own city heading, it will appear under the city nearest to its location. In these cases, the address and town appear in parenthesis immediately following the name of the establishment.*

Motels

★ ★ **BEST WESTERN CIVIC CENTER.** *364 Ninth St (94103), in Civic Center area.* 415/621-2826; FAX 415/621-0833. 57 rms, 2 story. No A/C. May-Oct: S $68-$85; D $75-$95; each addl $7; under 13 free; lower rates rest of yr. Crib free. TV; cable. Heated pool. Complimentary coffee in rms. Restaurant 7 am-2 pm. Ck-out noon. Coin lndry. Airport transportation. Refrigerators. Cr cds: A, C, D, DS, ER, JCB, MC, V.

🏊 🔥 **SC**

★ ★ **BUENA VISTA MOTOR INN.** *1599 Lombard St (94123), at Gough, in Cow Hollow.* 415/923-9600; res: 800/835-4980; FAX 415/441-4775. 50 rms, 3 story. Mid-May-mid-Oct: S $80; D $85; under 12 free; suite $140; lower rates rest of yr. Crib free. TV. Complimentary coffee in rms. Ck-out noon. Airport transportation. Cr cds: A, C, D, DS, MC, V.

D 🚫 🔥 **SC**

★ **CHELSEA MOTOR INN.** *2095 Lombard St (94123), at Fillmore St, in Marina District.* 415/563-5600; FAX 415/567-6475. 60 rms, 3 story, no ground floor rms. S $73; D $78-$86; each addl $7; under 5 free. Crib free. TV; cable. Complimentary coffee in rms. Restaurant nearby. Ck-out noon. Free covered parking. Airport transportation. Cr cds: A, C, D, MC, V.

D 🚫 🔥

★ ★ **COLUMBUS MOTOR INN.** *1075 Columbus Ave (94133), in North Beach.* 415/885-1492; FAX 415/928-2174. 45 rms, 5 story. S, D $92-$110; each addl $7-$10. Crib free. TV; cable. Complimentary coffee in rms. Restaurant nearby. Ck-out noon. Free covered parking. Fisherman's Wharf 4 blks. Cr cds: A, C, D, MC, V.

🚫 🔥

★ **COVENTRY MOTOR INN.** *1901 Lombard St (94123), in Marina District.* 415/567-1200; FAX 415/921-8745. 69 rms, 3 story. S $73-$86; D $78-$86; each addl $7; under 6 free. Crib free. TV; cable. Complimentary coffee in rms. Restaurant nearby. Ck-out noon. Free covered parking. Cr cds: A, C, D, MC, V.

🚫 🔥

★ ★ **COW HOLLOW MOTOR INN.** *2190 Lombard St (94123), in Marina District.* 415/921-5800; FAX 415/922-8515. 117 rms, 2-4 story, 12 suites. S $73; D $78; each addl $7; suites $175-$245; under 5 free. Crib free. TV; cable. Restaurant adj 7 am-2:30 pm. Ck-out noon. Free covered parking. Meeting rm. Health club privileges. Cr cds: A, C, D, MC, V.

D 🚫 🔥

★ ★ **DAYS INN.** *2600 Sloat Blvd (94116), south of Union Square.* 415/665-9000; FAX 415/665-5440. 33 rms, 2 story. July-mid-Sept: S $80-$100; D $85-$105; suites $130; under 12 free; lower rates rest of yr. Crib free. TV; cable. Complimentary continental bkfst, coffee. Restaurant nearby. Ck-out 11 am. Refrigerators. Cr cds: A, C, D, DS, JCB, MC, V.

D 🚫 🔥 **SC**

✔★ **DAYS INN-DOWNTOWN.** *895 Geary St (94109), at Larkin, west of Union Square.* 415/441-8220; FAX 415/771-5667. 73 rms, 4 story. S, D $60-$100; each addl $10; under 12 free. Crib free. TV. Complimentary continental bkfst. Complimentary coffee in lobby. Ck-out noon. Free garage parking. Airport transportation. Cr cds: A, C, D, DS, MC, V.

🚫 🔥 **SC**

★ ★ **HOWARD JOHNSON.** *580 Beach St (94133), at Fisherman's Wharf.* 415/775-3800; FAX 415/441-7307. 128 rms, 4 story. S $89-$129; D $99-$139; suites $130-$160; under 17 free. Crib free. Covered parking $4.50/day. TV; in-rm movies. Restaurant 7-11 am. Ck-out noon. Coin lndry. Bellhops. Valet serv. Minibars. Cr cds: A, C, D, DS, ER, JCB, MC, V.

D 🚫 🔥 **SC**

★ **LOMBARD MOTOR INN.** *1475 Lombard St (94123), in Cow Hollow.* 415/441-6000; res: 800/835-3639; FAX 415/441-4291. 48 rms, 3 story. May-Sept: S $78-$95; D $78-$97; each addl $6; under 11 free; lower rates rest of yr. Crib free. TV. Complimentary coffee in rms. Ck-out noon. Airport transportation. Cr cds: A, C, D, MC, V.

🚫 🔥 **SC**

★ ★ **PACIFIC HEIGHTS INN.** *1555 Union St (94123), in Cow Hollow.* 415/776-3310; res: 800/523-1801; FAX 415/776-8176. 40 rms,

2 story, 17 kits. No A/C. S, D $65-$89; suites $79-$98; family rates. Crib free. TV; cable. Complimentary continental bkfst. Complimentary coffee, newspaper in rms. Restaurant opp open 24 hrs. Ck-out noon. Bellhops. Refrigerators; some in-rm steam and whirlpool baths. Cr cds: A, C, D, DS, MC, V.

⊠ 🔥 SC

★ ★ PHOENIX. 601 Eddy St (94109), at Larkin St, in Civic Center area. 415/776-1380; res: 800/248-9466; FAX 415/885-3109. 44 rms, 2 story. No A/C. S, D $89; suites $129-$139; under 12 free. Crib free. TV; cable. Heated pool; poolside serv. Complimentary continental bkfst. Restaurant 6-10 pm; wkends to 11 pm; closed Mon. Rm serv. Bar from 5 pm. Ck-out noon. Meeting rms. Concierge. Sundries. Health club privileges. Some refrigerators. Private patios, balconies. Cr cds: A, C, D, DS, MC, V.

≈ 🔥 SC

✔★ ★ ROYAL PACIFIC. 661 Broadway (94133), in Chinatown. 415/781-6661; res: 800/545-5574; FAX 415/781-6688. 74 rms, 12 A/C, 5 story. Apr-Nov: S, D $72-$76; each addl $5; suites $89-$99; lower rates rest of yr. Crib $5. TV; cable. Complimentary coffee in rms. Restaurant nearby. Ck-out noon. Coin lndry. Sauna. Refrigerators avail. Some balconies. Cr cds: A, C, D, MC, V.

⊠ 🔥

★ SEAL ROCK INN. 545 Point Lobos Ave (94121), at 48th Ave, west of Union Square. 415/752-8000; FAX 415/752-6034. 27 rms, 4 story, 11 kit. units. Mid-May-mid-Sept: S $78-$104; D $86-$112; deposit required wkends; each addl $8; kit. units $5 addl; under 16, $4; lower rates rest of yr. Crib $2. TV; cable. Pool. Complimentary coffee in rms. Restaurant 6:30 am-4 pm; Sat & Sun to 6 pm. Ck-out 11 am. Sundries. Covered parking. Lawn games. Refrigerators; some fireplaces. Ocean view. Near Golden Gate Park. Cr cds: A, C, D, MC, V.

≈ 🔥

★ VAGABOND INN-MIDTOWN. 2550 Van Ness Ave (94109), in Russian Hill. 415/776-7500; FAX 415/776-5689. 132 rms, 5 story. No A/C. S $75-$120; D $85-$150; each addl $5; suites, kit. units $125-$150; under 19 free; higher rates special events. Crib free. TV; cable. Heated pool. Complimentary coffee in rms. Complimentary continental bkfst. Restaurant open 24 hrs. Bar 5 pm-midnight. Ck-out noon. Meeting rm. Valet serv. Airport transportation. Some refrigerators. Some balconies. Cr cds: A, C, D, DS, ER, MC, V.

D ≈ ⊠ 🔥 SC

★ ★ WHARF. 2601 Mason St (94133), at Fisherman's Wharf. 415/673-7411; res: 800/548-9918; FAX 415/776-2181. 51 rms, 3-4 story. No A/C. May-Oct: S, D $88-$140; kit. suite $225-$295; lower rates rest of yr. Crib free. TV; cable. Complimentary coffee, newspaper in lobby. Restaurant nearby. Ck-out 11 am. Concierge. Airport transportation. Some balconies. Cr cds: A, C, D, DS, MC, V.

⊠ ⊠ 🔥 SC

Motor Hotels

★ ★ BEST WESTERN AMERICANIA. 121 Seventh St (94103), in Civic Center area. 415/626-0200; FAX 415/626-3974. 143 rms, 4 story, 24 suites. No A/C. June-Sept: S $87-$99; D $99-$115; each addl $10; suites $110-$175; under 12 free; lower rates rest of yr. Crib free. TV; cable. Heated pool. Coffee in rms. Restaurant 6:30 am-10 pm. Rm serv. Bar 11 am-midnight. Ck-out noon. Coin lndry. Meeting rms. Valet serv. Exercise equipt; weight machine, stair machine, sauna. Some refrigerators. Cr cds: A, C, D, DS, ER, JCB, MC, V.

≈ 🕴 ⊠ 🔥 SC

★ ★ BEST WESTERN CANTERBURY HOTEL & WHITE-HALL INN. 750 Sutter St (94109), near Taylor St, on Nob Hill. 415/474-6464; FAX 415/474-5856. 250 rms in 2 bldgs, 4 & 10 story, 14 suites. S, D $79; each addl $10; suites $99; under 18 free; wkend, honeymoon plans. Garage parking $12 in/out. TV; cable. Pool privileges. Complimentary coffee in rms. Restaurant 6:30 am-10:30 pm. Rm serv. Bar;

entertainment. Ck-out noon. Meeting rms. Gift shop. Airport transportation. Exercise equipt; weight machine, bicycles. Many refrigerators. Cr cds: A, C, D, DS, JCB, MC, V.

D 🕴 ⊠ ⊠ SC

★ ★ BEST WESTERN MIYAKO INN. 1800 Sutter St (94115), in Japantown. 415/921-4000; FAX 415/923-1064. 125 rms, 8 story. S $83-$91; D $93-$101; each addl $10; suites $160-$260; under 18 free. Crib free. Garage parking $6.50. TV. Restaurant 7 am-10 pm. Bar. Ck-out noon. Bellhops. Valet serv. Airport transportation. In-rm steam baths. Balconies. Cr cds: A, C, D, DS, JCB, MC, V.

⊠ ⊠ 🔥 SC

★ ★ HOLIDAY INN-FISHERMAN'S WHARF. 1300 Columbus Ave (94133), at Fisherman's Wharf. 415/771-9000; FAX 415/771-7006. 580 rms, 2-5 story. June-Nov: S $140-$185; D $145-$190; each addl $5; suites $300-$400; under 19 free; lower rates rest of yr. Crib free. Pet accepted. Parking $8. TV; cable. Heated pool; poolside serv. Restaurant 6:30 am-10 pm. Bar 4-11:30 pm. Rm serv. Ck-out noon. Coin lndry. Meeting rms. Bellhops. Valet serv. Sundries. Some refrigerators. Cr cds: A, C, D, DS, JCB, MC, V.

D 🐾 ≈ ⊠ 🔥 SC

★ ★ ★ HYDE PARK SUITES. 2655 Hyde St (94109), at Fisherman's Wharf. 415/771-0200; res: 800/227-3608; FAX 415/346-8058. 24 kit. suites, 3 story. No A/C. S, D $165-$220; each addl $10; under 12 free. Garage in/out $12. TV; cable. Complimentary continental bkfst. Ck-out noon. Coin lndry. Concierge. Airport transportation. Refrigerators, honor bars. Private patios; some balconies. Ghirardelli Square 1 blk. Cr cds: A, C, D, DS, JCB, MC, V.

🔥 SC

★ ★ RAMADA HOTEL AT FISHERMAN'S WHARF. 590 Bay St (94133), at Fisherman's Wharf. 415/885-4700; FAX 415/771-8945. 232 rms, 4 story. May-Oct: S $135-$170; D $150-$185; each addl $15; suites $240-$255; under 19 free; lower rates rest of yr. Crib free. Garage in/out $8. TV; cable. Restaurant 6:30 am-10 pm. Rm serv. Bar 4 pm-midnight. Ck-out noon. Meeting rms. Valet serv. Sundries. Gift shop. Refrigerator in suites. Cr cds: A, C, D, DS, ER, JCB, MC, V.

D 🕴 ⊠ 🔥 SC

★ ★ ★ SHERATON AT FISHERMAN'S WHARF. 2500 Mason St (94133), at Fisherman's Wharf. 415/362-5500; FAX 415/956-5275. 524 rms, 4 story. S, D $129-$200; each addl $20; suites from $275; under 17 free; package plans. Crib free. Garage $12. TV; cable, in-rm movies. Heated pool. Restaurant 6:30 am-10 pm; Fri, Sat to 11 pm. Rm serv 24 hrs. Bar; entertainment Fri, Sat. Ck-out noon. Convention facilities. Valet serv. Concierge. Gift shop. Barber, beauty shop. Health club privileges. Cr cds: A, C, D, DS, ER, JCB, MC, V.

≈ ⊠ 🔥 SC

★ ★ TRAVELODGE HOTEL. 250 Beach St (94133), at Fisherman's Wharf. 415/392-6700. 250 rms, most rms with shower only, 4 story, 4 suites. Some A/C. S, D $95-$155; each addl $10; suites $150-$300; under 17 free. Crib free. TV; in-rm movies. Heated pool. Complimentary coffee, newspaper in rms. Restaurant adj. Ck-out noon. Meeting rm. Gift shop. Airport transportation. Refrigerators avail. Balconies. Opp bay. Cr cds: A, C, D, DS, MC, V.

D ≈ ⊠ ⊠ SC

Hotels

✔★ ALEXANDER INN. 415 O'Farrell St (94102), at Taylor St, west of Union Square. 415/928-6800; res: 800/843-8709; FAX 415/928-3354. 48 rms, 6 story. No A/C. S, D $58-$78; under 12 free. TV. Complimentary continental bkfst. Coffee in rms. Ck-out 11 am. Coin lndry. Airport transportation. Cable car turntable 2 blks. Cr cds: A, D, DS, JCB, MC, V.

⊠ 🔥 SC

★ ★ ★ **ANA.** *50 Third St (94103), south of Union Square.* 415/974-6400; res: 800/ANA-HOTE; FAX 415/543-8268. 667 rms, 36 story. S $170-$235; D $180-$270; each addl $25; suites $350-$1,500; under 12 free; wkend rates. Crib free. Valet, garage parking $22. TV. Restaurant 6:30 am-10:30 pm. Bar 11-1:30 am; entertainment (exc Sun & Mon). Ck-out noon. Convention facilities. Concierge. Gift shop. Tennis privileges. Exercise equipt; weight machine, bicycles, sauna, steam rm. Bathrm phones, minibars. Cr cds: A, C, D, DS, ER, JCB, MC, V.

D 🏃 🏋 🛪 🔥 SC

✔★ **ATHERTON.** *685 Ellis St (94109), at Larkin St, west of Union Square.* 415/474-5720; res: 800/227-3608; FAX 415/474-8256. 74 rms, 6 story. No A/C. S, D $61-$81; each addl $10; under 12 free. Crib free. TV. Restaurant 7 am-2:30 pm, 5-10:30 pm. Bar 4 pm-2 am. Ck-out noon. Meeting rm. Airport, RR station, bus depot transportation. Cr cds: A, C, D, DS, ER, JCB, MC, V.

🔥

★ **BEDFORD.** *761 Post St (94109), 3 blocks west of Union Square.* 415/673-6040; res: 800/227-5642; FAX 415/563-6739. 144 rms, 17 story. No A/C. S, D $119; each addl $10; 2-bedrm family unit $175; under 12 free. Crib free. Valet parking $15. TV; cable, in-rm movies. Coffee in rms. Restaurant 7-10 am. Bar 5 pm-midnight. Ck-out 1 pm. Meeting rms. Refrigerators, honor bars. Cr cds: A, C, D, DS, ER, JCB, MC, V.

🛪 🔥 SC

★ **BERESFORD.** *635 Sutter St (94102), north of Union Square.* 415/673-9900; res: 800/533-6533; FAX 415/474-0449. 114 rms, 7 story. No A/C. S $79; D $89; each addl $10; family units $94-$104; under 12 free. Pet accepted, some restrictions. Garage parking $15 in/out. TV; cable. Complimentary continental bkfst. Restaurant 7 am-2 pm, 5:30-10:30 pm; Sun & Mon to 2 pm. No rm serv. Bar 7-1 am, Sun to 2 pm. Ck-out noon. Airport transportation. Health club privileges. Refrigerators, honor bars. Cr cds: A, C, D, DS, JCB, MC, V.

🐾 🛪 🔥 SC

★ **BERESFORD ARMS.** *701 Post St (94109), west of Union Square.* 415/673-2600; res: 800/533-6533; FAX 415/673-5349. 96 rms, 8 story, 40 kit. units. No A/C. S $79; D $89; each addl $10; suites $105-$135, under 12 free. Crib free. Valet parking $15 in/out. TV; cable. Complimentary continental bkfst in lobby, also tea & refreshments 4:30-5:30 pm. Ck-out noon. No rm serv. Airport transportation. Some bathrm phones, in-rm whirlpools, honor bars. Cr cds: A, C, D, DS, JCB, MC, V.

D 🛪 🔥 SC

✔★ ★ **BRITTON.** *112 7th St (94103), near Civic Center area.* 415/621-7001; res: 800/444-5819; FAX 415/626-3974. 79 rms, 5 story. June-Sept: S $59-$69; D $61-$80; each addl $7; suites $78-$83; lower rates rest of yr. Crib free. TV. Restaurant 6 am-10 pm. Ck-out noon. Coin lndry. Union Square transportation. Barber. Convention Center 3 blks. Cr cds: A, C, D, DS, ER, JCB, MC, V.

D 🛪 🔥 SC

★ **CALIFORNIAN.** *405 Taylor St (94102), at O'Farrell St, west of Union Square.* 415/885-2500; res: 800/227-3346; FAX 415/673-5784. 244 rms, 17 story. No A/C. S $85; D $95; each addl $10; suites $95-$159; under 12 free. Crib free. TV; cable. Complimentary coffee in rms. Restaurant 7 am-3 pm; dining rm 6:30 am-11 pm. Bar 11 am-midnight. Ck-out noon. Meeting rms. Barber. Cr cds: A, C, D, JCB, MC, V.

🛪 🔥 SC

CAMPTON PLACE. *(4-Star 1994; New general manager, therefore not rated) 340 Stockton St (94108), on Union Square.* 415/781-5555; res: 800/235-4300; FAX 415/955-5536. 120 rms, 7-17 story, 10 suites. S, D $200-$350; suites $450-$850; under 18 free. Crib free. Valet parking $20/24 hrs. Pet accepted; $25. TV; cable, in-rm movies avail. Restaurant (see CAMPTON PLACE). Rm serv 24 hrs. Bar 10 am-11 pm; Fri & Sat to midnight. Ck-out 1 pm. Meeting rms. Concierge 24 hrs. Butler services. Airport transportation; complimen-

tary morning limo service downtown. Health club nearby, by arrangement. Bathrm phones; honor bar. Rooftop garden. Lavish decor; antiques, artwork. A small luxury hotel in the European tradition. Cr cds: A, C, D, JCB, MC, V.

D 🐾 🛪 🔥 🐾

★ ★ **CARLTON.** *1075 Sutter St (94109), north of Union Square.* 415/673-0242; res: 800/227-4496; FAX 415/673-4904. 165 rms, 9 story. No A/C. S, D $114; 3rd person in rm $12 addl; under 12 free. Crib free. TV; in-rm movies. Coffee in rms. Complimentary afternoon tea, evening wine. Restaurant 7-11 am, 5-9 pm. Ck-out 1 pm. Meeting rm. Airport, RR station, bus depot transportation; free Financial District and civic center transportation. Honor bars. Cr cds: A, C, D, DS, JCB, MC, V.

🛪 🔥 SC

★ ★ **CARTWRIGHT.** *524 Sutter St (94102), at Powell St, north of Union Square.* 415/421-2865; res: 800/227-3844; FAX 415/421-2865. 114 rms, 34 A/C, 8 story. S $99-$119; D $109-$129; suites $150-$170; under 3 free. Crib free. Parking in/out $13. TV; cable. Complimentary afternoon tea, cakes. Restaurant 7-11 am. Ck-out 1 pm. Meeting rm. Airport transportation. Game rm/library. Many refrigerators. Antiques. Originally opened 1915. Cr cds: A, C, D, DS, ER, JCB, MC, V.

🛪 🔥

★ ★ **CHANCELLOR.** *433 Powell St (94102), south of Union Square.* 415/362-2004; res: 800/428-4748; FAX 415/362-1403. 140 rms, 16 story. No A/C. S $97; D $114; each addl $20; suites $165. Crib free. Garage 1/2 blk $16. TV; cable. Restaurant 7 am-3 pm, 5-9:30 pm. Bar 11-1 am. Ck-out noon. Meeting rm. Gift shop. Airport transportation. Tallest building in the city when constructed (1914) after the San Francisco earthquake in 1906. Cr cds: A, C, D, DS, ER, JCB, MC, V.

🛪 🔥 SC

✔★ **COMFORT INN-BY THE BAY.** *2775 Van Ness Ave (94109), north of Union Square.* 415/928-5000; FAX 415/441-3990. 134 rms, 11 story. Mid-June-Oct: S, D $69-$129; each addl $10; under 19 free; lower rates rest of yr. Crib free. Garage parking in/out $8. TV; in-rm movies avail. Complimentary continental bkfst. Ck-out noon. Meeting rm. Airport transportation. Exercise equipt; bicycle, rower. Cr cds: A, C, D, DS, ER, JCB, MC, V.

D 🏋 🛪 🔥 SC

★ ★ **DIVA.** *440 Geary St (94102), west of Union Square.* 415/885-0200; res: 800/553-1900; FAX 415/346-6613. 110 rms, 7 story. S, D $119; each addl $10; suites $129-$300; under 12 free. Crib free. Valet parking, in/out $16. TV; in-rm movies. Complimentary California continental bkfst. Restaurant 11:30 am-10 pm; Fri, Sat to 11 pm; Sun 1-9 pm. Rm serv 7 am-10 pm. Ck-out noon. Meeting rms. Concierge. Exercise equipt; weight machines, bicycles. Bathrm phones, refrigerators, honor bars. Cr cds: A, C, D, DS, ER, JCB, MC, V.

D 🏋 🛪 🔥 SC

★ ★ ★ **THE DONATELLO.** *501 Post St (94102), 1 block west of Union Square.* 415/441-7100; res: 800/227-3184; FAX 415/885-8842. 94 rms, 14 story. S, D $175-$225; each addl $25; suites $325-$525; under 12 free; wkend rates. Crib free. Garage, in/out $16. TV; cable, in-rm movies avail. Restaurant 7-10:30 am, 5:30-10:30 pm. Bar 5 pm-1 am. Ck-out noon. Meeting rms. Concierge. Exercise equipt; weights, bicycles, whirlpool, sauna, steam rm. Bathrm phones; some refrigerators. Some balconies. Spacious rms with plants. Complimentary newspaper, shoeshine. Italian Renaissance decor; antiques; classic elegance. Grand piano in lobby; pianist. Cr cds: A, C, D, DS, JCB, MC, V.

D 🏋 🛪 🔥

✔★ ★ **ESSEX.** *684 Ellis St (94109), at Larkin St, west of Union Square.* 415/474-4664; res: 800/453-7739 (exc CA), 800/443-7739 (CA); FAX 415/441-1800. 96 rms, 7 story. No A/C. S $49; D $59; each addl $10; suites $79; under 12 free. TV. Complimentary coffee in lobby.

Ck-out noon. Airport transportation. Some balconies. Civic Center 3 blks. Cr cds: A, MC, V.

⊠ SC

★ ★ ★ **FAIRMONT HOTEL & TOWER.** *California & Mason Sts (94106), on Nob Hill.* 415/772-5000; FAX 415/781-4027. 600 rms, 8 & 24 story. S, D $150-$299; each addl $30; suites $475-$6,000; under 13 free; wkend rates. Crib free. Garage, in/out $25/day, valet. TV; cable. Restaurant 6 am-11 pm. Rm serv 24 hrs. Bars; entertainment, dancing. Ck-out 1 pm. Convention facilities. Concierge. Shopping arcade. Barber, beauty shop. Free financial district transportation. Exercise rm; instructor, weight machine, weights, sauna. Bathrm phones, minibars, in-rm whirlpools. Some suites with private patio. Spacious lobby. Outside glass-enclosed elvtr to Fairmont Crown Room. Panoramic view of city; rooftop garden. Cr cds: A, C, D, DS, JCB, MC, V.

⊠ ⊠ ⊠ ⊠

★ ★ ★ ★ **FOUR SEASONS CLIFT.** *495 Geary St (94102), at Taylor St, west of Union Square.* 415/775-4700; FAX 415/441-4621. 329 rms, 17 story. S $215-$330; D $215-$360; each addl $30; suites $365-$690; under 18 free; wkend rates. Crib free. Pet accepted. Valet parking $22. TV; cable. Restaurant (see FRENCH ROOM); lobby tea service Mon-Sat 3-5 pm. Rm serv 24 hrs. Bar 11-2 am; pianist 6 pm-1:30 am, Sun to 10 pm; also lobby lounge Mon-Fri 3-10 pm. Ck-out 1 pm. Valet serv 24 hrs. Concierge. Free limo to financial district. Exercise equipt; bicycles, treadmill. Bathrm phones, refrigerators, minibars. Tastefully furnished rms; lovely large suites. Specialized child's amenity package. In-rm FAX avail. Hotel with Old World charm; personalized service. Cr cds: A, C, D, ER, JCB, MC, V.

⊠ ⊠ ⊠ ⊠ ⊠

★ ★ **GALLERIA PARK.** *191 Sutter St (94104), in Financial District.* 415/781-3060; res: 800/792-9639; FAX 415/433-4409. 177 rms, 8 story. S, D $105-$150; suites $155-$375; family, wkend rates. Garage in/out $16. TV; cable, in-rm movies avail. Restaurant 7 am-11 pm. Bar. Ck-out noon. Meeting rms. Concierge. Shopping arcade. Airport transportation. Refrigerators, honor bars. Atrium lobby with unique sculptured fireplace. Cr cds: A, C, D, DS, ER, JCB, MC, V.

⊠ ⊠ ⊠ ⊠ SC

★ ★ ★ **GRAND HYATT SAN FRANCISCO.** *345 Stockton St (94108), on Union Square.* 415/398-1234; res: 800/233-1234; FAX 415/392-2536. 690 rms, 36 story, 33 suites. S, D $195-$240; each addl $25; suites $350-$1,550; under 19 free; honeymoon, hol and other package plans. Crib free. Valet parking, garage in/out $24. TV; cable, in-rm movies avail. Restaurant 6:30 am-11 pm. Rm serv 24 hrs. Bar 11-2 am; entertainment. Ck-out 3 pm. Convention facilities. Concierge. Shopping arcade. Barber, beauty shop. Airport, RR station, bus depot transportation. Complimentary limo serv. Tennis privileges. Exercise equipt; weight machine, bicycles. Masseuse. Refrigerators, minibars; many bathrm phones; some wet bars. **LUXURY LEVEL : REGENCY CLUB.** 60 rms, 7 suites, 3 floors. S, D $205-$275; suites $350-$950; wkend plans. Concierge. Private lounge, honor bar. In-rm movies, wet bar in suites. Complimentary continental bkfst, refreshments. Cr cds: A, C, D, DS, ER, JCB, MC, V.

⊠ ⊠ ⊠ ⊠ ⊠ SC

✔ ★ **GRANT PLAZA.** *465 Grant St (94108), in Chinatown.* 415/434-3883; res: 800/472-6899; FAX 415/434-3886. 72 rms, 6 story. S $39-$45; D $42-$65; each addl $7; under 10 free. Crib $7. Garage $8.50. TV. Restaurant adj open 24 hrs. No rm serv. Ck-out noon. Cr cds: A, C, D, ER, JCB, MC, V.

⊠

★ ★ ★ **HANDLERY UNION SQUARE.** *351 Geary St (94102), west of Union Square.* 415/781-7800; res: 800/843-4343; FAX 415/781-0269. 376 rms, 8 story. Some A/C. S, D $125-$135; each addl $10; suites $155-$320; under 15 free. Crib free. Garage in/out $13.50. TV; cable, in-rm movies avail. Heated pool; sauna, poolside serv. Complimentary morning coffee & tea. Restaurant 7 am-11 pm. Rm serv 7-10:30 am, 5-10 pm. Bar 10 am-11:30 pm. Ck-out noon. Meeting rms. Concierge. Gift shop. Barber, beauty shop. Airport transportation.

LUXURY LEVEL : HANDLERY CLUB. 93 rms, 8 floors. S $150; D $160; each addl $10; suites $300-$480. Private lounge. Minibars. Complimentary coffee & tea. Cr cds: A, C, D, DS, ER, JCB, MC, V.

⊠ ⊠ ⊠ ⊠ SC

★ ★ **HARBOR COURT.** *165 Steuart St (94105), in Financial District.* 415/882-1300; res: 800/346-0555; FAX 415/882-1313. 131 rms, 5 story. Apr-mid-Nov: S, D $99-$165; wkend rates; lower rates rest of yr. Crib free. Parking in/out $15. TV; cable. Indoor pool; lifeguard. Restaurant 7 am-11 pm. Rm serv 5-9 pm. Bar to 2 am; entertainment exc Sun. Ck-out noon. Concierge. Free Financial District transportation Mon-Fri. Exercise rm; instructor, weights, bicycles, whirlpool, sauna. Refrigerators, minibars. Victorian decor. On waterfront. Cr cds: A, C, D, DS, ER, JCB, MC, V.

⊠ ⊠ ⊠ ⊠ ⊠ SC

★ ★ ★ **HILTON & TOWERS.** *333 O'Farrell St, south of Union Square.* 415/771-1400; FAX 415/771-6807. 1,891 rms, 19, 23 & 46 story. S $175-$225; D $200-$250; each addl $25; suites from $300-$2,000; wkend packages. Garage, in/out $22. TV; cable. Pool on 16th floor in garden court. Restaurants 6 am-midnight. Bars 10:30-1:30 am; dancing. Ck-out noon. Convention facilities. Shopping arcade. Barber, beauty shop. Exercise equipt; weights, bicycles, sauna. Masseuse. Balconies. Some penthouse suites with solarium. 16th floor lanai rms; some rms on floors 17-19 overlook pool area. 46-story tower with distinctive rms. **LUXURY LEVEL : TOWER.** 130 units, 4 suites, 2 floors. S $250; D $275. Concierge. Private lounge. Minibars. Complimentary continental bkfst, refreshments. Cr cds: A, C, D, DS, JCB, MC, V.

⊠ ⊠ ⊠ ⊠ ⊠

★ ★ **HOLIDAY INN-CIVIC CENTER.** *50 8th St (94103), at Market St, in Civic Center area.* 415/626-6103; FAX 415/552-0184. 389 rms, 14 story. S $94-$134; D $104-$144; each addl $15; suites $200-$350; under 19 free; wkend rates. Crib free. TV; cable; in-rm movies. Heated pool. Restaurant 6 am-2 pm, 5-10 pm. Bar 4-midnight. Ck-out noon. Coin lndry. Meeting rms. Gift shop. Free garage parking. Airport transportation. Health club privileges. Balconies. Cr cds: A, C, D, DS, JCB, MC, V.

⊠ ⊠ ⊠ ⊠ SC

★ ★ **HOLIDAY INN-GOLDEN GATEWAY.** *1500 Van Ness Ave (94109), at California St, in Russian Hill.* 415/441-4000; FAX 415/776-7155. 499 rms, 26 story. June-Oct: S, D $115-$140; each addl $15; suites $185-$460; under 19 free; lower rates rest of yr. Crib free. Parking in/out $11. TV; cable, in-rm movies avail. Heated pool. Restaurant 6:30 am-10:30 pm. Bar. Ck-out noon. Convention facilities. Gift shop. Airport transportation. Some refrigerators. On cable car line. Cr cds: A, C, D, DS, JCB, MC, V.

⊠ ⊠ ⊠ ⊠ SC

★ ★ ★ **HOLIDAY INN-UNION SQUARE.** *480 Sutter St (94108), north of Union Square.* 415/398-8900; FAX 415/989-8823. 400 rms, 30 story. May-Oct: S $145-$185; D $160-$200; each addl $15; suites $175-$750; under 19 free; wkend rates; lower rates rest of yr. Crib free. Parking in/out $18. TV; in-rm movies avail. Restaurant 6:30 am-10:30 pm. Bar; pianist Tues-Sat. Rm serv. Ck-out noon. Convention facilities. Bellhops. Valet serv. Gift shop. Exercise equipt; treadmill, bicycle. Refrigerator in suites. Cr cds: A, C, D, DS, JCB, MC, V.

⊠ ⊠ ⊠ ⊠ SC

★ ★ **HOTEL MILANO.** *55 5th St (94103), south of Union Square.* 415/543-8555; FAX 415/543-5843. 108 rms, 8 story. S $125-$165; D $135-$165; each addl $10; under 12 free; wkend & hol rates. Crib free. Parking $17. TV; cable. Restaurant 6:30 am-2 pm. Rm serv 24 hrs. Bar 11-2 am. Ck-out noon. Meeting rms. Concierge. Exercise equipt; treadmill, stairmaster. Minibars. Cr cds: A, C, D, DS, JCB, MC, V.

⊠ ⊠ ⊠ ⊠ SC

★ ★ **HOTEL NIKKO.** *222 Mason St (94102), west of Union Square.* 415/394-1111; FAX 415/421-0455. 522 rms, 25 story, 33 suites. S $185-$245; D $215-$275; each addl $30; suites $375-$1,300;

under 18 free; wkend rates. Crib free. Covered parking, in/out $23; valet. TV; cable, in-rm movies. Indoor pool; poolside serv. Complimentary bkfst, refreshments. Restaurant 6:30 am-10 pm. Rm serv 24 hrs. Bar 11-2 am. Ck-out noon. Convention facilities. Concierge. Drugstore. Barber, beauty shop. Free transportation to financial district. Exercise rm; instructor, weight machines, bicycles, whirlpool, steam rm, sauna. Full-service fitness center. In-rm steam baths, minibars. 2-story marble staircase in lobby frames cascading waterfall. *LUXURY LEVEL* : **NIKKO FLOORS.** 68 rms, 14 suites, 3 floors. S $245; D $275; suites from $475. Private lounge. Wet bars. Cr cds: A, C, D, DS, ER, JCB, MC, V.

⊡ ≋ ✕ ⊠ 🔥 SC

★ ★ ★ **HOTEL TRITON.** *342 Grant Ave (94108), east of Union Square. 415/394-0500; res: 800/433-6611; FAX 415/394-0555.* 140 rms, 7 story. S, D $119-$139; each addl $10; suites $189-$239; under 16 free. Crib free. Valet, in/out parking $18. TV; cable, in-rm movies avail. Complimentary morning coffee & tea, evening wine. Restaurants 6:30 am-midnight. Rm serv 24 hrs. Bar from 11 am. Ck-out noon. Meeting rm. Airport transportation. Exercise equipt: stair machine, bicycle. Health club privileges. Minibars. Whimsical sophisticated design; showcase for local artists. Cr cds: A, C, D, DS, ER, JCB, MC, V.

⊡ ✕ ⊠ 🔥 SC

★ ★ **HOTEL UNION SQUARE.** *114 Powell St (94102), west of Union Square. 415/397-3000; res: 800/553-1900; FAX 415/399-1874.* 131 rms, 6 story. S, D $99-$109; each addl $10; suites $129-$280; under 12 free. Garage in/out $16. TV; in-rm movies. Complimentary continental bkfst. Restaurant adj 11 am-11 pm. Bar 11 am-9 pm. Ck-out noon. Airport transportation. Honor bars; some wet bars. Penthouse suites with refrigerator, deck. Cr cds: A, C, D, DS, ER, JCB, MC, V.

⊠ 🔥 SC

★ ★ ★ **HUNTINGTON.** *1075 California St (94108), top of Nob Hill. 415/474-5400; res: 800/227-4683 (exc CA), 800/652-1539 (CA); FAX 415/474-6227.* 100 rms, 12 story, 40 suites. No A/C. S $165-$215; D $185-$235; suites $250-$660; under 6 free. Crib free. Garage, in/out $20. TV; cable. Restaurant (see THE BIG 4). Rm serv 6 am-midnight. Bar 11:30-12:30 am; pianist. Ck-out 1 pm. Meeting rms. Concierge. Free downtown, financial district & Fisherman's Wharf transportation. Health club privileges. Minibars. Wet bar in most rms; some kits. Complimentary tea or sherry upon arrival. Exquisite rms, individually decorated; many rms with view of city, bay. Built 1924; site of the Tobin house. Cr cds: A, C, D, DS, MC, V.

⊠ 🔥

★ ★ ★ **HYATT AT FISHERMAN'S WHARF.** *555 North Point St (94133), at Fisherman's Wharf. 415/563-1234; FAX 415/749-6122.* 313 rms, 5 story. Apr-Oct: S $155-$185; D $180-$210; suites $275-$525; under 19 free; wkend rates; lower rates rest of yr. Crib free. Garage $14 in/out. TV; cable, in-rm movies. Heated pool. Restaurant 6:30-11 am, 6-10 pm; Fri & Sat to 11 pm. Bar 4:30 pm-midnight, Fri & Sat noon-1 am. Ck-out noon. Coin lndry. Meeting rms. Concierge. Gift shop. Airport transportation. Exercise equipt; weights, bicycles, whirlpool, sauna. Some bathrm phones. Cable car line opp. Cr cds: A, C, D, DS, ER, JCB, MC, V.

⊡ ≋ ✕ ⊠ 🔥

★ ★ ★ **HYATT REGENCY.** *5 Embarcadero Center (94111), Market & Drumm Sts, in Financial District. 415/788-1234; FAX 415/398-2567.* 803 rms, 15 story. S $149-$245; D $215-$245; each addl $25; suites $350-$995; under 18 free; package plans. Crib free. Covered parking, valet $20. TV; cable, in-rm movies. Coffee in rms. Restaurant 6-1:30 am. Rm serv 24 hrs. Bars; entertainment; revolving rooftop restaurant/bar. Ck-out noon. Convention facilities. Concierge. Shopping arcade. Airport, RR station, bus depot transportation. Exercise equipt; bicycles, stair machine. Health club privileges. Refrigerators. Balconies. Spacious 17-story atrium in lobby. *LUXURY LEVEL* : **REGENCY CLUB.** 54 rms. S $215-$295; D $245-$295. Private lounge,

honor bar. Complimentary continental bkfst, refreshments. Cr cds: A, C, D, DS, JCB, MC, V.

⊡ ✕ ⊠ 🔥

★ ★ ★ **INN AT THE OPERA.** *333 Fulton St (94102), in Civic Center area. 415/863-8400; res: 800/325-2708 (exc CA), 800/423-9610 (CA); FAX 415/861-0821.* 30 rms, 7 story, 18 suites. No A/C. S $110-$160; D $120-$170; suites $165-$210. Crib free. Parking $18. TV; cable; in-rm movies. Complimentary bkfst. Restaurant 7-10 am, 11:30 am-2 pm, 5:30-10:30 pm; Sun brunch 7-10:30 am. Rm serv 24 hrs. Bar to 10 pm, Fri & Sat to 1 am; entertainment Tues-Sat. Ck-out noon. Concierge. Refrigerators, minibars. Elegant European decor. In Performing Arts Center. Cr cds: A, MC, V.

⊡ ⊠ 🔥

★ ★ **JULIANA.** *590 Bush St (94108), north of Union Square. 415/392-2540; res: 800/328-3880; FAX 415/391-8447.* 106 rms, 9 story. S, D $134-$170; suites $150-$170; monthly rates. Crib free. TV; cable. Complimentary coffee, tea, fruit in lobby. Restaurant 7-11 am, 5:30-11 pm. Bar. Ck-out noon. Free Financial District transportation. Health club privileges. Refrigerators, honor bars. Cr cds: A, C, D, DS, ER, JCB, MC, V.

⊡ ⊠ 🔥 SC

★ ★ **KENSINGTON PARK.** *450 Post St (94102), west of Union Square. 415/788-6400; res: 800/553-1900; FAX 415/399-9484.* 86 rms, 12 story. S, D $89-$115; each addl $10; suites $160-$350; under 13 free. Crib free. Valet parking $16. TV. Complimentary continental bkfst, also tea/sherry in afternoon. Ck-out noon. Meeting rms. Bathrm phones; some refrigerators. Renovated 1924 hotel, guest rms on floors 5-12. Grand piano in lobby. Traditional English decor. Theater in building. Cr cds: A, D, DS, ER, JCB, MC, V.

⊡ ⊠ 🔥 SC

★ ★ **KING GEORGE.** *334 Mason St (94102), west of Union Square. 415/781-5050; res: 800/288-6005; FAX 415/391-6976.* 143 rms, 9 story. No A/C. S $110; D $120; each addl $10; suites $185; under 12 free; 2-night packages. Crib free. Garage, in/out $15.50. TV; cable, in-rm movies avail. Continental bkfst, afternoon tea. Restaurant 7-10 am, 3-6:30 pm. Rm serv 24 hrs. Bar; entertainment. Ck-out noon. Meeting rms. Concierge. Airport, RR station, bus depot transportation. Health club privileges. Union Square 1 blk. Cr cds: A, C, D, DS, ER, JCB, MC, V.

🔥 SC

★ **LOMBARD.** *1015 Geary St (94109), at Polk St, west of Union Square. 415/673-5232; res: 800/777-3210; FAX 415/885-2802.* 101 rms, 6 story. No A/C. S, D $99; each addl $10; under 12 free. Crib free. Valet parking in/out $10/day. TV. Complimentary coffee, tea, sherry. Restaurant 7-11 am. Ck-out noon. Meeting rm. Airport, bus depot transportation. Free downtown transportation. Game rm. Some refrigerators. Cr cds: A, C, D, DS, ER, JCB, MC, V.

⊠ 🔥 SC

★ ★ ★ **MAJESTIC.** *1500 Sutter St (94109), at Gough St, in Pacific Heights. 415/441-1100; res: 800/869-8966; FAX 415/673-7331.* 58 rms, 5 story. S, D $125-$160; each addl $15; suites $250. Covered parking $15. TV. Restaurant 7 am-2 pm, 5:45-10 pm; closed Mon lunch. Bar 11 am-midnight; pianist. Ck-out noon. Meeting rms. Concierge. Free downtown transportation. Many fireplaces; some refrigerators. Each rm individually decorated with antiques, custom furnishings. Restored Edwardian hotel (1902); antique tapestries. Cr cds: A, D, MC, V.

⊡ ⊠ 🔥

★ ★ ★ **MANDARIN ORIENTAL.** *222 Sansome (94104), between Pine & California Sts, in Financial District. 415/885-0999; res: 800/622-0404; FAX 415/433-0289.* 160 rms, 11 story; on floors 38-48 of the twin towers in the First Interstate Center. S, D $255-$390; suites $540-$1,200; under 12 free; wkend rates. Crib free. Covered parking $21. TV; cable, in-rm movies avail. Restaurant (see SILKS). Rm serv 24 hrs. Bar 11 am-11 pm; entertainment from 3 pm exc Sun. Ck-out noon. Meeting rms. Concierge. Health club privileges. Bathrm phones, refrigerators, minibars. Unique location; all guest rms occupy twin towers of Center and are linked on each floor by a spectacular sky bridge; panoramic view of bay and skyline. Lobby level business center. Cr cds: A, C, D, DS, JCB, MC, V.

[D] [≈] [⚒]

★ ★ ★ ★ **MARK HOPKINS INTER-CONTINENTAL.** *1 Nob Hill (94108), on Nob Hill.* 415/392-3434; *res:* 800/327-0200; *FAX* 415/421-3302. 391 rms, 19 story. S $180-$250; D $200-$280; each addl $30; suites $410-$2,000; under 14 free; wkend rates. Crib free. Garage, in/out $22/day. TV; cable, in-rm movies. Restaurant 6:30 am-11 pm (also see LEGENDS). Rm serv 24 hrs. Bars noon-2 am. Ck-out 1 pm. Convention facilities. Concierge. Airport transportation. Complimentary limo service 7:30 am-noon. Exercise equipt; bicycles, treadmill. Minibars. Some balconies. Complimentary newspaper, shoeshine. California landmark; on site of the Mark Hopkins mansion. Panoramic view from glass-walled Top of the Mark. *LUXURY LEVEL :* CLUB INTER-CONTINENTAL. 19 rms, 3 suites. S $275; D $305; suites $375-$1,000. Concierge. Private lounge, honor bar. Wet bar, in-rm movies in suites. Complimentary continental bkfst, refreshments. Cr cds: A, C, D, ER, JCB, MC, V.

[D] [🏃] [≈] [⚒]

★ ★ ★ **MARRIOTT.** *55 4th St (94103), opp Moscone Convention Center, south of Union Square.* 415/896-1600; *FAX* 415/896-6175. 1,500 rms, 39 story, 133 suites. S, D $169-$225; each addl $20; suites $300-$2,000; under 18 free. Crib free. Garage $24, in/out 24 hrs. TV; cable, in-rm movies. Indoor pool; poolside serv. Restaurant 6:30 am-11 pm; Fri, Sat to midnight. Bar 10:30-2 am. Ck-out noon. Convention facilities. Concierge. Gift shop. Airport, RR station, bus depot transportation. Exercise equipt; weight machine, bicycles, whirlpool, sauna, steam rm. Minibars; some bathrm phones. Refrigerator, wet bar in suites. Some balconies. Six-story atrium lobby. *LUXURY LEVEL :* CONCIERGE LEVEL. 86 rms, 6 suites, 2 floors. S $185; D $205; suites $350-$650. Private lounge, honor bar. Wet bar. Bathrm phones. Complimentary continental bkfst, refreshments. Cr cds: A, C, D, DS, ER, JCB, MC, V.

[D] [≈] [🏃] [≈] [⚒] [SC]

★ ★ ★ **MARRIOTT FISHERMAN'S WHARF.** *1250 Columbus Ave (94133), at Fisherman's Wharf.* 415/775-7555; *FAX* 415/474-2099. 255 rms, 5 story. S, D $129-$189; each addl $15; suites $235-$495; under 16 free; wkend rates. Crib free. Valet parking in/out $16. TV; cable, in-rm movies. Restaurant 6:30 am-10 pm. Bar 2 pm-midnight. Ck-out noon. Meeting rms. Gift shop. Free morning downtown transportation (Mon-Fri). Airport transportation. Exercise equipt; weight machine, bicycles, sauna. Honor bars; bathrm phones. Marble floor in lobby. Cr cds: A, C, D, DS, ER, JCB, MC, V.

[D] [🏃] [≈] [⚒] [SC]

★ ★ ★ **MIYAKO.** *1625 Post St (94115), in Japantown.* 415/922-3200; *res:* 800/533-4567; *FAX* 415/921-0417. 218 rms, 5 & 16 story. S $109-$129; D $129-$159; each addl $20; suites $189-$279; under 18 free. Crib free. Garage in/out $15. TV; cable, in-rm movies. Restaurant (see ELKA). Bar 10-1 am. Ck-out 1 pm. Meeting rms. Concierge. Shopping arcade. Airport transportation. Health club privileges. Minibars. Refrigerator in suites; sauna in suites. Balconies. Shiatsu massage avail. Japanese decor; authentic Japanese furnishings in most rms. Cr cds: A, C, D, DS, ER, JCB, MC, V.

[D] [≈] [⚒] [SC]

★ ★ **MONTICELLO INN.** *127 Ellis St (94102), south of Union Square.* 415/392-8800; *res:* 800/669-7777; *FAX* 415/398-2650. 91 rms, 5 story, 36 suites. S, D $120-$135; suites $145-$280. Crib free. Valet parking $25. TV; cable. Complimentary continental bkfst. Restaurant 11 am-midnight. Ck-out noon. Concierge. Airport, downtown transportation. Refrigerators. 18th-century decor. Renovated hotel built 1906. Cr cds: A, C, D, DS, ER, JCB, MC, V.

[D] [≈] [⚒] [SC]

★ ★ **NOB HILL LAMBOURNE.** *725 Pine St (94108), on Nob Hill.* 415/433-2287; *res:* 800/274-8466; *FAX* 415/433-0975. 20 kit.

units, 3 story, 6 suites. No A/C. S, D $125; suites $199; family, monthly rates. Crib avail. Garage; valet, in/out $18. TV; cable, in-rm movies. Complimentary continental bkfst. Complimentary coffee in rms. Restaurant opp 6:30 am-11 pm. No rm serv. Ck-out noon. Concierge. Airport, RR station, bus depot transportation. Health club privileges. Wet bars. Balconies. Cr cds: A, C, D, DS, MC, V.

[≈] [≈] [SC]

★ ★ ★ **ORCHARD.** *562 Sutter St (94102), north of Union Square.* 415/433-4434; *res:* 800/433-4434; *FAX* 415/433-3695. 94 rms, some A/C, 7 story. S, D $110-$130; each addl $10; suites $195-$225. Crib free. Garage $15 in/out. TV; cable. Complimentary coffee, newspaper in rms. Complimentary afternoon refreshments in lobby. Restaurant 7 am-noon. Bar 4:30-10 pm, closed Sun & Mon. Ck-out noon. Concierge. Airport transportation. Health club privileges. Minibars. Renovated hotel; many furnishings imported from Europe. Cr cds: A, C, D, DS, JCB, MC, V.

[D] [⚒] [SC]

✔ ★ **PACIFIC BAY INN.** *520 Jones St (94102), between O'Farrell St and Geary Blvd, west of Union Square.* 415/673-0234; *res:* 800/445-2631; *FAX* 415/673-4781. 84 rms, 7 story. No A/C. S, D $49; wkly rates. Covered parking, in/out $12. TV. Restaurant 7 am-2 pm; closed Tues. No rm serv. Ck-out 11 am. Airport, RR station, bus depot transportation. Some refrigerators. Cr cds: A, D, DS, MC, V.

[D] [≈] [⚒] [SC]

★ ★ ★ ★ **PAN PACIFIC.** *500 Post St (94102), west of Union Square.* 415/771-8600; *res:* 800/533-6465; *FAX* 415/398-0267. 330 units, 21 story, 19 suites, 2 with kit. S, D $185-$325; suites $350-$1,500; under 18 free; special wkend rates. Crib free. Garage, in/out $22; valet parking. Pet accepted, some restrictions. TV; cable. Supervised child's activities. Restaurant 6:30 am-10 pm (also see PACIFIC GRILL). Rm serv 24 hrs. Bar 11 am-11:30 pm; pianist 5-10 pm. Ck-out 4 pm. Meeting rms. Personal valet serv. Concierge. Gift shop. Airport transportation; limo serv avail. Exercise equipt; weights, bicycles. Health club privileges. Minibars, bathrm phones. Complimentary newspaper. Third-floor atrium lobby highlighted by spectacular 17-story skylight; extensive use of marble; 2 fireplaces; fountain; commissioned sculptures. Cr cds: A, C, D, ER, JCB, MC, V.

[D] [✦] [🏃] [≈] [⚒]

★ ★ ★ **PARC FIFTY-FIVE.** *55 Cyril Magnin St (94102), Market at 5th St, south of Union Square.* 415/392-8000; *FAX* 415/392-4734. 1,008 rms, 32 story. S $155-$175; D $170-$190; each addl $15; suites $340-$1,200; under 19 free; wkend rates. Crib free. Garage, in/out $22. TV; cable. Restaurants 6:30 am-11 pm. Bar 11 am-1 am; pianist. Ck-out noon. Convention facilities. Concierge. Drugstore. Exercise equipt; weights, bicycles, sauna. Bathrm phones. *LUXURY LEVEL :* CONCIERGE CLUB. 86 rms, 15 suites. S $195; D $210; suites $450-$1,200. Private lounge, honor bar. Some in-rm whirlpools. Complimentary continental bkfst, refreshments. Cr cds: A, C, D, DS, ER, JCB, MC, V.

[D] [🏃] [≈] [⚒] [SC]

★ ★ ★ ★ **PARK HYATT.** *333 Battery St (94111), at Clay St, in Financial District.* 415/392-1234; *FAX* 415/421-2433. 360 rms, 24 story, 37 suites. S, D $240-$290; each addl $25; suites $295-$2,000; under 18 free; wkend rates. Crib free. Pet accepted, some restrictions. Covered valet parking, in/out $20. TV; cable. Restaurant (see PARK GRILL); afternoon tea and evening caviar service. Rm serv 24 hrs. Bar 11-1 am; entertainment. Ck-out noon. Meeting rms. Concierge. Airport transportation; complimentary downtown transportation. Exercise equipt available for in-rm use. Health club privileges. Bathrm phones, minibars. Some balconies. Reference library with national and international publications. Complimentary newspaper, shoeshine. Located in Embarcadero Center. Offers neoclassical formality. Cr cds: A, C, D, DS, ER, JCB, MC, V.

[D] [✦] [≈] [⚒] [SC]

★ ★ **QUALITY HOTEL CATHEDRAL HILL.** *1101 Van Ness Ave (94109), at Geary Blvd, west of Union Square.* 415/776-8200; *res:* 800/227-4730 (exc CA), 800/622-0855 (CA); *FAX* 415/441-2841. 400

rms, 8 story. S $105-$180; D $125-$200; each addl $20; suites $200-$400; under 18 free; wkend package. Crib free. Garage parking $10 in/out. TV; cable. Heated pool. Restaurant 6:30 am-10:30 pm. Bar 11-1 am. Ck-out noon. Convention facilities. Concierge. Shopping arcade. Barber, beauty shop. Airport transportation. Many bathrm phones; some refrigerators. Balconies; some private patios. Cr cds: A, C, D, DS, JCB, MC, V.

⊡ ≋ ⊠ 🔥 SC

★ ★ **RAPHAEL.** 386 Geary St (94102), west of Union Square. 415/986-2000; res: 800/821-5343; FAX 415/397-2447. 152 rms, 12 story. S $99-$124; D $109-$134; each addl $20; suites $145-$225; under 18 free. Crib free. Parking in/out $16. TV; cable, in-rm movies avail. Complimentary morning coffee. Restaurant 7 am-11 pm. Bar 11 am-midnight. Ck-out 1 pm. Airport transportation. Bathrm phones. Cr cds: A, C, D, DS, MC, V.

⊠ 🔥

★ ★ ★ ★ ★ **THE RITZ-CARLTON, SAN FRANCISCO.** 600 Stockton St (94108), at California St, on Nob Hill. 415/296-7465; FAX 415/296-8559. 336 rms, 9 story, 44 suites. S, D $225-$345; suites $450-$3,000; under 18 free; wkend packages. Crib avail. Garage; valet $25, in/out $25. TV; in-rm movies. Indoor pool. Supervised child's activities. Restaurant 6:30 am-11 pm (also see THE DINING ROOM). Rm serv 24 hrs. Bar; entertainment. Ck-out noon. Convention facilities. Concierge. Gift shop. Complimentary limo service within city. Exercise equipt; weight machine, stair machine, treadmills, whirlpool, sauna. European spa service. Bathrm phones, minibars; some wet bars. Elegant furnishings. Rooms surround outdoor inner courtyard. Public areas decorated with fine art and antiques. Located at a cable car stop on the eastern slope of Nob Hill, this neoclassical building achieved San Francisco city landmark status in 1984 and is included on the list of Architecturally Significant Structures. **LUXURY LEVEL : RITZ-CARLTON CLUB.** 67 rms, 15 suites, 2 floors. S, D $345-$500. Concierge. Private lounge, honor bar. Complimentary continental bkfst, afternoon refreshments. Cr cds: A, C, D, DS, ER, JCB, MC, V.

⊡ ≋ 🕴 ⊠ 🔥 SC

★ ★ ★ **SAVOY.** 580 Geary St (94102), 3 blks west of Union Square. 415/441-2700; res: 800/227-4223; FAX 415/441-2700, ext. 297. 83 rms, 7 story. No A/C. S $99-$109; D $109-$119; each addl $10; suites $149-$189; under 14 free. Crib free. Valet parking in/out $16. TV. Complimentary continental bkfst. Afternoon tea, cookies, sherry. Restaurant 6:30-10 am, 5:30-10:30 pm; wkends 6:30-10:30 am, 5:30-11 pm. Bar. Ck-out noon. Meeting rm. Concierge. Cr cds: A, C, D, DS, ER, JCB, MC, V.

⊠ 🔥 SC

✔★ **SHEEHAN.** 620 Sutter St (94102), west of Union Square. 415/775-6500; res: 800/848-1529; FAX 415/775-3271. 68 rms, 58 with bath, 6 story. No A/C. S $45-$80; D $55-$99; each addl $10; under 12 free. Crib free. Garage $12. TV; cable. Indoor pool; lifeguard. Complimentary continental bkfst. Tea rm 7 am-9 pm. No rm serv. Ck-out 11 am. Meeting rms. Beauty shop. Airport transportation. Exercise equipt; weight machines, rowers. Cr cds: A, C, D, DS, JCB, MC, V.

⊡ ≋ 🕴 ⊠ 🔥 SC

★ ★ ★ **SHERATON PALACE.** 2 New Montgomery St (94105), at Market St, east of Union Square. 415/392-8600; FAX 415/543-0671. 550 rms, 8 floors. S $225-$285; D $245-$305; each addl $20; suites $450-$2,500; family, wkend rates. Crib free. Valet parking, in/out $20. TV; cable, in-rm movies. Indoor pool; poolside serv. Restaurant 6:30-1 am. Rm serv 24 hrs. Bar from 11 am; entertainment. Ck-out noon. Convention facilities. Concierge. Shopping arcade. Airport transportation. Exercise rm; instructor, weights, treadmill, whirlpool, sauna. Health spa. Bathrm phones, refrigerators. Cr cds: A, C, D, DS, ER, JCB, MC, V.

⊡ ≋ 🕴 ⊠ 🔥 SC

★ ★ ★ **SIR FRANCIS DRAKE.** 450 Powell St (94102), north of Union Square. 415/392-7755; res: 800/227-5480; FAX 415/677-9341. 417 rms, 21 story. S, D $140-$180; each addl $15; suites $300-$600;

under 18 free; wkend rates; package plans. Crib free. Pet accepted; deposit. Valet parking in/out $23. TV; cable, in-rm movies avail. Restaurant 6:30 am-10 pm. Bar 11:30-1 am, Sun to 10 pm; dancing. Ck-out noon. Meeting rms. Concierge. Shopping arcade. Airport, bus depot transportation. Exercise equipt; weights, bicycles. Some honor bars. Cr cds: A, C, D, DS, JCB, MC, V.

⊡ 👊 🕴 ⊠ 🔥 SC

★ ★ ★ ★ **STOUFFER RENAISSANCE STANFORD COURT.** Nob Hill (94108). 415/989-3500; res: 800/227-4736 (exc CA), 800/622-0957 (CA); FAX 415/391-0513. 402 rms, 8 story. S $195-$295; D $225-$325; each addl $30; 1-bedrm suites $325-$1,750; 2-bedrm suites $475-$2,000; under 18 free. Crib free. Pet accepted. Valet parking, in/out $22/day. TV; cable, in-rm movies. Restaurant 6:30 am-2:30 pm (also see FOURNOU'S OVENS). Afternoon tea in lobby. Rm serv 24 hrs. Bars 11-1 am. Ck-out noon. Meeting rms. Concierge. Shopping arcade. Free limo service. Health club privileges. Marble bathrms with phone, TV & special amenities. Antiques. Lavish hotel with glass-domed courtyard carriage entry. Antiques & artwork in lobby. Cr cds: A, C, D, DS, JCB, MC, V.

👊 ⊠ 🔥

★ ★ ★ **TUSCAN INN AT FISHERMAN'S WHARF.** 425 North Point St (94133), at Fisherman's Wharf. 415/561-1100; res: 800/648-4626; FAX 415/561-1199. 221 rms, 4 story, 12 suites. S, D $158-$178; each addl $20; suites $198-$218; under 19 free; package plans avail. Crib free. Garage in/out $15/day. TV; cable, in-rm movies. Complimentary continental bkfst. Restaurant 7 am-10 pm. Bar. Ck-out noon. Meeting rms. Concierge. Airport transportation. Free Financial District transportation Mon-Fri. Health club privileges. Minibars. European-style "boutique hotel" following the tradition of a classic inn. 3 blks from Pier 39. Cr cds: A, C, D, DS, JCB, MC, V.

⊡ ⊠ 🔥 SC

★ ★ **VILLA FLORENCE.** 225 Powell St (94102), south of Union Square. 415/397-7700; res: 800/553-4411; FAX 415/397-1006. 180 rms, 7 story, 36 suites. S, D $134; suites $149-$154; under 16 free; Christmas, honeymoon package plans. Crib free. Garage parking in/out $17. TV; cable. Coffee in rms. Restaurant 7 am-midnight. Bar. Ck-out noon. Meeting rms. Concierge. Free Financial District transportation. Airport transportation. Refrigerators. Cr cds: A, C, D, DS, ER, JCB, MC, V.

⊠ 🔥 SC

★ ★ **VINTAGE COURT.** 650 Bush St (94108), north of Union Square. 415/392-4666; res: 800/654-1100; FAX 415/433-4065. 106 rms, 65 A/C, 8 story. S, D $119-$149; each addl $10; under 12 free. Crib free. Garage in/out $15. TV; cable, in-rm movies avail. Complimentary continental bkfst 7-10 am. Complimentary coffee, wine in lobby. Restaurant 6-9:30 pm. Bar 6-10 pm. Ck-out noon. Meeting rm. Airport transportation. Health club privileges. Refrigerators. Sitting area each floor. Built 1912. Cr cds: A, C, D, DS, ER, JCB, MC, V.

⊡ ⊠ 🔥 SC

★ ★ ★ **WARWICK REGIS.** 490 Geary St (94102), west of Union Square. 415/928-7900; res: 800/827-3447; FAX 415/441-8788. 80 rms, 8 story. S, D $99-$225; each addl $10; suites $150-$225; under 16 free. Crib free. Valet parking in/out $18. TV; in-rm movies avail. Complimentary continental bkfst. Restaurants 7-10 am, 6-10 pm. Bar 11-2 am. Ck-out 1 pm. Meeting rms. Refrigerators; some fireplaces. Balconies. Louis XVI decor. Built 1911. Cr cds: A, C, D, DS, ER, JCB, MC, V.

⊡ ⊠ 🔥 SC

★ ★ ★ **THE WESTIN ST FRANCIS.** 335 Powell St (94102), on Union Square. 415/397-7000; FAX 415/774-0124. 1,200 rms in hotel & tower, 12 & 32 story. S $150-$230; D $180-$280; each addl $30; suites $300-$1,500; under 18 free. Crib free. Pet accepted, some restrictions. Garage in/out, valet parking $22. TV; cable. Restaurants 6 am-midnight. Rm serv 24 hrs. Bars 11-2 am; entertainment, dancing. Ck-out 1 pm. Convention facilities. Concierge. Barber, beauty shop. Shopping arcade. Airport transportation. Refrigerators, minibars; bathrm phone in suites. Attractively furnished rms. Landmark hotel built 1904, on Union

Square. 32-story tower with outside glass-enclosed elvtrs. Cable car stop. Cr cds: A, C, D, DS, JCB, MC, V.

[D] [🤚] [⛤] [⛤] [SC]

★ ★ **YORK.** *940 Sutter St (94109), lower Nob Hill.* 415/885-6800; res: 800/808-9675; FAX 415/885-2115. 96 rms, 7 story. S, D $95-$110; each addl $10; suites $175; under 12 free; lower rates Nov-mid-Apr. Valet parking $12. TV; cable. Complimentary continental bkfst. Complimentary coffee in rms, afternoon refreshments. Bar 5 pm-midnight, closed Sun, Mon; entertainment. Ck-out noon. Meeting rm. Airport, RR station transportation. Free wkday morning downtown transportation. Exercise equipt; weights, treadmill. Honor bars; some refrigerators. Renovated 1922 hotel; marble floors, ceiling fans. Hitchcock's Vertigo filmed here. Cr cds: A, C, D, DS, ER, JCB, MC, V.

[🏃] [⛤] [⛤] [SC]

Inns

★ ★ **ALAMO SQUARE.** *719 Scott St (94117), west of Union Square.* 415/922-2055; res: 800/345-9888; FAX 415/931-1304. 15 rms in 2 bldgs (10 with shower only), 3 story. No A/C. S, D $85-$175; each addl $25; suites $150-$275; wkly rates; higher rates wkends (2-night min). Crib free. TV in some rms; cable. Complimentary full bkfst, coffee, tea, wine. Restaurant nearby. Ck-out noon, ck-in 2-6 pm. Concierge. Bellhop. Airport transportation. Health club privileges. Some balconies. Picnic tables. Inn complex includes two restored Victorian mansions, 1895 Queen Anne and 1896 Tudor Revival, located in historic district. Antique furnishings, some wood-burning fireplaces; stained-glass skylight. Garden. Overlooks Alamo Square; panoramic view of city skyline. Totally nonsmoking. Cr cds: A, C, D, JCB, MC, V.

[⛤] [⛤]

🖝★ ★ **ALBION HOUSE.** *135 Gough St (94102), south of Union Square.* 415/621-0896; FAX 415/621-0154. 8 rms, 2 story. S, D $75-$160; suite $180. TV. Complimentary full bkfst 8:30-10:30 am, afternoon tea. Restaurant nearby. Ck-out noon, ck-in 2 pm. Built 1906; individually decorated rms, antiques; piano in parlor. Cr cds: A, MC, V.

[⛤] [SC]

🖝★ **AMSTERDAM.** *749 Taylor St (94108), west of Union Square.* 415/673-3277; res: 800/637-3444; FAX 415/673-0453. 34 rms, some share bath, 3 story. No elvtr. S $45-$69; D $50-$79; each addl $10; under 11 free. Crib free. Garage $13 in/out. TV; cable. Complimentary continental bkfst. Restaurant nearby. Ck-out 11 am, ck-in noon. Cr cds: A, MC, V.

[⛤] [⛤]

★ ★ **ANDREWS HOTEL.** *624 Post St (94109), west of Union Square.* 415/563-6877; res: 800/926-3739; FAX 415/928-6919. 48 rms, 7 story. No A/C. S, D $82-$106; each addl $10; suites $119. Parking adj, $13 in/out. TV. Complimentary continental bkfst on each floor, wine. Dining rm 5:30-10 pm. Ck-out noon, ck-in 3 pm. European decor; impressionist prints. Former Turkish bathhouse built 1905. Cr cds: A, D, MC, V.

[⛤] [⛤]

★ ★ **ARCHBISHOPS MANSION.** *1000 Fulton St (94117), at Steiner St, south of Union Square.* 415/563-7872; res: 800/543-5820; FAX 415/885-3193. 15 rms, 3 story. S, D $115-$189; each addl $20; suites $205-$385. TV; cable. Complimentary continental bkfst, coffee, tea, evening refreshments. Restaurant nearby. Ck-out 11:30 am, ck-in 3 pm. Bellhops. Concierge. Stained-glass skylight over stairwell. Built 1904; antiques. Individually decorated rms. Smoking in common areas only. Cr cds: A, MC, V.

[⛤]

★ ★ ★ **INN AT UNION SQUARE.** *440 Post St (94102), west of Union Square.* 415/397-3510; res: 800/288-4346; FAX 415/989-0529. 30 rms, 6 story. No A/C. S, D $120-$170; each addl $15; suites $170-$300. Crib free. Valet parking in/out $18. TV; cable. Complimentary continental bkfst, refreshments. Afternoon tea. Rm serv 5-9:30 pm.

Ck-out noon, ck-in 2 pm. Bellhops. Concierge. Sitting area, fireplace most floors; antiques. Robes in all rms. Penthouse suite with fireplace, bar, whirlpool, sauna. Totally nonsmoking. Cr cds: A, D, JCB, MC, V.

[D] [⛤] [⛤] [SC]

★ ★ ★ **THE INN SAN FRANCISCO.** *943 S Van Ness Ave (94110), in Mission District.* 415/641-0188; res: 800/359-0913; FAX 415/641-1701. 22 rms, 17 baths, 3 story. No A/C. S, D $75-$195; each addl $20; suites $165-$195. Limited parking avail; $10. TV. Complimentary continental bkfst, coffee, tea, sherry. Restaurant nearby. Ck-out noon, ck-in 2 pm. Airport transportation. Whirlpool. Refrigerators. Balconies. Library. Italianate mansion (1872) near Mission Dolores; ornate woodwork, fireplaces; antique furnishings; garden with redwood hot tub, gazebo; view of city, bay from rooftop sun deck. Cr cds: A, C, D, DS, MC, V.

[⛤]

★ ★ **MANSIONS HOTEL.** *2220 Sacramento St (94115), in Pacific Heights.* 415/929-9444; res: 800/826-9398; FAX 415/567-9391. 21 rms, 3 story. No A/C. S $89-$225; D $129-$350. Pet accepted. Complimentary full bkfst. Dining rm (res required) 6-9 pm. Rm serv 7:30 am-midnight. Ck-out noon, ck-in 2 pm. Bellhops. Airport transportation. Game rm. Music rm. Evening magic concerts. Some balconies. Old mansion (1887); Victorian memorabilia, antiques. Garden; fresh flowers in rms. Large collection of Buffano sculptures. Cr cds: A, C, D, DS, MC, V.

[⛤] [⛤]

🖝★ ★ **MARINA INN.** *3110 Octavia St (94123), at Lombard St, north of Union Square.* 415/928-1000; res: 800/274-1420; FAX 415/928-5909. 40 rms, 4 story. S, D $65-$85; each addl $10. TV; cable. Complimentary continental bkfst, afternoon sherry. Ck-out noon, ck-in 2 pm. Bellhops. Barber, beauty shop. Restored 1928 bldg; English country ambiance. Cr cds: A, MC, V.

[D] [⛤]

★ ★ **MILLEFIORI.** *444 Columbus Ave (94133), in North Beach.* 415/433-9111; FAX 415/362-6292. 15 rms, 2-3 story. S $65-$95; D $85-$130; each addl $10; under 5 free. TV. Complimentary continental bkfst. Restaurant adj 7-1 am. Ck-out noon, ck-in from 7:30 am. Individually decorated rms. Cr cds: A, C, D, MC, V.

[⛤] [⛤]

★ ★ ★ **PETITE AUBERGE.** *863 Bush St (94108), north of Union Square.* 415/928-6000; FAX 415/775-5717. 26 rms, 5 story. No A/C. S, D $110-$160; each addl $15; suite $220. Crib free. Valet parking in/out $17. TV; cable. Complimentary full bkfst, coffee, tea refreshments. Ck-out noon, ck-in 2 pm. Bellhops. Airport transportation. Some fireplaces. French country inn ambiance. Cr cds: A, D, MC, V.

[⛤] [⛤]

★ ★ ★ **THE PRESCOTT HOTEL.** *545 Post St (94102), west of Union Square.* 415/563-0303; res: 800/283-7322; FAX 415/563-6831. 166 rms, 7 story, 12 suites. S, D $165; each addl $10; suites $215-$600; hol rates. Crib free. Covered valet parking, in/out $17. TV; cable, in-rm movies avail. Pool privileges. Dining rm (see POSTRIO). Complimentary morning coffee and tea, evening wine and hors d'oeuvres. Rm serv 6 am-midnight. Bar 11-2 am. Ck-out noon, ck-in 3 pm. Concierge. Airport transportation. Free morning Financial District transportation. Health club privileges. Minibars; some wet bars. Lobby has hearth-style fireplace, red fir wainscoting and alabaster chandeliers. Union Square shopping 1 blk. *LUXURY LEVEL : CLUB LEVEL.* 55 rms, 24 suites, 4 floors. S, D $185; suites $235. Concierge. Private lounge, honor bar. Complimentary use of exercise equipt (stationary bike or rower) for in-rm use. Complimentary continental bkfst, refreshments, shoeshine. Cr cds: A, C, D, DS, ER, JCB, MC, V.

[D] [⛤] [⛤] [SC]

★ ★ **QUEEN ANNE.** *1590 Sutter St (94109), west of Union Square.* 415/441-2828; res: 800/227-3970; FAX 415/775-5212. 49 rms, 4 story. No A/C. S, D $99-$175; each addl $10; suites $175-$275; under 12 free; wkly rates. Parking in/out $12. TV; in-rm movies. Crib

$10. Complimentary continental bkfst, afternoon tea & sherry. Ck-out noon, ck-in 3 pm. Meeting rm. Bellhops. Bathrm phones; some wet bars, fireplaces. Restored boarding school for young girls (1890); palms, stained glass, many antiques, carved staircase. Cr cds: A, C, D, DS, JCB, MC, V.

✔★ **SAN REMO.** 2237 Mason St (94133), in North Beach. 415/776-8688; res: 800/352-7366; FAX 415/776-2811. 62 rms, shared baths, 2 story. No rm phones. S $35-$55; D $55-$85; wkly rates. Parking $8. Ck-out 11 am, ck-in 2 pm. Lndry facilities. Italianate Victorian bldg; antiques, art. Cr cds: A, C, D, JCB, MC, V.

★ ★ ★ **SHERMAN HOUSE.** 2160 Green St (94123), Pacific Heights, north of Union Square. 415/563-3600; res: 800/424-5777; FAX 415/563-1882. 14 rms, 4 story. No elvtr. S, D $235-$375; suites $550-$750; under 18 free. Garage $16. TV; cable. Dining rm (by res) 7 am-2 pm, 5:30-9:30 pm. Rm serv 24 hrs. Ck-out noon, ck-in 2 pm. Concierge. Butler service. Bathrm phones; many wet bars. Roman tub, whirlpool in some rms. Private patios, balconies. Built 1876. Each rm individually designed, furnished in French Second Empire, Biedermeier or English Jacobean motifs & antiques. Marble, wood-burning fireplaces; canopy beds; private garden. Cr cds: A, D, MC, V.

★ ★ ★ **STANYAN PARK.** 750 Stanyan St (94117), in Haight-Ashbury. 415/751-1000; FAX 415/668-5454. 36 rms, 3 story, 6 kits. No A/C. S, D $83-$103; suites $130-$180. Municipal parking lot $5. TV. Complimentary continental bkfst, afternoon coffee, tea & cookies. Ck-out noon. Bellhops. Refrigerator in suites. Restored Victorian hotel. Cr cds: A, C, D, DS, MC, V.

★ ★ ★ **VICTORIAN INN ON THE PARK.** 301 Lyon St (94117), in Haight-Ashbury. 415/931-1830; res: 800/435-1967; FAX 415/931-1830. 12 rms, 4 story. No A/C. No elvtr. S, D $99-$159; each addl $20; suites $159-$315. Parking $9. TV in lounge, rm TV avail. Complimentary continental bkfst, coffee, sherry & refreshments. Ck-out noon, ck-in 2 pm. Some fireplaces. Historic building (1897); Victorian decor throughout. Cr cds: A, D, DS, MC, V.

★ ★ **WASHINGTON SQUARE.** 1660 Stockton St (94133), in North Beach. 415/981-4220; res: 800/388-0220; FAX 415/397-7242. 15 rms, 11 with bath, 2 story. No A/C. S, D $85-$180; each addl $10. Valet parking $17. TV avail. Complimentary continental bkfst, afternoon tea, wine. Bkfst rm serv on request. Ck-out noon, ck-in 2 pm. Bellhops. Concierge. Individually decorated rms with English & French country antiques. Opp historic Washington Square. Totally nonsmoking. Cr cds: A, D, JCB, MC, V.

★ ★ ★ **WHITE SWAN.** 845 Bush St (94108), north of Union Square. 415/775-1755; FAX 415/775-5717. 26 rms, 5 story. S, D $145-$160; each addl $15; suites $195-$250. Crib free. Valet parking in/out $17. TV; cable. Complimentary full bkfst, evening refreshments. Restaurant nearby. Ck-out noon, ck-in 2 pm. Airport transportation. Refrigerators. Country English theme; antiques, fireplaces. Each rm individually decorated. Gardens. Totally nonsmoking. Cr cds: A, D, MC, V.

Restaurants

★ ★ **A. SABELLA'S.** 2766 Taylor St, at Fisherman's Wharf. 415/771-6775. Hrs: 11 am-11 pm. Closed Dec 25. Res accepted. Bar. Wine list. A la carte entrees: lunch $7.25-$13.75, dinner $15-$35. Child's meals. Specializes in fresh local seafood. Own cakes, cheese-

cake. Pianist evenings. Dinner theater Fri & Sat (7:30 pm). 1,000 gal crab tank. Overlooks wharf. Family-owned. Cr cds: A, D, JCB, MC, V.

D

★ ★ **ABIQUIU.** 129 Ellis St (94102), south of Union Square. 415/392-5500. Hrs: 11:30 am-3 pm, 5-11 pm. Closed Dec 25. Res accepted. Southwestern menu. Bar to midnight. A la carte entree: lunch $7.95-$16.95, dinner $10.95-$16.95. Specialties: rattlesnakes of caviar, salmon painted desert, enchilada of lamb saddle. Street front dining. Modern decor. Cr cds: A, D, DS, MC, V.

D

★ ★ **THE ACORN.** 1256 Folsom St, south of Union Square. 415/863-2469. Hrs: 11:30 am-2:30 pm, 6-10 pm; Sat from 6 pm; Sat brunch & Sun 10:30 am-2:30 pm. Closed Mon; Jan 1, Dec 25. Res accepted. No A/C. Wine, beer. A la carte entrees: lunch $6.50-$13, dinner $13-$20. Sat & Sun brunch $6-$14. Specializes in fresh organic produce, seafood, pastas. Menu changes daily. Patio dining. Two dining rms. Totally nonsmoking. Cr cds: A, DS, MC, V.

★ ★ **ACQUERELLO.** 1722 Sacramento St, in Russian Hill. 415/567-5432. Hrs: 6-10:30 pm. Closed Sun, Mon; most major hols. Res accepted. Regional Italian menu. Wine, beer. A la carte entrees: dinner $7-$30. Specializes in pasta, seafood. Menu changes every 6 wks. Intimate dining in restored chapel (ca 1930); high-beamed ceiling decorated with gold foil. Local artwork on display. Totally nonsmoking. Cr cds: A, C, D, DS, MC, V.

D

★ ★ ★ **AGUA.** 252 California St, in Financial District. 415/956-9662. Hrs: 11:30 am-2:30 pm, 5:30-10:30 pm; Fri & Sat to 11 pm. Closed Sun; most major hols. Res accepted. Bar. A la carte entrees: lunch $12-$15, dinner $20-$31. Complete meals: dinner $55. Specialties: medallions of ahi tuna (rare) with foie gras in wine sauce, Dungeness crab cakes. Valet parking (dinner). Totally nonsmoking. Cr cds: A, D, MC, V.

D

★ ★ **ALEJANDRO'S.** 1840 Clement, in Richmond District. 415/668-1184. Hrs: 5-10 pm; Fri & Sat to 11 pm; Sun 4-10 pm. Closed Tues; Jan 1-2, Thanksgiving, Dec 25-26. Res accepted. Mexican, Spanish, Peruvian menu. Bar. A la carte entrees: dinner $9-$20. Specialties: paella marinera, paella Valenciana, tapas. Flamenco guitarist/vocalist exc Sun. Spanish decor; pottery display. Cr cds: A, C, D, DS, MC, V.

D

★ ★ ★ **AMELIO'S.** 1630 Powell St, in North Beach. 415/397-4339. Hrs: 5:30-10:30 pm. Closed Dec 25; also 1st 2 wks Jan. Res accepted. No A/C. French menu. Bar. Wine cellar. A la carte entrees: dinner $13-$25. Prix fixe: dinner $70. Specialties: woven pasta with shellfish, Maine lobster, Grand Marnier soufflé in orange shell. Own baking. Valet parking. Traditional San Francisco dining. Intimate, distinctive. Jacket.Totally nonsmoking. Cr cds: A, C, D, DS, JCB, MC, V.

★ **ANGKOR PALACE.** 1769 Lombard St, in Marina District. 415/931-2830. Hrs: 5-10:30 pm. Closed Jan 1, Dec 25. Res accepted wkends. Cambodian menu. Wine, beer. A la carte entrees: dinner $6-$40. Complete meals: dinner $20. Specialties: stuffed chicken legs, barbecued jumbo river prawns, mixed seafood curry platter, royal fire pot of beef, squid, prawns, clams, octopus, fish slices and vegetables. Cambodian decor; gold canopy throne, highly polished wood, antiques. Cr cds: A, MC, V.

D

★ ★ **ANJOU.** 44 Campton Pl, off Stockton St, north of Union Square. 415/392-5373. Hrs: 11:30 am-2:30 pm, 5:30-10 pm. Closed Sun & Mon. Res accepted. French menu. Bar. A la carte entrees: lunch $8-$17, dinner $15-$30. Specialties: Chilean sea bass, confit of duck leg, honey-roasted chicken. Bi-level dining area, high ceilings, modern decor. Cr cds: A, MC, V.

★ ★ **ARIANA'S.** 659 Merchant St, in Financial District. 415/981-1177. Hrs: 11:30 am-2 pm, 5:30-10:30 pm; Fri to 11 pm; Sat 5:30-11 pm. Closed Sun; July 4, Thanksgiving, Dec 25. Res accepted. A la carte entrees: lunch $8.50-$13.95, dinner $11.50-$18.50. Specializes in California cuisine with Mediterranean influence. Pianist Thurs & Fri. Valet parking. Cr cds: A, C, D, DS, MC, V.

✔ ★ **BALBOA CAFE.** 3199 Fillmore St, in Marina District. 415/921-3944. Hrs: 11 am-11 pm; Sat & Sun brunch 10:30 am-3 pm. Bar to 2 am. A la carte entrees: lunch, dinner $7.95-$14.95. Sat, Sun brunch $7-$14.95. Built 1897. Cr cds: A, C, D, DS, MC, V.

★ **BALISTRERI'S.** (1922 Palmetto Ave, Pacifica) 8 mi SW on I-280 to CA 1, then 4 mi S to Palmetto Ave. 415/738-0113. Hrs: 5:30-10 pm. Closed Mon; Jan 1, July 4, Thanksgiving, Dec 24-25. Res accepted wkends. No A/C. Italian menu. Wine, beer. Semi-a la carte: dinner $9.25-$16.95. Child's meals. Specializes in veal, pasta, seafood. Totally nonsmoking. Cr cds: MC, V.

D

✔ ★ ★ **BASTA PASTA.** 1268 Grant St, at Vallego St. in North Beach. 415/434-2248. Hrs: 11:30-1:45 am. Closed some major hols. Res accepted. Italian menu. Bar. Semi-a la carte: lunch $6.95-$14.25. A la carte entrees: dinner $7-$15.25. Specializes in pizza baked in wood-burning oven, pasta, veal, chicken. Valet parking. Outdoor (rooftop) dining. Main dining rm on 2nd floor. Cr cds: A, C, D, DS, JCB, MC, V.

D

★ ★ ★ **THE BIG 4.** (See Huntington Hotel) 415/771-1140. Hrs: 7-10 am, 11:30 am-3 pm, 5:30-10:30 pm; Sat & Sun 7-11 am, 5:30-10:30 pm. Res accepted. Bar 11:30-12:30 am. Wine cellar. Contemporary continental cuisine. A la carte entrees: bkfst $4-$11.95, lunch $7.50-$14.50, dinner $8.50-$28.50. Complete meal: bkfst $15. Specialties: seasonal wild game dishes, lamb sausage with black pepper papardelle noodles, petrale sole with sweet corn and sun-dried tomatoes. Pianist evenings. Valet parking. Turn-of-the-century atmosphere. Cr cds: A, C, D, DS, JCB, MC, V.

★ ★ **BIX.** 56 Gold St, in Financial District. 415/433-6300. Hrs: 11:30 am-11 pm; Fri to midnight; Sat 5:30-midnight; Sun 6-10 pm. Closed major hols. Res accepted. Bar to 1 am. A la carte entrees: lunch $10-$15, dinner $14-$24. Specializes in classic American dishes, seafood. Jazz nightly. Valet parking (dinner). Art deco decor with grand piano; some seating on balcony. Cr cds: A, C, D, DS, JCB, MC, V.

D

★ **BOBBY RUBINO'S.** 245 Jefferson St, at Fisherman's Wharf. 415/673-2266. Hrs: 11:30 am-11 pm. Res accepted. No A/C. Bar. A la carte: lunch $3.95-$12.50, dinner $5.95-$16.95. Child's meals. Specializes in barbecued dishes, fresh fish. Casual, family dining, on two levels. View of fishing fleet. Cr cds: A, D, DS, JCB, MC, V.

SC

✔ ★ ★ **BONTÀ.** 2223 Union St, in Cow Hollow. 415/929-0407. Hrs: 5:30-10:30 pm; Fri & Sat to 11 pm; Sun 5-10 pm. Closed Mon; some major hols. Res accepted. No A/C. Italian menu. Wine, beer. A la carte entrees: dinner $9.50-$15.75. Child's meals. Storefront dining rm. Totally nonsmoking. Cr cds: MC, V.

★ ★ **CAFE PESCATORE.** 2455 Mason St (94133), at Fisherman's Wharf. 415/561-1111. Hrs: 7 am-10 pm; Fri & Sat to 11 pm. Closed Dec 25. Res accepted. Italian, Amer menu. Bar. A la carte entrees: bkfst $5.95-$8.95, lunch $6.95-$12.95, dinner $8.75-$15.95. Child's meals. Specialties: tonno saltimbocca, pollo arrosto. Outdoor dining. Trattoria-style dining with maritime memorabilia. Cr cds: A, C, D, DS, JCB, MC, V.

D

✔ ★ **CAFE RIGGIO.** 4112 Geary Blvd (94118), in Richmond District. 415/221-2114. Hrs: 5-10 pm; Fri & Sat to 11 pm; Sun from 4:30

pm. Closed some major hols. Res accepted. Italian menu. Bar. A la carte entrees: dinner $7.50-$14.50. Child's meals. Specializes in veal, fish, pasta. Casual atmosphere. Cr cds: MC, V.

D

✔ ★ **CAFFE ROMA.** 414 Columbus Ave, in North Beach. 415/391-8584. Hrs: 7 am-11:15 pm; Fri & Sat to 1:15 am; Fri, Sat & Sun brunch to 2 pm. Closed Dec 25. Res accepted. Italian menu. Bar. A la carte entrees: bkfst $3.80-$8, lunch, dinner $5.25-$10. Brunch $3.25-$8.50. Specializes in pizza, pasta dishes, oversize salads. Outdoor dining. Murals on ceiling & walls. Cr cds: MC, V.

D

★ ★ ★ **CAMPTON PLACE.** (See Campton Place Kempinski Hotel) 415/955-5555. Hrs: 7 am-2:30 pm, 5:30-10 pm; Fri to 10:30 pm; Sat 8 am-2:30 pm, 5:30-10:30 pm; Sun 8 am-2:30 pm, 4:30-10 pm. Res accepted. Contemporary American cuisine with regional emphasis. Bar 10 am-11 pm; Fri, Sat to midnight. Extensive wine list. A la carte entrees: bkfst $9-$15, lunch $11-$18, dinner $18-$28. Prix fixe: Sun dinner $29. Sun brunch $9-$16.50. Child's meals. Own baking. Menu changes frequently to reflect fresh seasonal ingredients. Valet parking. Brass wall sconces; Oriental antiques. Jacket (dinner). Cr cds: A, C, D, DS, JCB, MC, V.

D

★ ★ ★ **CARNELIAN ROOM.** 52nd floor of Bank of America Center, 555 California St, in Financial District. 415/433-7500. Hrs: 6-10 pm; Sun brunch 10 am-2:30 pm. Closed Jan 1, Labor Day, Thanksgiving, Dec 25. Res accepted. Bar from 3 pm; Sun from 10 am. Wine cellar. A la carte entrees: dinner $19-$36. Prix fixe: dinner $32. Sun brunch $22.50. Vintage 18th-century decor; antiques. 11 dining rms. Panoramic view of city. Jacket. Cr cds: A, C, D, DS, JCB, MC, V.

D

★ **CHIC'S PLACE.** Pier 39, at Fisherman's Wharf. 415/421-2442. Hrs: 9 am-11 pm. Res accepted. No A/C. Bar. Semi-a la carte: bkfst $4.50-$6.95, lunch $6.95-$10.95, dinner $8.95-$17.95. Specializes in seafood. Own desserts. Parking (Pier 39 garage). View of bay, Alcatraz, Golden Gate Bridge. Cr cds: A, C, D, DS, JCB, MC, V.

★ **CHINA MOON CAFE.** 639 Post St, west of Union Square. 415/775-4789. Hrs: 5:30-10 pm. Closed major hols. Res accepted; required before theater. Chinese menu. Wine. A la carte entrees: dinner $25-$30. Specialties: pot-browned noodle pillow, spring rolls. Art deco cafe. Totally nonsmoking. Cr cds: A, MC, V.

★ ★ **CIAO.** 230 Jackson St, at Front St, in Financial District. 415/982-9500. Hrs: 11:30 am-11 pm; Fri & Sat to midnight; Sun 4-10:30 pm. Closed Thanksgiving, Dec 25. Res accepted. No A/C. Italian menu. Bar. A la carte entrees: lunch, dinner $8-$15. Specializes in mesquite-grilled fresh fish and meats, homemade pasta. Cr cds: A, D, MC, V.

D

★ ★ **CIRCOLO.** 161 Sutter St, in Financial District. 415/362-0404. Hrs: 11:30 am-3 pm, 5-10 pm; Sat from 5 pm. Closed Sun; most major hols. Res accepted. Northern Italian, Mediterranean menu. A la carte entrees: lunch, dinner $8-$15. Specializes in fresh pasta. Jazz Mon-Fri 5-9 pm. Outdoor dining. Elegant fine dining. Cr cds: A, C, D, MC, V.

D

★ ★ ★ **CYPRESS CLUB.** 500 Jackson St, in Financial District. 415/296-8555. Hrs: 5:30-10 pm; Fri & Sat to 11 pm. Closed Jan 1, July 4, Dec 25. Res accepted. Contemporary Amer menu. Bar 4:30 pm-2 am. Wine list. A la carte entrees: dinner $17-$25. Menu changes daily. Whimsical, 1940s-style design. Cr cds: A, D, JCB, MC, V.

D

★ ★ ★ **THE DINING ROOM.** (See The Ritz-Carlton, San Francisco Hotel) 415/296-7465. Hrs: 6-11 pm. Closed Sun. Res accepted. Bar. Wine cellar. Semi-a la carte: dinner $8-$23. Child's meals. Specializes in regional Northern California and French cuisine. Entertainment. Valet parking. Totally nonsmoking. Cr cds: A, C, D, DS, ER, JCB, MC, V.

D

★ **DYNASTY FANTASY.** 6139 Geary Blvd, at 25th Ave, in Richmond District. 415/386-3311. Hrs: 11:30 am-10 pm. Closed Mon; Thanksgiving, Dec 25. Res accepted; required hols. Chinese menu. Wine, beer. A la carte entrees: lunch, dinner $6.50-$20. Specialties: apple chicken, trout in ginger & scallion sauce, Grand Marnier prawns. 3 floors. Cr cds: A, DS, JCB, MC, V.

D

✔★ ★ **ELEVEN.** 374 11th St, at Harrison St, in Civic Center area. 415/431-3337. Hrs: 6-11 pm; Fri & Sat to midnight. Closed Sun; major hols. Res accepted. Italian menu. Bar from 6 pm. A la carte entrees: dinner $7-$12.95. Specializes in pasta, pizza, fresh seafood. Rustic Italian courtyard atmosphere; faux stone walls, trompe l'oeil grapevines, antique wrought-iron gates. Cr cds: A, D, MC, V.

D

★ ★ ★ **ELKA.** (See Miyako Hotel) 415/922-7788. Hrs: 6:30 am-10 pm. Res accepted; required Thurs-Sat (dinner). Franco-Japanese menu. Bar. Wine cellar. A la carte entrees: bkfst $6.50-$9.50, lunch $7-$12, dinner $14-$24. Specializes in distinctive seafood. Parking. Mix of modern American and Oriental decor. Cr cds: A, D, MC, V.

D

★ ★ ★ **EMPRESS OF CHINA.** Top floor of China Trade Center Bldg, 838 Grant Ave, in Chinatown. 415/434-1345. Hrs: 11:30 am-3 pm, 5-11 pm. Chinese menu. Res accepted. Bar. A la carte entrees: lunch $7.50-$10.50, dinner $12.50-$29. Complete meals (for 2 or more persons): lunch $9.50-$16.95, dinner $16.95-$33.95. Specialties: regional delicacies of China. Oriental decor; ancient art objects. View of city, Telegraph Hill. Jacket (dinner). Cr cds: A, D, JCB, MC, V.

✔★ **ENRICO'S SIDEWALK CAFE.** 504 Broadway, in North Beach. 415/982-6223. Hrs: noon-11 pm; Fri & Sat to midnight. Closed Jan 1, Dec 25. Res accepted. No A/C. Mediterranean menu. Bar. A la carte entrees: lunch $8-$10, dinner $8-$15. Jazz. Outdoor dining. Bistro with glass wall, large terrace. Local artwork. Smoking at bar only. Cr cds: A, MC, V.

D

★ ★ **ERIC.** 121 Spear St (94105), in Rincon Center II, in Financial District. 415/777-0330. Hrs: 11:30 am-2:30 pm, 5:30-11:30 pm; Sat from 5:30 pm. Closed Sun; some major hols. Res accepted. Bar. A la carte entrees: lunch $7.50-$14, dinner $10-$19.50. Specialties: rack of lamb, charcoal grilled filet mignon. Valet parking (dinner). Mythological figures painted on ceiling. Totally nonsmoking. Cr cds: A, C, D, JCB, MC, V.

D

★ ★ ★ ★ ★ **ERNIE'S.** 847 Montgomery St, in Financial District. 415/397-5969. Hrs: 6-10:30 pm. Closed Sun; major hols; also 1st 2 wks Jan. Res accepted. Contemporary French cuisine. Bar from 5:30 pm. Wine cellar. A la carte entrees: dinner $24-$30. Prix fixe: dinner $38-$68. Specialties: Dungeness crab & asparagus cake with tomato gelee, roast rack of lamb with spring vegetables, fricasse of Maine lobster with ginger and sauternes, grilled salmon with sweet mustard. Own baking. Valet parking (dinner). Parisian decor. Popular with celebrities. Jacket. Totally nonsmoking. Cr cds: A, C, D, JCB, MC, V.

★ ★ **FINO.** 1 Cosmo Place, south of Union Square. 415/928-2080. Hrs: 5:30-10 pm. Closed major hols. Res accepted. Italian menu. Bar. Semi-a la carte: dinner $8.50-$16.95. Specializes in fresh seafood, fresh pasta. Valet parking. Descending staircase leads to dining area; marble fireplace. Totally nonsmoking. Cr cds: A, D, MC, V.

★ ★ **FIOR D'ITALIA.** 601 Union St, in North Beach. 415/986-1886. Hrs: 11:30 am-10:30 pm. Closed Thanksgiving. Res accepted. No A/C. Northern Italian menu. Bar. A la carte entrees: lunch, dinner $7-$22. Specializes in veal, risotto, homemade pasta. Valet parking. On

Washington Square Park; Tony Bennett memorabilia. Family-owned. Totally nonsmoking. Cr cds: A, C, D, DS, JCB, MC, V.

D

★ ★ ★ ★ **FLEUR DE LYS.** 777 Sutter St, north of Union Square. 415/673-7779. Hrs: 6-10 pm. Closed Sun; Jan 1, July 4, Thanksgiving, Dec 25. Res required. French menu. Bar. Wine list. A la carte entrees: dinner $26-$32. Prix fixe: dinner $62.50. Vegetarian: $50. Specialties: salmon baked in tender corn pancake topped with caviar, oven-roasted lamb loin, chocolate creme brulée. Valet parking. French provincial decor; unusual tapestry ceiling. Jacket. Totally nonsmoking. Cr cds: A, C, D, MC, V.

D

★ **FLOWER LOUNGE.** 5322 Geary Blvd, at 17th Ave, in Richmond District. 415/668-8998. Hrs: 11 am-2:30 pm, 5-9:30 pm; Sat & Sun from 10 am. Res accepted. Chinese menu. Bar. A la carte entrees: lunch $1.80-$7.50, dinner $4-$20. Complete meals: dinner (for 4) $78. Oriental decor. Cr cds: A, D, MC, V.

D

★ ★ **FOG CITY DINER.** 1300 Battery St, in Financial District. 415/982-2000. Hrs: 11:30 am-11 pm; Fri & Sat to midnight. Closed July 4, Thanksgiving, Dec 25. Res accepted. No A/C. Bar. A la carte entrees: lunch, dinner $9-$20. Specializes in seafood. Outdoor dining. Railroad dining car atmosphere. Cr cds: D, DS, JCB, MC, V.

D

✔★ ★ **FOUNTAIN COURT.** 354 Clement St (94118), in Richmond District. 415/668-1100. Hrs: 11 am-3 pm, 5-10 pm. Closed Thanksgiving. Res accepted. Chinese menu. Wine, beer. A la carte entrees: lunch $4-$4.50, dinner $5.50-$9.50. Specializes in Shanghai cuisine, braised catfish, vegetarian chicken. Two-tiered dining rm; modern decor. Cr cds: A, D, MC, V.

D

★ ★ ★ **FOURNOU'S OVENS.** (See Stouffer Renaissance Stanford Court) 415/989-1910. Hrs: 6:30 am-2:30 pm, 5:30-10 pm; Fri & Sat to 10:30 pm; Sun brunch 10 am-2:30 pm. Res accepted; required hols. New American cuisine. Bar. Extensive wine cellar. A la carte entrees: bkfst, lunch $7.50-$13.50, dinner $9-$28. Table d'hôte: dinner $25-$45. Sun brunch $12-$16. Child's meals. Specializes in rack of lamb, farm-raised meats, nightly poultry & fish selections. Own breads, pasta. Valet parking. Several dining areas. On Nob Hill; view of cable cars from dining room. Cr cds: A, C, D, DS, JCB, MC, V.

D

★ ★ **FRANCISCAN.** Pier 43½, at Fisherman's Wharf. 415/362-7733. Hrs: 11 am-10:30 pm; Fri & Sat to 11 pm. Closed Thanksgiving, Dec 25. Res accepted. Bar. A la carte entrees: lunch, dinner $8.50-$30. Child's meals. Specialties: bouillabaisse, halibut à la Florentine, prawns Marsala. Own cheesecake. Announcement of passing ships. View of bay, city. Cr cds: A, MC, V.

D

★ **FRASCATI.** 1901 Hyde St, in Russian Hill. 415/928-1406. Hrs: 5-10:30 pm. Closed Dec 25. Res accepted. No A/C. Roman, Northern Italian menu. Wine list. A la carte entrees: dinner $7.50-$17.95. Specialties: stuzzicarello della casa (appetizer plate), petti di pollo al funghi de bosco, fresh pastas, risotto. Valet parking. Outdoor dining. Storefront location; bistro atmosphere. Cr cds: A, DS, MC, V.

D

★ ★ ★ **FRENCH ROOM.** (See Four Seasons Clift Hotel) 415/775-4700. Hrs: 6:30 am-11 pm; Sat, Sun from 7 am; Sun 10 am-2:30 pm. Res accepted; required Sun & hols. California continental menu. Bar. Award-winning wine list. A la carte entrees: bkfst $8-$12, lunch $10-$20, dinner $22-$35. Prix fixe: 4-course dinner $35. Sun brunch $23. Child's meals. Specializes in beef, veal, lamb, fresh seafood specials. Pianist. Valet parking. Classic decor. Jacket. Cr cds: A, C, D, ER, JCB, MC, V.

D

✔★★ **FRINGALE.** *570 Fourth St, south of Union Square.* 415/543-0573. Hrs: 11:30 am-3 pm, 5:30-10:30 pm; Sat from 5:30 pm. Closed Sun; some major hols. Res accepted. No A/C. French menu. Bar. A la carte entrees: lunch $3-$11.75, dinner $3-$14.75. Upscale bistro fare. Atmosphere of European country cafe. Totally nonsmoking. Cr cds: A, MC, V.

D

★★ **GABBIANOS.** *1 Ferry Plaza (94111), at foot of Market St, in Financial District.* 415/391-8403. Hrs: 11:30 am-2 pm, 5-9 pm; Sun brunch 10:30 am-2 pm. Res accepted. Italian, Amer menu. Bar. A la carte entrees: lunch $6.95-$14.95, dinner $12.25-$19.50. Sun brunch $19.95. Specializes in fresh seafood, pasta. Valet parking. Patio dining. Waterfront views of Alcatraz, Oakland and Mt Tamalpais. Cr cds: A, C, D, DS, JCB, MC, V.

D

★★ **GAYLORD INDIA.** *900 North Point St, in Ghirardelli Square, at Fisherman's Wharf.* 415/771-8822. Hrs: 11:45 am-1:45 pm, 5-10:45 pm; early-bird dinner Mon-Thurs 5-6:30 pm; Sun brunch noon-2:45 pm. Closed Thanksgiving, Dec 25. Res accepted. Indian menu. Bar. Semi-a la carte: lunch $9.25-$13.25, dinner $9.95-$21. Complete meals: dinner $22-$28.75. Specializes in tandoori dishes, Indian desserts. Parking. Spectacular view of bay. Totally nonsmoking. Cr cds: A, C, D, DS, JCB, MC, V.

★★ **GOLDEN TURTLE.** *2211 Van Ness Ave, at Broadway, in Russian Hill.* 415/441-4419. Hrs: 11:30 am-3 pm, 5-11 pm. Closed Mon. Res accepted. Vietnamese menu. Wine, beer. A la carte entrees: lunch $7.50-$17.95, dinner $8.50-$18.95. Specialties: imperial beef, spicy calamari sauté, chili chicken, lemon-grass beef & pork, pan-fried Dungeness crab. Carved wooden panels depict scenes of Vietnamese culture. Cr cds: A, MC, V.

D

✔★★ **GREENS.** *Building A at Fort Mason, in Marina District.* 415/771-6222. Hrs: 11:30 am-2 pm, 5:30-9:30 pm; Mon from 5:30 pm; Fri & Sat 11:30 am-2:15 pm, 6-9:30 pm; Sun brunch 10 am-2 pm. Closed Jan 1, July 4, Thanksgiving, Dec 25. Res accepted. Vegetarian menu. Wine, beer. A la carte entrees: lunch $7-$12, dinner $9-$12.50. Prix fixe: dinner (Fri & Sat) $36. Sun brunch $7-$11. Parking. View of bay. Totally nonsmoking. Cr cds: DS, MC, V.

D

★★★ **HARBOR VILLAGE.** *4 Embarcadero Center, in Financial District.* 415/781-8833. Hrs: 11 am-2:30 pm, 5:30-9:30 pm; Sat from 10:30 am; Sun & hols from 10 am. Res accepted. Chinese menu. Bar. Wine list. A la carte entrees: lunch $2.40-$26, dinner $8-$26. Specializes in Hong Kong-style seafood. Parking. Formal Chinese decor. Cr cds: A, C, D, JCB, MC, V.

D

★★ **HARRIS'.** *2100 Van Ness Ave, in Pacific Heights.* 415/673-1888. Hrs: 6-10 pm; Sat & Sun from 5 pm. Closed Jan 1, Dec 25. Res accepted. A la carte entrees: dinner $16.95-$23.50. Specializes in beef, fresh seafood, Maine lobster. Jazz Fri & Sat. Valet parking. Cr cds: A, D, DS, JCB, MC, V.

D

★★ **HARRY DENTON'S.** *161 Steuart St (94105), in Financial District.* 415/882-1333. Hrs: 7-10 am, 11:30 am-2:30 pm, 5:30-10 pm. Sat & Sun brunch 8 am-3 pm. Cover charge Wed-Sat $3-$10. Closed most major hols. Res accepted. Bar. A la carte entrees: bkfst $2.75-$8, lunch $7.25-$15.95, dinner $7.25-$16.95. Sat & Sun brunch $5.75-$10.95. Specializes in pot roast, fresh seafood, pasta. Entertainment. Valet parking (dinner). Jazz club atmosphere. Cr cds: A, C, D, DS, MC, V.

D

★★ **HAYES STREET GRILL.** *320 Hayes St, in Civic Center area.* 415/863-5545. Hrs: 11:30 am-2 pm, 5-9:30 pm; Fri to 10:30 pm; Sat 6-10:30 pm; Sun 5-8:30 pm. Closed Sun; major hols. Res accepted. Bar. A la carte entrees: lunch $9.50-$17, dinner $13-$25. Specializes in fresh seafood, salads, charcoal-grilled fish. Cr cds: A, D, DS, MC, V.

D

★★★ **HOUSE OF PRIME RIB.** *1906 Van Ness Ave, at Washington St, in Russian Hill.* 415/885-4605. Hrs: 5:30-10 pm; Fri & Sat from 5 pm; Sun from 4 pm; hols from 3 pm. Res accepted. Bar. Wine list. A la carte entrees: dinner $17.95. Semi-a la carte: dinner $18.75-$22.25. Child's meals. Specializes in corn-fed, 21-day aged prime rib of beef, seafood. Prime rib carved at table. Valet parking. Early American decor. Cr cds: A, D, MC, V.

D

✔★ **HUNAN.** *924 Sansome St, in Financial District.* 415/956-7727. Hrs: 11:30 am-9:30 pm. Closed Jan 1, July 4, Thanksgiving, Dec 25. Res accepted. No A/C. Hunan menu. A la carte entrees: lunch, dinner $5-$9.95. Specializes in smoked Hunan dishes. Chinese decor. Cr cds: A, C, D, DS, MC, V.

D

★★ **I FRATELLI.** *1896 Hyde St at Green, in Russian Hill.* 415/474-8603. Hrs: 5-10 pm. Closed major hols, Dec 31. Italian menu. Bar. A la carte entrees: dinner $8-$15. Child's meals. Specializes in homemade pasta. Cafe atmosphere; photos of Italian street scenes. Cr cds: MC, V.

D

★★★ **JULIUS CASTLE.** *1541 Montgomery St, on Telegraph Hill, in North Beach.* 415/362-3042. Hrs: 5-10 pm. Res accepted. No A/C. Contemporary French & Italian menu. Bar. A la carte entrees: dinner $20-$30. Specializes in veal, rack of lamb, seafood. Own pastries, pasta, ice cream. Valet parking. Turreted castle overlooking San Francisco Bay. Totally nonsmoking. Cr cds: A, C, D, DS, MC, V.

★★ **KHAN TOKE THAI HOUSE.** *5937 Geary Blvd, in Richmond District.* 415/668-6654. Hrs: 5-11 pm. Closed Labor Day, Thanksgiving, Dec 25. Res accepted. Thai menu. Wine, beer. A la carte entrees: dinner $4.95-$12.50. Complete meal: dinner $14.95. Specialties: pong pang (seafood), haa sa hai (chicken and beef). Thai classical dancing performance Sun (8 pm). Thai decor and furnishings. Totally nonsmoking. Cr cds: A, MC, V.

D

★★ **KULETO'S.** *221 Powell St, south of Union Square.* 415/397-7720. Hrs: 7-10:30 am, 11:30 am-11 pm; Sat & Sun from 8 am. Closed Labor Day, Thanksgiving, Dec 25. Res accepted. Northern Italian menu. Bar 10 am-midnight. Complete meals: bkfst $4.50-$8.95. A la carte entrees: lunch, dinner $7.50-$16.95. Specializes in grilled fish, chicken, pasta. Italian decor. Cr cds: A, C, D, DS, ER, JCB, MC, V.

D

✔★★ **LA FIAMMETTA.** *1701 Octavia St (94109), in Pacific Heights.* 415/474-5077. Hrs: 5:30-10 pm; Fri & Sat to 10:30 pm; Sun 5-9:30 pm. Closed Mon; Thanksgiving, Dec 25. Res accepted. Italian menu. Wine, beer. A la carte entree: dinner $8.50-$14.50. Specializes in southern Italian & Sicilian cuisine. Trattoria-style dining in corner storefront. Totally nonsmoking. Cr cds: A, D, DS, MC, V.

✔★★ **LA PERGOLA.** *2060 Chestnut St, in Marina District.* 415/563-4500. Hrs: 5:30-10:30 pm; Fri & Sat to 11 pm. Closed most major hols. Res accepted. Northern Italian menu. Wine, beer. A la carte entrees: dinner $12-$15. Cr cds: A, D, JCB, MC, V.

D

★★★ **LE CLUB.** *(4-Star 1994; New owner and chef, therefore not rated) 1250 Jones St, at Clair, on Nob Hill.* 415/771-5400. Hrs: 5-10 pm. Closed Mon; major hols. Res accepted. French, Mediterranean menu. Bar. Wine list. A la carte entrees: dinner $18-$25. Child's meals. Specialties: grilled sea bass, roasted rack of lamb. Valet parking. Florentine mirrors, wood paneling. Jacket. Totally nonsmoking. Cr cds: A, C, D, MC, V.

D

★ ★ ★ **LEGENDS.** (See Mark Hopkins Inter-Continental Hotel) 415/616-6944. Hrs: 6:30 am-11 pm. Res accepted. Bar. A la carte entrees: bkfst $5-$15, lunch $7.50-$19, dinner $18-$26.50. Prix fixe: dinner $25. Child's meals. Specialties: steamed or grilled salmon, sautéed duck foie gras, grilled lamb. Valet parking. 19th-century club atmosphere; oak-paneled walls. Cr cds: A, C, D, ER, JCB, MC, V.

D

★ ★ ★ **LIBERTÉ.** 248 Sutter St, north of Union Square. 415/391-1555. Hrs: 11:30 am-2:30 pm, 5:30-10 pm; Fri & Sat 5:30-11 pm; Sun 5-9 pm. Closed major hols. Res accepted. French, Amer menu. Bar. Wine cellar. A la carte entrees: lunch $8-$17, dinner $12-$18. Specializes in lobster macaroni & cheese, cumin roasted lamb. Own pastries. Fireplace. Smoking in bar only. Cr cds: A, D, MC, V.

D

★ **LOLLI'S CASTAGNOLA.** 286 Jefferson St, at Fisherman's Wharf. 415/776-5015. Hrs: 9 am-11 pm. Closed Dec 25. Bar. Semi-a la carte: bkfst $3.95-$9.95, lunch, dinner $7-$26.45. Child's meals. Specializes in seafood. Valet parking lunch. Outdoor dining. View of fishing fleet. Cr cds: A, C, D, DS, JCB, MC, V.

★ ★ **MAC ARTHUR PARK.** 607 Front St, in Financial District. 415/398-5700. Hrs: 11:30 am-3:30 pm, 5-10 pm; Fri to 11 pm; Sat from 5 pm; Sun 4:30-10 pm. Closed Thanksgiving, Dec 25. Res accepted. No A/C. Bar. A la carte entrees: lunch, dinner $7.95-$18.95. Specializes in barbecued ribs, mesquite-grilled fish. Valet parking. Outdoor dining. Cr cds: A, C, D, MC, V.

D

★ ★ **MANDARIN.** 900 North Point St, in Ghirardelli Square, at Fisherman's Wharf. 415/673-8812. Hrs: 11:30 am-11 pm. Closed Thanksgiving, Dec 25. Res accepted. Northern Chinese, mandarin menu. Bar. Semi-a la carte: lunch $8.95-$13, dinner $13-$35. Complete meals: dinner $16-$38. Mandarin banquet for 8 or more, $25-$38 each. Specialties: minced squab, beggar's chicken (1-day notice), Peking duck (1-day notice). Valet parking. Chinese decor; beautifully tiled floor, artifacts. 19th-century structure. View of bay. Cr cds: A, C, D, JCB, MC, V.

★ ★ **MARRAKECH MOROCCAN.** 419 O'Farrell St, south of Union Square. 415/776-6717. Hrs: 6-10 pm. Res accepted. Moroccan menu. Bar. Prix fixe: dinner $19.95-$23.95. Specialties: chicken with lemon, lamb with honey, couscous fassi, b'stila. Belly dancing. Valet parking. Seating on floor pillows or low couches. Moroccan decor. Unusual dining experience. Cr cds: A, DS, MC, V.

★ ★ ★ **MASA'S.** (See Vintage Court) 415/989-7154. Hrs: 6-9:30 pm. Closed Sun & Mon; 2 wks in Jan & 2 wks in July. Res accepted. French menu. Bar. Wine cellar. Prixe fixe: dinner $68 & $75. Specialties: foie gras sautéed with Madeira truffle sauce, lobster salad with crispy leeks and truffle vinaigrette, sautéed medaillions of New Zealand venison. Valet parking. Intimate dining in elegant surroundings. Cr cds: A, C, D, DS, JCB, MC, V.

D

★ ★ **MOOSE'S.** 1652 Stockton St, between Union & Filbert Sts, in North Beach. 415/989-7800. Hrs: 11:30 am-2:30 pm, 5:30-10 pm; Fri & Sat to 11 pm; Sun brunch 10:30 am-3 pm. Closed some major hols. Res accepted. Bar. Wine cellar. A la carte entrees: lunch $4.75-$13.75, dinner $4.75-$24. Sun brunch $2.95-$12.95. Child's meals. Specializes in Mediterranean, Italian cuisine with California elements. Jazz pianist evenings. Valet parking. Exhibition kitchen. Dining rm accented with terrazzo tile and ceramics; expansive views of Washing-

ton Square Park. Large bronze "moose" near entry. Cr cds: A, D, MC, V.

D

★ ★ **NEW JOE'S.** 347 Geary St, west of Union Square. 415/397-9999. Hrs: 7 am-11 pm. Res accepted. Contemporary Italian menu. Bar. A la carte entrees: bkfst $5-$8, lunch $6-$14, dinner $10-$19. Child's meals. Specialties: linguine Portofino, bisticca con Pepe, pizza margharita. Mahogany paneling and moldings. Mural of city. Cr cds: A, C, D, DS, JCB, MC, V.

D

★ ★ ★ **NORTH BEACH.** 1512 Stockton St, at Columbus, in North Beach. 415/392-1700. Hrs: 11:30-1 am. Closed some major hols. Res accepted. Northern Italian menu. Wine cellar. A la carte entrees: lunch $8.50-$24, dinner $10.75-$29. Complete meals: lunch, dinner from $22.95. Specializes in fresh fish, veal, pasta. Valet parking. Cr cds: A, C, D, DS, JCB, MC, V.

★ ★ **NORTH INDIA.** 3131 Webster St, at Lombard St, in Marina District. 415/931-1556. Hrs: 11:30 am-2:30 pm, 5-11 pm; Sat from 5 pm; Sun 5-10 pm. Res accepted. Northern Indian menu. Bar. Semi-a la carte: lunch $6.95-$9.95, dinner $9.95-$22.50. Child's meals. Specializes in tandoori seafood, lamb & poultry, fresh vegetables. Own desserts. Paintings of Moghul and Bengal lancers. Kitchen tours. Cr cds: A, C, D, DS, MC, V.

D

★ ★ ★ **PACIFIC GRILL.** (See Pan Pacific Hotel) 415/771-8600. Hrs: 6:30 am-10 pm; Sun brunch 10 am-2 pm. Res accepted. Bar 11 am-11:30 pm. Wine list. A la carte entrees: bkfst $5-$10, lunch $7.50-$14, dinner $15-$22. Sun brunch $10-$15. Child's meals. Specializes in Pacific Rim cuisine with French accent. Pianist. Valet parking. Modern decor; atrium setting in lobby of hotel. Cr cds: A, C, D, DS, ER, JCB, MC, V.

D

✔★ ★ **PACIFIC HEIGHTS BAR & GRILL.** 2001 Fillmore St, in Pacific Heights. 415/567-3337. Hrs: 11:30 am-9:30 pm; Fri & Sat to 10:30 pm; Mon & Tues 5:30-9:30 pm. Closed Thanksgiving, Dec 24 & 25. Res accepted. Bar 11:30 am-midnight; Fri & Sat to 1 am. A la carte entrees: lunch $5.95-$9.95, dinner $9.95-$15.95. Specializes in bistro-style food. Oyster bar. Own pastries. Cr cds: A, C, D, MC, V.

★ ★ **PALIO D'ASTI.** 640 Sacramento St, at Montgomery St, in Financial District. 415/395-9800. Hrs: 11:30 am-9:30 pm; Thurs & Fri to 10:30 pm; Sat 5:30-10 pm. Closed Sun; major hols. Res accepted. Italian menu. Bar. A la carte entrees: lunch $9-$16.50, dinner $9-$18.75. Child's meals. Speciaizies in risotto, seafood, mezzelune alla monferrina. Valet parking. Exhibition pasta-making and pizza-making kitchens; wood-burning ovens. Cr cds: A, C, D, DS, MC, V.

D

★ ★ ★ **PARK GRILL.** (See Park Hyatt Hotel) 415/296-2933. Hrs: 6:30 am-11 pm; Sun brunch 10 am-2:30 pm. Res accepted. Bar 11-1 am. Wine list. A la carte entrees: bkfst $7-$12, lunch $8-$16, dinner $8-$16. Sun brunch $21.50. Child's meals. Specializes in mixed grills. Own baking. Pianist. Valet parking. Outdoor dining. Club rm atmosphere; original art. Cr cds: A, C, D, DS, ER, JCB, MC, V.

D

★ ★ ★ **POSTRIO.** (See The Prescott Hotel) 415/776-7825. Hrs: 7-10 am, 11:30 am-2 pm, 5:30-10 pm; Sat & Sun from 5:30 pm; Sat & Sun brunch 9 am-2 pm. Closed July 4, Thanksgiving, Dec 25. Res required. California, Oriental menu. Bar 11:30-2 am. Wine list. A la carte entrees: bkfst $5-$15, lunch $10-$18, dinner $20-$35. Specialties: Chinese duck, roasted salmon. Own baking. Valet parking. Bi-level seating under skylight; custom Oriental light fixtures. Cr cds: A, C, D, MC, V.

D

★ **THE POT STICKER.** *150 Waverly Place, in Chinatown.* *415/397-9985.* Hrs: 11:30 am-9:45 pm. Closed Thanksgiving; also Dec 20-25. Res accepted. No A/C. Hunan/Mandarin menu. A la carte entrees: lunch, dinner $5.25-$18. Complete meals: lunch $3.50-$4.95, dinner $7.95-$9.95. Specialties: pot stickers, Szechwan crispy fish, orange spareribs. Cr cds: A, MC, V.

★ ★ **PREGO.** *2000 Union St, in Cow Hollow. 415/563-3305.* Hrs: 11:30 am-midnight. Closed Thanksgiving, Dec 25. Res accepted. Northern Italian menu. Bar to 1 am. A la carte entrees: lunch, dinner $5.75-$17.95. Specialties: carpaccio, agnolotti d'aragosta, pizza baked in wood-burning oven, meats & fowl cooked on a rotisserie. Cr cds: A, C, D, MC, V.

D

✔ ★ **RAMIS CAFE.** *1361 Church St, in Mission District.* *415/641-0678.* Hrs: 11:30 am-3 pm, 4-10 pm; Sat & Sun from 4 pm; Sat & Sun brunch 8 am-4 pm. Closed Thanksgiving, Dec 25. Res accepted. Middle Eastern, California menu. Wine, beer. A la carte entrees: lunch $4.50-$9.95, dinner $9.95-$14.95. Sat & Sun brunch $4.50-$8.95. Specialties: sesame chicken pasta, cheese blintzes. Patio dining. Built 1903; changing art display monthly. Totally nonsmoking. Cr cds: A, DS, MC, V.

D 🚭

★ ★ **RUE LEPIC.** *900 Pine St, at Mason St, on Nob Hill.* *415/474-6070.* Hrs: 11:30 am-2:30 pm, 5:30-10 pm; Sat 5:30-10 pm; Sun 5:30-10 pm. Closed most major hols. Res accepted; required wkends. French menu. A la carte entrees: lunch $6-$17, dinner $17-$21. Complete meals: dinner $31-$35. Specialties: roast medallion of veal with mushroom sauce, Maine lobster, roasted rack of lamb with garlic. Totally nonsmoking. Cr cds: A, MC, V.

★ **SCHROEDER'S.** *240 Front St, in Financial District.* *415/421-4778.* Hrs: 11 am-9 pm; Sat from 4:30 pm. Closed Sun; major hols. Res accepted. German, Amer menu. Bar. Semi-a la carte: lunch $7.50-$16, dinner $9.50-$18.50. Child's meals. Specializes in baked chicken & noodles, sauerbraten, Wienerschnitzel. Menu changes daily. German decor, murals. Established 1893. Family-owned. Cr cds: A, D, DS, MC, V.

SC

★ **SCOMA'S.** *Pier 47, at Fisherman's Wharf. 415/771-4383.* Hrs: 11:30 am-10:30 pm; Fri, Sat to 11 pm. Closed Thanksgiving, Dec 24, 25. Italian menu. Bars. A la carte entrees: lunch $11-$44. Child's meals. Specialties: calamari, cioppino, scampi. Valet parking. View of fishing fleet. Originally fisherman's shack. Family-owned. Cr cds: A, C, D, DS, JCB, MC, V.

D

★ ★ **SCOTT'S SEAFOOD GRILL AND BAR.** *2400 Lombard St, in Marina District. 415/563-8988.* Hrs: 11:30 am-10:30 pm; Fri & Sat to 11 pm; Sun brunch 11 am-3 pm. Closed Thanksgiving, Dec 25. Res accepted. Bar. A la carte entrees: lunch $7.50-$16.50, dinner $8.50-$18.50. Sun brunch $6.50-$16.50. Specializes in fresh seafood. Cr cds: A, D, MC, V.

D **SC**

★ ★ **THE SHADOWS.** *1349 Montgomery St, on Telegraph Hill, in North Beach. 415/982-5536.* Hrs: 5-10 pm. Closed Mon-Thurs. Res accepted. No A/C. Country French menu. Bar. A la carte entrees: dinner $18-$24. Specializes in duck, lamb, fresh seafood. Own pastries, pasta, ice cream. Valet parking. Chalet overlooking San Francisco Bay. Cr cds: A, C, D, DS, MC, V.

★ ★ **SILKS.** *(See Mandarin Oriental Hotel) 415/986-2020.* Hrs: 7-10:30 am, 11:30 am-2 pm, 6-10 pm. Res accepted. Bar 11 am-11 pm. Wine list. A la carte entrees: bkfst $6.75-$19, lunch $15-$25, dinner $25-$40. Prix fixe: dinner $48. Specializes in California cuisine with Asian accents. Own pastries. Valet parking. Original paintings by local artists. Cr cds: A, C, D, DS, JCB, MC, V.

D

★ ★ **SPLENDIDO.** *Embarcadero Center Four, promenade level, in Financial District. 415/986-3222.* Hrs: 11:30 am-2:30 pm, 5:30-10 pm; Thurs-Sun to 10:30 pm. Closed major hols. Res accepted. Mediterranean menu. Bar. A la carte entrees: lunch $11.50-$15.75, dinner $13-$17.95. Specializes in seared pepper tuna, baked goods. Own pasta, sausages, ice cream. Outdoor dining. Cr cds: A, C, D, DS, MC, V.

D

★ ★ ★ **STARS.** *150 Redwood Alley, at Van Ners Ave, in Civic Center area. 415/861-7827.* Hrs: 11:30 am-2:30 pm, 5:30-11:30 pm; Sat from 5:30 pm. Closed Thanksgiving, Dec 25. Res accepted. Bar from 11 am; wkends from 4 pm. A la carte entrees: lunch $8-$18, dinner $19.50-$28. Pianist. Daily changing menu. Oyster bar. Bistro decor. Cr cds: A, D, MC, V.

D

★ ★ **SWISS LOUIS.** *Pier 39, at Fisherman's Wharf. 415/421-2913.* Hrs 11:30 am-10 pm; Sat & Sun brunch 10:30 am-3:30 pm. Closed Dec 25. Res accepted. No A/C. Italian menu. Bar. Semi-a la carte: lunch $9.50-$15, dinner $11.50-$25. Sat & Sun brunch $10.50. Child's meals. Specializes in veal dishes, seafood. Own desserts. View of bay, Golden Gate Bridge. Cr cds: A, C, D, DS, JCB, MC, V.

D

★ **TADICH GRILL.** *240 California St, in Financial District.* *415/391-1849.* Hrs: 11 am-9 pm; Sat from 11:30 am. Closed Sun; major hols. Bar. A la carte entrees: lunch, dinner $12-$25. Child's meals. Specializes in fresh seafood. Also counter serv. Turn-of-the-century decor. Established in 1849; family-owned since 1928. Cr cds: MC, V.

D

★ ★ ★ **TOMMY TOY'S.** *655 Montgomery St, in Financial District. 415/397-4888.* Hrs: 11:30 am-3 pm, 6-10 pm; Sat & Sun from 6 pm. Closed Jan 1, Dec 25. Res accepted; required wkends. Chinese menu. Bar. A la carte entrees: lunch $11.95-$14.95, dinner $14-$17.95. Table d'hôte: lunch $11.95. Prix fixe: dinner $38-$48. Specializes in seafood, breast of duckling. Valet parking (dinner). 19th-century Chinese decor. Antiques. Jacket. Cr cds: A, C, D, DS, MC, V.

D

✔ ★ ★ **TUBA GARDEN.** *3634 Sacramento Ave (94118), in Pacific Heights. 415/921-8822.* Hrs: 11 am-2:30 pm; Sat & Sun from 10 am. Closed Dec 25. Res accepted. Continental menu. Wine, beer. Semi-a la carte: lunch $8-$10. Child's meals. Specializes in chicken salad Hawaii, cheese blintzes, Belgian waffles. Own desserts. Outdoor dining. Victorian house with original art. Smoking in garden only. Cr cds: A, C, D, MC, V.

★ ★ **WATERFRONT.** *Pier 7, the Embarcadero at Broadway, in Financial District. 415/391-2696.* Hrs: 11:30 am-10:30 pm; Sun brunch 10 am-3 pm. Closed July 4, Dec 25. Res accepted. No A/C. Bar 11 am-10:30 pm. A la carte entrees: lunch $9-$22, dinner $12-$39. Sun brunch $7.95-$12. Specializes in seafood from around the world, including fresh abalone. Valet parking. Outdoor dining. View of harbor. Cr cds: A, C, D, DS, MC, V.

D

★ ★ **WU KONG.** *101 Spear St, in Rincon Center, south of Union Square. 415/957-9300.* Hrs: 11 am-2:30 pm, 5:30-10 pm. Res accepted. Chinese menu. Bar. A la carte entrees: lunch $5.95-$15.95, dinner $7.95-$20. Complete meals: lunch $8-$12, dinner $15-$30. Specializes in dim sum & Peking duck. Valet parking. Outdoor dining. Oriental decor. Atrium with fountain. Cr cds: A, D, JCB, MC, V.

D

★ ★ **YAMATO.** *717 California St, in Chinatown. 415/397-3456.* Hrs: 11:45 am-2 pm, 5-10 pm. Closed Mon; Jan 1, Thanksgiving, Dec 25. Res accepted. Japanese menu. Bar. A la carte entrees: lunch, dinner $7.75-$23. Complete meals: lunch $7.75-$11.75, dinner $10.50-$23. Specializes in sukiyaki, tempura, chicken or steak teriyaki. Sushi bar. Traditional Japanese decor. Indoor gardens.

Some rms with floor & well seating. Family-owned. Cr cds: A, C, D, JCB, MC, V.

✔★ ★ **YANK SING.** *427 Battery St, in Financial District.* *415/781-1111.* Hrs: 11 am-3 pm; Sat & Sun 10 am-4 pm. Res accepted. Chinese menu. Bar. Semi-a la carte: lunch $12-$15. Specialties: dim sum cuisine. Tableside carts in addition to menu. Cr cds: A, D, MC, V.

★ **YOSHIDA-YA.** *2909 Webster St, in Cow Hollow.* *415/346-3431.* Hrs: noon-2 pm, 5-10:30 pm; Fri to 11 pm; Sat 5-11 pm; Sun 5-10:30 pm. Closed Jan 15, July 4, Thanksgiving eve & Thanksgiving Day, Dec 25. Japanese menu. Bar. Complete meals: dinner $20-$25. Specialties: sushi, yakitori. Oriental decor; traditional dining upstairs. Cr cds: A, C, D, DS, JCB, MC, V.

D

★ ★ **ZUNI CAFE.** *1658 Market St, in Civic Center area.* *415/552-2522.* Hrs: 7:30 am-midnight; Sun to 11 pm; Sun brunch 11 am-3 pm. Closed Mon; some hols. Res accepted. Bar. A la carte entrees: bkfst $3-$5, lunch $7.50-$16, dinner $20-$35. Sun brunch $7.50-$15. Own desserts. Pianist Fri & Sat. Outdoor dining. Changing art displays of local artists. Cr cds: A, MC, V.

D

Unrated Dining Spots

CAFÉ LATTÉ. *100 Bush St, 2nd fl, north of Union Square.* *415/989-2233.* Hrs: 7-9:30 am, 11:30 am-3 pm. Closed Sat, Sun; major hols. No A/C. Nouvelle California/northern Italian menu. Wine, beer. Avg ck: bkfst $3.50, lunch $7. Specializes in fresh fish, fresh pasta, salads. Stylish cafeteria in landmark art deco skyscraper; mirrored deco interior with marble counters, tray ledges, floors. Cr cds: A, C, D, MC, V.

DAVID'S. *474 Geary St, west of Union Square.* *415/771-1600.* Hrs: 7-1 am; Sat, Sun from 8 am. Closed Jewish high hols. Jewish deli menu. Beer, wine. Semi-a la carte: bkfst $3.35-$9.75, lunch $4.95-$9.95, dinner from $6.95. Complete meal: dinner $16.95. Specializes in chopped chicken liver, stuffed cabbage, cheese blintzes. Cr cds: A, C, D, JCB, MC, V.

DOTTIE'S TRUE BLUE CAFE. *522 Jones St, west of Union Square.* *415/885-2767.* Hrs: 7:30 am-2 pm. No A/C. Wine, beer. Semi-a la carte: bkfst $3-$7.50, lunch $3.50-$7.50. Specializes in all-American bkfst. Traditional coffee shop. No cr cds accepted.

GHIRARDELLI CHOCOLATE MANUFACTORY. *900 North Point St, on grounds of Ghirardelli Square, at Fisherman's Wharf.* *415/771-4903.* Hrs: 10 am-midnight; winter to 11 pm; Fri, Sat to midnight. Closed Thanksgiving, Dec 25. Soda fountain & chocolate shop. Specializes in ice cream sundaes, premium chocolates. Own candy making, ice cream toppings. Parking. Located in former chocolate factory; built in late 1890s. Totally nonsmoking. Cr cds: MC, V.

ISOBUNE. *1737 Post St, in Japantown.* *415/563-1030.* Hrs: 11:30 am-10 pm. Closed Jan 1-3, Thanksgiving, Dec 25. Japanese sushi menu. Wine, beer. A la carte entrees: lunch $5-$8, dinner $10-$12. Specializes in sashimi. Dining at counter; selections pass in front of diners on small boats. Cr cds: MC, V.

JUST DESSERTS. *3 Embarcadero Center, in lobby, in Financial District.* *415/421-1609.* Hrs: 7 am-6 pm; Sat 9 am-5 pm. Closed Sun; most major hols. A la carte entrees: pastries, cakes, muffins $2.50-$4. Specializes in cheesecake. Own baking. Outdoor dining. Modern cafe atmosphere. Cr cds: MC, V.

D SC

MIFUNE. *1737 Post St, in Japantown.* *415/922-0337.* Hrs: 11 am-9:30 pm. Closed Jan 1-3, Thanksgiving, Dec 25. Japanese menu. A la carte entrees: lunch, dinner $3.50-$13. Specializes in noodle dishes. Own noodles. Validated parking. Cr cds: A, C, D, DS, MC, V.

MO'S GOURMET HAMBURGERS. *1322 Grant Ave (94133), in North Beach.* *415/788-3779.* Hrs: 11:30 am-10:30 pm; Fri,

Sat to 11:30 pm. Closed Dec 25. Wine, beer. Semi-a la carte: lunch, dinner $4.75-$7.75. Specializes in grilled or charbroiled hamburgers. Casual dining with art deco design. Kitchen with rotating grill over lava rocks at front window. Cr cds: MC, V.

D

SALMAGUNDI. *442 Geary St, west of Union Square.* *415/441-0894.* Hrs: 11 am-11 pm; Sun & Mon 11 am-9 pm. Closed Thanksgiving, Dec 25. Wine, beer. Soup, salad, roll $3-$7; dessert extra; pasta torte. Specialty: oven-baked onion soup. Own soups. Cr cds: A, MC, V.

D SC

TRIO CAFE. *1870 Fillmore St, in Pacific Heights.* *415/563-2248.* Hrs: 8 am-6 pm; Sun 10 am-4 pm. Closed Mon; Easter, Thanksgiving; also Dec 24-Jan 2. Eclectic menu. Bar. A la carte entrees: bkfst, lunch $4-$6. Outdoor dining in cafe setting. Store front entrance. Totally nonsmoking. No cr cds accepted.

San Francisco Airport Area

Motels

★ ★ **COMFORT SUITES.** *(121 E Grand Ave, South San Francisco 94080)* 2 mi N on US 101, E Grand Ave exit. 415/589-7766; FAX 415/588-2231. 165 suites, 3 story. S $59-$69; D $69-$89; each addl $10; under 18 free. TV; cable, in-rm movies. Complimentary continental bkfst. Coffee in rms. Ck-out noon. Meeting rms. Valet serv. Free airport, RR station transportation. Whirlpool. Health club privileges. Refrigerators. Grill. Cr cds: A, C, D, DS, ER, JCB, MC, V.

D ✈ 🏊 SC

★ ★ **COURTYARD BY MARRIOTT.** *(1050 Bayhill Dr, San Bruno 94066)* 1½ mi N on US 101 to jct I-380 W, then 1 mi W to El Camino Real South (CA 82), then 1 blk S to Bayhill Dr. 415/952-3333; FAX 415/952-4707. 147 rms, 2-3 story. S $95-$105; each addl (after 4th person) $10; suites $115-$125; under 13 free; lower rates wkends. Crib free. TV; cable, in-rm movies. Indoor pool. Complimentary coffee in rms. Restaurant 6:30 am-1 pm, 4 pm-11 pm. Ck-out 1 pm. Coin lndry. Meeting rms. Valet serv. Sundries. Free airport transportation. Exercise equipt; weight machine, bicycles, whirlpool. Balconies. Cr cds: A, C, D, DS, MC, V.

D 🏊 🏃 ✈ 🚭

✔★ ★ **MILLWOOD INN.** *(1375 El Camino Real, Millbrae 94030)* 1 mi SE on US 101, then ½ mi W on Millbrae Ave to El Camino Real (CA 82), then 1 mi NW. 415/583-3935; res: 800/345-1375; FAX 415/875-4354. 34 rms, 2 story. S $54-$64; D $58-$68; suites $66-$82; kit. units $54/wk addl; wkly rates exc summer. Crib $4. TV; cable. Complimentary continental bkfst. Coffee in rms. Restaurant nearby. Ck-out 11 am. Coin lndry. Bathrm phones, refrigerators. Cr cds: A, C, D, DS, ER, JCB, MC, V.

D ✈ 🚭 SC

★ ★ **RAMADA HOTEL AIRPORT NORTH.** *(245 S Airport Blvd, South San Francisco 94080)* 2 mi N on US 101, off S Airport Blvd exit. 415/589-7200; FAX 415/588-5007. 319 rms, 2 story. S $70-$100; D $73-$110; each addl $10; under 18 free; wkend rates. Crib free. Pet accepted, some restrictions. TV; cable, in-rm movies. Pool. Restaurant 6 am-10 pm. Rm serv. Bar. Ck-out 2 pm. Coin lndry. Meeting rms. Bellhops. Gift shop. Barber shop. Airport transportation. Cr cds: A, C, D, DS, ER, JCB, MC, V.

Motor Hotels

★ ★ **BEST WESTERN EL RANCHO INN.** (1100 El Camino Real, Millbrae 94030) 1 mi SE on US 101, then 1/2 mi W on Millbrae Ave to El Camino Real (CA 82), then 1 mi NW. 415/588-8500; FAX 415/871-7150. 300 rms, most A/C, 1-3 story. S $74-$84; D $84-$94; each addl $5; kit. units, suites $110-$150; under 18 free. Crib free. Pet accepted, some restrictions. TV; cable, in-rm movies. Heated pool. Coffee in rms. Restaurant 6 am-11 pm. Rm serv. Bar. Ck-out 1 pm. Coin lndry. Meeting rms. Bellhops. Valet serv. Sundries. Free airport transportation. Exercise equipt; weights, bicycles, whirlpool. Some refrigerators. Cr cds: A, C, D, DS, ER, JCB, MC, V.

D ✦ ≋ 🏃 ✈ ⛷ 🔥 SC

★ ★ **RAMADA-AIRPORT.** (1250 Old Bayshore Hwy, Burlingame 94010) 1 mi SW on US 101. 415/347-2381; FAX 415/348-8838. 145 rms, 3 story. S $88; D $98; each addl $10; suites $120-$160; under 18 free; wkend rates. Crib free. TV; cable. Heated pool. Restaurant 6:30 am-10 pm. Rm serv 6:30-9:30 am, 6-10 pm. Bar 11 am-10 pm; entertainment. Ck-out noon. Meeting rm. Bellhops. Valet serv. Concierge. Free airport transportation. Health club privileges. Refrigerators avail. Wet bar in suites. Cr cds: A, C, D, DS, ER, JCB, MC, V.

D ≋ 🏃 ✈ ⛷ 🔥 SC

Hotels

★ ★ ★ **CLARION-SAN FRANCISCO AIRPORT.** (401 E Millbrae Ave, Millbrae 94030) 1 mi SE on US 101, then E on Millbrae Ave. 415/692-6363; FAX 415/697-8735. 440 rms, 2-6 story. S $90-$125; D $110-$135; each addl $10; suites $175-$250; under 16 free; wkend rates. Crib free. TV; cable. Heated pool. Restaurant 6 am-11 pm. Bar 10-2 am. Ck-out noon. Convention facilities. Gift shop. Free airport transportation. Exercise equipt; weights, bicycles, whirlpool. Refrigerator in suites. Some private patios, balconies. Cr cds: A, C, D, DS, ER, JCB, MC, V.

D ✦ ≋ 🏃 ✈ ⛷ 🔥 SC

★ ★ ★ **CROWN STERLING SUITES-SOUTH SAN FRANCISCO.** (250 Gateway Blvd, South San Francisco 94080) 2 mi N on US 101, E Grand Ave exit, then N on Gateway Blvd. 415/589-3400; FAX 415/876-0305. 312 suites, 10 story. S $119-$129; D $129-$139; each addl $10; under 12 free; wkend rates. Crib free. TV; cable, in-rm movies. Indoor pool; whirlpool, sauna. Complimentary full bkfst. Complimentary coffee in rms. Restaurant 11 am-11 pm. Bar 11-1 am; entertainment. Ck-out 1 pm. Coin lndry. Meeting rms. Gift shop. Free airport transportation. Health club privileges. Refrigerators. Balconies. Cr cds: A, C, D, DS, ER, JCB, MC, V.

D ≋ ✈ ⛷ 🔥 SC

★ ★ **DOUBLETREE.** (835 Airport Blvd, Burlingame 94010) 2 mi S on US 101. 415/344-5500; FAX 415/340-8851. 291 rms, 8 story. S $99-$129; D $109-$139; each addl $10; suites $150-$300; under 17 free. Crib free. Pet accepted, some restrictions; $20 non-refundable. TV; cable. Restaurant 6:30 am-10 pm. Bar 11 am-11:30 pm. Ck-out noon. Meeting rms. Gift shop. Free airport transportation. Exercise equipt; weight machine, bicycles. Refrigerator, wet bar in suites. Cr cds: A, C, D, DS, ER, JCB, MC, V.

D ≋ 🏃 ✈ ⛷ 🔥 SC

★ ★ ★ **HILTON SAN FRANCISCO AIRPORT.** (Box 8355, San Francisco 94128) At San Francisco Intl Airport. 415/589-0770; FAX 415/589-4696. 527 rms, 3 story. S $145-$165; D $165-$185; each addl $20; suites $275-$500; family, wkend rates. Crib free. TV; cable. Heated pool; poolside serv. Restaurant 6 am-11 pm. Bar; entertainment. Ck-out noon. Convention facilities. Concierge. Free airport transportation. Exercise equipt; weights, bicycles, whirlpool. Minibars; bathrm phone in suites. Balconies. Cr cds: A, C, D, DS, ER, JCB, MC, V.

D ≋ 🏃 ✈ ⛷ 🔥 SC

★ ★ ★ **HOLIDAY INN-CROWNE PLAZA.** (600 Airport Blvd, Burlingame 94010) 1 1/2 mi S on US 101 to Broadway exit, then E to Airport Blvd, then 1 mi along bay. 415/340-8500; FAX 415/343-1546. 405 rms, 15 story. S $119-$124; D $124-$134; each addl $10; suites $250-$300; under 18 free; wkend rates. Crib free. TV; cable, in-rm movies. Indoor pool. Restaurant 6 am-midnight. Bar 11-1:30 am; entertainment. Ck-out noon. Coin lndry. Meeting rms. Gift shop. Free covered parking. Free airport transportation. Exercise equipt; weights, bicycles, whirlpool, sauna. Refrigerators avail. **LUXURY LEVEL : CROWNE LEVEL.** 30 rms, 2 suites. S $119; D $129; suites $300. Wet bar. Complimentary continental bkfst, refreshments, newspaper. Cr cds: A, C, D, DS, JCB, MC, V.

D ≋ 🏃 ✈ ⛷ 🔥 SC

★ ★ ★ **HYATT REGENCY-SAN FRANCISCO AIRPORT.** (1333 Bayshore Hwy, Burlingame 94010) Off US 101 Broadway exit. 415/347-1234; FAX 415/696-2669. 793 rms, 9 story. S $129-$205; D $154-$230; each addl $25; suites $200-$720; under 18 free; wkend rates. Crib free. Valet parking $9. TV; cable. Heated pool. Supervised child's activities (Fri, Sat evenings). Restaurant 6:30 am-11 pm. Rm serv 24 hrs. Deli open 24 hrs. Bar 11-1 am. Ck-out noon. Convention facilities. Concierge. Gift shop. Free airport transportation. Exercise equipt; weight machine, bicycles, whirlpool, sauna. Some bathrm phones, wet bars. Refrigerators avail. Atrium. **LUXURY LEVEL : REGENCY CLUB.** 72 rms, 4 suites. S $180; D $180-$205; suites $600-$720. Private lounge, honor bar. Bathrm phones. Complimentary continental bkfst, evening refreshments. Cr cds: A, C, D, DS, ER, JCB, MC, V.

D ≋ 🏃 ✈ ⛷ 🔥 SC

★ ★ ★ **MARRIOTT AIRPORT.** (1800 Old Bayshore Hwy, Burlingame 94010) 1 mi SE on US 101, then E on Millbrae Ave to Old Bayshore Hwy, then SE on San Francisco Bay. 415/692-9100; FAX 415/692-8016. 683 rms, 11 story. S $159; D $179; suites $450-$600; under 18 free; wkend, wkly rates. Crib free. Pet accepted, some restrictions. Valet parking $10. TV; cable, in-rm movies. Indoor pool; poolside serv. Restaurant 6 am-11 pm. Rm serv 24 hrs. Bar; entertainment, dancing. Ck-out noon. Coin lndry. Convention facilities. Concierge. Gift shop. Free airport transportation. Exercise equipt; weights, bicycles, whirlpool, sauna. Some bathrm phones, refrigerators. **LUXURY LEVEL : CONCIERGE LEVEL.** 55 rms. S, D $179. Private lounge. Wet bar. Bathrm phones. Free bkfst, refreshments. Cr cds: A, C, D, DS, ER, JCB, MC, V.

D ✦ ≋ 🏃 ⛷ ✈ ⛷ 🔥 SC

★ ★ **RADISSON.** (1177 Airport Blvd, Burlingame 94010) 1 1/2 mi S on US 101 to Broadway exit, then E to Airport Blvd. 415/342-9200; FAX 415/342-1655. 301 rms, 10 story. S $100-$130; D $110-$140; each addl $10; suites $175-$250; under 16 free; wkend rates. Crib free. Pet accepted, some restrictions. TV; cable, in-rm movies. Indoor/outdoor pool. Restaurant 6 am-11 pm. Bar; entertainment. Ck-out 1 pm. Coin lndry. Convention facilities. Concierge. Gift shop. Barber, beauty shop. Free airport transportation. Free covered parking. Exercise equipt; weights, bicycles, whirlpool. Cr cds: A, C, D, DS, ER, MC, V.

D ✦ ≋ 🏃 ✈ ⛷ 🔥 SC

★ ★ ★ **THE WESTIN-SAN FRANCISCO AIRPORT.** (One Old Bayshore Hwy, Millbrae 94030) 1 mi SE on US 101, then E on Millbrae Ave to Old Bayshore Hwy. 415/692-3500; FAX 415/872-8111. 388 rms, 7 story. S, D $155-$185; each addl $20; suites $375-$475; under 18 free; wkend rates. Crib free. Pet accepted, some restrictions. Valet parking $7. TV; cable. Indoor pool; poolside serv. Restaurant 6 am-10 pm. Rm serv 24 hrs. Bar 11 am-midnight; entertainment. Ck-out 1 pm. Convention facilities. Concierge. Gift shop. Free airport transportation. Exercise equipt; weight machine, bicycles, whirlpool, sauna. Refrigerators, minibars. **LUXURY LEVEL : EXECUTIVE CLUB.** 78 rms. S, D $180-$200; each addl $20. Private lounge. Complimentary continental bkfst, refreshments. Cr cds: A, C, D, DS, ER, JCB, MC, V.

D ≋ ✦ ≋ 🏃 ✈ ⛷ 🔥 SC

Restaurant

★ ★ ★ **EMPRESS COURT.** *(433 Airport Blvd, Burlingame) 1¹/₂ mi SE on US 101 to Broadway exit, then NE to Airport Blvd, then 1 mi E along bay.* 415/348-1122. Hrs: 11:30 am-2:30 pm, 5-10 pm; Fri & Sat to 9:30 pm. Res accepted. Chinese menu. Bar. Complete meals (4 or more): lunch from $5.95, dinner $14.25-$32. A la carte entrees: dinner from $9.95. Peking banquet for 4, $27.95 each. Specialties: barbecued baby quail and minced squab, Szechwan spice beef, lemon chicken. Parking. Lavish Sung dynasty decor; aviary, pond. On 5th floor; view of bay. Cr cds: A, DS, MC, V.

[D]

Seattle

Founded: 1852

Pop: 516,259

Elev: 125 feet

Time zone: Pacific

Area code: 206

Seattle is among the youngest of the world's major cities. Nestled between Puget Sound and Lake Washington, the city grew up along the shores of Elliott Bay, a natural harbor that today welcomes more than 2,000 commercial deep-sea vessels a year.

Named for a friendly Native American chief, Seattle offered a great harbor and seemingly unlimited stands of timber. Soon a sawmill and a salmon-canning plant were in operation. Isolated at the fringe of the continent, Seattle had great resources but few women, an obvious threat to the growth of the community. Asa Mercer, a civic leader and first president of the territorial university, went east and persuaded 11 proper young women from New England to sail back with him to take husbands among the pioneers; the idea proved so successful that Mercer repeated the trip, this time recruiting 100 Civil War widows. Today many of Seattle's old families proudly trace their lines to the "Mercer girls."

When a ship arrived from Alaska in 1897 carrying a "ton of gold," the great Yukon Gold Rush was on, converting Seattle into a boomtown. Seattle has remained the natural gateway to Alaska because of the protected Inland Passage. The commercial interests of the two have remained tightly interwoven. The 1915 opening of the Panama Canal nearly halved the passage time between the East and West coasts, creating a tremendous stimulant to Seattle's economy.

Seattle has prospered from the products of its surrounding forests, farms and waterways. It continues to serve as a provisioner to Alaska and the Orient. In recent years, it has acquired a new dimension from the manufacture of jet aircraft, missiles and space vehicles, which are among the city's most important products.

Business

There are more than 2,200 industrial firms located in the city, but industry represents only about one-fourth of the city's economy. The Boeing Company, still the largest manufacturer of commercial aircraft in the world, employs the greatest number of people.

About 15 million tons of cargo are handled each year in the Port of Seattle. The city has become a major container port for the Pacific Rim.

Convention Facilities

Seattle Center is a network of buildings where any convention, meeting or banquet can be accommodated.

The Arena is a multipurpose room seating as many as 6,100 people. The exhibit area has 15,600 square feet of space. Banquets for as many as 1,500 people can be arranged.

The Coliseum, measuring 125,000 square feet and with a capacity of 15,000, is used for concerts, exhibitions, conventions and trade shows.

The Exhibition Hall has 40,000 square feet for display; for dining, the seating capacity is 3,500 persons. This hall can also be converted into a ballroom.

The Flag Pavilion seats 1,200 for meetings and has 17,000 square feet for exhibition space.

The Opera House is a beautifully constructed, modern theater seating more than 3,000 people; in addition there are 7 separate conference areas of various sizes. The lower level, the Mercer Forum, has 8 meeting rooms, each seating as many as 285.

The playhouse, a smaller theater with a seating capacity of 900, provides an artistic setting for imaginative convention utilization. The Bagley Wright Theater has a seating capacity of 850. Throughout the complex, there are a number of meeting rooms, with seating capacities of 180 to 750 persons. They can be used either singly or in combination with any major Seattle Center structure.

The 204,000-square-foot Washington State Convention and Trade Center accommodates more than 10,000 people. It also boasts a 50,000-square-foot convertible exhibition space on its upper level.

The Seattle Trade Center, near Pier 70, has trade show and banquet facilities. Its 55,000-square-foot area is divided into booths of varying sizes surrounding an atrium.

The multipurpose Kingdome is located across town from the Seattle Center. In addition to a 65,000-seat stadium, it has 153,000 square feet of floor space, making it the largest exhibit hall in the Pacific Northwest.

Sports and Recreation

Seattle's spectator sports are centered in the all-weather Kingdome. Playing their home games here are the NFL Seattle Seahawks and the American League Seattle Mariners. The NBA Supersonics play in the nearby Coliseum.

Seattle offers superb outdoor opportunities and spectacular scenery. The freshwater lakes and inlets of Puget Sound are ideal for waterskiing and freshwater and saltwater fishing, and the nearby mountain ranges offer hunting, backpacking and skiing.

Entertainment

Seattle has an international reputation for its fine arts organizations. Among them are the Seattle Symphony Orchestra and the Seattle Opera, both of which perform at the Opera House. The Pacific Northwest Ballet presents a mixed repertoire in the Opera House. Performing at the Bagley Wright Theater is the Seattle Repertory Theatre. A Contemporary Theatre (ACT) presents innovative pieces.

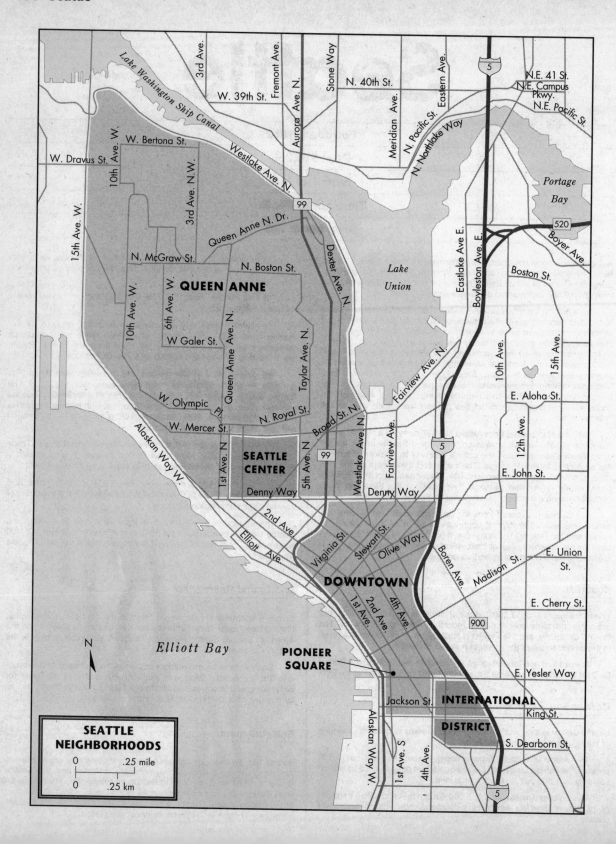

QUEEN ANNE

SEATTLE CENTER

DOWNTOWN

PIONEER SQUARE

INTERNATIONAL DISTRICT

Lake Union

Portage Bay

Elliott Bay

SEATTLE NEIGHBORHOODS

0   .25 mile

0   .25 km

N

SEATTLE / TACOMA INTERNATIONAL AIRPORT

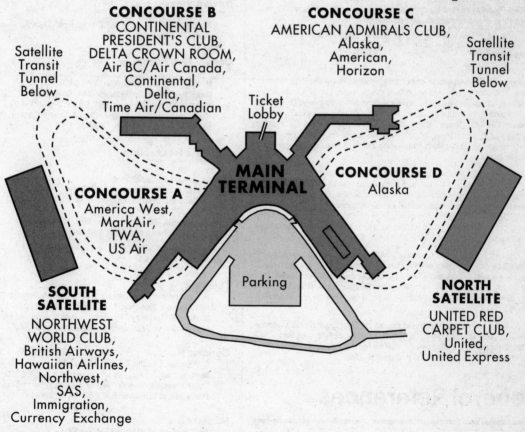

Terminals
Parking Lot

CONCOURSE B
CONTINENTAL
PRESIDENT'S CLUB,
DELTA CROWN ROOM,
Air BC/Air Canada,
Continental,
Delta,
Time Air/Canadian

CONCOURSE C
AMERICAN ADMIRALS CLUB,
Alaska,
American,
Horizon

Satellite
Transit
Tunnel
Below

Satellite
Transit
Tunnel
Below

Ticket
Lobby

**MAIN
TERMINAL**

CONCOURSE A
America West,
MarkAir,
TWA,
US Air

CONCOURSE D
Alaska

Parking

**SOUTH
SATELLITE**

NORTHWEST
WORLD CLUB,
British Airways,
Hawaiian Airlines,
Northwest,
SAS,
Immigration,
Currency Exchange

**NORTH
SATELLITE**

UNITED RED
CARPET CLUB,
United,
United Express

Historical Areas

Pioneer Square is Seattle's most historic neighborhood. In the middle and late 1800s this was an area of prosperity. After the Klondike Gold Rush in 1897 and 1898, the entire section became known as "skid row," a term that originated in Seattle for an area once used to skid logs. The term later came to describe streets peopled with derelicts. In 1954 a group of interested citizens began restoring the Pioneer Square area. By 1970, the city recognized the district as Seattle's birthplace and an historic site that had to be preserved. This area of Old Seattle is thriving again as the Pioneer Square Historic District.

Pioneer Square is a mélange of art galleries, antique stores, bookshops, saloons, cafes and restaurants. The Klondike Gold Rush Museum details the history of the gold rush and its effect on Seattle.

The Museum of History and Industry tells the story of the city's first hundred years. Exhibits include an old-time fashion gallery, mementos of the Alaskan Gold Rush and souvenirs of the Alaska-Yukon-Pacific Exposition of 1909. The museum also displays old cable cars, Native American canoes, early vehicles and firefighting equipment.

Pike Place Market is a seven-acre maze of craft tables, fish, meat and produce stalls, musicians and painters.

Sightseeing

Because of its hill-and-water geography, Seattle is an exciting town to explore. The city's park system offers many recreational areas. Freeway Park is a five-acre oasis built over a downtown freeway. Discovery Park contains more than 391 acres of urban wilderness and is home for the Indian Cultural Center. Stroll through the International District for authentic Far Eastern food, goods and celebrations. Take the waterfront streetcar under Alaskan Way along Elliott Bay to see ships of all nations in port.

Southeast of Seattle is Mount Rainier National Park. Majestic Mount Rainier towers 14,410 feet above sea level and is part of the 378-square-mile park, which contains 34 waterfalls, 62 lakes, about 40 glaciers, centuries-old trees and hundreds of subalpine meadows lush with wildflowers. The park offers mountain climbing—for expert mountaineers only—and 300 miles of hiking trails, which lead to primitive wilderness sections.

Olympic National Park, within a half day's drive, occupies 1,400 square miles of wilderness on the Olympic Peninsula. The west side of the park receives excessive rainfall, creating a moss-covered rain forest of Sitka spruce, western hemlock, Douglas fir and western red cedar. Glacier-capped mountains contrast with miles of unspoiled beaches.

Lying between the northwest corner of Washington and Vancouver Island, British Columbia, are 172 islands called the San Juan Islands, famous for their history as well as for their beauty. Ferries from Anacortes make stops at the four largest islands.

General References

Founded: 1852 **Pop:** 516,259 **Elev:** 125 feet **Time zone:** Pacific **Area code:** 206

Phone Numbers

POLICE & FIRE: 911
FBI: 622-0460
POISON CONTROL CENTER: 526-2121
TIME: 976-1616   **WEATHER:** 526-6087

Information Source

Seattle/King County Convention and Visitors Bureau, 520 Pike St, Suite 1300, 98101; 461-5840.
Parks & Recreation Department, 684-4075.

Transportation

AIRLINES: Air Canada; Alaska; America West; American; British Airways; Continental; Delta; Hawaiian; Northwest; SAS; Thai; TWA; United; USAir; and other commuter and regional airlines. For the most current airline schedules and information consult the *Official Airline Guide,* published twice monthly.
AIRPORT: Sea-Tac International, 431-4444.
CAR RENTAL AGENCIES: (See Toll-Free Numbers) Avis 433-5238; Budget 243-2400; Dollar 433-6766; Hertz 682-5050; Thrifty 246-7565.
PUBLIC TRANSPORTATION: Metro Transit System 553-3000.
RAILROAD PASSENGER SERVICE: Amtrak 800/872-7245.

Newspapers

Seattle Daily Journal of Commerce; Seattle Post-Intelligencer; Seattle Times.

Convention Facilities

Kingdome, 201 S King St, 296-3128.
Seattle Center, 305 Harrison St, 684-7200.
Seattle Trade Center, 2601 Elliott Ave, 441-3000.
Washington State Convention & Trade Center, 800 Convention Place, E of 7th & Union, 447-5000.

Sports & Recreation

Major Sports Facilities
Arena, Seattle Center, 684-7200.
Coliseum, Seattle Center, 684-7200 (Supersonics, basketball, 281-5800).
Kingdome, 201 S King St, 296-3128 (Seahawks, football, 827-9777; Mariners, baseball, 628-3555).

Cultural Facilities

Theaters
A Contemporary Theatre (ACT), 100 W Roy St, 285-5110.
5th Avenue Theater, 1308 5th Ave, 625-1900.
Seattle Repertory Theater, Seattle Center, 443-2222.
University of Washington theaters, 543-4880.

Concert Halls
Coliseum, Seattle Center, 684-7200.
Meany Hall, University of Washington, 543-4880.
Opera House, Seattle Center (Opera & Symphony), 684-7200.
Paramount Theatre, 907 Pine St, 682-1414.

Museums
Burke Memorial-Washington State Museum, Univ of Washington, 17th Ave NE & NE 45th St, 543-5590.
Children's Museum, Center House, Seattle Center, 441-1768.
Coast Guard Museum, Pier 36, 1519 Alaskan Way S, 217-6993.
Museum of Flight, 9404 E Marginal Way S, 764-5720.
Museum of History and Industry, 2700 24th Ave E, north side of WA 520, 324-1125.
Nordic Heritage Museum, 3014 NW 67th St, 789-5707.
Pacific Science Center, Seattle Center, 200 2nd Ave N, 443-2001.
Puget Sound & Snoqualmie Valley Railroad, Snoqualmie Falls, 746-4025.

Art Museums and Galleries

Charles and Emma Frye Art Museum, 704 Terry Ave, 622-9250.
Davidson Galleries, 313 Occidental Ave S, 624-7684.
Northwest Craft Center and Gallery, Seattle Center, 728-1555.
Seattle Art Museum, 100 University St, 654-3100.
William Traver Gallery, 110 Union St, 587-6501.
Woodside & Braseth Galleries, 1533 9th Ave, at Pine St, 622-7243.

Points of Interest

Historical

Klondike Gold Rush National Historical Park, 117 S Main St, 553-7220.
Pioneer Square, S edge of downtown area, bounded by 1st Ave, James St & Yesler Way.

Other Attractions

Alki Beach Park, Alki Ave SW & 59th Ave SW.
Center House, Seattle Center, 305 Harrison St, 684-7200.
Chateau Ste Michelle Winery, 15 mi NE, via WA 405, at 14111 NE 145th St in Woodinville, 488-1133.
Discovery Park, 3801 W Government Way, 386-4236.
Evergreen Floating Bridge, on WA 520, near Montlake Pl.
Fisherman's Terminal, seen from Ballard Bridge.
Freeway Park, 6th & Seneca.
Fun Forest Amusement Park, 305 Harrison St, in Seattle Center, 728-1585.
Golden Gardens Park, N end of Seaview Ave NW.
Green Lake and Park, Aurora Ave (WA 99), between N 65th & 72nd Sts, 684-4960.
Hiram H. Chittenden Locks, NW 54th St, Ballard.
Indian Cultural Center, Discovery Park, 285-4425.
International District, 4th Ave to I-5 & Yesler Way to S Dearborn St.
International Fountain, Seattle Center.
Lake Washington Floating Bridge, seen from Lake Washington Blvd & from Lakeside Ave.
Monorail, Seattle Center, runs between Center House and Westlake Center, 684-7340.
Mount Baker-Snoqualmie National Forest, E & S of city, reached via I-90, 220-7450.
Mt Rainier National Park, S via I-5.
Myrtle Edwards/Elliott Bay Parks, N of Pier 70.
Pike Place Market, 1st Ave & Pike St, 682-7453.
Seattle Aquarium, Pier 59, Waterfront Park, 386-4320.
Seattle Center, 305 Harrison St, 684-7200.
Shilshole Bay Marina, 7001 Seaview Ave NW, 728-3385.
Smith Cove, seen from Elliott Ave & W Garfield St.
Snoqualmie Falls, 30 mi E via I-90.
Space Needle, Seattle Center, 443-2111 or 800/937-9582.

Tillicum Village, Blake Island State Park, 443-1244.
University of Washington, 17th Ave NE & NE 45th St, 543-9198.
Warren G. Magnuson Park, NE 65th & Sand Point Way NE.
Washington Park Arboretum & Japanese Garden, both sides of Lake Washington Blvd between E Madison & Montlake, 543-8800.
Waterfront Drive, Alaskan Way along Elliott Bay.
Waterfront Park, Alaskan Way, Pier 57 to Pier 59.
Woodland Park Zoological Gardens, Phinney Ave N between N 50th & N 59th Sts, 684-4800.

Sightseeing Tours

Bill Speidel's Underground Tour, 610 1st Ave, 682-1511.
Ferry Trips, Seattle Ferry Terminal, Colman Dock, foot of Madison St, 464-6400 or 800/843-3779 (WA).
Gallant Lady Cruises, Lake Union, 463-2073.
Gray Line bus tours, 720 S Forest, 624-5813 or 800/426-7532.
Seattle Harbor Tours, from Pier 55, foot of Seneca St, 623-4252

Annual Events

Folklife Festival, Seattle Center. Memorial Day wkend.
Pacific Northwest Arts & Crafts Fair, 4 mi E in Bellevue. Late July.
Seattle Seafair, events throughout the city. Late July-early Aug.
Bumbershoot, Seattle Center. Labor Day wkend.

City Neighborhoods

Many of the restaurants, unrated dining establishments and some lodgings listed under Seattle include neighborhoods as well as exact street addresses. A map showing these neighborhoods can be found immediately following the city introduction. Geographic descriptions of these areas are given, followed by a table of restaurants arranged by neighborhood.

Downtown: South of Denny Way, west of I-5, north of S King St and east of Alaskan Way and Elliot Bay. **North of Downtown:** North of E Denny Way. **South of Downtown:** South of Dearborn St. **East of Downtown:** East of I-5.
International District: Southeast of Downtown; south of Yesler St, west of I-5, north of S Dearborn St and east of 4th Ave S.
Pioneer Square: Downtown area on and around Pioneer Square, bounded by 1st and James Sts, Yesler Way and 1st Ave S.
Queen Anne: South of W Nickerson St and Washington Ship Canal, west of Aurora Ave N, north of Denny Way and east of Elliot Ave W and 15th St W.
Seattle Center: South of Mercer St, west of 5th Ave N, north of Denny Way and east of 1st Ave N.

Lodgings and Food

SEATTLE RESTAURANTS
BY NEIGHBORHOOD AREAS

(For full description, see alphabetical listings under Restaurants)

INTERNATIONAL DISTRICT

Four Seas. 714 S King St

Linyen. 424 7th Ave S

DOWNTOWN

Campagne. 86 Pine St

Clippers. 409 Olive Way

Cutter's Bay House. 2001 Western Ave

Dahlia Lounge. 1904 Fourth Ave

Elliott's Oyster House. 1203 Alaskan Way

Franco's Hidden Harbor. 1500 Westlake Ave N

Fuller's (Sheraton Hotel & Towers). 1400 6th Ave

Georgian Room (Four Seasons Olympic Hotel). 411 University St

Hunt Club (Sorrento Hotel). 900 Madison St

Il Bistro. 93A Pike St

A Jays. 2619 First Ave

Labuznik. 1924 1st Ave

Maximilien-In-The-Market. 81A Pike Place

Metropolitan Grill. 820 2nd Ave

McCormick & Schmick's. 1103 First Ave

McCormick's Fish House. 722 Fourth Ave

Old Spaghetti Factory. 2801 Elliott Ave

Painted Table (Alexis Hotel). 1007 1st Ave

Palomino. 1420 5th Ave

Prego (Stouffer Madison Hotel). 515 Madison St

Ruth's Chris Steak House. 800 5th Ave

Tlaquepaque. 1122 Post Ave

Union Square Grill. 621 Union St

Wild Ginger. 1400 Western Ave

NORTH OF DOWNTOWN

Arnie's Northshore. 1900 N Northlake Way

Ave! Al Ristorante Italiano. 4743 University Way NE

Cactus. 4220 E Madison

Chinook's. 1900 W Nickerson

Cucina! Cucina!. 901 Fairview Ave N

Hiram's At The Locks. 5300 34th St NW

Ivar's Indian Salmon House. 401 NE Northlake Way

Le Gourmand. 425 NW Market St

Ray's Boathouse. 6049 Seaview Ave

Serafina. 2043 Eastlake Ave E

Stella's Trattoria. 4500 9th Ave

Surrogate Hostess, A Seasonal Kitchen Cafeteria. 746 19th Ave E

Tatsumi. 4214 University Way NE

EAST OF DOWNTOWN

Rover's. 2808 E Madison St

PIONEER SQUARE

Al Boccalino. 1 Yesler Way

F.X. McRory's Steak, Chop & Oyster House. 419 Occidental Ave S

Trattoria Mitchelli. 84 Yesler Way

QUEEN ANNE

Adriatica. 1107 Dexter N

Canlis. 2576 Aurora Ave N

Kaspar's. 19 W Harrison St

Latitude 47. 1232 Westlake N

Reiner's. 1106 Eighth Ave

SEATTLE CENTER

Space Needle. 203 Sixth Ave N

Note: *When a listing is located in a town that does not have its own city heading, it will appear under the city nearest to its location. In these cases, the address and town appear in parenthesis immediately following the name of the establishment.*

Motels

★ ★ **BEST WESTERN LOYAL INN.** *2301 8th Ave (98121), at Denny Way, downtown.* 206/682-0200; FAX 206/467-8984. 91 rms, 4 story. July-Sept: S $82; D $88; each addl $6; suites $185; under 12 free; lower rates rest of yr. Crib $4. TV; cable. Restaurant opp open 24 hrs. Ck-out noon. Meeting rms. Whirlpool; sauna. Some refrigerators, wet bars. Cr cds: A, C, D, DS, MC, V.

★ **DAYS INN.** *2205 7th Ave (98121), at Blanchard St, downtown.* 206/448-3434; FAX 206/441-6976. 90 rms, 3 story, no ground floor rms. S $80; D $85-$110; each addl $7; under 18 free. Crib free. Pet accepted, some restrictions; $3. TV; cable. Restaurant 6:30 am-10 pm. Bar 11 am-midnight. Ck-out noon. Cr cds: A, C, D, DS, JCB, MC, V.

★ ★ **QUALITY INN CITY CENTER.** *2224 8th Ave (98121), downtown.* 206/624-6820; FAX 206/467-6926. 72 rms, 7 story. May-Oct: S $80-$90; D $88-$98; each addl $10; suites $135-$155; under 18 free; lower rates rest of yr. Crib free. Pet accepted. TV; cable. Continental bkfst. Ck-out 1 pm. Meeting rms. Valet serv. Sundries. Whirlpool, sauna. Some refrigerators. Balconies. Cr cds: A, C, D, DS, ER, JCB, MC, V.

✔ ★ **TRAVELERS INN.** *(4710 Lake Washington Blvd NE, Renton 98056)* S on I-405, exit 7. 206/228-2858; res: 800/633-8300; FAX 206/228-3055. 117 rms, 2-3 story. No elvtr. S $34.95; D $41.95; each addl $4; suites $55.95; under 12 free. Crib free. TV; cable. Heated pool. Complimentary coffee in lobby. Restaurant adj open 24 hrs. Bar 11-2 am. Ck-out 11 am. Cr cds: A, D, DS, MC, V.

✔ ★ ★ **TRAVELODGE BY THE SPACE NEEDLE.** *200 6th Ave N (98109), at Seattle Center.* 206/441-7878; FAX 206/448-4825. 88 rms, 4 story. June-Sept: S $65-$95; D $81-$119; each addl $6; under 18 free; lower rates rest of yr. Crib free. TV; cable. Heated pool; whirlpool. Complimentary continental bkfst. Coffee in rms. Restaurant nearby. Ck-out noon. Valet serv. Cr cds: A, C, D, DS, ER, JCB, MC, V.

Motor Hotels

★ ★ **BEST WESTERN EXECUTIVE INN.** *200 Taylor Ave N (98109), at Seattle Center.* 206/448-9444; FAX 206/441-7929. 123 rms, 5 story. S $92-$118; D $103-$143; each addl $10; suites $125-$175; under 12 free. Crib free. TV; cable. Restaurant 6:30 am-10 pm; wkend from 7 am. Rm serv. Bar 11-2 am. Ck-out noon. Meeting rms. Bellhops. Valet serv. Sundries. Airport, RR station, bus depot transportation avail. Exercise equipt; weight machine, rowing machine, whirlpool. Some refrigerators. Cr cds: A, C, D, DS, JCB, MC, V.

D ⟨icons⟩ SC

★ ★ **DOUBLETREE INN.** *205 Strander Blvd (98188), I-5, I-405 Southcenter exit, south of downtown.* 206/246-8220; FAX 206/575-4749. 200 rms, 2 story. S $84-$94; D $94-$104; each addl $10; suites $102-$112; wkend rates. Crib free. Pet accepted, some restrictions; $20 non-refundable. TV; cable. Heated pool; poolside serv. Playground. Restaurant 6:30 am-10 pm. Rm serv. Bar 11-2 am; entertainment, dancing Fri, Sat. Ck-out noon. Meeting rms. Bellhops. Valet serv. Free airport transportation. Health club privileges. Some refrigerators; wet bar in suites. Some private patios, balconies. Cr cds: A, C, D, DS, ER, JCB, MC, V.

D ⟨icons⟩ SC

★ ★ ★ **EDGEWATER INN.** *2411 Alaskan Way (98121), Pier 67 (98121), west of downtown.* 206/728-7000; res: 800/624-0670; FAX 206/441-4119. 237 rms, 4 story. S $115-$145; D $120-$200; each addl $15; suites $250; under 18 free. Crib free. Valet parking. TV; cable. Restaurant 6 am-10 pm. Rm serv. Bar 11-12:30 am; entertainment Tues-Sat. Ck-out noon. Meeting rms. Bellhops. Valet serv. Gift shop. Exercise equipt; bicycles, rowing machine. Health club privileges. Guest bicycles. Minibars. Some balconies. Built entirely over water; adj to ferry terminal. Cr cds: A, C, D, DS, ER, JCB, MC, V.

D ⟨icons⟩ SC

✔ ★ ★ **SIXTH AVENUE INN.** *2000 6th Ave (98121), downtown.* 206/441-8300; res: 800/648-6440; FAX 206/441-9903. 166 rms, 5 story, no ground floor rms. S $79-$83; D $94-$100; each addl $12; suites $132; under 17 free. Crib free. TV; cable. Restaurant 6:30 am-10 pm. Rm serv 7 am-9 pm. Bar 11 am-midnight. Ck-out noon. Meeting rms. Bellhops. Valet serv. Sundries. Cr cds: A, C, D, MC, V.

⟨icons⟩ SC

★ ★ **UNIVERSITY INN.** *4140 Roosevelt Way NE (98105), north of downtown.* 206/632-5055; res: 800/733-3855; FAX 206/547-4937. 102 rms, 4 story. S $75-$95; D $85-$109; each addl $10; under 18 free; wkly rates. Crib free. TV; cable. Heated pool. Complimentary coffee in rms. Complimentary continental bkfst. Restaurant nearby. Ck-out noon. Meeting rms. Valet serv. Exercise equipt; weight machine, stair machine, whirlpool. Balconies. Cr cds: A, D, MC, V.

D ⟨icons⟩ SC

Hotels

★ ★ ★ **ALEXIS HOTEL.** *1007 1st Ave (98104), downtown.* 206/624-4844; res: 800/426-7033; FAX 206/621-9009. 54 rms, 4 story. S, D $170-$205; suites $220-$325; under 12 free; some wkend rates. Crib free. Covered valet parking $13/day. TV; cable. Complimentary continental bkfst. Restaurant 6:30 am-3 pm (also see PAINTED TABLE). Rm serv 24 hrs. Bar 11-1 am. Ck-out 1 pm. Meeting rms. Concierge. Shopping arcade. Tennis privileges. Health club privileges. Steam bath. Bathrm phones; refrigerators. Wet bar, beverages, whirlpool in suites. Some balconies. 15 languages spoken. Rms individually decorated; 6 wood-burning fireplaces. All serv charges included, no tipping allowed for hotel serv; bar & restaurant tipping recommended. Complimentary newspaper. A unique, small hotel. Cr cds: A, C, D, DS, MC, V.

D ⟨icons⟩

★ ★ ★ **DOUBLETREE SUITES.** *16500 Southcenter Pkwy (98188), I-5 Southcenter exit, south of downtown.* 206/575-8220; FAX 206/575-4743. 221 suites, 8 story. S $125-$135; D $140-$150; each

addl $15; under 18 free; wkend rates. Crib free. Pet accepted, some restrictions; $20 non-refundable. TV; cable. Indoor pool; outdoor pool privileges in summer. Complimentary bkfst. Restaurant 6:30 am-10 pm; wkends 7 am-11 pm. Rm serv. Bar 11-2 am. Ck-out noon. Meeting rms. Gift shop. Free airport transportation. Exercise equipt; weight machine, bicycles, whirlpool, sauna. Racquetball. Refrigerators. Atrium lobby. Cr cds: A, C, D, DS, ER, JCB, MC, V.

D ⟨icons⟩ SC

★ ★ ★ ★ **FOUR SEASONS OLYMPIC HOTEL.** *411 University St (98101), downtown.* 206/621-1700; FAX 206/682-9633. 450 rms, 13 story. S $195-$225; D $225-$255; each addl $20; suites $245-$1,150; under 18 free; wkend rates. Crib free. Valet parking $15. TV; cable. Indoor pool; poolside serv. Restaurant (see GEORGIAN ROOM). Rm serv 24 hrs. Bar 11-2 am; dancing Fri & Sat. Ck-out 1 pm. Convention facilities. Concierge. Shopping arcade. Barber, beauty shop. Airport transportation. Exercise rm; instructor, weight machine, bicycles, whirlpool, sauna. Massage. Bathrm phones, minibars; some refrigerators. Complimentary newspaper. Historic landmark. Cr cds: A, C, D, ER, JCB, MC, V.

D ⟨icons⟩

★ ★ ★ **HILTON.** *Box 1927 (98111), 6th Ave & University St, W of I-5 Seneca-Union exit, downtown.* 206/624-0500; FAX 206/682-9029. 237 rms, 28 story. S $159-$184; D $174-$199; each addl $10; suites $295-$395; under 18 free; some wkend rates. Crib free. Garage $9.50. TV; cable. Restaurant 6 am-10 pm; dining rm 5:30-10 pm. Rm serv 24 hrs. Bar 11-2 am; pianist. Ck-out 1 pm. Meeting rms. Concierge. Gift shop. Exercise equipt; weight machines. Refrigerator in suites. View of Puget Sound. Cr cds: A, C, D, DS, ER, JCB, MC, V.

D ⟨icons⟩

★ ★ **HOLIDAY INN CROWNE PLAZA.** *1113 6th Ave (98101), at Seneca St, downtown.* 206/464-1980; FAX 206/340-1617. 415 rms, 34 story. S $130-$150; D $150-$170; each addl $20; suites $168-$300; under 18 free; wkend rates. Crib free. Covered valet parking $13. TV; cable. Restaurant 6 am-10 pm. Bar 11-2 am. Ck-out noon. Meeting rms. Concierge. Exercise equipt; weight machine, bicycles, whirlpool, sauna. Refrigerators avail. *LUXURY LEVEL : CONCIERGE FLOORS.* 36 rms, 5 suites, 3 floors. S,D $168-$188; suites $300-$500. Private lounge. Complimentary bkfst, refreshments. Cr cds: A, C, D, DS, JCB, MC, V.

D ⟨icons⟩ SC

★ ★ ★ **HOTEL VINTAGE PARK.** *1100 Fifth Ave (98101), at Spring St, downtown.* 206/624-8000; res: 800/624-4433; FAX 206/623-0568. 129 rms, 11 story. S $165-$185; D $180-$200; under 12 free; wkend rates; honeymoon, Seahawks football, theater plans. Crib free. Garage parking $15; valet. TV; cable. Restaurant 7 am-2:30 pm, 5-10:30 pm. Rm serv 24 hrs. Ck-out noon. Meeting rms. Concierge. Exercise equipt delivered to rms. Health club privileges. Bathrm phones, minibars. Renovated 1922 European-style hotel combines luxury of upscale hotel with the personality of a bed and breakfast. The parlor-style lobby features a marble fireplace. Winery theme is carried throughout; each guest rm is named after a Washington vineyard or winery and decorated in rich vineyard shades. Wine tasting (Washington wines) in lobby Tues-Sat. Cr cds: A, C, D, DS, ER, JCB, MC, V.

D ⟨icons⟩

★ ★ **INN AT THE MARKET.** *86 Pine St (98101), downtown.* 206/443-3600; res: 800/446-4484; FAX 206/448-0631. 65 rms, 4-8 story, 9 suites. S $100-$180; D $110-$180; each addl $15; suites $106-$225; under 16 free; some wkend rates. Crib free. Parking $12; valet. TV; cable. Complimentary coffee in rms. Ck-out noon. Meeting rm. Shopping arcade. Beauty shop. RR station, bus depot transportation. Health club privileges. Bathrm phones, refrigerators. Overlooks Elliott Bay. Cr cds: A, C, D, DS, JCB, MC, V.

D ⟨icons⟩ SC

★ ★ **INN AT VIRGINIA MASON.** *1006 Spring St (98104), east of downtown.* 206/583-6453; res: 800/283-6453; FAX 206/223-7545. 79 air-cooled rms, 9 story. S,D $85-$125; suites $129-$190. TV; cable.

Restaurant 7 am-2 pm, 5-9 pm. Ck-out noon. Concierge. Health club privileges. English country-style apartment house (1928); Queen Anne-style furnishings. Cr cds: A, D, DS, JCB, MC, V.

⊡ ⊠ ⊠ SC

★ ★ ★ **MAYFLOWER PARK.** 405 Olive Way (98101), downtown. 206/623-8700; res: 800/426-5100; FAX 206/382-6997. 173 rms, 12 story. S $110; D $120; each addl $10; suites $160-$380; studio rms $116-$125; under 17 free. Crib free. Covered valet parking $10. TV; cable. Restaurant 6:30 am-10 pm. Rm serv 24 hrs. Bar. Ck-out noon. Meeting rms. Cr cds: A, C, D, DS, MC, V.

⊡ ⊠ ⊠ SC

✔★ ★ **MEANY TOWER.** 4507 Brooklyn Ave NE (98105), E of I-5 exit 45th St, north of downtown. 206/634-2000; res: 800/648-6440; FAX 206/634-2000. 155 rms, 16 story. S $69-$78; D $79-$88; each addl $10; under 14 free. Crib free. TV; cable. Restaurant 6:30 am-10 pm. Bar 11 am-midnight. Ck-out noon. Meeting rms. Exercise equipt; bicycles, stair machine. Game rm. View of mountains, lakes, city. 2 blks from Univ of WA campus. Cr cds: A, C, D, MC, V.

⊡ ⊼ ⊠ ⊠ SC

★ **PACIFIC PLAZA.** 400 Spring St (98104), downtown. 206/623-3900; res: 800/426-1165; FAX 206/623-2059. 160 rms, 8 story. S, D $78-$98; each addl $10; under 18 free; wkend rates. Crib free. Garage parking $9 in/out. TV; cable. Complimentary continental bkfst. Ck-out 11 am. Cr cds: A, C, D, DS, ER, JCB, MC, V.

⊠ ⊠ SC

★ ★ **PLAZA PARK SUITES.** 1011 Pike St (98101), downtown. 206/682-8282; res: 800/426-0670 (exc WA); FAX 206/682-5315. 194 suites, 9 story. Studio $130-$180; 1 bedrm $175-$250; 2 bedrm $260-$275; under 18 free. Crib free. Valet parking $5. TV; cable. Heated pool. Complimentary continental bkfst. Complimentary coffee in rms. Restaurant nearby. Ck-out noon. Coin lndry. Meeting rms. Gift shop. Exercise equipt; weights, bicycles, whirlpool. Refrigerators; many in-rm whirlpools, fireplace. Balconies. Picnic tables. Cr cds: A, C, D, DS, ER, JCB, MC, V.

⊡ ⊠ ⊼ ⊠ ⊠ ⊠ SC

★ ★ ★ **SHERATON HOTEL & TOWERS.** 1400 6th Ave (98101), downtown. 206/621-9000; FAX 206/621-8441. 840 units, 35 story. S, D $185; suites $250-$575; under 17 free; honeymoon, wkend rates. Crib free. Pet accepted, some restrictions. Covered valet parking $15. TV; cable. Indoor pool. Restaurant 6 am-midnight (also see FULLER'S). Rm serv 24 hrs. Bar 11-2 am; entertainment, dancing. Ck-out noon. Convention facilities. Concierge. Drugstore. Barber. Exercise rm; instructor, weights, bicycles, whirlpool, sauna. Minibars; some bathrm phones. Rms with original Northwest art. *LUXURY LEVEL : SHERATON TOWERS.* 98 rms, 12 suites, 4 floors. S, D $205; suites $450-$575. Private lounge. Wet bar in some suites. Complimentary continental bkfst, refreshments, newspaper. Cr cds: A, C, D, DS, ER, JCB, MC, V.

⊡ ⊠ ⊠ ⊼ ⊠ ⊠ SC

★ ★ ★ ★ **SORRENTO.** 900 Madison St (98104), I-5 N James, S Madison exits, downtown. 206/622-6400; res: 800/426-1265 (exc WA); FAX 206/343-6155. 76 rms, 6 story, 42 suites. S, D $155-$185; each addl $15; suites $185-$450; under 16 free; wkend rates. Crib free. Covered parking; valet $10. TV; cable. Restaurant (see HUNT CLUB). Bar 11:30-2 am. Ck-out noon. Meeting rms. Concierge. Complimentary limo serv to downtown area. Health club privileges. Refrigerators; many bathrm phones. Complimentary shoeshine, newspaper. Cr cds: A, C, D, DS, JCB, MC, V.

⊡ ⊠ ⊠

★ ★ ★ **STOUFFER MADISON.** 515 Madison St (98104), I-5 S Madison St exit, downtown. 206/583-0300; FAX 206/622-8635. 553 rms, 28 story. S,D $154-$174; suites $194-$800; wkend rates. Crib free. Covered parking $12. TV; cable. Indoor pool. Complimentary coffee in rms. Restaurant 6:30 am-10 pm; Fri, Sat to 11 pm. (also see PREGO). Rm serv 24 hrs. Bars 11-2 am. Ck-out 1 pm. Convention

facilities. Concierge. Barber, beauty shop. Exercise equipt; treadmill, bicycles, whirlpool. Refrigerators, minibars. *LUXURY LEVEL : MADISON CLUB.* 62 rms, 2 floors. S, D $194; suites $194-$800. Concierge. Complimentary continental bkfst and evening refreshments. Cr cds: A, C, D, DS, ER, JCB, MC, V.

⊡ ⊠ ⊼ ⊠ ⊠ SC

★ ★ ★ **WARWICK.** 401 Lenora Ave (98121), at 4th Ave, downtown. 206/443-4300; res: 800/426-9280; FAX 206/448-1662. 230 units, 19 story. S $140-$170; D $155-$185; each addl $15; suites $275-$500; under 18 free. Crib free. Covered valet parking $9. TV; cable. Indoor pool. Restaurant 6:30 am-2 pm, 5:30-10 pm. Rm serv 24 hrs. Bar 11-2 am; pianist Thurs-Sat. Ck-out 1 pm. Meeting rms. Airport transportation; free RR station, bus depot, downtown transportation. Exercise equipt; weight machine, bicycles, whirlpool, sauna. Bathrm phones; many refrigerators, wet bars. In-rm whirlpool in suites. Balconies. Fireplace in lobby. Cr cds: A, C, D, DS, ER, JCB, MC, V.

⊡ ⊠ ⊠ ⊼ ⊠ ⊠ SC

★ ★ **WESTCOAST CAMLIN.** 1619 9th Ave (98101), at Pine St, downtown. 206/682-0100; res: 800/426-0670; FAX 206/682-7415. 136 rms, 36 A/C, 4-11 story. S, D $83-$114; each addl $10; suites $175; under 18 free. Crib free. TV. Pool. Restaurant 7-10:30 am, 11:30 am-2 pm, 5:30-10:30 pm. Bar; entertainment Tues-Sat. Ck-out noon. Meeting rms. Some refrigerators. Some balconies, lanais. Motor entrance on 8th Ave. Cr cds: A, C, D, DS, JCB, MC, V.

⊠ ⊠ ⊠ SC

★ ★ ★ **THE WESTIN.** 1900 5th Ave (98101), at Westlake, downtown. 206/728-1000; FAX 206/728-2259. 865 rms, 40-47 story. S $98-$170; D $175-$200; each addl $25; suites $300-$1,100; under 18 free; wkend, winter rates. Crib free. Garage $14. TV; cable. Heated pool. Restaurant 6 am-10 pm. Rm serv 24 hrs. Bar; entertainment exc Sun. Ck-out 1 pm. Convention facilities. Concierge. Shopping arcade. Barber, beauty shop. Exercise equipt; weight machines, bicycles, whirlpool, sauna. Masseur. Refrigerators, minibars. Sun deck. Tower rms with panoramic view. Cr cds: A, C, D, DS, ER, JCB, MC, V.

⊡ ⊠ ⊼ ⊠ ⊠

Inns

✔★ **BEECH TREE MANOR.** 1405 Queen Anne Ave N, in Queen Anne area. 206/281-7037. 7 rms, 2 share bath, 2 story. No A/C. No rm phones. June-Sept: S $49-$79; D $59-$79; suite $95; each addl $10; wkly rates; lower rates rest of yr. Pet accepted. TV in sitting rm; cable. Complimentary full bkfst. Restaurant nearby. Ck-out 11 am, ck-in 4-7 pm. Street parking. Turn-of-the-century mansion (1903) furnished with many antiques. Totally nonsmoking. Cr cds: MC, V.

⊠ ⊠ ⊠

★ ★ **CHAMBERED NAUTILUS.** 5005 22nd Ave NE (98105), north of downtown. 206/522-2536. 6 rms, 4 with bath, 3 story. No A/C. No rm phones. S $67-$90; D $75-$99; each addl $15. Children over 12 yrs only. Complimentary full bkfst, afternoon tea. Restaurant nearby. Ck-out 11 am, ck-in 4-6 pm. Street parking. Georgian colonial house (1915); library/sitting rm with fireplace. Cr cds: A, C, D, MC, V.

⊠ ⊠

★ ★ **CHELSEA STATION.** 4915 Linden Ave N (98103), north of downtown. 206/547-6077. 6 rms, 2 story, 3 suites. No A/C. Many rm phones. July-Aug: S $84; D $89; each addl $10; suites $104; lower rates rest of yr. Children over 11 yrs only. Complimentary full bkfst, coffee & tea. Restaurant nearby. Ck-out 11 am, ck-in 3-7 pm. Street parking. Colonial-style brick house (1920); antiques. Near Woodland Park Zoo. Totally nonsmoking. Cr cds: A, C, D, DS, MC, V.

⊠ ⊠

✔★ ★ ★ **GASLIGHT.** 1727 15th Ave (98122), east of downtown. 206/325-3654; FAX 206/324-3135. 15 rms (4 with shower only, 3 share bath), 3 story, 6 suites. No A/C. Some rm phones. S, D $62-$94; suites $88-$98. TV; cable. Heated pool. Complimentary continental bkfst.

Complimentary coffee, tea in library. Restaurant nearby. Ck-out 11 am, ck-in 3-6 pm. Luggage handling. Refrigerators. Picnic tables. Two buildings; one built 1906. Many antiques. Cr cds: A, MC, V.

★ ★ **ROBERTA'S BED & BREAKFAST.** *1147 16th Ave E (98112), east of downtown.* 206/329-3326; FAX 206/324-2149. 5 rms (4 with shower only), 3 story. No A/C. No rm phones. S $73-$88; D $80-$105; each addl $15. Complimentary full bkfst. Complimentary coffee in rms. Ck-out 11 am, ck-in by arrangement. Built 1903; many antiques. Extensive library. Totally nonsmoking. Cr cds: MC, V.

★ **SALISBURY HOUSE.** *750 16th Ave E (98112), east of downtown.* 206/328-8682; FAX 206/720-1019. 4 rms (3 with shower only), 2 story. No A/C. No rm phones. Mid-May-mid-Sept: S $69-$87; D $79-$97; each addl $15; lower rates rest of yr. Children over 12 yrs only. Complimentary full bkfst. Complimentary coffee, tea in library. Restaurant nearby. Ck-out noon, ck-in 4-6 pm. Built 1904; wraparound porch. Many antiques. Totally nonsmoking. Cr cds: A, D, MC, V.

Restaurants

★ ★ ★ **ADRIATICA.** *1107 Dexter N, in Queen Anne.* 206/285-5000. Hrs: 5-10 pm; Fri, Sat to 11 pm. Closed Jan 1, Thanksgiving, Dec 24, 25. Res accepted. Southern Mediterranean menu. Bar 5 pm-2 am. Wine list. Semi-a la carte: dinner $13.50-$22.50. Specializes in lamb, pasta, seafood. Own pastries. Parking. Outdoor dining. Built 1922. European villa decor. Cr cds: A, D, MC, V.

★ ★ **AL BOCCALINO.** *1 Yesler Way, in Pioneer Square.* 206/622-7688. Hrs: 11:30 am-2 pm, 5-10:30 pm; Sun 4:30-9:30 pm. Closed major hols. Res accepted. No A/C. Italian menu. Semi-a la carte: lunch $6-$10, dinner $9-$19.50. Specializes in fresh seafood, rissotto saddle of lamb. Bistro atmosphere. Cr cds: A, D, MC, V.

★ ★ **ARNIE'S NORTHSHORE.** *1900 N Northlake Way, opp Gas Works Park, north of downtown.* 206/547-3242. Hrs: 11:30 am-9 pm; Sat 5-10 pm; Sun 10 am-9 pm; early-bird dinner Sun-Fri 5-6 pm; Sun brunch to 2:30 pm. Closed Dec 25; also lunch Memorial Day, July 4, Labor Day. Res accepted. Bar to 2 am. Semi-a la carte: lunch $5.95-$9.95, dinner $10.95-$17.95. Sun brunch $5.95-$9.95. Specializes in Northwest seafood. Own sauces. Parking. Contemporary decor. Panoramic view of Lake Union, Seattle skyline. Cr cds: A, MC, V.

✔★ ★ **AVE! AL RISTORANTE ITALIANO.** *4743 University Way NE (98105), north of downtown.* 206/527-9830. Hrs: 11:30 am-2:30 pm, 5-10 pm; Fri & Sat 11 pm. Closed July 4, Thanksgiving, Dec 25. Res accepted. Italian menu. Wine. Semi-a la carte: lunch $4.75-$7.95, dinner $6.95-$13.50. Child's meals. Specializes in pizza, pasta. Open cooking area. Murals of Italy. Cr cds: A, DS, MC, V.

✔★ ★ **CACTUS.** *1220 E Madison, east of downtown.* 206/324-4140. Hrs: 11:30 am-2:30 pm, 5-10:30 pm; Sun 5-9 pm. Closed some major hols. Hispanic menu. Serv bar. Semi-a la carte: lunch $4.95-$8.50, dinner $5.95-$12.95. Child's meals. Specializes in flan, tapas, Yucatan fish. Outdoor dining. Southwestern atmosphere. Cr cds: DS, MC, V.

★ ★ ★ **CAMPAGNE.** *86 Pine St, downtown.* 206/728-2800. Hrs: 11:30 am-2 pm, 5:30-10 pm; Sun from 5:30 pm; Oct-May from 5:30 pm. Closed some major hols. Res accepted. French menu. Bar to 2 am. A la carte entrees: lunch $6-$16, dinner $12-$24. Specializes in fresh seafood, rack of lamb. Valet parking. Outdoor dining. View of Elliott Bay. Cr cds: A, C, MC, V.

★ ★ ★ **CANLIS.** *2576 Aurora Ave N, in Queen Anne.* 206/283-3313. Hrs: 5:30-10:30 pm. Closed Sun; major hols. Res accepted. Bar 5 pm-12:30 am. Extensive wine list. Semi-a la carte: dinner $18-$34. Specializes in seafood, steak. Own sauces. Piano bar from 7 pm. Valet parking. Fireplace. Open-hearth grill. Panoramic view of Lake Union, cascade mountains. Formal dining. Family-owned. Jacket. Cr cds: A, C, D, JCB, MC, V.

✔★ ★ **CHINOOK'S.** *1900 W Nickerson, in Fisherman's Terminal, north of downtown.* 206/283-4665. Hrs: 11 am-10 pm; Fri to 11 pm; Sat 7:30 am-11 pm; Sun 7:30 am-10 pm. Closed Thanksgiving, Dec 25. Bar to midnight. Complete meals: bkfst $4.25-$8.95. Semi-a la carte: lunch $4.95-$10.95, dinner $4.95-$14.95. Child's meals. Specializes in Northwest seafood, salmon, halibut. Parking. Outdoor dining. On Fisherman's Wharf. Nautical decor. Cr cds: A, C, D, DS, MC, V.

★ ★ **CLIPPERS.** *409 Olive Way, downtown.* 206/382-6999. Hrs: 6:30 am-2:30 pm, 5:30-10 pm; Sat & Sun 6:30 am-10 pm. Res accepted. Bar 11-2 am. Semi-a la carte: bkfst $5-$10, lunch $5.95-$10, dinner $11-$20. Specializes in prime rib, seafood, steak. Original modern art on display. Cr cds: A, C, D, DS, MC, V.

✔★ ★ **CUCINA! CUCINA!** *901 Fairview Ave N, north of downtown.* 206/447-2782. Hrs: 11:30-2 am. Closed Thanksgiving, Dec 25. Res accepted (lunch). Italian menu. Bar. A la carte entrees: lunch $4.95-$10.95, dinner $4.95-$14.95. Child's meals. Specializes in pizza, pasta, salads, desserts. Valet parking. Outdoor dining. Italian bicycles hang from ceiling. Cr cds: A, D, DS, JCB, MC, V.

★ ★ **CUTTER'S BAY HOUSE.** *2001 Western Ave, downtown.* 206/448-4884. Hrs: 11 am-10 pm; Sat, Sun from 4:30 pm. Closed Thanksgiving, Dec 25. Res accepted. Bar to 1 am. Semi-a la carte: lunch $5.95-$16.95, dinner $6.95-$24.95. Child's meals. Specializes in fresh Northwest seafood. Parking. View of Elliott Bay. Cr cds: A, D, DS, MC, V.

★ ★ ★ **DAHLIA LOUNGE.** *1904 Fourth Ave, downtown.* 206/682-4142. Hrs: 11:30 am-2:30 pm, 5:30-10 pm; Fri, Sat to 11 pm; Sun 5-9 pm. Closed major hols. Res accepted. Semi-a la carte: lunch $6.50-$12, dinner $9.95-$19.95. Child's meals. Specialties: crab cakes, gnocchi, roasted crispy duck. Eclectic decor. Cr cds: A, C, D, DS, MC, V.

★ ★ **ELLIOTT'S OYSTER HOUSE.** *1203 Alaskan Way, Pier 56, downtown.* 206/623-4340. Hrs: 11 am-11 pm; Fri, Sat to midnight. Res accepted. Bar. Semi-a la carte: lunch $5.95-$15.95, dinner $9.95-$27.95. Child's meals. Specializes in broiled salmon, fresh Dungeness crab, fresh oysters. Outdoor dining. View of bay. Cr cds: A, C, D, DS, JCB, MC, V.

★ ★ **F.X. McRORY'S STEAK, CHOP & OYSTER HOUSE.** *419 Occidental Ave S, opp Kingdome, in Pioneer Square.* 206/623-4800. Hrs: 11:30 am-2 pm, 5-11 pm; Sat noon-11 pm; Sun from 3 pm. Closed some major hols. Res accepted. Bar to 2 am. Semi-a la carte: lunch $6-$12, dinner $10-$25. Child's meals. Specializes in steak, oysters, prime rib. Oyster bar. Outdoor dining. 1920s atmosphere. Cr cds: A, C, D, DS, MC, V.

✔★ **FOUR SEAS.** *714 S King St, in International District.* 206/682-4900. Hrs: 10:30-2 am; Sun to midnight. Res accepted. Cantonese, mandarin menu. Bar. Semi-a la carte: lunch $5.95-$7.95, dinner $5.25-$15.95. Specialties: Hong Kong dim sum, garlic spareribs, moo goo gai pan, hot & spicy chicken. Parking. Hand-carved Oriental screens. Cr cds: A, MC, V.

[D]

★ ★ **FRANCO'S HIDDEN HARBOR.** *1500 Westlake Ave N, north of downtown.* 206/282-0501. Hrs: 11 am-10 pm; Fri & Sat to 11 pm; Sun noon-10 pm. Closed Dec 25. Res accepted. Northwestern menu. Bar to 1 am; Sun 1-10 pm. Semi-a la carte: lunch $5-$11, dinner $11-$30. Child's meals. Specializes in fresh seafood. Valet parking. Outdoor dining. Waterfront dining overlooking yacht harbor. Cr cds: A, C, D, DS, MC, V.

[D]

★ ★ ★ **FULLER'S.** *(See Sheraton Hotel & Towers)* 206/447-5544. Hrs: 11:30 am-2 pm, 5:30-10 pm; Sat from 5:30 pm. Closed Sun; most major hols. Res accepted. Bar. Wine list. A la carte entrees: lunch $7-$11.95, dinner $15.95-$22. Child's meals. Specializes in Northwest seafood, fowl, Ellensberg lamb, prime beef. Own soufflés, sauces. Valet parking. Formal dining. Water fountain; original works of art by Northwest artists; Pilchuck glass collection. Totally nonsmoking. Cr cds: A, C, D, DS, ER, JCB, MC, V.

[D]

★ ★ ★ **GEORGIAN ROOM.** *(See Four Seasons Olympic Hotel)* 206/621-7889. Hrs: 6:30 am-2 pm, 5:30-10 pm; Fri to 10:30 pm; Sat 6:30 am- noon, 5:30-10:30 pm; Sun 6:30 am-1:30 pm, 5:30-10 pm; Sun brunch (exc Memorial Day-Labor Day) 11:30 am-2 pm. Res accepted. Bar. Wine cellar. A la carte entrees: bkfst $4.50-$12.50, lunch $7.50-$14.75, dinner $14.50-$33. Sun brunch $7.75-$15.25. Specializes in Pacific Northwest seafood, rack of lamb. Own pastries, walnut bread, onion bread. Pastry chef. Italian Renaissance decor; elegant dining. Jacket (dinner). Cr cds: A, C, D, JCB, MC, V.

[D]

★ ★ ★ **GERARD'S RELAIS DE LYON.** *(17121 Bothell Way NE, Bothell)* NE on I-405, exit 23 to WA 522. 206/485-7600. Hrs: 5-9 pm. Closed Mon. Res accepted. No A/C. French menu. Serv bar. Wine list. Semi-a la carte: dinner $21-$27. Complete meals: dinner $38.50-$48. Specializes in lamb, seafood. Own desserts. Parking. Outdoor dining. Turn-of-the-century French decor. Original artwork, antiques. Cr cds: A, C, D, DS, MC, V.

[D]

★ ★ **HIRAM'S AT THE LOCKS.** *5300 34th St NW, north of downtown.* 206/784-1733. Hrs: 11 am-3 pm, 4:30 pm-closing; Sun brunch 9 am-2:30 pm. Res accepted. Bar to midnight. Semi-a la carte: lunch $5.95-$11.95, dinner $12.95-$19.95. Sun brunch $16.95. Child's meals. Specializes in salmon, steak, oysters. Parking. Outdoor dining. Overlooks Chittendon Locks. Family-owned. Cr cds: A, C, D, DS, JCB, MC, V.

[D] [SC]

★ ★ ★ **HUNT CLUB.** *(See Sorrento Hotel)* 206/343-6156. Hrs: 7 am-2:30 pm, 5:30-10 pm; Fri & Sat to 11 pm; Sat, Sun brunch 10 am-2:30 pm. Res accepted. Bar 11:30-2 am. A la carte entrees: bkfst $5-$10, lunch $9-$15, dinner $19-$28. Sat & Sun brunch $8-$16. Specializes in seafood of the Northwest, rack of lamb. Valet parking. Outdoor dining. European decor; English hunt motif. Cr cds: A, C, D, DS, MC, V.

[D]

★ ★ **IL BISTRO.** *93A Pike St (98101), downtown.* 206/682-3049. Hrs: 11:30 am-3 pm, 5:30-10 pm; Fri & Sat to 11 pm; Sun from 5:30 pm. Closed some major hols. Res accepted. Italian menu. Bar to 2 am. A la carte entrees: lunch $3.50-$12.50, dinner $9.95-$26.50. Specializes in fresh seafood, pasta, rack of lamb. Valet parking Thurs-Sat. Original art. Cr cds: A, C, D, DS, MC, V.

[D]

★ ★ **IVAR'S INDIAN SALMON HOUSE.** *401 NE Northlake Way, on N shore of Lake Union, north of downtown.* 206/632-0767. Hrs: 11 am-2 pm, 4:30-10 pm; Sat from 4 pm; Sun 4-10 pm; Sun brunch 10

am-2 pm. Closed Thanksgiving, Dec 25. Res accepted. Bar 11 am-11 pm. Semi-a la carte: lunch $6-$11, dinner $10-$18. Sun brunch $13.95. Child's meals. Specializes in smoked salmon. Parking. Indian long house decor. View of lake. Family-owned. Cr cds: A, MC, V.

[D] [SC]

★ ★ ★ **KASPAR'S.** *19 W Harrison St (98119), in Queen Anne.* 206/441-4805. Hrs: 5-10 pm; Fri also 11:30 am-2 pm. Closed Sun & Mon; Jan 1, July 4. Res accepted. Bar. A la carte entrees: lunch $7-$11, dinner $13-$19. Child's meals. Specializes in Northwestern cuisine, vegetarian dishes. Own ice cream & sorbets. Valet parking. 2 levels. Smoking at bar only. Cr cds: A, MC, V.

[D]

★ ★ **LABUZNIK.** *1924 1st Ave (98101), downtown.* 206/441-8899. Hrs: 4:30 pm-midnight. Closed Sun & Mon; major hols; also closed spring break & 3 wks July. Res accepted. Continental menu. Bar. Semi-a la carte: dinner $15-$35. Child's meals. Specializes in veal, pork, roast duck. Dining on 2 levels; sliding doors open to street. Original art. Cr cds: A, D, DS, MC, V.

[D]

★ ★ ★ **LATITUDE 47.** *1232 Westlake N, north of downtown.* 206/284-1047. Hrs: 11:30 am-2:30 pm, 5-9:30 pm; Fri, Sat 5-10 pm; Sun 3-9 pm; Sun brunch 10 am-2 pm. Closed Dec 25. Res accepted. Bar to 2 am. Wine list. Semi-a la carte: lunch $5.75-$9.50, dinner $10-$18.50. Sun brunch $13.95. Child's meals. Specializes in seafood. Valet parking. Entertainment. Outdoor dining. Enclosed patio overlooks Lake Union; moorage. Cr cds: A, D, DS, MC, V.

[D]

★ ★ ★ **LE GOURMAND.** *425 NW Market St, at 6th Ave, north of downtown.* 206/784-3463. Hrs: 5:30-11 pm. Closed Sun-Tues; Easter, Thanksgiving, Dec 24, 25. Res accepted. French, Amer menu. Wine, beer. Complete meals: dinner $18-$28. Specialties: poached salmon with gooseberry & dill sauce, roast duckling with black currant sauce. Original artwork. Totally nonsmoking. Cr cds: A, C, D, MC, V.

[D]

✔★ **LINYEN.** *424 7th Ave S, in International District.* 206/622-8181. Hrs: 10:30-2 am. Res accepted. Chinese menu. Bar. Semi-a la carte: lunch $2.80-$6, dinner $5.95-$15.25. Specializes in fresh Northwest fish and vegetables, lemon chicken. Valet parking. Cr cds: A, D, DS, MC, V.

[D]

★ ★ **MAXIMILIEN-IN-THE-MARKET.** *81A Pike Place, Pike Place Market, downtown.* 206/682-7270. Hrs: 7:30 am-10 pm; Sun 9:30 am-4 pm. Closed Jan 1, Thanksgiving, Dec 25. Res accepted. French menu. Bar. Semi-a la carte: bkfst $3-$10, lunch $5.50-$13, dinner $11.50-$24. French family supper Mon-Fri: $13.25-$24. Sun brunch $5.50-$13. Specializes in French-style Northwest seafood. French marketplace decor; antiques. View of bay, mountains. Cr cds: A, C, D, MC, V.

[D]

★ ★ **McCORMICK & SCHMICK'S.** *1103 First Ave, downtown.* 206/623-5500. Hrs: 11:30 am-11 pm; Sat from 5 pm; Sun 5-10 pm; early-bird dinner Mon-Fri 5-6 pm. Closed Thanksgiving, Dec 25. Res accepted. Bar to 1 am; Fri & Sat to 2 am; Sun to midnight. Semi-a la carte: lunch $2.95-$7.95, dinner $8.95-$20. Specializes in fresh seafood. Beamed ceilings, Irish bar. Original art. Cr cds: A, C, D, DS, JCB, MC, V.

[D]

★ ★ **McCORMICK'S FISH HOUSE.** *722 Fourth Ave, downtown.* 206/682-3900. Hrs: 11 am-11 pm; Fri to midnight; Sat 5 pm-midnight; Sun 5-11 pm. Closed Memorial Day, Thanksgiving, Dec 25. Res accepted. Bar. Semi-a la carte: lunch $5.95-$11.95, dinner $5.95-$22.95. Specializes in fresh seafood. Oyster bar. Outdoor dining. Vintage 1920s and 30s atmosphere; tin ceilings. Cr cds: A, C, D, DS, MC, V.

D

★ ★ ★ **METROPOLITAN GRILL.** *820 2nd Ave, at Marion St, downtown.* 206/624-3287. Hrs: 11 am-3:30 pm, 5-11 pm; Sat from 4:30 pm; Sun 4:30-10 pm. Closed Thanksgiving. Res accepted. Bar. Wine list. Semi-a la carte: lunch $6.95-$15.95, dinner $10.95-$26.95. Child's meals. Specialties: 28-day dry aged steak, Northwest seafood dishes. Cr cds: A, C, D, DS, JCB, MC, V.

D

✔★ **OLD SPAGHETTI FACTORY.** *2801 Elliott Ave (98121), downtown.* 206/441-7724. Hrs: 11:30 am-2 pm, 5-10 pm; Fri to 11 pm; Sat noon-11 pm; Sun noon-10 pm. Res accepted. Closed Thanksgiving, Dec 24 & 25. Italian menu. Bar. Semi-a la carte: lunch $3.35-$7.95, dinner $4.25-$9.25. Child's meals. Specializes in spaghetti, lasagne. Parking. Many turn-of-the-century antiques and collectibles; Tiffany-style lamps; booths made from iron and oak bedsteads. Family-owned. Cr cds: DS, MC, V.

D

★ ★ ★ **PAINTED TABLE.** *(See Alexis Hotel)* 206/624-3646. Hrs: 6:30-10 am, 11:30 am-2 pm, 5:30-10 pm; Sat & Sun 7 am-noon, 5:30-10 pm. Res accepted. Bar. Wine list. A la carte entrees: bkfst $3.50-$9.50, lunch $6.95-$14.95, dinner $7.95-$18.95. Specializes in Northwest regional cuisine. Own pastries, sauces. Valet parking. In historic building (1901). Totally nonsmoking. Cr cds: A, C, D, DS, ER, JCB, MC, V.

D

★ ★ **PALOMINO.** *1420 5th Ave, on 3rd floor of Pacific First Center, downtown.* 206/623-1300. Hrs: 11:15 am-9:30 pm; Fri & Sat to 10:30 pm; Sun 5-9:30 pm. Closed some major hols. Res accepted. Mediterranean menu. Bar to 12:30 am. Semi-a la carte: lunch $6.50-$12.95, dinner $6.95-$19.95. Specializes in grilled salmon, spit-roasted chicken, wood oven-roasted prawns. Parking. Overlooking atrium. Cr cds: A, D, DS, MC, V.

D

★ ★ **PREGO.** *(See Stouffer Madison Hotel)* 206/583-0300. Hrs: 11:30 am-2 pm, 5:30-10 pm; Fri & Sat 5:30-11 pm. Closed Dec 25. Res accepted. Italian menu. Bar. Semi-a la carte: lunch $9.75-$15.95, dinner $12.95-$25.95. Specializes in seafood, pasta, veal. Views of skyline, Puget Sound. Cr cds: A, C, D, DS, ER, JCB, MC, V.

D

★ ★ ★ **RAY'S BOATHOUSE.** *6049 Seaview Ave, north of downtown.* 206/789-3770. Hrs: 11:30 am-2 pm, 5-10 pm; early-bird dinner 5-6 pm. Closed Jan 1, Dec 25. Res accepted. Bar to midnight. Wine cellar. Semi-a la carte: lunch $5.95-$9.95, dinner $10.95-$25. Child's meals. Specializes in Northwest seafood. Valet parking. Outdoor dining. View of Olympic Mts. Cr cds: A, D, MC, V.

D

★ ★ ★ **REINER'S.** *1106 Eighth Ave, downtown.* 206/624-2222. Hrs: 11:30 am-2 pm, 5:30-9 pm; Sat 5:30-9:30 pm. Closed Sun, Mon; some major hols; also first 3 wks Jan. Res accepted; required Fri & Sat. Continental menu. Serv bar. Wine list. A la carte entrees: lunch $7.75-$10, dinner $13.75-$22. Specializes in rack of lamb, crab cakes, calf's liver. Outdoor dining. Intimate dining in European atmosphere. Totally nonsmoking. Cr cds: A, D, MC, V.

★ ★ ★ **ROVER'S.** *2808 E Madison St, east of downtown.* 206/325-7442. Hrs: 5:30-9 pm. Closed Sun & Mon; most major hols. Res accepted. French menu. Wine list. A la carte entrees: dinner $22.50-$37.50. Complete meals: dinner $44.50 & $54.50. Specializes in seafood, Northwest game, vegetarian dishes. Outdoor dining. Herb & edible flower garden. Totally nonsmoking. Cr cds: A, D, MC, V.

★ ★ **RUTH'S CHRIS STEAK HOUSE.** *800 5th Ave, downtown.* 206/624-8524. Hrs: 5-11 pm. Closed some major hols. Res

accepted. Bar. A la carte entrees: dinner $25-$30. Specializes in steak, seafood. Valet parking. Cr cds: A, D, MC, V.

D

✔★ **SERAFINA.** *2043 Eastlake Ave E (98102).* 206/323-0807. Hrs: 11:30 am-2 pm, 5:30-10 pm; Sat & Sun from 5:30 pm. Closed some major hols. Res accepted. Italian menu. Bar. A la carte entrees: lunch $2.25-$8.95, dinner $5.95-$14.95. Specializes in rustic Italian dishes. Entertainment. Outdoor dining. Murals. Cr cds: MC, V.

D

★ ★ **SPACE NEEDLE.** *203 Sixth Ave N, in Seattle Center.* 206/443-2100. Hrs: 7 am-11 pm; Sun from 8 am. Res accepted. Bar 1 pm-midnight. Semi-a la carte: bkfst $9.95-$13.95, lunch $12.95-$16.95, dinner $18.95-$30.95. Sun brunch $16.50-$19.95. Child's meals. Specializes in regional dishes. Valet parking. Revolving dining rm. Family-owned. Totally nonsmoking. Cr cds: A, D, DS, ER, JCB, MC, V.

D

✔★ **STELLA'S TRATTORIA.** *4500 9th Ave, northeast of downtown.* 206/633-1100. Open 24 hrs. Sun brunch 4-11 am. Closed Thanksgiving, Dec 25. Italian, Amer menu. Semi-a la carte: bkfst $2.95-$5.50, lunch $5.25-$7.50, dinner $6-$13. Sun brunch $2.95-$6.50. Child's meals. Outdoor dining. Lively atmosphere. Totally nonsmoking. Cr cds: A, DS, MC, V.

D

★ ★ **TATSUMI.** *4214 University Way NE, north of downtown.* 206/548-9319. Hrs: 11 am-2 pm, 5-9:30 pm; Sat noon-3 pm, 5-9:30 pm; Sun 5-9:30 pm. Closed some Sun; some major hols. Res accepted. Japanese menu. Semi-a la carte: lunch $4.95-$13.95, dinner $6.50-$16.45. Specializes in sushi, tempura & teriyaki dishes. Indoor garden. Cr cds: MC, V.

D

✔★ **TLAQUEPAQUE.** *1122 Post Ave, downtown.* 206/467-8226. Hrs: 11:30 am-11 pm; Fri to 11:30 pm; Sat 1-11:30 pm; Sun 1-10 pm. Closed Jan 1, Dec 25. Res accepted. Mexican menu. Bar. Semi-a la carte: lunch $5.95-$8, dinner $7-$12.50. Specializes in regional cuisine, camerones Tocino, steak fajitas. Entertainment Wed, Fri & Sat. Lively atmosphere. Cr cds: A, C, D, DS, MC, V.

✔★ **TRATTORIA MITCHELLI.** *84 Yesler Way, in Pioneer Square.* 206/623-3883. Hrs: 7-4 am; Sat from 8 am; Sun 8 am-11 pm, Mon to 11 pm. Closed Dec 25. Res accepted Sun-Thurs. No A/C. Italian menu. Bar 11-2 am. Semi-a la carte: bkfst $2.50-$6.95, lunch $3-$8.95, dinner $5-$15. Child's meals. Specializes in pizza, pasta, chicken. Outdoor dining. Antique furnishings. Cr cds: A, DS, MC, V.

D

★ ★ ★ **UNION SQUARE GRILL.** *621 Union St, downtown.* 206/224-4321. Hrs: 11 am-3 pm, 5-10 pm; Fri to midnight; Sat 5 pm-midnight; Sun 5-10 pm. Closed some major hols. Res accepted. Bar. Semi-a la carte: lunch $6.95-$15.95, dinner $13.95-$27.95. Specializes in steak, Northwestern seafood. Valet parking. Extensive beer selection. Several dining areas; mahogany furnishings, dividers. Cr cds: A, C, D, DS, JCB, MC, V.

D

★ ★ **WILD GINGER.** *1400 Western Ave, downtown.* 206/623-4450. Hrs: 11:30 am-11 pm; Fri, Sat to midnight; Sun 5-11 pm. Closed Thanksgiving, Dec 25. Res accepted. Southeast Asian, Chinese menu. Bar. Semi-a la carte: lunch $6.95-$12.95, dinner $9.95-$19.95. Specializes in fresh seafood, curry. Satay bar. Near Pike Place Market. Cr cds: A, D, DS, MC, V.

D

Unrated Dining Spots

A JAYS. *2619 First Ave, downtown. 206/441-1511.* Hrs: 7 am-11 pm; Sun & Mon to 3 pm. Closed Thanksgiving, Dec 25. Deli menu. Wine, beer. Semi-a la carte: bkfst $2.99-$7.95, lunch $4.25-$8.25, dinner $10-$20. Specializes in pancakes, pastrami sandwiches, matzo ball soup. Cr cds: MC, V.

D

SURROGATE HOSTESS, A SEASONAL KITCHEN CAFETERIA. *746 19th Ave E, north of downtown. 206/324-1944.* Hrs: 6 am-9 pm. Closed Jan 1, Dec 25. No A/C. Northwest country cooking. Wine, beer. Avg ck: bkfst $3-$7, lunch $4-$7, dinner $4-$11. Specializes in fish, salads, desserts. Parking. Outdoor dining. Totally nonsmoking. No cr cds accepted.

D

Seattle-Tacoma Intl Airport Area

Motels

★ ★ **BEST WESTERN AIRPORT EXECUTEL.** *(20717 International Blvd, Seattle 98198) 1 mi S on WA 99, at S 207th St. 206/878-3300; FAX 206/824-9000.* 138 rms, 3 story. June-Sept: S $85-$109; D $99-$129; each addl $10; suites $125-$305; under 12 free; lower rates rest of yr. TV; cable. Indoor pool. Complimentary coffee in rms. Restaurant 5:30 am-10:30 pm. Bar 3 pm-2 am. Ck-out noon. Meeting rms. Bellhops. Valet serv. Airport transportation. Exercise equipt; weights, bicycle, whirlpool, sauna. Some refrigerators. Some balconies. Cr cds: A, C, D, DS, JCB, MC, V.

D ≈ ⅋ ✈ ⊠ ♨ SC

★ ★ **COMFORT INN.** *(19333 International Blvd, Seattle 98188) 1 mi S on WA 99, at S 193rd St. 206/878-1100; FAX 206/878-8678.* 119 rms, 4 story. S $65-$75; D $75-$85; each addl $10; suites $105-$150; under 18 free. Crib free. TV; cable. Continental bkfst. Complimentary coffee. Restaurant adj open 24 hrs. Ck-out noon. Meeting rms. Bellhops. Valet serv. Sundries. Free covered parking. Free airport transportation. Exercise equipt; weight machine, bicycles, whirlpool. Refrigerator in suites. Cr cds: A, C, D, DS, ER, JCB, MC, V.

D ⅋ ✈ ⊠ ♨ SC

★ ★ **HAMPTON INN-SEATTLE AIRPORT.** *(19445 International Blvd, Seattle 98188) 1 mi S on WA 99, at S 194th St. 206/878-1700; FAX 206/824-0720.* 131 rms, 4 story. S $65-$67; D $75-$77; under 18 free. Crib free. TV; cable. Pool. Complimentary continental bkfst, coffee. Restaurant nearby. Ck-out noon. Meeting rm. Bellhops. Valet serv. Free airport transportation. Exercise equipt; weight machine, bicycles. Cr cds: A, C, D, DS, JCB, MC, V.

D ≈ ⅋ ✈ ⊠ ♨ SC

✔ ★ ★ **HAMPTON INN-TUKWILA.** *(7200 S 156th St, Tukwila 98188) Just S of I-405, exit 1. 206/228-5800; FAX 206/228-6812.* 154 rms, 4 story. S $58-$67; D $68-$76; under 18 free. Crib free. Pet accepted. TV; cable. Heated pool. Complimentary continental bkfst, coffee. Restaurant nearby. Ck-out noon. Meeting rm. Valet serv. Free airport, mall transportation. Exercise equipt; weight machine, bicycles, whirlpool. Cr cds: A, C, D, DS, MC, V.

D ⚓ ≈ ✈ ⊠ ♨ SC

★ **HERITAGE INN.** *(16838 International Blvd, Seattle 98188) ¼ mi S on WA 99, at S 168th St. 206/248-0901; res: 800/845-2968; FAX 206/242-3170.* 148 rms, 3 story. S $74; D $84; each addl $10; suites $94; under 12 free. Crib free. TV; cable. Complimentary continental bkfst. Restaurant 4 am-10 pm; Sat, Sun 7 am-2 pm, 5-9

pm. Rm serv. Meeting rm. Ck-out noon. Bellhops. Sundries. Free airport transportation. Balconies. Cr cds: A, C, D, DS, ER, JCB, MC, V.

✈ ⊠ ♨ SC

✔ ★ **LA QUINTA.** *(2824 S 188th St, Seattle 98188) 1 mi S on WA 99, at S 188th St. 206/241-5211; FAX 206/246-5596.* 142 rms, 6 story. S, D $58-$81; each addl $8; under 18 free. Crib free. Pet accepted, some restrictions. TV; cable. Pool. Complimentary continental bkfst. Restaurant opp open 24 hrs. Ck-out noon. Coin lndry. Meeting rm. Valet serv. Sundries. Free airport transportation. Exercise equipt; weights, rower. Cr cds: A, D, DS, MC, V.

D ⚓ ≈ ⅋ ✈ ⊠ ♨ SC

✔ ★ **SEA-TAC CREST MOTOR INN.** *(18845 International Blvd, Seattle 98188) 1 mi S on WA 99, at S 188th St. 206/433-0999; res: 800/554-0300; FAX 206/248-7644.* 46 rms, 4 story. S $38-$45; D $42-$49; suites $59-$69. Crib $3. TV; cable. Complimentary continental bkfst, coffee, tea. Ck-out noon. Meeting rms. Bellhops. Airport transportation. Some refrigerators. Balconies. Cr cds: A, C, D, DS, ER, MC, V.

D ✈ ⊠ ♨ SC

✔ ★ **TRAVELODGE.** *(2900 S 192nd St, Seattle 98188) 206/241-9292; FAX 206/242-0681.* 104 rms, 3 story. S, D $34-$80; each addl $5; under 18 free. Crib free. TV; cable, in-rm movies. Complimentary coffee in rms. Restaurant adj open 24 hrs. Ck-out noon. Coin lndry. Meeting rms. Free airport transportation. Sauna. Cr cds: A, C, D, DS, ER, JCB, MC, V.

D ✈ ⊠ ♨ SC

Motor Hotels

★ ★ ★ **HILTON SEATTLE AIRPORT.** *(17620 International Blvd, Seattle 98188) International Blvd (WA 99) at S 176th St. 206/244-4800; FAX 206/248-4495.* 173 rms, 2-3 story. S, D $105-$120; suites $275-$350; under 18 free; wkend rates. Crib free. TV; cable. Heated pool; poolside serv. Complimentary coffee in rms. Restaurant 6 am-11 pm. Rm serv. Bar 11 am-midnight. Ck-out 1 pm. Meeting rms. Bellhops. Valet serv. Sundries. Free airport, mall transportation. Exercise equipt; weight machine, bicycles, whirlpool. Private patios. Garden setting. Cr cds: A, C, D, DS, ER, JCB, MC, V.

D ≈ ⅋ ✈ ⊠ ♨

★ ★ ★ **HOLIDAY INN SEATTLE-TACOMA AIRPORT.** *(17338 International Blvd, Seattle 98188) On International Blvd S at S 173rd St. 206/248-1000; FAX 206/242-7089.* 260 rms, 12 story. S,D $114-$124; each addl $10; family, some wkend rates. Crib free. TV; cable. Indoor pool. Restaurant 6 am-10:30 pm; Sat, Sun from 7 am. Rm serv. Bars 11 am-midnight. Ck-out noon. Coin lndry. Meeting rms. Bellhops. Sundries. Gift shop. Free airport transportation. Exercise equipt; weight machine, bicycle, whirlpool. Revolving rooftop dining rm. Cr cds: A, C, D, DS, JCB, MC, V.

D ≈ ⅋ ✈ ⊠ ♨ SC

★ ★ ★ **MARRIOTT SEA-TAC.** *(3201 S 176th St, Seattle 98188) International Blvd (WA 99) to S 176th St. 206/241-2000; FAX 206/248-0789.* 459 rms. S, D $111-$132; suites $200-$450; under 18 free; wkly, wkend rates. Crib free. Pet accepted. TV; cable; in-rm movies. Indoor pool; poolside serv. Restaurant 6 am-11 pm. Rm serv. Bar 11-2 am. Ck-out 1 pm. Convention facilities. Bellhops. Valet serv. Shopping arcade. Free airport transportation. Exercise equipt; weight machines, bicycles, whirlpool, sauna. Game rm. 21,000-sq ft atrium with trees, plants, totem poles, waterfall. *LUXURY LEVEL : CONCIERGE LEVEL.* 61 rms. S $132; D $144. Concierge. Private lounge. Complimentary continental bkfst, refreshments. Cr cds: A, C, D, DS, ER, JCB, MC, V.

D ⚓ ≈ ⅋ ✈ ⊠ ♨ SC

★ ★ ★ **RADISSON SEATTLE AIRPORT.** *(17001 International Blvd, Seattle 98188) N on International Blvd (WA 99) at 170th St. 206/244-6000; FAX 206/246-6835.* 165 rms, 2 story. S $99-$129; D $109-$139; each addl $10; under 18 free; wkend rates. Crib free. TV;

cable. Heated pool; poolside serv. Restaurant 6 am-11 pm. Rm serv. Bar 11-2 am; entertainment. Ck-out noon. Convention facilities. Bellhops. Valet serv. Sundries. Free airport, mall transportation. Exercise equipt; stair machines, bicycles, sauna. Some bathrm phones; wet bar in some suites. *LUXURY LEVEL : EXECUTIVE CLUB LEVEL.* 20 rms, 2 suites. S $129; D $139; suite $145-$275. Concierge. Private lounge, bar. Wet bars. Complimentary coffee in rms. Complimentary continental bkfst, refreshments. Cr cds: A, C, D, DS, ER, JCB, MC, V.

⊡ ≋ 🏃 ✈ 🛏 🔥 SC

★ ★ ★ **RED LION HOTEL-SEATTLE AIRPORT.** *(18740 International Blvd, Seattle 98188) International Blvd (WA 99) at S 188th St.* *206/246-8600; FAX 206/242-9727.* 850 rms, 14 story. S $115-$135; D $120-$140; each addl $5; suites $275-$450; under 18 free; wkend rates. Crib free. TV; cable. Heated pool; poolside serv. Restaurant 6 am-midnight. Rm serv 24 hrs. Bars 11:30-2 am; entertainment, dancing. Ck-out 1 pm. Convention facilities. Bellhops. Valet serv. Concierge. Sundries. Barber, beauty shop. Free airport transportation 24 hrs. Exercise equipt; weight machines, stair machine. Many bathrm phones. Private patios, balconies. Many rms with view of lake, mountains. Outdoor glass-enclosed elvtrs. On 28 acres. Cr cds: A, C, D, DS, ER, JCB, MC, V.

⊡ ≋ 🏃 ✈ 🛏 🔥

★ ★ **WESTCOAST SEA-TAC HOTEL.** *(18220 International Blvd, Seattle 98188) On International Blvd (WA 99) at 182nd St.* *206/246-5535; res: 800/426-0670; FAX 206/246-5535, ext. 135.* 146 rms, 5 story. S $80-$89; D $85-$99; each addl $10; suites $150; under 18 free; some wkend rates. Crib free. TV; cable. Heated pool; whirlpool, sauna. Restaurant 6 am-10 pm. Rm serv. Bar 11:30-2 am. Ck-out noon. Meeting rms. Bellhops. Valet serv. Free valet parking. Airport transportation. Minibar in suites. Cr cds: A, C, D, DS, ER, JCB, MC, V.

⊡ ≋ ✈ 🛏 🔥 SC

Bellevue

Motels

★ ★ **BEST WESTERN BELLEVUE INN.** *11211 Main St (98004), just W of I-405 exit 12.* *206/455-5240; FAX 206/455-0654.* 179 rms, 2 story. S $80; D $90; under 18 free; some wkend rates. Crib free. Pet accepted; $30 non-refundable. TV; cable. Heated pool. Restaurant 6:30 am-2:30 pm, 5-10 pm. Rm serv. Bar; entertainment Thur-Sat. Ck-out noon. Meeting rms. Bellhops. Valet serv. Sundries. Some refrigerators. Balconies. Cr cds: A, C, D, DS, ER, JCB, MC, V.

⊡ 🐾 ≋ 🛏 🔥 SC

★ ★ **RESIDENCE INN BY MARRIOTT.** *14455 NE 29th Place (98007), off WA 520 148th Ave N exit.* *206/882-1222; FAX 206/885-9260.* 120 suites, 2 story. S, D $144-$199. Crib $5. Pet accepted; $50 non-refundable and $5 per day. TV; cable, in-rm movies avail. Heated pool. Playground. Complimentary continental bkfst, coffee. Ck-out noon. Coin lndry. Meeting rms. Valet serv. Sundries. Health club privileges. Lawn games. Bathrm phones, refrigerators. Private patios, balconies. Picnic tables, grills. Cr cds: A, C, D, DS, JCB, MC, V.

⊡ 🐾 ≋ 🛏 🔥

Motor Hotel

★ ★ **WESTCOAST BELLEVUE HOTEL.** *625 116th Ave NE (98004), E of I-405, NE 8th St exit.* *206/455-9444; FAX 206/455-2154.* 176 rms, 6 story. S $61-$65; D $71-$75; each addl $10; suites $85-$95; under 18 free. Crib free. TV; cable. Heated pool; poolside serv. Complimentary coffee in rms. Restaurant 6:30 am-10 pm; Sat & Sun from 7 am. Rm serv. Bar 4-11 pm. Ck-out noon. Meeting rms. Sundries.

Exercise equipt; stair machine, bicycles. Health club privileges. Cr cds: A, C, D, DS, ER, MC, V.

≋ 🏃 🛏 🔥 SC

Hotels

★ ★ ★ **HILTON.** *100 112th Ave NE (98004), just off I-405 NE 4th St exit.* *206/455-3330; FAX 206/451-2473.* 180 rms, 7 story. S $95-$111; D $115-$121; each addl $10; suites $160-$235; family, wkend rates. Crib free. TV; cable. Indoor pool; whirlpool, sauna. Restaurants 5:30 am-10 pm. Bar 10-2 am. Ck-out 1 pm. Meeting rms. Concierge. Health club privileges. Some wet bars. Cr cds: A, C, D, DS, ER, JCB, MC, V.

⊡ ≋ 🛏 🔥 SC

★ ★ ★ **HYATT REGENCY.** *900 Bellevue Way NE (98004), at Bellevue Place.* *206/462-1234; FAX 206/646-7567.* 382 rms, 24 story, 30 suites. S $150-$169; D $170-$189; suites $200-$1,000; under 18 free. Crib free. Garage $7; valet parking $12. TV; cable. Indoor pool privileges. Supervised child's activities (Fri, Sat evenings). Restaurant 6 am-10:30 pm. Bar 11-2 am. Ck-out noon. Convention facilities. Concierge. Shopping arcade. Barber, beauty shop. Health club privileges. Some bathrm phones, refrigerators. Hotel connected to office/retail complex by enclosed walkway. 6-story glass atrium lobby. *LUXURY LEVEL : REGENCY CLUB.* 17 rms, 5 suites, 2 floors. S $175; D $200. Concierge. Private lounge, honor bar. Complimentary continental bkfst, refreshments, newspaper. Cr cds: A, C, D, DS, ER, JCB, MC, V.

⊡ 🛏 🔥 SC

★ ★ ★ **RED LION.** *300 112th Ave SE (98004), just W of I-405 exit 12.* *206/455-1300; FAX 206/455-0466.* 353 rms, 10 story. S, D $115-$135; each addl $15; suites $250-$495; under 18 free; wkend rates. Crib free. TV. Heated pool, poolside serv. Restaurant 6 am-11 pm. Bar 11-2 am; dancing. Ck-out noon. Convention facilities. Gift shop. Barber, beauty shop. Exercise equipt; weight machine, bicycles, whirlpool. Some bathrm phones. Balconies. Glass-enclosed elvtrs in lobby; multistory glass canopy at entrance. *LUXURY LEVEL : EXECUTIVE LEVEL.* 45 rms. S,D $135-$155. Concierge. Private lounge. Complimentary continental bkfst, refreshments. Cr cds: A, C, D, DS, ER, JCB, MC, V.

⊡ ≋ 🏃 🛏 🔥

★ ★ ★ ★ **WOODMARK HOTEL AT CARILLON POINT.** *(1200 Carillon Point, Kirkland 98033) N on Bellevue Way, continue onto Lake Washington Blvd NE.* *206/822-3700; res: 800/822-3700; FAX 206/822-3699.* 100 units, 4 story, 21 suites. June-Oct: S $160-$195; D $170-$205; suites $225-$900; under 18 free; lower rates rest of yr. Crib free. Overnight parking $9; valet. TV; cable, in-rm movies. Complimentary coffee in rms, late night snacks. Restaurant 6:30 am-10 pm, Sat & Sun from 7 am. Bar 11 am-midnight; entertainment Wed-Sun. Ck-out noon. Meeting rms. Concierge. Free van service to downtown Seattle and local areas. Health club privileges. Refrigerators, honor bars. Balconies. Complimentary newspaper, shoeshine. On the shores of Lake Washington with swimming beach, marina, pier, shoreline promenade; 3 lakeside parks; stream with trout and salmon. Panoramic views of the lake and mountain ranges. Cr cds: A, D, MC, V.

⊡ 🐟 🏃 🛏 🔥 SC

Inn

🡥 ★ ★ ★ **SHUMWAY MANSION.** *(11410 99th Place NE, Kirkland 98033) I-405N, exit 20A, then 1 1/2 mi west.* *206/823-2303; FAX 206/822-0421.* 8 rms, 2 story. No A/C. Rm phone avail. S, D $65-$85; each addl $10; suite $95. Children over 12 yrs only. TV avail. Complimentary full bkfst; evening refreshments. Restaurant nearby. Ck-out 11 am, ck-in 3 pm. Health club privileges. Balconies. Picnic tables, grills. A 24-rm historic mansion (1909), restored and moved to present site in 1985. Overlooks Juanita Bay. Totally nonsmoking. Cr cds: A, MC, V.

 🛏 🔥

Restaurants

★ ★ ★ **BISTRO PROVENÇAL.** *(212 Central Way, Kirkland)* I-405 Kirkland exit. *206/827-3300.* Hrs: 5:30-10:30 pm; Sun to 9:30 pm. Closed major hols. Res accepted. French menu. Serv bar. Semi-a la carte: dinner $11.95-$23.50. Complete meals: dinner $18-$19.50. Specializes in seafood, rack of lamb. Own baking. French country inn decor. Casual elegance. Fireplace. Cr cds: A, C, D, MC, V.

★ ★ **KAMON OF KOBE.** *2444 Bel Red Rd NE. 206/644-1970.* Hrs: 11:30 am-2 pm, 5-10 pm. Closed some major hols. Res accepted. Japanese menu. Bar from 4:30 pm. Semi-a la carte: lunch $4.50-$13.95, dinner $6.75-$21.95. Specializes in hibachi chicken, teriyaki steak. Parking. Overlooks walled garden. Cr cds: A, D, MC, V.

D

 ★ ★ **SPAZZO MEDITERRANEAN GRILL.** *10655 NE Fourth St (10655), on 9th floor of Key Bank Bldg. 206/454-8255.* Hrs: 11 am-3 pm, 4-10 pm; Fri & Sat to 11 pm; Sun 4-10 pm. Closed Dec 25. Res accepted. Mediterranean menu. Bar. Semi-a la carte: lunch $5.95-$11.95, dinner $6.95-$15.95. Child's meals. Specializes in Italian, Greek and Spanish dishes. View of Lake Washington and downtown. Cr cds: A, D, MC, V.

D

Tampa

Settled: 1824

Pop: 281,837

Elev: 57 feet

Time zone: Eastern

Area code: 813

St Petersburg

Founded: 1876

Pop: 250,000

Elev: 44 feet

Time zone: Eastern

Area code: 813

Third largest city in Florida and home to a Spanish, Cuban and Italian enclave of 30,000, Tampa, meaning "sticks of fire," is indeed a hot spot on the west Florida coast. More than any other major city in the state, Tampa retains the Latin color and flavor that attest to its Spanish origins.

The fourth largest city in the state and second only to Miami as a winter resort, St Petersburg is host to a half million visitors each year. St Petersburg wears a fringe of beaches, parks and yacht basins along Tampa Bay and a string of resort-occupied islands on the Gulf of Mexico, connected to the mainland by causeways. These islands form the St Petersburg Beach area.

Tampa and St Petersburg are the gateway cities to Florida's southwest Gulf Coast area. Together, the two cities, along with seven other nearby coastal communities, comprise the Suncoast, a popular vacation destination area.

Business

While tourism is an important factor in the economy of the Tampa-St Petersburg metropolitan area, there is considerable industry as well. The Port of Tampa, the seventh largest in the nation, handles more than 52 million tons of shipping a year. The city is a major manufacturing center for cigars; two large breweries, two citrus-processing plants and a variety of other industries are also here. Some 800 small-to-medium-sized manufacturers operate in Tampa.

Hillsborough County is one of Florida's most diverse agricultural counties, with citrus fruit, beef cattle, dairy products, vegetables and ornamental horticulture the main commodities. Some 2,600 Hillsborough County farms produce more than $400 million worth of farm goods each year. In the Greater Tampa area are a large number of feed, fertilizer and insecticide manufacturers, paper and metal container fabricating plants and food processing plants. Some of the world's

largest phosphate mines are nearby. The county is the second largest egg producer in the state and is also second in milk production. Some 350 vegetable farmers cultivate more than 15,000 acres of vegetables and strawberries.

Tampa is the transportation center for the west coast of Florida, as well as a center of banking, insurance and investment. The city is also growing as a medical and high technology center.

Convention Facilities

The Tampa Convention Center, overlooking the Hillsborough River, includes 200,000 square feet of exhibit space and features a 36,000-square-foot ballroom and 42,000 square feet of meeting rooms.

There are 22 meeting rooms with seating capacities from 40 to 1,000. Parking space for 450 cars is located under the building, with an additional 5,000 parking spaces available within a 4-block area.

The Florida State Fairgrounds, located six miles from downtown Tampa, provides versatile facilities for year-round use. The exposition hall has 93,000 square feet of floor space, with a seating capacity of 12,500 or space for 322 exhibits or concessions. The air-conditioned structure has a 45-foot ceiling, enabling it to be used for circuses and sports events as well as trade shows.

The 325-acre complex has numerous other exhibition buildings and entertainment centers, campsites with rest rooms and showers and parking for 16,500 cars with room for expansion.

The Florida Suncoast Dome in downtown St Petersburg contains 152,000 square feet of unobstructed floor space and an additional 22,000 square feet of meeting space. On-site parking is available for 7,500 cars with 32,500 spaces available within a mile.

St Petersburg's Bayfront Center is one of the finest entertainment complexes in the nation. Its auditorium and arena provide space for

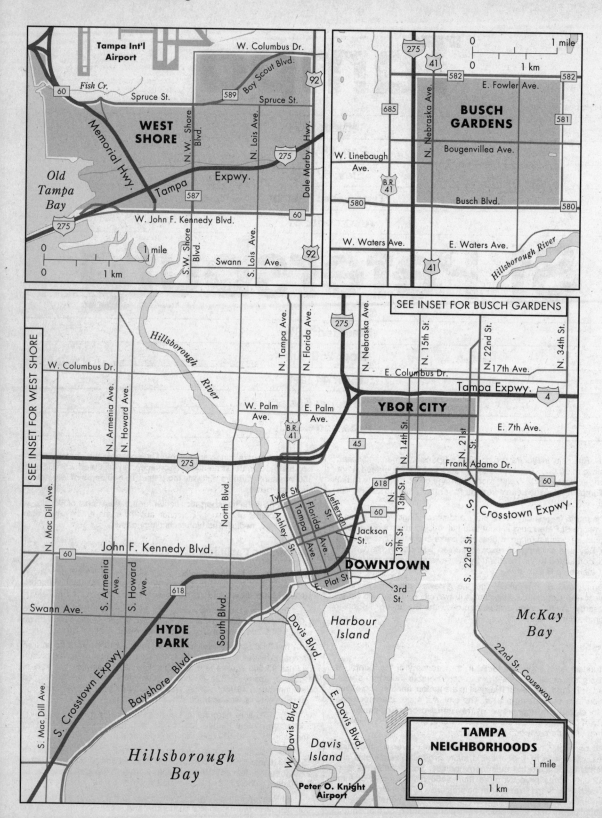

Tampa Int'l Airport

W. Columbus Dr.

Boy Scout Blvd.

589 · 92

Spruce St.

Fish Cr.

Spruce St.

60

WEST SHORE

Memorial Hwy.

Tampa Expwy.

275

Old Tampa Bay

587

275

W. John F. Kennedy Blvd.

Swann Ave.

N.W. Shore Blvd.

N. Lois Ave.

Dale Marby Hwy.

60

92

S.W. Shore Blvd.

S. Lois Ave.

0 — 1 mile
0 — 1 km

275

---

275 · 41

582

E. Fowler Ave. · 582

685

581

BUSCH GARDENS

W. Linebaugh Ave.

Bougenvillea Ave.

N. Nebraska Ave.

B.R. 41

580

Busch Blvd. · 580

W. Waters Ave.

E. Waters Ave.

Hillsborough River

41

0 — 1 mile
0 — 1 km

SEE INSET FOR WEST SHORE

SEE INSET FOR BUSCH GARDENS

Hillsborough River

W. Columbus Dr.

N. Armenia Ave.

N. Howard Ave.

N. Tampa Ave.

N. Florida Ave.

275

N. Nebraska Ave.

N. 15th St.

N. 22nd St.

N. 34th St.

E. Columbus Dr.

N. 17th Ave.

Tampa Expwy. · 4

W. Palm Ave.

E. Palm Ave.

B.R. 41

YBOR CITY

E. 7th Ave.

N. 14th St.

N. 21st St.

45

275

Frank Adamo Dr.

60

618

N. 13th St.

60

S. Crosstown Expwy.

Tyler St.

Jefferson St.

S. 13th St.

S. 22nd St.

North Blvd.

John F. Kennedy Blvd.

60

S. Armenia Ave.

S. Howard Ave.

Ashley St.

Tampa St.

Florida Ave.

Jackson St.

DOWNTOWN

3rd St.

McKay Bay

N. Mac Dill Ave.

618

South Blvd.

E. Plat St.

Swann Ave.

HYDE PARK

Bayshore Blvd.

S. Crosstown Expwy.

Davis Blvd.

Harbour Island

22nd St. Causeway

S. Mac Dill Ave.

W. Davis Blvd.

E. Davis Blvd.

Davis Island

Hillsborough Bay

Peter O. Knight Airport

TAMPA NEIGHBORHOODS

0 — 1 mile
0 — 1 km

Broadway shows, ice shows, circuses and concerts, as well as for conventions, exhibitions and trade shows.

The Tampa/Hillsborough Convention and Visitors Association lists more than 50 hotels that together contain more than 210 meeting rooms with capacities of 15 to 1,820 people. All hotels can accommodate banquets for medium-sized groups; all have food service and cocktail lounges; and most have exhibit space.

Sports and Recreation

All of the activities that draw tourists to Florida are available in the Tampa/St Petersburg area; among them are golf, boating, tennis, fishing, swimming, shuffleboard, playgrounds and parks.

Tampa/St Petersburg city officials are attempting to lure a major league baseball franchise to its new Florida Suncoast Dome, a stadium with capacity of 43,000, specifically designed for baseball. In addition, the stadium plays host to college basketball, ice shows, motor sports, indoor tennis, indoor soccer and concerts. The stadium's roof is cable-supported rather than air-supported, thus allowing "self-contained" areas of the stadium to be moved.

In addition, the St Louis Cardinals have spring training in St Petersburg's Al Lang Stadium; the Cincinnati Reds in Plant City Stadium. The Tampa Bay Buccaneers play professional football games in Tampa Stadium, and the Tampa Bay Lightning play professional hockey at the Expo Mall at the State Fairgrounds. There is also horse racing, jai alai, college sports, auto racing, golf tournaments, dog racing, various festivals and the Florida State Fair.

Entertainment

Each year Tampa enjoys the bright and colorful tradition of the Gasparilla pirate invasion, when a fully rigged pirate ship sails into the bay and "captures" the city. In March, St Petersburg hosts an ocean racing event, and from late March to mid-April the Festival of States features parades and band competitions.

Close by St Petersburg's Bayfront Center is the Pier. The revitalized area contains shops and restaurants and offers fishing and other water sports. Nearby are a marina, beach, yacht club, the Fine Arts Museum, the Salvador Dali Museum, the Historical Museum and Great Explorations Museum.

Some of the most famous restaurants in the South, serving everything from Spanish cuisine to fresh seafood, are in this area, and many clubs and nightspots feature live entertainment.

Historical Areas

Ybor City is the Latin Quarter of Tampa where Cuban immigrants established residences and businesses—the most important of which was the cigar industry.

A complex of brick buildings that once housed the largest cigar factory in the world, Ybor Square has been converted into a thriving center containing a nostalgic marketplace, restaurants, old-fashioned ice cream parlor and a variety of shops and boutiques. The original factory was built by Vincente Martinez Ybor in 1886 and employed more than 4,000 cigar makers for 5 decades. This was the original center of Ybor City and was not only a place of employment, but an educational center for the workers as well. The facades of the buildings are being restored to their original 19th-century appearance.

Today Ybor City is still a thoroughly Cuban community, with wrought-iron balconies, multicolumned buildings, plazas, arcades and sidewalk coffee shops.

An interesting restoration in St Petersburg Beach is that of the Don CeSar, an elegant and striking "pink palace," which was a favorite resort of the members of café society during the 1920s. The Don CeSar was used as a hospital during World War II and for federal offices for some years after. It was later restored and reopened as a resort.

Sightseeing

Within the Tampa/St Petersburg area are Busch Gardens Tampa, a zoological park and garden featuring rides, attractions, animal shows and big game; Adventure Island, a 13-acre water theme park; and Florida's Sunken Gardens, which are especially beautiful in early spring when the camellias, gardenias, azaleas and rhododendrons are in bloom.

Major Tampa shopping areas include Tampa Bay Center, Westshore Plaza, University Mall, Old Hyde Park Village and Eastlake Square Mall. Major St Petersburg shopping areas include Tyrone Square Mall and Pinellas Square Mall. Harbour Island Marketplace is connected to downtown Tampa by monorail.

City Environs

Just north of Tampa/St Petersburg, on the Gulf Coast, is Tarpon Springs, a town settled largely by Greek fishermen. Today, this area is a sponge market center. Spongeorama features an audiovisual sponge-diving show and displays. Approximately 30 miles farther north is Weeki Wachee Spring with its spectacular underwater show.

South from St Petersburg, is the sparkling city of Sarasota, where the Ringling Museums are worth a stop of several hours. Still farther south along the coast is Fort Myers, where Thomas Edison and several of his industrialist friends lived and worked; Sanibel Island, one of the less commercial beach areas to be found in the state; and Naples, home of Jungle Larry's Zoological Park at Caribbean Gardens.

To the east and northeast, within driving distance of the Tampa/St Petersburg area, are Cypress Gardens in Winter Haven, Bok Tower Gardens in Lake Wales, Sea World near Orlando and, of course, the vacation kingdom of Walt Disney World.

General References Tampa

Settled: 1824 **Pop:** 280,015 **Elev:** 57 feet **Time zone:** Eastern **Area code:** 813

Phone Numbers

POLICE & FIRE: 911
FBI: 228-7661
POISON CONTROL CENTER: 253-4444
TIME: 976-1111 **WEATHER:** 976-1111

Information Sources

Tampa/Hillsborough Convention & Visitors Association, 111 Madison St, Suite 1010, 33602; 223-1111, ext 44 or 800/44-TAMPA. Greater Tampa Chamber of Commerce, 801 E Kennedy Blvd, PO Box 420, 33601; 228-7777.

Transportation

AIRLINES: Air Canada; American; America West; British Airways; Cayman; Continental; Delta; Northwest; TWA; United; USAir; and other commuter and regional airlines. For the most current airline schedules and information consult the *Official Airline Guide,* published twice monthly.
AIRPORT: Tampa International, 870-8700.
CAR RENTAL AGENCIES: (See Toll-Free Numbers) Avis 276-3500; Budget 877-6051; Dollar 276-3640; Hertz 874-3232; National 276-3782.
PUBLIC TRANSPORTATION: RTA 254-4278.
RAILROAD PASSENGER SERVICE: Amtrak 800/872-7245.

Newspaper

Tampa Tribune.

Convention Facilities

Florida State Fairgrounds, 4800 US 301, 621-7821.
Tampa Convention Center, 333 S Franklin St, 223-8511.

Sports & Recreation

Major Sports Facilities
Expo Mall, Florida State Fairgrounds, 4800 US 301, 229-2658 (Tampa Bay Lightning, hockey).
Plant City Stadium, Park Rd, 2 mi S of I-4 on Park Rd, 752-1878 (Cincinnati Reds, baseball, spring training).
Tampa Stadium, 4201 N Dale Mabry Hwy, 879-2827 (Tampa Bay Buccaneers, football).

Racetracks
Tampa Bay Downs, 11 mi NW on FL 580, then 1 mi N on Race Track Rd, Oldsmar, 855-4401 (horse racing).
Tampa Track, 8300 Nebraska Ave, 932-4313 (greyhound racing).

Jai Alai
Tampa Fronton, 5125 S Dale Mabry Hwy at Gandy Blvd, 831-1411.

Cultural Facilities

Theaters and Concert Halls
Tampa Bay Performing Arts Center, 1010 N MacInnes Place, 221-1045.
Tampa Theatre, 711 N Franklin, 223-8981.

Museums
Children's Museum of Tampa at Lowry Park, 7550 N Boulevard, 935-8441.
Henry B. Plant Museum, 401 W Kennedy Blvd, Univ of Tampa, 254-1891.
Hillsborough County Historical Commission Museum, County Courthouse, Room 250, Pierce St between Kennedy Blvd & Twiggs St, 272-5919.
Museum of African-American Art, 1308 N Marion St, 272-2466.
Museum of Science and Industry, 4801 E Fowler Ave, 987-6300.
Tampa Museum of Art, 601 Doyle Carlton Dr, 223-8130.
Ybor City State Museum, 1818 E 9th Ave, 247-6323.

Points of Interest

Adventure Island, 4545 Bougainvillea Ave, 987-5660.
Bok Tower Gardens, 50 mi E, just N of Lake Wales, 676-1408.
Busch Gardens Tampa, 3000 Busch Blvd, entrance on 40th St, 987-5082.
Cypress Gardens, 2 mi SW of Winter Haven on FL 540, 324-2111.
Hillsborough River State Park, 30 mi NE via US 301, in Zephyrhills, 987-6771.
Lowry Park Zoo, 7530 N Boulevard, 932-0245.
Municipal Beach, Courtney Campbell Causeway, FL 60.
University of Tampa, John F. Kennedy Blvd at Hillsborough River, 253-3333.
Waterfront, from Davis Island, Water St or 13th St.
Ybor City, between I-4, 5th Ave, Nebraska Ave & 22nd St.
Ybor Square, 1901 N 13th St, 247-4497.

Sightseeing Tours

Around the Town, 3450 W Busch Blvd, Suite 115, 932-7803.
Gray Line bus tours, PO Box 145, St Petersburg 33731; 273-0845.
Tampa Tours, 5805 N 50th St, 621-6667.

Annual Events

Gasparilla Festival of Tampa Bay, waterfront. Early Feb-early Mar.
Florida State Fair, Florida State Fairgrounds and Expo Park. Early-mid-Feb.
Florida Strawberry Festival, Plant City. Late Feb-early Mar.
(For further information contact the Tampa/Hillsborough Convention & Visitors Association.)

St Petersburg

Founded: 1876 **Pop:** 238,629 **Elev:** 44 feet **Time zone:** Eastern **Area code:** 813

Phone Numbers

POLICE & FIRE: 911
POISON CONTROL CENTER: 253-4444
FBI: 581-9938 or 228-7661
TIME: 976-1111 **WEATHER:** 976-1111

Information Sources

St Petersburg-Clearwater Area Convention & Visitors Bureau, Florida Suncoast Dome, 1 Stadium Dr, Suite A, 33705; 892-7892 OR 800/951-1111.
St Petersburg Area Chamber of Commerce, 100 2nd Ave N, PO Box 1371, 33731; 821-4715.
Suncoast Welcome Center, 2001 Ulmerton Rd, 573-1449.
Dept of Leisure Services, 893-7207.
The Pier, 800 2nd Ave NE, 821-6164.

Transportation

AIRPORTS: St Petersburg/Clearwater International, 535-7600 or 531-1451; Tampa International, 870-8700.
AIRLINES: American Trans Air; Canadian Intl; Southwest; and other commuter and regional airlines. For the most current airline schedules and information consult the *Official Airline Guide*, published twice monthly.
CAR RENTAL AGENCIES: (See Toll-Free Numbers) Avis 530-1406; Budget 576-4011; Hertz 531-3774; National 530-5491.
PUBLIC TRANSPORTATION: St Petersburg Transit Dept 530-9911.
RAILROAD PASSENGER SERVICE: Amtrak 800/872-7245.

Newspaper

St Petersburg Times.

Convention Facilities

Bayfront Center, 400 1st St S, 893-7211.
Florida Suncoast Dome, 204 16th St S, 825-3100.

Sports & Recreation

Major Sports Facilities

Al Lang Stadium, 1st St S & 2nd Ave S, 822-3384 (St Louis Cardinals, baseball, spring training).
Florida Suncoast Dome, 204 16th St S, 825-3333.

Racetracks

Derby Lane-St Petersburg Kennel Club, 10490 Gandy Blvd NE, 576-1361 (greyhound racing).
Sunshine Speedway, 9 mi N on I-275, then 3 mi W on FL 688, in Pinellas Park, 573-4598 (auto racing).
Tampa Bay Downs, N on US 19, E on FL 580, then 1 mi N on Race Track Rd, Oldsmar, 855-4401 (horse racing).

Cultural Facilities

Theater & Concert Hall

Bayfront Center Theater, 400 1st St S, 892-5767 (Florida Orchestra).

Museums

Great Explorations, 1120 4th St S, 821-8885.
St Petersburg Historical Museum, 335 2nd Ave NE, 894-1052.

Art Museums

Museum of Fine Arts, 255 Beach Dr NE, 896-2667.
Salvador Dali Museum, 1000 3rd St S, 823-3767.

Points of Interest

Historical

Coliseum Ballroom, 535 4th Ave N, 892-5202.
Don CeSar Hotel, 3400 Gulf Blvd, St Petersburg Beach, 360-1881.

Other Attractions

De Soto National Memorial, S on US 41 to Bradenton, then 2 mi N off FL 64, on Tampa Bay, 792-0458.
Florida's Sunken Gardens, 1825 4th St N, 896-3186.
Fort De Soto Park, Mullet Key, 866-2484.
Lake Maggiore Park, 9th St S.
Planetarium, St Petersburg Jr College, 6605 5th Ave N, 341-4320.

Ringling Museums, 25 mi S via US 10, 41, Sarasota, 355-5101.
Science Center of Pinellas County, 7701 22nd Ave N, 384-0027.
Spongeorama, 510 Dodecanese Blvd, Tarpon Springs, 942-3771.
Suncoast Seabird Sanctuary, 18328 Gulf Blvd, Indian Shores, 391-6211.
Weeki Wachee Spring, 30 mi N via US 19, at jct FL 50, 904/596-2062.

Sightseeing Tours

Gray Line bus tours, 6890 142nd Ave N, 34641; 535-0208

Annual Events

International Folk Fair. Mar.
Renaissance Festival. Mar.
Festival of States. Late Mar-mid-Apr.
St Anthony's Tampa Bay Triathlon. Apr.
Artworks Festival. May.

City Neighborhoods

Many of the restaurants, unrated dining establishments and some lodgings listed under Tampa include neighborhoods as well as exact street addresses. A map showing these neighborhoods can be found immediately following the city introduction. Geographic descriptions of these neighborhoods are given, followed by a table of restaurants arranged by neighborhood.

Tampa

Busch Gardens: West of Busch Gardens amusement park; south of Fowler Ave, north of Busch Blvd and east of I-275.
Downtown: South of Tyler St, west of Jefferson St, north of Water St and Harbour Island and east of Ashley St. **North of Downtown:** North of US 275. **South of Downtown:** South of FL 618. **West of Downtown:** West of Hillsborough River.
Hyde Park: South of Kennedy Blvd, west and north of Bayshore Blvd and east of S MacDill Ave.
West Shore: On Old Tampa Bay south of Courtney Campbell Pkwy and Tampa Intl Airport, west of Dale Mabry Hwy and north of Kennedy Blvd.
Ybor City: South of I-4, west of 22nd St, north of 7th Ave and east of Nebraska Ave.

Lodgings and Food Tampa

TAMPA RESTAURANTS
BY NEIGHBORHOOD AREAS

(For full description, see alphabetical listings under Restaurants)

DOWNTOWN

Harbour View (Wyndham Harbour Island Hotel). 725 S Harbour Island Blvd

NORTH OF DOWNTOWN

A.J. Catfish. 8751 N Himes Ave

Rumpelmayers. 4812 E Busch Blvd

Sukothai. 8201 A North Dale Mabry Hwy

WEST OF DOWNTOWN

Briedy's. 8501 W Hillsborough

Consuelo's. 3814 Neptune

Donatello. 232 N Dale Mabry Hwy

Malios. 301 S Dale Mabry Hwy

HYDE PARK

Bern's Steak House. 1208 S Howard Ave

Cactus Club. 1601 Snow Ave

Colonnade. 3401 Bayshore Blvd

Jimmy Mac's. 113 S Armenia Ave

WEST SHORE

Armani's (Hyatt Regency Westshore Hotel). 6200 Courtney Campbell Causeway

YBOR CITY

Columbia. 2117 E 7th Ave

Spaghetti Warehouse. 1911 N 13th St

Note: *When a listing is located in a town that does not have its own city heading, it will appear under the city nearest to its location. In these cases, the address and town appear in parenthesis immediately following the name of the establishment.*

Motels

(Rates may be higher during state fair, Gasparilla Festival)

★★ **COURTYARD BY MARRIOTT.** 3805 W Cypress St (33607), I-275, exit 23B, near Intl Airport, in West Shore. 813/874-0555; FAX 813/870-0685. 145 rms, 4 story. Jan-Apr: S, D $95-$115; suites $115; under 18 free; lower rates rest of yr. Crib free. Pet accepted; $50 non-refundable. TV; cable. Heated pool. Complimentary coffee in rms. Bkfst avail. Ck-out noon. Coin lndry. Meeting rms. Valet serv. Free airport transportation. Exercise equipt; weight machine, bicycles, whirlpool. Refrigerator, minibar in suites. Balconies. Cr cds: A, C, D, DS, MC, V.

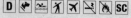

✔★ **DAYS INN-BUSCH GARDENS NORTH.** 701 E Fletcher Ave (33612), near Busch Gardens. 813/977-1550; FAX 813/977-6556.

238 rms, 3 story. Jan-Apr: S $37-$55; D $40-$60; each addl $5; family, monthly rates; varied lower rates rest of yr. Crib free. Pet accepted, some restrictions; $5. TV; cable. Pool. Restaurant 6 am-1 pm, 5-9 pm. Ck-out noon. Coin lndry. Meeting rms. Sundries. Cr cds: A, D, DS, ER, MC, V.

★ **DAYS INN-FAIRGROUNDS.** 9942 Adamo Dr (FL 60) (33619), east of downtown. 813/623-5121; FAX 813/628-4989. 100 rms, 2 story. Jan-Apr: S $49-$58; D $53-$60; each addl $5; under 12 free; lower rates rest of yr. Crib free. TV; cable. Pool. Complimentary continental bkfst. Coffee in rms. Restaurant opp 10:30 am-10 pm. Ck-out noon. Meeting rm. Cr cds: A, C, D, DS, MC, V.

✔★ **ECONOMY INNS OF AMERICA.** 6606 E Dr Martin Luther King Blvd (33619), I-4 exit 4, east of downtown. 813/623-6667. 128 rms, 2 story. Jan-mid-Apr: S $33.90; D $39-$51; each addl $6; lower rates rest of yr. Pet accepted. TV; cable. Heated pool. Complimentary coffee in lobby. Restaurant nearby. Ck-out 11 am. Cr cds: A, MC, V.

★★ **HAMPTON INN.** 4817 W Laurel St (33607), near Intl Airport, in West Shore. 813/287-0778; FAX 813/287-0882. 134 rms, 6 story. Jan-Apr: S $62-$69; D $72-$79; under 19 free; higher rates special events; lower rates rest of yr. TV; cable. Pool. Complimentary continental bkfst, coffee. Ck-out noon. Valet serv. Sundries. Free airport transportation. Cr cds: A, C, D, DS, MC, V.

★★ **HOLIDAY INN BUSCH GARDENS.** 2701 E Fowler Ave (33612), near Busch Gardens. 813/971-4710; FAX 813/977-0155. 400 rms, 2 story. Jan-Apr: S, D $79-$89; each addl $8; under 18 free; lower rates rest of yr. Crib free. TV; cable. Pool; poolside serv. Restaurant 6-1 am. Bar 11-2 am. Ck-out noon. Coin lndry. Meeting rms. Bellhops. Free Busch Gardens transportation. Tropical garden. Opp shopping mall. Cr cds: A, C, D, DS, JCB, MC, V.

★★ **HOLIDAY INN EXPRESS-STADIUM.** 4732 N Dale Mabry Hwy (33614), north of downtown. 813/877-6061; FAX 813/876-1531. 200 rms, 1-2 story. Late Dec-early Apr: S, D $65-$81; each addl $10; under 18 free; higher rates special stadium events; lower rates rest of yr. Pet accepted; $20 non-refundable. TV; cable. Pool. Complimentary continental bkfst. Restaurant 11 am-11 pm. Rm serv. Bar to 2 am. Ck-out noon. Meeting rms. Bellhops. Valet serv. Free airport transportation. Picnic table. Cr cds: A, C, D, DS, JCB, MC, V.

✔★ **LA QUINTA INN.** 2904 Melbourne Blvd (33605), I-4 exit 3, east of downtown. 813/623-3591; FAX 813/620-1375. 129 rms, 3 story. S $43-$58; D $50-$58; each addl $7; suites $78; under 18 free. Crib free. Pet accepted. TV; cable. Heated pool. Complimentary continental bkfst. Ck-out noon. Guest lndry. Meeting rms. Sundries. Cr cds: A, C, D, DS, MC, V.

★ **RED ROOF INN.** 5001 N US 301 (33610), near I-4 exit 6A, east of downtown. 813/623-5245; FAX 813/623-5240. 109 rms, 2 story. Mid-Jan-mid-Apr: S, D $49.99; under 18 free; lower rates rest of yr. Pet accepted, some restrictions. TV; cable. Complimentary coffee. Restaurant adj open 24 hrs. Ck-out noon. Cr cds: A, C, D, DS, MC, V.

★★ **RESIDENCE INN BY MARRIOTT.** 3075 N Rocky Point Dr (33607), near Intl Airport, west of downtown. 813/281-5677. 176 kit. units, 1-2 story. Jan-Apr: S, D $105-$150; family rates; lower rates rest of yr. Crib free. Pet accepted; $100 non-refundable and $6 per day. TV. Pool; whirlpool. Complimentary continental bkfst 6:30-9:30 am; Sat & Sun 8-10 am. Ck-out noon. Meeting rms. Bellhops. Valet serv. Airport transportation. Some balconies. On Tampa Bay. Cr cds: A, C, D, DS, MC, V.

[D] [icons] SC

★ ★ **SAILPORT RESORT.** 2506 Rocky Point Dr (33607), west of downtown. 813/281-9599; res: 800/255-9599; FAX 813/281-9510. 237 kit. suites (1-2 bedrm), 4 story. S, D $97-$149; under 12 free; monthly, wkly rates. Crib $5; TV; cable. Heated pool. Complimentary continental bkfst, coffee. Ck-out 11 am. Meeting rms. Coin Indry. Valet serv. Covered parking. Lighted tennis. Private patios, balconies. Some grills. On bay; dock; all waterfront rms. Cr cds: A, D, MC, V.

[icons] SC

✔ ★ **TAHITIAN INN.** 601 S Dale Mabry Hwy (33609), Westshore. 813/877-6721; res: 800/876-1397; FAX 813/877-6218. 79 rms (18 with shower only), 2 story. Mid-Jan-mid-Apr: S $44-$50; D $48-$59; each addl $5; under 12 free; higher rates football games; lower rates rest of yr. Crib $5. Pet accepted. TV; cable. Heated pool. Restaurant 7 am-2:30 pm; Sat & Sun 8 am-1:30 pm. Rm serv. Ck-out noon. Meeting rm. Bellhops. Sundries. 18-hole golf privileges; green fee $30. Balconies. Picnic tables. Cr cds: A, C, D, DS, MC, V.

[D] [icons] SC

★ **TRAVELODGE AT BUSCH GARDENS.** 9202 N 30th St (33612), near Busch Gardens. 813/935-7855; FAX 813/935-7958. 146 rms, 3 story. Mid-Jan-Apr: S $50; D $54; each addl $4; suites $70; under 18 free; lower rates rest of yr. Crib free. Pet accepted; $10 refundable. TV; cable. Pool. Restaurant adj 7 am-11 pm. Ck-out 11 am. Coin Indry avail. Meeting rm. Sundries. Gift shop. Game rm. Cr cds: A, D, ER, MC, V.

[D] [icons] SC

Motor Hotels

★ ★ **COLONY RESORT-BUSCH GARDENS.** 820 E Busch Blvd (33612), near Busch Gardens. 813/933-4011; FAX 813/932-1784. 261 rms, 2-4 story. Jan-Apr: S $59-$99; D $79-$99; suites $119-$159; under 12 free; wkly, wkend rates; higher rates special events; lower rates rest of yr. Crib free. TV; cable. 2 heated pools, 1 indoor. Restaurant 6:30 am-10 pm. Rm serv. Bar 11-1 am; dancing Tues-Sat. Ck-out 11 am. Coin Indry. Convention facilities. Bellhops. Valet serv. Sundries. Gift shop. Free Busch Gardens transportation. Lighted tennis. Exercise equipt; weights, bicycles, sauna. Game rm. Cr cds: A, C, D, DS, ER, JCB, MC, V.

[D] [icons] SC

★ ★ **QUALITY SUITES.** 3001 University Center Dr (33612), near Busch Gardens. 813/971-8930; FAX 813/971-8935. 150 suites, 3 story. Suites $69-$159; each addl (1-4 persons) $10; under 18 free. Crib free. TV; cable, in-rm movies. Heated pool; whirlpool. Complimentary full bkfst. Complimentary coffee in rms. Restaurant 6-10 am; wkends 7-11 am, 4-7 pm. Ck-out noon. Coin Indry. Meeting rms. Bellhops. Valet serv. Sundries. Gift shop. Balconies. Cr cds: A, C, D, DS, ER, JCB, MC, V.

[D] [icons] SC

Hotels

★ ★ ★ **EMBASSY SUITES-WEST SHORE.** 555 N Westshore Blvd (33609), near Intl Airport, in West Shore. 813/875-1555; FAX 813/287-3664. 221 kit. suites, 16 story. Jan-Apr: S, D $139-$159; under 18 free; monthly, wkly, wkend rates; lower rates rest of yr. Crib free. Pet accepted, some restrictions. TV; cable. Heated pool; poolside serv. Restaurant 6:30 am-2 pm, 5-10 pm; Sat & Sun 7 am-2 pm. Bar noon-midnight. Ck-out noon. Coin Indry. Meeting rms. Gift shop. Free covered parking; valet. Free airport transportation. Exercise equipt; stair machine, bicycles, whirlpool, sauna. Balconies. Cr cds: A, C, D, DS, ER, JCB, MC, V.

[D] [icons] SC

★ ★ ★ **GUEST QUARTERS ON TAMPA BAY.** 3050 N Rocky Point Dr W (33607), at Courtney Campbell Causeway, near Intl Airport, west of downtown. 813/888-8800; FAX 813/888-8743. 203 suites, 7 story. Oct-Apr: S $149; D $169; each addl $20; under 13 free; wkend rates; lower rates rest of yr. Crib free. TV; cable. Heated pool. Restaurant 6:30 am-10 pm. Bar 11 am-midnight. Ck-out noon. Coin Indry. Meeting rms. Free airport transportation. Exercise equipt; weights, bicycles, whirlpool, sauna. Refrigerators. Sun deck. Library. On Tampa Bay. Cr cds: A, C, D, DS, MC, V.

[D] [icons] SC

★ ★ ★ **HILTON AT METROCENTER.** 2225 Lois Ave (33607), near Intl Airport, in West Shore. 813/877-6688; FAX 813/879-3264. 238 rms, 12 story. Jan-Apr: S $105-$155; D $115-$165; each addl $10; suites $150-$350; family, wkend rates; lower rates rest of yr. Crib free. TV; cable. Heated pool; poolside serv. Restaurant 6:30 am-11 pm. Bar 11-2 am; pianist evenings. Ck-out noon. Meeting rms. Gift shop. Free airport transportation. Lighted tennis. Exercise equipt; bicycle, stair machine, whirlpool. Cr cds: A, C, D, DS, ER, JCB, MC, V.

[D] [icons] SC

★ ★ **HOLIDAY INN ASHLEY PLAZA CONVENTION CENTER.** 111 W Fortune St (33602), adj to Performing Arts Center, downtown. 813/223-1351; FAX 813/221-2000. 312 rms, 14 story. Jan-mid-Apr: S $89.50; D $99.50; each addl $10; suites $179; under 18 free; wkend rates; lower rates rest of yr. Crib free. TV; cable. Pool. Restaurant 6:30 am-11 pm. Bar 3 pm-1 am; entertainment Thurs-Sat. Ck-out 11 am. Convention facilities. Gift shop. Free airport transportation. Exercise equipt; weights, bicycles, whirlpool. Some refrigerators. Cr cds: A, C, D, DS, ER, JCB, MC, V.

[D] [icons] SC

★ ★ ★ **HOLIDAY INN CROWNE PLAZA.** 700 N Westshore Blvd (33609), near Intl Airport, in West Shore. 813/289-8200; FAX 813/289-9166. 272 rms, 11 story. Jan-Apr: S $130; D $145; each addl $15; under 18 free; wkend rates; lower rates rest of yr. Crib free. Pet accepted, some restrictions. TV; cable. Heated pool. Restaurant 6:30 am-10:30 pm. Bar 11-2 am; entertainment. Ck-out noon. Convention facilities. Airport transportation. Gift shop. Exercise equipt; weights, bicycles, whirlpool, sauna. *LUXURY LEVEL : EXECUTIVE LEVEL.* 26 rms. S $145; D $160; suites $175-$350. Concierge. Private lounge. Bathrm phones. Cr cds: A, C, D, DS, MC, V.

[D] [icons] SC

★ ★ ★ **HOLIDAY INN CROWNE PLAZA-SABAL PARK.** 10221 Princess Palm Ave (33610), at I-75 exit 52 S, east of downtown. 813/623-6363; FAX 813/621-7224. 265 rms, 5 story, 41 suites. Mid-Jan-mid-Apr: S, D $125-$175; suites $145-$500; under 18 free; wkend rates; higher rates special events; lower rates rest of yr. Crib free. Pet accepted, some restrictions. TV; cable. Heated pool; wading pool. Restaurant 6 am-11 pm. Bar 11-2 am. Ck-out noon. Convention facilities. Concierge. Gift shop. Barber, beauty shop. Free airport transportation. Lighted tennis. Exercise equipt; weights, bicycles, whirlpool. Refrigerator in suites. Private patios, balconies. Bldg with distinctive bowed structure located on 9 acres; 3-story atrium lobby with waterfall. *LUXURY LEVEL : CONCIERGE LEVEL.* 67 rms, 12 suites. S, D $145-$175; suites $165-$500. Ck-out noon. Private lounge. Wet bars. Complimentary continental bkfst, refreshments. Cr cds: A, C, D, DS, JCB, MC, V.

[D] [icons] SC

★ ★ ★ **HYATT REGENCY.** 2 Tampa City Center (33602), off I-275 Ashley exit, bear left onto Tampa St to Jackson St, downtown. 813/225-1234; FAX 813/273-0234. 518 rms, 17 story. S $169; D $184; each addl $15; 1-bedrm suites $200-$490; 2-bedrm suites $280-$590; under 18 free; wkend rates. Crib free. TV; cable. Heated pool. Restaurant 6:30 am-11 pm. Rm serv 24 hrs. Bar; entertainment. Ck-out noon. Meeting rms. Concierge. Garage, valet parking. Exercise equipt; weights, bicycles, whirlpool, sauna. Massage therapy. *LUXURY LEVEL : GOLD PASSPORT LEVEL.* 105 rms, 7 suites, 4 floors. S $169;

D $184; suites $280-$590. Private lounge. Complimentary beverages, newspapers. Cr cds: A, C, D, DS, ER, JCB, MC, V.

[D] [≈] [✕] [✈] [✕] [🔥] [SC]

★ ★ ★ ★ **HYATT REGENCY WESTSHORE.** 6200 Courtney Campbell Causeway (33607), on the shores of old Tampa Bay, near Intl Airport. 813/874-1234; FAX 813/281-9168. 400 rms in main bldg, 14 story, 24 suites, 45 casita villas. Main bldg: S $169; D $194; each addl $25; suites $275-$640; casita villas: S $179; D $204; suites (1-3 bedrm) $275-$515; under 18 free; wkend rates; lower rates May-Sept. Crib free. Covered parking; valet parking $7/night. TV; cable. 2 heated pools; poolside serv. Restaurant 6:30 am-11 pm (also see ARMANI'S). Rm serv 24 hrs. Bar noon-1 am; pianist. Ck-out noon. Convention facilities. Concierge. Gift shop. Free airport transportation. Tennis. Exercise rm; weights, bicycles, whirlpool, sauna. Massage. Racquetball. Lawn games. Some refrigerators, minibars. On Tampa Bay; boat dock. Elaborate landscaping; courtyard with fountains. Nestled amidst a 35-acre nature preserve. **LUXURY LEVEL : REGENCY CLUB.** 30 units, 5 suites. S $194; D $219; suites $390-$640. Private lounge, honor bar. In-rm movies. Wet bar, whirlpool in some suites. Complimentary continental bkfst, refreshments. Cr cds: A, C, D, DS, ER, JCB, MC, V.

[D] [☞] [🖐] [≈] [✕] [✈] [✕] [🔥] [SC]

★ ★ ★ **MARRIOTT TAMPA AIRPORT.** At Tampa Intl Airport (33607), 1½ mi N of jct FL 60 & I-275, in West Shore. 813/879-5151; FAX 813/873-0945. 300 rms, 6 story. Jan-Apr: S, D $144-160; each addl $15; suites $250-$600; under 18 free; wkend rates; lower rates rest of yr. Crib free. TV; cable. Pool; poolside serv. Restaurant 6 am-11 pm. Bar 11-1 am. Ck-out 1 pm. Meeting rms. Gift shop. Exercise equipt; weights, bicycles. Refrigerator in suites. Golf nearby. **LUXURY LEVEL :** 55 rms, 4 suites. S $149; D $164; suites $250-$400. Concierge. Private lounge. Wet bar. Complimentary continental bkfst, refreshments, newspaper. Cr cds: A, C, D, DS, ER, JCB, MC, V.

[D] [≈] [🖐] [✕] [✈] [✕] [🔥] [SC]

★ ★ ★ **MARRIOTT TAMPA WEST SHORE.** 1001 N Westshore Blvd (33607), near Intl Airport, in West Shore. 813/287-2555; FAX 813/289-5464. 310 rms, 14 story. S, D $144-160; suites $400; under 18 free; wkend rates. Crib free. TV; cable. Indoor/outdoor pool. Restaurant 6:30 am-11 pm. Bar 11-2 am. Ck-out 1 pm. Convention facilities. Gift shop. Free airport transportation. Exercise equipt; weights, bicycles, whirlpool, sauna. Game rm. Balconies. Golf, tennis nearby. **LUXURY LEVEL : CONCIERGE LEVEL.** 18 rms, 2 suites. S $139; D $154. Concierge. Private lounge. Complimentary continental bkfst, refreshments. Cr cds: A, C, D, DS, ER, JCB, MC, V.

[D] [≈] [🖐] [✕] [✈] [✕] [🔥] [SC]

★ ★ ★ **RADISSON BAY HARBOR INN.** 7700 Courtney Campbell Causeway (33607), west of downtown. 813/281-8900; FAX 813/281-0189. 257 rms, 6 story. Jan-Apr: S, D $95-$130; each addl $10; suites $150-$475; under 18 free; lower rates rest of yr. Crib free. TV; cable. Heated pool; poolside serv. Restaurant 7 am-midnight. Bar 11 am-midnight, Sun from 1 pm. Ck-out noon. Meeting rms. Barber, beauty shop. Free airport transportation. Lighted tennis. Golf privileges. Exercise equipt; weight machines, bicycles. Game rm. Private patios, balconies. On Tampa Bay; private beach. Cr cds: A, C, D, DS, MC, V.

[D] [🖐] [🖐] [≈] [✕] [✕] [SC]

★ ★ ★ **SHERATON GRAND HOTEL.** 4860 W Kennedy Blvd (33609), near Intl Airport, in West Shore area. 813/286-4400; FAX 813/286-4053. 324 rms, 11 story. Jan-Apr: S $135-$169; D $145-$179; each addl $10; suites $240-$550; under 18 free; wkend rates; lower rates rest of yr. Crib free. TV; cable. Heated pool; poolside serv. Coffee in rms. Restaurant 6 am-11 pm. Rm serv 24 hrs. Bar 11-2 am; entertainment. Ck-out noon. Meeting rms. Concierge. Shopping arcade. Free airport transportation. Exercise equipt; weights, stair machines. Some bathrm phones, refrigerators. **LUXURY LEVEL : GRAND CLUB.** 32 rms, 2 suites. S $159; D $169; suites $240-$375. Concierge. Private

lounge. Bathrm phones. Complimentary continental bkfst, refreshments, newspaper. Cr cds: A, C, D, DS, ER, MC, V.

[D] [≈] [🖐] [✈] [✕] [✕] [🔥] [SC]

★ ★ ★ **SHERATON INN & CONFERENCE CENTER.** 7401 E Hillsborough Ave (33610), east of downtown. 813/626-0999; FAX 813/622-7893. 276 rms, 6 story. Jan-Apr: S $105-$115; D $115-$125; each addl $10; suites $175-$275; under 17 free; wkend rates; lower rates rest of yr. Crib free. Pet accepted; $25 non-refundable. Pool. Restaurant 6:30 am-10:30 pm. Bar 11-2 am. Ck-out noon. Convention facilities. Gift shop. Airport transportation. Exercise equipt; weights, bicycles, whirlpool. Private patios, balconies. Cr cds: A, C, D, DS, JCB, MC, V.

[D] [☞] [≈] [🖐] [✕] [✕] [🔥] [SC]

★ ★ ★ ★ **WYNDHAM HARBOUR ISLAND.** 725 S Harbour Island Blvd (33602), downtown. 813/229-5000; res: 800/822-4200 (US), 800/631-4200 (CAN); FAX 813/229-5322. 300 rms, 12 story. S $149-$209; D $160-$229; each addl $10; suites $295-$850; under 18 free; wkend rates. Crib free. TV; cable. Heated pool; poolside serv. Coffee in rms. Restaurants (also see HARBOUR VIEW). Rm serv to 2 am. Bar; entertainment wkends. Ck-out noon. Convention facilities. Concierge. Shopping arcade. Free airport transportation. Tennis privileges. Health club privileges. Bicycle, boat rentals. Minibars, wet bars; some bathrm phones; refrigerator in suites. Complimentary newspapers Mon-Fri. Formal furnishings. Picturesque bay views, panoramic views of Tampa. Cr cds: A, C, D, DS, ER, JCB, MC, V.

[D] [☞] [🖐] [≈] [✕] [✕] [🔥] [SC]

Resort

★ ★ ★ ★ **SADDLEBROOK RESORT.** (5700 Saddlebrook Way, Wesley Chapel 33543) 25 mi N of Tampa Airport on I-75, exit 58 then 1 mi E on FL 54. 813/973-1111; res: 800/729-8383; FAX 813/973-4504. 530 units, 2 story, 393 with kits., 131 hotel rms, 157 1-bedrm condos, 242 2-bedrm condos. Mid-Jan-Apr: S, D $175-$325; each addl $20; under 13 free; lower rates rest of yr. TV; cable. 4 pools, 1 heated. Playground. Free supervised child's activities. Dining rm (public by res) (see CYPRESS RESTAURANT AND TERRACE ON THE GREEN). Rm serv 6:30-1 am. Box lunches, snack bar. Bar 11-1 am; entertainment, dancing. Ck-out noon, ck-in 3 pm. Convention facilities. Concierge. Grocery 1 mi. Package store. Gift shop. Barber, beauty shop. Valet parking. Airport transportation. Sports dir. Tennis, 45 courts, 5 lighted, pro. 36-hole golf designed by Arnold Palmer & Dean Refram, pro, putting green, driving range. Home of Arnold Palmer Golf Academy. Nature walks. Bicycle rentals. Game rm. Exercise rm; instructor, weight machines, bicycles, whirlpool, sauna, steam rm. Massage therapy. Minibars. Many refrigerators. Private patios, balconies. Luxury resort secluded on 480 acres of woodlands, lakes, and rolling hills. Accommodations and activities center designed as a walking village. Cr cds: A, C, D, MC, V.

[☞] [✕] [🖐] [🖐] [≈] [✕] [🖐] [🔥]

Restaurants

★ **A.J. CATFISH.** 8751 N Himes Ave, north of downtown. 813/932-3474. Hrs: 11:30 am-10:30 pm; Sat to 11 pm; Sun 5-10 pm. Closed Mon; most major hols. Semi-a la carte: lunch $2.95-$8.95, dinner $7.95-$14.95. Child's meals. Specializes in steak, seafood, pasta. Parking. Outdoor dining. Cypress wood interior, 2nd floor balcony. Cr cds: A, MC, V.

[D]

★ ★ ★ **ARMANI'S.** (See Hyatt Regency Westshore Hotel) 813/281-9165. Hrs: 6-10 pm; Fri & Sat to 11 pm. Closed Sun; some major hols. Res accepted; required Fri & Sat. Northern Italian menu. Bar 5-11 pm; Fri & Sat to midnight. Semi-a la carte: dinner $12-$25. Child's meals. Specialties: veal Armani, lobster ammiraglia. Antipasta bar. Own baking, desserts. Pianist. Valet parking. Outdoor terrace overlooks bay; on rooftop. Jacket. Cr cds: A, C, D, DS, ER, JCB, MC, V.

Ⓓ

★ ★ ★ ★ **BERN'S STEAK HOUSE.** *1208 S Howard Ave, 4 blks N of Bayshore Blvd, in Hyde Park. 813/251-2421.* Hrs: 5-11 pm. Closed Dec 25. Res suggested. Bar. Wine cellars. Semi-a la carte: dinner $15-$45 (serv charge). Specializes in own organically grown vegetables, aged prime beef, variety of roasted and blended coffees. Own baking, ice cream, sherbet, onion soup. Pianist/accordionist. Valet parking. Antiques, paintings, statuary. Chef-owned. Cr cds: A, C, D, DS, MC, V.

Ⓓ

★ **BRIEDY'S.** *8501 W Hillsborough (33615), west of downtown. 813/886-8148.* Hrs: 11 am-11 pm; Fri, Sat to 12:30 am. Closed Thanksgiving, Dec 25. Res accepted. Italian, Irish, Amer menu. Bar; wkends to 3 am. Semi-a la carte: lunch $3.95-$6, dinner $5.95-$17.95. Child's meals. Specialties: Irish pizza, sirloin strip steak, Italian pastas. Entertainment Wed-Sat. Casual, pub-like atmosphere. Cr cds: A, DS, MC, V.

Ⓓ

✔★ ★ **CACTUS CLUB.** *1601 Snow Ave, in Old Hyde Park Shopping Center, in Hyde Park. 813/251-4089.* Hrs: 11 am-midnight; Fri, Sat to 1 am; Sun to 11 pm. Closed Thanksgiving, Dec 25. Southwestern menu. Bar. Semi-a la carte: lunch, dinner $5.95-$11.95. Child's meals. Specialties: bluesburger, tacobrito, Texas pizzas. Patio dining. Southwestern decor; ceiling fans. Cr cds: A, C, D, MC, V.

Ⓓ

✔★ ★ **COLONNADE.** *3401 Bayshore Blvd, in Hyde Park. 813/839-7558.* Hrs: 11 am-10 pm; Fri, Sat to 11 pm. Closed Thanksgiving, Dec 25. Bar. Semi-a la carte: lunch $4.95-$6.95, dinner $4.95-$11.95. Child's meals. Specializes in fresh seafood, steak, prime rib, desserts. Parking. Nautical decor. Overlooks Tampa Bay. Family-owned. Cr cds: A, C, D, DS, MC, V.

Ⓓ

★ ★ ★ **COLUMBIA.** *2117 E 7th Ave (33605), in Ybor City. 813/248-4961.* Hrs: 11 am-10 pm; Fri, Sat to 11 pm; Sun noon-9 pm. Res accepted. Spanish menu. Bar. Wine cellars. Semi-a la carte: lunch $4.95-$7.95, dinner $6.95-$16.95. Cover charge $5 (in dining room with show). Child's meals. Specialties: paella a la Valenciana, snapper alicante, filet mignon steak Columbia. Flamenco dancers (dinner) exc Sun. Valet parking. Built 1905; balcony surrounds interior courtyard. Family-owned. Cr cds: A, C, D, DS, MC, V.

Ⓓ

✔★ **CONSUELO'S.** *3814 Neptune, west of downtown. 813/253-5965.* Hrs: 11:30 am-10 pm; Sat 4-11 pm; Sun 3-9 pm. Closed Thanksgiving, Dec 25. Mexican menu. Bar. A la carte entrees: lunch $4.75-$12.95, dinner $7.25-$13.95. Child's meals. Specialties: stuffed jalapeños, enchiladas. Strolling guitarists. Cr cds: A, MC, V.

Ⓓ

★ ★ ★ **CYPRESS RESTAURANT AND TERRACE ON THE GREEN.** *(See Saddlebrook Resort) 813/973-1111.* Hrs: 6:30 am-3 pm, 6-10 pm; Fri 6-11 pm; hrs may vary seasonally. Res accepted. Continental menu. Bar 11-1 am. Semi-a la carte: bkfst $5-$10.50, lunch $8-$14, dinner $19-$24.50. Serv charge 18%. Child's meals. Specializes in steak, veal, seafood buffet. Pastry shop. Entertainment. Valet parking. Creative food presentation. Contemporary decor. Lakeside terrace dining overlooking golf course. Cr cds: A, C, D, MC, V.

★ ★ ★ **DONATELLO.** *232 N Dale Mabry Hwy (33609), west of downtown. 813/875-6660.* Hrs: noon-3 pm, 6-11 pm; Sat, Sun from 6 pm. Closed Jan 1, Memorial Day, July 4, Dec 25. Res accepted. Northern Italian menu. Bar. Wine list. Semi-a la carte: lunch $5.95-$11.95, dinner $15.95-$23.95. Specializes in hand-rolled

pasta, veal chops, fresh seafood. Own breads, desserts. Valet parking. Some tableside cooking. Cr cds: A, C, D, DS, MC, V.

Ⓓ

★ ★ ★ **HARBOUR VIEW.** *(See Wyndham Harbour Island Hotel) 813/229-5001.* Hrs: 6:30 am-2 pm, 6-11 pm; Sun brunch 10:30 am-2 pm. Res accepted. Serv bar. A la carte entrees: bkfst $5.25-$9.75, lunch $7-$11.50, dinner $16.50-$24.95. Sun brunch $19.95. Pasta bar (Mon-Fri) $9.75. Child's meals. Specializes in contemporary regional cuisine featuring fresh pasta, fresh seafood. Own baking. Valet parking. Waterfront view. Cr cds: A, C, D, DS, ER, JCB, MC, V.

Ⓓ

★ **JESSE'S.** *(5771 Fowler Ave, Temple Terrace) W via Busch Blvd, in Terrace Walk Shopping Center. 813/980-3686.* Hrs: 11 am-midnight; Sun noon-10 pm. Closed some major hols. Bar. Semi-a la carte: lunch $5.75-$6.75, dinner $5.75-$18.50. Child's meals. Specializes in steak, seafood, prime rib. Extensive beer collection. Two aquariums; fireplace. Cr cds: A, MC, V.

Ⓓ

★ **JIMMY MAC'S.** *113 S Armenia Ave, in Hyde Park. 813/879-0591.* Hrs: 11:30-2 am; Sat from 11 am; Sun 11 am-11 pm. Closed most major hols. Res accepted. Bar 11:30-3 am. Semi-a la carte: lunch $4-$7.75, dinner $6.50-$17. Specializes in grilled seasonal seafood, hamburgers. Entertainment Fri-Sat. Parking. Eclectic decor. In 2 restored houses. Cr cds: A, D, DS, MC, V.

★ ★ **MALIOS.** *301 S Dale Mabry Hwy (33609), west of downtown. 813/879-3233.* Hrs: 11:30 am-2:30 pm, 5-11 pm; Fri, Sat 5-11:30 pm. Closed Sun; most major hols. Res accepted. Bar 11:30-2:30 am. A la carte entrees: lunch $4.95-$6.95, dinner $8.95-$22.95. Specializes in steak, seafood, pasta. Entertainment. Parking. Large central lounge with entertainment. Cr cds: A, C, D, DS, MC, V.

Ⓓ

★ ★ **RUMPELMAYERS.** *4812 E Busch Blvd, in Ambassador Square Shopping Center, north of downtown. 813/989-9563.* Hrs: 11 am-11 pm. Res accepted. German menu. Serv bar. Complete meals: lunch $3.75-$9.25, dinner $7.50-$16.50. Child's meals. Specialties: Wienerschnitzel, sauerbraten, Black Forest cake. Accordionist evenings. Parking. Extensive German beer selection. Cr cds: A, C, D, DS, MC, V.

✔★ **SPAGHETTI WAREHOUSE.** *1911 N 13th St (33605), in Ybor City. 813/248-1720.* Hrs: 11 am-10 pm; Fri to 11 pm; Sat noon-11 pm; Sun noon-10 pm. Closed Thanksgiving, Dec 25. Res accepted. Italian menu. Bar. Semi-a la carte: lunch $2.95-$6.95, dinner $4.10-$8.95. Specialties: lasagne, veal & chicken parmigiana, cannelloni alla Florentina. Parking. Antiques; authentic trolley. Cr cds: A, C, D, DS, MC, V.

Ⓓ

★ ★ **SUKOTHAI.** *8201 A North Dale Mabry Hwy, north of downtown. 813/933-7990.* Hrs: 11 am-11 pm; Sat, Sun from 5 pm. Closed Labor Day, Thanksgiving, Dec 25. Res accepted. Thai menu. Wine, beer. Semi-a la carte: lunch $4.95-$6.95, dinner $8.95-$17.95. Specializes in seafood. Original Thai tables, pillows. Parking. Cr cds: A, C, D, DS, MC, V.

Ⓓ

St Petersburg

Motels

✔★ ★ **COMFORT INN CENTRAL.** *1400 34th St N (33713). 813/323-3100; FAX 813/327-5792.* 78 rms, 3 story. Dec-Apr: S $45-$62; D $51-$68; family, wkly rates; lower rates rest of yr. TV. Heated pool; whirlpool. Complimentary full bkfst. Restaurant 6:30-11 am. Ck-out 11 am. Coin lndry. Meeting rms. Cr cds: A, D, DS, MC, V.

D ≈ ⊷ SC

★ **DAYS INN.** 2595 54th Ave N (33714). 813/522-3191; res: 800/325-2525; FAX 813/527-6120. 155 rms, 2 story. Feb-mid-Apr: S $45-$55; D $49-$65; each addl $4; under 12 free; lower rates rest of yr. Crib free. TV; cable. Pool; wading pool. Complimentary continental bkfst. Ck-out 11 am. Coin lndry. Meeting rm. Lawn games. Picnic tables. Cr cds: A, C, D, DS, JCB, MC, V.

D ≈ ⊷ SC

★★ **DAYS INN MARINA BEACH RESORT.** 6800 Sunshine Skyway Lane (33711). 813/867-1151; FAX 813/864-4494. 157 rms, 2 story, 20 kits. Feb-mid-Apr: S, D $69-$123; each addl $10; suites; townhouses $121-$190; under 16 free; lower rates rest of yr. TV; cable. 2 pools; whirlpool, poolside serv. Playground. Restaurant 7-11:30 am, 5-10 pm. Bar; entertainment Thurs-Sat. Ck-out 11 am. Coin lndry. Meeting rms. Valet serv. Sundries. Gift shop. Lighted tennis. Game rm. Lawn games. Many refrigerators; bathrm phone in suites. Private patios, balconies. On bay; water sports, private beach. Marina sailing school, boat charter, deep sea fishing. Attraction tours. Cr cds: A, C, D, DS, JCB, MC, V.

D ⊷ ⊷ ≈ ⊷ ⊷ SC

★ **LA MARK CHARLES.** (6200 34th St N, Pinellas Park 34665) ½ mi S of FL 694, off I-275. 813/527-7334; res: 800/448-6781; FAX 813/526-9294. 93 rms, 1-2 story, 35 kits. Feb-Apr: S, D $60; each addl $5; suites $65-$70; kit. units $65-$75; under 12 free; lower rates rest of yr. Crib $3. Pet accepted; $35 ($25 refundable). TV. Heated pool; whirlpool. Restaurant 7-10 am. Ck-out 11 am. Meeting rm. Coin lndry. Sundries. Refrigerators avail (3-day min). Cr cds: A, DS, MC, V.

⊷ ≈ ⊷ ⊷ SC

★★ **LA QUINTA INN.** 4999 34th St N (33714). 813/527-8421; FAX 813/527-8851. 120 rms, 2 story. Mid-Jan-Apr: S $59; D $69; each addl $10; lower rates rest of yr. Pet accepted, some restrictions. TV; cable. Heated pool. Complimentary continental bkfst. Ck-out noon. Coin lndry. Meeting rm. Exercise equipt; weights, bicycles. Spanish decor. Elaborately landscaped; fountain, palm trees, jasmine & gardenia bushes. Cr cds: A, C, D, DS, MC, V.

⊷ ≈ ⊷ ⊷ ⊷ SC

★★ **SUNCOAST EXECUTIVE INN AND ATHLETIC CENTER.** 3000 34th St S (33711). 813/867-1111; FAX 813/867-7068. 117 rms, 3 story. Feb-Apr: S, D $60-$65; each addl $5; suites $80-$85; under 18 free; lower rates rest of yr. Crib free. TV; cable. Heated pool. Restaurant 7-2 am. Rm serv. Bar. Ck-out 11 am. Coin lndry. Meeting rms. Beauty shop. Tennis, pro. Some refrigerators. Refrigerator, wet bar in suites. Some balconies. Cr cds: A, C, D, DS, MC, V.

D ⊷ ≈ ⊷ ⊷ SC

✔★ **VALLEY FORGE.** 6825 Central Ave (33710). 813/345-0135; FAX 813/384-1671. 27 rms, 8 kits. Mid-Jan-mid-Apr: S, D $45-$65; lower rates rest of yr. Crib $5. Pet accepted; $3. TV; cable. Pool. Coffee. Restaurant nearby. Ck-out 11 am. Lawn games. Refrigerators. Private patios. Cr cds: A, D, MC, V.

⊷ ≈ ⊷

Hotel

★★★ **HILTON.** 333 1st St S (33701). 813/894-5000; FAX 813/894-7655. 333 units, 15 story, 31 suites. S $94-$119; D $104-$129; each addl $10; suites $129-$454; under 18 free. Crib free. TV; cable. Heated pool; poolside serv. Restaurant 6:30 am-10:30 pm. Bar. Ck-out noon. Convention facilities. Concierge. Valet parking. Exercise equipt; weights, stair machine, whirlpool. Game rm. Refrigerators avail. Picnic tables. Opp Tampa Bay. *LUXURY LEVEL : EXECUTIVE LEVEL.* 44 units, 3 suites, 2 floors. S from $129; D from $139; suites $139-$449. Private lounge. In-rm movies. Bathrm phones. Kit. area in suites.

Complimentary continental bkfst, refreshments. Cr cds: A, C, D, DS, JCB, MC, V.

D ≈ ⊷ ⊷ ⊷

Resort

★★★★ **STOUFFER VINOY RESORT.** 501 Fifth Ave NE (33701), off I-275 onto I-375, then 4th Ave to Beach Rd, left one block, downtown. 813/894-1000; FAX 813/822-2785. 360 units, 7 story, 27 suites. Mid-Jan-mid-Apr: S, D $229-$289; suites $500-$2,000; under 18 free; wkend packages; golf & tennis plans; lower rates rest of yr. Crib free. Garage, overnight; valet parking $9, self-park $6. TV; cable. 2 heated pools; poolside serv. Supervised child's activities. Complimentary coffee & newspaper in rms. Restaurants 6 am-11 pm (also see TERRACE ROOM/MARCHAND'S GRILL). Rm serv 24 hrs. Bar 10-2 am, Sun 1 pm-midnight; entertainment. Ck-out noon. Lndry facilities. Convention facilities. Concierge. Gift shops. 14 tennis courts, 8 lighted, 4 different surfaces, including grass and clay. 18-hole golf, greens fee $80 (incl cart), pro, putting green, driving range. Exercise rm; instructor, weight machine, bicycles, whirlpool, sauna, steam rm. Masseuse. Complete fitness center. Croquet courts. Minibars. Wet bar in suites. Restored historic landmark (1925) blends the best of the old and the new. Stenciled cypress beams in lobby; leaded-glass windows, hand-painted ceilings and wall murals in the original dining wing; tropical gardens. Situated on a 14-acre site overlooking Tampa Bay; swimming beach; 74-slip private marina. Cr cds: A, C, D, DS, ER, JCB, MC, V.

D ⊷ ⊷ ⊷ ⊷ ≈ ⊷ ⊷ ⊷

Restaurants

★★ **BASTA'S.** 1625 4th St S (33701). 813/894-7880. Hrs: 5-11 pm. Closed Jan 1, Thanksgiving, Dec 25. Res accepted. Northern Italian menu. Bar. A la carte entrees: dinner $13-$24. Specializes in fresh seafood, veal, pasta. Guitarist & mandolinist Fri & Sat. Parking. Italian atmosphere; artwork, mural. Hand-painted ceiling in main dining area. Cr cds: A, MC, V.

D

✔★ **CHINA DELIGHT.** 1198 Pasadena Ave S. 813/347-0000. Hrs: 11:30 am-10 pm; Fri to 11 pm; Sat noon-11 pm; Sun 4-10 pm; early-bird dinner Mon-Fri 2:30-5 pm. Closed Thanksgiving. Res accepted. Chinese, Amer menu. Semi-a la carte: lunch $3.95-$4.95, dinner $5.25-$10.95. Child's meals. Specialties: sesame chicken, seafood bird nest. Parking. Decorated with Chinese accents. Cr cds: A, C, D, MC, V.

D

★★ **KEYSTONE CLUB.** 320 4th St N. 813/822-6600. Hrs: 11 am-2:30 pm, 5-10 pm; Fri to 11 pm; Sat 5-11 pm. Closed Sun; major hols. Res accepted. Bar. Semi-a la carte: lunch $3.95-$6.50, dinner $8.95-$19. Child's meals. Specializes in prime rib, pork chops, fresh fish. Parking. Club-like atmosphere. Cr cds: A, D, MC, V.

D

★★ **LEVEROCK'S.** 4801 37th St S. 813/864-3883. Hrs: 11:30 am-10 pm; early-bird dinner 3-6 pm. Closed Thanksgiving, Dec 25. Bar. Semi-a la carte: lunch $3.75-$6.95, dinner $5.95-$19.95. Child's meals. Specializes in grouper, Florida fish. Parking. Overlooks bay. Cr cds: A, C, D, MC, V.

D

✔★ **SMOKEY'S TEXAS BAR-B-QUE.** (8180 49th St N, Pinellas Park) N via 49th St to 82nd Ave. 813/546-3600. Hrs: 11 am-10 pm. Bar. Semi-a la carte: lunch, dinner $3.50-$12. Specializes in hickory-smoked ribs, prime rib, steak. Parking. Southwestern decor. Cr cds: A, MC, V.

D

★★★ **TERRACE ROOM/MARCHAND'S GRILL.** (See Stouffer Vinoy Resort) 813/894-1000. Hrs: 6 am-3 pm, 5:30-11 pm; early-bird dinner Sun-Thurs 5:30-6:30 pm; Sun brunch 9:30 am-3 pm. Res accepted. Mediterranean menu. Bar 11 am-midnight; wkends to 1 am. Wine list. A la carte entrees: bkfst $5-$7.50, lunch $7.25-$15, dinner $12.50-$21.50. Sun brunch $29. Child's meals. Specialties: tortellini with 4 cheeses, bouillabaisse, Caribbean-style snapper. Contemporary jazz band Tues-Sat eve. Valet parking. In historic building; flower and griffin designs on the high ceiling and just above the column were hand-painted as part of an extensive restoration process. The windows are replicas of the original 1920s leaded-glass windows. Cr cds: A, C, D, DS, ER, JCB, MC, V.

D

Notes

Notes

Notes

Notes

Notes

Notes

Notes

Mobil Travel Guide

Order Form

If you would like other editions of the MOBIL TRAVEL GUIDES that might not be available at your local bookstore or Mobil dealer, please use this order form or call the toll-free number below.

Ship to:

Name _____

Address _____

City _____ State _____ Zip _____

☐ My check is enclosed.

☐ Please charge my credit card

☐ VISA ☐ MasterCard ☐ American Express

Credit Card # _____

Expiration _____

Signature _____

Please send me the following 1995 Mobil Travel Guides:

☐ 0-679-02851-X
California and the West (Arizona, California, Nevada, Utah)
$13.95 (Can $18.95)

☐ 0-679-02852-8
Great Lakes (Illinois, Indiana, Michigan, Ohio, Wisconsin, Canada: Ontario)
$13.95 (Can $18.95)

☐ 0-679-02853-6
Mid-Atlantic (Delaware, District of Columbia, Maryland, New Jersey, North Carolina, Pennsylvania, South Carolina, Virginia, West Virginia)
$13.95 (Can $18.95)

☐ 0-679-02854-4
Northeast (Connecticut, Maine, Massachusetts, New Hampshire, New York, Rhode Island, Vermont, Canada: New Brunswick, Nova Scotia, Ontario, Prince Edward Island, Québec)
$13.95 (Can $18.95)

☐ 0-679-02857-9
Northwest and Great Plains (Idaho, Iowa, Minnesota, Montana, Nebraska, North Dakota, Oregon, South Dakota, Washington, Wyoming, Canada: Alberta, British Columbia, Manitoba)
$13.95 (Can $18.95)

☐ 0-679-02855-2
Southeast (Alabama, Florida, Georgia, Kentucky, Mississippi, Tennessee)
$13.95 (Can $18.95)

☐ 0-679-02856-0
Southwest & South Central (Arkansas, Colorado, Kansas, Louisiana, Missouri, New Mexico, Oklahoma, Texas)
$13.95 (Can $18.95)

☐ 0-679-02858-7
Frequent Traveler's Guide to Major Cities (Detailed coverage of 46 major U.S. cities, plus airport maps)
$14.95 (Can $19.95)

Total cost of book(s) ordered $ _____

Shipping & Handling (please add $2 for first book, $.50 for each additional book) $ _____

Add applicable sales tax* $ _____

TOTAL AMOUNT ENCLOSED $ _____

*To ensure that all orders are processed efficiently, please apply sales tax in Canada and in the following states: CA, CT, FL, IL, NJ, NY, TN and WA.

Please mail this form to:

Mobil Travel Guides
Random House
400 Hahn Rd.
Westminster, MD 21157
or call toll-free, 24 hours a day 1-800-533-6478

M⊙bil Travel Guide

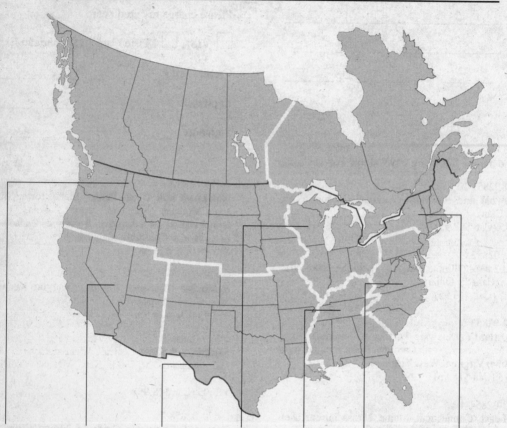

Northwest and Great Plains

Idaho
Iowa
Minnesota
Montana
Nebraska
North Dakota
Oregon
South Dakota
Washington
Wyoming

Canada:

Alberta
British Columbia
Manitoba

California and the West

Arizona
California
Nevada
Utah

Southwest and South Central

Arkansas
Colorado
Kansas
Louisiana
Missouri
New Mexico
Oklahoma
Texas

Great Lakes

Illinois
Indiana
Michigan
Ohio
Wisconsin

Canada:

Ontario

Southeast

Alabama
Florida
Georgia
Kentucky
Mississippi
Tennessee

Middle Atlantic

Delaware
District of Columbia
Maryland
New Jersey
North Carolina
Pennsylvania
South Carolina
Virginia
West Virginia

Northeast

Connecticut
Maine
Massachusetts
New Hampshire
New York
Rhode Island
Vermont

Canada:

Atlantic Provinces
Ontario
Quebec

YOU CAN HELP MAKE THE *MOBIL TRAVEL GUIDES* MORE ACCURATE AND USEFUL

ALL INFORMATION WILL BE KEPT CONFIDENTIAL

Your Name_____
(Please Print)

Street_____

City, State, Zip_____

Were children with you on trip? ☐ Yes ☐ No

Number of people in your party _____

Your occupation_____

1.

Establishment name_____

Hotel ☐ Resort ☐ Cafeteria ☐
Motel ☐ Inn ☐ Restaurant ☐

Street_____City_____ State _____

Do you agree with our description? ☐ Yes ☐ No If not, give reason_____

Please give us your opinion of the following:

ROOM DECOR	CLEANLINESS	SERVICE	FOOD
☐ Excellent	☐ Spotless	☐ Excellent	☐ Excellent
☐ Good	☐ Clean	☐ Good	☐ Good
☐ Fair	☐ Unclean	☐ Fair	☐ Fair
☐ Poor	☐ Dirty	☐ Poor	☐ Poor

1995 *GUIDE* RATING _____★

CHECK YOUR SUGGESTED RATING BELOW:
☐ ★ good, satisfactory ☐ ★★★★ outstanding
☐ ★★ very good ☐ ★★★★★ one of best
☐ ★★★ excellent in country
☐ ✓ unusually good value

Comments:_____

Date of visit_____

First visit? ☐ Yes ☐ No

2.

Establishment name_____

Hotel ☐ Resort ☐ Cafeteria ☐
Motel ☐ Inn ☐ Restaurant ☐

Street_____City_____ State _____

Do you agree with our description? ☐ Yes ☐ No If not, give reason_____

Please give us your opinion of the following:

ROOM DECOR	CLEANLINESS	SERVICE	FOOD
☐ Excellent	☐ Spotless	☐ Excellent	☐ Excellent
☐ Good	☐ Clean	☐ Good	☐ Good
☐ Fair	☐ Unclean	☐ Fair	☐ Fair
☐ Poor	☐ Dirty	☐ Poor	☐ Poor

1995 *GUIDE* RATING _____★

CHECK YOUR SUGGESTED RATING BELOW:
☐ ★ good, satisfactory ☐ ★★★★ outstanding
☐ ★★ very good ☐ ★★★★★ one of best
☐ ★★★ excellent in country
☐ ✓ unusually good value

Comments:_____

Date of visit_____

First visit? ☐ Yes ☐ No

3.

Establishment name_____

Hotel ☐ Resort ☐ Cafeteria ☐
Motel ☐ Inn ☐ Restaurant ☐

Street_____City_____ State _____

Do you agree with our description? ☐ Yes ☐ No If not, give reason_____

Please give us your opinion of the following:

ROOM DECOR	CLEANLINESS	SERVICE	FOOD
☐ Excellent	☐ Spotless	☐ Excellent	☐ Excellent
☐ Good	☐ Clean	☐ Good	☐ Good
☐ Fair	☐ Unclean	☐ Fair	☐ Fair
☐ Poor	☐ Dirty	☐ Poor	☐ Poor

1995 *GUIDE* RATING _____★

CHECK YOUR SUGGESTED RATING BELOW:
☐ ★ good, satisfactory ☐ ★★★★ outstanding
☐ ★★ very good ☐ ★★★★★ one of best
☐ ★★★ excellent in country
☐ ✓ unusually good value

Comments:_____

Date of visit_____

First visit? ☐ Yes ☐ No

FOLD AND TAPE (OR SEAL) FOR MAILING–DO NOT STAPLE

95

Revised editions are now being prepared for publication next year:

California and the West: Arizona, California, Nevada, Utah

Northeast: Connecticut, Maine, Massachusetts, New Hampshire, New York,
Rhode Island, Vermont; Eastern Canada.

Mid-Atlantic: Delaware, District of Columbia, Maryland, New Jersey, North Carolina,
Pennsylvania, South Carolina, Virginia, West Virginia.

Southeast: Alabama, Florida, Georgia, Kentucky, Mississippi, Tennessee.

Great Lakes: Illinois, Indiana, Michigan, Ohio, Wisconsin; Ontario, Canada.

Northwest: Idaho, Iowa, Minnesota, Montana, Nebraska, North Dakota, Oregon,
South Dakota, Washington, Wyoming; Western Canada.

Southwest: Arkansas, Colorado, Kansas, Louisiana, Missouri, New Mexico, Oklahoma, Texas.

Frequent Traveler's Guide to Major Cities: Detailed coverage of 46 Major Cities, plus airport maps.

Mobil Travel Guides are available at Mobil Service Stations, bookstores, or by mail from Mobil Travel
Guides, Random House, 400 Hahn Rd., Westminster, MD 21157, or call toll-free, 24 hours a day,
1-800-533-6478.

HOW CAN WE IMPROVE *MOBIL TRAVEL GUIDES*?

Mobil Travel Guides are constantly revising and improving. All attractions are updated and all listings are
revised and evaluated annually. You can contribute to the accuracy and usefulness of the guides by
sending us your reactions to the places you have visited. Your suggestions for improvement of the guides
are also welcome. Just complete this prepaid mailing form or address letters to: *Mobil Travel Guide,* 4709
West Golf Rd., Suite 803, Skokie, IL 60076. The editors of the *Mobil Travel Guides* appreciate your useful
comments.

Have you sent us one of these forms before?   ☐ Yes   ☐ No

Please make any general comment here. Thanks! _____

_____

_____

_____

Mobil Travel Guide®

The Guide That Saves You Money When You Travel.

FREE ONE CAR CLASS UPGRADE

This coupon entitles you to a Free One Car Class Upgrade on a leisure rental. Call 1-800-654-2210 for reservations. Request PC# 52021 to receive the upgrade. In Canada call 1-800-263-0600 and request PC# 62020. See reverse for important rental information.

Restrictions apply. Advance reservations required.

OFFER EXPIRES DECEMBER 31, 1995

CHOICE HOTELS INTERNATIONAL

10% OFF

The next time you're traveling, call **1-800-4-CHOICE** and request "Mobil Travelers' Discount." You'll save 10% at participating Comfort, Quality, Clarion, Sleep, Econo Lodge, Rodeway and Friendship hotels. 1,400 Choice Hotels will provide a free continental breakfast and children under 18 stay free when they share a room with their parents.

Advance reservations are required through 1-800-4-CHOICE. Discounts are based on availability at participating hotels and cannot be used in conjunction with any other discounts or promotions.

OFFER EXPIRES DECEMBER 31, 1995

50% OFF

Sbarro invites you to enjoy 50% off one entree when a second entree of equal or greater value is purchased.

Valid at any of the 600 Sbarro locations nationwide. This coupon may not be used in conjunction with any other discounts or promotions.

OFFER EXPIRES DECEMBER 31, 1995

BUSCH ENTERTAINMENT UP TO $18.00 OFF

Busch Entertainment invites you to enjoy $3.00 off per person. Present this coupon at any ticket window for your discount. One coupon is good for your entire group.

Not valid with any other discount, special event, special pricing or on purchase of multi-party/multi-visit, annual or season pass. Not for sale. Valid at Sea World of California, Florida, Ohio and Texas; Busch Gardens and Adventure Island of Tampa, FL; Busch Gardens and Water Country USA of Williamsburg, VA; Cypress Gardens of Winter Haven, FL; and Sesame Place of Langhorne, PA. © 1993 Busch Entertainment Corp.

9780A   9779C

OFFER EXPIRES DECEMBER 31, 1995

FREE FANNY PACK

Yours free when you join NPCA now! Join NPCA and save our national treasures! We are offering a special one-year introductory membership for only $15! Enjoy the many benefits of an NPCA membership and receive: a free National Parks and Conservation Association Fanny Pack, a free PARK-PAK, travel information kit, an annual subscription to the award-winning National Parks magazine, the NPCA discount photo service, car rental discounts and more. See reverse for order form.

OFFER EXPIRES DECEMBER 31, 1995

---

pierre cardin $20 OFF

5 Piece Luggage Set

Introducing the Pierre Cardin 5-piece tweed luggage collection. It's lightweight, attractive, and very affordable! Retails for $99. You send only $79.99 plus shipping and handling of $11.99. Choose from black tweed, green tweed or gray tweed. Set includes: 44″ garment bag, 25″ wheeled pullman, 21″ carry on bag, 17″ roll bag and 14″ flight bag. See reverse for order form.

OFFER EXPIRES DECEMBER 31, 1995

ONE FREE REGULAR OR LARGE CUP OR CONE

I Can't Believe It's Yogurt® invites you to enjoy one free regular or large cup or cone when a second regular or large cup or cone of equal or greater value is purchased.

Valid at all participating full-sized stores. One coupon per customer per visit. May not be used in conjunction with any other offer. Offer good for soft serve frozen yogurt only. Waffle cones and tax extra.

OFFER EXPIRES DECEMBER 31, 1995

ONE HOUR MOTOPHOTO®   50% OFF

One Hour MotoPhoto invites you to enjoy 50% off processing and printing.

Valid at all participating locations nationally. Limit one. Coupon must be presented at time of processing. May not be used in conjunction with any other discount or special promotion.

OFFER EXPIRES DECEMBER 31, 1995

Read each coupon carefully before using. Discounts only apply to the items and terms specified in the offer at participating locations. Remove the coupon you wish to use.

CHOICE HOTELS
INTERNATIONAL

Sleep • Comfort • Quality • Clarion
Friendship • Econo Lodge • Rodeway

With your 10% Mobil Traveler's Discount, the Choices - and savings - are better. So, call **1-800-4-CHOICE** today!

TASTE PUBLICATIONS INTERNATIONAL

Terms and Conditions: 1) Receive a One Car Class Leisure Upgrade when you reserve a Compact 2-Door (Class A) through Full Size 2-Door (Class D) car on any Hertz Leisure daily, weekly or weekend rate. 2) Maximum upgrade is from Full Size 2-Door (Class D) to Full Size 4-Door (Class F). 3) This offer is redeemable at participating Hertz corporate airport locations in the U.S. and participating licensee locations, subject to vehicle availability, and advance reservation is required. Request PC# 52021 at time of reservation. 4) Standard blackout dates apply. 5) This coupon has no cash value, must be surrendered at the time of rental pick-up and may not be used with any other coupon, offer, promotion, or discount. 6) Hertz rate and rental conditions for renting location apply and the car must be returned to that location. 7) Minimum rental age is 25 and Hertz standard driver qualifications apply. 8) Only one coupon will be honored per rental transaction; taxes and optional items, such as refueling are extra. 9) Coupon expires December 31, 1995.

TASTE PUBLICATIONS INTERNATIONAL

Sea World
California • Florida • Ohio • Texas

BUSCH GARDENS
TAMPA
WILLIAMSBURG

SESAME PLACE

TASTE PUBLICATIONS INTERNATIONAL

TASTE PUBLICATIONS INTERNATIONAL

Mail check for $91.98* for each set to: Merchandise Order Center, 929 N Plum Grove Road, Schaumburg, IL 60173-9797 1-800-788-1808 (8am - 4pm CT)

Name: _____

Address: _____

City: _____ State: _____ Zip: _____

VISA   MasterCard   (please circle one)

Acct. #: _____

Exp. Date: _____ Signature: _____

TASTE PUBLICATIONS INTERNATIONAL

Please indicate: Black, Green, or Gray
* IL residents add sales tax.   004   109/82

❏ Yes! I want to preserve and protect our National Parks by becoming a National Parks and Conservation Association Member.
  ❏ I enclose a check for $15 for my one-year membership.
  ❏ Charge my annual dues to my ❏ Visa ❏ MasterCard ❏ Amex

Acct. #: _____

Signature: _____

Name: _____

Address: _____

City: _____ State: _____ Zip: _____

Phone: _____

Make checks payable and mail to:
NPCA, 1776 Massachusetts Ave. NW
Washington, DC 20036-1904   **GRA95**

TASTE PUBLICATIONS INTERNATIONAL

ONE HOUR MOTOPHOTO®

TASTE PUBLICATIONS INTERNATIONAL

TASTE PUBLICATIONS INTERNATIONAL

Mobil Travel Guide®
The Guide That Saves You Money When You Travel.

The Place

Where Fresh is the Taste.™

TASTE PUBLICATIONS INTERNATIONAL

Plazas · Hotels · Park Square Inns · Lodges · HoJo Inns

THE COMFORTABLE LANDMARK™

TASTE PUBLICATIONS INTERNATIONAL

Offer valid on an Intermediate (Group C) through a Full Size 4-door (Group E) car for a 5 day rental. Certificate must be surrendered at time of rental; one per rental. May be used in conjunction with Taste Publications International rates and discounts. May not be used in conjunction with any other coupon, promotion or offer. Certificate valid at Avis corporate and participating licensee locations in the contiguous U.S. Offer not available during holiday and other blackout periods. Offer may not be available on all rates at all times. Cars subject to availability. Taxes, local government surcharges and optional items, such as LDW, additional-driver fee and refueling, are extra. Renter must meet Avis age, driver and credit requirements. Minimum age is 25. Offer expires December 31, 1995.

Rental Sales Agent Instructions:

At Checkout: In AWD, enter A291806   In CPN, Enter MUGC150.

Complete this information: RA# _____

Rental Location: _____

Attach COUPON to tape.   © 1994 Wizard Co., Inc.

TASTE PUBLICATIONS INTERNATIONAL

Museum of Science and Industry

Some of the Latest Exhibits at the Museum of Science and Industry • Chicago

"**Navy: Technology at Sea**" -Step on board partial recreations of three ships, then fly on a top-gun mission in our F-14 Tomcat flight simulators.

"**IMAGING: The Tools of Science**" -See sound, marvel at 6-foot thermal images of yourself and experience virtual reality.

"**Take Flight**" -An actual 727 inside the museum provides a unique setting for learning the principles of flight.

MOP 07

TASTE PUBLICATIONS INTERNATIONAL

No matter where you travel, there is a Six Flags Theme Park near you.

Houston Six Flags AstroWorld (713) 799-8404	NJ/NY/Philadelphia Six Flags Great Adventure (908) 928-2000	Los Angeles Six Flags Magic Mountain (805) 255-4100
Atlanta Six Flags Over Georgia (404) 948-9290	St. Louis Six Flags Over Mid-America (314) 938-5300	Dallas/Fort Worth Six Flags Over Texas (817) 640-8900

Chicago/Milwaukee Six Flags Great America
(708) 249-1776

TASTE PUBLICATIONS INTERNATIONAL

TASTE PUBLICATIONS INTERNATIONAL

RAMADA LIMITEDS · INNS · HOTELS · RESORTS · PLAZA HOTELS

Ramada Limiteds, Inns, Hotels, Resorts and Plaza Hotels offer you the value and accommodations you expect... And so much more! Over 700 convenient locations. Children under 18 always stay free. Non-smoking and handicap rooms available. Four people can share a room for the price of one at participating locations. For reservations call 1-800-228-2828.

TASTE PUBLICATIONS INTERNATIONAL

Pro Football Hall of Fame

Prices effective January 1, 1994:
Adult - $6.00 • Child - $2.50

TASTE PUBLICATIONS INTERNATIONAL

Mobil Travel Guide®

The Guide That Saves You Money When You Travel.

Please note: All offers may not be available in Canada.
Call (410) 825-3463 if you are unable to use an 800 number listed in the coupons.

The Best Value Under The Sun Just Got Better.

DAYS INN
The Best Value Under The Sun.™

TASTE PUBLICATIONS INTERNATIONAL

UNITED ARTISTS **GENERAL CINEMA THEATRES** **LOEWS**

Send payment and form to: Taste Publications International,
1031 Cromwell Bridge Road, Baltimore, MD 21286
A self-addressed stamped envelope must be enclosed to process your order.
No refunds or exchanges. Mail order only, not redeemable at box office.
Passes have expiration dates, generally one year from purchase.
Allow 2-3 weeks for delivery.

Name: _____
Address: _____
City: _____ State: _____ Zip: _____

TASTE PUBLICATIONS INTERNATIONAL

SAFE FIT™

TASTE PUBLICATIONS INTERNATIONAL

Las Vegas **TRAVEL**

1-800-992-7454 - One toll-free call gives you all these:

Luxor ♦ Maxim ♦ Tropicana ♦ MGM Grand ♦ Caesar's Palace
Sands ♦ Ballys ♦ Bourbon Street ♦ Hacienda ♦ Plaza ♦ Stardust
Imperial Palace ♦ Aladdin ♦ Sahara ♦ Westward Ho
Holiday Inn ♦ Excalibur ♦ Flamingo Hilton ♦ Las Vegas Hilton
Hollywood ♦ Rio Suites ♦ San Remo and so many more!

TASTE PUBLICATIONS INTERNATIONAL

CRUISE AMERICA   KOA   CRUISE CANADA

KOA has over 550 locations throughout the U.S. and Canada.

Cruise America and Cruise Canada have over 100 rental centers.

TASTE PUBLICATIONS INTERNATIONAL

Credit card orders call (615) 584-2626.
For further information (615) 584-2626.

Enclosed is $9.95 - shipping and handling included.
Rush my camera and film offer to:

Name: _____
Address: _____
City: _____ State: _____ Zip: _____

Enclose $9.95 payment (check or money order) and coupon -
mail to: **U.S. Express**,
7035 Middlebrook Pike, P.O. Box 51730, Knoxville, TN 37950

TASTE PUBLICATIONS INTERNATIONAL   **AUTH #347**

Terms and conditions: Subject to availability; reservation must be made
in advance. Offer valid through December 22, 1995; some dates may be
unavailable. Must be at least 21 years old. One coupon per person. Offer
not valid with any other promotion. No cash value. Program subject to
change or cancellation without notice. The following information must be
completed prior to redemption.

Name: _____
Street Address: _____
City: _____ State: _____ Zip: _____
Date of Birth: _____   **MB2**

TASTE PUBLICATIONS INTERNATIONAL   Gambling problem? Call 1-800-GAMBLER.

DØLLAR
RENT A CAR

TASTE PUBLICATIONS INTERNATIONAL

Mail this coupon to: National Audubon Society, Membership Data Center, P.O. Box 52529, Boulder, CO 80322-2529

Yes! Please enroll me as a 1-year member for $20 to the National Audubon Society.

Check one: _____ Payment enclosed. _____ Bill me later.

Name: _____

Address: _____

City: _____ State: _____ Zip: _____

Please allow 4-6 weeks for receipt of magazine and 8-10 weeks for receipt of backpack. $10.00 of dues is for AUDUBON magazine.

TASTE PUBLICATIONS INTERNATIONAL   5MBL9

TITLES:	RETAIL PRICE:	YOUR DISCOUNTED PRICE:
Touring America's National Parks	$29.95	$14.98
Hidden Treasures of America's National Parks	$29.95	$14.98
Touring America's Ghost Towns	$29.95	$14.98
Symphony to America's Natural Wonders	$29.95	$14.98
The Story of America's Crown Jewels	$24.95	$12.48
The Story of America's Classic Ballparks	$19.95	$9.98

Shipping and handling $4.50 on each order.

Questar Video Inc.

P.O. Box 11345 • Chicago, IL • 60611-0345

TASTE PUBLICATIONS INTERNATIONAL

Audio Diversions offers one of the broadest collections of Literature for Listening currently available. With more than 1,800 titles carefully drawn from among the latest travelbooks and the best in adventure, mystery, biography, business, motivational, inspirational and self help books, Audio Diversions is sure to have what you need to purchase or rent. Rentals come with addressed and stamped packages for easy return.

$4.95 for shipping and handling.

Call 1-800-628-6145.

TASTE PUBLICATIONS INTERNATIONAL   Ask for CLUB 3B.

Taxes, optional CDW at $12.99 per day or less, fuel, young renter fee, airport imposed taxes or fee, and other optional items are extra. Rental subject to driver record review. A 24-hour advance reservation is required. Availability is limited.

TASTE PUBLICATIONS INTERNATIONAL